P9-CRT-993

The Second World War: Europe and the Mediterranean

Thomas B. Buell
Clifton R. Franks
John A. Hixson
David R. Mets
Bruce R. Pirnie
James F. Ransone, Jr.
Thomas R. Stone

Thomas E. Griess
Series Editor

DEPARTMENT OF HISTORY
UNITED STATES MILITARY ACADEMY
WEST POINT, NEW YORK

Wayne, New Jersey

Illustration Credits

Page

6 Air-Armor Cooperation as Practiced in England: Photo: Courtesy of *Army Ordnance* magazine (now *National Defense* magazine) from Vol. X, p. 327 (July-August, 1929).

12 The German Battleship, *Scharnhorst*. Photo: Courtesy of Cassell and Company, Ltd. (Friedrich Ruge, *Sea Warfare, 1939-1945*, 1957).

13 Wever's Vision: The Ural Bomber. Photo: Courtesy of Alfred Price (*Pictorial History of the Luftwaffe*, 1969).

14 The *Luftwaffe* Was a Tactical Air Force. Photo: Courtesy of Alfred Price (*Pictorial History of the Luftwaffe*, 1969).

16 A Fiesler Storch–The Eyes of the *Panzers*. Photo: Courtesy of Alfred Price (*Pictorial History of the Luftwaffe*, 1969).

17 The Cutting Edge of the *Blitzkrieg*. Photo: Reprinted from *German Tank and Antitank*, by E.J. Hoffschmidt and W.H. Tantum IV, by permission from Paladin Press, Boulder, Colorado.

32 Marshal of France, Phillipe Petain. Photo: Harlingue-Viollet.

39 French Infantry Carrier. Photo: Courtesy of *Army Ordnance* magazine (now *National Defense* magazine), from Vol. XIV, p. 330 (May-June, 1934).

64 Hurricane, Spitfire, and Messerschmitt. Illustrations: *World Encyclopedia of Military Aircraft*, © 1980 Arnoldo Mondadori Editore, Italy.

65 Hawker Hurricanes of the RAF in Flight. Photo: Courtesy of Imperial War Museum.

119 Moscow Under Siege. Photo: Courtesy of Ullstein Bilderdienst.

121 Freezing Germans Surrender to Russians. Photo: Pix Inc., LIFE Magazine © 1945, Time, Inc.

131 General Vasili Ivanovich Chuikov. Photo: Novosti.

147 The German Main Battle Tank, Panzerkampfwagen IV. Illustration: Courtesy of Profile Books, Ltd.

148 The German Heavy Tank, Panzerkampfwagen VI. Illustration: Courtesy of Profile Books, Ltd.

230 Landing Craft Carry 3rd Infantry Division Troop Toward Beach. Photo: Wide World Photos.

231 German Dive Bombers Attacking Allied Fleet. Photo: Wide World Photos.

267 Railway Destruction, May 1944. Map: Reproduced with the permission of the Controller of Her Brittanic Majesty's Stationery Office from L.F. Ellis, *Victory in the West* (London, 1962), Vol. I, p. 112.

268 V-1 Flying Bomb. Photo: Black Star.

268 V-2 Rocket. Photo: Courtesy of Imperial War Museum.

294 Glider-Borne Reinforcements. Photo: Courtesy of Imperial War Museum.

All other illustrations are reprinted courtesy of the U.S. Armed Forces and the U.S. National Archives.

Series Editor, Thomas E. Griess.
In-House Editor, Joanne Abrams.
Cover design by Martin Hochberg.

ISBN 0-89529-242-4

10 9 8 7 6 5 4 3 2

Printed in the United States of America

Contents

To the Corps of Cadets at the United States Military Academy,
whose preparation for the military profession
is enhanced by the study of military history.

Illustrations

Chapter 5

Chapter 6

Chapter 7

Chapter 8

Chapter 9

Chapter 10

Chapter 11

Chapter 12

Chapter 13

Chapter 14

Chapter 15

Chapter 16

Chapter 17

Acknowledgements

In writing this volume on the European and Mediterranean Theaters, we have attempted to offer cadets succinct, readable narratives, that weave the complexities of the Second World War into the broader fabric of warfare over the years. But as with other attempts to simplify the complex and abbreviate the lengthy, our work suffers at times in clarity and felicity of phrase. We also admit to drawing heavily on the historical research and writing of others, in part because of the time limitations that constrain the writer–instructor at West Point. Neither a comprehensive treatise nor a product of exhaustive research in original sources is intended. Given those limitations, whatever merits the reader can discern are rightfully shared with many people.

Our utmost gratitude goes to the Head of the Department of History, Colonel Thomas E. Griess. As editor–in–chief, he gave purpose and coherence to this volume; as editor, he polished our narratives, pointing out those vague passages and instances of troubled syntax that authors are unable to see for themselves.

Since original thinking is rare and a synthesis of the ideas of others is more often the case, we are very much indebted to our military colleagues in the Department of History and to the department's Visiting Professors for sharing their views on the Second World War. In comparable measure, we are grateful to the official historians of the United States Army, United States Army Air Force, and the United Kingdom. Besides relying on their extensive research and excellent writing, we have been guided in our work by several historians in the U.S. Army Center of Military History.

Our appreciation extends to members of the USMA Library, for assisting in gathering research material; Mr. Edward J. Krasnoborski, for preparing supporting maps; the Department of History's administrative staff, headed by Mrs. Sally L. French, for typing innumerable drafts and final manuscripts; and our families for sustaining us through times that were indeed demanding but satisfying.

Thomas B. Buell
Clifton R. Franks
John A. Hixson
David R. Mets
Bruce R. Pirnie
James F. Ransone, Jr.
Thomas R. Stone

West Point, New York

Foreword

Cadets at the United States Military Academy have studied military campaigns and institutions for almost a century in a course entitled History of the Military Art. Beginning in 1938, that study of history was supported by texts and maps which were prepared by departmental faculty under the direction of T. Dodson Stamps, then Head of the Department of Military Art and Engineering. The first integrated treatment of the Second World War under this scheme was introduced in 1953 with the publication of *A Military History of World War II*, a departmental text which was jointly edited by Stamps and Vincent J. Esposito. That work, with an accompanying atlas which depicted the military operations described in the text, served cadets until 1959, when Esposito adopted the commercially published *The West Point Atlas of American Wars*. Departmentally prepared and edited by Esposito, *The West Point Atlas of American Wars* included coverage of World War II.

New texts and supporting atlases were required when I modified the scope of the course in the History of Military Art in 1967. Two years later the course came under the direction of a newly created Department of History, wherein it was structured around themes which broadened the coverage of the course in order to accommodate new events and the need to teach more than purely operational military history. Cadets were urged to:

> study military history in depth to get beneath the historian's necessarily imposed pattern of seeming orderliness and to try to understand what war is really like; in breadth to understand the flow of events and the existence of continuity or discontinuity therein; and in context to appreciate the political, social and economic factors that exercise important influences on the military part of the equation.[1]

To help the cadets organize their inquiries and study of the military art, the department proposed that they use a device called the "threads of continuity."

While the threads of continuity have no inherent worth, they can provide students with a way of getting at information, and serve as a lens through which they can examine events and place them in perspective. The military past can be envisioned as a carpet of mankind's activities, ideas, and discoveries, which is woven from strands representing major factors or themes. The carpet is a complex one, and it is in a constant state of subtle change. Focusing on these factors, which are the threads of continuity, can help students understand the meaning of the past and why changes have occurred. The importance of individual factors will vary from one era to another, for the strands in the tapestry of the military past fluctuate in size as their importance to the tapestry as a whole dictates. The threads which the Department of History adopted are: military thought and doctrine, strategy, tactics, generalship, logistics and administration, military professionalism, political factors, social factors, economic factors, and technology.[2]

Participating in a project which extended over a decade and a half, faculty members of the Department of History researched and wrote the texts which support the 1967 instructional concept just described. They also devised the maps which depict the military campaigns described in the texts. Although occasionally resorting to primary source materials, for documentation they relied largely upon sound secondary sources, particularly the excellent official histories of the various wars. Working under my guidance, the authors took pains to emphasize pertinent threads of continuity; in this endeavor, they were guided by a departmentally constructed blueprint of

[1]Thomas E. Griess, "A Perspective on Military History" in John E. Jessup and Robert W. Coakley (eds.), *A Guide to the Study and Use of Military History* (Government Printing Office: Washington, D.C., 1979), p. 39. The author is indebted to Michael Howard for the conceptualization regarding the study of military history.

[2]For a more detailed discussion of the threads of continuity see: John F. Votaw, "An Approach to the Study of Military History" in Jessup and Coakley (eds.), *Guide to Military History*, pp. 47-48; John I. Alger, *Definitions and Doctrine of the Military Art: Past and Present* (Department of History: West Point, New York, 1979), pp. 5-11.

the evolution of the art of war, which was collectively discussed and carefully structured and revised before writing commenced. The authors tried to bring breadth and context to their narratives by developing strategic and political themes and by emphasizing institutional factors; they sought to achieve depth of coverage by periodicially examining a particular military operation in some detail.

The reader of *The Second World War* will quickly perceive that the text is essentially a narrative of the military campaigns of the war. In the text devoted to the war in Europe, ground operations are emphasized; in the text which narrates events pertaining to the war between Japan and the Allies, naval operations predominate, but there is still considerable coverage of ground actions. In both works, the vital role played by airpower is stressed, and the political aspect of the war is highlighted in appropriate places. With regard to the latter, Chapter 8, "The Grand Alliance," in *The Second World War: Europe and the Mediterranean*, is particularly important; the reader should refer to it repeatedly in order to understand the subtle nuances associated with the higher direction of the war. Also, for its background on the United States military services, Chapter 2, "From Versailles to Pearl Harbor," in *The Second World War: Asia and the Pacific*, is recommended for frequent reference. Finally, the maps which depict operations should be studied as carefully as the narrative. They illustrate the importance of terrain, the vastness of space in some of the campaigns, the ebb and flow of battle, and the crucial importance of mobility in fighting forces. At the same time, the reader should recognize that maps can depict military operations too neatly. It must not be assumed that as the battle raged, any military leader saw things as clearly as the maps now represent them—and, lest the reader forget, the small red and blue arrows depict flesh and blood men, who were usually tired, hungry, dirty, scared, and unaware of the larger human drama which was unfolding around them.

Nine faculty members of the Department of History shared in the writing of this military history of the Second World War. Thousands of graduated cadets and the department are indebted to them for their efforts, which were performed under the pressure of time and with minimal resources. They pioneered in the development of unique texts which were designed to be used in the teaching of an unusual course in military history. Their work contributes to the literature on the history of World War II. In the text on the European and Mediterranean Theaters of Operation, John A. Hixson sets the stage in the opening chapters by relating how far-reaching German thinkers harnessed technology so as to unleash mobile elements which spearheaded the early German conquests. David R. Mets and Thomas B. Buell respectively treat the important roles air and sea power played, particularly in the pivotal battles. Bruce R. Pirnie describes the events which took place in the vast eastern theater and shows how Russia, just barely able to absorb the German onslaught, recovered and developed her own form of *blitzkrieg*. Clifton R. Franks recounts the story of the entry of the United States into the war in North Africa, and then illustrates how the vagaries of coalition strategy influenced the course of the war in Italy. Commencing with the highly complex invasion of Normandy, Thomas R. Stone surveys the advance of the western Allies into Germany, highlighting the importance of logistics and the running argument over campaign strategy. James F. Ransone, Jr., describes how the most successful coalition in history planned the war at the highest levels, and coincidentally illustrates the global nature of the Second World War. John H. Bradley was the primary author of *The Second World War: Asia and the Pacific*. His sweeping narrative captures the essence of the war which was fought over the vast reaches of the Pacific Ocean, stressing the interrelationship between land, sea, and air forces. Jack W. Dice prepared the chapter on the war in the "forgotten theater" of China-Burma-India, emphasizing China's difficult role, the importance of logistics, and how critical the proper training of military forces can be when war comes. Each of these authors also conceptually contributed to the design of supporting maps. The project would have faltered, however, but for the work of Edward J. Krasnoborski and his assistant, George Giddings. An unusually gifted cartographer, Mr. Krasnoborski made innumerable suggestions regarding the depiction of operations, supervised the drafting effort, and personally drew most of the maps. His skill is imprinted everywhere upon the finished product.

This present edition of *The Second World War* is essentially the text which was produced at the Military Academy as described above. As editor, however, I have attempted to clarify certain passages for the general reader, amplify purely military terminology, and improve the evenness of the narrative. Also, in an occasional instance, I have added material which was not available when the original text was written. The best example of this aspect of editing is the inclusion of the Allied intelligence effort known by its product as ULTRA. The editor is grateful for the advice and suggestions which were tendered by Rudy Shur and Joanne Abrams of Avery Publishing Group, Inc. Their assistance was timely and helpful. Ms. Abrams immeasurably improved the narrative through her painstaking editing, corrections of lapses in syntax, and penetrating questions related to clarity of expression.

Thomas E. Griess
Series Editor

Introduction

The First World War did not end the twentieth-century struggle for dominance over Europe. The treaties signed near Paris in 1919 resulted only in a 20-year truce—an uneasy peace lasting until the western European countries, waiting almost too long, attempted once more to turn back a resurgent Germany. This time, however, Germany was in league with Italy, which was led by the opportunistic Mussolini. Ironically, when the Second World War ended in 1945, no European power dominated Europe. Instead, within a few years, the United States and Russia confronted each other across an "iron curtain" that divided ancient battlefields and redrew those national boundaries in eastern Europe which had been realigned at Versailles. The two world wars were connected in another way.

The technological promises of The Great War were fulfilled during World War II. The tank and the airplane, teamed in *blitzkrieg*, prevented the bloody stalemate of the 1916 Western Front. France fell after a swift campaign in 1940, and those Balkan countries which opposed Hitler shared a similar fate in the following year; then, armies surged back and forth across Russia and western Europe until the war ended. Advocates of airpower took great strides toward achieving the military promise of the airplane. Meanwhile, on the high seas the potential of the submarine to blockade a nation was developed with frightening efficiency. Naval power, in its totality, however, proved equal to the menace of the underseas raider; it also projected its combat muscle ashore, all the while sustaining ground forces and helping to give them essential mobility. Technology, however, proved to be a two-edged sword. If it did not allow another stalemate to develop, it enabled the belligerents to spill even more blood. In effect, the devastation of trench warfare shifted to the homes and hearths of Europe's civilians. In the end, the tragic cost in lives during the Second World War was twice that of the First World War.

The world still lives with the results of World War II. Lines on the map that traced the final advances of the victors in Europe were quickly converted to the front lines of the Cold War. But the detonation of "Little Boy" over Hiroshima some six months after V-E Day created a new military environment. The Second World War was probably the last world war, because mankind seems to realize that the use of the terrifyingly unlimited military power which technology has spawned is capable of ending not only war but civilization as well. World War II also was probably the last war in which the belligerents could fight to a clear-cut decision. The goal of unconditional surrender, nurtured by Allied strength and Hitler's intransigence, is unlikely to be duplicated in an era when the power of nuclear weapons must dictate limitation of force. Clausewitz, the wise nineteenth-century Prussian military philosopher, understood what his more modern counterparts did not—the anomaly which unlimited military force freed from political restraint can create.

In the final analysis, the Second World War in Europe is the story of an unusually successful Allied coalition bringing crushing force to bear on an astonishingly resilient Germany, which was led to ruin by a short-sighted dictator. While the Allied coalition won a conclusive victory in three short years, German mistakes must share in the credit. Hitler and his partners failed to create a militarily effective Axis coalition, which might have coped more realistically with the problem of keeping the United States out of the war and thereby precluded, at least for a longer time, that country's great contribution to the Allied cause. In the end, moreover, Italy proved to be more of a burden than an asset to the Axis cause. Hitler's mistaken belief that he could fight a war whose duration could be measured in months was fatal. This belief, which was based upon Hitler's overestimation of the effectiveness and staying power of the *blitzkrieg*, largely dictated the German failure to build an industrial base capable of sustaining a large military establishment. Relying excessively upon intuition and trusting too much in amateurs, Hitler also made strategic errors and allowed a conceptually flawed airpower thesis to gain credence. Finally, perhaps the most telling German error was becoming ensnared in a two-front war. German mismanagement, however, should not be allowed to dim the Allied accomplishment.

In general, coalitions come together slowly, influenced by each member's self-interest and suspicions, but spurred on by a commonly perceived danger. So it was with the Allies. The unusual degree of trust, willingness to compromise, and genuine cooperation displayed by the United States and Great Britain, however, represents a significant landmark in the history of coalitions. Moreover, that harmonious relationship did not greatly deteriorate later, as is wont to be the case when coalition members can sense victory and an end to the common threat. Such was not the case in the relationship between the two western Allies and Russia, the third Ally. Suspicion of Soviet goals and intentions developed in 1944, particularly on Churchill's part. In the beginning, however, after the collapse of France and before the Grand Alliance was forged, Great Britain stood alone.

Although the British margin of survival in those harrowing months in 1940 and 1941 was narrow, it was enduring. Comprehension of this fact requires an understanding of the strengths and weaknesses of the military forces which Hitler unleased upon an unprepared Europe in 1939. The story begins, accordingly, with a prostrate Germany in 1919. In that country, which was then reeling from defeat in The Great War, a few nationalistic leaders took steps to preserve and perpetuate a martial spirit and to lay the foundation upon which Hitler built his war machine.

Birth of the Blitzkrieg

1

The High Command deliberately adopted the position of refuting the responsibility for the armistice . . . it was vital to keep the armour shining and the general staff free of burdens for the future.

Lieutenant General Wilhelm Groener

On September 29, 1918, General Erich Ludendorff informed the Kaiser that Germany must sue for peace and establish a new government based on democratic principles. The offensive that Ludendorff had begun in March had dissipated into unproductive attacks, whereupon the Allies had initiated their own offensive. Germany did not have the means to halt it. Moreover, among Germany's allies, Austria-Hungary was disintegrating, Bulgaria had already sued for an armistice, and Turkey was on the verge of collapse. On the German home front leaders were plagued with riots, strikes, and spreading revolution. The future was not promising, and the people were not prepared for it; for years they had been fed on the hope of a "victor's peace."[1] A primary consideration in the minds of the generals was to avoid being blamed for the defeat and subsequent acceptance of Allied terms, which were bound to be harsh. To shed this mantle of responsibility, these military men were anxious to shift that blame on to the political leaders. Ironically, President Woodrow Wilson unwittingly played into their hands by intimating "that he could not negotiate with a government which was not in the process of democratizing itself."[2]

General Wilhelm Groener replaced Ludendorff as First Quartermaster-General on October 26, 1918. Ludendorff's intense radical nationalism, growing megalomania, and reversal of his earlier plea to seek terms from the Allies had made him a liability in the peace negotiations then being conducted by the new government, headed by the liberal Prince Max of Baden. For these reasons, his resignation had been promptly accepted. Now it fell to Groener to tell the Kaiser the unvarnished truth, and what course of action he proposed to follow. Bluntly stated, this was to bring about the abdication of the Emperor, march the Army home under its own officers, and thereby preserve the unity of the *Reich* and the Army. The initial scenes in the drama unfolded much as Groener had outlined. William II abdicated on November 9, and a republic was proclaimed on the same day. Two days later the war ended.

November 9 and 10 were busy days for Groener. Hardly had the Kaiser departed for Holland when the general began to take steps to insure that the Army would continue to be an important factor in Germany's future. The government of President Friedrich Ebert's new German socialist republic was weak and disunited, and the country was on the verge of disintegration because of pressure from left-wing Independents and Spartacists (Communists). Ebert's relief was great on the evening of the tenth when the secret phone connecting the Chancellory with *Oberste Heeresleitung* (OHL) in Cassel rang and he heard Groener's voice. The general had called to make the new president an offer. He stated that the officer corps looked to the Government to combat bolshevism, and that they were putting themselves at its disposal for that very purpose. In return, however, they expected the Government to assist in maintaining discipline in the Army and to help in getting it back to Germany. Although this was a tacit recognition of the new republic, it was also a conditional arrangement. Ebert had nowhere else to look for a source of strength. Anxious to prevent a bolshevist-inspired revolution in Germany, he readily accepted Groener's offer. The rebuilding program desired by the Army was underway, even though the war would not end for two more days.[3] The new Government had an ally, not a servant.

The Rebuilding of the Army

The problem of maintaining an effective army, however, was not to be easily solved. Once the troops had re-entered Germany, the Army simply collapsed. The individual soldier's desire for demobilization and the increasing effect of pacifist and revolutionary propaganda took their toll. If the social and economic fabric of the *Reich* was to be repaired and its territorial integrity preserved, internal order had to be restored.[4] Not surprisingly, therefore, maintenance of the Government's authority remained the objective of the Army's leadership. Since the old army was no longer an effective instrument for re-establishing internal order, an expedient was adopted—the raising of volunteer units known as *Freikorps* (Free Corps). During the period from November 1918 to March 1920, these *Freikorps* ensured the domestic peace which was necessary to re-establish firm governmental control. They also provided the link between the old Imperial Army and the new *Reichswehr* which was created in March of 1920.* Because the *Freikorps* were by their very nature difficult to control, it had been decided by the general staff and other high-ranking army officers to replace them with a regular army as soon as possible.[5] Accordingly, on March 6, 1919, the Constitutional Assembly in Weimar laid down the basis for a provisional *Reichswehr* to be formed from *Freikorps* units. This organization was to be an interim step toward the creation of a regular *Reichswehr*, whose organization was still being worked out by OHL.†

In the midst of this governmental turmoil, the Allied powers presented Germany the draft of the Treaty of Versailles. (*See Map 1, in Atlas.*) By its terms, Germany was to have an army of not more than 100,000 men, including 4,000 officers; and it would be deprived of heavy artillery, tanks, and airplanes. All equipment and ammunition stocks were to be reduced to below normal levels. The general staff was to be dissolved, while all military schools, with the exception of one for each of the main arms, would be closed. All apparatus and preparations for a mobilization base were prohibited. The Navy was similarly limited, to include the prohibition against building or possessing submarines and a reduction in strength to 15,000 personnel.[6]

These military clauses and the so-called "honor clauses" were felt by the *Reichswehr* to be intolerable. After all, the Imperial Army had not been defeated in the field; there had been no hostile shots fired within the territory of the *Reich*; and, besides, who in Germany had sought peace—not the Army.** Attempts to persuade the Allies to modify the terms, especially the "honor clauses," were of no avail. Elements within the Army and Navy advocated resistance; but it was clear to Hindenburg, Groener, and General Hans von Seeckt, Chief of the *Truppenamt* (Troops Office), that effective resistance was impossible and that the treaty must be accepted. The Government's implementing order of March 6, 1920, to begin reduction of the *Reichwehr*, nevertheless, caused the abortive Kapp *Putsch* which lasted just three days.†† The failure of this *putsch* resulted not only in the elimination of those elements implacably against the Versailles Treaty and the republic but also in the sidelining of Gustav Noske, the socialist War Minister, and General Walter Reinhardt, the Chief of the Army Command. Thus, the control of the Army fell into the hands of Seeckt who would fashion a new German military machine from the ashes, as had Scharnhorst and Gneisenau before him.

General Hans von Seeckt combined in his person the best traditions of the Prussian military caste along with a broad outlook and a flair for political matters which was unusual in the German officer corps. The son of a Prussian general, descending from a family of noble Pomeranian stock whose sons had served Prussia well as civil servants and soldiers, Seeckt was born in 1866; he entered the Army in 1885 after finishing school in Strasbourg. He was posted early to the general staff, and the outbreak of World War I found him as Chief of Staff of the Third Army Corps. He so distinguished himself in operations near Soissons that he was sent as Chief of Staff to Mackensen's Eleventh Army in the East where he helped direct the great break-through at Gorlice in May of 1915. For this effort, he received the coveted *Pour la Merite* (Blue Max) and the reputation as a perfect chief of staff. His display of strategic skill and diplomatic ability during this campaign and in the subsequent conquest of Serbia led to his appointment as Chief of Staff for coordination of the Central Powers on the Eastern Front. Ultimately he became Chief of the Turkish General Staff.[7]

In appearance Seeckt was the stereotype of the Prussian general. He was of medium height and slight of build, with a severe, emaciated look to his facial features. Here the resemblance ended, for behind this Prussian facade was a mind which combined precision and accuracy with the vision and imagination of a creative artist. His manner was reserved, and his disinclination for talk earned him the title of "The Sphinx." Moreover, his officers and associates in the Government found him inapproachable, critical, and highly opinionated. In fact, in the Army there was only "Seeckt's opinion" on any matter.

*The *Freikorps* were formed throughout Germany by various former officers and non commissioned officers from the Imperial Army. They were formed for a variety of social and political reasons.

†The term *Reichswehr* refers to the armed forces of Germany, but it is most commonly used in connection with the Army only.

**The "honor clauses" demanded that Germany admit responsibility for causing the war and surrender her leaders for trial by an Allied tribunal.

††The Kapp *Putsch* was a monarchial *coup* which led to the seizure of government buildings in Berlin. It collapsed as a result of a general strike of the trade unions.

Notwithstanding his rather forbidding appearance and demeanor, he was highly respected both in and out of the Army for his breadth of vision and military expertise. He entered the office as Chief of the Army Command with two objectives clear in his mind: to strengthen and preserve the German *Reich* and to rebuild the Army. To manage the latter, he would rely upon the pillars of Prussian tradition, strict discipline, and loyalty—to Seeckt as the Army Commander. Both of these objectives he accomplished in such expert fashion, while apparently remaining within the restrictions of the Treaty of Versailles, that the various general staffs in Europe regarded him with awe and felt that there was definitely a "foxlike" aspect to his makeup.[8]

An anti-liberal and nonrepublican, Seeckt was an avowed monarchist, but he was pragmatic enough to take advantage of the opportunities offered by the Treaty of Versailles and the Weimar Constitution. By virtue of the fact that it was imposed upon Germany—an undefeated Germany—the Treaty provided a means of unifying a badly divided country. It also insured that the new German Army would be a high quality organization, one which would have to look to new ways to create a creditable military posture. The Constitution cleared away the old royal and aristocratic governmental superstructure. Although the Army had sheltered under the royal shield of the Kaiser, there had been many shortcomings in this relationship which had impaired service effectiveness. With their removal, opportunity for change beckoned.[9]

Seeckt's first move was to consolidate his position as Chief of the Army Command. The Constitution specified that the President was the Commander-in-Chief of all German forces. But Seeckt insisted on and was granted the right to exercise the power of command over the Army. As a result, the Minister of Defense, his nominal superior, would have little authority in military affairs. Subordinate to Seeckt's personal command were the Personnel Office, Troop Office (i.e., the clandestine general staff), Ordnance Office, the Office of the Inspectors of Weapons and Training, and the line of the Army. He wielded greater powers, therefore, than had any German military commander prior to this time. Unlike his predecessor, General Reinhardt, who had attempted to unify and centralize the control of Germany's armed forces, Seeckt sought to retain and reinforce the independent position of the Army.[10]

The new *Reichswehr* under Seeckt was designed as a dual purpose force. It was to be capable of operating as an efficient professional army of 100,000 or serving as the basis for an expanded national army, of at least three times its normal size. Although the Treaty of Versailles had specified a defensive mission for the new army, the doctrine was to be offensive in the German tradition of the elder Moltke and Schlieffen. Seeckt felt that the strategic concept which sought the destruction of the enemy's military forces was still valid, and that the experience of World War I dictated that this could best be achieved with mobile forces. The watchword of the new force was to be quality not quantity.[11]

The new army was to be a *Fuhrerheer*, an army of leaders, with only high quality personnel being recruited and retained. The officer selection process eliminated three out of every four, with preference being given to members of the general staff corps. The Treaty of Versailles stipulated that if an officer remained on duty he had to serve to age 45, or if he had enlisted he must serve for 25 years. The requirements for those aspiring to commissions were made more stringent than before. A young man had to be a graduate of a *Hochschule*. He then had to undergo a four-and-a-half-year training course successfully before he was considered for a commission. This did not end the selection process. If he subsequently failed to pass the examinations for the next higher grade, he was dismissed from the service. While in service, he had to apply himself to his profession and obey his superiors without question. No political activity or expression was tolerated. The *Reichswehr* was going to be a nonpolitical army, a clear manifestation of the reaction to the effects of political agitation in 1917-18.

These restrictions and personnel criteria, of course, presented recruiting problems. What could the officer candidate expect in the way of benefits for entering this Spartan program? First of all, he would enjoy a certain prestige. The Allies had tried but failed to destroy the spirit and prestige of the German Army completely. Its actions in helping to restore internal order in Germany immediately following the war greatly enhanced its relationship with the civilian community. Second, upon discharge the officer automatically received a civil service certificate, and if he entered government employ his military time counted toward retirement—war service counted double. Third, special lump sum payments were arranged for those who desired to enter business upon completion of service. Finally, compensation was granted for service-connected disabilities, and the disabled were accorded priority in the allocation of "low-cost housing."[12]

Just as the officer corps was a select group, so was the noncommissioned officer corps. Not only were the NCOs retained from the remnants of the Imperial Army, but others who were not selected for retention as NCOs were allowed to remain and serve in a lower grade. Therefore, the *Reichswehr* had a trained and experienced non commissioned officer corps far greater in numbers than that indicated by their authorized strength. As in the officer program, the standards were raised. A man had to serve three years to be eligible to take the promotion examinations. He could not, however, be promoted before his fourth year of service. Promotion was considerably more difficult in the *Reichswehr* than in the old Imperial Army, and the general level of intelligence and education of the NCOs was raised considerably.

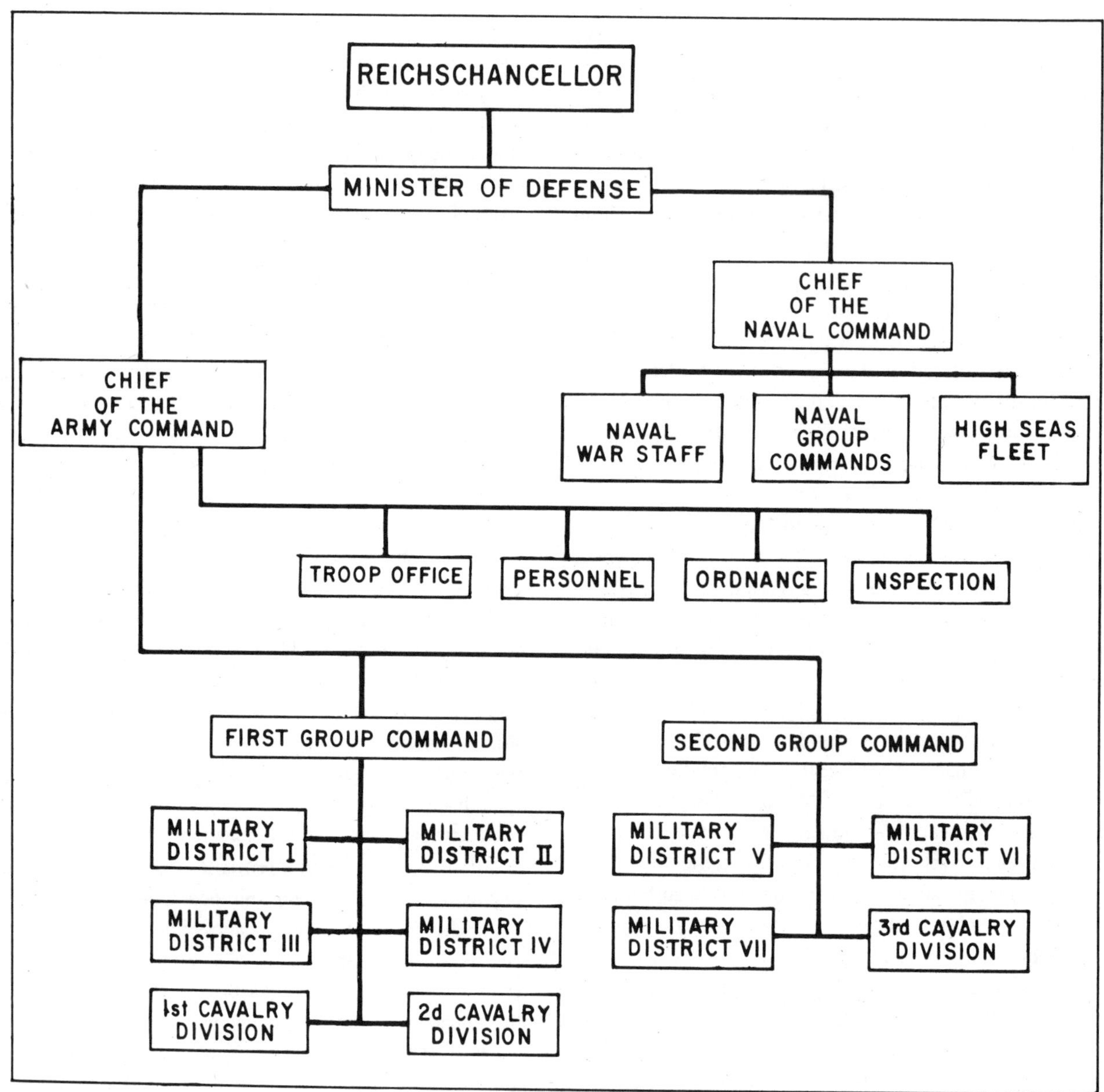

Organization of the *Reichswehr,* 1920-1935

Changes were also made which affected the soldier in the ranks. Emphasis was placed on obtaining recruits from rural areas and from the families of old soldiers, men who were in good physical condition and untainted with the bolshevism of the large urban areas. That recruit could expect better food and barracks, a higher pay scale, fewer restrictions on his personal movements, and a more liberal leave policy than had been experienced by his predecessor in the old Imperial Army. Discipline remained strict, but the idea was to treat the soldier as a human being rather than as a second-class citizen, which had formerly been the case.

Although the preservation of military traditions was to be a major factor in Seeckt's rebuilding of the Army, it was not allowed to stand in the way of needed reforms. Traditions determined to have little value were discarded. On the other hand, traditions which contributed to the development of spiritual strength and esprit were retained.[13]

The personnel program for the new Army would have been worthless without an effective training program by which Seeckt intended to create his army of leaders. The major efforts in this training program were directed toward mental and spiritual rearmament, the one area which the Allies were powerless to control. All ranks were encouraged to take an interest in the problems of national defense.

The enlisted man received thorough training in the use of weapons, small unit leadership, and tactical principles. Care was taken to prevent the training cycle over the 12-year enlistment from becoming merely repetitive and monotonous. Athletic training and competition, therefore, constituted a major portion of the training program. Steps were taken to identify early those men who displayed intelligence and ability and to develop them to their full capabilities. The mobile warfare of the Eastern Front and the infiltration tactics utilized in 1917-18 in the West had highlighted the need for resourceful and strong small unit leaders. The mobile doctrine which Seeckt envisioned would again require quality leadership at all levels. The squad would truly be the basic building block of the new Army.

Officer training was even more intensive and varied than the enlisted program. The stress was on combined-arms operations, officers being rotated among units throughout Germany to give them varied experience. New subjects, such as military geography and psychology, were introduced into the program of professional studies, and continued stress was placed on the study of military history and tactics. Training on modern arms, such as aircraft and tanks, was hindered because of treaty restrictions, but to compensate partially for this lack, the experiences and experiments of other countries with these weapons were studied. The reading, therefore, of foreign military books, regulations, and periodicals was encouraged. New ideas discovered in this manner were introduced into theoretical and practical exercises by means of mockups and other improvisations. Finally, and above all else, the officer was called upon continually to prove himself worthy of his rank and responsibilities.[14]

In the years prior to the First World War the German officer corps was viewed by foreigners as being a group of stiff, military martinets of whom the general staff officer was the archetype. That this view presented a paradox, most observers failed to notice, because they equated organization with bureaucracy and innovative efficiency with systematic routine. As the war continued, however, some perceptive western soldiers began to realize that perhaps they had only seen the facade of the German system. A British officer in 1915 wrote to his brother on this subject:

> The remarkable thing, as a soldier said to me the other day, is this—that when the war began we were all prepared for the Germans to be successful *at first* owing to their study of war and scientific preparation, but we argued that very soon we should become much better than they, not being hide-bound by a system. The exact contrary has been the case. The Germans with their foundation of solid study and experience have been far quicker to adapt themselves to the changed conditions of war and the emergencies of the situation than either we or the Russians have been—possibly even more so than the French.[15]

With the dictation of terms at Versailles, the old Great General Staff was replaced by the *Truppenamt*, and many of the old general staff agencies had to be hidden in other civilian offices in the Government.* The *Kriegsacademie* (War Academy), the foundation stone of the General Staff Corps, was also abolished. Seeckt felt that the select group of future high level commanders and staff officers, who formed the very core and spirit of the German Army, had to be preserved and their future existence guaranteed. The successful accomplishment of this goal may have been Seeckt's greatest contribution to the new *Reichswehr*.

Provisions of the treaty which abolished the *Kriegsacademie* also provided the loophole for its re-establishment, albeit in a different form. The *Reichswehr* was authorized two corps and ten divisional headquarters, and it was also permitted to train staff officers to fill vacancies which occurred in these staffs. Quite logically, therefore, a two-year general staff training course was established at each of the seven *Wehrkriese* (Military District) headquarters. This was followed by a third year of training for the student officer in Berlin through the subterfuge of "attaching" him to the Defense Ministry.

All army officers were required to take the entrance examination for general staff training. This normally took place when the officer had reached the rank of senior first lieutenant or junior captain. Preparation for this examination was an individual matter, and the emphasis was on applied tactics. Officers who passed the entrance examinations with a sufficiently high score—all were expected to pass—were given a choice of either tactical or technical training. The tactical (general staff) training was conducted at the *Wehrkriese* headquarters while the technical students were sent to the *Technische Hochschule* in Berlin. The general staff trainees served a "practical year" with troops between their second and third years of theoretical training; and during their summer months they also gained practical experience by serving with units in the various branches of the Army.[16]

*The historical and archival section was moved into a seven-story building in Potsdam and renamed the *Reichsarchiv*. The topographical section moved to the Ministry of the Interior, the railway section to the Ministry of Transport.

Air-Armor Cooperation as Practiced in England, 1927

This general staff training program was designed to provide a quality product which had passed through vigorous selective and attritive processes. The candidate was screened initially by the entrance examination and then again after each year and summer of the *Wehrkriese* courses. He was also evaluated on his performance during the "practical year." And, finally, he was scrutinized personally by either the Chief of the Army Training Department or the Chief of the *Truppenamt*. Failure at any point meant the officer's elimination and return to his parent unit. The system, obviously, was not designed to produce a large number of trained staff officers. Only about 14-17 officers completed the three-year program annually.

Another selection criterion, which carried as much weight as the evaluation of the student's performance in the classroom and in the unit, was the quality of his character. Great emphasis was placed upon selecting only those who displayed a willingness to work and shoulder responsibility. The general staff candidate had to display initiative, talent for improvisation and organization, decisiveness, ability to work independently, modesty and reserve. In short, he had to be a living example of the motto of the General Staff: "To be, rather than appear to be." These requirements were ideal, to be sure, and they were not always fully met; but they tended to stimulate a high level of performance.

The goal of the entire training program was to provide the young officer with the military knowledge which would enable him to be an effective high-level assistant chief of staff or commander later in his career. The main emphasis was placed on developing a uniform tactical view and command technique. Little time was devoted, therefore, to the problems of national policy, logistics, intelligence, joint military operations, or the solution of pending military problems. This was probably due to Seeckt's efforts to keep the army nonpolitical and his traditional view of the Army's role *vis-a-vis* the Navy and Defense Ministry. The result was that the young general staff officer was well grounded in tactical and operational matters but weak in many of the other important aspects of a modern military education.[17]

An officer's training was not considered complete when he donned the wine-red stripes of the General Staff. Seeckt felt that many of the failures in the First World War had resulted not from faulty doctrine or planning but because commanders and general staff officers at divisional levels and higher had not remained true to their theoretical training. He, therefore, instituted a policy of rotating general staff officers between command and staff assignments on a regular basis to prevent them from becoming too oriented on theory, thereby forgetting what units were actually capable of accomplishing. To further the idea that no one could afford to rest on his laurels, he instituted a series of tactical field trips to be attended annually by three special groups of commanders and staff officers. The first of these was called the *Wehrkriese* Trip. This exercise was under the supervision of each *Wehrkriese* commander. Included in this group were junior general staff officers who were performing troop duty or were waiting to become unit commanders. The Chiefs-of-Staff Trip constituted the second exercise. This exercise was under the direction of the Chief of the *Truppenamt* and was attended by general staff officers slated to be unit chiefs of staff. The third group, consisting of high level commanders and those slated for such positions, attended what was called the Commander's Trip. This exercise was under the personal direction of the Commander-in-Chief of the Army. The scope of the tactical problems increased at each level. During these trips, the officers were required to make their decisions and issue orders independently, without recourse to an operations officer or chief of staff. In this way, Seeckt was able to get a better feel for his commanders, forcing them to perform alone without their usual assistants.[18]

Another reason for Seeckt's insistence that commanders at all levels be capable of standing on their own two feet was that the role of the General Staff during The Great War had become exaggerated. This had been due in part to the old imperial system of appointing commanders who might or might not be qualified and backing them with good general staff officers. Under the new republic this was no longer a problem. Also, all commanders in the new army, beginning at division level, would be graduates of the general staff program. Seeckt reinforced the policy by stating that henceforth there would no longer be a sharing of responsibility between the commander and his chief of staff. The commander alone was responsible.

The technique of command in the German Army was one of its strongest and most representative characteristics. It was a technique which emphasized decisiveness, accuracy, clarity, brevity, and freedom of action.[19] The German General Staff and the products of its training have popularly been viewed as automatons because of their emphasis on uniformity of thinking. Nothing could be further from the truth. Uniformity in thinking resulted from the emphasis placed upon the requirement for all commanders and staff officers to base their decisions upon the overall concept of the operation. The idea was to keep free of any formal systematization which could develop into a dogma and impede the offensive spirit of the Army. Orders were issued in the form of a directive. This directive contained an estimate of the situation so that the subordinate could understand the logic of the order and also determine if the situation had changed and demanded new measures. A second paragraph stated his mission. How this mission was to be carried out was left strictly up to the subordinate commander. His training enforced the idea that he must make a quick, accurate estimate of the situation; decide how his mission could be accomplished; and settle upon the contents of a clear and brief directive. There were no approved solutions.[20]

In addition to devoting time to recruiting and training matters, Seeckt made major efforts in the fields of technological development and mobilization planning. In spite of restrictions, he undertook to keep Germany abreast of technological advances and planning for the economic mobilization necessary to support an Army, Navy, and potential Air Force. From the beginning, Seeckt took steps to preserve the nucleus of an air force. A subsection within the *Truppenamt* was staffed by flying officers and charged with keeping abreast of current air developments as well as the status of former military pilots. Another group (*Sondergruppe* R) was established in 1921 to handle the secret *Reichswehr*-Red Army agreements. The Treaty of Rapallo (April 1922) opened the way for the German military establishment to effect close military collaboration with the Russians.[21]

The Reichswehr wanted the Red Army to provide areas for testing aircraft, mechanized troops, and techniques associated with chemical warfare. They also wished to test ground weapons and to experiment with tactical theories. When the Russians concurred, it was agreed that they were to receive as payment access to all technical, tactical, and theoretical results obtained. Germany thereupon established an air training center in the Lipetsk-Voronezh-Borisoglebsk area south of Moscow which utilized Fokker planes purchased in Holland; similarly, a tank school was opened at Kama, near Kazan, in 1929. German officers also attended a Russian school for heavy artillery.

In the field of military-industrial collaboration, large amounts of ammunition were produced under German technical supervision in Soviet plants at Zlatoust in the Urals and the Tula plant in Leningrad. The old German firm of Krupp established an arms plant and an experimental tractor station on the Manych River near Rostov. The military-industrial arrangements were handled by the Trade Enterprises Development Company, an allegedly commercial firm established in 1921 with offices in Moscow and Berlin. The agreement with the Russians remained in force until Hitler ended it in 1935.[22]

Krupp was busy in places other than in Russia. The Allied Control Commission kept a close watch on its operations in Germany, but it was not completely successful in preventing the firm from circumventing the Treaty of Versailles. Krupp ingeniously began to manufacture items which appeared to be completely unrelated to the production of armaments, such as padlocks, cash registers, and trash carts. The secret, of course, was that the machinery and machinists who made these items could be rapidly shifted to arms production. This type of activity led to a rash of jokes, such as the one which alleged that a Krupp baby carriage could be taken apart and reassembled as a machinegun. The Navy was also using Krupp to keep abreast of submarine technology. The firm established a dummy company in Holland which built submarines for foreign navies, all the while utilizing German technicians and crews for construction and testing. A similar arrangement was negotiated with the Swedish firm of Bofors for the manufacture of artillery and tanks.[23]

In the matter of clandestine rearmament, however, the Navy and the Army essentially went their separate ways. The Army, even though it had no love for the revolutionary ideology espoused by the Soviets, recognized in Russia a potential collaborator. For its part, Russia, which had not signed the Treaty of Versailles and was ostrasized by the French and British, was receptive to the idea of re-establishing the frontiers of 1914. The Navy, on the other hand, looked toward a rapprochement with the British Navy. Any agreements reached with the Russians would solve none of the traditional strategic problems of the German Navy. That service believed that Great Britain was the leader of western culture—the United States was too far away and too little interested. Believing that the British would recognize enemies of bolshevism as allies, the Navy simply saw Russia as a political ploy to play off against England. This situation highlights the failure of the German leadership to establish an effective armed forces command which could coordinate military and naval activities with national policy.[24]

The treaty provisions prohibiting the formation and training of reserves were evaded in several ways. District commissioners (usually former officers) were appointed by Seeckt and charged with encouraging military virtues among the people of their respective districts. These officers, in effect, served as the basis for organizing a reserve officer corps. *Arbeits Kommandos* (labor troops) were formed for the ostensible purpose of locating and destroying contraband arms; in actuality, they comprised an army reserve which was financed, billeted, trained, and commanded by the *Reichswehr*. These labor battalions were soon superseded by a police organization called the *Schutzpolizei*; under the guise of being police, these units soon assumed a military character and were commanded by former army officers. They also took part in military maneuvers.[25]

The necessity for secrecy in all these operations prevented the Germans from training large groups of personnel, testing full-sized units, or accumulating large reserves of equipment and munitions. What they did accomplish was the design and development of work on weapons systems and the training of a core of officers and technicians in their use. As a result, when Hitler renounced the Treaty of Versailles in 1935, Germany was ready to proceed with a modern armaments program.

Transition from Reichswehr to Wehrmacht

On April 26, 1925, Field Marshal Paul von Hindenburg, the 78-year-old hero of Tannenberg, was elected President of the German Republic. Almost immediately Seeckt's star began to wane. With Hindenburg in office, the President as Commander-in-Chief of the armed forces was clothed in reality. His great reputation in Germany and in the Army made his replacement of Seeckt as the "royal shield" of the Army an easy transition for the officer corps. Moreover, Seeckt compounded his problem in the autumn of 1926 by stupidly allowing the next in line of royal succession, the grandson of the Kaiser, to appear in uniform at military maneuvers. Not unexpectedly, Seeckt's resignation was accepted on October 9, 1926. As noted above, he had accomplished much in his years as Commander-in-Chief of the Army. But not all of his influence was good. His retention of older, sometimes unproductive staff officers as well as some traditions contributed to a bureaucratic attitude at high levels; and his emphasis on an independent and nonpolitical army both hurt the development of a unified armed forces command and led to neglect of the study of national policy and economic mobilization by officers.[26]

The crash of the American stock market and the subsequent worldwide depression revived in Germany all the troubles of the early 1920s, only in a more virulent form. During these pre-depression years, the morale of the Army had declined because of its seemingly hopeless situation. To some extent, some army personnel were no longer willing to remain aloof and nonpolitical. They actively supported whatever political party seemed to offer a solution to the current chaos and the promise of stability and return to a normal life. In spite of Seeckt's attitude, the Army had gradually become more politicized; it thus provided fertile soil for the policies and ideas of Adolf Hitler, named German Chancellor on January 30, 1933.

By openly trying to revive a virile spirit of nationalism in the German people, the National Socialists under Hitler attracted the sympathies of many army officers. They advocated a repudiation of the Treaty of Versailles, German military parity, respect for the Army, and recognition of that service as the principal instrument of German defense. Following the elections of March 1933, the Nazis solidified their control of the governmental machinery. Hitler won further support from military circles by increasing the tempo of clandestine rearmament and linking the National Socialist revolution with the military traditions of Prussia.[27] On June 30, 1934, this relationship with the Army was further heightened by the purging of the leadership of the *Sturmabteilung* (SA), the military arm of the party.

On March 16, 1935, expansion and reorganization of Germany's military forces began. In a proclamation to the German people, Hitler repudiated the Treaty of Versailles, reintroduced conscription, and announced the expansion of the Army to 36 divisions and 12 corps. The *Reichswehr* was to be known henceforth as the *Wehrmacht*. The Minister of Defense was now titled the Minister of War and also Commander-in-Chief of the Armed Forces. The head of each armed service was designated as the Commander-in-Chief of his respective service. As things began to move again, a deep and genuine enthusiasm for Hitler's policies pervaded the military ranks. He wasted little time, following President Hindenburg's death, in consolidating his authority over the new *Wehrmacht*. On August 20, 1934, all officers and men took the required personal oath to serve Adolf Hitler:

> I swear by God this sacred oath, that I will render unconditional obedience to Adolf Hitler, the Fuehrer of the German Reich and people, Supreme Commander of the Armed Forces, and will be ready as a brave soldier to risk my life at any time for this oath.[28]

When the *Wehrmacht* was created and the shackles of Versailles cast off, a battle began between the armed forces and the office of the War Minister. The cause of this internecine fray was the question of the allocation of responsibilities among these various agencies. General Werner von Blomberg, the War Minister, felt that he should exercise command; that an armed forces general staff should be established to control the operations of the Army, the Navy, and the Air Force during wartime; and that certain agencies for ordnance and administration should be centralized under the control of the War Ministry to effect better utilization of resources.

The major protagonist against this proposal was the Army. Commander-in-Chief, General Freiherr von Fritsch, and his

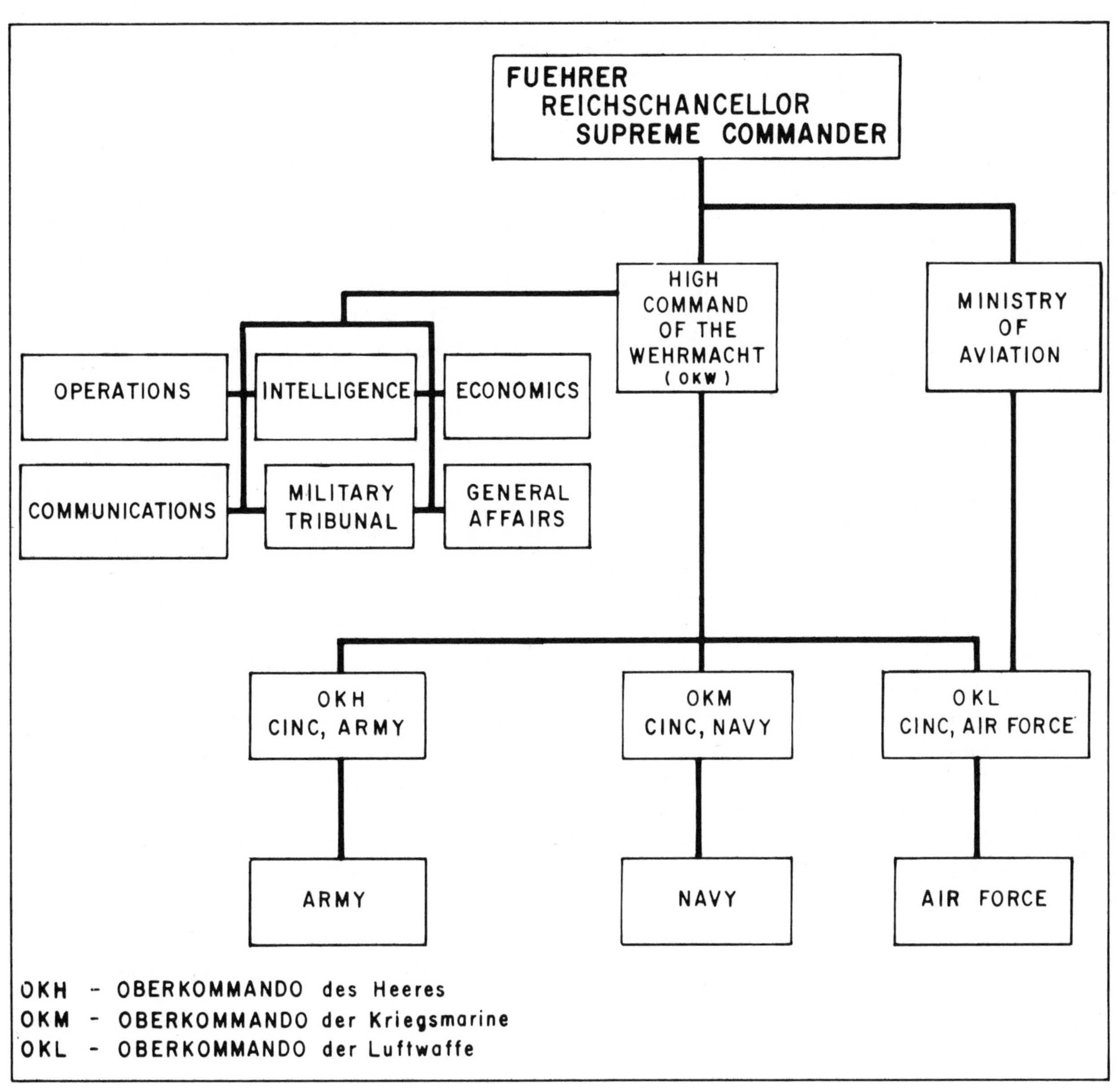

Hitler's Reorganization of the Command Structure

brilliant Chief of the General Staff, General Ludwig Beck, ably presented the counter argument. The Army's position was that any future war, be it offensive or defensive, would be decided by land battles. The Navy would carry out its predetermined mission and the Air Force would assist the Army. The army high command should, therefore, assume the functions of an advisory staff to the armed forces commander and plan all joint operations.[29] Although the Navy also opposed the creation of an armed forces general staff, it did not entirely agree with the Army's line of reasoning. General Hermann Goering, Commander-in-Chief of the *Luftwaffe*, felt that he could not share control of the *Luftwaffe* or the aeronautical industry with any outside agency.*

There was another aspect to this conflict aside from the questions of military precedence and prerogatives. During their rise to power, the National Socialists had actively courted the favor of the Army and Navy. As a result, the armed services had retained an autonomous position within the German state. The Nazis had needed their support in the past, and Hitler would require their services in the future. He did not, however, intend that the armed forces should occupy a position which could challenge his ultimate authority.

On November 5, 1937, Hitler laid his cards on the table and announced to his service chiefs his "irrevocable decision to solve the German problem of living space no later than 1943-45, possibly even as early as 1938 and by force."[30] Generals Blomberg and Fritsch challenged his stand. As a result, each was out of a job by February of the following year. Blomberg was relieved ostensibly because of his marriage to a woman of ill repute, and Fritsch was accused of homosexual practices.[31] Hitler's relief of Blomberg and Fritsch eliminated their active opposition to his plans and resolved the question of who would exercise supreme command. The post of Minister of War was abolished (on February 4, 1938), and Hitler exercised supreme command, utilizing Blomberg's old staff—now called the *Oberkommando der Wehrmacht* (OKW)—and thereby earning the enmity of a number of army and navy officers.

Hitler had now combined the positions of Supreme Commander and Commander-in-Chief of the Armed Forces in his own person. The Commanders-in-Chief of the armed services were now directly subordinate to the head of state. Although unity of command over the entire *Wehrmacht* had been established, it might be questioned how satisfactory the arrangement appeared—even at that time. Hitler would be hard-pressed to find time to devote to the multiplicity of responsibilities he had now taken under his personal purview. He was simultaneously the Chief of State, head of the Nazi Party, Minister of War, and Supreme Commander—a sizable job for any man, even with competent help. Hitler's primary assistant for armed forces matters was General Wilhelm Keitel, Chief of the OKW. Keitel had no independent prerogatives of command—he was the executive agent for Hitler, essentially an administrative assistant.† Fritsch's replacement as Commander-in-Chief of the Army was the more malleable General Walther von Brauchitsch. The portent for the future was clear for those who paused to reflect—Hitler intended to exercise command of the armed forces and control over the conduct of operations personally.

While the battle raged over the prerogatives and responsibilities within the *Wehrmacht* high command, the separate services began their precipitate expansion. This rush to rearm would create a force which, because of its apparent strength and capability, would cow many of Germany's potential adversaries. Moreover, in its first real test in battle, that force would not reveal its major flaws.

Hitler's announced 1936 expansion target of 36 divisions and 12 corps hit the Army General Staff like a thunderbolt. The staff planners preferred to follow Seeckt's guideline of an initial expansion to 21 divisions, firmly convinced that quality could only be retained by a slower pace of expansion. But since Hitler was determined to have the Army ready for war by 1940—or at the latest by 1942-1943—the tempo of rearmament had to be increased. There was another conflict in philosophy. The more conservative members of the army high command, such as Fritsch and Beck, tended to think along traditional lines; they were not very enamored of the new ideas on mechanization, armor, and aircraft. The *Fuehrer* felt otherwise.

Between 1936 and 1939, the expansion program made considerable progress. Three *panzer* (armored) divisions had been authorized in 1935, and two years later four motorized infantry and one light division were added. By 1939, the active army numbered approximately 750,000 and included 54 divisions; there were also about 1,100,000 men in reserve, organized into 51 infantry divisions.[32] The reserve, which was incorporated into a revised mobilization plan in 1938, also furnished headquarters personnel and service support units. The new mobilization plan was designed to be implemented in four phases over seven days, at the end of which a new headquarters would be ready to direct functions within Germany, freeing *Oberkommando des Heeres* (OKH) to guide wartime operations.

*Goering also held cabinet rank as Minister of Aviation. He and Heinrich Himmler, Chief of the *Schutzstaffel* (SS), both aspired to the position of Commander-in-Chief of the Armed Forces. The subsequent sordid events which led to the relief of Blomberg and the resignation of Fritsch were the product of their conspiratorial machinations. They desired to discredit the leadership of the general officer corps. With this accomplished, each hoped that he would be named Commander-in-Chief.

†Although Keitel was a member of the General Staff Corps, he was not highly regarded by his fellow officers. He was frequently referred to as the "nodding ass" or "the supine Keitel" because of his reticence to challenge Hitler's directions and curb his flights of fancy.

As had been the case with his immediate predecessors, Grand Admiral Erich Raeder, Commander-in-Chief of the Navy from 1929 to 1943, was confronted with the problem of what the strategic doctrine of the new Navy should be. In short, a choice needed to be made between a battle fleet or a naval coastal defense force. Under the Treaty of Versailles, the German fleet was restricted to: six 10,000-ton heavy cruisers armed with 11-inch guns; six 6,000-ton cruisers with 6-inch guns; 24 torpedo boats; and a number of auxiliary craft. No aircraft, aircraft carriers, or submarines were allowed. Restrictions on personnel were the same as those imposed on the Army. The vessels in being were of World War I vintage. The Navy, therefore, like the Army, could afford to—and did—think along new strategic lines, unfettered by an inventory of obsolete and aging equipment.

Who were Germany's potential enemies during the 1920s and early 1930s? The Treaty of Versailles had resulted in Poland being considered a potential threat, with France and Russia being added later. *(See Map 1, in Atlas.)* The Navy, particularly under Raeder, forbade any planning or wargaming aimed at Great Britain as an adversary. The Royal Navy was viewed as a potential ally. A naval coalition which included Germany's recognized enemies as well as Great Britain presented to German naval commanders a hopeless situation.[33] The objective, therefore, of any major rebuilding of the Navy must be to create a fleet which would be of value to the British as an ally. But German naval planners also wanted a balanced fleet, one which could threaten French commerce in the Atlantic and thereby disperse her naval strength. At the same time, the German Navy could bring the badly needed imports through the North Sea into the German Baltic ports, assisted, one supposes, by the assumed British ally. The first step along these lines was taken in 1931 with the launching of the pocket battleship *Deutschland.* In 1933, however, the new German government was in no hurry to expand the Navy, primarily because Hitler did not wish to antagonize the British during his revitalization of Germany's strength and international position.

The London Naval Treaty of June 1935 created options for Germany and gave Raeder the way to build his balanced fleet. It also quite possibly strengthened the wishful thinking of the German Naval Staff that Great Britain would be an ally in the next war. By the terms of this treaty, Germany could build up to 35 percent of British tonnage in all categories except submarines; for the latter, the limit was 45 percent of British submarine tonnage. The Germans could, however, by giving special notice, build just submarines, up to 100 percent of their total authorized tonnage.* Germany commenced work immediately on her first increment, including the battleships *Scharnhorst* and *Gneisenau*, 3 heavy cruisers, 16 destroyers, 28 U-Boats, and various fleet auxiliaries. The battleships *Bismarck* and *Tirpitz* followed shortly thereafter.

*On the surface, this appears to be a rather singular agreement, considering the havoc created by the German submarine fleet in World War I.

	1932	1935	1936	1937	1938	1939
ARMY GROUPS	2	3	3	4	6	6
CORPS	—	11	13	14	21	21
INFANTRY DIVISION	7	24	36	32	35	36
INFANTRY DIV (Motorized)	—	—	—	4	4	4
LIGHT DIV (Motorized)	—	—	—	1	4	4
PANZER DIVISION	—	3	3	3	5	7
MOUNTAIN DIVISION	—	1	1	1	3	3
CAVALRY DIVISION	3	2	—	—	—	—
CAVALRY BRIGADE	—	1	1	1	1	1
ACTIVE DIVISIONS	10	31	41	42	52	54
RESERVE DIVISIONS	—	—	—	29	40	51

Expansion of the German Army, 1932-39*

*Sources disagree as to the size and strength of the German Army during the period 1932-1939. This chart was composed from the following sources which are in relatively close agreement: Burkhart von Mueller-Hillebrand, *Das Heer Bis Zum Kriegbegnin* (Darmstadt, 1954), p. 25; Telford Taylor, *Sword and Swastika* (New York, 1952), p. 325; Robert M. Kennedy, *The German Campaign in Poland* (Washington, 1956), p. 25.

The German Battleship, *Scharnhorst*

Captain Karl Doenitz was placed in charge of U-Boat development, training, and operations. Doenitz had the first increment of 24 submarines ready within a year, and then developed a method of concentrating them against heavily defended convoys. This controlled operation would be known as "wolf pack tactics" in World War II. Improved radio equipment on the new boats made the tactic possible by allowing them to be directed by a scout (another submarine, a disguised merchantman, or aircraft). Doenitz, in 1937, urged the expansion of the U-Boat fleet because he felt war with Great Britain was not far off. Raeder, however, did not agree, and the concentration on large surface elements continued.[34]

In 1938 Hitler shattered Raeder's plans by telling him that he now considered war with England a definite possibility. Thus caught in mid-stride in the naval expansion program, Raeder offered Hitler a choice of two plans. One, assuming war to be imminent, called for emphasis on commerce-raiding weapons: U-Boats, surface raiders, mine layers, and coastal defensive forces. The other, known as Plan Z, was a long-range plan which assumed another ten years of peace. It envisioned building a battle fleet which could wrest control of the seas from the Royal Navy. Hitler endorsed Plan Z. Whatever his reason for this decision, he left the Navy in no position to fight a war; on September 1, 1939, the German Navy had 2 battleships and 3 pocket battleships in commission, 2 more battleships building, 3 heavy cruisers and 6 light cruisers, a respectable number of destroyers and fleet auxiliaries, 56 submarines, and no aircraft carriers.[35]

The fact that there were no aircraft carriers in the German fleet by the autumn of 1939 is significant. As early as 1932 there had been plans to create a naval air arm complete with its own carriers. The Navy, like the Army, had given up a number of good men to help flesh out the fledgling German Air Force (*Luftwaffe*), and it expected to receive in return 62 squadrons by 1942. In anticipation of eventually creating a naval air arm, the carrier *Graf Zepplin* was laid down; it was never completed because Goering claimed responsibility for *all* air operations, over land or sea. Goering's position in the party and the Government added weight to his views. In January 1939, the Navy and the *Luftwaffe* reached an agreement which gave the Navy responsibility for controlling sea-air reconnaissance and air operations during contact between naval forces; all other air operations were to be the concern of the *Luftwaffe*. As with many other things, Goering did not understand the sea and made no effort to come to grips with the problems of naval air operations. He fared a little better with organizational problems in the Air Force.

When Seeckt resigned in 1926, he left an air force which totaled four flying sqûadrons. This small beginning of what was to become the famous *Luftwaffe* had been made possible by the Treaty of Rapallo with Russia in 1922. A large number of Germany's future air leaders (to include Albert Kesselring, Hugo Sperrle, and Hans Stumpf, who would command the three fleets in the Battle of Britain) passed through the Russian flying school at Lipetzk. Kurt Student, the future German airborne-operations expert, also received his initial training in Russia.

Although the treaty ban on the German construction of civil aircraft was lifted in 1922, there were still formidable obstacles to the development of a military air arm. Restrictions on size and performance still remained, and this impacted on the German aircraft-engine industry which could thus acquire no experience with heavy aircraft engines. Accordingly, like the Army, the fledgling airmen had to rely on foreign technical journals and visits to foreign aircraft factories. This situation was eased by the Paris Air Agreement of 1926, which lifted the additional restrictions on the construction of civil aircraft. Moreover, the development and testing of aircraft was in the hands of a civilian agency, the Air Transport Ministry.[36] But the amalgamation of Germany's two financially unstable airlines into *Lufthansa* in effect provided the fledgling air force with a training school in Germany.* To this school were sent the most promising pilots discovered in the *Deutscher Luftportsverband*, a sport glider program under the direction of Student, now a member of the Air Technical Branch of the *Reichswehr*.[37] Although a marginal training and technical development program for Germany's clandestine military air force had been established by the late 1920s, the fundamental problem as to what type of air force it should be, nevertheless, remained to be resolved.

*The use of *Lufthansa* resulted in positive military advantages. Instrument flying, long distance flights, and flights over foreign territory could only be conducted with the aid of the *Lufthansa* organization.

While the majority of military thinkers favored the creation of a tactical air force, there was a minority, led by Lieutenant General Walther Wever, which advocated a more balanced force with both strategic and tactical capabilities. Consideration also had to be given to defining the relationship of the new Air Force to the Army and Navy. The Army leadership felt that it should remain as an integral part of the Army. In direct opposition to this view was a group, led by ex-army pilot Hermann Goering, which advocated the establishment of a separate air force. The Navy also envisioned creating its own air fleet.

Shortly after assuming the Chancellorship, Hitler directed Goering to create a new German Air Force secretly and in the shortest possible time. Goering accepted the challenge and never seemed to consider that his successful role as a fighter pilot in World War I might not necessarily have qualified him to be a brilliant air strategist. This was to be the *Luftwaffe*'s greatest problem—lack of effective direction of the entire aviation program. Goering's fatal weakness seemed to be that he had trouble concentrating on any one subject for extended periods of time. He was simultaneously to be Hitler's successor-designee, Aviation Minister, Prussian Minister of the Interior, *Reichsjaegermeister*, Commissioner for the German Four Year Economic Plan, Commander-in-Chief of the *Luftwaffe*, and frequent dabbler in diplomacy. He has been compared, by Germans, to Henry VIII. There may, indeed, be some similarity: if Henry had too many wives, Goering had too many jobs. Another factor which contributed to the problems of the expanding *Luftwaffe* was Goering's declining health. He suffered from weight and glandular problems; he took large amounts of various tonics, pills, and medicines; and he was still prone to morphine injections, a result of the Beer Hall Putsch of 1923.[38] His frequent bouts of illness often kept him from attending to his various responsibilities.

Although the German aviation industry made great strides during the late 1920s and early 1930s, the progress was along the lines of invention and in the development of prototypes rather than in the construction of an air force around a solid body of strategic thought. In the initial stages of the *Luftwaffe*'s development, there was the beginning of a comprehensive air strategy. The man responsible for this was Walther Wever, Chief of Staff of the new *Luftwaffe*, and the man considered by many to be its best brain. He embraced many of the ideas of the Italian air theorist, Giulio Douhet, an exponent of the value of the heavy bomber and strategic bombing. Under Wever's guidance, two prototypes of four-engine heavy bombers were developed by the Dornier and Junkers aircraft firms, the DO-19 and JU-89. This promising line of development came to a halt, however, with Wever's death in an air crash near Dresden in 1936. Wever had clearly seen the interrelationship between air weaponry and strategy, but he was not followed by anyone else of comparable vision and ability.

Wevers's Vision: The Ural Bomber

Wever's death highlights the main problem of the *Luftwaffe*—finding qualified personnel to plan and direct its development. Upon its official creation as a separate service of the *Wehrmacht* in 1935, the *Luftwaffe* turned for its personnel, in the main, to the Army and the Navy, services which were also feeling the personnel strains of Hitler's armed forces expansion. Goering induced several of his old comrades from the Richthofen Flying Circus of World War I fame to accept positions in the new *Luftwaffe*, but upwards of three-quarters of the top-ranking leaders came from the Army or, to lesser degree, the Navy. Most of these officers were not pilots and had little knowledge of air theory or technology.[39] The hierarchy of the *Luftwaffe* thus comprised an odd assortment of personalities, experience, and varying service allegiances. In 1936, the pressure on the newest service began with the reoccupation of the Rhineland and the loss of Wever's steadying and guiding hand.

The Spanish Civil War (1936-1939) gave the Germans their first opportunity to test a large number of their personnel and aircraft in combat. It was in Spain that the Condor Legion, the name given to the German fighting men and support troops sent by Germany to aid the Spanish Nationalists, developed specialized dive-bombing techniques. The *Luftwaffe* entered the Spanish Civil War with a solid doctrinal background in tactical support of ground forces which had been developed for the *Schlachstaffeln* (Battle Flights) of the German Air Force in 1917 and 1918.[40] Therefore, its adoption of the Junkers 87, a specialized dive bomber which proved to be an effective close support aircraft, is hardly surprising. The apparent ineffectiveness of Spanish Republican air defenses, both ground and air, furthered the trend of developing the light bomber (Dornier DO-17 and Heinkel HE-111) as the real backbone of the

The *Luftwaffe* Was a Tactical Air Force

Luftwaffe. The Messerschmitt BF-109 also demonstrated its worth in Spain as a short-range fighter, and the Germans developed the new finger-four formation for fighters during this period.* In addition, there was a concentrated effort on developing the use of radio communications between tanks and supporting aircraft to speed up the reaction time from target identification to attack.[41] But the specialized operations in Spain blinded the Germans to other eventualities. They failed to consider that a large theater of operations would require deep penetrations with the danger of constant and sustained attack by enemy fighters and antiaircraft guns. Other factors overlooked were capabilities for logistical support and transport of troops demonstrated by the Junkers JU-52 and the need for an effective early warning system for air defense.

The *Luftwaffe* got little rest or time to train between 1936 and September 1939. The occupation of the Rhineland in 1936, the annexation of Austria in 1937, and the Sudetenland crisis of 1938 called for exaggerated displays of strength by the German Air Force.† As a result, the organization was in early continuous use. Although the *Luftwaffe* had 4,303 operational aircraft available on September 1, 1939, and was the world's most powerful air force, it was a short-ranged and short-winded tactical air force.[42] Goering added to these organizational and operational problems by insisting that the new airborne units and the air defense artillery formations come under the command of the *Luftwaffe*..

*The standard V formation was found to be unsuited for the faster modern fighters. As a result, the finger-four formation, which resembles the ends of the hand's four fingers, extended close together, was adopted.

†Much of the reported strength of the *Luftwaffe* was pure fiction. The picture of great depth in numbers of aircraft and trained personnel was created by an elaborate deception. Aircraft were moved from one airfield to another, squadron markings were changed, unserviceable aircraft were rolled out for display as flyable machines, and ground personnel were paraded in flying togs as trained air crewmen.

Economic Preparation for War

In an address to a capacity crowd in Hamburg in 1936, Hermann Goering put the question of rearmament squarely to the German people and the world:

> We have no butter, my friends, but I ask you—would you rather have butter or guns? Shall we import lard or metal ores? Let me tell you—preparedness makes us powerful. Butter merely makes us fat![43]

The crowd howled with laughter at Goering's reference to obesity, and roared their approval of his answer to the question. If he had wanted a form of public approval, Hitler now had his answer; rearmament on a more intensive scale could begin.

The extensive rearmament accredited to Germany beginning with Hitler's accession to power, however, is largely a myth. The Nazis were proceeding cautiously although Hitler asserted that it was Germany's lot to defend Europe against bolshevism and that only more *lebensraum* (living space) could solve the German food problems. War, therefore, was inevitable, as he saw it. The German Propaganda Ministry, the speeches of the Nazi hierarchy, and the guided tours of German industry conducted for the benefit of visiting foreign dignitaries and military leaders tended to create the impression of a much vaster program than in reality existed. Actual German production of aircraft and tanks in 1939 was 60 and 45 percent respectively of western intelligence estimates.[44]

In the prewar period, the German economy catered both to guns and to butter. The expenditure on armaments from 1933 to 1938 was only about 10 percent of the gross national product. The civilian consumer industries and government nonwar expenditures equalled the peak years of the 1920s. Obviously, if war was a strong possibility, German leadership did not harness the economy in the prewar years to prepare for it. These leaders, however, clearly recognized their insufficiency in such war essential materials as iron ore, ferro alloys, oil, copper, rubber, aluminum, and foodstuffs. But on the eve of World War II, a stockpiling program found Germany with only a six-months' supply of estimated needs on hand. Only in rubber and foodstuffs did Germany ever achieve a substantial degree of self-sufficiency. And the labor force was increased only to the extent necessary to eliminate unemployment.

With the danger of war imminent, why did the Germans not fully prepare their economy to fight it? A complete answer to this question may never be found, but any analysis must take into consideration several plausible reasons. First, Hitler's view of the coming conflict did not include a protracted war of attrition against a coalition of major powers. The lessons of World War I clearly pointed out Germany's inability to win a war of this nature. He planned on a series of small wars against isolated opponents, who were to be overcome by subversion, by intimidation, and, finally, if necessary, by a short, quick military campaign. This was to be accomplished before the other powers could decide on intervention. The military force he visualized for this type of strategy need only comprise 50 or 60 first-line divisions with a supporting air force of 2,000 combat aircraft. Second, the Nazi government was unwilling to increase rearmament funding by deficit spending. The party, still in the process of consolidating gains, wanted to retain and increase its popular support. Deficit spending would cause loss of confidence in the currency and lead to inflation. Third, the alternative to deficit spending was higher taxes. Since this would reduce the purchasing power of the average German, the people looked upon this with disfavor. It was, accordingly, not a real alternative. Fourth, there was no real central agency responsible for coordinating the materiel demands of the German armed forces. The armed forces competed against each other throughout the war, a phenomenon not peculiar to Germany. Finally, Hitler failed to subordinate the various Nazi Party programs to his own desires. The industrialists, for example, had interests which were never completely controlled. Hitler's decision, therefore, was to use the existing industrial base rather than expand it. Building or modifying an economy to fight a prolonged war would have required a postponement of military operations until 1943. This Hitler would not accept. Moreover, he felt that between campaigns priorities in armaments could be shifted within the industrial base to provide for what was needed for the next limited campaign (e.g., emphasis on tanks and aircraft one time, U-boats and ships the next).[45]

Doctrinal Development

The September 25, 1939, issue of *Time* magazine described the German campaign in Poland as "a war of quick penetration and obliteration—*Blitzkrieg*, lightning war." It further accurately stated that this form of mobile warfare was not new, but merely its implements: the tank, the airplane, and mechanized infantry. To better understand why the Germans first successfully developed this form of *Bewegungskrieg* (mobile warfare), it is necessary to go back in German military history to the time of the elder Moltke. Here begins the very core of German strategic and tactical doctrine and the creation of the intellectual environment in which this doctrine was progressively developed.

Helmuth von Moltke's theory of operations, if it may be termed that, can be summarized as "the development of the original leading idea [objective sought] in conformity with ever changing circumstances in order to achieve maximum strategic results."[46] The desired strategic result, in Moltke's view, was the realization of the dictum "that the most imperative objective in war is the annihilation of the enemy's combat forces."[47] Here begins the central idea behind German doctrinal development, the idea of decisive annihilation. But Moltke was realist enough to see that to destroy the enemy in one decisive battle might not always be practicable. In other words, if it was a goal to be aimed at, in practice it would probably seldom be achieved. His advice was that the commander should base his future actions upon his recent successes even though they did not conform to his original thoughts. Use of common sense, then, was Moltke's doctrinal guideline. His legacy to future German commanders was that they should seek the quick and decisive solution by one blow at the enemy's front and flank if possible; but, understanding the impact of technology, they must determine the best ways and means of accomplishing this, always recognizing that the risks would be great.[48]

Count Graf von Schlieffen, Chief of the German General Staff from 1892 to 1905, imbued Moltke's ideas with special significance. Schlieffen's solution to the problem of how to defeat the superior forces of Germany's enemies was to attack their flank and rear in an attempt for a quick solution. The development of the machinegun and quick-firing field gun provided the necessary means to compensate for lack of troops. Firepower would hold the enemy front while the main attack moved against the flank and rear. Schlieffen emphasized that the blow should fall suddenly and thus cause the surprised enemy to change front—at a disadvantage. Moreover, Schlieffen recognized that Germany faced the probability of a two-front war. It would have to fight a war of maneuver, seeking quick decisive victories; the maneuver ideally should be to turn the enemy's flank. But Schlieffen was pragmatist enough to recognize that turning the flank of an entire army might not be possible; in that case, a penetration and smaller encirclements might be dictated. The basic tenet still held, however—attempt to turn the enemy's flank and quickly destroy him.[49]

The trouble was that postwar German planners faced the reality that the 1914 Schlieffen Plan had failed. Seeckt's reappraisal of the war's campaigns, however, led to the conviction that usually it was the command echelon which had failed, not the basic doctrine. If there had been problems with logistics, mobility, and communications, the central concept was still sound. Destruction of the enemy forces in quick, decisive, offensive battles, accordingly, remained the keystone of German strategic and tactical doctrine. Seeckt felt that success could not be insured by reliance upon a weapons system because the same technology which created it would also create the appropriate defense. The answer lay in the intellectual application of new weapons to the battlefield and not in the materiel itself. Only in thought and application could real surprise and success be achieved. The officers must be imbued with the spirit of boldness and action which the doctrine demanded.[50]

The strategic and tactical doctrine under which an army fights, however, is the result of the interrelationship of many factors. Because of Germany's geographic location the problem of a two-front war was still present. Moreover, the Army was charged by the Treaty of Versailles with a mission of defense, further complicated by limits on weapons, no mobilization base or reserves, budgetary restrictions, and the requirement to defend an irregular border several hundred miles long. The logical doctrine to adopt was a mobile one which emphasized a form of maneuver that led to quick decisions and incorporated surprise, quick local concentrations, and heavy firepower.[51]

Seeckt, because of his experience on the Eastern Front, naturally favored mobile operations. While he did not think mechanized units possessed the flexibility and mobility of cavalry, he early began experiments with motorized forces. His idea initially was to gain greater mobility and logistic support through motorization rather than through the increased use of armored vehicles. He also placed great emphasis on the close support of ground operations by aircraft. The maneuvers of 1925 and 1927 began to draw attention to the significance of the tank. Even Seeckt began to see that it had its own distinct role. But what this role would be was as yet unclear.

In 1928, Heinz Guderian, who had been an early advocate of the use of armor, got his chance. The *Reichswehr*'s Motor Transport Service expanded its training program to include tactics, the employment of tanks, and their cooperation with other arms. Guderian was charged with giving the lecture course on tank tactics. Here he could be a creator since there was no doctrinal background in existence in the German Army. The German tank school at Kazan, Russia, did not become fully operational until 1929, and then it was mainly concerned with prototype testing. Guderian, therefore, had to rely for his lecture material on the German evaluation of World War I experiences, the reports on field maneuvers of motorized and armored formations in Great Britain and France, and the works of such military writers as J. F. C. Fuller, Basil H. Liddell Hart, Giffard Martel, and later Charles DeGaulle.* Guderian was not the only advocate of armor in the German Army; but he was the most vocal, an attribute which periodically got him into trouble with the more traditional thinkers in the Army.[52]

The idea that the next war would see continuous fronts was nearly universal. Any attempt, therefore, to create a fluid situation on the battlefield which offered the opportunity for decisive action through maneuver would have to begin with a penetration of the enemy front. Wheeled and tracked vehicles could provide the necessary speed and mobility for troop and logistic concentration and movements. Armored vehicles could pro-

*Guderian, in his works on armored warfare published prior to World War II, speaks frequently of Fuller and DeGaulle but makes no mention of Liddell Hart.

A Fiesler Storch–The Eyes of the *Panzers*

The Cutting Edge of the *Blitzkrieg*

vide the necessary fire support which could be reinforced by close support aviation. And the radio permitted widespread operations to be more effectively directed and coordinated. The requisite means were now at hand to place the battle of annihilation within reach. Whose idea it was originally to use armor in deep penetrations is difficult to say. In all likelihood, it was an amalgamation of parallel thought and developments which crystallized in Germany rather than in some other country. These ideas came to fruition in Germany, rather than in France or Great Britain, because they fitted into Seeckt's concept of the new mobile army, supplemented traditional German doctrine of the offense, and would attract Hitler's attention in 1938 as a fitting tool of his foreign policy.[53]

The combination of the World War I experience, foreign and local thought, and recognition of technological advances were combined by the Germans into the doctrine of the *blitzkrieg*. Simply stated, it was a system of weapons and tactics capable of piercing an enemy's front and then encircling and destroying all or part of his forces. It was characterized by speed, violence, and retention of the initiative. In practice, the *blitzkrieg* featured extensive and continuous reconnaissance to locate weak points followed by the rupture of continuous fronts at several points called *schwerpunkt* (thrust points). Powerful *kampfgruppen* (combat teams) were to be concentrated on a narrow frontage. The Germans felt that deception of the enemy for any length of time was highly unlikely due to modern means of reconnaissance; therefore, the essential element of surprise could only be preserved through mobility and rapidity in execution of the attack. Prepared positions which could not be bypassed were to be ruptured by successive attack impulses, and the enemy command was to be dislocated and confused by the rapidity of the advance. Initial objectives were specifically designated, but the guideline for subsequent advance was primarily to deepen the penetration. While the armored combat teams forced their way deeper into the enemy's rear, follow-on units (normally infantry) would conduct the *aufrollen* maneuver—that is, expand the breaches in the enemy line and fan out to encircle bypassed enemy units and strongpoints and destroy them. The combat team or local concentration at each *schwerpunkt* was to be continually maintained by units pressing up from the rear through the breaches in the enemy defensive position. Although communications means had improved to the point where reconnaissance information could be readily evaluated, local concentrations quickly ordered, and new attack orders issued, the whole doctrinal concept of the *blitzkrieg* rested on the training and initiative of the unit leaders. This held true from squad to corps level.[54]

A unit capable of conducting this type of an operation was not in existence until 1935 in the German Army. Fritsch had not been convinced up to this time that a division could be so controlled as to adapt itself to the quick ebb and flow of the *blitzkrieg* battle as envisioned by Guderian and other armored proponents. But the maneuvers of August 1935, featuring the control of an armored division by radio, cleared away Fritsch's doubts. The *panzer* division was born.[55] Guderian concluded that tanks alone were highly vulnerable and would be faced with situations which called for assistance from other specialized arms. The German *panzer* division, therefore, consisted not only of tanks and motorized infantry but also of mechanized reconnaissance, engineer, antitank, artillery, and signal units. The French came to the same conclusion, but they devised a different solution, as we shall see. In addition to the *panzer* divisions, four light divisions were organized, and four standard infantry divisions were fully motorized. The light divisions contained one tank battalion which was transported on trailers, thus giving the unit a uniform speed capability.

Believing that a smaller organization represented less of a threat, the Allies had forced the triangular division on the German Army through the Treaty of Versailles. If the Allies felt they were discommoding the Germans by this, they were mistaken. The Germans had adopted this division in 1917 because it was a more flexible organization and better suited infiltration tactics. Now the triangular organization was adopted throughout the Army up through the corps level. This gave each level of command two units to commit and one held in reserve as a maneuver element with which to meet rapidly changing situations. In short, it exactly fitted the aggressive tactics which permeated German doctrine.

The other unique feature of German military organization was the nearly universal application of the *Einheit* principle. Simply speaking, this was an attempt to make standard units independent and self-sustaining. Sufficient weapons and manpower, coupled with the necessary supply and administrative means, were given to each battalion, regiment, and division so that they could carry on their respective roles when forced to operate independently. Special emphasis was placed upon heavy weapons for the infantry. It was felt that the regiment should have sufficient firepower to deal with hostile automatic weapons, without constantly calling for artillery support. The *Einheit* principle also lessened the need for making unit attachments and detachments, because no major reorganization of support elements was required. The principle was also extended to the logistics system by arranging loads of ammunition and supplies in *Einheits*. This allowed the division and army supply trains, which were standardized at 30 and 60 tons respectively, to arrive at a railhead supply point, to load, and then to transport a standardized 30- or 60-ton *Einheit* with a minimum of labor and loss of time. The German view of future

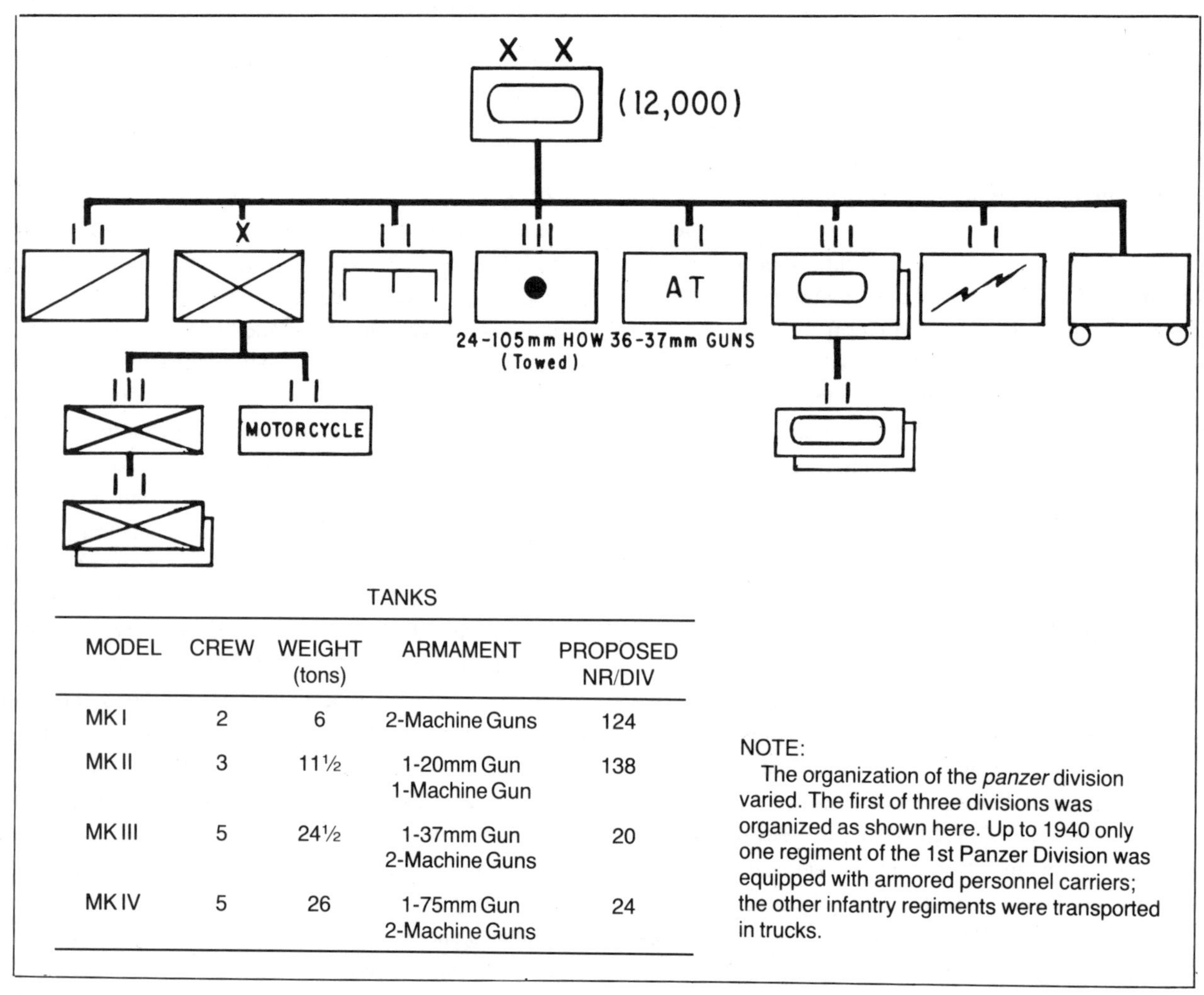

TANKS

MODEL	CREW	WEIGHT (tons)	ARMAMENT	PROPOSED NR/DIV
MK I	2	6	2-Machine Guns	124
MK II	3	11½	1-20mm Gun 1-Machine Gun	138
MK III	5	24½	1-37mm Gun 2-Machine Guns	20
MK IV	5	26	1-75mm Gun 2-Machine Guns	24

NOTE:
The organization of the *panzer* division varied. The first of three divisions was organized as shown here. Up to 1940 only one regiment of the 1st Panzer Division was equipped with armored personnel carriers; the other infantry regiments were transported in trucks.

Organization of *Panzer* Division, 1939-1940

battle foresaw rapidly moving fluid situations which would demand quick adjustments in organization and the conduct of decentralized operations over wide areas. The *Einheit* concept was meant to facilitate these adjustments and was designed to solve the continuing problem of logistic support for mobile operations. Nonetheless, good road and railroad networks were still essential to the German Army's logistics system.[56]

All doctrinal thought was not devoted to the offense. The doctrine of the mobile defense developed in the First World War was retained. For the Germans, the purpose of defense was to weaken the attacker as quickly as possible and thereby attain a shift in relative combat power which would provide the opportunity to go on the offensive. Defensive thinking stressed firepower, deep organization of mutually supporting positions, and the retention of strong mobile reserves for counterattack. The German Siegfried Line (West Wall), constructed in 1938 to shield the Ruhr industrial area and the rear of the German Army, was built around these doctrinal principles.

The standard German infantry division was organized and equipped in such a manner as to make it an effective defensive as well as offensive unit. The relatively large number of divisional antitank guns highlights the importance which the Germans felt armor would play in the coming war. The division position in a defensive situation was organized in depth in front of a Main Line of Resistance (MLR). Reverse slope positions were utilized where possible, and 300- to 400-yard fields of fire were deemed sufficient to halt an enemy attack. The mission of the mutually supporting strong points, which included antitank guns deployed in depth in front of the MLR, was to weaken, disorganize, channelize, and slow down the enemy attack. Hopefully this attack would break down in front of the MLR from where the counterattack would be launched. The MLR was the only position which had to be retained. Commanders of outlying outposts and strong points enjoyed great latitude as to how they conducted their actions within their defensive sectors.[57]

The German Army which took the field in Poland in 1939 was a compromise between Seeckt's "small army of quality and maneuver" and a modernized version of the 1917-18 Imperial Army. Beck, Chief of the General Staff, believed that the new mechanized and armored forces could be used to trigger the encirclements, but that the real strength of the army would remain with the standard infantry divisions with their combined foot, horse, and vehicular mobility. A fully motorized army was out of the question. No European industrial power during the 1920s and 1930s could have provided such a force. Guderian and other armor advocates were critical of Beck's conservatism and what they felt was undue cautiousness. But Beck was a firm adherent to Moltke's dictum of "Erst wägen, dann wagen" (first consider, then venture). He was perfectly willing to take a risk, but only after due consideration. His main concern was that whenever the war started he would have to fight with what he had. Prudence, therefore, dictated that the old standard division be improved and modernized rather than be scrapped to rebuild the Army along entirely new lines.

Most German Transport Was Horse-Drawn

The Wehrmacht's Initial Trials

Hitler's strategy to acquire the necessary *lebensraum* for Germany by use of bluff, subversion, and intimidation against small isolated neighbors worked well from 1936 through 1938. *(See Map 2, in Atlas.)* The Rhineland, Austria, and part of Czechoslovakia were occupied without resort to war during this period, which is often referred to as the *Blumenkrieg* or flower war. (In truth, the German troops were bombarded with floral missiles when they marched into the Rhineland, Austria, and the Sudetenland.) The subsequent German seizure of the remainder of Czechoslovakia in March 1939, however, changed the temper of the times. The Poles, who had shared in the exploitation of Czech territory, now realized that it was their turn. So did Great Britain and France.

Hitler's foreign policy had caused increasing apprehension and tension not only throughout Europe but also in the High Command of the German Army. The occupation of Austria, although peaceful, had revealed technical weaknesses in the new *panzer* forces and problems in the mobilization of reserve units. Blomberg and Fritsch, as previously mentioned, had been sacked for opposing Hitler's aggressive intentions. It was now Beck's turn. General staff studies of the OKW directive for the Czechoslovakian occupation had caused Beck to conclude that its implementation ran great risk of foreign intervention leading to general war and ultimate German defeat. When Hitler rejected Beck's views, he resigned. His replacement, as Chief of the General Staff, was General Franz Halder, a Bavarian, and the last Chief of the General Staff to represent the old German military tradition. Halder assumed his new duties on September 1, 1938.[58] He believed that since Hitler could not be persuaded from continuing his current foreign policy of aggression, he had to be removed from power. The subsequent Green Plot to accomplish this end never reached fruition. Hitler's triumph at Munich in September 1938 cut the ground from under the plotters.

Although Hitler now enjoyed great prestige and confidence in Germany because of his bloodless conquests, he was still aware of the opposition within the army high command over his plans for Poland. This opposition had been weakened in 1938 by the voluntary or involuntary retirement of 16 of the 30 top-ranking generals in the Army. These retirements still left the hierarchy of the Army with an ambitious, energetic, and highly skilled group of general officers. Within this group, however, there was little breadth of outlook or unity of purpose. There was no individual personality, such as Fritsch or Beck, who could rally general support from the officer corps in the event of a crisis. Moreover, Hitler took further steps to reduce the apprehensions of the armed forces by holding two conferences with his commanders at his mountain retreat, the *Obersalzberg*, in August 1939. He emphasized the necessity for taking a risk now because of the unreadiness of France and England and the hostility of Russia toward Poland. He added, moreover, that he now enjoyed the confidence of the whole German people; that Germany could expect the support of Italy and at least passive neutrality from Spain; and that he had eliminated the possibility of Russian help to the Anglo-French by the conclusion of a nonaggression pact with the Soviet Union. Poland was now isolated and Germany did not stand alone.[59]

The preliminaries to the German conquest of Poland were largely diplomatic. During October 1938, Hitler began to exert pressure on Poland over Danzig and the Polish Corridor. Poland refused any concessions and in March 1939 implemented a partial mobilization. But others were easier to cajole; Hitler persuaded Lithuania to return the one-time German port of Memel, and he pressured Rumania into a pact guaranteeing Germany most of the Rumanian oil production. *(See Map 2, in Atlas.)*

Poland is a vaster Belgium—an open, level country with few natural obstacles to the passage of large armies. *(See Map 3, in Atlas.)* Like Belgium, much of its history has been that of a roadway and a battleground for contending powers. Its only natural defenses are: the Tatra-Carpathian Mountains on the south; the lines of the Vistula, Narew, and San Rivers; and the Pripet Marshes on the east. None is particularly formidable. The mountains reach heights of 8,700 feet, but there are several good passes—the Jablunka and the Dukla are the most important—traversed by road and rail lines. The rivers are generally broad and slow, practically impassable when in flood after heavy rains, but frequently low at the end of a hot summer. The winter of 1938-39 had been dry, and the subsequent autumn remained warm and dry. Rivers were low and the ground was hard, making a perfect arena for the German mechanized troops. Advanced airfields could be eaily improvised as the German advance swept forward.[60]

Among the difficulties confronting the Polish command were the shape of their western frontier and the location of their major industries. *(See Map 3, in Atlas.)* If the Poles massed their troops west of the San-Vistula line, they occupied a salient, its flanks exposed to German advances from East Prussia and Slovakia. If they retired behind the rivers, they gave up the richest and most productive area of their country, as well as their only seaport, Gdynia.

Poland's fatal weakness, however, was its isolation. Its seaport faced the Baltic, which the Germans could easily block with mines, submarines, and aircraft against Allied entry. To the south, Germany was allied with Slovakia, and Hungary and Rumania were semi-vassals of the Germans. To the east waited an unfriendly Russia. To the north, Lithuania had an old score to settle with Poland over possession of Vilna. Under these circumstances, England and France could help Poland only indirectly—by exerting pressure on Germany in the West. Neither was prepared, militarily or emotionally, for such an effort. Memories of the Somme, of Flanders, of Verdun and Champagne had convinced them that the defense was the decisive form of warfare—a conviction that the French had embodied in the concrete and steel of the Maginot Line. Hitler's West Wall might be of unproved strength and garrisoned largely by second-rate troops, but no French or British statesman or general was willing to chance a major offensive against it.

One thing became certain, however, as war crept closer during the hot days of August: the Poles would fight. They had seen the fate of Czechoslovakia, which had elected to surrender without a struggle. Their army might be small, its equipment scanty and antiquated, its mobilization seriously delayed as the result of heeding a final, futile sputter of Franco-British appeasement; but Poland had never lacked tough infantry and gallant cavalry. The Germans were an ancient enemy; the rains would surely come to bog down the German tanks; England and France would not fail their ally. But—whatever came—it was better for one to die on his feet than to live on his knees.

The final German plan provided that Army Group North (General Fedor von Bock) would mount two major attacks. *(See Map 4, in Atlas.)* Its Fourth Army (General Guenther von Kluge) would advance immediately on Graudenz, cutting the Polish Corridor at its base and establishing communications between Germany proper and East Prussia; it would also seize

Gdynia. The Third Army (General George von Kuechler) would make its main effort toward Warsaw, and also launch a second attack westward to help the Fourth Army seize the Vistula crossings. Once the Corridor was secured, Bock's entire force would drive on Warsaw.

Army Group South (General Gerd von Rundstedt) was the stronger of the two army groups. It would make its main attack toward Warsaw with its Tenth Army (General Walther von Reichenau), covered on its left flank by the Eighth Army's (General Johannes Blaskowitz) drive on Lodz, and on its right by the Fourteenth Army (General Wilhelm List), which would move on Cracow and through the Carpathian passes. The link-up of Army Group North and the Tenth Army at Warsaw could cut off a large part of the Polish forces west of the San-Vistula-Narew line. (Note that most of the *panzer* units were with the Fourth and Tenth Armies.)

The area between the two army groups was largely filled by the Oder Quadrilateral fortified area. Frontier guards, reinforced by some reserve units, were concentrated here with instructions to carry out local attacks—both to deceive the Poles as to German intentions and to tie down as many Polish units as possible. Other frontier guard units covered the flank of the Third Army. Local reserve units, supported by the German Navy, were to secure Danzig. The Navy would also provide a small force to blockade the Polish coast, attack Polish naval installations at Gdynia and Hela, keep open the sea lanes to East Prussia, capture or destroy Polish shipping, and give Bock's forces all possible assistance. Against the possible threat of Franco-British intervention, Hitler had deployed the greater part of the Navy in the North Sea and the Atlantic. The West Wall was garrisoned by infantry units only, which were supported by relatively light air forces. *(See Map 5, in Atlas.)*

The Polish defense plan was at best a compromise. It was clear that the only real tenable defensive line lay behind the Narew-Vistula-San Rivers. To withdraw eastward behind this line initially would surrender the richest part of Poland to the Germans at little cost to Hitler. To man the frontier positions would double the length of the defensive line and place the Army within the suspected gigantic German pincers closing in on Warsaw. The determining element was time—time in which the Anglo-French could mobilize and come to the aid of the Poles. The resulting Plan "Z," therefore, featured a deployment along the common frontiers with the idea of quickly engaging the German forces, slowing their advance, and conducting a slow withdrawal to the optimum defensive position behind the Vistula. *(See Map 4, in Atlas.)* A large number of the available Polish divisions were to be held in reserve for use in a counteroffensive. The Poles—like their allies—expected to fight a World War I-type of war, which would give them time to complete their mobilization. Also, they undoubtedly believed that French and British pressure in the West would limit the strength of the German invasion armies. They had almost no armored forces. Field fortifications were hastily erected along the frontier, but these were weak and incomplete.

Without bothering with the formality of declaring war, Hitler struck early on September 1. At 4:30 A.M. the *Luftwaffe* raided airfields all across Poland; almost simultaneously, an old German battleship, which had been visiting Danzig, took nearby Polish fortifications under fire, and the German Army surged across the frontier. Despite the long preliminary period of tension—or, possibly, because of it—the invasion took the Poles completely by surprise. Their Air Force did not effectively intervene in the battle, and Danzig fell almost without a struggle. A few Polish warships escaped to England; the rest were soon sunk or driven into Swedish harbors and there interned.

On the first day, the Fourth Army made good progress. *(See Map 6, in Atlas.)* The Third Army's I Corps was checked by a fortified Polish area around Mlawa, but Kuechler reinforced Corps Wodrig (which broke through farther east the next day) with all his armor and swung it westward to bypass the town. Rundstedt's armies were equally successful, some units advancing up to 15 miles by late afternoon of the first. The Poles relied on their rear guards and demolitions to slow the German advance; but *panzer* units, supported by dive bombers, were usually able to bypass such obstacles. Jablunka Pass was rapidly cleared, and by September 2 it was apparent that the Poles intended to stand on the line of the Warta River.

By September 3, the Third and Fourth Armies had joined hands to cut the Corridor, which was rapidly being cleared, the remaining Polish units there being driven toward Gdynia. Polish resistance had been tough and desperate, some of their cavalry riding at German tanks with lance and saber. (Unofficial contemporary reports suggest these troopers had been told

The Polish Cavalry–Here Shown During 1939 Maneuvers–Was No Match for the *Panzers*

that the German tanks were fakes, "armored" with canvas or papier-mâché.) Both the Pomorze and Modlin Armies had suffered heavy losses. Polish cavalry from the Narew Group had made several short incursions into East Prussia, but they had not slowed the Third Army's advance. To the south the Tenth Army took the fortified industrial city of Czestochowa on the morning of September 3 and moved on to seize several bridgeheads over the Warta. The next day, its *panzer* units drove beyond Radomsko. Several Polish units were cut off and destroyed; the rest retired hurriedly, pressed by ground elements and harassed by the *Luftwaffe*.

Deploying some 1,400 fighters and bombers, the *Luftwaffe*'s mission was the establishment of air superiority. Close support of ground operations was second in the order of precedence. The Poles were reported to have 900 first-line operational aircraft, including 150 bombers and 315 fighters. (In fact, they had only 396 aircraft, 160 being fighters.) While the *Luftwaffe* had struck heavily at Polish air installations on the first two days of the campaign, they had hit largely an empty bag. The Poles had dispersed and hidden their meager air force, which would continue to operate—albeit ineffectively—until September 16. Inferiority in quality and numbers of aircraft prevented any serious challenge to German air superiority from the outset of the campaign. Close support of the ground forces began on a random basis with the *Luftwaffe* finding its own targets, which at times turned out to be friendly elements. The system of air force liaison officers equipped with their own communications vans moving with ground units was not initially in effect. This omission was soon rectified, and a more effective use of support aircraft was instituted.[61]

The Fate of the Polish Air Force

Bock now prepared to shift the Fourth Army well to the east so that it could attack southward through Lomza; this advance was to begin on September 4. However, this plan was vetoed by Brauchitsch, who feared an Anglo-French attack in the West and wanted to move no deeper into Poland than necessary to destroy the Polish Army. Bock's protestations pried loose only Guderian's XIX Panzer Corps and the 10th Panzer Division for the move. Three days later he was allowed to shift the XXI Corps as well. Meanwhile, Rundstedt's three armies had steadily advanced, meeting the most resistance west of Cracow. *(See Map 6, 5 Sept. blue line, in* ***Atlas.****)* On September 6, elements of the Tenth Army raced across open country toward Warsaw while Rundstedt, worried about the relatively intact Polish Poznan Army, moved two reserve divisions to the north of the Eighth Army to protect his open flank. Almost everywhere the situation of the Polish Army had grown increasingly desperate, most reserves having been committed by now.

In the north, by September 9 Bock had two corps advancing beyond Lomza, and two days later he began pushing the Third Army toward Koch-Wlodawa. This latter drive, designed to link up with the Fourteenth Army units previously ordered to drive on Radymno-Kock and thereby complete a second, more eastward closing of pincers, was dictated by reports that the Polish Government was trying to establish a line along the Bug River. Farther south, meanwhile, the XVI Panzer Corps had reached Warsaw on September 9, but had to remain in the suburbs until more infantry could be brought up to help with the street fighting.

It was on September 10 that the Poznan Army struck a blow for Poland. Moving out of the Kutno area, it surprised the poorly directed 30th Division and forced the rest of the X Corps to change the direction of their drive to the north. But the Germans quickly reinforced—air transport was used in part—and swung the XI Corps north and west to entrap the attacking Poles. Then the Eighth and Fourth Armies relentlessly compressed the elements of three Polish armies—about one-third of the entire Polish Army—into an ever-shrinking pocket around Kutno.

Continuing German advances on all fronts gave the enemy no chance to reorganize, and it was only a matter of days before the fragmented Polish centers of resistance were forced to capitulate. The Tenth Army overcame bitter resistance at Radom and forced 60,000 Poles to surrender on September 11. The Fourteenth Army seized the dominant heights around Lwow two days later, while, in the north, the Third and Tenth Armies tightened the noose around Warsaw and Modlin. *(See Map 7, in* ***Atlas.****)* The Eighth Army continued to compress the Kutno pocket, assisted by the Tenth Army. Throughout these operations, the Germans showed great flexibility in switching control of corps from one army to another as the fluid situation dictated, even moving the Fourth Army's headquarters eastward to direct the occupation of Bialystok. On that same flank, Guderian's *panzers* raced southward, took fortified Brest on September 17, and established radio contact with units of the IV Corps south of Wlodawa. That same day, the Tenth Army finally snuffed out Polish resistance at Kutno, taking 52,000 prisoners; it also fought its way into Lublin. In the southeast, the Fourteenth Army took Lwow on the twenty-first of September and blocked the attempted flow of Polish government officials and troops into Rumania.

Warsaw and Modlin now came under heavy artillery and aerial bombardment, but the Poles refused to capitulate. Finally, an Eighth Army attack on September 27 forced the defenders of Warsaw, already plagued by typhoid and facing starvation, to surrender. The next day Modlin fell. A total of 164,000 Polish troops were taken prisoner. The isolated coastal fortress of Hel capitulated on October 1, and, five days later, the Tenth Army subdued the last organized Polish force at Kock.

Final operations were complicated by the Russian advance into Poland. The agreement of August 23 had secretly assigned to the Russians all territory east of the Narew, San, and Vistula (later changed to all territory east of the Bug). The Russians, however, were coy about occupying eastern Poland, apparently preferring to let the Germans conquer it for them. Eventually, after extremely short notice, they advanced on September 17. Great confusion developed, especially in the south where some German units were hotly engaged with die-hard Polish forces and had considerable trouble extricating themselves. There were a number of minor clashes between Germans and Russians during this period, but all were settled by the local commanders.

Even before the campaign was fully over, Hitler had begun transferring forces to the West. It had been a spectacular accomplishment, from which he managed to wring full propaganda value. The cost to the *Wehrmacht* was relatively cheap: 10,761 men killed and 285 aircraft lost. The new *panzer*-air team had proved itself, although both members still had much to learn. The main burden of the battle, however, had fallen—all unnoticed—on the hard marching German infantry and their largely horse-drawn artillery and trains.

The campaign had not caught the Polish Army in a large pocket west of the Vistula, as the Germans had planned. It had been destroyed in several smaller battles of encirclement with a large number escaping east and south of the Vistula River. Even with motorized and armored units equipped with radio and supported by aerial artillery, the classic Schlieffen double envelopment (pincers) was still elusive. The disparity in means of mobility between the few motorized infantry and *panzer* divisions and the remainder of the German Army allowed the stoutly resisting Poles to take advantage of the gaps between the advance and follow-up units to make good their withdrawals.

Logistic weaknesses were not readily apparent, although there were several instances of armored units running out of fuel, being cut off, and having to be resupplied by air. The main battle area west of the Vistula contained a good rail and road network which compared favorably to and dovetailed with the German road and rail system. These facilities were put to good use by the Germans even though the Poles used demolitions extensively. Another consideration for those who cared to reflect carefully was that the extent of the German advance was only about 250 miles.

Both strengths and weaknesses were revealed in equipment, organization, and training. The light tanks were of marginal value, particularly against fixed positions; they needed to be replaced by heavier models. Infantry weapons, with the exception of the machinegun, were satisfactory. But the motorized infantry division was too cumbersome and the light divisions had little staying power. Both types were to be reorganized. Because the infantry displayed little of its 1914 aggressive spirit, officer casualties were high. The German critique noted that there was too much preparation and caution exercised in the conduct of the attack; as a result, many opportunities had been missed.[62]

Possibly the most significant result of the campaign was that Hitler had apparently been right again. He began to consider himself a military genius, and the influence of his professional military advisors declined still further. Moreover, he did not wait for the final conclusion of the Polish campaign before announcing his plans for further conquests. On September 27, 1939, he made known his intention to launch an attack in the West at the earliest possible moment.

Notes

[1]Robert R. Palmer and Joel Colton, *A History of the Modern World*, 4th ed. (New York, 1971), p. 748.

[2]Frances L. Carsten, *The Reichswehr and Politics, 1918 to 1933* (Oxford, 1966), p. 5; Gordon A. Craig, *Politics of the Prussian Army, 1640-1945* (New York, 1970), p. 343.

[3]Carsten, *The Reichswehr*, pp. 10-12.

[4]Harold J. Gordon, Jr., *The Reichswehr and the German Public, 1919-1926* (Princeton, 1957), p. 51; Craig, *Politics of the Prussian Army*, pp. 350-355.

[5]Gordon, *Reichswehr*, p. 54.

[6]U.S. Congress, *Treaty of Peace With Germany*, 66th Cong., 1st Session, 1919, No. 85, pp. 191-219.

[7]Herbert Rosinski, *The German Army* (New York, 1966), p. 162; Carsten, *The Reichswehr*, p. 104.

[8]Carsten, *Reichswehr*, pp. 103-105; John W. Wheeler-Bennett, *The Nemesis of Power* (London, 1961), pp. 85-86.

[9]Carsten, *Reichswehr*, pp. 95-96.

[10]*Ibid.*, pp. 107-113.

[11]Craig, *Politics of the Prussian Army*, pp. 396-397; Hans von Seeckt, *Thoughts of a Soldier*, trans. by Gilbert Waterhouse (London, 1930), p. 55.

[12] Craig, *Politics of the Prussian Army*, pp. 385-393; Gordon, *Reichswehr*, pp. 174, 211-212; Wilhelm List, "The German General Staff," MS #P-031b, Vol. XIV, Center of Military History, Washington, D.C., 1954, pp. 8-9.

[13]Gordon, *Reichswehr*, pp. 202-212.

[14]*Ibid.*, p. 299.

[15]Stephen Gwynn, *The Anvil of War* (London, 1936), p. 113.

[16]Erich Brandenburger, "The German General Staff," MS #P-031a, Vol. XXX, Center of Military History, Washington, D.C., 1954, pp. 9-12.

[17]Brandenburger, "German General Staff," pp. 35, 41; List, "German General Staff," p. 27.

[18]List, "German General Staff," pp. 28-30.

[19]Herman Foertsch, *The Art of Modern Warfare* (New York, 1940), p. 190.

[20]List, "German General Staff," pp. 31-33; author's interview with General Albert C. Wedemeyer, at United States Military Academy, West Point, N.Y., on April 25, 1973.

[21]Gordon, *Reichswehr*, pp. 179, 299; Wheeler-Bennett, *Nemesis of Power*, p. 143.

[22]John Erickson, *Soviet High Command* (London, 1962), pp. 151-156.

[23]Telford Taylor, *Sword and Swastika* (New York, 1952), pp. 43-46.

[24]Carsten, *The Reichswehr*, pp. 238-245.

[25]Craig, *Politics of the Prussian Army*, pp. 401-405.

[26]Rosinski, *The German Army*, p. 213.

[27]Robert J. O'Neill, *The German Army and the Nazi Party, 1933-1939* (New York, 1966), pp. 4-5, 31-53; Sir John Wheeler-Bennett, *Hindenburg: The Wooden Titan* (New York, 1967), p. 443.

[28]Taylor, *Sword and Swastika*, p. 81.

[29]O'Neill, *The German Army*, pp. 106-112; Walter Warlimont, *Inside Hitler's Headquarters* (New York, 1964), pp. 3-8.

[30]Taylor, *Sword and Swastika*, p. 140.

[31]*Ibid.*, pp. 145-161.

[32]Robert M. Kennedy, *The German Campaign in Poland 1939* (Washington, 1956), pp. 24-25.

[33]Friedrich Ruge, *Sea Warfare: 1939-1945* (London, 1957), pp. 13-14, 18-21.

[34]*Ibid.*, pp. 23-24.

[35]Elmer B. Potter and Admiral Chester W. Nimitz (eds.), *Seapower* (Englewood Cliffs, N.J., 1960), p. 492.

[36]John Killen, *A History of the Luftwaffe* (New York, 1968), pp. 40-41; Werner Baumbach, *The Life and Death of the Luftwaffe* (New York, 1960), pp. 17-19.

[37]Edward Jablonski, *Air War* (3 vols.; Garden City, N.Y., 1971), I, 9-11.

[38]Asher Lee, *Goering* (New York, 1972), pp. 40-41, 72.

[39]Baumbach, *Life and Death*, p. 20; Craig, *Politics of the Prussian Army*, pp. 482-83; Taylor, *Sword and Swastika*, pp. 106-107.

[40]Peter Gray and Owen Thetford, *German Aircraft of the First World War* (London, 1962), pp. xv-xxiii.

[41]Herbert Molloy Mason, Jr., *The Rise of the Luftwaffe, 1918-1940* (New York, 1973), p. 237; Asher Lee, *Air Power* (New York, 1955), p. 116.

[42]Kennedy, *German Campaign in Poland*, p. 35; Lee, *Goering*, pp. 60-61, 73.

[43]Willi Frischauer, *The Rise and Fall of Hermann Goering* (Boston, 1951), p. 123.

[44]Burton H. Klein, *Germany's Economic Preparations for War* (Cambridge, 1959), pp. 19-20.

[45]The foregoing account of the German pre-World War II economic preparations is based primarily on Klein, *Germany's Economic Preparations for War*, pp. 17-20, 76-82 and Gordon Wright, *The Ordeal of Total War, 1939-1945* (New York, 1968), pp. 44-47.

[46]Rudolph von Caemmerer, *The Development of Strategical Science During the 19th Century*, trans. by Karl Donat (London, 1905), p. 212.

[47]*Ibid.*, p. 213.

[48]Wolfgang Foerster, *Count Schlieffen and the World War*, trans. by W. J. Berry (2 vols.; Berlin, 1921), II, 1-6; Rosinski, *The German Army*, p. 296.

[49]Foerster, *Count Schlieffen*, II, 84-88.

[50]Seeckt, *Thoughts of a Soldier*, p. 12.

[51]Michael Howard (ed.), *The Theory and Practice of War* (New York, 1966), pp. 145-147.

[52]Heinz Guderian, "Representations of Armored Interests," MS #P-041p, Center of Military History, Washington, D.C., 1952, pp. 1-2; Howard, *Theory and Practice*, pp. 149-151.

[53]William Balck, *Development of Tactics in the World War*, trans. by Harry Bell (Ft. Leavenworth, 1922), pp. 266-281; Lieutenant Colonel Lucas, *The Evolution of Tactical Ideas in France and Germany, 1914-1918* (Paris, 1923), pp. 131-132.

[54]Heinz Guderian, *Armored Forces and Their Cooperation with Other Arms*, trans. by F. W. Mertin (Washington, D.C., 1937), pp. 13-14; Albert C. Wedemeyer, "Wedemeyer Report, German Kriegsacademie 1936-1938" (unpublished report, Washington, D.C., 1938), p. 40; Ferdinand O. Miksche, *Blitzkrieg* (London, 1941), pp. 17-19; Howard, *Theory and Practice*, pp. 151-152.

[55]Brandenburger, "German General Staff," pp. 27-28.

[56]Wedemeyer, pp. 142-143; T. Denis Daly, "The German Will to War Must Be Broken," *Army Quarterly,* XLIV (August 1942), 218.

[57]Howard, *Theory and Practice*, p. 153; U.S. War Department, Military Information Division, *German Doctrine of the Stabilized Front* (Washington, D.C., 1943), pp. vii-ix, 5-7; U.S. Command and General Staff School, "Organization and Tactical Employment of a Modern Division (German Army)" (unpublished report, Ft. Leavenworth, 1933), pp. 31, 68-70; Ritter Wilhelm von Leeb, *Defense* (Harrisburg, Pa., 1943), pp. viii-ix.

[58]Larry H. Addington, *The Blitzkrieg Era and the German General Staff, 1865-1945* (New Brunswick, N.J., 1971), pp., 49-59; Kennedy, *German Campaign in Poland*, p. 1-5, 138-139.

[59]Taylor, *Sword and Swastika*, pp. 244-247, 291-300.

[60]The following account of the campaign in Poland is based upon Vincent J. Esposito (ed.), *The West Point Atlas of American Wars* (2 vols.; New York, 1960), II, Section 2, 3-7, except where otherwise noted.

[61]Cajus Bekker, *The Luftwaffe War Diaries* (Garden City, N.Y., 1968), pp. 29-31, 59.

[62]Franz Halder, "The Private War Journal of Generaloberst Franz Halder," trans. by Arnold Lissance, unpublished journal, Office of the Chief Counsel for War Crimes (9 vols.; Nuremburg, 1947), II, 5-22.

Blitzkrieg in the West

2

Build we straight, O worthy Master!
Staunch and strong, a good vessel,
That shall laugh at all disaster,
And with wave and whirlwind wrestle!
Henry Wadsworth Longfellow

Even before the successful campaign in Poland was concluded, an impatient Hitler was thinking of turning on the western Allies. His intention to attack in the West at the earliest possible date, made known in the autumn of 1939, did not find widespread support within the high command of the German Army, where grave reservations existed as to the capability of the Army to force a decision on the Anglo-French forces. Both Brauchitsch and Halder made it patently clear that the Army was neither adequately trained nor sufficiently equipped to carry out the task at that time, especially if the fighting should extend into a winter campaign. Moreover, the senior German commanders all vividly recalled the fighting capabilities of the British and French, as well as the deadly stalemate of World War I. Hitler, however, would not be deterred; instead, he increased the pressure to force the army high command to abandon its defensive strategy in the West and begin intensive preparations for the offensive. By mid-October, he declared that his decision to attack was irrevocable and set November 12 as the date for the beginning of the offensive. However, bad weather, the unsatisfactory state of the hurried planning and preparations, and the continued lack of enthusiasm of many senior officers caused it to be postponed.* Aware of the distinct resistance of his generals against the offensive, Hitler assembled them at the Reichs Chancellory on November 23 in order to clear up their doubts, to give them an insight into his plans for the future, and to explain why it was imperative to attack France and Great Britain at an early date.[1]

In his review of the situation, the *Fuehrer* began with the rise of National Socialism and subsequent creation of the *Wehrmacht*. By linking these two events, he was reminding his generals that they owed their positions and allegiance to him. Hitler went on to explain the problems which remained, and why he was so insistent that the *Wehrmacht* move quickly against France and Great Britain. The problem of German *lebensraum* was still to be settled. Czechoslovakia and Poland were only the beginning. Russia, although militarily weak and bound by treaty to Germany, entertained expansionist ideas in the Baltic and the Balkans. Germany, therefore, must be in a position to thwart these moves when they occurred. (Russia, in fact, invaded Finland on November 30, 1939.) The elimination of Poland and the Russian treaty protected the rear of the German Army, and for the first time since the Franco-Prussian War the *Wehrmacht* need not fear a war on two fronts. Hitler further pointed out that the French and British had remained behind their fortifications since their declaration of war on September 3. How much longer they would remain static was problematical. Of particular worry to him was the increase in military strength which the British had managed in the past six months. An attack in the West now would take advantage of Germany's present military superiority,† provide naval and submarine bases on the Channel to carry the war to England, protect the vital industrial heart of Germany (the Ruhr), take advantage of the present American neutrality, and hopefully induce Mussolini to come into the war on the side of Germany.[2] The *Fuehrer* concluded his harangue with a call for unflagging determination and a warning that he would take strong action against any who opposed his will.

*Bad weather was the primary cause of the postponement. This was the first of 29 such postponements between October 1939 and May 1940.

†Anglo-French estimates as of March 1939: Anglo-French: 90 divisions, 86 of which were French, and 2,634 aircraft of all types; Germany: 100 divisions and 3,700 aircraft; Italy: 20 divisions and 1,400 aircraft.

A Temporary Diversion: Denmark and Norway

One of the major fears Hitler had voiced at his November 23 meeting was the possibility of France and England seizing the initiative. If allowed time, they just might markedly alter the military situation by making a strategic move into Belgium or Scandinavia, thereby confronting Hitler with hard choices. Indeed, there was pressure on the British and French governments to come to the aid of Finland during the winter war of 1939-1940. Hitler, fearing that the Anglo-French would use aid to Finland as a ruse to gain control of Narvik and Lulea *(see Map 8A, in Atlas.)*, directed OKW in December 1939 to study the problem of occupying Norway.[3]

Remembering the World War I Allied naval blockade, Admiral Erich Raeder, Commander-in-Chief of the German Navy (OKM), had informed the *Fuehrer* in early October 1939 that if the German fleet was to be effective, access to the Atlantic had to be assured. As long as Norway remained neutral or was in German hands this access was assured. Failing this, the Navy would again occupy "the dead angle of a dead sea."[4] Moreover, the German armament industry depended upon steady imports of Swedish iron ore. During the winter months, when the Gulf of Bothnia was frozen, much of this ore went by rail from Kiruna to Narvik; there it was picked up by German freighters, which utilized the Leads, thereby remaining in Norwegian waters.* Fearful that the British might block this traffic, or even occupy Norway as a base for future operations against Germany, Hitler decided, by early February, to seize Norway itself.† A small joint staff began preliminary planning for the operation now entitled WESERUEBÜNG and expanded to include the seizure of Denmark.

On February 21, 1940, Hitler designated General Nikolaus von Falkenhorst as commander of all German forces involved in the operation.** Falkenhorst was to exercise his command directly under the control of OKW. In light of the fact that this was the first joint operation involving all three services, Hitler reserved overall command to himself.[5] The Commanders-in-Chief of the three services were consulted neither as to the proposed operation nor the command organization; they were

General Nikolaus von Falkenhorst, Hitler's Intended Joint Commander for the Norwegian Operation

merely notified to furnish the requisite forces. This apparent attempt by Hitler to make this a strictly OKW-sponsored and directed operation and thereby increase his control of military operations was thwarted by the Army and the *Luftwaffe* during early March. OKH saw it as a diversion of forces from the planned western offensive and a further infringement upon command prerogatives. Goering, speaking for the *Luftwaffe*, raged about being kept in the dark concerning the *Fuehrer*'s plans and condemned the proposed command structure. To appease them, Hitler modified the organization by making Falkenhorst the senior of the three service commanders; he also postponed FALL GELB (Plan Yellow—code name for the western offensive) pending completion of the Scandinavian operations.

In his final review of the plans for WESERUEBÜNG on April 1, Hitler stated that the purposes of the operation were to forestall British action in Scandinavia, to secure the Swedish ore supply, and to broaden the base line for future air and naval operations against Great Britain.[6] The plan and subsequent operations for the conquest of Norway and Denmark were both bold and imaginative.

Denmark and Norway were to be invaded simultaneously. *(See Map 8a, in Atlas.)* In order to provide air support for the invasion forces in Norway, it was imperative that the airfields around Aarlborg, Denmark, be seized quickly. This was to be accomplished by small airborne and air-landed elements which were to be reinforced rapidly by two motorized infantry regiments. In Norway, the six coastal cities of Oslo, Kristiansand, Stavanger, Bergen, Trondheim, and Narvik were to be attacked simultaneously. The major planning problem to be

*The Leads was a coastal waterway from the North Cape to Stavanger, passing for much of the distance between offshore islands and the mainland and for all its length well within Norwegian territorial waters.

†Hitler's decision resulted directly from the *Altmark* incident. The *Altmark*, while in Norwegian territorial waters, was boarded by sailors from the British destroyer, *HMS Cossack*, on February 16. To Hitler this constituted a slap in the face and a further indication of aggressive British intentions in Scandinavia.

**Falkenhorst was selected because of his experience in amphibious operations during World War I. He had served as a general staff officer in the Ostee Division which had made landings on Oesel and Dagoe Islands in the Gulf of Riga and later in Finland.

solved was how to transport and land the six-division invasion force. To have approached the problem in a conventional manner would have meant using close to a half-million tons of transport shipping, convoyed by all available German warships. An armada of this size, even if the shipping were available, would have alerted the British long before the Germans could have reached their objectives.

Planning, therefore, emphasized secrecy, speed, and deception. Due to the greatly varying distances to be traveled and the need to strike simultaneously, the departure of the assault groups had to be staggered. The assault echelon was loaded upon warships. Their major equipment and initial reinforcements, however, preceded them in transport vessels which were disguised to resemble merchant or coal ships; these were to lie in wait in Norwegian harbors. The major reinforcements were not due until three to five days after the initial assault and would be introduced through Oslo. Their mission was to drive overland and link up the separate beachheads.[7]

The German task force weighed anchor late on April 7. By coincidence, the British were then preparing to mine the entrance to Narvik harbor. Scattered naval clashes on April 8 indicated a major German operation, but bad weather hindered British reconnaissance. Although warned, the Norwegian Government failed to act decisively: coastal defense units were alerted, but they were forbidden to lay defensive mine fields; nothing was done to defend key airfields; reservists were called up by ordinary mail. (Despite excited contemporary accounts, Vidkun Quisling's tiny pro-German party contributed very little to Norway's downfall.)

Early on April 9, German warships put small, lightly equipped army units ashore at Oslo, Kristiansand, Bergen, Trondheim, and Narvik. Airborne troops seized Sola airport and Stavanger. Meanwhile, Denmark was swiftly overrun, providing the *Luftwaffe* with the necessary advance bases to support the Norwegian operation.

If surprised, the Norwegians nevertheless fought hard. At Oslo, the German naval expedition was stopped, with heavy losses, by the coast defenses. This delay enabled the Norwegian Government and royal family to escape, but Falkenhorst met the crisis by airlifting troops into Fornebu airport hours ahead of schedule. This handful of Germans overawed Oslo until the harbor forts were knocked out. Kristiansand and Bergen were captured after lively fighting; Stavanger, Trondheim, and Narvik fell quickly. A second wave, composed of supply ships and tankers, followed the naval task forces with heavy weapons and equipment. Subsequent naval engagements (at Narvik and elsewhere) cost the Germans heavily in warships and supply vessels, but Falkenhorst poured in reinforcements by sea and air, particularly into the Oslo area. German columns pushed out to link up their isolated forces and crush the mobilizing Norwegian Army. *(See Map 8b, in Atlas.)*

The campaign became a race against Allied efforts to reinforce the Norwegians. Rapid *Luftwaffe* utilization of Danish and Norwegian airfields gave the Germans air superiority from the start. Cooperation between Falkenhorst and the local German air and naval commanders was generous and effective. By April 16, they had practically cleared southern Norway, and the British Navy had been forced by constant air attacks to withdraw its major ships north of Trondheim. Meanwhile, Allied troops—they were hastily assembled and poorly equipped—had landed at the minor ports of Andalsnes and Namsos in an effort to recapture Trondheim.

Almost immediately, however, the Andalsnes column was diverted southward to reinforce the Norwegians. En route on April 19, it captured a pocket of German paratroopers at Dombas, but the column was turned back just south of Lillehammer. The Namsos column was defeated on April 21 by the Trondheim garrison at Steinkjer. Despite stubborn Allied resistance in both cases, German superiority in armor, air support, artillery, training, and equipment was too great. By May 3, the Allies had been forced out of central Norway; Norwegian forces remaining there soon surrendered.[8] Some fighting continued around Narvik. *(See Map 8a, in Atlas.)* Allied forces recaptured that town, driving the Germans back into the mountains. But they were withdrawn early in June because of the desperate situation in France.

The Norwegian campaign brought Germany immense prestige, insured her supply of iron ore, and secured air and submarine bases in Norway which helped to loosen the British blockade. On the other hand, the Germans were faced with the requirement for providing a strong air, sea, and land garrison for Norway. The serious naval losses inflicted on the Allies by

German Mountain Troops in Norway, 1939

land-based German aircraft clearly demonstrated for the first time the vulnerability of naval vessels unprotected by airpower. Conversely, the Norwegian campaign also crippled the German Navy for months.*

German success had been achieved by surprise and the early establishment of air superiority. Of equal importance was the slow and vacillating approach of the Anglo-French to the German attack. The fact that the operation went so well is directly attributable to the thoroughness of the German planning and preparation and the coordination of effort effected by Falkenhorst with the air and sea component commanders. Nor did the Anglo-French try to coordinate and direct their operations by means of a joint command. The introduction of forces into Scandinavia was thought to be an Army problem, with the Navy providing only convoy protection and the Royal Air Force token support. Minor as it was, the lessons learned from the Norwegian experience later formed the basis of Allied joint planning for the return to the Continent in 1944.

The French Quandary and Compromise

There had been a desultory exchange of information between the British and French General Staffs since 1936, but meaningful conversations had been avoided. Closer coordination of military matters at an earlier date might have been interpreted by the Germans as a military alliance between Great Britain and France. While the policy of appeasement was still in effect, therefore, neither were formal staff talks allowed nor formal military commitments made. German actions following the Munich agreement, however, clearly indicated the future trend of events and that Great Britain and France would again fight as allies against Germany.[9] On March 29, 1939, therefore, Anglo-French staff conversations began in earnest.

A broad strategic policy for the two Allies resulted from these staff conversations which were based upon an appreciation of the probable German course of action. It was felt that the Germans, clearly recognizing the defensive strength of the Maginot Line, would probably try to achieve success by turning this barrier with an attack through Holland and Belgium. The Dutch and Belgians would likely be quickly overcome while still in the process of mobilization; and by bold exploitation the Germans would be able to close the Franco-Belgian frontier, seize the Channel coast of the Low Countries, and thereby put the *Luftwaffe* within striking distance of vital French and British targets. The Allies recognized that they would be unable to help the Dutch; but, time permitting, an advanced line might be occupied in Belgium upon which the German advance could be held. The French clearly stated that in the initial phases their strategy would be purely defensive. The idea was to force a repetition of the static warfare of 1914-1918 upon the Germans to give the Anglo-French time to build up their strength for an offensive. While the Allies clearly realized the value of a quick offensive, their initial strategic policy was based on a realistic evaluation of the capabilities of their respective armed forces and the apparent strengths of Germany and Italy. The British, having little in the way of land forces to contribute to the battle on the Continent, accepted the French view of the proposed action.

Initially, the British were to furnish only air and naval forces. Visions of the Somme and Passchendaele still haunted them. This policy was later modified to include an expeditionary force of two corps with a supporting air component. In addition, an advanced Air Striking Force, which would strike German targets from French airfields, was also to be sent. The two countries also reached an agreement on the roles to be assigned to the respective naval forces. The Royal Navy was to insure control of the North Sea, the English Channel, and the world-wide sea lines of communication. The French Navy generally was to be responsible for the western Mediterranean and for any action necessary to combat enemy commerce raiders in the eastern Atlantic.[10]

The French Army in the spring of 1939 was a mere shadow of the formidable force which had turned back the German onslaught on the Marne in 1914. Although still impressive on paper and enjoying a reputation based on its performance in the First World War, the Army of the late 1930s was in reality a flawed shield which would shatter at the first shock of combat. When Winston Churchill shouted, "Thank God for the French Army," during a debate on British disarmament in the House of Commons on March 23, 1933, he was merely voicing the widely held belief that the French Army was still the most formidable force in Europe.[11] That he and the western world were mistaken in this belief would become only too apparent in the summer of 1940. Behind this decline of French military power was a sort of "malaise militaire" which engulfed the French armed forces and nation during the two decades between the World Wars.[12] The causes and symptoms of this malady are varied and extensive, encompassing not only military developments but also social, economic, and political factors which impinged upon the mission, organization, composition, and doctrine of the French armed forces and the capability of the French nation to defend itself.

A general spiritual lassitude gripped the war-weary French people following the conclusion of The Great War. That war had solved nothing. The terrible cost in treasure, lives, and

*Because of heavy losses in Norway and the subsequent damaging of the battleships *Scharnhorst* and *Gneisenau*, Germany had only one heavy cruiser and four destroyers fit for service by the end of June 1940.

property only intensified the old prewar problems. There was no longer a symbol, such as "the country in danger," about which to rally the many factions in the French political spectrum. The intellectual element which might have stimulated the creation of a new spirit and purpose in the French people was missing.

With the war over, the dominant middle-class French politicians and intellectuals rapidly returned to their prewar preoccupations. They reaffirmed their bourgeois ideals of private property and low taxation, and advocated that massive reparations be paid by the Germans. The intellectuals, as middle class as the politicians, forgot their emotional talk during the war about the sickness of society and the need for reform. Instead they returned to the moral problems of the individual, only a few of them posing social and political questions. The factions of the political Left opposed this trend, influenced by the revolution in Russia and recognizing the militant strain developing in the French working class as a result of efforts by the Socialist Party and labor unions. This lack of national spirit and purpose manifested itself in great governmental instability.* Although this instability resulted from squabbles over internal affairs, it would have dire effects on the French foreign and military policies.[13]

The French fear of a resurgent, vengeful Germany was very real. French foreign policy was, therefore, motivated by a search for guaranteed security from any future German aggression. This policy, due to internal instability, was never consistent. It ran the gamut, during the 20 years between the World Wars, from harsh insistence on compliance with the provisions of the Treaty of Versailles, to *rapprochement*, to outright appeasement from 1933 to 1939. The practical purpose of the Treaty of Versailles and the League of Nations was to insure the security of Europe. While France continued to operate within the context of the treaty and the League, she also attempted to secure her future with bilateral alliances.

In 1920, the French concluded an agreement with Belgium under which the two countries would coordinate their military efforts for mutual defense. Failure to secure an Anglo-American guarantee at about the same time, however, prompted France to look to the east in search of a new ally to replace a suspect Russia as the traditional counterbalance to Germany. The search resulted in Poland becoming a French ally in 1921, soon to be followed by the states of the Little Entente (Czechoslovakia, Yugoslavia, and Rumania). The French had thus created a *cordon sanitaire* around Germany. The effectiveness of this alliance would depend upon the development of a common purpose, a military force capable of insuring its integrity, and diplomatic efforts to prevent the formation of a coalition between Germany and Russia or Germany and Italy.[14]

*Between 1919 and 1939 France had 43 changes in government, an average of less than six months per cabinet.

In addition to looking for allies, France sought to prevent Germany from rebuilding her strength. Various means were used: forcing payments of reparations due, long-term occupation of the Rhineland, attempts to lure the Ruhr and Saar regions away from Germany, and advocating reduction of the *Reichswehr* to a militia. This French policy was bankrupt by 1932. The French invasion of the Ruhr in 1923 was frowned on by the Anglo-Americans, as were the French attempts to create separate states from the Ruhr and Saar regions. The occupation of the Rhineland ended in 1930, rather than in 1935 as stipulated, also because of American and British desires. The Dawes Plan of 1924 helped to revitalize the German economy, which made rapid gains by 1929. The decade of the 1920s was filled with attempts to insure the settlement of future international disagreements through means other than war, such as the Locarno Treaty and the Pact of Paris (Kellogg-Briand Pact), concluded in August of 1928.[15] But the Geneva Disarmament Conference in the summer of 1932 demonstrated to the French that their attempts to keep Germany militarily and economically inferior had failed. The Germans, backed by the British, demanded parity in all matters of armaments. In this they signalled their intention to scrap the military clauses of the Versailles Treaty and rearm.[16] The point of no return had been reached. Six months later Adolf Hitler became the German Chancellor. He wasted little time making known his aggressive intentions. In March 1935, Germany withdrew from the League of Nations, renounced the Treaty of Versailles, reintroduced conscription, and overtly began to rearm. These actions were closely followed by the reoccupation of the Rhineland in March of the following year. The situation demanded firm action but none was taken, primarily because France's military strength had not kept pace with her aggressive foreign policy.

World War I had driven home two great lessons to the French. The first of these was that war had now truly become total—materiel and manpower were equally important. French industry and resources had neither been efficiently organized nor effectively utilized; as a result, orders for supplies and equipment had still required from six to eighteen months to be filled in 1918. With an industrially and demographically superior Germany viewed as the only likely future aggressor, what was needed was a complete organization of the French nation for the demands of modern war. The search for an acceptable legal basis which would provide the foundation for peacetime war planning began in 1924 and ended in July of 1938.

The second great lesson was that the reservist had proven his mettle, in spite of the fact that the professional had provided the necessary skeleton and brain. The role of the latter, however, became submerged in the glorification of the citizen soldier during the post-World War I period. Because of the traditional importance of the French Army in the history of the nation, French political parties have always held strong and even violent views on military affairs. The success, therefore, of an army of conscripts in World War I completely validated the French concept of the "Nation-in-Arms." At least it did to those whose political views placed them left of center in the French political spectrum.[17]

Basically, the term "Nation-in-Arms" implies the principle of universal and compulsory military service. Since the French Revolution this concept has been a part of the French military heritage. While seemingly a fairly simple concept, great controversy over its application raged throughout French political circles during the 20 years between the World Wars. The reason for this controversy was that this concept was seen to be no less a part of French political heritage than it was of the military tradition, involving as it does questions of recruitment, organization, effectiveness, and loyalty. As a result, a Frenchman's perception of this concept was colored by his particular political views. The Left saw the citizen army as a curb to undue military influence over civil institutions and the only kind of army which fulfilled the needs of a democracy. The Right, favoring a long-service professional force, saw the citizen army as politically unreliable, militarily ineffective, and a threat to social stability and internal order. Between these two extremes, there existed an almost infinite number of views. Prior to 1914, the concept had concerned itself only with the military relationship between the state and its male citizens. After 1918, however, it became a body of thought which dealt with the organization of every phase and aspect of French life in time of war. Political controversy thus arose over what kind of an army France would have and what authority would be allowed the central government to organize the nation's defense.[18]

These problems of national defense were closely linked with domestic and foreign policy issues. Increasing industrialization and the loss of vitality in the middle classes due to war losses caused increased tension between the Right and Left. Economic and financial issues replaced the old dynastic and clericalist issues of prewar France. In this political climate, which alternated between seasons of the Right and Left, the French leadership devised policies and enacted legislation which assisted in realizing that which they attempted to prevent—a new war with Germany. Since it was impossible for the contending political factions to find a common basis for cooperation, the *modus operandi* became "compromise." In other words, political action became a search for the form of government that divided Frenchmen the least.[19]

Reflecting this political accommodation, the new French Army established by law in 1927-1928 was based upon a compromise between the principle of the Nation-in-Arms and a professional force. In 1923, Marshal Phillippe Pétain, Commander-in-Chief designate of the French Army and vice president of *Conseil Superieur de la Guerre* (Superior War Council), had insisted that the Army needed a minimum strength of not less than 32 divisions consisting of 100,000 regulars, 200,000 colonial troops, and 100,000 conscripts serving for an 18-month period.[20] This force would constitute the *couverture* (frontier guard) which would keep the enemy, the Germans, at bay while the nation mobilized behind them. Pétain's estimate was based upon the French belief that the 100,000-man *Reichswehr*, reinforced by police and other secret organizations to a total strength of 400,000, could launch an *attaque brusque* (sudden attack) at a moment's notice, against the French frontiers. Outwardly, the new legislation reflected Pétain's estimates of the necessary strength required to insure French security. In reality, it destroyed the organizational cohesion and offensive capacity of the Army. Moreover, the 1927-1928 law reduced service time for conscripts from 18 to 12 months, a goal of the Left in an attempt to create a national militia. This shortened term of service would naturally result in a smaller number of peacetime effectives, so a compromise was necessary. The annual call-up was set at 240,000, rather than Pétain's 100,000, and the number of long-service regulars was increased to 106,000. Not all of these regulars, however, would be assigned to combat units. Some were assigned to the *couverture* force. The remainder were divided between a

Marshal of France, Phillippe Petain

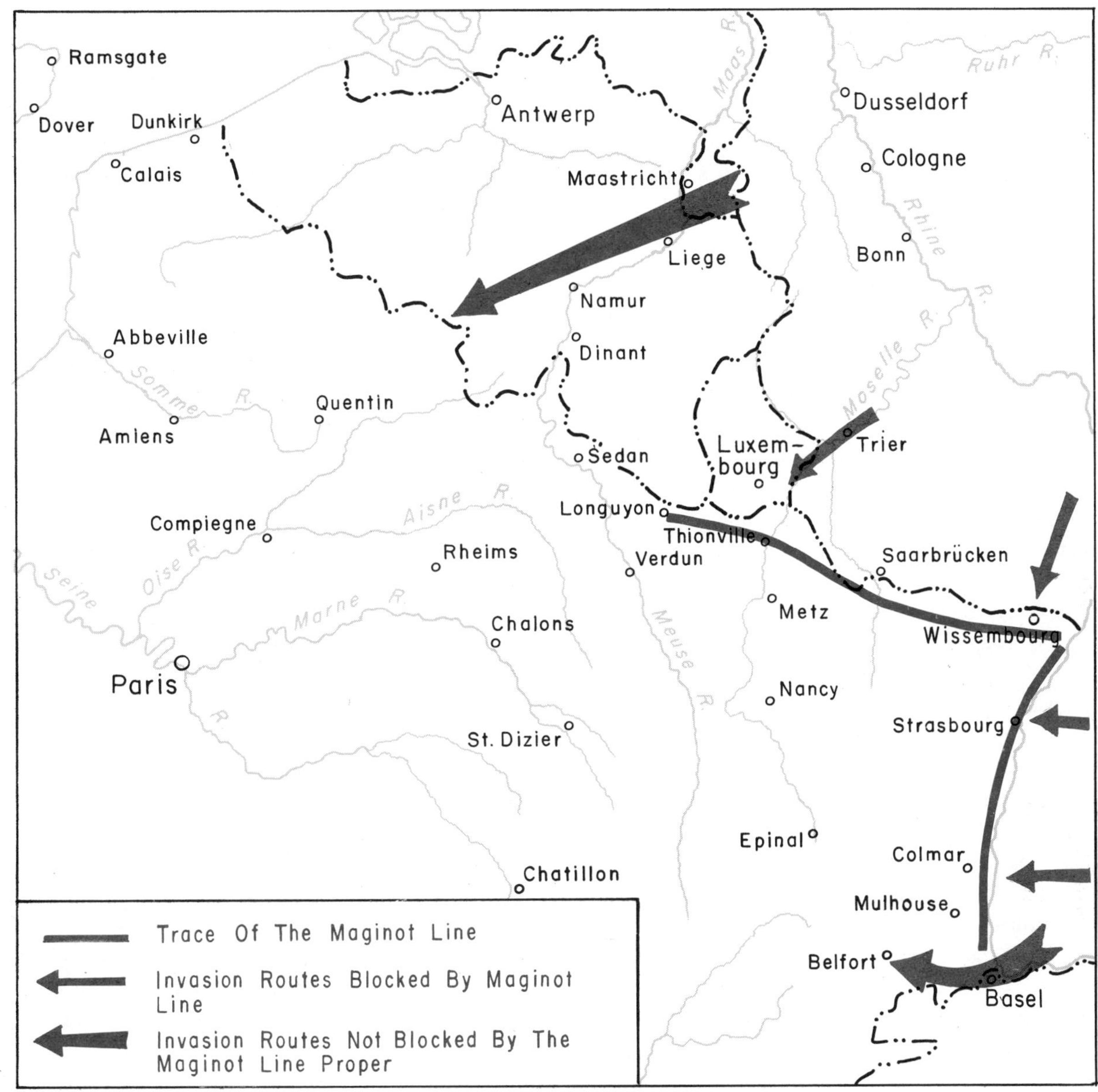

Maginot Line and Invasion Routes

training element, for instructing the annual conscript class, and a staff organization responsible for mobilization planning and maintaining the framework of units to be filled by masses of trained reserves. The remaining necessary force would be provided by the incorporation of approximately 200,000 colonial troops into the metropolitan army.[21]

During the 1920s, French strategy gradually took on more of a defensive orientation for several reasons. Pétain's goal of 32 divisions had not been achieved under the previous conscription law of 1923. Exemptions from service and the necessity to retain a large number of colonial troops in North Africa for the campaigns against the Riffs resulted in many divisions being skeletonized and rendered ineffective. By 1926, the estimate of the number of divisions necessary to ensure the *couverture* had risen to 40. It was impossible, however, to maintain 40 divisions on active duty with the strength available. Immediately upon declaration of mobilization, cadres of regulars from the active duty divisions would form the organizational framework of the second 20 divisions. The remaining vacancies in all 40 divisions were then to be filled by reservists. These divisions would then constitute the frontier covering force.[22] The French Army was, therefore, essentially a potential force. It had little immediate offensive capability.[23] Until 1929, the French war plans envisaged that the *couverture* force in the Rhineland would conduct a delaying action back to the French frontier.[24] But the imminent loss of the Rhineland buffer zone, the reduction in the strength of the active forces due to the colonial wars, the shortening of the required service time, and the impending advent of the *Années Creuses* (hollow years) heightened French fears of a German *attaque brusque* in the late 1920s.* These fears led to the French parliament voting the first appropriations for construction of a permanent *couverture*—the Maginot Line. French strategy had, therefore, begun to assume a definite defensive orientation which would continue until 1940. The Army was fast becoming a national militia—a force intended for defense only—which would have little offensive capability.

Construction of the fortified works along the northeastern frontier of France, which popularly came to be known as the Maginot Line, began in 1929. The decision to build these works was not new and novel. France's use of fortifications for defense of her frontiers goes back to the time of Vauban. Prior to 1914, the doctrine of the offensive had caused the fortifications constructed by General Sere de Rivieres after the Franco-Prussian War to be looked upon with disfavor. The Battle of Verdun, however, had done much to demonstrate the value of well-prepared concrete and steel fortifications in modern war. As a result, a commission headed by Marshal Joseph J. C. Joffre had been formed in 1922 and charged with studying France's defensive organization.[25] *(See Map: Maginot Line and Invasion Routes, page 33.)*

Because Joffre's group did not arrive at any definite solution to the fortification problem, a new commission under General Charles Alexandre Guillaumat was formed in 1925 to study the same problem. This commission directed its attention to the northern and eastern frontiers of the reclaimed provinces of Alsace and Lorraine. These two provinces were the most exposed to any German aggression. They contained the traditional invasion routes through the Moselle Valley and the Wissembourg Gap, they had industrial centers of great value, and they lay on the shortest land route between the German frontier and the political and spiritual center of France—Paris.[26] Although agreement was reached on assigning priority to the defense of these two provinces, there was considerable disagreement as to the form this defense should take.

Both sides in this argument rested their respective cases upon the experience acquired during the Battle of Verdun. Marshal Pétain and his supporters claimed that the German advance had been arrested by hastily constructed field fortifications. They therefore advocated the construction of a continuous, linear, deep defensive zone. The defensive works would consist of concrete-lined trenches behind deep fields of barbed wire obstacles. The trench system was to be modeled after those of World War I, containing protected observation posts, command centers, supply points, and communications facilities. The opposition, led by General Guillaumat, pointed to the same experience and claimed that Verdun had shown concrete forts to be relatively inviolable. This group pressed for the construction of fortified regions, 60 to 80 kilometers in length. Between these fortified regions, carefully chosen gaps would remain which could be used by a maneuver force to trap and destroy an enemy force penetrating the frontier, or as a sally port through which to launch an offensive thrust.[27] The proposed fortifications were, therefore, seen by Guillaumat to be something more than ancillary to defensive operations. As far as the French Parliament was concerned, however, the real selling point was the economy in manpower and materiel to be realized from Guillaumat's proposal as opposed to that of Pétain. Paul Painleve, the French War Minister, accepted the recommendations of Guillaumat and began experimental sites in 1928.

By 1929, however, Guillaumat's concept of the fortifications was already being modified. In that year, André Maginot became War Minister and began the job of acquiring the necessary funds for construction of the proposed fortifications. In this he was successful, but in the process he was forced to modify the concept of the defense. The idea of leaving gaps in the frontier defenses appeared dangerous to the French parliamentarians who feared that adequate protection would not be afforded along the entire exposed frontier. Maginot accepted their arguments and took steps to fill the gaps. The whole fortification scheme was, therefore, considerably modified.† Of more significance perhaps was the fact that now both civilians and some military personnel began to perceive the fortifications as a continuous and strictly defensive front.[28] This perception would grow from 1930 into what would be known by 1939 and in the postwar years as the Maginot Line Complex:

> A psychological pillow and an almost mystical belief in the efficacy of the fortified shield. This was a civilian phenomenon, not a military one. The unfortunate fact was that the army for the most part was reservist and the fears and attitudes of the civilians were reflected by their army, for it was literally "their" army.[29]

*While the French occupied the Rhineland, any German attempt to regain territories lost under the Treaty of Versailles was unlikely. The French, therefore, not only provided for their own defense, but also for that of Poland, Czechoslovakia, and Austria. With the evacuation of the Rhineland, however, there was no attempt to create a means by which France could continue to play the role of guarantor of European security. The predominant theme became that of how the French could buy time in which to mobilize their forces. The *Années Creuses* were the years 1935-1939. High French casualties during the period 1915-1917 had so reduced the French birth rate that only half the usual number of conscripts were available during the latter half of the 1930s.

†In general, the Maginot Line was a succession of casemates (bunkers). Along the Rhine no other fortification was used; elsewhere these casemates were reinforced every 3-5 miles by very powerful, underground fortresses. Even with Maginot's concession to building a continuous line, interval troops were still considered necessary to insure security. These units were fully equipped with all weapons, including field artillery, and charged with repelling any enemy penetration of the fortified line. There was, then, little economy of force (emphasize the principal effort and restrict the strength of secondary efforts) exercised.

In plain fact, the fortified shield existed only along the French northeastern and eastern frontiers. It extended from Longuyon (near the junction of Belgium, France, and Luxembourg) to Basle, Switzerland. It did not cover the entire French frontier, but only the exposed eastern provinces. The common frontier with Belgium was not fortified along the same lines.

Pétain had earlier stated, and most military experts agreed, that the only real defense for northern France lay inside Belgium. There were no natural defensive positions along that frontier, and the high ground water table precluded the construction of the tremendous fortresses to be found in the Maginot Line. The fact that all along this common border there existed large industrial and mining centers also made it impracticable to build lines of fortified bunkers, antitank ditches, and obstacles through these industrial complexes; any defensive line would thus have to be located behind them, thereby negating the purpose for which it was intended. In addition, the French had concluded a defense pact with Belgium in 1920, and, therefore, any fortification of their common frontier would be bound to produce an adverse effect on the Belgians. Finally, the estimated cost precluded a more extensive program. The initial cost estimate for the Alsace-Lorraine fortifications was approximately $323,000,000, a tremendous sum for defense spending in that period. *(See Map 10, in Atlas.)* As a result of these considerations, the Belgian border would be covered only by two lines of small casemates or bunkers. A mobile force would be created which, at the first hint of danger, would advance into Belgium to the line of the Meuse, and thereby cover the principal invasion route not covered by the Maginot Line.[30] In the center, between the Maginot Line and the mobile wing, lay the wooded Ardennes. The French did not see this area as a likely invasion route. Pétain voiced the military's view of the Ardennes while serving as Minister of War in 1934:

> Beginning at Montmedy are the Ardennes forests. They are impenetrable if certain preparations (*Amenagements*) are made. As this front would have no depth, the enemy will not deploy there. If he should, we shall close the pincers as he emerges from the forests. This sector, therefore, is not dangerous.†

Originally conceived as part of a balanced defensive-offensive scheme of national defense, the Maginot Line thus came to wield an unfortunate psychological and economic influence upon the French Army and the French people.

†Vivian Rowe, *The Great Wall of France* (London, 1959), p. 61. In all fairness to Marshal Pétain, it must be remembered that the deep trench of the Meuse Valley was viewed as part of the Ardennes obstacle. Furthermore, the Belgian declaration of neutrality in 1936 prevented French forces from entering Belgium prior to the initiation of hostilities and making those "certain preparations" stipulated by Pétain in 1934.

Simultaneously with the actions to reorganize the Army and provide a new *couverture*, the French undertook the reorganization of national agencies responsible for the preparation and conduct of war. How to achieve necessary centralization of authority in defense matters caused much parliamentary debate and several reorganizations of French defense agencies before a solution was agreed upon in 1938. While it was clearly recognized that the civil government should retain control over the higher preparation for and general direction of war, and that the military should exercise control of the actual conduct of operations, there was no consensus as to the actual authority to be granted each and their proper relationship to each other. The military and political Right favored reforms which gave the central government wide powers and organizational unity because of the increased complexity and totality of modern war; the Left argued that the military was seeking to expand its authority and that the granting of extensive powers to the Government was an infringement on the rights of Frenchmen. Not unexpectedly, the problem was resolved by compromise. The resulting national defense organization divided responsibilities for military thought and action into three phases (general direction of war, military direction of war, and the conduct of military operations). *(See Chart, page 36.)*

The general direction of war was the responsibility of the Council of Ministers who would determine national objectives and ensure adequate means. This Council would be provided advice on how to mobilize the nation's resources by the Superior Council of National Defense, composed of the civilian cabinet ministers of Army, Navy, and Foreign Affairs. But because by 1929 the latter council's membership included all cabinet ministers, the Council of Ministers in effect called itself together to give itself advice on mobilization matters.[31]

To provide military direction of a war, the Ministry of National Defense was reinstituted in 1936. The minister was charged with approving all actions of the armed forces, direction of the armaments program, industrial mobilization, and expenditures of defense funds. The same decree which re-established the defense ministry also created the Permanent Committee of National Defense. This committee was chaired by the Defense Minister and further composed of the Ministers of War, Navy, and Air and the Chiefs of Staff of the three services. In time of war, this body was to be redesignated the War Committee and would retain overall military direction of the nation's armed forces and ensure coordination of the nation's military efforts by providing instructions to the Chief of the General Staff of National Defense (who was to become Commander-in-Chief of the Armed Forces upon mobilization). This arrangement thus neatly confused the higher direction of war with the conduct of operations. A further weakness of the organization was that the Chief of the General Staff of National Defense was not provided with a joint general staff, a General

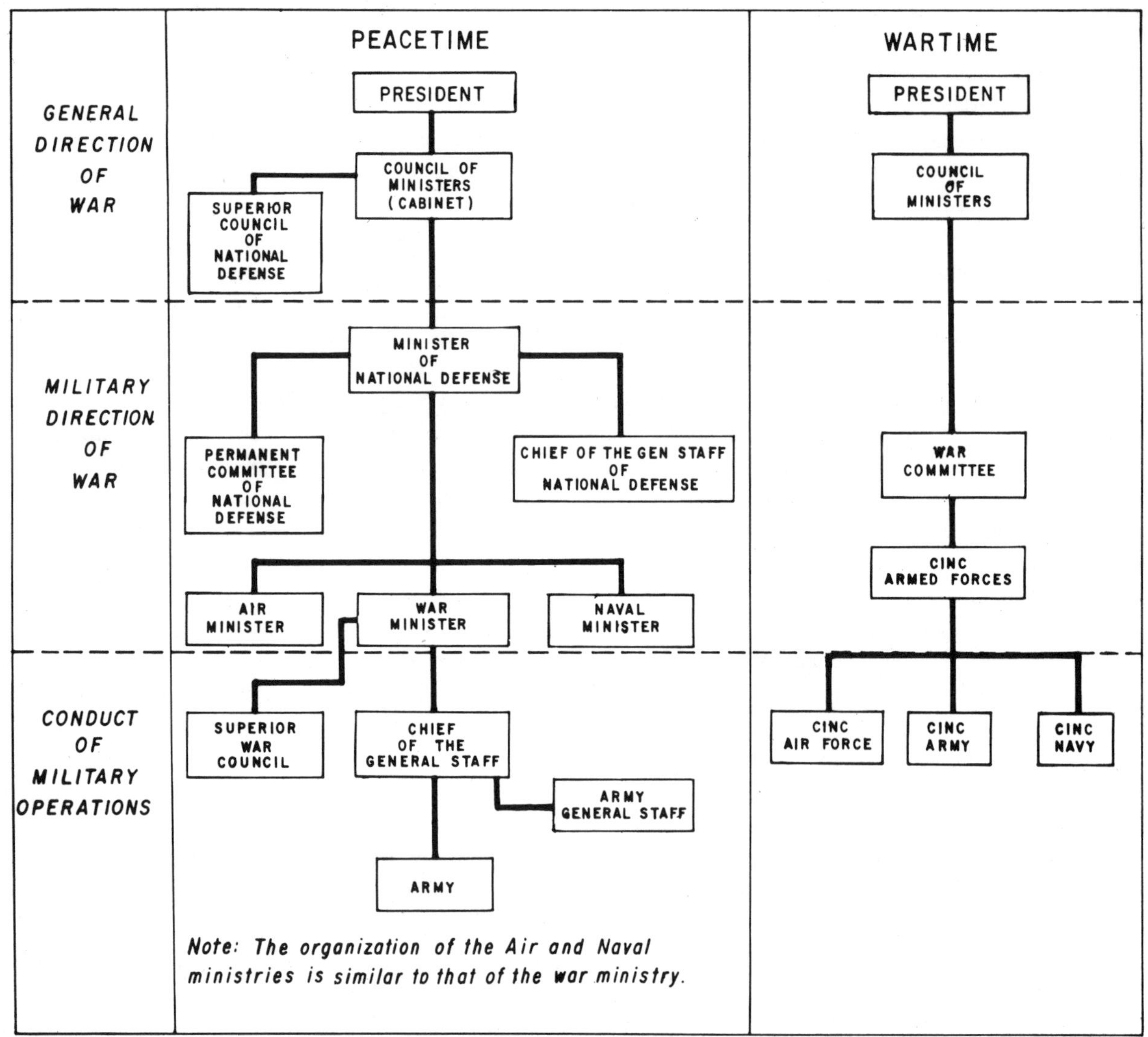

French National Defense Organization, 1938-1940
(Based upon Jean Vial, "The National Defense: Its Organization Between the Two Wars," *Revue d'Histoire de la Deuxieme Guerre Mondiale*, No. 18 [April, 1955], 11-32.)

Staff for National Defense. The necessary staff organizations which could effectively ensure joint cooperation and planning during peacetime and coordinate operations in time of war did not exist. Military direction was to come from a council and be effected through a supreme headquarters which would have to be organized upon mobilization.[32]

For the conduct of military operations, considering the Army as a model, the War Minister was advised by the Superior War Council. The president of the council was the minister himself; the vice-president was the general designated to be the Commander-in-Chief of the French Army in time of war. The remainder of the council consisted of nine generals who in time of war would command army groups or armies, and also any Marshals of France who were still living. The members of the Superior War Council acted as Inspectors General of the Army. In this capacity, they exercised some influence over units which would come under their command upon mobilization. The individual having major responsibility for preparing the Army for war, however, was the Chief of the General Staff. He directed the day-to-day operation, administration, and training of the Army and was assisted by the General Staff of the Army (*Grand Quartier General*). This staff, however, became the staff of the Army Commander-in-Chief upon mobilization. The army high command thus reflected the same imperfections in organization which existed at the higher levels of national defense. Military expertise and ideas on strategic, organizational, and equipment matters could only be introduced as advisories to the War Minister, who was neither obligated to accept them nor to use them. The designated wartime commander neither exercised control over his command during peacetime nor had an adequate staff organization around which to build his future headquarters.[33]

While seemingly attempting to centralize authority and define responsibility for the national defense, the French had actually weakened their defense organization by a democratic diffusion of authority and responsibility. It was a command organization which relied upon the leadership of councils, bodies of men which are seldom capable of quick decision. This organization was probably adequate for the tempo at which the First World War had been fought; it was criminally cumbersome for the coming war with Germany.*

French Armed Forces

Traditionally, popular opinion and historical accounts have attached primary importance to military thought as the main cause of a defeat. To say that the quality of a nation's military thought is not a major factor would also be a gross exaggeration. The true cause of any defeat can only be determined by careful appraisal of the complex array of historical, political, economic, social, psychological, technological, and military factors which interacted to produce it. None of these factors can be completely isolated because they constantly interact with and upon one another. The result of any investigation as to the cause of a defeat will, therefore, be a composite of the various factors rather than the determination of a single cause. French military thought and the resulting doctrine which evolved during the interwar period were no exceptions to this phenomenon.

Although Pétain, as Vice-President of the Superior War Council until his retirement in 1931, was not directly responsible for doctrine, his influence on the French Army during the interwar years was predominant.† He headed the committee which in 1921 devised the regulations for tactically handling divisional and larger formations. These regulations reflected his views on the inviolability of organized fronts and the pre-eminence of firepower in both offensive and defensive operations.[34] The attack and defense were both to be conducted carefully, methodically, and under centralized control. The doctrine of the impulsive all-out offensive espoused prior to World War I had been completely discredited. Pétain claimed that "the individual soldier realized his frailty. He recognized the folly of certain sacrifices and . . . demands the support of a powerful materiel. . . ."[35] No attack, therefore, was to be ordered which could not be adequately supported by artillery and armor. The idea was to wear down the enemy first and spare casualties among the attacking infantry. It was a time-consuming process and very much on the model of Pétain's successful attacks at Verdun and Malmaison in 1917.[36]

In the defense, Pétain's *Instructions* outlined a scheme designed to counter the 1918 German penetration tactics. The defensive position would be organized 2,000-4,000 yards in depth. By the use of extensive automatic weapons and artillery fire, the enemy was expected to be halted at, or shortly within, the forward edge of the position. To a large extent, maneuver became movement of fire rather than of units.[37] In the 1936 revision of the *Instructions*, the role of firepower was again emphasized. It was seen as further dominating the battlefield because of developments in aerial bombardment and the increased range of artillery weapons. Offensive operations were characterized by intensive reconnaissance, detailed preparation of supporting fires, and an extreme caution which sacrificed speed and surprise. This doctrine is best characterized by the slogan then in current use in the French Army, "Lavish with steel; Stingy with blood."[38]

Developments in mechanized warfare also caused changes in the previous defensive doctrine. Meeting engagements (going into battle immediately from the formation used to advance on the enemy's presumed location) were to be avoided as much as possible. Aerial and distant ground reconnaissance were expected to give adequate warning of approaching enemy mechanized columns. A defensive position behind a stream line would then be chosen and prepared. Selection of such a position would take precedence over observation and fields of fire. The bank of the stream was to be defended by only enough infantry, automatic weapons, and antitank guns to prevent a surprise crossing by light enemy elements. The obstacle created by the stream would prevent a large mass of armor from being introduced quickly into the defensive zone. The enemy infantry, therefore, would be isolated and forced to fight the real battle on ground of French choosing, several thousand yards in front of the stream, with his artillery firing at extreme ranges. Tanks were also to be utilized in the defense. The *Instructions* called for them to be deployed well forward in the defensive zone, to act either on their own or in conjunction

*Some Frenchmen, of course, were aware of the shortcomings of their command organization. Attempts to enact legislation which would more effectively centralize authority inevitably met stiff political opposition and failed to pass or were so modified in passage that they failed to accomplish their intended purpose. Aggressive German moves in the late 1930s caused a certain streamlining of the organization by allowing General Maurice Gamelin and Edouard Daladier to hold several positions simultaneously. Gamelin combined in his person the positions of Chief of the General Staff for National Defense, Vice-President of the Superior War Council, and Chief of the General Staff. Daladier was, at the same time, Minister of National Defense and War Minister. The value of this expedient is debatable, considering the many responsibilities of each position; its further weakness is evident when it is noted that neither Gamelin nor Daladier were strong advocates of centralization of command.

†Pétain's retirement in 1931 did not end his influence in military affairs. He was named Inspector General of Air Defense, and as a Marshal of France, he continued serving on the Superior War Council. In 1934, he was Minister of War in the Doumergue government.

with an infantry counterattack to restore the position or destroy enemy tanks which had penetrated it.[39]

A defensive mindedness began to develop in the French Army during the interwar period and spread as time passed, even though the *Instructions* for 1936 reiterated that "the offensive is the supreme form of action."[40] For the French not to have taken this view would have meant the complete rejection of their doctrinal heritage dating all the way back to Napoleon. Pétain realized that it was only through offensive operations that decisive results could be achieved; but it was to be a cautious, methodical offensive, not a bold, slashing attack with its attendant risks and probable heavy casualties.

Generals Jean Estienne and Edmond Buat had earlier seen in the tank the means by which a penetration of an enemy position might be accomplished, thereby reducing the tremendous artillery and ammunition requirements necessary for a successful offensive operation. They believed in capitalizing on the three advantages offered by armored fighting vehicles: protection, firepower, and mobility. The development of the antitank gun and the land mine, however, convinced the high command that these weapons posed too much of an obstacle for the tank. The developing doctrine of tank supremacy was therefore checked, and the tank returned to its World War I role as an infantry-support weapon. Use of masses of tanks would also help economize on infantrymen. This mission, of course, required that the tank advance into the enemy's antitank defenses. To resolve this problem, the French designed heavier tanks with thicker armor which mounted large caliber cannon.[41] This trend enhanced the protective and offensive aspects of the armored fighting vehicle, but it seriously compromised its mobility. Since the tank was to be essentially a support weapon for the infantry, the majority of them were organized into separate tank battalions and assigned to field armies for employment. (In May 1940, the French had 468 tanks in three armored divisions; 582 in three light mechanized divisions; 110 in five light cavalry divisions; and 1,125 in 25 separate tank battalions.)

Upon Pétain's retirement in 1931, General Maxime Weygand succeeded him as vice-president of the Superior War Council and Commander-in-Chief-designate of the French Army. The position of Chief of the General Staff was filled by General Maurice Gamelin. Weygand's and Gamelin's policy was to modernize the Army once the main Maginot fortifications in Alsace and Lorraine were complete.[42] Standing in the way of this intended program were three major problems.

The first was the loss of effectiveness in the active forces, particularly the *couverture*, due to the one-year conscription introduced in 1928 and the difficulties encountered in recruiting professional soldiers. The problem was acute in 1932 and was viewed as being nearly hopeless by the advent of the "lean years" in 1936. Largely because of opposition from the political Left, it was not until 1936, just one month before the German reoccupation of the Rhineland, that two-year service was reintroduced.[43]

General Jean Estienne: Founder of French Armored Forces

The reduction in appropriations for military purposes, drastically influenced by the world-wide depression, created the second problem. Requests for the development and production of new weapons had to be balanced against day-to-day requirements. In 1933, for example, 51 percent of the total French budgetary cuts were from the national defense sector, and 50 percent of this was borne by the Army.[44] Weygand could not proceed with the motorization of the cavalry divisions, although in 1933 he tested a mechanized division at Rheims, leading to the creation in 1934 of the *Division Légére Mecanique* (Light Mechanized Division or DLM).* Although this unit resembled what was to become an armored division, it was a cavalry formation and given a standard cavalry mission. The motorization of five infantry divisions was also begun. (Eventually there were a total of seven.) These two steps toward modernization were taken because arguments for their creation could be couched in terms of economy of manpower and a more effective defense. They, therefore, found acceptance in the eyes of the political Left. No such argument could be made for the creation of an armored division.

*This division consisted of a mixed battalion of armored cars and motorcycles, a brigade of tanks, a brigade of motorized infantry, artillery, and engineers.

French Infantry Carrier, 1939

Weygand and Gamelin were also burdened with maintaining an army and modernizing it in the face of popular demands for disarmament and pacifism, the third major problem. In 1934, Lieutenant Colonel Charles De Gaulle published his now famous work, *Vers l'armée de metier*. De Gaulle's book, while calling for the creation of needed armored, mobile forces, could not have been less timely. Given the current antimilitary feeling in France and the tradition of the "Nation-in-Arms," his call for the creation of an elite, professional armored corps triggered a violent reaction from the political Left, led by the Radical Socialist, Leon Blum. Weygand's careful efforts to work within the political system to establish a general reserve of maneuver and reinstill an aggressive spirit in the Army suffered a major setback.[45] As a result, when Gamelin requested authority to create an instrument of attack (armored division) in 1936 in order to be able to counter further German aggressive moves, he was refused.* De Gaulle's book created additional problems within the Army because the traditional arms saw it as an attempt to create an "all-tank army" at their expense. Therefore, when large-scale tank production began in 1935, priority was given to infantry-support tanks and the mechanization of the cavalry divisions. A second light mechanized division was organized in 1938, and a third in August 1939. In the winter and spring of 1939-1940, five light cavalry divisions were created, with each containing one horse brigade and one mechanized brigade.[46]

*The political Left saw the armored division as an offensive instrument which had no place in an army with a defensive mission. After the Sudetenland crisis in 1938, the decision was made to form two *Division Cuirassies* (armored divisions or DCR). No agreement could be reached concerning their composition, however. As a result, only a test organization was in existence when war broke out on September 1, 1939. On January 15, 1940, this test organization was split to form the First and Second Armored Divisions. A third was created on April 6, 1940, and a fourth on May 15, 1940. The organization, which was probably adopted from British experience and tests, was unsatisfactory.

The delay and the piecemeal creation of these mechanized units further prevented the organization and field testing of large mobile formations of corps size in which their true combat potential could be seen. However, the significance of such testing is questionable, because Pétain and the advocates of the continuous front felt that:

> Bold enemy irruptions would necessarily uncover both flanks of the invader. The defensive strike force need only dash with similar boldness into the flank and rear of the attack to cause its precipitate retreat in all probability.[47]

This clearly illustrates that there was little grasp in French military circles of the true potential of a massive attack by mechanized, combined-arms units. The continuous front had worked in World War I, and it would hold again and allow time for reinforcements to be moved to the threatened point. The army which France mobilized in 1939 was, therefore, for the most part a recreation of the French Army of 1914-1918, prepared to fight the new war at the tempo of World War I. The French Army, moreover, was not alone in this doctrinal miasma because similar events had affected the Air Force and, to a lesser degree, the Navy.

The *Armée de l'Air* (French Air Force), like the Army, was adversely affected by the political turmoil in France which worked a debilitating influence on aircraft production. By con-

Brigadier General Charles De Gaulle, 1940

centrating their industrial efforts on a few types, the Germans had increased aircraft production by 1939 to close to 3,000 a year. In contrast, the French had over 20 different types of fighter, attack, and bomber aircraft in production; as a result, they were producing only about 600 aircraft per year.[48] Although French designers had created modern fighters and bombers by the mid-1930s, the Air Force was still equipped with obsolescent aircraft. The problem was not one of design but of quantity production.

The depression emphasized the appalling plight of the worker in many industries. If management could ignore it, the politician could not. In May of 1936, the French Radicals formed common cause with the Communists and, spurred on by Hitler's occupation of the Rhineland in March, swept the *Front Populaire* into office. Failure of the Front to give immediate relief to the French workers, however, sparked a wave of wildcat strikes which severely crippled the aircraft industry. The ensuing agreement, moreover, failed to provide for an increased industrial output to balance the cost of reforms.[49] The *Front Populaire* opposed the introduction of the assembly line because they felt it created unemployment. As a result, aircraft and other military equipment were nearly all built by hand. Until 1937, the French aviation industrial complex was in reality little more than many small workshops—only one plant was equipped for mass production. Illustrative of the French primitive means of aircraft production is the fact that the Germans could build a BF-109 fighter with 6,000 man-hours of labor, while the French needed 18,000 man-hours to produce the Morane 406, a less sophisticated fighter aircraft.[50]

Rapid and frequent changes in government during the period 1934-1939 made its mark on the French Air Force. Because aircraft manufacturers wielded considerable power through means of political lobbies, successive Air Ministers found their proposals hard to resist. Contracts for prototypes were let without determining the need for a particular type aircraft. This would be followed by an order for an uneconomically small number of aircraft. The next player in the game of "musical ministers" would repeat the process. This type of activity created an inventory of aircraft of many varied types in small numbers. In 1938, the new Air Minister, Guy le Chambre, viewed the accumulated chaos of the preceding 18 years with alarm and tried to fill the gap between the *Armée de l'Air* and the *Luftwaffe* with large-scale purchases from the United States. His efforts were too little and too late.[51] But political activity alone was not responsible for the chaos in French military aviation; two other factors which contributed to the confusion were lack of a comprehensive air doctrine and absence of energetic direction at the highest command levels.

The effect of air action on the strategic movements of the Army was the only consideration dealt with to any degree in official doctrinal publications and instruction. This use of airpower was essentially to be one of interdiction of the battle zones, following logically from the French concept of first halting the aggressor, weakening his forces, and then attacking. Airpower was to diminish the speed and force of the enemy attack by attacking his key communications centers and railroad-switching facilities. This action would be accompanied by day and night raids on rail lines, trains, reserves, and air-landed commando operations in the enemy rear. The whole operation was aimed at "starving" the attacking enemy elements by preventing their reinforcement and resupply.[52] This mission called for a fast, twin-engine, medium bomber. Yet, or perhaps as a result, the French between 1930 and 1939 were testing, producing, and purchasing no less than eight different types of twin-engine bombers.

The French saw only dimly other uses of military aviation. Instruction in military schools rarely failed to mention the effect of attacking the enemy's war-making potential; but this was thought of in terms of factories and warehouses only, not population centers. The French, unlike Douhet, did not see these attacks as producing any cataclysmic effect on the enemy population, and therefore only belatedly began developing a heavy, four-engine bomber.[53]

There was little realization in French military thought as to the tactical impact of the airplane. Its value for reconnaissance and adjustment of artillery fire was appreciated by the Army, which required mainly observation aircraft; being the senior and largest service, it got its wish. In May 1940, the French had several hundred reconnaissance aircraft in service and three new types under development, a number all out of proportion to their actual needs. Official regulations and school instruction rarely envisioned tactical aircraft attacking enemy elements engaged in combat; nor were they envisioned as cooperating with armor except in a reconnaissance role. The *Ecole Superieur de Guerre* noted in the late 1930s that high losses were to be expected in aircraft which engaged in the strafing of enemy ground formations. It was, therefore, only justified in extreme situations.[54] Aircraft which could perform the close support missions had been developed, but they were not being produced in quantity because of the Army's view of the role of tactical air support.

General Gamelin, as Chief of the Defense Staff, was responsible for insuring air and naval preparedness as well as that of the Army. He was, however, a thoroughly conservative Army man, his views on airpower were limited, and he had little interest in new ideas on airpower. The Commander-in-Chief of the *Armée de l'Air*, General Joseph Vuillemin, an elderly ex-bomber pilot and a man not overly endowed with personal dynamism, obliged Gamelin by not bothering him with new ideas on airpower. There was, therefore, no spirit or force at work within the French Air Force which was capable of clarifying the doctrine, determining the type and number of aircraft needed to meet the defense needs of France, and directing aircraft production and development. From this welter of confusion emerged an air force that was impossible to support logistically; that lacked the necessary mass of trained personnel, modern aircraft, and ground organization necessary to conduct sustained operations; and that had only an imperfect concept as to the role of airpower in modern war.

Although fronting on the North Sea, the English Channel, the Atlantic Ocean, and the Mediterranean, France traditionally has devoted only secondary efforts to maritime development. The reason for this, of course, is that France historically has been engaged in an almost ceaseless series of struggles on the Continent. The role of the Navy in the French national defense structure was misunderstood as a result of the Franco-Prussian War and the First World War. In the former, it had played no part; and in the latter, although putting forth a tremendous effort, it concerned itself with the essential, but mundane, tasks of convoy escort and blockade. Again, attention focused on the role played by the Army and little thought was given in high governmental circles as to how the necessary men and supplies had reached France. While the other principal naval powers emerged from World War I with greatly increased fleets, the French Navy actually declined in fighting strength by approximately 40 percent.[55]

Significantly, this decline in French naval strength highlights the fact that the Navy's role in national defense was considered to be minor. As a result, the strength of the Navy was never established by law as was that of the Army. While the Navy sought the enactment of such a law, which would provide a solid basis for fleet construction and for negotiation at the disarmament conferences of the 1920s and 1930s, no legislation was forthcoming. In reality, this probably worked to the Navy's benefit over the two decades between the World Wars, because although it suffered budgetary restrictions—receiving generally only about 21 percent of the total defense purse—it proceeded largely unhindered to build a strong, modern fleet. Factors contributing to the Navy's ability to keep free of the political storms which circled about the Army and Air Force were: its relative invisibility to the French public at large, its small size, and a nonpolitical tradition. While the strength of the Army rested upon conscription and a vast reserve system, 86 percent of the Navy's strength was composed of new volunteers and long-service regulars.[56]

British Armed Forces

Traditional British opposition to the creation and maintenance of a large army reawakened at the end of World War I and continued into 1939. The British Army, up to the time of the Haldane Reforms (1905-1910), had been a small, professional, volunteer organization which served as an imperial police force. But the creation and dispatch of a large expeditionary force to France in 1914 (with its 744,702 dead) was viewed as a tragic mistake not to be repeated.[57] As a result, the British Army, during the two decades between the World Wars, was a recreation of the colonial *gendarmerie* of the 1890s. England withdrew behind the moat of the English Channel and once again placed its confidence for security in the Royal Navy, the traditional first line of defense. This trend was furthered by a widespread hope and reliance on the effectiveness of the Treaty of Versailles, the League of Nations, and the French Army to deal with emergencies on the European continent. Reinforcing this trend was a widespread popular belief in disarmament and pacifism.[58]

This was not an environment in which an army could easily lead a creative and forceful existence. To begin with, the British Army was small, being reduced to a field force of 5 divisions and a territorial force of 12 divisions. Until 1939 Army defense expenditures were directed toward re-equipping these divisions and not toward the development of new concepts or the creation of the organization for creating a mass army. In spite of this, the British led the other world powers in the development of armored combat vehicles and tactical concepts until the early 1930s.

Major General J. F. C. Fuller, the Chief of Staff of the Royal Tank Corps in 1918, was pre-eminent in attempting to

Type	In Commission	Under Construction
Battleships	7	2
Aircraft carriers	2	1
Cruisers	19	—
Destroyers	71	8
Submarines	76	10

French Naval Strength, 1939

maintain the momentum developed in The Great War toward the mechanization of the British Army. Fuller's ideas attracted others, such as the military commentator Basil H. Liddell Hart, and army officers Charles Broad, Percy Hobart, George Linday, F. A. (Tim) Pile, and Gifford le Q. Martel. These men fought for and furthered the development of the British armored forces and doctrine in the interwar period. Three things essentially worked against Fuller and his disciples in their attempts to create a modern mobile force: the mission of the British Army, the availability of funds, and intraservice rivalries. There was no requirement for large armored forces in an army charged with maintaining order in the colonies of the British Empire, although uses were found, particularly in India, for armored cars and light tanks. The Navy, being the first line of defense, received the major portion of the defense budget. The advocates of airpower made their presence felt by successfully arguing for the creation of a bomber force as an instrument of retaliation against expected devastating enemy air attacks upon British population centers. The bomber program, therefore, had a higher priority than the re-equipping of the Army. A second blow to the Army's hopes was the development of radar in 1935; now the Royal Air Force (RAF) had the means by which it could effectively intercept the German bomber fleets, and as a result, it acquired approval and funds to build a vast fighter force.

The advocates of mechanization might have enjoyed greater success had they couched their proposals in more accurate terms. Fuller and his followers had a tendency to refer to tracked self-propelled artillery and armored infantry carriers as tanks. This tendency created in the minds of the officers of the traditional arms the vision of an all-tank army and a takeover bid by the Royal Tank Corps. As a result, their proposals met with continual opposition from the vested interests of the older established arms.[59] These problems were manifested by the fact that no armored division, or Mobile Division as they were first called, appeared in the British Army on a permanent basis until 1938, when the trend of world events left little doubt as to the danger of another world war.

Although the British had established an early lead in the development of mechanized forces, they had fallen behind German developments by the latter half of the 1930s. The principal cause was their failure to create an armored force which could be used constantly to develop and test new ideas and equipment. A further setback to the development of the tank emanated from a review of military actions in the Spanish Civil War. This review seemed to indicate that the tank was vulnerable to small, easily concealed, high velocity antitank guns. This caused several of the former advocates of the tank, including Liddell Hart, to have second thoughts. What resulted, therefore, was a trend by the British, similar to the French, toward more heavily armored and, therefore, slower tanks which

British Equipment During Mechanized Exercise on Salisbury Plain, 1934

would aid the advance of the infantry.[60] The light and medium tanks would avoid close contact with the enemy and perform a cavalry mission. By 1938, British official doctrine for the Mobile Division stated:

> Tactical employment of the armored division.
>
> (a) Only on infrequent occasions which may be in the nature of a manifest crisis should the armored division, as a unit, be used on an independent mission.
>
> (b) The mission of this unit is to reconnoiter, to cover, to seize positions, and in the exceptional cases to strike a powerful blow, or to be launched against an enemy flank or rear to insure victory. It is not contemplated that at any time it be employed to smash into the enemy in frontal attack.
>
> (c) In its relationship to the infantry division, it is a force of light and heavy cavalry, and should follow the general usage of that arm, being drawn off to a flank as the main masses come together, so as not to become involved in the melee.
>
> (d) When the armored division is operating as part of a larger force, the division should not be held back in reserve for use at a critical moment. Instead, some of the cavalry component (light tanks) should be used for screening and reconnaissance, while the heavy tanks (tank brigade) should be held behind until needed as a striking force.[61]

The British Army, accordingly, did not envision the armored division as playing a decisive role in its own right. Rather, it was assigned the traditional role of cavalry. Separate tank brigades, equipped with heavily armored infantry tanks, were created to cooperate with the infantry. Aircraft were seen as another aid to the infantry; but, following the French practice, they were utilized only for reconnaissance and artillery fire direction. The RAF had been developed as a strategic bomber and air defense force. This left little room in the tight defense budgets for the development of tactical air support equipment or doctrine. Furthermore, the Royal Air Force resisted this kind of role, even after the outbreak of the war in France in 1940.[62]

In the spring of 1939, the British finally abandoned their belief in a war of "limited liability" and began to prepare a strong field army that was to be sent to France.* The Territorial Army was to be expanded to 26 divisions, which with 6 regular divisions would make a field army of 32 divisions. The British Expeditionary Force (BEF) of 1939 bore little resemblance to its predecessor of 1914. The BEF of 1914 had been in a state of preparation for ten years and arrived in France within two weeks of mobilization ready to fight. Its successor was created as a result of the failure of the Munich Agreement in 1938 and had an organization, equipment, and tactical doctrine that was far from adequate or complete. It clearly reflected the rush in which it had been established.

In March 1939, the British informed the French that their initial contribution of two regular divisions to the Allies' ground force would be reinforced with two more infantry divisions in 11 months' time. In 1938, they had promised to send two armored divisions in addition to the two infantry divisions. But a year later they had to renege on the promise of armor, claiming that these units would not be ready before September 1940. French pressure, which caused the above-mentioned expansion of the Army, also resulted in the commitment of an expeditionary force of two corps, each comprised of two divisions. An RAF component was attached to each of the corps within 33 days of mobilization.† No further promises were made beyond assuring that additional divisions would be sent to France as they became available.[63]

The actual condition of the BEF is aptly described by Major General Bernard L. Montgomery, the commanding general of the British 3rd Infantry Division:

> In the year preceding the outbreak of war no large-scale exercises with troops had been held in England for some time. Indeed, the Regular Army was unfit to take part in a realistic exercise. The Field Army had an inadequate signals system, no administrative backing, and no organisation for high command; all these had to be improvised on mobilisation. The transport was inadequate and was completed on mobilisation by vehicles requisitioned from civilian firms. Much of the transport of my division consisted of civilian vans and lorries from the towns of England; they were in bad repair and, when my division moved from the ports up to its concentration area near the French frontier, the countryside of France was strewn with broken-down vehicles.
>
> The antitank equipment of my division consisted of 2-pounder guns. The infantry armament against tanks was the .8-inch rifle. Some small one-pounder guns on little hand-carts were hurriedly bought from the French and a few were given to each infantry battalion. Apart from these, a proportion of the 25-pounders of my Divisional Artillery was supposed to be used in an antitank role, firing solid shot.
>
> There was somewhere in France, under G.H.Q., one Army Tank Brigade. For myself, I never saw any of its tanks during the winter or during the active operations in May. And we were the nation which had invented the tank and were the first to use it in battle, in 1916.[64]

*The strategy of "limited liability" was based on British reluctance to again commit major forces to a land war in Europe, and a belief that in the event of a major war Great Britain would have strong allies. The British contribution to the alliance would be a strong navy, a powerful air force, and limited ground forces. It was obviously a defensive strategy, and one which could hardly be expected to find favor with the French. It did not.

†By May 10, 1940, the BEF contained five regular and four territorial divisions. The British Army had two armored divisions: the Seventh in Egypt and the First still training in England. The armor available to the BEF in France was some 300 light, 300 medium, and 20 heavy tanks organized into one army tank brigade, two light armored reconnaissance brigades, and three divisional cavalry regiments.

The Campaign in the West, 1940

Although the Anglo-French had been unable to prevent or slow the catastrophe in Poland because of military and psychological unpreparedness, they viewed the situation in late 1939 with a certain complacency.[65] The French mobilization and the deployment of the BEF had proceeded to completion without hindrance. By May 1940, the French had mobilized some 5,000,000 men who were organized into an army of 99 divisions. The BEF in France numbered 394,165 personnel, assigned to 9 divisions as well as air force and supporting units.[66] The Allies, therefore, decided to rely upon a strategy directed toward first weakening Germany by blockade, economic strangulation, and defensive military operations, while continuing to build up military strength and popular support for the final offensive. The Allies felt that time was ultimately in their favor and continued to follow a policy of restricting military operations against Germany.

Hitler also held the view that time was on the side of the western Allies. Logically, his decision to pre-empt them in Scandinavia in the early spring of 1940 in no way distracted him from his ultimate aim of forcing an early decision in the West.

Except for patrol clashes, the fall and winter of 1939-1940 passed uneventfully. The expected German offensive did not materialize, although there were several alerts. The war acquired an unreal aspect for the Allied troops and became known as the "sitzkrieg" or phony war. A combination of the severe winter weather, reluctance of the German generals, dis-

Preparation for the German Offensive in the West

satisfaction with the proposed plan, loss of a portion of the plan to the Belgians on January 10, and finally, the operation in Norway and Denmark, caused the offensive to be postponed until spring. This delay in launching the offensive, paradoxically, worked to the advantage of the Germans. To OKH, the respite was heaven-sent. Despite the severe winter weather and the OKW directive to maintain all units in their attack positions, the army high command launched a vigorous training program in the conduct of mobile operations. New divisions were created, equipped, and trained; old divisions were re-equipped, reorganized, and given additional training. The experience gained in Poland was evaluated and disseminated throughout the Army. While the Germans were taking advantage of the prolonged break in operations to improve their forces and further develop their campaign plans, the French Army went into a period of decline.

The Allied policy of restricting military operations, the spirit of complacency, and the failure of the Germans to attack created a general atmosphere of inactivity. The French Army was above average, but it was a potential force which needed to be toughened. Failure to conduct even limited offensive operations prevented it from developing an aggressive spirit. As a result, the troops spent the severe winter building fortifications along the Franco-Belgian border, mounting guard, and loafing. This limited activity, supplemented by Communist agitators and German propaganda, led to a widespread attitude of apathy in the French forces and a consequent decline in morale. The reservists—the majority of the French Army—were more susceptible to this debilitating process than were the regular units of the French Army and the BEF. More serious, perhaps, was that there was no impulse from the French high command to halt this obvious trend and to repair the damage that had been caused.[67]

It was the intent of General Gamelin, Commander-in-Chief of the Allied forces, to move his four leftmost armies into Belgium if the Germans invaded the Low Countries. *(See Map 10, in Atlas.)* Gamelin's plan was based upon two strategic considerations paramount in French thinking since 1919: conserve French manpower and keep the war away from French soil. In keeping with French doctrine, he intended to avoid a direct confrontation and to meet the German offensive in a prepared defensive position behind a river line. This would allow the power of the French artillery to be fully employed. Originally the Escaut River had been picked as the position, but a more forward position (the Dyle River Line) was selected in November 1939. The Dyle Line was shorter, it covered Brussels, and it protected more of Belgium. It also had more depth. The added distance raised the question as to whether it could be reached and prepared before the Germans penetrated the Belgian defenses on the Albert Canal-Meuse River Line. It was assumed that the Belgians would be able to hold up the German advance for at least five days. While this plan would aid the Belgians, it offered no assistance to the Dutch. In late November, therefore, Gamelin began to study the possibility of extending the Dyle position north of Antwerp. On March 20, 1940, he directed that upon the initiation of the German offensive, the Seventh Army of General Giraud would advance north along the coast into Holland to the vicinity of Breda-Moerdijk. The Seventh Army would establish a connecting link between the Dyle Line and Fortress Holland, in effect creating a "continuous front" from the Zuider Zee to Basle, Switzerland.* The BEF and the French First Army would move to the Dyle River and cover that line from Antwerp to Namur. General Corap's Ninth Army would advance to the Meuse between Namur and Sedan.[68]

On October 19, 1939, OKH published its first plan (code name FALL GELB—Plan YELLOW) for the offensive in the West. *(See Map 9a, in Atlas.)* This plan involved only the capture of the Belgian and Dutch channel coast, intending it as an air-naval base for operations against England. It was solely a reflection of Hitler's fear of Allied occupation of the Low Countries and the attendant threat to the vital Ruhr, just as his invasion of Norway had been prompted, in part, by fear that England would get there first. This plan has often been misdescribed as a copy of the Schlieffen Plan of 1914. The only similarities between the OKH plan and the Schlieffen Plan were that the advance was to move through Belgium and that the main attack (*Schwerpunkt*) was on the right. Because of the

*The Dyle Plan committed 19 Allied divisions to the advance into Belgium. The addition of the Breda Variant added another 11, for a total of 30. The inclusion of the Seventh Army into the advance removed the only reserves from the left of the Allied line. These forces included all three French DLM's, one of the three DCR's, and 5 of the 7 motorized infantry divisions.

necessity of eventually turning to the Eastern Front, the plan devised by Schlieffen was intended to first produce a decisive defeat of the French Army in one operation. The OKH plan had no such objective and was not concerned with the problem of a two-front war. It was hurriedly prepared and distributed, and as a result, no one was satisfied with it. The army high command, as pointed out, did not want an offensive at the time. Hitler started revising his thinking on the offensive almost as soon as the first plan was distributed, and the more aggressive generals, such as Heinz Guderian and Erich Manstein, disapproved of it because it promised no decisive results.[69]

Throughout the winter of 1939-1940, the debate over and the repeated revision of the plan continued. *(See Maps 9a, b, d, in Atlas.)* General Erich Manstein, Chief of Staff of Army Group A, is generally credited with having conceived the idea of attacking through the Ardennes. Although more than anyone else he was responsible for its conception and adoption, the final plan was still a modification of the original and not a totally new strategic concept.* The final plan was the result of the interaction of many factors, the most important of which was time. *(See Map 10, in Atlas.)* The continual postponement of the offensive allowed time for the rebuilding and expansion of the German mechanized formations, the conduct of war games, and evaluation of their results and observation of the probable reaction by the Anglo-French forces. For the attack through the Ardennes to be successful, it was necessary to cross this obstacle and reach open terrain across the Meuse before encountering a major Allied counterattack. During the winter, the western Allies had been able to learn of several of the German scheduled attack dates. Their reactions to this intelligence were closely observed by the Germans, who were able to learn two facts which greatly influenced the development of their plans. First, it was clear that the Allies intended to advance into Belgium with their best units. Second, this advance would not begin until after the Germans launched their offensive. The Germans, therefore, could anticipate crossing the Ardennes without meeting major enemy formations in passage.[70] This factor was crucial to the success of the German plan. An encounter with major enemy forces while German formations were constricted in the Ardennes could spell disaster for the German hopes for a speedy and decisive campaign.[71]

By February 1940, Plan YELLOW had been drastically revised and now had a decisive objective: to cut off and destroy Allied forces north and west of Sedan. The major effort, spearheaded by 7 *panzer* and 3 motorized divisions, was to be made by Army Group A (45 divisions) through the Ardennes Forest, while Army Group B (30 divisions) applied frontal pressure in the north, and Army Group C (19 divisions) remained on the defensive in the south. The *Luftwaffe* was to establish air superiority, provide tactical air support, and furnish airborne troops to Army Group B. One question, however, still remained to be settled—if and when the *panzers* crossed the Meuse and broke through the French defenses, what was to be done next? Hitler reserved this decision for later, pending the crossing of the Meuse.

Numerically, the opposing armies were about equal, but the Germans had been combat tested and, most important, they were influenced by a few key, progressive leaders who appreciated tactical air power, the importance of mobility and speed, and the shock action of massed armor. Germany had 2,439 tanks, the Allies, 2,689; but Hitler's were concentrated for use in mass, while those of the Allies were dispersed all along the front. The Allies had 2,000 combat aircraft in France; the German offensive was to be supported by 3,700. Lastly, German esprit was superior to that of their foes—particularly the French.

Shortly after midnight on the evening of May 9, 1940, Hitler struck. Intensive aerial bombardments of principal Allied airfields were followed at dawn by swift ground attacks across the border and airborne assaults in Holland and Belgium.

The conquest of Holland took only five days. Kuechler's Eighteenth Army (about 10 divisions, including 1 *panzer*) advanced in three columns, while paratroopers and other airlanded elements arrived at The Hague, Rotterdam, Moerdijk,

Commencement of German Invasion, May 10, 1940

*Presenting his concept on October 25, 1939, Hitler was, in fact, the first person to raise the question of the feasibility of attacking through the Ardennes. He was also the first to suggest a mechanized attack along the Arlon-Sedan axis, originally making the proposal on October 30, 1939. Hitler's reference to Sedan, however, can more likely be attributed to the significance which it had as a demonstration of past Teutonic superiority than to his strategic insight. He shared a similar view on Verdun, in that he felt that its early capture was necessary in order to blot out the German failure there in World War I.

and Dordrecht, seizing airfields and key bridges. *(See Map 11, in Atlas.)* Recovering from their surprise, the Dutch struck back at the airheads, but the Germans, superbly supported by the *Luftwaffe*, held on to most of their gains. *(See Map 10, in Atlas.)* The northernmost column reached Afsluit Dyke late on May 11. The center column reached the Grebbe Line late on May 10; here the Dutch were able to maintain their position until May 13, when events farther south forced their withdrawal. The southern column, Kuechler's main effort, seized the Gennep railroad bridge intact, and by nightfall on May 10 had forced the Dutch evacuation of the Peel Line. On May 12, *panzer* units of the southern column linked up with the airborne elements holding the key bridges at Moerdijk and Dordrecht. En route at Breda they had brushed aside advance elements of the French Seventh Army, which had moved north to support the Dutch. On May 13, the French withdrew to Antwerp, and the Dutch Government departed for England. Isolated, with their cities threatened with destruction, the Dutch surrendered on May 14. That day, the bulk of the French Seventh Army began moving south.

Army Group B's main attack was made by the Sixth Army (23 divisions, including two *panzer*) through the restricted Maastricht-Liége area. *(See Map 11, in Atlas.)* In a brilliantly executed operation, the Germans utilized airborne forces to capture Fort Eben Emael as well as key bridges over the Albert Canal, thus allowing armored elements to drive toward Liége and the Dyle River. On May 11, the Belgians withdrew to the Dyle River, to which position the French and British advanced on May 12. At Hannut the next day, *panzer* elements defeated General Piroux's cavalry corps (2nd and 3rd DLMs), which was screening the Allied advance to the Dyle; by May 15 the Germans were probing the Dyle Line. The Allies had 35 of their best divisions—including practically all of the BEF—between Namur and Antwerp, in the mistaken belief that the German main attack would be there. But by that night it was clear that the real threat lay farther south on the Ardennes front, where the weak French Second and Ninth Armies had been shattered. The Allies now elected to withdraw westward to the Escaut River.

While Bock was overrunning Belgium, the powerful German main attack force (Army Group A) moved by three routes to the Meuse River, arriving there by nightfall on May 12. French cavalry and the rugged Ardennes terrain had only imperceptibly slowed the march. Leading the advance were General Ewald von Kleist's Armored Group (five *panzer* divisions under Guderian and Reinhardt, and three motorized divisions) and General Hermann Hoth's Armored Corps (two *panzer* divisions). The leading German elements arrived on the Meuse north of Sedan at about the same time that the advance troops of General André-Georges Corap's largely foot-mobile Ninth Army were arriving.* Although the French had destroyed the bridges over the river, the Germans immediately began crossing infantry and reconnaissance elements to secure a bridgehead on the west bank. On May 13, the river was forced at Houx, Monthermé, and Sedan. The crossings at Houx and Monthermé were accomplished primarily by ground means alone. The crossing at Sedan by the three *panzer* divisions of Guderian's XIX Corps, however, was supported by a tremendous aerial attack by medium bombers and Stuka dive bombers, which kept up a constant bombardment of the French artillery positions while the crossings were being made. The next day the bridgeheads were expanded against frantic French resistance and repeated air attacks. German armor poured across, and Guderian, securing high ground to the south, turned westward toward Montcornet. The following infantry divisions also arrived at Sedan on May 14. French counterattacks at Donchery and Stonne were unsuccessful. That night, Corap ordered a withdrawal, but it was a futile gesture. General Charles Huntziger decided, almost simultaneously with Corap, to withdraw his left.† He felt that Guderian's *panzers* at Sedan intended to make a shallow envelopment of the unprotected northwestern end of the Maginot Line. Also on May 14, Guderian had decided to change his direction of advance to a more westerly one. As a consequence of these three decisions, when Guderian renewed his attack on May 15, he found the "door" between the Second and Ninth French Armies ajar with only open space beyond.[72] Corap's Ninth Army and the left of the Second were shattered and unable to form a new line—a 50-mile gap yawned invitingly. By May 16, German spearheads had reached the line shown, and Rundstedt's infantry divisions were making forced marches to close up.

Meanwhile, on May 12, General Gamelin had ordered divisions from his general reserve to the Ardennes area; moving slowly, however, they had been too late. On May 15, he ordered divisions from the right of his line to the critical sector and activated Touchon's Sixth Army headquarters to command the troops which, being assembled, would supposedly close the gap. The units assigned to the Sixth Army were scattered, and those from the Second and Ninth Armies had already been roughly handled by Reinhardt's and Guderian's

*Corap was not scheduled to be fully in position until D + 5, or May 14. This was based on Gamelin's assumption that the Germans could not concentrate strong enough forces—primarily heavy artillery—until D + 9 to force a crossing of the Meuse. It is of interest to note that General Halder shared Gamelin's view.

†On May 13, Huntziger's Second Army had been removed from Billotte's First Army Group and placed under CINC, Northeast Front. Georges was not fully aware of the situation at Sedan, and as a result Corap's and Huntziger's moves were not coordinated.

The *Luftwaffe* Was Used in the Artillery Counter-Battery Role

*panzers.** As a result, only one regiment was in position to meet Guderian's lunge to the west. By dark on May 15, the German bridgehead was 62 miles wide and steadily increasing in depth.[73] French attempts to counter the German thrusts from the outset of the campaign were always too late. In part, this was due to their reliance on telephone communications; this form of communication quickly became submerged under the demands placed upon it, suffered heavily from the actions of the *Luftwaffe*, and was completely severed by the advancing *panzer* columns. Road and rail movement, upon which so much depended, was extremely difficult, due again to *Luftwaffe* activity and the masses of fleeing refugees.

Fear of a French counterstroke from the Verdun-Chalôns area unnerved Army Group A and OKH on May 17. *(See Map 12, in Atlas.)* As a result, Guderian, impatient to drive his divisions to the coast, was peremptorily ordered to halt. After a violent altercation with Kleist, which List had to come forward to resolve, Guderian received permission to conduct a "reconnaissance in force." It was during this advance that the French Ninth Army made one last futile effort to halt the onslaught. Also, Brigadier General Charles de Gaulle, commanding the 4th DCR, launched counterattacks against Guderian's south flank, but his weakened armored division could not hold the limited gains made. Meanwhile, to the north, Hoth's corps, spearheaded by Rommel's division, drove forward and seized Cambrai. In Belgium, Bock's depleted armies—his armor had already been dispatched to aid Rundstedt's drive to the coast—followed up the retreating Allies, and by May 18 had reached the Dender River. By the nineteenth of May, infantry from the Twelfth and Sixteenth Armies had lined the southern flank of the breakthrough as far west as Montcornet, and OKH then lifted the restrictions on Kleist's advance. Guderian, closely followed by the motorized infantry corps of Kleist's group, raced along the Somme River toward Abbeville. Late on May 20, that town surrendered, and the corridor to the sea, though tenuous, was a reality. The BEF, its communications with Cherbourg severed, was forced to switch its base to the Dunkirk area. By May 21, Kleist's other *panzer* corps had reached the line shown on *Map 12, in Atlas.* Guderian had seized bridgeheads across the Somme River; the motorized infantry had closed up to relieve the *panzers* on the south flank; and infantry from the Second and Ninth Armies was rapidly moving westward to strengthen the extended south flank.

But on the north side of the penetration, German success was slower and was achieved at greater cost. After crossing the Meuse, in contrast to Kleist's drive in the south, Hoth still had to fight his way through the border fortifications prepared during the winter. Rommel burst through relatively easily, but Kluge's following infantry corps had some bloody fighting in the "mop-up." Then, as they pushed toward Cambrai, the French First Army put up vigorous resistance and took a heavy

*The French 3rd DCR was ordered to support the Second Army on May 12. Rather than attacking Guderian's bridgehead, the division was dispersed in a 12-mile-long defensive line south of Stonne. Rommel's 7th *Panzer* Division destroyed the French 1st DCR while they were refueling on May 14. The French 2nd DCR was destroyed by Reinhardt's *panzers* on May 15 while moving by road and rail between St. Quentin and Hirson to support the Ninth Army.

Refugees Clogged the Major Routes

toll of German troops. Thus, when Guderian plunged forward on May 19, Hoth restrained Rommel at Cambrai until more infantry could close up to protect the north flank. Early the next morning, Rommel pushed his leading elements to the vicinity of Arras. After closing up his division, he resumed his westward advance the afternoon of May 21, soon colliding with the British attack being made by "Frankforce."

As Rundstedt's troops exploited their decisive breakthrough and the BEF withdrew to the Escaut River line, General Viscount John Gort, Commander-in-Chief of the BEF, had realized that the French First Army could not protect his right and rear. Thus he had stationed some of his communications-zone troops in the gap between the Somme and the Scarpe, hoping to slow Guderian, and he had begun organizing the canal line from Douai on the Scarpe to Watten. He also formed "Frankforce" (parts of two infantry divisions and a tank brigade) and gave it the mission of reinforcing Arras and blocking east-west roads to the south of it. On May 19, Weygand relieved Gamelin. Now London ordered the BEF to move to the Somme, but Gort convinced his superiors of the impracticability of the move. The Allied high command then urged a joint French-British attack south toward the Somme, and the French agreed to aid "Frankforce" with an attack toward Cambrai. "Frankforce" was too weak to do more than bloody Rommel's nose. Hoth massed his other divisions and forced the British back to Arras on May 22. The British attack disturbed OKH, however, and led to undue emphasis being placed upon securing Arras. Reinforcements were sent to the area, and Bock was ordered to transfer the main Sixth Army effort farther south to the Maulde area. Having driven "Frankforce" back into Arras on May 22, Hoth pressed his attack northward. *(See Map 13, in Atlas.)* On that day, the Allied Supreme War Council approved the "Weygand Plan," converging attacks on May 23 toward Bapaume from both Arras and the Somme. The decision was made without knowledge of the complete failure of the "Frankforce" attack on May 21 and of the tremendous power the Germans had stationed in the salient west of Cambrai-Péronne. Under these circumstances, the plan was decidedly unrealistic. On the twenty-third of May, Hoth forced the British back to Béthune; that day, the French counterattacks on the Somme failed. Still, as late as May 25, Weygand persisted in his plan.

Meanwhile, Guderian—lacking part of his force, as it was held back by OKH directives—fought his way against stiff resistance northward to Boulogne and Calais. Boulogne was captured on May 23, but Calais, recently reinforced from England, held out until the twenty-seventh of May. By May 24, five *panzer* divisions were exerting pressure on the canal line. Gort had reinforced this makeshift line with combat-tested troops from the Escaut line, but the chances of successfully holding the *panzers* appeared slim. Now, however, Hitler and Rundstedt intervened and halted the attack of the armored elements for two days, allowing the British to stiffen their canal defenses and begin a withdrawal to the Dunkirk beachhead. The halt order, one of the most controversial decisions of the war, was issued by Hitler over the protests of OKH; but the record reveals that Rundstedt, probably influenced by Kluge and List, had recommended to the *Fuehrer* on May 24 that the infantry continue to attack alone. The reasons for this incredible halt order are not clearly established, but it seems that Rundstedt, more cautious than the *panzer* leaders, was concerned with readying his troops for the campaign in southern France. Also Hitler considered the Dunkirk area unsuitable for armor; furthermore, he seemed almost frightened by the magnitude of his success. Underestimating the British, he considered the *Luftwaffe* capable of completing their destruction.*

A French Armored Division Was Immobilized Through Lack of Fuel

*There has been a great deal of speculation by historians over this halt order of May 24. British military historians have tended to feel that the counterattack at Arras on May 21 jolted the assurance of the German commanders and made them more cautious. Others have put forward the idea that the *Fuehrer* wanted to offer the BEF a "golden bridge" in hopes of inducing the British to negotiate a settlement. It is also possible that Goering, using the fearful toll of Polish troops destroyed by the *Luftwaffe* in the Kutno Pocket as a precedent, persuaded Hitler to give the Air Force the mission of completing the destruction of the trapped Allied forces. Whatever the reason, the decision to halt was a grave mistake for it allowed the British to save their Regular Army. Loss of the entire BEF would have placed the British in a position from which they would have had few options other than a settlement with Hitler.

The Bulk of the German Army Had a Struggle Keeping Pace with the Mobile *Panzers*

In the north, King Leopold had withdrawn by the night of May 23 to the Lys River and had taken over the front south to Menin, in order to allow the BEF to create a reserve with which to implement its part in the Weygand Plan. On May 24, Bock launched a powerful offensive with the Sixth Army, which, on May 25, created a gap between the Belgian right and the British left. Gort now committed all his available forces—none remained for the Weygand Plan—to an unsuccessful effort to close the gap. On May 26, he decided to withdraw to Dunkirk, and that night the Royal Navy was ordered to begin evacuation of the BEF. That day, Leopold warned the Allies of the impending collapse of the Belgian Army. The next day, as his army was being pushed back toward Ostend, he asked Hitler for terms; on May 28, he surrendered unconditionally.

Late on May 26, Hitler's halt order was lifted, and the *panzer* divisions attacked the canal line. Near the coast, the improved defenses and flooded country held Guderian to negligible gains; but in the better terrain near Béthune, Rommel's penetration, linking up with a Sixth Army column, sealed the fate of half of the French First Army whose leaders had rebelled at the idea of withdrawal. By May 30, most of the British and some French were within the Dunkirk perimeter; the previous day, most of the German armor had been withdrawn, and the reduction of the pocket was left to the *Luftwaffe* and 10 infantry divisions under Kuechler's control. Now the well-organized evacuation proceeded under the cover afforded by the Royal Air Force, which, in general, kept the *Luftwaffe* from having its accustomed free hand. By June 5, when the Germans finally reached Dunkirk, the Allies had evacuated 338,226 British, French, and Belgian troops.

South of the Somme, meanwhile, the French were lethargically preparing defenses along the river lines for the coming Battle of France. The Allies launched counterattacks at Abbeville and Amiens in an attempt to wipe out the German bridgeheads, but achieved only temporary gains.

The Battle of France began early on June 5, just one day after the British had completed the Dunkirk evacuation. *(See Map 14, in Atlas.)* In the short period since disengagement at Dunkirk, the German forces had been redeployed along the Somme and the Aisne and readied for the offensive. This was a remarkable achievement, for, in addition to the shifting of forces, considerable re-equipping and reorganization were necessary.

Hitler had received the initial German battle plan as early as May 20, but it was not finalized until the twenty-eighth of that month. Under this plan, Rundstedt, with about 45 divisions, would make the main attack east of Paris on June 9 to separate Army Groups 2 and 4 and to pin the former against the Maginot Line. Guderian, with four *panzer* divisions, was to spearhead this attack. The major secondary attack, led by Bock and his 50 or so divisions, was to be launched west of Paris on June 5. It was to drive rapidly to the Seine River, after which a decision would be made as to the ultimate direction of its attack. Bock was allocated six *panzer* divisions—two directly subordinated to the Fourth Army and four under Kleist; the Eighteenth Army, mopping up the Dunkirk area, was also part of his command. Another secondary attack, itself consisting of two attacks, was to be launched on June 14 by the 24 divisions of Army Group C against the Maginot Line at Saarbrücken and Colmar. This attack was designed to link up with the main attack in the encirclement of the French behind the Maginot Line. Thus, about 120 divisions, backed up by 23 others in general reserve, would participate in the operations. To combat this seasoned and formidable host, the French had only about 65 divisions—including three reconstituted armored divisions—of which 17 were either Maginot Line fortress troops or second-line reserve formations. Many were understrength, and some needed equipment; morale was generally low. The British had units equivalent to two divisions in line on the lower Somme. Under these conditions the odds were greatly against the Allies.

Weygand had attempted to build up a defense in depth behind the Somme and the Aisne.* However, lack of time and

*This was the same type defensive system, called the *Quadrillage*, that Weygand had urged be built along the Franco-Belgian border in 1932. Its defense utilized the many farm buildings, small villages, stone walls, hedges, and clumps of trees found throughout France. Various combinations of these obstacles were made into a deep system of infantry and artillery strong points. French weakness in armored units and tactical aircraft, however, prevented effective mobile counterattack groups from being formed or employed. Weygand also created in late May a number of *Groupes Franc* (unattached groups). These were essentially company-sized, mobile units equipped with medium tanks, armored cars, antitank guns, motorcycles, and a high ratio of machineguns. These groups were primarily intended to block vital roads.

materiel and the *Luftwaffe*'s constant harassment of French troop movements prevented the Weygand Line from being made very strong, except in a few areas. Bock's Fourth Army took one day to establish a firm grip south of the Somme, then plunged headlong for the Seine. By June 9, the *panzers* and General Erich von Manstein's corps had reached it. Now the German armor was directed westward to cut off the French IX Corps, which had been slow in withdrawing from the Somme west of Abbeville. On June 12, Rommel accepted the surrender of the bulk of this corps at St. Valéry-en-Caux. The Sixth Army found the Weygand Line more difficult to penetrate in its zone, and Kleist's tanks, leading the assault, were unable to achieve a clean breakthrough. As a result, on June 8, although some of his troops had reached Clermont, OKH directed the shifting of Kleist's group eastward to the Ninth Army sector, where passage seemed easier. (On June 11, the Eighteenth Army moved into line directly north of Paris.) Meanwhile, Weygand, his Tenth Army shattered and the Seventh Army falling back, ordered Army Group 3 to withdraw to the Seine on June 8. Already the French were reeling, and now, on June 9, Rundstedt attacked.

The French Fourth Army, defending in depth and making judicious use of local counterattacks, prevented List's Twelfth Army from securing a large enough bridgehead across the Aisne to accommodate the *panzers* until late in the day, when Guderian was able to cross west of Rethel. The French launched armored counterattacks against his columns during the next two days and slowed their advance. But to the west, the French Sixth Army had been forced back and the Fourth Army, bending its left back to maintain contact, became overextended. On June 12, Guderian broke through at Chalôns and raced southward; to his right, Kleist's armor had crossed the Marne at Château Thierry and also was surging southward. The fate of the French armies was sealed. With Kleist's forcing of the Marne and Guderian's drive southeast from Châlons, the French retreat became a rout. The Germans at once launched the pursuit. As early as June 12, Weygand had requested the Government to seek an armistice, but not until Pétain became Premier on the sixteenth was a surrender considered favorably.

Meanwhile, Bock's armies fanned out to the southwest while Rundstedt moved south and southeast. *(See Map 15, in Atlas.)* Hoth's *panzer* divisions overran Brittany and Normandy, arriving at Brest and Cherbourg on the dates shown. At Cherbourg, Rommel had a brisk encounter with the British, who were evacuating troops debarked there as recently as June 14, when hope had still flickered for the French cause. In the meantime, Weygand had withdrawn his troops south of Paris on the thirteenth, and the Eighteenth Army moved into the city the following day. By June 17, the remnants of the French armies had reached the general line shown on *Map 15, in Atlas,* but they had neither the time nor inclination to organize it for an effective defense. On that date, *panzer* elements from Kleist's and Guderian's groups—both were now operating under Rundstedt—reached the Loire River at Nevers and the Swiss border, respectively. Thus the French troops in and behind the Maginot Line were isolated. Guderian now turned his divisions north and east to assist in herding these forces into a pocket around Epinal. Kleist's troops drove on southward.

Between Hoth's *panzers* to the west and Kleist's group to the east, the infantry corps of five German armies pressed southward in a solid mass. (For purposes of clarity, only routes of representative corps are shown.) Farther east, List's Twelfth Army followed Guderian, and the Sixteenth Army swung in behind the Maginot Line to link up with the First Army, which had broken through the line at Saarbrücken on June 14. The following day, the Seventh Army also broke through to assist in the ensuing encirclement operations. The Army Group C attacks on the Maginot Line, made against a weakened garrison lacking mobile reserves, were extremely successful and less costly than might have been expected. The Germans utilized large quantities of artillery, bypassed strong points, and achieved surprise at Colmar by an unorthodox midmorning attack.

The last week of the campaign was an anticlimax. Pétain asked for an armistice on the seventeenth. It was signed with Germany on June 22, but hostilities did not cease until after Italy had also signed on June 25. Mussolini—eager to share in the spoils—had declared war on June 10, but it was the twentieth before his generals were able to attack. Stalled at the border by the much weaker but more determined French, the Italians begged Hitler to advance German troops from Grenoble toward the border. Only a halfhearted effort was made, and Italy went to the conference table without military conquests.

So ended the Campaign in the West. In six weeks, the Allied armies in Western Europe had been shattered and pursued

The Final Humiliation: Compiegne, June 21, 1940

with a vengeance reminiscent of Napoleon. Although the campaign had taken six weeks, the French and British had lost control of it by May 16. Until then there had been a chance to maintain the "continuous front" and stabilize the situation. Once the German *panzers* broke into the clear, however, the Allied high command, which still thought and acted in time with the clock of the First World War, found the pace too fast to cope with. Although hesitant at times, the German leadership in the main adhered steadfastly to the idea of maintaining the speed and momentum of the offensive once it was launched. The Allied commanders were, therefore, faced with a constant succession of surprises. The disaster which befell the Anglo-French forces was the cumulative effect of many mistakes:

> One glaring characteristic is, however, common to all of them. Our leaders, or those who acted for them, were incapable of thinking in terms of a "new" war. In other words, the German triumph was, essentially, a triumph of intellect—and it is that which makes it so peculiarly serious.[74]

The 1940 Campaign in the West was the first German experience against a numerically equal enemy with modern equipment. Evaluation of this campaign convinced the Germans that their tactical concepts for the conduct of mobile warfare were correct.[75] The experimental use of the independent *panzer* groups in decisive operations had worked well and would be retained. The campaign conducted over a front of several hundred miles and up to a depth of approximately 200 miles, however, had revealed some shortcomings in the German war machine. By the autumn of 1940, the German Army was emphasizing in its training programs for the regular and motorized divisions such things as:

(1) Strict traffic discipline. (The movement through the Ardennes and the redeployment of units for the attack south across the Somme-Aisne Line had been characterized by massive traffic jams.)

(2) Attack against fortified positions. (The Germans had only carried one fort [La Férte near Sedan] in the Maginot Line by direct assault, and it was only a minor outwork unsupported by others.)

(3) Cooperation with assault artillery. (The fast-moving, mobile operations in France had further convinced the army high command of the necessity for having mobile assault guns to accompany the infantry. The idea for this type weapon had originally been put forward by Manstein while he was serving as the Deputy Chief of the General Staff. Concentration on this weapon and failure to strengthen further their divisional and corps artillery would work to German disadvantage later when they were faced with a stabilized front in Russia.)

(4) Day and night marches of up to 60 kilometers. (The failure and the inability of the following infantry formations to keep up with the advancing *panzers* had placed those valuable armored formations in jeopardy on several occasions.)

(5) Antitank combat in both attack and defense. (The campaign in France had given the Germans their first real taste of combating enemy tanks. The results had not been all that good. The British counterattack at Arras had given the German command a particularly severe shock.)

The new training program for armored divisions emphasized quick reorganization and attacks to exploit success, independent operations, and march exercises of several days duration under simulated combat conditions, with special emphasis on maintenance. By the time that the *panzer* divisions had reached the Channel coast on the twenty-second and twenty-third of May, the men were reeling from fatigue, and units had lost from 30 percent to 50 percent of their vehicles. General Schaal's 10th Panzer Division, for example, reached Calais on May 22 after a trip from its initial assembly area of approximately 275 miles; since May 10, the division had lost one-third of its motor transport and more than half of its armored vehicles. Most of the vehicular losses were due, however, to mechanical failure, not enemy action.[76]

Luftwaffe operations in the West had, with the exception of Dunkirk, been crowned by success. The initial attacks against Allied airfields on May 10 had destroyed the Belgian and Dutch air forces and seriously weakened Anglo-French air strength. The airborne operations in Holland and along the Albert canal had made possible the resulting rapid advance of the ground forces and the early capitulation of the Netherlands. The drive to the Channel had been materially aided by the close support given the advancing *panzer* formations by the dive-bombers and the flank protection afforded by reconnaissance and attack aircraft. This continuous and aggressive air support created an impression of German air supremacy that had a deep psychological effect on the French troops and people. Throughout the campaign, the air strength of the *Luftwaffe* had been concentrated and logically employed.[77]

Hitler now sought to inveigle Britain into suing for peace. When rebuffed, he ordered plans prepared for an invasion of England (Operation SEALION). A plan was developed and changed several times, amidst constant bickering between the Army and Navy; but it was never destined to be implemented, because the vital requirement for air superiority could not be met. In the critical Battle of Britain (July 10-October 31) the *Luftwaffe* was unable to sweep the Royal Air Force from the sky. On the contrary, Goering's vaunted air force, operating against newly developed radar and superior fighter planes and employed less skillfully than it might have been, suffered a decisive defeat. The courage and sacrifices of the valiant handful of British fighter pilots spared England the ordeal of an invasion.

The attention of Hitler was now drawn eastward, where his partner in the dismemberment of Poland posed the only threat to German dominance of the Continent.

Notes

[1]Hans A. Jacobsen and J. Rahwer (eds.), *Decisive Battles of World War II: The German View* (New York, 1965), p. 32.

[2]*Ibid.*, pp. 29-31

[3]James L. Moulton, *A Study of Warfare in Three Dimensions* (Athens, Ohio, 1967), pp. 45-48.

[4]T. K. Derry, *The Campaign in Norway* (London, 1953), pp. 16-17.

[5]Greiner Diaries: "Western and Northern Europe, 1940," MS #C-065d, Center of Military History, Washington, D.C., pp. 19, 20-21.

[6]Moulton, *A Study of Warfare*, p. 61.

[7]*Ibid.*, pp. 61-68.

[8]Vincent J. Esposito (ed.), *The West Point Atlas of American Wars* (2 vols.; New York, 1959), II, Section 2, 11.

[9]Lionel F. Ellis, *The War in France and Flanders, 1939-1940* (London, 1953), pp. 3-4.

[10]*Ibid.*, pp. 4-5, 6-10.

[11]Alistair Horne, *To Lose a Battle: France 1940* (Boston, 1969), p. 22.

[12]Irving M. Gibson, "Maginot and Liddell Hart: The Doctrine of Defense," in *Makers of Modern Strategy*, ed. by Edward Mead Earle, 1st ed. (Princeton, 1971), p. 367.

[13]Horne, *To Lose a Battle*, pp. 17-19.

[14]Donald J. Harvey, *France Since the Revolution* (New York, 1968), pp. 202-203, 212.

[15]C. L. Mowat (ed.), *The New Cambridge Modern History*, Vol. XII, 2 ed.

[16]Judith M. Hughes, *To the Maginot Line* (Cambridge, 1971), pp. 231, 236, 239.

[17]Richard D. Challener, *The French Theory of the Nation in Arms, 1866-1939* (New York, 1955), pp. 184-187, 193-195, 216-218.

[18]*Ibid.*, pp. 6-8.

[19]David Thomson, *Democracy in France* (Oxford, 1954), pp. 179-191.

[20]Stephan Ryan, *Pétain the Soldier* (New York, 1969), p. 220.

[21]Gibson, "Maginot and Liddell Hart," pp. 370-371; Guy Chapman, *Why France Fell*, (New York, 1969), pp. 10-12.

[22]Ryan, *Pétain the Soldier*, pp. 222-223.

[23]*Ibid.*, p. 243.

[24]Hughes, *To the Maginot Line*, pp. 192-193.

[25]Vivian Rowe, *The Great Wall of France* (London, 1959), pp. 59-60; Ryan, *Pétain the Soldier*, pp. 245-246.

[26]Ryan, *Pétain the Soldier*, pp. 222-223.

[27]*Ibid.*, p. 248; Hughes, *To the Maginot Line*, pp. 196-201; Rowe, *The Great Wall of France*, pp. 42-43.

[28]Hughes, *To the Maginot Line*, pp. 206-207.

[29]Ryan, *Pétain the Soldier, p. 271.*

[30]*Ibid.*, pp. 263-266; Rowe, *The Great Wall of France*, pp. 60-61.

[31]Ryan, *Pétain the Soldier*, pp. 192-193, 195, 201-202; Jean Vial, "The National Defense: Its Organization Between the Two Wars," *Revue d'histoire de la deuxième guerre mondiale*, 18 (April 1955), 11-15.

[32]Vial, "The National Defense," pp. 18-22; Ryan, *Pétain the Soldier*, p. 38.

[33]Ryan, *Pétain the Soldier*, pp. 195-196.

[34]Guy Chapman, *Why France Fell*, pp. 9-10; Donald J. Harvey, "French Concepts of Military Strategy, 1919-1939" (unpublished dissertation, Columbia University, 1953), pp. 9, 15.

[35]Chapman, *Why France Fell*, p. 10.

[36]French Ministry of War, *Instructions for the Tactical Employment of Large Units* (Paris, 1936), trans. by LTC Richard U. Nicholas, 1937, pp. 7-8.

[37]U.S. Army Command and General Staff School, *Organization and Tactical Employment of a French Division* (Ft. Leavenworth, 1933), pp. 42-43, 48; Army War College, *Trends in Tactics and Technique in the Armies of Great Britain, France, Germany, Japan, Italy, and Russia* (Washington, D.C., 1938), pp. 21-22.

[38]Army War College, *Trends*, p. 21.

[39]Ralph C. Smith, *Report on French Tactical Doctrine, Organization and Material* (Ecole Superieure de Guerre, 1937), pp. 2-4.

[40]Kenneth J. Macksey, *Tank Warfare*, (New York, 1972), p. 89.

[41]Smith, *Report*, pp. 3-5; Macksey, *Tank Warfare*, p. 87.

[42]Philip Charles Bankwitz, *Maxime Weygand and Civil Military Relations in Modern France* (Cambridge, 1967), p. 150.

[43]Ryan, *Pétain the Soldier*, pp. 241-242.

[44]Bankwitz, *Maxime Weygand*, pp. 87-88.

[45]*Ibid.*, pp. 154-155.

[46]Macksey, *Tank Warfare*, pp. 104-105; Chapman, *Why France Fell*, pp. 342-343.

[47]Alvin D. Coox, "General Narcisse Chauvineau: False Apostle of Prewar French Military Doctrine," *Military Affairs*, XXXVII (February 1973), 16.

[48]Horne, *To Lose a Battle*, p. 83; Joe Miziahi, "Farewell to the Falcons of France," *Wings*, I (December 1971), 45.

[49]Horne, *To Lose a Battle*, pp. 63-70.

[50]Miziahi, "Farewell to the Falcons of France," pp. 32, 65.

[51]Horne, *To Lose a Battle*, pp. 82-83; Miziahi, "Farewell to the Falcons of France," pp. 32, 53.

[52]Harvey, *French Concepts of Strategy*, pp. 169-171.

[53]*Ibid.*, pp. 168-169; Miziahi, "Farewell to the Falcons of France," p. 55.

[54]Harvey, *French Concepts of Strategy*, pp. 173-175; Miziahi, "Farewell to the Falcons of France," pp. 46-47, 54-55.

[55]Paul Auphon and Jacques Mordal, *The French Navy in World War II* (Annapolis, 1959), pp. 1-10.

[56]*Ibid.*, pp. 11, 18.

[57]Correlli Barnett, *Britain and Her Army, 1509-1970* (New York, 1970), p. 411.

[58]*Ibid.*, p. 412.

[59]*Ibid.*, pp. 417-418; Kenneth Macksey (ed.), *The Guinness Book of Tank Facts and Feats* (Enfield, 1972), p. 72; Gibson, "Maginot and Liddell Hart," pp. 375-376.

[60]Macksey, *The Guinness Book*, p. 76; Kenneth Macksey, *Armoured Crusader* (London, 1967), pp. 131-132.

[61]Army War College, *Trends*, pp. 10-11.

[62]Barnett, *Britain and Her Army*, pp. 418, 421.

[63]Ellis, *The War in France and Flanders*, pp. 5-7; Macksey, *The Guinness Book*, p. 110.

[64]Bernard L. Montgomery, *Memoirs* (New York, 1958), p. 47.

[65]The following account of the Campaign in the West, 1940, is largely drawn from Vincent J. Esposito (ed.), *The West Point Atlas of American Wars*, II, Section 2, 12-17, except as otherwise noted.

[66]A. Goutard, *The Battle of France* (London, 1958), p. 23; J. R. M. Butler, *Grand Strategy* (London, 1957), II, p. 20.

[67]Goutard, *The Battle of France*, pp. 72, 76-77, 79-82.

[68]Horne, *To Lose a Battle*, pp. 124-128.

[69]Telford Taylor, *The March of Conquest* (New York, 1958), pp. 156-163.

[70]Kenneth Strong, *Men of Intelligence* (London, 1970), pp. 79-84.

[71]Guenther Blumentritt, *Von Rundstedt* (London, 1952), pp. 66-67; Basil H. Liddell Hart, *The Other Side of the Hill* (London, 1951), pp. 168-170.

[72]Horne, *To Lose a Battle*, pp. 331, 341-342.

[73]*Ibid.*, pp. 366-367.

[74]Marc Bloch, *Strange Defeat* (New York, 1968), p. 36.

[75]Erich Rochricht, "Duties of the Army Training Branch," MS #P-041g, Center of Military History, Washington, D.C., 1952, p. 24.

[76]*Ibid.*, pp. 28-29; Airly Neave, *The Flames of Calais* (London, 1972), pp. 68-69.

[77]Littleton, B. Atkinson (ed.), *German Air Force Operations in Support of the Army*, USAF Historical Studies No. 163, USAF Historical Division, June 1962, pp. 155-157.

The Battle of Britain

3

. . . we must regard the next week or so as a very important period in our history. It ranks with the days when the Spanish Armada was approaching the Channel, and Drake was finishing his game of bowls; or when Nelson stood between us and Napoleon's Grand Army at Boulogne. We have read all about this in the history books; but what is happening now is on a far greater scale and of far more consequence to the life and future of the world and its civilization than those brave old days.

Winston Churchill, September 11, 1940

Once the crises have passed, brave words like those of Churchill have ever been a challenge to "debunkers." In the years which have gone by since 1940, the Battle of Britain has taken its place alongside those of Gettysburg and Waterloo as favorite topics of historians and buffs alike. By now, some of the brave words have come to seem exaggerated: maybe the few were not so few, maybe everything was not owed to them alone, maybe SEALION (the German plan for the invasion of Britain) would have failed even if the Royal Air Force (RAF) had been defeated. But for all of that, the Battle of Britain must ever remain an epic in the annals of warfare. It was the first great, pure air battle. It was the first great test of the theories of Giulio Douhet, William Mitchell, and Hugh Trenchard; and, if it is true that the Germans could have been stopped in the Channel or on the beaches or in the streets of London, the fact remains that the Royal Navy and the civil defenses were never put to the test. The Germans, however, were stopped by the Royal Air Force.

The Battle of Britain is interesting in another way. It provides an excellent vehicle—a laboratory if you will—for the examination of the topics of military theory, technology, strategy, generalship, and principles of war. In extension of this point, the battle is treated in this chapter under two broad topics: the foundations of air doctrine and the application of air doctrine. Under the former, the intellectual heritage of World War I and the evolution of the ideas of Douhet and, especially, Trenchard will be covered; under the latter, the way in which the leaders on both sides attempted to apply these ideas to solve the problems of organizing and employing air forces in the Battle of Britain is examined.

The Foundations of Air Doctrine

Be it a tank, an airplane, or a longbow, the appearance of a new weapon has traditionally posed a fundamental question to the minds of military thinkers: shall it be used as an auxiliary to an older mode of fighting, or shall the new instrument be used as a main striking force in its own right? In the typical case, the first answer has been that the new weapon should constitute an auxiliary to the older tools of war. Then, as the technology of the new system improves, there gradually emerges a body of thought which advocates its use in organizations which have independent offensive missions of their own. So it was with the airplane. The Wright brothers themselves gave some thought to the ways in which the new vehicle could be used in war.

The first impulse in the days before World War I was to consider the airplane as a new and better horse, or, at the very most, as a better kind of long-range artillery. Even before the war started, the armies of the world had conceived of reconnaissance and artillery spotting roles for their aircraft and had developed rudimentary organizations for the accomplishment of those missions. The development of the artillery spotting role was handicapped by the difficulty in communications between the observer and the battery commander, but the reconnaissance mission produced immediate and important results. In the preliminaries to the first Battle of the Marne, the gap which developed between Kluck and Bülow was spotted by aerial reconnaissance and so reported to Joffre—with highly detrimental effects for the German war effort. As the war went on, practically all of the present-day roles and missions of the air forces were tried or at least contemplated, but reconnaissance and artillery spotting remained the most important. So much so, in fact, that the ground commanders began to demand an air defense organization to help win air superiority over the front and thus deny the enemy knowledge of friendly movements and plans. Thus, the air superiority role first germinated in the minds of the ground commanders—not the airmen—on both sides. Though reconnaissance, formerly a cavalry function, was clearly the most important air role in World War I, a considerable strategic bombing effort was mounted on both sides of the Western Front.

The Germans led the way in the development of an independent mission for airpower. Count Graf von Zeppelin had been an observer on the Union side in the American Civil War and had consequently observed the balloon operations of Professor T. S. Lowe. Though those operations certainly did not have an appreciable impact on that war, Count Zeppelin carried the idea back to Germany where he brought it a giant step further by developing the rigid dirigible. At the outset of the war, the Germans led the world in airship development and had a very considerable fleet of such vehicles. The first bombing raids completely independent of the battle on the ground came early in 1915 when the Germans launched their initial zeppelin missions against the British homeland. But there were serious technical difficulties inherent in the zeppelin operation. First, the lifting gas was hydrogen, a highly inflammable and very dangerous substance. Almost as important, the art of aerial navigation and bomb-aiming was in its infancy. Finally, the low airspeed and awkward handling characteristics of the airships made them particularly vulnerable to the vagaries of the European weather—a very serious fault given the primitive state of the science of meteorology. Thus, the direct impact of the zeppelin raids was relatively small, for they hardly killed a thousand Britons through the entire course of the war; and, when the English finally mounted a partially effective air defense, in 1917, the cost of the operation became so high that it had to be curtailed.

By 1917, the German heavier-than-air strategic bombing effort was well under way. The force was composed of two multi-engine aircraft types, the Gotha and the Giant. The latter had a wing span in excess of that of the Second World War's Flying Fortress and an endurance of eight hours. The bomb loads were so light and poorly aimed, however, that the campaign was never a serious threat to the national security of Great Britain and it, too, caused hardly more than a thousand British deaths and correspondingly light material damage. For all of that, the zeppelin and Gotha raids did have some important indirect effects. They caused such a panic in London that considerable air resources were recalled from the front and the world's first independent air arm, the RAF, was organized in the spring of 1918. Thus, though Douhet has been blamed for everything from the evacuation of the little children from London to the vaporization of Hiroshima, none of his ideas were entirely original—they all had been conceived before or during World War I.[1]

Though neither Billy Mitchell nor "Boom" Trenchard were particularly generous in crediting Douhet with the origin of their thought, it has been shown that both officers were at least indirectly aware of his existence and the nature of his ideas. Douhet's thought is important to our study because many leaders of the *Luftwaffe* have openly proclaimed their debt to the Italian theorist.* Any sociological study of the first generation of airmen would certainly reveal that a disproportionate share of them came from the artillery branches of their respective armies. That was the case with Giulio Douhet, a career soldier of long service when World War I broke out. During the war, he had been imprisoned as a result of insubordinate criticism of his seniors, but he was later exonerated and restored to a high position in the Italian armed forces. It was only at this later stage, from 1921 onwards, that he came to compose the writings which are supposed to have had such a profound effect on our times.[2]

What were some of the main ideas of Douhet? First and foremost he argued that airpower is a decisive instrument of war in its own right and has a role completely independent of the army and navy. That idea is really the crux of all of the interwar struggles between the airmen and their brethren on the ground; once the proposition of independent roles is accepted, then everything else would necessarily follow. Some of the corollaries flowing therefrom would include:

1. Armies and navies, because of limitations on their avenues of approach and on their speed of movement, must ever be relegated to defensive roles.
2. Airpower is inherently offensive because of its speed and flexibility.
3. The problems of interception in the vast reaches of the atmosphere are insuperable and, therefore, the bomber will always get through.
4. Because the bomber will always get through, the ideal independent air force should be composed wholly of bombers

*There is a nice little irony here since both the United States Army Air Force and the Royal Air Force governed their organization and operations with a doctrine that had much more in common with the theories of Douhet than was the case with the *Luftwaffe*.

and reconnaissance aircraft—there is no room for fighter aircraft.

5. Because the bomber will always get through, the principle of mass demands that it be made as large as possible and that it must carry as large a bomb load as possible. Speed is not particularly important to the bomber; but, because in rare instances the bomber might be attacked by defending aircraft, it should be a battleplane carrying heavy defensive armament.
6. Because the decisive element in all future wars will be airpower, all such wars must necessarily begin with a struggle for air superiority. Because the problem of airborne interception is unsolvable, the battle for air superiority cannot be an air-to-air struggle. It must, therefore, be an air-to-ground struggle carried out by means of heavy bomber attacks against the elements of the enemy's airpower: his aircraft factories, his airfields, and his air force *on the ground*.
7. Once the unchanging initial objective is achieved (the destruction of enemy airpower), then the victorious air force will be free to exploit its air superiority at its leisure. The most fruitful form of exploitation would be an attack on the enemy's population centers because civilian morale is inherently fragile. This is really the most humane form of warfare, as well, because it avoids the bloodbath such as the one Europe endured on the western front in World War I. Moreover, the civilian morale is *so* fragile that not very much death and destruction will be required before the populace revolts against its leadership and forces the latter to sue for peace—perhaps the mere threat of bombing attacks will suffice.

That, in a nutshell, is the theology which Adolf Galland claimed had a profound impact on the organization and employment of the *Luftwaffe*.[3]

There can be little doubt that the ideas of Douhet had considerable impact on *Luftwaffe* philosophy, although perhaps not as much as Galland claimed. Douhet wrote his *Command of the Air* in 1921, and it was translated into German during the 1920s; it did not appear in English, however, until the Second World War was underway.* The impact might have been greater but for an accident. The first Chief of Staff of the *Luftwaffe*, General Walther Wever, was a Douhetist of the first order despite his long career as a soldier and his late conversion to the flying business. Wever, the intellectual leader of the "big bomber men" of the *Luftwaffe*, developed two prototypes of what he called the "Ural Bomber"; but they might just as well have been named "battleplanes." Unfortunately for the *Luftwaffe*, however, disaster struck Wever on June 3, 1936, during a visit to Dresden; suffering a case of "gethomeitus" because of a late departure for Berlin, he neglected the walk-around preflight inspection of his brand new Heinkel 70 and left the aileron lock in place. He crashed on take-off. The prospects for a German strategic bombing force died with him.[4]

The evolution of thought and hardware in the Royal Air Force, meanwhile, had a much smoother road though it was certainly not free of bumps. Trenchard was in at the birth of the RAF. When it was created in the spring of 1918, he was recalled from his job as the Commander of the Royal Flying Corps in France to serve as the first Chief of Air Staff of the RAF. He soon ran into difficulties with the Air Minister, Lord Rothmere, and resigned. After a very short time, however, he was appointed to command the new strategic bombing force in France, the Independent Air Force which had been created to retaliate for the Gotha raids on Great Britain. When the war ended before this force could do much damage to the German homeland, Trenchard shortly again became the Chief of the Air Staff. He served in that capacity throughout the 1920s and was a profound influence on RAF thinking all through the next two decades. Thus, Trenchard was one of the intellectual fathers of the Royal Air Force.[5]

What were the ideas which governed Trenchard and his staff as they built the RAF during his long tenure? At the outset there was not much talk of strategic bombing. The war to end all wars had just been concluded. The chief antagonist had been subdued and completely disarmed in the air. Only France had a considerable air force on the Continent, and a war with her was at first unthinkable. It seemed, therefore, that the Royal Air Force had emerged from the Great War without a mission. Trenchard's first problem, then, was not to create a body of doctrine to govern strategic bombing operations, but rather to find justification for the continued separation of the air arm from the elder services. He did this by selling the Government on the idea that airpower could maintain proper order in the colonies at a much lower price than was possible for the ground forces. Presently, in 1923, the unthinkable became thinkable in that Anglo-French relations took a definite turn for the worse over the application of the terms of the Versailles Peace Treaty and the French occupation of the Ruhr industrial area. Though the unpleasantness was ultimately overcome as a result of the diplomacy of Gustav Stressman and the conclusion of the Locarno Treaty, the whole incident gave impetus to the development of a strategic air doctrine in the Royal Air Force.

If similar in many respects to the ideas of Douhet, the body of thought which emerged clearly owed much to Trenchard and differed from that of the Italian airman in significant ways. Trenchard, like Douhet, was a "big bomber man." He was

*A mimeographed copy was produced at the Air Corps Tactical School at Maxwell Field, Alabama, as early as 1932, and some of the copies were later given to some Congressmen. It is uncertain as to what extent these copies were read, nor do we know their effect on Air Corps and Congressional thinking.

convinced that the interception problem would be a very serious one and that the air weapon could strike at the heart of enemy strength; because it could be decisive in its own right, he was sure that any war would have to begin with a struggle for air superiority. Trenchard allowed, however, that there would be need for fighters and attack planes as well as the bombers and reconnaissance planes required by Douhet. Further, though Trenchard agreed that it would be highly desirable to destroy as much as possible of the enemy airpower *on the ground*, he nevertheless supposed that a part of the struggle for command of the air might take place in the form of air-to-air action. While some writers have held that Trenchard assigned a greater potential in the exploitation phase to the possibility of defeating the enemy through destroying his *means* to fight, as opposed to his *will*, it is nevertheless true that he shared Douhet's idea that civilian morale was a fragile, legitimate, and decisive target.[6] Because Trenchard's doctrinal influence was so strong, the air marshals of 1935 to 1940 were "big bomber men" who paid him unabashed homage.[7]

In the decade following 1923, the situation changed radically. Trenchard had retired, Japan had gone on the rampage in the Far East, and Hitler had come to power in Germany. The British air marshals, in the main, were slow to adjust their thinking to meet the new situation. They persisted in maintaining a force structure of two bombers for every fighter and in preaching a doctrine that the best defense is a good offense against the enemy homeland—despite the fact that the potential enemy's homeland was no longer as accessible as it once had been.[8] Fortunately, however, the establishment had its maverick.

The noncomformist of the RAF was Hugh C. T. Dowding, then the member of the Air Staff in charge of Research and Development. Although Prime Minister Stanley Baldwin, along with most of the Air Staff, was still advocating that "the bomber will always get through," Dowding felt that the bombers might never have a chance to prove it unless the RAF saw to the security of the base.* Once the *Luftwaffe* was unveiled in 1935 and Hitler began his string of conquests, there was a rising opinion in Britain in favor of doing something to improve the defensive side of the RAF. This tendency was abetted by the fact that Douhet's model assigned the public the role of enduring whatever blows the enemy could deliver until the offensive air force had won the battle for air superiority. Obviously, such a role could have but little appeal to the people of Great Britain. This rising opinion, along with certain technological improvements led the political authorities to impose a modification of the ideas of Trenchard on their air marshals. The famous Inskip decision of 1937 decreed that the priorities of the Bomber and Fighter Commands be reversed and that everything possible be done to build up the air defenses of Great Britain in the shortest possible time.[9]

Air Chief Marshal Sir Hugh Dowding

Nevertheless, the air marshals were not swayed from their convictions. Indeed, in 1937, all through the Battle of Britain, and down to the end of the Second World War and beyond, most of them remained steadfast in their commitment to the big bomber idea.

The British Application of Air Doctrine

Theory and doctrine are practically identical in that they are both bodies of ideas about war. The difference between the two is that doctrine is merely approved theory—that is to say, doctrine is a body of ideas about war which has been approved, by duly constituted authority, as that which will govern the organization and employment of military force. In that regard, the doctrine and equipment of the *Luftwaffe* was well suited to its projected role as an auxiliary of the ground forces; because this was so, some spectacular results were achieved in Poland, Norway, and France. When one examines the attempt to turn this specially tailored force to strategic ends, however, strains

*In a remarkable parallel, similar events were taking place at the same time at the Air Corps Tactical School in the United States. There, the conventional wisdom also was strongly committed to the big bomber idea and held that the air defense problem was insoluble. The maverick was Major Claire Chennault, who later went to China to prove his point and to make a name for himself.

become apparent. At the same time, it is essential to consider the ways in which air doctrine was applied to the organizational problems facing the RAF in the waning days of peace.

If during World War II the appearance of radar seemed to be a manifestation of black magic, the idea of measuring distance by means of emitting a signal and measuring the time required for it to travel to the target and to return was not a particularly new one. As early as 1920, the Germans tried to use it in an acoustical device designed to measure an airship's absolute altitude above the surface.[10] But perhaps more than anyone else, it was Sir Robert Watson-Watt who was responsible for the timely invention of radar.* As a meteorologist, he became interested in the electronic measurement of weather phenomena. In the beginning he undertook his studies in the hope of developing a device which would measure the bearing and distance of thunderstorms. As many a lost aviator will testify, the radio compass will point at the closest thunderstorm; and that was the initial direction of Watson-Watt's research—in order to create a radio-direction finding device which would deliver the desired data. As early as 1927, however, he had taken a long step in the direction of the radar principle when he succeeded in bouncing a radio wave off the ionosphere. By 1934, the Government was receiving intelligence indicating that the emergence of a great, new German air force was imminent—an ominous possibility which accelerated British interest in the solution of the air defense problem. H. E. Wimperis, Scientific Advisor to the Air Ministry, inquired of Watson-Watt whether the development of an electronic death ray might be practical as a way of defeating incoming bomber attacks. When Watson-Watt replied that although no such device seemed possible, the idea of radio location of bombers did have some promise, the government encouraged him.[11] He went to work on a demonstration device.

Typical "Chain Home" Radar Station Antenna

A "Chain Home" Receiver Room. The Receiver Is at the Left and the Console at the Right

Sir Robert Watson-Watt gave Dowding, still in charge of Research and Development for the Air Ministry, a successful demonstration of the new device in February 1935. Promptly, Dowding recommended that the Air Ministry give substantial support to the radar program long before it had gone through the normal testing cycle. Ten thousand pounds was provided for the purpose that spring.[12] More than any single event, Dowding's action in this case accounts for the outcome of the Battle of Britain.

What did the development of radar mean to the doctrine of the Royal Air Force? Verily, World War I and the Spanish Civil War had amply proved that Douhet, Trenchard, and even Stanley Baldwin had all been correct *in their own time*. Indeed, the Gothas and the Giants had suffered many more losses to accidents than to anything that the British did. And in the opening years of the Spanish War, the Russian SB-2 medium bomber could run away from any fighter the Germans and the Italians could launch after it; similarly, in the latter part of that war, the Heinkel III roamed the skies without much fear of any air opposition. Why was this so?

Prior to the days of radar, the offense invariably enjoyed the advantages of surprise and mass. The avenues of approach for a bomber force were practically infinite. The approach was so rapid, and the climb rates of the fighters were so low, that the bombers had every prospect of reaching the target area and releasing their bombs long before the fighters could be alerted and climb to altitude—even in those rare instances where the ground observers were able to spot the incoming raid. The only alternative for the defenders was to mount combat air patrols over all their important targets during all the hours of daylight; there was no point in doing it at night, as visual interception was completely out of the question. This procedure is the air equivalent of the cordon defense (trying to defend everywhere)

*A distant descendant of the James Watt who invented the steam engine.

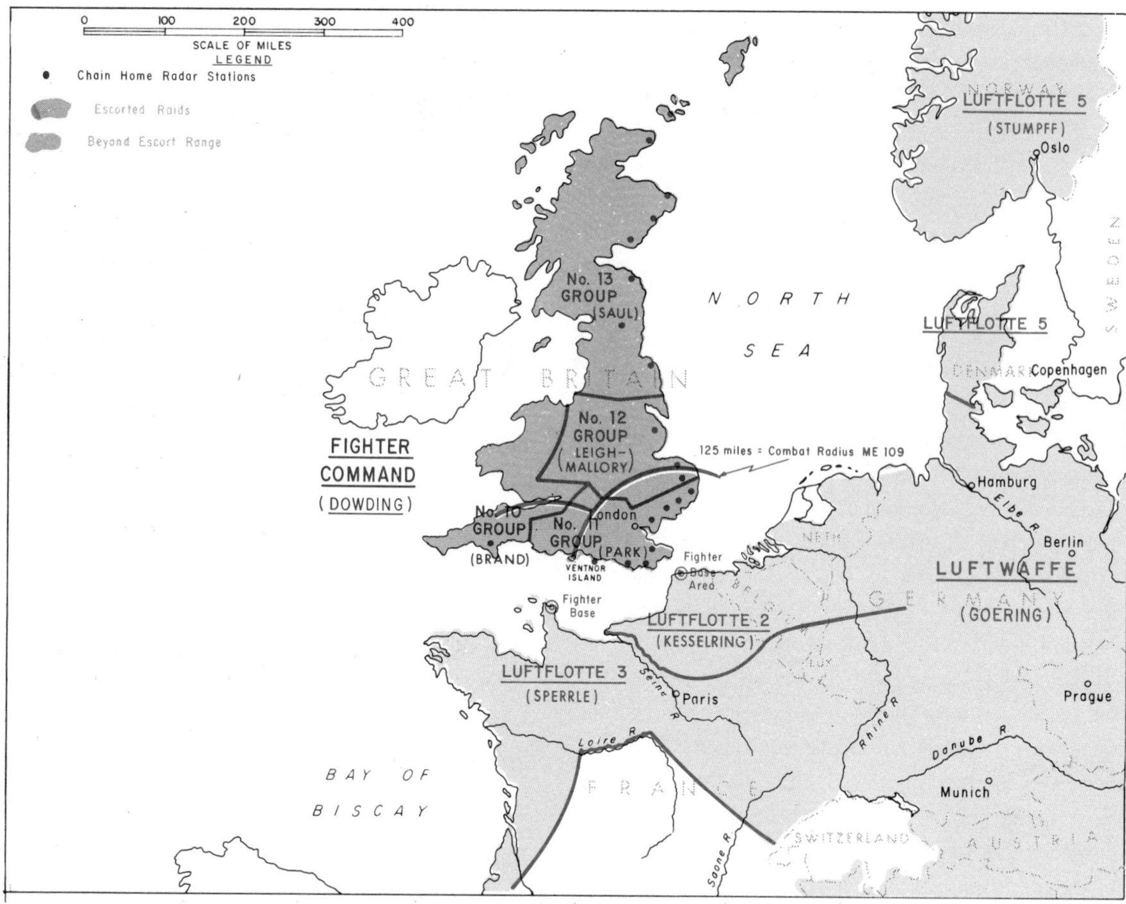

German Fighter Range and British Radar Deployment

and constitutes a gross violation of the principles of mass (concentration of power) and economy of force (emphasize the principal effort and restrict the strength of secondary efforts). Such tactics would inevitably be very expensive and result in a few fighters being outnumbered by bomber raids while many other defenders roamed fruitlessly over targets not to be attacked. The advent of radar brought a new dimension.

First, radar removed the element of surprise. By 1940, the British had established a chain of stations along the coast which had a range of up to 100 miles. *(See Map, above.)* Since the effective combat radius of the German fighters was but 125 miles, and their rendezvous procedures were clumsy and primitive, this allowed the British the capability of watching every move of the assaulting force during its assembly phase. Moreover, since it is far easier to spot a pip of light on a darkened scope than it is to find an aircraft visually in the "footless halls of space," radar made it improbable that even the smallest raids could sneak in undetected. Because the British could now know *when* the enemy attack was coming, they could avoid the violation of economy of force entailed in flying continuous combat air patrols; because they could now know *where* the attack would penetrate, it became possible to obey the principle of mass by vectoring all their interceptors towards the threatened point rather than spreading them all around the periphery. Air defense had now become possible; and if their fame were to rest on no other achievement, the development of radar by itself would suffice to guarantee Dowding and Watson-Watt a place in British history. However, there is a long journey between the invention of a device like radar and the fielding of a fully integrated weapons system.

Hugh Dowding's second great contribution to the victory in the Battle of Britain was his development of a command and control system. It was necessary to devise efficient means to translate the information detected by the radar into meaningful directions for the interceptors and to deliver instructions to the flyers soon enough for them to launch, to climb to altitude, and to make the interception before the bombers had reached their targets. This was no simple task. First, the initial generation of radar sets was so bothered by ground clutter that the equipment was of little use over land. Thus, once the incoming bombers passed the coast line, additional tracking information would have to be gathered by visual or acoustical means. This entailed the creation of a vast ground observer corps and the associated complex communications net. Second, it was then necessary to devise a system for taking the information gathered from the various sources and collating it into a usable form. Finally, it was necessary to create the command structure and the technology for delivering the directions to the fighter force, both while it was on ground alert and after it became airborne.

During the spring of 1936, the RAF was reorganized into several functional commands of which Fighter Command was but one. The others included Bomber Command, Coastal Command, and several others organized on a geographical basis. In connection with this reorganization, Hugh Dowding was transferred from his work in research and development to take charge of the new Fighter Command.[13] Thus, he became one of the principals in the effort to integrate the new radar into the interceptor weapons system, and in this capacity it was necessary for him to work closely with many other agencies. The Post Office had the responsibility for building and maintaining the land lines which connected the radar stations and the observer posts to the command posts. Local government also was brought into the scheme, because the ground observers were made a part of the local constabulary as far as housekeeping was concerned. They were raised, organized, equipped, paid, and trained by the constabulary.[14]

The new system for command and control which Dowding devised was logical, reasonably simple, and effective. The radar return would provide the initial input at the stations along the coast. The direction and distance, and later the numbers and altitudes, of incoming airplanes would then be reported to the command posts at both Fighter Command and Number 11 Group Headquarters. As the radar operators became more experienced, they were even able to identify the types of aircraft. Dowding did not take much of a hand in the tactical direction of the battle, so the information going to Fighter Command was used mainly to keep him abreast of the situation. Air Marshal Keith Park was the key man during the battle itself. He was the Air Officer Commanding, Number 11 Group, and it was in his command post that the information from various sources was collated and the launch orders thereby generated. Besides the radar system, the other important source of information was the Royal Observer Corps. Its members were responsible

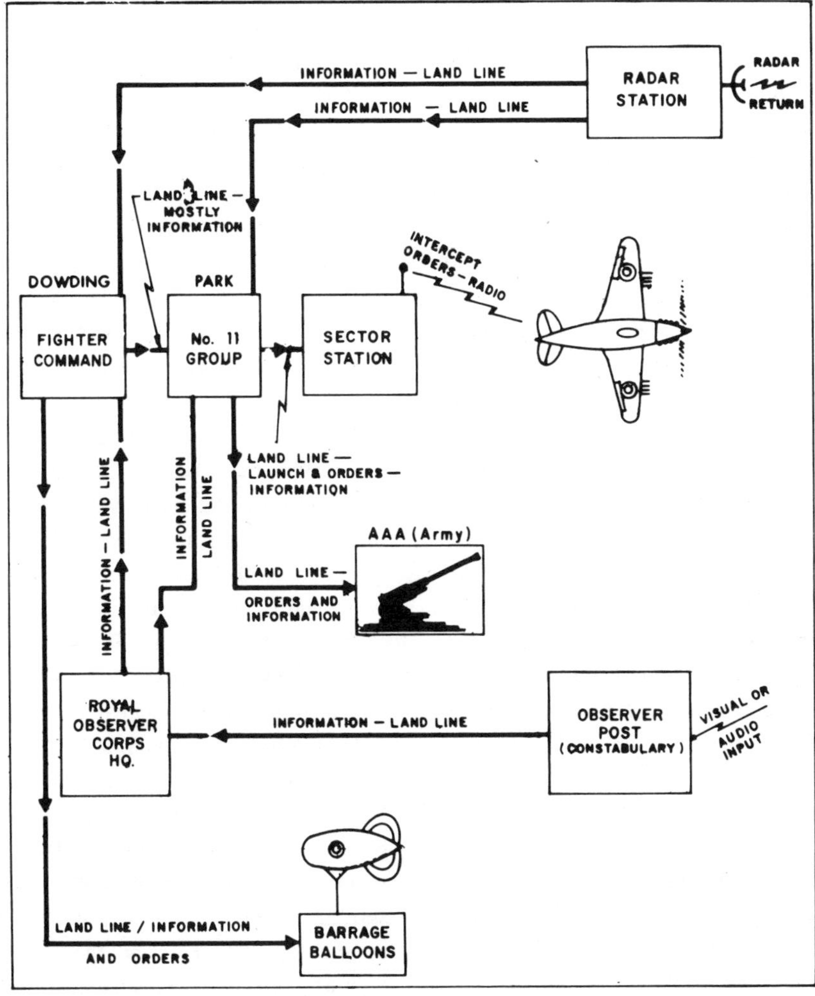

British Command and Control System, Battle of Britain, 1940

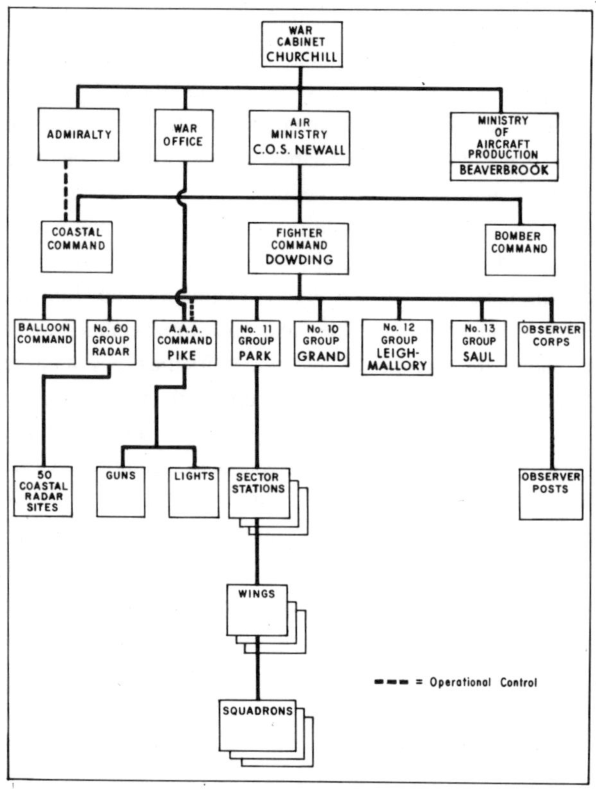

British Organization for Air Defense, 1940

for tracing the raiders once they had crossed the coastline. These observers became remarkably adept as the battle wore on. It is said that they were ultimately able to identify aircraft at night by the sound of their engines. All of the command posts at Fighter Command, Group Headquarters, and Sector Stations were equipped with large, horizontal plotting boards. Continuous plots of the incoming raids and the interceptor forces were maintained on these boards. At the Group headquarters, this information was used to make the decisions as to which fighter forces to launch and when to launch them. Once the aircraft were airborne, the operational control reverted to the next lower level, the Controller at the Sector Stations. This Controller was responsible for issuing vectors, climb instructions and recall orders. He had control up to the time of visual contact. Once the airborne fighter commander had called his "tallyho," the flyer took control and completed the attack by visual means. When the intercept was completed, the Sector Controller on the ground again took over and guided the pilots back to their recovery bases—very often different from the fields from which they had launched.

The key units during the battle were the Group and Sector command posts. Fighter Command did not play a very active role, although it did have occasion to intervene from time to time when Number 11 Group became saturated and had launched all its aircraft. Then it would call upon one of the other groups to send reinforcements into the Number 11 Group area. During the battle, Dowding delegated a part of this function to Park when he gave the latter the authority to call directly upon Leigh-Mallory's Number 12 Group for reinforcements. Even the antiaircraft artillery came under the operational control of the Group Air Officer Commanding. This air defense artillery, although it belonged to the Army for administrative purposes, was placed under the operational control of the Fighter Command which delegated the function down to the Group level.

The Balloon Command was a part of the Air Force. Though the balloons could not carry a heavy enough cable high enough to wreck many German aircraft, they, nevertheless, performed a valuable indirect service. They forced the German aircraft to fly at a higher altitude and thus complicated their bomb-aiming problem. Further, forcing the attackers up to medium altitudes made them more vulnerable to antiaircraft artillery than they would have been at low level, because the artilleryman's rate of change of azimuth was so high for low-flying aircraft that the gunners had trouble tracking them properly.[15]

Though Dowding's command and control system was the best that the world had yet seen, it was not without its deficiencies. First and foremost, a considerable part of it, especially the sector command posts, was above ground and thus vulnerable to bombing attack.[16] The radar towers were absolutely vital to the functioning of the system, and they were so tall and obviously located that they should have been highly vulnerable, too. Most of the land lines were also above ground. The early radar had difficulty tracking targets over land, measuring the altitude of raids, and distinguishing between friendly and enemy targets. This latter difficulty was partially overcome by the invention of "pip squeak," an early form of IFF (Identification, Friend or Foe), but that device was plagued with technical difficulties.[17] Though there were remarkably few breakdowns in the system during the battle, perhaps it did tend to violate the principle of simplicity. The liaison between the several Group Headquarters was imperfect, and it was sometimes difficult to control properly the reinforcements from other groups once they entered the Number 11 Group area.[18] Notwithstanding these faults, it is worth re-emphasizing that the virtues of the command and control system were absolutely vital to the successful air defense of Great Britain.

One of the chief virtues of the system was that the Germans did not know anything about it. They fully understood that the British had been working on radar and they were aware that the Britons also had a couple of good fighters coming on the line; but they did not understand that the British defense in the air would be effectively controlled from the ground and that, by itself, this system of control might be a decisive advantage in the upcoming battle. It was not that the *Luftwaffe* did not try to obtain information on the system. Before the war, for example, the Graf Zeppelin had been sent on a couple of ELINT (Electronic Intelligence) missions against the English radar system. The British, of course, could hardly miss such a fine target on their scopes and were fully aware of the proceedings. When it seemed likely that the craft was about to pick up some good data, the English merely shut down the system and maintained radio silence. The German airship was supposed to have remained over international waters and its commander thought it had done so. The British, however, had positive radar information which showed that the German bad weather navigation was not as fine as was supposed. The Graf Zeppelin had been plotted over English territory; but the British could not lodge a complaint because to have done so would have revealed some of the very information the Germans had been seeking.[19] Thus, at the outset of the battle, the Germans knew about the existence of British radar, but, partly through the arrogant assumption that the British shopkeepers could not possibly be more technologically advanced than the German radar scientists, they grossly underestimated its potential. At the same time, they knew little or nothing about the British GCI (Ground Controlled Intercept) system.[20] The Germans were therefore assuming that they would have the advantage of surprise, when in actuality a technological surprise of the first order was about to be sprung upon them.

The third major element of the British air defense system was the weapons platform—the Hurricane and the Spitfire. The doctrinal thinkers of the 1920s assumed that the bomber would always get through because its performance in those days was nearly equal to that of the fighter. A biplane fighter with a ten-knot speed advantage might spot a bomber 15 miles away, but would take an hour and a half to close to machine-gun range. Since its endurance would hardly permit that, it is no wonder that Douhet, Trenchard, Mitchell, and so many others assumed that there was little future for air-to-air combat. Moreover, were the fighter fortunate enough to be so placed as to try a head-on firing pass, the guns of the day were so few in number and so low in rate of fire, that a bomber would have been shot down only as a result of a lucky shot. Accordingly, even with first-class detection and command and control systems, the air defense of Great Britain in 1939 would still have posed a very tough problem unless the British could develop a fighter with a substantial performance advantage over bombers. The story of that development is a fascinating one.

Great Britain emerged from World War I in dire financial straits. Some hoped to solve this problem by squeezing reparations out of the Germans. When the depression came early to Britain, there was precious little defense money to be had. Moreover, it was assumed that there would be no war in Europe for a long time to come; the most likely threat would come from Japan in the Far East. Thus, building up the great base at Singapore had a high priority in the British scheme of things. Add to this the fact that the Chief of the Air Staff firmly believed that the best air defense is a good offense, and it is easy to see why the government spent little money to develop fighter aircraft. Yet important technological gains were made.

In the 1920s, there was an annual speed contest—the Schneider Cup Race—which captured the imagination of the public the world over. It came to be so important that many governments believed that winning carried sufficient prestige to justify the support of national entries with public funds. So it was with England. Each year a special RAF flight trained for and competed in the races. The team had considerable success in the early part of the decade and then again towards its end. In 1927, the British entry, a Supermarine seaplane, won with an average speed above 300 mph while a sister aircraft took the runner-up position. In 1929, the British won again in a Supermarine, this time at a speed of 357 mph. By 1931, the RAF hoped that it would be able to take the trophy for the third consecutive race and thus retire it. The Great Depression, however, was by then in full swing and the Government did not feel justified in spending the money on an air race. At that point, Lady Houston volunteered 100,000 pounds, and the British did, indeed, retire the trophy. By the end of that year, they had clocked their Supermarine 6B at 407 mph and its Rolls Royce engine had been perfected to the point where it could develop 2,300 hp for short periods. This Supermarine 6B was a direct ancestor of the famous Spitfire, the plane which would prove so invaluable to Britain when the crisis came in 1940.[21]

The rise of Hitler, the initial attempt at the *Anschluss*, the discarding of the armament features of the Treaty of Versailles, the German withdrawal from the League of Nations, and the unveiling of the new *Luftwaffe* all caused the British Government to renew its interest in fighter aviation by the spring of 1935. During the previous year, it had laid down specifications for a whole new generation of fighter aircraft—single-seat monoplanes with a performance far in excess of anything then flying. Two entries first flew in 1935, and came to be known as the Spitfire and the Hurricane. Air leaders ordered both types into production without waiting for the completion of the normal testing cycle.[22] First shown in public in 1936, these aircraft began to reach the squadrons in numbers two years later.

A vital technical advance, which complemented the development of the single-seat monoplane gun platform, was a radical improvement in the guns themselves. All through World War I and the 1920s, airmen had thought it necessary to mount the machine guns on the cowling to make them accessible for in-flight maintenance. As the Spitfires and Hurricanes emerged, a new Browning Caliber .303 was designed which was so reliable that it could be placed out of the reach of the pilot. This permitted enclosing the cockpit, moving the guns outside of the propeller's arc, and mounting several of them on each wing. The specifications for both the new fighters called for eight machine guns.[23] As the Battle of Britain approached, then, not only did the fighter enjoy a much greater speed advantage over the bomber than it had ten years earlier, but also it could lay down a storm of lead in a burst of a very few seconds.

Thus it happened that the combination of a new system of detection, an effective system of command and control, and the evolution of a much better interceptor aircraft had made Douhet's dictum that the bomber would always get through a very shaky proposition by 1940.

Readiness of the British for the Coming Battle

In the coming trial for the British, the main issue would be the struggle for air superiority over southern England. In the end, it is probable that the relative qualities and quantities of single-seat fighters decided this issue. Under these terms, the British were not in the disadvantageous position that they appeared to be in at the time. A tabular comparison of the key fighter aircraft clarifies this statement.

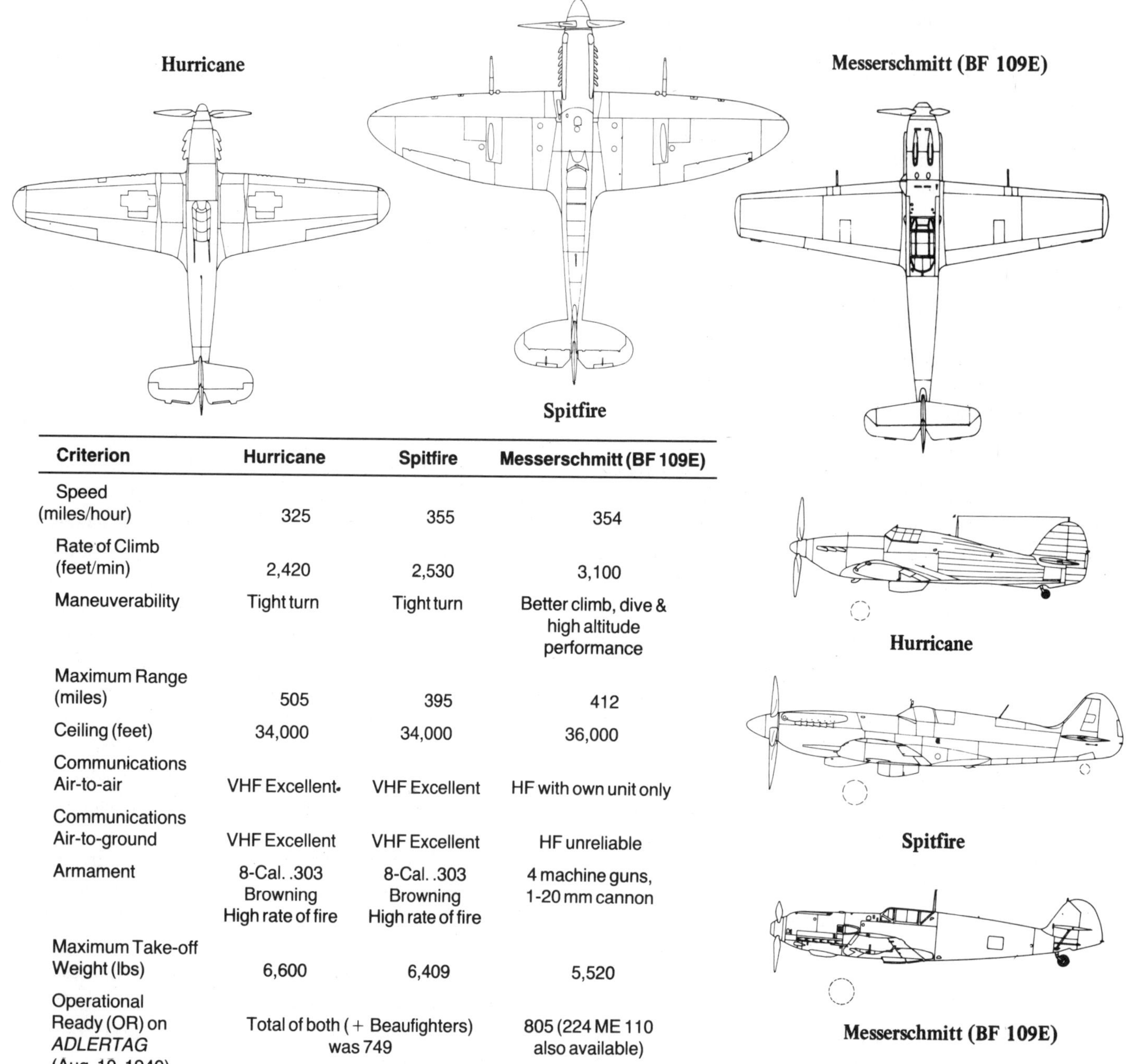

Criterion	Hurricane	Spitfire	Messerschmitt (BF 109E)
Speed (miles/hour)	325	355	354
Rate of Climb (feet/min)	2,420	2,530	3,100
Maneuverability	Tight turn	Tight turn	Better climb, dive & high altitude performance
Maximum Range (miles)	505	395	412
Ceiling (feet)	34,000	34,000	36,000
Communications Air-to-air	VHF Excellent	VHF Excellent	HF with own unit only
Communications Air-to-ground	VHF Excellent	VHF Excellent	HF unreliable
Armament	8-Cal. .303 Browning High rate of fire	8-Cal. .303 Browning High rate of fire	4 machine guns, 1-20 mm cannon
Maximum Take-off Weight (lbs)	6,600	6,409	5,520
Operational Ready (OR) on *ADLERTAG* (Aug. 10, 1940)	Total of both (+ Beaufighters) was 749		805 (224 ME 110 also available)

Comparison of Fighters Employed in Battle of Britain, 1940[24]

Hawker Hurricanes of the RAF in Flight

The tabulation shows that the BF 109E had a definite qualitative edge over the Hurricane, and that it was the rough equivalent of the Spitfire. Its superior climb rate and diving performance,* all other things being equal, would have given the Germans a slight edge. The chief fault of the Messerschmitt, however, was its range—a problem which the Americans would face again at the outset of their strategic bombing campaign aimed at the German homeland. The table also shows that the British enjoyed an advantage in the volume of fire, and probably in the total weight of fire as well. The Germans knew of this before the battle, but felt that the caliber of the British guns was too small and that the weight of their individual rounds was too light to do the required damage to the enemy aircraft. The German aircraft, on the other hand, were equipped with cannon and thus had an advantage in terms of the weight of the individual round. The communications equipment of the British aircraft was far and away superior to that of the German. Comparing the two British aircraft, the Hurricane had some advantages: it was sturdier, more easily maintained and repaired, more quickly produced, and available in greater numbers than was the Spitfire.

On the surface, the tabulation indicates that the Germans had an advantage in numbers of fighters. On August 10 that part of the *Luftwaffe* which was engaged in the battle had 1,029 operationally ready (OR) fighters. Of these, only 805 were the single-engine BF 109E, the remainder being the Messerschmitt 110, a two-engine aircraft which was so clumsy and slow that it was more of a burden than a help in the struggle for air superiority. Opposed to this fighter force was the Fighter Command with 749 operationally ready aircraft on the same date. Included in that figure, however, are some Beaufighters (a twin-engine aircraft used for night fighting) and some Bolton Paul Defiants (two-seaters so vulnerable that they were quickly withdrawn from the daylight contest). This left somewhat over 600 Hurricanes and Spitfires at Dowding's disposal for immediate launch.

*The BF 109E had a direct injection engine while the British fighters had float-type carburetors which prevented them from following when the 109 pilots pushed the stick forward to enter a power dive. The negative G's so generated would cause the floats to cut off the fuel flow in the British Merlin engines.

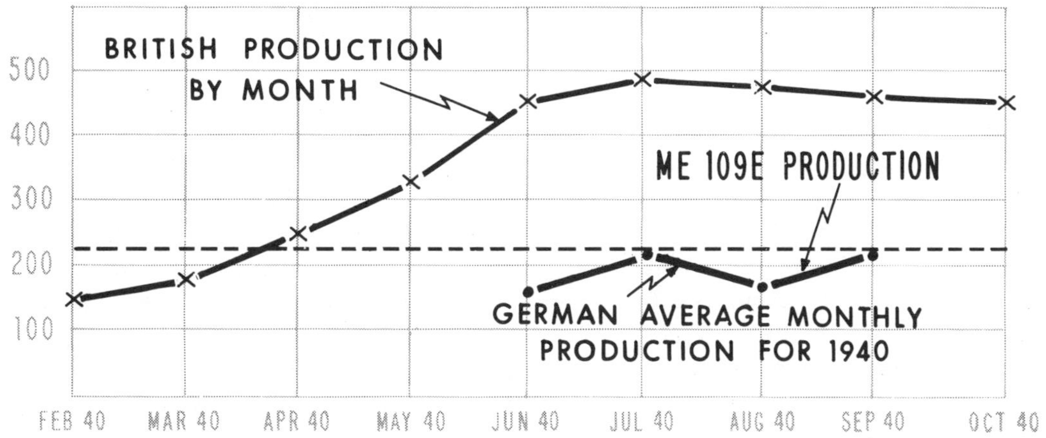

But when one considers production as well as forces on hand at the outset of the battle, the two sides had almost equal capabilities. British industry was more thoroughly mobilized for war at that point. Aircraft production figures had been rising rapidly in recent months; this was particularly true in the category of single-engine fighters. Lord William Beaverbrook had been appointed as the Minister of Aircraft production during the spring of 1940, and though a large part of that increase in production arose from measures undertaken before the beginning of his tenure, his ruthless measures had an important impact. He has been criticized for the effect that his unorthodox methods had on bomber production, but, even if that charge is granted, during the summer of 1940 the output of fighters was the decisive element in the struggle for air superiority—and here he succeeded.[26] A plotting of aircraft production figures in Germany and Great Britain shows that during 1940 the rate was increasing much more rapidly in England than it was in Germany, and this was especially true in the decisive single-engine fighter category. From April 1940 onwards, British fighter production (not to mention total combat aircraft production) exceeded that of the Germans. That, however, was not the extent of the British advantage. By 1940, their system for the restoration of battle-damaged aircraft—and they were to be able to recover more of such aircraft during the battle than were the Germans—was far more sophisticated than was that of their enemy.[27] Thus, although the Germans started the battle with greater numbers of fighters and, perhaps, with a slight qualitative edge, the British were far more capable of replacing their losses in aircraft because their industrial base was more thoroughly mobilized and because they had a superior system for recovering battle-damaged equipment.

As has been pointed out above, the British also had a decided edge in the command and control system and in electronics equipment. At the start of the battle, they had just completed their Chain Home radar system consisting of 20 long-range radar installations. These radar installations did not have a low altitude capability, but they were supplemented with 30 additional sites which provided a short-range capability at low altitude. In general, both high and low altitude systems were concentrated around the southeastern British Isles; coverage in the west and north was not nearly as thorough–not a serious fault given the limited range of the German aircraft, especially fighters.[28] The British, therefore, enjoyed one of the decisive advantages of air warfare: they were fighting in their own radar environment. Of course, this would have done them little good had they not simultaneously acquired the efficient command and control system along with the multi-channel VHF (Very High Frequency) communications airborne transceivers and IFF (Identification–Friend or Foe?) sets–yet another important technological advantage.

On the personnel side of the equation, the British had some important advantages over the *Luftwaffe*. First, the RAF had enjoyed a continuous development since the days of World War I and before. All of the top leaders in Fighter Command had accumulated considerable combat flying experience in The Great War. Keith Park, for example, had been wounded twice in the Gallipoli Campaign and had later served as a squadron commander on the Western Front. Dowding himself had won his wings before World War I and had served as a squadron and wing commander in the war in France. But combat experience alone did not distinguish the RAF leadership from the German. The English were able to carry on a continuous development of their service based upon the experience of The Great War, while the Germans—their clandestine efforts in Russia between wars notwithstanding—suffered a serious hiatus in the evolution of their air force as a result of the disarmament features of the Treaty of Versailles. While the British were attending their staff colleges and accumulating command experience in colonial assignments, many of the Germans were in civilian life trying to make a living in various other ways. Goering, though a fighter "ace" in the war, became involved in politics and civilian aviation; Udet, another "ace," spent a long period as a stunt pilot. Moreover, although the officers on both sides, in many cases, had their origins in the army, the army tradition was much stronger in Germany; accordingly, the tendency among the British to accept an auxiliary role for their air force was far weaker than was the case in Germany. Finally, even though politics always has an important impact on the development of armed forces, this was a far greater problem in Nazi Germany than it was in Great Britain. Goering was second in the National Socialist hierarchy. While many of the officers in the *Luftwaffe* were somewhat independent of mind and avoided political involvement, it is nevertheless true that ardent Nazism was even more helpful to an ambitious officer in the flying service than it was in the other German armed forces.[29] If the British had an advantage in the quality of their leaders, however, the combat flyers on both sides were about equal. In the words of the Air Officer Commanding Number 11 Group: "During the first half of this three-month battle the courage of the German pilots was not inferior to that of my RAF pilots."[30]

Other considerations involving personnel do not appear to have favored either side inordinately. If the British air service had enjoyed a more continuous development, the Germans had more recent combat experience. If the Britons had the morale advantage of fighting for hearth and home, the Germans came into the battle with the momentum of a long winning streak. If the British enjoyed reinforcements from the Dominions and from the remnants of the Polish and Czech Air Forces, the Germans had a greater population base upon which to draw. If the

British had a good and growing system of air reserves, the Germans enjoyed the fruits of a forced-draft civilian sports flying program and the highest personnel priority of any of the German armed services.

Finally, even if the *Luftwaffe* had achieved air superiority, the Royal Navy would have been a formidable adversary. The argument as to whether German air superiority would have guaranteed the success of SEALION (seaborne invasion) still continues. On the face of things, the record of the *Luftwaffe* in Norway against the line of communications with Russia, and the record of the Japanese air units against the *Repulse* and *Prince of Wales* as well as at Pearl Harbor, seems to suggest that the invasion might have succeeded if Goering had been able to clear the skies. Yet, the complexity of amphibious operations, the lack of German expertise and equipment for such operations, and the undoubted willingness of the Royal Navy to pay any price to stop the invasion would have imposed a monumental toll on Hitler's legions as they tried to cross the Channel.

If the quality of RAF personnel, especially its flying personnel, was high, perhaps the chief weakness was in the number of fighter pilots. An aircraft can be designed and built in a matter of a few years; once the production lines are rolling, there are many things which can be done to accelerate the process. Then the craft can be produced in days. Beyond a certain point, however, there is not much that can be done to accelerate the training of a pilot. Even given an ample supply of high quality human resources, the training program cannot be cut much below nine months—to do so reduces the quality of the product to the point where the pilot might as well not be trained at all, for he will kill himself before the enemy has a chance to do so. Comparison of the graph which gives the pilot inventory of Fighter Command during the Battle of Britain with the one which depicts the reserve aircraft available to Dowding, demonstrates that the supply of pilots was the limiting factor during the darkest hours of the battle. Although aircraft reserves reached a low of about 125 during early September, when it is remembered that each squadron had earlier been issued an extra flight of aircraft, it is clear that the personnel situation was the more critical. When it is further recalled that the replacement pilots, because of a serious want of experience, were in no way equal to the pilots who had been lost in battle, the leveling off depicted on the graph between the middle of August and September 7 becomes all the more critical.

Lastly, though fighting for one's own home generates some advantages in terms of morale, there is also a detrimental aspect to standing on the defensive. Though radar had reduced this disadvantage radically, it remained true that the Germans had the prerogative of choosing the time and place of battle and thereby were sometimes able to achieve an advantage in numbers.

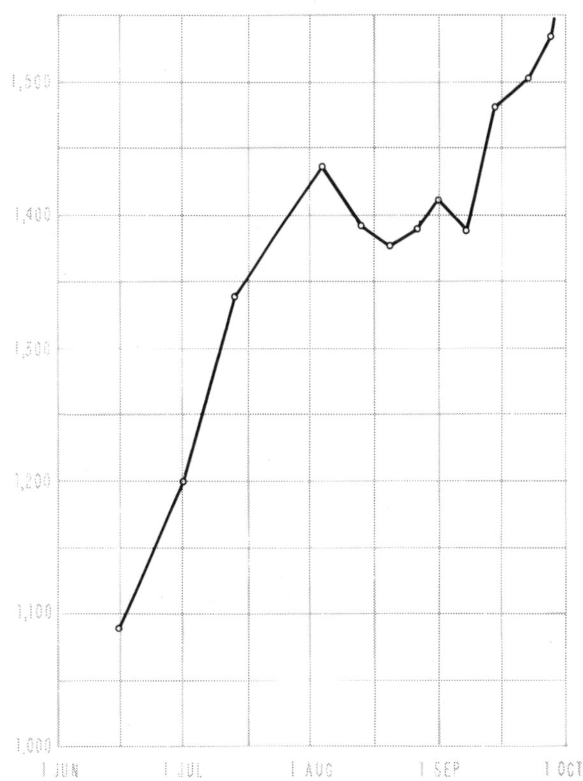

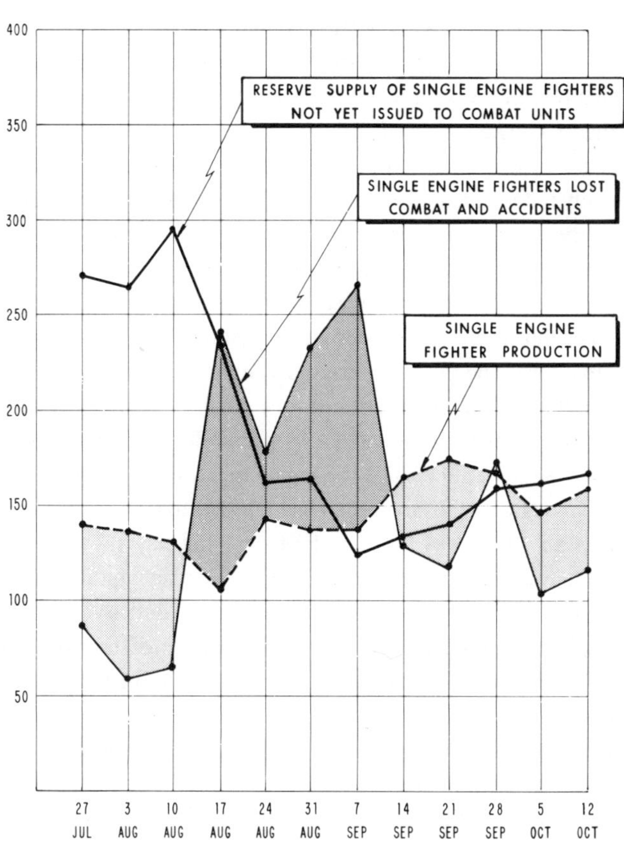

RAF Weekly Aircraft Summary, 1940[32]

German Air Doctrine and Relationship to Strategy in World War II

Many of the German air leaders, like Werner Baumbach, gave much of credit to Giulio Douhet as the source of many of the ideas which formed the base of the organization of the *Luftwaffe*. It is true that the Germans did accept much of the theory of the Italian airman, but the doctrine which emerged in the German Air Force was something quite different from the complete theory of Douhet.[34]

What did German technology and organization owe to Douhet? After the death of Wever, the Germans accepted the propositions that the bomber would always get through and that the first step of any campaign was necessarily winning the struggle for air superiority. Moreover, they tended to agree with Douhet that the most efficient way to win that struggle was to destroy the enemy air arm *on the ground*. The result was the creation of a force in which the bomber predominated and in which fighter development was neglected.* Tending to accept Douhet's dictum that air defense is a hopeless proposition, the Germans were, therefore, far behind the British in this regard; they remained behind for a long time to come, although they achieved some good results against the United States Eighth Air Force and the British Bomber Command in 1943.

But the *Luftwaffe* departed from Douhet in so many ways that it really was quite a different instrument from the one the theorist had envisioned. Douhet looked upon the army as a defensive, secondary arm. He felt that the air battle would be entirely independent of events on the ground and that the function of the Army would merely be to hold off the enemy ground forces until the offensive air arm had had time to do its work. The *Luftwaffe* doctrine was entirely opposed to this theory, since the Germans were convinced that the Army was the principal force and the Air Force must be the auxiliary. They were convinced that the air arm must be a kind of a highly flexible artillery which would enhance the mobility of ground forces because it would reduce the requirement to move guns along the roads with the advance. The *Luftwaffe* agreed with Douhet that air superiority was the first step, but beyond that point there was a departure from his theory. Douhet would have exploited his air superiority with an attack directly upon the civilian population centers for the purpose of breaking the enemy's *will* to fight; the *Luftwaffe* would exploit its command of the air by shifting to interdiction and close air support operations which were expected to break the enemy's *means* to resist. Thus, while Douhet would have urged creating a fleet of long-range battleplanes and developing the art of area bombing, the German air leaders were devoted to the creation of a

German Junkers JU-87 "Stuka" Dive Bombers in Flight Over France, 1940

vast fleet of small bombers with a precision bombing capability. Since they did not have the requisite skill in manufacturing the bomb sight for this, they compensated by demanding that all their bombers have a dive-bombing capability. This latter criterion not only led to the development of the Stuka but also made it practically inevitable that Germany would not develop a good, long-range, heavy bomber.[35]

The Spanish Civil War did nothing to change the German divergence from Douhet's ideas. They experimented with bombing population centers, but achieved no significant results. This seemed to confirm their conviction that airpower was necessarily an auxiliary to ground power, if, however, a very vital auxiliary. As so often is the case, the "lessons" which were drawn from the war in Spain were not accompanied with the qualifications which arose from the special nature of that particular episode. The astounding accuracy of the Stuka was cited without the qualification that it was operating in a permissive environment. Its ability to penetrate enemy airspace and the low losses of the Heinkel 111 bomber were noted approvingly, without the qualification that there was no first class air force in opposition—especially after the Russians began to withdraw in 1937. The kill ratio of the Messerschmitt 109 was lauded without the qualification that the battle took place very close to its airfields and that the Russian I-15s and I-16s were in no way comparable to the Spitfire and the Hurricane.[36]

*In fact, it was largely due to accident that the *Luftwaffe* wound up with a fighter, the Messerschmitt 109, which had any hope at all of competing with the Spitfire. The *Luftwaffe* procurement people were not at all interested in single-engine fighters and were concentrating on dive bombers and medium bombers. Willy Messerschmitt, on his own initiative, conceived and developed the famous 109, and the German Air Ministry somewhat reluctantly accepted the fruits of Willy's brain.

Thus, the theories of Douhet had only a partial application in the evolution of *Luftwaffe* doctrine and organization. If the German theorists emphasized the role of the bomber and the achievement of air superiority through an attack on enemy airpower on the ground as the first phase of any campaign, they also departed from Douhet's tenets in that the Air Force was organized, equipped, and trained to exploit its command of the air through operations in more or less direct support of the Army and not through an independent attack on the more remote sources of enemy power. Likewise, the theory of Douhet had a limited application to the strategy of the *Luftwaffe* during the Battle of Britain.

Even before the Second World War broke out, the Germans were condemned to suffer from a violation of the principle of the objective (the direction of one's efforts towards a clearly defined, decisive, and attainable objective). Hitler never really developed a grand strategy which clearly enunciated the objectives of his policy. The German General Staff had gradually been reduced from its former greatness, and there was no other agency which was capable of defining overall objectives. Some of the military planners used *Mein Kampf* for guidance on grand strategy while others went their own ways.

During the summer of 1940, however, it seems plain enough that the objective of Hitler's grand strategy was not the subjugation of Great Britain. For the time being, at least, he apparently merely desired British acquiescence for German policy in eastern Europe. That is to say, had Churchill been willing to give Hitler a free hand in the development of the *lebensraum* in the east, Hitler said he would make no great demands outside of Europe—beyond the return of the former German colonies. Of course, these demands did not seem so reasonable to Churchill; rather they appeared to entail the disruption of the European balance of power, the preservation of which had been a main objective of British foreign policy since the time of Louis XIV.

Although the objective at the level of grand strategy was reasonably clear, there was difficulty in translating grand strategy into specific, pragmatic strategy for the armed forces. It was not just that British acquiescence had to be won, but also that it had to be won soon. From the outset, German organization and strategy had to be based upon a presumption of a short war. In any prolonged war, the superior human resources of the British Empire (and potentially of the United States and Russia, as well) would doom Hitler to failure. Hitler had assured the German generals time and again that the Kaiser's main mistake was that he had permitted the development of a two-front war and that the *Fuehrer* would not repeat that unpardonable error. How was Hitler to win the desired approval for German expansion in the east?

From one point of view, Hitler had five possible alternatives. He could have done absolutely nothing and allowed time to work on the British determination to carry on the war to the bitter end. But even if that alternative were politically and psychologically possible for Hitler, it flew in the face of the requirement that the war be a short one. Or he might have brought off a diplomatic settlement. However, the prospects for this, as events were to prove, were pretty remote. Even had the British been able to accept the humiliation entailed, they could hardly allow German hegemony on the Continent.[37] Neither one of those alternatives seemed very promising to Hitler, and, as hope for them faded, he moved towards the selection of one of three military strategies: (1) mount an amphibious invasion of the British home islands and dictate a conqueror's peace; (2) break the British *will* to continue the fight by bombing them into submission *a la* Douhet; (3) undertake a combined air/sea blockade which would deny the enemy the means to continue the struggle and starve the English into submission. Unfortunately for Germany, prior to the fall of France, little or no thought had been given to the question of which of the three, or what combination of the three, if any, would most nearly support the objectives of Hitler's grand strategy.

Hitler had believed that once the conquest of Poland was complete the British would resign themselves to the new situation and would be unwilling to take any big risks, as had happened so many times before. Although he was disappointed that this did not happen, he did not fully think out the implications of the British decision to continue fighting. Of the German leaders, only Grand Admiral Erich Raeder gave some forethought to the problem and had his staff make some preliminary studies of the feasibility of invading Britain, should that become necessary. Throughout these early studies in the fall of 1939, and then again before and during the Battle of Britain in 1940, Raeder and the other naval leaders remained unenthusiastic about the prospect of crossing the Channel. This want of enthusiasm became even more pronounced after the Norwegian campaign because of the losses suffered by the German Navy. In absolute terms, the casualties were no worse than those suffered by the Royal Navy, but, relatively speaking, the impact on Germany was much greater than it was on Great Britain. The prospect for maintaining the temporary command of the sea essential to a successful crossing was very dim from the beginning, but once Germany had lost almost half of her modern destroyers in Norway, that hope was almost completely extinguished. At any rate, Raeder and the naval staff insisted that air superiority over the Channel was an absolute prerequisite for a successful crossing.[38]

When it arrived on the Channel, the Army, which had given no thought to the problem, was at first enthusiastic for the crossing—some thought it to be only another river crossing. Even after Hitler had set the Army planners to work and they discovered some of the problems entailed, they nevertheless maintained more hope for SEALION than they did for either a blockade or a strategy of strategic bombing.

Like the Navy, the soldiers were quick to insist that air superiority over the Channel and the beaches was necessary to the safety of the movement, but they ran into disagreement with their maritime colleagues when the details of the crossing were considered. The Army, concerned over the problem of the security of the beachhead *after* landing, wanted a crossing on as broad a front as possible. The Navy, concerned with security *during* the crossing, held that it could not spread its resources far enough to cover the broad-front landing. Rather, it would have to be a narrow front or nothing. A compromise solution was imposed on the two services, but that does not much concern us here since SEALION was never executed. In fact, there is considerable doubt that Hitler ever intended to execute it. Some authors have maintained that the whole invasion threat was a gigantic bluff.[39] They argue that Hitler was merely trying to use the threats of bombing and invasion to achieve another of the great psychological victories he had brought off when he conquered Czechoslovakia, Austria, and the Rhineland. The opponents of this theory[40] generally argue that Hitler's expenditure in blood and treasure was simply too great for it to have been a mere bluff—too great even for him. He destroyed the flower of his air force in the Battle of Britain, and severely dislocated the German economy by disrupting its internal transportation system in collecting vast numbers of invasion barges in the Channel ports. Whatever the answer to the question, it could have made little difference to the British. They had to assume the worst case and prepare accordingly; and the preparation would have been about the same for them whatever the German strategy, since all of their options demanded air superiority as a prerequisite.[41]

It is hard to say where Hermann Goering stood on the question of the feasibility of SEALION. He did not take much interest in the planning for the operation; he never went to the joint planning conferences himself, and his representatives were absent more often than not. Apparently to him it was not a question of whether SEALION was or was not feasible; rather, as an advocate of the second strategic alternative, he believed SEALION was simply unnecessary because the *Luftwaffe* would be able to bring about the capitulation of the British without any help from the Army and Navy—a very Douhetian view for the commander of an air force without any battleplanes![42] The problems of that kind of strategy were apparent even to some of the *Luftwaffe* officers of the time—if you can believe their postwar testimony. Kesselring, writing in 1953, said:

> The air battle for England also suffered from the muddleheadedness of the *Sea-lion* programme. It was clear to every discerning person, including Hitler, that England could not be brought to her knees by the Luftwaffe alone . . . permanent air supremacy was impossible without the occupation of the island, for the simple reason that a considerable number of British air bases, aircraft and engine factories were out of range of our bombers. For the same reason only a few of their ports were open to our attack. The range limitations of our fighter aircraft increased the difficulty.[43]

General Hellmuth Felmy made similar objections explicit well before the Battle of Britain—and in so doing ruined his credit with *Luftwaffe* Headquarters (OKL). Not only did he suggest that Great Britain could not be beaten with the air weapon alone, but also he counselled his superiors against opening an air campaign, as it might call up retribution from the Bomber Command, for which Germany was not prepared.[44]

During the interwar period, Mitchell, Trenchard, and Douhet had all agreed that once air superiority had been achieved the next step should be the exploitation. In that phase, however, there was a divergence of views. Mitchell's theory, as further developed by his intellectual heirs at the U.S. Air Corps Tactical School, pointed towards the destruction of the enemy's *means* to continue the battle. Douhet, at the opposite pole, desired an assault on the enemy *will* to persist with the struggle. Trenchard, perhaps, was somewhere between the two, but he leaned toward Douhet. The Mitchell theory would have demanded precision attacks on vital industrial and military targets in the enemy homeland; that of Douhet would have required area bombing of the great urban

General Field Marshal Hermann Goering Decorating One of His Fliers With the Iron Cross, 1940

areas in the hope of demoralizing the citizens of the enemy nation. Where did Goering, and the others who thought the *Luftwaffe* could win alone, stand on this issue?

There seems to have been a certain confusion in German strategic thinking as to just what the objectives of the exploitation phase should be. If all the influential leaders were agreed that the air superiority phase must come first, most of them, including Hitler, thought that they might be able to use psychological means to bring about the British capitulation. Time and again they spoke of breaking the British *will*, but they were not really talking about a Douhetian campaign aimed directly at civilian morale. Rather, they often said they would break the British *will* through the destruction of their airframe factories, the engine plants, the docks, and other such targets. Whose *will*? One would think that such a campaign would be aimed at the will of the military and political leaders, but the Germans disclaimed such an intention. Yet, from the outset of the campaign, terror bombing attacks were forbidden by Hitler (and Goering).[45] At the very beginning, the objectives were confused. The target selection was not, therefore, in accord with the theories of Douhet. It is doubtful that Goering would have been able to say just what sort of targets Douhet would have selected; the commander had been so far removed from military aviation in the 1920s and so involved with politics, economics, and diplomacy in the 1930s, that it is doubtful that he ever gave much study to the subject.[46] The indecisiveness at the highest level was reflected in the planning all summer long and continued when the issue finally came to a head in late August and early September.

Field Marshal Albert Kesselring After His Capture by U.S. Army Units in 1945

As will be discussed in detail later, some of the German air leaders felt that air superiority had been achieved, or nearly achieved, and the time to switch targets had come. Hugo Sperrle of Guernica fame* argued against switching to the bombing of London; he thought the campaign against the sector stations and other elements of British airpower should be continued. Kesselring, who had thought that airpower had no chance of independently defeating the British, now urged the switch to the bombing of the British capital—but not for the purpose of breaking civilian morale. He was convinced that the British were pulling their air forces out of the airfields in the southeastern part of England and locating them at bases outside the range of the German fighters. In his mind, the only way to force the British fighter force into the decisive battle for air superiority was to attack the one target they would have to defend—London.[47] Adolf Galland illustrated another strain of *Luftwaffe* thought when he wrote:

> We therefore had to get used to the fact that our offensive could only be directed against a small and extraordinarily well-defended sector of the British Isle. But this sector included the capital, the heart of the British Empire, London. The seven-million-people city on the Thames was of exceptional military importance as the brain and nerve center of the British High Command, as a port, as a center for armament and distribution.[48]

Be it noted that there is nothing in that particular passage which suggests either the goal of collapsing civilian morale or of attracting the British fighter force into the decisive, final battle. Then there were those among the *Luftwaffe* leaders who from the beginning had felt that the experiences of bombing Warsaw and Rotterdam suggested that there might be something in Douhet—perhaps the morale of the Londoners was the most vulnerable part of the British defense.[49] Hitler, however, was inconsistent on the point. Sometimes the object of the bombing campaign seemed to be merely to pave the way for invasion; at other times he seems to have hoped that the psychological impact of the bombing campaign and the threat of invasion would be enough to break the *will* of the British *leaders*. The famous incident which started with the accidental bombing of London by a wayward *Luftwaffe* crew, continued with an immediate retaliation on Berlin at the orders of Churchill, and resulted in Hitler's *Sportspalast* speech wherein he promised to exterminate London in revenge, has also been offered as an explanation of the basis of German strategy.

What does seem certain is that even in the *Luftwaffe* there was no unanimous opinion that the struggle could be won by airpower alone—still less was there any consensus as to how that result might be brought about.[50] Even had there been a

*Sperrle had been in command of the Condor Legion in Spain when he ordered the deliberate bombing of the market place in Guernica, and later boasted of it.

unity of purpose behind the German effort, the equipment and training of the *Luftwaffe* was not at all well-suited for the proposed strategic campaign and a large part of the British Isles was well beyond its reach. If both SEALION and an independent air campaign were fraught with difficulties, what were the prospects of the last alternative: a blockade?

The experience of the First World War, during which Germany had been subjected to a fairly complete blockade, suggests that such an operation is not an easy one, and that even where it can be decisive, it is very slow to have its effect against a major industrial nation with a fairly well-balanced economy. An island power, however, whose economy is based on industry and dependent upon overseas sources of food, would seem to be more vulnerable. One of the most decisive factors in the victory over Japan in 1945 was the very effective submarine campaign carried on against her overseas commerce. Yet, the situation of Japan was different from that of England in significant ways. First, time was against Japan whereas it was on the side of Great Britain. For the Japanese, there was no hope for help from the outside; for the English, there were already signs that the United States (the Cash-and-Carry revision of the Neutrality Acts, the growing sentiment for the peacetime draft, Roosevelt's "stab-in-the-back" speech of June 1940) would ultimately deliver whatever material aid was required—if there was time, and time is what a blockade takes. Further, Japan enjoyed neither air superiority nor command of the seas; Great Britain clearly dominated the waves, and Dunkirk suggested that perhaps the *Luftwaffe* was not invincible after all.

Since Hitler had promised that there would be no war against Great Britain many times, it seemed to the German planners that any war would necessarily be fought out on the plains of northern Europe. Thus, they logically devoted the bulk of German resources to land power and a tactical air force designed specifically to give close support to that land power. Consequently, Germany lagged in the construction of the submarine fleet which would have been required. Moreover, there was no chance of Hitler being able to build a surface fleet equal to the task—not while it remained necessary to maintain a great army as a guarantee of the good behavior of the giant in the east! Submarines had seriously hampered the Allies in the First World War, and in World War II they crippled Japanese industry. What were the prospects for an underseas campaign against the extended British line of communications on the high seas? This might have been a hopeful option, but Hitler's promise that the *Wehrmacht* would not have to fight Great Britain caused the German Navy to face the Battle of Britain with few more than 50 submarines. To build more would take time, and that time could be used by America and Great Britain to build up the antisubmarine forces more rapidly than a respectable U-Boat fleet could be brought to bear.

Perhaps the principle of mass should have dictated the cutting off of British overseas commerce where it was most concentrated—in the ports. Might not this be done with the great bomber fleet of the *Luftwaffe*? First, the *Luftwaffe* was worn down as a result of the three victorious campaigns against Poland, Norway, and France.* Further, the German air industry was far from completely mobilized. Moreover, the destruction of the heavy port installations of Great Britain and the ships within them would have required greater numbers of aircraft, heavier bomb loads, and better antimaritime doctrine and training than were then possessed by the *Luftwaffe*. Finally, Goering's flyers would have had to defeat the RAF to close the ports of the English—if for no other reason than because most of the ports were beyond the range of the only effective escort fighter available, the Messerschmitt BF 109E.[51]

No matter what the opinions of Admiral Raeder, then, and no matter how grim the alternatives, the blockade strategy was also fraught with difficulties. It, too, was one in which the odds would have been very much against the Germans.

To do nothing was politically and psychologically impossible for Hitler. The British would not acquiesce in his diplomatic program. The cross-Channel movement seemed beyond the capabilities of the Navy and the *Luftwaffe*. The *Luftwaffe* had neither the equipment nor the doctrine to break the British with a bombing campaign—assuming that such a thing were possible at all in 1940. The blockade was beyond the abilities of the Navy and Goering's air force. What was to be done? It seemed that all of the alternatives, and any combination of them, were bad for Germany—Hitler, in other words, was faced with a dilemma. His apparent solution was simply to drift along with events, sometimes hoping that the British would suffer a moral collapse. Since he appears to have tried all strategies from time to time, he so diluted the impact of each of them that none ever really got a full test. In the words of Telford Taylor:

> As for the Fuehrer, his was the greatest sin, for he permitted—nay, encouraged—both Eagle (Code Name for the air attack on Great Britain) and Sea Lion without making them part of a considered strategy. At times he treated them as a primarily psychological offensive, the shock of which might bring the British to their senses and persuade them to yield to the inevitable before suffering utter defeat. At others, he hoped or pretended that Eagle alone might beat them into helplessness. On one occasion, as we have seen, he even advanced the preposterous notion of using the Sea Lion invasion fleet to lure

*Asher Lee, in his *The German Air Force*, p. 68, says:

> . . . The Luftwaffe did not escape its triumph without suffering substantial losses, and some 2,000 aircraft were lost or so badly damaged that they had to be sent back to Germany. . . . But the ardors of the previous six weeks, the air drubbing received at Dunkirk, the need to reform and refit, made such a lightning venture impractical [immediate invasion].

the British Navy to destruction at the hands of the Luftwaffe.[52]

If Hitler was unable to conceive and apply a viable and consistent strategy in an attempt to neutralize England, the German efforts would likely turn to expediency and improvisation. It is to this development and application in the Battle of Britain that the narrative now turns, after a brief review of the previous campaigns of the *Luftwaffe* in World War II.

Preliminaries to the Battle of Britain

The *Luftwaffe* was spectacularly successful during the campaigns in Poland, Norway, and France. In each instance, it was used in the role for which it had been designed—as an auxiliary for the tactical support of the Army. The governing doctrine, as far as it went, was sound and is as valid today as it was then. In each campaign, the *Luftwaffe* began with an attack on the enemy's airpower—mainly on the ground—and quickly went on to achieve unquestioned air superiority. Once that was done, it exploited its command of the air with interdiction operations designed to prevent the enemy's arrival on the battlefield or, later, his departure therefrom. It also performed close air support missions, which partially substituted for artillery and thus greatly improved the mobility of the ground columns by relieving them of the necessity of transporting the paraphernalia of the gunners.

At Dunkirk, however, where it appeared that the annihilation of the BEF was inevitable, the *Luftwaffe* performance was something less than striking. Given a largely free hand by Hitler's controversial halt order, it failed to achieve its objective in the face of first-class air opposition (the RAF).[53] After Goering's bold promises, one would think that the Germans might have become more introspective following that experience. Instead, additional successes in the final days of the battle for France led to an unfounded euphoria and the frittering away of precious time.[54] That time was put to good use by Beaverbrook and Dowding in an attempt to restore the fighter strength that the British had lost in Norway and France. In that effort they were only partially successful, because the drain on fighter resources had been so great.

Dowding's shortage of aircraft for Fighter Command was severely aggravated by the requirements of the battle on the Continent. In 1939, before the war had begun, the British had planned that Fighter Command would have a strength of 52 squadrons, and that four first-line fighter squadrons would accompany the 10 attack bomber squadrons and the BEF to the Continent. Dowding had understood that only one Hurricane squadron would accompany the first wave of the BEF to France, and that until Fighter Command had reached its full complement of 52, no more squadrons would be dispatched across the Channel. At the outset of the war, the misunderstanding immediately came to light when four squadrons of Hurricanes were sent. Dowding lodged his protest but without much satisfaction, and, through the winter of the "Sitzkrieg," a trickle of fighters was drawn from Fighter Command's reserves to replace losses on the Continent—all this with Fighter Command still far below planned strength. When Hitler began his Campaign in the West, the trickle became a stream, so that by the middle of May, when Dowding's force stood at nine squadrons below its allotted strength, the equivalent of 12 or 13 squadrons had been dispatched to France.[55]

As the battle wore on, the losses increased and the pleas of French Premier Paul Reynaud for additional fighters became louder. Dowding, convinced that the security of the base was paramount, set himself against the sending of additional strength. He felt that to honor Reynaud's requests for an additional 10 squadrons would irreparably damage Fighter Command, and that these fighters could not affect the outcome of the ground battle in France. The aircraft were not equipped for close support work, and the pilots were trained only for air defense, not escort or ground attack. When it appeared that the Cabinet was about to support the French with the airplanes they desired, Dowding requested an audience with the statesmen. He personally presented his case on May 15, and the next day dispatched his famous letter to the Prime Minister in which he stated that were Fighter Command so weakened he could not guarantee the safety of the homeland.[56]

Anguished over the desperate cries of the French, the Cabinet was reluctant to go along with Dowding's request. Still, the losses of pilots and aircraft were appalling, and the resources previously sent seemed to have done little to stem the onslaught. Of the 261 Hurricanes sent to France, only 61 ever came back. During May and June of 1940, the RAF lost 25 percent of its fighter strength—432 Hurricanes and Spitfires.[57] Finally, on May 19, Churchill made the painful decision; he proclaimed that no more fighters would go to France.

Another source of difficulty for the Fighter Command was the constant requirement to provide protection for Channel convoys against German air attack. Because the Germans could arrive on the scene before the Ground Control Intercept system could launch and get the fighters out over the Channel, the British were forced into flying a continuous combat air patrol over the convoys—an early-day version of the airborne alert and likewise extremely costly in terms of flying time, maintenance, and crew effort. As was the case with the requirement to dispatch forces to France, Dowding repeatedly protested this requirement, but with less success. The drain on Fighter Command was continued until after the commencement of the Battle of Britain when the air superiority mission *had* to take precedence. By then, the convoys had been pulled out of the Channel and were sent to west coast ports.[58]

The Battle of Britain

Through the latter part of July and into August, the *Luftwaffe* restricted itself to antimaritime operations, in daylight at least. The targets were the English convoys steaming up the Channel and the ports in the southeastern part of England. This choice of targets illustrates the aimlessness or confusion in the German strategy. The proper application of air doctrine demanded that priority be given the air superiority role, although that was certainly one of the purposes of the antishipping operations. While the targets would be maritime in nature, it was hoped that the Fighter Command would rise to the challenge and accept battle over the Channel, where the Germans would be closer to their bases than they would if the conflict were fought out over England. Had the battle been fought there, it would have been on much more equal terms because the Spitfires and the Messerschmitts would then have had roughly equal amounts of combat time per airplane *in the battle area*. Further, the selection of the ports, instead of those radars, airfields and aircraft plants near the coast, constituted a certain dilution, a violation of the principle of mass. Douhet had decreed that all efforts be initially directed at the destruction of enemy airpower on the ground, and that nothing else be done until command of the air had been achieved.

The German effort violated the principle of mass in yet another way. The *Luftwaffe* had been engaged in intensive operations for some weeks, and it was impossible for its squadrons to switch to British targets immediately. It would take time to develop the new French bases and to mass German strength on them. Meanwhile, Goering thought it would be beneficial to keep some pressure on the British through night raids and attacks on their commerce and simultaneously to obtain some experience in strategic air operations for the crews and the commanders. The defect in this scheme, however, was that it benefited the British more than it did the Germans. The English losses in ships were minimal, and another month of aircraft production and pilot training was gained. Most important, the air defense system got some extremely good practice at a low intensity, allowing many of the defects to be discovered and eliminated before the real crisis came. Further, the bombing accuracy of the *Luftwaffe* at night was too poor to do much damage. Finally, the Germans gave away the advantage of technological surprise in their night attacks. They had invented a method of bomb-aiming called *Knickbein*, which promised to make their efforts more productive. The British quickly became aware that the Germans were using such a device, and before the latter had gone over to massive night attacks, countermeasures were devised. (The *Knickbein* device was based upon the use of two radio beams, one for course and one for distance. It never could have achieved pinpoint accuracy, but it certainly would have improved the work of the *Luftwaffe* at night.) The British answer was to jam the beam electronically, and to light bonfires in fields, confirming to the German crews that the information they derived from their radios was erroneous. Thus, the later bombing waves would drop their loads on fires, which had supposedly been set by their predecessors. Had the Germans waited until they could put more muscle into their night attacks before they employed *Knickbein*, it might have had a greater effect.[59]

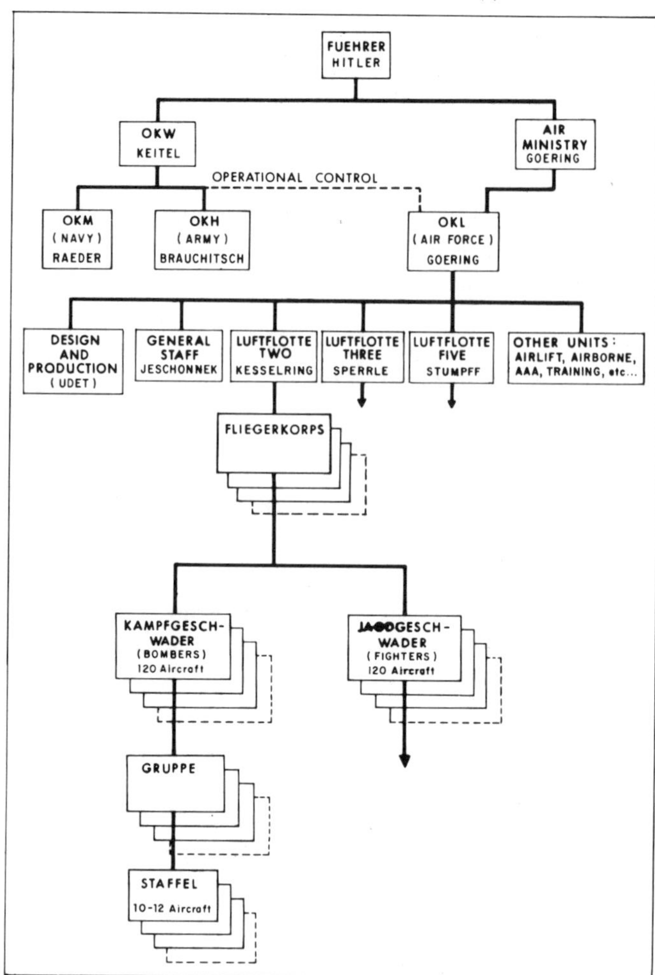

***Luftwaffe* Organization for Battle of Britain, August 1940**

The antishipping phase of the battle was not intended to be decisive by the Germans, but the British, nevertheless, achieved a kind of victory by passive methods. The generalship of Dowding was as decisive as anything else during this phase. He avoided the German trap by resisting the deployment of any more combat power than was necessary to escort the convoys by urging upon the political leaders the withdrawal of merchant marine units from the Channel; by instructing the Fighter Command pilots to avoid contact with German fighters and to concentrate on the bombers; and by ordering his flyers to break off pursuit at the coastline.[60] Goering was not much perturbed over Dowding's restrictive measures, for he was sure that things would be set aright by the *Luftwaffe* as soon as *Adlertag* (Eagle Day) arrived. The day would have to come soon if SEALION was ever to be launched, for German meteorologists were fully aware that the climate would prohibit any crossing after the middle of September. (*Adlertag* was the code name for the commencement of the campaign designed to sweep the British fighters from the sky and thereby gain air superiority.)[61]

By early August, *Luftflotten* 2 and 3 were poised for *Adlertag* on the airfields of northeastern France. The opening blow was supposed to have fallen on August 10, but weather delayed the great day until the thirteenth. The struggle against the RAF, and especially against its Fighter Command, went on until September 7, when the *Luftwaffe* was directed to shift its objective to the city of London.

Adlertag got the campaign off to a rough start. The weather at the outset was marginal, and the inferiority of the German command and control system caused trouble from the very beginning. The decision to commence the operation was the subject of debate several times during the early hours, but the command finally decided to launch—and then reversed itself, but only after a part of the force was already airborne. Recall, given the inadequate air-ground and air-to-air communications equipment, was a tough proposition; only a part of the force got the word. One Messerschmitt 110 outfit milled around for a time looking for the bomber force it was supposed to escort. There was no chance of finding the bombers since they had gotten the word that the attack had been called off. Whereupon the fighter commander, in a magnificent display of dedication, decided to go to England even though he did not have any bombers to escort—and got his organization quite badly bloodied in the process.[62] Many such incidents occurred that morning. One bomber pilot, not being equipped with the capability of talking to any aircraft not in his own group, wondered why a fighter was zooming at his formation and rocking its wings. Concluding that it was due to the exhilaration of the day and natural to fighter pilots in any event, he went on with the mission.

The afternoon sorties had a little better results, but the weather limited the effects of the bombs. The score for the first day showed that the *Luftwaffe* lost 45 out of 1,485 sorties while the Fighter Command did not recover 13 of the 727 they dispatched. It would not have been a very encouraging day for the "Fat One" had he known what the real figures were.[63] He would have been even more shocked had he known that the British had access to his most secret communications.

In the 1970s it came to light that from the beginning of the war the British—and later the Americans—had an important advantage over their enemies. Just before the outbreak of war, British intelligence had pulled off a highly significant coup in that they broke the German coding system. Achieved through a combination of espionage and brilliant technical innovation, the accomplishment permitted the British to read most of the German message traffic. The decoded messages were transmitted only to the top-level British leadership (including Dowding) under an intelligence source known as ULTRA; they gave Fighter Command additional leverage to supplement the impact of radar in combatting the inherent German advantages of mass and surprise.[64] Equally important was the fact that the British managed throughout the war to deny to the Germans that the code had been broken.

A strong case can be made for the role ULTRA played in the Battle of Britain. Ronald Lewin states:

> . . . it was on radar that the actual fighting depended, and the Germans' gravest error was to under-value its power. But radar revealed only what was immediately happening or soon likely to happen. It was not a long-term predictor, able to forecast the pattern of a whole day's operations. Here was Ultra's opportunity. Whenever Bletchley could provide in advance deciphered German orders for a complicated series of attacks, stretching over many hours, Dowding was able to plan and orchestrate his response with ample foreknowledge instead of having to think from minute to minute, as was the case whenever radar alone supplied his intelligence. Such occasions were inevitably few, but *Adler Tag* offers a classic example.[65]

Group Captain F. W. Winterbotham argues that if radar was the first key to survival of the RAF, ULTRA was probably the second. It enabled Dowding to pinpoint the locations of German air units and read their orders; it also provided some indication of the *Luftwaffe*'s true losses from the calls for replacement aircraft and pilots.[66] But if the organizational, technical, and intelligence advantages that the British were able to gain were significant, German errors also contributed to the outcome of the battle.

Hermann Goering made one of his most serious blunders just after the beginning of the battle. Radar denied the Germans the advantage of surprise, and allowed the British to implement the principles of mass and economy of force in their defense. On Eagle Day, the *Luftwaffe* had succeeded in knocking the Ventnor radar station off the air, incapacitating it for 11 days. This was serious enough for the British; but had Goering recognized the importance of radar and the vulnerability of the radar towers, the battle might have gone the other way. The magnetron had not yet been made practical for air defense radar, and the equipment was still operating on a relatively low frequency with correspondingly long wave length. This, of course, required very high towers which were easily found and quite fragile. There were but 20 of these towers, and some of them were not much involved in the main battle. During a commanders' conference which Goering held on August 15, he remarked that he did not think that the radar sites were profitable targets; in the *Luftwaffe*, this statement was the equivalent of an order not to attack them. Thus, the Germans neglected one of the greatest vulnerabilities of the Fighter Command when they failed to gouge out its eyes by destroying the radar stations.[67]

Goering, along with most officers in the *Wehrmacht*, was fully aware that air superiority was an essential prerequisite to further steps no matter which of the military strategies was pursued. Yet, the *Luftwaffe*'s approach to that goal was certainly not as direct as it might have been. The fault arose more from faulty intelligence than it did from any defects in doctrine. In the commanders' conference on the fifteenth, Goering again emphasized the need to concentrate on the RAF, but the intelligence was not distinct enough to permit the massing on Fighter Command, which was the essence of the resistance in the air. It was bad enough that the German intelligence grossly underestimated the output of the British fighter factories; but when it could not distinguish between them and the bomber plants, it led to a good deal of dispersion of effort. On August 15, for example, the *Luftwaffe* hit the Stirling factory. This was a serious setback to the Bomber Command, but not to the air defense of Great Britain, especially since the bombers were not then engaged in a campaign against the *Luftwaffe*'s bases and factories. There was a Spitfire factory quite close to the Stirling establishment; it came through the battle untouched.[68]

Faulty target selection hurt the Germans in other ways. They made attacks on Coastal Command and on Bomber Command Bases; and, on one occasion, they wrecked a fleet of Tiger Moths assigned to a training base, but they did not get the pilot trainees who were in short supply and vitally important to the struggle for air superiority. But perhaps the most serious mistake in this area was the failure to mass against the sector station airfields. The control rooms at these stations were absolutely vital to the conduct of the battle because they were in direct tactical control of the flying forces once the latter were airborne. Soon after the beginning of the battle the Germans suspected that the command and control system had been grossly underestimated and that the British fighters were being effectively controlled from the ground. Yet the German intelligence system never imagined that these control rooms were above ground and therefore vulnerable. It is true that the *Luftwaffe* did strike some of these command posts with bombs aimed at other targets on some of the sector station airfields; but had they understood the situation, they doubtless could have deprived the Fighter Command of mass and economy of force by punching out its brains in its control rooms.[69]

Despite the Zeppelin and Gotha experience in World War I, strategic bombing was puzzlingly new, and the *Luftwaffe* had its troubles developing tactics during the campaign, especially escort tactics. The Stuka quickly showed itself to be unsuited to a strategic campaign when it suffered very grievous losses early in the air superiority phase. For a short time, Goering tried to give the dive bombers fighter protection; but the fighters could not accompany the Stukas during their dives, and the Hurricanes found the bombers to be most vulnerable just after they had pulled out. The pride of the *Luftwaffe* had been brought low. Because of the Stukas' small bomb load and short range, Goering thought their protection not worth the price and pulled them out of the battle before August had ended.[70]

When it came to the problem of escorting the bombers, Goering found himself in an even more difficult dilemma. From the beginning of the battle, the Germans had suffered much higher losses among their bombers than anticipated. Crew members were considerably upset and took out their chagrin on their brethren of the fighter force. The bomber men claimed that the fighter pilots were merely cavorting about the footless halls of space and leaving the former alone to face the wrath of the Fighter Command. As August wore on, Goering became more and more insistent that the fighters fly close escort for the bombers and this created a storm of protest among the single-engine men. They claimed that doing so would give away the principle advantages of the fighter aircraft. The essence of such a craft is surprise. Surprise is achieved through the characteristics of flexibility and high speed. Adolf Galland and others argued that when the fighters were forced to fly formation with the bombers, they were also forced to start the struggle from a position known to the enemy and from an airspeed and an altitude which were much lower than those of the enemy. Thus, a basically offensive weapon was forced into the tactical defense and could not serve its function of achieving air superiority. But Goering insisted because there was something reassuring to the bomber men about being able to see their escorts. However, even though one of the three fighter wings accompanying each one of the bombers was required to fly "close" escort, the pilots of this unit often interpreted this to mean that they would have to remain near, but that they could do so by weaving rather than by flying in a conventional formation with the bigger and slower aircraft. This, at least, would permit them to maintain their speed, though they would still be starting their battles from an altitude disadvantage. The other fighter wings in the attack formation were not as tightly controlled. One of them was assigned the mission of flying ahead of the bomber unit to clear the target area, and the other was used for top cover.[71]

Despite Goering's initial restrictions on fighter tactics, the high losses continued through August and into September. Towards the end of August, the Reichsmarschall decided that more had to be done to cut the losses. He had been getting falsely encouraging reports about the night raids, so he decided to switch Hugo Sperrle's *Luftflotte* 3 over to the night attack, thus releasing its fighters from escort duties. These fighters were then shifted northwards to the service of Kesselring's continuing daylight offensive, and the additional combat power did have a beneficial effect on the relative loss rates of the two air forces.

The favorable trend for the *Luftwaffe* did not last long. The British, too, were improving with experience. The radar observers were delivering better information to the controllers, and the latter were becoming more expert at the deployment and employment of their forces. Thus, early in September, the argument over tactics in the German Air Force was revived. The bomber men argued that the weaving was carrying the fighters too far away from the bomber formations, and the fighter pilots restated their arguments of the previous month. Goering again took the side of the bomber men even at the vigorous opposition of the fighter leaders—if one can believe the memoirs of the latter. This time his reaction was to limit the fighters further by insisting that the weaving come to an end and that the BF 109s remain in conventional formation with the bombers.[72]

Meanwhile, the British were also evolving a tactical doctrine by trial-and-error. They had started the war with the formation which had been used by the Royal Flying Corps against the Central Powers a generation earlier: elements of three ships, flying in an inverted "V" and in close formation. When he is flying in such a formation, the wing man cannot for even a moment remove his eyes from the leader. To do so would be to risk a midair collision. The Germans, on the other hand, had evolved a "finger four" formation in the battles of the Spanish Civil War. That is to say that four fighters would fly in a formation similar to the tips of the fingers of one's right hand. There were two elements of two ships each, and the spacing was much wider than it was in the old three-ship group. This allowed the wing man in each element to remain in support of his leader, but it also permitted him to turn his eyes to clear the area *behind* the formation. Thus, the Germans had implemented both the principle of mass and the one of security in that they were better able to protect the rear while still increasing the firepower of the basic tactical unit by 33 percent. The British quickly perceived the advantages of the German method and adopted an identical tactical formation.[73]

The British were not so quick to implement the principle of mass in another sense. All through the battle, a tactical argument raged in the higher reaches of the RAF. The question was whether the individual squadrons should be committed to the fray as soon as possible, or whether a delay should be tolerated for the sake of massing squadrons into "Big Wings" for the purpose of increasing the weight of the strike on the German attacking formations. At first glance, the answer would seem obvious—that the "Big Wing" was the thing. But Air Vice Marshal Park, commander of Number 11 Group and proponent of the immediate commitment of forces, argued that his primary mission was not the destruction of the maximum number of German aircraft. Rather, it was to protect England from the bombs of the invader. He admitted the theoretical value of large formations and the possibility of their imposing a higher attrition upon the *Luftwaffe*. But, he argued that this attrition would be imposed on the Germans during their withdrawal *after* they had delivered the bombs. To conduct the battle that way might well result in defeat because the Germans could possibly destroy the RAF on the ground *before* the *Luftwaffe* was destroyed in the air.[74]

Douglas Bader, then a squadron commander in Number 12 Group, was one of the proponents of the "Big Wing." His argument was that the radar could immediately spot the German formations as they began their join-up over the French coast. As soon as this happened, he advocated that the fighters of Number 12 Group, at least, be launched and have time to join up in "Big Wings" and to climb to altitude so that they could dive out of the sun onto the German formations as the latter crossed the English coast. After the "Big Wings" had broken up the German formations, then the fighters of Number 11 Group, which had been launched later, could enter the fray and destroy the fragments.

In a fateful meeting at the Air Ministry, the Air Officer Commanding of Number 11 Group, Air Vice Marshal Park, rebutted the arguments of Bader and his commander, Air Vice Marshal Trafford Leigh-Mallory. Park held that the Germans would immediately react with a countermeasure which would put the RAF in a bad way. The *Luftwaffe* would launch a dummy raid which would go through the normal join-up procedures on its side of the Channel. This would trigger the launch of the Number 12 Group fighters. Then, at about the time the British fighters were returning to base for fuel, the Germans could launch the real attack which would catch the RAF on the ground with disastrous results. No matter what the theoretical advantages of mass were, Park argued that the security of the base had to come first; the "Big Wing" tactic was impractical because of that.[75]

Unfortunately, there were overtones in the argument that were unbecoming to the RAF. Implications were drawn that Park's resistance was due to his desire to gather all the glory unto himself. It was suggested that the controllers of Number 11 Group were purposely delaying the alert to Number 12 Group and the commitment of that Group to the battle merely to sustain the tactical views of the commander. On the other side, those loyal to Park argued (and still argue) that Leigh-Mallory and Sholto Douglas (then a member of the Air Staff) were excessively ambitious and that they were jealous of Park whose Group was located at the vortex of the battle. Mindful of how important it was to protect the priceless secret of ULTRA, Dowding, to his credit, refused to point out that his conduct of the battle was influenced by knowledge of German plans gained from ULTRA, access to which Leigh-Mallory did not have.[76]

Whatever the merits of the case on both sides—and both sides did have some valid arguments—Park and Dowding were both relieved in November at the end of the battle. Leigh-Mallory took the helm of Number 11 Group in the place of Park.* The "Big Wing" scheme was then implemented, but that really proved nothing because the battle was over and the mission had changed. Perhaps the Combined Bomber Offensive against Germany (1943 to 1945) did offer some insight into the matter. For a time, then, the Germans tried to mass fighter forces against the Allied bombers; but they found that the big fighter formations were too inflexible and too slow in responding, and reverted to the use of smaller units. Again the situation was not entirely analogous with that in Great Britain in 1940.

In the latter days of August, although Beaverbrook was managing to replace aircraft losses, the *Luftwaffe* was hurting the RAF in the attacks on the sector stations. Losses in pilots were going up as a consequence, and the crew inventory was declining in both numbers and experience level. Things looked bad for the British.

At the darkest hour, Hermann Goering came to the relief of the RAF. Fighter Command was beginning to stagger, but the Reichsmarschall released his grip on the British throat by perpetrating a gross violation of the principle of the objective. Just at the moment the *Luftwaffe* seemed to be about to attain the decisive objective of the destruction of the Fighter Command and the acquisition of air superiority, it was switched to a campaign which might have been decisive had it been attainable: the attack on London. Convention views this as an emotional reaction on the parts of Hitler and Goering.

A Heinkel HE-111 Bomber Takes off for a Raid Against England, 1940

There was indeed an element of emotion in the basic decision to switch targets. From the outset of the battle, Hitler's crews had the strictest instructions not to engage in terror attacks; he reserved the decision to undertake such attacks to himself. Why? It was not that the *Fuehrer* had any great humanitarian regard for the women and children of London. Rather, he fancied himself as an expert on mass psychology, and he felt that his totalitarian system was based on the rather fragile morale of the German people. He feared, once terror bombing was started, that the English would retaliate against the German cities with disastrous results for the totalitarian regime. (German morale later proved to be much more durable than Hitler thought.) On the other side, the British Bomber Command also was very much against terror raids. From the beginning the crews had strict orders not to attack anything but purely military targets only along the coast of Europe.[77] But this tacit arms control agreement, such as it was, came to an end on the night of August 24, quite by accident. On the twenty-fourth of August, a *Luftwaffe* bomber crew was briefed to make a night attack on an airfield slightly to the south of London. Normally, the London area was one of the few where night navigation was not a serious problem. The Thames flows through the center of town in such a way that the metropolis is practically unmistakable, even at night. But that night the weather was marginal and a mistake was made; the bombs fell on the city rather than on the airfield. Naturally, the crew did not report it because they thought that they had bombed the designated target. Churchill ordered the Bomber Command to retaliate against the German capital on the very next night. Those interpretations which suggest that he did this specifically to draw the *Luftwaffe* off of the Fighter Command are exaggerated and give the Prime Minister credit for wisdom which was even greater than that which he did possess. The leaders of the Bomber Command were opposed to the idea, but the Prime Minister insisted; the mission was launched as ordered. Only a few of the British planes made it to the target area, and their bomb loads were neither very heavy nor well-aimed. The damage was minimal and the casualties light. Yet the psychological impact was very considerable. Goering was made to appear a fool. He had long bragged that Germany was invulnerable to air attack and had also publicly boasted that if even one British airplane appeared over Germany, then his name was "Meier." Hitler was supposed to have been outraged. There was no way for him to know that the Berlin attack had been a retaliation, so

*Dowding retired after a liaison trip to America, Leigh-Mallory was killed in an airplane accident in 1944, and Park later commanded the air defense of Malta and was living in New Zealand in 1975.

it was easy to assume that the British had committed an unprovoked "atrocity." In a speech in the *Sportspalast* on September 4, he promised he would retaliate for the bombing of German cities with the total annihilation of the British metropolis. This, then, was one of the important reasons for the decision to bomb London.[78]

Albert Kesselring was also in favor of bombing London. He was an old soldier of the German Army who had come over to aviation only quite late in life. An efficient and logical man, he was not much given to emotional reactions. His conduct of the defense of Italy later in the war showed him to be a soldier of some competence. Why would he desire the attack on London? His opposite number, the commander of *Luftflotte* 3, Hugo Sperrle, very much desired to continue the attack on Fighter Command because he did not feel that air superiority had been won. Kesselring argued that it could never be won with an attack on the RAF airfields in southern England. Such a campaign could be won only with the assault on *all* the English airfields. He felt that Dowding would never accept defeat in southern England as long as the option remained of withdrawing his fighter forces to the fields north of London. And these fields were beyond the escort range of the BF 109. The bombers could not attack them in the daytime without escort because the losses would be excessive; they could not attack them at night because they could not then see them. Therefore, Kesselring argued, the only way to complete the destruction of the Fighter Command was to take the indirect approach: attack a target within range of the BF 109 which was so vital to Dowding that he would *have* to commit his last reserves to the battle. Once these last reserves had been destroyed, then the way would be open for SEALION. Curiously, while Goering was still convinced that airpower would do it alone, one of his principal subordinates, Kesselring, believed the whole thing to be but a prelude to the invasion. At any rate, where would one find such an objective? Napoleon hoped that the Imperial Russian Army would stand and fight in front of Moscow in 1812. Would the RAF fight to the last man over London?[79]

From another point of view, perhaps the switch in targets was not as revolutionary an act as it appeared to some. First, Douhet and all the other theorists of strategic bombing had dictated the achievement of air superiority as the first step and the exploitation of that superiority as the second. The German intelligence system was so bad that many of the airmen of the *Luftwaffe* fully believed that they had already achieved air superiority. Thus, it would have been perfectly reasonable, according to the Douhet logic, to move on to an attack on the morale of the British people. Further, a glance at the map will reveal that the Germans had started with an assault along the periphery and gradually moved towards targets farther inland. London was only one more step in that direction.

Whatever the logic or illogic behind the shift in targets, the great 300-bomber attack on the capital on September 7 gave Fighter Command more than it could handle, in spite of a forewarning through ULTRA. Goering saw his men off to the attack from his luxury train, which had been drawn to the coast. He watched the assault pass overhead late in the afternoon. Park had deployed his units against further attacks against the sector stations to the south and east of London, and, though many of them were able to join the fight before the withdrawal was complete, their attacks on the Germans generally came only after the bombs had been laid on the metropolis. Great fires were started among the docks and fuel storage tanks along the Thames. Thus, the bombers lit a beacon which would guide comrades for the night assault. Although the Germans lost 40 aircraft that day, 26 English fighters went down. The latter figure was exaggerated by Goering's returning flyers, and many of the *Luftwaffe* leaders were encouraged to believe that another important step towards air superiority had been taken.[80]

In English eyes, even at the time, the defeat was a tactical one; however, in the strategic sense, some felt that the Germans had blundered. In the words of Churchill, written after the war:

> . . . Biggin Hill Sector Station, to the south of London, was so severely damaged that for a week only one fighter squadron could operate from it. If the enemy had persisted in heavy attacks against the adjacent sectors and damaged their operations rooms or telephone communications, the whole intricate organization of Fighter Command might have been broken down. This would have meant not merely the maltreatment of London, but the loss to us of the perfected control of our own air in the decisive area. . . . I was led to visit several of these stations, particularly Manston (August 28), and Biggin Hill. . . . they were getting terribly knocked about, and their runways were ruined by craters. It was therefore with a sense of relief that Fighter Command felt the German attack turn on to London on September 7, and concluded that the enemy had changed his plan. Goering should certainly have persevered against the airfields, on whose organisation and combination the whole fighting power of our air force at this moment depended. By departing from the classical principles of war, as well as from the hitherto accepted dictates of humanity, he made a foolish mistake.[81]

Though he could hardly have much confidence in future trends in numbers of pilots at the time, Churchill's analysis was essentially correct, assuming that the supply of fighter pilots in Fighter Command was *the* critical factor. The number of pilots assigned peaked in early August, declining thereafter until the beginning of September. At just about the time of the initial assault on London, the curve was reversed and the issue was never again in doubt.

The figures available to the OKL staff could hardly have been as accurate as those supplied to Churchill, even if the German crews had not exaggerated their claims. The situation in OKW headquarters was all the more complicated because the hour of decision was approaching. Since the determination as to what strategy was being pursued had never really been made, there were those who still believed that SEALION was to be launched. Were that the case, the initial moves had to be made no later than mid-September. Admiral Raeder demanded a minimum of 10 days warning so that the Navy's preparations could be completed. It would take that long to make the final concentration of the vessels required, and to lay the protective mine fields on both sides of the invasion route. The target date for the warning order was set as September 11 for a landing which would commence no later than the twenty-first. After that the worsening Channel weather would prohibit any landing. Yet, all concerned agreed that nothing more could be done until air superiority had been achieved, and that issue was still in doubt in most German minds. Though Dowding and Park had suffered a tactical defeat on the seventh, they quickly reacted to the change in German air strategy, and the fights on the following days were less one-sided.[82] As one wit has said, in effect the Germans were using their bombers as bait to catch the British fighters. The rub was that the lure tended to be more valuable than the fish.

In the meantime, the British Bomber Command had been directed to attack the growing concentration of German invasion shipping in the Channel ports. Although the bombers did achieve about 10 percent attrition upon the collected shipping before September was over, the direct strategic effect in the first half of the month was not that apparent. Perhaps the indirect psychological impact was significant. At a time when *Luftwaffe* enthusiasts were arguing that they were on the verge of achieving the dreamed-of air superiority, the doubting Thomases saw the Bomber Command return to the offensive night after night.[83]

Thus, when the hour of decision came on September 11, there was enough dissent from the *Luftwaffe* party line to make Hitler unsure. Certainly the Navy remained unconvinced. Unable to make up his mind, Hitler postponed his decision to the fourteenth. On that date, he again hesitated, and promised Admiral Raeder a firm decision on the seventeenth.[84] On September 11, the *Luftwaffe* suffered fewer losses than did the RAF. Three days later, on the fourteenth, both sides lost the same number of aircraft. It was going to be close. Optimistic reports were reaching Goering from the German Attaché in Washington and the Japanese Attaché in London.[85]

Then came Sunday, September 15. Privileged with the first look at the eastward march of the North Atlantic weather, the British forecasters knew long before the Germans that it would be another fine day for the aerial assault. Visibility in the blue

A Dornier DO-17 Under Attack From a Spitfire. The German Caption Claimed that the Spitfire Was Downed

September sky would be unlimited, and only scattered cumulus would hamper the bombers' aim. There was little deception, and Park had plenty of time to make his deployments. No longer could the *Luftwaffe* concentrate on the way to the battlefield. The initial wave of bombers, in the late morning, first flew to the fighter base area at Calais; only after the rendezvous had been made, did the fighters and bombers set out to cross the Channel. Since the whole assembly was conducted in full view of the British electronic eye, Park was able to budget his strength on the ground until the very last minute. No diversionary raids were flown. As the massive German formations lumbered up the Thames Estuary, the squadron pairs of Number 11 Group stormed through their ranks. Some of the Germans fell, others turned back. But most advanced onward towards London. Then, over the city itself, the "Big Wing" of Number 12 Group crashed into the staggering German swarm. More of the *Luftwaffe* aircraft went down, and the bombs of the rest were scattered far and wide across the face of the great metropolis; then the assault began to recede. The remnants of the attack were harried all the way to the Channel. Then came a nervous lull, as the "Hurries" and "Spits" were recalled to their airdromes where their ground crews struggled to replenish them in time for the second assault that everyone knew would come.[86]

The two-hour respite was all that Fighter Command needed. The afternoon battle was more of the same. There were no real diversions—only a head-on approach by a few more than 100 bombers, escorted by hundreds of Messerschmitts. Again, the squadron pairs of Number 11 Group weakened the attacking force on its inbound leg; again, the massive wing of Leigh-Mallory's Group collided with the Germans over the city; again, the impact of the attack was ruined because the bombs were strewn far and wide; again, the bomber crews bent their throttles in gradual power dives to escape the harassment of Park's fighters; and, again, there was the seemingly endless struggle to stretch the last gallon of fuel to escape the unfriendly grasp of the Channel.[87]

Winston Churchill chose that day to visit the command post of Number 11 Group. As the battle wore on, the Prime Minister saw more and more of the squadron status lights indicate that their units had engaged the enemy. And Churchill, in his eloquence, described the moment of crisis:

> . . . I became conscious of the anxiety of the Commander (Park), who now stood still behind his subordinate's chair. Hitherto I had watched in silence. I now asked, "What other reserves have we?" "There are none," said Air Vice-Marshal Park. In an account which he wrote about it afterwards, he said that at this I "looked grave." Well I might. What losses should we not suffer if our refueling planes were caught on the ground by further raids of "40 plus" or "50 plus!" The odds were great; our margins small; the stakes infinite.[88]

Still exhilarated from the battle, the Fighter Command pilots came down to report 185 victories, and that was the figure which the Prime Minister used to announce to the world a great victory. And a victory it was. Although later, postwar figures prove that the *Luftwaffe* losses were much less than that, they were nevertheless substantial.[89] But perhaps more important was the psychological shock of the thing. For days, the propagandists and *Luftwaffe* optimists had been harping on the fact that the Fighter Command was down to its last 50 aircraft, and *Luftwaffe* intelligence supported that view. One more assault, they said, would consume those last 50. Yet, on September 15, the German flyers could see for themselves that Fighter Command could still assault them with 300 fighters at one time. The conclusion was inescapable. Air superiority had not been won. Even if Goering would not admit it, the *Fuehrer* saw this truth. Two days later, on the seventeenth, he postponed SEA-LION at least until October—which was the same as never.*

Thus ended the Battle of Britain. Although the British did not immediately recognize that the crisis had passed and the *Luftwaffe* continued its painful night attacks for a long time, the struggle for air superiority was over. The British had won it. Without command of the air, there could be no invasion of Britain. Without an invasion, Britain probably could not be defeated. Without such a defeat, the war could not be a short one.

The rest of the story is anticlimactic. At the end of the month, Goering finally admitted that the daylight offensive was too expensive and his bomber wings went over to the night assault. Once the decision to go over to a night campaign for the sake of security was made, it became inevitable that the bombing accuracy would be too bad to have decisive effects. As for the daylight fighter-bomber raids, the weight of bombs was too light to have much of an impact, even if they were delivered accurately. The main effect of these latter raids was to bend the morale of the German fighter pilots for they considered it a gross misapplication of their weapons system. Once a bomb was hung on a BF 109, even the Hurricane could compete with it on equal terms.[90]

Like Gettysburg and Waterloo, the Battle of Britain has been analyzed and reanalyzed from practically every possible angle. There have been German accounts, British accounts, and neutral accounts; there have been memoirs, official histories, popular histories, documentary films, popular films, articles, and historical novels. In fact, the battle was so complex, and so much has been written about it, that a complete analysis here is out of the question. This critique, accordingly, is only an explanation of the outcome of the battle in terms of the faults in the theory of airpower itself, and also in terms of faults in the way that that theory was applied to the Battle of Britain.

First, and probably foremost, Douhet, and the German air leaders after him, theorized that the bomber would always get through. They had some sound historical precedents for that view. The Gothas had penetrated British air space during World War I with impunity. Even in the use of the clumsy Zeppelins many more craft were lost to accidents than to the air defenses of London. There was little that the defenses could do to stop the bombers in the Spanish Civil War. But the whole theory depended upon the inability of the defenses to locate incoming attacking forces before it was too late. All of this was changed with the coming of radar. This technological surprise, married as it was to an effective command and control system and first-class interceptor aircraft, was the single most important reason for the failure of the German air offensive. To this must be added the considerable contribution made by ULTRA-supplied intelligence.

Next, Douhet grossly overestimated the effects of high explosive bombs. He assumed that they could be delivered in neat geometrical patterns with small errors and that they would easily knock down urban structures. The raids on London proved that the metropolis was capable of absorbing a good deal more punishment than was thought. The reinforced concrete structures of modern European cities could not be tumbled without a good deal more bomb weight than had been predicted by Douhet and his German followers.

Douhet, and Trenchard to some extent, assumed that the experience of London in World War I was indicative of the future. They felt that civilian morale was a legitimate and fragile target. Douhet, especially, held that an attack on that morale was really a humane form of warfare because it would quickly

*Weather would have prohibited any landing after the end of September, and Hitler fully realized that British mobilization and American aid would certainly cause the British strength to grow more rapidly during the winter than could the German power to invade. He nevertheless persisted with night attacks and with day fighter-bomber raids to mask the German failure and to hide his intent to invade Russia the following year.

Characteristics	HE-111	B-29
Maximum Weight	*27,400 lbs.*	*105,000 lbs.*
Range	*760 miles with 4,400 lbs. bombs*	*More than 3,000 miles on Hiroshima trip (10m lbs. bomb)*
Maximum Speed (mph)	*255*	*365*
Total Horse Power	*2,400*	*8,800*
Total Guns	*3 machineguns*	*10 machineguns + 20-mm cannon*
Service Ceiling	*25,500 ft.*	*31,850 ft.*

Comparison of World War II Bombers

bring about such a decisive result that the prolonged blood bath would be avoided. But the morale of Londoners in World War II proved to be much more sturdy than expected. Their spirit did not crack, and many have argued that it became even tougher under the rain of German bombs.

The German approach to strategic air warfare was also blemished because few of their leaders fully appreciated the corollaries to Douhet's theorems. First, decisive results could not be achieved if the target could not be located and hit. Yet the Germans, even though they concentrated on the production of bombers, were so oriented toward tactical operations in support of the armies that they neglected the vital area of long-range navigation. This hurt their daylight campaign to some extent, and it had a deadly effect on the night bombing which accompanied and finally replaced it. Nor did the Germans find the answer to the bomb-aiming problem. The Americans produced a technical answer in the Norden bombsight, and the British solution was a combination of tactical and technical steps in their pathfinder operations and the development of airborne radar. The Germans, however, attempted a tactical resolution of the difficulty. Ernest Udet's trip to the Cleveland Air Races in the early 1930s, among other things, caused an overcommitment to the dive-bombing answer.* Hitler dictated that all bombers, even those with four engines, would have a dive-bombing capability. This turned out to be a gross violation of mass in that it guaranteed that the weight of the bomb load would never be sufficient to achieve decisive results. A proper interpretation of Douhet would have produced the corollary that accurate bomb-aiming and navigation must be developed for *heavy* bombers.

Another corollary which probably should have emerged from Douhet's emphasis on bombers was that such planes should not only be numerous but also big and strong. In an obvious analogy to the monstrous battleships of his day, Douhet himself called them "battleplanes." Yet the line bombers of the *Luftwaffe* were too small, too short-legged, too lightly armored, too lightly armed, and they had too small a carrying capacity. Compare, for example, the main line bomber of the Battle of Britain to the B-29 which attacked Hiroshima just five years later. Thus, even if Douhet's theories had not had their faults, the German interpretation and amplification of those ideas was defective. In fact, there were enough defects that it would have been remarkable had the application of the theory to the problems of the Battle of Britain been successful.

The most serious German fault in the employment of airpower lay in the area of generalship. Leaving aside the prewar errors, Goering committed two monumental blunders during the course of the battle itself. We have seen how the idea that the bomber would always get through was valid in the days of Douhet and how the thought was invalidated by the invention of radar. That need not have defeated the Germans. On *Adlertag*, the *Luftwaffe* partially blinded Fighter Command through the destruction of the radar station on Ventnor Island; the job might have been completed had the Germans persisted in their attacks on the electronic eyes of the British. Had they succeeded, they might have restored the validity of Douhet's theorem. But Goering's decision to call off the assault on the towers allowed a great opportunity to slip by.

Goering made his second great blunder in the application of the principle of objective when he ordered the attack on London before the Fighter Command had been destroyed. The British were in serious trouble because of the declining numbers and experience levels of pilots. The gradual destruction of the command and control system of Fighter Command could only have made this problem worse. When Goering called off

*The main originators of dive-bombing were the flyers of the U.S. Navy and Marine Corps. A kind of glide-bombing technique had been developed in the First World War, and the Marines steepened the dive to about 65 degrees in their operations against the Nicaraguan revolutionaries in 1927. The technique proved so effective against small targets in jungle clearings that in 1928 Martin Company was commissioned to design a dive bomber specifically for the task. The Navy picked up the idea in the early 1930s because it seemed impractical to hit a moving ship with level bombing. Experiments on the West Coast in the early thirties were so successful that the Navy decided to demonstrate the technique at the Cleveland Air Races in 1933. Udet happened to be there, and he was so impressed that he purchased two American dive-bombers and had them shipped back to Germany. This was said to have been one of the most important origins of the *Luftwaffe*'s overcommitment to the dive-bombing idea. For further details, see David R. Mets, "Dive Bombing Between the War," *Air Power Historian* (July, 1965), 62-65.

the attacks on the sector stations, he gave up on an objective which was decisive and might have been attainable in favor of an objective which was not attainable. He thus threw away the *Luftwaffe*'s last chance for victory.

The high command of the *Luftwaffe* also violated the principles of war in the creation of a system of command and control. It was insufficiently simple. The command decisions were made before the attack was launched, sometimes the day before. They were handed down to the operating personnel in briefings before take-off. There could be little modification of the preflight briefings once the assault was airborne because of the primitive state of German radio communications. Accordingly, German pilots went into the battle over London with information that was at least three hours old and which had been filtered down from the decision makers through several layers of intermediaries. In the British case, the sector controller made the tactical decisions based on almost instantaneous information from the radar stations and was able immediately to issue these decisions to the flight commanders over the VHF radios. In the latter case, the decision maker and the operating personnel were in immediate voice contact, a much simpler and more efficient system.

The *Luftwaffe* also violated the principle of mass in its deployment of *Luftflotte* 5. The location of this unit in Norway placed it out of supporting distance of the main attacking units. It was done to impose a kind of cordon defense upon the British by forcing Dowding to protect the northeastern shores of Great Britain as well as those in the south. The Germans did not realize that Dowding was not much burdened by this requirement because he felt it necessary to rotate some of the fighter units out of the main battle area to quieter sectors to enable them to recuperate—no matter what the deployment of *Luftflotte* 5. Moreover, because the distance between Norway and England was too much for the BF 109, Stumpf's one and only attack was a disaster for the Germans.

Most of these German misapplications of the principles of war arose, in part, from a very faulty intelligence system. The *Luftwaffe* grossly underestimated British fighter production, overestimated RAF combat losses, misunderstood the vulnerability of the British command and control system, denigrated the toughness of British civilian morale and—most important—failed to appreciate the extent to which radar would enable the defense to apply the principles of war in what had formerly been a hopeless situation.[91]

Perhaps it would be fair to say that the British won partly because they were more intelligent than were the Germans in the application of the principles of war in the evolution of tactical doctrine. On the other hand, one might well argue that Goering failed partially because he did not apply the principles of war properly to the tactical problems of the day.

Legacy of the Battle of Britain

Since World War II, the fifteenth of September has been celebrated in England as Battle-of-Britain Day, and it has become a part of the cultural heritage of the English, much as Gettysburg has come to be a symbol of a great turning point in the history of the American people. But for our purposes, the legacy of the battle is important in other ways—what it meant to the continuing and expanding war and how it affected the evolution of airpower theory and doctrine.

Many scribes argue that the British victory led more or less directly to the cancellation of SEALION. There are those who hold that was not the case because Hitler never seriously intended to invade Great Britain. Some of the German soldiers have so argued; and, as we have seen above, J. F. C. Fuller looked upon SEALION and the Battle of Britain as the biggest bluff in the history of world politics. If the argument regarding Hitler's intentions can never be settled, one thing is fairly certain—whatever Hitler's plans for England, air superiority was an essential prerequisite. That this is true for a blockade, invasion, or a Douhetian strategy is quite obvious; what is less obvious is that it was also true for a bluff. The defeat of the RAF was essential to make the bluff credible. Thus, although the Royal Navy might well have stopped SEALION had the RAF been beaten, the fact remains that the RAF did not suffer defeat. What is important here is that whether Hitler's intention was to win by invading or bluffing or taking whatever came his way, the RAF must receive credit for his frustration. Given the ambiguous results of subsequent air campaigns against Germany, Japan, North Korea, and North Vietnam, it is probably fair to say that the Battle of Britain was the single most decisive air campaign in history.

If a conclusion regarding the frustration of SEALION must remain shrouded in uncertainty, it is more clear that Hitler's desire for a short war was frustrated by British resistance. On countless occasions, especially in *Mein Kampf*, Hitler said that Germany could only fight a short war because of her limited resources. The threat of the *Luftwaffe* had been instrumental in the quick collapse of Austrian and Czechoslovakian resistance. This time there was no quick collapse to substantiate Hitler's fundamental premise. The Battle of Britain, like the Battle of the Marne in the Kaiser's day, denied Hitler the short war he so ardently desired.

Another fundamental premise of the *Fuehrer* was that a two-front war was suicide for Germany and had to be avoided. In *Mein Kampf* he had pointed to this as a fundamental cause for Germany's defeat in the First World War. Yet, even as the Battle of Britain was approaching its climax, Hitler began preparing to invade Russia; and when the battle was over, it became yet another reason impelling Hitler to launch such an attack. Germany was committed to gaining *lebensraum* in the east. Perhaps Hitler believed that Great Britain was hanging on beyond the bounds of reason in the vain hope that Joseph Stalin would come to her aid; thus Hitler could solve both of these problems by issuing one great "puff" which would blow down the whole Bolshevik house in a flash of German fury. In so doing, however, he forgot his own warning about the perils of a two-front war.

Perhaps the most important effect of the Battle of Britain was the least tangible, the least obvious at the time. General George Marshall remarked that, "It is not enough to fight. It is the spirit which we bring to the fight that decides the issue." On another occasion he observed that "the refusal of the British and Russian peoples to accept what appeared to be inevitable defeat was the great factor in the salvage of our civilization."[92] Perhaps the moral effect of the Battle of Britain was paramount. Up until September 15, 1940, the *Wehrmacht* had never been denied an important objective, and until then the *Luftwaffe* had been used to cowing people all over Europe, time and again. For the first time, it became obvious that the German air force was beatable. This knowledge itself helped turn the tide.

Hitler was privy to that knowledge. Yet he failed to act upon its implications. A long war would call for more and better armaments, and a two-front war would call for greater numbers of tanks and airplanes. Yet Germany lolled along on a one-shift economy for another two years. She kept her housewives in the kitchen. The British victory meant that the "big bomber men" on the Air Staff would have their day. Without extant fighters to meet that threat, Germany would have to abandon her emphasis on bombers in order to guarantee the command of her own skies. Yet Hitler dragged on and on with the bomber idea in the face of a growing volume of advice crying for the buildup of the air defense system.[93]

The battle gave the airpower theorists their first test. It tended to deny that the bomber would always get through—at least not with acceptable losses. Rather, air defense was shown to have a far greater potential than had been predicted, and the British methods were copied the world over. Targets were much harder to destroy than Douhet had thought. Civilian morale, in the British case at least, seemed to be much tougher than the "big bomber men" had supposed. The battle certainly seemed to imply that armies and navies were much more than the defensive instruments described by Douhet. The difficulties inherent in the command and control of air forces were shown to be much more complex than predicted by any of the theorists. Target selection was a serious problem unforeseen by the bomber men. The collection and especially the interpretation of intelligence proved to be a very difficult task. In general, then, those who followed Goering, Kesselring, and Sperrle were made aware of an experience which seemed to say that the strategic bombing idea had failed its first test. Those men who would later head the Allied Combined Bomber Offensive only dimly perceived some of the lessons of the struggle. If the German experience over Great Britain provided some signposts for them, many others had to be relearned in the "school of hard knocks" over Ploesti and Schweinfurt.

In the last analysis, the Battle of Britain bought time—time which was precious to the Allies and deadly to Hitler. It would probably be going too far to say that the battle made the defeat of Germany inevitable; but, together with the success of the Soviet Army, it did make a major contribution to that result. Time was what America needed to mobilize her men and materiel; time was what the Royal Navy, and later the United States Navy, needed to make the blockade effective; time was what the Allies needed to mount the Combined Bomber Offensive against the German homeland; time was what was essential to the building of the invasion base in the British Isles. On the other side, Hitler could not afford a long war. He would run out of oil; he would run out of metals; and he thought that the German people would run out of the will to endure a long war. Perhaps those orators who espouse superlatives on the anniversary of the Battle of Britain are not too far off the mark when they cite the struggle as one of the great turning points of World War II.

Notes

[1]The authority on strategic bombing in World War I is Raymond Fredette, *The Sky on Fire: The First Battle of Britain* (New York, 1966). See the entire work, but especially "The Fearson Legacy," pp. 231-251.

[2]The English version of Douhet's work is Giulio Douhet, *Command of the Air* (New York, 1942); on the *Luftwaffe* commitment to Douhet see examples in Werner Baumbach, *The Life and Death of the Luftwaffe* (New York, 1960), p. 60, and Adolf Galland, "Defeat of the Luftwaffe: Fundamental Causes," *Air University Review,* VI (Spring 1953), 23.

[3]Galland, "Defeat of the Luftwaffe," 23.

[4]Herbert Malloy Mason, *The Rise of the Luftwaffe* (New York, 1973), pp. 214-215.

[5]Paul C. Phillips, "Decision and Dissension—Birth of the RAF," *Aerospace Historian,* XVIII (March 1971), 33-39.

[6]Material on Trenchard, his theory and his struggle to maintain the independence of the RAF may be found in the scholarly biography of Andrew Boyle, *Trenchard* (New York, 1962), chapters 8-18. An equally scholarly work, but one more favorable to the naval view of things, is: Stephen Roskill, *Naval Policy Between the Wars*, Vol. I: *The Period of Anglo-American Antagonism* (New York, 1968), chapters VI, X, XIII, and XV. An important work, which is largely devoted to the subject, is Robin Higham's *The Military Intellectuals in Great Britain, 1918-1939* (New Brunswick, N.J., 1966), book two.

[7]Basil Collier, *The Defence of the United Kingdom* (London, 1957), p. 64; J. W. R. Taylor and P. J. R. Moyes, *Pictorial History of the R.A.F.* (London, 1968), p. 13.

[8]George Quester, *Deterrence Before Hiroshima* (New York, 1966), pp. 61-70.

[9]Basil Collier, *The Battle of Britain* (New York, 1962), pp. 19-23.

[10]Monte Duane Wright, *Most Probable Position: A History of Aerial Navigation to 1941* (Lawrence, Kansas, 1972), pp. 27, 142-143.

[11]Peter Wykeham, *Fighter Command* (London, 1960), pp. 34-37.

[12]Collier, *Defence of the United Kingdom*, pp. 37-38.

[13]Robert Wright, *The Man Who Won the Battle of Britain* (New York, 1969), p. 27.

[14]Collier, *Battle of Britain*, p. 27.

[15]Taylor and Moyes, *History of the RAF*, p. 28.

[16]Peter Townsend, *Duel of Eagles* (New York, 1971), p. 307.

[17]Alan C. Deere, *Nine Lives* (New York, 1959), p. 37.

[18]William Sholto Douglas, *Years of Command* (London, 1966), p. 90.

[19]Derek Wood and Derek Dempster, *The Narrow Margin* (New York, 1961), pp. 18-20.

[20]Asher Lee, *Goering: Air Leader (New York, 1972), pp. 65, 75.*

[21]Wykeham, *Fighter Command,* pp. 59-62.

[22]Collier, *Defence of the United Kingdom*, pp. 42-43.

[23]Wykeham, *Fighter Command*, p. 61.

[24]Figures in table are based upon Francis K. Mason, *Battle Over Britain* (New York, 1969), pp. 560, 562, and 573, and Wood and Dempster, *Narrow Margin*, pp. 420, 426, and 446.

[25]Graph is based upon Wood and Dempster, *Narrow Margin*, p. 462; Cajus Bekker, *The Luftwaffe War Diaries* (New York, 1966), p. 556; and Richard Collier, *Eagle Day* (New York, 1964, p. 255.

[26]A. J. P. Taylor, *Beaverbrook* (New York, 1973), pp. 428-431.

[27]Lee, *Goering*, p. 52.

[28]Edward Jablonski, *Air War*, Vol. I; *Terror From the Sky* (Garden City, N.Y., 1971), pp. 89-92.

[29]Collier, *Battle of Britain*, pp. 28-29; Lee, *Goering*, p. 52; Richard Suchenwirth, *Historical Turning in the German Air Force War Effort* (Maxwell AFB, Alabama: Air University, USAF Historical Study No. 189, 1959), pp. 1-19; Sir Thomas Elmhirst, "The German Air Force and Its Failure," *Journal of the Royal United Service Institute,* XVI (1946), 503-504.

[30]Sir Keith R. Park, letter to the author, Auckland, New Zealand, August 19, 1973.

[31]Figures based upon Wood and Dempster, *Narrow Margin*, p. 470.

[32]Figures based upon Denis Richards, *Royal Air Force, 1939-1945*, Vol 1: *The Fight at Odds* (London, 1953), p. 171.

[33]Basil H. Liddell Hart, *History of the Second World War* (New York, 1970), p. 93.

[34]Baumbach, *The Life and Death of the Luftwaffe*, p. 60.

[35]Suchenwirth, *Turning Points*, pp. 28-31.

[36]John F. Guilmartin, "Aspects of Airpower in the Spanish Civil War," *Air Power Historian*, IX (April 1962), 83-85.

[37]Telford Taylor, *The Breaking Wave* (New York, 1967), pp. 33-39.

[38]Collier, *Defence of the United Kingdom*, pp. 175-183.

[39]J. F. C. Fuller, *A Military History of Western World*, Vol. III: *From the Seven Days Battle, 1862, to the Battle of Leyte Gulf, 1944* (New York, 1956), p. 410, is one of those who have called it a great bluff—and evidence in support of the idea is easy to find since many of the German generals have testified that they never took the whole thing seriously. Since much of this testimony was given at the Nuremburg trials, it is open to question. See also, H. A. DeWeerd, "Hitler's Plans for Invading Britain," *Military Affairs*, XII (Fall 1948), 142-148.

[40]Peter Fleming, *Operation Sea Lion* (New York, 1957), p. 240. Fleming is among the majority of scholars who feel that it was not a bluff when he says: "Hitler was slow to admit that invasion was a strategical necessity and almost equally slow to realize that it was a tactical impossibility. . . . But no respectable evidence, indeed no evidence at all, supports the view that Hitler never really meant to carry out the invasion for which elaborate and costly preparations were made." Air Chief Marshal Sir Keith R. Park gave his opinion on the matter: "I agree that Hitler firmly intended to invade England when he had obtained air superiority by destroying Royal Air Force Fighter Command in 1940." But then, Park, like most of the other RAF people, who are almost unanimously of that opinion, would not like to admit Fuller's proposition for to do so would be to dim their splendid achievement in fighting off the *Luftwaffe*. (The quote from Park is in a letter to the author dated August 19, 1973, Auckland, New Zealand.)

[41]One of the best discussions of the evolution of the invasion strategy, and the consideration of the other strategic alternatives as well, is contained in Taylor, *The Breaking Wave*, pp. 34-43. Anthony Cave Brown's recent revelations that the British were reading much of the high-level German message traffic really doesn't resolve this argument. While ULTRA was informing Churchill that invasion preparations were underway and that if a victory were won by the Germans in the air on September 15 the invasion would be launched, there is still not conclusive proof one way or another. Hitler was a master at the bluff, and it is not at all inconceivable that he never really intended to

sail no matter what he said and did, even within his innermost circles. For additional details on ULTRA, see Anthony Cave Brown, *Bodyguard of Lies* (New York, 1975), Chapters 1 and 2.

[42]Collier, *Defence of the United Kingdom*, p. 181.

[43]Albert Kesselring, *Kesselring: A Soldier's Record* (New York, 1954), p. 72. Testimony from sources like this might sometimes be suspect because of the natural desire of the old soldiers to put the blame for the German failure on the shoulders of the politicians–usually Hitler, but in this case it would be Goering.

[44]Karl Bartz, *Swastika in the Air: The Struggle and Defeat of the German Air Force, 1939-1945* (London, 1956), p. 58.

[45]Kesselring, *Soldier's Record*, p. 73.

[46]Lee, *Goering*, p. 92.

[47]Richard Collier, *Eagle Day* (New York, 1966), p. 15; Cajus Bekker, *The Luftwaffe War Diaries*, trans. Frank Ziegler (New York, 1964), p. 240.

[48]Adolf Galland, *The First and the Last*, trans. Mervyn Savill (New York, 1954), p. 32.

[49]Wood and Dempster, *Narrow Margin*, p. 330.

[50]*Ibid.*, p. 332; Taylor, *Breaking Wave*, p. 293; Kesselring, *Soldier's Record*, p. 72; Fleming, *Operation Sealion*, pp. 124-127.

[51]For a short discussion of the defects of the blockade strategy, see Erich von Manstein, *Lost Victories* (Chicago, 1958), pp. 157-158 or the longer treatment in Taylor, *Breaking Wave*, pp. 34-43.

[52]Taylor, *Breaking Wave*, p. 293.

[53]Lee, *Goering*, p. 85.

[54]*Ibid.*, p. 86.

[55]Wykeham, *Fighter Command, pp. 93-94;* Taylor and Moyes, *History of the R.A.F., p. 23.*

[56]Basil Collier, *Leader of the Few* (London, 1957), pp. 188-189.

[57]Taylor and Moyes, *History of the R.A.F.*, pp. 23-24; Collier, *Defence of the United Kingdom*, p. 111.

[58]Collier, *Defence of the United Kingdom*, pp. 92, 164; Higham, *Military Intellectuals*, p. 119.

[59]E.B. Addison, "The Radio War," *Journal of the Royal United Services Institute*, XVII (February 1947), 31-34.

[60]Fleming, *Operation Sea Lion*, p. 218.

[61]Bekker, *Luftwaffe War Diaries*, p. 181.

[62]Collier, *Defence of the United Kingdom*, p. 186.

[63]*Ibid.*, p. 188. The debriefings of aircrew members have been notoriously inaccurate down through history. It seems that in the Battle of Britain exaggeration affected intelligence estimates on both sides, but more so on the German side. Not only were the German errors larger, but also they had a more serious effect because of the nature of the situation. The British, once the battle began, had very few strategic decisions to make. Their only real option was to fight on, no matter how accurate or erroneous their estimates of the remaining enemy strengths were. The Germans, however, did have some very significant decisions to make, especially in the field of target selection. Here they were vulnerable to very serious errors arising from false estimates of British air strength. This was a contributing factor to the bad decision to switch the target prematurely to the city of London. Some German leaders felt that because of the false figures the air superiority battle had been won, and that it was time to turn to the exploitation phase.

[64]Cave Brown, *Bodyguard of Lies*, pp. 17-24, 36; F. W. Winterbotham, *The Ultra Secret* (New York, 1974), pp. 10-16.

[65]Ronald Lewin, *Ultra Goes to War* (New York, 1978), p. 87.

[66]Winterbotham, *The Ultra Secret*, pp. 46, 50, 61-62.

[67]Lee, *Goering*, pp. 106-107.

[68]*Ibid.*, p. 106.

[69]Bekker, *Luftwaffe War Diaries*, pp. 198, 209.

[70]John Killen, *A History of the Luftwaffe* (Garden City, N.Y., 1967), pp. 128-129.

[71]John E. Johnson, *Full Circle* (New York, 1964), pp. 137-141.

[72]*Ibid.*, p. 160.

[73]Townsend, *Duel of Eagles*, p. 361.

[74]Wright, *Man Who Won the Battle of Britain,*, pp. 225-236.

[75]Paul Brickhil, *Reach for the Sky* (New York, 1954), pp. 207-209.

[76]*Ibid.*; Wright, *Man Who Won the Battle of Britain*, pp. 225-236; Lewin, *Ultra Goes to War*, p. 90; Winterbotham, *The Ultra Secret*, pp. 62-63.

[77]Quester, *Deterrence Before Hiroshima*, p. 106.

[78]Collier, *Defence of the United Kingdom*, pp. 233-234.

[79]Jablonski, *Terror from the Sky*, p. 122; Bekker, *Luftwaffe War Diaries*, pp. 241-253.

[80]Wood and Dempster, *Narrow Margin*, pp. 334-339; Winterbotham, *The Ultra Secret*, pp. 54-55.

[81]Winston Churchill, *Their Finest Hour*, Vol. II of *The Second World War* (6 vols.; Boston, 1948-53), p. 331.

[82]Asher Lee, *The German Air Force* (New York, 1946), p. 81.

[83]Collier, *Defence of the United Kingdom*, pp. 225-226.

[84]*Ibid.*

[85]Taylor, *The Breaking Wave*, pp. 160-161.

[86]Francis Mason, *Battle Over Britain*, pp. 386-391.

[87]Wood and Dempster, *Narrow Margin*, pp. 350-354; Bekker, *Luftwaffe War Diaries*, pp. 242-246.

[88]Churchill, *Their Finest Hour*, pp. 335-336. Basil Collier has said that some of the witnesses indicate that the above interchange between Churchill and Park could not have taken place because all of the aircraft of Number 11 Group were never airborne all at one time [*The Battle of Britain* (New York, 1962), p. 149.] The author of the present work inquired of Air Marshal Park as to the accuracy of the Prime Minister's description of the event. His reply of August 19, 1973, stated:

> In reply to your letter Basil Colliers (sic) book on Battle of Britain is incorrect. I did in fact tell Mr. Churchill that all my available squadrons had already been dispatched and were engaging the Germans.

[89]Francis K. Mason, *Battle Over Britain*, pp. 391-395, in his authoritative recent work on the subject cites the losses as 27 for the RAF versus 61 for the *Luftwaffe*. It is important to remember that many of the German aircraft were bombers which carried several crew members, but all of the British aircraft were single-seaters. The German losses were, therefore, even more serious than those figures indicate. This, incidentally, was not the most deadly day of the battle. That distinction belongs to the fifteenth of August when the RAF lost 29 and the *Luftwaffe* 71.

[90]Galland, *The First and the Last*, p. 42.

[91]The effects of these factors are all the more important when considered in the light of recent revelations that the British were reading the transmissions of the German high command throughout the battle, and that the latter did not suspect that their communications had been compromised. Cave Brown, *Bodyguard of Lies*, pp. 36-44.

[92]John Bartlett, *Familiar Quotations*, Fourteenth Edition, ed. Emily Beck (Boston, 1968), p. 959.

[93]Lee, *Goering*, p. 102.

Hitler Triumphant: The Balkan Campaign and Operation BARBAROSSA 4

Before the last [gliders] had touched ground, they were followed by the parachutists, each of them now entering into their common experience, first the lurch into the void, then the giant tug as the parachute opened, followed by the fall, twisting and turning in the wind, a glimpse of snowcapped mountains, and of the furrowed sea with its rim of surf—at last, in quick succession, the green hills and squat white houses, fields and plantations, trees, rocks and sand. All were sharing the ruthless hazard of the parachutist, the time when skill and courage are of no avail, when chance rules all, the journey with no return. The fire crackled up at them with an intensity far beyond their fears. For many this brief climax of exaltation and terror was to be their last moment of life.

Ian M. Stewart, The Struggle for Crete

The Non-Aggression Pact signed between Germany and Russia in August 1939 not only took the world by surprise, but also was the result of expedient policies on the part of the opportunistic and callous leaders of the signatory powers. Although Hitler did not recant in his belief that Germany needed living space in the east, he had not expected Great Britain to be so recalcitrant; hence, his options for alliance (with the British or the Russians) could be reversed, since to Hitler any alliance was only a temporary expedient. In that way, already determined to subjugate Poland, he could avoid a two-front war and also provide for the uninterrupted flow of strategic war materials—the concomitant Russo-German economic agreement ensured that Russia could be dealt with later, in keeping with Hitler's long-range designs. In spite of these advantages to Germany, however, it was Stalin, more than Hitler, who consistently took the initiative in trying to develop better relations between the two countries.

In the final analysis, Stalin wanted to conclude a pact with Hitler because he feared Germany, desperately felt the need for a western buffer zone, and had little confidence in his ability to secure an advantageous alliance with the Anglo-French. He suspected that if Hitler could not reach an agreement with Poland, the *Wehrmacht* would crush the Poles and then possibly overrun the Baltic states, bringing German arms dangerously close to Leningrad. Ultimately, therefore, although the Soviet leader allowed Russian talks with Great Britain and France to continue up into August, he placed his greatest hope on reaching agreement with Hitler, properly recognizing that the Anglo-French would not consent to a Russian free hand at the expense of their Baltic neighbors. Hence, ideological disagreements between Germany and Russia notwithstanding, the coldly opportunistic Stalin acquired over half of Poland simply through a pact with Hitler and the dispatch of an occupying force. He also gained agreement from Hitler that the Soviet sphere of influence would encompass the Baltic states—including Finland—as well as Bessarabia, a part of Rumania.

Even before Hitler's legions had completed snuffing out the heroic Polish resistance, Stalin began to pressure states in the new Soviet sphere of influence. Latvia, Estonia, and Lithuania were brutally compelled to grant the Russians military bases by early October 1939. Then it was Finland's turn, although Stalin proceeded a little more cautiously, fully expecting the patriotic Finns to be more difficult to bend to his will. The Soviet demands were: a mutual assistance pact; a new border on the Karelian Isthmus, only 20 miles from the city of Viipuri; a lease on the Hango Peninsula, at the entrance to the Gulf of Finland; and cession of the western part of the Rybachi Peninsula, on the Barents Sea. *(See Map 16a, in Atlas.)* The Finns saw little alternative to outright resistance.[1]

An independent Finland had emerged from a civil war fought between Communist and anti-Communist forces in 1918. During the following year, the Finns had fought Communist Russia over conflicting claims in Karelia, and during the 1930s they had successfully resisted native fascist movements. Proud of their democratic government, the Finns were very suspicious of Soviet intentions.[2] On November 26, 1939, they rejected Stalin's demands. Four days later, Russia attacked suddenly without a declaration of war. Girding themselves against the overwhelming odds, the Finns defended their freedom and independence gallantly against their gigantic, totalitarian neighbor.

The Winter War

Russia's vast preponderance of strength led it to underestimate the difficulties of a winter campaign in Finland. The military planners expected to overwhelm the Finns by forcing them to defend every vital area: their only Arctic port of Petsamo, the communications over the narrow waist of Finland from Kemi on the Gulf of Bothnia to the Soviet border, and the city of Viipuri (Vyborg) on the Gulf of Finland.[3] At first, this wide-ranging mission was assigned to the Leningrad Military District alone.[4] Additionally, the Soviets tried to appeal to Communist sentiment in Finland by creating a "People's Government" which would be installed in Helsinki when that city was "liberated." This appeal was wasted on the Finns, who saw the Russians as oppressors and had confidence in their ability to resist.

To oppose the Soviet attack, the Finns had only 300,000 men under arms with an additional 100,000 trained reservists and about the same number of women auxiliaries, called *Lotta Svärd* after the heroine of a patriotic epic.[5] The indispensable "Lottas" performed medical, quartermaster, air defense, and administrative and signal duties, freeing men for combat. The Finns employed the "Suomi" submachinegun, which was excellent for forest engagements, but they lacked almost every other modern weapon and equipment. They had only a few obsolete tanks, a miniscule air force, little field artillery, and very limited stocks of ammunition. The well-known Mannerheim Line, blocking the approaches to Viipuri, consisted only of concrete machinegun emplacements in mutual support.[6] Yet, despite the hopeless odds, the Finns closed ranks to defend their country. On the day of the Soviet attack, Baron Carl Gustav Mannerheim, a former Czarist officer who had led Finland's earlier war for independence against Russia, became Commander-in-Chief again. On December 1, a national coalition government was formed with Vaino Tanner, the Social Democratic leader, as Prime Minister. Domestic politics faded into insignificance in the face of the Soviet threat.

Although the Finns could not hope to win a protracted war, they had some immediate advantages. Rather than await the summer campaigning season, the Russians had chosen to fight a winter war. This winter proved exceptionally severe with temperatures down to –30° Centigrade and heavy snowfalls which hampered cross-country movements.[7] Such weather reduced the Soviet advantage in modern equipment and favored the Finns, who were trained for winter fighting and accustomed to deploy on skis. Finland is also admirably suited by nature for defense. Seventy percent of the country is thickly forested, and 55,000 lakes of various sizes create a watery maze. The Russians needed exceptionally good leadership to cope with these extremes of weather and terrain, but here lay their weakness. During the purges of 1937 and 1938, Stalin had removed over half the brigade commanders and even higher percentages of the more senior officers.[8] Not surprisingly, Soviet military leadership would be badly deficient during the first months of the war.

The Russians began the war with air attacks on Helsinki and Viipuri, amphibious assaults on the southern coast, and ground operations in Karelia. *(See Map 16a, in Atlas.)* Since they lacked strategic bombers, the Soviets accomplished little more from the air than occasional disruptions of communications. Their amphibious assaults along the Gulf of Finland failed entirely. Along the Mannerheim Line in Karelia, the Russians tried repeated mass attacks without regard for losses, yet they failed to breach the defenses. Poor coordination of infantry, artillery, and armor contributed heavily to the failure.[9] Artillery fires did not properly support the attacks, and often either infantry or armor attacked separately, rather than giving mutual support. Although they could employ only approximately 100 Bofors 37-mm antitank guns, the Finns destroyed many Russian T-26 light tanks when these attacked without supporting infantry.[10]

North of Lake Ladoga, the Red Army at first enjoyed greater success, because the Finns lacked the force to halt the massive attacks on the Mannerheim Line and still defend north of the lake. But after breaking through, the Russian units lacked the staying power and mobility to exploit success. By February, the Soviets had lost an entire division near Pitkaranta and two more near Tolvajarvi. *(See Map 16a, in Atlas.)* In these northern regions, the Russians could operate only on cleared roads or across frozen lakes. They quickly stalled or became disoriented if they attempted to move through the trackless forests. The Russian soldier endured much, but he was demoralized by *Bielaja Smert*, the "White Death" brought by Finnish ski troopers in white uniforms.[11] Confronted by a powerfully armed but sluggish and badly led opponent, the Finns developed a tactic they called *motti* (wood stacked up for chopping). They moved around the extended flanks of the Russians strung out along the roads, harassing, raiding supply

Finnish Ski Troopers, 1940

columns, and making limited attacks. Then they attacked in force at several locations, dividing the Russians into smaller groups. Finally, they encircled and annihilated these groups immobilized in the snow.

The Finns won their greatest victory of the war by employing the *motti* tactic in the battle fought around Suomussalmi in December and January.[12] *(See Map 16b, in Atlas.)* Elements of the Finnish 9th Division made contact with the Russian 163rd Division near Suomussalmi on December 11, 1939, and quickly blocked the road east of the town. Unable to maneuver or bring up supplies, the Soviet division set up an all-around defense and awaited relief. On December 22, the Russian 44th Motorized Division approached Suomussalmi from the east, but Finnish ski troops pinned it down on the road. Now both the Soviet divisions tried repeatedly to break out, but the Finns blocked their retreat. By the end of December, nothing remained of the 163rd Division. During the first week of January, the Finns systematically sliced up and annihilated the 44th Division. Approximately 27,500 Russian soldiers suffered the "White Death," and they lost over 50 tanks and all the artillery and motor transport for the two divisions, while only 900 Finns were killed.[13] The western democracies greeted this victory with enthusiasm, but it gave a misleading impression of Finland's chances in the war. The Finnish leaders were under no illusions. They knew that the Russians would certainly win, if they were willing to pay the price.

As the Suomussalmi battle was ending, the Russians prepared for a new offensive towards Viipuri. On January 7, 1940, a Northwestern Front was organized with General Semion Konstantinovich Timoshenko in command. (The Soviet "front" corresponded roughly to the army group headquarters used by the western Allies.) A cavalryman during the First World War and a regimental commander during the Russian Civil War, Timoshenko was a reserved and painstaking officer, in fact a martinet. He trained his troops on replicas of Finnish fortifications, emphasizing the coordination of all arms.[14] Using the roads and railways leading north from Leningrad, Timoshenko assembled 12 divisions opposite Viipuri. In typical Russian style, he massed troops and artillery on narrow sectors intended for breakthroughs. Continual Soviet air strikes and heavy artillery fire prevented the Finns from reinforcing or resupplying during daylight.[15]

On February 1, 1940, the Russian Karelian offensive began with a heavy artillery preparation adjusted from balloons. *(See Map 16c, in Atlas.)* After almost two weeks of continuous attacks spreading all along the line, the Russians finally broke through the Finnish defensive line. By March, they were attacking Viipuri both overland and across the frozen Gulf of Finland where the ice was thick enough to support tanks.[16] Having lost almost 25,000 men killed to date, the Finns were nearly exhausted.[17] On March 7, Mannerheim advised the Government to ask for peace terms.

In the resulting Treaty of Moscow signed on March 12, 1940, the Finns ceded their portion of the Ribachi Peninsula west of Murmansk, a large triangle of territory east of Salla opposite the Murmansk railway and a wide strip of land around Lake Ladoga including the city of Viipuri. The Finns also agreed to lease the Russians a naval base at Hangö on the entrance to the Gulf of Finland. Stalin obviously intended these cessions to secure his entire northwestern frontier from Murmansk to Leningrad. Over 400,000 Finns, roughly 10 percent of the country's entire population, made their homes in the 16,100 square miles annexed by Russia. Many of these people had fled during the war, but approximately 200,000 had to be evacuated within only 12 days.[18] On the other hand, the Finns still retained the Petsamo area, and they were relieved that Stalin did not insist on a military alliance, as in the Baltic countries. Russian losses in the winter war are unknown, but they may have totaled almost 200,000 dead.[19]

The Finns' brave defense of their liberties against great odds aroused sympathy in the west. On December 14, 1939, the League of Nations found the Soviet Union guilty of aggression and expelled the Soviet delegation. England and France wished to send aid, but Sweden and Norway would not compromise their neutrality status by granting transit rights. Nor did the Finns make a formal appeal for aid, because they feared the outcome of an enlarged war.[20] France eventually sent some pre-World War I artillery, but the principal aid came from Sweden in the form of rifles, automatic weapons, and antitank guns.[21] In retrospect, the western democracies lacked the power to save Finland; moreover, any attempt to intervene might have impelled the Soviet Union into Hitler's war with the Anglo-French. When the Finns fought again in 1941, they received substantial aid, but on this occasion it came from Germany.

The indirect effects of the winter war between Russia and Finland are difficult to assess. Because of its slow start and heavy casualties, foreign observers tended to underrate the Red Army's true power. Yet Hitler thought the Russians' poor showing was attributable to climate and supply difficulties.[22] He underrated the Red Army largely on racial grounds, believing that the Slavic races lacked soldierly virtues. Thus his ultimate decision to invade Russia was not influenced by the winter war. From a strategic point of view, the Russians made a great mistake in provoking war with the Finns. A neutral Finland would have been very welcome in the years that lay ahead. As events proved, the new border in Karelia added little to the defense of Leningrad, while renewed war with Finland diverted troops from the main effort against Germany. On the other hand, the winter war may have prompted the Russians to overhaul their army, especially equipment for winter fighting, and to coordinate their combat arms better.[23] Certainly they had expected an easy victory and were shocked to discover their weakness. Possibly the humiliations of the winter war encouraged Stalin to propitiate and appease Hitler. In the end, appeasement would serve no purpose, for the German dictator, although in March he was involved in preparing to smash France, would not abandon his long-avowed goal of attacking Russia in due time.

Operations Deferred: *SEALION and FELIX*

In the summer of 1940, a triumphant Hitler stood at the height of his power. No conqueror since Napoleon had enjoyed similar hegemony in Europe. German troops occupied western Poland, Norway, Holland, Belgium, and northern France, while in southern France the Vichy government was friendly to Germany. Generalissimo Francisco Franco's conservative government owed its existence to the Fascist powers, and Benito Mussolini was a German ally. Moreover, Hungary, Rumania, and Bulgaria would prove increasingly susceptible to German influence. Awed by German power, the Soviet Union offered no threat for the foreseeable future. Hitler's only immediate concern was the state of hostility with Great Britain. If the war dragged on too long, an Anglo-American alliance might ensue, but isolationist sentiment was strong in America.[24]

His triumphs gave Hitler great freedom of action. The initiative lay with him and he could choose from a variety of strategies, all offering good prospects for final victory. But he had to choose. Fortunately for mankind, the German dictator could not make rational strategic decisions.[25] His untrained, disorderly, and highly subjective mind simply could not formulate a clear strategic conception. At first, he imagined that the collapse of France would impel the British to ask for peace, making a strategic choice unnecessary. In a *Reichstag* speech on July 19, 1940, Hitler made a peace offer to Great Britain, yet he had already asked his general staff to prepare invasion plans.[26]

The proposed invasion of Britain, called SEALION, required the close cooperation of all three services. Army planners thought the British would offer bitter resistance and insisted that the Navy guarantee the rapid passage of very large forces. On August 27, 1940, Hitler terminated the interservice discussion by deciding that 25 divisions would be sufficient.[27] Thirteen of these divisions would land in the first assault. Grand Admiral Erich Raeder, Commander-in-Chief of the German Navy, thought the Navy could transport this force, but only if the *Luftwaffe* could assure air cover. And that was far from a sure thing, because just then Goering's airmen had their hands full trying to dominate the Royal Air Force in the Battle of Britain. During an attack on London on September 15, 1940, the *Luftwaffe* lost 56 aircraft.[28] Two days later Hitler postponed SEALION indefinitely, although still continuing the preparations. Soon these preparations served only to fix British troops in anticipation of landings, and finally they helped to conceal the buildup for the invasion of Russia.[29] Although it offered the optimum solution to his immediate problem, Hitler was always halfhearted about SEALION and ignored the project after December 1940. In the last analysis, Hitler had scant interest in conquering Great Britain, because he was obsessed by dreams of a great empire in the east.

A logical and obvious alternative to an invasion of Great Britain was an attack on the British position in the Mediterranean. Raeder outlined such a strategy in a discussion with Hitler on September 26, 1940.[30] The inaction since the fall of France in June made the admiral anxious, because he anticipated American entry into the war. When and if the Americans became belligerents, Raeder expected that the British, in cooperation with the Americans and the Free French, would attack Italy from bases in North Africa. To prevent this eventuality, Germany should secure Gibraltar and Suez, thus dominating the Mediterranean area. Raeder was offering Hitler an unclouded glimpse of the future, but the admiral's arguments for a Mediterranean strategy had a fundamental flaw. The German Navy was too weak to confront the Royal Navy or to exploit victories in the Mediterranean area. Unless submarines alone could win a protracted battle of attrition in the Atlantic, the German fleet would remain hopelessly inferior. Hitler indicated general agreement with Raeder's arguments; but, mentioning difficulties with Vichy France and Spain, he reserved his decision.

At first sight, no operation seemed more obvious, easier, and more profitable for the Germans than the seizure of Gibraltar. For one thing, Franco was indebted to the Axis powers for their aid during the Spanish Civil War. From Spanish bases, German airpower could frustrate any British attempt to resupply the Gibraltar garrison from the sea. Once in possession of Gibraltar, the *Luftwaffe* could interdict the western entrance to the Mediterranean. The Operations Section of the *Oberkommando der Wehrmacht* (German High Command, abbreviated OKW) produced a plan to assault Gibraltar, later code-named FELIX, in August 1940.[31] After Hitler gave approval, Colonel-General Franz Halder, the Army Chief of Staff, submitted a list of troop requirements on October 17.[32] Halder thought surprise was impossible due to inadequacies of the Spanish rail and road nets. He anticipated a set-piece attack, estimating that two regiments would suffice. He proposed using the elite and heavily reinforced infantry regiment *Grossdeutschland* plus one mountain regiment. One or two motorized divisions would cover the coast against British landings. Twenty-six German artillery batteries, some firing directly on the embrasures, would neutralize the British guns on Gibraltar.

On October 23, Hitler conferred with Franco in a small French town just south of Biarritz.[33] He asked that Spain enter the war and cooperate in an attack on Gibraltar, offering Franco Gibraltar and additional territory in North Africa. Franco demurred, citing the damage caused by the Civil War, Spain's dependence on imported foodstuffs, and the poor equipment of his army. He also made extensive territorial demands, which Hitler could not satisfy without alienating Vichy France. Although the conference ended without agreement, German interest in FELIX continued. *Fuehrer* Directive Number 18, published on November 12, outlined the preparations.[34] Four days later, the German staff set the air requirement at 800 aircraft, which would operate primarily from Seville.[35] Since Gibraltar's small air strip would not accept modern fighters, the Germans expected uncontested air superiority. Hitler was only waiting for Franco's approval, but the Spanish dictator refused every blandishment. In a last attempt to convince him, Admiral Wilhelm Canaris, Chief of Military Intelligence, who had conducted the first reconnaissance, returned to Madrid. Referring again to the terrible destruction caused in the Civil War, Franco alleged Spain was too weak to wage war and refused to set a date for Spanish belligerency. After Canaris reported the failure of his mission, FELIX was postponed indefinitely on December 10.[36] Canaris, who was executed in 1944 for his part in the abortive German resistance movement against Hitler, may have done something to sabotage the plan, but the basic difficulty was Franco's reluctance to join a war against Great Britain before she was clearly defeated.

The Hollow Legions: Mussolini's Attack on Greece

In the meantime, the Italians had been more aggressive than their German ally. During the summer, they advanced into the Sudan and British Somaliland from Ethiopia. On September 13, 1940, the Italian Army in Libya invaded Egypt, an operation which would end disastrously for the junior member of the Axis.* Mussolini wanted to invade Yugoslavia as well, but Hitler opposed this scheme.[37] Instead, the Italian dictator turned his attention towards Greece. When the German Foreign Minister, Joachim von Ribbentrop, visited Rome on September 19 and 20, Mussolini argued strongly that Greece was an accomplice of Great Britain, implying the necessity for military action.[38] On October 4, Hitler and Mussolini met at the Brenner Pass, their first meeting since June.[39] Hitler indulged himself in a long, rambling monologue about the difficulty of invading England. The Italians later claimed that Hitler approved an invasion of Greece, but perhaps they only interpreted his silence on this topic as tacit approval. Mussolini may have mentioned Greece obliquely, anxious to avoid another German veto of his plans.

While Hitler was traveling in his special train to meetings with Franco and Marshal Henri Philippe Pétain, the Italians prepared to invade Greece. Mussolini dispatched a backdated letter to Berlin on October 22, which finally reached Hitler in

*See Chapter 7.

France three days later.[40] The German dictator could have contacted Mussolini immediately, if he was strongly opposed to the invasion, but instead he simply rerouted his train to Italy. When he met Mussolini in Bologna on the morning of October 28, the invasion was already in progress. If Hitler was irritated by Mussolini's duplicity, he had only himself to blame. Failure to coordinate with Italy would cost the Germans a superfluous campaign and perhaps delay the invasion of Russia.

General John Metaxas, the virtual dictator of Greece, was not so pro-British as Mussolini claimed. Metaxas was chiefly interested in avoiding war, and but for Mussolini's ambitions he would have succeeded.[41] The Greek Army had no tanks, no modern aircraft, and few antitank or antiaircraft guns.[42] Hoping to avoid provocation, the Greeks had only three-and-a-half divisions on active duty to counter an Italian invasion from Albania. But the Greeks were skilled in mountain warfare, and they occupied excellent defensive positions on the mountainous border. Their morale was high, and they hoped to delay the Italians until the remainder of the Greek Army mobilized for a counteroffensive.

The Italian Commander-in-Chief, Marshal Pietro Badoglio, and most of the Italian generals feared the risks of a Grecian campaign and had tried unsuccessfully to dissuade Mussolini from invading. Italy obviously lacked the resources to invade Egypt and Greece simultaneously. The Italian Army accomplished such planning as was done, failing to consult the Navy even though it would have to provide logistical support across the Adriatic Sea.[43] As a result, the vital Albanian harbor of Durazzo became hopelessly clogged with shipping during early November. *(See Map 17, in Atlas, for orientation; Italo-Greek operations in 1940 are not shown, however.)* The Italian commander in Albania, General Visconti Prasca, divided his 11 divisions into 4 columns which he sent through the rugged Pindus Mountains. Within a week, the column attacking along the Adriatic coast reached the Kalamas (Thiamis) River. If the Italians could have exploited this success, they might have deployed on the plains of Epirus; but they were badly disorganized and hampered by autumn rains which turned the narrow roads to mud. The Greek Commander-in-Chief, General Alexander Papagos, quickly brought up several fresh divisions and began a general counteroffensive during the second week of November. Soon the Italian forces fell into a disorganized retreat all along the front. As winter began, the Greeks advanced into Albania and the Italians felt lucky to stabilize the front. After reinforcing his army to a total of 25 divisions, Prasca attempted a new offensive in early March, 1941. This offensive quickly degenerated into senselessly repeated frontal assaults, and the Italians made no progress until Germany entered the war. From a German point of view, the Italians had caused what they were supposed to prevent: British engagement in Greece. On October 31, 1940, the British had landed troops on the strategic island of Crete, and beginning on November 4, they had sent a small Royal Air Force contingent to support the Greek counteroffensive.

Germans to the Rescue: Operation MARITA

By November 1940, Hitler was wondering whether he should come to Mussolini's rescue in North Africa or in Greece. On the fourth, he ordered the *Oberkommando des Heeres* (Army High Command, abbreviated OKH) to prepare plans for the invasion of northern Greece.[44] Apparently Hitler had three motives. His immediate concern was to help Mussolini and restore the prestige of the Axis. He also wanted to deny the British air bases for an attack on the Rumanian oil fields, which were vital to German industry. Finally, he may have wished to clear his right flank for the invasion of Russia, an operation which had been under study since July. Of course, had Mussolini never attacked, a neutral Greece which refused to admit British forces would have served German purposes well. By attracting British attention, Mussolini had drawn the Germans into an unwanted campaign. It was a classic instance of the tail wagging the dog. *(See Map 17, in Atlas.)*

To reach Greece by land, the Germans needed transit rights either through Yugoslavia or through Hungary, Rumania, and Bulgaria. They acquired the latter route without much difficulty. On August 30, 1940, Italy and Germany had mediated Hungary's claim on Rumania, resulting in Hungary's acquisition of northern Transylvania and earning that country's gratitude. Also, during the 1930s, Hungarian politics had become increasingly nationalistic and anti-Semitic as the Magyar majority turned towards Fascist ideals, manifested by the Arrow-Cross organization. For these reasons, Hungary joined the Tripartite Pact on November 20, thus declaring solidarity with Germany, Italy, and Japan. By the terms of the Russo-German Non-Aggression Pact, the Soviets were promised Bessarabia, the province between the Prut and Dniester Rivers which Rumania had acquired after the First World War. After issuing an ultimatum, Russia occupied Bessarabia in June 1940. The loss of so much territory threw Rumania into a political crisis. The Iron Guard, a violent, Neo-Fascist organization, terrorized the country's politicians. Following the King's abdication, General Ion Antonescu came to power and welcomed German troops into his country. On November 23, Rumania allied with the Axis by signing the Tripartite Pact. The Bulgarian Government inclined towards the Germans, but delayed joining the Pact until March 1, 1941, for fear of exciting opposition within the country. Gaining the cooperation of Yugoslavia, however, was another matter.[45]

The Germans could conduct their invasion of Greece without troubling Yugoslavia, but Hitler hoped to gain this more direct route. On November 28, 1940, he offered to give the Yugoslavians Salonika on the Aegean Sea and to secure Italian withdrawal from the Dalmatian coast, if Yugoslavia would sign a nonaggression pact with the Axis. The Yugoslavs declined.[46] Even after the invasion of Greece (code-named MARITA by the Germans) had been planned without reference to Yugoslav territory, Hitler still wished the Yugoslavs to join the Tripartite Pact for reasons of prestige. On condition that the Germans demand no military cooperation, the Yugoslavian Government finally signed the pact on March 25, 1941. The pro-German Croats were pleased, but the Serbians in Belgrade were so incensed they overthrew the Government. Although the Serbs did not denounce their treaty obligations, Hitler fell into a foolish rage and ordered preparation of concentric attacks on Yugoslavia from the neighboring countries.[47] The ensuing redeployment forced the Germans to postpone MARITA for a few days.

The British felt a strong political and moral obligation to help Greece. They wished to honor a pledge given in April 1939 to defend Greek independence, and they feared the effect on British prestige if Greece should succumb to the Axis powers alone and unaided. On November 4, 1940, following the Italian invasion, Prime Minister Winston Churchill directed General Sir Archibald Wavell, the Army Commander-in-Chief, Middle East, to send five Royal Air Force squadrons, which were immediately dispersed on the Albanian front to allay German apprehensions over the Rumanian oil fields. At that time, the British were anxious about the Italian invasion of Egypt and had no troops to spare for Greece. But on December 9, the Commonwealth forces in Egypt initiated COMPASS, an offensive which drove the Italians from Egypt in three days. Wavell continued the advance through Cyrenaica, reaching El Agheila by early February. Now the British could assemble an expeditionary force to send to Greece, not against the Italians, who were already defeated, but to counter a German initiative. Naturally assuming that the Axis powers coordinated their strategy, the British had expected German intervention in the Balkans ever since the Italian invasion of Greece.[48]

In January 1941, Churchill directed Wavell to consider what force might be assembled for Greece. Intent on his own offensive in Cyrenaica and anxious not to disperse his force, Wavell suggested that the Germans might feign an attack in the Balkans while they struck elsewhere. But Churchill immediately sent a stiff rejoinder, taking full responsibility for the decision and demanding prompt compliance.[49] When Wavell flew to Athens and conferred with Metaxas on January 14 and 15, 1941, he had only a few regiments to offer. Metaxas estimated Greece would need the help of 10 divisions to stop Germany and declined to accept a small force which would provoke the Germans without helping the Greeks.[50] But Metaxas died on January 29, leaving command of the Greek armed forces to the more optimistic Papagos, who had directed the counteroffensive against Italy. Late in February, the British Foreign Secretary, Sir Anthony Eden, and the Chief of the Imperial General Staff, General Sir John Dill, arrived in Cairo to determine British policy in the Balkans. Eden's instructions spoke of prompt aid to Greece, but Churchill carefully instructed him not to approve an enterprise likely to fail, as had the British expedition to Norway in the spring of 1940.[51]

Eden, Dill, and Wavell flew to Athens and conferred with Papagos on February 22 and 23. Now the Greek Government formally accepted the British offer of a strong corps intended to thwart the Germans. Unfortunately, political considerations clouded the military discussions. The British thought both sides were agreed on defending the general line of the Aliakmon River, rather than the fortified Metaxas Line covering Salonika *(See Map 17, in Atlas.)* But Papagos believed that Greek deployment on the Aliakmon line depended upon the attitude of the Yugoslavs, who could be resupplied only through Salonika.[52] Of course, the British also hoped to gain Yugoslavian cooperation, but informal contacts brought very discouraging results. In Ankara, Eden found the Turks similarly reluctant to risk conflict with Germany and almost as fearful of the Soviet Union's intentions. By the end of February, it had become clear that Greece and Britain could not forge a Balkan coalition against Hitler. To make matters even worse, the British delegation discovered upon its return to Athens on March 2 that the Greeks were still on the Metaxas Line. By this time, the Germans were already in Bulgaria and across the Danube, making redeployment too dangerous.[53] Only three Greek divisions would be available on the Aliakmon line under General Sir Henry Maitland Wilson's command. Churchill became increasingly alarmed and anxious that the expedition not prove a fiasco. On March 6, he telegraphed Eden in Cairo that he could no longer see any reason for expecting success, but would attach importance to the opinions of Wavell and Dill.[54] Eden reassured Churchill that the military commanders-in-chief were unanimous in their approval, whereupon the British Cabinet decided to send the expeditionary force to Greece.

After the Belgrade *coup d'état* on March 27, Yugoslavia's defense became vital to the Greeks and British. If the Yugoslavs could hold their southern frontier and deny the Germans use of the mountain passes over Prilep-Bitola (Monastir) and along the Vardar River, then the Greeks and British had a better chance of holding their own lines against the Germans. But if the Germans came through Yugoslavia, they would immediately outflank the Greek and British positions. Unfortunately, the Yugoslavian state was so rent with dissension between Croats and Serbs that the new Government could not appear to sacrifice the northern part of the country.[55] Instead of coordinating with the Greeks or adopting a flexible defense, the Yugoslavs tried to cordon their frontiers, without depth or strong reserves. Such deployment was wholly inappropriate to defend against German *blitzkrieg* tactics.

Hitler and the OKH wildly overestimated the resistance they would encounter from the million-man Yugoslavian Army. *(See Map 17, in Atlas.)* In a remarkable display of flexibility and good staff work, the Germans quickly turned the bulk of the Twelfth Army, already deploying for MARITA, west against the Yugoslavs. In addition, the German Second Army deployed to advance south from Austria and Hungary. On April 6, 1941, the Germans bombed Belgrade, killing 17,000 civilians and disrupting communications between the Yugoslavian general headquarters and the field armies.[56] The German Second Army, with a mountain corps, two infantry corps, and a *panzer* corps, quickly overran northern Yugoslavia. The Croats welcomed the Germans as liberators from Serbian oppression and declared Zagreb the capital of an independent Croatia. The XLI Panzer Corps with the 2nd SS Motorized Division and the elite overstrength regiment *Grossdeutschland* attacked from Rumania directly south on Belgrade, arriving at the city on April 12. Most alarming of all, the XL Panzer Corps with the 9th Panzer Division and the SS Division *Adolf Hitler* assigned to the Twelfth Army, attacked west towards Skopje and then south towards the Yugoslavian-Greek border. By April 9, the SS Division *Adolf Hitler* reached Prilep-Bitola (Monastir), threatening the British expeditionary force on the left flank. At the same time, the XVIII Mountain Corps advanced to the Vardar River valley, outflanking the Greek forces on the Metaxas Line. Thus both the Greek and British positions became untenable before the fighting even began in Greece.

Panzergrenadiers During the Advance Through Serbia, April 1941

The Yugoslavian Government capitulated unconditionally on April 17. Its military forces had collapsed from within after offering little resistance to the invader. Of the 12 German divisions committed against Yugoslavia, only 4 saw action while the others were practically on maneuvers.[57] In this parody of *blitzkrieg*, the Germans suffered only 558 casualties, including only 151 listed as killed in action.[58] The Second Army was little the worse for wear and the Germans had gained the invaluable mountain passes from Yugoslavia into Greece. The British had fervently hoped for Yugoslavian participation, yet it actually seemed to benefit the Germans. In their haste to move on, the Germans left the Yugoslavs more stunned than defeated. Many Yugoslavian soldiers had never seen their enemy, and some were even left with their weapons. At first the Germans garrisoned Serbia with three regular divisions; later they used poor quality security divisions.[59] Soon partisans grew strong in the mountains and forests. Distracted by other concerns, the Germans were unable to destroy these irregular forces, then or in later years.[60]

As with Yugoslavia, the Germans attacked Greece suddenly and without any warning on April 6. They faced a Greek Army without modern arms or equipment already strained by the war against Italy. They also faced the British Commonwealth forces deployed between March 7 and 31. These forces consisted of the British 1st Armoured Brigade of the 2nd Armoured Division, the Australian 1st Corps Headquarters, the Australian 6th Division, and the New Zealand Division; with supporting troops, the force totaled over 31,000 men.[61] The Australian 7th Division was expected to follow, but it remained in Egypt when General Erwin Rommel began a thrust from Cyrenaica on March 30.[62] The Commonwealth forces were deployed along the Aliakmon line extending from the Gulf of Salonika to the area of Edhessa in the Vermion Mountains. *(See Map 17, in Atlas.)* The rugged terrain offered good defensive positions, but the Commonwealth forces had little or no time to prepare their defense and insufficient force to organize deep defensive zones. For lack of better alternatives, the Commonwealth commanders simply placed their units on high ground and prepared for all-around defense.[63] With 12 divisions deployed against Italy and 4 divisions on the Metaxas Line, the Greeks had only 3 remaining divisions to take positions on the Aliakmon line. Germany's Twelfth Army, deploying the XL Panzer Corps, the XVIII Mountain Corps, and the XXX Infantry Corps, constituted an overwhelming force, although an additional corps had been diverted to the Second Army, and still another corps was detraining in Rumania.

The German air attack on Piraeus during the night of April 6 exploded a munitions ship, causing extensive damage to the

German Troops at a Dynamited Section of Road Near Klisoura in Northern Greece, 1941

vital harbor facilities.[64] General Wilson, commanding the Commonwealth forces, learned on April 8 that the Germans were headed for the Prilep-Bitola (Monastir) pass, so he ordered the 1st Armoured Brigade to move back from Edhessa and build a front facing north.[65] On the following day, Wilson decided to retreat back to the next defensible line extending from Mount Olympus back over the mountain range paralleling the Aliakmon River on the east. In the knowledge that the Greeks had been outflanked and the Yugoslavs were crumbling, Wilson had no other choice. At approximately the same time, the Greeks terminated their offensive against the Italians in order to move troops towards the Yugoslavian frontier. None of these movements could seriously delay the very rapid German advance. While the XVIII Mountain Corps breached the Metaxas Line in three days of hard fighting, the 2nd Panzer Division outflanked the Greeks by moving through the southeast corner of Yugoslavia, then drove south and captured Salonika against no resistance on April 9. Its position wholly untenable, the Greek Second Army in Thrace surrendered the same day. The Greeks now paid the full price for their earlier failure to coordinate properly with the Commonwealth forces.

Field Marshal Wilhelm List, commanding the German Twelfth Army, now organized his attack into two major thrusts. *(See Map 17, in Atlas.)* The XVIII Mountain Corps, including two mountain divisions, was to advance through the very rugged terrain in the Mount Olympus area, while the strong XL Panzer Corps advanced through the Kozani valley onto the Plain of Thessaly.[66] On April 12, the Greek First Army in Albania began a general retreat too late to have any effect on the German operations.[67] In the only tank battle of the war, the 33rd Panzer Regiment of the 9th Panzer Division maneuvered boldly through a swamp and defeated elements of the British 1st Armoured Brigade near Kozani.[68] Only lack of fuel and ammunition prevented the Germans from immediately exploiting their advantage. Although only the 1st Brigade had been heavily engaged to this point, Wilson could not run the risk of encirclement, and decided during the night of April 13 to withdraw another hundred miles south to the area of Thermopylae.[69] His forces moved virtually alone because command and control were deteriorating in the Greek forces, which also lacked motor transport. With two German corps in pursuit, the Commonwealth forces had no chance of holding any defensive position long.

On April 16, the Greek Commander-in-Chief, General Alexander Papagos, suggested that the British withdraw from Greece to spare the country unnecessary destruction.[70] Churchill promptly approved the evacuation, but stipulated that Crete must be held in force. By April 20, the ANZAC Corps, as the 6th Australian and the New Zealand Division were called in memory of the World War I Gallipoli Campaign, had withdrawn through the covering force to positions across the famous Pass of Thermopylae. Although the Pass of Thermopylae had been but a few yards wide when Leonidas fought and died in 480 B.C., river deposits had widened it to well over a mile by the twentieth century. On April 20, the Greek First Army surrendered to the Germans and a *Luftwaffe* strike on the Athens air fields destroyed most of the few Hurricane fighters which remained in Greece. From this time on, the Germans enjoyed uncontested air superiority, interdicting road and rail movements at will. Well supported from the air, the 5th Panzer Division broke the ANZAC line at Thermopylae on April 24,

**Armored Reconnaissance Vehicles in Greece, 1941
(On the right: Sd Kfz 231 with 20-mm Gun)**

and three days later the swastika flag flew over the Acropolis in Athens.

The British evacuation of Greece took place from April 24 to 29. Over 50,000 men were taken from various harbors and beaches, 21,000 being transported only to Crete.[71] The Germans made a bold attempt to cut off the retreat by landing paratroops near the Corinth Canal bridge on April 26. The paratroopers captured the bridge intact, but two British officers apparently fired on the charges and detonated them, dropping the bridge 150 feet into the canal.[72] The 5th Panzer Division captured about 7,000 Commonwealth troops in Kalamata on the Peloponnese before they could be evacuated.[73] In all, the Commonwealth forces suffered over 2,000 battle casualties and lost 10,000 men as prisoners of war.[74] Total German casualties for the entire Balkan campaign now came to 2,500 killed in action, 3,100 missing, and 5,800 wounded.[75] The Germans could consider themselves very fortunate to have accomplished so much with so few losses.

Blitzkrieg had enjoyed another brilliant success in the Balkans, while the Commonwealth forces suffered the losses and humiliation of a second Dunkirk. The Germans deserve credit for a bold campaign through terrain well-suited for defense, but no real trial of arms had taken place. They defeated two armies which lacked modern arms and pursued a Commonwealth force hopelessly inferior in strength. As had been the case in France, they made aggressive thrusts with armored columns under commanders who stayed well forward. They exploited every advantage rapidly and with little regard for flank security. Under the circumstances, these tactics were correct. But they could be disastrous against an equally strong opponent.

In terms of strategy, both sides were probably wrong to fight in the Balkans. Hitler had first thought to secure Greek neutrality through political agreement. Even after Mussolini attacked Greece, Hitler might still have used his influence to reach a peaceful solution and bring about the departure of the British. Had he done so, the German Army would have been spared a diversion from preparing for the attack on Russia and a protracted war against irregular forces in Serbia. But by the end of 1940, Hitler preferred military solutions and had lost such political talent as he might have possessed. As events turned out, the British decision to support Greece was also a mistake. The British commanders badly miscalculated the amount of resistance Yugoslav and Greek troops could offer to a modern army. They also overestimated the difficulty of employing armor in mountainous terrain, especially when enjoying air superiority. The deployment of troops to Greece was morally justified and perhaps even politically fruitful, but it was militarily wrong. With the same effort, the British Commonwealth forces might well have expelled the Axis from North Africa.

Grave of German Paratroopers: Operation MERCURY

Although committed to preparing to invade Russia, Hitler permitted himself a last hurried operation in the Mediterranean: an airborne assault on Crete. This island, lying across the entrance to the Aegean Sea about 60 miles from the tip of Greece, is 160 miles long, but only 7 to 36 miles in width. It is formed of submerged mountain ranges, whose peaks still thrust five to eight thousand feet above sea level. *(See Map 18, in Atlas.)* Crete has only one good natural harbor for large vessels, Suda Bay near the town of Khania. Herakleion is the only other major port. On the southern coast are only a few fishing villages difficult to reach from the north. As a result, the Royal Navy had to operate north of the island, exposed to the full onslaught of the *Luftwaffe* operating from Greek bases. In 1941, Crete had three landing strips located at Maleme, Rhethymnon, and Herakleion. These three air strips were widely separated and connected only by a single east-west road, which would be extremely vulnerable to strafing. The island had no railways of tactical importance, and extremely rough terrain hampered all inland movement. Vineyards and groves of olive and almond trees on the northern coast gave concealment against air reconnaissance. Early summer in Crete brings bright sun and clear skies, perfect flying weather.

Although the British had been on Crete since November 1940, they had not materially improved the defenses of the island. Preoccupied with other operations, the British had done

Calm Before the Storm: A Lewis Gun Positioned Above Suda Bay, Crete, 1940

little to develop communications and prepared no landing facilities on the southern coast. Nor did they arm the inhabitants of Crete on a large scale or prepare to destroy the air strips, although the Germans could obviously extend their air superiority over the island.[76] By May 20, 1941, the entire garrison of Crete numbered about 42,000 men, including 10,000 Greeks.[77] Of the Commonwealth troops, 21,000 had recently been evacuated from Greece, bringing little heavy equipment with them. They had little artillery and armor and only a few antiaircraft guns. For example, artillery in the Maleme sector consisted of only two batteries totaling 12 tubes, including captured German and Italian guns.[78] The entire Suda Bay sector had only 24 heavy artillery pieces and 16 Bofors antiaircraft guns.[79] The Commonwealth strength on Crete was organized into the New Zealand division, deployed from Maleme to Khania; the Australian 19th Brigade, deployed east of Rhethymnon; and the strong British 14th Brigade, deployed in the Herakleion area. *(See Map 18, in Atlas.)* The 14th Brigade mustered almost 8,000 men and included the 2nd Battalion of the famous Black Watch Regiment. The New Zealand Division had two of its own brigades, plus a brigade improvised from troops out of Greece for a total of 7,700 men. The Greek units were poorly armed, lacking even rifles.[80]

The Germans had long contemplated an airborne operation in the Mediterranean area. They would have gained more by capturing Malta, but that operation also appeared more hazardous. In spite of the fact that their Greek bases would serve almost equally well, by capturing Crete the Germans believed that they could keep the Royal Air Force farther from the Rumanian oilfields, gain new bases to interdict British shipping and fleet movements, and secure their right flank for the invasion of Russia, code-named BARBAROSSA. In addition to these strategic considerations, Goering and General Kurt Student were simply eager to find employment for the airborne forces. Student developed the first plans in early April.[81] He originally contemplated seven landing zones, a dangerous dispersion of effort which would probably have caused defeat.[82] In the final plan, the paratroopers were still expected to seize all three airstrips by landing in the areas of Maleme, Suda Bay, Rhethymnon, and Herakleion. On April 25, 1941, Hitler issued Directive 28 for the operation against Crete, code-named MERCURY[83]

The Germans assembled over 22,000 troops for MERCURY, half from the 7th Airborne Division with its elite *Sturmregiment*. (Of the two German airborne divisions in being, one was stationed in Rumania and could not assemble quickly enough.) The 5th Mountain Division contributed two regiments, and the 6th Mountain Division one regiment.[84] According to plan, only about 10,000 men would parachute into Crete, while the remainder would arrive by air-landing or sea. Air Force elements were organized into the VIII Air Corps with over 700 fighters and dive-bombers and the XI Air Corps with over 500 transport aircraft.[85] The Germans were certain to have unchallenged air superiority, but they had no naval force worth mentioning. They hoped to conduct their sea landings at night, using captured Greek boats escorted by a few Italian destroyers. German intelligence badly underestimated the Allied strength at one division of two brigades plus an unknown number of troops lately evacuated from Greece.[86] It also advanced the optimistic assumption that the Allies were dispirited and exhausted. Finally, German aerial reconnaissance failed to reveal the Commonwealth positions, which were well camouflaged and had been inspected from the air by the defenders.[87]

Having broken the German Enigma code, the British had excellent intelligence (ULTRA) concerning MERCURY.[88] On May 1, a message from the War Office arrived in Crete announcing that the German attack was certain.[89] The British expected airborne and seaborne operations to begin simultaneously, and even slightly exaggerated the forces available to the Germans. The ULTRA intercepts were detailed and gave the British accurate information on units, plans, and timing. Churchill was elated at the fine opportunity to destroy the German paratroopers.[90]

The overall commander on Crete was Major General Bernard Freyberg from New Zealand, one of the Commonwealth's most distinguished soldiers. In the First World War, Freyberg had fought on Gallipoli and in Flanders, where he won the Victoria Cross. Still youthful and vigorous in 1941, Freyberg was a soldier's general, a natural leader of astonishing personal courage. Yet, dismayed by the lack of arms and equipment on Crete, Freyberg was uncertain that he could defend the island. Finally, he signaled on May 16: "With the help of the Royal Navy I trust Crete will be held."[91] Not privileged to have access to ULTRA intelligence, Freyberg nevertheless was given all the details on the German plan and received firsthand guidance from Wavell, who visited Crete shortly before the battle began. Freyberg instructed his officers to secure the airfields and to counterattack rapidly when the Germans parachuted, but he was equally concerned about seaborne landings.

The Germans began MERCURY by bombing and strafing Crete from bases in Greece as little as 75 miles away. On May 17, Freyberg sent the last British Hurricanes and Gladiators back to Cairo, rather than sacrifice them to the swarms of Messerschmitt 109s over Crete.[92] During daylight, German air interdiction made even infantry movements dangerous. The airborne assault began three days later, on the morning of May 20, 1941. *(See Map 18, in Atlas.)* Some paratroopers fell directly on Commonwealth positions and were killed while still airborne or hunted down moments after landing. Due to the parachute harnesses then in use, the paratroopers jumped carrying only knives, sidearms, and Schmeisser submachine guns. Their survival depended on landing unobserved or

German Airborne Troops Falling Near New Zealand Trenches on Crete, 1941

reaching their weapons canisters quickly.[93] The commanding general of the 7th Airborne Division died during the approach flight, and the commander of the Maleme group was shot in the chest shortly after landing. The slaughter of German airborne troops on May 20 must have exceeded Churchill's expectations. But some paratroopers landed unopposed or even unobserved.

The Germans failed to capture the airstrips at Rhethymnon and Herakleion, but they won the battle of Crete by seizing the airstrip at Maleme. Here the *Sturmregiment* confronted the New Zealand 5th Brigade. Arriving by parachute and glider, the 2nd, 4th, and elements of the 1st Battalion landed safely west of the Tavronitis River or along its dry bed; but the 3rd Battalion jumped over New Zealand positions and was annihilated. *(See Map on page 99.)* The Maleme air strip was defended by the New Zealand 22nd Battalion deployed with its westernmost companies on the east bank of the Tavronitis. The battalion headquarters was located on the reverse side of Hill 107, a key terrain feature because it dominated the air strip from the south. German bombing destroyed the wire communications, forcing the New Zealanders to rely on a radio link between battalions and the brigade. Despite vigorous attacks by the German 2nd and 4th Battalions during the day, only Company C of the New Zealand 22nd Battalion, deployed around the airfield, was partially overrun during the day. The other New Zealand companies remained largely intact and in position, but the battalion commander could not communicate with his companies and feared the worst. He decided to withdraw during the night and so informed the brigadier, who failed to order counterattacks with either the 21st or 23rd Battalion even though these units had been only lightly engaged. Infiltrating during the night, the German paratroopers crawled into empty New Zealand trenches on Hill 107.

The New Zealanders could have won the battle for Maleme during the night of May 20. As Student later said, the survivors of the *Sturmregiment* were extremely tired and short of ammunition.[94] But the battle was only one day old and Freyberg remained tentative in his judgments. He had ample strength to destroy the *Sturmregiment* in a night assault and reoccupy positions around the airstrip. During the night a staff officer arrived at his headquarters with an order captured from the 3rd Regiment, 7th Airborne Division, which had landed south of Khania. The order was marked "not to be carried into battle" and gave the objectives for the first two German assault echelons.[95] Ironically, Freyberg failed to realize that the landing strips were crucial objectives.[96] He incorrectly supposed that the Germans could parachute many more troops or even crash land if necessary. Actually a crash landing on Crete away from a cleared surface was nearly suicidal, and the Germans had sent almost all their paratroopers in the first assault echelon. If they could not capture and use an airstrip soon, they faced almost certain defeat.

At dawn on May 21, the Germans were in a very difficult position. They had had no success anywhere but at Maleme, and even there approximately 2,000 paratroops confronted 7,000 New Zealand infantry with nearly 6,000 ancillary British troops within striking distance. During the afternoon, Freyberg decided to counterattack with the New Zealand 20th Battalion, then east of Galatos *(see Map 18, in Atlas)*, and the 28th (Maori) Battalion at Palatanias. *(See Map, page 99.)* This strength was inadequate and the battalions started so late that they failed to reach Maleme before daybreak of May 22. If Freyberg had ordered a larger attack to begin promptly at dusk, when the Germans lost the advantage of air support, he might have enjoyed the finest victory of his career.[97] Earlier, on the morning of the twenty-first, Student had dropped his few remaining paratroopers east of Maleme, but they landed too close to the New Zealanders, who immediately shot them to pieces. Then, in desperation, he had sent a formation of Junkers 52 transports carrying 800 mountain troops to make forced landings at Maleme, even though the airstrip still lay under light artillery fire. This willingness to sacrifice aircraft might have suggested to Freyberg that the Germans had no good alternative. But he hesitated to concentrate on the paratroopers, because he still anticipated seaborne attacks. During the night of May 21, the British Force D, consisting of three light cruisers and four destroyers, did in fact discover a convoy of German troops in Greek cargo vessels escorted by a single Italian destroyer. Although the Italian destroyer fought gallantly, the British rammed and sank with gunfire about half the cargo ships. Almost none of the German troops reached Crete.[98]

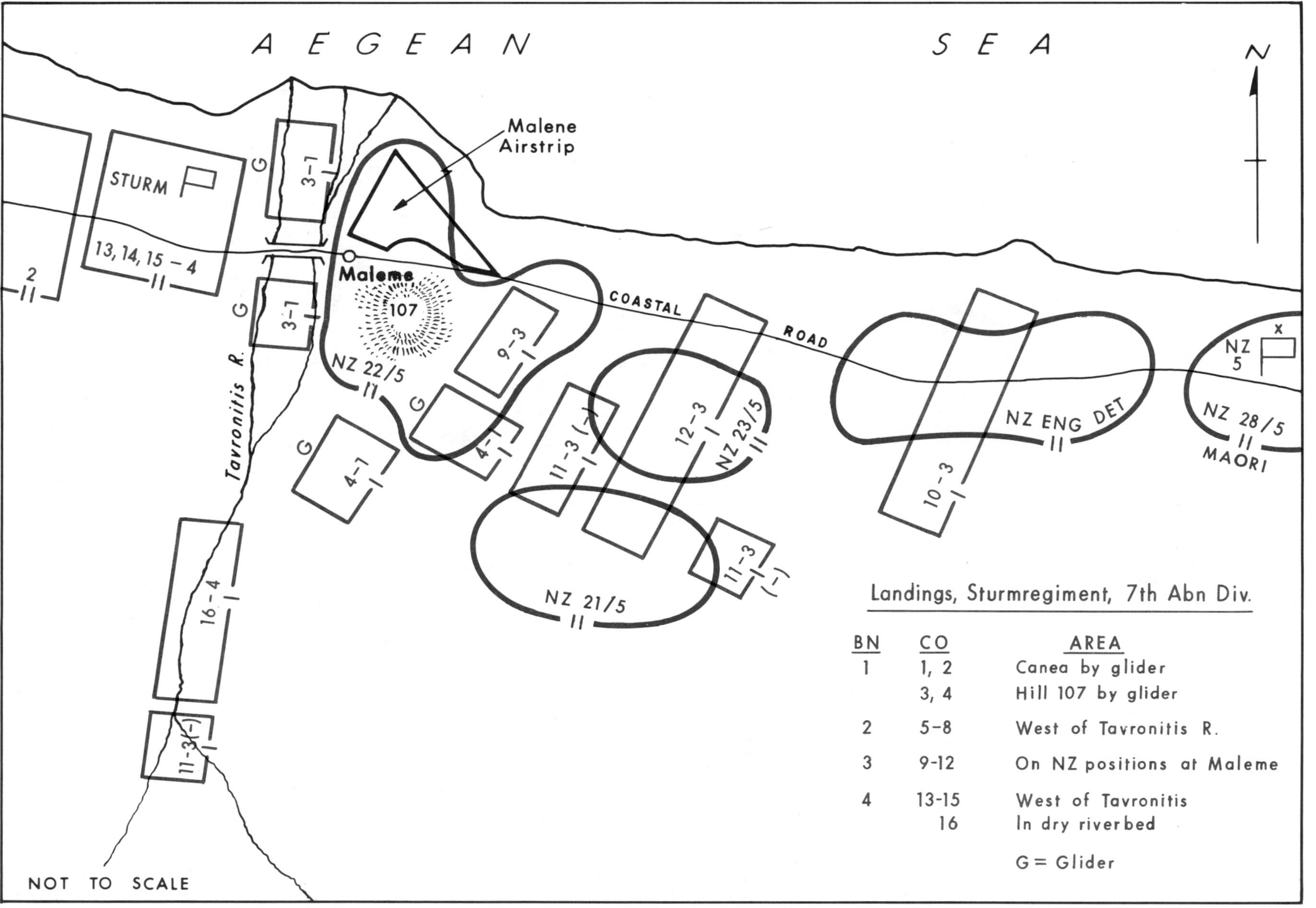

German Landings and Allied Dispositions, Vicinity of Maleme, Crete, May 20, 1941

The Royal Navy operated at extreme peril in the Aegean Sea. Since the British air assault on the Italian fleet in the Taranto harbor on November 11, 1940, and the sea battle off Cape Matapan on March 28, 1941, the British had had no naval rival in the Mediterranean. But experience in the North Sea had already proven that surface ships were extremely vulnerable to concentrated bombing. Since the middle of May, the *Luftwaffe* had interdicted all traffic in Suda Bay during daylight. The round trip from Alexandria to Crete is about 900 miles, so a British ship then cruising the Aegean ran short of fuel very quickly. To guard the island against seaborne assault, ships of the Royal Navy remained north of Crete during the entire night of May 21. At dawn, the *Luftwaffe* swarmed over the ships and sank two cruisers and a destroyer. As losses continued, the Navy quickly approached the limits of endurance. Vice Admiral Sir Andrew Cunningham, the Naval Commander-in-Chief in the Mediterranean, reported to the Chiefs of Staff on May 24: "The experience of three days in which two cruisers and four destroyers have been sunk, and one battleship, two cruisers and four destroyers severely damaged, show what losses are likely to be. Sea control in the eastern Mediterranean could not be retained after another such experience."[99]

German Troops Moving From a Junkers 52 Aircraft Towards Hill 107 at Maleme, Crete, 1941

After the failure of the counterattack at Maleme, the Commonwealth position west of Khania deteriorated rapidly, while the garrisons at Rhethymnon and Herakleion continued to control their areas. On the evening of May 22, Freyberg decided to withdraw the New Zealand 5th Brigade and leave Maleme to the Germans. By May 24, the New Zealand general was convinced his choice now lay between defeat and withdrawal from Crete.[100] That evening, German radio first mentioned the battle, a sign that the Germans at last felt confident of success.[101] Next day, the German 3rd Regiment attacked north from Prison Valley and breached the New Zealand line before Galatos, ending the last hope for an effective counterattack. *(See Map 18, in Atlas.)* On the afternoon of May 26, Freyberg decided to march south and evacuate his force through the little fishing village of Sfakia on the southern coast. Surprisingly ill-informed considering their air superiority, the Germans attempted an envelopment of Khania the following day. Despite the great risk to his ships, Cunningham decided to attempt evacuation rather than desert the Army on Crete.

Until May 28, the Germans did not realize that the Commonwealth forces were retreating to Sfakia and even then they were more anxious to relieve their own hard-pressed troops at Rhethymnon and Herakleion than to pursue the retreating enemy. On the same day, 4,000 British troops were evacuated from Herakleion, but two destroyers were lost in the operation.[102] Because Freyberg had no communications to Rhethymnon, the Australian 19th Brigade never learned of the retreat and ultimately surrendered. By this time some of the troops at Sfakia had become rabble, and the last units to embark had to secure the beach with fixed bayonets.[103] In all, about 12,000 men remained as German prisoners of war when the Royal Navy ended the evacuation on May 31.

The casualties on Crete show the intensity of the fighting. Of the British Commonwealth troops, 1,750 died, and 1,740 wounded were evacuated. Probably about 2,000 of the prisoners of war were also wounded.[104] The Royal Navy lost 1,800 men killed in action in operations around Crete. Three cruisers and 6 destroyers were lost, while 17 other ships were damaged.[105] From German reports, it appears that about 4,000 men were killed on Crete, over half of these during the initial landings.[106] The *Luftwaffe* lost over 200 aircraft during the entire operation. Crete was the grave of the German paratrooper. The Germans retained airborne units in service, but never employed them again in a major airborne assault. Hitler left a small garrison on Crete and turned to invade Russia, expecting to return to the Mediterranean after a quick victory. Apart from some partisan activity, nothing occurred thereafter on Crete until the Germans withdrew voluntarily late in the war.

Both combatants made serious mistakes during the battle for Crete. The Germans should never have assaulted Crete at all, since they could dominate the Aegean Sea as easily from their Greek bases. Even Student's modified plan of operation was too ambitious. Instead of attempting to seize all three landing strips simultaneously, he should have concentrated on one objective to assure success. Student did not clearly understand how quickly paratroops would be destroyed if they landed too close to battle-ready infantry. As for the seaborne landings, they might better have been attempted in full daylight under heavy air cover. On the Commonwealth side, the failures lay in communications and leadership. For lack of communications, the New Zealand commanders practically lost control of their units once they were committed to battle.[107] Just 100 radios, correctly distributed and employed, might have saved Crete. But even when they could communicate, the New Zealand officers in the Maleme area above company level often reacted too slowly to events. They could have defeated the *Sturmregiment* through aggressive leadership, especially by counterattacking in sufficient force at the earliest opportunities. In fairness to these officers, they made errors in judgment but never lacked courage. For his part, Freyberg, who had received the highly accurate ULTRA intelligence, misinterpreted that information and failed to perceive that holding the airfield at Maleme was crucial, not guarding against seaborne landings.

The rank and file on both sides fought tenaciously on Crete, and in the end the Germans could claim only a pyrrhic victory. The 7th Airborne Division was squandered for an objective of dubious worth, but its success deserves admiration. The Germans accomplished an unusual feat of arms. Few troops of any nation could have fought as the German paratroopers did after the casualties sustained on May 20, 1941.

Why Was BARBAROSSA *Delayed?*

In his directive for the invasion of Russia, dated December 18, 1940, Hitler demanded that all lengthy preparations be complete by May 15, 1941, thus implying an intention to begin the operation about this time. On subsequent occasions he spoke of commencing the invasion in the middle or at the end of May.[108] Yet the Germans actually invaded on June 22, and then failed to capture Leningrad or Moscow before winter. At first glance, MARITA does not seem responsible for the delay, since both operations were planned simultaneously in late 1940. But the Germans did not originally plan to advance all the way down the Grecian peninsula. Hitler ordered this advance on March 17, 1941, to drive the Commonwealth forces out of Greece. At the time, the OKH Chief of Staff, General Franz Halder, thought the MARITA forces would now be unable to meet the BARBAROSSA deadline.[109] If Halder was right, then the British decision to help the Greeks might inadvertently have helped the Russians. But Hitler dispensed with the plan to attack on the right flank of Army Group South and ordered a holding action in Moldavia instead, so that the Twelfth Army no longer played a vital role in BARBAROSSA.[110] In any case, the Germans left only two mountain divisions and one infantry division to garrison Greece, freeing the other MARITA forces for early participation in BARBAROSSA.[111]

At the time he decided to smash Yugoslavia, Hitler announced that BARBAROSSA would be postponed for a month. Unfortunately, no other clear statement from Hitler on the subject has been preserved, right down to the final selection of June 22.[112] In late March, Hitler thought the Yugoslavian operation would force a postponement, but did he continue to think so? The invasion of Yugoslavia caused only a four- to five-day postponement of MARITA. The German divisions which paraded through Yugoslavia suffered few casualties and little wear, leaving them fresh for BARBAROSSA. Only the armored units required a few weeks to refit. In addition, the invasion of Yugoslavia made MARITA much easier because the Germans could outflank their enemies. If Hitler wanted an early start for BARBAROSSA, it is hard to see why the Yugoslavian operation should have deterred him.

The impact of the entire Balkan operation is not easy to assess. The BARBAROSSA planning involved a grand total of 152 divisions and 29 of these were deployed in the Balkans. Three of these divisions remained stationed in Greece, and 11 others were drawn from the OKH reserve for BARBAROSSA.[113] Thus, only 15 divisions and the VIII Air Corps had to redeploy quickly from the Balkans to assembly areas for BARBAROSSA. Apart from the assault on Crete, the Balkan campaign ended in April, leaving a month to prepare these divisions for BARBAROSSA. But the Germans were executing a complicated movements plan which left little transport available to move the MARITA forces.[114] Even so, they could certainly have initiated BARBAROSSA in May at the cost of committing some MARITA divisions to operations already in progress. The last obstacle to BARBAROSSA was the operation against Crete. This operation required the entire VIII Air Corps (fighters and dive-bombers) which the *Luftwaffe* needed to support the invasion of Russia. Not until May 29 did Hitler finally set June 22 as the firm date for BARBAROSSA.[115]

Available records also suggest that OKH accepted the delay of BARBAROSSA for two reasons unrelated to German movements. Once they learned of German intentions, Rumania and Finland needed additional time to prepare to participate in the invasion. In addition, a late thaw in spring 1941 caused flooding and wet conditions well into June.[116] Of course, at the time neither Hitler nor his generals were much disturbed by the delay. Hitler's intention to begin in May was not very firm, and he changed his mind easily under the press of events. Although no single segment of the Balkan campaign forced the Germans to delay BARBAROSSA, obviously the entire campaign did prompt them to wait. On the other hand, the Germans could have begun earlier had they thought it important. In the last analysis, anticipation of *blitzkrieg* success in Russia influenced German thinking more than the Balkan campaign did.

Hitler Invades the Soviet Union: Operation BARBAROSSA

Long before he came to power, Hitler had speculated on Germany's need to crush the Soviet Union in a great war. His motives fell into two categories: the elimination of Communism, and territorial expansion towards the east. Hitler posited that the German nation required more land and raw materials to support an expanding population. He did not arrive at this idea through any rational calculation. He simply felt that nations should live like animals in a jungle, that the strong had the right and even the duty to prey on the weak. The catchword *lebensraum* clothed a primitive desire to conquer and oppress. Hitler's feelings about Communism were more sinister and even less rational. He believed that Communism was an outgrowth of an international Jewish conspiracy, that the Jews secretly manipulated the capitalist states but had openly seized power in Russia. His rabid anti-Semitism was thus conjoined with anti-Communism. Certainly the former motive was dominant. Hitler's deepest, most sincere belief was an utter delusion: the international conspiracy of Jews against "Aryan" peoples and especially against Germany. His war against Russia was a war against the Jews.[117]

Previously, the Germans had overestimated their enemies, but in the general euphoria following the collapse of France, they went to the opposite extreme. Buoyant with success, Hitler even thought he could conclude an invasion of Russia in 1940. On July 21, 1940, Hitler directed Field Marshal Walter von Brauchitsch, the OKH Commander-in-Chief, to advise him on a fall campaign.[118] After Hitler was dissuaded of this idiocy, the OKH staff began to plan an invasion of Russia for 1941. With whatever sincerity, Hitler told his generals that Stalin was only awaiting a favorable opportunity to ally with Great Britain and attack Germany. Hitler may have taken his argument seriously, but there is no historical evidence to suggest that Stalin had any such intention. Hitler also stressed economic and political objectives: to protect German industry and the Rumanian oilfields by creating Baltic and Ukrainian states under German influence. On July 29, the OKH Chief of Staff General Franz Halder directed General Erich Marcks, the Eighteenth Army Chief of Staff temporarily assigned to OKH, to prepare a concept of operations quickly.[119] To this point, the OKH had planned campaigns against known opponents on familiar terrain, but intelligence concerning Russia was very sparse. The German staffs were entering *terra incognita*.

Marcks submitted his plan on August 5, 1940. *(See Map, page 103.)* Essentially, he foresaw a quick victory in *blitzkrieg* style followed by a vast exploitation. He distinguished four phases of the operation, each lasting two to four or even six weeks, depending upon Soviet resistance. In the first phase, the Germans would break through and pursue the Russians back to the forests and rivers forming natural barriers on the approaches to Moscow. Here the Red Army would accept battle, and the German Army would win decisive victories in the general area of the Dvina and Berezina Rivers. In the third phase, the Germans would advance against scattered resistance to Moscow, Leningrad, and deep into the Ukraine. Finally, the Germans would continue virtually unopposed to the Volga River and the Northern Dvina emptying into the White Sea. The entire operation would require only 9 to 17 weeks. In retrospect, Marcks' plan appears absurdly optimistic, but it reflected accurately the German optimism after the victory in France. The Russian performance in World War I, Stalin's purges of the Soviet officer corps, and the very unimpressive showing against Finland all indicated that Russia was a less formidable opponent than France.

With Halder's approval, Marcks made Moscow the major terrain objective of the campaign. He pointed out that the road net was best in northern Russia, permitting rapid if somewhat constricted movement. Moscow was a center of communications, transportation, and government whose capture might lead to the collapse of coordinated resistance. On the way to Moscow, the German forces would encounter and destroy the greater part of the Red Army. At the same time, a secondary effort towards the Ukraine would protect the Rumanian oil fields from a Soviet thrust. Once Moscow fell, the main German force might swing south, forcing the Soviet forces in the Ukraine to fight on an inverted front. To accomplish such a vast operation, Marcks thought the Germans would have to mass their forces boldly and maneuver them very rapidly, giving the Soviets little time to react. He massed 75 percent of the available armor north of the Pripet marshes to ensure superiority in the decisive battles of White Russia. Realizing that transport would be difficult, he called for special efforts in road and bridge construction and in the collection of cartographic information. Neither roads nor maps had posed problems in France as they would in Russia. Marcks made no provision for a winter campaign because he confidently expected the Russians to collapse before bad weather began. All subsequent planning shared this basic assumption.

On October 29, Halder's operations division prepared a summary which pointed out some of the risks inherent in a Russian campaign and outlined a clear strategic conception.[120] The summary estimated Soviet strength at 170 divisions plus a large reserve, an estimate then thought generous but actually too low. The German forces would be numerically inferior and would have to rely on mass, maneuver, and superior training, morale, and leadership. The Soviet soldier might be very tough, but his officers were demoralized by the purges and inexperienced in mobile war. The Soviets might or might not defend on the frontier, but in any event the Germans must prevent

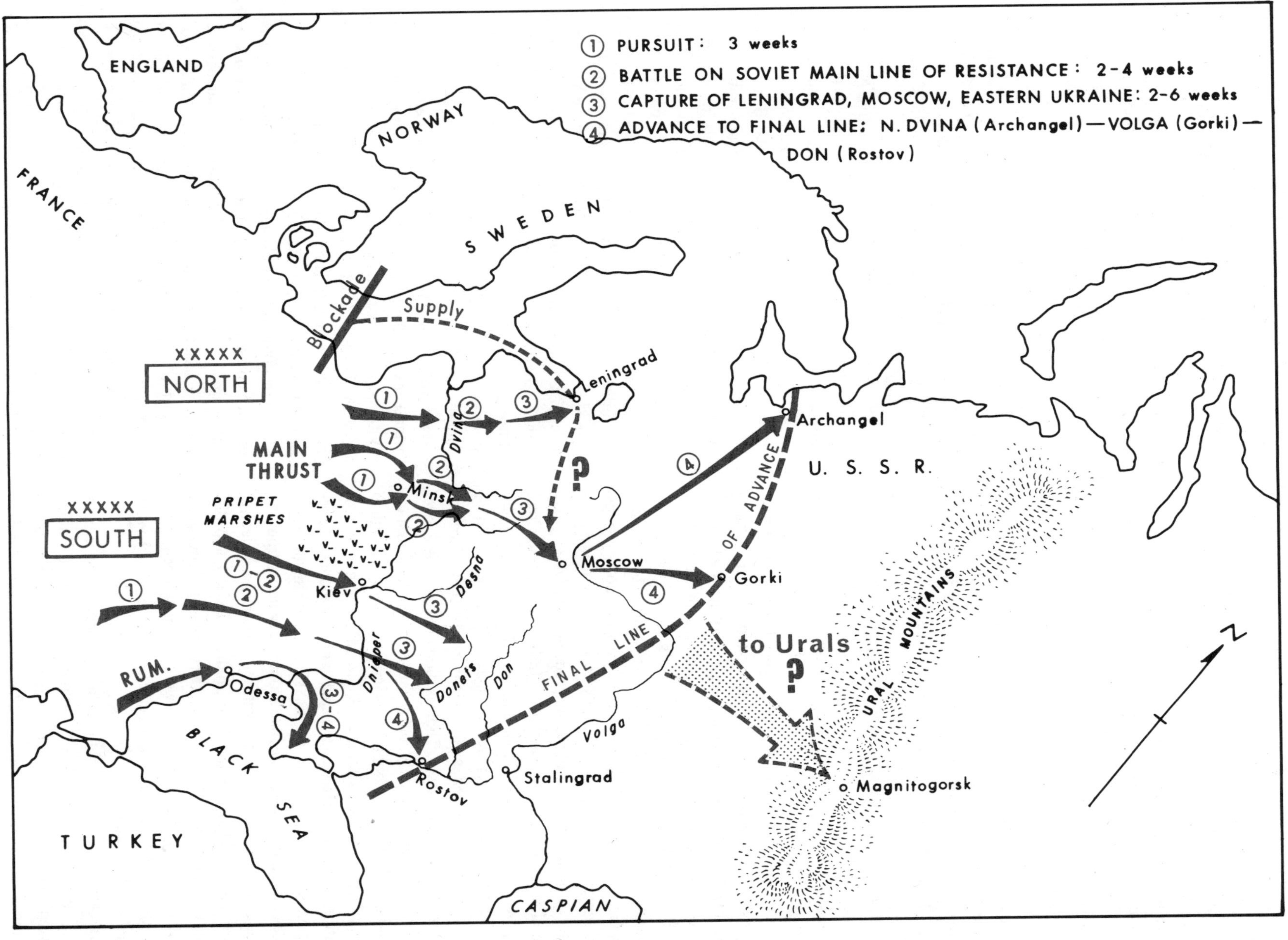

Marcks' Plan, August 5, 1940

them from making orderly withdrawals. The Germans must encircle and destroy the Red Army before it could retreat into the vast spaces of European or even Asiatic Russia. Suitable campaigning weather would last only from May to October. No army could invade through the Pripet Marshes, and an advance through the Ukraine would be difficult due to river barriers and the lack of west-east roads and rail lines. The major economic objectives, especially the Donets industrial area, lay in the south, but only in the north could the Army expect to win a quick decisive campaign. Whether this analysis was correct or not, it at least offered a coherent plan, and both von Brauchitsch and Halder consistently advocated a *Schwerpunkt* on the Minsk-Smolensk-Moscow land bridge. Although emphasizing Moscow's importance as an objective, their reasoning was essentially military. In northern Russia they saw better bases, better roads, fewer river obstacles, and shorter distances, resulting in the best chance to fix and destroy the Red Army quickly.

During the fall of 1940, the operations division and the economic office of OKW prepared studies independently of OKH. Although in organizational theory OKW should have assumed responsibility for overall strategy, it actually functioned as just another agency serving Hitler's whims.[121] The operational plan submitted to the Chief of OKW Staff, General Alfred Jodl, on September 19, also placed the *Schwerpunkt* north of the Pripet Marshes for an advance to Moscow. The German forces would be deployed in three army groups. The center group attacking towards Moscow might assist the northern group in capturing Leningrad, an idea which reappeared in the BARBAROSSA directive. In November, the Chief of the economic office (*Wirtschafts-und Rüstungsamt*), General Georg Thomas, prepared an interesting survey outlining the effects of an invasion on Soviet industry.[122] If the Germans occupied European Russia, Thomas did not expect the Soviet industry to collapse entirely, but he did anticipate the Russians would lose 75 percent of their heavy industry, surely enough to render them harmless. Thomas failed to imagine a massive relocation of industry into the Ural area or greatly increased production outside of European Russia. He did not think that Germany could anticipate immediate economic benefits from the occupation, due to difficulty with transportation, electric power, and the supply of petroleum products. Indeed, to profit at all, Germany would have to seize the Caucasus oil fields on the Caspian Sea. These oil fields were not mentioned in the BARBAROSSA directive, but they became the chief objective of Hitler's 1942 strategy.

On December 5, 1940, Hitler held a major conference with the chiefs of OKW and OKH.[123] Von Brauchitsch and Halder stressed the advantages of advancing straight toward Smolensk and then on to Moscow, but Hitler remained unimpressed. In his opinion, the Baltic area and the Ukraine offered more vital objectives. He agreed with his generals in emphasizing the rapid encirclement of the Red Army before it could retreat beyond the operational reach of the invading forces, but he considered the Russians to be extremely poor soldiers, who also lacked efficient officers and modern armored vehicles. He assured his generals that the Russians would collapse even more rapidly than the French had. Having now lost interest in SEALION, Hitler wished the invasion of Russia to commence in May 1941. OKW then prepared a directive outlining the responsibilities of all the services, and submitted it to Hitler on December 17. On his own initiative and contrary to all the advice he had received, Hitler altered the directive, giving Leningrad rather than Moscow first priority.[124] He argued that the capture of Leningrad would secure the Baltic Sea for resupply and effect junction with the Finns, who would be co-belligerents.

On December 18, Hitler signed Directive Number 21 for the invasion of Russia, now code-named BARBAROSSA.[125] This directive reflected Hitler's amateurism in its rambling, imprecise language and form. *(See Map, page 106.)* The Navy was to remain fully committed against Great Britain, while also blockading the Baltic Sea. The *Luftwaffe* was to continue the air war against England while providing tactical support to the Army in Russia. Although Hitler denied it, these divided responsibilities showed Germany embarking on a two-front war. According to the BARBAROSSA plan, the German Army would annihilate the Red Army in bold operations and then pursue quickly to the general line of Archangel to the Volga River. A central group of armies would destroy the Soviet forces in White Russia and subsequently cooperate with a northern army group in capturing Leningrad. Leningrad was the first priority objective, but if the Russians were to collapse very rapidly, the Germans might advance on Leningrad and Moscow simultaneously. At the same time, a southern army group would envelop the Russian forces west of the Dnieper River. With Russian resistance virtually ended, the Germans would seize the Donets industrial area and Moscow, if the city were not already captured. The Rumanians would assist by fixing Soviet forces in the Ukraine, and the Finns would attack either west or on both sides of Lake Ladoga, thus assisting in the capture of Leningrad. OKW-OKH acquiesced in Hitler's strategy but retained their preference for Moscow, a latent difference which surfaced during the actual campaign. Hitler had taken his most important and perhaps his last important decision.

After December 1940, the plan for BARBAROSSA changed in only two respects: the German offensive in northern Finland received more emphasis, and Army Group South was no longer to attempt a double envelopment. Hitler hoped to forestall British landings by rapidly seizing Murmansk on the Barents Sea and mining the harbor of Archangel on the White Sea. Both these operations later proved to be beyond German capabilities. Conscious of the Ukrainian river barriers and concerned over British intervention in Greece, Hitler decided on March 17, 1941 that Army Group South should concentrate its attack on its left flank, advancing towards Kiev. The Eleventh Army on the right flank should guard the Rumanian oil fields, while the Sixth Army and First Panzer Group on the left flank attempted a single envelopment by following the Dnieper from Kiev to the Black Sea.[126] Even in the optimistic atmosphere of 1941, the success of such a gigantic single envelopment appeared doubtful, yet OKH made no objections. During the actual campaign, this change proved fateful because Hitler was prompted to discard the single envelopment in favor of cooperation between Army Groups Center and South, an operation foreseen in none of the formal BARBAROSSA plans.

German planning for BARBAROSSA on the OKW-OKH level lacked clear strategic design. OKW had been largely excluded from the planning up to the preparation of Directive 21, and, in any case, neither the OKW Commander-in-Chief (Field Marshal Wilhelm Keitel) nor his Chief of Staff (General Alfred Jodl) could offer strong leadership. The strongest personality in the German high command was the OKH Chief of Staff, Halder, but he was limited to planning the initial phases of the operation and to unsuccessful advocacy of Moscow as the primary objective. Hitler had the worst effect on planning because he lacked the intelligence to combine political, economic, and military considerations into a clear strategy. But Hitler does not bear the sole responsibility for misplanning BARBAROSSA. Although harboring faint misgivings, virtually all the highest German officers cooperated willingly and even enthusiastically in the planning. None expected the Russians would prove more dangerous than the French and none anticipated a long war. The latest differences between Hitler and his generals were obscured by their common anticipation of *blitzkrieg* success that would make a clear strategy or any strategy unnecessary. Hitler was too undisciplined to adhere to a plan anyway, and he abandoned his own priorities once the campaign began.

Politically, Hitler did little to prepare for BARBAROSSA beyond enlisting the Finns and the Rumanians. The Finns saw the opportunity to renew their earlier war against the Soviet Union and recover their losses. But they would not go beyond these aims by attacking Leningrad, the only objective in northern Russia of vital interest to the Germans. Rumania had become Germany's client, but her army had almost no modern equipment. The obvious ally against Russia was Japan, signator of the Tripartite Pact of September 27, 1940, with Germany and Italy; yet Hitler preferred to see Japan exert herself in the Pacific area. In a conference with his generals on January 9, 1941, Hitler said that German success in Russia would encourage Japan to attack America, thus keeping the United States out of the Anglo-German war. With rather more wisdom, he added that Germany would be invulnerable once she defeated the Soviet Union.[127] When the Japanese Foreign Minister visited Berlin on March 27, 1941, von Ribbentrop suggested strongly that Japan should attack the British in Singapore, while he said nothing of the impending attack on the Soviet Union. After these talks, the Japanese diplomat went on to Moscow and promptly concluded a Russo-Japanese neutrality pact.[128] The Italians had as little advance notice of BARBAROSSA as the Japanese. Neither the Axis nor the Tripartite Pact constituted a military alliance. Hitler was not even interested in fighting a coalition war. Arrogant in his own strength, he let Italy and Japan go their own ways. As a result, he had to underwrite a series of Italian disasters in the Mediterranean area and to fight America because Japan had attacked her. It would be difficult to imagine a policy more inept or more damaging to German interests.

Hitler planned the invasion not simply as a war of conquest, but as a war of annihilation. On March 30, 1941, he ordered the senior army commanders to have Soviet commissars and Communist Party officials summarily executed or given to special *Schutzstaffel* (SS) groups for execution.[129] Many of the officers must have felt that this order was dishonorable, but few dared to complain. During the campaign, many would feign compliance, while ignoring the killings done by the special SS groups. These *Einsatzgruppen* were formed in May 1941 under the supervision of Reinhard Heydrich, then chief of the *Reichssicherheitshauptamt* (RSHA), the central security agency.[130] Four *Einsatzgruppen* were raised, each of about battalion strength, totaling approximately 3,000 men. Although attached to the Army for administrative purposes, they remained under Heydrich's operational control. Their primary mission was to murder the civilian Jewish population as soon as the German Army had occupied an area. By tolerating this deliberate inhumanity, the German officers became accomplices in Hitler's crimes and compromised the traditional honor of their service.

Prior to the invasion of Russia, German industry mirrored the *blitzkrieg* style of war. The Germans neglected to initiate all-out war production, despite the impression they gave abroad. Instead, German factories produced relatively modest amounts of first one weapon, then another, in response to the various needs of several campaigns. Even as BARBAROSSA began, Hitler was planning a shift to production of planes and ships to defeat Great Britain. As a result, the Germans were unprepared for a protracted war in Russia.[131] To take the most important example, they did not produce the armor which would be needed. The *Panzerkampfwagen* III equipped with a short 50-mm gun, which served as the main battle tank during 1941, was produced so slowly that only 1,090 were ready for the invasion. At the same time, over 800 PzKw I (with dual machineguns) and over 1,000 PzKw II (with a 20-mm gun) re-

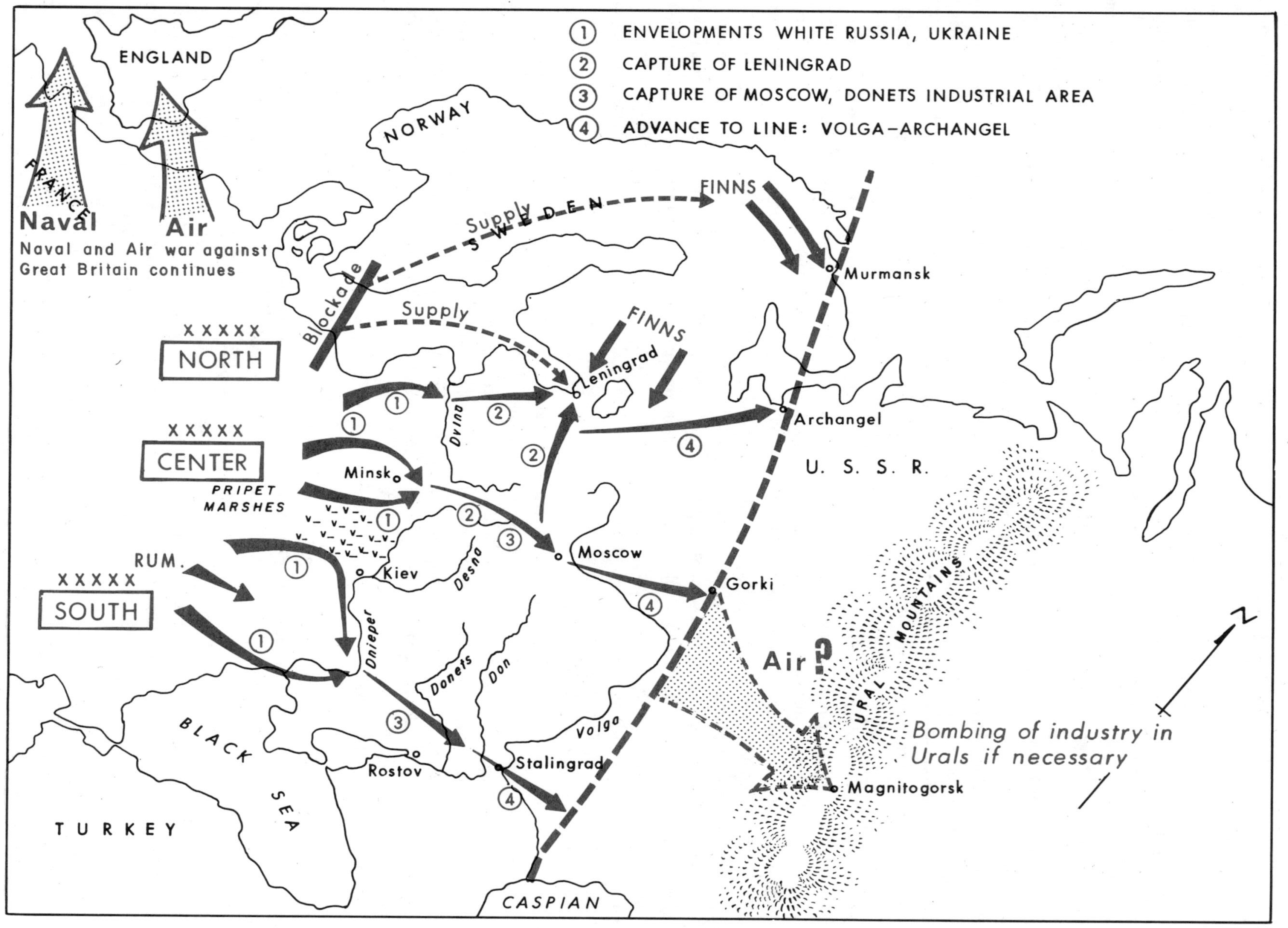

Operation BARBAROSSA (Dir. 21), December 18, 1940

mained on active service, although the Germans knew them to be obsolete. Although it was already in service during the summer of 1940, only about 550 PzKw IV, mounting a 75-mm gun, were ready for BARBAROSSA.[132]. Rather than produce more armor, the Germans expanded their force by reducing the authorized strength of a *panzer* division. Each 1940 *panzer* division gave up one regiment which formed the nucleus of a new *panzer* division which was authorized only 190 tanks.[133] Other crucial arms and equipment fared even worse than armor. The Germans produced few tracked prime movers, and their production of heavy infantry weapons and field artillery even declined during 1941.[134]

In discussions with his generals, Hitler denied that he was undertaking a two-front war. But the German dispositions in 1941 tell a different story. Thirty-nine divisions remained in France and seven in Norway, where Hitler feared another British landing. Eight divisions were still in the Balkan area and two more were fighting the British in North Africa.[135] The *Luftwaffe* had only 4,300 firstline aircraft and 1,530 of these remained at western air bases when BARBAROSSA began.[136] Despite these diversions, the force assembled to invade Russia was the largest ever to invade on a single command. The German strength totaled 119 infantry divisions, 19 *panzer* divisions, and 15 motorized divisions, in all over three million men and 600,000 motor vehicles.[137] In view of German tactics, the armor strength was less impressive: only about 3,500 tanks of all types.[138] The Germans brought about as many horses as motor vehicles into Russia, but both would be used largely for supply and to move heavy equipment. The infantry march would largely determine the tempo of the German advance. The Germans had the support of 12 Rumanian divisions and 18 Finnish divisions plus a few Slovakian and Hungarian units.[139]

Russian strength in 1941 is difficult to estimate. The Five Year Plans, whatever their human cost, had been enormously successful. While the capitalist countries suffered depression during the 1930s, the Soviet Union sustained very rapid growth.[140] Without this forced expansion of heavy industry, the Soviet Union could not have survived the Germar onslaught. At the same time, the Soviet armed forces grew tremendously and may have totaled nearly five million men in 1941.[141] Perhaps 2.5 million men were stationed in the five western military districts and about one million remained in the Far East to defend against Japan. The Red Army had approximately 20,000 tanks, by far the largest armored force in the world, but most of these tanks were obsolete in 1941.[142] But the Russians were producing a new generation of armored vehicles unknown to the Germans. In 1941, the Soviets already had approximately 1,000 T-34 tanks, the best armored vehicles then available anywhere in the world, but these new tanks were just being introduced to the field army when the Germans struck. The Soviets had a large air force mustering 7,000 combat aircraft, but most of these were biplanes or other obsolete types hopelessly inferior to their German counterparts. Soviet training and efficiency must have been far below the German standard, and of course Soviet troops lacked the Germans' experience in mobile war.

Although they took pains to conceal their preparations, the Germans did not imagine they could achieve tactical surprise.[143] The Soviets knew everything the Germans did, yet Stalin gave his army no warning. Here is an enigma. The Soviets received excellent intelligence from a variety of sources. Since 1940, the British had been deciphering German radio communications (ULTRA). Although the Germans were not so careless as to transmit operations orders regularly, the mass of logistical information clearly revealed their dispositions. After several previous warnings, the British finally called the Soviet Ambassador to the Foreign Office on June 10, 1941, and presented him with the German order of battle for BARBAROSSA, showing the movement of each division into its assembly area.[144] Rudolf Rossler (best known by his code name "Lucy"), operating from Switzerland, gave Soviet intelligence information on BARBAROSSA, including the date; so did Richard Sorge, an agent operating within the German embassy in Tokyo.[145] The Germans gave warning through their reconnaissance flights, which ranged as far as Minsk and Kiev at heights up to 39,000 feet. The Soviets protested against these flights on three occasions, citing hundreds of violations of their air space.[146] As the date approached, the Germans ordered their merchant ships to leave Soviet harbors, and even evacuated women and children from the Moscow embassy.[147] Stalin undoubtedly feared the *Wehrmacht* and was anxious to avoid any provocation; but his failure to alert the Red Army may always remain something of a mystery.

BARBAROSSA began at 3:00 A.M. on June 22, 1941, with an artillery preparation and air strikes, followed by full-scale attacks. Despite all warnings, Stalin had issued only a vague alert notice during the night and even that notice failed to reach all units before they were attacked.[148] Some units did not have their basic loads of ammunition and other supplies, and others had sent their organic artillery to distant firing ranges.[149] The Russians had no time to execute their mobilization plans and had to rush units into combat without full equipment. The *Luftwaffe* destroyed approximately 800 Soviet aircraft on the ground and a total of 1,200 during the first day.[150] Many Soviet soldiers surrendered too quickly, yet others fought tenaciously against any odds. The Russian high command in faraway Moscow made the disaster worse by ordering counterattacks where the choice lay between retreat and annihilation.[151] Most military experts thought the Germans would win a quick victory. Yet on the evening of June 22 Churchill broadcast from London: "We shall give whatever help we can to Russia and the Russian people. We shall appeal to our friends, and allies in every part of the world to take the same course, and pursue it, as we shall, faithfully and steadfastly to the end."[152]

Notes

[1]The account in this and the preceding two paragraphs is based upon: Sidney Aster, *1939, The Making of the Second World War* (London, 1973), p. 280*ff*; John Lukacs, *The Last European War, September 1939/December 1941* (Garden City, N.Y., 1976), pp. 30-31, 40-44, 64-65; Vincent J. Esposito (ed.), *A Concise History of World War II,* (New York, 1964), pp. 32-33, 42; Robert Cecil, *Hitler's Decision to Invade Russia, 1941* (London. 1975), pp. 56, 60.

[2]John Henry Wuorinen, *A History of Finland* (New York, 1965), p. 246*ff*; William Richard Mead, *Finland* (New York, 1968), p. 149*ff*.

[3]Allen F. Chew, *The White Death, The Epic of the Soviet Finnish Winter War* (Lansing, Mich., 1971), p. 7.

[4]*Ibid.*, p. 2.

[5]Vincent J. Esposito (ed.), *The West Point Atlas of American Wars* (2 Vols.; New York, 1959), II, Section 2, 8; Baron Mannerheim, *The Memoirs of Marshal Mannerheim* (New York, 1954), p. 360; Chew, *White Death*, pp. 26-27, 223.

[6]Mannerheim, *Memoirs*, p. 371.

[7]Chew, *White Death*, p. 19.

[8]Otto Preston Chaney, Jr., *Zhukov* (Tulsa, Okla., 1971), p. 31.

[9]Mannerheim, *Memoirs*, p. 367.

[10]Chew, *White Death*, p. 19.

[11]*Ibid.*, p. 80.

[12]*Ibid.*, pp. 97-125.

[13]Hans-Adolf Jacobsen, *Kriegstagebuch des Oberkommandos der Wehrmacht, Band I* (Frankfurt am Main, 1965), p. 1156; Chew, *White Death*, p. 123.

[14]Chew, *White Death*, pp. 140-144.

[15]*Ibid.*, p. 139.

[16]*Ibid.*, p. 157*ff*; Mannerheim, *Memoirs*, p. 357.

[17]Mannerheim, *Memoirs*, p. 370; Chew, *White Death*, p. 216; Mead, *Finland*, p. 172.

[18]Anthony Upton, *Finland, 1939-1940* (London, 1974), p. 148*ff*; Chew, *White Death*, p. 206*ff*.

[19]Sir Basil H. Liddell Hart (ed.), *The Red Army* (New York, 1956), p. 85; Chew, *White Death*, p. 212.

[20]Chew, *White Death*, p. 204.

[21]Mannerheim, *Memoirs*, p. 377; Chew, *White Death*, p. 188.

[22]Chew, *White Death*, p. 213.

[23]*Ibid.*, p. 214.

[24]See Andreas Hillgruber, *Hitler's Strategie 1940-1941* (Frankfurt am Main, 1965).

[25]Walter Warlimont, *Inside Hitler's Headquarters 1939-45* (New York, 1964), p. 104*ff*.

[26]Jacobsen, *Kriegstagebuch*, I, 1170.

[27]Ronald Wheatley, *Operation Sea Lion* (Oxford, 1958), pp. 71-72; Jacobsen, *Kreigstagebuch*, I, 1175.

[28]Jacobsen, *Kriegstagebuch*, I, 1177.

[29]Barton Whaley, *Codeword Barbarossa* (Boston, 1973), pp. 172-175; Wheatley, *Sea Lion*, pp. 86-89, 97-98.

[30]Charles B. Burdick, *Germany's Military Strategy and Spain in World War II* (Syracuse, N.Y., 1968), p. 46; Hillgruber, *Hitler's Strategie*, pp. 189-190.

[31]Burdick, *Strategy and Spain*, pp. 35-40.

[32]*Ibid.*, pp. 55-56.

[33]Walter Ansel, *Hitler and the Middle Sea* (Durham, N.C., 1972), pp. 37-39; Burdick, *Strategy and Spain*, pp. 51-52.

[34]Burdick, *Strategy and Spain*, pp. 69-70.

[35]*Ibid.*, pp. 73-74.

[36]Martin van Creveld, *Hitler's Strategy 1940-41, The Balkan Clue* (Cambridge, 1973), p. 87; Burdick, *Strategy and Spain*, pp. 98-105; Ansel, *Middle Sea*, p. 73.

[37]Creveld, *Balkan Clue*, pp. 3-13.

[38]*Ibid.*, pp. 31-32.

[39]Ansel, *Middle Sea*, p. 33; Burdick, *Strategy and Spain*, pp. 49-50; Creveld, *Balkan Clue*, p. 35.

[40]Creveld, *Balkan Clue*, pp. 44-47; I.S.O. Playfair, *The Mediterranean and the Middle East* (London, 1954), p. 226.

[41]Playfair, *Middle East*, p. 228.

[42]*Ibid.*, pp. 334-335.

[43]Mario Cervi, *The Hollow Legions* (New York, 1971), p. xix; Henri Michel, *The Second World War* (New York, 1975), p. 187.

[44]Barry A. Leach, *German Strategy Against Russia 1939-1941* (Oxford, 1973), p. 165; Creveld, *Balkan Clue*, p. 58.

[45]See Robert Lee Wolff, *The Balkans in Our Time* (Harvard University, 1974).

[46]Creveld, *Balkan Clue*, p. 80.

[47]Hillgruber, *Hitler's Strategie*, pp. 406-410; Creveld, *Balkan Clue*, pp. 146-147; Leach, *German Strategy*, p. 165.

[48]Llewellyn Woodward, *British Foreign Policy in the Second World War* (London, 1962), p. 144.

[49]Winston Churchill, *The Grand Alliance* (London, 1950), pp. 16-17.

[50]W. G. McClymount, *To Greece* (Wellington, N.Z., 1959), p. 96.

[51]Churchill, *Grand Alliance*, pp. 59-62.

[52]Sir Henry Maitland Wilson, *Eight Years Overseas 1939-1947* (London, 1948), pp. 69-72; Playfair, *Middle East*, pp. 379-380.

[53]Ian McDougall Steward, *The Struggle for Crete* (Oxford, 1966), pp. 25-28; Playfair, *Middle East*, pp. 382-383.

[54]Churchill, *Grand Alliance*, p. 90.

[55]Playfair, *Middle East*, pp. 74-75; Creveld, *Balkan Clue*, pp. 157-158; George E. Blau, *German Campaigns in the Balkans* (Washington, 1953), p. 35.

[56]Blau, *German Campaigns*, p. 49; Creveld, *Balkan Clue*, p. 158.

[57]Creveld, *Balkan Clue*, p. 166.

[58]Blau, *German Campaigns*, p. 64.

[59]Creveld, *Balkan Clue*, p. 165.

[60]Wolff, *Balkans in Our Time*, pp. 207-213; Robert M. Kennedy, *German Antiguerrilla Operations in the Balkans 1941-1944* (Washington, D.C., 1954), p. 10.

[61]Playfair, *Middle East*, p. 79.

[62]McClymont, *To Greece*, pp. 160-161.

[63]*Ibid.*, pp. 136-146.

[64]Playfair, *Middle East*, p. 86; Wilson, *Eight Years*, p. 85.

[65]Wilson, *Eight Years*, p. 85; McClymont, *To Greece*, p. 169.

[66]Blau, *German Campaigns*, pp. 89-90.

[67]Playfair, *Middle East*, p. 87.

[68]Blau, *German Campaigns*, pp. 93-94; McClymont, *To Greece*, p. 214.

[69]McClymont, *To Greece*, pp. 217-218; Wilson, *Eight Years*,

pp. 89-90.

[70]Playfair, *Middle East*, p. 89.

[71]McClymont, *To Greece*, p. 486.

[72]Creveld, *Balkan Clue*, p. 164; McClymont, *To Greece*, pp. 417-419; Playfair, *Middle East*, p. 101.

[73]Blau, *German Campaigns*, p. 111; McClymont, *To Greece*, pp. 448-468.

[74]McClymont, *To Greece*, p. 486.

[75]Jacobsen, *Kriegstagebuch*, I, 1204.

[76]Playfair, *Middle East*, p. 124; Stewart, *Crete*, p. 36.

[77]David Marcus Davin, *Crete* (Wellington, N.Z., 1953), p. 480; S. W. C. Pack, *The Battle for Crete* (London, 1973), p. 20.

[78]Davin, *Crete*, p. 482.

[79]Stewart, *Crete*, p. 112.

[80]*Ibid.*, p. 97.

[81]Hans-Adolf Jacobsen (ed.), *Decisive Battles of World War II: The German Point of View* (New York, 1965), p. 102.

[82]Donald E. Cluxton, Jr., "Concepts of Airborne Warfare in World War II" (Unpublished M.A. Thesis; Duke University, Durham, N.C., 1967), pp. xxiii-xxv.

[83]Walter Hubatsch, *Hitler's Weisungen für die Kriegführung, 1939-1945* (Frankfurt am Main, 1962), pp. 115-116.

[84]Blau, *German Campaigns*, p. 126; Davin, *Crete*, p. 85; Playfair, *Middle East*, pp. 128-129; Pack, *Crete*, p. 21.

[85]Blau, *German Campaigns*, pp. 125-126; Davin, *Crete*, p. 85; Playfair, *Middle East*, p. 129; Stewart, *Crete*, p. 79.

[86]Davin, *Crete*, p. 83.

[87]Stewart, *Crete*, pp. 89-90; Jacobsen, *Battles*, pp. 117-118.

[88]Frederick W. Winterbotham, *The Ultra Secret* (New York, 1974), pp. 67-68; Ronald Lewin, *Ultra Goes to War* (New York, 1978), pp. 157-159.

[89]Stewart, *Crete*, p. 60.

[90]Churchill, *Grand Alliance*, p. 281.

[91]Stewart, *Crete*, p. 140.

[92]*Ibid.*, pp. 130-132.

[93]Alan Clark, *The Fall of Crete* (London, 1962), p. 56; Joseph F. Cody, *28 (Maori) Battalion* (Wellington, N.Z., 1956), p. 90; Stewart, *Crete*, pp. 147-153.

[94]Davin, *Crete*, p. 182; Jacobsen, *Battles,* p. 123.

[95]Stewart, *Crete*, pp. 226-228.

[96]*Ibid.*, p. 228.

[97]Cody, *28 Battalion*, pp. 101-107; Stewart, *Crete*, pp. 346-347.

[98]Pack, *Crete*, pp. 31-32; Stewart, *Crete*, pp. 279-281.

[99]Pack, *Crete*, p. 54.

[100]Davin, *Crete*, p. 294.

[101]Stewart, *Crete*, p. 377.

[102]Pack, *Crete*, p. 73; Stewart, *Crete*, pp. 448-449.

[103]Davin, *Crete*, pp. 434-435; Stewart, *Crete*, p. 439; Cody, *28 Battalion*, p. 132.

[104]David A. Thomas, *Crete 1941* (London, 1972), p. 18 and Appendix C; Davin, *Crete*, pp. 486-488 and Appendix V; Playfair, *Middle East*, p. 147.

[105]Stewart, *Crete*, p. 474; Pack, *Crete*, pp. 84-85.

[106]Davin, *Crete*, p. 488; Jacobsen, *Battles*, p. 130; Blau, *German Campaigns*, pp. 140-141.

[107]Davin, *Crete*, p. 228; Stewart, *Crete*, p. 102.

[108]Helmuth Greiner, *Die Oberste Wehrmachtführung* (Wiesbaden, 1951), pp. 325-326; Franz Halder, *Kriegstagebuch* (6 vols.; Stuttgart, 1961-64), II, 213.

[109]Halder, *Kriegstagebuch*, II, 318-319.

[110]Hillgruber, *Hitler's Strategie*, p. 503; Jacobsen, *Kriegstagebuch*, I, 361.

[111]Creveld, *Balkan Clue*, p. 171.

[112]Hillgruber, *Hitler's Strategie*, p. 505.

[113]Creveld, *Balkan Clue*, p. 171.

[114]Halder, *Kriegstagebuch*, II, 387.

[115]Halder, *Kriegstagebuch*, II, 435; Hillgruber, *Hitler's Strategie*, p. 507.

[116]Hillgruber, *Hitler's Strategie*, p. 505; Blau, *German Campaigns*, p. 150.

[117]Adolf Hitler, *Mein Kampf* (Munich, 1924); Henry Picker (ed.), *Hitler's Tischgespräche in Führerhauptquartier 1941-42* (Stuttgart, 1963); Hillgruber, *Hitler's Strategie*, pp. 207 and 519; Karl Dietrich Bracher, *The German Dictatorship* (New York, 1970), pp. 407-408.

[118]Halder, *Kriegstagebuch*, II, 32, 49; Hillgruber, *Hitler's Strategie*, pp. 216-218.

[119]George E. Blau, *The German Campaign in Russia—Planning and Operations (1940-1942)* (Washington, D.C., 1955), p. 4.

[120]*Ibid.*, pp. 14-17.

[121]Walter Warlimont, *Inside Hitler's Headquarters, 1939-45* (New York,1964), pp. 156-157.

[122]Blau, *Campaign in Russia*, pp. 20-21; Hillgruber, *Hitler's Strategie*, pp. 267-268.

[123]Ansel, *Middle Sea*, pp. 68-70; Hillgruber, *Hitler's Strategie*, p. 363; Leach, *German Strategy*, pp. 107-112; Jacobsen, *Kriegstagebuch*, I, 205; Halder, *Kriegstagebuch*, II, 211-214.

[124]Warlimont, *Headquarters*, pp. 138-139.

[125]Hubatsch, *Weisungen*, pp. 84-88.

[126]Hillgruber, *Hitler's Strategie*, p. 503; Blau, *Campaign in Russia*, p. 34; Warlimont, *Headquarters*, p. 414.

[127]Hillgruber, *Hitler's Strategie*, p. 364.

[128]Leach, *German Strategy*, pp. 178-179; Hillgruber, *Hitler's Strategie*, p. 418.

[129]Warlimont, *Headquarters*, pp. 148-171; Hillgruber, *Hitler's Strategie*, pp. 526-532; Albert Seaton, *The Russo-German War 1941-45* (New York, 1970), p. 54.

[130]Raul Hilberg, *The Destruction of the European Jews* (Chicago, 1961), pp. 177-190; Heinz Höhne, *The Order of the Death's Head* (New York, 1967), pp. 410-412.

[131]Alan S. Milward, *The German Economy at War* (London, 1965).

[132]F. M. von Senger und Etterlin, *German Tanks of World War II* (New York, 1964), Appendix II.

[133]Seaton, *Russo-German War*, p. 71.

[134]Milward, *German Economy*, p. 45.

[135]Leach, *German Strategy*, p. 94.

[136]*Ibid.*, p. 130.

[137]Jacobsen, *Battles*, p. 140; Hillgruber, *Hitler's Strategie*, p. 537; Leach, *German Strategy*, p. 192.

[138]Richard M. Ogorkiewicz, *Armor, A History of Mechanized Forces* (New York, 1960), p. 214.

[139]Hillgruber, *Hitler's Strategie*, p. 537.

[140]G. Warren Nutter, *Growth of Industrial Production in the Soviet Union* (Princeton, 1962), p. 289.

[141]Nutter, *Industrial Production*, p. 210; Hillgruber, *Hitler's Strategie*, p. 438; Albert Seaton, *The Battle for Moscow* (New York, 1971), p. 30.

[142]Kenneth Macksey, *Tank, A History of the Armoured Fighting Vehicle* (New York, 1971), p. 193; Seaton, *Russo-German War*, p. 30.

[143]Whaley, *Codeword Barbarossa*, p. 19.
[144]*Ibid.*, pp. 114-116, 157.
[145]*Ibid.*, pp. 70-73, 98-103.
[146]*Ibid.*, pp. 31-32.
[147]*Ibid.*, pp. 109-111.
[148]Vladmir Petrov (ed.), *June 22, 1941, Soviet Historians and the German Invasion* (Columbia, S.C., 1968), pp. 217-218.
[149]Konstantin Rokossovski, *A Soldier's Duty* (Moscow, 1970), p. 9.
[150]Petrov, *22 June*, p. 222; Richard C. Lukas, *Eagles East* (Tallahassie, Florida, 1970), pp. 9-10.
[151]Adam B. Ulam, *Stalin* (New York, 1973), p. 539; Vasily Ye. Savkin, *The Basic Principles of Operational Art and Tactics* (Moscow, 1972) (US Air Force translation), p. 269.
[152]Charles Eade (ed.), *The War Speeches of the Rt. Hon. Winston S. Churchill* (3 vols.; London, 1946), I, 453.

Cannae on a Vast Scale: The Russo-German War to Stalingrad

5

The Nazi regime is indistinguishable from the worst features of Communism. It is devoid of all theme and principle except appetite and racial domination. It excels all forms of human wickedness in the efficiency of its cruelty and ferocious aggression. No one has been a more consistent opponent of Communism than I have for the last twenty-five years. I will unsay no word that I have spoken about it. But all this fades away before the spectacle which is now unfolding.

Winston S. Churchill,
Radio Broadcast, June 22, 1941

The World Holds Its Breath:
BARBAROSSA

As the Germans invaded the Soviet Union, they had only a vague grand strategy as reflected in the BARBAROSSA directive of December 18, 1940, but their mechanized and armored forces were initially concentrated in the Second and Third Panzer Groups (later Armies) assigned to Field Marshal Fedor von Bock's Army Group Center.[1] *(See Map 19, in Atlas.)* This concentration suggested a continuing offensive over the land bridge to Moscow (through Minsk, Smolensk and Vyazma), the strategy most German generals favored. On June 22, Army Group Center plunged into White Russia north of the Pripet Marshes, an area of heavy forests, sparse population and few roads. Many roads were only narrow tracks through the forests, and few bridges were of solid construction capable of bearing armor.[2] Infantry divisions on the march occupied over 20 miles of road and often slowed the motorized formations despite strict traffic control.[3] Nevertheless, Bock's Army Group advanced rapidly with the *panzer* groups on its flanks. On the left, the Third Panzer Group struck from East Prussia, while the Second Panzer Group moved past Brest-Litovsk, on the right flank. *(See Map 19, in Atlas.)* Bock and his armored commanders, General Hermann Hoth—commanding the Third Panzer Group—and General Heinz Guderian—commanding the Second Panzer Group—wanted to join the armored pincers in the Smolensk area at an operative depth of approximately 600 kilometers. General Franz Halder, the OKH Chief of Staff, approved this plan, but Hitler thought his commanders were too bold and refused to take the risk.[4] Instead, the enveloping forces converged on the White Russian capital, Minsk, arriving there on June 27.[5] The large Russian pocket west of Minsk contained the Soviet Third and Tenth Armies and elements of three other armies, a total of 290,000 prisoners of war.[6]

Surprised by superior forces, the Soviets were certain to lose the opening phases of the war, but inept leadership made their defeats the greater. It appears that Stalin may have suffered a brief emotional collapse before recovering his nerve.[7] Even the operations section of the Soviet General Staff in Moscow was crowded into unsuitable quarters and had poor communications to the Front headquarters.[8] ("Front" was the Soviet term for an army group. Roughly speaking, all Soviet formations were smaller than their nominal German equivalents.) The Red Army relied almost entirely on wire communications suspended from poles, which became extremely unreliable under combat conditions. The Soviets had very few radios and their radio code system was almost unworkable.[9] Relying on such communications, Soviet officers rapidly lost control of their formations, even at the highest levels. The Soviet commander of the West Front in White Russia had so little combat intelligence that he did not know his forces were surrounded until the Germans broadcast the news.[10] He was

German Machinegun Crews in a Russian Village, 1941

tried by court martial and executed; meanwhile, Marshal Semen Konstantinovich Timoshenko, who had won the winter war against Finland, assumed command of the West Front.[11] Through this injustice, Stalin tried to divert the blame for his own incompetence. Such influence as he exerted on operations was generally disastrous because he insisted on static defense.[12] Admittedly, the Red Army lacked the training and experience to fight a mobile war in 1941, but at least the Soviet forces might have fought their way out of encirclement. Mistakes in leadership sacrificed men and equipment in very large quantities, making the German task easier.

After the Minsk pocket was cleared in early July, Army Group Center resumed its advance with the Fourth Army, to which Hoth's and Guderian's *panzer* groups were now subordinated.[13] The Ninth Army and Second Army moved behind the spearheads and fanned out to cover the flanks of the advance. In contrast to the Minsk operation, this new advance was conducted with less intention to envelop the Russians[14] and greater concern for flank security because the Fourth Army no longer had the Pripet Marshes on its right flank and Army Group North lacked the armored strength to keep pace. While German engineers were converting the Soviet railways to European gauge (or beginning operation with captured or converted rolling stock), they had to supply the armored spearheads by truck transport from depots far behind the front.[15] Although the infantry marched up to 30 miles a day, it could hardly keep pace with the armor.[16] This affected the German advance because decisive engagement depended upon the staying power of the infantry divisions.

In spite of reinforcing the West Front from the Smolensk area, the Soviets were wholly unable to halt the German advance. On occasion, Soviet discipline collapsed at the sight of German armor, leaving the officers to collect stragglers and improvise a defense.[17] Advancing on a fairly wide front, Hoth's Third Panzer Group reached Vitebsk by mid-July and passed north of Smolensk; Guderian's Second Panzer Group crossed the Dnieper at Mogilev on July 10.[18] *(See Map 19, in Atlas.)* The Russians counterattacked desperately on the flanks of the German advance, even recapturing Rogachev on the Dnieper on July 13.[19] But the Germans held their flanks and entered Smolensk on the sixteenth.[20] The Soviet Sixteenth and Twentieth Armies were trapped west of Smolensk and attacked towards the city, while other West Front armies tried to relieve them. The Germans held the ring, however, and cleared the Smolensk pocket by August 5, taking approximately 300,000 prisoners.[21]

In two great battles of encirclement, Bock's Army Group Center had destroyed the armies defending White Russia and taken about 600,000 prisoners. Here was *blitzkrieg* success on a grand scale. Confidence ran high among the Germans, who felt they must be nearing the end of the campaign. Even the cautious and deliberate Halder confided to his diary: "It is no exaggeration, when I claim that the Russian campaign was won in fourteen days. Of course it is not yet ended. The great distances and the bitter resistance will concern us for many weeks to come."[22] Expecting the Germans to continue towards Moscow, the Russians brought up still more armies and counterattacked vigorously throughout August. When Army Group Center went on the defensive, the Soviets imagined they had won a victory,[23] but the explanation lay elsewhere.

Army Groups North and South could not conduct spectacular double envelopments like the Minsk and Smolensk operations, because they lacked enough *schnelle Verbände* (the mechanized and armored troops). These Army Groups were one-armed, in the sense of having only one *panzer* group each. Of the two, Army Group North had the easier mission. Its assembly areas were on German territory in East Prussia, and the populations of the Baltic countries in its path were hostile to the Russian government. However, the wooded and swampy Baltic lowlands offer little terrain suitable for maneuver.[24] This terrain and its own lack of armor prevented Army Group North from making the spectacular progress of Army Group Center. Still, the Germans easily destroyed counterattacking armor and crossed the Dvina River on June 26.[25] From this point, operations were somewhat hampered by disagreements between Field Markshal Ritter von Leeb, commanding the Army Group, and General Erich Hoepner, commanding the Fourth Panzer Group. Leeb was a conservative officer, who failed to grasp all the possibilities of a dynamic use of armored forces, while Hoepner was an impetuous commander very similar to the aggressive Guderian.[26] Leeb wished the Fourth Panzer Group to cover his right flank by advancing towards Lake Ilmen through swamp and forest, while Hoepner preferred to advance rapidly over the best route to Leningrad. *(See Map 19, in Atlas.)* Because neither view prevailed entirely, the armored formations could have been better employed.[27] As usual, Hitler feared the boldness of his armored commanders. Afraid that Hoepner would attempt a dangerous race for Leningrad, he began to interfere daily with operations, exasperating Halder.[28] Despite these divided counsels, Army Group North advanced into Estonia and beyond Lake Peipus by mid-July.

Waffen SS Light Machinegunner, Russia 1941

A Secondary Road in Russia, 1941

Army Group South was least well-prepared and had the most difficult mission. Originally, Hitler had planned a double envelopment converging on the Kiev area, but in mid-March he decided that the Army Group should mass its strength on the left in an advance towards Kiev.[29] This decision was sound because Army Group South had only five armored divisions and even these were a bit worn from the Balkan campaign. The Rumanian Fourth Army, which would attack Bessarabia on the right flank, lacked modern equipment, including armor and antitank guns. Moreover, the Rumanian border had to be strongly defended in order to keep the Russians away from the Ploesti oil fields. On the other side, the Soviets had assembled their strongest formations in the Ukraine, expecting that an invader would concentrate his force there.[30] This Soviet strategy was sound for several reasons. First, industry was concentrated in the bend of the Donets River, much as German industry was concentrated in the Rhineland. *(See Map 19, in Atlas.)* Approximately 60 percent of Russia's coal and 30 percent of her iron came from this region. In addition, an invasion of the Ukraine could cut Russia off from the great Baku oil fields on the Caspian Sea, which then produced 70 percent of the country's oil.[31] To make the situation worse, the Ukrainians chafed under Soviet Russian rule and might help the invader. Finally, the wide, often featureless Ukrainian plain offers the best tank country in European Russia. For all these reasons, the Russians were justified in thinking the Germans would make their main effort in the Ukraine.

Field Marshal Gerd von Rundstedt, commanding Army Group South, planned to attack south towards Kiev and secure bridgeheads on the Dnieper River for subsequent operations, allowing the Pripet Marshes to cover his left flank. The Eleventh Army in Rumania would await the outcome of this operation, then advance cautiously into the Ukraine while the Rumanian Fourth Army advanced towards Odessa.[32] As the campaign actually developed, General Ewald von Kleist, commanding the First Panzer Group, advanced methodically, winning numerous small armor engagements and reached Zhitomir, about 90 miles from Kiev, on July 9.[33] As the German Eleventh Army moved over the Prut River into Bessarabia, Kleist's deep thrust endangered the Soviet armies still deployed close to the Polish and Rumanian borders. But, perhaps learning from the Minsk encirclement, the Soviet high command ordered the Southwest Front to withdraw quickly.[34] The Soviet Fifth Army took up a strong defensive position with its back to the Pripet Marshes and attacked vigorously along Rundstedt's left flank. *(See Map 19, in Atlas.)* This single Russian army was to have a profound effect on Hitler's direction of the campaign. Despite the earlier withdrawal, most of the Soviet Sixth and Twelfth Armies, about 20 divisions in all, were surrounded on August 2 in the Uman area. The Uman pocket yielded about 103,000 prisoners of war.[35]

The overall situation by the beginning of August was favorable to the Germans, but they had not obtained a major objective. As yet they did not menace Leningrad, Moscow nor the Donets Basin; nor had they enjoyed decisive military success, except in White Russia. On the other hand, they had won every major battle, overrun most of the Baltic countries, captured the land-bridge to Moscow through Smolensk, and were nearing Kiev. Although buoyant with success, the German generals began to realize that they could not press forward everywhere at once if Soviet resistance continued. They must pursue a grand strategy assuring economy of force.

Although appearing monolithic from the outside, National-Socialist Germany was confused and even chaotic when seen from the inside.[36] This state, which worshipped strong leadership, actually had less central direction than Churchill's England or Roosevelt's America. The vagueness and lack of definite priorities typical of National-Socialism showed even in the military sphere. The original BARBAROSSA directive of December 18, 1940, had emphasized the envelopment and annihilation of the Red Army, followed by the capture of Leningrad and Moscow in that order.[37] But this choice of objective reflected no more than Hitler's whim of the moment.[38] The vague planning merely concealed the disagreement between Hitler and his generals, who all tended to assume that the Red Army would collapse before a strategic decision became necessary. As Soviet resistance continued through the summer of 1941, the disagreement surfaced again. The direction of the war became fumbling and uncertain because Hitler, although he had no clear strategy in mind, refused to let his generals make their own decisions.

Hitler had never thought that Moscow was the most important objective. As between Leningrad and the Donets area, the longer he thought, the more he agreed with the Russians, who had always expected the main effort in the Ukraine. On July 4, Hitler told the OKW Chief of Staff, General Alfred Jodl, that he was debating whether to turn north or south after crossing the Dvina and Dnieper Rivers. Jodl at once asked Halder to study whether the Third and Second Panzer Groups should be diverted north and south respectively.[39]

Halder was in an unenviable position because his own ideas ran exactly counter to Hitler's. Above all else, Halder dreaded a shift to the positional warfare characteristic of the First World War, which would cancel the German advantage in mobile operations. Once both sides went into the trenches, the Russians would have time to raise new armies and subject the Germans to attrition. With the chance for a quick victory gone, the Germans might face the dreaded two-front war again, caught between Great Britain and Russia. To avoid a *Stellungskrieg* (trench warfare), Halder thought the Germans must retain the initiative by concentrating their forces and striking boldly into Russia. All other operations must be subordinated to a single great drive towards a primary objective, Moscow being the best choice. The Russians would commit all available force to defend the capital and the Germans would envelop and destroy the bulk of the Red Army on the approaches to the city. When Moscow fell, the Russians would also lose their political and administrative center and a transportation nexus. The country would be split in halves and Russian morale would be severely affected.[40] Based on this reasoning, Halder preferred to make no large diversions of the armored formations assigned to Army Group Center. Instead, Hoth and Guderian should advance on the flanks of a drive towards Moscow and close yet a third pincer around the defending armies.

Hitler contemptuously disregarded Halder's rather unimaginative but very sound advice. Instead, he issued directives on July 19 and 23 for an entirely different strategy.[41] In a flush of optimism, Hitler proposed to advance everywhere at once. Hoth's Third Panzer Group would drive northeast, cut the communications between Moscow and Leningrad, and assist Army Group North in Leningrad's capture. Guderian's Second Panzer Group would swing south and cooperate with Army Group South in destroying the Soviet Fifth Army and all Soviet armies still west of the Dnieper River. Then the First and Second Panzer Groups would lead the way through the industrial city of Kharkov over the Don River and into the Caucasus. Now stripped of its armor, Army Group Center would clear out Soviet resistance in the Smolensk area and advance towards Moscow with infantry alone. This strategy only made sense if the Russians were on the verge of a total collapse. And Hitler's generals did not share this delusion. Field Marshal Walther von Brauchitsch, the Army Commander-in-Chief, said frankly that these objectives were unattainable, especially for Army Group Center.[42]

Persuaded that his strategy was unfeasible for the moment, Hitler issued a new directive on July 30 which cancelled the previous directives.[43] Without assistance from the Third Panzer Group, Army Group North was to continue the advance on Leningrad with the *Schwerpunkt* north of Lake Ilmen. Army Group South was to destroy the Soviet Fifth Army and the remaining armies west of the Dnieper without help from the Second Panzer Group. Army Group Center was to take up defensive positions, withdraw its armored formations from the front, and bring them up to strength. In the preamble to the directive, Hitler admitted frankly that the Soviet resistance in the area of Army Group Center and logistical difficulties had forced the change in plans. By deferring his ultimate decision on strategy, Hitler at least gave the armored divisions a much-needed chance to refit, but of course the Russians had the same time to reinforce. In early August, Hitler visited the headquarters of Army Groups Center and South, probably more to convince Bock and Rundstedt than to hear his generals' opinions. By this time, he had at last sorted out his own ideas, retaining his preference regarding objectives for Leningrad, then the Ukraine, with Moscow a distant third.[44] His generals remained unconvinced.

On August 7, Halder tried to enlist the support of OKW by discussing strategy with Jodl.[45] Halder argued that the Soviet forces in the Korosten area, that is the Fifth Army *(See Map 19, in Atlas)* should not dictate German strategy. Rather than disperse strength by replying to this minor flank attack, the Germans should seek a decision in wide-reaching operations. Following this discussion, Jodl submitted an OKW memorandum to Hitler, arguing for an all-out drive on Moscow.[46] By this time, a decision was overdue. The Germans had already suffered more than 260,000 casualties in the campaign. Ominously, they had also identified approximately 360 Soviet divisions as compared to the 200 they had anticipated.[47] Hope for a decisive victory in 1941 rode on a bold strategy. On August 18, Halder made a last attempt to convince Hitler that Army Group Center should start at once for Moscow.[48] Halder pointed out that this operation would require the Second and Third Panzer Groups, that these groups could complete only one great operation before winter, and that a Moscow operation should not continue beyond October. To exploit their qualitative superiority, Halder argued, the Germans should attack exactly where the Russians were massing their forces—that is, in front of Army Group Center. In its own memorandum of the same date, OKW supported an operation towards Moscow with similar arguments.[49]

Utterly heedless of this professional advice, Hitler reasserted his own ideas. On August 20, he ended the controversy over strategy by announcing that he entirely disagreed with his generals. Moscow was not the most important objective. The first priority objectives fell to Army Groups North and South. Army Group North was to besiege Leningrad and make contact with the Finns. Army Group South was to reach the Crimea and the Donets industrial area, then cut off the supply of oil from the Caucasus.[50] During August, Army Group Center had captured Gomel and Army Group South had reached the Dnieper River, thus creating a huge salient in the Russian line. Hitler laid special emphasis on attacking this salient upon both flanks and thus surrounding the Soviet Fifth Army which was still defending north of Kiev.

On August 23, Halder held a conference at Army Group Center headquarters and heard Guderian argue against diverting his *panzer* group into the Ukraine. In view of the expected logistical problems and the extremely poor road conditions, Guderian doubted that his armor could operate in the Ukraine and still participate in a subsequent attack on Moscow. In the hope of impressing Hitler, Halder brought Guderian to the OKW-OKH headquarters near Rastenburg in East Prussia (now Ketrzyn in Poland). Guderian conferred with Hitler on the evening of August 23 and strongly advocated an advance on Moscow, emphasizing that his soldiers were eager to continue the advance on the Soviet capital. Hitler listened to Guderian, but refused to change his mind. In rejoinder, he described the natural riches of the Ukraine and observed:[51] "My generals know nothing about the economic aspects of war." With no one from OKH present, Guderian found himself alone in opposition to Hitler and felt obliged to carry out the dictator's decision loyally. When he learned on the following day that Guderian had abandoned his opposition to the Kiev operation, Halder became bitter and confided to his diary that Guderian lacked strength of character.[52] In fact, very few officers could match Halder's honest determination and sense of duty. (In November 1942, Halder lost his position and was later imprisoned by Hitler, while Guderian, although relieved of field command, served Hitler to the end.)

Following Hitler's orders, the Germans began a great battle of encirclement in the western Ukraine on August 25.[53] The Second Army and Guderian's Second Panzer Group attacked south from the Gomel area, crossed the Desna River and quickly penetrated the Soviet Twenty-First and Fortieth Armies on their front.[54] The advance was somewhat risky for Guderian, whose group was attacked on both flanks.[55] *(See Map 20, in Atlas.)* Despite the earlier opportunity to refit, Guderian's best *panzer* division was at 80 percent strength, while the others averaged about half strength.[56] As Guderian's troops moved south, General Kleist's First Panzer Group broke out of its Dnieper bridgeheads and drove north, seeking a junction with Guderian's troops about 150 miles east of Kiev. Meanwhile, the German Sixth Army assaulted the Soviet Fifth Army and crossed first the Dnieper, then the Desna River. As so often before, Stalin reacted tardily to the threat and failed to authorize a general retreat in time.[57] His generals were still trying to extract a decision from him when Guderian and Kleist joined their forces at Lokhvitsa on September 16. The enormous Kiev pocket contained the Soviet Fifth Army, which had long obstructed the advance of Army Group South, together with the Twenty-First, Twenty-Sixth, Thirty-Seventh, and elements of the Thirty-Eighth and Fortieth Armies, a total of 665,000 prisoners according to German records.[58] Here was a tactical success so great as to seem strategic in its consequences. By the end of September, OKW estimated that Russian losses in the campaign must total 2.5 million men, 22,000 guns and 18,000 tanks.[59] How much longer could the Russians sustain losses on this scale?

Did Hitler make a serious error by detaching the Second Army and Second Panzer Group to assist Army Group South in the Kiev encirclement? This question has been much debated. At the time, Brauchitsch, Halder, Bock, Guderian and Jodl all thought Army Group Center should continue its advance towards Moscow. With varying emphasis, they argued that a diversion towards the south would be an undesirable dispersion of effort. To fully realize their advantage in mobile war, the Germans should concentrate their forces for bold thrusts; moreover, the best killing ground lay on the approaches to Moscow. In opposing his generals, Hitler used a number of convenient, but often contradictory arguments. At times he argued for the quick envelopment of the Soviet Fifth Army, as though this tactical concern were paramount. He was undoubtedly irritated by Fifth Army's defensive success and wished to destroy it. On the other hand, Hitler advanced a fundamental argument for the primacy of economic objectives in modern war. Here he was on much more solid ground and his preference for the Ukraine over Moscow made considerable sense. Certainly the Donets industry was more important to the Soviet war effort than was Moscow. But after the Kiev envelopment, Hitler promptly ignored his own priorities and reverted to the advance on Moscow which his generals wanted. The generals' thinking is clear, but Hitler's motives are hard to define. Probably he was not clear in his own mind and let himself be swayed by impulses of the moment and reports of tactical success or failure. Perhaps Jodl was right in suspecting that Hitler had an instinctive aversion to Moscow because of the Napoleonic campaign.[60]

It would have been extremely odd if one emotionally unbalanced amateur had shown more wisdom than OKW, OKH, and experienced field commanders combined. Hitler was probably wrong and his generals were probably right. However, Hitler's interference may have had only a marginal effect on the campaign.[61] After all, the Kiev encirclement was one of the greatest German victories of the war. It destroyed entire Soviet armies and opened the rich Ukraine to German invasion. If Hitler had listened to his generals and continued toward Moscow, the city would have fallen, but the Soviets would certainly have continued the war. Even in possession of Moscow, the Germans would still have been overextended in winter. Because Moscow presented a definite objective within striking distance which the Soviets had to defend, the generals were right to prefer it; but Germany was not likely to end the war in 1941, whatever strategy was adopted. The decision to continue the advance on Moscow during November was the disastrous decision, but the generals concurred in it, despite some misgivings. Strangely enough, Hitler deserves the full credit for the Kiev victory but not the full blame for continuing the Moscow offensive after the weather had broken.

If no diversion had been made, Army Group Center could have renewed its advance towards Moscow in mid-August rather than at the end of September. In other words, the diversion cost Army Group Center about six weeks and thus saved Moscow. It also caused great wear on the mechanized equipment. But timetables do not tell the whole story of the campaign. Every step the Germans took in Russia cost them men and equipment. At the beginning of August, the Germans had lost 213,000 officers and men in combat.[62] By the end of September, combat losses totaled 534,950 officers and men or about 15 percent of the 3.4 million men in Russia.[63] Only about half these losses could be promptly replaced. The losses and shortfall were naturally greatest in the *panzer* and first-line infantry divisions. Even when replacements arrived, they usually lacked the combat experience of the men they replaced. Losses in equipment were still heavier, through wear as much as combat. At the beginning of the Kiev encirclement, the German divisions had less than half their authorized tank strength available for combat.[64] At the end of September, only the Fourth Panzer Group was at authorized strength, while the First and Third Panzer Groups were at 70 to 80 percent strength.[65] Guderian's Second Panzer Group was at only 50 percent strength after the Kiev battle and received only 100 replacement tanks.[66] German armor production was insufficient to replace the losses, even when the supply system functioned adequately. The German forces experienced similar shortages in motor vehicles, petroleum products, and even weapons. As the campaign progressed, they took increasing amounts of Soviet artillery and antitank guns into service. All these shortages pointed to the need for a clear and definite strategy that economized force, but Hitler continued to grasp for every objective like a greedy child.

In the meantime, the Germans and their Finnish co-belligerents converged on Leningrad in the north, the objective given first priority in the BARBAROSSA directive. In mid-July, Army Group North reached the Luga River east of Lake Peipus, but there the attack stalled. *(See Map 19, in Atlas.)* By the end of July, the German Eighteenth Army had reached Lake Ilmen,[67] but the wooded and swampy terrain in this area was totally unsuited for the employment of Hoepner's Fourth Panzer Group.[68] South of Lake Ilmen, in the area of Staraya Russia, the Russians attacked so strongly in mid-August that

Leningrad as Seen From the German Trenches

Hitler detached the XXXIX Motorized Corps from the Third Panzer Group to ward off danger.[69] With this reinforcement, Leeb's Army Group went over to the offensive in late August. *(See Map 20, in Atlas.)* The Eighteenth Army captured Novgorod and advanced towards Tikhvin over difficult terrain against increasing resistance. The Sixteenth Army reached Demyansk near the Valdai Hills in early September. The Soviets reacted by reorganizing their commands and committing fresh armies. The Leningrad, Karelian and Northwest Fronts were subordinated directly to the Soviet high command (*Stavka*) in Moscow which sent General Georgi Konstantinovich Zhukov to command the Leningrad Front during September.[70] Leningrad was the first front-level command for Zhukov, who would become Russia's foremost soldier.

Now fighting against favorable odds, the Finnish Karelian Army attacked on July 10 and quickly drove the Soviet Seventh and Twenty-third Armies back over the 1939 frontier. Just 30 miles north of Leningrad, the Finns went on the defensive. *(Operations not shown on map.)* The Germans pleaded and threatened in an attempt to induce them to cross the Svir River east of Lake Ladoga and link up with Army Group North or to attack Leningrad from the north. But the Finns refused to interest themselves in Leningrad and came to a halt just south of the Svir. Having accomplished their war aims, the Finns would not advance farther. But neither would they negotiate with the Russians, whose defeat they expected. In northern Finland, General Nikolaus von Falkenhorst commanded the German Army of Norway, comprising two corps. The Mountain Corps attacked on June 29 from the Petsamo area towards Murmansk, an important seaport.[71] At the same time, the XXXVI Corps attacked towards Salla with the intention of reaching the Murmansk railway at Kandalasha. The Soviet Fourteenth Army defended Murmansk successfully against the Mountain Corps and the XXXVI Corps made little progress beyond Salla. Due to the extremes of climate and the often thickly wooded terrain, the Army of Norway (in November, designated the Army of Lapland under General Eduard Dietl) never accomplished much. Perhaps the Germans might have done better in Finland had they concentrated on one objective instead of attacking in such widely separated areas.[72]

Apparently, Hitler's decision to make Leningrad a primary objective was irrational, springing from blind hatred for the home of the Russian Revolution. Had he wished to use the city as an assembly area and depot for ship transport over the Baltic Sea, he would have wished to capture it intact. Instead, he ordered Leningrad encircled and attacked from the air with the express purpose of destroying the city and its inhabitants.[73] At the time, Hitler argued that the Germans could not accept the casualties incurred through combat in built-up areas, nor assume responsibility for feeding the urban population in winter. On September 8, the German Eighteenth Army reached the southwestern end of Lake Ladoga, cutting the land route to Leningrad.[74] Two days later, the XXXI Panzer Corps captured high ground about seven miles from the city permitting visual observation; but then the Corps was returned to Army Group Center control and the attack came to a halt.[75] Following Hitler's wishes, the Eighteenth Army proceeded to bombard Leningrad, but it lacked the heavy artillery to do great damage.[76] The *Luftwaffe* soon curtailed its attacks on Leningrad because the planes were needed to support the renewed attack of Army Group Center. Without the strength to capture Leningrad, Army Group North dug positions for a long siege, expecting to starve the city. Even the siege positions were not ideal. The Soviet Eighth Army (Coastal Command) still clung to the Baltic coast opposite the Kronstadt naval base and the Russians could still reach Leningrad across Lake Ladoga. *(See Map 20, in Atlas.)* Content with these half measures, Hitler gave his attention to the impending operations of Bock's Army Group.

Flucht Nach Vorn: *The Attack on Moscow*

Since early August, Bock's Army Group Center had fended off the counterattacks of Timoshenko's West Front, while armored strength was diverted to the adjacent army groups. In his restless, illogical way, Hitler neglected the Ukraine following the Kiev encirclement and returned to the objective his generals had originally advocated. Although Rundstedt lost the support of the Second Panzer Group, his weakened Army Group South was still expected to seize the Crimea and advance to Rostov on the Don. Earlier, OKH had insisted that an advance on Moscow must begin in early September to avoid the autumn rains. Desperate to reach some objective before winter, the German Army staff now planned this operation for the end of September, as outlined by Hitler's Directive 35 of August 6.[77] The OKH plan, code-named TYPHOON, foresaw yet another great envelopment, similar to the earlier one in the Minsk area. The northern pincer was formed of the Ninth Army and Hoth's Third Panzer Group. The southern pincer consisted of the Fourth Army and Hoepner's Fourth Panzer Group, which had been detached from Army Group North for the operation. The two *panzer* Groups were to close at Vyazma, approximately 80 miles behind the Soviet forces facing Smolensk. Since Guderian's Second Panzer Group could not return from the Ukraine in time, it was ordered to attack with the Second Army from the Glukhov area northeast towards Tula south of Moscow. *(See Map 20, in Atlas.)* To provide sufficient force for TYPHOON, OKH took five *panzer* and two motorized divisions from Leeb and nine divisions, including two *panzer* and two motorized divisions, from Rundstedt.[78] As a natural result, Army Groups North and South soon ran into difficulties. In all, Army Group Center now had over 70 divisions, including 14 *panzer* and 8 motorized divisions.[79] Although many of these units were well below authorized strength, the Germans undoubtedly enjoyed a numerical advantage at the initiation of TYPHOON. General Albert Kesselring's Second Air Force was to provide tactical air support with approximately 1,000 aircraft. The *Luftwaffe*'s losses in Russia had been so great that on September 6 less than 2,000 aircraft were combat-ready on the entire front.[80]

Despite their appalling losses, the Russians still had some causes for hope. After a poor start, Stalin had slowly emerged as a competent wartime leader because he had enough sense to seek and follow good advice. The *Stavka*, a Soviet counterpart to the German General Staff, served both as staff and as a pool of gifted and experienced commanders, who took up front or theater commands as necessary. In this flexible system, the *Stavka* planned operations in close cooperation with front headquarters. The Russians had also contrived to salvage some industry from the occupied areas. By their own statistics, they relocated over 1,300 industrial plants, 93 steel mills and 150 machine tool factories into areas outside the German grasp.[81] However this may have been, the Russians certainly possessed an astonishing war industry in the Urals, Western Siberia, Kazakhstan, and the Volga Basin. During 1941, the Soviets were just going into mass production of the famous T-34, a tank superior to any the Germans then deployed.[82] The Russians could also take faint hope from the attitudes of Great Britain and the United States. Churchill had immediately announced his full support for the Soviet Union. Of course, the British had practically nothing to spare at the time, but help might be forthcoming. President Franklin D. Roosevelt sent his personal advisor, Harry Hopkins, to Moscow on July 30 to confer with Stalin about American aid.[83] On August 18, the President approved 145 million dollars of military shipments,[84] and one week later Soviet and British troops occupied Iran, which might provide a supply route.[85] But this route was not open yet, nor did America have the shipping or the war industry to render substantial aid. For the moment, the Russians' most important advantage was their determination to make any sacrifice before surrendering. Many Russians must have secretly hated Stalin's misrule, but most were determined to resist the Germans who represented a worse tyranny. The Soviet state was more resilient and durable than anyone had believed. Lastly, the Russians knew that their climate would soon end the campaigning season and give them respite from the German armored tactics.

In late September, the Germans completed the Kiev operation and assembled their forces for TYPHOON with great speed and secrecy, often moving at night. Apparently, Hitler's haphazard direction of the war had one advantage: the Soviets were caught off balance because they had ceased expecting Bock to renew offensive operations.[86] *(See Map 20, in Atlas.)* On September 30, Guderian's armor broke through Russian defenses and advanced rapidly through open country while fending off flank attacks by the Soviet Thirteenth Army. By October 3, Guderian's columns had reached Orel, approximately 130 miles into the Soviet rear area.[87] At the same time, the German Second Army advanced through Bryansk to the north, enveloping elements of the Soviet Third, Thirteenth, and Fiftieth Armies. The Germans took about 50,000 prisoners in the Bryansk pocket, but resistance continued until October 25.[88] TYPHOON itself began on October 2 in fine weather and over hard ground. Although General Georg-Hans Reinhardt's Third Panzer Group contained only three *panzer* divisions, he broke through immediately, crossed the upper Dnieper and advanced rapidly on Vyazma. Hoepner's Fourth Panzer Group enjoyed similar success, enabling Army Group Center to close the ring around Vyazma by October 7. As before, the Soviets reacted sluggishly to events, tried at first to defend all along the front and began a general withdrawal too late. As command and control broke down again among the Soviet forces, the *Stavka* only added to the confusion by attempting a complicated regrouping. The Vyazma pocket contained the Soviet Nineteenth, Twentieth, Twenty-fourth, and Thirty-second Armies from the West Front, a total of 45 divisions. Within a week, the Germans cleared the pocket, taking 650,000 prisoners of war.[89] They had conducted another classic battle of encirclement, a modern Cannae, and annihilated the defenders of Moscow. Halder had proven his contention that an attack towards Moscow would yield a great victory. Although no one could have suspected it at the time, the Germans had also won their last great victory in Russia. Now the rains began.

On October 7, the fine weather over the central Russian plain gave way to mixed snow and rain. Heavy autumn rains occur regularly in European Russia and have an especially strong effect in the poorly drained central region. As the poor weather continued, the unimproved roads became morasses impassable to trucks and difficult even for tracked vehicles. In some places, the roads resembled rivers of mud, difficult to imagine for anyone who had not seen them with his own eyes.[90] Because they were dependent on motor transport beyond the rail depots, the German supply system began to break down. The small, high-axled Russian farm wagon, called by the Germans *panje*, was one of the few vehicles to retain some mobility. The Germans used these vehicles in large numbers, giving their forces the appearance of a pre-industrial army. Infantry marches slowed to a painful crawl as the mud stuck to the men's boots in thick, viscous masses. Already exhausted, the infantry suffered further for lack of warmth and shelter. Even during lulls in fighting the *landser* (common soldier) could find little shelter in this sparsely populated and primitive region. Although the Soviet defenders also suffered from the weather, it was their ally because it cancelled the Germans' technical advantages and prevented them from dominating the battlefield through rapid maneuver.

On October 9, as the rains were falling, the German official press announced Russia's defeat as a result of the Vyazma encirclement.[91] In Germany the news was readily believed and even the *landser* in all his misery expected to see Moscow before winter. *(See Map 20, in Atlas.)* By mid-October, the Germans reached Kalinin on the upper Volga and Kaluga on the Oka River, but here the advance became mired.[92] The operational maps at higher headquarters gave a misleading picture of the campaign, showing imposing arrays of units at locations actually reached by a few ragged, half-starved men. On October 12, Hitler ordered the Army not to accept the surrender of Moscow. Bock was to destroy the city through artillery fire and bombing, permitting the population to flee east.[93] By these methods, Hitler hoped to prevent German casualties and cause chaos in eastern Russia. On October 15, panic occurred in Moscow as the diplomatic corps was evacuated.[94] The next day, part of the Soviet General Staff left the city, while another part remained to direct its defense.[95] Although prepared to continue the war after losing Moscow, Stalin remained in the

Moscow Under Siege: Russian Antiaircraft-Gun Fire, 1941

A Road in the German Army Group North Area During Rains

city to set an example. The civilian population built rings of antitank ditches and field fortifications around the city while still more Soviet armies were assembled into a new reserve. Both sides in this vast conflict sensed an impending crisis.

Not only Hitler, but Brauchtsch and Halder as well, believed the attack on Moscow must continue.[96] They felt the Russians must be nearly exhausted and final victory very close. They recalled vividly the first Battle of the Marne in the First World War, lost, they thought, because the Imperial German Army had not pressed its attack home at the crucial moment. The attack on Moscow had also become a *Flucht nach vorn* ("fleeing towards the front") for the German officers who were afraid to remain where they were with winter approaching. Accordingly, the Germans regrouped their forces, resupplied them as best they could, and resumed the offensive in mid-November, attempting to encircle Moscow. The Third Panzer Group attacked towards Klin against the Soviet Thirteenth Army of General Ivan S. Konev's Kalinin Front. On November 16, the Fourth Panzer Group attacked in a sector defended by the Soviet Sixteenth Army, commanded by General Konstantin K. Rokossovski. (Both these officers were to end the war as Marshals of the Soviet Union.) These attacks brought the Germans to the Moscow-Volga Canal, about 25 miles from the city. *(See Map 20, Inset, in Atlas.)* Meanwhile, Guderian's Second Panzer Army (formerly designated a Group) approached Tula but failed to capture the city and came to a halt short of the Oka River. Guderian's troops felt panic for the first time in the campaign when the Soviets counterattacked with the new T-34 tanks.[97] This tank had 45 millimeters of well-sloped frontal and turret armor, making it impervious to the Germans' standard 37- and 50-mm antitank guns.[98] The T-34 had appeared earlier, but now the Russians could deploy sufficient numbers to win large engagements. The Germans were the more shocked because they had become accustomed to thinking of themselves as the masters of armored warfare.

Tactically speaking, the German November offensive on Moscow was little more than a frontal assault. As the armor resources were badly depleted, Bock placed Reinhardt's Third Panzer Group and Hoepner's Fourth Panzer Group together on the left. Logistical problems and the tough Soviet resistance kept Reinhardt and Hoepner from breaking through, so that their advance slowly degenerated into a series of bitterly fought local attacks. At their farthest advance, Hoepner's troops were just north of Moscow, but wholly unable to threaten an encirclement. Directly west of Moscow stood General Günther von Kluge's Fourth Army with command over Hoepner's Group. For some reason, perhaps because of reluctance to leave a thin line of prepared positions, Kluge failed to attack until December 1.[99] In the meantime, an indignant Hoepner had to sustain the operation virtually unaided except for Reinhardt's help on the flank. When Kluge did attack, he failed to make any progress against the Soviet West Front, commanded by Zhukov since October 9. Undoubtedly Zhukov did his best to keep pressure on Kluge, but there is no reason to suppose that the Fourth Army was in greater difficulty than the Fourth Panzer Group. Of course, Guderian's Second Panzer Army should have formed the right pincer arm around Moscow, but following the Kiev operation Guderian had been too far south to return for TYPHOON. These deployments and Kluge's hesitation made the Soviets' tactical problem easy. It is quite likely, however, that the German troops were too exhausted and ill-supplied to conduct a much wider maneuver anyway.

German Troops Digging Positions in the Snow, Winter 1941

The long Russian winter, always harsh but unusually cold in 1941, began in November. The Germans had been so confident of a quick victory that not even winter uniforms were ready for the front-line troops. The *landser* stuffed newspapers into his summer uniform and foraged civilian clothing—especially coats, mittens and headgear. The leather-soled, hobnailed German Army boot offered little insulation and soon frostbite cases exceeded battle casualties. (Frostbite was punishable in the Red Army because the soldier was presumed able to prevent it.) Exhaustion and undernourishment made the Germans even more vulnerable to cold. When temperatures fell to –20° and –30° Centigrade, much German equipment began to malfunction. Lubricants became too viscous and even froze, causing automatic weapons and artillery to misfire. As a field expedient, the *landser* often removed all lubrication from his weapons. The tanks' gunsights fogged over in the cold and became useless. To start a vehicle at all, the crews often had to light fires under the engines. The deep ruts in the autumn mud froze solidly, creating a surface rough enough to jolt vehicles to pieces. The ground became rock hard, making field fortifications practically impossible to construct, even when using explosives.[100] The Russian soldier also suffered these hardships, but he was better adapted and better equipped for the cold. Furthermore, the winter reduced the Germans' qualitative advantages, making the battle for Moscow an infantry fight with roughly equal weapons.

Soviet losses from June to December had been fantastically high (perhaps five to six million men, including over three million prisoners of war),[101] yet the Soviet Union could still raise fresh armies. The Soviet will to resist was strengthened by the knowledge that captivity brought death, for the Germans deliberately permitted their prisoners to die of exposure, illness, and starvation. This will was also strengthened by the example of 2.5 million Communist Party members, who organized rear area services and carried on an effective propaganda or served as political commissars, regular officers, and non commissioned officers.[102] Finally, it was reinforced by deep feelings of patriotism and abhorrence for the invader. In the face of shocking losses, the people told themselves: "Mother Russia has many sons." The slogan during the battle of Moscow was: "Russia is vast, yet there is nowhere to retreat, for behind us lies Moscow."[103] As the Germans drew closer to Moscow, Soviet problems of supply and control were alleviated. On November 7, Russian troops celebrated the 1917 Revolution with a parade on Red Square and heard Stalin evoke the names of Alexander Nevsky, Alexander Suvorov, and Mikhail Kutusov, then continued their march directly to the front.[104] On that same day, Roosevelt made Russia eligible for lend-lease assistance by announcing that he judged the defense of the Soviet Union vital to American defense.

Incessant Russian counterattacks, so often merely wasteful of men, now began to show an effect. In early December,

Freezing Germans Surrender to Well-Clothed Russians Near Moscow, 1941

Kluge withdrew the Fourth Army to the Nara River rather than risk envelopment. Far back in his East Prussian headquarters, Hitler at first refused to understand the situation, then at last abandoned the offensive towards Moscow on December 8.[105] At first the *Stavka* had no particular strategy, just the determination to attack everywhere and fix the Germans in place. The Red Air Force began to appear again over Moscow and Soviet artillery began to deliver heavy preparatory fires. Soviet fires sometimes included 82 and 132-mm rockets delivered from truck-mounted launchers. The *Katyusha*, as Soviet troops called these weapons, were fin-stabilized and fired in salvos off open rails. They gave good area coverage at ranges up to 8,500 meters and were heartily disliked by the *landser*.[106] Soviet tactics still relied on massed troops and resulted in heavy losses to defensive fires; still the Russians continued to press home the attacks. Soon Army Group Center could no longer maintain a continuous line of resistance and the Germans were forced to concentrate upon road junctures, villages and key terrain features. In response, Zhukov instructed his commanders to bypass and encircle the German strong points.[107] The Soviets also employed infiltration tactics to penetrate into the German rear areas. *(See Map 21, in Atlas.)* Spread over a 700-mile front, Army Group Center could no longer contain the Russians.[108]

Even while the battle of Moscow was fought, Army Group South advanced into the Ukraine and the Crimea in a hazardous dispersion of effort. *(See Map 20, in Atlas.)* The advance continued as soon as the Germans had cleared the enormous Kiev pocket in late September. General Erich von Manstein, who was to emerge as the best German strategist of the war, commanded the Eleventh Army in an offensive over the Perekop Isthmus leading to the Crimea. As Manstein was making some progress against the Soviet Fifty-first Army, the Rumanian Third Army on his left flank buckled, forcing him to divert some units in support. But then Kleist's First Panzer Army (formerly Group), returning from the Kiev operation, attacked south into the rear area of the Soviet South Front and joined with Manstein's Eleventh Army on October 6 near the Sea of Azov. This operation encircled elements of the Soviet Ninth and Eighteenth Armies and brought the Germans another 100,000 prisoners of war.[109] Manstein then resumed his offensive over the flat Perekop Isthmus in bitter fighting against the strongly emplaced Russians. After suffering heavy losses, the German infantry finally broke through and occupied the Crimea with the exception of Sevastopol by the end of November. Meanwhile, after a staunch defense against the Rumanian Fourth Army, the Soviets finally surrendered the Black Sea port of Odessa, evacuating by sea on October 16.[110]

Throughout October, Rundstedt's Army Group South maintained a general advance eastwards, forcing the Second Army to sideslip south in order to maintain contact with the Sixth Army. For this reason, the Second Army could not support Guderian in his attack towards Tula. The Germans did not have sufficient force to cover a front which was growing longer as they fanned out across Russia. The Second Army entered Kursk on November 2, but there its progress ended.[111] During the heavy October rains, Rundstedt's armies continued to advance through the Ukraine, while the Russians worked frantically to evacuate industrial equipment from the Donets region. The Sixth Army entered the industrial city of Kharkov, a center of Soviet armor production, on October 25, but could advance only a little farther.[112] Kleist brought his First Panzer Army to the Mius River north of Taganrog and thus stood at the entrance to the Donets region. But at this point Army Group South had reached the logistical limit of its advance, particularly since alternate rain and frost had begun to break up the supply columns. The Soviet South Front and Southwest Front, the latter commanded by Timoshenko, had retreated in fairly good order and still offered strong resistance. Despite the obvious dangers, Rundstedt continued the advance, hoping to reach the Donets River.

During freezing weather and using more *panje* wagons than motor vehicles,[113] the First Panzer Army attacked the Soviet Fifty-sixth and Ninth Armies and entered Rostov on the Don River on November 20.[114] Hitler needed Rostov as an assembly area for a campaign in the Caucasus, under study by OKH since October.[115] But in reaching Rostov the Germans had created a long salient, allowing three Soviet armies to attack the First Panzer Army from the north. This Soviet force included five tank brigades, largely equipped with the T-34.[116] Seeing the First Panzer Army threatened by envelopment, Rundstedt quickly ordered a withdrawal from the Don, and the Germans had already left Rostov when a countermanding order arrived from Hitler.[117] A distinguished officer whose long career had begun in 1893, Rundstedt asked to be relieved of duty if the First Panzer Army were not allowed to withdraw to the Mius River.[118] As a result the Sixth Army commander replaced Rundstedt as Commander-in-Chief of Army Group South on November 30, but he could do nothing to alter the situation. On December 1, elements of the Soviet Ninth Army broke through the positions of the SS Division *Leibstandarte*, forcing a withdrawal to the Mius River line which Hitler now approved.[119] Hitler's foolish interference had cost the Germans time, troops, and the services of Rundstedt,[120] who would never command in Russia again.

During September, Army Group North had curtailed its attack on Leningrad because its *panzer* divisions were needed for TYPHOON. *(See Map 20, in Atlas.)* On Hitler's orders, the Sixteenth Army continued towards Tikhvin to secure the bauxite plants in that area and to link up with the Finns on the Svir River east of Lake Ladoga. It captured that city on November 8, cutting the railway used to bring supplies to the shore of

We Are Defending Lenin's City! (Soviet Poster)

Lake Ladoga for shipment to Leningrad. Alert to Tikhvin's importance, the *Stavka* gave General Kirill A. Meretskov, a former Chief of General Staff, overall command of the forces in that area. Attacking primarily with the Fourth Army, Meretskov soon forced Leeb's exhausted troops to take up defensive positions.[121] As Meretskov pressed ahead, the Tikhvin salient became untenable, compelling a German withdrawal in early December. *(See Map 21, in Atlas.)* The battles for Rostov and Tikhvin were the first real Soviet victories of the war and sure indications that the Germans had reached the limits of their advance.

As events transpired, the Germans would never capture Leningrad, but they still retained a few miles of shore on the southwestern tip of Lake Ladoga. The Soviets had stockpiled neither food nor fuel in Leningrad and now 2,500,000 people were trapped in the besieged city.[122] Army Group North settled down to the siege, assuming that the population of Leningrad would starve and freeze to death during the winter; but, by the end of November, the Russians began transporting supplies by truck over the ice on Lake Ladoga. Despite German bombing and fire from heavy artillery, the Russian trucks moved steadily over an 18-mile road on ice. Later the Soviets constructed a railway over the same route. By recapturing Tikhvin on December 8, they gained much better access by rail to Lake Ladoga.[123] Despite this success, the siege caused terrible suffering. In Leningrad, food was rationed at near starvation levels, and the inhabitants could not heat their homes in sub-zero weather. As many as a million citizens of Leningrad ultimately perished in the worst siege of human record. Yet the civilian population still succeeded in constructing almost 100 miles of antitank ditch and escarpment plus countless infantry trenches around the city.[124] The male citizens not engaged in war production served in hastily formed *opolchenie* (militia units). This tenacious defense of Leningrad had great military value because it held a large besieging force immobile.

Why Did the German Blitzkrieg Fail in Russia?

By December 1941, the German Army was on the defensive everywhere in Russia and Army Group Center was retreating from the Moscow area under heavy Soviet counterattack. Despite success on a tremendous scale in such envelopments as Minsk, Smolensk, Kiev, and Vyazma, *blitzkrieg* had still failed to defeat the Russians. Why had it failed? Clearly the outstanding causes were the Red Army's unexpected toughness, the Russian climate and geography, the inadequate German preparation, and faulty German strategy. The German strategic blunders were the most obvious yet perhaps the least important cause of the failure. German strategy was faulty, not because Hitler chose Leningrad and the Ukraine over Moscow, but because he reached his decisions too late and then failed to carry them out. Had Army Group Center continued to advance on Moscow in August, the Russians would have lost their capital before winter. But they would not have surrendered. Without Moscow as a base, however, the Russians could not have launched such a powerful winter offensive against Army Group Center. On the other hand, Hitler was probably right in preferring to seize the Donets region and interdict the Russian supply of Caucasian oil. Had the Germans concentrated on these objectives and taken up good defensive positions elsewhere, they would at least have begun the next campaigning season with a clear advantage. Dazzled by success and expecting the Russians to collapse as the French had, Hitler and OKW-OKH squabbled, vacillated, and ended by choosing all the possible objectives, creating an intolerable strain on the Army. Of all the highest echelon leaders, Halder had the firmest grip on reality, but Hitler would not listen to Halder—or to anyone else for that matter. In the last analysis, German strategy in 1941 amounted to a general advance all across Russia, heading for every possible objective. The worst choice was not to choose at all. Obviously, Hitler had the worse influence on strategy, but most of the generals first shared his optimism and then did little to avert the impending crisis. Right up to Moscow, the expectation of Soviet collapse lured them on and clouded their judgment.

Inadequate preparation for war defeated the Germans more surely than their faulty strategy. Astonishing as it sounds, the German *Reich* had not begun all-out wartime production prior to the inception of BARBAROSSA. The director of the German

Trucks on the Ice of Lake Ladoga

Four Year Plan inaugurated in 1936 was Hermann Goering, an indolent and vainglorious man largely ignorant of economics.[125] In addition, since 1939 armament production had been supervised by a branch of OKW called the *Wirtschafts-und Rüstungsamt*, which tried to centralize planning but lacked the authority. Hitler did not help by wrenching the economy around through personal commands rather than organizing production in depth.[126] So little did he appreciate the needs of the Russian campaign that Hitler ordered priority for naval and air force requirements in July 1941, anticipating new operations against Great Britain.[127] Moreover, prior to 1941 German factories generally operated on a single shift, thereby badly underusing the available machinery.[128] Thus, despite their proverbial industry and great technical sophistication, the Germans fell behind their enemies in armaments production. In 1941, they produced fewer aircraft than Great Britain[129] and tanks obviously inferior to the new Soviet T-34. In a typical gesture, Hitler made his personal architect the top industrial planner in February 1942. By a lucky chance, Albert Speer happened to be a highly intelligent and able manager, who used Hitler's authority to initiate full war production. As a result the Germans produced in 1944, under difficult circumstances, about five times as many armored vehicles as they had in 1941.[130] Such production earlier would have sufficed to keep the *panzer* divisions at their 1940 authorization of over 300 tanks each. The Germans also failed to produce the transport they needed for the Russian campaign, even though they fully realized that the roads would be impassable to wheeled vehicles during rain. The Germans needed good tactical vehicles and plenty of tracked prime movers, but they entered Russia with a miscellaneous truck park, including many types suitable only for paved surfaces.[131]

Russian climate and geography were no secrets, but the Germans underestimated the effects of distance on their operations and never planned for a winter campaign at all. Obviously, they would have defeated the Russians if the Soviet Union were as shallow as France. Paris was but 300 kilometers from the German border; the same penetration into Russia brought the Germans only to Minsk. Army Group North marched over 800 kilometers in straight-line distance from Königsberg to Leningrad; shorter marches over better roads had brought the Germans clear across France to the Bay of Biscay. Moscow lay 1,000 kilometers from the then-Polish border and Rostov 900 kilometers from the Rumanian. The still largely unmechanized German Army could not cover such distances except in laboriously prepared multiple operations. In addition, the Germans had to deploy over an unimaginably wide front. By the time Manstein entered the Crimea, the German front extended over 1,700 kilometers in straight line distance from Leningrad to Sevastopol. The forests and swamps of northern Russia and the general lack of hard surfaced roads added greatly to the Germans' problems. Although unusually severe in 1941, the European Russian winter is not appreciably worse than the winter in the north-central United States or southern Canada, just longer.[132] But even such a winter was catastrophic for troops without proper clothing and equipment.

Russian authors emphasize the accomplishment of the Red Army in 1941, and certainly it was both larger and more durable than anyone had imagined. After all, the Germans knew Russian geography and controlled their own production and strategy. Only the Red Army was an unknown quantity and it was the surprise of the war. At the outset, the Red Army seemed merely to provide statistics for the *Wehrmacht* reports of continual victories. It had all the predicted failings: poor coordination of arms, lack of control, fear to use initiative, communications as bad as the Germans could have wished, inept leadership that wasted resources, weak discipline, a fatal tendency to commit unsupported infantry in repeated frontal attacks, obsolete armor and aircraft, and a sluggish high command. Several times, the Germans thought they had finally defeated this primitive opponent, yet he still remained in the field. Mere survival would have been an accomplishment in 1941, yet the Red Army actually seemed to improve. Just as the T-34 replaced the obsolete BT series of tanks, so more competent commanders—men like Zhukov, Rokossovski, Konev, and Meretskov—appeared at all echelons. So often betrayed by incompetent leadership, the Red Army soldier showed his worth when he had a fighting chance under good commanders. Soviet units varied wildly in quality from raw militia to units as experienced as their opponents, but they exacted a price for every German advance. By December 1941, the cumulative price was too high to pay. It would be invidious to say that either Mother Russia or her sons primarily accomplished this feat; both were necessary, but the most astonishing contribution was that of the sons. The German *blitzkrieg* presupposed a qualitative superiority the Germans no longer enjoyed in the winter of 1941. As the first to master a particular style of war, the Germans were the first to demonstrate its limits.

As the Russians began their counterattacks on Army Group Center, Hitler took the decision which assured his ultimate defeat. Although the Japanese had not consulted him prior to attacking Pearl Harbor, Hitler promptly declared war on the United States in a *Reichstag* speech on December 11. He made this declaration without seeking advice from OKW[133] and apparently without rational motive.[134] In June 1941, Hitler had been the master of Europe and there had been little prospect of a world war. By December, the Germans were hopelessly overextended and Hitler's destruction was virtually assured in a war against three of the world's foremost powers. While Stalin's neutrality pact with Japan permitted the Soviet dictator to use over 15 Siberian divisions in the defense of Moscow,[135] Hitler saw himself forced to station over 40 divisions outside of Russia. Simultaneously with the Russian campaign, Hitler conducted an air war against Great Britain, garrisoned western Europe against invasion, conducted a submarine war in the Atlantic, and waged a small war in North Africa. All these efforts were secondary to the war against Russia, and all diverted German strength needed there. At a time when his resources were already strained, Hitler had declared war on the world's foremost industrial power, that same power which had assured Germany's defeat in the First World War. Hitler may well be the most evil man ever to lead a great nation; he certainly was the most foolish.

The Red Army and "General Winter"

By mid-December, total German casualties in Russia had mounted to 775,000, or almost one-quarter of the average strength engaged.[136] Since June, the Germans had expected the Russians to collapse, but now a German collapse seemed more likely. In this crisis, Hitler ordered "fanatic resistance" wherever his armies stood.[137] At the time, some of his generals felt this order was justified to prevent a rout, but there is no evidence to prove them right. In fact, German troops retreated up to 200 miles in five weeks under Soviet pressure, without losing their discipline.[138] Later the German Army made many long retreats under extremely difficult conditions without being routed. Given this historical evidence, it seems very unlikely that flexible defense in the winter of 1941 would have produced any confused flight of German troops. Hitler's stand-fast order did not prevent the Germans from retreating, but only from planning their retreats enough to organize rear positions in advance and break contact with the enemy.

Hitler's other reaction to the crisis was to dismiss officers, like Rundstedt, who felt they should exercise some professional judgment. For having ordered a tactical withdrawal, Guderian was relieved on December 26. Hoepner was relieved of his command over the Fourth Panzer Army on January 8, 1942, for a similar reason. These aggressive armor commanders were especially alert to the futility and danger of static defense. Although his authority had already degenerated into mere liaison between the Army and Hitler, the December 19 dismissal of the Army Commander-in-Chief, Brauchitsch, for ill health had important consequences. Halder wished to couple his own fate with that of his friend, but Brauchitsch convinced him to remain OKH Chief of Staff in order to keep the Army well represented.[139] To Halder's astonishment, Hitler himself now assumed the post of Army Commander-in-Chief. Hitler felt contempt for the traditions of the German officer corps, and he ranked his intuition higher than the best professional opinion. For all of Germany's proud military history, the German general officer had come to enjoy less discretion than his counterpart in Great Britain, America, or even the Soviet Union.

The Soviet winter offensive began as a series of counterattacks to save Moscow.[140] In early December, the armies of Konev's Kalinin Front and Zhukov's West Front achieved numerous local successes which showed clearly that the Germans had overextended themselves. *(See Map 21, in Atlas.)* As the Soviet attacks mounted, the German commanders adopted the expedient of *Igel* (hedgehog) tactics. Rather than try to defend along the entire line, they concentrated on all-around defense of selected strong points. This tactic worked best when the Soviets stubbornly continued their attacks on the strong point, worst when they deliberately by-passed and surrounded the *Igel*. Encouraged by the signs of German weakness, Stalin planned a general offensive, although Zhukov argued strongly in favor of limiting the offensive to the West Front.[141] For this offensive, Stalin intended to commit the large *Stavka* reserve, carefully built up and saved until this crucial moment. In early December, Kovev's Kalinin Front crossed the frozen Volga River and attacked the German Ninth Army, while Zhukov's West Front attacked the German Third and Fourth Panzer Groups, both far below strength.[142] Finding the Istra River still only half frozen over, troops from Rokossovski's Sixteenth Army crossed on logs, pieces of fences and torn-off doors.[143] Due to Hitler's stand-fast order, the German troops soon found themselves in nearly untenable positions. By early January 1942, the Soviets were attacking the neck of a huge salient containing the German Ninth Army and Fourth Panzer Army (formerly Group). Zhukov and Konev were anxious to capture Vyazma and close the trap, but their armies were too exhausted.[144] In desperation, the *Stavka* dropped paratroopers (the 8th Brigade, IV Airborne Corps) near Vyazma beginning on January 16.[145] *(See Map 21, Inset, in Atlas.)* The Soviet Thirty-third Army and the I Guards Cavalry Corps established contact with the paratroops and partisans in the Vyazma area, but all these forces were themselves encircled when the Fourth Panzer Army regained contact with the Fourth Army outside the salient.[146] At the end of March, Zhukov made a last attempt to reach the encircled troops, but his offensive quickly spent its force during the spring rains. With the return of good weather, Army Group Center systematically destroyed the encircled Russians.

To keep the Germans from reinforcing Army Group Center and in the hope of provoking a general collapse, the Russians also launched winter offensives in the north and south. On January 7, Meretskov's Volkhov Front mounted an attack through heavy forests and waist-deep snow.[147] The Soviet Fifty-fourth and Second Shock Armies attempted to envelop the German I Corps assigned to the Eighteenth Army, but the Second Shock Army itself became encircled and was finally destroyed in June 1942. *(See Map 21, in Atlas.)* The Northwest Front offensive had greater success, trapping about 90,000 German troops in the area of Demyansk below Lake Ilmen. The Germans supplied these troops by air from February 8 until a corridor was opened on April 21. Although the airlift never reached the minimum requirement of 300 tons daily and the *Luftwaffe* lost 262 aircraft in the operation, Goering thought he had proven the feasibility of supplying large units by air.[148] Hitler argued at the time that salients or even encirclements of German troops were advantageous, because they kept large numbers of Soviet troops occupied in holding the perimeters. His generals took the more orthodox view that a salient should be held under pressure only if needed for further operations.

In the south, South West and South Fronts attacked across the Donets River in mid-January, gaining a large bridgehead west of Izyum.[149] This bridgehead offered a good assembly area for an offensive against Army Group South. *(See Map 21, in Atlas.)* In the meantime, the Russians attempted to relieve the garrison of Sevastopol by landing on the Kerch Peninsula and near Feodosita in late December 1941. To avoid being trapped east of Feodosita, General Graf von Sponeck, commanding the German XLII Corps, ordered a retreat on his own authority. At Hitler's urging, Sponeck was tried by court-martial and sentenced to death, but the sentence was commuted to life imprisonment. (He was shot to death without trial in 1944, following the attempt on Hitler's life.) Manstein's Eleventh Army counterattacked in mid-January and drove the Soviet armies back into the Kerch Peninsula.

During February 1942, the Soviet offensive began to taper off and the Germans realized they had survived the crisis. Russian strategy, like the German, had been too ambitious and should better have concentrated on one objective, perhaps the destruction of Army Group Center as Zhukov had urged. On the other hand, continuous pressure over the entire front kept the Germans in a permanent crisis and prevented them from resting troops or building reserves.[150] The Russians had changed *blitzkrieg* into a gigantic war of attrition. They accepted terrible losses, allowing their infantry divisions to fall from authorized strengths of 8,000 to 9,000 men to one-half or even quarter strength.[151] While the Soviets still had the manpower to replace these losses in men, the German Army never recovered entirely from the first winter in Russia. German battle casualties, from mid-November 1941 to the end of March 1942, totaled over 370,000 men,[152] while another half million men were lost to sickness and frostbite.[153] Due to losses during the winter, the Germans had to begin a new campaigning season with approximately the same armored strength as a year earlier, despite increased production;[154] they had lost almost 75,000 motor vehicles and 180,000 horses.[155] The real success of the Soviet winter offensive lay in this sapping of German strength.

A Dilettante in War: Hitler's 1942 Campaign

Hitler had long wished to capture the Soviet oil fields in the Caucasus. On July 31, 1940, at the very inception of BARBAROSSA planning, he had spoken of an advance to Baku on the Caspian Sea after the defeat of the Red Army.[156] The economic officer of OKW (*Wirtschafts-und Rüstungsamt*) noted in November 1940 that Germany would need the Caucasian oil to exploit the captured Soviet industry.[157] Hitler had also planned to invade the Caucasus as part of the continuing war against Great Britain. Directive 32, issued on June 11, 1941, concerned the period following BARBAROSSA and envisioned a three-pronged attack on the British position through Libya, through Turkey, and over the Caucasus through Iran, if circumstances permitted.[158] The first detailed operational plan had emerged from OKH in October 1941.[159] It assumed a total force of three motorized and two mountain corps, which would cross the Caucasian Mountains in June 1942 and occupy the Transcaucasus to the Soviet border with Iran by September. The Germans would have to seize the lower Volga in a preliminary operation to secure the flank of the advance. Retreating from his earlier optimism, Hitler told Brauchitsch on November 7, 1941, that the Caucasus operation would have to wait for 1942 and even then it would not continue beyond the Russian border.[160] On November 19, he confirmed to Halder that the Caucasus would be the first objective in 1942.[161] This decision reflected Hitler's insight into the economic nature of modern war, but it also posed some difficult military problems.

In the spring of 1942, Army Group South was in a poor position to begin a Caucasian operation. First Panzer Army was still no farther east than the Mius River, and even this position was threatened by a large Soviet bridgehead around Izyum on the Donets River. *(See Map 21, in Atlas.)* Furthermore, the Soviets still held Sevastopol and the Kerch Peninsula. Jodl submitted a draft directive embodying the OKH recommendations to Hitler on April 4, but Hitler rewrote and amended the draft before signing it the following day.[162] The resulting Directive 41 was jumbled, unclear and embarrassingly amateurish.[163] It mingled propaganda about the alleged success of the winter's fighting with insulting admonitions concerning the correct employment of armor. As objectives for 1942, Hitler set the capture of Leningrad and the advance into the Caucasus, the latter having priority. In preliminary operations, Army Group South would capture Sevastopol and Kerch, and destroy the Soviet forces around Iyzum. It would then destroy the forces remaining west of the Don and capture the Caucasian oil fields. To secure the long left flank of the Caucasian operation, the Army Group South would conduct three mutually supporting operations along the Don River. These three operations, later code-named BLUE, began with an envelopment converging on Voronezh. *(See Map, Directive 41, April 5, 1942, page 128.)* During the second operation, an armored force would advance south along the Don and meet another force attacking east from the Kharkov area. In the third operation, the Germans would continue along the Don into the Stalingrad area. At the same time, another force would attack from the Mius position north of the lower Don towards Stalingrad, thus enveloping the Soviet forces still in the Don bend. Hitler specified that Army Group South should either capture Stalingrad or destroy its industry and transportation by artillery fire. As it advanced, the southernmost force would also try to acquire Don bridgeheads for the subsequent advance into the Caucasus, the real purpose of the campaign. Hitler showed concern over the lengthening flank on the Don from Voronezh to the Stalingrad area, but he expected Hungarian, Italian, and Rumanian armies to hold it through the winter.

The Germans began the 1942 campaign still in weakened condition. In the spring, the infantry divisions of Army Group South were at 50 per cent strength and those of the other army groups averaged 35 percent.[164] Halder naturally tried to fill the Army Group South divisions prior to beginning the offensive, but the replacements were often 19-year-old draftees without military experience. According to an OKW study, the 225 divisions in Russia were 625,000 men short of authorized strength in May.[165] The shortage of armor was even more critical. As of March 30, the 16 *panzer* divisions in Russia had a total of 140 tanks deployed—less than the authorized strength of a single division.[166] By refitting divisions from recent production, the Germans would have over 3,000 tanks for the 1942 campaign, about the same number originally available for BARBAROSSA.[167] The new tanks were primarily PzKw III with the long barreled 50-mm gun. Again, armor replacements went largely to Army Group South where each *panzer* division was to have one regiment of three battalions or somewhat more than 150 tanks. Armored divisions in the other two army groups, which could not be removed from the front for rehabilitation, would have only one battalion of 40 to 50 tanks.[168] Shortages of motor vehicles were so great that even fully rehabilitated divisions in Army Group South would only have 85 percent of authorization when the offensive began. Army planners calculated that Army Group South's stockpile of petroleum products would be exhausted by mid-July, forcing it to rely on current shipments.[169] Nor was the *Luftwaffe* in better condition. Its units averaged only 50 to 60 percent of authorized strength in aircraft during May.[170] Hitler was paying for his failure to initiate a full war economy in 1939 to 1941.

In 1941, the Russians had generally expected an invader to concentrate on the Ukraine. In 1942, Stalin was convinced the Germans would renew their offensive on Moscow, and he was wrong again.[171] As during the winter, Stalin favored a general offensive and overrode Zhukov who advocated a modest effort against Army Group Center. Apparently because they detected the offensive preparation in the area of Army Group South, the Soviets prepared their first effort as a double envelopment north of the Iyzum salient to converge on Kharkov. This spoiling attack had no chance to succeed because German intelligence gave notice of the Soviet intentions and Army Group

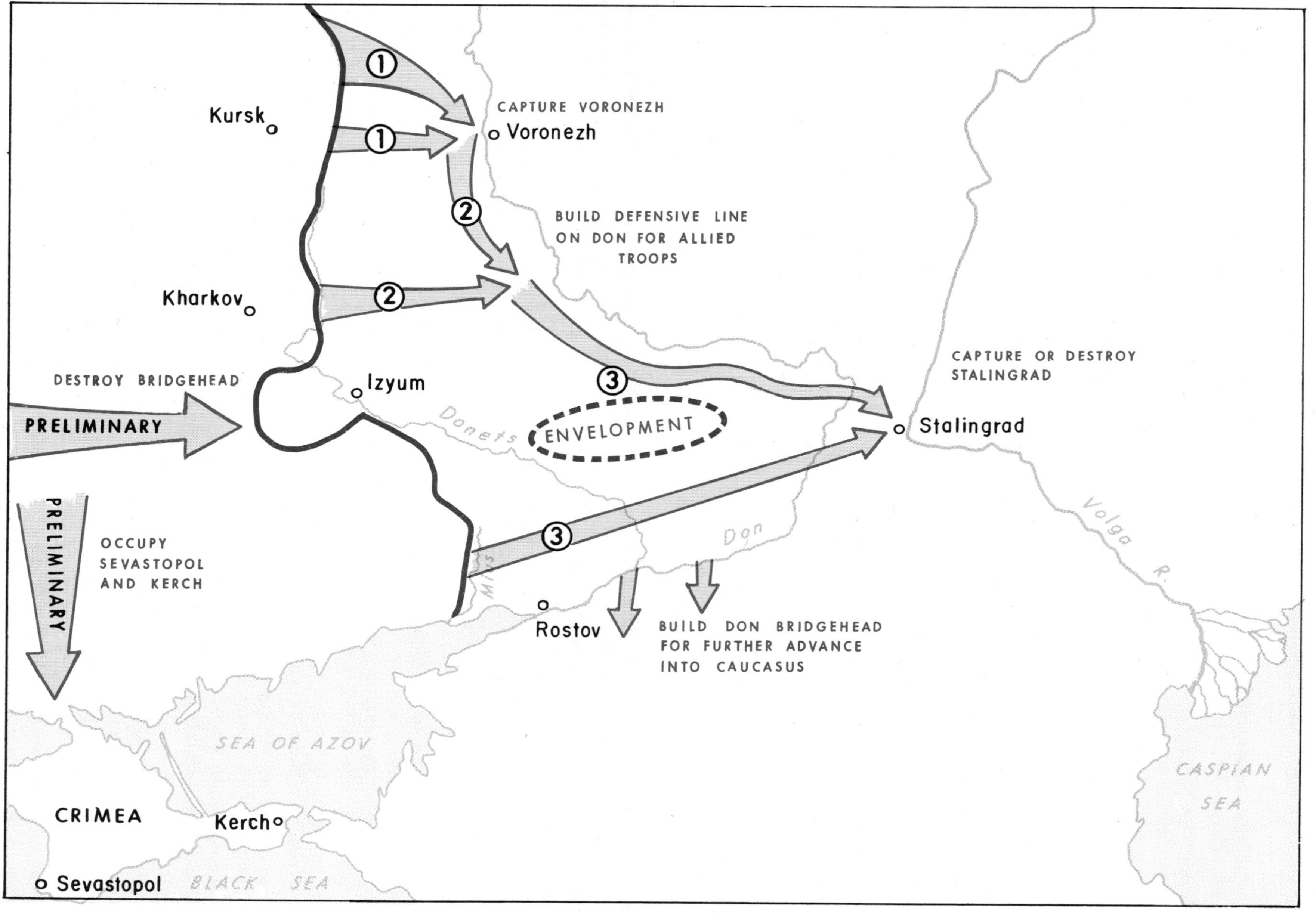

Directive 41, April 5, 1942

South was already prepared for its own attack on the Izyum bridgehead.[172] *(See Map 22, in Atlas.)* The Soviet Southwest Front, subordinated to Timoshenko's Southwest Theater, began its offensive on May 12. This attack fell on General Friedrich Paulus' Sixth Army which was hard-pressed until Kleist's First Panzer Army attacked on May 17—one day earlier than originally planned—and captured Izyum in two days. Stalin failed to see the danger and ordered Timoshenko to continue his offensive.[173] Kleist's forces broke through the southernmost Soviet army and made contact with the VIII Corps of the Sixth Army attacking from the north. This maneuver sealed off the salient and enveloped the southern arm of the Soviet offensive, including the entire Soviet Sixth and Fifty-seventh Armies. In clearing the Izyum pocket, the Germans took 214,000 prisoners.[174] The Russian northern enveloping force managed to withdraw. This defeat weakened and demoralized the Russians, making Operation BLUE much easier than it would otherwise have been. Stalin was very brash to attempt a spoiling attack, if that had been his intention. Like Hitler, he never seems to have appreciated the advantages of the counterattack, even though the Red Army's first successes were all counterattacks.

After defeating the three armies of the Soviet Crimean Front on the Kerch Peninsula and taking 170,000 prisoners during May, Manstein began an assault on Sevastopol in June.[175] *(See Map 22, in Atlas.)* The Sevastopol garrison occupied deeply echeloned fortifications, including clusters of concrete bunkers. The terrain was excellently suited for defense, ranging from ridges and thick shrubs to steep cliffs and mountains. The German VIII Air Corps continually attacked the city and harbor of Sevastopol while heavy siege artillery fired on the fortifications. This artillery included two 600-mm guns and the monstrous 800-mm Krupp gun called "Gustav," the largest ever constructed.[176] Manstein's infantry and engineers advanced painfully against bitter Soviet resistance and counterattacks. By June 26, the nearly exhausted Eleventh Army had reached the last Soviet defensive ring. During the night of June 28, two German divisions crossed the harbor in assault boats, outflanking the strong Soviet positions on the Sapun Heights east of Sevastopol.[177] After Sevastopol fell on July 1, Hitler made Manstein a field marshal and later decided to employ his Eleventh Army in assaulting Leningrad, rather than deploying it in the Kuban as planned. Four divisions from the Eleventh Army finally arrived in the Leningrad area, but were fully occupied just in repelling a Soviet offensive. Hitler's foolish decision deprived Army Group South of forces badly needed during the crisis of November 1942.[178]

On June 28, the great German summer offensive described by Directive 41 finally began.[179] In the first phase (BLUE I), the Second Army and Hoth's Fourth Panzer Army attacked towards Voronezh. On June 30 (BLUE II), Paulus' Sixth Army attacked from the Kharkov area towards the Don south of Voronezh. *(See Map 22, in Atlas.)* After breaking through the Soviet lines, the Second Army and the Sixth Army joined on July 2, encircling elements of two Soviet armies, but capturing only 30,000 prisoners. They reported a total of 73,000 prisoners up to July 8, an impressive total but not the decisive success the Germans were seeking.[180] The Fourth Panzer Army seized an almost undefended Voronezh on July 6, but encountered heavy resistance around the city. Stalin had ordered large reinforcements for the Bryansk and Voronezh Fronts, in part because he still thought the Germans were planning to develop their offensive north towards Moscow.[181] Because of this resistance, Bock showed reluctance to deploy Hoth's army southwards along the Don. Hitler, who arrived at Army Group South headquarters near Poltava on July 3, intervened on July 9 to send Hoth south in the hope of enveloping the Soviet forces still west of the Don. At the same time, the First Panzer Army attacked over the Donets River (BLUE III or CLAUSEWITZ) to form the right arm of this envelopment.

To facilitate control for the subsequent operations in the Don bend and into the Caucasus, Army Group South was reorganized in early July into Army Group B, comprising the Sixth Army and three allied armies, and Army Group A, comprising the Seventeenth Army, the First Panzer Army and, after July 13, the Fourth Panzer Army. Out of irritation with Bock, Hitler gave command of Army Group B to General Maximilian von Weichs on July 15, while Field Marshal Wilhelm List assumed command of Army Group A. The actual command over both groups resided primarily with Hitler, who increasingly interfered with operations down to corps level.[182] He maneuvered fitfully during the following weeks to encircle largely imaginary Soviet forces. *(See Map 22, in Atlas.)* First, he directed Hoth and Kleist, commanding the First Panzer Army, to perform an envelopment around Millerovo north of the Donets, but this maneuver yielded only 14,000 prisoners.[183] Then, on July 13, he ordered Hoth to cross the lower Don and advance towards Rostov, while Kleist recrossed the Donets to advance on the same city. In other words, Hitler sent both *panzer* armies west, thus halting Army Group B's advance towards Stalingrad; typically, Hitler had also abandoned his own previous planning for BLUE III. Breakdowns in the supply of motor fuel hampered all these movements. On July 17, Hitler tacitly admitted the cogency of Halder's criticisms by redirecting elements of the Fourth Panzer Army towards the Don bend to assist the Sixth Army. But in the meantime, the Russians had begun an orderly retreat, avoiding a large envelopment west of the Don. Hitler had also forfeited his chance to capture Stalingrad while the Soviets were still off balance.

On July 23, Hitler published Directive 45 for the further progress of the summer campaign.[184] His "directive" now had the character of a jumbled operational order which named specific units down to divisional level and small Russian towns. In the directive, Hitler announced a fictitious victory and directed Army Group A to seize Rostov, then to capture the entire eastern coast of the Black Sea, the passes through the Caucasus Mountains, and the coast of the Caspian Sea down to Baku. This absurdly ambitious series of operations bore the single code name EDELWEISS. Army Group B was to build defensive positions on the Don, seize Stalingrad and continue down the Volga River to its mouth at Astrakhan on the Caspian Sea. In a wildly optimistic mood, Hitler thus proposed to send the two army groups on widely divergent axes to accomplish missions well beyond those originally contemplated. If the original planning were already questionable, Directive 45 was practically a blueprint for disaster.

Hoth's Fourth Panzer Army now reverted to control by Army Group B and moved along the south bank of the Don towards Stalingrad, leaving a gap between the two army groups. *(See Map 23, in Atlas.)* Hoth made slow progress because his army had been reduced by various reassignments to just four German divisions. The First Panzer Army captured Rostov on July 23, but the Soviet South Front exploited a period of wet weather to escape encirclement. Kleist then pursued the retreating Soviets across the parched Caucasian plain and reached the Maikop oil fields by August 9, only to find them in flames.[185] At the same time, the Seventeenth Army captured Krasnodar and began a fruitless attempt to advance down the Black Sea coast against very strong resistance.[186] At the end of August, Kleist reached the Terek River and began an attack towards Mozdok near the foothills of the Caucasus, but here Soviet resistance stiffened. Although Mozdok fell, Kleist's few remaining *panzer* units could make no further progress towards Grozny against the Soviet Ninth and Thirty-seventh Armies. Ironically, he had run short of fuel just a few miles from the largest Caucasian oil fields. Although German light infantry and mountain divisions entered the Caucasian mountain passes, none succeeded in forcing a passage into the Transcaucasus. In a dramatic gesture that annoyed Hitler, mountain troops placed the swastika flag atop Mount Elbrus on August 21. The Soviets promptly removed it.[187] At the far end of an inadequate supply line through Rostov and facing determined resistance, List could go no farther. On September 6, he notified OKH that he would not accept responsibility for another advance. Enraged to be told of List's predicament, Hitler relieved him three days later and himself assumed command of Army Group A. The German dictator now gave orders to himself on various levels—as *Fuehrer*, as Army Commander-in-Chief, and as an army group commander.

Paulus's strong Sixth Army, comprising 18 German divisions, advanced slowly into the Don bend during late July, delayed by the confusions caused by Hitler's contradictory orders. At Stalin's express order, four Soviet armies continued to defend roughly on the line of the Chir River. Paulus caught the Soviet Sixty-second Army and the First Tank Army west of the Don near Kalach on August 7, causing heavy casualties and taking 57,000 prisoners.[188] Hoth's Fourth Panzer Army approached Stalingrad from the south, but Soviet armor stopped it well south of the city. *(See Map 23, in Atlas.)* Zhukov and General Alexander M. Vasilevsky, the new Soviet Chief of Staff, visited the Stalingrad area as *Stavka* representatives in early August to coordinate the defense. Nikita S. Khrushchev became political commissar to both the newly formed Stalingrad and Southwest Fronts. The Sixty-second and several other armies were rehabilitated, and a series of defensive rings were built around Stalingrad. Soviet counterattacks on Paulus's left flank delayed the Sixth Army's next attack, which finally began on August 23. While the VIII Air Corps gave tactical support and bombed Stalingrad, the XIV Panzer Corps from the Sixth Army broke through and reached the Volga north of the city. At the end of August, the Sixty-fourth Army and the reconstituted Sixty-second Army suddenly broke contact and retreated within the defensive positions around Stalingrad. Hitler had virtually ignored the city during early July when it might easily have been taken. As he began to realize that EDELWEISS could not possibly succeed, he made Stalingrad a main objective. Now began an epic struggle for the city.

Caucasus Mountains: The Pass at Alagir at the Farthest Point of German Advance

The Defense of Stalingrad and Operation Uranus

In some ways, Stalingrad was well suited for defense. Approaches to the city led over open steppes, deeply scored by ravines and dry river beds. The ruins left by German bombing, the cellars of the houses, and the thick concrete walls of new factory buildings all offered good positions for the defenders.

General Vasili Ivanovich Chuikov

On the other hand, the Russians could reach Stalingrad only across the wide Volga, subjected to German air attack and artillery fire during daylight. Among the key terrain features in the city were the hill Mamaev Kurgan between the old and new cities, and the large factory complexes (Red October and Barricades) in the northern half of the city. *(See Map, Dispositions at Stalingrad, November 18, 1942, page 132.)*

After the defeats west of the Don, the defenders of Stalingrad were disorganized and dispirited,[189] but on September 10 General Vasili Ivanovich Chuikov assumed command of the Sixty-second Army. Arriving from a post as Attaché in Chungking, China, Chuikov brought vigor and optimism to his new duties. He soon proved to have a sound grasp of tactics and unbreakable nerves.[190] After being bombed off Mamaev Kurgan, Chuikov established his headquarters in a bunker buried in the sandy west bank of the Volga. Many of Chuikov's units were badly depleted and he had practically no armor at all. Both flanks of the Sixty-second Army were finally forced back to the Volga, breaking Chuikov's communications with neighboring units. With their backs to the river and no place to retreat, Chuikov's soldiers fought grimly against each new onslaught of the Sixth Army.

Determined to capture the city before the Russians had too much time to prepare the defense, Weichs ordered Paulus to attack immediately into the center of Stalingrad.[191] On September 7, the LI Corps attacked towards Mamaev Kurgan and slowly fought to the Volga on a narrow sector. Farther south, the XLVIII Panzer Corps fought into the old city on September 10, separating the Soviet Sixty-second and Sixty-fourth Armies. After each German advance, the Soviets counterattacked or infiltrated the new German positions. Some tactical objectives, such as the main railway station, changed hands repeatedly, often during the same day. Thousands of small, intense battles were fought for cellars, sewers, or a few yards of rubble. The German *landser* called this a *Rattenkrieg*: a war among rats. By mid-September, the Sixth Army occupied the center of Stalingrad and most of the old city in the south, but Paulus was extremely anxious about his flanks.

The Sixth Army and the Fourth Panzer Army were now at the tip of a salient pointing at Stalingrad, their northern flank protected by Italian, Hungarian, and Rumanian armies, their southeastern flank by Rumanian units, where it was not simply left open. *(See Map 23, in Atlas.)* Like Army Group A, Army Group B was at the end of a very long and uncertain supply line. Although himself concerned about the Don flank, Hitler refused to brigade the Allied troops with Germans for political reasons and he had no German units to spare. Instead, he ordered redoubled efforts to capture Stalingrad, as though that would solve the problems of Army Group B. Long convinced that Hitler was absurdly underestimating Soviet strength, Halder accepted his dismissal by Hitler on September 24 with a feeling of resignation.[192] Since the battle for Moscow, he had served Hitler largely in the hope of preventing his worst excesses, an illusion as events had proven. Halder went into retirement after the greatest victories any German chief of staff every enjoyed, but with the foreboding of imminent disaster.

In obedience to Hitler's order, Paulus rotated burned-out divisions from Stalingrad with better divisions from his left flank and renewed the assault on the city. By the end of September, the LI Corps fought into the Barricades Factory section, and during October into the tractor factories in the northern part of the city. During their *blitzkrieg* campaigns, the Germans had maneuvered over hundreds of miles in a few weeks; now the Sixth Army fought for weeks to gain a few hundred yards of ruins. The battle for Stalingrad reached its climax in mid-October as Paulus tried to compress Chuikov's army by attacking south along the Volga.[193] Although split in half by the latest German advance, the Sixty-second Army continued to fight for every building. Unable to maneuver armor or bomb effectively because the forces were so closely engaged, the Germans employed special sapper companies, flamethrowers, and direct-fire artillery. The Soviets used their *Katyusha* rocket

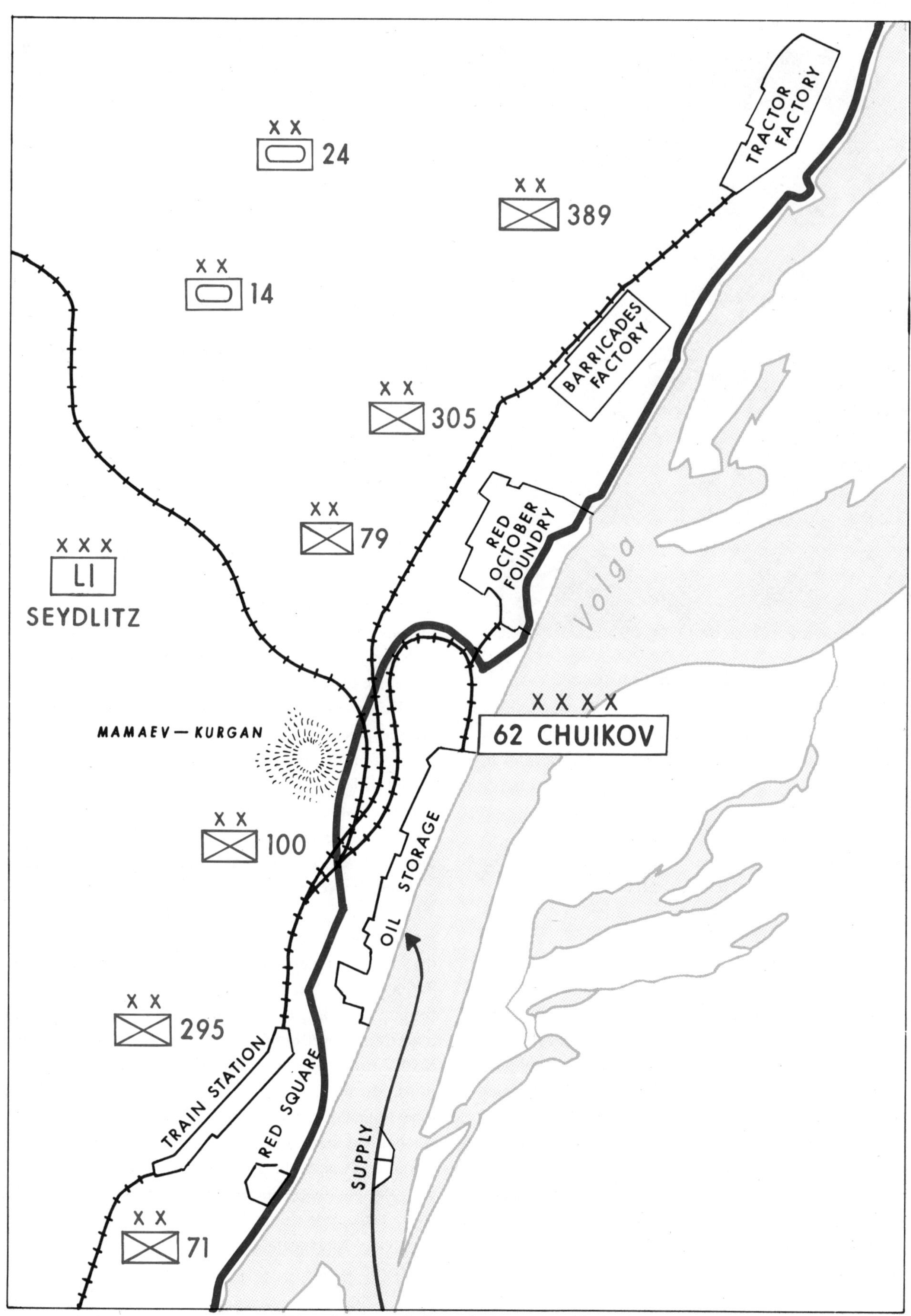

Dispositions at Stalingrad, November 18, 1942

launchers extensively and organized small centers of resistance that fought even when surrounded. By the end of October, Paulus's troops reached the Red October factory where fighting continued for several weeks, but the Sixth Army had become too exhausted to attempt another major assault. From the German point of view, the battle had ceased to have any strategic meaning; Stalingrad was simply a killing ground, like Verdun in the First World War. And this sort of battle favored the Red Army which fought best with its back to the wall. Chuikov still held just two narrow strips along the Volga and only one boat landing where reinforcements and supplies could arrive by night. But from the Russian point of view, the battle had great strategic value because it fixed the Sixth Army in a highly exposed position.

In imitation of his own stand-fast order in December 1941, which he firmly believed had saved the situation, on October 14, 1942 Hitler ordered that the entire German Army in Russia hold its positions until spring.[194] Badly miscast as a military leader, Hitler reverted to his older role of politician. On November 8 in Munich he triumphantly announced that Stalingrad had fallen.[195] On that same day, Great Britain and the United States landed in North Africa. A less intelligent man than Hitler might have seen that his position had become hopeless.

Zhukov and Vasilevsky had begun on September 12 to plan a massive counterattack against the flanks of the German salient. They were determined to build up their reserves sufficiently to mount a decisive operation, rather than fritter strength away in isolated attacks.[196] Although initially skeptical of so ambitious an operation, Stalin ultimately gave his approval as German exhaustion became apparent. Throughout October, while the battle for Stalingrad reached its climax, the *Stavka* assembled fresh forces, especially artillery and units of T-34 tanks, for the counteroffensive. The URANUS plan foresaw a double envelopment of the German forces in the Stalingrad area by the Southwest Front and the Stalingrad Front which would break through the thinly defended German flanks and join in the Kalach area.[197] *(See Map 24, in Atlas.)* The spearhead forces of the Southwest Front, the Fifth Tank Army and First Guard Army, would reach the line of the Chir in three days. Rokossovski's newly organized Don Front would mount supporting attacks. During late October and early November, Zhukov and Vasilevsky toured the area, coordinating the plan with front and army commanders and staffs. The Russian generals knew that the Rumanian units opposite the main thrusts were well below German standards.[198] Among other problems, the Rumanians were armed with discarded German 37-mm antitank guns that could not penetrate the T-34. As the massive build-up continued, the Russians used signallers to send trains one way at 15-minute intervals and laid 50 pontoon bridges across the Volga.[199] Although the Russians kept their intentions secret, preparations on this scale could not be concealed. By November 12, German intelligence reported an imminent attack on the Rumanian Third Army deployed on Paulus's left flank.[200]

Operation URANUS began on the morning of November 19. The Fifth Tank Army attacked from the Serafimovich bridgehead on the Don, broke through the Rumanian Third Army immediately, and swung southeast into the Don bend. *(See Map 24, in Atlas.)* The only substantial German force in the area, the XLVIII Panzer Corps, barely escaped encirclement by retreating west of the Chir River.[201] (This corps from the Fourth Panzer Army had been pulled out of Stalingrad earlier to back up the Rumanians when German intelligence warned of the build-up.) A lead detachment of the Fifth Tank Army boldly seized the Don bridge at Kalach during the night of November 22. The Twenty-first Army also broke through and joined with the Fifth Tank Army, creating a pocket which yielded 30,000 prisoners.[202] From the outset of URANUS, the Russians demonstrated tactics highly reminiscent of German *blitzkrieg*. Early on November 20, the Fifty-first and Fifty-seventh Armies of the Stalingrad Front broke through the Rumanian Fourth Army, whose troops fled in panic. Three days later, troops of the Southwest Front and the Stalingrad Front met near Kalach encircling the entire German Sixth Army and the IV Corps from the Fourth Panzer Army in a large pocket extending west from Stalingrad. Hoth, commanding the Fourth *Panzer* Army, had only his headquarters, one motorized division, and remnants of the Rumanian Fourth Army left outside the pocket. Paulus commanded three *panzer* divisions, but none had more than 60 tanks, and their weak counterattack was brushed aside by the Soviet Fifth Tank Army. Within just five days, the Germans in Stalingrad found themselves surrounded and far from any force strong enough to relieve them. On November 22, Paulus asked Weichs for

German Horse-Drawn Transport on the Steppe Near Stalingrad

permission to leave Stalingrad and the Army Group B commander promptly made this request of OKW-OKH, adding that otherwise the Sixth Army would starve. But on the twenty-fourth, Goering made an offhand promise to supply the Sixth Army by air, alleging that the Demyansk airlift had been a success.[203] Glad to avoid a retreat, Hitler declared Stalingrad a *Festung* and commanded Paulus to stay.

The Soviets had encircled 20 German and 2 Rumanian divisions in the Stalingrad area. With headquarters, corps, and army troops, approximately 250,000 men must originally have been surrounded.[204] To keep the Sixth Army supplied, the *Luftwaffe* had to land 300 JU-52 transport aircraft with 600 tons of cargo daily. General Wolfgang von Richtofen, commanding the Fourth Air Force, reported on November 25 that he could not meet this requirement and recommended that the Sixth Army break out, but Hitler brusquely refused.[205] In fact, the airlift subsequently averaged under 100 tons per day, condemning the Sixth Army to slow starvation. The *landser* listened to a personal message from Hitler on November 26, telling them to stand fast and promising help. To restore the situation, Hitler brought Manstein from the Leningrad area and gave him command over an Army Group Don created on November 20. The new group comprised the Sixth Army, the two Rumanian Armies (remnants), and the Fourth Panzer Army (elements not entrapped at Stalingrad); it would also include the 6th Panzer Division (arriving from western Europe) and four to five additional divisions.[206] Since Hitler gave orders directly to Paulus, Manstein was virtually a commander without troops. Manstein swiftly concluded that the Sixth Army would have to break out by attacking in a southeastern direction east of the Don, but he wished to wait until Hoth could mount a supporting attack.[207]

The *Stavka* planned an advance towards Rostov by the Vornezh and Southwest Fronts, code-named SATURN, but it hesitated to initiate this operation before the Sixth Army's destruction was certain.[208] Instead, these fronts were ordered to prepare LITTLE SATURN, an attack on the Italian Eighth Army still defending on the Don. *(See Map 24, in Atlas.)* At the same time, Manstein prepared his relief attempt, code-named WINTER STORM. On December 12, this attempt began with an attack by the LVII Panzer Corps east of the Don towards Stalingrad. *(See Map 25, in Atlas.)* This corps comprised two *panzer* divisions with a total of 230 tanks, most assigned to the fresh 6th Panzer Division.[209] The German tankers advanced unopposed until they encountered the Soviet Fifty-first Army and two mechanized corps equipped with the T-34. As the German advance slowly halted, the Soviets might simply have reinforced the Fifty-first Army, but instead they began LITTLE SATURN on December 16. The First Guards Army from the Southwest Front and the Sixth Army from the Voronezh Front immediately overran and routed the Italian Eighth Army. Several Soviet armies advanced rapidly across the open steppe and outflanked the weak Group Hollidt, which was comprised of the German XVII Corps and parts of various German and Rumanian divisions. LITTLE SATURN had torn away the right flank of Army Group B, completing the isolation of the forces in Stalingrad and threatening a further advance towards Rostov. If the Soviets reached Rostov, they could sever the supply line to Army Group A with incalculable consequences. On December 19, with the LVII Panzer Corps only 30 miles from the Stalingrad pocket, Manstein made a last appeal to Hitler for the Sixth Army to break out.[210] Hitler's refusal condemned the army he had promised to save.

The *Stavka* reassigned four armies to Rokossovski's Don Front and gave him the mission of destroying the German Sixth Army. After offering surrender terms, which were disregarded, Rokossovski began an attack from the west on January 10, 1943.[211] By this time, the *landser* had eaten their horses and were suffering from undernourishment aggravated by the extreme cold. Some wounded were flown out of Stalingrad, but most were left to die in cellars. As his troops advanced methodically on Stalingrad, Rokossovski tried to minimize his casualties by employing large artillery concentrations. For the German defenders, Stalingrad became a nightmare, perhaps the ultimate military horror of the Second World War. On January 26, armor from the Soviet Twenty-first Army penetrated to Mamaev Kurgan and met troops of Chuikov's Sixty-second Army.[212] This relief of the Stalingrad garrison brought tears to the Red Army men, who had survived a long ordeal. Hitler promoted Paulus to Field Marshal on January 31, probably hoping the honor would impel him to suicide. On the same day, Soviet troops captured the new Field Marshal in the basement of a ruined department store. Paulus died long after the war in East Germany, but approximately 90,000 survivors of his command left on a death march across the frozen steppe to labor camps. They suffered no worse fate than the countless Soviet prisoners taken by the Germans, but at least the Soviet soldier died defending his country. Both sides realized that Stalingrad was a turning point. The Germans no longer had any chance to defeat the Russians, and only a careful strategy could still gain them a stalemate.

Critique of the German 1942 Campaign

To critique the German strategy in 1942 is virtually to summarize the campaign, because every major decision was questionable or clearly wrong.[213] Hitler bears the primary responsibility because he personally devised the strategy and directed the operations in considerable detail. His generals cannot avoid censure for carrying out a ridiculous strategy, but of course their alternatives were retirement at best, a death sentence at worst. Like Halder, some served because they feared their successors might be more amenable to Hitler. On the other hand, some generals, including Paulus, believed Hitler had military talent. Generally speaking, the aims of the 1942 campaign were wholly out of proportion to the means available. Hitler gave the German Army impossible missions and abandoned it shamefully when it failed to accomplish them.

In the spring of 1942, the German Army was sadly weakened and depleted in every way. Before any large offensive, the Germans should have shortened their line and rehabilitated units on a large scale. Of course, the Soviets also would have benefited from this pause, but the Germans had to recover their qualitative superiority before attempting *blitzkrieg* again. Probably, Hitler should have chosen Moscow as the main objective in the hope of gaining a decisive military success. With the Anglo-American allies certain to cause trouble soon, it was already too late to think of long-term economic gains. Even more to the point, Moscow was within reach while the Caucasian oil was not. Choosing Leningrad and the Caucasus at both extremes of the front was grotesque and led to the mistake of moving the Eleventh Army to the north after its victory in the Crimea.

If Army Group South had executed the plan contained in Directive 41, more Russians might have been trapped in the Don bend. But by sending both *panzer* armies west in mid-July, Hitler gave the Russians an opportunity to escape. Once they did escape, Army Groups A and B could not possibly gain the objectives set by Directive 45. They could have seized Stalingrad *or* invaded the Caucasus, but not both, particularly in view of the logistical problems. Once the two army groups had fanned out, the flanks became intolerably long. Hitler was negligent in placing Hungarian, Italian, and Rumanian armies on the flanks. No one was more critical of these troops than the Germans, who knew perfectly well their poorly equipped allies could not stop a large Soviet offensive. Of course, Hitler did not need to capture Stalingrad at all; his fixation on the city merely kept the best units of Army Group B in an extremely dangerous position. In any case, the Germans, whose advantage lay in mobile war, should never have accepted protracted combat in a built-up area.

Once URANUS began, the Sixth Army and the Fourth Panzer Army should immediately have attacked west or southwest out of the Stalingrad area. They had no chance to survive on the Volga and would have been far more useful guarding the approaches to Rostov. Of course, Army Group A should have immediately withdrawn from the Caucasus. Unworkable command relationships hampered the German reaction to URANUS. Army Group A had no commander, or rather Hitler as a part-time substitute, while Weich's Army Group B was supposed to command three German and four allied armies, an impossible task. As the situation developed, Manstein's relief operation would probably have been more effective if the XLVIII and LVII Panzer Corps had operated together rather than in isolation. For both military and ethical reasons, the Sixth Army should have received permission to break out on December 18 or 19. Probably a good part of the army could have fought its way out.

By 1942, the German occupation policy and treatment of prisoners of war undoubtedly had some impact. Although captured Russians were treated correctly at the front, they were often left to die of disease, exposure, and starvation in the rear areas. Probably most Red Army men knew they might just as well fight to the death as surrender to the Germans. The German occupation was harsh and despotic in keeping with the racist ideology of National Socialism. His own evil motives worked against Hitler. He needed Russian help to conquer Russia, but his occupation policies discouraged this assistance. After being greeted as liberators in many parts of the Ukraine, for example, the Germans did nothing in 1942 to encourage Ukrainian nationalism. Curiously, for a man who had begun as a politician and propagandist, Hitler consistently preferred a military solution.

Since the 1942 campaign was Hitler's own, any criticism ultimately devolves to some description of his character and ability. He certainly had a retentive memory, an appreciation for technology, some flair for operations at approximately corps level, and an extraordinarily strong will.[214] With more military experience and more self-restraint, he might have become a competent corps commander, but he was a hopelessly inept strategist. He was incapable of adapting his plans to an objective reality of space, time, and opposing forces. Instead, he retreated into an infantile dream world, where his will alone was decisive. Because he refused to admit restraint on his own will, Hitler vastly overestimated the role of morale in warfare. Regardless of what tasks he set, if the Army failed he felt it must lack the will to overcome all obstacles. Hitler found it easy to make any demands because he had no real sympathy or affection for the soldiers whose lives he recklessly sacrificed. Probably no strategy could have brought decisive German success in 1942, but only a strategy as inane as Hitler's could have brought a disaster.

Notes

[1] Walter Hubatsch, *Hitler's Weisungen für die Kriegfuhrung 1939-1945* (Frankfurt am Main, 1962), pp. 84-88.

[2] Herman Mueller-Hillebrand, *German Armored Traffic Control*, Department of the Army Pamphlet 20-242 (Washington, 1952), p. 4.

[3] Albert Seaton, *The Russo-German War, 1941-45* (New York, 1971), p. 118.

[4] Franz Halder, *Kriegstagebuch* (6 Vols.: Stuttgart, 1961-64), III, 15; Seaton, *Russo-German War*, p. 214.

[5] Hans-Adolf Jacobsen, *Kriegstagebuch des Oberkommandos der Wehrmacht* (Frankfurt am Main, 1965), I, 497.

[6] Halder, *Kriegstagebuch*, III, 56; Seaton, *Russo-German War*, p. 125.

[7] Seweryn Bailer, *Stalin and His Generals* (New York, 1969), pp. 40-41; Albert Seaton, *Stalin as Military Commander* (New York, 1976), p. 104.

[8] Sergei M. Shtemenko, *The Soviet General Staff at War* (Moscow, 1970), p. 33.

[9] Pavel A. Zhilin, et al., *The History of the Great Patriotic War of the Soviet Union* (6 Vols.: Moscow, 1960-63), II, 49; Seaton, *Stalin*, pp. 101-103.

[10] Seaton, *Russo-German War*, p. 123.

[11] Seaton, *Stalin*, pp. 105-106.

[12] Albert Seaton, *The Battle for Moscow, 1941-1942* (New York, 1971), pp. 61-62.

[13] Seaton, *Battle for Moscow*, p. 45.

[14] Hermann Hoth, *Panzeroperationen* (Heidelberg, 1956), p. 78; Seaton, *Russo-German War*, p. 78.

[15] Department of the Army Pamphlet 20-240, *Rear Area Security in Russia* (Washington, 1951), p. 7.

[16] Seaton, *Russo-German War*, p. 128.

[17] Konstantin K. Rokossovski, *A Soldier's Duty* (Moscow, 1970), p. 21; Seaton, *Russo-German War*, pp. 127-128.

[18] Jacobsen, *Kriegstagebuch*, I, 517-518.

[19] *Ibid.*, 1218.

[20] *Ibid.*, 525.

[21] Seaton, *Russo-German War*, pp. 129-130; Jacobsen, *Kriegstagebuch*, I, 454-455.

[22] Halder, *Kriegstagebuch*, III, 38.

[23] Alexander Vassilevsky, "The Turning Point of the War," *Moscow-Stalingrad, 1941-42* (Moscow, 1970).

[24] Paul E. Lydolph, *Geography of the U.S.S.R.* (New York, 1970), pp. 127-128.

[25] Jacobsen, *Kriegstagebuch*, I, 496; Seaton, *Russo-German War*, pp. 103-104.

[26] Seaton, *Russo-German War*, p. 105.

[27] *Ibid.*, p. 107.

[28] Halder, *Kriegstagebuch*, III, 79.

[29] Andreas Hillgruber, *Hitler's Strategie, Politik und Kriegführung 1940-1941* (Frankfurt am Main, 1965), p. 503; George E. Blau, *The German Campaign in Russia–Planning and Operations (1940-1942)*, Department of the Army Pamphlet 20-261a (Washington, 1955), p. 34; Walter Warlimont, *Inside Hitler's Headquarters, 1939-45* (New York, 1964), p. 141.

[30] Adam B. Ulam, *Stalin* (New York, 1973), p. 543; Seaton, *Russo-German War*, pp. 134-135.

[31] Lydolph, *Geography of U.S.S.R.*, p. 489.

[32] Seaton, *Russo-German War*, p. 134.

[33] Jacobsen, *Kriegstagebuch*, I, 430.

[34] Seaton, *Russo-German War*, p. 137.

[35] Jacobsen, *Kriegstagebuch*, I, 551; Seaton, *Russo-German War*, pp. 140-141.

[36] Karl Dietrich Bracher, *The German Dictatorship* (New York, 1970).

[37] Hubatsch, *Weisungen*, pp. 84-88.

[38] Warlimont, *Hitler's Headquarters*, pp. 138-139.

[39] Blau, *German Campaign in Russia*, pp. 45-46.

[40] Jacobsen, *Kriegstagebuch*, I, 1031-1034; Blau, *German Campaign in Russia*, pp. 53-56; Halder, *Kriegstagebuch*, III, 121.

[41] Hubatsch, *Weisungen*, p. 140; Blau, *German Campaign in Russia*, pp. 50-53; Halder, *Kriegstagebuch*, III, 108; Seaton, *Russo-German War*, p. 142.

[42] Jacobsen, *Kriegstagebuch*, I, 1031; Blau, *German Campaign in Russia*, p. 53.

[43] Hubatsch, *Weisungen*, pp. 145-147; Blau, *German Campaign in Russia*, p. 61.

[44] Halder, *Kriegstagebuch*, III, 157-158; Blau, *German Campaign in Russia*, pp. 61-62.

[45] Halder, *Kriegstagebuch*, III, 159-160; Warlimont, *Hitler's Headquarters*, pp. 186-187.

[46] Blau, *German Campaign in Russia*, p. 63.

[47] Halder, *Kriegstagebuch*, III, 169-170.

[48] Jacobsen, *Kriegstagebuch*, I, 1055-1059; Blau, *German Campaign in Russia*, pp. 65-69.

[49] Warlimont, *Hitler's Headquarters*, p. 188.

[50] Warlimont, *Hitler's Headquarters*, p. 190; Blau, *German Campaign in Russia*, pp. 69-70.

[51] Heinz Guderian, *Panzer Leader* (New York, 1957), pp. 179-182.

[52] Halder, *Kriegstagebuch*, III, 194-195; Warlimont, *Hitler's Headquarters*, p. 191.

[53] Jacobsen, *Kriegstagebuch*, I, 1224.

[54] Seaton, *Russo-German War*, p. 145.

[55] Halder, *Kriegstagebuch*, III, 207.

[56] *Ibid.*, 202.

[57] Seaton, *Stalin*, pp. 110-116.

[58] Alan Clark, *The Russo-German Conflict, 1941-1945* (New York, 1965), p. 143; Jacobsen, *Kriegstagebuch*, I, 1230; Seaton, *Russo-German War*, p. 147.

[59] Clark, *Russo-German Conflict*, p. 145.

[60] Warlimont, *Hitler's Headquarters*, p. 187.

[61] Seaton, *Russo-German War*, pp. 216-217.

[62] Halder, *Kriegstagebuch*, III, 151.

[63] *Ibid.*, 260.

[64] Blau, *German Campaign in Russia*, p. 72.

[65] Seaton, *Russo-German War*, p. 172.

[66] Guderian, *Panzer Leader*, pp. 174-175.

[67] Jacobsen, *Kriegstagebuch*, I, 1221.

[68] Seaton, *Russo-German War*, pp. 113-114.

[69] Alfred Philippi and Ferdinand Heim, *Der Feldzug gegen Sowjet-Russland, 1941 bis 1945, Ein operativer Uberblick* (Stuttgart, 1962), p. 74; Halder, *Kriegstagebuch*, III, 178.

[70] Seaton, *Stalin*, p. 116.

[71] Jacobsen, *Kriegstagebuch*, I, 424.

[72] Seaton, *Russo-German War*, pp. 153-158.

[73] Hubatsch, *Weisungen*, p. 152; Halder, *Kriegstagebuch*, III, 53; Leon Goure, *The Siege of Leningrad* (Stanford, Calif., 1962), p. 85.

[74] Jacobsen, *Kriegstagebuch*, I, 621, 1226.

[75] Goure, *Leningrad*, p. 87; Jacobsen, *Kriegstagebuch*, I, 625.

[76] Goure, *Leningrad*, pp. 99-100.

[77] Hubatsch, *Weisungen*, pp. 150-153.

[78] Seaton, *Russo-German War*, p. 177.

[79] Philippi, *Feldzug gegen Sowjet-Russland*, p. 83.

[80] Seaton, *Russo-German War*, p. 178; Philippi, *Feldzug gegen Sowjet-Russland*, p. 83.

[81] Robert Huhn Jones, *The Roads to Russia* (Norman, Okla., 1969), p. 222.

[82] John Milsom, *Russian Tanks, 1900-1970, The Complete Illustrated History of Soviet Armoured Theory and Design* (New York, 1970), p. 104.

[83] T. H. Vail Motter, *The Persian Corridor and Aid to Russia (United States Army in World War II, The Middle East Theater)* (Washington, D.C., 1952), p. 2.

[84] George C. Herring Jr., *Aid to Russia 1941-1946* (New York, 1973), p. 15.

[85] Motter, *Persian Corridor*, p. 10.

[86] Seaton, *Russo-German War*, pp. 179-180; Vassilevsky, *Moscow-Stalingrad*, pp. 14-15.

[87] Halder, *Kriegstagebuch*, III, 266; Seaton, *Russo-German War*, p. 180.

[88] Seaton, *Russo-German War*, p. 181.

[89] Seaton, *Russo-German War*, p. 184; Philippi, *Feldzug gegen Sowjet-Russland*, p. 86.

[90] Guderian, *Panzer Leader*, p. 170.

[91] Hans-Adolf Jacobsen (ed.), *Decisive Battles of World War II: The German View* (New York, 1965), p. 150.

[92] Jacobsen, *Kriegstagebuch*, I, 715; Seaton, *Russo-German War*, p. 190.

[93] Blau, *German Campaign in Russia*, pp. 81-82; Jacobsen, *Kriegstagebuch*, I, 1070-1071.

[94] Herring, *Aid to Russia*, p. 21; Ulam, *Stalin*, pp. 553-554.

[95] Shtemenko, *Soviet General Staff*, p. 44; Vassilevsky, *Moscow-Stalingrad*, p. 17.

[96] Seaton, *Russo-German War*, p. 199; Halder, *Kriegstagebuch*, III, 305-307; Blau, *German Campaign in Russia*, p. 84; Jacobsen, *Battles*, p. 155.

[97] Guderian, *Panzer Leader*, p. 249; Seaton, *Russo-German War*, p. 205.

[98] Milsom, *Russian Tanks*, p. 171; Seymour Freidin, *The Fatal Decisions* (New York, 1956), p. 66.

[99] Seaton, *Russo-German War*, pp. 206-207.

[100] Department of the Army Pamphlet 20-291, *Effects of Climate on Combat in Russia* (Washington, D.C., 1952).

[101] Norman Rich, *Hitler's War Aims, The Establishment of the New Order* (New York, 1974), pp. 341-342; Jacobsen, *Kriegstagebuch*, I, 1106.

[102] Vladimir Katkoff, *Soviet Economy 1940-1965* (Baltimore, 1961), p. 91.

[103] Rokossovski, *Soldier's Duty*, p. 74; Vassilevsky, *Moscow-Stalingrad*, p. 19.

[104] Otto Preston Chaney, Jr., *Zhukov* (Norman, Oklahoma, 1971), p. 155.

[105] Hubatsch, *Weisungen*, pp. 171-174.

[106] Peter Chamberlain, *Mortars and Rockets* (New York, 1975), pp. 61-63.

[107] Chaney, *Zhukov*, p. 175.

[108] Jacobsen, *Kriegstagebuch*, I, 809; Seaton, *Battle for Moscow*, p. 193.

[109] Jacobsen, *Kriegstagebuch*, I, 679-681; Seaton, *Russo-German War*, p. 148; Philippi, *Feldzug gegen Sowjet-Russland*, p. 89.

[110] Jacobsen, *Kriegstagebuch*, I, 703.

[111] *Ibid.*, 739.

[112] *Ibid.*, 719.

[113] Elisabeth Wagner, *Der Generalquartiermeister* (Munich, 1965), p. 212.

[114] Jacobsen, *Kriegstagebuch*, I, 767.

[115] Blau, *German Campaign in Russia*, pp. 110-113.

[116] Seaton, *Russo-German War*, pp. 194-196.

[117] Jacobsen, *Kriegstagebuch*, I, 1236; Halder, *Kriegstagebuch*, III, 312-315; Seaton, *Russo-German War*, p. 196.

[118] Halder, *Kriegstagebuch*, III, 319.

[119] Zhilin, *Great Patriotic War*, III, 222-223; Seaton, *Russo-German War*, p. 198.

[120] Halder, *Kriegstagebuch*, III, 322; Seaton, *Battle for Moscow*, p. 173.

[121] Zhilin, *Great Patriotic War*, II, 224-225; Seaton, *Russo-German War*, p. 147.

[122] Goure, *Leningrad*, pp. 57-58.

[123] Halder, *Kriegstagebuch*, III, 334; Goure, *Leningrad*, pp. 145-148.

[124] Chaney, *Zhukov*, p. 132.

[125] Alan S Milward, *The German Economy at War* (London, 1965), pp. 19-21.

[126] Albert Speer, *Inside the Third Reich* (New York, 1970), Chapter 16; Milward, *German Economy*, pp. 22-25.

[127] Hillgruber, *Hitler's Strategie*, p. 269.

[128] Milward, *German Economy*, pp. 45-47.

[129] Hillgruber, *Hitler's Strategie*, p. 400 (Germany: 11,030, Great Britain: 20,100).

[130] F. M. von Senger und Etterlin, *German Tanks of World War II* (New York, 1969), Appendix 4, p. 211.

[131] B. H. Liddell Hart, *The German Generals Talk* (New York, 1948), p. 167.

[132] Lydolph, *Geography of U.S.S.R.*, p. 38.

[133] Warlimont, *Hitler's Headquarters*, pp. 207-210.

[134] Joachim Fest, *Hitler* (New York, 1974), pp. 655-666.

[135] Clark, *Russo-German Conflict*, p. 170.

[136] Halder, *Kriegstagebuch*, III, 345.

[137] Wilhelm Keitel, *The Memoirs of Field Marshal Keitel* (New York, 1965), pp. 166-168; Warlimont, *Hitler's Headquarters*, p. 207; Liddell Hart, *German Generals*, p. 108.

[138] Seaton, *Battle for Moscow*, pp. 199-201.

[139] Halder, *Kriegstagebuch*, III, 354.

[140] Seaton, *Battle for Moscow*, pp. 293-294.

[141] Georgi K. Zhukov, *Marshal Zhukov's Greatest Battles* (New York, 1969), pp. 90-92.

[142] Seaton, *Russo-German War*, p. 224.

[143] Vassilevsky, et al., *Moscow-Stalingrad*, p. 90 (article by Konstantin K. Rokossovski).

[144] Zhukov, *Greatest Battles*, pp. 98-100.

[145] Zhilin, *Great Patriotic War*, II, 327; John Erickson, *The Road to Stalingrad* (New York, 1975), pp. 314-316.

[146] Seaton, *Russo-German War*, p. 238.

[147] Zhilin, *Great Patriotic War*, II, 336-337; Seaton, *Russo-German War*, pp. 243-244.

[148] Seaton, *Russo-German War*, pp. 246-248.

[149] *Ibid.*, p. 250.

[150] Jacobsen, *Battles*, pp. 167-168; Chaney, *Zhukov*, pp. 177-179; Seaton, *Battle for Moscow*, p. 187.

[151] Rokossovski, *Soldier's Duty*, p. 106.

[152] Halder, *Kriegstagebuch*, III, 292, 418; Seaton, *Russo-German War*, p. 228.

[153] *Effects of Climate on Combat in Russia*, p. 6; Halder, *Kriegstagebuch*, III, 430.

[154] Blau, *German Campaign in Russia*, p. 36; Halder, *Kriegstagebuch*, III, 431.

[155] Halder, *Kriegstagebuch*, III, 431.

[156] Hillgruber, *Hitler's Strategie*, p. 226; Blau, *German Campaign in Russia*, p. 109.

[157] Hillgruber, *Hitler's Strategie*, p. 267.

[158] Hubatsch, *Weisungen*, pp. 129-133; Blau, *German Campaign in Russia*, p. 109.

[159] Blau, *German Campaign in Russia*, p. 110.

[160] *Ibid.*, p. 112.

[161] Halder, *Kriegstagebuch*, III, 295.

[162] Warlimont, *Hitler's Headquarters*, p. 231.

[163] Hubatsch, *Weisungen*, pp. 183-188.

[164] Blau, *German Campaign in Russia*, p. 135.

[165] Warlimont, *Hitler's Headquarters*, p. 240.

[166] Blau, *German Campaign in Russia*, p. 120.

[167] *Ibid.*, p. 136.

[168] Blau, *German Campaign in Russia*, p. 115; Warlimont, *Hitler's Headquarters*, p. 239.

[169] Blau, *German Campaign in Russia*, p. 128.

[170] Warlimont, *Hitler's Headquarters*, p. 240.

[171] Hanson W. Baldwin, *Battles Lost and Won, Great Campaigns of World War II* (New York, 1966), p. 160; Earl F. Ziemke, *Stalingrad to Berlin: The German Defeat in the East* (Washington, D.C., 1968), p. 32; Andrei Grechko, *Battle for the Caucasus* (Moscow, 1971), pp. 86-87; Joseph Stalin, *The Great Patriotic War of the Soviet Union* (New York, 1945), p. 60; Seaton, *Russo-German War*, p. 273.

[172] Erickson, *Road to Stalingrad*, p. 344.

[173] Zhilin, *Great Patriotic War*, II, 413-415; Erickson, *Road to Stalingrad*, p. 346; Seaton, *Russo-German War*, p. 261.

[174] Seaton, *Russo-German War*, p. 261.

[175] *Ibid.*, p. 259.

[176] Erich von Manstein, *Lost Victories* (Chicago, 1958), p. 245; John Batchelor and Ian Hogg, *Artillery* (New York, 1972), pp. 43-46.

[177] Zhilin, *Great Patriotic War*, II, 410; Seaton, *Russo-German War*, p. 264.

[178] Manstein, *Lost Victories*, pp. 260-265.

[179] Halder, *Kriegstagebuch*, III, 466; Blau, *German Campaign in Russia*, p. 143.

[180] Philippi, *Feldzug gegen Sowjet-Russland*, p. 135.

[181] Seaton, *Stalin*, pp. 147-148; Erickson, *Road to Stalingrad*, p. 351; Stalin, *Great Patriotic War*, p. 60.

[182] Philippi, *Feldzug gegen Sowjet-Russland*, p. 138.

[183] Seaton, *Russo-German War*, pp. 275-276.

[184] Hubatsch, *Weisungen*, pp. 196-200.

[185] Philippi, *Feldzug gegen Sowjet-Russland*, p. 148.

[186] Grechko, *Battle for Caucasus*, pp. 126-131; Seaton, *Russo-German War*, p. 285.

[187] Grechko, *Battle for Caucasus*, p. 142.

[188] Philippi, *Feldzug gegen Sowjet-Russland*, p. 156.

[189] Vasili I. Chuikov, *The Battle for Stalingrad* (New York, 1964), pp. 84-85.

[190] Erickson, *Road to Stalingrad*, p. 388.

[191] Philippi, *Feldzug gegen Sowjet-Russland*, p. 160; Seaton, *Russo-German War*, p. 296.

[192] Halder, *Kriegstagebuch*, III, 528.

[193] Zhilin, *Great Patriotic War*, II, 445-446; Chuikov, *Battle for Stalingrad*, pp. 182-191; Seaton, *Russo-German War*, p. 300.

[194] Philippi, *Feldzug gegen Sowjet-Russland*, p. 168.

[195] Jacobsen, *Battles*, p. 232; Seaton, *Russo-German War*, p. 305.

[196] Zhukov, *Greatest Battles*, pp. 139-144.

[197] Zhukov, *Greatest Battles*, p. 163; Erickson, *Road to Stalingrad*, pp. 449-450.

[198] Zhukov, *Greatest Battles*, pp. 168-169.

[199] Erickson, *Road to Stalingrad*, pp. 448-449.

[200] Reinhard Gehlen, *The Service* (New York, 1972), pp. 56-59; Seaton, *Russo-German War*, p. 310.

[201] Ziemke, *Stalingrad to Berlin*, p. 54.

[202] Zhukov, *Greatest Battles*, p. 175.

[203] Warlimont, *Hitler's Headquarters*, p. 284; Ziemke, *Stalingrad to Berlin*, p. 58; Seaton, *Russo-German War*, pp. 320-321.

[204] Seaton, *Russo-German War*, p. 336; Philippi, *Feldzug gegen Sowjet-Russland*, p. 183; Chuikov, *Battle for Stalingrad*, p. 263; Ziemke, *Stalingrad to Berlin*, p. 79; Henri Michel, *The Second World War* (New York, 1975), pp. 400, 406.

[205] Ziemke, *Stalingrad to Berlin*, p. 61.

[206] Manstein, *Lost Victories*, p. 301.

[207] *Ibid.*, pp. 304-307.

[208] Zhilin, *Great Patriotic War*, III, 42; Zhukov, *Greatest Battles*, p. 174.

[209] Seaton, *Russo-German War*, p. 326.

[210] Manstein, *Lost Victories*, pp. 334-335, Appendix 3.

[211] Zhilin, *Great Patriotic War*, III, 37-38; Rokossovski, *Soldier's Duty*, p. 164.

[212] Zhilin, *Great Patriotic War*, III, 60; Chuikov, *Battle for Stalingrad*, pp. 258-259.

[213] Manstein, *Lost Victories*, pp. 289-293; Blau, *German Campaign in Russia*, pp. 176-179; Seaton, *Russo-German War*, pp. 338-340.

[214] Manstein, *Lost Victories*, pp. 273-288.

New Masters of Blitzkrieg: The Russo-German War From Kursk to Berlin 6

In 1942 the enemy suffered decisive defeat on the Volga, and this was the climax and the turning point of the whole Second World War. The battle of Kursk in the summer of 1943, and then the forcing of the Dnieper by our troops and the liberation of Kiev, left Hitlerite Germany facing catastrophe.

. . . .

In spite of the fact that the Soviet Armed Forces were taking the offensive along a wide front, the fighting power of their armies and fronts was not diminished, since in these battles losses of arms and equipment were brought down to a minimum—they cannot even be compared with the losses sustained in 1941, when we were retreating. Added to which the liberated territories enabled reserves of manpower to be increased. Industry was supplying the front with all it required at ever-increasing rates of output. All this induced confidence in a speedy and complete victory over the foe.

Marshal Vasili I. Chuikov,
The Fall of Berlin

In their winter offensive of 1942-1943, the Soviets were not content merely to destroy the German Sixth Army in Stalingrad. They intended also to force the Donets River and converge on Rostov near the mouth of the Don, isolating the German Army Group A in the Caucasus. On January 12, the Voronezh Front began an offensive against the German Second and the Hungarian Second Armies. *(See Map 25, in Atlas.)* Like all Germany's allies, excepting only the Finns, the Hungarians were hopelessly inferior to the Soviets and quickly collapsed. With very light losses, the Soviet Third Tank Army pierced the Hungarian defenses and wheeled north to link up with the Soviet Fortieth Army. In addition to the bulk of the Hungarian Second Army, the German XXIV Panzer Corps and two other German divisions were surrounded west of Voronezh. The German troops saved themselves only by abandoning their heavy equipment. This Soviet success opened the way for an advance towards Kharkov, a center for German logistical support.

At Zhukov's urging, the Soviet offensive continued towards Kharkov in early February. As the Voronezh Front closed around the city, a partisan revolt broke out in Kharkov on February 14, forcing the II SS Panzer Corps to evacuate.[1] In the meantime, the Soviet Southwest and South Fronts advanced to the Donets and Mius Rivers where Manstein's Army Group Don made a stand. *(See Map 25, in Atlas.)* The frozen Donets proved no barrier to the Soviets who crossed on a broad front in the Izyum area and continued south towards Dnepropetrovsk, threatening to cut one of the two rail lines to the German armies defending on the Mius. As the First Guards Army approached Dnepropetrovsk from the northeast, Tank Group Popov moved south in the direction of Stalino. *(See Map 26, in Atlas.)* To all appearances, the Soviets were on the verge of enveloping Army Group Don (Group South after February 13) and gaining a greater victory than Stalingrad—perhaps even a decisive victory in the war.[2] Scenting blood, Stalin urged his commanders to continue.

Riposte on the Donets: Manstein's Spring Counteroffensive

On February 17, 1943, Hitler flew to Manstein's headquarters at Zaporozhye, a city almost within the range of Soviet tankers

German Armor in the Winter of 1942-1943: PzKw IV Tank in Foreground

roaming east of the Dnieper.[3] Irritated by Manstein's recent suggestion to appoint an overall chief of staff, Hitler came intending to dismiss him, but soon became too involved in the crisis facing Army Group South.[4] Manstein argued that his army group could not possibly defend the entire line. Instead, the Fourth and First Panzer Armies must first remove the threat of the Southwest Front to the Dnieper crossings and then deliver a rapid counterstroke towards Kharkov.[5] Hitler, on the other hand, underestimated the strength of the Soviet threat and preferred to concentrate on the earliest recapture of Kharkov, probably for reasons of prestige. After two days of discussions, Hitler finally permitted Manstein to draw troops from Army Group A and to concentrate armor on his northern flank for a counterstroke. Although a field marshal and Germany's most successful strategist, Manstein often had to obtain Hitler's approval to shift a corps or division.

On February 18, at the low point of Germany's fortunes, the propaganda minister Joseph Goebbels harangued a crowd of party members in Berlin and obtained thunderous approval for "total war." The next day, Manstein ordered Hoth's Fourth Panzer Army, recently reconstituted, to begin deploying for an attack northwards from the Dnepropetrovsk area. A few days later, the II SS Panzer Corps began attacking from the Krasnograd area into the rear of the Soviet First Guards and Sixth Armies. The elite SS *panzer* divisions *Das Reich* and *Totenkopf* made rapid progress and contacted the XLVIII Panzer Corps of the Fourth Panzer Army on February 22.[6] At the same time, the First Panzer Army employed the XL Panzer Corps, including the SS division *Wiking*, to envelop the Soviet Tank Group Popov which threatened to break the rail line near Stalino. At this point, the Soviet forces west of the Donets should have gone on the defensive, but the *Stavka* ordered the advance renewed. Fortunately for the Southwest Front, the Germans were not able to form continuous lines around the enveloped forces, and ultimately most of the encircled troops could escape.[7]

On February 28, as the spring thaw was already beginning, Manstein ordered an attack on Kharkov parallel to the Donets.[8] The Second SS Panzer Corps reversed its direction of attack and recaptured the city after heavy street fighting in mid-March. On March 18, the elite Panzergrenadier (Mechanized Infantry) Division *Grossdeutschland*, the only named division in the German Army, recaptured Belgorod. Although several of its units were destroyed, the Soviet Third Tank Army escaped from the Kharkov area and withdrew over the Donets. Manstein would have liked to cross the Donets, but he ordered a halt at this point to rest his exhausted troops. He had brought the Soviet winter offensive to a halt and even won a small but significant victory. Of course, a major share of the credit must be accorded the well-equipped and relatively fresh SS *panzer* divisions, which now each had one battalion of Mark VI (Tiger) tanks. The Soviets had been badly overextended west of the Donets and were vulnerable due to the rapidity of their own advance from the Volga and Don. Reflecting on his success, Manstein concluded that the advantage lay with the counteroffensive.[9] He thought that a mobile defense based on the counterstroke could still bring the war in Russia to a draw. He realized clearly that the Germans must exploit their superiority in mobile warfare in the defense as they once had in the attack. But Hitler rejected these tactics, arguing that Germany must hold the entire Donets industrial area for economic reasons.

German Troops Riding on a PzKw IV Tank in Russia, March 1943

The Caucasus and Leningrad

During early 1943, the Germans suffered reverses at both extremes of the immensely long front in Russia. Field Marshal Ewald von Kleist, the new commander of Army Group A, wished to withdraw the bulk of his force through Rostov.[10] This retreat would have brought Kleist's troops out of an untenable position and added weight to Manstein's counteroffensive, but Hitler refused to admit the utter failure of his grandiose Caucasus operation. *(See Map 25, in Atlas.)* He merely gave his tacit approval to withdrawal into a large defensive zone in the Kuban east of the Kerch Straits.[11] This half-measure left the Seventeenth Army where it could do the Germans no good and the Russians no harm. According to the *Stavka* plan, the North Group of the Transcaucasus Front was to mount a strong offensive towards Rostov, pinning Kleist's troops against the mountains.[12] This plan appeared risky to the Soviet field commanders who still feared a new German offensive towards Grozny and the Caspian Sea. Rather than developing a full offensive, they contented themselves with keeping pressure on the retreating Germans. Logistical difficulties also slowed the Soviet offensive, as they had the earlier German efforts. In places, the Soviets were compelled to use men to haul food and ammunition over poor roads.[13] The Transcaucasus Front lacked direct land communications with the heart of the Soviet Union and was supplied in everything but heavy weapons directly from the Caucasus region. Despite these difficulties, the Soviets entered Krasnodar on February 12 and their Forty-fourth Army reached the Rostov area in early February. Elements of four Soviet armies cooperated in encircling Rostov and finally captured the city on February 14. This important city had changed hands for the fourth and last time.

During the summer of 1942, the Russians evacuated almost a half million civilians from Leningrad over Lake Ladoga and brought in fresh supplies.[14] As a result, life became more bearable in the besieged city. The capture of Leningrad was Hitler's second priority objective in 1942 and to this end he had sent Manstein from the Crimea after the fall of Sevastopol. Manstein arrived with elements of the Eleventh Army and a train of siege artillery, but he succeeded only in repelling a series of violent Soviet attacks. Soon Manstein left to take command of Army Group Don in the Ukraine and the Soviets began to prepare a large offensive to relieve Leningrad. Behind their own lines they practiced assaulting replicas of the defensive positions built by Army Group North. Troops of the Leningrad Front equipped themselves with ladders, ropes and cleated boots to aid in crossing the frozen Neva River.[15] Finally, on January 12, 1943, the Leningrad Front attacked over the Neva, while the Volkhov Front attacked west towards Schlusselberg (Kirovsk), the key German position on Lake Ladoga. *(Actions not shown on map.)* On January 18, units from the two fronts met, breaking the siege. Emotions ran very high among the Red Army men and the civilians of Leningrad, who decorated their city with flags and cried in relief at the news.[16] Although, strictly speaking, the siege was now lifted, Leningrad continued a beleaguered existence. The offensive had opened only a very narrow corridor along the lake, which lay within German artillery range. Having achieved their own aims, the Finns offered no assistance during these battles, nor were the German units in Finland able to help. Army Group North remained condemned to static warfare with Leningrad just outside its grasp.

Farther south, in order to relieve some of the pressure on Army Groups North and Center, Hitler allowed his commanders to abandon two large salients. On January 31, after a long debate, Hitler authorized the evacuation of the Demyansk salient, so stubbornly and foolishly defended during the previous winter.[17] *(See Maps 21 and 27a, in Atlas.)* A week later, he reluctantly agreed to evacuate the large Rzhev salient near Smolensk, a relic of the first winter's confused fighting.[18] These long overdue withdrawals gave the Germans a shorter and more easily defended line.

Soldiers Without Uniforms: The Soviet Partisans

Brief as its existence was, the German government of conquered Russia convinced the citizens that even Stalin's government was preferable. Hitler's only plan for Russia was brutal exploitation of the people and natural resources.[19] The Baltic countries and White Russia constituted the *Reichskommissariat Ostland*, while a broad swath from the Pripet Marshes to the Crimea became *Reichskommissariat Ukraine*. Both territories were given to old Nazi Party members to administer, Erich Koch in the Ukraine being the worse of the two. Koch arrogantly refused cooperation with the Ukrainians, whom he described as slaves even in public speeches.[20] The Germans proved the viciousness of their regime by murdering the Jews in occupied Russia, usually in mass shootings before open graves. In a report to Hitler on December 20, 1942, the *Reichsführer SS* Heinrich Himmler indicated that 360,000 Jews had been murdered in occupied Russia during the previous four months. It seems likely that mobile operations conducted by special SS units (not the *Waffen SS* who served as soldiers) killed approximately 1,400,000 Russian Jews.[21] Meanwhile, a Russian resistance movement harassed German rear areas.

A Wartime Poster Depicts Soviet Partisans

Behind the German lines, the Soviet partisan movement gained strength. Exact numbers are unknown even to the Russians, but the partisans apparently grew from negligible strength in 1941 to 150,000 in the summer of 1942 and perhaps 200,000 by the summer of 1943.[22] These partisans had not come into being as the result of preparations begun prior to the invasion; nor can they be said to have risen spontaneously. Many of the original partisans were soldiers who escaped from the enormous battles of encirclement in 1941 but could not rejoin their units.[23] Other partisans were Communist Party members trapped behind German lines. As the movement grew in strength, Communists infiltrated or returned by aircraft to organize the resistance to the Germans.[24] In accordance with Communist ideology, Stalin called for widespread resistance in his radio address of July 13, 1941, but a central staff for the partisan movement was not organized until 1942.[25] During the second year of the war, the partisans were organized into brigades with strengths varying from 350 to 2,000 men. These brigades were subordinated directly to the nearest front (army group) headquarters. The brigades usually maintained radio contact with the fronts and often Red Army officers arrived on special assignment to train and lead the partisans.[26] Especially during 1943 and 1944, the Soviet commanders planned partisan activity to complement large offensive operations. The partisans' primary mission was usually the interdiction of German supply lines.

Having little manpower to spare, the Germans refused to permanently assign first-quality troops to antiguerilla operations. Instead, veterans of the First World War were drafted into active service and formed into security divisions equipped with light infantry weapons.[27] Even when supported by small SS formations or Army units on temporary assignment, the security divisions usually failed to destroy the partisans, especially when they could retreat into difficult terrain. If they ventured onto the open steppe, the partisans were in great danger, but they thrived in the trackless forests and marshes of White Russia. Occasionally they risked small fire fights in order to destroy a bridge or supply depot. For example, on the night of March 20, 1943, partisans fought a brisk engagement against a German guard detachment and succeeded in destroying the railway bridge over the Desna River on the line between Gomel and Bryansk.[28] But apart from these often spectacular exceptions, the partisans wisely avoided military confrontation and concentrated on intelligence gathering and widespread sabotage. The Germans relied almost entirely on rail transport and the tracks remained susceptible to sabotage, despite strenuous efforts to protect them. By summer 1943, Army Group Center was reporting over a thousand incidents of railway sabotage each month, involving tens of thousands of demolitions.[29] Although the Germans usually restored service within a few hours or days, railway sabotage had a cumulative effect and was especially dangerous when it coincided with a large Soviet offensive. In desperation, the Germans sent young Russians to forced labor in Germany, burned villages and publicly murdered hostages, but these measures alienated the civilian population and increased its support for the partisans.[30] In this war without rules, the partisans assassinated collaborators and the commanders of brigades exercised the right of summary execution over their men.[31]

The Sinews of War: Industry and Lend-Lease

Although nearly half the population and the great industrial region of the Donets remained under German occupation, the Soviets still found men for new armies and vastly increased war production. They defeated the Germans at Stalingrad almost entirely through their own efforts and would probably have won the same victory if they had received no assistance at all.[32] However, by the end of 1942, American lend-lease aid began arriving in sufficient quantity to be noticed, especially in field telephone wire and boots for the Russian infantry.[33] The Americans could offer the Soviets very few arms through 1942, either because American production was too small or because American arms were not needed in Russia. For example, the Sherman tank was not available until late 1942 when the Russians were already producing their own equally good or better T-34/85. Except in aircraft, American arms and weapons systems never made any large contribution to victory in Russia. But American aid in other categories began to arrive in abundance during 1943, increasing the tempo of Soviet offensives.

Soon American motor vehicles allowed the Soviets to rapidly exploit their success on the battlefield. In all, the Russians received over 40,000 jeeps, almost 150,000 one-and-one-half-ton trucks and over 180,000 two-and-one-half-ton trucks, all vehicles with good tactical mobility.[34] These vehicles were used primarily to accumulate stocks before a battle or to keep advancing troops supplied with ammunition and fuel. The Americans also delivered over 7,500 tractors and 1,900 steam locomotives, sorely needed because the Soviets virtually ceased to produce railway equipment during the war.[35] Having lost their fertile, black soil region of the Ukraine, the Russians especially welcomed large deliveries of wheat flour, sugar, fats and vegetable oil. Their communications owed much to the delivery of over 380,000 field telephone units and over a million miles of field wire.[36] They uniformed their armies with over 11 million yards of American and woolen cloth.[37] All of these deliveries complemented Soviet industry, which was forced to concentrate on armaments.

Although lend-lease was a great help from 1943 to the end of the war, the Soviets had no cause to feel unduly grateful. It had not arrived during their greatest peril, but only when they began to win the war anyway. Even when the goods were available in America, much time was lost in transport. There were just three practical routes, all of them difficult: across the Pacific to Valdivostok and through Siberia by rail; around Scandinavia through the Arctic Sea to Murmansk; or around Cape Horn, up the Persian Gulf and north by truck and railway. Although the Japanese did not molest merchant traffic to Vladivostok, the Russians lacked shipping and of course the Americans could not sail in Japanese waters after December 1941. From the beginning of the war, the British Royal Navy sent lightly armed merchantmen with destroyer escort on the Murmansk run. They were relatively safe during the long Arctic nights, but in the spring of 1942 the Germans interdicted this traffic with submarines and aircraft based in Norway.[38] After losing two-thirds of a convoy to enemy action in July 1942, Churchill felt compelled to suspend the Murmansk operations until fall when the days grew shorter.[39] There remained the route through Persia, occupied by the British and Soviets since August 1941. To make this route viable, the Americans had to improve the port facilities, roads and railways, but they were frustrated during 1942 by administrative confusion and conflicts among British, Persian and Soviet authorities.[40] Even in spring 1943, deliveries remained disappointing because of port congestion and heavy rains which washed away the roads.[41]

Communist ideology, which tends to equate human achievement with industrial production and emphasizes the effect of production on history, prompted the Soviets to seek victory in the factory. In this endeavor, they enjoyed astonishing success under very difficult circumstances. The Soviets argue that their production proves the superiority of Communist society over Fascist, which they regard as an inevitable outgrowth of a capitalist society in crisis. However this may be, Stalin's Russia did make better use of her resources than Hitler's Germany. The ruthless Five Year Plans had brought the Soviet Union about even with Germany during the interwar years when the capitalist countries were struck by depression. But during 1941 and 1942, the Germans conquered the Ukraine and the Donets Basin, captured Kharkov, destroyed Stalingrad, almost strangled Leningrad and interdicted shipments of Caspian oil, causing a crisis in Soviet industry. For example, the Soviets estimate that the Germans had conquered areas which accounted for over half the prewar metallurgy.[42] How were the Soviets able to overcome these losses and outproduce the Germans, whose generally unscathed industry could draw on a conquered or docile Europe?

According to the Soviets, plants and workers were relocated to the Urals, western Siberia, the Volga region, and Kazakhstan on a massive scale.[43] More important, the centralized Soviet state immediately sacrificed the entire civilian economy, including even agriculture and transportation, to the needs of heavy industry. This industry concentrated entirely on the production of a few proven weapons, such as the T-34 tank. The Soviets produced a few rugged and effective weapons in great quantity, in contrast to the Germans who developed a great variety of weapons and designed endless modifications. The Communist Party, long accustomed to administering the economy, proved an efficient conduit for Stalin's orders, unlike the Nazi Party in Germany. Of course, the Soviet Union also enjoyed vast reserves of natural resources, especially the open pit coal mines of the Ural region. Finally, the Soviets relied on women to carry on war industry. By 1944, over one-half of the entire industrial work force was composed of women.[44] Although their exploits as partisans, snipers, and combat pilots were better publicized, Soviet women made their greatest contribution in the factory.

Much of Soviet industry remained well beyond the German grasp. For example, although the T-34 was produced in Kharkov, Stalingrad, Voroshilovgrad, and Mariupol on the Sea of Azov, it was also assembled in Nizhni-Tagil and Chelyabinsk (both in the Urals), at Novo-Sibirsk in western Siberia, and even at Chita, east of Lake Baikal. Later, T-34 plants appeared at Gorki and Kirov, northeast of Moscow, and Saratov on the Volga.[45] The center of T-34 production lay in the Ural region, especially *Uralmashzavod* (Ural Tank Factory) at Nizhni-Tagil, which used machinery salvaged from Kharkov. Here, the Soviets first began to stamp T-34 turrets out of 45-mm steel plates.[46] Magnitogorsk, also in the Urals, was a great metallurgical center which developed high quality steel for armor plate and armor piercing shot.[47] Of course, the Soviets had to overcome immense difficulties in transporting raw materials to the plants and the weapons to the battlefields of European Russia.

Soviet industry survived severe shortages of electrical power and petroleum products in 1942 and early 1943, then began a general recovery during the last half of 1943. Although it failed to reach Baku, Hitler's Caucasus campaign caused a sharp decline in shipments of Caspian oil. By early 1943, half of all Soviet oil wells lay idle.[48] Despite this setback, the Soviets raised their overall output during 1943 by as much as 17 percent.[49] According to their figures, the Soviets produced 8.5 million tons of steel in 1943, and from this steel they fabricated 24,000 tanks and self-propelled guns and 130,000 guns of all calibers.[50] Of the armor production, no less than 14,000 were the T-34 main battle tank. Soviet production continued to increase up to 1945 but certainly 1943 was the crucial year, the year Soviet workers hammered out a victory. It is possible that the Soviet statistics are inflated, but the German sources depict an abundance of Soviet weaponry on the battlefield, especially in armor and artillery.

While the Soviets immediately shifted their full effort to the war against Germany, Hitler hesitated and procrastinated. Not only did his regime fail to curtail civilian production, but Hitler also failed to realize that the German economy must be wholly directed to winning the land war in Russia. As late as January 10, 1942, he issued a directive which reiterated the long-term goal of producing more airplanes and submarines for the war against Great Britain, and gave the Army precedence only for the time being.[51] But a set of fortuitous circumstances in early 1942 placed the German economy into more capable hands. On February 8, the munitions minister Fritz Todt, whose Organization Todt bore responsibility for a series of large building projects, died in an airplane crash.[52] With typical carelessness, Hitler named his architect Albert Speer as Todt's successor and gave him very wide but ill-defined powers over the German economy.[53] Speer happened to be an extremely competent administrator, and he succeeded in introducing central planning for the entire economy and fixed prices in place of a

"Each Blow a Hammer Blow Against the Enemy!" (Soviet Poster)

cost-plus system.[54] When he took power, Speer found that civilian production was just three percent below its prewar level and key industries still had only one work shift. He curtailed the civilian production and introduced two and three work shifts into crucial factories.[55] Speer sought to rationalize production by creating layers of committees responsible for particular industries. Even such a minister as Speer could not overcome some basic problems, such as a lack of skilled labor; a short supply of metals like copper, tungsten, lead and nickel; a dependence on foreign sources of petroleum; and a chronic shortage of high-grade steel.[56] But Speer did vastly expand Germany's output of armaments. As an example, tank production went from 4,198 units in 1942 to 5,996 in 1943, and reached 8,328 in 1944 despite the Allied bombing campaign. In fact, German industry produced 19,087 armored vehicles in 1944, including large numbers of turretless assault guns.[57] Most of these vehicles were lost during the endless German retreats of the last war years. After an extremely late start, the Germans had closed the gap quickly; but it came too late to stem the Allied tide.

The Greatest Tank Battle: Operation CITADEL

As the summer campaigning season approached in 1943, realistic Germans realized that they could no longer expect a decisive success in Russia. The choice lay between a defensive strategy and some limited offensive. Since the Japanese were obviously losing the initiative and Mussolini was pleading for peace with the Russians, Hitler felt that he needed a victory to signify to the world that the Germans were still powerful.[58] Finding himself on a 500-mile front with only 32 understrength divisions, Manstein was opposed to static defense and inclined to favor a strategy of counterattack.[59] But Hitler, his OKH Chief of Staff (General Kurt Zeitzler), and Field Marshal Günther von Kluge (commanding Army Group Center) agreed on a limited offensive, and finally Manstein accepted this idea.[60] At first, Hitler considered converging attacks over the Donets in the Izyum area, but on April 15 he decided in favor of Operation CITADEL, converging attacks south from the Orel area and north from the Kharkov area to cut off the Soviet salient around Kursk. *(See Map 27a, in Atlas.)* Even under the best circumstances, this plan entailed risks. Orel lay in a German salient with a long northern flank, and the Germans were not well established in the Kharkov area, having just recaptured the city in March. The operation was also a trifle over-obvious. To minimize the inherent risks, CITADEL demanded secrecy and speed of execution.

Hitler originally intended CITADEL to begin in early May, but when heavy rains forced postponement, he decided to call a conference in Munich on May 3 to discuss the operation. Manstein, Kluge, Zeitzler, and Speer were present, as was Guderian who had recently become the Inspector-General of the *panzer* forces. General Walter Model, the commander of Ninth Army, was not present, but he had sent a letter describing the very strong Soviet defenses, implying that CITADEL might fail. Manstein said the offensive would have had a better chance in April, and asked for two additional divisions. Kluge and Zeitzler favored the plan, but Guderian was strongly opposed. The latter had just decided to continue building the Mark IV tank because the much superior Mark V (Panther) could not be produced in sufficient quantity. He feared that armor losses in Russia would open Western Europe to Anglo-American invasion. Even Hitler was doubtful about CITADEL and decided to wait until larger numbers of the heavy Mark VI (Tiger) arrived at the front.[61] While Hitler hesitated, the *Afrika Korps* surrendered in Tunisia on May 13, leaving Italy extremely vulnerable to invasion by the western Allies. In light of this danger, on June 18 the OKW operations section recommended that CITADEL be abandoned. But, for the same reason, Hitler had become convinced that he must have some victory to bolster German morale and keep German allies faithful.[62] He ordered the operation to begin on July 5.

For CITADEL, the Germans assembled the bulk of their available armor and combat aircraft. Model's Ninth Army was to attack from the Orel salient with six *panzer* divisions and over 900 tanks; Manstein was to attack from the Kharkov area with the Fourth Panzer Army and Group Kempf, deploying five *panzergrenadier* divisions and approximately 1,000 tanks.

General (later Field Marshal) Walter Model With the Crew of an Assault Gun, January 28, 1943

The Fourth Panzer Army included the elite II SS Panzer Corps, which had been extremely successful during Manstein's spring counteroffensive. Approximately 1,700 aircraft were to support the operation. The Germans had never concentrated such large forces on such small fronts before. With their customary meticulosity, they made aerial photographs of the entire Soviet salient and took elaborate deception measures.[63]

Through intelligence sources and partisan reports of the German preparations, however, the Soviets were well informed of the impending attack.[64] Acting on this intelligence, the Russians worked from April through June to improve the defenses around Kursk. *(See Map 27b, in Atlas.)* Within the salient stood the Voronezh and Center Fronts, the latter commanded by General Konstantin K. Rokossovski, who had received Paulus's surrender. General Ivan S. Konev's Steppe Front with five armies was deployed in reserve across the neck of the salient. Always adept at field fortifications, the Soviets applied every lesson they had learned in the course of the war. The entire salient was covered by three defensive lines to a depth of 20 to 25 miles. Behind these continuous lines were extensive fall-back positions to a depth of more than 100 miles.[65] Each defensive line consisted of four to five sets of trenches, interconnected and provided with weapons pits and bunkers. Approaches were heavily mined and covered by mutually supporting antitank guns. The Soviet commanders took the risk of concentrating their forces at the neck of the salient where they anticipated the German attacks.[66] Marshal Georgi K. Zhukov, who was *Stavka* representative for the Kursk area, later estimated the Soviet forces as 1,330,000 men, 3,600 tanks, and 3,100 aircraft, figures which may be inflated.[67] Whatever their strength, the Soviets were at least equal and probably superior to the Germans in every major category. By the end of June 1943, Hitler could not have chosen a worse place than Kursk to mount an offensive.

Operation CITADEL began on July 4 with probing attacks by the XLVIII Panzer Corps against the Soviet Sixth Guards Army. *(See Map 27b, in Atlas.)* (The "Guards" designation in the Red Army indicated an elite formation honored for its good combat record. The Guards units enjoyed extra pay and had a slightly heavier table of organization and equipment.) Certain now that the main attack was imminent, the Voronezh Front fired heavy concentrations of preplanned fire during the night, hoping to strike the Germans in their assembly areas. Despite cloud bursts on the southern edge of the Kursk salient, the full assault began on July 5. On the northern flank, Model's Ninth Army penetrated the first Soviet line of defense to a depth of about six miles, but could not advance much farther. When their minefields were breached, Rokossovski's infantrymen appeared behind the German armor to sow more mines. Model's commanders concentrated heavy Tiger tanks and Ferdinand assault guns on narrow sectors, but the troops still failed to break the determined Soviet resistance. The German infantry took 10,000 casualties in two days, trying to clear the small towns and forests.[68] By July 8, Model clearly saw that his army was engaged in a battle of attrition, with little prospect of ever penetrating the Soviet defenses. Rokossovski's only fear was that he might be struck from the south where the Germans were making better progress.[69]

On the south side of the salient, the XLVIII Panzer Corps with the *Grossdeutschland* Division and the II SS Panzer Corps attacked together towards Kursk, while the III Panzer Corps attacked east of Belgorod. The Voronezh Front met this extremely heavy assault with a series of responses and field expedients. Neighboring formations counterattacked repeatedly on the flanks of the German advance. Armies on quiet sectors detached their artillery to stiffen the defensive lines threatened by the advance. The Soviet First Tank Army moved into the Sixth Guards Army defensive zone and dug its tanks into the ground rendering them immobile but difficult to destroy. The Fifth Guards Army and the Fifth Guards Tank Army from Konev's Steppe Front, which was in reserve, marched quickly to the area of Prokhorovka on the rail line between Belgorod and Kursk. Here, on July 12, the Fifth Guards Tank Army engaged the Second SS Panzer Corps in a great tank battle, while both sides fought for air superiority in the skies above the battlefield. The terrain was lightly wooded and cut by ravines, allowing the Soviet tankers opportunities to engage the heavier German tanks at close ranges.[70] Both sides suffered staggering armor losses in the largest tank-to-tank confrontation of the war. Hoping that the Soviets had committed their last reserves, Manstein ordered the XXIV Panzer Corps, which included the SS Division *Wiking*, to assemble in the Belgorod area and prepare to be committed. But at the same time, the Soviet Bryansk Front began a well-prepared offensive, which fell upon the XXXV Corps of the German Second Panzer Army in the Orel salient.

On July 10, 1943, as the battle of Kursk reached its critical phase, the Soviet Union's western allies began the invasion of Sicily. Hitler immediately became alarmed because he correctly surmised that the Italians had very little staying power. Fearful for the security of both Italy and the Balkans, he called Kluge and Manstein to his headquarters on July 13 and announced the termination of CITADEL.[71] Kluge agreed because Model's Ninth Army could make no progress and the Second Panzer Army was itself under attack, but Manstein argued that his Fourth Panzer Army was close to a tactical breakthrough. Manstein may have been correct, but it is hard to imagine what his exhausted troops could have accomplished even if they did briefly gain open country.[72] On July 17, Hitler ordered the II SS Panzer Corps out of the line in order to transfer it to Italy. Following Benito Mussolini's arrest on July 25, Hitler also decided to evacuate the Orel salient to release more troops for

Italy. Model, briefly commanding both the Second Panzer and Ninth Armies, began this planned retreat on August 1. At the same time, the Soviet West Front attacked towards Roslavl trying to outflank the Second Panzer Army or break into its fall-back positions. In July, the Germans had expected to cut off a Russian salient, but by August they were satisfied to evacuate their own Orel salient without serious losses. Begun too late against too strong an opponent, CITADEL was an utter failure that senselessly sacrificed German armor. It was also the last important German offensive in Russia.

The Apotheosis of War: Development of Armor to 1943

Armor had long been the dominant arm in the war in the East, and Kursk was the greatest armor battle of the war. A comparison of the equipment shows how far the contest for tank superiority had gone. In 1941, the Germans still employed *Panzerkampfwagen* (PzKw) I, armed merely with two machine guns, and PxKw II, which mounted only a 20-mm cannon. These early types had been useful in Poland and France, where any armored vehicles had caused apprehension among enemy troops and commanders and had gained the advantages of mobility. In Russia, however, such vehicles were employed only briefly for scouting and reconnaissance. The German main battle tank had become the PzKw III in the E variant, mounting a short 50-mm gun and almost vertical 30-mm armor on the hull. Even though this tank weighed only 20 tons, it was very slow off the roads and had to be refueled every 60 miles. In every respect except sighting equipment, it was inferior to the Soviet T-34 which appeared in late 1941. In response to this challenge, the Germans gave PzKw III a longer-barrelled 50-mm and later a 75-mm gun while also adding additional armor. When they realized that no 50-mm gun was sufficiently effective against the T-34, they began producing a high velocity 75-mm gun in 1942. The PzKw IV, which was already in production, was the only tank with a turret big enough for the new gun. As an interim measure, production of this tank was increased until sufficient Panthers could be produced—which never happened.

From 1943 to the end of the war, PzKw IV tanks remained the mainstay of German armored formations. In all, about 8,000 of these tanks left the assembly lines, more than any other German tank. In all its variations, PzKw IV mounted a 75-mm gun and carried a coaxial turret machine gun. Its armor was progressively increased to 50-mm or even more in hull and turret. The heaviest versions weighed just under 24 tons and had much better cross-country mobility than earlier tank types. Fuel resupply remained a problem becase the 300-horsepower gasoline V-12 engine had high consumption and little fuel could be carried within the hull. Although a highly serviceable tank, the PzKw IV owed much of its good combat record to the efficiency of its crews. If he could have produced PzKw V and VI tanks in sufficient numbers, Guderian would gladly have stopped PzKw IV production in 1943.[74] The chassis from types III and IV appeared in a variety of other vehicles, including 88-mm self-propelled guns and lightly armored troop carriers.

The German Main Battle Tank, the Panzerkampfwagen IV. This is Ausfuhrung A, the First Version of the Tank

Panzerkampfwagen V, better known as the Panther, is generally considered the best German tank and even the best tank on any side in the Second World War. Although the Germans experimented with tanks of its size as early as 1937, the first Panthers were produced in November 1942. With a combat weight of approximately 45 tons, the Panther was a heavy tank by the standards of the time. It had an excellent suspension, using transverse torsion bars to support the bogie wheels. With its 700-horsepower gasoline engine, the Panther traveled about 15 miles per hour off the roads, despite carrying an 80-mm glacis plate. The main armament was an extra-long, high-velocity 75-mm-gun. Turretless tank destroyers mounting the 88-mm gun were produced on the same chassis and known as *Jagdpanther* (Hunting Panther or tank destroyer). Over 1,700 Panthers were produced during 1943, and Manstein had about 200 for CITADEL.[75] But in their haste to gain armor superiority, the Germans had foregone field testing of the PzKw V. The transmission was barely adequate to the strain of the large engine, tracks were liable to break, and the engines were poorly ventilated, causing them to overheat and even catch fire. Most of the Panthers deployed for the Kursk battle broke down, and all the surviving vehicles had to be recalled for modification. In subsequent battles, the Panther proved its excellence—but much too late to save the Germans from defeat.

The celebrated PzKw VI, or Tiger, also made its first appearance in substantial numbers at Kursk. The Tiger was a formidable machine, reflecting Hitler's preference for very heavy tanks, but it was less effective than the Panther. It had 100-mm of glacis armor, enough to withstand direct hits from most antitank guns, but it could be pierced from the flank or have a track shot away. PzKw VI carried the well known 88-mm gun, first developed by the Germans for antiaircraft fire and eventually used for almost every purpose. Every tank design is a compromise, and the Tiger paid for its relative invulnerability with reduced speed and range. PzKw VI in the E variant traveled only 12 miles an hour cross country and often managed less than 40 miles on a tank of gas. The Germans also lacked the productive facilities and raw materials to mass produce the Tiger in sufficient numbers. Less than 650 of them were produced in 1943 and fewer than 1,400 during the entire war.[76] The first Tigers were heavy enough at 55 tons, yet Hitler finally increased the armor on one version to a ponderous 70 tons, the heaviest tank employed by any nation during the war. Despite the Tiger's great shock effect, the Germans would probably have done better simply to produce more Panthers. In the spring of 1943, Hitler inspected the model for a mobile fort weighing 188 tons. No less a designer than Ferdinand Porsche was responsible for this monster, whose turret alone would weigh almost as much as a Tiger.[77] This odd weapon obviously had no tactical value and never got beyond the prototype stage, but it illustrates Hitler's mania for size and his wild search for some miracle weapon to retrieve his fortunes.

The Soviets had long recognized the importance of armor and had conducted an extremely active program of tank development during the 1930s. They experimented with every extreme, from the five-turreted, 45-ton T-35 to the 14-ton BT-7 which had only 13-mm armor and traveled 45 miles an hour on the road. Unfortunately, they placed their faith in fast, lightly armored tanks which the German gunners destroyed in large numbers during 1941. But in late 1939, the Soviets had

The German Heavy Tank, Panzerkampfwagen VI ("Tiger"), Ausfuhrung E Shown

designed an entirely new medium tank, the justly famous T-34. This was the first fully successful modern tank, distinguished by a careful balance of heavy, sloped armor, large caliber turret gun, powerful diesel engine, and good cross-country mobility. The suspension was on the Christie pattern, with pivot arms resting on coil springs within the hull. Running on wide tracks well suited to the Russian terrain, the T-34 could manage 25 miles an hour cross-country and had a range of 130 miles. The engine was a standardized and reliable 12-cylinder, 500-horsepower diesel that the Soviets also employed in several other tanks and armored vehicles. After some initial problems with the transmission were overcome, the T-34 became very rugged. Originally, it mounted a 76.2-mm gun, larger than that of any German tank in 1941, but in 1943 it was up-gunned to 85-mm. The hull was welded throughout and sloped around the entire tank. The glacis armor was 45-mm thick and the side armor 40-mm, making the hull practically invulnerable to the standard German 37- and 50-mm antitank guns.[78] In all its variations, the T-34 ran from 26 to 31 tons in combat weight.[79] One weakness of the T-34 lay in its relatively primitive sighting equipment. The lack of a turret floor also posed some problems for the crew, especially for the commander who had to stay clear of the breech on recoil.[80] The Russians claim to have produced approximately 40,000 T-34s during the war.[81] Even if this statistic is exaggerated, the Soviets certainly produced enough to make the T-34 standard equipment, replace very heavy combat losses, and gain a clear armor superiority over the Germans by the summer of 1943. Given the chance, a T-34/85 crew could kill any German tank, except perhaps an up-armored Tiger.

The Soviets also maintained an interest in heavy tanks, often employed in breaking through strong defensive positions, but these tanks appeared in relatively small numbers. During 1938 to 1939, they designed the Klementy Voroshilov (KV) tank with 75-mm armor and a 76.2-mm gun. The KV tank helped to penetrate the Mannerheim Line during the winter war against Finland and later gave German antitank gunners a terrible shock when their rounds failed even to dent its massive armor. Through the KV the Soviets also gained the experience necessary to produce the Josef Stalin (JS) tank in late 1943. The JS tank appeared in three versions during the war and played a role similar to that of the Tiger in the German Army. JS-I mounted a 122-mm gun, much larger than the 88-mm weapon in PzKw VI, but not as efficient due to difficulty in storing and handling the semi-fixed ammunition. JS-I weighed under 45 tons, yet carried 90-mm of frontal armor. The last modification, JS-III, appeared in early 1945, too late to see much service. JS-III had two hull plates welded at the center and sloped sharply towards the rear plus an extremely low and well-rounded cast turret. With some justification, the Soviets confidently regarded JS-III as the best heavy tank of the Second World War.[82]

The First Soviet Summer Offensive: Back to the Dnieper River

Although Hitler had terminated Operation CITADEL after only 10 days, it had an important result. Had the Germans remained on the defensive during 1943 and built a reserve of armored divisions to contain breakthroughs, they might have gained a stalemate in Russia, as Manstein had thought possible.[83] Instead, by hurling their armor at the strongest Russian positions, the Germans had so depleted their force that they could no longer build a mobile reserve, especially when they had to defend Italy against an Anglo-American invasion. Having failed for the first time to break through the Russian lines in a major offensive, the Germans now found themselves compelled to adopt a defensive strategy under unfavorable conditions. The initiative passed to the Red Army, which never again relinquished it.[84] For the first time, the Russians could begin a large-scale offensive in good campaigning weather. For several reasons, they directed this offensive against Army Group South. First, they hoped to regain the industrial and agricultural regions of the Ukraine, which already supplied the Germans with some important ores. Then they hoped to trap large German forces in extended positions on the Donets and Dnieper Rivers. If the Soviet attack reached Kiev, the Russians might split the German front at the Pripet Marshes and threaten the rail communications between Army Group South and the *Reich*. Finally, the open steppe and farm land of the Ukraine is good tank country, presenting only a few large river barriers to an attacking force.[85]

Although assured of superiority, the Russians still used cautious tactics in 1943. Two years' experience with German envelopments had left the Soviet commanders with an acute concern for flank security. For the time, they preferred to exploit their superiority through a series of attacks along a broad front, rather than risk bold penetrations in the style of *blitzkrieg*. On July 17, the Soviet South and Southwest Fronts attacked across the Mius River north of Taganrog and in the Izyum area on the Donets River. *(See Map 28, in Atlas.)* Manstein countered this attack by bringing armored reinforcements from his own left wing. As a result, the left wing buckled quickly when the Voronezh Front and Konev's Steppe Front attacked south towards Belgorod on August 3.[86] The Soviet attackers enjoyed tactical surprise and achieved a breakthrough on the first day. At the same time, the Bryansk and Center Fronts continued to clear the Orel salient. When Orel and Belgorod were both captured on August 5, Stalin ordered the first victory salvo of the war fired in Moscow.[87] Realizing too late that his greatest danger lay in the Ukraine, Hitler ordered two divisions of the II SS Panzer Corps (*Das Reich* and *Totenkopf*) returned from Italy. He also directed all army groups in Russia to construct the Panther and Wotan positions, practically an East Wall analogous to the West Wall already under construction in France.[88] This defensive line was to extend from the Sea of Azov near Melitopol to the Dnieper River, along the river to a point north of Kiev and then over Vitebsk to Lake Peipus and the Finnish gulf. *(See Map 28, in Atlas.)* Hitler had refused this obvious precaution earlier out of mistrust for his generals, whom he thought too inclined to retreat. Now the measure came too late. In fact the Army would have to occupy part of the position before any fortifications could be constructed.

On August 23, the troops of the Steppe Front recaptured Kharkov. *(See Map 28, in Atlas.)* Shortly afterwards, they were counterattacked by the returning SS *panzer* divisions, but the Fifth Guards Tank Army restored the situation. Three days later, Rokossovski ordered his Center Front into the offensive and encountered stiff resistance from the German Second Army. Confident of his greater resources, Rokossovski widened the offensive and reached Glukhov by August 29.[89] In late August, the Fifth Shock Army of the South Front broke through the German Sixth Army positions on the Mius River, threatening to roll back Manstein's southern flank. In desperation, Manstein and Kluge flew to Hitler's East Prussian headquarters on September 3 to make far-reaching suggestions. They wished to end the OKW-OKH dualism which left the Russian front an OKH responsibility while OKW oversaw all other theaters. Instead, they proposed to create a new Army Chief of Staff with overall responsibility. Their candidate was Manstein himself, who would immediately have shortened the line in Russia and drawn heavily on the garrisons in the West in order to stop the Soviet offensives. As the generals must have foreseen, Hitler adamantly refused to share his own wide authority with a strong Army Chief of Staff, least of all with Manstein, whom he had long mistrusted.[90] On September 8, 1943, the same day the Italian surrender was made public, Hitler made his last visit to the Eastern Front. At Manstein's headquarters on the Dnieper, he gave his approval in principle to withdrawal into the Wotan position.[91]

Soviet Troops Crossing a Branch of the Dnieper River

By mid-September, Army Group South was racing with the Russians for the Dnieper River. Hitler ordered Manstein to carry off or destroy the industry and agriculture east of the river, but the Germans were too harassed to do this thoroughly.[92] For many German units, including the elite *Grossdeutschland* Division, the retreat soon became an exercise in survival.[93] Fighting by day and marching by night, most German units reached the west bank only by abandoning large quantities of heavy equipment. Under urgent orders to make a headlong crossing of the Dnieper, the Red Army men used any field expedient and affected numerous crossings before the end of September. On the other side, the German *landser* found few prepared positions or supplies awaiting them. On the northern flank of the Soviet advance, the Voronezh and Center Fronts approached the Dnieper on broad fronts and continued straight west, although Rokossovski would have preferred to swing south into the left flank of the Fourth Panzer Army.[94] On the southern flank, Hitler at last permitted the Seventeenth Army to withdraw from the Kuban into the Crimea. The Germans crossed the Straits of Kerch with small losses, but the troops of the North Caucasus Front maintained a very close pursuit, crossing the Straits themselves by the end of October.[95]

If the Germans had planned a defense of the Dnieper River line earlier and reached the river ahead of the Russians, they might have stopped the Soviet offensive there. On its lower reaches near Kremenchug the river is 2,500 feet wide, and near Kiev 300 foot cliffs guard the west bank.[96] But Army Group South had lost the race and during the fall the Soviets overran most of the planned Wotan position. On October 1, the Third Guards Army and Chuikov's Eighth Guards Army (the new designation of his Sixty-second Army) attacked the German bridgehead east of the Dnieper at Zaporozhye *(not shown on maps)* and forced the German First Panzer Army across the river in two weeks' fighting. During late October, the Fifty-first and Twenty-eighth Armies of the South (Fourth Ukrainian) Front captured Melitopol and broke the weak German Sixth Army defenses. The Sixth Army saved itself by retreating behind the Dnieper, leaving the Seventeenth Army isolated in the Crimea. The Seventeenth Army commander General Erwin Jaenecke protested vigorously against allowing his troops to be trapped in a positon which must ultimately become untenable.[97] Hitler argued blandly that the Soviets would use the Crimea to launch air strikes on the Rumanian oil fields and refused to consider a withdrawal. Of course, Jaenecke was right, and the Germans finally had to evacuate the Crimea under heavy losses.

On October 15, Konev's Steppe (Second Ukrainian) Front attacked out of its Dnieper bridgeheads near Kremenchug in the direction of Krivoi Rog. This latter city not only provided Germany iron ore, but also served as depot and railhead for the forces still in the lower Dnieper bend.[98] Konev's spearhead included the strong Fifth Guards Tank Army, which had been transferred from the Kharkov area. His troops entered the city on the twenty-fifth, but a sudden counterattack by the XL Panzer Corps drove them out, inflicting heavy losses. Perhaps the *Stavka* erred in not concentrating the southern offensive on this vital objective, but the strategy of shifting attacks all along the front had the advantage of keeping the Germans fixed by forcing them to defend everywhere. On November 3, the First Ukrainian Front attacked the Fourth Panzer Army and captured the Ukrainian capital, Kiev, in three days. The Soviets then advanced rapidly on a broad front south of the Pripet Marshes, reaching the line Korosten-Zhitomir by mid-November and cutting an important rail line. At this point, the Fourth Panzer Army counterattacked with the XLVIII Panzer Corps, including the SS *panzer* division, *Leibstandardte*, which had been rushed back from Italy. The First Ukrainian Front recoiled toward Kiev, but heavy rains and sheer exhaustion soon ended the German counteroffensive.[99]

Although their main effort in 1943 was against Army Group South, the Russians also attacked Army Groups Center and North, proving their superiority along the entire front. Rokossovski, now in command of the White Russian Front (combining the Center and Bryansk Fronts), broke out of his Sozh bridgeheads and backed the German Second Army into the Pripet Marshes, capturing Gomel on November 23, after a long struggle. Then he advanced into a gap between the Second and Ninth Armies and crossed the Dnieper on a wide front, forcing the Germans to abandon a large segment of the Panther position. At the same time, a West Front offensive captured Smolensk and Roslavl. Through these operations, the Russians split the Germans into two fronts, extending north and south of the Pripet Marshes where there was so little firm ground that neither side attempted to maintain a continuous front. They also gained good positions for operations along the traditional invasion route, the Minsk to Moscow landbridge. On October 6, the Kalinin (First Baltic) Front began a surprise attack towards Nevel at the boundary between the German Army Groups Center and North. Attack along unit boundaries was a favorite, oft-repeated Soviet tactic. The Soviet Third Shock Army immediately scattered a *Luftwaffe* field division and seized Nevel before the Germans could react. Then the First Baltic Front attacked along the flanks of the breakthrough, trying to pry the German Army Groups apart. Harassed by partisans in the rear areas, almost devoid of armor and unable to maneuver effectively through the lakes, woods, and forests of central Russia, the Germans could barely hold the line. The success of the Nevel attack gave the Soviets some conception of what they might expect from a major offensive in the area.[100]

The Tehran Conference and Winter Campaigning

Since 1941, Hitler had maintained strong German forces in the West to guard against invasion, particularly in France and Norway. By late 1943, 84 German divisions were deployed in western Europe and the German Army maintained almost as many men in foreign countries other than Russia as it did on the Eastern Front.[101] Had these forces always been available to fight Russia, Hitler would probably have won his war. Had they been available even as late as 1943, the Germans would have been able to defend themselves indefinitely against the Russians alone. Yet, in terms of men and materials, all the fighting in North Africa and Italy to this time was insignificant compared to the war raging in the Soviet Union. Ironically, the threat of an Anglo-American invasion was as important to Hitler's defeat as the landings themselves. When Stalin went to the first wartime conference with Churchill and Roosevelt at Tehran on November 28, 1943, he had the confidence of a man who knows he is winning; but he also had an overwhelming desire to see a second front in France, whatever the political consequences. At the Tehran Conference, the three great anti-German powers agreed for the first time on a mutually supporting military strategy. Stalin promised to initiate a great Soviet offensive to coincide with OVERLORD, the Anglo-American invasion then scheduled for May 1944. At Tehran, the Allies also agreed to accord recognition to Josip Broz Tito's Communist partisans fighting in Yugoslavia and to apply pressure on Finland to negotiate peace with the Soviet Union.[102]

As the war in Russia entered its third winter, nothing Hitler could do would prevent his defeat, but the decisions he did make hastened the end. In the military sphere, Hitler had never been more than an inspired, or simply lucky, amateur, and in adversity his incompetence became glaringly apparent. At the end of 1943, he had his last chance to shorten the line and build reserves to counter Soviet break-throughs. Instead, Hitler clung to a strategy of static defense, perhaps reverting to his personal memories of trench warfare. Static defense was a strategy most helpful to the Soviets, who still had some difficulty in maneuvering their forces on and beyond the battlefield. To force this bankrupt strategy on his generals, Hitler resorted to lies. He claimed, for example, that Germany must have manganese ore from Nikopol in the lower Dnieper bend, even though his economic minister Albert Speer denied this was so.[103] German defeats during 1943 were primarily due to lack of men and material, while discipline and even morale remained amazingly high. Yet Hitler, always more propagandist than soldier at heart, professed to believe that poor morale was the problem.[104] This slur on the German soldier was the more grotesque since Hitler no longer left his headquarters, the famous *Wolfsschanze* ("Wolf's Lair") in East Prussia, and took pains not to learn how morale really was, either among soldiers or civilians. Staff officers at the *Wolfsschanze* were oppressed by the atmosphere of suspicion and mistrust, by Hitler's total lack of concern for the troops, and an eerie sense of unreality.

Although the Russians had gained a narrow corridor to Leningrad in January 1943, the city was still virtually besieged by the German Eighteenth Army. During the fall of 1943, Army Group North prepared its section of the Panther position behind Lake Peipus, and evacuated most of the adult males living between the front and the Panther position to prevent their serving in the Red Army. By the beginning of 1944, the Germans were screening the Oranienbaum pocket west of Leningrad with weak *Luftwaffe* field divisions and non-German SS units, while straining to contain the Russian break-through in the Nevel area. *(See Map 29, in Atlas.)* Alert to his danger, the commander of Army Group North advised an early withdrawal into the Panther line; but Hitler procrastinated as always. On January 14, 1944, the Leningrad Front attacked simultaneously from the city and the Oranienbaum pocket, while the Volkhov Front began its own assault. After three days' fighting, the German defenses began collapsing before Leningrad and around Novgorod, north of Lake Ilmen. After joining in the Leningrad area, the Second Shock Army and the Forty-second Army attacked west towards Narva north of Lake Peipus. Despite the extremely poor weather and difficult terrain, the Soviet attacks continued with such intensity that on February 15 Hitler finally agreed to withdraw to the Panther line roughly along the Estonian-Latvian border. Command of Army Group North went to General Walter Model, an officer of Nazi sympathies who had acquired a reputation for tenacity in the defense. (At Hitler's bidding, Model continued his undertaking of a series of hopeless missions which finally ended with his suicide in 1945, as the commander of forces trapped in the Ruhr pocket.) In 1941 and again in 1942, Hitler had planned the destruction of Leningrad, but Soviet successes elsewhere had always saved the city. The Soviets rightly considered their defense of Lenin's city, the home of the Communist revolution, as an epochal achievement. After enormous privation and suffering, this greatest siege in history was finally lifted.[105]

On December 24, 1943, the First Ukrainian Front attacked west and south against the Fourth Panzer Army. *(See Map 29, in Atlas.)* Although their units were far under strength and an unseasonable thaw hampered their movements, the Soviets soon recaptured Zhitomir and approached the upper Bug River. The pressure on the Fourth Panzer Army was so great that Manstein feared his entire Army Group South might be cut off, but Hitler refused his urgent requests to evacuate the Dnieper bend and bring the Seventeenth Army out of the Crimea.[106] On January 5, Konev attacked southwest from the Cherkassy area with strong armored forces from his Second Ukrainian Front. Despite German counterattacks on his right flank, Konev pressed his offensive until his tankers encircled the German XI and XLII Corps in the Korsun area south of Cherkassy on January 28. Rapidly applying classic envelopment tactics, the Twenty-seventh Army and Fourth Guards Army built an inner ring, while the armored formations of the Sixth Tank Army and the Fifth Guards Tank Army faced outward to repel any relief attempt.[107] Fortune's wheel had come full circle, as the Soviets employed the same enveloping tactics the German Army had used in 1941. After trying to supply the Korsun pocket from the air, Hitler finally gave permission to break out on February 15. Most of the encircled soldiers immediately fought out of the Korsun pocket, leaving all their heavy equipment and most of their wounded behind. The survivors could not immediately return to combat, so Manstein had lost two corps from his already thinly defended line.[108]

Both belligerents found cavalry useful in this war over vast spaces and difficult terrain. Of course, the cavalrymen usually fought as highly mobile light infantry, and they had to avoid prolonged contact with units employing heavier fire power. Some of the partisan brigades were mounted, and the Germans raised indigenous cavalry to pursue them. Soviet cavalry corps infiltrated and raided throughout the war, especially under cover of poor weather. During January 1944, two Soviet cavalry corps, assisted by partisans, advanced through the forests and marshes on the left flank of the Fourth Panzer Army. On February 2, 1944, these troops captured Koch's headquarters at Rowne, putting an inglorious end to *Reichskommissariat Ukraine*.[109] At the same time, on the opposite German flank, the Third and Fourth Ukrainian Fronts converged on Nikopol, whose manganese ore Hitler had declared vital to the war effort. Despite knee-deep mud, the Soviet troops captured the city on February 7, and Krivoli Rog two weeks later. The German position in the Ukraine had become precarious before the summer campaigning season even began.

Spring and Summer 1944: Operation BAGRATION

In the spring of 1944, the Soviets enjoyed great numerical superiority over the Germans. Comparisons of units are meaningless because of great disparities in authorized strength and the tendency on both sides to let units fall well below authorized strength before sending replacements or disbanding them. In overall strength, the Soviets had 5.5 million men at the front in January 1944, with another 400,000 in *Stavka*-level reserve. At the same time, the Germans were frantically searching for more manpower. By the end of 1943, they had permanently lost over 2 million men in Russia, killed, missing, or disabled. As a result, the Army strength in Russia dropped to about 2.5 million men.[110] Of course, the Germans had always been outnumbered in Russia. They had often defeated superior numbers through greater facility in mobile war. By 1944, however, the Soviets had better mobility than the Germans. To their own broad-tracked, powerful T-34 tanks, they could add four-wheel-drive trucks from America, while their infantry continued to rely on the horse-drawn *panje* wagon.[111]

Determined to keep the initiative, the Soviets attacked in early March, surprising the Germans who expected them to wait until the ground dried out in summer. Zhukov, in temporary command of the First Ukrainian Front, attacked south between the Fourth and First Panzer Armies on the fourth. *(See Map 29, in Atlas.)* At the same time, Konev, commanding the Second Ukrainian Front, attacked southeast towards Uman. The Third Ukrainian Front joined the offensive with Chuikov's Eighth Guards Army in the vanguard. On March 8, as the German front began to crumble, Hitler issued an order establishing 26 *Festungen* (fortresses) in towns astride the German supply lines. These *Festungen* were to be held to the last man unless Hitler gave his personal consent to a withdrawal.[112] This order showed how strongly Hitler distrusted his officers, but the *Festungen* probably had little effect on the Soviet operations. By this stage in the war, the Soviet commanders had learned to by-pass centers of resistance in order to maintain the momentum of an attack. On March 21, Zhukov's First Tank Army attacked in the Tarnopol area, crossing the Dniester River within a week and penetrating far into the rear area of the First Panzer Army. Konev's forces split the First Panzer Army from the Eighth Army and reached the Prut River on the Rumanian frontier by March 26. At the same time, his Sixth Guards Tank Army made contact with Zhukov's First Tank Army, encircling the First Panzer Army north of the Dniester River. Recalling the horrors of Stalingrad, Manstein flew to Berchtesgaden on the twenty-fifth and convinced an angry Hitler to permit the encircled army to break out.[113] In the meantime, troops from the Third Ukrainian Front fought through the deep ravines across their front and forced the German Sixth Army to retreat to the west of the Bug River.

Hitler responded to these Soviet victories by relieving two of his ablest commanders. On March 30, he awarded Manstein and Kleist the Swords to the Knight's Cross of the Iron Cross, illustrating a peculiar inflation in Germany's highest military decorations; he then dismissed them from active service.[114] Due to his planning of the French campaign, his capture of Sevastopol, and his spring counteroffensive on the Donets River in 1943, Manstein enjoyed a high reputation. His successor was Model, the former Ninth Army commander, whom Hitler confidently expected would prove a lion on the defense. One of the German Army's few ardent Nazis, General Ferdinand Schörner, replaced Kleist as commander of Army Group A. In a ridiculous gesture, Hitler redesignated the Army Groups South and A as Army Groups North and South Ukraine on April 5. To the Russians' surprise, the First Panzer Army broke through Zhukov's forces in early April and escaped, but only at a heavy sacrifice in weapons and heavy equipment.[115] Schörner attempted to hold the Black Sea port of Odessa on Hitler's orders,[116] but during early April, the Third Ukrainian Front forced the Sixth Army to abandon the city in a hasty and confused retreat. Now the Soviets were again in undisputed possession of the entire Ukraine, including their richest agricultural and industrial areas, damaged as they were by battle and the invader.

Jaenecke's Seventeenth Army, which Hitler had refused to place at Manstein's disposal, still remained in the Crimea with seven Rumanian divisions. These 230,000 troops would have been very useful in the Ukraine, but they were inadequate to defend the Crimea, once the Soviets could bring their overwhelming strength to bear. As an officer who had served at Stalingrad, Jaenecke refused to sacrifice his command, but Hitler only replaced him with a more docile general. On April 8, two armies of the Fourth Ukrainian front attacked the north Crimean coast, while an independent army attacked from a bridgehead around Kerch. These Soviet assaults forced the Germans to abandon heavy weapons and equipment, falling back on the fortress of Sevastopol. On the twenty-first, Schörner flew to Berchtesgaden to ask permission to abandon the Crimea, but Hitler insisted that it must be held to keep Turkey neutral. The Soviet Fifty-first Army and Coastal Army began their last assault on May 5; in the ensuing rush to evacuate, approximately 30,000 German troops and nearly all the Seventeenth Army's remaining equipment were left behind.[117]

In 1944, the Germans still maintained 180,000 troops in northern Finland, organized as the Twentieth Mountain Army, although this force could not fulfill its mission of capturing Murmansk. *(Operations not shown on map.)* The Finns, who had remained on the defensive since 1941, watched uneasily as the Soviets forced Army Group North away from Leningrad. Perhaps because the Finns still rejected harsh peace terms, the Soviets opened a heavy offensive on June 9, employing the Karelian Front and two armies from the Leningrad Front. These forces rapidly drove the Finns back and occupied Viipuri (Vyborg) on June 21. As a condition for negotiations with the Soviet Union, the Finns agreed on September 2 to break relations with Germany and to ensure that all German troops left Finnish territory. Preoccupied by their own much larger offensive in White Russia, the Soviets made little effort to pursue the Twentieth Mountain Army; but when the Germans failed to depart on schedule, several clashes occurred between Germans and Finns.[118]

Operation BAGRATION, based on a proposal by Marshal Konstantin K. Rokossovski, was first formulated at the *Stavka* level on May 14, 1944.[119] This operation sought to destroy the German Army Group Center in White Russia. *(See Map 30, in Atlas.)* Marshal Alexander M. Vasilevsky was to coordinate a northern force composed of the First Baltic Front and Third White Russian Front, while Zhukov oversaw the Second White Russian Front and Rokossovski's own First White Russian Front. BAGRATION fell into two phases. During the first phase, tactical envelopments in the areas of Vitebsk on the Dvina and Bobruisk on the Berezina River would break the German defenses. In the second phase, the two attacking forces would pursue on parallel axes to encircle all German forces still east of the White Russian capital of Minsk.[120] After Stalin approved a final version of the plan on May 31, Vasilevsky and Zhukov went to the front headquarters where they supervised detailed preparations with front, army, and corps commanders and their staffs. According to the memoirs of Soviet officers, front and army commanders were allowed to suggest improvements in the planning and even to select the best axes of advance for their formations, although Stalin had to be informed of every important decision. Consonant with their own experience and temperament, the Soviet officers preferred face-to-face conversations and conferences spanning several levels of command to formal communications through command channels. The large discussions at front headquarters served as war games to test the planning. BAGRATION would cover 450 miles of front and employ about 1.2 million men in the 124 divisions scheduled for initial participation.[121] The heavy forests of White Russia would impede the advance of Soviet armor, but they also would canalize the German retreat. Moreover, the strongest and most active partisan brigades operated in White Russia.

Because Hitler and the OKH expected another Soviet offensive in the south, a *panzer* corps was transferred from Army Group Center to Army Group North Ukraine during May.[122] As a result, Army Group Center retained only two armored divisions while Army Group North had virtually no armor at all.[123] Following the retreats of the two flanking army groups, Army Group Center occupied a huge bulge, practically a salient with the right flank resting on the Pripet Marshes. *(See June 22 line, Map 30, in Atlas.)* The commander of Army Group Center asked permission to shorten his line during May, but after Hitler's refusal he loyally tried to conduct a static defense on the existing line and ordered fanatic resistance in the towns designated *Festungen*.[124] During June, the signs of an impending offensive multiplied. The Germans discovered the presence of elite Guards units on their front and learned that Zhukov had assumed command responsibilities. Partisan activity increased and the Soviets appeared to be massing aircraft, but German attention was so riveted to the south that all these indications were dismissed as deceptive measures.[125]

Beginning on April 7, 1944, the head of the American military mission in Moscow gave the Soviets a series of projected dates for OVERLORD (the invasion of France) so that the Soviets could time their own offensive to coincide.[126] After several delays, OVERLORD finally began on June 6, but the Soviets waited until June 22—the third anniversary of the German invasion—to initiate BAGRATION. Even so, they had prepared this immense operation in less than a month since formulating the plan. The Soviet commanders initiated the offensive with extensive probing attacks instead of throwing troops headlong at the German defenses in the old fashion. During 1941, the Soviet commanders had tended to repeat attacks mechanically and to commit fresh troops where resistance was heaviest. Now they committed second echelon troops in areas of light resistance and attempted to by-pass heavier resistance or neutralize it with large artillery concentrations. Although they enjoyed overwhelming armor superiority, the Soviets cautiously minimized tank losses by letting infantry, with some supporting tanks, break through the German lines, and then committing armor formations through the gaps. The Red Air Force quickly acquired full dominance over the *Luftwaffe*, which lacked both aircraft and stocks of aviation fuel. Operating under front command, the partisan brigades interdicted the railways with mines and demolitions, especially behind the German Third Panzer Army.[127]

Operation BAGRATION achieved immediate and crushing success all along the front of Army Group Center. The Soviet Forty-third and Thirty-ninth Armies joined west of Vitebsk on June 25, encircling the German LIII Corps which was totally destroyed. *(See Map 30, in Atlas.)* Rokossovski's armies quickly encircled two corps from the German Ninth Army in the area of Bobruisk, yet still continued to advance west of the Beresina River.[128] On June 28, Hitler gave Model command of Army Group Center, leaving him also in command of Army Group North Ukraine temporarily to facilitate the transfer of troops.[129] The situation was further complicated due to the Allied landing in Normandy and the large garrisons still stationed in Norway and Yugoslavia. Germany no longer had any strategic reserve. After crossing the upper Berezina, the Fifth Guards Tank Army from the Third White Russian Front captured Minsk on July 4 and joined with troops from Rokossovksi's First White Russian Front. Most of the German Fourth Army was encircled in the large Minsk pocket east of the Berezina. The German troops tried to retreat over the narrow roads littered with dead horses and burned-out vehicles while under heavy attack from the Red Air Force, but the

German Prisoners of War in Moscow, July 17, 1944

Soviet forces pushed them against the Berezina and took them under heavy artillery and *Katyusha* fires. Model could do nothing to relieve either the Ninth or Fourth Armies, which were largely destroyed. In less than two weeks, the Germans had lost 28 divisions, or approximately 300,000 men, in a disaster greater than Stalingrad.[130]

The roles these combatants had played in 1941 were now reversed. Partly due to Hitler's poor leadership and partly due to lack of armor and transport, the German Army futilely attempted static defense. In the inevitable retreats, they moved only at the rate of infantry march and horse-drawn wagon. By destroying the Ninth and Fourth Armies, the Soviets opened a 250-mile gap between the Pripet Marshes and the remnants of the Third Panzer Army, retreating from the Vitebsk area. The Soviet motorized columns advanced into open country, their operational freedom limited for the moment only by their striking range. Rokossovski's troops advanced almost unopposed in the direction of Brest, moving beyond the Pripet Marshes by the end of July. The Fifth Guards Tank Army attacked from the Minsk area northeast in pursuit of the Third Panzer Army. Forces from the First Baltic Front attacked into Lithuania and wheeled north, reaching the Gulf of Riga at the end of July. Army Group North, now commanded by the fanatic Schörner, lost contact with Army Group Center and began to waver under assault from the Second and Third Baltic Fronts. But on August 21, elements of the Third Panzer Army regained contact with the Sixteenth Army, winning a narrow corridor on the Baltic coast.[131] The time had obviously come to evacuate Army Group North from Latvia and Estonia, but Hitler predictably refused.[132] During August, the German defensive line began to stabilize, largely because the Soviet rear services needed time to restore the railways to operation and establish depots.

Meanwhile, on July 13, Konev's First Ukrainian Front had begun an offensive against Army Group North Ukraine with an exceptionally heavy artillery preparation and air strikes.[133] Confronted by German counterattacks in divisional strength, Konev's infantry armies failed to break through in two days' fighting. On the fifteenth, however, he committed the Third Guards Tank Army and the Fourth Tank Army on the same narrow sector. *(See Map 30, in Atlas.)* This Soviet armor opened a narrow corridor through the German defensive zone and reached open country. The Third Guards Tank Army quickly moved north and joined with the Third Guards Army to encircle the German XIII Corps in the Brody area, south of Kowel. Very few of the 40,000 encircled troops were able to escape.[134] After joining forces near Kowel during July, Rokossovski and Konev began to force the Vistula River over a broad front.

On July 20, 1944, an intensely patriotic German Army officer, Count Claus von Stauffenberg, almost succeeded in assassinating Hitler by leaving a time bomb under his briefing table at the *Wolfsschanze* headquarters. When lack of determination among senior commanders caused the conspiracy to fail, many officers fell victim to the ensuing purge. Field Marshal Günther von Kluge, who had commanded the Fourth Army and Army Group Center, committed suicide; the former commander of the Fourth Panzer Army, General Erich Hoepner, was executed; General Franz Halder, the former OKH Chief of Staff, was imprisoned. The German officers had long been the only men with the power to remove Hitler, but they lacked the will. Their narrow professionalism, more than Nazi sympathies, made most of them his obedient servants. The tradition of the German officers corps came to an end when the Army assisted civilian courts and the SS in purging those officers suspected of disloyalty to Hitler. Through special evidences of loyalty, Guderian supplanted Zeitzler as OKH Chief of Staff. Guderian was miscast in this role and could do little to improve the direction of the war.[135] Shortly after the bombing attempt, Reichsmarshal Hermann Goering and the OKW Commander-in-Chief, Field Marshal Wilhelm Keitel, an arrogant nonentity, demanded of Hitler that the armed services adopt the Nazi salute.[136]

Troops from both Rokossovski's and Konev's Fronts rapidly effected crossings of the Vistula, using ferries and pontoon bridges capable of carrying their heaviest tanks. Konev's Third Guards Army and Thirteenth Army built a large bridgehead east of Cracow, but then they were counterattacked by the Fourth Panzer Army. *(See Map 30, in Atlas.)* Chuikov's Eighth Guards Army, now assigned to the First White Russian Front, crossed the Vistula on August 1, followed by the Second Tank Army. On the next day, Rokossovski learned that an uprising had begun in Warsaw; he later claimed that he was simply unable to help the Polish patriots, but his government clearly showed its lack of sympathy for the revolt.[137] Although they had already raised a Polish army, recruited largely from the prisoners taken in 1939, the Soviets were not true friends of the Poles. In April 1943, the Germans had discovered the corpses of 4,300 Polish officers in the Katyn forest near Smolensk. Despite their denials, the Soviets undoubtedly murdered these officers, as well as another 10,000 whose bodies were never found.[138] Stalin was hostile to the Polish Government-in-exile in London, and he certainly did not care to see an independent Polish revolt succeed. For two months, the First White Russian Front remained in defensive positions on the west bank of the Vistula less than 60 miles from Warsaw, while the Germans suppressed the revolt with great cruelty.[139]

Juggernaut: Soviet Tactics in the Offense

By 1944, the Soviets had developed offensive tactics of breakthrough and exploitation reminiscent of *blitzkrieg*, but a Soviet offensive remained more ponderous than its German counterpart. While the Germans emphasized maneuver, the Soviets emphasized mass. After the Battle of Kursk in July 1943, the Soviets had the strength to mount a successful offensive anywhere. Their problem was to mass this strength effectively for rapid breakthroughs. To German observers, Soviet tactics seemed primitive and absurdly inflexible,[140] but the Red Army should not be judged solely by German standards. The Soviet commanders would have invited disaster had they accorded each echelon the scope for initiative traditional in the German Army. The Soviets did not reach German levels of efficiency, but the improvement in the Red Army throughout the war was astonishing.

The most effective arm at the beginning of an offensive was the artillery.[141] During the last years of the war, front commanders routinely planned concentrations of 200 to 250 tubes per kilometer of breakthrough front, counting mortars. Rather than try to gain surprise, the Soviets preferred to crush the first trace of German trenches with a heavy artillery preparation. The German officers tried to keep their troops out of range by screening the main line of resistance and preparing deep zones of defense with numerous fall-back positions.[142] The Soviets responded by using probing attacks to locate and fix the German defenders. The Soviet artillery preparation usually began with concentrations on particular targets and shifted to a single or double rolling barrage to a depth of three or four kilometers. The foremost regimental commanders kept the barrage moving just ahead of the attacking infantry. Sometimes the infantry advanced through narrow no-fire lanes while the artillery preparation continued undiminished around them. However, Soviet artillery was seldom able to displace forward rapidly enough during a successful offensive.[143]

The 1944 Soviet infantry divisions had no organic armor and only one regiment of artillery with 36 guns. The Soviets deliberately weakened the infantry divisions in this way in order to facilitate massing armor and artillery for the offensive. Infantry units also received the worst classes of replacements, often men with no training at all. As a result, infantry was the weakest Soviet arm, even declining in quality during the war.[144] Yet the Red Army infantryman was still a dangerous opponent. On occasion, he fought with incredible tenacity, even when all hope was gone. He effectively employed simple and rugged weapons, especially land mines, mortars, and submachine guns. As might be expected from men of their background, the Soviet soldiers could tolerate extremes of weather well, they were very adept at camouflage and field fortifications, and they endured hardship and wounds stoically.

On the narrow attack sectors, the front commanders echeloned their troops to accomplish mass. Every unit above company level might have two echelons, generally with two elements forward and one held back. At front level, entire armored corps and armies formed the second echelon. The second echelon was not simply a reserve—it regularly received its mission before the offensive began.[145] A front commander tried to commit his second echelon at just the right moment to secure a breakthrough and begin the exploitation phase. If the second echelon were committed prematurely, it might clog the battlefield or lose too much strength in the breakthrough phase. If it was committed too late, the front might fail to break through at all or penetrate the defensive zone so slowly that the Germans had too much time to react. Like their German counterparts, the Soviet commanders emphasized speed in the offensive—one to two days to break through, two to three weeks for an exploitation to a depth of several hundred kilometers. By 1944, the Soviets expected their armor to advance 20 to 30 kilometers per day during the exploitation. Like the Germans, the Soviets depended upon the railway for resupply, forcing them to stop and consolidate at a range of about five to six hundred kilometers, even if resistance were light.

During the exploitation, the Soviets sought to envelop, encircle, and destroy large bodies of troops, but they remained very sensitive, perhaps too sensitive, to their own flank security. Of course, as late as February 1943, the Germans successfully enveloped the Tank Group Popov south of the Donets; but by 1944 the German Army was too weak to contain any large Soviet force very long. In the Ukraine, the Soviets missed several chances to envelop German forces on the lower Dnieper, failed to destroy the troops in the Korsun pocket during February 1944, and let the First Panzer Army escape during April. On the other hand, BAGRATION destroyed most of the German Ninth and Fourth Armies, and the Soviets utterly destroyed a German Sixth Army twice—at Stalingrad in January

1943 and on the Prut River in August 1944. In retrospect, perhaps the Soviets should have been bolder, but they certainly were not timid.

The Soviet Balkan Campaign of 1944

During the fall of 1944, offensives by the Soviet Second and Third Ukrainian Fronts badly defeated Army Group South Ukraine while invading Rumania and Bulgaria. Once again, the Germans were caught in an overextended position, for Hitler hesitated to withdraw, even though the Rumanian dictator, Marshal Ion Antonescu, wished to evacuate Bessarabia.[146] *(See Map 31, in Atlas)* The Soviet offensive began on August 20, concentrating on the Rumanian formations, which constituted about half of the opposing army group.[147] The Rumanians broke and fled, leaving the Germans isolated. The Sixth Tank Army from the Second Ukrainian Front advanced rapidly through open country and joined with armies of the Third Ukrainian Front to encircle the German Sixth Army on the Prut River. Like its predecessor at Stalingrad, the reconstituted Sixth Army was almost entirely destroyed and most of the men never seen again.[148] On August 23, Antonescu was arrested and King Carol announced the end of hostilities with the Soviet Union. While the remaining German troops retreated in long forced marches, on August 30 the Soviet columns occupied Ploesti, whose oil fields had so long influenced Hitler's strategy.

Although Bulgaria reaffirmed neutrality, the Soviets declared war and the Third Ukrainian Front crossed the border without meeting resistance. On September 8, Bulgaria declared war on Germany and placed its armies under Soviet command. During October, the Germans swiftly evacuated Greece and began a retreat through Yugoslavia, harassed by American air attacks and pursued by Josip Broz Tito's partisans. Although he had narrowly escaped capture by SS paratroopers in May,[149] Tito was the most successful of all partisan leaders. During 1944, as many as 125,000 German troops were in Yugoslavia fighting partisans, and even more were immobilized by Tito's movement.[150] When the Hungarians had attempted to leave the war in March, the Germans occupied their country. Now, since the Germans no longer had the strength to hold the line of the Transylvanian Alps, an offensive by the Second Ukrainian Front in early October quickly reached the Hungarian plain. *(See Map 31, in Atlas.)* On October 15, the day after partisans and Soviet troops entered Belgrade, the Hungarian regent announced the cessation of hostilities, but the Germans quickly arrested him. On Hitler's orders, the Germans continued to defend Budapest, even after the city was surrounded by the Soviets in December. (After the failure of the SS divisions *Totenkopf* and *Wiking* to relieve the garrison, it attempted to break out in February 1945 and was annihilated.[151]) The capture of Budapest at last opened the Danube valley to further Russian advance.

Reaping the Whirlwind: Vistula to Oder and Berlin

In late September 1944, the Leningrad and the Second and Third Baltic Fronts cleared Estonia and part of Latvia, as Army Group North retreated south of the Gulf of Riga. *(See Map 31, in Atlas.)* During October, the First Baltic Front captured Riga and reached the Baltic Sea in the Memel area, isolating Army Group North in northern Latvia (Kurland), where it remained until the end of the war. At this point, the Soviets ceased operations on the northern front and began preparations for a winter offensive in 1945. In the meantime, Hitler built up a force in the Ardennes at the juncture of the British and American armies. The German offensive achieved such success that Churchill sent Stalin an urgent letter on January 6, 1945, expressing the hope that the Soviets might be able to quickly begin an offensive on the Vistula.[152] For whatever motives, Stalin obliged by advancing the date of his offensive, changing it to January 12.

Konev, Zhukov, and Rokossovski, commanding the First Ukrainian, First and Second White Russian Fronts respectively, were to conduct the offensive. Konev was a gruff, vigorous and very ambitious commander who had begun his career as a political commissar, later becoming a regular army officer. His First Ukrainian Front was expected to break out of its Vistula bridgeheads and advance into the Breslau area in Silesia. *(See Map 32, in Atlas.)* The efficient but extremely overbearing Zhukov, who had been preeminent among Soviet officers since the battle for Moscow, was to envelop Warsaw, attack towards Radom with two armies, and advance west into the Poznan area. Rokossovski was an intelligent, unassuming, and able commander whose career, like Zhukov's, had begun in the cavalry. His front was to cover Zhukov's right flank by closing to the Baltic in the Danzig area.[153] Operations beyond the Danzig-Poznan-Breslau line would depend on the situation. Just as the German armies had felt the strain as their front widened across Russia, so Soviet strength now became more concentrated as the front narrowed. The First Ukrainian and First White Russian Fronts together had 2.2 million men organized in 163 divisions with 6,400 tanks and self-propelled guns.[154] The Soviets deployed small numbers of the new JS-II tank, and their artillery concentrations reached 300 tubes per kilometer of breakthrough sector.[155] They enjoyed almost total air superiority, but coordination between ground and air elements remained a problem.[156]

By 1945 the German Army was hopelessly inferior to the Red Army, and no strategy could have postponed the inevitable Soviet victory very long. Ironically, German war industry had reached a peak in 1944, despite shortages of raw material and Anglo-American bombing. In fact, the Germans had produced enough arms to equip 250 infantry and 40 *panzer* divisions during 1944, yet their weapon strength actually declined because of the losses sustained through encirclements and retreats.[157] Moreover, Germany was so desperate for manpower that on September 25, 1944, Hitler had announced the formation of the *Volkssturm* (People's Assault Group), battalions of men from 16 to 60 years of age otherwise deferred from military service. Provided with the *Panzerfaust,* which was a hollow-charge grenade fired from a shoulder-held tube, and a miscellany of light infantry weapons, the *Volkssturm* had small military value.[158] Although they realized the war was lost, German soliders offered strong resistance, not out of fanaticism but from patriotic motives and because the war against Russia had never known any other rule but to kill or be killed.

As anticipated, the Soviet offensive enjoyed rapid success. The Germans had prepared very deep defensive zones with trench systems like those in France during the First World War, but they had no chance at all to stop the Soviet onslaught. After three-days' fighting, employing mostly infantry and 76-mm self-propelled guns, Rokossovski overran the German lines and advanced into East Prussia; from January 20 on, the bulk of his forces were moving northwest on *Stavka* orders.[159] As his armies became concentrated in the general area of Danzig, Rokossovski could no longer protect the right flank of Zhukov's fast moving First White Russian Front. The Germans abandoned Warsaw to Zhukov on January 17, causing Hitler to direct that every corps and divisional commander must notify him of all operational plans in sufficient time to permit review.[160] The German conduct of the war thus reached its *reductio ad absurdum*. At the same time, Hitler made the SS chief, Heinrich Himmler, the commander of Army Group Vistula, although his only qualification was obedience. With the First and Second Guards Tank Armies and Chuikov's Eighth Guards Army in his spearheads, Zhukov advanced well ahead of plan, reaching Lodz on January 20. Konev enjoyed a similar success, as his Third Guards Tank and Fourth Tank Armies attacked out of the Sandomierz bridgehead on the Vistula. When Konev's troops captured Auschwitz, the largest German annihilation camp, they found over 800,000 women's coats—proof not only of the wholesale slaughter that had taken place there, but also of the camp's practice of sorting and hoarding its prisoners' possessions.[161]

On January 25, Zhukov recommended to Stalin that his front continue the offensive on to Berlin without pause.[162] Stalin pointed out that Rokossovski and Konev would not be able to secure the flanks of a rapid advance, but Zhukov argued that any halt would only give the Germans time to prepare defenses in depth. *(See Map 32, in Atlas.)* At the end of January, the Soviet Fifth Shock Army and Chuikov's Eighth Guards Army closed on the Oder River in the area of Küstrin, and on February 2 Chuikov's guardsmen began to cross the river on the thin ice.[163] Within a few days, the Eighth Guards Army occupied a substantial bridgehead less than 40 miles from Berlin. But in the meantime, Zhukov removed the First and Second Guards Tank Armies from their sectors on the Oder and deployed them for an attack north into Pomerania. Although acting on *Stavka* orders, Zhukov later defended this maneuver, alleging that his right flank was seriously threatened.[164] The Germans did attempt to counterattack south from Pomerania, but with very little effect. In Operation SOLSTICE, the recently formed Eleventh SS Panzer Army of ten understrength divisions, attacked from February 14 to 18 before Himmler stopped the useless effort.[165] In mid-January, Hitler had precluded any major operations in Pomerania or on the Oder by transferring his only substantial reinforcement, the Sixth SS Panzer Army to Hungary for a fruitless attempt to recapture Budapest.[166] Zhukov quickly cleared Pomerania, capturing Kolberg on March 18, and loaned Rokossovski the First Guards Tank Army. In a more drawn-out battle, Rokossovski finally entered Danzig on March 30. Zhukov's wheeling movement towards the Baltic delayed the advance on Berlin until mid-April, giving the Germans time to build deep defensive positions opposite the Oder bridgeheads. Very likely, Zhukov's estimate of the situation on January 25 was correct and he could have captured Berlin in February, but it is easy to imagine why Stalin preferred to take no risks.

The February conference at Yalta produced agreement on zones of occupation in Germany, leaving General Dwight D. Eisenhower free to develop strategy according to military considerations. On March 28, he sent Stalin a message, informing him quite truthfully that the next major operation would be along the Erfurt-Leipzig-Dresden axis. Stalin at once suspected that his allies were trying to reach Berlin first. At a special conference in Moscow on April 1, he ordered Zhukov and Konev to prepare plans for the capture of Berlin and encouraged the two commanders to compete for the honor. The First White Russian and First Ukrainian Fronts, designations long overtaken by events, began their last offensive on April 16. *(Operations not shown.)* Zhukov appeared at Chuikov's command post to observe the assault across marshy flatlands to dislodge the Germans from high ground.[167] At the same time, Konev's troops made an assault crossing of the Neisse River

Festivities After US–USSR Meeting at Torgau, 1945

by boat and turned north towards Berlin. The Soviets surrounded Berlin on April 25, the same day that troops from the Fifty-eighth Guards Division (assigned to Konev's First Ukrainian Front) contacted a reconnaissance group from the American 69th Infantry Division on the Elbe River.[168] During the next few days, Chuikov's troops moved slowly towards the center of Berlin, encountering strong resistance along the rail lines and canals. The veterans in this army had fought in the winter cold at Stalingrad, across the burning steppe to the Dnieper, through the forests of White Russia, and out of the Oder bridgehead to arrive there.

Chuikov's troops were forcing the Landwehr Canal south of the *Tiergarten* as Hitler composed his last testament on April 29. In his parting words, he railed against an international Jewish conspiracy which he alleged had caused the war.[169] This vacuous and nearly insane individual was responsible for the horrid murders of six million Jews, the most sickening crime in human history.[170] He had also sacrificed the lives of two-and-a-quarter-million German servicemen in a war to conquer Russia.[171] The Russians discovered his burnt corpse in the rubble of Berlin on May 2, 1945. Nazi Germany's militarism and vicious racism thrived on victory, but they could not endure defeat, and collapsed utterly.

Russian losses are unknown, even to themselves, but they may have lost in military service almost half of those killed in the entire world war, approximately 12 million men and women.[172] Their war against the invader was the largest, most destructive, and most momentous ever fought. In 1942 the front line had been over 3,000 miles long. Both sides exhausted their manpower to keep eight to nine million men in the field for over four years. The Soviets destroyed or dismantled their own industry in retreat, as did the Germans, leaving the richest areas of Russia in ruins. Other countries swept into this war—especially Poland and Finland—suffered terrible losses. Despite tremendous mistakes, the Germans very nearly won the war. Had they won, Europe and much of Asia might be fascist today and Hitler's gutter philosophy would command the allegiance of millions. Although Hitler's two-front strategy made the Soviet victory possible, the Russians undoubtedly made the greatest contribution to his defeat. Had Hitler defeated the Russians, an Anglo-American invasion of Europe might never have been possible. As a result of the Russian victory, the Soviet Union became the greatest power in Europe and imposed a Communist system upon Eastern Europe—an unwelcome outcome, but one preferable to a German victory.

Notes

[1]Earl F. Ziemke, *Stalingrad to Berlin: The German Defeat in the East* (Washington, 1968), p. 90; Erich von Manstein, *Lost Victories* (Chicago, 1958), p. 422.

[2]Manstein, *Lost Victories*, p. 368.

[3]*Ibid.*, p. 423.

[4]Ziemke, *Stalingrad to Berlin*, p. 91.

[5]Manstein, *Lost Victories*, pp. 424-427.

[6]Albert Seaton, *The Russo-German War 1941-45* (New York, 1970), p. 349.

[7]Manstein, *Lost Victories*, p. 433.

[8]Ziemke, *Stalingrad to Berlin*, p. 96.

[9]Manstein, *Lost Victories*, pp. 443-446.

[10]Ziemke, *Stalingrad to Berlin*, p. 81.

[11]Seaton, *Russo-German War*, p. 345.

[12]Pavel A. Zhilin, et al., *The History of the Great Patriotic War* (6 vols: Moscow, 1960-1963), III, 82.

[13]Andrei Grechko, *Battle for the Caucasus* (Moscow, 1971), pp. 213, 262.

[14]Ziemke, *Stalingrad to Berlin*, p. 111.

[15]Zhilin, *Great Patriotic War*, III, 131; Kirill A. Meretskov, *City Invincible* (Moscow, 1970), pp. 63-65.

[16]Zhilin, *Great Patriotic War*, III, 139-140; Meretskov, *City Invincible*, p. 72.

[17]Ziemke, *Stalingrad to Berlin*, p. 112.

[18]*Ibid.*, p. 115.

[19]See Norman Rich, *Hitler's War Aims, The Establishment of the New Order* (New York, 1974) and Alexander Dallin, *German Rule in Russia* (New York, 1957).

[20]Rich, *War Aims*, pp. 359-360; Erich Hesse, *Der sowjetrussische Partisanenkrieg 1941 bis 1944 im Spiegel deutscher Kampfanweisung und Befehle* (Göttingen, 1969), pp. 186-187.

[21]Raul Hilberg, *The Destruction of the European Jews* (Chicago, 1961), p. 256.

[22]John A. Armstrong (ed.), *Soviet Partisans in World War II* (Madison, Wis., 1964), pp. 35-36, 151; Hesse, *Der Partisanenkrieg*, p. 197; Department of the Army Pamphlet 20-240, *Rear Area Security in Russia* (Washington, 1951), p. 36.

[23]Armstrong, *Soviet Partisans*, pp. 23-24.

[24]*Ibid.*, p. 145.

[25]Armstrong, *Soviet Partisans*, pp. 15, 98-100; Hesse, *Der Partisanenkrieg*, pp. 52-53; Josef Stalin, *The Great Patriotic War of the Soviet Union* (New York, 1945), p. 15.

[26]Armstrong, *Soviet Partisans*, pp. 91-92, 155.

[27]DA Pamphlet 20-240, p. 5; Armstrong, *Soviet Partisans*, pp. 27-28.

[28]Hesse, *Der Partisanenkrieg*, p. 198.

[29]DA Pamphlet 20-240, pp. 26-27; Hans Pottgiesser, *Die deutsche Reichsbahn im Ostfeldzug 1939-1944* (Neckargemünd, 1960), p. 85.

[30]Hesse, *Der Partisanenkrieg*, p. 258; Armstrong, *Soviet Partisans*, p. 30.

[31]Armstrong, *Soviet Partisans*, pp. 191-194.

[32]John R. Deane, *The Strange Alliance, The Story of Our Efforts at Wartime Co-operation with Russia* (New York, 1947), p. 87.

[33]George C. Herring, Jr., *Aid to Russia 1941-1946, Strategy, Diplomacy and the Origins of the Cold War* (New York, 1973), pp. 75-77.

[34]Robert Huhn Jones, *The Roads to Russia, United States Lend-Lease to the Soviet Union* (Norman, Okla., 1969), Appendix, Table IV.

[35]*Ibid.*, Appendix, Table IV.

[36]*Ibid.*, Appendix, Table V.

[37]*Ibid.*, Appendix, Table V.

[38]Earl F. Ziemke, *The German Northern Theater of Operations 1940-1945* (Washington, 1959), pp. 235-239.

[39]E. B. Schofield, *The Russian Convoys* (Philadelphia, 1964), p. 95; Ziemke, *Northern Theater*, pp. 239-241.

[40]T. H. Vail Motter, *The Persian Corridor and Aid to Russia (United States Army in World War II, The Middle East Theater)* (Washington, 1952), pp. 35-43.

[41]Joseph Bykofsky and Harold Larson, *The Transportation Corps: Operations Overseas (United States Army in World War II, The Technical Services)* (Washington, 1957), pp. 390-391.

[42]Zhilin, *Great Patriotic War*, III, 163.

[43]Vladimir Katkoff, *Soviet Economy 1940-1945* (Baltimore, 1961), p. 139.

[44]Zhilin, *Great Patriotic War*, IV, 661.

[45]Chris Ellis and Peter Chamberlain, *The Great Tanks* (New York, 1975), p. 60.

[46]Zhilin, *Great Patriotic War*, III, 167-168.

[47]*Ibid.*, III, 162.

[48]*Ibid.*, III, 155.

[49]Katkoff, *Soviet Economy*, p. 139.

[50]Grechko, *Battle for the Caucasus*, p. 309; Seaton, *Russo-German War*, p. 401; John Milsom, *Russian Tanks, 1900-1970* (New York, 1970), p. 182.

[51]Georg Thomas, *Geschichte der deutschen Wehr-und Rüstungswirtschaft* (Boppard am Rhein, 1966), pp. 483-487.

[52]Alan S. Milward, *The German Economy at War* (London, 1965), pp. 57-59, 131-132.

[53]Albert Speer, *Inside the Third Reich* (New York, 1970), p. 197.

[54]Milward, *German Economy*, pp. 69-70.

[55]Speer, *Inside Third Reich*, p. 222; Thomas, *Rüstungswirtschaft*, p. 355; Milward, *German Economy*, p. 151.

[56]Milward, *German Economy*, pp. 48, 110-111.

[57]F. M. von Senger und Etterlin, *German Tanks of World War II* (New York, 1969), p. 211.

[58]Ziemke, *Stalingrad to Berlin*, p. 49.

[59]Manstein, *Lost Victories*, p. 476.

[60]Seaton, *Russo-German War*, pp. 353-356.

[61]Heinz Guderian, *Panzer Leader (Erinnerungen eines Soldaten)* (New York, 1952), p. 277; Manstein, *Lost Victories*, pp.. 447-448; Seaton, *Russo-German War*, p. 356; Ziemke, *Stalingrad to Berlin*, pp. 129-130; Alfred Philippi and Ferdinand Heim, *Der Feldzug gegen Sowjet-Russland* (Stuttgart, 1962), pp. 208-211.

[62]Ziemke, *Stalingrad to Berlin*, p. 132.

[63]Seaton, *Russo-German War*, p. 358.

[64]Konstantin K. Rokossovski, *A Soldier's Duty* (Moscow, 1970), pp. 185-193; Martin Caidin, *The Tigers are Burning* (New York, 1974), pp. 72-74; Seaton, *Russo-German War*, p. 361; Georgi K. Zhukov, *Marshal Zhukov's Greatest Battles* (New York, 1969), pp. 214-215.

[65]Rokossovski, *Soldier's Duty*, p. 187; Zhukov, *Greatest Bat-*

tles, pp. 231-232; Ziemke, *Stalingrad to Berlin*, pp. 133-134.

[66]Rokossovski, *Soldier's Duty*, p. 186.

[67]Seaton, *Russo-German War*, p. 361.

[68]*Ibid.*, p. 364.

[69]Rokossovski, *Soldier's Duty*, p. 201; Ziemke, *Stalingrad to Berlin*, p. 136.

[70]Caidin, *Tigers*, pp. 214, 216-221; Seaton, *Russo-German War*, pp. 363-364.

[71]Ziemke, *Stalingrad to Berlin*, p. 137.

[72]Manstein, *Lost Victories*, p. 449; Seaton, *Russo-German War*, p. 367; Ziemke, *Stalingrad to Berlin*, pp. 137-138.

[73]Senger, *German Tanks*, pp. 43-45 and Appendix 3.

[74]*Ibid.*, p. 57.

[75]Seaton, *Russo-German War*, p. 358; Senger, *German Tanks*, pp. 63-65, 211.

[76]Seaton, *Russo-German War*, pp. 200-201, 211.

[77]Kenneth Macksey and John H. Batchelor, *Tanks, A History of the Armoured Fighting Vehicle* (New York, 1971), p. 133; Caidin, *Tigers*, p. 81; Senger, *German Tanks*, pp. 200-201.

[78]Seymour Freidin, *The Fatal Decisions* (New York, 1956), p. 66.

[79]Milsom, *Russian Tanks*, pp. 104-109, 171, 172.

[80]Caidin, *Tigers*, pp. 144-147.

[81]Milsom, *Russian Tanks*, p. 180.

[82]*Ibid.*, pp. 121-125, 176-179.

[83]Manstein, *Lost Victories*, p. 443.

[84]Alan Clark, *Barbarossa, The Russian-German Conflict, 1941-1945* (New York, 1965), p. 322; Basil H. Liddell Hart (ed.), *The Red Army* (New York, 1956), pp. 116-118; Seaton, *Russo-German War*, p. 368.

[85]Ziemke, *Stalingrad to Berlin*, pp. 143-144.

[86]Manstein, *Lost Victories*, pp. 450-454; Seaton, *Russo-German War*, p. 370; Ziemke, *Stalingrad to Berlin*, p. 138.

[87]Rokossovski, *Soldier's Duty*, p. 206; Ziemke, *Stalingrad to Berlin*, p. 151.

[88]Philippi, *Feldzug gegen Sowjet-Russland*, appended maps 21 and 24; Seaton, *Russo-German War*, p. 378.

[89]Rokossovski, *Soldier's Duty*, pp. 208-210.

[90]Philippi, *Feldzug gegen Sowjet-Russland*, pp. 215-216; Manstein, *Lost Victories*, pp. 460-462; Ziemke, *Stalingrad to Berlin*, pp. 163-164.

[91]Manstein, *Lost Victories*, pp. 462-464; Philippi, *Feldzug gegen Sowjet-Russland*, p. 216; Ziemke, *Stalingrad to Berlin*, pp. 164-165.

[92]Friedrich Wilhelm von Mellenthin, *Panzer Battles* (Norman, Okla., 1956), pp. 240-241; Ziemke, *Stalingrad to Berlin*, pp. 171-172.

[93]Guy Sajer, *The Forgotten Soldier (Le Soldat Oublie)* (New York, 1971), pp. 308-328; Seaton, *Russo-German War*, p. 375.

[94]Rokossovski, *Soldier's Duty*, p. 213; Philippi, *Feldzug gegen Sowjet-Russland*, p. 217.

[95]Grechko, *Battle for Caucasus*, pp. 328-349; Seaton, *Russo-German War*, p. 380.

[96]Department of the Army Pamphlet 20-201, *Military Improvisations during the Russian Campaign* (Washington, 1951), pp. 83-85; Ziemke, *Stalingrad to Berlin*, p. 174.

[97]Ziemke, *Stalingrad to Berlin*, pp. 179-181.

[98]Philippi, *Feldzug gegen Sowjet-Russland*, p. 218; Ziemke, *Stalingrad to Berlin*, pp. 181-184.

[99]Seaton, *Russo-German War*, pp. 381-384; Ziemke, *Stalingrad to Berlin*, pp. 186-189.

[100]Rokossovski, *Soldier's Duty*, pp. 222-223; Ziemke, *Stalingrad to Berlin*, pp. 191-205.

[101]Seaton, *Russo-German War*, p. 396.

[102]Maurice Matloff, *Strategic Planning for Coalition Warfare 1941-1942* (Washington, 1953), pp. 360-361, 366; Robert W. Coakley, *Global Logistics and Strategy 1943-45* (Washington, 1968), pp. 284-296.

[103]Speer, *Inside Third Reich*, pp. 315-317; Hans Adolf Jacobsen, *Decisive Battles of World War II* (New York, 1965), p. 358; Philippi, *Feldzug gegen Sowjet-Russland*, pp. 226-227, 231-232.

[104]Felix Gilbert (ed.), *Hitler Directs His War* (New York, 1950), pp. 92-93.

[105]Leon Goure, *The Siege of Leningrad* (Stanford, Cal., 1962), p. 299; Earl F. Zeimke, *The German Northern Theater of Operations 1940-1945* (Washington, 1959), pp. 272-273; Philippi, *Feldzug gegen Sowjet-Russland*, pp. 235-236.

[106]Department of the Army Pamphlet 20-233, *German Defense Tactics Against Russian Breakthroughs* (Washington, 1951), pp. 59-63; Manstein, *Lost Victories*, pp. 498-499.

[107]Seaton, *Russo-German War*, p. 417.

[108]Manstein, *Lost Victories*, pp. 515-517; Ziemke, *Stalingrad to Berlin*, pp. 226-238.

[109]Seaton, *Russo-German War*, p. 419; Ziemke, *Stalingrad to Berlin*, pp. 244-247.

[110]Ziemke, *Stalingrad to Berlin*, pp. 213-216.

[111]Seaton, *Russo-German War*, p. 421.

[112]Ziemke, *Stalingrad to Berlin*, p. 277.

[113]Manstein, *Lost Victories*, pp. 610-612; Mellenthin, *Panzer Battles*, p. 275.

[114]Manstein, *Lost Victories*, pp. 544-546.

[115]DA Pamphlet 20-233, p. 12; Seaton, *Russo-German War*, p. 426.

[116]Ziemke, *Stalingrad to Berlin*, p. 285.

[117]Seaton, *Russo-German War*, pp. 429-431.

[118]*Ibid.*, pp. 460-466; Ziemke, *Northern Theater*, pp. 20-27, 400-402; Carl Gustav Mannerheim, *The Memoirs of Marshal Mannerheim* (New York, 1954), pp. 475-476.

[119]Albert Seaton, *Stalin as Military Commander* (New York, 1976), p. 211.

[120]Zhilin, *Great Patriotic War*, IV, 181.

[121]Rokossovski, *Soldier's Duty*, p. 274; Seaton, *Russo-German War*, pp. 435-436.

[122]Jacobsen, *Decisive Battles*, p. 363; Philippi, *Feldzug gegen Sowjet-Russland*, p. 246; Ziemke, *Stalingrad to Berlin*, pp. 313-314.

[123]Seaton, *Russo-German War*, p. 432.

[124]Jacobsen, *Decisive Battles*, p. 361.

[125]Ziemke, *Stalingrad to Berlin*, p. 315.

[126]Deane, *Strange Alliance*, pp. 149-150.

[127]DA Pamphlet 20-240, pp. 149-150.

[128]Seaton, *Russo-German War*, pp. 438-439; Ziemke, *Stalingrad to Berlin*, pp. 322-323.

[129]Jacobsen, *Decisive Battles*, p. 376.

[130]Seaton, *Russo-German War*, pp. 381-382; Ziemke, *Stalingrad to Berlin*, p. 325; Jacobsen, *Decisive Battles*, pp. 381-382.

[131]Seaton, *Russo-German War*, p. 457.

[132]Ziemke, *Stalingrad to Berlin*, p. 343.

[133]Zhilin, *Great Patriotic War*, IV, 207; Mellenthin, *Panzer Battles*, p. 285.

[134]Seaton, *Russo-German War*, p. 449; Ziemke, *Stalingrad to*

Berlin, p. 449.

[135]Karl Dietrich Bracher, *The German Dictatorship* (New York, 1970), pp. 453-456; Walter Warlimont, *Inside Hitler's Headquarters 1939-45* (New York, 1964), pp. 440-442; Seaton, *Russo-German War*, p. 559.

[136]Joachim Fest, *Hitler* (New York, 1974), pp. 711-712.

[137]Rokossovski, *Soldier's Duty*, pp. 255-261; Seaton, *Russo-German War*, pp. 452-455; Herbert Feis, *Churchill, Roosevelt, Stalin* (Princeton, 1967), p. 387.

[138]Janusy Kazimierz Zawodny, *Death in the Forest, The Story of the Katyn Massacre* (Notre Dame, 1962), p. 24; Wladslaw Anders, *The Crime of Katyn* (London, 1965), pp. 270-271.

[139]Rokossovski, *Soldier's Duty*, pp. 255-256; Seaton, *Russo-German War*, pp. 453-456; Ziemke, *Stalingrad to Berlin*, p. 341.

[140]Department of the Army Pamphlet 20-230, *Russian Combat Methods in World War II* (Washington, 1950), pp. 24-26.

[141]A. A. Sidorenko, *The Offensive* (Moscow, 1970), pp. 27-28, 31, 125-129; DA Pamphlet 20-230, pp. 19-23.

[142]DA Pamphlet 20-230, pp. 36-40, 57-63.

[143]*Ibid.*, p. 20.

[144]*Ibid.*, pp. 17-19.

[145]Sidorenko, *Offensive*, pp. 97-99.

[146]Guderian, *Panzer Leader*, pp. 365-366; Seaton, *Russo-German War*, p. 473.

[147]Philippi, *Feldzug gegen Sowjet-Russland*, p. 259.

[148]Seaton, *Russo-German War*, p. 483.

[149]Robert M. Kennedy, *German Antiguerrilla Operations in the Balkans, 1941-1944* (Washington, 1954), pp. 65-66; Warlimont, *Inside Hitler's Headquarters*, pp. 416-417.

[150]Martin van Creveld, *Hitler's Strategy 1940-1941, The Balkan Clue* (Cambridge, 1973), p. 176; Kennedy, *Antiguerrilla Operations*, p. 49.

[151]Seaton, *Russo-German War*, pp. 500-501.

[152]Vasili I. Chuikov, *The Fall of Berlin* (New York, 1968), p. 76; Ivan S. Konev, *Year of Victory* (Moscow, 1969), p. 48; Seaton, *Russo-German War*, pp. 532-533.

[153]Otto Preston Chaney, Jr., *Zhukov*, (Norman, Okla., 1971), pp. 24-25, 345-346; Cornelius Ryan, *The Last Battle* (New York, 1966), pp. 244-246; Konev, *Year of Victory*, pp. 163-166; Rokossovski, *Soldier's Duty*, pp. 84-86.

[154]Chaney, *Zhukov*, p. 293; Rokossovski, *Soldier's Duty*, p. 309; Seaton, *Russo-German War*, p. 531.

[155]Milsom, *Russian Tanks*, pp. 122-125, 178-179; Konev, *Year of Victory*, pp. 9, 125-126; Liddell Hart, *Red Army*, pp. 344-345.

[156]Chuikov, *Fall of Berlin*, p. 90.

[157]Milward, *German Economy*, pp. 72-73, 104, 190-191.

[158]DA Pamphlet 20-201, pp. 95-97; A. J. Barker, *German Infantry Weapons of World War II* (New York, 1969), p. 57; Ryan, *Last Battle*, p. 383.

[159]Rokossovski, *Soldier's Duty*, pp. 277-283; Seaton, *Russo-German War*, p. 538.

[160]Warlimont, *Inside Hitler's Headquarters*, pp. 500-502; Ziemke, *Stalingard to Berlin*, p. 423.

[161]Hilberg, *Destruction of European Jews*, p. 632.

[162]Zhukov, *Greatest Battles*, pp. 270-271; Sergei M. Shtemenko, *Soviet General Staff*, p. 309; Chuikov, *Fall of Berlin*, pp. 115-121.

[163]Chuikov, *Fall of Berlin*, pp. 110-112.

[164]Zhukov, *Greatest Battles*, pp. 273-281; Shtemenko, *The Soviet General Staff at War* (Moscow, 1970), p. 307.

[165]Felix Steiner, *Die Armee der Geächteten* (Göttingen, 1963), p. 223; Seaton, *Russo-German War*, p. 540; Ziemke, *Stalingrad to Berlin*, pp. 445-448.

[166]Warlimont, *Inside Hitler's Headquarters*, p. 499.

[167]Chuikov, *Fall of Berlin*, pp. 145-152.

[168]Konev, *Year of Victory*, p. 172; Ryan, *Last Battle*, pp. 470-471; Seaton, *Russo-German War*, pp. 578-584.

[169]Robert Payne, *The Life and Death of Adolf Hitler* (New York, 1973), pp. 589-591.

[170]Hilberg, *Destruction of European Jews*, p. 670.

[171]Seaton, *Russo-German War*, p. 586.

[172]Ziemke, *Stalingrad to Berlin*, p. 500.

The Western Allies Seize the Initiative: North Africa 7

A tactician's paradise and a quartermaster's hell.

General von Ravenstein[1]

Throughout World War II the western Allies and the Axis powers fought along the shores of the Mediterranean Sea. Confrontation there began seven months before German troops occupied the Rhineland and ended only after Hitler lay dead in his Berlin bunker. Italian dictator Benito Mussolini began the conflict on October 20, 1935, when he dispatched an army to conquer Ethiopia. The League of Nations failed to punish that glaringly clear case of naked aggression; but relations between Italy and all other Mediterranean powers, as well as Germany, turned icy and formal.

As Hilter occupied the Rhineland and aggressively marched into Austria, the Sudetenland, and Czechoslovakia, the British government tried to improve relations with Italy. This seemed logical to the practical Englishman, for while war with Germany seemed inevitable, war concurrently with Italy would be foolish. Great Britain was unsuccessful diplomatically, but the four years between 1935 and 1939 were put to good use. Because Mussolini's conquest of Ethiopia had made the Egyptians more wary of Italian imperialism than of the British brand, England asked for and received permission to station large forces in the land of the Pharaohs. Meanwhile, the British and French divided responsibility for naval control of the Mediterranean Sea, and both countries signed agreements with Turkey, insuring her neutrality or cooperation in the event of war in the eastern Mediterranean. British officers surveyed Egypt and made plans for the establishment of a logistical system capable of serving the entire Mediterranean Fleet and a large army with its supporting air forces; however, construction of the facilities had just begun when war broke out.

The objects of all these diplomatic and military efforts, of course, were the Suez Canal and Mideast oil. Since World War I, the strategic importance of the area had grown. The Canal had always been the critical link with the Dominions, but by 1939 the importance of oil had increased immeasurably. All aircraft, warships, and tactical vehicles required oil; so did civilian economies. If England were to fight Germany successfully, she would need the oil and a secure route for it to be carried to England. Italy presented a potential problem in this regard unless Mussolini chose to remain neutral or become allied with the English; for from the naval base at Taranto and airfields on Sicily, Sardinia, and Pantelleria, Italian forces could block unfriendly east-west shipping. *(See Map 33, in* ***Atlas.****)* From the English viewpoint, Mussolini made the correct choice when Hitler invaded Poland in September 1939—he remained neutral. Then, nine months later, when Hitler invaded France, he watched. Finally, eager to share in the spoils, he declared war on France and Great Britain on June 11, 1940, just six days after the Dunkirk evacuation. President Roosevelt told the American people that "the hand that held the dagger has struck it into the back of its neighbor."[2] The stage was thus set for a clash between British and Italian forces in the Mediterranean.

The Adversaries and Their Background

Great Britain's principal concern was defense of the home islands. No reinforcements could be spared to hold Mussolini in the Mediterranean, where the situation looked bleak. Although the performance of Italian armed forces would turn out to be abysmal, in June 1939, Italy seemed formidable. In the Mediterranean she was significantly stronger than Great Britain in both ships and aircraft.

	SHIPS IN MEDITERRANEAN					AIRCRAFT IN EASTERN MEDITERRANEAN		
	Battle-ships	Aircraft Carriers	Cruisers	Destroyers	Subs	Bombers	Fighters	Other
Italy	6	0	19	50	108	140	101	72
Great Britain	4	1	8	20	12	96	75	34

Comparison of Strengths in Ships and Aircraft, June 1939

British Hurricane Over Mediterranean Beach, Coastal Road and Strip, and Beginning of Escarpment

Except for two Italian battleships, all ships of both belligerents had been launched prior to the First World War. The Italian ships were faster, type for type, than the British vessels. Generally, Italian aircraft were also faster and flew farther than corresponding British types. Thus, many British airfields were within range of Italian bombers, but the Italian bomber bases could not be reached by RAF bombers.[3]

Admiral Sir Andrew Browne Cunningham, Commander of the Mediterranean Fleet, had only three advantages. First, his fleet was known to be better trained and to have higher morale than that of the Italians. Second, Great Britain's possession of the Suez Canal and Gibraltar would contain the Italian Navy in the Mediterranean and allow the British fleet to be reinforced from the Atlantic. Third, the tiny British island of Malta sat right in the middle of Italian shipping lanes. Aircraft on Malta could be used to watch or strike the Italian fleet–if the island base were not crushed first.

If British ships and airplanes were inferior to Italian models, however, British ground divisions were decidedly superior. The Italian divisions contained only two regiments, fewer support troops, and far less equipment. Italy, however, was able to commit more of her divisions to North Africa than England could. In Libya, Marshal Rodolfo Graziani mustered 250,000 troops while General Sir Archibald P. Wavell had 100,000 men to defend Egypt, Palestine, and the Sudan.[4]

The surrender of France on June 25 threatened to throw the force in the Mediterranean further out of balance. What was to happen to the French fleet? If it were surrendered to Germany or Italy, Great Britain, the only nation then at war with the Axis, would be hopelessly outgunned. To insure that this did not occur, the Royal Navy impounded all French warships in British harbors and attacked warships in the French harbors of Oran, Casablanca, and Dakar, sinking five battleships.

The bulk of Graziani's and Wavell's combat forces faced each other across the Libyan-Egyptian border in the western desert, as inhospitable a battleground as any supply officer could imagine. The area from Mersa Matruh to El Agheila had one road, running along the coast and joining the region's only towns. *(See Map 33, in Atlas.)* Along the south shore of the Mediterranean lies a sandy coastal strip of varying width. There is an escarpment where the coastal strip abruptly ends and the 500-foot high Libyan Plateau begins. Without major engineer work, ascent of the escarpment for wheeled or tracked vehicles is possible at only a few passes. The plateau, while desert, is not a sea of sand but a bed of limestone thinly covered by sand. Often bare limestone shows through in large patches. Once on the plateau, vehicles can move about freely off the roads. The outstanding feature of the entire area, however, is the fact that it produces nothing—not even water with which to sustain life or military operations.

British Gun in Position With Escarpment in Background

First British Successes, August 1940-February 1941

Two main factors controlled the campaigns in the Mediterranean. The first of these was the interdependence of land, sea, and air forces caused by geography. As the fighting in Norway had demonstrated, control of the sea was difficult without control of the air above the sea. The Italian Navy had no aircraft carriers because land-based planes could cover the fleet throughout the central and eastern Mediterranean. Yet Italian air bases in the Dodecanese Islands depended on resupply by sea. Armies operating on any Mediterranean shore, particularly the south one, depended on supply by sea. An army could help its resupply by capturing the enemy's airfields, thus making the sea lanes safer. But the more land the army controlled, the greater the tonnage of supply required to sustain it. This interdependence was illustrated from the first Italian advance in 1940 to the Anglo-American capture of Rome in 1944.

In August 1940, Mussolini ordered Marshal Graziani to advance into Egypt, a movement Graziani reluctantly began a month later. *(See Map 34a, in Atlas.)* "Never has a military operation been undertaken so much against the will of the Commander," wrote Mussolini's chief of staff.[5] There was no battle; Graziani's four divisions motored past the battalion-sized British covering force, then stopped at Sidi Barrani prior to reaching Wavell's main body at Mersa Matruh. There he sat, obviously not intending to advance farther. Moreover, Mussolini, who had just begun his supposed conquest of Greece, failed to prod Graziani.

Yet, because of the interdependence of land, sea, and air forces, this seemingly minor gain altered the capabilities of all Italian and British services. There was an airfield at Sidi Barrani. Once Graziani owned it, the Italian Air Force was able to provide fighter escort to its bombers as far as Mersa Matruh. British bombers with a full bomb load could no longer reach the main Italian port of supply at Benghazi. The Royal Navy was denied land-based fighter cover from Sidi Barrani to Tobruk, reducing its ability to bombard the Italian line of communication. RAF planes with extra fuel tanks could no longer reach Malta, requiring the Royal Navy to use its aircraft carriers as resupply ships. The reduced effectiveness of Malta's air squadron gave more freedom to the Italian Navy and eased Italian supply problems.

The second factor controlling Mediterranean campaigns was their dependence on events in other theaters. The Mediterranean was always a secondary theater, even in 1941 and 1942 when it was the only European theater in which Anglo-American land forces were engaged. Being secondary, it always depended on the forces left over from other theaters. For example, prior to and during Graziani's advance, the British had been unable to send reinforcements to Egypt because the Battle of Britain was raging and invasion seemed imminent. Once the threat of invasion passed in October, Great Britain began to reinforce its Mediterranean forces. From September through December, 126,000 troops set sail for Egypt from India, Australia, New Zealand, and Great Britain. Naval reinforcements also arrived, the aircraft carrier *Illustrious* being particularly valuable. Meanwhile, Graziani received no reinforcements since Mussolini's campaign in Greece was proving disastrous.

While the reinforcements did not give the British numerical superiority, they did allow Cunningham and Wavell to take the offensive in late 1940. First, on November 11, Cunningham had HMS *Illustrious* launch a surprise air attack on the Italian fleet at its home base, Taranto. All six battleships were in port. Attacking aircraft destroyed one and inflicted damage on two others which required six months to repair. Overnight, Italy lost its superiority at sea.

Wavell used his reinforcements to attack on December 9. *(See Map 34a, in Atlas.)* The attack passed through an unfortified portion of Graziani's line, then turned and closed on his fortified outposts from the rear. The position crumbled, and the Italian Tenth Army fled back along the coastal road with Wavell's troops in pursuit. No Italian attempt to establish a new line succeeded. Finally, Wavell sent an armored division across the base of the Cyrenaican Peninsula, trapping the Italians at Beda Fomm on February 7, 1941. In two months of battle and pursuit, Wavell had advanced 500 miles and captured 130,000 Italians, 380 tanks, and 845 guns. His own force suffered only 1,928 casualties.[6]

German Intervention in North Africa

All North Africa lay open. But now the controlling factors, interdependence of theaters and interdependence of forces, combined to thwart Wavell. On February 22, Churchill decided to send troops to help the Greeks defend against impending German invasion.* Most of the troops dispatched came from the front in Cyrenaica, leaving Wavell only five brigades with which to defend Libya.

In the meantime, Hitler had decided to send forces to North Africa to help Mussolini. He neither wanted the Italians to lose control of the central Mediterranean nor the British free to reinforce Greece. On January 8, the first German unit, *Fliegerkorps X*, which had been specially trained in the attack of ships, arrived in Sicily from Norway. It made its debut five

*See Chapter 4 for a description of the German invasion of Greece.

days later by severely damaging HMS *Illustrious* and sinking the cruiser *Southampton*. For the following two months, this corps rained bombs on Malta, completely neutralizing it, while fresh troops and 220,000 tons of supplies moved unhampered to Tripoli.[7] Axis aircraft were also able to keep British ships away from Benghazi, necessitating a 450-mile overland haul from Tobruk to forward positions at El Agheila.

Four divisions crossed to Libya: an Italian mechanized division, an Italian armored division, a German motorized division, and a German armored division. But most important of all, on February 12, Lieutenant General Erwin Rommel crossed and assumed command of the German units, soon to be named the *Deutsches Afrika Korps*. ULTRA intercepts informed the British of Rommel's new appointment and also of the movement of the reinforcing divisions, thereby alerting Wavell to the fact that he would be considerably outnumbered. British intelligence knew very little about Rommel—but that would change radically in a short time.[8]

Rommel's First Advance

By March 1941 the situation was completely reversed. The Italo-German forces were numerically strong, well-equipped, adequately supplied, and superbly led, while Allied strength had degenerated. On March 24, Rommel raided positions at El Agheila. Upon finding them a hollow shell, he boldly converted his raid into a general attack in spite of Hitler's standing orders to remain on the defensive. *(See Map 34b, in Atlas.)* Soon the attack turned into a pursuit as British units, which had never experienced *blitzkrieg,* disintegrated.

During his first African advance, Rommel displayed the l;eadership and tactical skill that were to earn him the name, "desert fox." Within one month after his arrival, Rommel, whose combat experience had been in the mountains of Italy and the plains of France, could read the desert terrain like an Arab, using the slightest depression to hide antitank guns or seeing trafficable routes where others saw only obstacles. He was bold, not hesitating to convert a raid into a major advance. Using his private reconnaissance airplane and his armored staff car, he usually managed to be at the critical point at the front. He would often land his plane and personally tell a subordinate commander to take the covered route to the right, to move faster, to avoid the ambush ahead, to refuel, or to move to the support of another column.[9]

On April 14, Rommel halted at Salum, just inside the Egyptian border, stopped less by the reinforcements Wavell had rushed west than by the Royal Navy and the Australians at Tobruk. During the retreat, the 9th Australian Division had accepted siege in Tobruk, where it not only occupied a perfect flanking position but also denied Rommel use of the port. Axis forces required 50,000 tons of supplies at the front per month, and the port of Benghazi could accept only 29,000 tons. This meant that as long as the Australians held Tobruk, 21,000 tons of supplies would have to move a thousand miles from Tripoli to Tobruk by trucks—and these were scarce.

The Royal Navy caused other supply shortages. On March 26, the Italian fleet, which had so far contributed nothing to the Axis effort, put to sea to intercept British troop ships bound for Greece. Instead, it was itself intercepted by Cunningham's warships. Again, ULTRA had provided vital information about Italian plans and strength, enabling Cunningham to plan his ambush artfully.[10] In the ensuing Battle of Cape Matapan, the Italians lost five warships while the British lost only one airplane. With the Italian fleet reduced, Cunningham risked stationing four destroyers at Malta. Within two weeks those four warships had destroyed two convoys containing 300 vehicles and other supplies for Rommel. *Fliegerkorps X* quickly chased all destroyers from Malta, but the damage had been done.

There was now a brief operational interlude in which an emissary from OKW, Churchill, and ULTRA played roles. The German high command had been shocked at Rommel's rapid advance and was skeptical of his ability to take Tobruk, particularly after his first impetuous assault ended in failure. Accordingly, OKW sent General von Paulus—who would later surrender at Stalingrad—to inspect the situation. Paulus' gloomy report detailed Rommel's great shortages in fuel, ammunition, and vehicles, and commented on his weak position between Tobruk and British forces to the east. This report reached not only OKW but also the British through ULTRA intercept. Churchill, who had pushed the "Tiger" convoy (some 300 tanks and 50 Hurricane fighters) through the Mediterranean to Alexandria, was beside himself with joy. He badgered Wavell, stressing his overly optimistic assessment of Rommel's desperate situation, and urged a prompt British attack to relieve Tobruk. Wavell thought an attack was premature, but finally gave in to the pressure and launched Operation BATTLEAXE on June 15. It failed, and Wavell lost 91 of the new tanks, principally because of skillful German employment of antitank guns.[11] Wavell, who seemed destined to lead losing causes, was relieved on the twenty-first and replaced by General Sir Claude Auchinleck in July. Churchill sent Wavell to India, where he would head yet another losing cause against the Japanese.

Second British Advance

Churchill hounded Auchinleck to attack immediately, but Auchinleck delayed, knowing that during every day that passed his army gained strength while Rommel's grew weaker. In June, Hitler had launched his invasion of Russia, and the Eastern Front now demanded priority on German resources. Almost all *Luftwaffe* squadrons, except *Fliegerkorps X*, departed the Mediterranean for Russia. The Tenth then drastically reduced its attacks on Malta in order to provide air support for the entire central and eastern Mediterranean, including close air support of the *Afrika Korps*. Once freed from the *Luftwaffe's* attention, Malta's fighters and Cunningham's destroyers began to exact a 20 percent toll of Rommel's supplies as they crossed the sea. *(See Table, page 178.)*

At the same time, Hitler created a new German command in the Mediterranean in an attempt to dominate Italian planning. Field Marshal Albert Kesselring, a *Luftwaffe* officer, became Commander-in-Chief South. From Rome he controlled all German naval and air forces in the Mediterranean, but not Rommel. Since Italy depended on Germany for oil and gasoline, Kesslring could also influence the Italian Air Force and Navy.

By mid-November, Rommel had 414 tanks, 320 aircraft, and 9 divisions, 4 of which were besieging Tobruk. Auchinleck's strength had grown to about 700 tanks, 1,000 aircraft, and 8 divisions. He organized these divisions into the Eighth Army with General Alan Cunningham in command. Auchinleck remained head of the entire Middle East Command, but he spent most of his time looking over Cunningham's shoulder.[12]

Auchinleck launched his CRUSADER offensive on November 18 by attempting to envelop Rommel's inland flank with an armored brigade while the Tobruk garrison attempted to break out. *(See Map 35a in Atlas.)* Rommel countered with his armored reserve, and the battle raged for two weeks. He made better use of his tanks because he kept them concentrated by using antitank guns with his infantry. The British, while keeping some of their armor concentrated, insisted on stationing some tanks with all infantry formations to counter *panzers*. At first, Rommel's tactics succeeded. Cunningham, despairing over heavy tank losses, asked permission to stop the attack. Auchinleck immediately replaced him with Major General Neil Ritchie. By December 4, attrition had whipped Rommel, and he began a retreat across Cyrenaica. Although Hitler raged at him to stop the retreat, Rommel continued back to El Agheila, escaping encirclement and exhausting his pursuers.

Rommel's Second Advance

Even as the land battle swirled westward, events were occurring in other theaters, on the sea, and in the air that would again reverse the course of the land war. After the Royal Navy and RAF sank 62 percent of the supplies en route to Africa during November, Hitler ordered *Fliegerkorps II* from Russia to Sicily and 10 U-boats from the Atlantic to the Mediterranean. The *Fliegerkorps II* pounded Malta while the submarines announced their presence by sinking a carrier, a battleship, and a cruiser. Throughout December, Royal Navy losses mounted, climaxing on the nineteenth when Italian frogmen damaged four ships within Alexandria harbor. By the time Rommel had stopped his retreat at El Agheila, Cunningham's fleet consisted of three cruisers and a handful of destroyers, and Malta was reeling.

To insure that Rommel got supplies, the Italian Navy escorted a mid-December convoy of four merchant ships with 4 battleships, 5 cruisers, and 21 destroyers. Learning that this tactic insured that the supplies arrived safely, the Italians continued the "battleship convoys" throughout January, delivering 66,000 tons of supplies, including 54 tanks. On the other hand, the Japanese attack on Pearl Harbor and Malaya caused all British units then en route to the Middle East to be diverted to India and Singapore.

By January 21, 1942, Rommel was ready to strike again. Catching the Eighth Army overextended and deployed with its forward divisions beyond supporting distance of each other, his attack rolled the British back to Gazala before Ritchie could re-establish a front. *(See Map 35b, in Atlas.)* But then little happened for the next four months as each side sought to refit and replenish supplies faster than the other. Hitler had finally decided that Malta had to be captured, notwithstanding the Crete experience. His air force kept pounding it in preparation for an airborne assault. By the end of April, Malta had no ships and only four operational aircraft left. Unescorted Italian merchant ships sailed within 50 miles of the island.

Although Rommel's strength had increased by mid-spring, Auchinleck was also being resupplied, partially with new American equipment, and ULTRA was proving invaluable. The American M3 tank, christened the "General Grant," was particularly valuable because its 75-mm gun was more powerful than the gun in any British, German, or Italian tank. ULTRA, drawing on intercepts of messages from Rommel's logistical agency and from the *Luftwaffe*, kept the British apprised of Rommel's strength in armor and fuel and his concomitant concern, a situation which Churchill read much more optimistically than did Auchinleck. The Prime Minister, accordingly, continued to urge that Auchinleck attack. ULTRA, moreover, enabled the badly stretched British naval and air forces to pinpoint sailing times and locations of Italo-German supply convoys, which could then be attacked with minimal forces. All these things considered, Rommel felt by May that he could no longer delay an attack on the British Gazala line. ULTRA provided Auchinleck with sufficient warning of the impending attack (code-named VENEZIA), although it did not reveal operational details. Auchinleck sensed correctly that the key to the upcoming battle would be concentration of armor, and he advised Ritchie to keep his armored formations massed in the north, from which location they could strike *en masse* either at

American Instructing British Tankers in Egypt

a Rommel-attempted penetration of the line or a turning movement in the south. Unfortunately for the British, Ritchie disregarded this sound advice.[13]

The Battle of the Gazala-Bir Hacheim line is illustrative of World War II desert warfare. Both sides at this time were approximately equal in strength. Roles played by the air forces, the armor, and the infantry were typical. Resupply, not terrain, limited mobility. The loser ultimately lost because most of his tanks were destroyed. Finally, once retreat began, it did not end for hundreds of miles.

Initial dispositions are shown on *Map 36, in Atlas.* The British infantry occupied fortified positions behind an extensive minefield. The infantry positions (called "boxes") were organized for all-round defense, and the gaps between these positions were seeded with additional mines. In all, the position contained half a million mines within its 50-mile length. The line should have robbed Rommel of the chance to surprise his enemy, since a penetration or envelopment would require so much time to execute that the British would be able to concentrate their 700 tanks against his 544 tanks. However, Ritchie's tanks were split into five brigades under four division commanders. Armored units positioned near Gazala, the 32nd and 1st Army Tank Brigades, were armed with slow, heavy, infantry-support tanks.

During the afternoon of May 26, Rommel attacked South African and British positions south of Gazala with the Italian X and XXI Corps, and also feinted with his mobile units in the same area. But after dark he reversed the mobile columns and ran his vehicles south to get around Bir Hacheim before dawn. He succeeded, for at first light his four-division strike force brushed aside the green 3rd Indian Motorized Brigade. By 10:00 a.m., elements of the 90th Light Infantry Division had overrun an advanced command post of the British 7th Armored Division, but the two *panzer* divisions had run into the 4th Brigade, 7th Armored Division, armed with the new Grant tanks. The ensuing tank battle little resembled dashing cavalry charges of old, more closely copying the stereotyped, wild-west gunfight. Tanks, hunkering behind whatever cover was available, exchanged shots at 2,000 yards with enemy tanks also dug-in. Occasionally a company of tanks would scurry for a more advantageous position, thereby drawing a hail of tank and antitank shot as it moved. By noon the two German divisions had largely destroyed the one brigade and advanced northward where they met the 1st Armored Division's two tank brigades. The 1st Army Tank Brigade also struck at the 21st Panzer Division's left flank. This tank battle raged until dark, then continued at dawn.

Although he still retained the initiative, by noon the third day Rommel could advance no farther. He had lost over one-third of his tanks and, because British motorized raiding parties were ambushing convoys in his rear, his forward units were growing short of gasoline and ammunition. During the afternoon of the twenty-ninth, Rommel ordered all units to withdraw to a spot west of Knightsbridge where elements of the Italian X Corps, having side-slipped southward, had breached the minefields. After organizing a defense of his now consolidated penetration, he turned on the "box" within it and by June 2 had destroyed the 150th Brigade. He then set

General Grant Tank in North Africa

about repairing and resupplying his mobile units. British Tommies quickly nicknamed Rommel's position "the cauldron." *(See Map 37 in Atlas.)* For the next ten days, Ritchie destroyed 230 of his remaining British tanks by throwing them, a brigade at a time, into "the cauldron."

Meanwhile, Rommel had turned on Bir Hacheim, for without a safe southern flank he could not resume the offensive. The Allied troops at Bir Hacheim had already helped stop his first attack by raiding his supply line. For ten days (June 2 through 11) the war reverted from lightning tank thrusts to the infantry trench warfare of World War I. *(Actions not shown on map.)* The 1st Free French Brigade, fighting for the first time as a unit, defended the Bir Hacheim box. They had prepared their positions well and fought fiercely.* It required two Axis divisions (the 90th Light and Italian Trieste), 1,400 *Luftwaffe* sorties, and 10 days to wrest Bir Hacheim from the French. On the night of June 10, 2,700 Frenchmen broke through the German encirclement, leaving behind only 500 wounded and 400 dead. Rommel later praised the French resistance as an example of what a determined commander could do in a seemingly hopeless situation.

Throughout the entire battle the RAF and *Luftwaffe* supported their respective armies and dueled for control of the skies. British fighters pounced on *Stuka* dive bombers, shooting down 40 in a single day over Bir Hacheim. German fighters hunted high-flying British bombers. Fighter pilots who went low to strafe enemy vehicles on the wide open desert hurried aloft after a few passes lest they be caught in a disadvantageous position by enemy fighters. In spite of all the activity, however, the air battle must be called a draw.

Once his southern flank was cleared, his *panzers* resupplied, and his enemy weakened, Rommel charged out of the cauldron on June 11. *(See Map 37, in Atlas.)* The remaining British armor held off the *panzers* just long enough for the 1st South African and 50th Divisions to escape. By the Fifteenth, German tanks had reached the coast, after immobilizing all but 60 of Ritchie's tanks.[14] Two days earlier, Ritchie and Auchinleck had been debating whether the Eighth Army should retreat to Egypt and, if so, whether forces should be left to hold Tobruk; the decision was in the affirmative in both instances. Rommel, determined not be stopped again by a thorn in his flank, quickly assaulted and seized Tobruk on June 21. There he found 2,000 tons (two-and-a-half million gallons) of gasoline and 2,000 wheeled vehicles, all of which he desperately needed before moving into Egypt.[15]

Free French Troops at Bir Hacheim

As Rommel pursued the British and Commonwealth forces eastward, Auchinleck relieved Ritchie and assumed personal command of the Eighth Army. Upon reaching El Alamein, Auchinleck faced his army about and dug in. *(See Map 35b, in Atlas.)* The El Alamein-Qattara Depression line was an excellent choice of positions, aside from being the only choice left before the Nile River. For once, there were no flanks to turn. Rommel would have to meet the British Tommy, who was known as a dogged defender, head on. Additionally, his long supply line lay exposed to RAF attack. Although he tried all during July, Rommel was unable to penetrate the El Alamein position.

The longer Rommel remained before El Alamein the weaker he became. Hitler cancelled the invasion of Malta, for the island was no longer a serious threat, but two years of war had reduced the Italian merchant fleet to a third of its prewar size. Thus, by July 1942, Great Britain could resupply Egypt over long routes from England, India, Australia, and the United States faster than Italy and Germany could resupply their forces by the 600-mile route across the Mediterranean.† In August, for example, the Allies in Egypt received ten times as much supply tonnage as the Axis did.[16]

Desperately needing a victory for reasons of politics and morale, Churchill despaired that Auchinleck would be unable to give it to him. Not surprisingly, therefore, he replaced him in early August with two men: General Sir Harold R. L. G. Alexander, who took over Middle East Command, and Lieutenant General Bernard L. Montgomery, who assumed command of the Eighth Army. Like Auchinleck, however, neither of these two men would attack before accumulating an overwhelming advantage. Meanwhile, through ULTRA, the British read Rommel's account to Hitler of his greatly worsening supply and equipment situation. Better yet, they also learn-

*Rommel's chief of staff claimed that the box contained 1,200 separate positions and strong points.

†Of the supplies arriving in Egypt during the summer of 1942, 10 percent came 14,000 miles from the United Kingdom, 30 percent came 14,000 miles from Canada and the U.S., and 60 percent came 2,500 miles from India and other sources.[17]

ed of his plan to make a final attempt to smash the Eighth Army.

On the last day of August, Rommel gathered all his strength and attempted to crack the British position. Montgomery, forearmed with knowledge of the date of the attack and an understanding of Rommel's scheme of maneuver, prepared in-depth defenses and a trap for Axis armor. To protect the ULTRA secret, he had told his commanders of his intuition that Rommel would soon attack around the southern flank. The outcome of the Battle of Alam Halfa was never in doubt, as Montgomery fought a careful action and inflicted moderate to heavy casualties on his enemy. Rommel had no choice but to withdraw to his starting line. Montgomery let him go because he was not yet ready to launch his own offensive.[18]

Montgomery then spent most of September and October visiting his units, talking to his troops, improving the Eighth Army's morale, developing a plan of attack and checking its every detail, training, integrating the 300 Sherman tanks recently arrived from America, and moving equipment and supplies forward. His preparations reflected his personal principles of war: morale, balance, and tidiness.[19] He felt that time and energy invested in communicating with and caring for the troops would pay dividends in battle. By balance, he meant that like a boxer the army should always be in a position to shift its direction of movement or to ward off enemy blows. Attempting the single knockout punch left both the boxer and the army overextended, off balance, and vulnerable. Tidiness was a corollary of balance. Montgomery used the term to mean that a commander should know both his and his enemy's situation so that he could use his balanced unit, even if it meant delaying maneuver to simplify a complicated situation.*

* Later in Italy, some American commanders would be angered by Montgomery's slowness because they mistook tidy to mean a well-policed battlefield.

Sherman Tank

It is interesting to contrast Montgomery's technique with that of Rommel. The German thrived on untidiness because he felt that when all was confusion there would be many opportunities for the bold commander. He further believed in the knockout blow, for the decisive thrust could quickly win the battle with few casualties. If the blow was properly timed and vigorously executed, there was little danger of a successful counterstroke from a confused enemy.[20] To his troops, Rommel was cold and aloof. He was always called Rommel, never by a nickname like Monty, Auk, or Ike. Rommel's relations with his men and with civilians were exactly what one would expect from a German officer—formal, with concealed disdain for civilians and genuine admiration for his competent troops. He never gave pep talks or told his troops what his plans were. Few have claimed that his troops loved Rommel, but no one has denied that they would follow him anywhere. They followed because they trusted him; they believed that he would not risk their lives unnecessarily and that he would find a way to win with few casualties.[21]

Montgomery, on the other hand, worked at being identified with his men and sought their adoration in return. He spoke often to them, telling them of his plans and his confidence in them. He welcomed the press to increase his exposure. He exuded confidence. Indeed, he never admitted to ever having made a significant mistake. Yet Montgomery's leadership technique was appropriate for the British Eighth Army in late 1942. Unlike Rommel, he had no reputation upon which to base trust. He had never before led the Eighth in battle. If a trust founded on deeds was impossible, a trust based on words was the next best alternative. He was no doubt genuinely confident of his abilities and judgments, but he had to infuse that confidence into his army. This he accomplished through maximum exposure and communication, using both personal visits and the media. If Montgomery seems less sincere than Rommel, we must remember that Montgomery won the battle.

When the Eighth Army did attack on October 23, Montgomery had a three-to-one advantage in troops, tanks, guns, and airplanes. Through ULTRA, he knew that Rommel was ill and on sick leave in Germany when the battle began—he would return precipitately when his temporary successor was killed the first day. ULTRA, as well as providing excellent battlefield intelligence, also revealed to Montgomery how desperate Rommel's supply and equipment situation was. To the British commander's credit, however, is the fact that he fully understood how to use his great military intelligence advantage and was determined to fight a careful, set-piece battle which would sap Rommel's strength. Rommel defended determinedly, for he did not have enough fuel to maneuver properly and had never had enough material to construct alternate positions to the rear. His only advantage lay in the four-mile-thick minefield his men had laid across their front. After slugging it out for a fortnight, the *Afrika Armee* was reduced to 20 serviceable tanks while Montgomery still had 600. Then, through ULTRA, came confirmation of what Montgomery had hoped—Rommel was in dire straits and close to collapse. This information was obtained from a message Rommel sent to Hitler, asking permission to withdraw. It was refused at first and Hitler's orders were to "stand fast." Finally, on November 4, another exchange of messages prompted Hitler grudgingly to give his permission for Rommel to begin the withdrawal, which would not end for 1,400 miles.[22] *(See Map 38a, in Atlas.)* The Battle of El Alamein, taken in conjunction with the German debacle at Stalingrad, proved strategically decisive. Together, they marked a clear turning of the tide against the German march of conquest.

The Anglo-American Invasion of North Africa

Even as Rommel gave his withdrawal order, three large Allied task forces were at sea carrying British and American soldiers toward the invasion of northwest Africa. In October 1941, Churchill had considered landing forces in Morocco, Algeria, and Tunisia when Auchinleck's CRUSADER offensive approached Tripoli. In late December 1941, at the Arcadia Conference—the first Allied wartime conference—Roosevelt had agreed to provide additional shipping and troops for the seizure of Tunisia. Unfortunately, Auchinlech only reached El Agheila, 500 miles short of Tripoli. Planning for the invasion of Northwest Africa stopped.*

Roosevelt, however, insisted that American ground forces be committed somewhere in Europe during 1942. Since an invasion of France was not possible, the old plans for an invasion of northwest Africa were dusted off, revised, and renamed TORCH. The seizure of northwest Africa offered several advantages: it might provide some relief to the Russians by creating a second front; it would certainly drive Rommel from Africa; it would save millions of tons of shipping annually by replacing the long trip around Africa with a short trip through the Mediterranean under Allied air cover from the south shore; and, finally, it would strike at Germany without getting within reach of the entire *Wehrmacht*.

TORCH, however, had one serious disadvantage. Morocco, Algeria, and Tunisia were French, not Italian or German. During the war the French were generally divided into three factions. First, the French National Committee in London followed General Charles DeGaulle. His group, also known as the "Free French" and later as the "Fighting French," comprised both French refugees who had escaped to England, America, or the French colonies rather than accept German oppression at home, and also those patriots who remained in France and took part in the activities of the resistance groups. The 1st Free French Brigade, which fought so well at Bir Hacheim, demonstrated the determination and hatred of Germany which characterized DeGaulle's followers.

A second group, Frenchmen living in North Africa where open resistance would have brought sudden German occupation, succeeded in establishing an underground "French Liberation Movement." Although the aim of this group, like the Free French, was to liberate France, its members were operating under German surveillance, which to the outside world seemed to give a collaborationist tinge to their activities. General Henri Giraud, who had recently escaped from German custody, was to become the recognized leader of this group, which included some of the French military leaders in North Africa. The British sinking of part of the French Navy in North African ports had made this group almost as anti-British as anti-German.

The third group was made up of pro-Vichy French, men clinging with pathetic loyalty to old Marshal Pétain. This group comprised those unfortunates in France and Axis-dominated territories who believed that collaboration with the Germans was the best method of insuring the future of their country. Admiral Jean Darlan, who controlled the French Fleet, was Pétain's designated successor.

Bitter rivalry existed among the three groups. For example, DeGaulle and Pétain publicly accused each other of treason, DeGaulle for fleeing his homeland in its hour of need and Pétain for cooperating with Germany.

Allied planners debated how the French in North Africa would react. They had announced they would fight any invader, Allied or Axis, but would they? Some planners predicted that the French would have to fight an Allied invasion because Germany held the French homeland hostage. Others claimed that North African French would take up arms against Germany just as soon as they were given the oportunity. It was under the latter assumption that TORCH was planned, for if the French actively opposed the invasion, Hitler would have time to move sufficient forces to Africa to block the Allies somewhere in Algeria. Planners further assumed that the French would be more disposed to welcome Americans than Englishmen. Therefore, TORCH was designed to appear to be totally American.[23]

Soon after agreeing to conduct TORCH, the Combined Chiefs of Staff appointed the commander of U.S. Army elements in England, Lieutenant General Dwight D. Eisenhower, as Supreme Commander, Allied Expeditionary Force. To preserve the fiction of an all-American invasion, the Combined

*Chapter 8 discusses the interrelationship of Allied Mediterranean and European strategy.

Chiefs named Major General Mark W. Clark to be Eisenhower's deputy.*

Eisenhower insisted on unity of command for TORCH, thereby setting a precedent for the remainder of the war. All invasion task forces would be commanded by one man, no matter what the mix of U.S. Army, British Army, U.S. Navy, or Royal Navy elements. Additionally, he developed a new staff organization at his headquarters, Allied Force Headquarters (AFHQ). The operations and intelligence staffs were completely integrated, about half British and half American. On the other hand, because the personnel and logisitics systems of the British and Americans were based on service custom, military regulation, and national legislation, the administrative staffs could not be integrated. Eisenhower solved this problem by appointing a Chief Administrative Officer to coordinate and resolve difficulties between the two G-4s and the two G-1s.

When AFHQ began planning TORCH the major decision to be made was where to land. *(See Map 38b, in Atlas.)* The objective of the entire operation was the port complex in Tunisia (Bizerte and Tunis). From all-weather airfields near these two cities, Sicily could be bombed, convoys to Malta protected, and supply ships for Rommel sunk. But a landing at the objective was considered suicidal because of Axis aircraft on Sicily and Sardinia. One faction, mostly British, favored landing at Bone; most Americans, fearing Spanish intervention would close Gibraltar, wanted to land only on the Atlantic shores of Morocco. The compromise adopted called for landings at Algiers, Oran, and Casablanca. The latter two forces would stand ready to capture Spanish Morocco if Spain joined the Axis, while the Eastern Task Force would race overland to Tunis.

The entire force of 370 merchant ships and 300 warships was at sea before the final plan was published. The Western Task Force, composed of U.S. Army units and U.S. Navy ships, sailed directly from America to Casablanca. The Center Task Force, composed of U.S. Army units and Royal Navy ships, sailed from England for Oran. In the Eastern Task Force, the Royal Navy carried both American and British Army units from England to Algiers. Miraculously, German submarines failed to detect the convoys. Axis air reconnaissance reported the presence of the Central and Eastern Task Forces in the Mediterranean, but the German Admiralty assumed that they were convoys bound for Malta.

Before dawn on Sunday, November 8, 1942, Allied soldiers waded ashore in Morocco and Algeria. French reactions varied. At Algiers, pro-Allied Frenchmen helped seize the city so that by evening all fighting was over. At Oran, two days were needed to subdue unethusiastic Frenchmen. In Morocco, however, Major General George S. Patton's troops met tough resistance from French colonial units who stopped fighting only after three days and orders from superiors in Algiers.

Unfortunately, the superiors in Algiers were the wrong superiors. Admiral Jean François Darlan, commander of the Vichy armed forces, was in Algiers visiting his sick son when the Allies landed. Once captured and convinced of the hopelessness of further resistance, he ordered the French forces to return to their barracks. But the Allies needed active French cooperation, not neutrality. At a minimum, French forces had to patrol the line of communication from Algiers eastward and had to prohibit a German administrative seizure of Tunis. During the five days required to obtain Darlan's cooperation, German troops were air-landing in Tunis. When Darlan finally ordered active cooperation with the Allies it was too late, for the Axis already held Bizerte and Tunis. Hitler also occupied the remainder of France, but the French fleet at Toulon scuttled itself before Nazi troops could seize it.

*This was the only time during the war that one ally provided both the commander and deputy commander for an operation containing substantial numbers of both British and American troops.

American Troops Landing Near Algiers

The Race for Tunis

The campaign in Northwest Africa was now a transportation officer's battle to determine who could assemble forces in Tunisia the fastest. The Axis transported a German division from Sicily by air and ferryboat, while the British First Army moved east from Algiers by sea, road, and air. *(See Map 39, in Atlas.)* The First was an Army in name only, consisting of one incomplete British division, one armored task force, two battalions of British paratroopers, and one battalion of American airborne troops. The first clash occurred near Medjez el Bab on November 17, where the Germans pushed the Allies back a few miles. *(See Map 40a, in Atlas.)* More battalions reinforced each side. The First Army then advanced to within 30 miles of Tunis, but was forced back to Medjez el Bab by New Year's Day. Germany had won the race because the battlefield was near Tunis, making her supply lines short and all-weather airfields only 10 minutes flying time away. In opposition, Allied reinforcements had to travel overland 350 miles, and Allied fighters had only 10 minutes loiter-time over the battlefield, having flown all the way from Constantine.

In January, the winter rains began, turning the soil into a gelatinous goo that ensnared tanks, slowed infantry to a crawl, and rendered dirt airstrips useless. Eisenhower accepted the fact that no offensive in northern Tunisia was possible until the ground dried in March; he used the lull to improve the line of communication, build up a logistical base, sort out his mixed combat units, and establish a workable chain of command at the front. He placed the British First Army commander, Lieutenant General Sir Kenneth A. N. Anderson, in charge of the entire Tunisian front and established three corps under him (the British V, the French XIX, and the American II). Anderson searched for strong defensive positions in which to spend the next three months.

The terrain in northern Tunisia is a jumble of mountains with peaks over 3,000 feet high. The mountains are bisected by the Medjerda River Valley from Souk Ahras, through Medjez el Bab, to the ocean at a point halfway between Bizerta and Tunis. The mountains become more orderly in southern Tunisia where they divide into two chains, the Eastern Dorsal and the Western Dorsal. Both stretch south from Ousseltia like an inverted V. Between them lies a plateau. Since the Eastern Dorsal ends in a great impassable salt marsh, it made an ideal defensive position for the Allied southern flank. Anderson, therefore, disposed his American and French units at the mountain passes along the Eastern Dorsal. *(See Map 40b, in Atlas.)*

Even as Eisenhower worried about little things, like when the ground would dry, his superiors met at Casablanca to discuss his next strategic move. At this third wartime conference, Roosevelt, Churchill, and the Combined Chiefs of Staff abandoned plans for a cross-channel assault on France in 1943. Instead, they agreed to seize Sicily next, in order to secure the Mediterranean shipping route completely and, in Churchill's mind, hopefully to cause Italy to ask for surrender terms.*[24]

If the Allies assumed that North Africa would be cleared in time to invade Sicily in the summer of 1943, the Axis was unwilling to concede the point, for Hitler poured 140,000 troops, mostly German, into North Africa in the four months following TORCH.[25] The first task of General Curt von Arnim, German commander in Tunisia, was to keep open a route from his forces to Rommel. Fearing that from their positions along the Eastern Dorsal, Allied units might attempt to penetrate to the coast, Arnim struck a series of blows at the poorly equipped French units, seizing from them the passes at Pont Du Fahs, Fondouk, and Faid.† Counterattacks by Combat Command B, 1st Armored Division, failed to recapture the passes.** Rommel's backdoor was securely bolted.

Battle of Kasserine Pass

In late January 1943, Rommel's army crossed the Libyan-Tunisian border en route to a defensive position in the old French frontier fortifications at Mareth. It was an army which had just barely survived on several occasions during the long withdrawal from Egypt. *(See Map 38a, in Atlas.)* Its 10 divisions were at half strength—a total of 78,000 men—and could muster only 129 tanks, many of which were inoperable.[26]

Throughout the withdrawal, a dispirited Rommel seemed intent on reaching Tunisia and gaining succor for his equipment-starved forces, while Montgomery seemed to follow more than pursue. Constantly quarreling with his German and Italian superiors, who wanted him to turn and fight to save Libya—several times they proposed a counteroffensive—Rommel literally had to scrounge fuel to keep his tanks and vehicles running. When he did halt at the lines shown on the map, it was to gather supplies and to defer to direct orders to stand and fight; but he always slipped away before Montgomery could close a trap.

The British general also had problems keeping his large force supplied, but his failure to launch a hounding pursuit seems to have been more grounded in his determination to take no chances and always to have an overwhelming advantage before attacking any position. This was so in spite of the fact that

*The Casablanca Conference is fully discussed in Chapter 8.

†Many French units were serving in V and II Corps.

**A combat command was a tailored unit similar to a modern brigade and was used only by American armored divisions. Hereafter, combat command will be abbreviated CC.

ULTRA was providing him with fairly good information both about Rommel's deteriorating situation and about the orders Hitler sent the field marshal to stop and fight at certain locales.[27] In the end, a victorious army pushed a defeated one into Tunisia, where they had one final go at each other. Before that, however, Rommel tried to use the Axis central position in Tunisia to strike at the Americans.

By combining Arnim's forces with his own, Rommel had believed for some time that the Italo-German armies could mount stiff offensives either against Eisenhower or Montgomery. He hoped in that way to buy time for the Axis and, coincidentally, perhaps to achieve some strategic gain. Arnim, however, who had already been given one of Rommel's divisions (the 21st Panzer), was not enthused about parting with any troops; nor did he envision much more than small attacks as being necessary to secure the passes through the Eastern Dorsal. *(See Map 40b, in Atlas.)* For his part, Rommel clearly was wary of Montgomery's army to the east, and refused to pull the 15th Panzer Division from that front to participate in an attack on the Americans. The fact that Rommel and Arnim detested each other did not help matters. Finally, Kesselring ordered the two generals to meet him in Tunisia to resolve the impasse.

On February 9, 1943, the three commanders met and agreed upon a plan. Arnim would attack first through Faid Pass, and then would send the 21st Panzer Division to Rommel to help him seize Gafsa. *(See Map 41, in Atlas.)* But now, inexplicably, Rommel was more cautious regarding a full-blooded thrust to Tebessa; Kesselring, who did want a deep drive, accused Rommel of being timid. But even more inexplicably, he left the command arrangement muddled—there was no overall commander of the two attacks short of Kesselring in Rome—leading one to conclude that no one expected the operation to bring real strategic gain.

Arnim's attack on February 14 burst out of Faid Pass, bypassed the 168th Regimental Combat Team, and bounced CCA out of Sidi Bou Zid. *(See Map 41, in Atlas.)* With Faid compromised, the II Corps withdrew its units from Gafsa, and Rommel's troops entered the town on the fifteenth without requiring Arnim's 21st Panzer Division. That same day, the 1st Armored Division, hoping to rescue the trapped regimental combat team, counterattacked Arnim with CCC reinforced with part of CCB. The attacking force contained only one complete tank battalion. German dive bombers disorganized the attack, and the defenders enveloped the confused Americans. Most of the American infantry and artillery escaped, but only four tanks from the tank battalion left the battlefield.[28] The regimental combat team was later captured trying to withdraw as individuals across the treeless plateau.

As the remnants of CCC reformed around the old Roman town of Sbeitla, Anderson, with Eisenhower's approval, ordered the entire southern portion of the First Army line withdrawn to the Western Dorsal, even though this meant giving up the supply base at Sbeitla and the airfield at Thelepte. Before this order could be executed, Arnim's *panzers* reconnoitered Sbeitla. The exhausted, disorganized Americans panicked and fled rearward, bumper-to-bumper and hub-to-hub.

Aerial View of Faid Pass

Rommel's reactions to the combat on the opening days of the offensive had been decidedly mixed. When Arnim's troops routed CCC on the fifteenth, he had been at the Mareth Line, obviously quite preoccupied with readying things for Montgomery; he was relieved that the Americans evacuated Gafsa, thus eliminating the need for *Kampfgruppe DAK* to attack. When he rode into Gafsa on the sixteenth, however, he again became the dynamic leader, anxious to exploit every advantage. Now he wanted to push the Americans off the Western Dorsal as well, and strike deep into the Allied rear. But to do this he needed Arnim's troops, and Arnim did not agree to Rommel's scheme. He did agree, however, to reinforce his reconnaissance effort at Sbeitla. When Rommel discovered that Arnim was shifting the 10th Panzer Division to the northeast late on the seventeenth, he became incensed and the next morning radioed Kesselring, asking for control of the 10th and 21st Panzer Divisions so that he could drive on Tebessa. A tentative approval received shortly made Rommel jubilant; but the later official directive, apparently influenced by Arnim, gave Rommel the town of Le Kef as an objective. Rommel considered this objective to be too shallow and indecisive. *(See Map 40b, in Atlas.)* Still buoyant, however, he made plans for the attack on the nineteenth: from Feriana, an Italian group would "feel" toward Tebessa; *Kampfgruppe DAK* would force

Sbeitla, Tunisia and Surrounding Countryside

Kasserine Pass; and the 21st Panzer Division would advance on Sbiba, toward Le Kef. When he saw which force was making the most progress, Rommel would reinforce it with the 10th Panzer Division and take personal command of that effort. *(See Map 41, in Atlas.)*[29]

The "friction" about which the famous nineteenth-century German military philosopher Clausewitz warns combined with mediocre German leadership to compromise Rommel's plan. In the first place, the petty, German command-level bickering consumed valuable time, which the Americans used to dig in at Kasserine Pass. Then the 21st Panzer Division moved slowly over rain-mired roads and through mine fields only to encounter a stubbornly resisting 1st Guards Brigade; Rommel, however, thought that the 21st was not being aggressively led. Finally, the 10th Panzer Division dawdled in moving back to Sbeitla, where it arrived with neither two of its best tank battalions nor some newly-arrived Tiger tanks, all of which were being withheld by Arnim. A frustrated Rommel decided to use the 10th to reinforce at Kasserine, and ordered *Kampfgruppe DAK* to force the pass the night of February 19. The next morning, still without a breakthrough, Rommel personally went to the scene of action and pushed his commanders unmercifully. The Americans were forced back late on the twentieth, but then a lethargic Rommel wasted the morning of the twenty-first before ordering a resumption of the attack and then leaving the front. Returning on the twenty-second, he discovered that the 10th Panzer Division had failed to take Thala and that *Kampfgruppe DAK* could not budge the determined Americans. Time had run out—precious time which the Germans, including Rommel, had let slip away on February 21 and 22, when they had a chance for a breakthrough before Allied reinforcements could consolidate defenses. A weary and depressed Rommel now gave up; no amount of urging from Kesselring, who had arrived for a visit, could convince him to continue the offensive. Bitterly, and to a degree correctly, Rommel blamed the weather, the Axis high command in Italy, Arnim, his division commanders—everyone but himself. Moreover, Montgomery had arrived at Mareth, and undoubtedly that gave Rommel some concern. Thus, orders went out to halt the attack, hold, and then slowly withdraw. The confused and grateful Allies did not follow aggressively.[30]

The Battle of Kasserine Pass, as the entire affair from Sidi Bou Zid to Thala came to be called, was a bitter pill for the Americans to swallow. They had made many mistakes to which the British and even the French would allude in the following months. The II Corps commander and the 1st Armored Division commander had proved to be indecisive in crisis. American armor was employed piecemeal, not massed. Initial dispositions had been too dispersed, thereby sacrificing an entire regimental combat team. American tankers had been outwitted by the veteran Germans. The Army Air Force had been ineffectively coordinated. Units had been haphazardly mixed. Worst of all, American troops had fled in panic before the enemy. In actuality, American errors and reactions were no different from the reactions of the French along the Meuse River or the British at El Agheila when their green troops first encountered *blitzkrieg*. Nevertheless, Eisenhower was understandably unhappy over the whole affair and relieved the II Corps and 1st Armored Division commanders. He also asked the British to replace his Intelligence Officer, who had predicted that the offensive would come farther north with only a feint at Sidi Bou Zid. Ironically, that individual had relied *too* much on ULTRA information, while earlier Auchinleck's G-2 had been relieved for not relying sufficiently on ULTRA![31]

Allied Command Structure

When the Eighth Army entered Tunisia, the Allies revised their command arrangements in keeping with a decision made at the Casablanca Conference. Eisenhower was elevated to Supreme Commander of all Allied forces in the Mediterranean west of Tripoli. General Alexander relinquished command of the British Middle East Command and assumed two new jobs. He replaced Clark as Eisenhower's deputy, and he formed the 18th Army Group, which would directly control the First Army, Eighth Army, and II Corps. The French Corps remained part of the First Army, and Clark took command of the Fifth Army, still watching Spanish Morocco. Air Marshal Sir Arthur Tedder became Commander-in-Chief of all Allied air forces in the Mediterranean theater. Admiral Cunningham retained his position as commander of all Allied naval forces in the Mediterranean.

The Allied Command Team, 1943
Front row, left to right: Eisenhower, Tedder, Alexander, Cunningham

By March 1943, the western Allies had evolved the command system that they would use for the remainder of the war in Europe and the Mediterranean, except for minor modification.* Each theater would have a single commander of all services and forces of all nations within that theater. He was usually selected from the country providing the most troops. His staff would comprise members of all services and forces under his command, while his deputy would be from the nation providing the second largest troop contingent. Either the deputy or the supreme commander would retain command of the ground forces or an army group would be formed to control all ground forces. Under the supreme commander there served a commander of all naval forces and a commander of all air forces, who always turned out to be British.

Allied Victory in North Africa

After the Kasserine Pass offensive failed to damage the Allies permanently, the Axis position in Tunisia was hopeless, although Hitler failed to realize it and Kesselring refused to acknowledge it. Logistics still ruled the outcome. As Montgomery cleared the North African coast, resupply to Malta became easier. With the delivery of bombs and aviation gasoline, that island once again began exacting a toll of Italian shipping. In January, Rommel and Arnim reported that together they needed 150,000 tons of supplies per month. *Commando Supremo* promised to send 80,000 tons, of which 60,000 could be expected to arrive safely. Since they needed 70,000 tons for subsistence alone, no hope of increasing strength in relation to the Allies existed. In fact, only 166 replacement tanks arrived in North Africa from January to May 1943[32]

Commando Supremo's estimates proved remarkably accurate during January and February, when an average of 65,000 tons arrived while 23 percent was lost en route. *(See table on p. 178.)* However, in March and April sinkings rose dramatically as Allied air forces used their new bases in Algeria and Libya to keep constant watch over the short shipping lanes from Sicily to Tunisia, and began to bomb embarkation and debarkation ports. During the last two-and-a-half months of the compaign, the air forces flew over 13,000 antishipping sorties.[33]

Even though the logistical situation made the Italo-German position in Tunisia untenable, the local commanders fought on, prodded by Hitler and Mussolini, neither of whom would face reality, but instead grandiosely talked of providing ample supplies and reinforcements. As something of a sop, Rommel was appointed overall commander in Tunisia (Army Group Afrika) on February 23, but the appointment was largely meaningless, as Arnim continued to flaunt his independence. Without apprising Rommel, Arnim mounted Operation OCHSENKOPF toward Béja. *(See Map 42a, in Atlas.)* Rommel, who wanted any limited offensive that Axis forces could launch to be made under as favorable circumstances as possible, was furious and expected it to fail. It did. Between February 26 and March 3, Arnim gained some meaningless

*Arrangements in the Pacific were different because of the preponderance of American forces there.

ground at a cost of 71 tanks. Meanwhile, Rommel, anxious to square accounts with Montgomery, was contemplating an attack on the Eighth Army. He hoped to surprise and destroy Montgomery's advance elements at Medenine, thereby delaying a British assault on the Mareth Line. At a planning session with his commanders, Rommel proposed a pincers movement, arguing that Montgomery would not expect an attack from the coast; his generals objected strongly. Ultimately, Rommel gave in and allowed General Giovanni Messe (his successor at the army command level) to plan the maneuver as an envelopment from the south. And so the traditional attack was made on March 6, the date and many operational details being known in advance by Montgomery via ULTRA. Axis forces ran into a screen of skillfully deployed antitank guns, which exacted a toll of 50 tanks. The next day Rommel learned that Hitler had rejected his earlier proposal to shorten the defensive line in Tunisia by withdrawing from the Mareth Line. Disheartened, physically ill, and disgusted, he decided to go on sick leave in Germany at once. This had been pending for some time and was desired by several of his superiors, who thought he had lost his nerve and believed him to be too independent. On March 9, Rommel bid farewell to his immediate staff and left Africa, never to return. Arnim, who had originally been slated for the army group command, now took over direction of all Axis forces.[34] He would soon feel the pressure of the tightening Allied encirclement.

Patton had assumed command of the II Corps after Kasserine, and had immediately begun to rebuild its confidence and strength. He wanted to drive for the coast, but Alexander, not trusting American troops after Kasserine, authorized only a limited attack designed to pull forces from the Eighth Army front. This offensive succeeded not only in tying down the 10th Panzer Division, but also in giving American morale a boost. On the night of March 20, Montgomery inexplicably attempted a penetration of the Mareth Line. When it failed at considerable cost, he converted his attack into a movement around the southern flank, which succeeded. The Italian First Army fell back to the Wadi Akarit. Continued pressure from the II Corps and the Eighth Army then forced Messe to withdraw to Enfidaville on April 7.

Although ultimate victory in North Africa seemed certain, Eisenhower was beginning to feel the pinch of time. Now that the winter rains were over, he had to eliminate the Axis forces in time to invade Sicily in July. But before he could atttack, adjustments had to be made. Patton turned the II Corps over to Major General Omar N. Bradley so that he would be free to prepare for the invasion of Sicily. Bradley found himself commanding an inactive corps, for Messe's withdrawal pinched II Corps out of the encirclement. To keep Americans participating, Bradley asked for and received Eisenhower's permission to move II Corps north to the coast, allowing the First Army to concentrate its strength for the final push. Additionally, Montgomery lent Anderson an armored division.

Alexander planned to send his main attack down the Medjerda River Valley from Medjez el Bab to Tunis, while his other units launched supporting attacks to hold Axis troops facing them in place. *((See Map 42b, in Atlas.)* Montgomery attacked first, but his desert warriors were completely stymied by the mountainous terrain. He halted his attack, thereby allowing Arnim to switch units from his left to his right. Starting on April 22, the First Army inched forward against a tough defense by desperate Axis units. Against less opposition, both the II Corps and the French XIX Corps made impressive gains.

Anderson regrouped and borrowed two more divisions from Montgomery. Then, massing two infantry divisions, two armored divisions, and 442 guns on a 3,000-yard front, he smashed through the Axis line in eight hours on May 6.[35] Arnim's army crumbled. One week later the war in North Africa was over, and 240,000 prisoners milled around in makeshift POW compounds. Few Germans or Italians escaped, since Cunningham's fleet lurked off shore in Operation RETRIBUTION (for Dunkirk).

As he sat overlooking the Gulf of Tunis, some British Tommy must have wondered what had been accomplished by the campaign which had just ended after three years and nine months. The war was not over; in fact, there was every indication that it would last years longer. Yet the Allied victory bore substantial fruit. The Suez Canal and Middle East oil had been secured. The Allies could now use the Mediterranean as a secure shipping route. Three Axis armies totaling 620,000 men[36] had been destroyed: the Italian army which initially invaded Egypt, the Italo-German army which came to recoup that first loss, and the German army which came to defend Tunisia. At Kasserine, the American Army had suffered the bitter lessons of defeat without paying the price of disaster. The anti-German French factions had been united, rearmed, and incorporated into Allied forces. The Allies had developed a command system which would serve them well for the remainder of the war. The British had perfected the means of providing ULTRA information to high level commanders, and those men had begun to better understand how to use that information and integrate it with normally-generated intelligence. Finally, both the Americans and the British had found capable commanders such as Eisenhower, Cunningham, Tedder, Alexander, Montgomery, Patton, Bradley, and a hundred more, who would later lead Allied forces to victory.

Besides the 260,000 Allied casualties* suffered during the past four years, one factor detracted from the victory. Like a pool player, who after making a difficult shot finds himself at

*The British suffered 220,000 casualties in almost four years of fighting. The French suffered 20,000 and the Americans 19,000 in the last half year of fighting.[37]

the wrong end of the table for his next move, the Allies had almost a million men in North Africa with no way to strike directly at Germany and insufficient shipping to move them rapidly to another theater.

On the other hand, Germany's mistakes were major. Hitler had committed his forces in the wrong theater. North Africa was always a secondary theater. Campaigns in Russia, the Balkans, and even Crete enjoyed higher priority, particularly in *Luftwaffe* support. The German effort was always a gamble, an attempt to cause Great Britain major harm without risking anything more important to Hitler than a good commander and three German divisions. But Hitler's reluctance to accept defeat caused German losses to be significant. Starting at El Alamein, he forbade retreat. Once the Allies had landed in Algeria, he committed to North Africa a second army which he could not logistically support, refusing to withdraw gracefully. By May 1943, he had lost strong forces which he could more profitably have used in Russia, France, or Sicily.

Finally, the Italo-German alliance lacked naval power. The Italian Navy had been quickly cowed by the Royal Navy, and Hitler, having no surface navy, never committed sufficient air strength to negate the Royal Navy. In the end, Hitler lost because he fought a sea power overseas.

CARGO DISEMBARKED IN NORTH AFRICA
(in thousands of tons)

	Date	Tons	Percentage Lost En Route
June	1941	130.9	4½
July	1941	62.7	19½
August	1941	83.9	13½
September	1941	67.4	28
October	1941	73.6	20
November	1941	30	62
December	1941	39.	18
January	1942	66	less than 1
April	1942	150	less than 1
May	1942	86	7
June	1942	32.3	22
July	1942	91.5	6
August	1942	51.6	33
September	1942	77.2	20
October	1942	46	44
November	1942	94	18
December	1942	65	25
January	1943	70	23
February	1943	59	23
March	1943	43	41
April	1943	29	42
May	1943	3	77

Axis Supplies & Equipment Reaching North Africa[38]

Notes

[1] Vincent J. Eposito, (ed.), *The West Point Atlas of American Wars,* (2 Vols.; New York, 1959), II, Section 2, 73.

[2] James M. Burns, *Roosevelt* (New York, 1956), p. 421.

[3] I.S.O. Playfair, *The Mediterranean and Middle East* (4 Vols.; London, 1954, 1956, 1960, 1966), I, 91, 95, and 96.

[4] *Ibid.*

[5] *Ibid.*, p. 209.

[6] Esposito, *West Point Atlas,* II, 74.

[7] Playfair, *The Mediterranean,* I, 369.

[8] Ronald Lewin, *Ultra Goes to War* (New York, 1978), p. 160. F. W. Winterbotham, *The Ultra Secret* (New York, 1974), pp. 65-66.

[9] Ronald Lewin, *Rommel as Military Commander* (London, 1968), pp. 31-34.

[10] Lewin, *Ultra Goes to War,* pp. 196-197.

[11] Playfair, *The Mediterranean,* II, 171; Levin, *Ultra Goes to War,* pp. 162-163; Winterbotham, *The Ultra Secret,* pp. 69-70.

[12] Esposito, *West Point Atlas,* II, 75.

[13] Lewin, *Ultra Goes to War,* pp. 172-175, 177-178.

[14] Erwin Rommel, *The Rommel Papers* (New York, 1952), pp. 206-225; Playfair, *The Mediterranean,* III, 223-243.

[15] Playfair, *The Mediterranean,* III, 274.

[16] *Ibid.,* pp. 329-330.

[17] *Ibid.,* p. 371.

[18] Lewin, *Ultra Goes to War,* pp. 264-265; Winterbotham, *The Ultra Secret,* pp. 73-75.

[19] Bernard L. Montgomery, *Memoirs* (Cleveland, 1958), pp. 74-83.

[20] Rommel, *Papers,* pp. 198-201.

[21] Lewin, *Rommel,* pp. 163-185, 238-249.

[22] Rommel, *Papers* pp. 321, 323; Lewin, *Ultra Goes to War,* pp. 266-268; Winterbotham, *The Ultra Secret,* pp. 76-78.

[23] Mark W. Clark, *Calculated Risk* (New York, 1950), p. 42.

[24] Robert A. Devine, *The Reluctant Belligerent* (New York, 1968), p. 84.

[25] George F. Howe, *Northwest Africa: Seizing the Initiative in the West* (Washington, 1957), Appendix B.

[26] *Ibid.,* p. 379.

[27] David Irving, *The Trail of the Fox* (New York, 1977), pp. 236-263; Winterbotham, *The Ultra Secret,* p. 97; Lewin, *Ultra Goes to War,* p. 269; Ronald Lewin, *Montgomery as Military Commander* (New York, 1971), Chapters 5 and 6.

[28] Howe, *Northwest Africa,* p. 421.

[29] Irving, *Trail of the Fox,* pp. 268-271; Rommel, *Papers* pp. 398-402.

[30] Irving, *Trail of the Fox,* pp. 271-275; Rommel, *Papers* pp. 403-407.

[31] Lewin, *Ultra Goes to War,* pp. 273-274.

[32] Howe, *Northwest Africa,* p. 682; Playfair, *The Mediterranean,* IV, 274.

[33] Playfair, *The Mediterranean,* IV, 418.

[34] Lewin, *Ultra Goes to War,* p. 275; Irving, *Trail of the Fox,* pp. 276-284.

[35] Playfair, *The Mediterranean,* IV, 447.

[36] Ernest R. Dupuy, *World War II: A Compact History* (New York, 1969), p. 123.

[37] *Ibid.*

[38] Playfair, *The Mediterranean,* II, 281; III, 158, 189, 327; IV, 210, 250, 417.

The Grand Alliance 8

How it is that the plans of two great empires like Britain and the United States should be so much hamstrung and limited by a hundred or two of these particular vessels [LST] will never be understood by history.

Telegram, Prime Minister Churchill to General Marshall, April 16, 1944

As the British Prime Minister comfortably settled himself at the Anfa Hotel on the outskirts of Casablanca in January 1943, his mind may well have been reflecting on dismal times: Austria and Czechoslovakia, the sites of Hitler's early aggression; Poland, where Great Britain had drawn the line, but from too great a distance; and France, where the Germans had swiftly deprived the British of the only European ally available to play the primary land role in their strategy of British blockade combined with a continental sword to strike the enemy at the right moment. Then there had been the desperate months between the fall of France and the Japanese attack on Pearl Harbor when the Commonwealth stood alone, except for the retreating Russians, whose initial resistance to the German invasion of 1941 gave so little assurance to Great Britain that she was not alone.

The Beginnings of Coalition Strategy

The early war years had been truly dismal and desperate, but they had not been hopeless. Dunkirk was more a triumph than a trauma, the Battle of Britain was the "finest hour," the Battle of the Atlantic looked more like a draw than a loss, and in the Libyan desert the god Logistics had shorn Rommel of his mantle of invincibility. Although winning may still have seemed remote to Winston Churchill in late 1941, losing had been stricken from his list of possibilities.

With the Japanese attack on Pearl Harbor, Churchill concluded that the war could be won. The United States would replace France as the land power necessary to fulfill the last part of the British strategy of build-up, maintaining sea and air communications, closing the ring, eroding German strength, and returning to the Continent for the decisive offensive. Now the war would be won, unless the United States decided to deviate from the previously accepted strategy later to be recorded in history as Germany-first. Churchill realized that Germany-first made sense. The Atlantic was not as wide as the Pacific, and most of America's industry was in the east. Short lines of communications across the Atlantic led to Great Britain—an ideal base of operations. Across the English Channel were the Germans, and Germany was the more dangerous enemy. Nearby were the Russians, who needed help if they were to stay in the war. On the other hand, a Pacific war would be a naval war, and Pearl Harbor had left the United States short of warships. Also, the Japanese had limited strength, and it was unlikely that they could span the Pacific, even against a limited defense.

Obviously then, the chance that the United States would deviate from a strategy so sound as to be almost self-evident was not likely, though possible. It was possible because in the wake of Pearl Harbor the strategy of Germany-first was antithetical to American emotions. Intellect would triumph over emotion, but Churchill was not sure of this as he crossed the Atlantic[1] two weeks after "the day that will live in infamy."[2] And he was still anxious as he sat down in late December 1941 in Washington at the first wartime conference with the man who had so eloquently turned that phrase.

Soon after the ARCADIA Conference opened, Churchill's anxiety dissipated.* Infamy notwithstanding, President Franklin D. Roosevelt expressed more than adherence to Germany-first. He and the American Chiefs of Staff bought the British strategic package in its entirety, save for a phrase or two.

The plan that Prime Minister Churchill presented at ARCADIA reflected the evolution of British strategic thought from the outbreak of the war in 1939 to the beginning of the conference. Further, it spelled out rather accurately the scenario of the war from ARCADIA on; for the British strategic plan of December 1941 was, to a striking degree, the Allied strategy actually executed in the European war. Future American strategy would mesh with the British plan, but would not dominate it. The build-up of men and materiel had started and would continue; the major sea lanes would be kept open, although at great cost; the ring around the Axis would be closed by mid-1943; the erosion of German strength would be well along by 1944; and the return to the Continent would begin with the invasion of Italy in September 1943 and then be followed by landings in Normandy almost one year before the German surrender in May 1945.

This five-part British plan merits elaboration. Build-up meant expanding the production of armaments and protecting the main areas of war industry in the United States, Great Britain, and Russia. Maintaining communications meant securing the major sea and air lanes across both the Atlantic and Pacific and trying to open up the Mediterranean. Closing the ring meant stopping the German offensive and gaining control of the periphery running clockwise from Archangel-the Black Sea-Asia Minor-the northern seaboard of the Mediterranean to the western coastline of Europe. Further gaps in the ring were to be prevented, existing gaps closed, and platforms gained for future offensives. Erosion meant undermining and wearing down German resistance through air bombardment, blockade, assistance to Russia, and support of subversive movements in the occupied countries. Returning to the Continent meant crossing the Mediterranean, invading the Balkans via Turkey, landing simultaneously in several of the occupied countries in western Europe, or some combination of these three approaches.

Against Japan, the Allies would adopt a strategic defense. American planners had made this decision earlier, had recorded it in documents known as "Plan Dog" and RAINBOW 5, and had agreed to it with the British at the American-British Conversations (ABC-1) of March 1941. And to the satisfaction of Churchill and his entourage, they adhered to it at ARCADIA.

Why the Americans readily accepted a plan they would soon contest is open to conjecture. They were no doubt preoccupied with the present—with the Japanese offensive in the Pacific and the security of the Western Hemisphere. They were also aware that their concept of a single, massive cross-Channel assault seemed remote in the light of limited resources and the shipping losses being sustained in the Battle of the Atlantic.[3] And too, they were relatively unprepared at ARCADIA to counter British plans that had been thoroughly worked out in advance.

Even at this time, however, the Americans did modify the British proposal for returning to the Continent. "Simultaneous landings in several of the occupied countries of North-Western Europe," a reflection of Churchill's preference for peripheral operations, was incompatible with the American penchant for massing at the decisive point. This phrase was therefore replaced by "landings in Western Europe." But the cross-Mediterranean operation and a possible offensive in the Balkans were retained, so that the revised wording was still broad enough to embrace a major assault as well as several supporting operations. "A form of words had been found to which both parties could assent; but that did not necessarily mean that they had found a common strategy."[4].

After deciding on this strategic outline, vague as it was, Churchill and Roosevelt charged their military subordinates to devise a plan for the invasion of North Africa as part of closing the ring. Churchill had for some time wanted such an operation; with Auchinleck's offensive rolling on toward Tripoli, now seemed to be the time. The French might encourage an Allied occupation of North Africa; or, if not, the Allies might be able to stage a *coup de main*. More important, Roosevelt was interested in North Africa, for he wanted American troops committed actively somewhere across the Atlantic in 1942. Earlier in the ARCADIA Conference, both Churchill and Roosevelt had agreed to the shipment of American troops to Iceland and Ireland. British troops could then be released for duty in the Middle East—and perhaps in North Africa too. But cold Iceland and green Ireland were not active theaters. Roosevelt wanted more substantial involvement for 1942; he wanted a North African invasion almost as much as Churchill.

Having been told to produce a feasible plan for North Africa, the British and American planners soon found themselves at odds. The British desire for a *coup de main* was too bold for the Americans, even though it would take place in an area far removed from German strength. (Churchill must have recognized the anomaly when the Americans within a few months pressured the British to sally forth across the English Channel into an area of great German strength.) On the other hand, the American proposal for a large landing force required extensive logistical support, which was unavailable if other operations were to continue. The planners tentatively compromised on a sizable force, large enough to alleviate Ameri-

**Throughout this chapter various wartime code names are used. See Glossary, p. 203, and Maps 43 or 44, in Atlas, as appropriate, for definition.*

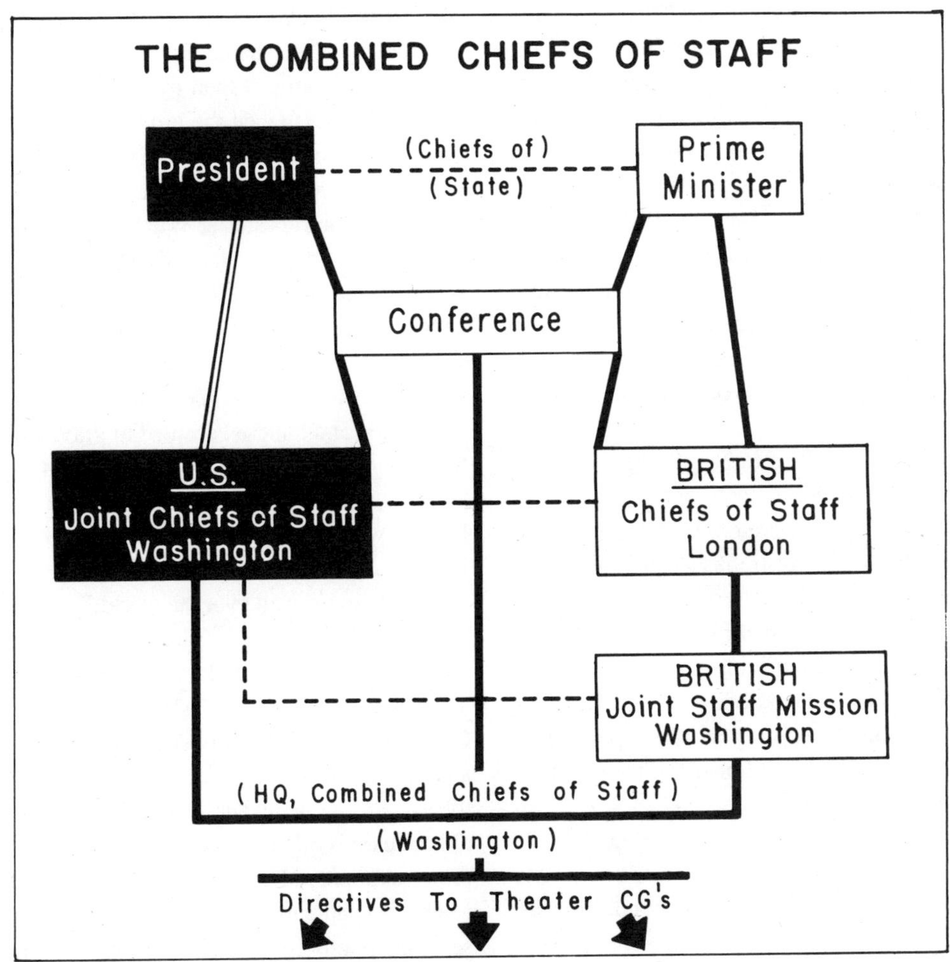

Organization of the Combined Chiefs of Staff

can fears that the operation might fail but not too large to be supported logistically. Troop shipping was the bottleneck and continued to be until the Allies gained the advantage in the Battle of the Atlantic in 1943. Now there was insufficient shipping to support simultaneously an American-size North African invasion, troop movements to Iceland and Ireland, and reinforcement of the Pacific in the face of continuing disaster there.[5] Churchill and Roosevelt had to choose, but first they needed to evaluate the Pacific carefully.

The panorama of events in the Pacific during the three-week ARCADIA Conference was increasingly unnerving. By late December 1941, the Japanese had seized Guam, Wake, Hong Kong, and Thailand, had started their invasions of Burma and the Netherlands East Indies, and had almost overrun Malaya. A week later they took Manila as General MacArthur declared it an open city and withdrew his forces to Bataan. It appeared to the British and Americans at ARCADIA that Australia and New Zealand had to be reinforced, or they too might fall before the Japanese offensive abated. At the same time, Churchill and Roosevelt wanted to retain the Iceland-Ireland agreement. Thus the choice was made by elimination, and plans for North Africa were deferred. They would come up again in a few months.

At ARCADIA, the Allies also took steps to achieve unity of effort. To control operations in the Pacific, General George C. Marshall, the Army's Chief of Staff, argued for a unified command; the British reluctantly agreed. The first step, therefore, was ABDACOM (Australian-British-Dutch-American Command), which encompassed the Philippines, the Netherlands East Indies, Malaya, and Burma. As a second measure, the Allies established procedures for coordinating the American and British Chiefs of Staff. Together, they became known as the Combined Chiefs of Staff and were responsible for coordinating strategy in all theaters and for allocating resources. But because neither the British nor the American Chiefs could operate continuously at one location, the British Chiefs would be represented by a party permanently assigned to Washington. This party, called the Joint Staff Mission, together with the American Chiefs, would act on a day-to-day basis in behalf of the Combined Chiefs.

ARCADIA thus ended in harmony. The Grand Alliance, like other alliances in the past, had many difficult coalition problems to face, but it had provided well for future compromise and resolution. The work of the Combined Chiefs of Staff and the Joint Staff Mission and the close cooperation and comradeship of Churchill and Roosevelt would smooth the way ahead.

As Prime Minister Churchill returned to England, the Japanese continued their expansion, contrary to Allied plans. It was all well and good to say at ARCADIA: let us hold the Malay Barrier and Burma and Australia; let us re-establish communications with Luzon through the Netherlands East Indies. But these were more hopes than plans. Yet they were hopes that moved troops and equipment to Australia and to the islands to the east that dotted the sea lines of communications back to Hawaii and the United States. They were hopes that initiated a build-up in the Pacific, a build-up out of tune with the anthem of the Grand Alliance—Germany-first.

The Japanese seemed to ignore the Allied build-up. Rabaul, keystone of the Bismarck Archipelago, fell on January 24, 1942. From there the Japanese leapfrogged south, reaching the Solomon Islands six weeks later. In Malaya all had been lost, including Singapore. Rangoon was evacuated on March 7; Tommy was retreating back to Mandalay—not exactly as Kipling had envisioned. For the Philippines, the Navy declined to attempt the impossible—to re-establish a line of communications to Luzon. President Roosevelt eventually acquiesced in the Navy's inaction, thereby writing off the Philippines. General Douglas MacArthur, perhaps too valuable to lose, was ordered to Australia to a new command in the southwest Pacific.

Elsewhere, the Allies were having mixed results. Rommel had started his second offensive and by early March was nearing Tobruk. German armies, having stalled earlier in front of Moscow, were now confronting the first Russian counteroffensive. Such was the military scene as important studies and policies were unfolding in Washington in early 1942.

There, organization was a dominant theme. ABDACOM, having lost most of its territory to the Japanese, was disbanded on February 25. President Roosevelt then sought and gained British approval to divide the world into three general areas: (1) the Pacific area, an American operational responsibility; (2) the Middle East and Far East, within British operational purview; and (3) the European and Atlantic area, shared by the United States and the United Kingdom. The Combined Chiefs of Staff would oversee all three areas and have operational responsibility in the shared European and Atlantic areas.

With the Pacific as their own, the American Joint Chiefs of Staff (JCS) next faced the problem of how to split it up. Although the principle of Unity of Command was understood by all, a dilemma remained: in the Pacific where water was preeminent, Admiral Chester W. Nimitz, the ranking naval commander, was not. He lagged behind General MacArthur in seniority and prestige. "There was no escape from the impasse except the creation of two commands."[6] The Navy was given control of the north, central, and south Pacific; the Army, specifically MacArthur, the southwest Pacific.

As men and materiel seemed to gravitate inexorably to the Southwest Pacific Command, General Marshall became concerned. Equally disturbed was Brigadier General Dwight D. Eisenhower of the War Plans Division. "We've got to go to Europe and fight," wrote Eisenhower, "We've got to quit wasting resources all over the world." Based on Eisenhower's studies, War Department planners drew up an invasion plan, later to be known as the Marshall Memorandum, that called for a build-up in the British Isles (BOLERO) to support a cross-Channel invasion of 48 divisions in 1943 (ROUNDUP). The plan also specified an emergency landing in 1942 (SLEDGEHAMMER) to save Russia or invade Germany in the unlikely event that either neared collapse. In record time, the Marshall Memorandum was approved, first by President Roosevelt and then, after Marshall hand-carried it to London, by the British. Although several options for returning to the Continent had been included in the ARCADIA plan, the British now agreed to the American choice for the main effort. The Americans would later suspect, however, that the agreement had been more apparent than real.

The core of the problem that developed was the emergency invasion, SLEDGEHAMMER. The British had agreed to SLEDGEHAMMER but did not like it. It could not be supported logistically, a shortcoming recognized by the Americans when they sold it and suspected by the British when they bought it.[7] The British were also averse to one of the contingencies for activating SLEDGEHAMMER. Should Russia appear to be collapsing, sending an inadequate force to the Continent to be sacrificed in expiation made no sense to the British, particularly when the sacrifice, because of shipping shortages, would be theirs to make.

As the British began to study SLEDGEHAMMER in detail, Roosevelt urged them to accept it, regardless of the condition of Russia or Germany. Meanwhile, Russian Foreign Minister V. M. Molotov visited Washington and got Roosevelt to commit himself to opening up a second front in Europe in 1942. Nonetheless, the British were determined that Roosevelt's second front would not be SLEDGEHAMMER. The Allies simply did not have the shipping nor the landing craft to send to the Continent a force large enough to survive against the German forces already in western Europe, much less to send a larger force that could draw off German forces from the Eastern Front. SLEDGEHAMMER was out; but whereas General Marshall and General Sir Alan Brooke, the Chief of the Imperial General Staff, were content to sit out 1942 and prepare for ROUNDUP in 1943, their political superiors who had voters to face, were not. Churchill and Roosevelt resurrected the idea of a North African invasion over the objections of Marshall. The Chief of Staff objected primarily because he foresaw that a North African invasion in 1942 would draw off BOLERO resources and would thereby delay ROUNDUP beyond 1943. He was partially correct. The cross-Channel attack *would* be delayed until 1944; and although the invasion of North Africa, soon to be named TORCH, would be a major cause, there were other contributing causes, such as the continuing attrition of Allied shipping in the Atlantic and an American offensive in the Pacific.

As the Allies struggled to refine their European strategy, the Japanese quickly revised their offensive plans for central and southwest Pacific After all, they had carried out their initial strategy with only minor setbacks, such as the delay in taking Bataan and Corregidor. Why not do more? Why not occupy Midway and the western Aleutians? That would bring about a decisive battle with the U.S. Pacific Fleet and would eliminate a repetition of Doolittle's earlier air raid on Tokyo. Why not isolate Australia? That could be accomplished by taking Port Moresby in southeastern New Guinea and Tulagi in the Solomons, thereby controlling the Coral Sea; by seizing islands farther east (New Caldedonia, Fiji, and Samoa); and by then establishing air bases for interdicting American shipping to Australia.

Positive answers to these questions brought about two major naval engagements. The Battle of the Coral Sea was fought in early May 1942; a tactical loss for the United States, it was a strategic victory since the invasion of Port Moresby was thwarted. The Battle of Midway, fought in early June, was a major tactical and strategic victory for the United States—a turning point in the war, for the Japanese permanently lost the initiative in the Pacific.

How to exploit Midway? Even before Midway the Navy had never considered accepting a static defense in the Pacific. RAINBOW 5, for instance, had called for limited offensives by the Pacific Fleet. On this basis, Admiral Ernest J. King, Chief of Naval Operations, had sought and, in spite of the Army's reluctance, gained approval to occupy portions of the Tonga Group and the New Hebrides to fortify the line of communications to Australia. The Army's attitude was clearly reflected in the speed with which its planners worked up the BOLERO-ROUNDUP plan and got it approved. The decision for ROUNDUP, the Army felt, would put a stop to further dissipative operations, particularly in the Pacific. But no one anticipated Midway and the momentum it would generate.

How to exploit Midway? MacArthur quickly presented a plan: assault New Britain and New Ireland, take Rabaul and control the Bismarck Archipelago. Needed for this operation, according to MacArthur, were two aircraft carriers and one additional division. King opposed the plan. Since the operations would be "primarily of a naval and amphibious character,"[8] the Navy considered the general manifestly unsuited for overall command. Further, the Navy objected to giving him control of even a single carrier. Still further, the Navy opposed a direct assault against the Bismarck Archipelago without first neutralizing Japanese land-based aircraft in the Solomons and New Guinea. MacArthur responded that he intended to reduce the land-based air threat to carriers, even though he had not included such details in his broad outline.

Army-Navy differences were therefore temporarily reduced to the problem of command, the basis of earlier and future disputes in the Pacific. The operation to secure the Bismarck Archipelago should be controlled by MacArthur, said MacArthur and Marshall; by Nimitz, said Nimitz and King. King then threatened to undertake the operation without Army support. Marshall restored reason and negotiated a compromise on July 2: Task One—an assault on Tulagi, controlled by Nimitz; Task Two—seizure of the northeast coast of New Guinea starting with Lae and Salamaua, as well as the remainder of the Solomons, controlled by MacArthur; Task Three—the final assault on Rabaul, controlled by MacArthur. King accepted the compromise with the stipulation that the final decision on the command relationships for Tasks Two and Three be deferred.

This JCS agreement, another step away from Germany-first, was in part a legacy of the Anglo-American differences regarding Europe. A month earlier the British had vetoed SLEDGEHAMMER, a veto that made their allegiance to ROUNDUP suspect in the eyes of Marshall and the American planners. If he could not convince the British to mass in the decisive theater, Marshall wanted to mass American forces in the secondary theater against the Japanese. Roosevelt quickly rejected his proposal. There would be no change in the official Allied strategy. But there was a change in Marshall, who was weakening as the staunchest proponent of Germany-first. In the future, he would give more support to King's desires for an active defense in the Pacific. He would also allow the Army planners to adopt the tacit principle that diversions in the Mediterranean would justify diversions in the Pacific. By the fall of 1942, the game of *quid pro quo,* the historic favorite among alliance members, would be well advanced.

Other events also shaped a larger role for the Pacific. When MacArthur in late June had initially proposed an offensive to take Rabaul, he had planned to do so in 14 days. But Japanese operations proved incompatible with his plans. In early July, a

Japanese force landed at Guadalcanal before the Americans could begin Task One against Tulagi; as a result, U.S. Marines were sent to both Tulagi and Guadalcanal. The Navy then suffered a small disaster—four cruisers lost off Savo Island in the Solomons, leaving the Marines stranded on Guadalcanal. Previously, MacArthur had planned to precede Task Two by marching overland from Port Moresby to Buna. But the Japanese in the meantime landed at Buna and were marching overland to Port Moresby. The Americans halted the Japanese but made little progress themselves. The jungle, the Japanese, and inexperienced American leadership combined to delay the Allied drive toward Buna. The Americans and Australians did not take Buna and Guadalcanal until early in 1943; they did not neutralize Rabaul until late that year. MacArthur's 14-day plan took 18 months to execute. One implication was clear: beginning an offensive meant providing the resources necessary for carrying it out.[9] That was the American way. But it was also the way to accumulate resources sufficient to make the Pacific a major theater, sufficient to give the Southwest Pacific Command a major role in future Pacific operations.

Emerging Strategic Disagreement

While awaiting President Roosevelt's arrival at Casablanca, the Prime Minister had completed his reflections on what had passed. The war was far from over. The Battle of the Atlantic was still best described as undecided, and even Churchill could not foresee that a turning point was only a few months away. But elsewhere, turning points abounded: Midway in the Pacific; El Alamein in North Africa; and Stalingrad on the Eastern Front. Operation TORCH had started well with successful landings in Morocco and Algeria. Optimism prevailed.

Still, the lessons of World War I suggested caution. Let us get on with the ARCADIA strategy, Churchill thought, but without repeating a Somme or Passchendaele on the way. Let us get on with wearing down the Germans and tightening the ring. Crossing the Channel could wait. But would the Americans prove difficult, as they had over SLEDGEHAMMER? If Churchill was apprehensive as he walked the 50 yards between his bungalow and Roosevelt's, he need not have been.

The Americans had come to Casablanca without an American position. Their final planning sessions before leaving for Casablanca had been deadlocked. Admiral King wanted to do more in the Pacific; General Marshall still favored a cross-Channel invasion for 1943. Roosevelt decided not to decide. Instead, he elected to allow King and Marshall to explain their dissident views to the British.

The British, on the other hand, were fully prepared. Churchill and his military chiefs had settled their differences and agreed on the invasion of Sicily as the next rung on the Mediterranean ladder; staff studies on every important issue had been prepared; and a ship full of staff officers had docked in Casablanca harbor to support the British Chiefs in the strategy debate that was to follow.

Shortly after the conference opened, Marshall argued for a reduced ROUNDUP in 1943, suggesting that superior air power operating from the United Kingdom could compensate for an inferiority in landing forces. General Alan Brooke countered Marshall's position by citing the shortage of landing craft, the paucity of available divisions (21), and the need to weaken Germany in 1943 by a continuation of the Mediterranean strategy. Italy should be knocked out of the war, Turkey brought in, the air offensive intensified. Then, in 1944 said Alan Brooke, the cross-Channel invasion should be launched.

Roosevelt, in effect, sided with the British, not by overruling Marshall outright but by revealing that he favored an extension of operations in the Mediterranean. Without presidential support, Marshall yielded and accepted the British proposal to invade Sicily (HUSKY). He was able, however, to rationalize his decision. After all, Eisenhower, while the Commanding General of European Theater of Operations, had wanted more resources for a cross-Channel invasion than could be made available in 1943. Troops already in the Mediterranean could be used there without wasting the shipping necessary to transport them to the British Isles. HUSKY would open up the Mediterranean, thereby saving shipping, assisting the buildup for an eventual cross-Channel invasion. In addition, Sicily was a good place to close out the Mediterranean strategy.

Having failed to halt operations in the Mediterranean, Marshall sided with King on the Pacific. King argued forcefully against a static defense and for a second "limited" drive that would seize the Marshall Islands and the Caroline Islands, to include Truk. He also wanted to continue the Southwest Pacific offensive: to retake the remainder of the Solomons, to capture Rabaul, and to secure New Guinea to the Dutch border. Although the British preferred to scale down the Southwest Pacific Command to the benefit of European operations, they agreed to King's proposal. A dual drive across the Pacific was recorded as Allied strategy; and the British proviso, that these operations be sustained with forces already assigned to the Pacific Theater, would soon be ignored.

In spite of this agreement on a limited dual drive across the Pacific, Anglo-American planners had not decided on a way to defeat Japan. At Casablanca, the Americans were still hoping that China's masses could help to defeat Japan. To accomplish this, the Allies needed to open up land communications with China; for large Chinese armies could never be armed and supplied with the limited tonnage that could be flown from India over the Himalayas—over the Hump. So Burma would have to be retaken.

Prior to Casablanca, the Americans had tried to interest the British and Chinese in such an operation. The British, who had started a limited offensive in north Burma in October 1942, were reluctant; the Chinese, unwilling. Generalissimo Chiang Kai-shek wanted the British to dominate the Bay of Bengal, occupy the Andaman Islands, and land forces at Rangoon as a prelude to challenging the Japanese in Burma. As a result, Japanese sea communications to Rangoon would be cut, and they would be vulnerable to attack from the south as well as from the north. The British understood Chiang's reasoning, but did not have the naval resources to comply. Both the British and Chinese saw in the boast of the American air commander in China, General Claire L. Chennault—that he could defeat Japan with 105 fighters, 30 medium bombers, and 12 heavy bombers—a hopeful substitute for their own inaction.[10]

At Casablanca, King did not let the British and Chinese off so easily. Lack of British naval strength and American landing craft, which were major obstacles, were not major obstacles according to King. He would make up the deficiencies. Consequently, the British agreed to plan for recapturing all of Burma (ANAKIM) and in the meantime to continue their limited offensive in north Burma.

How to use Allied air power was also a major issue at Casablanca. The Americans recited to the British their theory, by now turned dogma, developed in the early 1930s: daylight bombing without escorts could be sustained with acceptable losses and would be precise. The British, having lost too many bombers in daylight, urged the Americans to learn from their experiences and adopt instead area-bombing at night. The Americans persisted. Two diametrically opposed air strategies, daylight-precision and nighttime-area, were thus enjoined into round-the-clock bombing of Germany, called the Combined Bomber Offensive. Euphemism shrouded dissent; of such is coalition warfare made.

Speaking to the press after the conference had ended, Roosevelt announced the policy of unconditional surrender. Although he had discussed it with Churchill and although unconditional surrender may have been implied earlier at ARCADIA, still the British had not formally agreed to such a policy; and Churchill, as well as the American Chiefs of Staff, were completely and unknowingly abandoning the British historic balance-of-power approach to European wars. Americans applauded, not realizing that their security in the post-World War II period had been ransomed to bring about an end to the war, American-style.

Shortly after Casablanca, General MacArthur forced the Japanese from Buna, and Admiral William F. Halsey, Nimitz's subordinate in the south Pacific, drove the Japanese from Guadalcanal. MacArthur was now ready to begin Task Two (pincers around Rabaul); he was hopeful that this task, plus Task Three (the seizure of Rabaul) would be completed by the end of 1943.

At the Pacific Military Conference held in Hawaii in March 1943, MacArthur's representatives asked for the supplies and personnel to carry out his 1943 plans. As it turned out, they asked for more than could be hauled with available shipping. On this basis, they were turned down and had to reduce their expectations to accomplishing only Task Two, now called CARTWHEEL, in 1943. The conferees also wrestled with the command issue, which had been only tentatively resolved before. The Navy again objected to MacArthur's control of Tasks Two and Three; the Army objected to the Navy's objection. The resulting compromise was unusual. MacArthur received overall command, and Halsey was subordinated to him; but that part of Halsey's forces not specifically designated by the JCS to participate in the operation remained under Nimitz's control.

In the meantime, Army-Navy planners in Washington developed a strategic outline for the Pacific. They started with the premise that the Japanese might capitulate before an invasion became necessary if their sea lanes in the Far East were severed and if their vital centers—their industry and will to resist—were destroyed by an air offensive. China was the preferred base for the air offensive, but a port near China's coast and a direct sea line of communications would have to be opened to provide logistic support for the air offensive. Hong Kong was the best port. To secure it would require control of the South China Sea. The best approach to the South China Sea seemed to be through the Celebes Sea, a route that would also cut the Japanese line of communications to the Southern Resources Area. How to reach the Celebes? Across the central Pacific through Mindanao or by way of the Solomons and New Guinea? Both approaches had been entered in the ledger at Casablanca.

The joint planners decided to continue the two-pronged drive, even though they preferred the central Pacific route.[11] Since there were already substantial forces and considerable logistical back-up in the southwest Pacific, they reasoned that switching these forces to the central Pacific would cost time and shipping and would also release Japanese forces already tied down. Further, they believed that simultaneous advances on exterior lines would cause the Japanese to guard their entire perimeter and thereby weaken their advantage of interior lines. And last, they realized that Australia and New Zealand would object to the elimination of the southwest Pacific drive.

The planners then devised a five-phase outline, entitled the Strategic Plan for the Defeat of Japan, which not only included a dual drive across the Pacific, but related these operations to the Allied effort in the China-Burma-India (CBI) Theater. Believing that the British would no longer support operations to retake all of Burma, the planners reduced their goal for 1943 to taking north Burma. This would permit the construction of the

Ledo Road, which would connect India with the Burma Road and China. Properly supplied through land communications and air transport over the Hump, China could stay in the war and hold on to the air bases near her eastern coast that were necessary for the air offensive against Japan. Meanwhile, the dual drive across the Pacific would establish a more efficient sea line of communications to China, one that would augment the Burma supply lines. Both supply routes could provide enough logistic support to sustain the air offensive and the ground forces defending the air bases. So the essential features of the five-phase plan called for: (1) recapturing Burma and opening a line of communications to the Celebes Sea; (2) recapturing the Philippines; (3) gaining control of the South China Sea and capturing Hong Kong; (4) establishing air bases in China; and (5) conducting the air offensive against Japan. Prior to the next Allied conference, TRIDENT, a sixth phase, was added—the invasion of Japan, if required.

"We lost our shirts . . . we came, we listened, and we were conquered."[12] So said an American planner who best expressed the feeling of the JCS that they had done poorly at Casablanca. Now they were determined to best the British at TRIDENT. Primarily, they needed an American position. President Roosevelt was helpful. He agreed to support their call for the earliest possible cross-Channel invasion, which meant 1944. The Chiefs, on the other hand, assured Roosevelt that they would accept another limited operation in the western Mediterranean. They admitted the value of using the resources already in the area until needed for the cross-Channel invasion, of assisting the USSR and threatening southern France and Italy. They preferred the seizure of Sardinia. They would reject any operation requiring additional resources. They would oppose any operation in the eastern Mediterranean, which to them was suggestive of British imperial interests. These reservations marked the limits of any American compromise required to bring the British back to the cross-Channel fold.

The TRIDENT Conference, Prime Minister Churchill's third conference in Washington, opened on May 12, 1943, just as the Germans were surrendering in Tunisia and a month before the Allied invasion of Sicily. At the opening session, Roosevelt presented the American position and insisted on setting a date in the spring of 1944 for the cross-Channel invasion. Agreeing with his Joint Chiefs and anticipating the British position, he went on to express his reluctance to put large armies into Italy. An air offensive against Italy might suffice. Churchill then restated Britain's allegiance to a cross-Channel invasion provided there was a reasonable chance for success. But he was elated over Tunisia and wanted to continue the Mediterranean strategy by knocking Italy out of the war. To the British this meant invading the mainland. The advantage was clear: Italy would then have to withdraw her troops from the Balkans to defend the homeland; Germany would have to replace these Italian troops and thus weaken her eastern front and her forces in France. A reduction in German forces in France would improve the chances for a cross-Channel invasion in 1944. Invading Italy and tying down German divisions, according to British logic, was therefore a prerequisite for a successful landing in France.

Invading Italy, according to American logic, was a subsidiary operation that would drain resources and possibly prevent a cross-Channel attack in 1944. Using words very similar to those of the President, General Marshall said that an air offensive might cause Italy to collapse and would pin down German forces as well—the same results that the British sought. Obviously the coalition had agreed upon ends but not means.

So the impasse was turned over to the staff planners who were to determine if a 1944 invasion of western Europe and the extension of operations in the Mediterranean were mutually exclusive in terms of resources. Regarding western Europe, they concluded that by transferring seven divisions from the Mediterranean to the United Kingdom starting in November 1943, the Allies could cross the Channel in the spring of 1944 with 29 divisions. Sufficient landing craft would be available to support this force, substantially reduced from the ROUNDUP figure of 48 divisions. The operation was called ROUNDHAMMER—less ROUNDUP but more than SLEDGEHAMMER—and soon after became OVERLORD. The target date was May 1, 1944. Regarding Italy, the planners could not agree. The British got only a vague commitment from the Americans to plan for driving Italy out of the war. General Eisenhower would prepare the plans, subject to later approval by the CCS.

For the Pacific, the Americans presented their Strategic Plan for the Defeat of Japan. The British accepted it readily with the exception of provisions for land operations in Burma. As a result, the Pacific was no longer a theater for defense or limited offense; from now on, the Allied purpose was "to maintain and extend unremitting pressure against the Japanese."[13]

As the Americans expected, the CBI Theater turned out to be a contentious issue at TRIDENT; for the British would agree to no more, and wanted less, than a modified ANAKIN—a joint drive in north Burma by the British and by Chinese forces commanded by General Joseph W. Stilwell. They really wanted to avoid fighting in northern Burmese jungles and would have been content just to augment the air route to China. Roosevelt was willing to accept the British maximum—a modified ANAKIM; and he also favored increasing Hump tonnage while giving priority to General Chennault for his air offensive against the Japanese. But Chiang Kai-shek, who made his desires known through his ambassador in Washington, wanted both Chennault's air offensive and a full-blown ANAKIM—operations in both north and south Burma. Chiang lost the round. The compromise was Chennault's air offensive and a modified

ANAKIM.

Few, if any, at TRIDENT were pleased with this solution. Particularly disturbed was Marshall. He believed that a half-loaf ANAKIM would not open a land line of communications to Burma in time. The air offensive would fail because the Hump could not supply the air offensive plus the ground forces necessary to protect the airfields. The Japanese would quickly overrun Chennault's forces. On all counts, events were to prove Marshall correct.

The Americans ostensibly won the TRIDENT round, thanks to the determined presentation of a unified American position by Roosevelt and his military advisors, sound preparation (31 staff studies) for the conference, and frequent use of the bludgeon known as the "Pacific Alternative" (threatening to switch the main American effort to the Pacific). But whether or not there was any true winning or losing at TRIDENT on the major issues is moot, for the British throughout the conference expressed their fealty to a cross-Channel invasion for 1944. And although they did not get the Americans to agree to an invasion of Italy, they soon would.

To Invade Italy or Not

"I was extremely concerned that no definite recommendation had been made by the combined staff to follow up the conquest of Sicily by the invasion of Italy." Specifically, Prime Minister Churchill was fearful that the Americans would agree to no more than the taking of Sardinia, whereas he was intent on leading the Americans down the "garden path"[14] in the Mediterranean, at least as far as Rome. "The alternative between southern Italy and Sardinia involved the difference between a glorious campaign and a mere convenience."[15]

To insure that the Allies did not settle for a mere convenience, Churchill journeyed to Algiers to convince General Eisenhower, Allied commander in North Africa, that Italy should be invaded. General Marshall went along at Churchill's insistence. At their first meeting on May 29, 1943, Eisenhower posited that Italy should be invaded if the Sicilian campaign proved to be an easy one; Churchill said it would and predicted that the fighting in Sicily would be over by August 15. (The campaign was to end on August 17.) Marshall was more cautious. He realized that determined Axis resistance in Sicily would augur a difficult campaign for Italy, that a slugging match in Italy would turn the Mediterranean sump into an abyss and would eliminate the chance for a cross-Channel attack in 1944. He therefore told Eisenhower to plan for two operations, one to invade the mainland if HUSKY promised to be an easy success, and another for the seizure of Sardinia and Corsica if HUSKY proved difficult. The choice between the two would be made once the outcome of HUSKY was clear.

Meanwhile, Marshall's planners in Washington were arguing among themselves about further operations in the Mediterranean. General Henry H. Arnold, Commanding General of Army Air Forces, wanted bases in northern Italy; but some planners were opposed because the effort to secure the bases would drain OVERLORD resources. Thus an all-American debate was already underway as Allied forces landed in Sicily on June 10. Six days later, Marshall decided that the Sicilian landings were successful enough to justify the invasion of Italy, and he called for an amphibious operation in the vicinity of Naples. Churchill was delighted; but whereas Marshall wanted to advance to Rome but not beyond, Churchill now wanted more. "The Allies should march as far north as possible in Italy."[16] Coalition strategy had taken another turn. This time there was temporary agreement on the means, but not the ends. Disagreement over objectives as well as resources for Italy would thereafter fully test the Grand Alliance for the remainder of the war. Eisenhower in the meantime officially proposed an amphibious assault near Naples (AVALANCHE), which the CCS approved on July 20.

On July 25, King Victor Emmanuel dismissed Mussolini and had him arrested. As a result, Marshall became more enthusiastic for AVALANCHE; but he had yet to match the enthusiasm of some of his planners, who were now proposing to drop OVERLORD and shift the main effort to the Mediterranean[17]—precisely what many Americans thought the British were plotting. Marshall eventually overruled his planners, but the proposal and the reasoning behind it were significant. As the American planners looked back on Allied plans and operations, they concluded that SLEDGEHAMMER would have been suicidal, whereas TORCH and HUSKY had opened up the Mediterranean and placed Italy in a precarious position. As they looked ahead, they foresaw the advantages, articulated earlier by Arnold, of bombing Germany and Ploesti from Italian bases.[18] They could have well been saying to themselves: British strategy had been nearly perfect; only their motives were suspect.

Of further significance was the simultaneous work of British Lieutenant General Frederick Morgan, chief of the combined planning staff established at Casablanca. His plan for OVERLORD was completed in July. This anomaly resulted: while some Americans had been considering the abandonment of OVERLORD, a British officer had worked up the plan for its execution; while some Americans had wanted the Mediterranean as the main Allied effort, most Britishers still viewed it as a subsidiary operation. It was no wonder then that the forthcoming OVERLORD-Mediterranean debate would be a mix of mistrust and misunderstanding.

Having rejected the Mediterranean-first idea, the JCS approved the OVERLORD plan on August 9. For the Mediterranean they wanted: an invasion of Italy, followed by an advance to Rome and possibly Ancona; the capture of Sardinia and Corsica; and an invasion of southern France, called for in Morgan's plan as a diversion for OVERLORD.

For the Pacific, American planners tried to turn the TRIDENT agreement into operational plans. The Navy wanted to get the central Pacific drive under way and needed the three Marine divisions currently assigned to General MacArthur in the southwest Pacific for the invasion of the Marshalls. But Army planners and MacArthur considered the Marines essential to CARTWHEEL. The real issue—which drive should have priority, the Army's southwest Pacific or the Navy's central Pacific—was debated but not resolved. The Navy agreed to start its drive in the Gilbert Islands, an easier objective than the Marshalls, and to accept the Army's 27th Infantry Division, then in Hawaii, in lieu of two of the three Marine divisions in the Southwest Pacific; the Army agreed to transfer the third Marine division from the southwest Pacific to the central Pacific.

In deciding to give up this one Marine division to the Navy, Army planners thought it unneeded in the southwest Pacific if Rabaul could be bypassed. Marshall had for some time believed it possible to neutralize Rabaul and had told MacArthur so. MacArthur, though, considered Rabaul the only suitable naval base to support future operations. Also, he believed that operations beyond Rabaul would most likely fail if this Japanese stronghold was not eliminated first. Eventually, Marshall and the JCS overruled MacArthur and approved plans that called for neutralization rather than seizure.

Quadrant: Rebirth of a Unified Strategy

As Roosevelt and Marshall met on August 9, 1943, to prepare for the next Allied conference in Quebec, the President was still more Mediterranean-minded than the general. Although he assured the JCS that he was steadfast on OVERLORD and though he shared their view that operations in Italy should be terminated just north of Rome, Roosevelt wanted to replace the seven experienced divisions, which according to the TRIDENT ageement were to be transferred from the Mediterranean to Great Britain. Marshall at first argued that there was not enough troop shipping available to send seven new divisions from the United States to the Mediterranean. Roosevelt was not convinced. Marshall then sought the support of the JCS. Not only would the President's proposal waste shipping; but also, he told his colleagues, the British would use the seven replacement divisions to invade the Balkans. Marshall had for some time suspected that the British favored a ground operation in the Balkans. After all, British Foreign Minister Anthony Eden, at the post-TRIDENT conference with General Eisenhower at Algiers, had talked about "when our troops had reached the Balkans." Even though Churchill had immediately disavowed Eden, Marshall remained suspicious, as did Secretary of War Henry Stimson. At a second hearing with the President, Marshall, with the support of Stimson and the JCS, convinced Roosevelt that the seven experienced divisions should be removed from the Mediterranean without replacement. Thus the Americans, with difficulty, achieved a unified position on the eve of the QUADRANT Conference.

When the conference began on August 14, Marshall forcefully presented the American position, intimating that the British wanted to renege on OVERLORD. To ward off any further British proposals for the Mediterranean he declared that OVERLORD should be given "overriding" priority. Alan Brooke said the British agreed that OVERLORD was the main effort for 1944, but they did, in fact, want to renege on the TRIDENT decision to withdraw the seven veteran divisions from the Mediterranean. They therefore objected to "overriding," which seemed to foreclose all possibility of maintaining the existing troop strength in Italy.[19]

Somewhat reinforcing American suspicions, Churchill declared that he had never really favored SLEDGEHAMMER or ROUNDUP. Now, however, he strongly supported OVERLORD, if the Germans were weak enough and the Allies strong enough. He defined "weak" as no more than 12 mobile German divisions in northern France at the time of the invasion; "strong" meant that the Allies should increase their invasion forces by 25 percent. As a back-up for OVERLORD, he proposed JUPITER—the invasion of Norway. In Italy, he saw no need at present to go beyond the Ancona-Pisa line. In this way, Churchill's minimum position on Italy coincided with the American maximum. Contrary to the OVERLORD plan, he was reluctant to support the invasion of southern France, although he was in favor of seizing Sardinia and Corsica. With respect to the Balkans, he was interested in commando raids along the Dalmatian coast but not in an invasion.

After further debate, the Allies compromised. The OVERLORD plan was accepted. The "main object" was to allocate resources to ensure its success, but "overriding" failed to find its way into the script. The Mediterranean would have to make do with forces already allocated, "except insofar as these may be varied by decisions of the Combined Chiefs of Staff." JUPITER was given alternate status to OVERLORD. In Italy, the Allies would advance to Rome, and, "if feasible, further north"—a vague and open-ended goal that the Americans had tried to preclude. Sardinia and Corsica would be invaded. Landings would be made in southern France as a diversion for OVERLORD. For the Balkans, operations would be limited to supplying the guerrillas, conducting minor commando raids, and continuing with strategic bombing.[20]

Just as the Americans were about to insist, the Prime Minister suggested that a previous agreement with Roosevelt, which called for a British commander for OVERLORD, be set aside. Because there would be a predominance of American troops after the landings, Churchill avowed that the commander should be an American. The British would accept the consolation prize, command of the Mediterranean, the significance of which was not grasped at QUADRANT. For not too long afterward, British preoccupation with the Mediterranean came to exceed by far that dictated by their postwar political interests; neither did their desire to avoid a Somme or Passchendaele nor their insistence on diverting German forces from northern France prior to OVERLORD justify this preoccupation. Before the war ended, the British wanted to sustain the Mediterranean operation primarily because it was the only British show in town.[21]

With respect to the Far East, the British wanted to know what their role would be in the Pacific after Germany was defeated. Very small, said the Americans. Prodded by his military advisors, Churchill stated Great Britain's demands: "a share of the airfields, a share of the bases for the Royal Navy, and a proper assignment of duties to whatever divisions she could transport to the Far East after the Hitler business was finished." The argument became heated. The Combined Chiefs had their junior staffers leave the room. A shot was fired. "My God," said one staffer, "they've now started shooting." But of such, coalition warfare is not made. It was only Lord Louis Mountbatten, Chief of Combined Operations, firing at a new synthetic material to demonstrate its strength to the Americans.[22] In the end, the Americans gave ground and agreed that the CCS should determine a proper role for the British, implying that they should have one.

The British also pressed the Americans to accord primacy to one of the two drives across the Pacific, preferably to the Navy's central Pacific operation. Although King personally shared the British view and had tried before to convince the Army, he loyally defended the American compromise for two mutually supporting drives. The British then dropped the discussion, agreed to accept a target date for defeating Japan 12 months after the defeat of Germany, and approved the American timetable for Pacific operations. Two additional objectives, the Palau and Mariana Islands, were added to the central Pacific drive. The Marianas were a significant addition, since they would later serve as bases for the B-29 Superfortress, expected in quantity in 1944.

Less progress was made on the strategy for Burma. The British, having reluctantly started a ground offensive in the north that was now bogged down because of severe flooding, urged the Americans to change the Hump priority to favor General Stilwell's ground forces. Stilwell could then better support the lagging British drive. The Americans urged the British to reconsider an operation for south Burma. The British declined. In the end, the JCS yielded on both points. The Hump priority would be temporarily reversed; a decision on south Burma would be deferred until the next conference.

The Impact of Field Operations and Strategic Opportunism

By the end of QUADRANT, the Americans had mastered the intricacies of coalition strategy making. Preconference preparation and gradual experience were two reasons for their success. Another reason, becoming more and more apparent, was the growing American contribution to the Allied cause in manpower and materiel. By mid-1943, when the British contribution was peaking, the Americans had matched their ally's efforts and would soon become the predominant supplier of men and machines. An old English proverb, "He who pays the piper calls the tune," would soon become, if it had not already, a guiding maxim for control of the Anglo-American alliance.

In the case of the Aegean island of Rhodes, near Turkey, the payer had declined to support the Prime Minister in his quest to seize that island. Churchill had always been interested in it. Capturing Rhodes would help bring Turkey into the war, inflame the Balkans, and shorten the sea route to Russia—the same reasons proffered by the same man for undertaking the Dardanelles Campaign one world war earlier. Further, occupying Rhodes might also draw German troops into southern Greece.[23] Events in Italy now turned Churchill's mind once again to Rhodes, "so long the object of strategic desire." On September 3, 1943, an Allied army had crossed the Strait of Messina and invaded the Italian toe. On September 9, the main Allied force landed at Salerno, south of Naples. General Eisenhower announced Italy's surrender the same day, even though the Italians preferred to scrap their earlier agreement to cease fighting. Now was the time for Rhodes. "Improvise and dare," Churchill said in his cable to General Wilson, the British commander in the Middle East.[24] Wilson's improvisation—an air drop of a small force on Rhodes—was daring but abortive; for just before the drop, a few Germans seized control of the island from many Italians and were awaiting the British. Churchill's interest in Rhodes was dampened but not extinguished. This little Aegean island would flicker and flame as a major topic at the next Allied conferences at Cairo and Teheran.

As the battle over Rhodes temporarily subsided, the Allies battled the Germans on the Salerno beaches and nearly lost. More successful were operations against Sardinia and Corsica where Axis forces preferred evacuation to fighting. With respect to Italy, Hitler, after much equivocation, decided to defend south of Rome rather than withdraw to the Apennines as the Allies hoped for. As a result, Rome would be dearly bought. Although the Allies on the eve of the Cairo-Teheran Conferences had yet to perceive the final price, they had already determined that an amphibious end run around the German defensive line south of Rome would be necessary to break the stalemate.

Italy was also an important issue at the Moscow Conference, an assemblage of foreign ministers that preceded the meetings at Cairo and Teheran. Although the Russians had complained bitterly before about delays in launching a cross-Channel invasion and opening up a second front, they showed at Moscow an unexpected interest in Italy as constituting the second front. Russian reasoning, however, was obscure. The Anglo-Saxons could only ponder and infer. Perhaps the Russians were confident that they could end the war, since they had already recovered most of their territory from the Germans. Perhaps they wanted immediate action, a step-up of Mediterranean operations to draw more Germans away from the Eastern Front, and viewed the cross-Channel assault as a distant prospect. Perhaps they really wanted a belated OVERLORD, as a way of keeping the Allies out of Germany.[25] Regardless of Russian motivation, the Americans became concerned and began to refine their position against a possible British-Russian Mediterranean stand at Teheran.

In the Pacific, between QUADRANT and Cairo-Teheran, General MacArthur continued his pincer moves around Rabaul. Army forces took Lae and Salamaua in mid-September; the Marines invaded Bougainville in the Solomons two weeks later. On November 20, the Navy began the central Pacific drive by attacking Tarawa in the Gilberts.

Washington planning, however, was not keeping pace with Pacific operations. Having persuaded the British to accept the aim of ending the war against Japan within 12 months of the defeat of Germany, and now expecting the war in Europe could terminate as early as October 1944, American planners saw the need to reach agreement on a more explicit plan for defeating Japan. They failed to do so primarily because General Marshall, supported by Admiral King, was inclined toward an opportunistic—or rather, flexible—approach to Pacific operations. ("Opportunistic" was the derogatory label applied by the Americans to British Mediterranean operations, whereas "flexible" was the American word for what Marshall believed to be a policy of planned opportunism in the Pacific.)[26] Marshall's outlook was not unrealistic. China's status had changed. Because operations in Burma and China were lagging, because October 1945, or earlier, was the target date for defeating Japan, the war in the Pacific might well be ended before the Allies conquered Burma, resolved their logistic problems, and engaged large Japanese armies in China. Russia's status had also changed. At the Moscow conference, Molotov and Stalin had casually mentioned that Russia would enter the war against Japan once Germany had been beaten. With Russia in the war, who would need China?

Roosevelt had an answer, a political answer. China would be one of the "Four Policemen" in the postwar world.[27] It would be appropriate, though, for Chinese military performance to justify the subsequent political role. So Roosevelt would try once again at the next Allied conference to make the CBI an important theater. Yet he too probably realized that the war was passing China by and that he would eventually have to plead for a great power political status for China, unsupported by military capability and performance.

Cairo-Teheran: Maturity of Allied Strategy

The fifth and sixth Allied conferences of the war were held at Cairo and Teheran in late fall of 1943. The Americans, British, and Chinese met in Cairo from November 22 to 26; the Americans, British, and Russians in Teheran from November 28 to December 1; the Americans and British back in Cairo from December 3 to 7.

China's presence at Cairo was at President Roosevelt's instigation and to Prime Minister Churchill's displeasure. "The talks of the British and American staffs were sadly detracted by the Chinese story. . . . All hope of persuading Chiang and his wife to go and see the pyramids and enjoy themselves till we returned from Teheran fell to the ground, with the result that Chinese business occupied first instead of last place at Cairo."[28] (In a way, Churchill mistook the main issue. It was the landing craft business that was most important at Cairo—as it would continue to be until the Allies arrived on Normandy beaches in June 1944.)

The Chinese again said they would support land operations in north Burma but again insisted on simultaneous naval operations in the south. They still thought it necessary for the Allies to control the Bay of Bengal, to include an amphibious operation against the Andaman Islands, now called BUCCANEER. Roosevelt decided on BUCCANEER despite Churchill's objections to simultaneous land and sea operations. Since Churchill did not share Roosevelt's political-military reasons for bolstering China, he contended that BUCCANEER was an unnecessary drag on the supply of landing craft. He wanted the landing craft not required for OVERLORD for a flanking move to break the Italian stalemate and open the road to Rome and also for the invasion of Rhodes. Even if OVERLORD had to be postponed for a month or two, he still wanted Rome and Rhodes. The

Americans, on the other hand, would not stand for a postponement of OVERLORD. As in the past, they wanted Rome and opposed Rhodes. All agreed that there were not enough landing craft to conduct OVERLORD on schedule plus the three proposed secondary operations.

Surprisingly, a fifth operation requiring landing craft got scant consideration. After having agreed in principle to an invasion of southern France (ANVIL) at QUADRANT, both the Americans and British ignored the issue at Cairo. Perhaps both had achieved sufficient coalition expertness by QUADRANT to realize that agreeing in principle was a convenient method for reserving a veto in advance of detailed study. In any event, Churchill and Roosevelt went to Teheran with ANVIL far removed from their thoughts and with the realization that the Russian position would be the primary factor in settling British-American differences.

At Teheran, Roosevelt explained these differences to Stalin and then asked him how the Allies could best help the Soviet Union. Contrary to American fears and British expectations, Stalin sided with the American position. He wanted no delay in OVERLORD. He wanted ANVIL. He was totally uninterested in the eastern Mediterranean. He did not consider Rome important and preferred that the Allies switch to the defensive in Italy. After arduous arguing, the British conceded in part and affirmed OVERLORD and ANVIL. The target month was May 1944, rather than the specific date of May 1. The Americans hen agreed to an advance to the Pisa-Rimini line in Italy, and to the retention of sufficient landing craft in the Mediterranean to conduct an amphibious landing near Anzio in January. Both were content to postpone decisions on BUCCANEER and Rhodes until they returned to Cairo.

With ANVIL approved, the British selected it as the basis for attacking BUCCANEER when the conference resumed at Cairo. Now they contended that BUCCANEER and ANVIL were mutually exclusive because of the shortage of landing craft and that BUCCANEER therefore detracted from OVERLORD since a diversion in southern France was considered necessary. The Americans debated the problem among themselves. Although landing craft arithmetic supported the British position, General Marshall believed BUCCANEER was necessary because Chiang Kai-shek would not support the land offensive in north Burma without it and because the north Burmese offensive would fail without Chinese support. Roosevelt, however, decided to give in to the British and go back on his promise to Chiang. He then offered the Chinese a choice of either going ahead with the north Burma operation or delaying it until the fall of 1944, when landing craft used for OVERLORD would be available to undertake BUCCANEER. Shortly after the conference broke up, Chiang answered that he would accept the delay. The war had almost passed China by.

Whereas the Americans gave up BUCCANEER, the British, having faced strong American-Russian opposition, essentially gave up Rhodes and the eastern Mediterranean. Rhodes was put in the "desirable" category, provided it could "be fitted in without detriment to OVERLORD and ANVIL."[29] A month later, with the shortage of landing craft still acute and because Turkey still refused to enter the war, Churchill ruled out the operation.

At this point it is appropriate to review Churchill's interest in the eastern Mediterranean in 1943. He did not want to invade the Balkans.[30] He did want to bring Turkey into the war. He did want to employ British troops, statically deployed in the Middle East Command, in offensive operations. This was a political need, just as it was for political reasons that Roosevelt had insisted on getting American troops involved in 1942 in North Africa. Churchill also could not agree with the Americans on the landing craft problem. When he argued that the same landing craft could support Anzio in January, Rhodes in February, and ANVIL in May, he probably realized that this was not possible—that the combination of operational exigencies and the repair and replacement of damaged and destroyed landing craft would refute his hypothesis. But he also believed that too many landing craft were being sent to the Pacific and that through judicious allocation there would be enough for the Mediterranean, regardless of attrition and unforeseen operational difficulties. "I was sure that in the end enough landing craft would be found for all," Churchill said.[31] But he was surely wrong. Even though Admiral King eventually agreed to a shift of priority away from the Pacific, there would still be too few landing craft to support OVERLORD as well as Churchill's plans for the Mediterranean.

The Pacific received little attention throughout the Cairo-Teheran Conferences. Finally, back at Cairo, the British and Americans found time to identify the "main effort" against Japan as the dual drive in the Pacific and to classify operations in Burma and China as supporting and secondary. Although they did not belabor the issue of primacy in the Pacific, they did imply that the central Pacific drive was first among equals: "When conflicts in timing and allocation of means exist, due weight should be accorded to the fact that operations in the central Pacific promise at this time a more rapid advance toward Japan . . . ."[32] The combined planners by this time had also recognized the importance of the Marianas as a launching platform for B-29s. Accordingly, they moved the Marianas ahead of the Palaus in the schedule of central Pacific operations.

As the conference came to a close, Roosevelt announced the American commander for OVERLORD. Marshall had initially been the President's choice, but he wanted Marshall to have the prestige of controlling more than OVERLORD. He wanted Marshall as a grand overseer of both the cross-Channel and Mediterranean operations. Not unexpectedly, Churchill objected. He objected for many reasons, but primarily because he wanted the Mediterranean to remain under British control. He did not want the only British show in town to be produced and directed by their predominant ally. Confronted with this opposition and convinced that Marshall's presence in Washington was almost indispensable, Roosevelt decided on Eisenhower[33]—an unconscious first step in the making of the President, 1952.

Allied Strategy Tested

Cairo-Teheran was a watershed in Allied planning. Although the basic decisions of these conferences would still be challenged, the relative importance of each theater had been determined. Matching diversions in the Mediterranean with diversions in the Pacific no longer applied. The Pacific had become a major theater, the Mediterranean secondary. Operations in the CBI Theater would be limited, whereas OVERLORD's primacy was once again asserted. The strategy of the war had evolved substantially from Germany-first. Now there were two acknowledged grand theaters, Europe and the Pacific, with the priority of operations within each theater clearly established.[34]

With the overall strategy fairly well resolved, the Americans paused to recompute the forces necessary to carry it out. Previously, in the early days of the war, American planners had based their estimates on the possibility that the Soviet Union might collapse, leaving the burden of the land war to be borne by the western Allies. Consequently, they initially estimated that the Army would require 213 divisions. By the end of 1942, as the Russians were winning at Stalingrad, American planners realized that Russia would stay in the war and would continue to fight most of the German Army. At the same time, General Marshall was confident that strategic bombing would reduce the requirements for land forces. By late 1943, it was agreed that 89 divisions would suffice. But as the time for OVERLORD drew near, the doubters, civilian and military alike, surfaced. Secretary of War Stimson was the leading spokesman among those who believed that the United States would be fighting the Germans in France with too few forces. General Marshall, however, was not among the doubters; primarily because of his staunch defense, the decision for 89 divisions stood. He, therefore, deserves much of the credit for what became known as the 90-divison gamble—a gamble that minimized disruption of the American "guns and butter" economy and defied the military tradition of asking for more than is needed. But it was a gamble. Of the 89 divisions, 87 were deployed overseas and all but two saw combat.[36] How narrow the margin for error was would become apparent on the beaches of Normandy, in the hedgerows of France, and in the forest of the Ardennes.

Elsewhere, General Eisenhower faced a similar problem but came up with a dissimilar solution. Once he and General Bernard L. Montgomery, who initially was to command the ground forces involved in OVERLORD, began their detailed study of the invasion plan, they concluded that the lead assault was too weak. Both wanted five, instead of three, divisions in the initial phase. But the increase would require more landing craft. More landing craft would also be needed because of Anzio. Having landed there on January 22, 1944, the Allied force, somewhat in the tradition of Suvla Bay, consolidated the beachhead rather than moving inland. The Germans took advantage of this hesitation, assembled their forces, and counterattacked. Somewhat harshly, Prime Minister Churchill derided the American corps commander: "I hoped we were hurling a wildcat on the shore, but all we got was a stranded whale." Regardless of who was to blame, the Anzio forces remained stranded until late in May 1944. In the meantime, the landing craft that had brought them to Anzio now had to supply them and were therefore unavailable for ANVIL as originally planned.[36]

The increase in the assault forces for OVERLORD together with the unexpected retention of landing craft in the Mediterranean meant that there were insufficient resources to conduct OVERLORD and ANVIL simultaneously. This shortage was ameliorated by postponing OVERLORD from May 1 to May 31 to gain an extra month's production of landing craft, but still there was not enough. For this reason, the British proposed that ANVIL be cancelled. Concerned about changing an operation to which Stalin had agreed, the Americans resisted and began to search for the needed LSTs, the most critical type of landing craft. The search led to the Pacific, where most of them had gone—but it was too late. Even if the required ocean-going LSTs were immediately sent from the Pacific to Europe, they would be too late for OVERLORD. Meanwhile, total output was being allotted to Europe, and current productional facilities were already working at maximum capacity and could not be expanded in time. The United States, the paragon of mass production, could not make up the shortage of LSTs; and ANVIL, accordingly, had to be deferred indefinitely.[37]

After Cairo-Teheran, the status of the CBI further declined. Chiang's willingness to accept a one-year delay in Burmese operations was key in the sequence of frustrated efforts that eventually overtaxed American patience. Now American planners decided that it was simply too late to try to bring China's manpower into the war. They still wanted to open the Burma Road, but only to have another option if Pacific operations bogged down. They remained interested in China as a base for bombing Japan, but this interest would eventually dwindle also. Very soon, the problem of logistic support for B-29 operations in China would prove too formidable, and the bulk of the Superfortresses would be shifted to the Marianas. The war had passed China by.

For the Pacific, American planners wanted to turn their outline into a blueprint, but their reasons were less than selfless. In spite of the agreement at QUADRANT that the British should have a role in the Pacific, the Americans, in fact, decided to pre-empt British participation in Pacific planning and operations. The best pre-emption was to work up immediately a definitive plan excluding the British. But try as they would, American planners could not settle the existing Army-Navy differences and come up with a compromise. They were able, though, to agree on more immediate issues. Most important was the decision to bypass Truk, the major Japanese bastion in the central Pacific—a step made feasible by the withdrawal of the Japanese fleet from Truk after Nimitz's forces had invaded the Marshalls.[38] On the eve of OVERLORD, the central Pacific drive was nearing the Marianas and MacArthur's forces in the southwest Pacific were leapfrogging their way in a series of amphibious operations toward the northwestern edge of New Guinea. Yet the precise nature of follow-up operations was still to be determined.

On June 6, 1944, the American strategic dream, President Roosevelt's "mighty endeavor,"[39] began. Although part of the Normandy landings, specifically Omaha Beach, appeared for a while to be more like a nightmare, the beachhead was eventually secured. The Allied airman helped by isolating the battlefield and achieving almost total air superiority in the invasion area; the Allied sailor helped with accurate, devastating naval gunfire; the Allied soldier helped by fighting well. Hitler helped by restraining the only available force that could possibly have repulsed the landings. He insisted on keeping the 15th Army Group near Pas de Calais where he expected the main landings to be made by General Patton's fictitious army.

As in all wars, the fighting did not go according to plan. At D + 48, the Allies had achieved only the D + 5 objective line; but by D + 79, they had reached the Seine River, 11 days ahead of schedule. This initial delay followed by a rapid advance did not allow the engineers sufficient time to construct or reconstruct the necessary roads, railroads, and pipelines. The Germans also compounded Allied logistic problems by destroying the Brittany ports; and even the weather conspired against "the mighty endeavor" by stirring up the English Channel sufficiently to destroy one of the two artificial harbors devised by the Prime Minister himself. All told, the Allied logistical problems were severe enough to affect their strategy both in northern France and in the Mediterranean.

In the Mediterranean, the ANVIL debate resumed. The disputants remained the same; only the supporting arguments had changed. Whereas the Americans previously wanted ANVIL as a diversion for OVERLORD, now they saw it as the best way to alleviate the port shortage. ANVIL meant taking Marseilles, which they believed to be the best port available. Eisenhower also felt that a supporting attack in southern France was necessary to protect the flank of the Allied offensive in northern France. Churchill disagreed. He viewed current operations in Italy as the best diversion for OVERLORD. He also did not think the port problem so severe; but if it was, there were better ports available along the French Atlantic Coast. More important, Rome had fallen on June 4, but it had fallen to an American army whose commander had disregarded his assigned mission in order to get to Rome ahead of the British.[40] Regardless of who had taken Rome, there were prospects of exploiting its capture by moving not just to the Pisa-Rimini line, but through it into the Po Valley—if Allied strength in Italy was not sacrificed to satisfy ANVIL. There was also the possibility of a supporting attack across the Adriatic Sea into Istria near the Italian-Yugoslavian border. Then the offensive could be continued through the Ljubljana Gap and into Austria. These were the recommendations of Churchill's generals, whom he fully supported. National pride was his overriding motivation:

> Let us at least have a chance to launch a decisive strategic stroke with what is entirely British and under British command. I am not going to give way about this for anybody . . . We have been ill-treated [by the Americans] and are furious.[41]

Churchill also had other reasons for wanting to continue the Italian Campaign. A drive to Vienna through the outskirts of the Balkans would foster revolts against German rule. It would also give Britain temporary control of the port of Trieste and a secure line of communications to occupied Austria after the war. It would not, however, prevent postwar Russian dominance of the Balkans, as some writers were to allege after the war.[42] Regardless of how desirable the Allied occupation of the Balkans later came to appear, Churchill maintained after the war that he had never proposed to invade this area.[43] Not that he would not have liked to—both for military and political reasons. As one committed to applying pressure from multiple directions, he had wanted to precede OVERLORD with a supporting invasion of Norway and one launched from Turkey into the Balkans and through Europe's "soft underbelly."[44] Yet, in light of past and present operations, neither invasion was logistically feasible and therefore never formally proposed by the British. As an anti-communist, he also feared Russian domination of eastern Europe. Yet the armies of the western Allies had no chance of arriving there in advance of the Russians, and therefore the British never called for an attempt to do the impossible. Thus it is fair to state that when Churchill objected in the summer of 1944 to a belated ANVIL, now called DRAGOON at his insistence, he did so primarily because this operation would take away both personnel and landing craft from the only British campaign.[45] The Americans opposed Churchill with a plethora of both valid and invalid arguments, and in the end he rather bitterly agreed to DRAGOON. In his mind, he had been dragooned; but he still had much more to say about a drive to Vienna.

In the period after OVERLORD, little progress was made in Pacific planning. American differences at the CCS Conference in London on June 17 prevented any Anglo-American agreement on subsequent operations in the Pacific. Afterwards, the Americans debated various combinations among themselves. Although the debaters did not take sides solely on the basis of service affiliation, a majority of the Navy's planners wanted to invade Formosa, claiming that the Philippines could be bypassed, whereas most of their Army counterparts argued for retaking the Philippines, including Luzon. Although the Navy would not accept Luzon, they did agree to seize Leyte and to postpone the decision as to whether Luzon or Formosa would follow.

Army-Navy planners were also divided, essentially along service lines, on another issue: how to make the Japanese surrender. Many Navy planners thought that Japan could be strangled through blockade and air bombardment; many Army planners believed that only an invasion could bring Japan to her knees. The JCS finally agreed in principle to the need for an invasion, and the British Chiefs later concurred. This agreement, however, was to be continually questioned, with the answer remaining in doubt until the Americans entered the atomic age at Hiroshima and Nagasaki.

Octagon: The Emerging Primacy of Political Factors

The second Quebec Conference (OCTAGON) was the first of the Allied meetings that dealt primarily with political issues. From Quebec on, President Roosevelt, as the head of the nation providing most of the materiel for the war, would be predominant in Anglo-American circles. His biases, therefore, are significant. He was anti-imperialist and would oppose British and French colonial interests in a way that would influence the remaining course of operations in the Pacific and CBI—as well as the course of events in Asia in the postwar period. He became anti-French after viewing their early performance in the war and assessing their subsequent collaboration as criminal and traceable to their extreme decadence.[46] His prejudice would limit the role France would play in the last year of the war. He was opposed to balance-of-power politics, but neither his "Four Policemen" nor the United Nations would provide a valid substitute for achieving world order.

Prime Minister Churchill, as the leader of a nation slipping from first-rank status, was for imperialism and balance of power, two ways to stem the British descent from greatness. Understandably, he had not become the King's first minister "to preside over the liquidation of the British Empire." Also understandable was his agreement with Roosevelt at Casablanca to consign Germany to total defeat and harsh punishment; but, like Roosevelt, in 1943 he too had a faulty view of the postwar era as he helped eliminate an important weight in the European balance. At that time, Churchill may have thought that the postwar strength of Great Britain and France, plus the European interests of the United States, would offset the Soviet Union.[47] But Great Britain would turn out to be debilitated, France too destitute, and the United States too disinterested to balance the USSR in Europe as World War II ended. By OCTAGON, the problem of whether and how to restore the European balance of power without Germany was in clear view.[48] But since the President had already decided that balance-of-power politics were undesirable, the question of how became academic. Notwithstanding the idealism of Roosevelt and of Wilson before him, the concept of balanced power blocs would survive the war, with the United States applying it through the Truman Doctrine, Marshall Plan, and NATO.

In another way, OCTAGON and beyond reflected the growing importance of political factors in coalition decision making. Henceforth, the American Chiefs of Staff would face a difficult predicament. They fully understood that war is the servant of policy, but the declining Roosevelt failed to turn his idealism into policy guidance for his military subordinates. And though he eventually realized that the Russians would never measure up to his image of them, his last weeks were marked by ailing inaction. American military leaders, not wanting to establish policy themselves, would therefore base their decisions on how to win the war most expeditiously.[49] As a result, though not politically naive, they would seem to be so and would suffer the stigma of naiveté along with their political superior.

News of the war on the eve of the OCTAGON Conference was favorable in most respects. While slighting his severe logistical problems, General Eisenhower had pushed the army groups of Generals Bradley and Montgomery across the Seine and up to Germany's West Wall. DRAGOON had been a success, and the invasion forces had joined hands with the Allied armies in the north. Current intelligence estimates forecasted that the war would be over by December 1, 1944. In the Pacific, the Marianas had been taken, the Japanese Navy had suffered heavily in its defense during the Battle of the Philippine Sea, and B-29 bases were being readied in several of the islands for the bombing of Japan. Only in China was the picture bleak. There the Japanese, as General Marshall and others had predicted, were overrunning Chennault's air bases in the southeast.

Foreseeing a speedy victory, Roosevelt and Churchill early in the Quebec Conference discussed Germany's postwar fate. To prevent German rearmament, Roosevelt introduced a plan, conceived by Secretary of the Treasury Morgenthau, which would eliminate heavy industry, limit Germany to an agricultural economy, and hold down the standard of living to subsistence levels. This proposal was too harsh for Churchill; yet in the end he accepted it because the President had been "so insistent."[50] (Later, the Morgenthau Plan was tacitly renounced.)

Churchill's insistence on an amphibious operation across the Adriatic into Istria was equally effective. With DRAGOON now past, the Americans were willing to make available the necessary landing craft. In fact Churchill had more difficulty with his Chiefs, whom he accused of planning a "frame-up" with the American JCS to reduce the offensive in Italy to "secondary importance," than he did with the Americans.[51] The JCS, wanting before the conference to transfer the remainder of the U.S. Fifth Army from Italy to France, even agreed to defer this issue until the outcome of the current Italian offensive was known.

With respect to the CBI Theater, the British attitude had changed. Having acted before as a brake on Roosevelt's China policy, they now wanted to speed up operations in Burma. Now they believed that the conquest of Burma was a prerequisite for attacking Singapore, whose recovery would bolster British imperial prestige in the postwar years.[52] Consequently, it was agreed to schedule an amphibious operation for 1945 in the Bay of Bengal against Rangoon with landing craft to be transferred from the Mediterranean after the Istrian operation. The Americans, however, categorically refused to assist the British in Burma with ground forces, ostensibly because there were no divisions to be spared from Europe and the Pacific. Not mentioned but equally important in the refusal was their neutral attitude that politically-motivated operations of the British should be neither helped nor impeded.[53]

In discussing the Pacific Theater, the British overcame American evasive tactics designed to prevent or at least minimize British participation. Again, for purposes of postwar politics and prestige, they wanted a supporting role in the central Pacific, which they considered the main effort, rather than a subsidiary part in General MacArthur's operations. Overruling his Chiefs, Roosevelt agreed to a role for a balanced and self-supporting British fleet in the central Pacific drive, but the nature of that role was yet to be determined.

American plans for future operations in the Pacific remained as indefinite as the British role. American planners had not resolved the Luzon-Formosa issue prior to the conference, and their major proposal was to accelerate the invasion of Leyte by two months, from December to October 1944. The difficult decision of what to do after Leyte was postponed.

Operational Interlude

There were two important operational issues in the fall of 1944. The first was the long-standing Luzon-Formosa dispute, finally resolved in October. For some time, General MacArthur had been the Army's foremost spokesman. He argued persuasively that the United States had a moral obligation to liberate the entirety of the Philippines and that there were sound military reasons, moreover, for seizing Luzon. Yet it was not the strength of MacArthur's position for invading Luzon but the gradual weakening of the rationale for invading Formosa that determined the decision. After all, the Japanese had just overrun southeastern China, thus countering the American plan to bomb Japan from Chinese bases. Taking Formosa as a means of reaching China's coast and and controlling the South China Sea was therefore less essential. And though B-29s could still bomb Japan from bases in western China, the Marianas were better situated. Formosa could also provide air bases; but unless the whole of the island could be quickly conquered, the air forces would face the prospect of operating from insecure bases in the southern half. Northern Luzon, on the other hand, had more room for B-29 fields and was less vulnerable to air attack. Also, the Navy, by going into Leyte early, could now invade Luzon before the end of 1944. Giving way to this logic, the Navy planners, with Admiral King as the final holdout, eventually agreed to MacArthur's taking Luzon. The JCS did not formally rule out a subsequent operation against Formosa, but after Luzon there would be few advocates for it.

The second operational issue concerned the European Theater. There the Allies debated how their armies, operating with grave logistical deficiencies, should continue their advance against a retreating, deteriorating German army. In early September, General Montgomery claimed that a single, concentrated thrust of American-British-Canadian armies under his command could break through the northern extremity of the West Wall, cross the Rhine River, drive toward Berlin, and end the war in the fall of 1944. In the process, some American forces, including General Patton's Third Army, would have to be grounded to afford the single thrust with sufficient logistic support. General Eisenhower believed the logistical situation to be more critical, and German deterioration less severe, than did Montgomery. He consequently chose to approach the West Wall cautiously with both main and secondary attacks and at the same time to maintain a continuous front. Although Montgomery's plan to drive to Berlin was farfetched,[54] a single thrust, Eisenhower was later to admit, might have given the Allies a northern bridgehead across the Rhine in September 1944.[55] But it can also be argued that Eisenhower's broad-front plan might have been equally productive had Generals Bradley and Patton completely supported his decision to give logistical priority to Montgomery's main effort, or had the later Allied vertical envelopment of the West Wall (MARKET-GARDEN) been more professionally planned and executed.

In any event, Eisenhower's armies did not break through the West Wall in September; and after shoring up their logistics for a renewed effort, they faced a strengthened German army that finished their hopes for an end to the war in 1944. In difficult fighting throughout the fall, the Allied armies made several minor breaches in the West Wall but failed to cross the Rhine. Then on December 16, German forces attacked through the Ardennes, surprising the Allies and achieving initial success. But they failed to reach the Meuse River, and after two months of bitter fighting the Battle of the Bulge ended with the Germans back in their original position, though in a critically depleted condition.

While Hitler was playing his last hand in the Ardennes, the Combined Bomber Offensive was reducing the German capacity to carry on the uneven struggle by obliterating their industry. The bombers were now virtually unopposed, but it had not always been that way. Without fighter escorts, the Americans had to cease their daylight bombing of interior Germany in the fall of 1943 because of prohibitive losses. Without fighter escorts, the British in March 1944 had to halt their nighttime bombing of Berlin. Early in 1944, with escorts, the Americans began the attrition of Germany's defensive air forces. By the summer of 1944 the Allies were bombing both day and night against negligible opposition. By mid-December the bombing had affected Germany's war potential to the extent that German *panzer* divisions moving through the Ardennes did not know the source of their next liter of fuel.

As the Big Three assembled in February 1945 for their next-to-last conference of the war, the end for Nazi Germany was clearly in sight.

Yalta, Political Predominance, and Victory in Europe

If the end of World War II was clearly in sight at Yalta, the beginning of its replacement, the Cold War, should have been evident as well. To many, it was; to President Roosevelt, possibly not. Many issues were settled at Yalta: German reparations, the spoils to be given to Russia at the expense of China and Japan, membership and voting differences regarding the United Nations, an occupation zone for France, and more. Yet the most prophetic issue was Poland. As far back as August 1944, Russia had flown its postwar colors by halting its armies near Warsaw. Expecting the Russians to help in their liberation, the Poles rose against the occupying German troops. But the Russians stood on the sidelines while the Germans eliminated thousands of underground fighters who were in political opposition to Russia's potential puppet, the Lublin Committee. Then in October Prime Minister Churchill went to Moscow to get agreement on a representative government for Poland. But the Russians refused Churchill and two months later unilaterally recognized the Lublin Committee. At Yalta, Churchill and Roosevelt accepted this *fait accompli* and also agreed to alter Poland's eastern boundary to Russia's benefit, and her western border to Germany's detriment. For Poland and other potential satellites, their right to self-determination was expressed in the "Declaration of Liberated Europe," which soon proved in the face of Russian *realpolitik* to be no more than diplomatic pablum.

Although his conduct at Yalta has been much debated, Roosevelt was more pragmatic than naive.[56] Russia occupied Poland, had the manpower to help defeat Japan, and could subvert his plans for the United Nations. He could not deny Stalin what Russian armies had gained, but he could jeopardize chances for Russian participation in the Pacific war and in the United Nations by taking a hard line on Poland. For Roosevelt, choosing was difficult, yet future choices would be equally difficult to make. The nuances of the Polish question—the reality of Russian power and American hopes for a reasonable use of that power—would appear frequently in the incoherent pattern of strategic decision making that marked the last months of the war.

While the Yalta Conference was taking place, the Allies resumed the offensive in western Europe. But before deciding on the form of the offensive, they had re-fought the battle over "broad front" versus "single thrust." General Montgomery had once again opposed a continuous front and favored a single, Montgomery-controlled operation north of the Ruhr; General Eisenhower had insisted on secondary attacks in addition to the main British effort but had assured the British that their armies were and would continue to be involved in the main drive. Still not satisfied with Eisenhower's assurance, the British took the dispute to the CCS; but the American Chiefs would not agree to override Eisenhower's strategy. They did, however, comply with the British request to record in writing that Montgomery's main effort in the north would be supported with maximum strength.

Meanwhile, the actual fighting continued. The Allies started their Rhineland Campaign in January 1945. The Germans defended well. So it was not until early March that an

American force in the Allied center crossed the Rhine at Remagen. In the south, American armies were overrunning the Saar. In the north, British and American forces were capturing the Ruhr and by late March were in position to begin the final drive across the north German plain toward Berlin, 200 miles away. Closer to Berlin were the Russians. The Soviet armies at this time had reached the east bank of the Oder River, some 30 miles away from the German capital, and were building up for their final offensive.

With the Allies so far from Berlin and the Russians so close, should the Allies change their plans? Eisenhower thought so. Since the Russians would certainly get to Berlin first, he felt there were good reasons for shifting the main effort from Montgomery in the north to Bradley in the center. In front of Bradley was Germany's last important industrial area. Also, Eisenhower believed Allied intelligence sources reporting a German intent to build a vast fortress, a "National Redoubt," in Bavaria and Austria, and he wanted to forestall this possibility.

Of course, the British objected to Eisenhower's change in plans. They doubted that the "Redoubt" existed; they interpreted the change as a breach of faith and felt their forces were being given a static role; and they believed that the Germans might hold off the Russians long enough for the western Allies to get to Berlin first. Churchill in particular had political fears. He was afraid that the Russians might hold on to part of the occupation zones assigned to the western Allies at Yalta. The best counter, he felt, would be to have Eisenhower's forces liberate as much of the Russian occupation zone as possible. Then if the Russians balked at withdrawing to their own area, the western Allies could bargain from strength.[57] Since the Russians did not balk, Churchill's fears turned out to be unfounded. Regardless, Eisenhower's superiors—the JCS and Roosevelt, and Truman after Roosevelt's death in April—backed him. He therefore went ahead and ordered his armies, after they had reached the Elbe River, to turn north to the Baltic ports and south to the nonexistent "Redoubt." Had they continued to Berlin, the western Allies might have arrived there ahead of the Russians, since the Russians did not begin their drive from the Oder until the U.S. Ninth Army reached the Elbe, about 50 miles from Berlin.

As the American armies moved south along the Elbe, it became apparent that they could reach Prague ahead of the Russians. Eisenhower, however, decided not to do so, again for military reasons, but also because the Russians had already said that they would drive to the Elbe and overrun western Czechoslovakia. Churchill objected. He believed that liberating as much of Czechoslovakia as possible "might make the whole difference to the postwar situation in Czechoslovakia, and might well influence that in nearby countries." Although Eisenhower understood Churchill's rationale, he was determined to base his plans entirely on military reasoning unless he received political guidance from the President. None was forthcoming. Truman said the deployment of Eisenhower's troops was a "military matter." Clearly the matter was more than just military, but Eisenhower's adherence to the military view in the absence of political contradiction or guidance cannot be logically challenged.[58]

As the war ended, Churchill's vision of postwar Soviet aggression was clear and correct; his view of how to counter the reality of Russian power, however, was not clear. He did foresee the "Iron Curtain" descending; he did want the western Allies to stand temporarily in place until a Big Three Conference could be held to discuss the political problems of eastern Europe.[59] But he did not recommend that the western Allies stand indefinitely in place or threaten force to achieve the fulfillment of the Yalta agreements.[60] Given the determination of the Russians to shape the political structure of eastern Europe, given the disinclination of Churchill, Roosevelt, and Truman to contest the Russians by force, it seems in retrospect that Eisenhower's military decisions regarding Berlin and Prague were not politically senseless. But the speed of the American withdrawal from Europe after the war is another matter; the lack of an Allied corridor to Berlin, still another.

While the major Allied effort was succeeding in western Europe, operations in Italy were proceeding at a rate commensurate with the difficult terrain and the now-accepted secondary nature of the Mediterranean theater. Earlier, in the fall of 1944, the plan for landings in Istria had been discarded. The availability of landing craft had ceased to be the problem; the problem had become one of insufficient troop strength. The British were shorthanded; for when the Germans had withdrawn from Greece, Churchill had felt compelled to send in troops to prevent a takeover by Greek communists. The Americans were shorthanded, for the 90-division gamble was not a misnomer. So the British could support the Istrian landings only by taking forces away from the Italian Front. But dividing forces this way was risky, as Anzio had clearly demonstrated. Discouraging the British further, the Russians were moving through the Balkans fast enough to make it unlikely that the British could win the race to Vienna.

The British also considered a landing farther south along the Dalmatian coast; but as the Russians drew geographically near the Yugoslavs, their leader Tito drew psychologically away from the British and let it be known that a Dalmatian operation would not be welcome. At this point, both the British and the Americans readily agreed to cancel all amphibious plans and confine their efforts in the Mediterranean theater to the Italian Front.

Fighting along that front continued during the last months of the war much the same as it had before. The Italian campaign continued to be a war of attrition over difficult terrain.

But now it was a forgotten war of attrition. Forces had been taken away from Italy in August 1944 to take part in DRAGOON, in the fall to prevent a communist takeover in Greece, and in January 1945 in response to the Ardennes fighting and in anticipation of the final Allied offensive. Even the mission had been reduced to limited offensives intended only to hold down existing German forces in northern Italy (a mission that might have been appropriately assigned much earlier). Regardless, the Allied commanders in Italy persisted in their quest to defeat the German armies outright, which they did shortly before the curtain came down on Nazi Germany.

The curtain that has yet to come down is historical. Historians and military analysts have yet to agree on whether the Anglo-American strategies for the European Theater were opposed or complementary, whether the British wanted the cross-Channel attack as the main effort or as the *coup de grace* or at all. One revisionist historian even argues that there was only one Allied strategy: the ARCADIA strategy.[61] More significant than this debate is the question: Was there a better way to fight the war than the strategy that was in fact executed? Some say yes, but to date no one has presented a valid case.[62]

The End in the Pacific

On October 20, 1944, the U.S. Sixth Army landed on Leyte. The command structure in the Pacific, which had for so long violated the principle of Unity of Command, almost led to disaster. Admiral "Bull" Halsey, in a manner befitting his nickname, chased the Japanese lure, a fleet of carriers without airplanes, north. Inadequate naval forces were left to defend General MacArthur's landing force. The Japanese, however, made offsetting mistakes, and the American Navy won the Battle of Leyte Gulf by a slim margin. Soon after, Luzon was invaded and Manila fell, Iwo Jima in the Volcano Islands was bitterly fought for but taken, and by early April 1945 the Allies were landing on Okinawa. Elsewhere, the British were rapidly moving south toward Rangoon, and the long-awaited amphibious landing took place on May 2. The Australians, one day before, invaded Borneo in the Netherlands East Indies.

These events passed quickly but not, from the standpoint of the Allied coalition, smoothly. As was true in Europe, the Allies, seeing the end in sight, became less enthusiastic about subordinating their individual interests to that of the coalition as a whole. Most unhappy were the Australians. During the early days of the war, they had done much of the very difficult fighting in New Guinea. But when it came time to return to the Philippines, they were given a minor role. At the same time, they wanted to mop up the Japanese in their own yard—in the Solomons and in New Guinea. Not surprisingly, accordingly, they felt that General MacArthur's plan to use their forces to take Borneo detracted from their ability to eliminate the Japanese in places closer to home. They could not see the logic in MacArthur's decision to mop up the Philippines entirely while assigning much less effort to doing the same thing in the Solomons and New Guinea. Also, after American troops came to outnumber Australia's in the southwest Pacific, MacArthur subordinated Australian units to American commanders. Even though he had valid reasons for the way he handled the Australians, they could not help feeling at the time that their interests had been slighted.[63]

The British also had their differences with the Americans. They particularly opposed the Borneo invasion since their fleet would have to support it and their role in the final operations against Okinawa and Japan would be reduced. Also, they wanted a voice in the strategy for the last months of the war and proposed that the CCS assume general control over operations in the Pacific in place of existing unilateral control by the Americans. But the British hand held only a low pair. They "did most of the proposing and the Americans did most of the disposing."[64] Still the British were pragmatists. In the end: "What was good enough for the United States would certainly be good enough for the British."[65] So said Prime Minister Churchill.

Among themselves, the Americans also differed. A foreseeable problem was how to alter the command structure as the two drives across the Pacific converged on the Philippines and Okinawa. Again, mixing MacArthur and Nimitz proved insoluble. The compromise gave MacArthur control over all land forces and Nimitz responsibility for all naval forces; the JCS would directly control the strategic air forces and would attempt to oversee the operations of all three services from Washington.

Once Germany had been defeated, the Americans had to decide whether or not an invasion of Japan was necessary. On this very important issue, the ranking military men held to their service views. Admiral King and General Arnold thought that Japan could be defeated by a continuation and intensification of the naval blockade and air bombardment; Generals Marshall and MacArthur insisted that an invasion was necessary. In mid-June 1945, President Truman did not pass the buck and decided on the Army view. There were, however, other possible alternatives to invasion. Russia's entry into the war might cause the Japanese to capitulate. But the Americans at this point had an ambivalent attitude toward Russia. They would not oppose her entry, but neither would they seek it, so they did not even consider waiting for the effect of Russia's eventual declaration of war.[66] One alternative that they did consider was the atomic bomb. They would use the bomb if the Japanese did not respond to a demand for unconditional surrender. This ultimatum was issued from Potsdam, the site of the last Big Three Conference, on July 26. Although the Emperor and some Japanese officials were willing to accept, the military were not; and the Japanese Premier's statement to the press that the Potsdam Declaration would be ignored was taken by the Americans as a rejection. On August 6, the bomb was dropped on Hiroshima. On August 9, just as the Japanese discerned the nature of the first explosion, a second bomb hit Nagasaki. Russia declared war on Japan the same day. On August 10, Japan asked for peace.

In retrospect, some Americans have viewed Hiroshima and Nagasaki with misgivings. Why didn't the ultimatum mention the bomb and the intent to allow the Japanese to keep their Emperor? Why wasn't the bomb held in abeyance until the effect of Russia's declaration of war became clear? Why Nagasaki so soon after Hiroshima? Why the bomb at all? All the answers are not known, and some that are known are less than satisfying. What is known by all is that the Second Great War ended with awesome portent.

Epilogue

On the eve of the British elections in July 1945, Prime Minister Churchill had a premonition that he was to be denied the "power to shape the future" of the nation he had led in World War II.[67] Rejected by British voters the next day, he was instead given ample time in the years ahead to reflect on how well he had helped to shape Great Britain's past.

How did he view the Mediterranean strategy in retrospect? Perhaps he assured himself that Allied operations in Italy had tied down enough German forces and thereby made it possible for OVERLORD to succeed. Still, was there a less costly or a more effective way of tying down the Germans? After Italy had been driven from the war, would it have been sufficient to switch to a strategic defensive south of Rome, coupled with occasional limited offensives? Or was Rome the place to stop? Or could more Germans have been tied down by secondary operations in either southern France or the Balkans? Or conversely, would it have been better, both militarily and politically, to launch a major drive through Italy at the expense of OVERLORD? Granted, the Americans would have rejected some of these approaches, and others Churchill himself would not have proposed. But was there a better way?

Perhaps a more important question regarding the Mediterranean pertained to British prewar strategy. For on the eve of the war in the west, Great Britain had reversed the priorities of the Far East and Mediterranean, relegating the Japanese threat to third place behind Germany and Italy. "Italy would offer prospects of early results," it was felt.[68] But were the prospects worth the risks? Just what was the cost of sending an offensive force to Egypt and a defensive force to Greece? What if Great Britain had instead fortified her position in the Far East? Would the Japanese have been dissuaded from launching their aggression? But had they persisted, could they have been stopped short of Malaya and Singapore? Was it possible, through a different allocation of resources, to prevent the Japanese from exploding the myth of western superiority? Would the extension of the myth have also extended the lease on the colonial empires of Great Britain and France?

Most likely, Churchill mentally revisited the Pacific on another count. The American dual drive had never appealed to him. Scaling down or cancelling the drive in the southwest Pacific would have freed manpower and materiel for Europe, and a greater effort in Europe might have led to Germany's defeat in 1944. On the other hand, what if the CBI Theater had been emphasized more and the Pacific less? This was a question Churchill, among others, might have asked himself in 1949 as Chiang Kai-shek and his battered armies sailed toward Formosa. Had Chiang received more help, his regime might have survived. Without a communist China to support insurgencies throughout Asia, what then would have been the lot of western colonialism? What would have been the effect on Great Britain's status as a world power?

If Churchill questioned himself this way, he must also have reflected on Germany-first. Was it the correct strategy? A minor effort in Europe would have depleted the British less and the Russians more; and if Russia had persisted in a death struggle with Germany, would there not have been a stronger Great Britain in the postwar period to help balance a weaker Russia? On the other hand, if Russia had carried a greater burden successfully, would she have demanded greater spoils?

Perhaps the best course of action would have been to support the German resistance to Hitler. But this implied a negotiated settlement and contravened Churchill's own "victory at all costs"[69] and Roosevelt's "unconditional surrender." Perhaps there was no choice. Perhaps total war inevitably leads to total victory. But if not, what were the costs of Great Britain's six-year struggle that ended in total victory? No doubt it was disheartening for Churchill to come to realize that Great Britain was the world's largest debtor nation at the end of the war, and that the structure of colonialism was about to crumble. Great Britain's painful retreat from greatness was underway and would soon be apparent to all. Like the *ancien régime* of Louis XIV many centuries before, Great Britain had depleted herself by warring beyond her strength.[70] If total victory is not the predestined effect of total war, had Churchill's "victory at all costs" been too costly? If another choice was possible, how ironic for a descendant of Marlborough, of one who had contributed to France's fateful decline from greatness, not to have made it.

Notes

[1]James M. Burns, *Roosevelt: The Soldier of Freedom* (New York, 1970), pp. 179, 231; Winston S. Churchill, *The Grand Alliance* (Boston, 1950), p. 641.

[2]Franklin D. Roosevelt, speech of December 8, 1941, to Congress, as quoted in Burns, *Roosevelt: The Soldier of Freedom*, p. 165.

[3]J. M. A. Gwyer, *Grand Strategy*, Part I, (London, 1964) Vol. III, pp. 349, 358; Maurice Matloff and Edwin M. Snell, *Strategic Planning for Coalition Warfare, 1941-1942* (Washington, 1953), p. 97 (hereafter referred to as *Strategic Planning, 1941-1942).*

[4]Gwyer, *Grand Strategy*, Part I, Vol. III, p. 360.

[5]Matloff and Snell, *Strategic Planning, 1941-1942*, pp. 112-113.

[6]Louis Morton, *Strategy and Command: The First Two Years* (Washington, 1962), p. 244 (hereafter referred to as *Strategy and Command*).

[7]Winston S. Churchill, *The Hinge of Fate* (Boston, 1950), p. 324; Matloff and Snell, *Strategic Planning, 1941-1942* p. 192.

[8]Admiral Ernest J. King, as quoted in Morton, *Strategy and Command*, p. 296.

[9]Morton, *Strategy and Command*, p. 324.

[10]Charles F. Romanus and Riley Sunderland, *Stilwell's Mission to China* (Washington, 1953), pp. 252, 261.

[11]Morton, *Strategy and Command*, pp. 450-451; Philip A. Crowl and Edmund G. Love, *Seizure of the Gilberts and Marshalls* (Washington, D.C., 1955), p. 14.

[12]Brigadier General Albert C. Wedemeyer, as quoted in Maurice Matloff, *Strategic Planning for Coalition Warfare, 1943-1944* (Washington, D.C., 1959), p. 106 (hereafter referred to as *Strategic Planning, 1943-1944*).

[13]Matloff, *Strategic Planning, 1943-1944*, p. 138; Morton, *Strategy and Command*, pp. 458, 648.

[14]Churchill, as quoted in Trumbull Higgins, *Soft Underbelly* (New York, 1968), p. 61.

[15]Churchill, *The Hinge of Fate*, p. 825.

[16]Winston S. Churchill, *Closing the Ring* (Boston, 1951), p. 36.

[17]Matloff, *Strategic Planning, 1943-1944*, p. 165.

[18]*Ibid.*, p. 177.

[19]Higgins, *Soft Underbelly*, p. 101; Matloff, *Strategic Planning, 1943-1944*, pp. 220-221.

[20]John Ehrman, *Grand Strategy* (London, 1956), Vol. V, pp. 9-10; Matloff, *Strategic Planning, 1943-1944*, pp. 227-229.

[21]Higgins, *Soft Underbelly*, pp. 219-221; Michael Howard, *The Mediterranean Strategy in the Second World War* (New York, 1968), pp. 53, 70.

[22]Churchill, *Closing the Ring*, pp. 90-91.

[23]W. G. R. Jackson, *The Battle for Italy* (New York, 1967), p. 162.

[24]Churchill, *Closing the Ring*, p. 205.

[25]Burns, *Roosevelt: The Soldier of Freedom*, p. 399.

[26]Matloff, *Strategic Planning, 1943-1944*, pp. 336-337.

[27]Robert E. Sherwood, *Roosevelt and Hopkins: An Intimate History* (New York, 1950), p. 717.

[28]Churchill, *Closing the Ring*, p. 328.

[29]Ehrman, *Grand Strategy*, Vol. V. p. 189.

[30]*Ibid.*, p. 112.

[31]Churchill, *Closing the Ring*, pp. 345-346, 378.

[32]Morton, *Strategy and Command*, pp. 668-669.

[33]Churchill, *Closing the Ring*, pp. 335-340; Ehrman, *Grand Strategy*, Vol. V., pp. 118-121; Matloff, *Strategic Planning, 1943-1944*, pp. 338-339.

[34]Matloff, *Strategic Planning, 1943-1944*, pp. 383-385.

[35]Maurice Matloff, "The 90-Division Gamble," in Kent Roberts Greenfield (ed.), *Command Decisions* (Washington, D.C., 1968), pp 366-381, *passim*.

[36]Robert W. Coakley and Richard M. Leighton, *Global Logistics and Strategy, 1943-1945* (Washington, D.C., 1968), 338-340; Matloff, *Strategic Planning, 1943-1944*, p. 422.

[37]Matloff, *Strategic Planning, 1943-1944*, pp. 413-424, *passim*.

[38]*Ibid.*, pp. 433-453, *passim*; Higgins, *Soft Underbelly*, p. 47.

[39]Franklin D. Roosevelt, statement on D-Day, June 6, 1944.

[40]Charles B. MacDonald, *The Mighty Endeavor*(New York, 1953), pp. 691-692.

[41]Winston S. Churchill, *Triumph and Tragedy* (Boston, 1953), pp. 691-692.

[42]Hanson W. Baldwin, *Great Mistakes of the War* (New York, 1949), p. 25; Trumbull Higgins, "The Anglo-American Historians' War in the Mediterranean, 1942-1945," *Military Affairs*, XXXIV, No. 3 (October 1970), 86; Chester W. Wilmot, *The Struggle for Europe* (New York, 1952), pp. 446-447.

[43]Churchill *Triumph and Tragedy*, p. 65.

[44]Churchill describes his use of the term, "soft underbelly" in *The Hinge of Fate*, pp. 281-282; Matloff, *Strategic Planning, 1943-1944*, pp. 427-428.

[45]Higgins, *Soft Underbelly*, p. 178; Howard, *The Mediterranean Strategy in the Second World War*, p. 65.

[46]Gaddis Smith, *American Diplomacy During the Second World War* (New York, 1965), pp. 76, 92, 133-134.

[47]Pinpointing the time when Churchill came to realize that the European balance of power was being destroyed is open to question. Wilmot suggests in *The Struggle for Europe*, pp. 141-142, that as late as the Teheran Conference Churchill still may not have realized the eventual extent of Russian dominance; Matloff, *Strategic Planning, 1943-1944*, pp. 287-288, discusses the awareness of this problem by the U.S. Army staff as early as March 1943.

[48]Matloff, *Strategic Planning, 1943-1944*, pp. 523-524.

[49]*Ibid.*, pp. 528-534.

[50]Churchill, *Triumph and Tragedy*, p. 156.

[51]Higgins, *Soft Underbelly*, p. 187.

[52]Churchill, *Triump and Tragedy*, p. 152; Matloff, *Strategic Planning, 1943-1944*, p. 513.

[53]Matloff, *Strategic Planning, 1943-1944*, pp. 514, 527-528.

[54]MacDonald, *The Mighty Endeavor*, p. 517; Wilmot, *The Struggle for Europe*, p. 489.

[55]Dwight D. Eisenhower, *Crusade in Europe* (Garden City, N.Y., 1948), p. 306.

[56]Burns, *Roosevelt: The Soldier of Freedom*, p. 572; *cf.*, among others, Wilmot, *The Struggle for Europe*, pp. 628-659 *passim*. Smith in *American Diplomacy During the Second World War*, p. 131, suggests that the issue of Roosevelt's naivete at Yalta is still moot.

[57]John Ehrman, *Grand Strategy* (London, 1956), Vol. VI, p. 150; Harry S. Truman, *Years of Decision* (Garden City, N.Y. 1955), p. 212.

[58]Forrest C. Pogue, "The Decision to Halt at the Elbe," in *Command Decisions*, p. 492.

[59]Churchill, *Triumph and Tragedy,* pp. 571-573.

[60]Ehrman, *Grand Strategy,* Vol. VI, p. 150; Herbert Feis, *Churchill, Roosevelt, Stalin* (Princeton, 1957), pp. 633-641.

[61]Richard M. Leighton, "OVERLORD Revisited: An Interpretation of American Strategy in the European War," *The American Historical Review,* LXVIII, No. 4 (July 1963), 919-937 *passim.*

[62]Howard, *The Mediterranean Strategy in the Second World War,* p. 71.

[63]Gavin Long, *The Final Campaigns* (Canberra, Australia, 1963), pp. 45-57 *passim.*

[64]Admiral William D. Leahy, as quoted in Ehrman, *Grand Strategy,* Vol. VI, p. 272.

[65]Churchill, as quoted in Ehrman, *Grand Strategy,* Vol. VI, p. 273.

[66]Ehrman, *Grand Strategy,* Vol. VI, p. 291.

[67]Churchill, *Triumph and Tragedy,* pp. 674-675.

[68]J. R. M. Butler, *Grand Strategy* (London, 1957), Vol. II, p. 13.

[69]Winston S. Churchill, *Their Finest Hour* (Boston, 1949), p. 26.

[70]Correlli Barnett, *Britain and Her Army, 1509-1970* (New York, 1970), p. 475.

GLOSSARY

ABC-1: American-British Conversations held in Washington, January-March 1941.

ABDACOM: Australian-British-Dutch-American Command.

ANAKIM: Plan for the recapture of Burma.

ANVIL: Initial plan for the invasion of southern France.

ARCADIA: American-British conference held in Washington, December 1941-January 1942.

AVALANCHE: Invasion of Italy, vicinity of Salerno, September 1943.

BOLERO: Buildup of American forces and supplies in the United Kingdom for the cross-Channel attack.

BUCCANEER: Plan for an amphibious operation against the Andaman Islands in the Bay of Bengal.

CARTWHEEL: Converging drives on Rabaul by South Pacific and Southwest Pacific Area forces.

CBI: China-Burma-India Theater.

CCS: Combined Chiefs of Staff.

CIGS: Chief of the Imperial General Staff.

DRAGOON: Final code name for the invasion of southern France, August 1944.

HUSKY: Allied invasion of Sicily, July 1943.

JCS: Joint Chiefs of Staff.

JUPITER: Plan for an invasion of Norway.

OCTAGON: American-British conference held in Quebec, September 1944.

OVERLORD: Allied cross-Channel invasion of northwest Europe, June 1944.

QUADRANT: American-British conference held in Quebec, August 1943.

RAINBOW 5: One of several American war plans prepared between 1939 and 1941; included the concept of defeating Germany and Italy first.

ROUNDHAMMER: A cross-Channel operation smaller than ROUNDUP but larger than SLEDGEHAMMER.

SLEDGEHAMMER: Contingency plan for a limited cross-Channel attack in 1942.

TORCH: Allied invasion of northwest Africa.

TRIDENT: American-British conference held in Washington, May 1943.

The Battle of the Atlantic

9

The only thing that ever really frightened me during the whole war was the U-boat peril.
Winston S. Churchill, Their Finest Hour

The Battle of the Atlantic was a war at sea. Paradoxically, it was fought between a great land power, Germany, and two great sea powers, the United States and Great Britain. The battle was protracted, lasting more than five years with varying intensity and success. It was fought over millions of square miles of ocean, from the Barents Sea in the Arctic to the South Atlantic, and from the shores of the American continents to the continental shores of Europe and Africa.

The battle was fought for elemental reasons. Beginning in September 1939, Germany was at war with Great Britain, France, and their allies. The Germans defeated the British armies during the fall of France in the summer of 1940, forcing them to retreat to the security of the British Isles. Though weakened, the defiant British, going it alone, continued to resist German arms. The Battle of Britain convinced Hitler that England was too strong to invade—the Royal Navy could prevent an amphibious assault across the English Channel, and the Royal Air Force controlled the air, albeit tenuously.

With but few natural resources, Great Britain, as an island nation, historically had been almost entirely dependent upon seaborne commerce for her sustenance. Consequently, she always had been vulnerable to sea blockade, compelling her over the centuries to maintain the most powerful navy in the world to protect her sea lines of communication. Hitler's surface fleet was inferior to the Royal Navy and therefore unsuitable for blockade, so the Germans chose to use their submarines to attack Allied shipping going to and from the British Isles. If the submarines sank enough shipping, Great Britain no longer would be able to fight Germany.

The defeat of Great Britain would have been a calamity to western civilization, for her survival was the key to the ultimate defeat of Germany. After the fall of France, Great Britain was the sole nation continuing to fight Germany for almost a year. After Russia entered the war in mid-1941, her capability to continue fighting Germany depended in great measure upon seaborne war materiel from the United States via Great Britain. When America eventually did take up arms against the Axis, Great Britain was essential as the major base for the eventual invasion of the Continent. Thus the Allies' first priority during the Second World War became a victory in the Battle of the Atlantic. Until that battle was won, the Allies would be unable to defeat Germany.

Background to Conflict

Great Britain had been the world's greatest sea power for centuries when the Second World War began in September 1939. There were many historical reasons why she had become the supreme sea power; these had been analyzed by Rear Admiral Alfred Thayer Mahan, United States Navy, a famous naval philosopher, historian, and strategic theorist. Mahan was born at West Point in 1836, the son of Dennis Hart Mahan, the Military Academy professor after whom the Academy's Mahan Hall is named. (Admiral Mahan's middle name was chosen to honor his father's friend and mentor, Sylvanus Thayer.) Young Mahan chose the Naval Academy rather than West Point, graduated just before the Civil War, and became a career naval officer. An intellectual and a student of history, in 1890 he published a monumental book entitled *The Influence of Sea Power Upon History*. In his book he stated that England had developed the most powerful navy in the world in order to protect her sea lines of communication so that her merchant ships could ply the seas safely.

Mahan studied other major historical periods, as well, such

Alfred Thayer Mahan

as the Wars of Napoleon. Great Britain, a great sea power, often was alone in fighting a great land power, France. Unable to invade Great Britain, France chose to attack British merchant shipping to exploit her vulnerable dependence upon seaborne commerce. The French Navy avoided decisive battle with the Royal Navy and instead, together with privateers, sought out and destroyed whatever unprotected British merchantmen it could intercept along the world's trade routes. This type of naval warfare was called *guerre de course*.

The upshot was that the French mauled the British merchant marine but failed to defeat either the Royal Navy or Great Britain. There were too many British merchantmen too widely scattered about the world, and France could not sink enough of them. Although *guerre de course* caused the British people to suffer economic harships, the British nation continued to make war against France and finally won with the assistance of her continental allies.

Mahan concluded that an enemy nation could not defeat a great sea power by commerce raiding alone, maintaining that France failed because her warships were unable to defeat Great Britain's warships. He concluded that a sea power could be conquered only after her battle fleet was destroyed in a decisive battle, called a "fleet action." Mahan's theories on sea power were popularly embraced by many nations, and these nations transformed his concepts into powerful new battle fleets. A quarter century after *The Influence of Sea Power* was published, the European powers tested his doctrine as the First World War began. The German surface fleet, although much enlarged and strengthened, still was inferior to the Royal Navy. After the indecisive Battle of Jutland, the German High Seas Fleet withdrew to protected waters for the war's duration. The Germans had misnamed their fleet, for "High Seas" implies warships that could range about the oceans of the world. In reality, the German battle fleet had limited endurance and was restricted in radius to no more than several hundred miles from its home ports on the Continent.

Thus Great Britain's uninhibited seaborne commerce traversed to and from the home islands, carrying the materiel that sustained the United Kingdom in its war against Germany. The land war on the Continent became a stalemate, and a desperate Germany searched for other means to defeat Great Britain. Her battle fleet impotent, Germany tried the submarine.

The newly developed submarine seemed a puny weapon compared to the bulk, power, and majesty of a battleship. With only several hundred tons displacement, it was fragile, cramped and uncomfortable, often unsafe and unreliable, and it was untested in war. Its greatest asset was its ability to submerge and thereby approach a surface target while undetected. Although slow and with limited underwater endurance, if it could by stealth approach to within a half mile of a target, it could launch a submerged torpedo, whose large high explosive warhead would blast open a ship's side and sink the ship.

Such were the submarine's capabilities, but the submarine was so new and so primitive that there were no well-developed tactics and doctrine for its wartime employment. International law was another complication. For example, civilized countries fought by Rules of War, and one rule was that unarmed merchantmen and passenger ships were not to be sunk without warning—even if they belonged to the enemy. Therefore, a submarine would be forced to expose itself to ramming and hidden gunfire if it obeyed international law by surfacing and warning its intended victims to abandon ship prior to its attack.

Another complication was neutral shipping carrying cargo destined for Great Britain. By international law, German submarines were obliged to surface and dispatch a boarding party to search the neutral merchantman for possible contraband. Again, the submarine would have to lie exposed on the surface, vulnerable to surprise attack, while her position almost certainly was being broadcast to the world by the merchantman's radio operator.

It soon became apparent in the First World War that the old rules at sea did not apply to modern naval warfare. In time, an indignant United States, whose ships and citizens were imperiled as they crossed the Atlantic to England, forced Germany to equivocate her submarine policy, for Germany wanted to appease America and thereby keep her neutral. But the war on the Continent continued to go against Germany, and finally an increasingly desperate Kaiser declared unrestricted submarine warfare in hopes of weakening Great Britain. In response, America went to war. Soon the German submarines effected enormous losses, and the Allies were confronted for the first time in history with the real possibility of losing Great Britain to a submarine-enforced maritime blockade.

The principal problem was whether to convoy merchantmen or allow them to transit individually. Merchantmen are independent by nature, accustomed to setting their own schedules, courses, and speeds that will most economically route them to their various ports of call. Sailing in convoy, therefore, is understandably an anathema to the master of a merchantman. His ship must conform to the actions of the group as a whole. For example, he must waste valuable time in port waiting for the convoy to assemble. Once underway, he is grudgingly subject to the orders of the convoy commodore. His ship must keep station within a formation, a task for which his watch officers are unaccustomed, and which is doubly hazardous because of the unpredictable handling characteristics of the cumbersome merchantmen. Finally, on arriving at the convoy's destination, he perhaps must wait—this time to unload—because of the congestion caused by everyone arriving at once.

But beyond these considerations was the more germane question of whether sinking losses could be reduced by using convoys. One argument propounded that convoys simplified the submarines' task by concentrating the merchantmen into large, attractive, easily detected targets. Better to let the merchantmen randomly scatter about the ocean, went the argument, in order to complicate the submarines' detection problems.

Naval tradition begun by Admiral Lord Nelson was another factor, for Nelson's aggressiveness was a revered historical precedent. The Royal Navy's task was *offensive*: to protect the sea lines of communication, to maintain control of the sea, and to seek out and destroy the submarines. Convoy escort duty was passively *defensive* and unworthy of the Royal Navy.

Statistics eventually proved that the convoy method was best. The navies of the United States and Great Britain could not find the submarines, however aggressively their patrols searched the ocean. Meanwhile, the submarines were torpedoing over one-fourth of the independent merchantmen on certain sea lanes where merchantmen habitually followed established routes. Yet when an escorted convoy system was substituted, the loss rate dropped to less than one percent. Moreover, the convoy served to attract the submarines to within range of the escort ships, which hitherto had been unable to find the submarines; and so the Germans lost more and more submarines while the Allies lost fewer and fewer merchantmen.

The Allies also developed new weapons such as the depth charge, essentially a barrel filled with several hundred pounds of high explosive which detonated at a pre-set depth. It was dropped overboard near a submarine's assumed position, and if it exploded close enough to the submarine, it would crush its hull. Aircraft and crude hydrophone listening devices aided in detecting submarines. In the end, the German submarine, still undeveloped and rudimentary, could not overcome the convoy system.

But it had been a near thing. Most naval historians believe that the German submarine blockade almost won the First World War for the Central Powers. The submarine proved to be the perfect commerce raider, and the surprised Allies had no immediate countermeasures. Indeed, the Germans sank well over 5,000 allied merchantmen, displacing over 12 million tons. They also sank 10 battleships, 18 cruisers, 20 destroyers, and 9 submarines. The Germans, in contrast, lost only 187 submarines.[1]

Between Wars, 1918-1939

The distinguishing feature of this period was the emphasis on naval disarmament. The predominant mood during the 1920s was pacifism, and the world powers agreed to limit the sizes of their navies in order to save money and presumably to avoid future wars. But the western nations deceived themselves with wishful thinking, for by the mid-1930s Germany and Japan renounced all disarmament treaties and began to rearm their navies, concentrating on the creation of large surface warships. So also did Great Britain and the United States in response to these potential threats. Regarding the Japanese Navy as the main threat to the United States, the American Navy used what limited construction funds it received from Congress to build carriers, battleships, cruisers, and large destroyers. Anti-submarine warfare (ASW) received low priority, although the U.S. Navy did experiment with underwater, echo-ranging equipment during the mid-1930s.

The reasons for the neglect of ASW are understandable. Senior American naval officers were inculcated with Mahan's theories, and in their minds a future naval war with Japan would be won by the classic fleet action using large surface warships. Neither Japan nor the United States, according to the disciples of Mahan, could be defeated by commerce raiding. Submarines would be used as scouts, and they were not envisioned as operating independently against enemy merchant shipping. That was the traditional task of light cruisers, fast 7,000-ton surface warships with 6-inch guns and long cruising radii.

Furthermore, most American naval officers scorned submarines, based upon past experiences within the American submarine force. Submarines were mechanically unreliable, ill-designed, and given to accidents. Many had sunk during the inter-war years, either from collision or from shipboard malfunctions. Thus it was difficult for most in the United States Navy to respect the submarine.[2] The corollary to this thinking was that German and Japanese submarines were not considered as too great a threat, and ASW research and development was correspondingly lethargic.

The other major reason for slighting ASW was want of funds. Despite President Roosevelt's invigorating programs to build a new Navy, construction and research funds still were limited. Owing to the scarcity of ASW sponsors within the Navy Department, little money was appropriated for what the Navy regarded as a low priority. Thus the United States Navy largely neglected ASW through the 1920s and well into the 1930s. The Americans tacitly assumed that the Royal Navy would handle whatever ships the German Navy would be able to muster in the Atlantic. The United States would focus on Japan.

The Germans built battleships and cruisers but relatively few submarines during the 1930s. Given the submarine's ineffectiveness against convoys during the First World War, many naval planners still did not regard them as a serious threat. Yet the British were realists, and they were prescient enough to develop an underwater detection device called "asdic."* This acoustic sensor emitted bursts of underwater sound energy ("pings"), then detected the returning echoes bouncing from a submerged hull at ranges up to a half mile. The asdic operator could then determine the submarine's range and bearing, information which allowed the speedy destroyer to close and pass over the much slower submarine and to destroy it with depth charges.

Many Americans and British naval officers mistakenly assumed that asdic (and the American version called "sonar"†) provided surface ships with a comfortable superiority over submarines in a war at sea. It was not generally appreciated that many complex variables (such as water temperature, salinity, and pressure, as well as marine life) could degrade sonar and asdic performance. Operator training and experience levels also were crucial to successful ASW operations, but peacetime training exercises with submarines were infrequent and unrealistic.[3]

Interestingly enough, Germany correspondingly was unprepared to use submarines against the Allies. According to historian Samuel Eliot Morison:

> Military men are often accused of planning every new war in terms of the last one. Now, the pattern of World War II in the Atlantic turned out to be very similar to that of World War I; yet nobody planned it that way. Hitler had endeavored to build up a high-seas fleet and neglected U-boats; while Britain, France and the United States were far better prepared to deal with a surface than with an underwater navy. . . . Submarine warfare was unwanted and unexpected by Hitler, unprepared for by the German Navy; when adopted perforce it was improvised until well into 1943 when all German naval effort and a large share of production were concentrated on making it a success.[4]

The War Begins

When war began in September 1939, Germany had less than 50 submarines in its Navy. Hitler simply had not believed he would ever need them; he intended to depend upon the army and Air Force. Morison commented:

> Fortunately for the Allied nations, the Fuehrer had slight appreciation of the significance of sea power and only faint glimmerings of naval strategy. He was *landsinnig* (land-minded), obsessed with a geopolitical theory very similar to that of the *blocus continental* with which Na-

*An acronym for *Anti-Submarine Detection Investigation Committee*.
†*Sound Navigation and Ranging*.

> poleon had hoped to strangle England. If he could bring the European "Heartland" under his domination or influence, the maritime powers would be stalemated. . . . Hitler was almost wholly preoccupied with thoughts of glorious continental victories as the one means necessary to achieve world domination.[5]

The German Navy thus was unprepared for war when it began in September 1939, having been misled by Hitler's assurances that he did not intend to go to war until at least 1945, thereby allowing Germany time to build a fleet that one day could challenge the Royal Navy. Inferior at war's outbreak in surface warships to the Royal Navy and with too few submarines for commerce warfare, the German Navy initially was too weak to contest British sea power and withdrew to the safety of German waters.

Grand Admiral Erich Raeder commanded the German fleet. Although a competent professional naval officer, he did not advocate a total commitment to submarine warfare to the exclusion of his small yet growing surface fleet. His main concern was to conserve his warships, to avoid rather than to seek battle. His submarine commander was Rear Admiral Karl Doenitz, an ambitious, unscrupulous flag officer in his late forties, who was an innovative and imaginative naval strategist and tactician. Impatient and frustrated, Doenitz deplored the older Raeder's conservatism and strove to convince Hitler that Germany should forsake surface ships and use all of Germany's naval resources for a massive campaign of unrestricted submarine warfare.

Hitler gradually accepted Doenitz's arguments and authorized an intensified submarine construction program. Still, the German submarine campaign against British shipping was indecisive through the summer of 1940, as Hitler concentrated on seizing France and threatening the British Isles. The British convoy system of the First World War still seemed to be working. But when the Battle of Britain in the fall of 1940 proved England invulnerable to invasion, Hitler authorized Doenitz to loose the German submarines in full force against Britain's seaborne commerce.

By the fall of 1940 Doenitz enjoyed two advantages. French and Norwegian ports became available to German submarines, shortening the transit distance to the western Atlantic sea lanes and increasing the numbers of submarines that could be maintained on station. The other factor was that Great Britain had too few destroyers in other assignments. Smaller, makeshift escorts—such as trawlers and corvettes—tried to substitute but had little success.

Doenitz also established an ingenious command and control system. From headquarters in Lorient, France, he organized his submarines into task forces called "wolfpacks." Using radio communications he dispersed them in wide search formations across known shipping lanes to locate British con-

Grand Admiral Erich Raeder

Grand Admiral Karl Doenitz

U-Boat at Full Speed

American Destroyer Attacks

Depth Charges Seek U-Boat

voys. Upon discovering a likely convoy, a submarine would radio its location to Doenitz who then would order nearby submarines to rendezvous for an attack. Other times Doenitz deployed his submarines based upon intelligence gathered from intercepted Allied radio traffic.[6]

When the wolfpack had assembled and intercepted the convoy, Doenitz would pass tactical command to the senior submarine commander present. Sometimes as many as 20 submarines would converge around an approaching convoy for a coordinated attack. Lacking in air cover, the convoy escorts were outnumbered and the submarines could attack almost with impunity, both surfaced and submerged. The escorts could not simultaneously fight all the submarines, which attacked with a persistent boldness that achieved devastating success. Attacks often would last for days, with the submarines sometimes contemptuously shadowing the convoy in full view of the exhausted escorts, much as a pack of wolves stalk on the fringes of a herd.

The typical German submarine had a cruising radius of 8,500 miles without refueling. She carried 14 torpedoes in fore and aft launching tubes and could dive to 350 feet. Her 220-foot hull was strong and resilient, able to withstand repeated depth charge attacks unless the weapons exploded close aboard. The captain and his crew of 50 were equally tough and durable, all highly motivated to take risks to sink enemy ships. The slow, deep-draft merchantmen were normally their principal targets, because the lively escorts were difficult to hit.

The submarine was most vulnerable to aircraft, whose speed and range allowed them to search and patrol much larger areas than that of an escort ship. If an aircraft could patrol above a convoy, the attacking submarine would be forced to submerge for self-protection, thereby preventing it from maneuvering on the surface. But ASW aircraft based on the British Isles and Canada had a limited range and could not cover the middle North Atlantic.* Bad weather and darkness also handicapped ASW air operations. New methods of providing air coverage were obviously needed in the early 1940s.

The submarine's greatest weakness was the limited endurance of its batteries, which restricted speeds to less than seven knots when submerged, and then only as long as the battery lasted—usually no more than several hours. Thus a submarine preferred to operate while surfaced, using her diesel engines either to charge her batteries or to attain speeds up to 17 knots in order to maneuver and attack. Her low silhouette allowed an undetected surfaced approach during cover of darkness or weather. At times a frantic escort would chase a surfaced submarine in a wild melee amongst the columns of lumbering merchantmen, the hound chasing the wolf under the sputtering glare of flares and burning ships.

Doenitz enjoyed stupendous success from July 1940, when his submarines had begun to operate from French ports, until

*For much of 1940, Great Britain and Canada could not provide escort ships, as well, in the mid-Atlantic.

1940 came to an end; the Germans sank 217 merchantmen, displacing over a million tons with the loss of only 6 submarines. But in November and December he was forced to withdraw most of his submarines for maintenance and repair, and German shipyards were not yet geared for rapid replacements. Both sides paused, ready to renew the Battle of the Atlantic in 1941.[7]

1941: America's Undeclared War

During 1940, President Roosevelt decided that it was in the best interests of the United States to aid Great Britain in her war against Germany. However, the United States was ostensibly neutral, so by international law Roosevelt was restricted in the ways and means that he could support British war efforts. Moreover, the United States was decidedly isolationist, and Congress was reluctant to become involved in the European war. As Great Britain's struggle became increasingly desperate, however, Roosevelt resolved to do whatever was necessary to keep her in the war, and he worked to influence public opinion accordingly. Thus, Roosevelt and Congress became less and less "neutral," pledging to give all aid "short of war."[8]

The greatest problem was to get American-supplied war materiel across the Atlantic to England against the opposition of the German submarines. In late 1939, Roosevelt had warned Great Britain and Germany to keep their sea wars on their side of the Atlantic, and the American Navy had established a token force called the Neutrality Patrol to enforce the President's proclamation. But, as the Battle of the Atlantic worsened for Great Britain, Churchill boldly asked Roosevelt to provide American warships to escort British convoys across the western Atlantic. In mid-1940 the United States already had agreed to loan 50 old destroyers from her mothball fleet; these were delivered in April 1941. Actually escorting British convoys, however, unquestionably violated all recognized rules of neutrality, and could provoke a justifiable declaration of war by Germany. Roosevelt was willing to accept the risk in order to help England survive. Hitler, however, wanted to avoid war with the United States, because Germany soon was to become entangled in its invasion of Russia. Thus, despite Roosevelt's provocations throughout 1941, Hitler was not prepared to declare war on the United States.

Increasing American involvement in the Battle of the Atlantic created terrible uncertainties for the navies of both the United States and Germany. The governments of both countries provided only vague guidance respectively to the captains of the American escorts and German submarines who soon would be meeting at sea. For example, could a German submarine attack a convoy escorted by American destroyers? If a British merchantman were torpedoed, could an American destroyer attack the German submarine? What if a German battleship appeared on the horizon (such as the *Bismarck*) to attack the convoy? When survival at sea is threatened, no responsible warship captain of any nationality wants to be fired upon first. Both navies wanted clearly defined rules of engagement. None were forthcoming.

President Roosevelt's Navy was handicapped also because it was unprepared to implement the President's decision to escort Atlantic convoys. Most of the American fleet was in the Pacific in order to deter Japanese military expansion. The few ships then in the Atlantic, designated the Atlantic Patrol Force, were entirely inadequate in numbers and readiness for major escort duties. The Navy hurriedly transferred to the Atlantic what ships it could spare, recommissioned those mothballed destroyers for which manpower was available, and prayed for new destroyers to arrive from the building yards. Although most of the destroyers carried sonar, the fleet had little experience in using and maintaining the complex equipment. Worse yet, the escorts were without radar and were essentially blind in searching for surfaced submarines at night. For political and personal reasons Roosevelt was reluctant to ask Congress to authorize enough personnel to man the Navy's expanding fleet adequately. Thus, the Atlantic escorts were shorthanded, as well, and suffered accordingly.

Given these difficulties, Roosevelt needed an exceptional senior naval officer to make things work. The President found him in Admiral Ernest J. King, who commanded the makeshift ASW force in early 1941. This force soon was redesignated the U.S. Atlantic Fleet in light of its expanding operations and responsibilities. Then 62 years old and nearing mandatory retirement, King was a widely experienced officer with 40 years of naval service in aviation, submarines, and surface ships. Although brilliant, innovative, and with a record of successful commands for 18 consecutive years, he was not without enemies. His standards of performance were exacting, and he often enforced them with an arbitrary harshness that could create bitterness and resentment. His hot temper, intellectual arrogance, impatience, and tactlessness also alienated others. Few questioned his extraordinary professional competence and ability to get things done, but he had not been a member of Roosevelt's clique of favored senior naval officers. In 1939, the President had to choose a new Chief of Naval Operations (CNO), and a hopeful, ambitious King was both qualified and eligible. But the President never seriously considered him and chose Harold R. Stark.

A despondent King went to Washington to serve on the General Board, considered to be a dead-end job for passing time until retirement. Meanwhile, America's undeclared war in the Atlantic intensified, and a strong naval leader was

Fleet Admiral Ernest J. King

needed to direct it. Both Secretary of the Navy Frank Knox and Admiral Stark appreciated King's talent for high command, and they asked the President to order King to the post of Commander-in-Chief, U.S. Atlantic Fleet (CINCLANT). Roosevelt approved, and King broke his flag aboard USS *Texas* at Norfolk on December 17, 1940. A year later he would become Commander-in-Chief, U.S. Fleet (COMINCH) and Chief of Naval Operations.

Rescued from limbo and delighted with his restoration to sea duty and a concurrent promotion to full admiral, King was the perfect man for the job. Realizing that there were shortages in men and ships for the task Roosevelt had given him, King's pragmatic policy was to "make the best of what you have."[9] He shocked the somnolent Atlantic Fleet like a wrathful fury, ordering his ships to consider themselves at war and to act accordingly. Twenty years of peacetime routines are not easy to change on short notice, but the Atlantic Fleet soon was darkening ships, manning its guns, practicing damage control, and mentally preparing for war. Six weeks after King had taken command, Secretary Knox sent him an approving letter. "I am not at all surprised," he wrote, "but I am gratified, to know that the Commander-in-Chief of the Atlantic Fleet recognizes the existence of an emergency and is taking proper measures to meet it. I knew you would."[10]

King pushed his ships to exhaustion as the United States assumed increasing responsibilities for protecting convoys in the western regions of the Atlantic. The Americans began as novices in ASW and remained so through much of 1941. The Germans and British concentrated in the battle areas of the eastern Atlantic, and naturally the fighting centered in those regions. The Germans, in obedience to Hitler's orders, avoided the western Atlantic, so the American escorts spent wearing days at sea escorting convoys through empty ocean. Under these conditions the Americans neither had time to train nor the benefit of battle experience achieved only through fighting German submarines. Neither did they have time to repair their ships nor to rest ashore; there were too few ships and too much to do. Thus the Atlantic Fleet expended its limited resources with little benefit in return.

Throughout the late summer and early fall, however, the Atlantic Fleet edged eastward closer to the battle area, and inevitably Germans and Americans met at sea. Initially the Americans only tracked the German submarines and reported their positions to the British. A submerged German submarine with an aggressive American destroyer overhead became understandably nervous, especially when the Americans summoned British ships and aircraft to the scene. Still Hitler ordered restraint. The uncertainty ended in early September,

1941, when a German submarine fired a torpedo at the American destroyer USS *Greer*, which had been tracking the submarine on sonar for several hours. *Greer* evaded the torpedo, counterattacked with depth charges, and an undeclared war had begun at sea between the United States and Germany.

American inexperience became manifest during the remainder of 1941. German submarines torpedoed two American destroyers in October, *Kearny* and *Reuben James*, the latter sinking with great loss of life. The Americans, however, neither sank any German submarines nor prevented the Germans from continuing to sink merchantmen in convoy. On the other hand, the American presence did allow the British to concentrate their own forces in other areas threatened by submarines, such as Gibraltar and West Africa.

As the winter of 1941 approached, the Atlantic Fleet neared the end of its endurance. The older destroyers suffered in the cruel weather of the North Atlantic, and ships needing repairs and maintenance could not be spared from operations at sea.[11] Morison observed:

> Autumn and winter escort work in the North Atlantic was arduous and exhausting for men and ships. Winds of gale force, mountainous seas, biting cold, body-piercing fog and blinding snow squalls were the rule rather than the exception; U-boats could escape this by submerging, but the escorts had to face it. . . . The continual rolling and pitching, coupled with the necessity of constant vigilance night and day, not only for enemy attack but to guard against collisions with other escort vessels and the convoy, wore men down.
>
> The strain was not only physical but psychological. These officers and men were enduring all the danger and hardship of war; yet it was not called war, and for the most part they were escorting ships under foreign flags. Forbidden to talk of their experiences ashore, or even to tell where they had been or what they were doing, their efforts were unknown to the American people. They had none of the satisfaction derived from public recognition.[12]

The Navy Department, however, sought to compensate these men with appropriate medals and commendations, and the Department asked King for his comments on these proposals. King's response was emphatic and set the tone for his attitude throughout the Second World War.:

> Personally, I do not favor such awards unless the incidents indicate clearly deeds which are "above and beyond the call of duty." I sincerely hope that there will be no repetition of certain awards made during the last war where people were, in effect, decorated when they lost their ships. This is not to say that they were to blame for losing their ships, but certainly there was no cause whatever for commendation . . . I suggest that we "go slow" in this matter of making heroes out of those people who have, after all, done the jobs they are trained to do. The earlier incidents [the torpedoing of *Kearny* and *Reuben James*] loom large by contrast with peacetime conditions—but can be expected to become commonplace incidents as we get further along.[13]

The Second World War began for the United States less than a month later.

German Maritime Strategy: 1942

When the United States and Germany finally went to war in December 1941, Admiral Doenitz already had acquired over two years' experience in the strategic direction of his country's submarine campaigns. In developing his grand strategy, he first had to determine his principal objective. Initially, that objective had been to blockade Great Britain so that she eventually would become unable to wage war against Germany. The method by which Doenitz would achieve his objective was to sink as many merchantmen entering or leaving Great Britain as possible.

Doenitz then faced the problem of determining how well he was progressing in achieving that objective. This ostensibly became a matter of statistical analysis through compiling data on numbers of ships sunk and total tonnage sunk over a given period. After a two-year effort the Germans had sunk over 1,300 ships, totaling over 7 million tons.[14] Astronomical figures, and yet Great Britain somehow was still in the war. Worse yet for Germany, so now was the United States.

These statistics used alone suggest that they were not the most accurate indication of how well the German submarine campaign was progressing. For example, they did not classify the kinds of cargo that a sunken ship had been carrying. Obviously a ship filled with tanks and guns was more vital to the war effort than a ship filled with coal. The submarines, however, normally did not have time to discriminate between ships within a convoy and were likely to shoot at the nearest target. Even given time, they could not discern the cargo being carried, nor would the Allies announce their own shipping losses to aid the German analysts. Therefore this lack of data for selective analysis undoubtedly misled Doenitz's own assessments.

Another complication was the uncertainty faced by the submarine captains in estimating the displacements of the ships they had torpedoed. Often they had only a glimpse of their victims before attacking; afterwards, if the submarines were too busy evading escort counterattacks, they could not always verify that their targets had even been sunk. The captains also were coerced by Doenitz into achieving a tonnage quota during each war patrol, so they naturally tended to overestimate the sizes and numbers of ships they sank.

When a particularly vital convoy had to be protected, such as the movement of troops and their equipment, the Allies would select their fastest transports accompanied by a powerful screening force that usually included an aircraft carrier to provide air cover. This kind of convoy invariably was immune from submarine attack in the Atlantic. Fast ocean liners, such as the *Queen Mary* and *Queen Elizabeth*, were converted to troop carriers and steamed safely alone, outrunning both submarines and escorts. Thus, in varying degrees, the Allies would assign escort and air cover in direct relationship to the priority and importance of the cargo being transported.

When German submarines attacked the more powerful convoys they normally suffered heavy losses, and losses were not tolerated by Doenitz. It was his nature to conserve his submarines, so his tendency was to withdraw the ships to safer waters whenever the Allies sank them in unacceptable numbers in a defended area of the ocean. Once in safe waters his submarines no longer were threatened by Allied ASW forces. On the other hand, neither were they sinking Allied merchantmen. So Doenitz eventually would have to reassign his submarines to renew their attacks, but the question was where and against what shipping.

Doenitz in effect abandoned his attacks against well-defended convoys and conceded that their vital cargoes would be allowed to pass unscathed. By early 1942, he had evolved a strategic concept called, for want of a better term, his "tonnage theory." This theory held that if German submarines could sink merchantmen at a greater rate than the Allied building yards could replace them, concentrating in those areas where merchantmen were many and escorts few, the Allies eventually would be without enough shipping anywhere in the world. The Allies had too few ASW resources to protect their merchantmen everywhere. Doenitz would so deploy his submarines so that they would find plenty of easy targets while avoiding concentrations of Allied ASW forces. He decided that American shipping transiting between the United States and Central and South America would be one of his first targets.

Submarine Warfare Comes to America: 1942

Before December 1941, the United States naval forces in the Atlantic had been concerned with protecting convoys destined for Great Britain. That country's dependence upon seaborne commerce already has been discussed and is easily understood. One glance at a map reveals the geographic fact that Great Britain is a small island nation; ergo, she must depend upon the sea and ships for her survival.[15]

The United States, in contrast, is a huge land area abounding with natural resources; theoretically, she should be self-sufficient. In reality, however, America depended heavily upon seaborne imports for her economic welfare (as she, of course, still does today). Thousands of merchantmen of all descriptions transited along sea lanes from Newfoundland to Brazil. As a highly industrialized nation, the United States required great quantities of raw materials to sustain her factories, as well as her population. Moreover, the United States had become the principal manufacturer and supplier of arms and munitions for the Allied armies, navies, and air forces. Thus, as a consequence of war, the need for raw materials intensified enormously.

Much of this material came from South and Central America and was imported by sea. Oil, for example, came from fields in the Netherlands West Indies and from Venezuela and thither to the eastern United States and Great Britain. Bauxite (the basic ingredient for aluminum aircraft fuselages) was mined in the Guianas and Brazil for oceanic shipment to America. Basic foodstuffs such as coffee and sugar were imported via sea.

Moreover, raw materials and bulk commodities produced in the United States often were transported via coastal sea lanes to industrial centers on the east coast. Texas oil was loaded into tankers in ports in the Gulf of Mexico for shipment north. The great eastern cities depended upon coastal shipping to provide bulk commodities such as coal, iron, cement, and lumber. The nation's railroads and highways simply did not have the capacity to substitute for ships should they be unable to steam safely at sea.

Doenitz shrewdly calculated that the United States lacked sufficient escort ships and aircraft to protect this vital inter-America shipping, and, furthermore, that the United States would be shocked, confused, and distracted by the recent attack against Pearl Harbor. So he planned a "Pearl Harbor" of his own: *blitzkrieg* submarine attacks off the very coast of the eastern United States. On December 12, 1941, Hitler approved Operation *Paukenschlag* ("Roll on the Drums").[16]

It was a bold scheme, sending German submarines thousands of miles across the Atlantic to American shores. Initially none were in the western Atlantic in obedience to Hitler's orders to stand clear of that area during 1941. Owing to commitments elsewhere, Doenitz initially could deploy only five submarines to the United States—but they were five too many. When they arrived, the submarine skippers could hardly believe what they found. America was acting as if there were no war. Unprotected coastal shipping was steaming independently under peacetime conditions, lights showing at night, and there were neither convoys nor air and surface ASW forces to oppose the

Torpedoed Oil Tanker

submarines. They fell upon the merchant ships like ravenous wolves upon flocks of sheep.

Paukenschlag was a massacre. Merchantmen were torpedoed within sight of bathers at Miami Beach, and resort areas such as Virginia Beach were covered with oil and debris and bodies of merchant seamen. Great pillars of smoke from burning ships were a common sight off New York, Boston, and Charleston. Americans refused to darken their cities at night, and German submarines could see and sink merchantmen silhouetted against the lights ashore. Eventually, the Germans became so audacious that they remained surfaced even by day and used their deck guns to sink ships in order to conserve torpedoes. Off the east coast during the first four months of 1942, the Germans sank 87 ships, totaling 515,000 tons. During March alone, 28 ships of some 160,000 tons were sunk off America's Atlantic shores.[17] The psychological effect on American morale was devastating.

In retrospect, Doenitz had been quick to recognize and to act upon the opportunity to strike at America's unprotected seaboard. Although Japan's attack on Pearl Harbor had been a surprise to the Germans, Doenitz, five days later, had proposed his *Paukenschlag* plan to Hitler. However, Hitler had earlier decided to send more than 50 submarines to the Mediterranean to support Rommel's offensive in North Africa, so only 5 were available for deployment to North American waters. It took them nearly a month to get on station, and throughout the first months of 1942 there probably were no more than a dozen in east coast waters at any one time. It is astonishing that so few submarines could create such havoc. If Hitler had sent his other 50 submarines to the western Atlantic in early January rather than one-tenth that number, the Germans could have paralyzed American eastern industry.[18]

Further, Hitler's decision to concentrate his submarines in the Mediterranean was a mistake. Although they did succeed in sinking or damaging several important British warships in late 1941, they did not alter the eventual outcome of the war in North Africa. Had they remained in the Atlantic—as Raeder and Doenitz had urged—they might very well have immobilized the United States throughout 1942. They also probably would have prevented the Allied landings in North Africa in November 1942.

The United States Navy seemed helpless before the few submarines that entered the western Atlantic. The unthinkable had happened: the Navy had lost control of the sea in its own home waters. Ugly questions were being asked and answers demanded. Congress had appropriated hundreds of millions of dollars under the Roosevelt Administration for ships and aircraft during the 1930s; furthermore, the United States had been aware of German submarine capabilities ever since September 1939. Now it was early 1942. Had we ignored a two-year warning? Where were our ships? Where were our planes? Why weren't we ready?

The United States Navy had no excuse for its desperate shortage of ASW escorts in early 1942. Many had foreseen the need in the late 1930s, yet Navy Department indecision and administrative inertia had delayed any action. President Roosevelt, once an Assistant Secretary of the Navy, was a naval expert who saw perhaps better than anyone that some kind of escort ship, smaller and less expensive than a destroyer, would be needed. Indeed the President had even arranged for a prize to be offered for the best design of antisubmarine patrol craft.[19]

The Navy had reacted to Roosevelt's suggestions with disdain. For example, in 1938 the President was discussing future naval appropriations with Congressman Carl Vinson, the powerful chairman of the House Naval Affairs Committee, and the CNO, Admiral William D. Leahy (later Roosevelt's wartime chief of staff). Roosevelt avidly collected ship models, and he showed his visitors a model of a 110-foot subchaser. "This is something we worked up in the last war," he remarked, and he went on to suggest a feasibility study for its possible future use. Vinson noted Leahy's facial expression and later asked the admiral's opinion of the President's proposals. Replied Leahy: "They weren't worth a damn."[20]

After the war in Europe began in 1939, Admiral Stark (the new CNO) and his senior advisors still could not agree on the characteristics needed for an ASW escort.[21] It was agreed that a 2,000-ton destroyer had more capability than what was needed, but Roosevelt's proposed wooden-hulled subchasers of 500 tons and less were too small for open ocean warfare. What was needed was a destroyer-type escort of from 1,000 to 1,500 tons displacement—less powerful and less expensive than a full-sized destroyer, yet with enough range and armament to enable them to escort convoys around the world and to fight submarines. If properly designed so as to be simple and inexpensive, they could be mass produced and completed in a relatively short time. Thus the concept of the destroyer escort (DE) was created, but studies and discussions within the Navy Department dragged on indecisively as December 1941 approached. "We were just plugging along to find out what sort of anti-submarine craft we wanted in case we needed them," said one naval officer, "and then all of a sudden, by God, we were in the war!"[22]

The impetus of war finally jarred the DE construction program into motion in 1942, although delays of many kinds slowed production. For example, King, in his capacity as COMINCH, constantly had to establish priorities within the building yards, such as whether the production of amphibious

American Destroyer Escort (DE)

shipping for the planned North African landings in the fall of 1942 would take precedence over the DEs. It did.

Normally, however, King did not get involved in the details of wartime production—that was the job of the Congress and the Secretary of the Navy. He simply wanted them to get on with it at full speed. In early January 1942, Vinson wrote King that he and his Naval Affairs Committee were concerned that east coast industries were vulnerable to attack by German aircraft and surface ships, and he asked King what measures he was taking to defend them. King, avoiding a direct answer by replying that the matter was under "study and consideration," went on to tell Vinson what King expected of *him*. "We must," wrote King, "turn out every plane and ship and accompanying munitions that the *present* productive capacity of the country is capable of."[23]

Another matter which threatened the DE production program was a debate within the Navy Department in early 1942 over establishing building priorities between merchantmen and DEs. Some naval officials sensed the thrust of the Doenitz "tonnage theory" and concluded that the way to beat Doenitz was to build replacement merchantmen faster than Doenitz could sink them. The counter argument was to build enough DEs so that the Allies could sink submarines at a faster rate than the Germans could build replacements. Said King: "The answer appears obvious."[24] The DE building program was pressed with all the support King could bring to bear. Nevertheless, by June 30, 1943—20 months after the United States had been at war with Germany—only 25 DEs had been commissioned.[25] By war's end, however, some 498 had been built by American shipyards, and they were crucial to the eventual Allied victory in the Battle of the Atlantic.[26]

American east coast ASW aircraft similarly were as scarce as escort ships in early 1942. The story behind this grievous shortage also was complex and long-standing.[27]

For many years before the Second World War there had been a prolonged series of disputes in the United States over the organization, command, and control of naval and military aircraft. In the early 1920s, Brigadier General Billy Mitchell and his followers had argued that all military and naval aircraft should be organized into a separate service, independent of the Army and the Navy. Congress rejected Mitchell's ideas and authorized each service to have its own integral air arm.

There then arose a question as to the missions of each service's air forces. Clearly, Navy aircraft would fly from carriers and Army aircraft would fly from land bases—but whose aircraft would be responsible for coastal defense and surveillance? The Navy wanted to control land-based, long-range aircraft for patrolling the ocean waters adjacent to the United States. The Army objected, contending that any combat aircraft operating from a land-based airfield had to be under Army control. If the Navy wanted their own long-range patrol aircraft they would have to use seaplanes. The Army won its case in Congress. The Navy subsequently built a limited number of seaplanes authorized by Congress. By January 1942, there were far too few to provide ASW air protection over the thousands of miles of sea lanes in the Western Hemisphere that the Germans were threatening.

King quickly realized that he needed the Army Air Force to augment east coast ASW air protection. He asked General George C. Marshall, Army Chief of Staff, for help. Thus, in 1942 the Army allocated 84 medium bombers to assist the Navy in protecting shipping and to conduct ASW. Eventually the Army Air Force provided over 300 aircraft to assist naval aircraft on the east coast, in the Gulf of Mexico, and in the Caribbean.

It was not a harmonious arrangement. The Army pilots were not trained either for ASW or for open water navigation. Furthermore, the patrols usually were long and boring, and the Army pilots would have much preferred the excitement of bombing German factories, the mission for which their aircraft and their training had been intended. Disagreements on tactics and command-and-control procedures were not infrequent, and both Army and Navy were eager to get the Army out of the ASW business. King and General H. H. Arnold, the Army Air Force commander, had some particularly acrimonious arguments.[28] Eventually Arnold agreed to turn over a portion of his Army bombers to the Navy, to be flown by Navy pilots, and the Navy then progressively relieved the Army Air Force of its ASW responsibilities. Both services undoubtedly were happy once they could get on with what they considered to be their primary missions in the war against Germany.

The Americans Fight Back

When the German submarines began their attack in early 1942, the United States Navy lacked not only ASW ships and planes but plans as well. Already shocked by Pearl Harbor, the Navy was mentally unprepared for *Paukenschlag*. As a result, Doenitz achieved a stunning surprise, and the American response was muddled and uncoordinated.

To exacerbate the disorder, a major reorganization disrupted the Navy Department during the weeks immediately after the Pearl Harbor attack. Admiral King was brought to Washington from his Atlantic Fleet command and promoted to the post of Commander-in-Chief, U.S. Fleet. Thus King was the top commander of all forces afloat, but Stark remained as CNO, whose job it was to provide long-range planning and strategy, to provide logistical support to the Fleet, and generally to coordinate the activities of the shore establishment. In the past, the office of CNO also had been senior to COMINCH, who normally had remained at sea in a flagship. Thus it was that Stark was senior to King.

Now King changed everything. Although he maintained a nominal flagship at the Washington Navy Yard, King immediately established his headquarters ashore in the Navy Department. Starting essentially with little more than an empty office, he was forced to begin assembling his staff from scratch. Confusion was compounded when it soon became evident that there was no clear definition of authority and responsibility between King, Stark, and their respective staffs. The two admirals liked and respected each other, and they tried diligently to establish a sound working relationship. Similarly their staffs strived to get organized, yet intolerable delays and conflicts persisted. Japan was conquering the Pacific, and German submarines were off America's shores. The President solved the problem in March 1942 by sending Stark to Europe and making King both COMINCH *and* CNO.

King's immediate priorities were to stop Japan and, together with Marshall, to work with the British Chiefs of Staff to develop a unified Allied strategy. Given the many wartime crises demanding his attention, the admiral could give only a portion of his time to the Battle of the Atlantic. Accordingly, he delegated the immediate responsibility for fighting submarines in American waters to Vice Admiral Adolphus Andrews, an Annapolis classmate who commanded the Eastern Sea Frontier headquartered in New York City. The actual ships and planes that would have to fight the submarines, however, were commanded by Admiral Royal R. Ingersoll, who had relieved King as CINCLANT.

This arrangement was unwieldy and manifested the difficulty of defending against a well-coordinated submarine campaign. Andrews' staff was unprepared for its task; it initially had been organized almost solely for the general supervision of the Third Naval District's mundane shore establishments. The headquarters, in downtown New York City, had neither the control nor the communication facilities necessary to effectively deploy the polyglot air and surface ASW forces scattered from Maine to Florida. Ingersoll never could give Andrews the numbers of forces the latter requested because of Atlantic Fleet commitments to escort trans-Atlantic convoys and later to support amphibious operations in North Africa. On the other hand, Andrews was reluctant to return his assigned ships to Ingersoll without a direct order from King. Furthermore, Ingersoll, following Navy tradition, had established his headquarters on a small flagship that frequently was underway, thereby complicating communications with Washington and New York.* Much like Andrews' New York headquarters, Ingersoll's flagship was not equipped with the command and control facilities for coordinating the American ASW effort.[29]

*In contrast, Nimitz as CINCPAC recognized that a flagship was impractical and established his headquarters ashore at Pearl Harbor.

By the end of February 1942, Doenitz's small submarine force had sunk some 31 ships off the east coast.[30] Admiral Andrews would not form convoys because he had nothing with which to protect them, so merchantmen continued to steam independently at the mercy of the submarines. Tankers in particular were frequent victims. The frustrated American ASW forces—such as they were—had not sunk a single submarine, owing to their haphazard employment by Andrews.[31] Worried oil company representatives asked to meet with the War and Navy Departments to discuss the status of their diminishing fleet of oil tankers. The meeting convened on March 4, 1942.

The civilians showed slight confidence in Navy and Army efforts thus far and correctly suspected that the services still did not comprehend the magnitude of the submarine threat. Accordingly, they began by stating that tankers were being sunk faster than they could be replaced and that ships delayed sailing because their crews feared going to sea. Sooner or later, they insisted, there would be a "real shortage" of oil on the east coast. Only so much could be delivered by means other than tankers. Could not more protection be provided?

The service representatives replied that adequate ASW escorts and aircraft were unavailable. The existing forces were needed elsewhere for high-priority commitments. They argued that everything possible was being done. The representatives of the oil companies were doubtful, and they cited some rather elementary measures that would protect the tankers, yet not require ships and planes. For example, the coastal cities were still brightly illuminated at night, thereby silhouetting passing ships. Couldn't the Army and Navy get them darkened? The service spokesmen countered that there was no federal law, and that so far the cities had been uncooperative. Miami Beach, for example, did not want to inconvenience its visitors during the peak tourist season.

The civilians persisted. If the services could not protect the merchantmen, could not the Navy at least route them closer to the coast and allow them to enter protected harbors at night? The Navy responded that it "would look into it." Finally, another civilian announced that he was forming a volunteer corps of civilian fliers to "combat the submarine menace." Although they would be unarmed, they could at least report any submarines they saw as well as increase the morale of the tanker crews, "who now complain that they seldom see any protecting aircraft." The Army responded that it had no objection.[32]

The remarkable aspect about this conference is that these initiatives came from oil company civilians rather than from professional naval and army officers. In any event, by mid-May the services were able to enforce coastal blackouts, and by early April a partial convoy system was established whereby merchantmen were escorted by small craft by day and stayed overnight in protected anchorages. Also as a result of

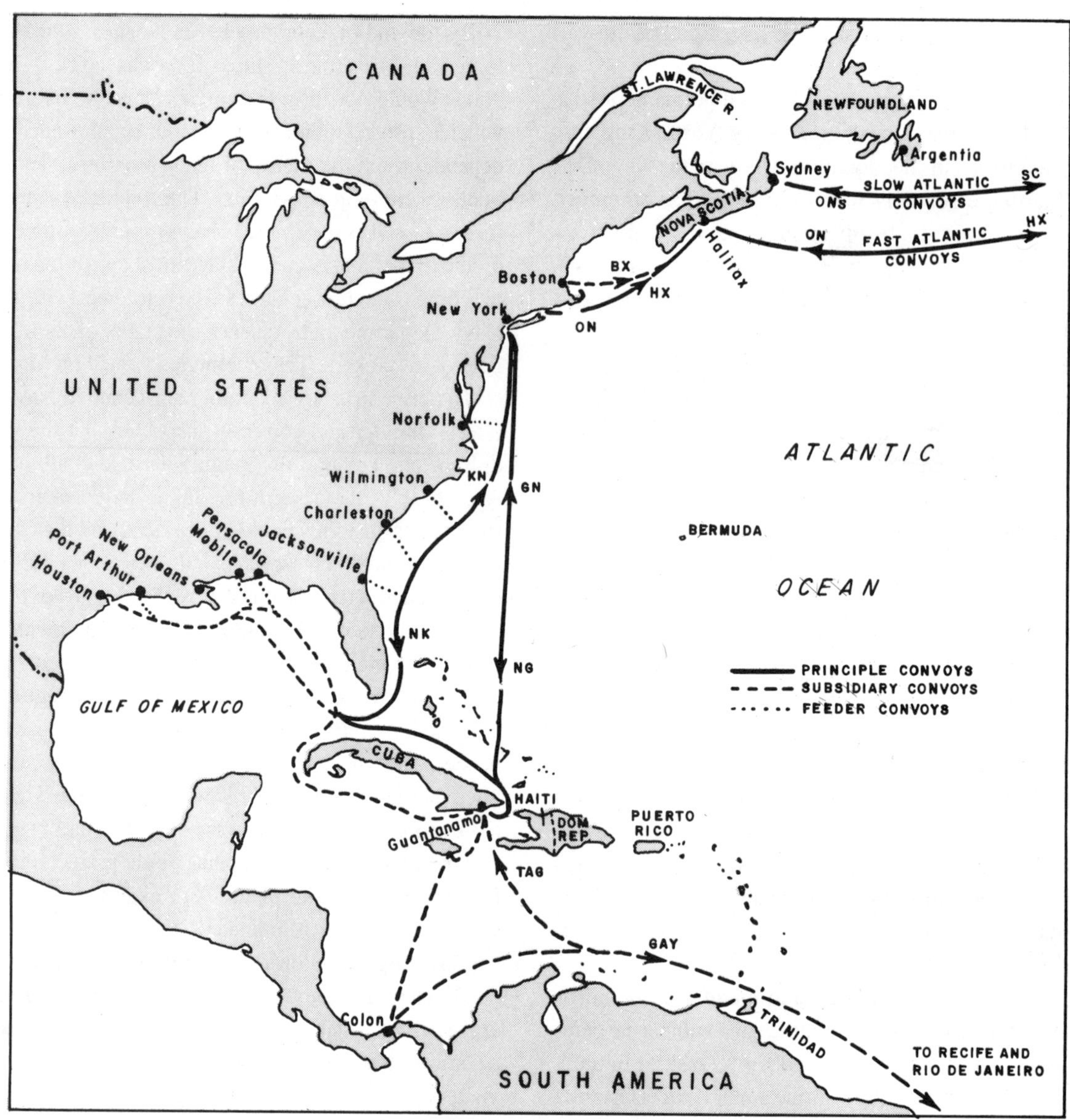

The Interlocking Convoy System, 1942

this meeting the War Department volunteered to loan its aircraft to help protect coastal shipping,[33] the effects of which were described earlier.

Soon after the meeting with the oil companies (and perhaps prodded by their suggestions) Admiral King appointed an informal board consisting of representatives from his own staff and from the major commands primarily involved with ASW. He charged them with developing a comprehensive plan for organizing convoys in the Western Hemisphere. King was convinced that a system of escorted convoys was mandatory. "Escort is not just one way of handling the submarine menace," he maintained, "it is the only way that gives any promise of success. The so-called hunting and patrol operations have time and again proved futile."[34]

In late March the board submitted recommendations which King subsequently approved and ordered implemented. The plan, known as the Interlocking Convoy System, made optimum use of the available ASW protection, matching it to the numbers of merchantmen that had to be protected. The Interlocking Convoy System was controlled by a schedule that resembled that used by railroads. The plan was a complex yet ingenious matrix that was designed to provide maximum protection with a minimum amount of delay in delivering cargoes to their destination.

It probably was the best possible plan under the circumstances, yet it still could not compensate for lack of ASW escorts and aircraft nor the strategy of Doenitz to shift his forces about in conformance with his tonnage theory. German submarines soon were operating in the Gulf of Mexico and the Caribbean, and Allied shipping losses throughout 1942 continued to be astronomical. As the east coast ASW forces became stronger and better organized, Doenitz was forced to

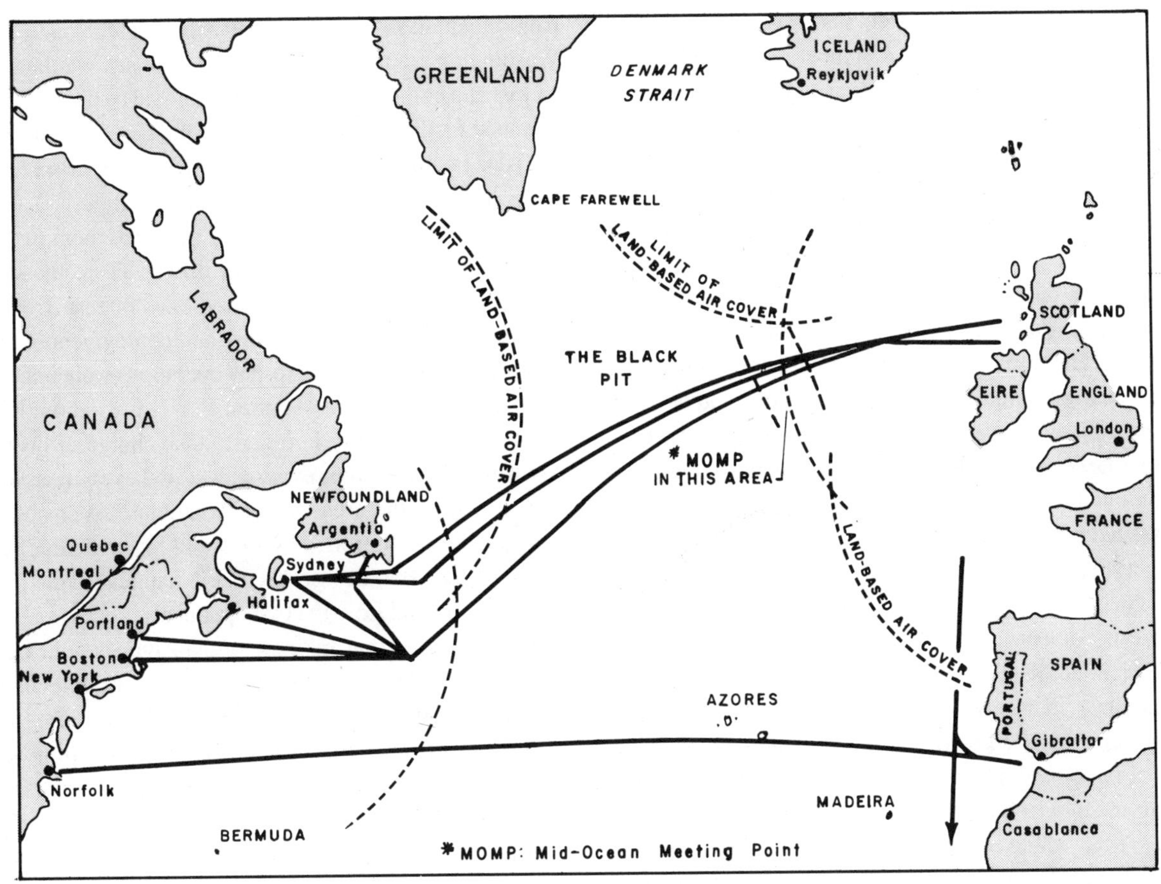

North Atlantic Convoy System, 1942

back off from the coastal convoys, but Allied shipping losses throughout the Atlantic progressively worsened.

Without question, Doenitz was winning the 1942 Battle of the Atlantic, at least statistically. In the Atlantic and Arctic Oceans, German submarines sank over 1,000 merchantmen at a loss of only 106 German and Italian submarines worldwide. Total allied shipping losses worldwide for all causes was 8.33 million tons, with some 5.7 million of this to submarines in the Atlantic. Merchantman construction lagged destruction, as Doenitz had hoped.

Meanwhile, Doenitz was building submarines at the rate of one per day by July 1942, and during a nine-month period in mid-1942 he averaged 75 submarines on station in the Atlantic. During all of 1942, American efforts to sink German submarines had been futile—only 16 destroyed in 12 months.[35] To King and the other naval leaders it was clear that the Allies had to find a way to sink German submarines faster than the Germans could build replacements.

Winning the Battle: 1943

President Roosevelt, Prime Minister Churchill, and the Combined Chiefs of Staff (CCS) met at Casablanca in January 1943 to determine future strategy for the war against the Axis. The Battle of the Atlantic was a top priority item in their discussion.

The British and Canadians thus far had borne the greatest load in the Battle of the Atlantic. Their ASW equipment and techniques were similar to—and often better than—those of the Americans, but a detailed discussion of their campaigns is beyond the scope of this chapter. During 1942, the Allied ASW forces had suffered from a lack of coordination, which often wasted or misdirected their already meager resources. For example, senior commanders failed to confer on common strategy or to exchange intelligence information and technical data. A team effort was badly needed in order to defeat the German submarine force.

The crux of the problem was whether to combine the ASW forces for joint operations, or to assign each country a zone of responsibility in which to conduct independent ASW operations. King supported the latter alternative. Despite their similarities, there still existed far too many differences in naval doctrine and procedures between the navies of the three countries, differences which King believed would cripple joint operations. Let's work together, King advocated, but each in his own part of the ocean.

It was a terribly complex problem that was not going to be solved at Casablanca. The limited numbers of conferees had time only to agree that the problem was very serious indeed, and that a solution would require a great deal of additional study and effort. King, however, did offer some more immediate suggestions. He wanted to hit the submarines before they went to sea, and in his mind Great Britain had the available means in its long-range strategic bombing force. Great Britain was then engaged in a campaign of rather inaccurate nighttime bombing against German cities, which to King was a wasted effort. He urged instead that British bombers concentrate on attacking submarine factories, shipyards, and bases in order to get to them at their source. The Royal Air Force preferred other targets, considering them to be more strategically important, but it reluctantly agreed to divert some raids to submarine-related targets.[36]

A few weeks later, King's British counterpart, Admiral of the Fleet Sir Dudley Pound, wrote King about the initial results. British bombers had attacked the German submarine base at Lorient; although there was much superficial damage, the submarines themselves were unscathed because their moorings were protected beneath heavy bomb-proof concrete shelters. "I hope very much that we shall now go on to other ports," wrote Pound, "but there is a very strong party here who wants to get the whole bombing effort back again on to Germany."[37] Pound, however, was pleased that at Casablanca, King had recommended a joint conference to reorganize Atlantic convoy control in order to better coordinate Allied ASW efforts.

The so-called Washington Convoy Conference convened in great secrecy in Washington on March 1, 1943. There were perhaps a hundred participants, including a score of flag and general officers, all representing the navies and air forces of the United States, Great Britain, and Canada. They comprised their countries' finest ASW talent—commanders and staff officers who had been fighting German submarines for months and years. They had finally gathered together to discuss and develop a coordinated campaign that would win the Battle of the Atlantic. Ingersoll and his staff were conspicuously absent.

King opened the conference by stressing what he expected of the conferees; he was followed by other senior service representatives who had their say. King then withdrew and left them to their labors. When the conference ended 12 days later, the three countries had agreed to divide the ocean areas into zones of responsibility. Essentially, the British and Canadians retained control of North Atlantic convoys, and the United States became responsible for the central Atlantic as well as the Interlocking Convoy System. Other procedures which would insure Allied cooperation were agreed upon as well.[38]

The Battle of the Atlantic reached a crescendo in early 1943. Admiral King took control of American ASW forces from Ingersoll in order personally to direct the battle from his Washington COMINCH headquarters. The sea war had become so vast and complex that it no longer could be directed from the cramped facilities of Ingersoll's diminutive flagship.*

After taking tactical control of ASW away from Ingersoll, King assembled a specialized staff of about 50 men and women, officers and enlisted, and stationed them in a control room near his Navy Department office. There the staff collected intelligence on submarine movements from many sources, and directed the routing and deployment of convoys and ASW forces. The day-to-day operations were under the direct supervision of Rear Admiral F. S. Low, whom King had recalled from sea duty in order to take charge of his new organization. Every ship, every plane, and every merchantman that moved in the areas under American responsibility was monitored and controlled by Low and his staff. In effect, the Battle of the Atlantic had become a nautical game of chess, with Doenitz and Low the two opponents.

King decided that his new organization would be designated "Tenth Fleet," and that he would be the commander. Yet in reality it had not a ship to call its own, because the forces remained under Ingersoll's nominal command. But now Ingersoll had been reduced to the role of executor of orders emanating from Tenth Fleet headquarters.[39]

Allied technology and industry finally were providing the numbers of sophisticated ships and aircraft needed to overwhelm Doenitz. The North Atlantic convoys now enjoyed almost continuous land-based air protection. In those areas beyond range of land-based aircraft, increased numbers of convoy escorts fitted with radar and improved weapons rammed through the German wolfpacks. Thus, during May 1943, Doenitz lost 41 submarines, and withdrew his dwindling numbers into the relative safety of the central Atlantic. It was the final blow to his "tonnage theory." By July, merchantman production exceeded losses; it would continue to do so for the remainder of the war. As a result, during the 12 months preceding the invasion of Normandy, convoys bearing arms and men to the British Isles passed unopposed.

Doenitz continued to shift his forces from one area of the ocean to another, probing for a weakness in the Allied protection of its convoys. None could be found. Allied ships and aircraft seemed to be everywhere. Beginning in mid-1943, escort carriers provided air cover to convoys everywhere on the oceans. The carriers also operated offensively as "hunter-killer" groups, attacking German submarines which had betrayed their positions by radio transmissions.† In October 1944, Por-

*The remainder of this chapter will focus largely on the American effort, although British and Canadian ASW forces were correspondingly important.

†German submarines communicated excessively by low-frequency, long-range radio. The Allied radio detection stations intercepted the bearings of these transmissions and the Tenth Fleet staff then could plot the submarines' locations. Allied code breakers also were able to determine submarine locations by decrypting intercepted messages.

tugal allowed the Allies to construct airbases in the Azores to provide land-based air coverage in the central Atlantic, and the Allied landings in Normandy in June 1944 soon rendered untenable the submarine bases in France. Germany continued to sink allied shipping until war's end, but she had lost the Battle of the Atlantic by mid-1943.

Conclusions

Allied industry, science, and technology finally defeated the German submarine threat. It had been a battle for which neither side had planned and for which neither had been prepared.

In the beginning the Germans exercised the greatest initiative and were rewarded with initially great success. There would have been even greater success had Hitler understood the concepts of sea power. But under Raeder's influence he wasted valuable industrial resources on a surface fleet that never hoped to challenge the Royal Navy. All the German leaders—Hitler, Raeder, and Doenitz—failed to grasp the potential of submarine warfare. However, it is difficult to fault them too seriously, because the Allied professional naval strategists, as well, never could have predicted the effect of submarine warfare on the ultimate course of the Second World War.

Once the Battle of the Atlantic was underway, the American strategists initially were slow to perceive the dangers posed by the German submarines. But with time they saw all too clearly that the United States was losing control of the sea, and they instinctively drew upon all the resources inherent in a great sea power to develop whatever new weapons, tactics, and strategy were needed to defeat the submarine. The Allies were flexible and ingenious, willing to try new concepts and techniques, to exploit those that worked, and to discard those that failed. With sea power resources at their disposal and with intelligent, adaptable leaders who knew how to use these resources, it was inevitable that the Allies eventually would win the Battle of the Atlantic.

The German submarine was but a single weapon which changed little during the war. Allied technology eventually overcame the initial advantages enjoyed by the submarine. Allied technology developed radar, sonar, improved aircraft, and escort carriers—and all in quantity because of America's industrial capacity. German technology could not keep pace, and German submarine improvements (such as the snorkel*)

*An air intake and exhaust trunk that allowed the submarine to operate its diesel engines while submerged at periscope depth.

The Escort Carrier (CVE)

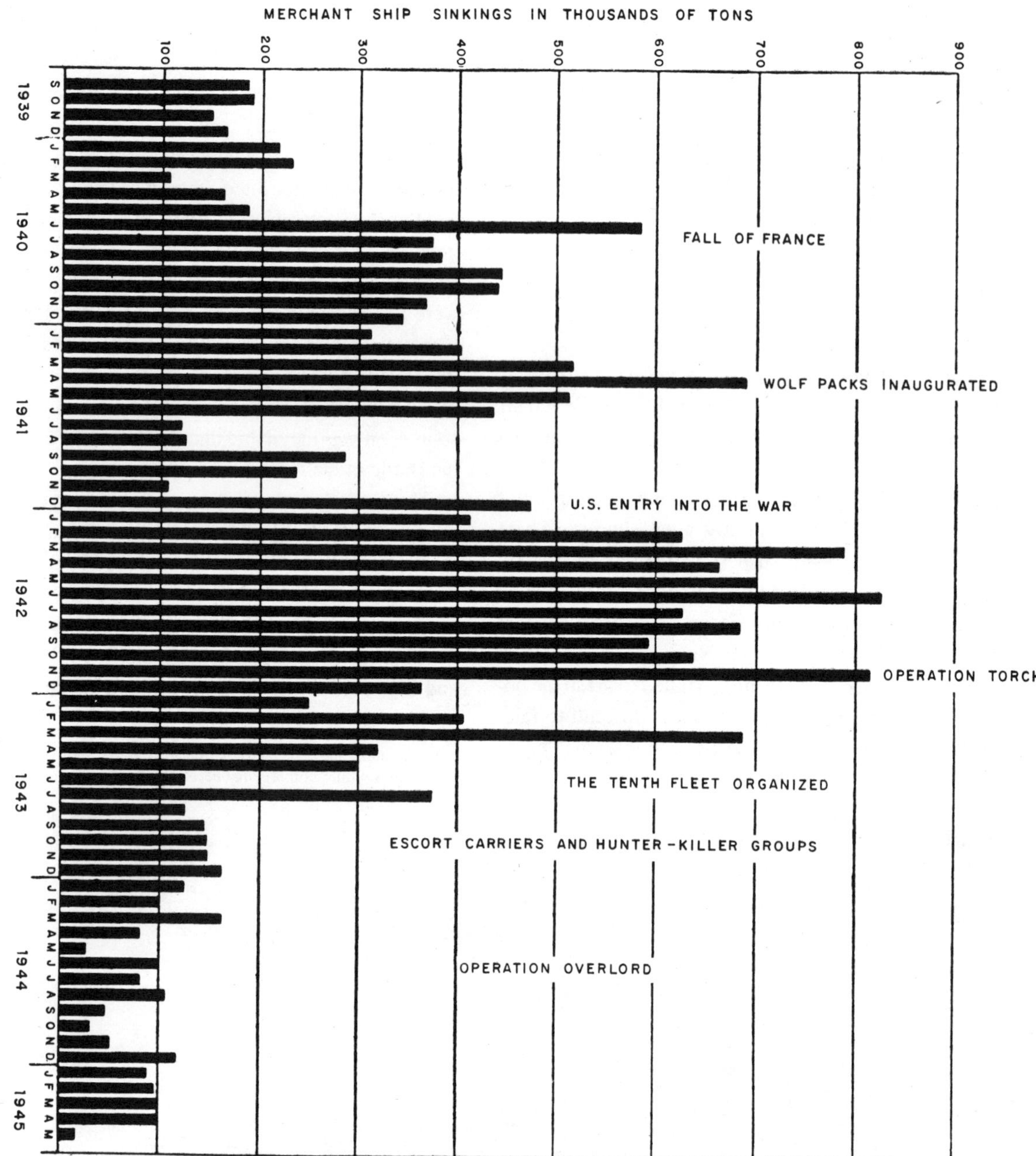

Merchant Ship Losses to U-Boats

were too few and too late. In the end, the submarine, alone and unsupported by the other elements of sea power, was overwhelmed by the quantity, diversity, and technical superiority of the Allied ASW forces.

One aspect of the Battle of the Atlantic which has received scant attention until recent years is the role played by ULTRA. One author, probably exaggerating, goes so far as to say that "Ultra was the hub of the whole Atlantic battle."[40] That it was important, however, cannot be denied. The critical breakthrough for the British came in May 1941, when a Royal Navy boarding party captured intact a U-boat's Enigma cipher machine and all its code books, which covered a three-month period. Shortly thereafter, the cryptanalysts penetrated the German Submarine Command's Hydra cipher which was used with Enigma. Exploiting this significant advantage, the British were now able to track many submarine locations and divert convoys from U-boat traps. Then and later, however, in both British and American circles, the operating commands had to be careful not to make diversions too obvious, lest the secret of ULTRA be compromised. Inevitably, this led to occasional merchant ships being sacrificed.

British joy turned to dismay in February 1942 when the Germans switched the U-boats to a new cipher called Triton. The British cryptanalysts were stymied until December, when

Triton was finally penetrated. Prior to December, Allied tonnages sunk drastically increased, partially due to the lack of ULTRA, but also as a result of the devastating German assault on American coastal shipping (PAUKENSCHLAG). During this time three interrelated events were unfolding and having an effect on the battle. The first of these was an inquiry into German signal security ordered by Doenitz in January 1943; the British seemed to have disconcertingly accurate information about U-boat locations, and Doenitz wanted to know its source. Fortunately for the Allies, that inquiry concluded that the Triton cipher had not been broken and that the British were obtaining their information from airborne radar and shore-based direction-finding equipment. About this same time, based on information gleaned from Triton intercepts, the British became convinced that the Germans had broken their convoy codes and were reading messages giving instructions to the convoys. Indeed they were, and had been doing so for some time. Accordingly, by May 1943, the convoy codes had been changed, drying up an important German source of intelligence. The third event was the American adoption of the British system for operational intelligence and submarine tracking in mid-1942. This was accompanied by the British sharing of ULTRA information with the newly created American tracking center and extremely close coordination between the intelligence apparatus of the two navies. Thus, by the middle of 1943, the Battle of the Atlantic had swung in favor of the Allies, affected in no small measure by ULTRA, but also due to the operational measures and technical advances previously discussed.[41]

Germany as a land power ultimately had to be defeated by decisive land battles on the Continent, but the western part of the land campaign could only succeed after the Allies gained control of the vital Atlantic sea lines of communication. It required overwhelming sea power to defeat the massive land power of Nazi Germany.

In retrospect, Mahan's theory of mercantile warfare was again proven to be valid. In the Wars of Napoleon I, the French had tried to defeat Great Britain by attacking her merchant marine; France failed and eventually lost the war. Doentiz's submarines similarly attacked unprotected merchantmen and avoided Allied warships, just as Napoleon's fleet had avoided Nelson's warships. Germany also failed and eventually lost the war to the Allies.

Doenitz never could have had enough naval power for a decisive fleet action. That, Mahan would have declared, was a virtual guarantee that Germany never could have hoped to defeat the United States and Great Britain. To be sure, the German submarines caused economic hardships, especially in Great Britain, and they undoubtedly prolonged the war; yet they never really threatened the ultimate outcome of the war. Allied victory was inevitable.

Notes

[1]E. B. Potter and C. W. Nimitz (eds.), *Sea Power: A Naval History* (Englewood Cliffs, 1960), pp. 474-475.

[2]Clay Blair, Jr., *Silent Victory: The U.S. Submarine War Against Japan* (Philadelphia and New York, 1975), Part I, pp. 46-69.

[3]Patrick Abbazia, *Mr. Roosevelt's Navy: The Private War of the U.S. Atlantic Fleet* (Annapolis, 1975), pp. 16-21, 160-161.

[4]Samuel Eliot Morison, *The Battle of the Atlantic* (Boston, 1948), pp. 3-4.

[5]*Ibid.*, p. 5.

[6]Ladislas Farago, *The Tenth Fleet* (New York, 1962), pp. 31-38.

[7]Potter and Nimitz, *Sea Power*, p. 547.

[8]*Ibid.*, p. 548.

[9]Ernest J. King and Walter M. Whitehill, *Fleet Admiral King: A Naval Record* (New York, 1952), pp. 324-326.

[10]Letter, Frank Knox to Ernest J. King, January 27, 1941, Ernest J. King Papers, Library of Congress.

[11]The above section was based principally upon Abbazia, *Mr. Roosevelt's Navy*.

[12]*Morison, Battle of the Atlantic*, pp. 95-98.

[13]Letter, Ernest J. King to C. W. Nimitz, November 10, 1941, King Papers.

[14]Data compiled from Potter and Nimitz, *Sea Power*, Chapter 30.

[15]This section is based largely upon data contained in Morison, *Battle of the Atlantic*, pp. 252-265.

[16]*Ibid.*, p. 126.

[17]Potter and Nimitz, *Sea Power*, pp. 552-553.

[18]*Ibid.*, pp. 552-553; Morison, *Battle of the Atlantic*, pp. 126-135.

[19]Robert C. Albion, "Makers of Naval Policy, 1798-1947" (Unpublished Manuscript, c. 1950), Harvard Univ. Library, p. 741. See also Morison, *Battle of the Atlantic*, p. 229.

[20]Albion, "Makers of Naval Policy," p. 741.

[21]Robert C. Albion and Robert H. Connery, *Forrestal and the Navy* (New York, 1962), pp. 116-120. See also Julius A. Furer, *Administration of the Navy Department in World War II* (Washington, D.C., 1959), pp. 675-676.

[22]Quoted in Morison, *Battle of the Atlantic*, p. 230.

[23]Letter, Ernest J. King to Carl Vinson, January 10, 1942, King Papers.

[24]Memorandum, Admiral King to all Bureaus and Offices of the Navy Department, May 4, 1942, King Papers.

[25]Morison, *Battle of the Atlantic*, p. 235.

[26]*The War Reports of Fleet Admiral Ernest J. King* (Philadelphia and New York, 1947), p. 758.

[27]Morison, *Battle of the Atlantic*, pp. 237-251.

[28]AAF ASW folder, Buell-Whitehill Collection, in the permanent possession of the author.

[29]Morison, *Battle of the Atlantic*, pp. 205-209, describes this organization but is far too charitable in his assessment of its effectiveness.

[30]*Ibid.*, p. 413.

[31]Potter and Nimitz, *Sea Power*, p. 553.

[32]Memorandum, R. S. Edwards to Ernest J. King, March 4, 1942, King Papers.

[33]*Ibid.*

[34]Quoted in Potter and Nimitz, *Sea Power*, p. 553.

[35]Morison, *Battle of the Atlantic*, pp. 410-415. For building rates, see Potter and Nimitz, *Sea Power*, p. 556.

[36]Minutes of King conference with newsmen, February 19, 1943, Buell-Whitehill Collection.

[37]Letter, Dudley Pound to Ernest J. King, February 18, 1943, King Papers.

[38]Conference Report, March 1-12, 1943, White House Map Room Collection, Box 169, File A/16-3, Franklin D. Roosevelt Library, Hyde Park, New York.

[39]Farago, *The Tenth Fleet*, gives the most detailed account of the Tenth Fleet.

[40]F. W. Winterbotham, *The Ultra Secret* (New York, 1974), p. 84.

[41]Anthony Cave Brown, *Bodyguard of Lies* (New York, 1975), pp. 251-259; Ronald Lewin, *Ultra Goes to War* (New York, 1978), pp. 204-220, 243-244.

Allied Victory in the Mediterranean: Sicily and Italy 10

The tyrant OVERLORD *dominated every action in the Italian theater.*

W. G. F. Jackson, The Battle for Italy

Long before the Axis troops in Tunisia surrendered, the Allies had decided on their next move. When the President, Prime Minister, and Combined Chiefs of Staff (CCS) met in Casablanca in January 1943, the British had convinced the Americans that ROUNDUP was not possible that year.* Since the stated Allied goal could not be obtained in 1943, the strategists had to find another way to fight Germany for the next 12 months.

Several alternatives had previously been studied and were reconsidered at Casablanca: (1) no land combat with the Axis, (2) an invasion of Sardinia, Sicily, Italy, Greece, or the Dodecanese Islands. *(See Map 33, in Atlas.)* While General George C. Marshall had said he would be content to avoid combat in 1942 and prepare for ROUNDUP in 1943, that option had been rejected by the heads of state. Americans were suspicious of British interest in the Balkans and vetoed action there. No one thought the Allied armies were strong enough to invade Italy; so only Sardinia and Sicily were left. The CCS believed that the capture of Sardinia would be easier, would place Allied forces in a position which would threaten both Rome and southern France, and would allow more effective bombing of Italian industrial areas. The capture of Sicily, on the other hand, would make the Mediterranean safe for shipping, would engage and destroy more German divisions, would capture more and better airfields from which to bomb southern Italy, and might cause the Italian Government to seek peace.

**See Chapter 8, p. 186.*

The Capture of Sicily

The CCS ultimately selected Sicily as the next target, but the reasons behind that selection differed between the Americans and the British. The Americans felt that the capture of Sicily would save shipping, use troops already in the theater, and provide a suitably final objective for campaigning in the Mediterranean—the Americans were anxious to get on with the invasion of France. The British liked Sicily as an objective because it would save shipping, would punish Italy, and might eliminate Italy from the war. At no time during the Casablanca debate was an invasion of Germany through Italy raised as a serious option. Previous staff studies had already discarded that route as too easily defended and too long.*[1]

Agreement on Sicily as the target had masked the Allies' differing fundamental approaches to strategy. The British believed in mobilizing strength and then using it as the situation dictated. Theirs was a flexible strategy which could take advantage of unexpected enemy weaknesses. The question to be answered at each decision point was, "What can we do next that will most hurt the Axis?" The Americans, on the other hand, approached the war using backward planning. Their ultimate goal was to defeat Germany, which could be accomplished by destroying the German Army. That Army could be forced to fight if the Fatherland were threatened with conquest, and the Fatherland could most easily be threatened with conquest from northwest Europe. Therefore, all mobilization should be directed toward the task of the invasion and the gigantic Napoleonic battle which would follow. To the American Chiefs, such strategic planning was necessary to guide American mobilization and allocation.[2]

*Churchill's famous phrase, "soft underbelly," was first coined by him to explain to Stalin why the Allies had launched TORCH, not as a name for a proposed route to Germany.

The Americans accepted Sicily as an objective because its capture would save the shipping so necessary for ROUNDUP. It also appeared to be a dead end; after Sicily was conquered, the Mediterranean would stop diverting strength from ROUNDUP. The British accepted it because it seemed to be a feasible operation and one that would most weaken the enemy at that time. At Casablanca, Marshall asked if Sicily was an end to operations in the Mediterranean or the first step to somewhere else. The British Chiefs were not prepared to say.[3] There was strength in the British logic, for it hardly seemed worthwhile to let good combat divisions lie idle for a year after Sicily was captured and before ROUNDUP could be launched. Failure to look further ahead at Casablanca was to cause the Allies to fight in Italy, when some other place in the Mediterranean might have been better.

There was no corresponding debate between Mussolini and Hitler. After the fall of Tunis, Italy was completely dominated by Germany, upon whom she depended for equipment, fuel, and even reinforcements. Italy no longer controlled her own destiny; she had become a German pawn, and her only escape was to negotiate with the Allies—whose only terms were unconditional surrender.

Within the German armed forces there were two major opinions on German strategy in the Mediterranean for 1943. The Rommel school believed that the Italians were a worthless asset and that once the Allies made their next move, Germany should abandon Sardinia, Sicily, most of Greece, and all of Italy below the Pisa-Rimini Line. *(See Map 51, in Atlas.)* The troops released by the withdrawal could be thrown against Russia. Fieldmarshal Albert Kesselring, Commander-in-Chief South (the Mediterranean area), led the opposite school. Being an airman, he did not want to give freely to the Allies airbases within range of German industry and Rumanian oilfields. He believed the Italians would fight for their homeland, and that with a little equipment and a few German divisions the Italian Army would keep the Allies far away from southern Germany.

Hitler made no decision on Sicily and Italy, but he refused to consider abandoning Greece. He ordered 6 new divisions into the Balkans, raising the garrison there to 13. Since he hated to lose territory, Hitler was disposed toward Kesselring's ideas. He reconstituted the 90th Division in Sardinia and the 15th Panzer Division in Sicily. Both divisions had been destroyed in Tunis. The Hermann Goering Panzer Division and the 16th Panzer Division—new divisions named for ones destroyed at Stalingrad—were also sent to southern Italy. Having received hints that the Italians might surrender, however, he ordered a plan for the disarming of all Italian divisions to be followed by a German occupation of northern Italy to the Pisa-Rimini Line. Rommel was notified that he would command German forces in Italy if plan ACHSE were executed. Ger many thus awaited the next move of the Allies, with Kesselring in command of forces positioned to defend in accordance with his concept but with a detailed plan and a new commander in case the Rommel school of thought proved correct.[4]

Immediately after the Casablanca Conference, General Dwight D. Eisenhower's planners began detailed planning of the assault on Sicily—known as HUSKY. These men, who were responsible for planning the first major opposed amphibious operation since Gallipoli, considered three requirements essential for success: control of the sea, control of the air, and quick seizure of port facilities. The first caused no problem, for the Royal Navy reigned supreme in the Mediterranean. Sicily contained 30 airfields located in three groups. Because Allied fighters would be operating at extreme range, it would be necessary to seize these complexes as soon as possible. The planners estimated that the Allies would need a port capacity of 6,000 tons per day to sustain its ground and air forces ashore. The solution to the air control and port problems constituted a dual assault, one on the western tip and one on the southern tip. That was what the original plan proposed. *(See Map, p. 229).*

The CCS had selected the HUSKY commanders at Casablanca. General Eisenhower would be supreme commander. Admiral Sir Andrew B. Cunningham would command all naval forces, and Air Chief Marshal Sir Arthur Tedder would direct all air forces. General Sir Harold R. L. G. Alexander would command the 15th Army Group consisting of two Armies, the Seventh (under fiery Major General George S. Patton) and the Eighth (under methodical General Sir Bernard L. Montgomery). Unfortunately, when the planners produced their scheme, all the future HUSKY commanders were busy fighting the campaign in Tunisia, and each was located at a different headquarters.[5]

When Montgomery saw the plan, he strongly objected to a dual assault. In essence, he claimed that to satisfy the logisticians and airmen the armies were to be landed beyond mutual supporting distance and would be dangerously weak, inviting defeat in detail. Cunningham and Tedder disagreed with him, but Montgomery's reputation as the only winning Allied commander to date was such that, after much controversy, HUSKY was altered to consist of a single strong assault on Sicily's southern tip.[6] *(Final plan and order of battle are shown on Map 45, in Atlas.)*

In Sicily, the Italian Sixth Army under General Alfredo Guzzoni theoretically consisted of eight coastal divisions, four Italian mobile divisions, and two German divisions. (The Hermann Goering division had crossed to Sicily in June.) In reality, the German liaison officer to the Sixth Army, Lieutenant General Fridolin von Senger und Etterlin, controlled the German divisions and dominated Guzzoni. Additionally, Hermann Goering took special interest in "his" division and often sent orders directly to it. The worthless coastal divisions, composed of local troops, could be relied on only to report a land-

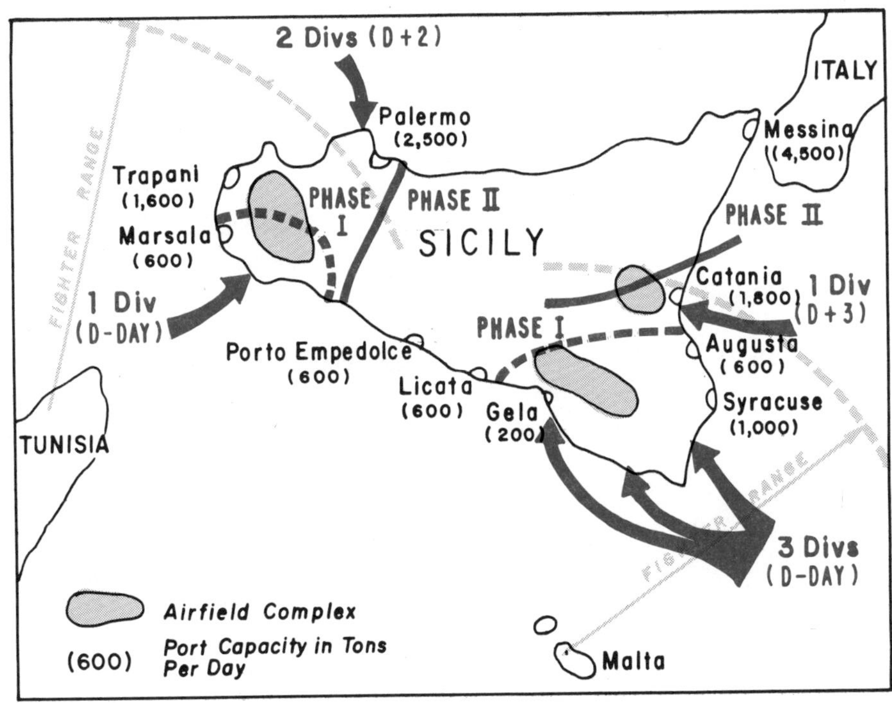

Airfield Complexes, Port Capacity, and Initial Allied Plan for Invasion of Sicily

ing and to fire a few shots before fleeing; therefore, the main defensive problem was determining where to position the six mobile divisions.[7] It was the same quandary that would befuddle the Germans one year later at Normandy. Should the invading divisions be destroyed by local reserves as they were trying to establish a beachhead, or should the defender wait to determine the main attack, then counterattack it with all his reserves from a central position? Senger und Etterlin favored the latter, Kesselring the former. Accordingly, the mobile divisions were dispersed *(See Map 45, in Atlas)* and ordered to launch immediate counterattacks on any Allied landing. That dispersal had been furthered by an Allied deception plan which simulated an assault at Trapani and caused movement of the 15th Panzer Grenadier Division to the west.

On July 9, 1943, as Allied convoys from Tunisia, Algeria, Egypt, United Kingdom, and United States rendezvoused in the central Mediterranean, a strong wind whipped up a choppy sea, placing the airborne and amphibious landings in jeopardy. The meteorologist predicted improved weather, and Eisenhower, paralleling his famous later Normandy decision, ordered the landings executed. Transport aircraft and ships headed toward Sicily.

Both tactical commanders had decided to use their airborne resources against tactical objectives which would facilitate the seaborne assaults. Patton chose the high ground behind Gela for the 505th Parachute Regiment, and Montgomery chose the Ponte Grande Bridge between his landing beaches and German reserves in Syracuse for the Airlanding Brigade of the British 1st Airborne Division. The airborne units attacked about 2:30 A.M. on July 10. Both fared badly. High winds, poor navigation techniques, and improperly trained air crews scattered the 226 planeloads of the 505th all over southeastern Sicily, placing only one-eighth in their planned drop zones. Only 12 of the 137 British gliders being towed by USAAF C-47s and RAF bombers landed near the bridge. Tragically, 47 were released too early and fell into the sea with great loss of life. The few paratroopers who did reach their objectives delayed the movement of Axis reserves toward the landing beaches, but they could not stop them. Ironically, although ULTRA had pinpointed the location of the two German divisions, strict dissemination rules, which allowed access to such intelligence only at high levels, precluded Colonel James Gavin (commanding the 505th) being informed that his unit was jumping within striking distance of the *panzers*.[8]

Meanwhile, the ships in modern history's largest amphibious assault* approached their assigned debarkation points without incident. Just 15 minutes after the paratroopers jumped, soldiers waded ashore. The landing encountered all the problems associated with night amphibious operations in a high wind and swell: ships lowered the landing craft too far at sea, boat waves formed late, many boats missed their assigned beaches, some stuck on off-shore sandbars, and others capsized in the surf. In spite of these difficulties, the landings were

*Seven divisions in the amphibious assault echelon, as opposed to five divisions at Normandy.

remarkably successful because there was almost no resistance from the Sicilian coastal divisions.

In accordance with Axis defense plans, the Livorno and Hermann Goering Divisions counterattacked the American beaches, but with no success. Italian resistance, except for those four mobile divisions held in reserve, collapsed. The Syracuse garrison surrendered without firing a shot, and the Augusta garrison began destroying the harbor-defense guns even before British ships appeared. The Napoli Division was unable even to slow the Eighth Army. The only significant opposition came from Axis air elements, which harassed the American beaches throughout the day, sinking a destroyer and a minesweeper and hampering unloading operations on the beach.[9]

Although ashore, the 15th Army Group was not out of danger. Guzzoni planned a coordinated counterattack against the Americans at Gela the following day (July 11). The Livorno and Hermann Goering Divisions began attacking at 6:00 A.M. and made good progress until, by noon, German tanks were within 2,000 meters of the beach, firing on unloading parties. *(See Map 46, in Atlas.)* Determined resistance and, most important, massive naval gunfire stopped the attack and forced the Axis units back, with the loss of one-third of their tanks. Kesselring's strategy of stopping the invasion at the beaches with immediate counterattacks had failed; but in the words of Wellington, it was "the nearest-run thing you ever saw in your life."[10]

Patton ordered that the remainder of the 82nd Airborne Division be flown that night from its reserve location in Tunis and dropped on the beach to reinforce his Seventh Army. This simple plan led to one of the most tragic administrative mistakes of the war. As the transport aircraft approached the beach, they passed over the fleet which was still at battle stations following a German bomber attack 45 minutes earlier. One antiaircraft gun fired, followed quickly by all the other AA guns on ship and shore. Some of the 144 transports pressed on, some turned back, and 6 were shot down before dropping their paratroopers. Seventeen others were shot down on the return trip, and 37 were badly damaged.[11]

The following day Guzzoni, with Kesselring's approval, began a slow and systematic withdrawal to the San Stefano Line, with the ultimate intention of evacuating Sicily after achieving as much delay as possible. *(See Map 46, in Atlas.)* Hitler, in far off East Prussia, decided to take personal charge of operations in Sicily but, surprisingly, did not issue one of his infamous hold-at-all-cost orders. After German losses at Stalingrad and in Tunisia, German manpower was scarce. Hitler, appreciating this scarcity, ordered maximum delay consistent with the preservation of German strength. He sent air, antiair, and armored units to Sicily with instructions that they not be trapped there.[12] Thereafter, Axis forces delayed along a series of six lines as they withdrew toward Messina.

Alexander's original intention had been for the Eighth Army to conduct the main attack up Sicily's eastern coast while the Seventh Army covered the left flank and rear of the Eighth. But Montgomery's progress was slow because the majority of the German strength was astride that obvious avenue of approach, and because the lower slopes of Etna Volcano provided excellent defensive positions. On July 17, Patton, who was unhappy with his subordinate mission, presented Alexander with a plan for the Seventh Army to overrun western Sicily and capture the port of Palermo. Considering Montgomery's difficulties and Patton's aggressiveness, Alexander approved the plan. Encountering only Italian coas-

WIDE WORLD

Landing Craft Carry 3rd Infantry Division Troop Toward the Beach at Licata, Sicily

German Dive Bombers Attacking Allied Fleet Strike an Ammunition Ship

tal defense units—ULTRA had given Patton a pretty good idea of German dispositions—the Seventh Army entered Palermo on July 22, and captured the western tip of Sicily the following day. Alexander than placed the Seventh on line with the Eighth and gave it the mission of advancing along the northern coast to Messina.

On July 26, the Italian King, sensing the war weariness of his people, demanded Mussolini's resignation, placed him under arrest, and appointed an ex-chief of *Commando Supremo*, Marshal Pietro Badoglio, to replace him. With this unstable political situation at his rear, Kesselring ordered the evacuation of Sicily the following day. The Germans conducted a classic withdrawal, delaying on the San Stefano Line, then the San Fratello Line, and finally the Tortorici Line. The actual passage of German troops from Sicily to Italy began on August 11 while the Germans held on the Tortorici Line. As troop departures reduced on-line strength, they withdrew to a shorter line.

The Allies were unable to interfere significantly with the evacuation. Although they did force abandonment of the Tortorici Line 24 hours sooner than planned, the Germans held an extra day on Line 1. Eisenhower, assuming that the evacuation would be at night, did not concentrate heavy bombers over the Straits of Messina except at night. Actually, most boats crossed during the day under thick antiaircraft protection that kept fighters and light bombers at a safe distance. When the withdrawal ended on August 17, the results surpassed those at Gallipoli or Dunkirk, for the Germans had not only evacuated all their men and equipment, they had also carried with them all their supplies and even some local mules.*

The Invasion of Italy

While Alexander and Guzzoni were fighting the Sicilian campaign, Eisenhower and Hitler were wrestling with strategic decisions which would lead to long and indecisive combat in Italy. Because the Italian campaign was difficult and unrewarding, it spawned much postwar debate, critical opinion falling generally into two schools. British critics contend that the commitment of just a few more divisions and landing craft would have resulted in significant success, perhaps even opening a supplemental southern route of invasion into Germany.[14] American critics charge that the Italian campaign required too many resources which were needed for OVERLORD, and therefore should have been halted prior to the Normandy landing—at Naples or at Rome.[15]

*The Germans safely evacuated 39,569 Germans, 9,605 vehicles, 94 guns, 47 tanks, 1,100 tons of ammunition, 970 tons of fuel, and 15,700 tons of miscellaneous supplies. Italians evacuated 70,000 men, 250 vehicles, 75 artillery pieces, and 12 mules.[13]

To choose intelligently between these two extremes, one must first understand the strategic considerations that changed the Germany-first strategy into an Italy-first accomplishment. The TRIDENT conference met on May 12, 1943, just as the last Axis armies in Tunisia were surrendering. The well-prepared American delegates soon secured British agreement for a cross-channel invasion in May 1944, but the question of what to do with the troops already in the Mediterranean, of which OVERLORD would require only seven divisions, remained. The British Chiefs proposed eliminating Italy from the war, as that seemed to be a feasible course that would most harm the Axis during the remainder of 1943. The American JCS agreed that it would be desirable to force Italy to surrender, for that would require Germany to replace the Italian divisions in Russia, the Balkans, and Greece with German divisions and to form a defensive line somewhere in Italy. Thus, an Italian collapse might contribute substantially to the success of OVERLORD.

At the time of TRIDENT, however, the CCS were unable to plan the specific steps required to eliminate Italy, for futher operations in the Mediterranean depended on many unknowns that could only be answered after Sicily was invaded. Would the Italians fight determinedly in defense of their homeland? Would Allied amphibious doctrine prove adequate, or would it have to be significantly altered prior to the next landing? How many precious landing craft would be lost to surf and shell? The CCS decided to delay choosing the next Mediterranean target until such questions could be answered. Instead, they ordered Eisenhower to plan "such operations in exploitation of HUSKY as are best calculated to eliminate Italy from the war and to contain the maximum number of German forces."[16] Churchill and Marshall then flew to Eisenhower's headquarters to explain that the CCS anticipated either an invasion of Italy or an invasion of Sardinia followed by the bombing of Italy. The theater commander initiated several plans for both contingencies.

By July 17, Eisenhower had decided that the answers to the critical questions were favorable. The will of the Italian Army was broken; amphibious doctrine was sound; and landing craft losses in Sicily had only reduced the Allied lift capability from seven to six divisions.[17] He ordered his planners to concentrate on plans for an invasion of Italy.

At first, the planners were very cautious, predicting that a drive up the toe would reach only to the Castrovillari Isthmus by Christmas. The news of Mussolini's downfall, however, caused much bolder leaps to be considered. On August 16, the last full day of the Axis evacuation of Sicily, Eisenhower selected the most ambitious of the eight plans his staff had prepared for the invasion of Italy—AVALANCHE. Montgomery would launch BAYTOWN as a supporting attack. The CCS approved this plan at the QUADRANT Conference that opened in Quebec the next day.[18]

Shortly after deciding on AVALANCHE, Eisenhower learned that Italian emissaries were negotiating with Allied ministers in Portugal. Italy sought to switch sides in the war to avoid the consequences of unconditional surrender.[19]

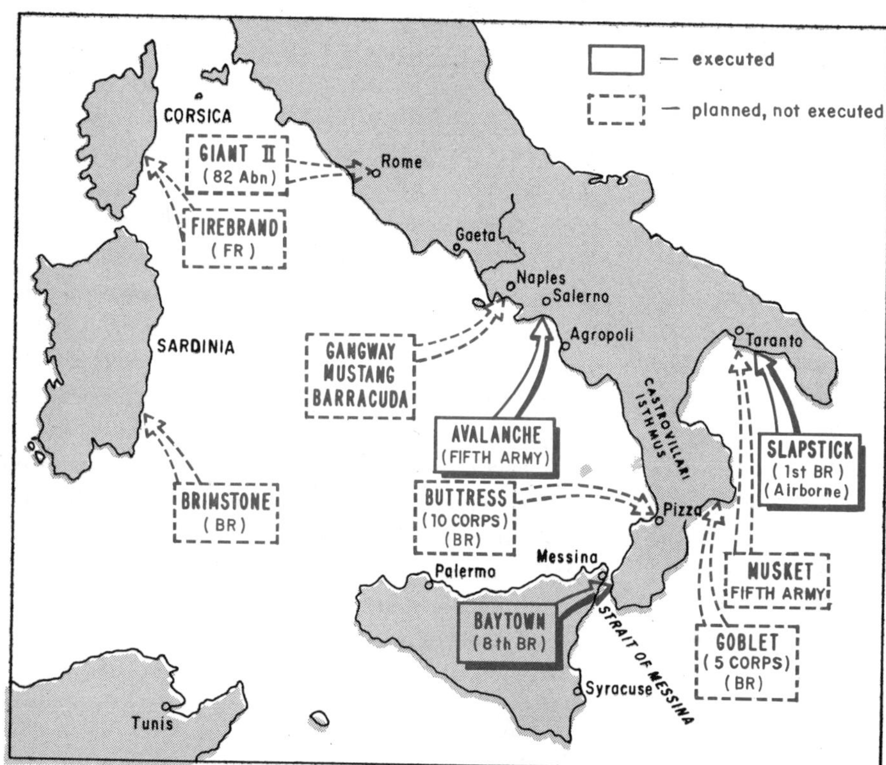

Post-HUSKY Contingency Plans

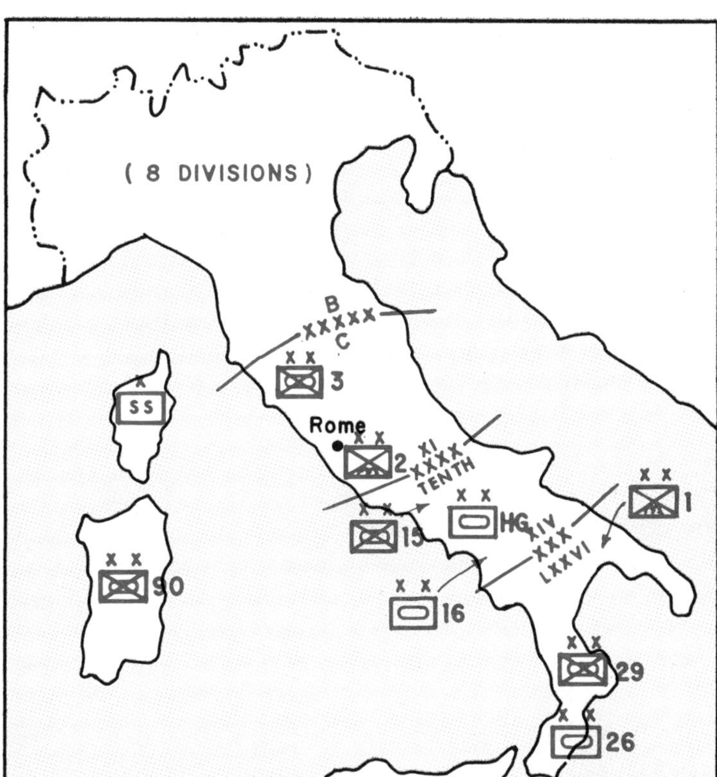

German Dispositions, September 3, 1943

Although the Italian surrender was signed on September 3, it was not to be announced until the eve of AVALANCHE. The Germans, however, were well aware of Italy's desire, if not intention, to quit the war. Accordingly, Hitler infiltrated German units into Italy. On the day the Italians signed the surrender, 16 German divisions were positioned in Italy. Five of these were reformed Stalingrad divisions which should have returned to the Eastern Front, one had been withdrawn intact from the Eastern Front, and ten had come from northwestern Europe. Thus, even before the landings, the Allies had accomplished their objective of drawing divisions from the OVERLORD area and the Eastern Front.[20]

The 16 German divisions in Italy were divided equally between Army Group B, commanded by Rommel, and Army Group C, later renamed Southwest and commanded by Kesselring. Each army group had two tasks. First, in the event of an Italian surrender, each was to disarm nearby Italian units and seize their equipment. Additionally, Rommel was to keep open the Alpine passes so that Kesselring's forces would not be trapped. Kesselring's second mission was to defeat any Allied landing. The Gela counterattack experience had convinced Kesselring that Allied landings must be defeated either during the landing itself or inland, beyond the range of Allied battleships. Therefore, he planned to deploy his units around the most likely beaches. In case defense at water's edge failed, he planned a series of defensive positions astride the Italian peninsula from which he would defend until able to counterattack. He was determined to give up nothing until forced, but if necessary, to withdraw slowly from position to position up to the Pisa-Rimini Line.[21] *(See Maps 47 and 51, in Atlas.)* Although Kesselring envisioned a determined fight in southern Italy, Hitler had accepted Rommel's philosophy on the uselessness of southern Italy. Consequently, he planned to withdraw to the Pisa-Rimini Line if the Italians defected and Kesselring was unable to prevent an Allied landing in strength.

On September 3, Montgomery's Eighth Army crossed the Straits of Messina (BAYTOWN). *(See Map 47, in Atlas.)* The Eighth advanced slowly north, delayed by thorough demolitions, mines, and a weak German rearguard. Kesselring, who felt certain that BAYTOWN was a supporting effort, continued to prepare for the main attack. That attack was scheduled to land at Salerno Bay on September 9. Salerno had been chosen because it was the furthermost suitable beach that could be covered by fighters based in Sicily. The rapid capture of a large port was essential to the Allied plan, since most landing craft had to be released for movement to England by November 1. An assault on Naples itself was infeasible because that port was heavily fortified. The Gulf of Gaeta, north of Naples, offered the best terrain for inland maneuver, but it had to be rejected because of its shallow beach gradient and distance from fighter bases in Sicily. Unfortunately for the Allies, the Germans had analyzed the situation exactly as had Eisenhower's planners; therefore, they had deployed the 16th Panzer Division in the hills overlooking Salerno Bay.[22]

In many ways, AVALANCHE was the most daring Allied amphibious operation in Europe up to that time. The enemy was stronger and better equipped, even after the Italian defection, than he had been anytime during TORCH. The assault forces were less than half the strength of the assault forces at Sicily, with three divisions in the initial landing and two follow-up divisions. Air support for AVALANCHE was less than that provided for Sicily because Eisenhower had been required to send three medium bomber groups to England for the combined bomber offensive. There were fewer landing craft available, and neither the Fifth Army commander, Lieutenant General Mark W. Clark, nor his two corps commanders had had experience in amphibious command.

At 6:30 P.M. on September 8, as Clark's Fifth Army steamed toward Salerno, Eisenhower announced the Italian surrender over radio. The Italian announcement followed at 7:45 P.M. over Rome radio. Invasion-bound troops began to relax; surely the Italian surrender would insure an easy landing. With luck one might even keep his feet dry. Ashore, however, the German Army executed plan ACHSE. Like most German general staff plans, ACHSE was executed rapidly and efficiently. By 3:30 A.M., September 9, when the invasion fleet began transloading to landing craft in Salerno Bay, the 16th Panzer Division, having disarmed and dispersed the Italian division in its area, sat waiting behind its guns. *(See Map 47, in Atlas.)*

Naval execution of AVALANCHE was much improved over the ragged Sicilian assault. Landing craft loaded quickly, kept station well, and arrived at shore on time and usually at the right spot. Clark's two corps commanders, Major General Ernest T. Dawling and Lieutenant General Sir Richard L. McCreery, had decided to forego pre-invasion bombardment to obtain both tactical and strategic surprise. Unfortunately, they were to have neither. A shore battery opened up on the X Corps as it was loading into landing craft. Warships immediately answered with a prearranged contingency bombardment on the X Corps beaches, but Dawling still refused to bring fire on his beaches since they were 10 miles south of the British beaches, and he hoped that he had not lost surprise.

In an eerie silence, the 36th Division's landing craft ground ashore. As coxswains dropped boat ramps, the Germans responded with a hail of fire, fortunately most of it too high. All during that day both the X Corps and the 36th Division crawled ahead, but neither reached its D-Day objective.[23]

The Battle of Salerno fell into three general phases. The first comprised the landings, successful though costly, for even without surprise one *panzer* division could not defend 30 miles of beach against three reinforced divisions. The second phase, September 10-13, was a reinforcement race to determine which side could bring the most strength to bear at the critical point. During September 10 and 11, each Allied commander took positive action to move more combat power to Salerno. Clark landed the floating reserve division. The CCS diverted to Salerno 18 Landing Ship, Tank (LST) already en route to England. Alexander ordered Montgomery to speed his advance up the toe; however, Monty failed to comply. Cunningham steamed two cruisers and two battleships into the bay to provide additional fire support, and employed smaller warships as troop transports. On September 13, Clark asked Major General Matthew B. Ridgway to bring his 82nd Airborne Division to Salerno, by dropping administratively on the beach behind the American lines. Ridgway arranged transport and jumped that night, this time avoiding the Navy in his approach to the drop zones. Eisenhower asked for and received CCS permission to place strategic bombers in direct support of the beachhead.[24]

On the German side, Kesselring ordered the 26th Panzer and the 29th Panzer Grenadier Divisions to leave only rearguards facing the Eighth Army and to move to Salerno. He also ordered the 15th Panzer Grenadier Division down from Rome. The *Luftwaffe* increased its air attacks on Allied ships in the bay, for the first time using radio-controlled glide bombs. These "smart bombs" heavily damaged three cruisers and one battleship.

The third phase of the Battle of Salerno, the counterattack, began on September 12, reached its highest intensity on the fourteenth, and ended on the sixteenth. During this phase, Kesselring threw his three *panzer* divisions and three *panzer grenadier* divisions against the five Allied infantry and airborne divisions. He probed the entire beachhead, but the main attack struck the American VI Corps astride the Sele River. German armor pushed the Allies back to their D + 1 positions. Although Kesselring had managed to move more and heavier divisions to the battlefield than had the Allies, his counterattacks were eventually shattered by strategic bombers, massive naval gunfire, and a determined stand by Allied forces that included field artillery and shore engineer batallions in the front lines. *(See Map 47, in Atlas.)* On the sixteenth, Kesselring gave up his attempts to throw the Fifth Army into the sea, and authorized a general withdrawal to the Volturno River. This was sanctioned by Hitler, whose message to Kesselring was read through ULTRA. The message revealed as well that Hitler thought he had administered such a threshing as to preclude further Allied invasions, and that the *Fuehrer* had now decided to defend Italy south of Rome. On the nineteenth, the Eighth Army's lead divisions reached Potenza, due east of Salerno.[25]

Kesselring intended to move slowly up the boot, giving his engineers time to destroy the Port of Naples and his reserve units time to prepare defensive positions along the Volturno and Biferno Rivers. He ordered the Volturno River Line held until October 15 so that reserve troops could prepare the Reinhard Line by November 1. In the meantime, German engineers, using labor battalions and impressed Italian civilians, began work on the Gustav Line from which Kesselring hoped to hold the Allies south of Rome at least until the Spring of 1944.[26]

After the breakout from the Salerno beachhead, the Allies, much reinforced, pushed Kesselring's troops northward without hurrying them appreciably. *(See Map 48, in Atlas.)* The Eighth Army captured the Foggia airfields on September 27 and plodded on to the Biferno River, where they met determined resistance. Once German engineers had completed their destruction of the port of Naples, Lieutenant General Heinrich von Vietinghoff gennant Scheel, Kesselring's Tenth Army commander, pulled back to the Volturno, allowing the British 7th Armoured Division to enter Naples on the first of October.

The reopening of Naples by Allied engineers was not only a magnificent accomplishment but also illustrated the logistical organization of the Allied armies that enabled fighting forces to maintain their strength as they moved forward, rather than becoming weaker as the *Wehrmacht* had done during the invasion of Russia. When the 7th Armoured Division reached the port, 30 major wrecks protruded above the water. Below the surface more than a 100 large and small vessels lay scuttled. Many sunken vessels had been piled with dynamited locomotives, trucks, or cranes before scuttling, creating jagged steel hazards for Allied divers. All piers and wharves were masses of rubble. Of 73 cranes on the docks, only one was standing, and it was badly damaged. Warehouses and railroads were in ruin and piles of coal were burning. Finally, the entire harbor had been laced with booby traps and time bombs.

Engineers required three days just to extinguish the fires in the coalpiles. But by the fourth day divers had cleared a narrow channel, and the first Liberty ship docked at the first cleared pier and began unloading. On the fifth day salvage crews opened the first rail line from Pier A to the main rail line out of Naples. Nine days later, in spite of booby traps and time bombs, stevedores at Naples unloaded 3,500 tons of cargo, the equivalent of five Liberty shiploads. Within another two weeks that figure had doubled. In clearing the harbor, engineers used many ingenious solutions, such as laying new piers on top of sunken ships.[27]

Allied soldiers continued to push the Germans back from delay position to delay position, until they arrived at the rain-swollen Volturno River on October 7. Meanwhile, Kesselring had ordered the 90th Panzer Division on Sardinia and the SS Brigade on Corsica back to Italy. French warships ferried about 800 French troops from North Africa to Sardinia to harry the evacuation, which was completed on October 3.[28]

The Allies had now attained all their objectives in Italy. The air forces could bomb Germany from Foggia; Italy was out of the war; southern France could be threatened from Corsica; and 19 German divisions had been tied down in Italy. *(See Table on page 249.)* There was, however, no thought of ending the campaign at the Volturno.[29] As noted earlier, throughout the campaign to date the Allies had been privy to the thoughts of Hitler, Rommel, and Kesselring through ULTRA intercepts. They knew that Hitler was equivocating in his choice of strategy, but that, after Salerno, he had decided to defend Italy along a line north of Naples.[30] Eisenhower expected to be in Rome by the end of October,[31] and Alexander had even issued a directive on September 21 to seize Rome.

Pier at Naples, 1943

Hitler's vacillation in strategy seems to have been primarily associated with his unwillingness to give ground without a fight. Should he follow Rommel's advice and withdraw to the Pisa-Rimini Line, or should he follow Kesselring's advice and defend as far south as possible? He was fully conscious of the possibilities for disaster that lay in deploying an army far down a long, narrow peninsula, when the Allies had already demonstrated an amphibious capability. Yet he hated to give up land, and Kesselring's arguments about keeping Allied bombers far from Germany made sense. On the other hand, he trusted Rommel's judgment in spite of his Tunisian setbacks. Hitler probably preferred to put Rommel in charge of executing Kesselring's strategy, but it would have been poor psychology to require a commander to execute a plan in which he had no faith. Instead, he vacillated. In September, he had refused to give Kesselring two of Rommel's divisions to attack the Salerno beachhead, but in early October he transferred three divisions to Kesselring for use along the Volturno-Biferno Line.[32]

On to Rome

Eisenhower now reassessed the situation and concluded that the Volturno-Biferno Line was too close to Naples and Foggia to provide adequate security to those vital installations. To gain the necessary depth, the Allies believed they would have to push the enemy at least back to a line north of Rome. Furthermore, if they were to contain the maximum number of German divisions in the Mediterranean, it was desirable to occupy the Po Valley, from which southern France, the Balkans, and even Germany itself would be threatened.[33] In light of the change in Hitler's intentions, Eisenhower recommended the abandonment of a Churchillian plan to invade Rhodes, and requested that four air-transport squadrons, two landing ships, and one regiment of the 82nd Airborne Division, all scheduled for movement to England, be retained in the Mediterranean.[34] He later asked to keep even more landing craft in readiness.

When the CCS disapproved the request for the additional airborne and amphibious resources, Eisenhower retorted, "This shortage will force us into frontal attacks which will undoubtedly be strongly contested and prove costly."[35] Even though the requirements of OVERLORD prevented allocating additional assets to the Mediterranean, the mission of protecting Foggia and tying down German divisions remained, so Alexander's directive of September 21 for the seizure of Rome stood.[36]

Unfortunately, Eisenhower's assessment that the Allies would be forced into frontal attacks was accurate, for terrain dictated the tactics. The Italian peninsula is divided north to south by the Apennine Mountains. Their ridges divide the country into a series of valleys containing swift rivers, flowing generally perpendicular to the Allied route of advance, each river dominated by nearby ridges, hills, or mountains. The Apennines also limited the road network. *(See Map 48, in Atlas.)* There were just four roads south of Rome and north of Naples capable of supporting a corps advance. Route 7, the Appian Way, paralleled the coast. Route 6 traversed the Liri Valley to the west of the Apennines. Route 17 twisted and turned through the eastern slopes of the Apennines, while Route 16 paralleled the eastern shore. Of these, only Route 6 offered a reasonable axis of advance to Rome. Route 7 could easily be blocked or destroyed as it crossed the Pontine Marshes. Route 17, with its many cliffs, bridges, and tunnels, could be almost completely destroyed with little demolition effort. To reach Rome over Route 16 would require the Allies to turn west along Route 5 after reaching Pescara and attack over the Apennine Mountains, hardly an appealing prospect. Route 6 was selected as the main axis of advance, not because of its advantages but because it had fewer disadvantages, for it was flanked along its entire length by dominating mountains, the names of which would later become infamous: Sammucro, Cesima, Camino, Lungo, Majo, Mignano, and Cassino. It was on these mountains and along Route 6 that Kesselring positioned his defenses.[37]

Montgomery tallied the first success in the long fight to Rome when he turned the Biferno River line with an amphibious end-run by his commando brigade on the night of October 2. Kesselring reacted violently to this threat to the position he planned to hold until October 15 by ordering the 16th Panzer Division to counterattack. After a slow start, the division road-marched 95 miles to Termoli and counterattacked, but it was too late to repulse the commandos, who had already linked up with other elements of the Eighth Army.[38] The battle raged until October 6, when the 16th Panzer Division withdrew; but Montgomery did not follow because he felt his army was overextended. Instead, he turned his attention to his usual methodical preparations for continuing the attack on October 22, well beyond Kesselring's scheduled withdrawal date.

Although lead battalions of Clark's Fifth Army closed on the Volturno on October 7, the rain, which had swollen the river and turned the approaches into quagmires, caused the assault crossing to be delayed twice until the night of October 12. Even after the assault elements secured a bridgehead, accurate artillery fire directed from the dominating hills prevented the engineers from building a 30-ton bridge the following day. During the following night more infantry crossed, and under cover of smoke the engineers erected the bridge on the fourteenth. They constructed another on the fifteenth. As tanks crossed to the north bank on the new bridges, Kesselring, having met his schedule, began slowly to withdraw to his next delay position, the Barbara Line. *(See Map 47, in Atlas.)*[39]

The Allies had now entered the Winter Position, the name they gave the area between the Volturno River and the Gustav Line. On Kesselring's map there were two delay lines in the area, the Barbara and Reinhard. His subordinate corps commanders had added intermediate delay lines of their own. Naturally, German commanders at lower echelons had added outposts and reserve blocking positions, so that to the GI and Tommy, attacking through the area seemed like attacking one big defensive zone. All hill masses were occupied. Positions had been sighted to provide each other covering small arms fire. Engineers had constructed some of the major bunkers of concrete. They had cut others from solid rock with pneumatic drills. Infantrymen had improved the less critical positions by rolling large rocks around their foxholes. Because of the treeless mountains, artillery forward observers had overlapping, unobstructed views of the approaches to other mountains in the area. The towns that dotted the valley floors, such as San Pietro, San Vittore, and Cassino, were converted into strong points in which the thick masonry walls provided protection for the defenders. Valley floors, naturally cut by gullies, offered innumerable positions for the emplacement of antitank guns.[40]

German Bunker on Monte Lungo

Kesselring correctly counted on the aid of the Italian winter weather. Rains begin in "sunny Italy" in early October and last through February. It is not unusual for it to rain almost every day in December, the height of the rainy season. Rainfall runs immediately off the steep mountainsides into the many rivers. Although most Italian rivers are fordable in summer, by winter these same rivers are rushing seaward and spilling over their banks. In many cases the valley floor on each side of the river constituted the greatest obstacle to military movement during the winter of 1943. The saturated land created a quagmire which absolutely prohibited vehicular movement off the roads and occasionally even made human and animal movement next to impossible. By the end of December the higher mountains would be covered with snow.[41]

The ultimate difficulty was, of course, the German infantryman, whose morale was high and who was glad to be ending his Army's 2,000-mile retreat from El Alamein, through Tunis and Sicily, to the Gustav Line. The fighting in the east coast town of Ortona in the Eighth Army sector provides a perfect example of the German's skill in defense. *(See Map 48, in Atlas.)* Since Route 16 passed through Ortona, the town could not be bypassed. The 2nd Battalion, 3rd Regiment, 1st Parachute Division, commanded by Captain Liebschev, was responsible for the defense of the small town. Liebschev meticulously prepared his defenses. He chose to defend only the northern half of the town. In the southern half he destroyed enough to create a massive obstacle of rubble that prohibited tank movement, or even rapid human movement, through the streets. The remaining houses were all traps of one sort or another. Some were dead ends, providing entrance but no exit, most were mined and booby-trapped, and others seemed to provide cover but were actually targets for large German guns. In the standing half of Ortona every house was defended, fields of fire were carefully cleared and coordinated, and interior passages were opened from one house to the next. The 2nd Brigade of the 1st Canadian Division attacked on December 20 on a 250-yard front; it required 9 days and 650 casualties to force the paratroopers from the town.[42]

The combination of terrain, weather, and German tactical proficiency presented the Allies an unenviable challenge. Cloud cover usually prevented close air support. The steep mountain slopes and the valley mud confined armor to the roads, where it was easy prey for German artillery and anti-tank guns. Even the artillery's effectiveness was reduced. The inadequate road net, washed-out bridges, and mud limited the amount of ammunition that could be carried forward to the guns, and the typical German position was secure against all but a direct hit.[43] Infantry units were plagued by even more difficult transport problems, which they solved by organizing mule-skinner units in early November. Each regiment on line required 250 mule loads per day to keep it supplied.[44]

Techniques used to overcome these defenses were similar. The air force kept the sky clear of the *Luftwaffe*, and Allied artillery, directed by Pipercub "Grasshoppers," concentrated on smothering German artillery with counter-battery fire. It was, therefore, relatively easy to approach to within small arms

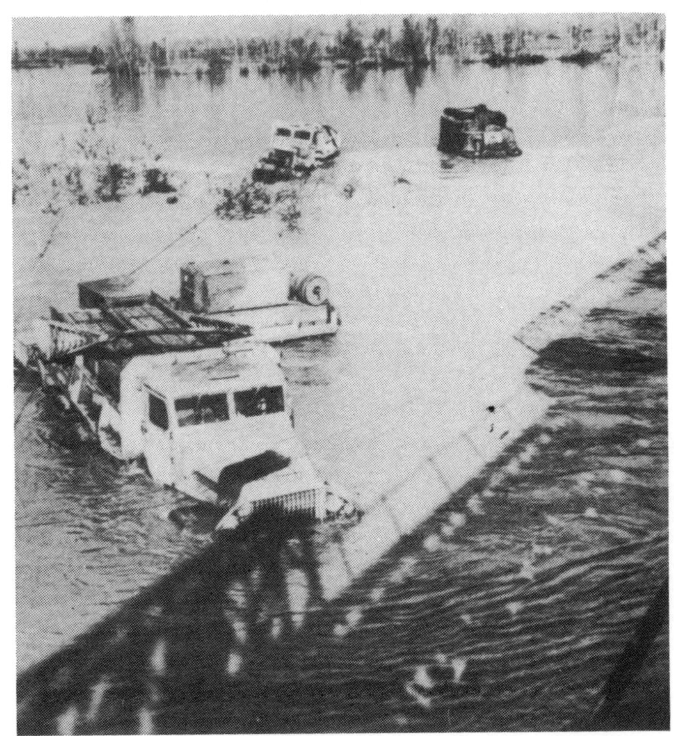

The Volturno River in Flood

range of the German positions, unless a river had to be crossed en route. Artillery fire on the enemy positions, using sometimes as many as 40 battalions at one time, saturated the objective area and surrounding hills while the infantry climbed the steep hillsides.[45] Once infantry units were on the upper slopes, they had to reduce each enemy position individually with grenades and small arms fire, a task that usually required several days. A German soldier described these tactics from his point of view in a local troop newspaper:

> The Americans use quasi Indian tactics. They search for the boundary lines between battalions or regiments, they look for gaps between our strong points, they look for the steepest mountain passages (guided by treacherous civilians. . . .) They infiltrate through these passages with a patrol, a platoon at first, mostly at dusk. At night they reinforce the infiltrated units, and in the morning they are often in the rear of a German unit, which is being attacked from behind, or also from the flanks simultaneously.[46]

Such tactics cost casualties, and Allied soldiers paid the price. In six days in early December on Monte la Difensa, the 1st Special Service Force, a mixed Canadian-American brigade-sized unit, suffered 511 casualties (73 killed, 9 missing, 313 wounded, and 116 hospitalized for exhaustion). The 1st Special Service Force, however, was an elite and experienced unit. Inexperienced units paid an even heavier toll. The 6th Armored Infantry Regiment entered combat for the first time in Italy in January 1944 on Monte Porchia. After 10 days of combat, its killed and wounded were about the same as the 1st Special Service Force—66 and 379 respectively—but the regiment was missing 480 men and had had 516 more evacuated for trench foot and exposure.[47] Losses were naturally not evenly distributed over branches and grades; for example, the turnover in infantry lieutenants in VI Corps from October to January was 115 percent.[48]

By January 15, 1944, the Allies possessed the Winter Position and were closing on the Rapido River, the forward edge of the Gustav Line. Yet the Germans had won the battle, even though they had lost the ground. Not once had the Allies forced them off a delay line before the time scheduled for its abandonment. During their four-month withdrawal, Kesselring's troops had accomplished all the classic tasks of a delaying action. The Allies arrived at the defensive position exhausted, punished, harassed, and having consumed much valuable time getting into an unfavorable situation. Alexander now faced an enemy determined to withdraw no more and entrenched in a formidable defensive position.

The Allies, however, had no intention of battering their way through the main German line in a simple frontal assault, for Alexander still held an ace in the hole—the navy with its amphibious capability. As early as October, Eisenhower's staff had begun to explore plans to turn the Gustav Line. It quickly encountered three problems. First, the shipping and landing craft not being used to build up and sustain forces in southern Italy could lift only one brigade. Second, all suitable beaches behind the Gustav Line were too far north to permit a linkage within 48 hours, the period that a single brigade could survive alone behind enemy lines.[49] Third, after the build-up of forces in southern Italy was completed, 80 percent of the LSTs and 67 percent of the landing craft in the Mediterranean were to return to England in preparation for OVERLORD, scheduled to take place in just five more months.

On November 3, Eisenhower told Alexander, Clark, and Montgomery that if the Fifth Army could quickly reach the Gustav Line, crack it, and advance 25 miles beyond, he would authorize an amphibious operation (to be code-named SHINGLE) of division size just south of Rome.[50] In anticipation of the opportunity, Eisenhower had requested that 68 LSTs be retained in the Mediterranean until December 15, but it soon became apparent that the Fifth Army would not even reach the Gustav Line by the deadline.[51]

At the Cairo-Tehran Conference during the last weeks of November 1943, the relationship of Italy to OVERLORD was a major topic of debate. Churchill desired to seize both Rome and the island of Rhodes before conducting OVERLORD. The Americans wanted nothing to do with Rhodes. They did want to take Rome, but most of all, they wanted a firm commitment to OVERLORD and its supporting invasion of southern France, ANVIL. The American position was little compromised during the debates. Rhodes was stricken from the list of objectives. Rome was to be taken, but not at the expense of OVERLORD and ANVIL, which were rescheduled for some time in May. In essence, then, by changing the OVERLORD D-Day from May 1 to anytime during May, Alexander received an extra month to take Rome. But the landing ships and craft could not be kept past January 15, for the heads of state agreed to "undertake nothing elsewhere that will jeopardize" OVERLORD and ANVIL.[52]

To Clark and Montgomery, whose armies were slowly crawling northward through the mud of the Winter Position, the 30-day extension for the use of landing craft gave little hope. It would require 20 days to mount an amphibious operation, and it was already obvious that neither army would meet the necessary precondition of cracking the Gustav Line by the end of 1943. Accordingly, on the eighteenth of November, Clark recommended to Alexander that SHINGLE be cancelled.[53]

While flying home after the Cairo Conference, Churchill fell ill with pneumonia. He lay sick and inactive at Tunis from December 11 to 18. Clark's recommendation for the cancellation of SHINGLE arrived just as Churchill was recovering a little of his old vigor. Clark's message shocked him into understanding that the realities of the situation in Italy were going to undo his efforts at Cairo to postpone OVERLORD a month so that Rome could be captured. Churchill immediately aroused himself to action to save SHINGLE. He fired a telegram to his Chiefs of Staff, calling the situation "scandalous," and then called a Christmas Eve conference with the senior British officers in the Mediterranean Theater. At that conference, the officers decided that if the 15th Army Group could not advance far enough to make a rapid link-up with one division, the landing should be made more self-sustaining. Everyone agreed that a two-division landing launched about January 20 would be sufficient. Of course, the departure of the LSTs would have to be delayed again. On Christmas Day, Churchill held another conference at which he presented his plan; this time the British commanders and Eisenhower and his staff were present. The conference was a rubber stamp of the previous evening's decision, for the British commanders had already agreed, and Eisenhower was reluctant to express an opinion since he was to depart for England in six days to command OVERLORD. The only man known to be against the plan, Eisenhower's intelligence officer, Brigadier K. W. D. Strong, was not allowed to speak until after a consensus had been reached. Churchill then turned to Strong and said, "Well, we may as well hear the seamy side of the question."[54] With that introduction, Strong's interpretation of the difficulties sure to be encountered made little impression.[55] Churchill then telegraphed Roosevelt, telling him of the plan and the consensus and asking him to agree to keep the LSTs in the Mediterranean until February 5, explaining that otherwise "the Italian battle [will] stagnate and fester on for another three months."[56] Three days later Roosevelt agreed.

Anzio and Cassino

After receiving the political go-ahead, Alexander issued his plan for SHINGLE and ordered it to be executed as soon after January 20 as possible. Basically the plan required the VI Corps under command of Major General John P. Lucas to land at Anzio and drive inland to seize the Alban Hills, control of which would sever Highways 6 and 7 and all rail lines to Kesselring's forces on the western end of the Gustav Line. *(See Map 49, in Atlas.)* Five days before the VI Corps' landing, the Fifth Army would cross the Garigliano and Rapido Rivers and assault the Gustav Line to achieve three purposes: to hold the enemy forces in the Gustav Line away from Anzio, to draw reserves from the Rome area to the Gustav Line, and to penetrate the Gustav Line to be in position to link up with the SHINGLE forces.

The task did not promise to be easy. The Gustav Line had more natural strength than the other lines farther south, for it overlooked the Rapido and Garigliano Rivers. In addition, its engineer-constructed improvements far surpassed those on earlier positions. Its bunkers were more substantial, including even steel-covered machine gun positions. It contained far more barbed wire and mines—mostly wooden box mines that would not register on metallic mine detectors. Kesselring waited for the Allied attack with confidence.[57]

Kesselring's first test came on January 17, 1944, when the British X Corps, using landing craft, launched its attack across the mouth of the Garigliano River. After two days of hard fighting, the two assaulting divisions had established a two-mile deep bridgehead. Two days later, X Corps attempted a second crossing with the 46th Division near Sant'Ambrogio. That attempt failed. To the north, the American II Corps attempted to send the 36th Division across the Rapido River on the following night. The attack was ill planned, the assault troops unwilling, the proper equipment unavailable, and the leadership uninspiring. After the division had been punished by the German defenders for 48 hours, Major General Geoffrey Keyes, the II Corps commander, halted the attempt.

In spite of the two failures, the one successful crossing on the lower Garigliano had accomplished two of the Fifth Army's purposes, for Kesselring had not only kept his Gustav Line garrison in place, he had also moved two reserve divisions (the 29th and 90th Panzer Grenadier) toward the Gustav Line, away from Rome and the SHINGLE beaches.

Although feasibility planning for SHINGLE had been underway for months, there was an incredibly short time to prepare for the operation itself. In a period of 24 days the selected troop units had to reorganize, pull out of line or reserve, assemble, draw special equipment, maintain their organic equipment, undergo amphibious training, move to Naples, embark, rehearse, correct rehearsal errors, sail to Anzio, and land. Accomplishment of all these tasks was impossible; naturally, it was training and maintenance which were omitted.

The rehearsal near Naples on January 18 was disastrous. The Navy seemed to have forgotten all it had learned about small boat seamanship and control of landing craft waves. Forty-three landing craft (DUKW's) were lost in the surf with their cargoes, 19 105-mm howitzers and 9 antitank guns. The losses were rapidly replaced by taking guns and DUKWs from units in X and II Corps, but there was no time for another rehearsal. It is not surprising that General Lucas sailed for Anzio full of trepidation.[58]

But the poor rehearsal was not the worst of the Allied problems. Alexander, Clark, and Lucas each had a different understanding of the mission of VI Corps. Alexander wanted the corps to cut the German main line of communications and to threaten Kesselring's rear. His intelligence officer forecast that the initial assault would be unopposed and that Kesselring could react to the landing only with two uncommitted divisions, which would arrive at the beachhead decimated by Allied air attacks. These were the two reserve divisions, which Alexander hoped would have been drawn to the Gustav Line by the earlier attacks—as we have seen they were. Beyond that, Alexander, drawing upon good intelligence, including ULTRA, expected that the Germans could only initially bring parts of divisions to Anzio. Kesselring's troops at Anzio, therefore, would be easily dominated by the VI Corps. But the first two days would be crucial because it was in that time frame that VI Corps would be able to stake out a hold on the Alban Hills and, in conjunction with Clark's attacks, seize the initiative and force Kesselring to withdraw.[59] Clark, on the other hand, had told Lucas first to seize and secure a beachhead and then to "advance on" the Alban Hills. Clark's choice of the phrase "advance on" was deliberate, for he intended VI Corps either to threaten or to seize the hills, as the situation allowed. Clark's G-2 expected Kesselring to react to the landing with five divisions, despite having ULTRA information; and Clark, remembering Salerno, wanted Lucas to be established ashore firmly before taking risks. Finally, Lucas understood his mission to be to threaten the German rear, which could be accomplished by his corps simply occupying a strong position at Anzio. He also expected a strong reaction from Kesselring.[60] The difference between the army group commander's concept and that of the corps commander was striking. Alexander expected VI Corps to be the main attack in a turning movement, but Lucas expected his corps to comprise a supporting attack designed to draw German strength away from the main attack on the Gustav Line.

The assault convoy carrying 40,000 men and 5,200 vehicles, the equivalent of three divisions, dropped anchor off Anzio at five minutes after midnight on January 22, The landing, two hours later, was a complete tactical surprise. Only a few coastal artillery and antiaircraft guns opposed the first waves, and those guns were quickly silenced by naval gunfire. In less than 24 hours, 90 percent of the assault personnel and equipment, along with a large quantity of supplies, were ashore; Anzio harbor was captured and operational; offshore mines had been swept; beach minefields had been cleared; and the corps front was established three miles inland—all at a cost of only 13 killed.[61]

On the German side, Kesselring had decided within three hours that SHINGLE was a major threat to his defensive line south of Rome. Although he had no reserve—it had already been committed against the X Corps bridgehead across the Garigliano—he began assembling units in a race against time to contain VI Corps. Shortly before daylight he ordered several replacement battalions and the 4th Parachute Division, which was in the process of being activated near Rome, to block the road from Anzio to the Alban Hills. He then asked OKW for reinforcements, and it responded later in the day by ordering to Italy a division from France, another from Yugoslavia, and the equivalent of a third from Germany. Next he ordered the Fourteenth Army in northern Italy to start parts of three divisions on the long march to Anzio; two days later he would order that army headquarters to the area to control his collection of troops. Finally, and with considerable reluctance, Kesselring told Vietinghoff to send a corps headquarters and what troops he could spare from the Gustav Line; the Tenth Army commander responded by getting the equivalent of two divisions on the way before the day was over, and late in the day pulled parts of two more divisions from the line near the Adriatic Sea as further reinforcements. But by then Vietinghoff doubted his ability to hold the Gustav Line and recommended a withdrawal to Kesselring, who refused him.

Thus, by the end of January 22, Kesselring had reacted quickly to the landing, more quickly in terms of getting locally positioned troops on the move to Anzio than Alexander's intelligence officer had expected. Nor were the Germans as harassed by Allied air as Alexander had expected would be the case, because they moved mostly at night. Nevertheless, Kesselring was very concerned because he did not expect to be able to hold a VI Corps attack to the Alban Hills if it were made before January 25, the day when he hoped to have enough strength in position to contain it. (Units from northern Italy began to arrive on the twenty-sixth and those sent by OKW even later.) Alexander's prediction about the criticalness of the first two days was proving correct, as Kesselring was very relieved to note that Lucas did little more than slightly increase the size of the beachhead on Janaury 23. Now he began to hope that he could not only avoid withdrawing from the Gustav Line but also perhaps eliminate the troublesome Allied beachhead.[62]

By the thirtieth, Lucas, having been reinforced with the follow-up divisions, felt strong enough to attack. Unfortunately, Kesselring had elements of eight divisions at Anzio by then, with five more divisions en route. The two-pronged attack toward Campleone and Cisterna met strong resistance. The British seized Campleone but could go no farther. The Americans began their attack towards Cisterna by infiltrating two ranger battalions of 767 men through the German lines.[63] The Germans discovered the infiltrators and killed or captured all but six men. After two days of bloody fighting Lucas halted the attack, which had reached only a little beyond Cisterna. General Eberhard von Mackensen's Fourteenth Army then counterattacked, and in four days pushed the British back out of Campoleone.[64]

At the conclusion of the counterattack, the Anzio beachhead was essentially a fortress besieged by the German Fourteenth Army. The entire beachhead was within range and observation of German artillery. Only the scarcity of German artillery ammunition and the presence of Allied air cover prevented its slow destruction.[65] Any breakout would have been difficult, but to storm the fortress would have required a major Axis effort.

Hitler felt that the Battle for Anzio Beachhead would be one of the most important battles in 1944. If the Allies succeeded in breaking out of the beachhead, the loss of southern Italy would be assured. On the other hand, if the Germans could destroy the beachhead, the Allies would have second thoughts about launching the cross-Channel attack on France which he felt would come in the spring of 1944. He therefore ordered Kesselring to eliminate the Allied "abscess"; but he kept tactical control in his own hands, down to dictating axes of attack and locations of units.[66]

Unknown to Hitler, the containment at Anzio had already affected OVERLORD. The LSTs used to put the troops ashore now had to keep them supplied. Obviously, these LSTs could not be released for OVERLORD on the promised date, February 5. Although the final decision was delayed until March 20, by mid-February planners knew that OVERLORD's supporting attack, ANVIL, would have to be cancelled.[67]

The Fourteenth Army began the attack to remove the Anzio "abscess" on the sixteenth of February. *(See Map 49, in Atlas.)* Hitler ruled out attacks on the Allied flanks because the attacking forces would be subject to enfilading fire from Allied ships, for which he now had a healthy respect. This left only one course—penetrations against the head of the salient. The weather that had prevented cross-country movement of Allied tanks in the Winter Position now kept the *panzers* roadbound. Winter weather in Italy definitely favored the defense. The fierce battle lasted four days, during which VI Corps was driven back to its last defensive line (the original beachhead line) but no farther. The Allies used artillery and air in quantities which literally staggered the Germans. On the afternoon of February 17 alone, Allied air forces flew 700 sorties in direct support of VI Corps. Casualties on both sides were heavy.[68] Ironically, Clark replaced Lucas with Major General Lucian K. Truscott, Jr. after Lucas had won the battle that he had long predicted and prepared for.

Hitler demanded that Kesselring try again. If the largest concentration of German strength in the West since the summer of 1940 could not destroy a small beachhead, he fumed, the Army and the homefront would lose confidence in their ability to keep the Allies off the continent. Mackensen reorganized, received reinforcements, prepared a detailed plan, and attacked again from February 28 to March 3, but without success. Kesselring then convinced Hitler to stop the offensive and begin constructing the Caesar Line to be used to hold the Allies south of Rome if the Gustav Line fell. *(See Map 50, in Atlas.)* Both sides had suffered about 20 percent casualties in the month since the landing. Because the combat elements

First Battle of Cassino

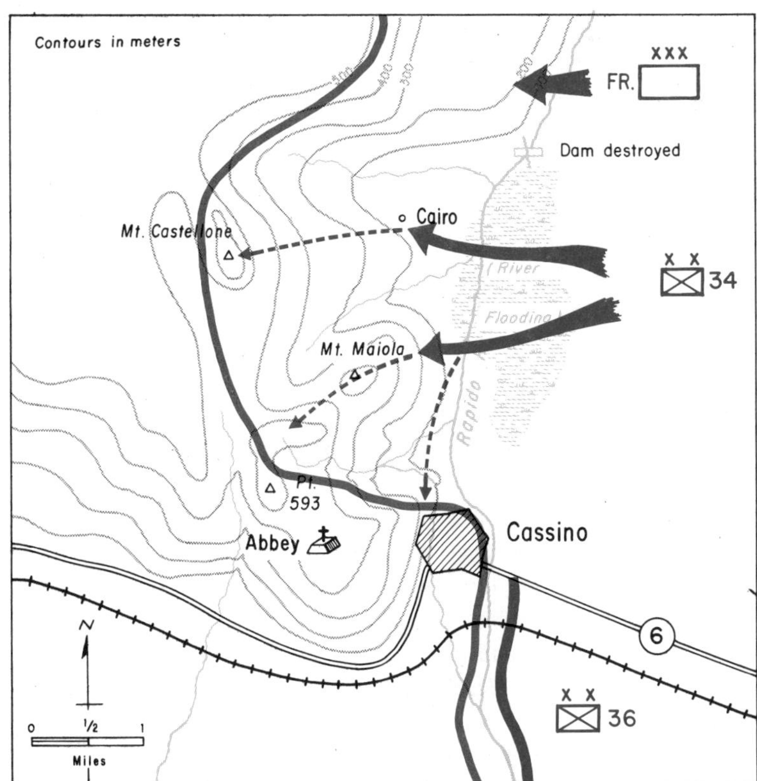

Monte Cassino as Seen From Across the Rapido River, Looking West (Abbey at Top Center)

had sustained a disproportionate number of those casualties, both sides were exhausted and incapable of further attacks. The Battle for Anzio Beachhead ended in a draw.

Of course, the Allies had not sat idly in front of the Gustav Line while the troops at Anzio fought for their lives. There was no escaping the fact that operations at Anzio and actions at the Gustav Line were part of the same battle. The first attack against the Gustav Line had been made across the Garigliano and Rapido Rivers just five days before the Anzio landing; although failing, it had assisted SHINGLE by attracting German reserves. After that attack, Alexander and Clark determined that the high ground to the north of the Liri Valley would have to be captured before the river could be bridged, much less the valley used. This high ground started with a finger just above Highway 6 called Monte Cassino, which dominated the crossing sites over the Rapido River, the river valley, Highway 6, and the Liri Valley. *(See Map 50, in Atlas.)* Unfortunately, the Abbey Montecassino, built by Saint Benedict about 529 A.D. and now home of the Benedictine Order, sat atop that finger, and with its six-foot thick walls formed a perfect fort. North of the Abbey, the ground rose steadily through a series of peaks to 1669-meter-high Monte Cairo. *(See Map, p. 241.)*

Kesselring could not be allowed to switch more units from Cassino to Anzio after the defeat of the first attack on the Gustav Line. So three days later, on the night of January 24, the U.S. 34th Division crossed the upper Rapido where the river was fordable. Clark planned for the 34th to seize Monte Castelleone and Point 593, then take Monte Cassino (Monastery Hill) from the rear. The muddy valley floor, however, proved to be as big an obstacle as the Rapido itself had been farther downstream. After infantry units had secured a shallow toehold west of the river, the engineers required five days to lay a corduroy road to get tanks across the quagmire to the far shore. In a few more days, the 34th had seized Monte Castelleone and lay only a few hundred yards from Point 593. The attackers continued to inch forward through rain and snow until, after another week, they lay only 70 yards from Point 593. There they were relieved by the 4th (Indian) Division. Many of the 25 percent of the regiment that had almost reached Point 593 had to be carried off the mountain by the relieving Indians, for although they were not wounded, they were too weak to walk. Even though the weather at the lower elevation was not so debilitating, the regiment attacking the town of Cassino had made no better progress. Even after using 1,500 grenades a day, the regiment could not enter Cassino.[69]

Meanwhile, Alexander had pulled two divisions from the Eighth Army sector, formed them into a provisional New Zealand Corps with Lieutenant General Bernard Freyberg in command, and positioned them behind the 36th Division ready to exploit into the Liri Valley. When the 34th failed, Alexander let Clark use the New Zealand Corps (the 4th Indian and the New Zealand 2nd Divisions) to try breaching the Gustav Line. In the second battle of Cassino, the New Zealand 2nd Division would attack the town from a different direction. Prior to resumption of the attack, Freyberg insisted that the abbey be bombed. Accordingly, the historic building was leveled on February 15, providing a propaganda victory for the Germans, who had never used it. In the subsequent attack, that did not begin until 24 hours after the bombing, the Indians got no closer to Point 593. The New Zealanders crossed the Rapido on the night of February 17, but were unable to construct a bridge before dawn. Using a thick smoke screen to conceal themselves from German forward observers, they remained in a shallow bridgehead without armor. Unfortunately, smoke conceals foe as well as friend. German *panzers* assembled just outside the bridgehead, then drove the New Zealanders back across the river.[70]

The Allies paused to rest and devise a different plan of attack for the third battle of Cassino. Monastery Hill had never been attacked frontally, so Freyberg decided to give that route a try. He planned to start the attack with a massive air and artillery bombardment of the town.* Freyberg's Corps was ready to attack by February 24, but constant rain prevented the bombing. Finally, on March 15, the sky cleared enough to allow the Allies to drop 1,184 tons of bombs and 196,000 artillery shells on Cassino. In the meantime, the German 1st Parachute Division had moved from the Adriatic front and taken up positions in and around the town. Although one battalion of the division was destroyed in the high explosive holocaust, the remaining battalions emerged from their underground shelters little hurt. The attacking New Zealanders not only had to contend with the paratroopers but also with their own bomb craters, some of which were so large that the engineers were unable to fill them and had to bridge them instead. By March 23, Alexander admitted defeat and halted the attack.[71] *(See Map, page 244.)*

After three months of hammering at the Gustav Line and an attempt to turn it, the Allies had spent 52,130 casualties, kept LSTs from OVERLORD, caused ANVIL to be postponed, and used up all infantry replacements available in Europe.[72] In return, they had gained three toeholds across water obstacles: one at Anzio, one across the lower Garigliano, and one across the upper Rapido.

General Sir Henry Maitland Wilson, Eisenhower's replacement as Commander-in-Chief of all Allied forces in the Mediterranean, could not quit. As the date for OVERLORD approached, he somehow had to draw German divisions from France to Italy. The obvious way to accomplish that mission was to destroy the forces in the Gustav Line and then pursue the Germans to Rome and beyond, causing Hitler to shift divisions to Italy. But how? He decided that if Alexander began his attack two months before OVERLORD, there would be time to draw divisions to Italy prior to D-Day in France. This gave him one month to reorganize, rest, retrain, reinforce, and resupply. By mid-April the rains would have stopped, allowing the ground to dry, Allied air forces to fly, and the rivers to subside.

Arranging his priorities accordingly, Wilson forwarded a recommendation that ANVIL be cancelled. His rationale was that there would be insufficient shipping and troops available to support both ANVIL and Italy, and that the ferocity of the fighting in Italy was diverting more German forces than had been anticipated when ANVIL was scheduled. The British Chiefs of Staff agreed. Eisenhower, who wanted ANVIL's landing craft for OVERLORD, also agreed. But the American Chiefs of Staff demanded that ANVIL be postponed only until July 1944. The American Chiefs did agree to the reallocation of landing craft from the Mediterranean to OVERLORD, and offered to send 26 LSTs and 40 landing craft from their Pacific fleet to the Mediterranean in order to make a July landing in southern France possible.† Although the debate over cancellation versus postponement of ANVIL would continue, at least there was agreement that a spring offensive in Italy would have priority, a change in the Cairo-Teheran decision "to undertake nothing elsewhere that will jeopardize" ANVIL. In April, the British Chiefs of Staff ordered General Wilson "to give the greatest possible assistance to OVERLORD by destroying or containing the maximum number of German formations in the Mediterranean."[74]

Alexander now began preparation for Operation DIADEM, the fourth battle of Cassino. The reorganization alone involved moving every division in front of the Gustav Line. Reinforcing divisions arrived from the United States and from other depots in the Mediterranean. Alexander assembled all British and British-equipped divisions (Indian, New Zealand, Canadian, and Polish) under the Eighth Army, and all American and American-equipped divisions (French) under the Fifth Army. Eighth Army took over responsibility for Cassino and the Liri Valley. Fifth Army retained responsibility for Anzio and the western part of the Gustav Line. *(See Map 50, in Atlas.)* The DIADEM plan called for Eighth Army to launch the main attack up the Liri Valley while Fifth Army conducted a supporting attack through the Aurunci Mountains west of the Liri Valley. VI Corps at Anzio was to attack on order, expected to be about D + 4, to seize the Alban Hills and trap the German Tenth Army.

To deceive the enemy, 15th Army Group made it appear that it was planning for an amphibious landing near Rome and gave indications that the reorganization would not be completed until June. Kesselring fell for the deception, for he ordered his forces to complete their own rest and refitting by the end of May and pulled three of his *panzer* and *panzergrenadier* divisions out of the Gustav Line, placing two of them in reserve near Rome.[75] He also prepared a new line, the Hitler Line, about six miles behind the Gustav Line.

When DIADEM began on May 11, the Allies outnumbered the Germans three to one in the vital Cassino sector and two to one north of the Liri Valley.[76] DIADEM started with a 2,000-gun preparation at 11:00 P.M. All units made some progress the first day, but on the second day the Germans limited the British XIII Corps to its newly won bridgehead into the Liri Valley and held the Polish Corps short of the elusive Point 593.

*This would be the first of the carpet bombings that would later be used at St. Lô and Caen in France.

†The British were a little peeved that the Americans could come up with landing craft from the Pacific for their pet projects but not for any British pet projects.[73]

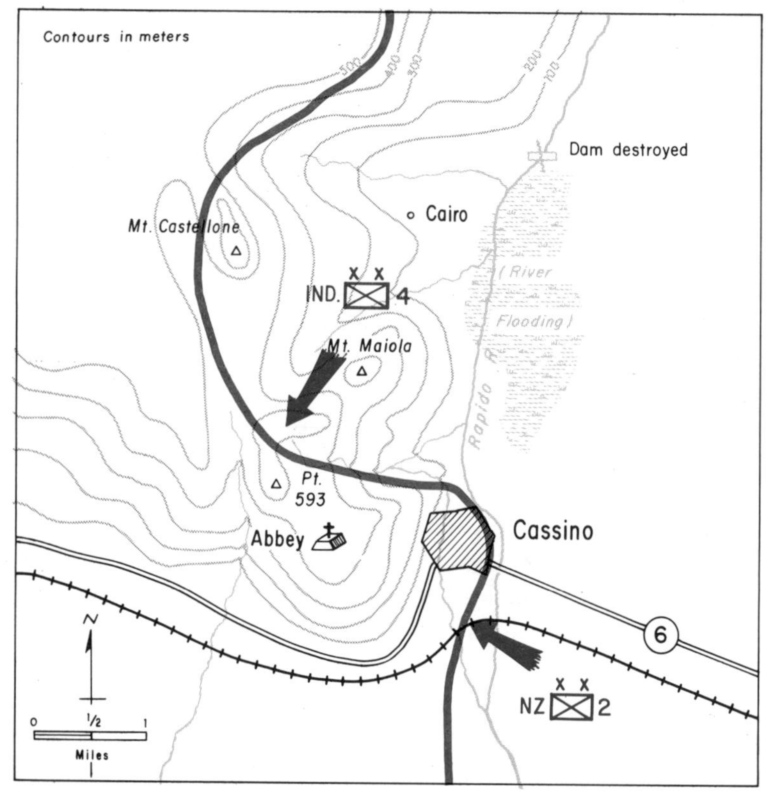

Second Battle of Cassino

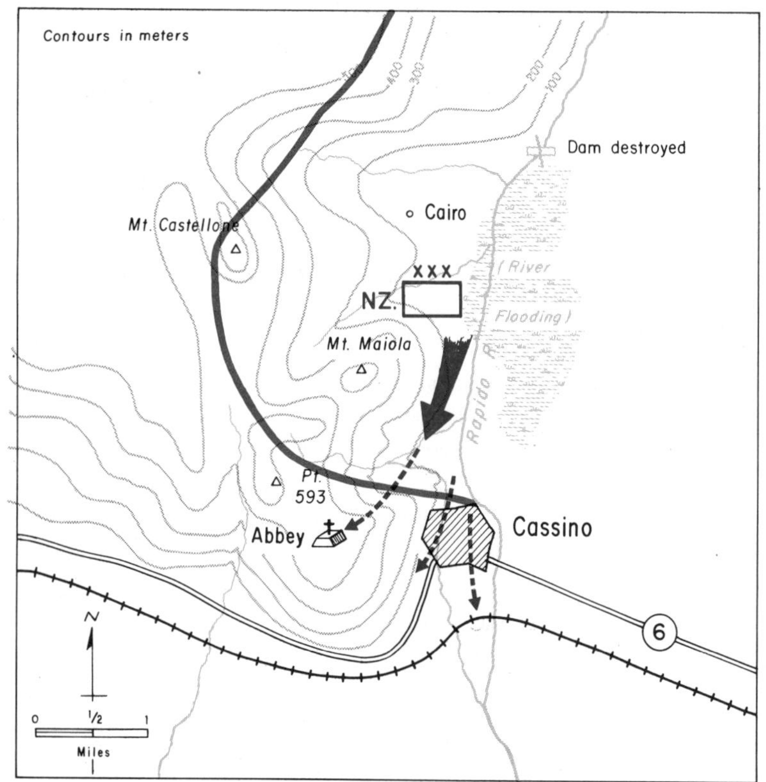

Third Battle of Cassino

Dramatic success, however, came in an unexpected sector. The French, whom Kesselring himself three months earlier had called the best Allied troops in Italy,[77] attacked along seemingly impassable routes through the Aurunci Mountains, routed the defenders, and broke through the Gustav Line. General Alphonse Juin, the French Corps commander, then used his famous Goumiers to move through the Hitler Line seven miles ahead. In the Cassino sector, a second effort by the Polish Corps carried Point 593 on May 17. The following day, the Poles raised their flag over the monastery ruins, and then attacked eastward to penetrate the Hitler Line before it could be manned. With the mountains on either side of the Liri Valley in Allied hands, British XIII Corps and the Canadian Corps thrust their armor up the valley toward Rome. In attempting to stem the advance, Kesselring recalled his reserve divisions from the Rome area. The deterioration of his front at several points, the pressure on all other points, and Allied air activity caused him to withdraw a division from Anzio and commit it and three reserve divisions piecemeal, accomplishing nothing except their placement in the trap that VI Corps was about to spring from Anzio.

Alexander ordered Clark to break out of the Anzio beachhead on May 23 and seize the town of Valmontone, south of the Alban Hills, in order to block the escape of the German Tenth Army. *(See Map 50, in Atlas.)* He had excellent information of the enemy, including many ULTRA intercepts, and thus must have been aware of how Vietinghoff's army was unravelling. Clark preferred instead to penetrate the Caesar Line before it could be manned, and then capture Rome. After VI Corps smashed out of the beachhead and linked up with II Corps, Clark sent one division toward Valmontone and four northeastward toward Rome. The Fifth Army entered Rome on June 4, but the one division sent to Valmontone had been stopped cold by three German divisions. Clark's desire to see the Eternal City captured by Americans resulted in the escape of most of the German Tenth Army.[78]

To the Po

Although given a temporary reprieve by Clark's decision, Kesselring's troubles were not over. Because his poorly mechanized forces could not hope to compete with Allied armor and air on the rolling plains north of Rome, he had to withdraw to his next mountain position, the Gothic Line. *(See Map 51, in Atlas.)* But construction on this line was not finished. Kesselring consequently instituted a delay along a series of lines beginning at Lake Trasimene, 50 miles south of the Gothic Line. He ruthlessly sacrificed his second-rate units in those delay positions in order to keep his better units fit for the upcoming defense.[79]

The Allies pushed northward, punishing but not breaking Kesselring's formations. No one knew how far north they would go, for no terrain objective had ever been established for the Italian Campaign, although the capture of Rome had been an implied objective. Wilson's mission remained to tie down as many enemy divisions as possible. As the miles of advance rolled by faster than ever before, commanders, both British and American, began to visualize breaking into the Po Valley and then turning left into southern France or right through northern Yugoslavia to Vienna. The British, holding the upper two echelons of command in Italy, were the ones who articulated those dreams. More importantly, Churchill, who had long desired to open active combat in the Balkan area, supported the idea of advancing toward Vienna through the Lubjubljana Pass.

While Roosevelt and the American Chiefs of Staff had always opposed operations in the Balkan area, the immediate problem was allocation of resources. As agreed by the CCS in April, four French and three American Divisions had been scheduled to leave Italy as soon as Rome was captured to participate in ANVIL, recently renamed DRAGOON. On June 18, Wilson asked Marshall to reconsider that decision. Marshall replied that France was the decisive front and that southern French ports were logistically essential to that front.

On June 28, Churchill made one last effort to cancel DRAGOON and keep Alexander's divisions for him. He cabled Roosevelt:

> The deadlock between our Chiefs of Staff raises most serious issues. Our first wish is to help General Eisenhower in the most speedy and effective manner. But we do not think this necessarily involves the complete ruin of all our great affairs in the Mediterranean, and we take it hard that this should be demanded of us. . . .[80]

Roosevelt replied with a long, reasoned cable in which he firmly stated, "I cannot agree to the employment of United States troops against Istria and into the Balkans. . . ."[81]

As the debates over the Mediterranean strategy again subsided, Wilson issued instructions to Alexander, clearly stating that DRAGOON would receive priority and requiring him to have the seven divisions at their embarkation ports by the specified loading date. Within that constraint, 15th Army Group was "to advance over the Apennines and to close to the line of the River Po, . . . subsequently to cross the Po to the line Venice-Padua-Verona-Brescia.[82]

The Allied advance halted on August 4, after reaching Florence, an advance of 270 miles in 64 days. Alexander had originally hoped to move through the Gothic Line just as he had through the Hitler Line, but stiffening German resistance indicated that Army Group Southwest was not sufficiently disorganized to give his weakened force any hope of success. Alexander used the next three weeks to close up his units, improve the lines of communication, plan a coordinated attack, and reposition his strength along the Adriatic coast. His plan envisioned Eighth Army attacking in the east on August 25; Fifth Army would attack in the center on order, around August 30.

Eighth Army's night attack by the Polish Corps, the Canadian Corps, and the large V Corps caught the Germans in the midst of relieving two on-line divisions. *(See Map 51, in Atlas.)* In the confusion, the Eighth had little trouble closing the 20 miles to the Gothic Line. Kesselring, learning through a captured order that this was the main effort, raced units to man the Gothic Line, which he had not expected to have threatened for another three days.[83]

During the night of August 29, V Corps crossed the Foglia River, the forward edge of the Gothic Line. After three days of tough fighting, the leading elements of the corps sat atop the ridges overlooking the Foglia. The Gothic Line had been pierced along a 10-mile front more easily than anyone had expected. Progress across the remaining mountain ridges, however, slowed appreciably as Kesselring shifted seven divisions to his threatened Adriatic sector. The next 10-mile advance, to the Marano River, required 14 days, resulting in 8,000 casualties.

Meanwhile, Mark Clark prepared his Fifth Army attack. The terrain ahead was as formidable as any he had faced: a 50-mile mass of jumbled mountains, with peaks in excess of 5,000 feet and the steepest portion of each mountain generally on the south side. There was only one natural weakness in the entire Fifth Army area—the Futa Pass, 20 miles north of Florence. This pass, however, contained formidable man-made defenses, including concrete bunkers, minefields, concrete-emplaced Panther tank turrets, a three-mile-long antitank ditch,[84] and two of the five German divisions opposite Fifth Army. Clark, aware of the enemy strength through ULTRA radio intercepts, wisely chose to make his main attack through the narrower and steeper, but less well-defended, Il Giogo Pass.

When Clark's Fifth Army attacked on September 10, enemy resistance was weak because, in addition to Kesselring's having shifted seven divisions to the Adriatic Sector, Hitler had recalled the four best divisions of Army Group Southwest to France once he learned that the Allies were withdrawing units from Italy. The Fifth closed the 20 miles to the Gothic Line in three days. Clark then threw three divisions at Il Giogo Pass and ruptured that position within another three days.* By mid-September, the vaunted Gothic Line had been penetrated in both the Adriatic and Central Sectors, and the British had advanced 14 miles beyond it.

*The difficulty of achieving mass in mountain warfare is illustrated by the fact that even though three divisions were attacking, no more than 1,000 men could be in contact with the enemy at any given time.[85]

German Antitank Ditch in Futa Pass

With his strongest position shattered, Kesselring's situation was desperate. If the armor-heavy Allied armies broke into the plains of the Po Valley, his army group was doomed. His chances of saving his armies looked bleak, for the Germans labored under many disadvantages. Since July, partisans had been inflicting as many as 5,000 casualties per month on his rear-area forces. Additionally, Allied air power prohibited all movement during daylight. One war correspondent dramatically described the effect:

> Nothing was more striking, to anyone who flew on a daylight sortie in Italy, than the complete contrast between the two sides of the front line. As your aircraft flew north to bomb you could look down on a busy countryside. Great columns of lorries moved on the roads, traffic jams formed on the outskirts of the towns and jeeps raced everywhere, even on the narrow tracks in the mountains.
>
> You crossed the line of smoke that always marked the front line and looked down on another world. On the German side the roads were deserted, the railway lines empty. Nothing moved in a dead and lonely landscape. The shadow of air power lay over it all.[86]

Furthermore, the Germans were outgunned by Allied artillery that interdicted almost any portion of the front lines at will. Together, Allied air and artillery created such a formidable counterattack problem that General Vietinghoff explained to Kesselring, "If the reserves are kept near the front they are decimated by the preparatory fire; if held further back they are dispersed by attacks from the air."[87] Finally, Kesselring could expect no reinforcements from Germany.

On the other hand, Kesselring enjoyed several advantages. He had one more division in Italy than Alexander had, the remaining mountains still offered ideal defensive terrain, and the winter rains would begin in late September or early October, bringing the Allied advance to a muddy halt as they had before the Gustav Line the previous winter. On the Allied side, 15th Army Group held the initiative but, like the Germans, could expect no reinforcements. To both sides, then, the war became a race against time. Could the Allies break out of the mountains before the rains began?

The Fifth and Eighth Armies continued their bloody, slow progress from ridge to ridge. By September 21, the Americans had advanced five more miles and owned a few more mountain peaks. The British, however, broke out of the mountains at Rimini but found it difficult to exploit their gains. That section of the Lombardy Plain between Rimini and Lake Comacchio is reclaimed swampland, traversed by nine rivers and hundreds of streams and drainage canals. Eighth Army sloshed ahead, beginning the Battle of the Rivers.

The day before, September 20, the first heavy rain had fallen. Drizzle and showers continued for the next seven days. Heavy rain began again on September 29 and continued until October 9. Then, after four days of clear skies, the rain resumed. Kesselring had won the race with the weather.[88]

Fifth and Eighth Armies continued to attack under appalling conditions. Roads washed out; all bridges over the Foglia River and on the Allied lines of communication washed downstream; artillery could be towed only by bulldozers; and there was no air support. Finally, troops began psychologically and physically to deteriorate from the discomfort.

Since neither side could expect reinforcements, the war in Italy had become a war of attrition. Who would run out of infantrymen first? The Allies did. Fifth Army suffered 17,388 American battle casualties from September 10 to October 28, most of them in its four US infantry divisions.[89] British units in Fifth Army and the Eighth Army suffered similar casualties, causing Leese to convert his 1st Armoured Division to infantry, disband two infantry brigades, and reduce each British infantry battalion from four to three rifle companies. The Germans also lost heavily. On September 25, Vietinghoff reported to Kesselring that of his 92 infantry battalions, 10 were "strong" (more than 400 men), 18 were "fairly strong" (300 to 400 men), 26 were "average" (200 to 300), and 38 were "weak" (less than 200).[90] The Germans, however, were not attacking.

The final straw came in late October when the Allies exhausted the available artillery ammunition in Italy.[91] On October 28, Clark ordered the Fifth Army to go over to the defensive. Leese attacked once more in early December, then stopped the Eighth for the winter.

Both sides now settled down to wait out the rain and snow of winter. The Germans strengthened their front line positions and built five more lines, the last one on the Adige River. *(See Map 51, in Atlas.)* The 15th Army Group thinned its line, then planned, rested, resupplied, and trained for a spring offensive. In spite of Alexander's having to send two more divisions to France, 15th Army Group grew steadily stronger throughout the winter as it received the U.S. 92nd Infantry Division, U.S. 10th Mountain Division, a Brazilian Division, and individual replacements. There was only one minor battle during the four-month-long winter, but its social results surpassed its insignificant tactical results. Mussolini, who had been heading a puppet government behind the German lines for over a year, decided to ape Hitler's Ardennes Offensive by striking for the Port of Leghorn through the American sector. Like the planners of the Ardennes Offensive, planners in Italy chose to make the penetration in a quiet sector occupied by a new division, in this case the 92nd Division, the only one of the three black divisions to see front-line combat in World War II. Unlike the Ardennes Offensive, however, the Allies learned through radio interceptions of the impending attack on the 92nd by elements of two Italian Divisions and one German Division. As a precaution, Alexander ordered the 8th Indian Division to prepare a second line of defense behind the 92nd. When the enemy attack came the day after Christmas, one regiment of the 92nd "melted away," but the 8th Indian held firm, ending the offensive just two days after it began.[92]

Because this defense was the first major combat action by a black division in World War II, it received far too much attention in the American press and even attracted an investigating team from the War Department. Almost everyone expressing an opinion on the causes of the defeat reached one of three general conclusions. The first was that blacks would never be good combat soldiers and should be used only in combat service support units. The second was that the division had not received sufficient training and contained too many category IV and V personnel.* The third was that the 92nd had performed no worse than had the 106th Division, which had borne the initial onslaught of the Ardennes Offensive and had also "melted away." Furthermore, the third conclusion continued, blacks had no reason to fight bravely as long as they were treated as second class citizens, given unimportant missions, denied high command positions in their own division, and disgraced by segregated officer and NCO clubs. Fifth Army, at the time, accepted the second conclusion, replacing 1,265 officers and men in the division and then returning the 92nd to combat;

*Personnel in World War II were classified into five categories, based on their scores on their entrance examinations.

eventually, the third conclusion was accepted, leading ultimately to President Truman's order in 1951 to integrate the Army.[93]

The long prepared-for, final Allied offensive in Italy began on April 1, 1945, with a minor supporting attack by the 92nd Division along the west coast, followed on April 9 by a major supporting attack by Eighth Army on the east coast. *(See Map 52, in Atlas.)* Eighth Army's attack began with a carpet bombing using 175,000 twenty-pound fragmentation bombs, and was followed by five 42-minute artillery preparations, the first four being false ones reminiscent of the Somme offensive in 1916. The assaulting forces were well supported by flame-throwing tanks and used amphibious armored personnel carriers that enabled some units to cross lakes, much to the Germans' surprise. They quickly penetrated into the German battle positions. When Fifth Army launched the main attack five days later, all German reserves had been committed against the two secondary attacks. By April 20, both the Fifth and Eighth Armies had ruptured the mountain and river defenses and were racing across the Po Valley.[94]

Army Group Southwest had always counted on the Po River as another defensive line, but because Allied aircraft had by now destroyed all the Po bridges, it became instead a trap. Many German troops escaped across the Po by small boat or by swimming, but almost all heavy equipment had to be abandoned. The Allies, with bridging equipment well forward, bounded across the Po and sped toward the major communications centers and the Alpine passes. By April 28, all the passes were under Allied control, prohibiting any escape. The following day, Vietinghoff, who had replaced Kesselring, agreed to unconditional surrender of his army group, effective on May 2.[95] The Italian Campaign was over.

Summary

After the shooting war in Italy ended, a verbal war continued for years. The major postwar argument centered on the political "if." If 15th Army Group had received more resources and had not been required to give up seven divisions in the autumn of 1943 and another six the following autumn, the Allies could have pushed to the Alps in late 1944, swung right through the Ljubljana Gap, and conquered Austria, thereby denying the Russians control of Eastern Europe.[96]

That argument is more wishful than factual. Aside from the fact that Soviet postwar policies were unknown in 1944, the Russians had already conquered all of Rumania, half of Poland, most of Hungary, and one-third of Czechoslovakia by the end of that year. In December of 1944, Russian armies were 130 miles east of Vienna while Allied armies would have been 230 miles from Vienna, even if they had conquered all of Italy by then.

American extremists, on the other hand, have claimed that excessive involvement in the Mediterranean caused the invasion of France to be postponed from 1943 to 1944, ultimately extending the war against Germany one year.[97] This argument is also wishful thinking. In General Marshall's view, an invasion of Normandy in the summer of 1943, before the Battle of the Atlantic had been won and before sufficient American armies had been raised and deployed, probably would have been smashed.[98]

At the tactical level, the German defense and delay were noteworthy. The campaign remains one of history's outstanding retrograde operations.

There is, also, little argument about the wisdom of invading Sicily. The conquest of that island secured the precious Allied shipping route through the Suez Canal and caused the withdrawal of Italy from the war, thereby increasing the strain on German manpower.

Although most contention has swirled around the controversies of OVERLORD *versus* Italy, and Allies *versus* Russia, a significant military question remains. Could the Mediterranean mission to contain the maximum number of German divisions possibly have been accomplished with fewer casualties, or accomplished more effectively by a strategy which did not involve an attack up the Italian boot? Certainly the mission was a valid one and certainly German divisions and manpower needed elsewhere were drawn into Italy. *(See Chart at end of chapter.)* In spite of the cost in casualties to the Allies (312,000), the Germans suffered more (536,000) because of superior Allied air and artillery.[99]

This is not to say, however, that a different course of action would not have occupied more German divisions and cost fewer Allied casualties. Alexander claimed that 55 German divisions were tied down in the Mediterranean in June 1944 when Normandy was assaulted.[100] Since only 26 of these divisions were in Italy, obviously 29 were in the Balkans and southern France. Thus, a significant number of German divisions were committed to occupation and security duties. Could the same number of divisions, or more, have been tied down if the Allies had invaded the Balkans or southern France instead of Italy, or even if the Allies had conducted continuous feints along the north shore of the Mediterranean? No one has examined the campaign in that light. Unfortunately, the question was never raised during 1943 and 1944.

Unlike the Allied invasion over the Normandy beaches, the Anglo-American offensives in Italy did not stem from a single strategic decision. Having committed forces in the Mediterranean to secure North Africa and capture Sicily, the Allies had troops available to further opportunistic plans to force Italy from the war. These troops could not be used in combat in

France in 1943; but if they were used in Italy they could pin down German divisions *away* from France. What the Allies had not anticipated, however, was the skillful way in which Kesselring would defend every mile up the Italian boot, extracting heavy casualties and causing an excessive drain on Allied manpower. Thus it came about that at every time for a critical decision the CCS had little choice but to continue fighting in Italy—if Hitler was to be *prevented* from reinforcing France.

The Allied armies which fought the tenacious German in Italy were always destined to play a secondary role in overall Allied strategy. From its inception, the Italian campain was expected to sap German strength so that the landings in Normandy could be successful. Moreover, the Italian Theater was envisioned by many Allied planners as being a source of troops to strengthen the more important effort in northwestern Europe. There, commencing in Normandy, the long-awaited, full-blooded, head-on assault against Hitlerite Germany would be made; there, over the easier and most direct invasion route into Germany, the western Allies would destroy Hitler's armies by applying overwhelming power. What gains Alexander's armies could make in Italy would be helpful, but only of secondary importance. The western Allies expected to win the war in northwestern Europe. It is to a description of the campaigns in that part of Europe that the narrative now turns—first, reverting in time to the early planning for the invasion of Normandy and then relating the story of the liberation of France and the subjugation of western Germany.

Summary of Allied Divisions in Fifteenth Army Group and German Divisions in Army Group Southwest

Period	**Date**	**In Italy**								**In Combat Zone**			
		Allied Divisions											
		Br.	U.S.	Commonwealth	Polish	French (Brazilian)	Total	German	Allied Superiority	Allied Div	German Div	Allied Superiority	Reinforcements and Withdrawals
Salerno	Oct 43	8	9	2			19	19	0	16	12	+4	
Winter Line	Dec 43	4	5	3		1	13	18	–5	13	11	+2	7 allied div w/d for OVERLORD
Gustav Line Anzio	Jan 44	5	5	5	1	2	18	23	–5	18	15	+3	3 Gr div formed 2 Gr div from Fr. and Balkans.
Winter Stalemate	Mar 44	5	6	5	2	3	21	24	–3	21	17	+4	
DIADEM	May 44	5	7	7	2	4	25	23	+2	25	18	+7	
Rome	Jun 44	5	7	7	2	4	25	26	–1	25	19	+6	4 Gr div arrived from other fronts. 1 disbanded.
Battles of Gothic Line	Aug 44	6	5	7	2		20	26	–6	20	22	–2	4 Fr and 2 US div to DRAGOON
Winter Interlude	Dec 44	4	6	6	2	1	19	27	–8	19	20	–1	1 Br div disbanded 1 Br & 1 Commonwealth div to Greece. 1 US div from US.
Final Offensive	Apr 45	3	7	4	2	1	17	23	–6	17	19	–2	Canadian Corps & 1 Br div to France. 1 Br div to Greece. 1 US div from US. 4 Gr div to East & Western Fronts.

Notes

[1] Albert N. Garland and Howard M. Smyth, *Sicily and the Surrender of Italy* (Washington, 1965), p. 3.

[2] *Ibid.*, p. 5; William G. F. Jackson, *The Battle for Italy* (New York, 1967), p. 12.

[3] Garland and Smyth, *Sicily* p. 10.

[4] *Ibid.*, pp. 50-51.

[5] *Ibid.*, pp. 54-55.

[6] *Ibid.*, p. 58.

[7] Jackson, *Battle for Italy*, pp. 41-42.

[8] Donald E. Cluxton, Jr., "Concepts of Airborne Warfare in World War II" (Unpublished MA thesis; Duke Univesity, Durham, 1967), pp. 59-62; Ronald Lewin, *Ultra Goes to War* (New York, 1978), p. 280.

[9] Vincent J. Esposito, *The West Point Atlas of American Wars* (2 vols.; New York, 1959), II, Section 2, 91.

[10] Robert D. Heinl, *Dictionary of Military and Naval Quotations* (Annapolis, MD, 1966), p. 357.

[11] Garland and Smyth, *Sicily*, pp. 181-182.

[12] Jackson, *Battle for Italy*, pp. 57-58.

[13] Garland and Smyth, *Sicily*, pp. 410, 416.

[14] Winston S. Churchill, *Triumph and Tragedy* (London, 1954), pp. 88-91; Jackson, *Battle for Italy*, p. 318.

[15] Samuel E. Morison, *Strategy and Compromise* (Boston, 1958), p. 47; Dwight D. Eisenhower, *Crusade in Europe* (Garden City, NY, 1952), p. 199.

[16] Michael Howard, *Grand Strategy*, Vol. IV (London, 1972), p. 432.

[17] Jackson, *Battle for Italy*, p. 86.

[18] *Ibid.*, p. 87.

[19] *Ibid.*, p. 88.

[20] Albert Kesselring, *Kesselring: A Soldier's Record* (New York, 1954), pp. 219-220; Jackson, *Battle for Italy*, p. 97.

[21] Kesselring, *Kesselring*, pp. 207-222; Jackson, *Battle for Italy*, p. 100.

[22] Esposito, *West Point Atlas*, II, Section 2, 95.

[23] Martin Blumenson, *Salerno to Cassino* (Washington, 1969), pp. 54-57, 73-90.

[24] *Ibid.*, pp. 119, 120, 124, 126, 147; Jackson, *Battle for Italy*, p. 113.

[25] Jackson, *Battle for Italy*, p. 118; Lewin, *Ultra Goes to War*, p. 284.

[26] Rudolf Bohmler, *Monte Cassino*, translated by R. H. Stevens (London, 1964), pp. 69-70.

[27] Blumenson, *Salerno to Cassino*, pp. 168-169.

[28] *Ibid.*, pp. 152-153.

[29] Alfred D. Chandler (ed.), *The Papers of Dwight David Eisenhower*, Vol. III (Baltimore, 1970), pp. 1411, 1459, 1476, 1479; Francis L. Lowenheim (ed.), *Roosevelt and Churchill, Their Secret Wartime Correspondence* (New York, 1975), pp. 360-361, 372.

[30] F. W. Winterbotham, *The Ultra Secret* (New York, 1974), p. 113. Also see Lewin, *Ultra Goes to War*, p. 284.

[31] Chandler, *Papers of Eisenhower*, III, p. 1485.

[32] Mary H. Williams, *Chronology* (Washington, 1960), p. 139; Kesselring, *Kesselring*, pp. 227-228.

[33] Chandler, *Papers of Eisenhower*, III, pp. 1479, 1497.

[34] *Ibid.*, pp. 1496, 1497.

[35] *Ibid.*, p. 1505; Blumenson, *Salerno to Cassino*, p. 181.

[36] Jackson, *Battle for Italy*, p. 123.

[37] *Ibid.*, p. 131.

[38] Kesselring, *Kesselring*, p. 227.

[39] Blumenson, *Salerno to Cassino*, pp. 189-206; Jackson, *Battle for Italy*, pp. 133-135.

[40] Blumenson, *Salerno to Cassino*, pp. 183, 224-226.

[41] *Ibid.*, pp. 249, 265; Jackson, *Battle for Italy*, pp. 128, 146, 208.

[42] G. W. L. Nicholson, *The Canadians in Italy, 1943-1945*, Vol. II (Ottawa, 1957), pp. 324-333; Jackson, *Battle for Italy*, pp. 152-153.

[43] Blumenson, *Salerno to Cassino*, p. 265.

[44] Office of the Chief of Military History, *The War Against Germany and Italy: Mediterranean and Adjacent Areas: Pictorial Record* (Washington, 1951), p. 205.

[45] Martin Blumenson, *Anzio: The Gamble that Failed* (New York, 1963), p. 29.

[46] Blumenson, *Salerno to Cassino*, p. 289.

[47] *Ibid.*, pp. 267, 308-310.

[48] Blumenson, *Anzio*, p. 63.

[49] *Ibid.*, p. 32; Chandler, *Papers of Eisenhower*, III, p. 1545.

[50] Blumenson, *Anzio*, p. 34.

[51] Chandler, *Papers of Eisenhower*, III, p. 1545; John Ehrman, *Grand Strategy*, Vol. V (London, 1956), p. 73; Maurice Matloff, *Strategic Planning for Coalition Warfare, 1943-1944* (Washington, 1959), p. 365.

[52] Matloff, *Strategic Planning*, p. 364.

[53] Jackson, *Battle for Italy*, pp. 156-157; Blumenson, *Salerno to Cassino*, p. 294.

[54] Jackson, *Battle for Italy*, p. 49.

[55] Trumbull Higgins, *Soft Underbelly, the Anglo-American Controversy Over the Italian Campaign, 1939-1945* (New York, 1968), pp. 136-139; Blumenson, *Anzio*, pp. 45-50.

[56] Lowenheim, *Roosevelt and Churchill*, p. 471.

[57] Kesselring, *Kesselring*, pp. 230-232.

[58] Blumenson, *Anzio*, pp. 64-65.

[59] Blumenson, *Salerno to Cassino*, pp. 353-354; Lewin, *Ultra Goes to War*, p. 285.

[60] Blumenson, *Salerno to Cassino*, pp. 353-356.

[61] *Ibid.*, pp. 358-359.

[62] *Ibid.*, pp. 360-364.

[63] *Ibid.*, p. 391.

[64] Jackson, *Battle for Italy*, p. 190.

[65] Blumenson, *Anzio*, p. 109.

[66] Kesselring, *Kesselring*, pp. 234-235.

[67] Robert W. Coakley and Richard M. Leighton, *Global Logistics and Strategy, 1943-1945* (Washington, 1968), pp. 338-340.

[68] Blumenson, *Anzio*, pp. 138-139.

[69] Jackson, *Battle for Italy*, p. 191.

[70] *Ibid.*, p. 198; Blumenson, *Salerno to Cassino*, pp. 402, 417-419.

[71] John D. Forsythe and Chester G. Starr (eds.), *Fifth Army History*, Part IV, pp. 178-182.

[72] *Ibid.*, p. 188.

[73] Michael Howard, *The Mediterranean Strategy in the Second World War* (New York, 1968), p. 59.

[74] Ehrman, *Grand Strategy*, Vol. V, pp. 244-253.

[75] Jackson, *Battle for Italy*, pp. 225-226.

[76] *Ibid.*, p. 229.

[77] Bohmler, *Monte Cassino*, p. 137.

[78] Sidney T. Mathews, "General Clark's Decision to Drive on Rome," in Kent R. Greenfield (ed.), *Command Decisions* (Washington, 1960), pp. 361-363; Lewin, *Ultra Goes to War*, p. 290.

[79] Douglas Orgill, *The Gothic Line: The Italian Campaign, Autumn, 1944* (New York, 1967), pp. 27-29; Esposito, *West Point Atlas*, II, Section 2, 105.

[80] Ehrman, *Grand Strategy*, Vol. V, p. 352.

[81] *Ibid.*, p. 354.

[82] *Ibid.*, pp. 357-358.

[83] Orgill, *The Gothic Line*, pp. 37-48.

[84] *Ibid.*, pp. 163-164.

[85] *Ibid.*, p. 167.

[86] Wynford Vaughn-Thomas, *Anzio* (New York, 1961), p. 22.

[87] Nicholson, *The Canadians in Italy*, p. 548.

[88] Orgill, *The Gothic Line*, p. 161.

[89] *Fifth Army History*, Vol. VII, pp. 215-218.

[90] Nicholson, *The Canadians in Italy*, pp. 562-563.

[91] Coakley and Leighton, *Global Logistics*, p. 550.

[92] Ulysses Lee, *The Employment of Negro Troops* (Washington, 1966), pp. 562-567.

[93] *Ibid.*, pp. 572-579.

[94] Orgill, *The Gothic Line*, pp. 302-305, 309.

[95] *Ibid.*, p. 315; Esposito, *West Point Atlas*, II, Section 2, 110.

[96] Churchill, *Triumph and Tragedy*, pp. 691-692; Clark, *Calculated Risk*, pp. 347-352; Hanson W. Baldwin, *Great Mistakes of the War* (New York, 1949), p. 25.

[97] Morison, *Strategy and Compromise*, pp. 50-51, 57, 58.

[98] Matloff, *Strategic Planning*, p. 27.

[99] Jackson, *Battle for Italy*, p. 317.

[100] "The Despatch of Field-Marshal The Earl Alexander of Tunis to the Secretary of State for War," published in the *London Gazette*, June 12, 1950, cited in Jackson, *Battle for Italy*, p. 366.

No More Gallipolis: Planning and Preparing the Cross-Channel Attack 11

The pages of history are strewn with the wreckage of empires which collapsed as a result of an unsuccessful attempt at invasion. The British Empire was almost wrecked on the shores of Gallipoli. Napoleon's empire never recovered from the failure of his attempts to invade England. The Spanish empire faded with the wrecking of the Great Armada.

*Lieutenant General David A. D. Ogden**

Events in the Italian Theater of War were closely related to Allied strategy and planning for the invasion of France. Alexander's armies not only furnished some of the troops for the Normandy invasion but also prevented the Germans from shifting divisions westward. Moreover, many of the key planners and leaders who would serve under General Dwight D. Eisenhower came from the Mediterranean area, where they had gained valuable experience. That experience was put to use on the beaches of Normandy, at a time when the troops serving in the secondary theater in Italy were finally enjoying the heady experience of driving the Germans northward of Rome, after months of frustratingly slow progress up the Italian Peninsula. As would continue to be the case regarding events in Italy and northwestern Europe, however, the seizure of the Eternal City was overshadowed by news of the Allied landings in France. Those landings represented the culmination of many months of planning and preparation, which had begun well before the Allies invaded Sicily. An important step in that preparation phase had been the designation of Eisenhower to command the invasion force and the issuance to him of a directive which set forth his mission.

On February 12, 1944, the Combined Chiefs of Staff charged General Eisenhower with planning and executing one of the crucial operations of the Second World War. Eisenhower's directive read: "You will enter the continent of Europe and, in conjunction with the other United Nations, undertake operations aimed at the heart of Germany and the destruction of her armed forces."[1] The invasion of Normandy, which resulted from this directive, marked not only the start of the decisive western campaign against Germany but also the high point of cooperation between Great Britain and the United States during the war.[2]

If Eisenhower possessed advantages normally the preserve of the commander on the offensive, he also had an awesome responsibility. Should the D-Day invasion—or Operation OVERLORD as it was code-named—fail, and the Allied armies be defeated on the beaches, much time would be lost before another force, perhaps under a new commander, could be prepared. As Franklin D. Roosevelt was up for re-election in November, a new President—one who would not have suffered defeat on the beaches of France—might be in office. In the interim, the American war effort would no doubt be concentrated against Japan, and the priority of the European Theater would be altered. Secure in France, Hitler might concentrate his troops against Russia and eventually negotiate a settlement with Stalin. On the other hand, Stalin might be capable of launching a supreme effort which would crush German forces and result in Russian troops advancing to the Channel. The consequences of failure were great. Eisenhower's decision had to be correct.[3] That it was so is a personal tribute to the commanding general; but it is also a strong testimonial to the meticulous planning which had gone on in the years before the invasion.

*Cited in Robert D. Heinl, Jr., *Dictionary of Military and Naval Quotations* (Annapolis, 1966), p. 162.

Preliminary Planning: Realism, Imagination and Thoroughness

Even as British troops were being driven off the Continent in 1940, Prime Minister Winston Churchill was already considering ways to return. While preparing to counter German air and sea threats, he ordered raids against enemy-held shores and also directed that work begin on plans for building landing craft capable of transporting armored vehicles. By the end of the summer of 1940, a Combined Operations Headquarters to control offensive actions had been established. In October, Commodore Lord Louis Mountbatten was named its head, and charged not only with the conduct of coastal raids but also with solving technical problems related to amphibious assaults. The previous month the British Chief of the Imperial General Staff had issued orders to prepare a plan for an attack on the continent. The next year, in March 1941, an informal accord regarding strategy was reached with the United States should America be drawn into the war.* Already, the previous summer, a permanent American naval observer had gone to England; following the ABC-1 talks, Major General James E. Chaney, an Army Air Corps officer, took station in London as Special Army Observer for the United States.[4]

With the entry of the United States into the war in December 1941, the informal nature of alliance planning abruptly changed. The quickly convened ARCADIA conference confirmed the Germany-first strategy and resulted in the organization of planning staffs designed to achieve unity of effort.† Almost simultaneously, Chaney's small group was redesignated United States Army Forces in the British Isles (USAFBI), Headquarters, U.S. V Corps went to Northern Ireland, and advanced air elements arrived in England. Meanwhile, the British continued planning a cross-Channel assault, using for that purpose senior commanders of the three services (designated the Combined Commanders), later augmented by Mountbatten and, informally, by the Commanding General of the U.S. Army European Theater of Operations (ETOUSA).** In Washington, planning also progressed in the Army's War Plans Division, headed by Brigadier General Eisenhower. Eisenhower stressed the importance of launching an invasion from England in 1942 or, barring that, of massing Allied strength in the Mediterranean. Much to his surprise, General George C. Marshall sent Eisenhower to London in June and gave him the job of implementing his own draft directive for ETOUSA. He would pave the way for the future Supreme Commander for the invasion, possibly Marshall himself.[5] As events over the next year and a half would reveal, impatient Americans pushed to get the invasion going while most British, led by a Prime Minister who vividly recalled the costly frontal assaults of the First World War, repeatedly brought up the problems involved and advocated a weakening of Germany by attacks in other areas before the main thrust was launched.[6]

Allied soldiers planning operations in this war had a real advantage over those who had performed similar tasks in the First World War. Since the time of the Battle of France in 1940, progressively more and more of the coded radio messages sent by the German high commanders (including Hitler) as well as those transmitted by senior staff officers were being deciphered by the British. The particular Germany cypher machine used was called Enigma. Material based on Enigma intelligence was classified separately so that it would be treated with particular care. This category of information, called ULTRA, was divulged directly to only a limited number of people. Should ULTRA information indicate that the enemy was going to take an action which must be quickly countered, a cover story had to be rapidly constructed lest the Germans learn that their messages were being read. For example, if it was learned that a supply convoy was to leave a certain port, an aerial reconnaissance flight would be flown where it could not only see the convoy but also be seen and reported by the enemy. With that report in the logs when the quickly mounted Allied strike came, the Germans would assume that the attack

U.S. Troops With British Escort in Northern Ireland

*See Chapter 8, p. 182, for discussion of the ABC-1 talks.

†*Ibid.*, pp. 182-183, for details of ARCADIA and the Combined Chiefs of Staff.

**USAFBI was redesignated ETOUSA in June 1942.

was based on the information from the reconnaissance aircraft, and the secret of ULTRA would be preserved.

What ULTRA meant to all Allied operations is readily apparent. After Dunkirk, for example, Churchill could use his limited resources where they were most needed, an important factor in the successful conclusion of the Battle of Britain. When planning the invasion of France, Allied officers knew the locations and strengths of units as well as their shortages in equipment and men. Other messages revealed that the coastal area was being used to rehabilitate divisions transferred from the East. This information, coupled with that from other intelligence sources, virtually enabled the planners and their military and political leaders to see on both sides of the hill.[7]

The decision to invade North Africa in November 1942 inevitably had considerable impact on the planning and build-up for the invasion of France. For one thing, continuity of direction suffered. Eisenhower commanded both ETOUSA and the North African operations until February 1943; his ETOUSA replacement died in May in an aircraft accident and was in turn succeeded by Lieutenant General Jacob L. Devers, then Chief of the Armored Force at Fort Knox. Second, operations in North Africa drew upon ETOUSA resources. Depth of the drawdown in the United Kingdom can be seen by comparing the 188,000 men (including four divisions) who were massed there in September 1942 to the 108,000 at the end of February 1943. Three of the four divisions and a total of 150,000 men had gone south. Some replacements had come in to account for the difference, but it would be the fall of 1943 before a second division would arrive. About 1,100 airplanes and much equipment had also been shifted. Supplies arriving in February hit a low of 22,000 tons, a significant drop from the 270,000 tons which reached the United Kingdom in September 1942.[8]

Nevertheless, by the time Devers assumed his post, much cross-Channel planning had been accomplished, initially toward mounting simultaneous attacks at several different points in France, later toward studying a single main thrust into an area which could be expected to hold all the attacking troops and their logistical tail. This change, perhaps, was due to lessons learned during the Dieppe raid in August 1942. Dieppe, a reconnaissance in force, was designed by Mountbatten's Combined Operations Headquarters to test tactics and techniques of the type that would be used in the actual invasion, as well as to support a rumor campaign that was designed to help Russia by causing the Germans to think an invasion was coming somewhere on the Channel coast. German deception had convinced Allied intelligence that Dieppe was garrisoned by only 1,400 men, when actually over 5,000 troops were located there and ample reserves were nearby. Due to the efforts of a French traitor and the result of a naval action which took place in the Channel as the invasion force was en route, the operation was compromised and the garrison alerted. The cost in Allied lives was high. In addition, Dieppe called Hitler's attention to France; he ordered a more rapid construction of the Atlantic Wall. The raid also demonstrated the futility of making a frontal attack against a well-defended port as well as the need for secrecy and better intelligence. Future attacks, both in the Mediterranean and cross-Channel, would have to be conducted by an extremely powerful landing force supported by concentrated air and naval gun fire.[9]

The major and quite obvious problem confronting the planners was where to re-enter western Europe. Several considerations were important: sufficiently large and workable landing beaches and an adequate port located in their vicinity; an adequate transportation network leading inland; neutralizable German beach defenses; an area both within fighter aircraft range of British bases and also suitable for construction of air fields if none already existed; and specific climatic conditions (tides, prevailing winds, sea approaches). Considering all these factors, the Caen area in Normandy appeared best, if Cotentin beaches were also included to speed the seizure of the port of Cherbourg. *(See Map 53, in* ***Atlas.****)* Additional ports would be needed, but more planning was required before these could be selected.[10]

Meanwhile, at the Casablanca Conference, decisions were made which affected the build-up and planning for the cross-Channel attack.* Shipping was still scarce because the U-boats were sinking more tonnage than was being built, even though on land the tide was turning in favor of the Allies. Hence, the Battle of the Atlantic took first priority while round-the-clock bombing of Germany (Operation POINTBLANK) would sap German industry and morale, preparatory to a projected cross-Channel landing in 1944. Until then, Eisenhower could exploit the Mediterranean situation by seizing Sicily. Though it was deemed too early to name a Supreme Commander for the invasion, planning was to be intensified under a separate joint staff headed by British Lieutenant General Frederick E. Morgan, named Chief of Staff to the Supreme Allied Commander (designate). Morgan staff would be known as COSSAC.[11]

Planning Under COSSAC

By late April 1943, when he received his directive from the Combined Chiefs of Staff, Morgan was already hard at work with his U.S. Deputy, Major General Ray W. Barker, at Norfolk House, St. James Square, site of the birthplace of George III. They gave special care to the selection of staff members because it was commonly believed that this staff would become the core of the future Supreme Headquarters which

*See Chapter 8, pp. 186-187, for discussion of the Casablanca Conference.

would execute the cross-Channel plan. Morgan echoed this concept when he met officially with his key staff members on April 17. "The term, 'Planning staff,'" said Morgan, "has come to have a most sinister meaning—it implies the production of nothing but paper. What we must continue to do somehow is produce not only paper, but action."[12] There was no slackening of the issuance of paper, however, as COSSAC worked also on plans for diversionary operations to draw enemy forces away from critical operational localities.

At the TRIDENT Conference† a month later, the heads of state made several decisions which provided Morgan with more definitive guidance but, significantly, also required Eisenhower to make plans for driving Italy from the war. Morgan was told to plan to assault about May 1, 1944, with three infantry divisions. Two more infantry divisions would be afloat, constituting an immediate follow-up force, and two airborne divisions would also be available. Total strength in the United Kingdom at the time of the attack was projected to be almost 30 divisions. To form part of the cross-Channel force, seven battle-tested divisions (four U.S. and three British) would be transferred from the Mediterranean to England. Agreement was also reached on a plan to use the Combined Bomber Offensive to help pave the way for the cross-Channel invasion.[13]

During the early summer, with the decisions reached at TRIDENT in hand, Morgan's planning became more detailed, yet his product remained but an outline; thus, the Supreme Commander, when he arrived, would be free to make his own decisions. Searching for an invasion site, COSSAC reviewed the planning previously done by the Combined Commanders and looked at both the Pas de Calais and the Caen area in Normandy. *(See Map 54, in Atlas.)*

The Pas de Calais was closer to England, the excellent port at Antwerp, and the German homeland. It also contained a larger number of airfields than Normandy. On the other hand, the Pas de Calais was more strongly defended and more exposed to the sometimes violent Channel winds. Finally, the beaches had narrow exits guarded by natural and man-made obstacles, and there was no defensible terrain feature inland which could serve as the rim of a lodgment area. At Caen, the weaker German defenses could not be reinforced as rapidly as was true in the Pas de Calais area. There was shelter from winds, and the beaches were better for tank use and had more exits. Superior natural defenses existed inland, and except for the Caen-Bayeux area, the hedgerow-type terrain was unfavorable for armored counterattack. In mid-June, those COSSAC planners who had been working on an estimate and outline plan for a Pas de Calais attack reported agreement with the pro-Caen assessment made earlier by the Combined Commanders. By the end of July, all other areas were rapidly eliminated, and Caen was selected.[14]

As the Allied invasion force would probably have but a small numerical superiority, everything possible had to be done to improve the odds of success. Starting in June 1943, deception, psychological warfare, and other means would be employed. Plan FORTITUDE was designed to cause the Germans to array their forces against false threats and thus ease the way for the actual invasion. FORTITUDE was composed of two major parts. FORTITUDE NORTH, targeted against Norway and the other countries of Scandinavia, was designed to cause Hitler to keep his divisions in place to meet a joint British-American-Russian attack; FORTITUDE SOUTH, hopefully, would trick Hitler into believing that a fictitious army group—the First United States Army Group—was getting ready to conduct the Allied main attack on the Pas de Calais. German units fixed in the Scandinavian countries and in the Pas de Calais could not reinforce those which were defending Normandy. FORTITUDE also included a threat to the Marseilles area to fix the German Nineteenth Army, and another to the Biscay coast to draw the attention of the First Army. Many other operations would be simulated at various points, to include Italy and the Balkans, all designed to confuse the German leaders concerning the actual invasion site. FORTITUDE was but one part, though a major one, of Plan BODYGUARD (formerly called Plan JAEL) which was designed to use offensive intelligence, counterintelligence and security, special operations, political warfare, and deception to mislead Hitler about Allied global strategy. By use of ULTRA, the Allies could obtain feedback concerning the success of these deceptive efforts.[15]

The planners envisioned that airpower would play a vital role in preparations for the invasion. During the summer of 1943, German fighter strength in western German was rising fast; it had to be reduced to assure Allied air superiority. Deep raids on German aircraft production facilities could be expected not only to damage those plants, but also to cause enemy fighters to rise to their defense. Once in the air, hopefully, many of the fighters could be destroyed. Concurrently, attacks aimed at other key targets, including transportation and industry, would continue. A major aim of this air offensive was the reduction of the morale of German civilians.[16]

Morgan's Outline Plan forecast that the beachhead taken on D-Day (two British divisions assaulting the eastern beaches and one U.S. division attacking the western beach) would be expanded so that Cherbourg as well as the airfields southeast of Caen would be in Allied hands by D + 14. Then the Americans would probably strike toward the Brittany ports while the British and Canadians covered the operation by attacking to the east. COSSAC also wanted a diversionary assault launched against southern France by Eisenhower's Mediterranean forces, timed to coincide with the cross-Channel assault. The Seine and Loire Rivers bounded the final lodgment area which

†See Chapter 8, pp. 188-189, for discussion of TRIDENT.

was to be taken by D + 50. Here the Allies would prepare for the next push, which would include the taking of the Seine ports and Paris. Then another pause would ensue. Though a breakout at some point would be a pleasant occurrence, Morgan's assigned job was to plan to get the invasion troops ashore and to take a lodgment area. His plan, which had been approved by the Combined Chiefs of Staff, was presented to Churchill and Roosevelt at the QUADRANT Conference* in August 1943.[17] It was approved, but Morgan was also told to consider what he would do if the landing force was increased by 25 percent so that the beaches on the eastern coast of the Cotentin Peninsula could also be attacked.

By the end of September, COSSAC had restudied the entire invasion problem. Morgan stated that his first priority was the acquisition of sufficient landing craft to support the original scheme. After this had been accomplished, a fourth division, with landing craft, could be added. Under current conditions, many of the follow-up forces would have to be administratively loaded in regular vessels. "We already have far too high a proportion of our goods in the shop window," Morgan said, "[and] to consider any increase in this proportion without adequate stocking of the back premises would in my opinion be basically unsound." Thus, as it would be throughout the exercise, the subject of landing craft came to be the key factor in planning OVERLORD. Morgan also expressed concern over widening the assault areas onto the Cotentin because the Germans were beginning to flood inland areas on the peninsula—they might extend this work to the eastern beaches. The British Chiefs of Staff told him that a fourth (U.S.) division would attack and go in on the east Cotentin beaches.[18]

Morgan had other difficulties with which to contend. His original task had been accomplished, but now, as a staff officer, he had been charged with continuing the planning and supplying the details that had purposefully been omitted, pending the appointment of a Supreme Commander. Moreover, the chance always remained that when such a leader was selected, he might veto much of this planning. To add to his woes, Morgan, a relatively junior officer, would have to task the commanders of major units—subordinate to the Supreme Commander for OVERLORD—with appropriate planning responsibilities. Also, a decision had to be reached concerning which major headquarters should command the combined British-American ground forces. Unified command was necessary to control offensive operations while guarding against the possibility that an enemy counterattack along the national boundary might split the force. After much discussion lasting into the fall, it was decided that the British 21st Army Group Headquarters, which had been operational since midsummer and had played a role in COSSAC planning, would command all Allied ground forces in the assault and for the first part of the build-up. Under the 21st Army Group, the Second British Army would direct British forces and the U.S. First Army would be the senior headquarters for American troops. The First Army became operational in England in late October under the command of Lieutenant General Omar N. Bradley, who had been transferred from command of the II Corps in Sicily. As the invasion progressed and two U.S. armies became operational, a United States Army group would assume direction of the U.S. ground forces.[19]

In part to enable Morgan to issue his "Supreme Allied Headquarters" planning directive to key subordinate commanders who would execute it, two of these leaders were named early. Admiral Sir Bertram A. Ramsay, organizer of the Royal Navy for the Dunkirk evacuation, participant in the planning for the 1942 North African landings, and later commander of the British naval task force in the Sicilian invasion, was named Allied Naval Commander. Commander of the Allied Expeditionary Air Force would be Air Marshall Sir Trafford Leigh-Mallory, who had commanded a fighter group in the Battle of Britain and the Air Force element at Dieppe. By mid-December, Leigh-Mallory would have both U.S. and British tactical air elements under his command. Command of strategic air elements posed a major problem which would not be resolved until well into 1944. American planners, opposed to putting their big bombers under fighter expert Leigh-Mallory, proposed that the Supreme Commander command Allied strategic air forces in both the Mediterranean and European theaters. The British felt that the Supreme Commander should not have a major say in strategic air operations until the OVERLORD date was much closer. Up to that point, normal strategic missions should continue. In any case, the Supreme Commander during the cross-Channel attack would command the sea and air forces, possibly including strategic air elements, through British subordinates, while a British commander led the Allied ground forces in the initial stages. Thus, Morgan's directive, issued on November 29, went to the Air Commander-in-Chief, Allied Expeditionary Air Force, the Allied Naval Commander-in-Chief, and the Commanding General, 21st Army Group. Allied ground command would remain in the hands of the 21st Army Group commander until the American army group took over its sector. Then, on order from the Supreme Commander, both group commanders would have equal status.[20]

While Morgan was readying his planning directive, the Cairo-Teheran Conferences were being held.* As usual, the availability of landing craft was a crucial problem. At Tehe-

*See Chapter 8, pp. 190-191. Note that the decision to invade Italy had been made *before* QUADRANT (on July 20, 1943) and that the heads of state agreed that the cross-Channel Supreme Commander would be an American, but that the selection was delayed.

*See Chapter 8, pp. 192-194.

ran, Stalin pressed hard for getting on with OVERLORD and for the landing in southern France. He also wanted to know why the Supreme Commander had not been named. These were difficult questions, because the number of landing craft available dictated dates and strengths of assaults and because Roosevelt had not yet been able to decide who to name as commander. For his part, Stalin committed the USSR to aiding in deception schemes, part of Plan JAEL (BODYGUARD), designed to cause the Germans to believe that Scandinavia and the Balkans were threatened by major invasions and that the western Allies would not invade France until after the 1944 Russian offensive began. Starting date for the Russian attack, so the story went, was mid-July. If Hitler was deceived by this international effort, he would not dare move his forces until well after the invasion force had landed in France.[21]

Army Chief of Staff George C. Marshall had been the odds-on choice for the job of Supreme Commander, but Roosevelt, although believing he deserved the job and the prestige, had reservations. The President had wanted Marshall to command both the Atlantic and Mediterranean operations, but Churchill vetoed this idea of a super command. Now Roosevelt saw that with a rearrangement of the Combined Chiefs of Staff, Marshall, working for former subordinates, might appear to have been demoted. Moreover, his prestige and influence in Washington (with Congress and the Joint Chiefs of Staff) and with the British was enormous, and there was a real doubt as to whether he could be spared for the OVERLORD job. On December 4, the President, probably knowing that Marshall would never request the job, asked his unofficial advisor, Harry L. Hopkins, to determine Marshall's desire. On that occasion, as on the fifth when Roosevelt personally asked him, Marshall said he would abide by the President's decision. Marshall later recalled, "Then he evidently assumed that concluded the affair and that I would not command in Europe. Because he said, 'Well, I didn't feel I could sleep at ease if you were out of Washington.'"[22] Roosevelt thus reached the judgment that Eisenhower, who had been approved previously by Churchill as a possible commander, would be the best choice. He promptly informed Stalin of his decision and, on December 7 at Tunis, personally told Eisenhower of his appointment.[23] The Allies had taken a major step forward.

German Preparations for Defense Against Invasion

As the Allies planned and made ready to invade France, Hitler's troops across the Channel were busy also. Following the fall of France in 1940, German defensive efforts had focused on combatting British raids, but a force had also captured the British Channel Islands off the coast of France. *(See Map 54, in Atlas.)* From there, Axis forces could protect coastal shipping and the Bay of St. Malo. Although Hitler believed that the British might attempt to retake these islands for prestige reasons, and thus heavily garrisoned them, the British did not launch an attack. Instead, world attention shifted to Russia where the Germans struck in full fury on June 22, 1941. When the conflict on the Eastern Front dragged on and the United States became a belligerent, Hitler determined that something must be done to solve the dilemma of a two-front war.[24]

General George C. Marshall

Massing of forces on one of the fronts without being destroyed from the other direction was the problem. Hitler turned to an oft-tried solution, the construction of a wall. Both fronts were studied, and the Western Front was selected. Because better rail and road communications existed there, it would be easier to bring in the vast quantities of needed equipment and materials. Also, terrain in the West was more favorable for defense, and of course any enemy attack would have to be launched from the sea. Finally, there was less room for maneuver in the West. An Allied break-through would soon threaten vital areas of the *Reich*, whereas there were great expanses of terrain to trade in the East. Although the Chief of the General Staff, Generaloberst Franz Halder, advised that the wall should be sited inland beyond reach of Allied naval guns, Hitler overruled him—construction would be accomplished just off the beaches. If an attack came, the defenders could take refuge from any preliminary bombardment in the fortifications, and then emerge to repel the invaders.[25]

Up to this time—March 1942—each unit had been responsible for its own defenses, but now that Hitler had made his decision there was need for more effective coordination. One of the most well-known of the *Wehrmacht* commanders had just informed his leader that his health had been restored and that he desired a new assignment. In a week, 66-year-old Generalfeldmarschall Gerd von Rundstedt, veteran of the fighting in Poland (1939), in the West (1940 to 1941), and in Russia (1941), had been appointed *Oberefehlshaber West* (Commander-in-Chief West) (OB West). During his early months in command, Rundstedt travelled unarmed about the French countryside, distributed surplus food to French civilians, and did all he could to encourage good relations with the French, hoping that a real and lasting peace could be reached between France and Germany. He was not a fan of Hitler. In fact, he was overheard referring to his leader as a "Bohemian lance corporal." Hitler, aware of the experience and prestige of Rundstedt, seemed prepared to accept the less than complimentary remarks, for when he was told of Rundstedt's lack of respect, he was supposed to have replied, "As long as the Field Marshal grumbles, everything is all right."

Rundstedt had much to grumble about. He was short of guns, especially heavy ones, and German reserve stocks of large artillery pieces were low. Those large weapons that were in place were normally improperly positioned for use by the Army because the Navy was to control most of this large caliber fire until an invasion force landed, at which time the ground chain of command would take over. Even then the Navy retained responsibility for engaging sea targets. Naval gunners preferred direct fire, and their pieces were sited with this in mind. As they could see their targets on the sea, so also could they be seen; therefore, heavy protection was needed. Laid to guard against the deep-water naval threat, most of the heavy batteries were unable to cover either the coast or close-in approaches. When the enemy landed and command was passed, Rundstedt would gain an almost worthless asset. Seacoast artillery was not Rundstedt's only command problem, for he had but limited control of *Schutzstaffel* (Elite Guard or SS) parachute troops and many antiaircraft units. Worse yet, there was to be no real unity of command in the West. Rundstedt and the German commander in Denmark reported to OKW (*Oberkommando der Wehrmacht*—Armed Forces High Command) on coastal defense matters. In case of attack, naval and air units were to respond to "requests," but they would not come under Rundstedt's command. Hitler, as Chief of State, Supreme Commander of the Armed Forces, and Commander-in-Chief of the Army, was the only one in a position to exercise unity of command. Rundstedt complained to the OKW, and as these remarks concerned major deficiencies in the German defense, his personal messages were encoded. Material from these messages was passed with dispatch through ULTRA to the Allied planners.[27]

Shortly after his appointment, Rundstedt received Hitler's Directive No. 40, issued on March 23, 1942. Therein the *Fuehrer* set forth his philosophy of defense for the West. Enemy invading forces must be destroyed by quick counterattack shortly after they hit the beach. Should any German position or garrisons be bypassed, they should be prepared to hold out to the last. The construction of defenses would be in areas where a major force could land. This would surely be in the general vicinity of a major port, as its facilities would early be needed to support a growing lodgment area. The employment of artificial harbors was not mentioned. Even the experienced Rundstedt had not considered this possibility.[28]

Within a week after the publication of Directive No. 40, the British raided the port of St. Nazaire. *(See Map 54, in Atlas.)* Then, in August, came the great Dieppe Raid. Both sides learned lessons. Whereas the Allies tested amphibious doctrine, the Germans learned the immediate need for improved defenses for St. Nazaire, where the only dry dock in Europe large enough to handle the largest warships of the German Navy was disabled. German success in repelling the Allies at Dieppe helped to prove the soundness of emphasizing construction, and an even stronger defense was ordered. The primary area of concern was the *Kanalkueste*, or the area close to both England and the German industrial area. The *Kanalkueste* included the coast between the Somme and the Seine Rivers plus the Pas de Calais.[29]

Some of the pressure of impending invasion was relieved in early November 1942 when the Allies landed in North Africa. Hitler, believing that no cross-Channel invasion would be launched in the near future, approved the transfer of large numbers of troops out of Rundstedt's command. With a weakened defense force, control over occupied France became even more important. Though during the Dieppe raid local residents took care of wounded German soldiers, Hitler was unsure of the loyalty of the Vichy army should an invasion of southern France take place. The invaders would probably include French deserters from Vichy as well as British and American troops. Thus, the previously prepared plan to occupy the remainder of France was executed shortly after the Allied landings in North Africa. Now Rundstedt's task became even more difficult because he was responsible for a greater area, but the quality of the troops who were to fight the defensive battle had declined. Between April 1943 (when the Allies were finishing up their task in Tunisia) and December (when they took San Pietro and were closing on the Rapido River in Italy), 27 divisions, including 5 armored and 2 motorized, were transferred by the Germans out of the West. Their replacements were of a lower caliber, being mainly newly formed or reserve divisions.[30]

Some Germans believed that the *Vergeltungs* (vengeance) type weapon, which was to be fired from the Pas de Calais area, might compensate for the deficiency in the number and quality of troops. Construction of launch sites for these pilotless aircraft (V-1) and rocket (V-2) weapons was so secret that at first the local army commander was not allowed to enter the area. When he complained to OB West that this mysterious construction was attracting Allied air attacks, it was discovered that neither the staff nor Rundstedt himself knew what was being built. This oversight was corrected, and the building continued. Hitler thought these V weapons—the letter was chosen not only because it was the first in the word *Vergeltungs* but also to counter Allied use of the "V for Victory" slogan—would so damage England that any invasion must be launched in the area of the sites so as to destroy the weapons as soon as possible. Such thinking reinforced the prevalent feeling that the *Kanalkueste* would be attacked.[31]

German planners tried to foresee all contingencies. Seven counterattack plans were prepared, each of which considered an Allied attack in a different area. Once the main threat was determined—possibly the most difficult task—and the appropriate plan was selected, troops would shift from other areas for the counterattack. Though projected Allied air superiority caused some to question the feasibility of such a major counterattack, detailed planning as well as map exercises and alerts continued. Moreover, Rundstedt's troops were stretched so thin that he felt Hitler's attention must be drawn to this critical situation. The field marshal had tried to do just that in the spring of the year when he had been called from leave at Bad Toelz to Berchtesgaden to see the *Fuehrer*. But Hitler persisted in discussing other subjects, such as his future triumphs in the East, and would not talk of the Western Front. After this experience, Rundstedt decided to conduct a detailed inspection of coastal defenses and submit his findings in the form of a written report to OKW. He would ask that it be shown to Hitler. Late in October, he forwarded the document. There were, said Rundstedt, three Allied courses of action: first was an assault, "in the Channel, probably combined with an attack from the south against the French Mediterranean coast"; second "attacks against Normandy and Brittany to establish bridgeheads with good harbours and to eliminate submarine bases"; and third, a combined assault "from the south against the French Mediterranean coast and from the Bay of Biscay. . . ." Rundstedt knew that the Allies were making preparations to cross the Channel, and he felt that his widely spread, inferior quality forces could not repel an invasion. Lack of equipment was another problem, and gasoline was in such short supply that, except on rare occasions, regimental commanders had to inspect their commands on horse or bicycle. Rundstedt concluded that to accomplish his mission he must have better troops plus a strong mobile reserve which would operate under his orders.[32]

As Rundstedt's report was being analyzed, enemies of the *Reich* were pushing forward on both the Eastern and Italian Fronts, dictating particularly careful allocation of German resources. Hitler responded to the situation with top secret *Fuehrer* Directive No. 51, issued on November 3, 1943. A summary of the directive was obtained by the Allies through ULTRA, while a more complete text was gained from the interception and decrypting of a message from the Japanese Ambassador in Berlin to the Imperial Headquarters in Tokyo. The gist of the document is contained in the first three paragraphs:

> For the last two and one-half years the bitter and costly struggle against Bolshevism has made the utmost demands upon the bulk of our military resources and energies. This commitment was in keeping with the seriousness of the danger, and the over-all situation. The situation has since changed. The threat from the East remains, but an ever greater danger looms in the West: the Anglo-American landing! In the East, the vastness of the space will, as a last resort, permit a loss of territory even on a major scale without suffering a mortal blow to Germany's chance for survival.
>
> Not so in the West! If the enemy here succeeds in penetrating our defenses on a wide front, consequences of staggering proportions will follow within a short time. All signs point to an offensive against the Western Front of Europe no later than spring and perhaps earlier.
>
> For that reason, I can no longer justify the further weakening of the West in favor of other theaters of war. I have therefore decided to strengthen the defenses in the West, particularly at places from which we shall launch our long-range war against England. For those are the very points at which the enemy must and will attack; there—unless all indications are misleading—will be fought the decisive invasion battle.[33]

This battle would be fought in the water and on the beaches by a defense force to be equipped with more fixed weapons and protected by stronger fortifications than there existed at the time the directive was issued. If the enemy did get ashore, he would be destroyed by a counterattack executed by highly trained mobile reserves. Both command post and field exercises were ordered, but there was no reference as to who would control the counterattack. In an effort to upgrade the quality of the forces, Hitler personally retained authority to order the transfer of troops to the East, and also specified that support be given by the *Luftwaffe*, Navy, and SS. His last paragraph, quoted below, not only reiterated his feeling that a combined effort was needed, but also revealed much about interservice relationships within the German establishment:

> All authorities will guard against wasting time and energy in useless jurisdictional squabbles, and will direct all their efforts toward strengthening our defensive and offensive power.[34]

Though some troops were subsequently transferred to the East and the authorized heavy weapons strength in the West was reduced, an actual build-up did take place in early 1944. One indicator of a higher priority for the West was the assignment, in November 1943, of Generafeldmarschall Erwin Rommel and a small army group headquarters. Rommel had been in command of Army Group B in northern Italy until Generalfeldmarschall Albert Kesselring was designated theater commander. Rommel was now told to inspect the entire western coastal defense system and make appropriate recommendations. His inspection tour was announced via a message which went from OKW to German organizations stationed in the West and also, incidentally, via ULTRA to the British and American leaders. He was especially charged to render advice concerning the use of armor. Particular emphasis must be placed on the formation and employment of counterattack forces. Rommel would report not to Rundstedt, the theater commander, but instead to OKW. Rundstedt was told that Rommel's appointment in no way was to detract from the authority of OB West; instead it would allow theater headquarters to work on training and other tasks, to include the difficult job of occupying a conquered land. It is hard to believe that the theater commnder could accept, without some resistance, the presence of another field marshal, and one of Hitler's favorites at that, in his sector. On the other hand, Rommel's appearance along the coast would no doubt serve to raise morale. And, Rundstedt thought, Rommel's task of exploring counterattacks coupled with Hitler's discussion of mobile forces in his Directive No. 51 might open the way for the adoption of a more mobile form of defense.[35]

By the middle of December, Rommel, having completed the first phase of his inspection in Denmark, arrived in France and was briefed by the theater commander. Rundstedt's guess was that the invasion would come between May and September 1944, and that with their powerful air forces the Allies could concentrate an invasion fleet anywhere, although he did not feel seriously threatened by the possibility of attacks on the coast of Holland or in the Brittany Peninsula–Bay of Biscay area. He referred to the coastal defenses as a "Propaganda Wall," and observed, "Things look black!" When the two men agreed that Army Group B should report to OB West, Rundstedt forwarded such a recommendation. A decision was reached by the end of the year whereby Rommel—commander of Army Group B, which contained the Fifteenth and Seventeenth Armies as well as the German Armed Forces of the Netherlands, and charged with handling the anti-invasion operation—would assume his new position on January 15. The command status, however, was not as clear as it would appear. *(See Chart 1 at end of chapter.)* Rommel, like every field marshal, was authorized direct communication with Hitler; in matters not directly related to defense against the invasion, however, Rundstedt could bypass Army Group B and contact units directly.[36]

This tangled command arrangement contributed to the bleak situation that faced the Germans at the end of 1943. They had read newspaper accounts of the Teheran Conference and fully realized the massive potential that the Allies would bring to bear. The nearness of the invasion was emphasized on Christmas Eve 1943 when President Roosevelt told the world, via radio, of his selection of General Dwight D. Eisenhower as Supreme Commander.[37]

Eisenhower Assumes Direction of OVERLORD

Prior to his official assumption of command, Eisenhower had been picking his subordinate leaders and organizing his staff. During the latter part of December, he exchanged views with Marshall. For the commander who would direct the initial ground phase of the invasion, Eisenhower wanted General Sir Harold R. L. G. Alexander, then his deputy and commanding general of the 15th Army Group in Italy. To command the U.S. assault army under Alexander, he favored Bradley, who had both combat experience and the respect of the senior British commanders with whom he had worked. As the operation developed, a second U.S. army would come in, at which time an army group headquarters would be required. Eisenhower's selection for command of the additional army was Lieutenant General George S. Patton, Jr., while either a combat experienced corps commander or an army commander from the U.S. (such as Courtney H. Hodges or William H. Simpson) would take the U.S. First Army if Bradley were elevated to army group commander. Bradley, Patton, and Hodges were chosen, after many exchanges of messages between Marshall and Eisenhower. Both Bradley and Hodges would be observed, and later one would be selected as army group commander. Marshall was unsure about Patton's judgment because indiscretions already committed by the flamboyant leader had made headlines. Eisenhower assured Marshall that under no circumstances would Patton be promoted above army level.[38]

Administrative matters also had to be resolved. Eisenhower was slated to take Devers' job as the American Theater Commander as well as become the Allied Supreme Commander. He recommended that Devers be transferred to the Mediterranean to become the U.S. Theater Commander there. To handle much of the necessary detail in England, Eisenhower decided to name Major General John C. H. Lee as Deputy Theater Commander for Supply and Administration. Lee, who had been the Commanding General of the Services of Supply, would merge that command into theater headquarters and direct the administrative organization. Later, when the Allies were firmly established on the continent, Lee would also command the Communications Zone which would control the rear area functions needed to support the American fighting men.[39]

While Marshall and Eisenhower were resolving questions concerning U.S. high level command positions, Churchill reached a decision on who should command the ground forces (British 21st Army Group). He did not favor transferring Alexander from the Mediterranean, preferring to leave him in command of his army group there. General Sir Henry Maitland Wilson was his nominee to succeed Eisenhower as Supreme Allied Commander, Mediterranean Theater (SACMED). (With the naming of an American to head OVERLORD, it had been agreed that a British commander would direct Mediterranean operations.) For the OVERLORD ground command, Churchill chose General Bernard Law Montgomery, then commanding the British Eighth Army in Italy. Though Eisenhower had originally suggested Alexander for the job, Montgomery was well known and acceptable to him.[40]

Notified of his selection on December 24, Montgomery prepared to move quickly to England, arranging first, however, to visit Eisenhower on the twenty-seventh. Thanks to a visit by a COSSAC staff officer in late October, Eisenhower had already read the outline plan for OVERLORD. Now he indicated that until he arrived in London, Montgomery was to represent him and, with the aid of Eisenhower's Chief of Staff, Major General Walter B. Smith, study and change the plan as necessary. He made it clear that he felt the invasion front was too narrow; it should be increased so that Cherbourg could be taken faster. He also told Montgomery of his concern that the plan provide for the early capture of other large ports and for a quick build-up of a major force on the continent. Eisenhower also explained that he envisioned Montgomery and Leigh-Mallory controlling the initial tactical battle. They would move to France with a combined British/American headquarters as soon as possible. *(See Chart 2 at end of chapter.)* Later, when two army groups were needed, Montgomery would relinquish immediate control to Eisenhower. Of course, even before Eisenhower took the tactical reins, any major change of the OVERLORD plan would have to be cleared with him.[41]

Eisenhower continued preparing for his move to England, but finally gave in to repeated requests from Marshall and agreed to a short home leave prior to the assumption of his new duties. He needed the respite from weighty responsibilities which promised only to intensify. His trip, made under a very tight security blanket, included a visit to Kansas and a journey to West Point to see his son, John, then in his last year at the Academy. Arrangements for the latter visit almost approached the bizarre. Rested and anxious to get at the task, the Supreme Commander arrived in Scotland on January 15, 1944, to find a dense blanket of fog which required him to continue on to London by train. Though Eisenhower's arrival was clothed in secrecy, "Tate," a German spy controlled by the British XX (or "double cross" committee), was permitted to send this news to his controller in Hamburg. Such bits of information demonstrated, in German eyes, the importance of "their" agent and lent credibility to other messages designed to further the Allied deception plan.[42]

By the time that Eisenhower arrived in London, Montgomery had assumed command of the 21st Army Group from General Sir Bernard Paget, who had been named to replace General Wilson as Commander-in-Chief, Middle East. Paget had trained his troops intensively and realistically, and had prepared a fine body of men to turn over to Montgomery. The selection of Montgomery was widely hailed in England. Of him the British official historian L. F. Ellis later wrote:

> As one of Britain's best known and most successful soldiers, he had become "Monty" to the man in the street as well as to the troops of the Eighth Army. His personality inspired confidence and his picturesque figure was easily distinguishable; for although he was an infantryman, he wore when in battle-dress the black beret of the Royal Armoured Corps and with it the badge of the Royal Tank Regiment set beside the badge of his own rank.[43]

He established his headquarters in St. Paul's school, where he had been a student, and used the High Master's room as his personal office. Since he had never entered the room during his student days, it appeared to him that he had to reach the rank of a senior British army commander to gain entrance. Such stories, widely disseminated, tended to emphasize his ties to ordinary Englishmen and served to enhance his popularity with the man in the street.[44]

Montgomery and Smith had studied Morgan's outlined plan and agreed with Eisenhower that the assault should be enlarged. On January 21, several proposed revisions were submitted to the Supreme Commander in a meeting attended by Montgomery, Ramsay, and Leigh-Mallory, among others. Montgomery proposed that the frontage for the assault be increased from the present 25 miles to over 50 miles. This would enable more assault troops (five divisions as opposed to three) to land on a front which would include the eastern portion of the Cotentin Peninsula *(See Map 54, in Atlas)*, speeding the capture of Cherbourg. A stronger force would enable Montgomery to seize critical communication centers quicker and also use his increased armor to push out rapidly to good defensive positions, thus helping keep enemy reserves from striking into the growing lodgment area. Airborne units would be dropped on either flank. Some of the airborne troopers who landed in the Cotentin would be specifically charged with securing the causeways which spanned flooded areas and served as beach exits.

Leigh-Mallory questioned the use of airborne troops on the Cotentin Peninsula and predicted that the difficulty pilots would have in locating their drop zones, coupled with stiff antiaircraft fire, would result in casualties of 75 to 80 percent. Bradley, who would be the ground commander in the peninsular area, felt that airborne support was essential if the Cotentin landings were to succeed. Montgomery supported Bradley. Ramsay noted that if the expanded invasion plan were adopted, the additional seaborne assault forces would have to be launched at a greater distance from the objective than had originally been planned. He pointed out that the extra transit time would result in the need for extremely accurate long-range weather forecasting. After the discussion was concluded, Eisenhower, who realized the risk he was taking by committing his paratroopers, endorsed the requests made by his ground commanders. Airborne forces would be dropped on the Cotentin. The enlarged invasion was also approved by the Supreme Commander, fully aware of the crucial importance of OVERLORD to the Allied war effort.[45]

Extra divisions would require extra support. Air resources must be taxed for more fighters and transports. Two more naval assault forces would have to be formed, and extra supply ships located. Most difficult to deal with, however, was the need for more landing craft. Smith felt that the only source was the Mediterranean. Two major Mediterranean plans called for the use of landing craft: the Anzio assault (SHINGLE) and the invasion of southern France (ANVIL). ANVIL was timed to go in with OVERLORD. Montgomery, Smith, Morgan, and the British Chiefs of Staff agreed that ANVIL should be reduced from a major assault to a threat. Eisenhower, however, while strongly supporting an enlarged OVERLORD, wanted to keep ANVIL. He thought that ANVIL would prevent some German reinforcements from moving to Normandy, abide by the promises made to the Russians at Teheran, open French ports for supply use, and give many French soldiers a chance to become the liberators of a portion of their country. Three months of discussion, which took up much of Eisenhower's time, ensued. Churchill's statement that ". . . the destinies of two great empires . . . seem to be tied up in some God-damned things called LSTs," seemed to be true.[46]

By the end of March, several agreements had been reached. To gain an extra month of landing craft production, the target date for OVERLORD was postponed to June 1. While this change would result in the loss of a month of good campaigning weather in the West, it would gain time to gather and train the assault force, and also better the chances that the weather in the East would be good enough for the Russians to launch a major attack timed to coincide with OVERLORD. ANVIL would not be scheduled for the same time as OVERLORD, and its status would be reviewed later; thus, needed landing craft could be gained from the Mediterranean as well as from the diversion of some craft originally intended for the Pacific. With these reallocations, Eisenhower finally possessed the landing craft resources to put a strong force on the beaches of Normandy.[47]

A Landing Ship, Tank (LST)

SHAEF As An Allied Headquarters

By the first of April, much had been accomplished in preparing for OVERLORD, particularly in the development of a functioning headquarters. In March, Eisenhower had moved Supreme Headquarters, Allied Expeditionary Force (SHAEF) to Bushy Park, near Kingston-on-Thames. This was in conformance with his policy of keeping headquarters out of large cities. He later observed that the remoteness of SHAEF enhanced the closeness of its personnel.

SHAEF was a carefully integrated headquarters in which the experience gained in the Mediterranean was put to good use. A staff officer, irrespective of his nation or service, could handle matters affecting the forces of either country. Officers from the Mediterranean came north to join the COSSAC group, most of whom stayed if they could work in an Allied atmosphere.* The group from the south, of course, knew Eisenhower and his ways, and brought experience in dealing with problems such as recognition of French political authority, civil affairs, handling of the press, psychological warfare, and air-ground cooperation. Eisenhower too had become more experienced. Prior to the Mediterranean campaign he had never commanded men in action. Having demonstrated there his ability to act under pressure, he now emphasized the necessity of directing all the command's assets toward a common objective.[48]

*Morgan became Deputy Chief of Staff to Smith.

Headquarters' policy was set early by Eisenhower when, on January 19 in his first meeting with the SHAEF staff, he stressed his desire for Allied thinking. He emphasized that he did not want to be surrounded by "yes men." If he proposed something that had already been considered, he wanted to be told about it. It was obvious to all that OVERLORD now had its commander and that he had both responsibility and authority. Foch had wide authority in the waning days of the First World War, but it was limited to high level affairs, and no Allied staff was formed. Such was also the case in 1940, when a French commander controlled the British Expeditionary Force. Now, with a long campaign ahead, an integrated staff made up of men from both nations and all three services existed.[49]

Leadership talent was provided by both countries. Eisenhower, an American, was Supreme Commander, while his deputy, Air Chief Marshal Sir Arthur W. Tedder, was British. *(See Chart 2 at end of chapter.)* Tedder's last job had been Commander-in-Chief, Mediterranean Allied Air Forces, where he had gained Eisenhower's respect. Now Tedder, who like Eisenhower was a strong supporter of Allied staff integration, occupied a high SHAEF position. In time, he would assume the special task of coordinating all Allied air forces.[50] By the first week of February, German intelligence agencies had issued their appraisals of Eisenhower and Tedder. The following comments formed part of a *Luftwaffe* Academy lecture entitled "Invasion Generals, Careers and Assessments," which was presented on February 7, 1944. Of Eisenhower the speaker said:

> Eisenhower is an expert on operations of armored formations. He is noted for his great energy and for his hatred of routine office work. He leaves the initiative to his subordinates whom he manages to inspire to supreme efforts through kind understanding and easy discipline. His strongest point is said to be an ability for adjusting personalities to one another and smoothing over opposite viewpoints. Eisenhower enjoys the greatest popularity with Roosevelt and Churchill.[51]

Eisenhower's deputy was also characterized:

> Tedder is on good terms with Eisenhower, to whom he is superior in both intelligence and energy. The coming operations will be conducted by him to a great extent. He regards the Air Force as a "spearhead artillery" rendering the enemy vulnerable to an attack. His tactics in North Africa, Sicily and Italy, based on this theory, provided for air support for the advance of even the smallest Army units . . . under Tedder's influence the cooperation between the Air Force and Army has become excellent . . . Obviously we are dealing here with one of the most eminent personalities amongst the invasion leaders.[52]

As noted above, Eisenhower's chief subordinate commanders had been named before his arrival in London. He had also elected to keep his Mediterranean Chief of Staff, Major General Walter Bedell Smith, who had the ability to deal with all manner of individuals. So adept did he become that Bradley, who termed Smith, "brilliant, hard-working," recalled that Eisenhower once remarked when a mission for SHAEF came in that he didn't like, "Bedell, tell them to go to hell, but put it so they won't be offended."[53] Eisenhower's decision that there would be no *permanent* ground forces commander—after the initial phase when Montgomery directed these forces, Eisenhower would stay close to the situation and direct matters—would later create bickering and acrimonious exchanges on the Continent.

While staff and commanders were continuing to refine plans and make important decisions regarding OVERLORD, the crucial and massive Allied supply build-up continued. Supplies were rapidly filling all storage space. Road shoulders were converted into long narrow ammunition dumps. Planes were parked in every conceivable space. Men and supplies kept coming. The British railroad system was strained almost to the breaking point. Though troop training was strenuous, there was some unstructured time during which the comparatively wealthy Americans competed for the attentions of English girls. Some soldiers married their female friends, but some, such as one sergeant, did not. Even though his affair resulted in the birth of quadruplets, his American wife would not agree to a divorce. The attitude of British soldiers toward the antics of the Yanks was summed up by the remark that Americans were OK except that they were "overpaid, over-sexed, and over here." If there were some disagreements, however, when both groups worked at it, harmony could be achieved off duty as well as on.[54]

Fighters and Attack Bombers in Great Britain Ready for Final Assembly

Problems which stemmed from racial questions were not as easily resolved and caused considerable Allied concern. Eisenhower, on February 26, 1944, clearly stated a number of his policies in a letter which was to be read by or read to all American soldiers at the first formation, then repeated once a month in the future. Eisenhower proclaimed that: "Equal opportunities of service and of recreation are the right of every American soldier regardless of branch, race, color, or creed."[55]

The fact that Eisenhower said nothing about integration was not surprising, for the U.S. Army was then a segregated force. When a portion of the army, to include black soldiers, was placed in England where but a few blacks had lived and where segregation was not widely practiced, serious difficulties arose. As early as August 1942, British Foreign Secretary Anthony Eden had been supported by the War Cabinet in his recommendation that U.S. leaders keep the number of blacks sent to England as low as possible. But blacks continued to arrive, and by October 1943 their number had grown to some 40,000.

Conflicts arose when British restaurant owners served blacks and landlords rented to them. British girls publicly dated black soldiers frequently and evoked remarks from whites, precipitating fights. In an attempt to explain the peculiar American racial situation, closely held papers prepared by the British Secretary of State for War had been circulated among the members of the War Cabinet. Cabinet members learned that though white officers usually led black units, the U.S. policy was in effect a separation of the races and that should British troops, especially female members, violate this American arrangement, white soldiers would not understand and the offending British would lose their respect. Besides, the War Cabinet was told, black soldiers "probably" expected the same treatment as they had received at home.

Local British leaders in a "private and confidential" document had been advised in late 1942 to consider the U.S. position and try not to cause embarrassment, as the Americans were working at resolving their own social problems. These leaders were warned to be on the lookout for attempts, especially by enemy propagandists, to use racial matters to try to stir up trouble between the British and Americans. Many activities, both at work and play, came to be separated by race. Red Cross Clubs, for example, were not officially segregated; but some were staffed by blacks and some by whites, with obvious results.

Racial problems added to the load carried by commanders at all levels. Bradley, though he said he would take a black division once he was established on the Continent, remarked in May that racial difficulties were interfering with the ability of commanders to do their jobs, and thus with the war effort. Bradley's aide recorded that the general felt that the U.S. job in Europe was to win the war, not to support or deny American racial mores.[56] Invasion preparations continued, but many British citizens must have wondered at the validity of the American crusade for democracy which was to be waged with units separated by race and with soldiers who did not mix or discuss their mutual problems.

Meanwhile, units scheduled to participate in the invasion were receiving special amphibious training during which new techniques and devices were employed. A typical German beach area, complete with mines (both in the water and on land), barbed wire, pill boxes, and a 12- to 15-foot high concrete wall, with a wire-defended strongpoint behind it, had been built by the British. When Eisenhower visited in late January, items of special armored equipment were under test, including flame-throwing tanks, amphibious tanks, ramp tanks, plow tanks, and flail tanks. An earlier type of flail tank had seen action in the North African desert, where German engineers had countered it by placing detonators at a distance ahead of a mine just equal to the distance the flail beat ahead of the tank. The British considered this bit of German ingenuity to be less than sporting. Eisenhower, who availed himself of the opportunity to drive an amphibious tank, enjoyed the visit.[57]

Shortly after the Supreme Commander's trip to the simulated German defense area, the Initial Joint Plan was published by Montgomery, Ramsay, and Leigh-Mallory. This plan dealt with the assault phase of OVERLORD, code-named NEPTUNE. *(See Map 54, in **Atlas**.)* There would be an American sector on the right to facilitate direct resupply from the United States. Here were two U.S. landing areas, while on the left three areas would be used by British and Canadian units. The landing of build-up units would so swell the invasion force that before long the U.S. First and Third as well as the British Second and Canadian First Armies would be in action under two army groups. When the initial lodgment area had been expanded to the Seine, to include the Brittany Ports and the Loire River, Operation OVERLORD would be concluded. The plan emphasized that it was essential to the successful accomplishment of the assault that there be control of both air and sea, attainment of some measure of surprise, and rapidity in landing and build-up. Subordinate units were to use the Initial Joint Plan as a basis for their own more detailed NEPTUNE planning.[58]

Who Should Control Strategic Air Forces?

Although a plan had been issued, the important question of who would direct the operations of strategic bombers still remained unresolved. Eisenhower, a great believer in the principle of unity of command, wanted control of the "heavies" as the individual immediately responsible for OVERLORD. High level politicians and airmen disagreed, and a lengthy argument ensued. Also involved was an Eisenhower decision made late in March to use strategic air strikes against the French railroads over which much of the German war material and many troops traveled. The Supreme Commander felt that such attacks, collectively known as the Transportation Plan, would crucially contribute to slowing the enemy ability to mass against the invasion. Those who opposed the Eisenhower view reasoned that the German war effort would be more severely damaged by a continuation of strategic bombing of targets in Germany. High on the list would be the oil industry, which the *Luftwaffe* would quickly rise to defend, thus also enabling Allied air to destroy enemy fighters.

The meaningfulness of the latter argument was demonstrated in part by a series of massive air raids launched from both England and Italy on German air frame factories. Heavily escorted by fighters—17 groups accompanied one raid—these swarms of bombers triggered the desired enemy response as German fighters filled the air. Although the raids cost the Allies a total of some 500 planes of all types as well as 2,600 crewmen, Allied pilots destroyed more than 500 German fighters. This German loss, made especially critical due to a lack of experienced pilots, could not be made up easily. After "Big Week," as the airmen called it, German planes would only rise to defend especially critical targets. The *Luftwaffe*, though still able to muster forces for an occasional flare-up, was definitely hurting. This victory, won by Allied airmen, would contribute greatly to the success of OVERLORD.

Benefits of deep penetration raids were obvious. Attacks on the French transportation system, as Eisenhower desired, would probably do some good, but they would inevitably result in many casualties to French civilians. Most vitally concerned about these losses were politicians who were considering the effect they might have on the post-war French attitude toward the Allies. Finally, however, after Eisenhower went as far as to threaten to resign, his position was adopted, because the concern for the success of OVERLORD was paramount. All possible precautions were taken to limit French casualties, including the cancellation of strikes in population centers and the prior warning of the populace in some other areas. The Combined Chiefs of Staff approved the giving of "direction," a carefully chosen word selected to avoid the use of "command," of the strategic air effort to Eisenhower. The final compromise included an understanding that an effort would be made to continue the attack on German industry, and specified that the Supreme Commander's plan had to be agreed to by the Chief of the British Air Staff, Air Marshal Portal, as well as by the Combined Chiefs of Staff. Eisenhower assumed "direction" of the strategic air effort on April 14. His first priority was destruction of the German air force and its supporting installations; second was an attack on rail lines, especially those which led into the planned lodgment area. The Supreme Commander now had control of the elements he needed to accomplish his mission.[59]

Both Eisenhower and Tedder in their postwar writings stressed the contribuiton made by the Transportation Plan to the success of OVERLORD. The authors of the official U.S. Army Air Force history, on the other hand, questioned whether the result was worth the cost, both in the diversion of air resources and in damage to the French and Belgians. German Minister of War Production Albert Speer emphasized the devastating effect of bombing the German oil industry.[60] Supporters of both sides of the argument present valid points. Eisenhower, however, was responsible for the success of OVERLORD and he felt the Transportation Plan to be necessary. No one can tell what would have been the result had strategic air not hit transportation targets; surely, however, Eisenhower and his subordinate commanders were more confident of success when they launched OVERLORD, secure in the knowledge that the ability of the enemy to reinforce the beachhead area had been significantly reduced.

Statistics published after the war illustrate the effectiveness of the transportation bombing. The intensive program, coupled with sabotage and passive resistance by some French railroad employees, put a serious strain on the transportation system. Supplies destined for defensive construction were not shipped. By early May, 18,000 workers were diverted from such construction to repairing transportation damage, and

Transportation Plan Results

Map is reproduced with the permission of the Controller of Her Britannic Majesty's Stationery Office from L. F. Ellis, *Victory in the West* (London, 1962), Vol. I, p. 112. Original source was a German report, "The Anglo-American invasion of France in the summer of 1944," submitted to the Chief of Transport in the German Army High Command (OKH).

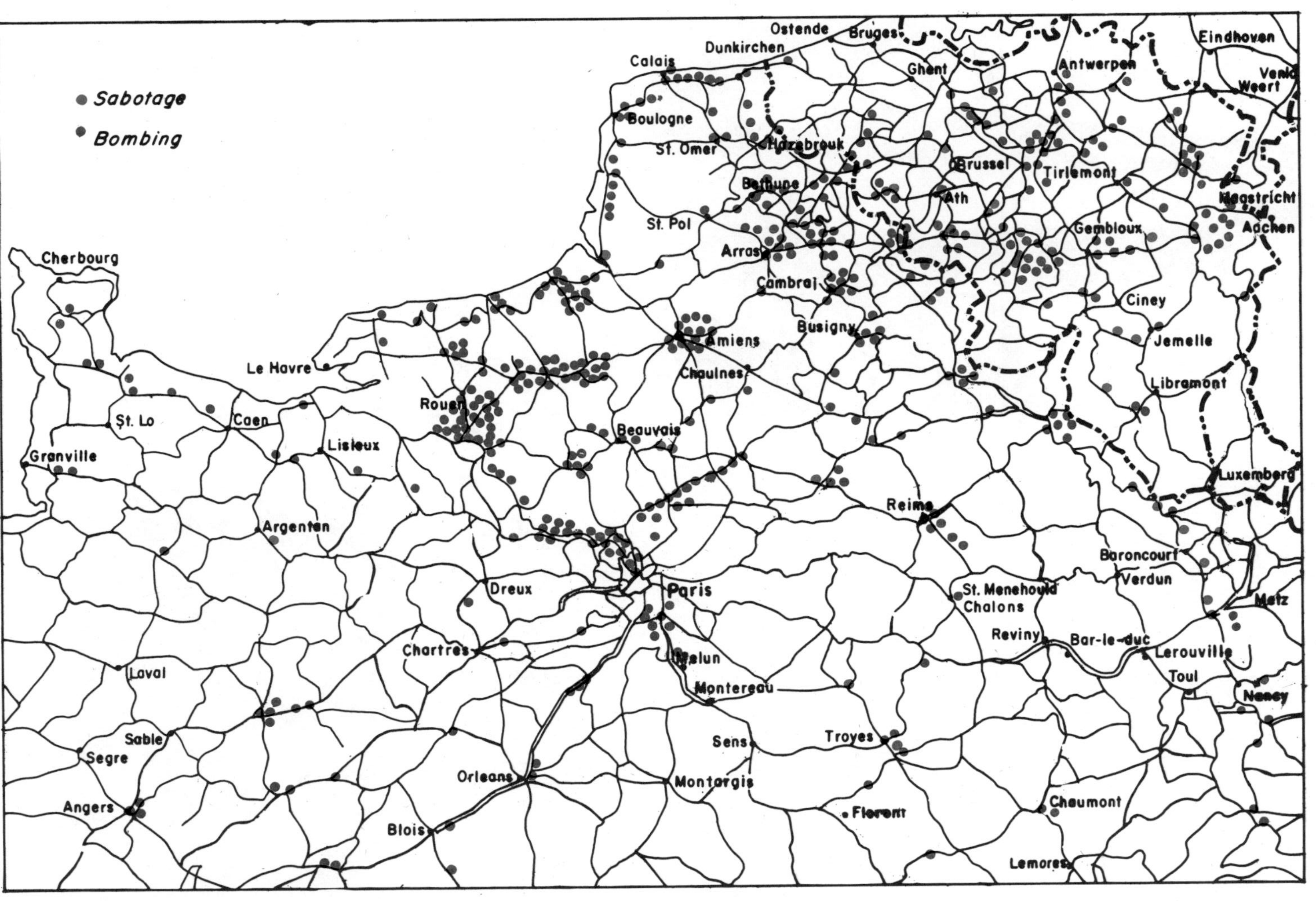

Railway Destruction, May 1944

OKW had approved the shifting of 10,000 more men. So good was Allied reconnaissance that when the Germans had almost readied a damaged bridge for traffic, it was hit again. Rail traffic was significantly reduced. Targeting was accomplished with the assistance of a French railroad official who, with his extremely pregnant wife, was flown out of France in an aircraft operated by a British intelligence agency. As information concerning the devastating results of the raids came back, the Frenchman grew more and more upset over the destruction he was helping to cause. Finally, in late May 1944, he refused to do any more work.[61]

V-2 Rocket in Firing Position

Hitler's Secret Weapons

As the invasion date drew nearer, the SHAEF staff became even busier than before. One of their problem areas was a German threat which worried Eisenhower, considering the massed troops and supplies in England. Information supplied by intelligence sources from time to time since 1939 had indicated that the Germans were working on long-range weapons. For example, in March 1943, two prisoners, both Afrika Corps generals, were put in a "bugged" room in a London mansion. One mentioned having seen rocket tests and expressed surprise that London had not already been destroyed. Soon an Allied expert in scientific intelligence deduced that the experimental site for some sort of flying bomb was located on the Baltic coast. He knew that during the First World War, when the Germans shelled Paris from a great distance, they had had trouble determining the trajectory of the rounds used. Now, with radar available, he felt that they would use their best radar units to follow the new bomb as it was tested. He expected that one of two companies would be selected, and alerted those who supplied the ULTRA information to watch for a movement of either company to the Baltic. Soon one did move, and it began to plot the bombs, using a code which was easily broken. The scientific intelligence expert used this data to locate the plotting stations and deduce the capabilities of the flying bomb. He located two points, Pennemünde, an island in the Baltic, and Zempin, nearby on the coast, and had a reconnaissance plane dispatched. When the photos were studied, both launch sites were identified, and a flying bomb was detected on a launch ramp at Pennemünde. Reconnaissance flights also disclosed large rocket-shaped objects.

V-1 Flying Bomb Being Pushed to Launching Ramp

On a moonlit night in August, British aircraft struck Pennemünde. Due to a clever deception scheme in which it appeared to the Germans that the main air attack was headed for Berlin, there was little interference with the attack. This raid caused much damage, killed key individuals (including some British intelligence agents who had infiltrated the installation), and destroyed important plans, thus setting production of what was to be called the V-2 rocket back a couple of months. The V-1 flying bomb program was also delayed. When launching later resumed in Poland, in an area virtually teeming with

British-controlled Polish intelligence agents, ULTRA picked it up, and intercepted messages were immediately passed to Allied officials. Manufacturing activities had been moved to a mammoth underground factory in the Harz mountains where 2,000 German technicians, 16,000 slave workers, and a number of employees of British intelligence went to work at their various tasks.

Agents reported that launching sites were being built near the coast in France. By late 1943, some 69 sites had been identified within 150 miles of London. Morgan considered this threat to be so serious that he discussed with the Combined Chiefs of Staff the possibility of moving the OVERLORD concentration areas in England to the west. They decided to make no change. German plans called for a stockpile of 5,000 V1s to be ready by mid-December so that they could be fired from 96 sites. The projected production rate of 5,000 per month would enable the rocket men to keep up a sustained attack. Actual December production did not reach 1,000, and to make matters worse for the Germans, early in the month Allied aircraft began to hit the sites. These air strikes were effective, and by February, 73 of the 96 sites had been hit so badly that the Germans felt that it would not be worthwhile to repair them. A switch was made to a new ramp which, while inferior, was easier to construct and camouflage. Still the air attacks continued and by D-Day over 32,000 sorties had been flown. ULTRA revealed in April the establishment by the *Fuehrer* of a new headquarters, the 155th Flak Regiment, scheduled to direct the V-1 attack. This headquarters was to be located near Amiens, France. By the end of May, even though he had been heavily bombed, the commander of the 155th Flak Regiment reported that he had 50 sites ready to go. The imminent start of the German rocket offensive was an important reason to launch OVERLORD as soon as possible. A few days after the invasion actually took place, the first V-1 was launched. [62]

As bombs rained on the V-sites, detailed invasion planning continued. By early April, Montgomery was prepared to brief all general officers of the four field armies which would come under his command. On the first day of a two-day exercise held at St. Paul's School, Montgomery, Leigh-Mallory, and Ramsay briefed the ground, air, and naval plans to an audience that included both Eisenhower and Churchill. During Montgomery's portion, the British commander illustrated his talk with a map, as wide as a city street, which had been spread on the floor. As he strode over the map, Montgomery explained that the attack would come in on a 60-mile front. *(See Map 55, in Atlas.)* The mission was to take and hold a beachhead so that a build-up for the battle for France could be accomplished. Once ashore, elements of the British Second Army were to get to the open area south of Caen as soon as possible. Not only was this terrain replete with airfield sites, but it was also good tank country. Taking Caen might be a tough task, as the prediction was that the enemy would try to hold the town to maintain a line of communication to the Pas de Calais area. Also anticipated was a stout German defense of the port of Cherbourg, a primary objective of the American forces. Another target for the Americans, whose left flank would be protected by the British, was the town of St. Lô. Later, American troops would move to the south to clear the Brittany Peninsula and take the vital ports located there. *(See Map 54, in Atlas.)* Then, after a protective force had been established on the Loire River to prevent a surprise enemy attack from the south, U.S. troops would pivot on the British and turn to the east to attack to the Seine River. Although phase lines were discussed, Montgomery said adherence to them was not essential as the situation was too uncertain. While but 5 seaborne and 3 airborne divisions would actually assault the coast, by the end of D-Day the equivalent of 11 divisions would be in the beachhead. This number would be built up to 39 by D plus 90.[63] Inexorably, events were moving toward the long-awaited assault of Hitler's Atlantic Wall.

The German Predicament Continues

On the other side of the English Channel, German preparations to repel an invasion were continuing. The major problem, of course, was trying to determine where and when the invasion would come. Only bits and pieces, a report of a military movement here or a convoy there, were available to the intelligence analyst. OB West estimated that the invasion would come in 1944, and more specifically that it would come after March 15 and probably in June. The significance of this accurate estimate should not be over-stressed, however, as the May-June period was the logical time for an invasion due to weather conditions at that time and the fact that several months of good campaigning weather remained before the fall rains and the cold of winter. OB West also raised the possibility of a landing in Mediterranean France, either shortly before or after the main invasion.

The Germans, like the Allies, considered several possible landing areas. Both Rundstedt and Rommel looked hard at the Pas de Calais. Rundstedt recalled after the war that even though he had a relatively strong defense in that area, he felt the attack would come there as it was nearer the key objectives of the Rhine River and the Ruhr industrial area. In addition, the V-weapon launching sites were located there. As it was closest to England, the shorter sea journey would give the Allies a better chance of a surprise assault and would make air support and resupply easier. Although the German leaders could plan ahead, once the actual invasion came, Rundstedt and Rommel would have to determine the location of the main Allied attack and then move against it. It was thought—and Allied deception schemes reinforced the idea—that the Allies might launch several attacks to fix German forces prior to the major assault. It appeared that Rundstedt would have to make do with forces then in the West (53 divisions in France and the Low Countries in January 1944), for no general reserve existed in Germany and the other divisions were committed elsewhere. It was extremely important to the German cause that once the main attack had been identified, all efforts be concentrated according to a well-designed plan to defeat the assault; yet Rundstedt and Rommel, both Field Marshals and both authorized direct access to Hitler, fundamentally disagreed on the course of action that should be followed.[64]

Hitler, of course, wanted the enemy kept far away from the German industrial base, and the best way to accomplish that was by a quick decisive defeat of any invasion attempt. He could then move up to 50 divisions to the East as the British and Americans would need some time before they could launch another invasion. All three senior leaders, Hitler, Rundstedt, and Rommel, agreed that the early hours of any invasion were critical. Both Dieppe and Sicily had demonstrated that the enemy was most vulnerable while still aboard ship and during the early landing phases. Rundstedt hoped that the main battle would be decided on or near the coast, but he also advocated the retention of a strong mobile reserve for use in case the enemy penetrated the coastal defenses. In this event, the defensive belt coupled with local reserves would slow the enemy long enough for the reinforcements to move to the threatened location and enter the fray. Rundstedt realized that such movements must be carried out under an air umbrella. Naval gunfire, shown to be extremely effective in the Sicily and Salerno landings, must be suppressed. Thus, Rundstedt pushed for a strong coastal defense coupled with a large mobile reserve. He had been assured that adequate air assets would be shifted to the West at an appropriate time.

By mutual agreement, Army Group B had been subordinated to OB West, but Rommel was still responsible for fighting the battle of the invasion. He believed that there would be no opportunity to move a reserve force any distance in time to affect the critical first phase of the battle. He knew from his African experience what it was like to fight an enemy who ruled the skies. Rommel summed up his defense philosophy during a visit to Hitler's headquarters in East Prussia. After a lengthy conference, he and the *Fuehrer* stepped outside where Armaments Minister Albert Speer was waiting for an appointment with Hitler. Speer later recalled hearing Rommel tell his leader:

> We must repulse the enemy at his first landing site. The pillboxes around the ports don't do the trick. Only primitive but effective barriers and obstacles all along the coast can make the landing so difficult that our countermeasures will be effective. If we don't manage to throw them back at once, the invasion will succeed in spite of the Atlantic Wall.[65]

Rommel felt the Allies must be prevented from securing a foothold, for once they were allowed to construct airstrips, Allied air superiority would be even more complete. Thus reserves would have to be moved close enough to the coast so that they could enter combat during the first 24 hours of the invasion. Yet they must stay far enough back to escape the inevitable pre-assault bombardment. Defenses, both on the beach and in the water, had to be strengthened and stakes planted in any likely air-drop or air-landing area. Rommel's ideas took into account the effect of overwhelming Allied air power, but by moving the reserves forward and specifying that they be committed during the first day, he imposed a requirement that an early decision concerning the identification of the main attack be made. Naturally, as he was to fight the battle, Rommel felt that the reserves should be placed under his direction.

In fact, Rommel, who already commanded two armies, asked not only for the reserves but for some say in the employment of Rundstedt's other two armies. Hitler initially agreed with Rommel's request, but after considering Rundstedt's written complaint, he decided that no officer should command the entire reserve. By mid-May, Rommel had a reserve of three *panzer* divisions; three others, plus a *panzer* grenadier division, were put in OKW reserve. It apparently appeared to Rundstedt that he would be able to employ the OKW divisions, for he incorporated them into his anti-invasion planning. (Essential elements of the reserve argument were well known to the Allies via ULTRA information. Secure in the knowledge that the OKW reserve would not be moved forward, as Rommel desired, the planners continued their work. They watched carefully for any ULTRA message which might indicate that these divisions or any from the Pas de Calais area were being moved.)

In an attempt to achieve better control, Rundstedt formed his southern two armies into Army Group G *(See Map 53, in Atlas)* and stated that he would allow the army group commanders maximum latitude in the accomplishment of their missions. As the invasion drew ever nearer, however, the German command system had become more and more confused. Though things looked fairly neat on paper, two field marshals—each holding a different view on counterinvasion techniques and both being authorized to appeal directly to the head of the Army—were charged with the defeat of the most powerful invasion force ever formed. Through the unwillingness of Hitler to make a firm decision, no clear policy had been selected.

Units charged with the defeat of the highly trained and well-equipped Allied force often were of low quality. Much of the top-grade equipment and the most experienced troops had been withdrawn bit by bit, or sometimes in great chunks, and fed into the eastern meat grinder. What was spit out in the form of worn-out units went to the West for rebuilding. Units in training could also be found in abundance. Though Hitler tried to halt the withdrawal in late 1943, by March 1944, with the Russians on the attack and an occupation force needed to keep Hungary in the German camp, two SS *panzer* divisions as well as the assault guns of four infantry divisions went East. In addition, other units previously slated to move from conquered countries to France when the invasion came were also sent. Though some rebuilding did take place before the Allied attack, units composing this German force, which was supported by less than 200 aircraft—about 100 were operational each day—were far different from the German Army which had been victorious in France only four years before. Yet the 58 combat divisions which formed Rundstedt's command could still pose many problems for the Allied attackers.[66]

As was expected, the Germans continued to work to improve all aspects of their defense. In February, the Allies learned of obstacles which were being built on the beaches in such a way that they would be under water when the tide was up. ULTRA provided valuable information concerning construction. In addition, night patrols often were landed on the French coast. Since assault waves would be landing as the tide rose, planners decided that the beach obstacles would have to be eliminated. Special demolition teams were trained for the task. Deftness in destruction would be essential, because experts predicted that the obstacles could not be effectively blown if they stood in more than two feet of water, and the tide rose four feet in an hour. As D-Day approached, more and more obstacles were detected. By the end of May, an observer off shore could count an average, if he totaled the various rows, of an obstacle every two to three yards. Some of the planners began to wonder if the gaps needed to bring in the precisely scheduled assault waves could be blown in time. If such paths could not be cleared, the possibility existed that the attack might turn into a tangled mass of impaled landing craft. So concerned was Eisenhower that he approved an earlier attack hour than had been originally planned to allow the demolition experts the maximum amount of time before the tide came in.[67]

Aerial reconnaissance and other intelligence sources also revealed that the Germans were trying to seal beach exits with more obstacles as well as with carefully sited weapons fire. Strong points had been constructed about every 1,000 yards. These positions were well-wired, mined, fortified, and manned by a force which varied in size from a platoon to a company. Mortars and an antitank gun or howitzer completed the typical strong point weapons complement. Often adjacent strong points were tied together with an antitank ditch. Cracking through such defenses would not be easy. Mines had been sown in the sand; gun emplacements, camouflaged as houses, contained weapons sited up and down the beaches. The Germans hoped that these defensive measures would disorganize any attack on the strong points before the invasion could really get started. Some areas featured hidden pipes fed from kerosene tanks. All it took was the push of a button to engulf an entire area and all attackers within it in flames.[68]

German Anti-Landing Obstacles Under Construction

Final Honing of the Sword of Invasion

While morale and physical fitness are important in a unit making a frontal attack, and instruction and practice in the attack of fortified positions is also necessary, exercise in the intricacies of an amphibious assault, including the transfer at night from transports to landing craft, is crucial. SHAEF planners and commanders did not overlook this matter. Those troops in the initial assault waves were to be brought ashore in landing craft which held approximately 30 men. Platoons in the American assault companies were temporarily split into two assault sections, each of which had 29 enlisted soldiers and one officer. A battalion of tanks, acting as artillery, was attached to each assault regiment to provide supporting fire. Both the assault infantrymen and their leaders and staff officers benefited from practice attacks which were held at regimental, divisional, and corps levels. Eisenhower made frequent troop visits, and in a letter to Marshall on April 17 said that, although many problems remained, much progress was being made. Two full-scale practices were scheduled, each including collecting, embarking, transporting, and finally unloading the troops so that they could experience a mock assault. These exercises played a part in the deception plan, as German intelligence agencies were led to believe through reports from agents under British control that these were the first of a series of exercises that would be conducted before the main invasion scheduled for July 20. For example, U.S. VII Corps units, spearheaded by the 4th Infantry Division, participated in Exercise TIGER held in late April. This corps was slated to hit Utah Beach on the Cotentin Peninsula. Similar exercises, called FABIUS, were run in early May for U.S. V Corps units. These practice attacks included the 1st and 29th Divisions, which were to attack Omaha Beach.[69]

Following completion of such exercises, the troops returned to their marshalling areas, which were located near the designated points of embarkation. Shortly before the large exercises, those units not already near the south coast of England moved to concentration areas where vehicles were waterproofed and special equipment needed for the amphibious operation was issued. As transportation space was at a premium, all men and equipment not absolutely required were separated temporarily from the assault units. Bradley's First Army G-4, for example, was deeply involved in the reduction of American overhead. One day when he was trying to juggle bridging equipment, gasoline, and ammunition, a Civil Affairs representative arrived and claimed it was essential that he be allotted a lift on D-Day to transport food for the French. Bradley later recalled that after the G-4 determined that the officer was serious, he stated: " . . . now listen closely. We'll fix you up for lift on D minus 1. There won't be another soul to bother you on the beach. You can feed all the Frenchmen you can find. And on the following morning you can wave a flag for us when we come in."[70].

Each week at platoon level an hour was specifically designated for the platoon leader to present a topic related to the task to come. One such topic was entitled "How Russians Kill Germans." Platoon leaders were provided with a little booklet, *Army Talks*, to use as resource material. Sixty thousand copies were distributed weekly. Studies made of those Americans who fought in the Mediterranean had revealed that up to half were not sure that it was worth it to fight the war; only a few felt a strong desire to continue to push the enemy. Also, as many did not realize the problems handled by junior officers, the troops did not show real confidence in their leaders. The necessary job done by support troops was misunderstood. As a result, SHAEF devised an orientation program, one part of which was the weekly discussion with the platoon leader. The program was supported by *Yank*, a weekly magazine, and *Stars and Stripes*, a daily newspaper, each with a circulation of 550,000 in the European Theater of Operations. It was also supported by the Armed Forces Network of 49 stations, each of which broadcast 12 hours per day.[71]

Tight security measures prevailed to prevent the Germans from learning the time or place of the attack. Troops who had participated in the invasion exercises did not know the actual locations they would assault nor when the attack would come. Once back in the marshalling areas they were sealed behind barbed wire and kept under the observation of 2,000 Counter Intelligence Corps agents. Briefings were conducted down to squad level so that each man might learn his assigned job and see how his task fit into the mission of his unit. When terrain features were disclosed, the general picture was still so vague, due to the use of false place names and map references, that the actual location of the beaches was concealed. This information would not be released until the invasion force was at sea. No visitors were allowed to enter the area along the coast where the camps were situated. Those who did happen to wander in were not allowed to depart. Families of those detained were informed that their relative was all right but that he would not be returning home for a time. Military units were not exempt from the restrictions. A quartermaster truck company, for example, got into the restricted area and was eventually sent to France rather than back to its old task. Some of the troops stayed in these restricted areas—where more rigid camouflage discipline was practiced than would ever be required after the campaign began—for almost a month. Finally, when on May 30 the first men moved out to the embarkation points, it still appeared that the secret was secure.[72]

Security for Overlord: Intentional and Unintentional

Although security was of major concern to the Allies, some slips were still made. In March, an American sergeant with German background sent a package of OVERLORD documents, which included data on a preliminary date, number of men, equipment, and locations, to his sister in Chicago. His wrapping was faulty, and the sensitive nature of the contents of the parcel was determined in the Chicago post office. At least 10 postal employees plus several people who worked for the Army saw the documents. An intensive interrogation of the sergeant revealed no attempt at espionage, but simply carelessness. His sister had been quite sick. When the sergeant addressed this package he was thinking of home and automatically wrote his sister's address. Errors were also made at higher levels. For example, on April 18, in a public dining room at Claridge's Hotel, a major general who was the Commanding General of the IX Air Force Service Command, remarked that the invasion would be launched before June 15, 1944. When others said he was wrong, the general said he would cover bets made against him. This discussion was reported to the Supreme Commander, and once Eisenhower was sure that he had his facts straight, he acted. Although the general was a West Point classmate and friend, Eisenhower reduced him to his permanent grade of colonel and shipped him home. Reduction and relief, this time done by British authorities, was also the fate of an English battalion commander who told some civilian friends that his unit was being specially trained to take a definitive objective. One who heard his conversation could easily deduce that the objective was in Normandy.[73]

If strict enforcement of security rules was an essential Allied requirement, the carefully organized and deliberate attempt to mislead the Germans was also important. This coordinated effort was known as Operation FORTITUDE. At Eisenhower's request, Churchill in late March had warned the English that there would be a series of exercises and feints. OVERLORD, hopefully, would be viewed as a feint; the Germans would think that the main effort was to begin with a mid-July attack launched from Scotland against southern Norway, followed by a maximum effort against the Pas de Calais. Allied leaders already knew that Rundstedt felt the main attack would come in the Pas de Calais. This plan would serve to reinforce his reasoning. Assaulting southern Norway would be the fictitious British Fourth Army, three corps strong, which was mainly simulated by radio signals. To further the deception, as had been done in the south of England, traffic was restricted in a part of Scotland. This threat of attack was kept alive long after the invasion, in fact until July, in an effort to fix German forces in the north so that they could not be shifted to meet the actual invasion. In one portion of the deception plan, German experience in fighting Patton in the Mediterranean was exploited. This part of the plan was geared to make the enemy believe that the main attack was to follow the Norway affair and would be led by Patton in command of a 12-division First Army Group, which would gradually expand to 50 divisions. Patton and his white bull terrier were seen everywhere in England. German double agents, controlled by the Allies, sent in reports which supported the deception plan. Various actual units were stationed in east and southeast England, and their numbers were increased by the careful use of radio simulation.

Although the Allies could mislead the Germans with a clear conscience, there were others, especially the families of the fighting men, who wanted to know what was going on. It was the job of war correspondents to give them that news, but it was the problem of the SHAEF staff to decide what news could be released and what could aid the enemy. Even the fact that a famous correspondent such as Ernie Pyle said in a dispatch that he had visited a certain area in England might cause the enemy to suspect major pre-invasion activity in that area. Yet much information was commonly available. B. H. Liddell Hart, the British military writer who studied enemy commanders and reported to Eisenhower on their skills and personalities, showed the Supreme Commander that by reading the major American and British newspapers, an individual could make a fairly accurate guess as to what the Allies had been planning to do between June 1943 and February 1944. As the days and weeks passed, more and more correspondents arrived, and the rumors flew. In early May, Eisenhower told his commanders to consider all SHAEF accredited correspondents as "quasi-staff officers," to help them when possible, and to allow them to talk to soldiers of all grades. A couple of weeks later Eisenhower personally presented an "off the record" briefing in which he told the correspondents about the forthcoming Allied effort. While press reports would continue to be censored, the correspondents had now been made a part of the operation. Eisenhower told them that he wanted the truth told. He said no report would be censored just because it criticized him. He hoped to retain the support of the informed public, for their opinion, he felt, was vital to a winning effort. "Without public opinion back of us," he said, "we would be nothing but mercenaries."[74]

Busy Days in May

Although the Allies geared all OVERLORD preparations toward the previously picked target date of June 1, Eisenhower had the flexibility to select any date between the first and a reasonable later date. Light, tide, and weather conditions would be major factors affecting his decision. It had already been decided that OVERLORD would be a daylight assault because control of the large force at night would be difficult and location and rapid destruction of beach defenses close to impossible in the dark. In addition, preparatory fires, both naval and air, could be much more accurately delivered in daylight. Thus the assault force would approach in darkness. An attack at low tide would give the engineers more time to destroy beach obstacles, but infantrymen would be required to cross a broad expanse of beach—in the case of Omaha some 300 yards. To enable the landing craft to return for the second wave, the tide needed to be rising. The best compromise seemed to be to attack about one hour after low tide. This would result in a realistic width of beach, while providing enough depth so that rocks in the British sector would not be a major problem; the landing craft could be refloated, and the water would not be too deep for the obstacles to be destroyed. Finally, the moon on the night preceding the assault would have to provide enough light for the ships to navigate and for the airborne landings to be executed properly. During June, a concurrence of all these conditions existed only on the fifth, sixth, and seventh. Considering everything, Eisenhower selected June 5 as D-Day, with the sixth and seventh as alternates in the event bad weather forced a postponement. When he informed the Combined Chiefs of Staff of his decision on May 17, he added that should none of these days be adequate, he would have to delay to June 19 and sacrifice the advantage of moonlight.[75]

Eisenhower realized that even if weather conditions favored the attack, his forces would have to overcome a tenacious defense. Perhaps Hitler would unveil new German weapons. Early in April, Major General Leslie R. Groves, commanding the Manhattan Project (development of the atomic bomb), had briefed Eisenhower concerning the possibility of Germany using radioactive poisons against OVERLORD. Eisenhower was also abreast of German progress on the development of weapons of atomic or bacteriological nature. He took care to bomb areas where it was thought that new weapons were being built. For fear of igniting an alarm which might sweep his command, however, he told only a few people of these dire possibilities. Commanders who were to be a part of OVERLORD were not briefed; but, by use of a cover story, medical authorities were alerted to some of the symptoms which might result.[76]

When the final plans were completed and subject only to modifications absolutely dictated by a change in enemy dispositions or weather considerations, Eisenhower and other senior commanders had to rely upon efficiency in execution of OVERLORD. Eisenhower understood that this factor was largely dependent on the morale of the lower-level units and troops and later wrote:

> Soldiers like to see the men who are directing operations; they properly resent any indication of neglect or indifference to them on the part of their commanders and invariably interpret a visit, even a brief one, as evidence of the commander's concern for them. Diffidence or modesty must never blind the commander to his duty of showing himself to his men, of speaking to them, of mingling with them to the extent of physical limitations. It pays big dividends in terms of morale, and morale, given rough equality in other things, is supreme on the battlefield.[77]

Between February 1 and June 1, the Supreme Commander visited 26 divisions, 24 airfields, 5 warships, and many other installations, including hospitals and depots. Not only did this provide an opportunity for the men to see him, but it also enabled him to assess the state of their training, morale, and equipment. Eisenhower also strongly encouraged his subordinate leaders to get out to see the troops. He concluded a May 14 letter to the senior U.S. commanders with the following: "This is not the time for long discussions on the roots and causes of war. Our soldiers have heard this before. What is required now is to impress on them that only hard and successful fighting will bring victory; and that the way home is via Berlin."[78]

As D-Day neared, precise knowledge about the locations of German units became even more important. French intelligence agents, posing as laundrymen, helped in this effort. Since their service was excellent and their prices low, they had much German business. When a unit would move, it would leave a forwarding address to which laundry could be sent when it was finished. Through this source, officers at SHAEF headquarters learned that neither the *panzer* division at Toulouse nor the one between Brussels and Antwerp *(See Map 53, in Atlas)* had moved as they most certainly would have done had the Germans discovered the actual invasion site.[79]

Late in May, however, an intelligence report revealed that the Germans had shifted reinforcements into the general area of the drop zones for the 82nd Airborne Division on the Cotentin Peninsula. At once an old argument was revived. As noted earlier, Leigh-Mallory had long opposed the extensive use of airborne units on the Cotentin, while Montgomery and Bradley had just as emphatically maintained that use of two American airborne divisions on that peninsula was essential. The opposing viewpoints of these senior commanders did not change with receipt of the new information, although Bradley did shift the drop zones for the 82nd, the new areas making glider landings even more difficult. Leigh-Mallory was so strongly against the use of airborne divisions that he protested to the Supreme Commander in a letter dated May 29, seven days before the scheduled D-Day, and followed it with a personal visit the next day. As before, he was concerned about the extremely heavy casualties he was sure the divisions would suffer; he wanted to cancel that part of the operation. Eisenhower had a difficult decision to make, knowing very well how essential the landing at Utah Beach was to OVERLORD and the importance Bradley attached to using airborne units to seize exits from the beaches. After careful deliberation, he decided to make no changes, in part influenced by his judgment that Leigh-Mallory was overestimating the danger. (As it turned out, the British airman had overestimated the hazards involved. After the mission, he called Eisenhower to say how glad he was that he had been wrong and to express regret over the added strain he had caused.) Later, Eisenhower wrote that he felt the pressure and responsibilty of command more in making this decision than he had when giving the final "go" order for OVERLORD.[80]

As the invasion date neared, the Allied air forces intensified their attacks, destroying material and disrupting facilities the Germans badly needed. The Transportation Plan, now in the final stages of execution, created real problems in movement for Rundstedt's forces. German airfields within 150 miles of Caen were also methodically kept under attack, making them useless and driving *Luftwaffe* units to fields as far removed from Normandy as were the Allied fields in England. On May 10, the Allies launched a series of air raids on radar sites and radio facilities. Through careful targeting, most radar sites were knocked out, while several were intentionally left operational so that at the appropriate time they could pick up the planned electronic deception measures. These measures included the use of special devices on a small group of ships or aircraft which caused a great number to be seen on a radar screen. When noise amplifiers were added and a smoke screen was employed, the presence of a large invasion fleet offshore could be simulated in sight and sound, as well as electronically.[81]

Strategic bombing forces also had a devastating effect on the German oil industry. On May 12, these forces launched 935 bombers with fighter escort in a raid which destroyed many German fighters* and severely damaged the ground targets. The German Minister of Armaments and War Production, Albert Speer, was impressed:

> I shall never forget the date May 12. . . . On that day the technological war was decided. Until then we had managed to produce approximately as many weapons as the armed forces needed, in spite of their considerable losses. But with the attack by nine hundred and thirty five daylight bombers of the American Eighth Air Force upon several fuel plants in central and eastern Germany, a new era in the air war began. It meant the end of German armaments production.[82]

Although production had been cut, Speer estimated that what remained, coupled with the reserves in hand, would fuel the German war effort for more than 19 months. The critical danger would come if the Allies continued to hit the oil targets. After conducting a personal inspection of the damage on May 19, Speer told Hitler:

> The enemy has struck us at one of our weakest points. If they persist at it this time, we will soon no longer have any fuel production worth mentioning. Our one hope is that the other side has an air force General Staff as scatterbrained as ours![83]

Speer thus seemed to support the position of those who several months earlier had opposed Eisenhower's Transportation Plan and favored an attack on the German oil industry. Had they been mounted, these attacks would certainly have created havoc, but their effect on OVERLORD cannot be adequately estimated.[84] Speer was also impressed with the accuracy of Allied bombing, and grew so concerned over the safety of the Rhine bridges that he had emergency repair materials brought to each site and ordered the construction of pontoon bridges.

In late May, the Allies did launch a major air campaign against a group of bridges—those over the Seine, however, not the Rhine. So successful were these attacks that by D-Day 18 of the 24 bridges on the Seine between Paris and the coast were destroyed, and the remaining 6 were blocked. This effectively separated much of Germany's Fifteenth Army from the Normandy area. The aerial campaign did not reveal the site of the invasion, however, because intelligence officers could easily assume that the bridges were destroyed to prevent a portion of the Fifteenth Army as well as all of the Seventh Army from coming to the rescue of those who were defending the Pas de Calais.[85]

Seine Railroad Bridge Destroyed by Allied Bombing

Between May 12 and 18, strategic bombers based in England were either used on OVERLORD-related missions or prevented from attacking oil targets due to weather conditions. Meanwhile, the Italian-based Fifteenth Air Force continued its anti-oil raids on Ploesti in Rumania. Bombers from England hit German synthetic oil plants once again on May 28 and 29. By this time Speer had raised his production level nearly back to where it was before the May 12 attack. These raids were even more effective than the earlier one and, coupled with the attacks on Ploesti, halved German oil production.[86]

Meanwhile, the airmen kept pressure on the enemy transportation system. So extensive was the damage that by June 3 the German Air Force Operations Staff reported that German railroad officials wondered if any more effort should be expended on repairs. Bombing raids had also caused a continual drain on German resources, because a large number of antiaircraft guns were built and many troops used to fill antiaircraft units. Significant damage of oil and airplane production facilities, lines of communication, and coastal fortifications had been achieved through the continuing air offensive. But the Allied cost was high. Between April 1 and June 5, 12,000 men

*The exact number of fighters destroyed was never resolved.

German Troop Dispositions, May 1944

Location	Inf. Divs.	Inf. Brigs.	Panzer Divs.	Panzer Brigs.	Misc. Divs.	Misc. Brigs.
Italy and Balkans	37	2	9		4	
Russian Front	122		25	1	17	1
Western Front to include the Netherlands, Norway, and Denmark	64	1 (regt)	12	2	12	
Reserves in Germany	3	1	1	2	4	2

were lost, along with 2,000 aircraft. In addition, many men were wounded and a large number of aircraft were damaged.[87]

As May drew to a close, much of Hitler's planned defensive system remained to be built. Still, the force which would meet the Allied thrust was a formidable one. According to SHAEF intelligence sources, on May 20, 58 German divisions were located in France, comprising about 750,000 men. Because Hitler had no central reserve, however, reinforcements for the Normandy area would have to come from another front or from an area of France not under attack. This is one reason why the intelligence report stressed the importance of Allied deception plans. If the Germans could be made to believe that an attack on Norway was probable, that the south of France was threatened, and that the main invasion would come in the Pas de Calais area, it would be difficult for Hitler to mass a sizable force to meet the Normandy invasion.[88]

Hitler reasoned that there probably would be preliminary attacks before the main assault. This belief, shared by many high-ranking German leaders, and reinforced by the Allied deception plan, caused him to search for attack sites other than the Pas de Calais. In February and March, accordingly, he had expressed his concern for the Normandy and Brittany areas. In May he directed the movement of units which resulted in the Cotentin build-up and required the displacement of landing zones for the 82nd Airborne Division discussed earlier. One *panzer* division also moved from Brittany to Caen, while a second came from Hungary to Chartres. This increased strength would be felt by the Allied forces on D-Day and immediately thereafter. Generally, however, the Allied deception scheme was working, as was confirmed by documents found in a German headquarters vehicle captured in Italy. The wide dispersal of German troop units, geared to meet the threats posed by the various facets of BODYGUARD, would not change prior to the invasion.[89]

As Eisenhower's forces stood poised to launch OVERLORD, the Germans continued to consider Normandy as a possible assault area; but their intelligence was so poor that insufficient evidence was available to determine that an invasion was imminent, much less where it would come. As late as June 5, those in Army Group B felt that the Allied bombing pattern indicated the main attack would be in the Pas de Calais area. Rundstedt, also on the fifth, commented in his weekly situation report:

> The systematic continuation and noticeable intensification of enemy air attacks indicate a more advanced state of readiness for the descent. The main front between the Scheldt and Normandy is still the most probable place of attack. Its possible extension along the north coast of Brittany, including Brest, is not excluded. Where within this entire sector the enemy will attempt a landing is still obscure. . . . As yet there is no immediate prospect of the invasion.[90]

Bad weather caused the cancellation of German naval patrols the night of June 5, but a Seventh Army map exercise scheduled for June 6 in Rennes remained scheduled. Rommel left France on the fifth, planning to stop for the night with his family in Germany while en route to see Hitler. With the invasion but hours away, the Allied secret was still secure.[91]

German Command in the West
Midnight, June 5-6, 1944

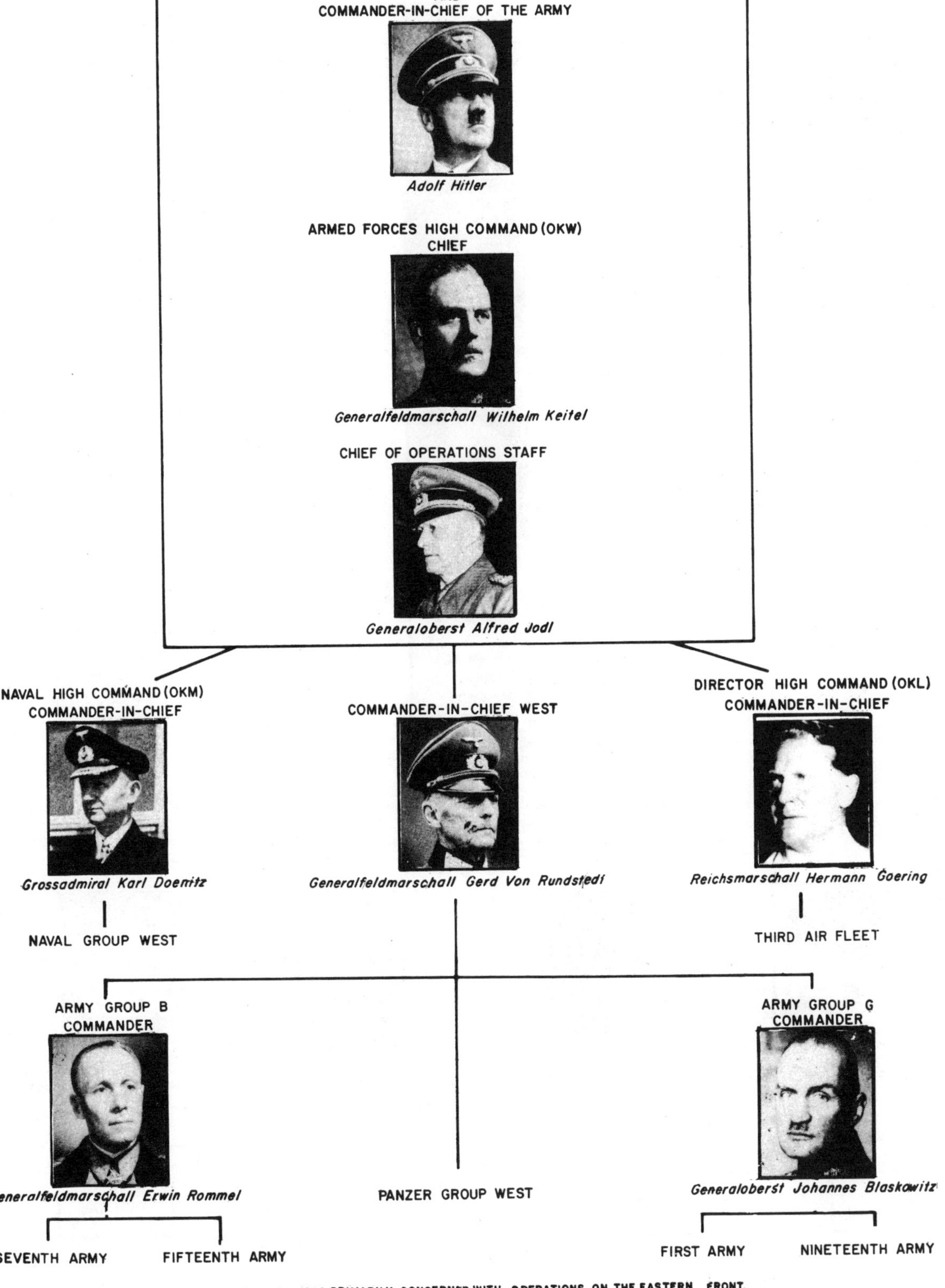
SUPREME COMMANDER OF THE ARMED FORCES
AND
COMMANDER-IN-CHIEF OF THE ARMY
Adolf Hitler
ARMED FORCES HIGH COMMAND (OKW)
CHIEF
Generalfeldmarschall Wilhelm Keitel
CHIEF OF OPERATIONS STAFF
Generaloberst Alfred Jodl
NAVAL HIGH COMMAND (OKM)
COMMANDER-IN-CHIEF
Grossadmiral Karl Doenitz
NAVAL GROUP WEST
COMMANDER-IN-CHIEF WEST
Generalfeldmarschall Gerd Von Rundstedt
DIRECTOR HIGH COMMAND (OKL)
COMMANDER-IN-CHIEF
Reichsmarschall Hermann Goering
THIRD AIR FLEET
ARMY GROUP B
COMMANDER
Generalfeldmarschall Erwin Rommel
SEVENTH ARMY
FIFTEENTH ARMY
PANZER GROUP WEST
ARMY GROUP G
COMMANDER
Generaloberst Johannes Blaskowitz
FIRST ARMY
NINETEENTH ARMY
NOTE: OKH, THE ARMY HIGH COMMAND WAS PRIMARILY CONCERNED WITH OPERATIONS ON THE EASTERN FRONT.

Chart 1

Allied Expeditionary Force
February 13, 1944

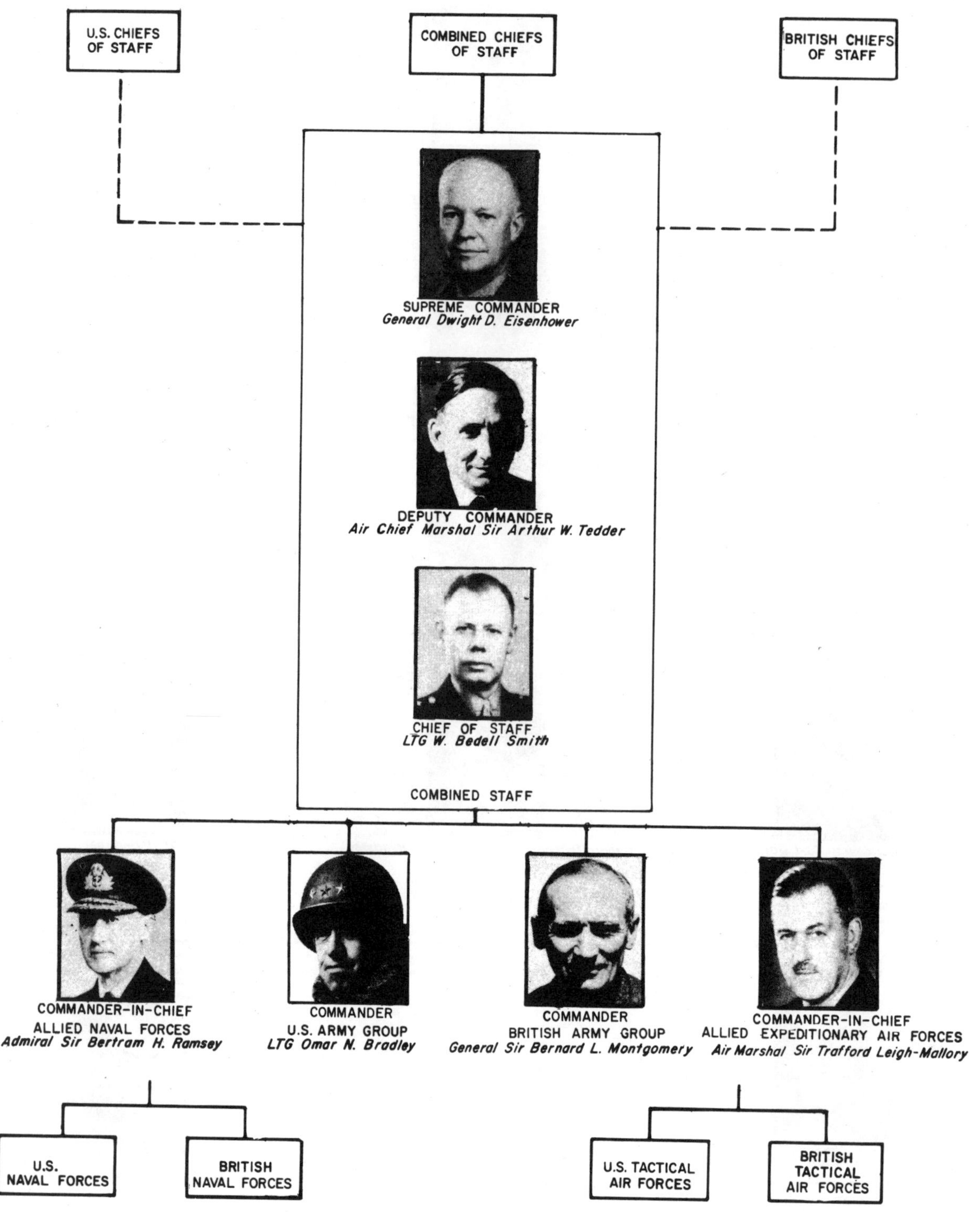

Chart 2

Notes

[1] Gordon A. Harrison, *Cross-Channel Attack* (Washington, 1951), p. 457.

[2] Forrest C. Pogue, *The Supreme Command* (Washington, 1954), p. 169; Pogue, "D-Day—1944" in *D-Day: The Normandy Invasion in Retrospect* (Lawrence, Kansas, 1971), p. 9.

[3] L. F. Ellis, *Victory in the West,* I, *The Battle of Normandy* (London, 1962), pp. xvii, 28; Stephen E. Ambrose, *The Supreme Commander: The War Years of General Dwight D. Eisenhower* (Garden City, 1970), p. 329; Anthony Cave Brown, *Bodyguard of Lies* (New York, 1975), p. 3.

[4] Pogue, *Supreme Command*, p. 98; Harrison, *Cross-Channel*, pp. 1-2, 5; Vincent J. Esposito (ed.), *The West Point Atlas of American Wars* (2 vols.; New York, 1959), II, Section 2, 26; Pogue, "D-Day," pp. 13-14.

[5] Pogue, *Supreme Command*, pp. 98-99; Harrison, *Cross-Channel,* pp.5-6, 22, 26; T. Dodson Stamps and Vincent J. Esposito (eds.), *A Military History of World War II* (2 vols.; West Point, 1956), I, 320; Ambrose, *Supreme Commander*, pp. 21, 30-33, 47-48.

[6] Harrison, *Cross-Channel*, pp. 10, 26, 31; Winston S. Churchill, *Closing the Ring* (Boston, 1951), p. 582; Ellis, *Normandy*, pp. 14-15; Maurice Matloff, "Wilmot Revisited: Myth and Reality in Anglo-American Strategy for the Second Front," in *D-Day: The Normandy Invasion in Retrospect* (Lawrence, Kansas, 1971), p. 113; Richard M. Leighton, "OVERLORD Revisited: An Interpretation of American Strategy on the European War, 1941-1944," *The American Historical Review*, LXVIII (July 1963), 922, 924.

[7] The discussion about ULTRA is based upon: F. W. Winterbotham, *The Ultra Secret* (New York, 1974), pp. 21, 24, 26, 89 and Cave Brown, *Bodyguard*, pp. 36, 52.

[8] Harrison, *Cross-Channel*, pp. 31-32, 46-47, 53; Stamps and Esposito, *Military History*, I, 320-321.

[9] Harrison, *Cross-Channel,* pp. 54-56; Ellis, *Normandy*, pp. 12-13, Charles B. MacDonald, *The Mighty Endeavor: American Armed Forces in the European Theater in World War II* (New York, 1969), p. 250; Earl Mountbatten of Burma, "Operation Jubilee: The Place of the Dieppe Raid in History," *Journal of the Royal United Services Institute for Defense Studies*, 119 (March 1974), 25, 27, 29-30; Cave Brown, *Bodyguard*, pp. 73, 83, 85-87, 90.

[10] Harrison, *Cross-Channel*, pp. 55-57; Ellis *Normandy*, p. 15.

[11] Harrison, *Cross-Channel*, pp. 38, 40, 45, 51; MacDonald, *Mighty Endeavor*, p. 228; Mary H. Williams (Comp.), *Chronology, 1941-1945* (Washington, 1960), pp. 83-88; Cave Brown, *Bodyguard*, pp. 247-249; Pogue, *Supreme Command*, p. 23.

[12] Harrison, *Cross-Channel,* pp. 48-49, 51 (Morgan's words appear on p. 51); Pogue, *Supreme Command*, pp. 15, 58.

[13] Harrison, *Cross-Channel*, pp. 48-49, 51, 64-70, 455; Matloff, "Wilmot Revisited," p. 111; Williams, *Chronology*, p. 110.

[14] Ellis, *Normandy*, pp. 15-16; Harrison, *Cross-Channel*, pp. 17-72; Pogue, "D-Day," p. 14; Stamps and Esposito, *Military History*, I, 333-335.

[15] Cave Brown, *Bodyguard*, pp. 4-8, 459-461.

[16] Harrison, *Cross-Channel*, p. 75; Alfred Goldberg, "Air Campaign OVERLORD: D-Day," in *D-Day: The Normandy Invasion in Retrospect* (Lawrence, Kansas, 1971), p. 57.

[17] Harrison, *Cross-Channel*, pp. 78-79; Ellis, *Normandy*, p. 17.

[18] Harrison, *Cross-Channel*, pp. 102-103.

[19] *Ibid.*, pp. 53, 105-106, 115-116.

[20] Pogue, *Supreme Command*, pp. 44-49; Ellis, *Normandy*, p. 32, Harrison, *Cross-Channel*, pp. 115-116; Omar N. Bradley, *A Soldier's Story* (New York, 1951), p. 204.

[21] Harrison, *Cross-Channel*, pp. 122-127; Matloff, "Wilmot Revisited," pp. 111-112; Cave Brown, *Bodyguard*, pp. 388-389; Pogue, *Supreme Command*, p. 30.

[22] Forrest C. Pogue, *George C. Marshall: Organizer of Victory* (New York, 1973), pp. 227-228, 263-264, 267, 272-273, 277, 319-321 (quote is on p. 321); Pogue, *Supreme Command*, pp. 3, 25, 27-32; Ambrose, *Supreme Commander*, pp. 306-307.

[23] Pogue, *Supreme Command*, p. 32; Ambrose, *Supreme Commander*, p. 308; Dwight D. Eisenhower, *Crusade in Europe* (Garden City, 1948), p. 207; Harry C. Butcher, *My Three Years with Eisenhower* (New York, 1946), pp. 452-453.

[24] Ellis, *Normandy*, pp. 52-53; Harrison, *Cross-Channel*, p. 131; Basil H. Liddell Hart, *History of the Second World War* (New York, 1970), p. 159; Treusch von Buttlar, MS#B-672: "Commentary on MS#B-308," in *OB WEST (Atlantic Wall to Siegfried Line), A Study in Command*, James F. Scoggin, Jr., ed. (Allendorf, Germany, 1946-1947), II, 24-25 (Buttlar was Chief of Army Operations, Armed Forces Operations Staff [WFST], June 12, 1942-November 15, 1944).

[25] Buttlar, "Commentary," II, pp. 21-24; Cornelius Ryan, *The Longest Day: June 6, 1944* (New York, 1959), p. 24.

[26] Bodo Zimmerman, MS#B-308, "OB WEST, Atlantic Wall to Siegfried Line, A Study in Command," in *OB WEST (Atlantic Wall to Siegfried Line), A Study in Command*, James F. Scoggin, Jr., ed. (Allendorf, Germany, 1946-1947), I, 15 (Zimmerman was Rundstedt's operations officer); Hans Speidel, MS#B-718: "Commentary on MS#B-308," in *Ibid.*, I, 13 (Speidel was Chief of Staff, Army Group B. This group later was assigned to the western theater); Buttlar, "Commentary," I, 14 (Buttlar recalled Hitler's words concerning Rudstedt); Harrison, *Cross-Channel*, pp. 131-133; Pogue, *Supreme Command*, p. 19.

[27] Harrison, *Cross-Channel*, p. 243; Esposito, *West Point Atlas*, II, Section 2, 48; Frederich Ruge, "German Naval Operations on D-Day," in *D-Day: The Normandy Invasion in Retrospect* (Lawrence, Kansas, 1971), p. 318; Frederich Ruge, "The Invasion of Normandy," in Hans-Adolf Jacobsen and Jürgen Rohwer (eds.), *Decisive Battles of World War II: The German View* (London, 1965), p. 159; Guenther Blumentritt, *Von Rundstedt: The Soldier and the Man* (London, 1952), pp. 122, 126-127 (Blumentritt became Rudstedt's Chief of Staff in September 1942); Winterbotham, *Ultra*, p. 121.

[28] Harrison, *Cross-Channel,* pp. 133, 135; Ellis *Normandy*, p. 53; Blumentritt, *Rundstedt*, pp. 121-122; Albert Speer, *Inside the Third Reich* (New York, 1971), p. 452; Pogue, *Supreme Command*, p. 175. (*Fuehrer* Directive #40 is reprinted as Appendix C in Harrison, *Cross-Channel*, pp. 459-463.)

[29] Harrison, *Cross-Channel*, pp. 135-138; Ellis, *Normandy*, p. 53; Ruge, "Invasion of Normandy," p. 319; Cave Brown, *Bodyguard*, p. 74.

[30] Ellis, *Normandy*, p. 53; Blumentritt, *Rundstedt*, pp. 134-138, 170-176; MacDonald, *Mighty Endeavor*, p. 101; Zimmerman, "OB WEST," p. 22; Ruge, "Invasion of Normandy," p. 319; Esposito,

West Point Atlas, II, Section 2, 36-37, 101-102.

[31] Harrison, *Cross-Channel,* pp. 70-71, 135, 140; Ellis *Normandy*, p. 54; Blumentritt, *Rundstedt,* pp. 162-163; Cave Brown, *Bodyguard*, pp. 325-326.

[32] Harrison, *Cross-Channel*, pp. 128, 140-141, 155-156; Zimmerman, "OB WEST," pp. 25-29; Blumentritt, *Rundstedt*, pp. 157-162; Ellis, *Normandy*, pp. 54-55 (quotations are on p. 54).

[33] Harrison, *Cross-Channel*, p. 464.

[34] This paragraph appears on p. 467 of Harrison, *Cross-Channel*. The entire directive can be found on pp. 464-467. Other references are: *Ibid.*, pp. 128, 148; Williams, *Chronology*, pp. 142-143; Cave Brown, *Bodyguard*, p. 356.

[35] Harrison, *Cross-Channel*, pp. 148-151; Winterbotham, *Ultra*, p. 121.

[36] Blumentritt, *Rundstedt*, pp. 196-198; Harrison, *Cross-Channel*, pp. 246-247; Ellis, *Normandy*, p. 56.

[37] Pogue, *Supreme Command*, p. 23; Harrison, *Cross-Channel*, p. 128; Esposito, *West Point Atlas*, II, Section 2, 97-101.

[36] Blumentritt, *Rundstedt*, pp. 196-198; Harrison, *Cross-Channel*, pp. 246-247; Ellis, *Normandy*, p. 56.

[37] Pogue, *Supreme Command*, p. 23; Harrison, *Cross-Channel*, p. 128; Esposito, *West Point Atlas*, II, Section 2, 97-101.

[38] Eisenhower, *Crusade in Europe*, p. 211; Alfred D. Chandler (ed.), *The Papers of Dwight D. Eisenhower: The War Years* (Baltimore, 1970), III: No. 1423, Eisenhower to Marshall, December 17, 1943; No. 1426, Eisenhower to McNarney for Marshall, December 23, 1943; No. 1440, Eisenhower to Marshall, December 27, 1943; No. 1449, Eisenhower to Marshall, December 29, 1943; Pogue, *Organizer of Victory*, p. 371; Maurice Matloff, *Strategic Planning for Coalition Warfare 1943-1944* (Washington, 1959), p. 406. Hereinafter, the Eisenhower Papers are cited as *EP*.

[39] *EP*, III: No. 1423, Eisenhower to Marshall, December 17, 1943; No. 1445, Eisenhower to Marshall, December 28, 1943; Pogue, *Supreme Command*, p. 74.

[40] *EP*, III: No. 1445, Eisenhower to Marshall, December 28, 1943; *EP*, V: p. 139; Pogue, *Supreme Command*, p. 66; Eisenhower, *Crusade in Europe*, p. 211. Eisenhower later wrote: "General Montgomery has no superior in two most important characteristics. He quickly develops among British enlisted men an intense devotion and admiration—the greatest personal asset a commander can possess. Montgomery's other outstanding characteristic is his tactical ability in what might be called the "prepared" battle. In the study of enemy positions and situations and in the combining of his own armor, artillery, air, and infantry to secure tactical success against the enemy he is careful, meticulous, and certain." (Eisenhower, *Crusade in Europe*, p. 211.

[41] *EP*, III; No. 1442, Eisenhower to Morgan, December 27, 1943; editor's note accompanying No. 1473, p. 1653; *EP*, V: p. 134; Eisenhower, *Crusade in Europe*, p. 217; Ellis, *Normandy*, p. 32; Walter B. Smith, *Eisenhower's Six Great Decisions* (New York, 1956), p. 30; Bernard Law Montgomery, *The Memoirs of Field Marshall The Viscount Montgomery of Alamein, K.G.* (Cleveland, 1958), pp. 184-185, 189; Pogue, *Supreme Command*, p. 107.

[42] Pogue, *Organizer of Victory*, pp. 326-328; Ambrose, *Supreme Commander*, pp. 317-318; John S. D. Eisenhower, *Strictly Personal* (Garden City, 1974), pp. 51-52, 397; Ellis, *Normandy*, p. 32; *EP*, V: pp. 139-140; Harry C. Butcher, *Three Years,* p. 468; Dwight D. Eisenhower, *At Eaśe: Stories I Tell to Friends* (Garden City, 1967), p. 269; Cave Brown, *Bodyguard*, pp. 59, 409.

[43] Ellis, *Normandy*, p. 32.

[44] *Ibid.*, p. 31; Pogue, "D-Day," p. 15; Montgomery, *Memoirs*, p. 192.

[45] *EP*, III: No. 1497, Eisenhower to Combined Chiefs of Staff and British Chiefs of Staff, January 23, 1944.

[46] Quoted in Ambrose, *Supreme Commander*, p. 350.

[47] Sources used for the above four paragraphs are: Pogue, *Supreme Command*, pp. 108-117, 121; Harrison, *Cross-Channel*, pp. 164-173; Ellis, *Normandy*, pp. 33-37, 120-121; MacDonald, *Mighty Endeavor*, p. 252; Smith, *Six Decisions,* pp. 33, 35; Montgomery, *Memoirs*, pp. 197-199; Arthur W. Tedder, *With Prejudice: The War Memoirs of Marshal of the Royal Air Force Lord Tedder G.C.B.* (Boston, 1966), pp. 505-506; Ambrose, *Supreme Commander*, p. 336; Butcher, *Three Years,* p.475; *EP*, III; editor's notes with No. 1473, p. 1653 and No. 1496, pp. 1672-1673; No. 1490, Eisenhower to Marshall, January 22, 1944; No. 1497, Eisenhower to Combined Chiefs of Staff and British Chiefs of Staff, January 23, 1944; No. 1531, Eisenhower to Marshall, February 6, 1944. Churchill, always opposed to ANVIL, did not give his final approval until early July. The invasion, renamed DRAGOON, took place on August 15.

[48] Pogue, *Supreme Command*, pp. 56-60, 96-97; *EP*, III: editor's note with No. 1585, p. 1767; Eisenhower, *Crusade in Europe*, pp. 210, 220; Smith, *Six Decisions,* p. 2; Ambrose, *Supreme Commander*, p. 324; Peter Lyon, *Eisenhower: Portrait of a Hero* (Boston, 1974), p. 266.

[49] Ambrose, *Supreme Commander*, pp. 338-339; Harrison, *Cross-Channel*, p. 158; Ellis, *Normandy*, pp. 37, 39.

[50] *EP*, III: No. 1310, Eisenhower to Smith, October 2, 1943; Pogue, *Supreme Command*, pp. 60-61, 123.

[51] Quoted in Pogue, *Supreme Command*, p. 34.

[52] *Ibid.*, p. 61.

[53] Bradley, *Soldier's Story*, p. 206; Pogue *Supreme Command*, p. 62.

[54] Lyon, *Eisenhower*, p. 279; MacDonald, *Mighty Endeavor*, pp. 246-247.

[55] *EP*, III; No. 1567, Eisenhower to Lee, February 26, 1947.

[56] Source material for the above discussion of racial matters was drawn from: Ulysses Lee, *The Employment of Negro Troops* (Washington, 1966), pp. 440-441, 626-627; Thomas E. Hachey, "Jim Crow with a British Accent: Attitudes of London Government Officials Toward American Negro Soldiers in England During World War II," *Journal of Negro History,* 59 (January 1974), 66-67, 71-74; Chester B. Hansen, "War Diary," Chester B. Hansen Papers, United States Army Military History Research Collection, Carlisle Barracks, Pa., entry of May 4, 1944.

[57] Harrison, *Cross-Channel*, pp. 162, 164; *EP*, III: No. 1522, Eisenhower to Percy Cleghorn Stanley Hobart (MG Hobart commanded the British 79th Armored Division charged with the development and testing of special armored equipment), January 29, 1944; editor's note with No. 1522, pp. 1697-1698; No. 1539, Eisenhower to George Catlett Marshall, February 9, 1944; Butcher, *Three Years*, p. 482.

[58] Harrison, *Cross-Channel*, pp. 173-174; Ellis, *Normandy,* pp. 63-65.

[59] The following sources were used for the above four paragraphs: Harrison, *Cross-Channel*, pp. 174, 220, 223; MacDonald, *Mighty Endeavor*, pp. 238-240, 253-255; Ambrose, *Supreme Commander*, pp 363, 366-368, 371-373; Ellis, *Normandy*, pp. 41-42, 94-95, 97-98; Eisenhower, *Crusade in Europe*, p. 222; Wesley F. Craven and James L. Cate (eds.), *The Army Air Force in World War II,* Volume III, *Europe: Argument to VE Day January 1944 to May 1945*

(Chicago, 1951), p. 173; Stamps and Esposito, *Military History*, II, 343-344; Goldberg, "Air Campaign," p. 59.

[60] Speer, *Third Reich*, p. 446; Eisenhower,*Crusade in Europe*, p 233; Tedder, *With Prejudice*, pp. 534-536; Craven and Cate, *Argument*, p. 73.

[61] Cave Brown, *Bodyguard*, pp. 517-519; Harrison, *Cross-Channel*, pp. 225, 227-228, 230.

[62] Material for the above three paragraphs was drawn from the following sources: Ellis, *Normandy*, pp. 105-107; Pogue, *Supreme Command*, pp. 134-136; Chester Wilmot, *The Struggle for Europe* (London, 1952), pp. 165-166; MacDonald, *Mighty Endeavor*, p. 255; Butcher, *Three Years*, pp. 478, 492; Winterbotham, *Ultra*, pp. 120-121; Cave Brown, *Bodyguard*, pp. 362-363, 365-370.

[63] Montgomery, *Memoirs*, pp. 210-211; Bradley, *Soldier's Story*, pp. 239, 241; Eisenhower, *Crusade in Europe*, pp. 243-244; Ellis, *Normandy*, pp. 78, 80-81.

[64] Source material for the above two paragraphs was drawn from: Ryan, *Longest Day*, p. 49; Blumentritt, *Rundstedt*, pp. 186-188, 190; Zimmerman, "OB WEST," pp. 36-39; MacDonald *Mighty Endeavor*, pp. 257, 260; Rundstedt, "Commentary," p. 37; Ellis, *Normandy*, p. 59.

[65] Speer, *Third Reich*, p. 454.

[66] Material for the above five paragraphs was drawn from: MacDonald, *Mighty Endeavor*, pp. 257-260; Harrison, *Cross-Channel*, pp. 151-154, 156-157, 242, 247-250; Blumentritt, *Rundstedt*, p. 150; Ruge, "Invasion," pp. 326-327; Ruge, "Naval," pp. 149-150; Speidel, "Commentary," pp.40-41; Zimmerman, "OB WEST," p. 51; Ellis, *Normandy*, pp. 119-120; Speer, *Third Reich*, pp. 453-454; Winterbotham, *Ultra*, pp. 125-128, 132.

[67] Ellis, *Normandy*, pp. 115-116; Bradley, *Soldier's Story*, pp. 260-261; George M. Elsey, "Naval Aspects of Normandy in Retrospect," in *D-Day: The Normandy Invasion in Retrospect* (Lawrence, Kansas, 1971), p. 177; *EP*, III: No. 1732, Memorandum, June 3, 1944; Winterbotham, *Ultra*, p. 125.

[68] Ellis, *Normandy*, pp. 104-105, 115-116; Ryan, *Longest Day*, pp. 78-79; Benjamin A. Dickson, "G-2 Journal: Algiers to the Elbe" (Devon Pa., n.d.), copy in Special Collections Division, USMA Library, p. 105.

[69] Harrison, *Cross-Channel*, pp. 190-192, 269-270; Pogue, *Supreme Command*, p. 166; Bradley, *Soldier's Story*, p. 236; *EP*, III: No. 1657, Eisenhower to Marshall, April 29, 1944; No. 1658, Eisenhower to Marshall, April 29, 1944; editor's note with No. 1658, p. 1839; Ellis, *Normandy*, p. 133; Butcher, *Three Years*, pp. 527-531; Cave Brown, *Bodyguard*, p. 545.

[70] Quoted in Bradley, *Soldier's Story*, p. 225; Harrison, *Cross-Channel*, pp. 269-270.

[71] "Orientation in E.T.O. Prior to Invasion," MG Frederick H. Osborn Papers, Special Collections Division, United States Military Academy Library.

[72] Bradley, *Soldier's Story*, p. 247; Harrison, *Cross-Channel*, p. 270; Pogue, *Supreme Command*, pp. 167-168; Dickson, "G-2 Journal," p. 116; Ellis, *Normandy*, pp. 136-137.

[73] Butcher, *Three Years*, p. 505; Ambrose, *Supreme Commander*, p. 403; Pogue, *Supreme Command*, p. 163; Ryan, *Longest Day*, p. 49; Cave Brown, *Bodyguard*, pp. 531-534.

[74] Pogue, *Supreme Command*, pp. 88-91, Eisenhower's words appear on p. 90; Cave Brown, *Bodyguard*, pp. 528-529.

[75] Harrison, *Cross-Channel* pp. 188-190; Ambrose, *Supreme Commander*, pp. 394-414; Ellis, *Normandy*, pp. 91, 140; Pogue, *Supreme Command*, p. 167.

[76] *EP*, III: No. 1683. Eisenhower to Marshall; editor's note with No. 1683, p. 1860; V, p. 149; Eisenhower, *Crusade in Europe*, pp. 229-230.

[77] Eisenhower, *Crusade in Europe*, p. 238.

[78] *EP*, III: No. 1689, (To Senior U.S. Commanders), May 14, 1944; Eisenhower, *Crusade in Europe*, p. 238; Pogue, *Supreme Command*, p. 158.

[79] Cave Brown, *Bodyguard*, p. 617.

[80] Eisenhower, *Crusade in Europe*, pp. 246-247; Ambrose, *Supreme Commander*, pp. 406-407; Pogue, *Supreme Command*, pp. 118, 120-121; Bradley, *Soldier's Story*, pp. 232-236; Ellis, *Normandy*, pp. 138-139; Smith, *Six Decisions*,pp. 18-19, 35-36.

[81] Harrison, *Cross-Channel*, p. 254; Tedder, *With Prejudice*, p. 535; Goldberg, "Air Campaign," p. 72; Gordon Wright, *The Ordeal of Total War, 1939-1945* (New York, 1968), p. 198; Ellis, *Normandy*, pp. 96-97, 101, 108, 111; Cave Brown, *Bodyguard*, pp. 524-527.

[82] Speer, *Third Reich*, p. 445.

[83] *Ibid.*, p. 446.

[84] *Ibid.*, pp. 445-446; Tedder, *With Prejudice*, p. 540; Craven and Cate, *Argument to V-E Day*, pp. 176-177.

[85] Tedder, *With Prejudice*, p. 537; Ellis, *Normandy*, p. 102.

[86] Craven and Cate, *Argument to V-E Day*, pp. 177-179; Speer, *Third Reich*, pp. 447-448.

[87] Ellis, *Normandy*, pp. 110-112.

[88] Harrison, *Cross-Channel*, pp. 262-263; Butcher, *Three Years*, p. 544; Ambrose, *Supreme Commander*, pp. 394-395.

[89] Buttlar, "Commentary," p. 66; Ellis, *Normandy*,p. 128; Smith, *Six Decisions*, pp. 44-45; Cave Brown, *Bodyguard*, pp. 616-617 (Material which appears on the chart is taken from p. 617).

[90] Quoted in Ellis, *Normandy*, p. 129.

[91] Harrison, *Cross-Channel*, p. 259; Ellis, *Normandy*, p. 129; MacDonald, *Mighty Endeavor*, p. 262.

Taking the Dare: The D-Day Assault 12

I double dare you to come over here.
I double dare you to venture too near.
Take off your high hat and quit that bragging.
Cut out that claptrap and keep your hair on.
Can't you take a dare on?

I double dare you to venture a raid.
I double dare you to try and invade.
And if your loud propaganda means half of what it says,
I double dare you to come over here.
*I double dare you.**

Early on June 4, 1944, as much of the OVERLORD assault force was en route to France, General Dwight D. Eisenhower postponed the long-awaited invasion and sent out an order which directed the ships to turn back. What had happened? Had the Germans learned of the attack? Had the massive invasion fleet been discovered? Was this just another dress rehearsal? These and many more questions filled the minds of numbers of Allied troops whose landing on the Normandy beaches had been delayed.

The invasion force had not encountered any enemy opposition and there did not seem to be anything awry with the meticulously prepared plans. To those men like Radioman Third Class Bernie Glisson of the destroyer *U.S.S. Corry*, who tuned to Radio Paris and heard the first record played by the sexy propagandist, Axis Sally, it must have seemed that the fleet had been discovered. Sally played the popular song, "I Double Dare You," but this morning her record featured new and ominous lyrics.[1]

In actuality, Eisenhower's decision was in no way influenced by German actions. The delay was due to events over which people have no control and for which the Supreme Commander had tried to prepare himself. The weather, quite simply, was so foul that "Ike" had decided to delay the assault one day, hoping to improve the Allied chance of success. There was nothing wrong with the OVERLORD plan; it would not be changed.

**"I Double Dare You," copyright 1937 by Shapiro, Bernstein & Co., Inc., New York, New York. Copyright renewed. Used by permission.*

The Last, Impatient Days of Waiting

Allied units and commanders were busy in the days just prior to the sailing of the invasion fleet, checking and rechecking plans and equipment. There could be no room for avoidable error. The entire Allied master plan depended upon OVERLORD being successful. Only if a beachhead could be seized and held against the almost certain German counterattack, could the necessary lodgment area be expanded to the Seine and used as a powerful base from which to launch forces to liberate France and invade Germany. *(See Map 53, in Atlas.)*

The mission which the Combined Chiefs of Staff had given Eisenhower directed him to destroy the German armed forces. He shaped his strategy to that end. In his mind, terrain features and cities were only important insofar as they affected the outcome of his attempt to defeat Hitler's armies. After the build-up was completed, Eisenhower's assault across the Seine would proceed along two distinct axes. *(See Map, page 284.)* The assault to the north—the main attack—would be made by Montgomery's 21st Army Group; this primary effort probably would be reinforced by an American corps or perhaps

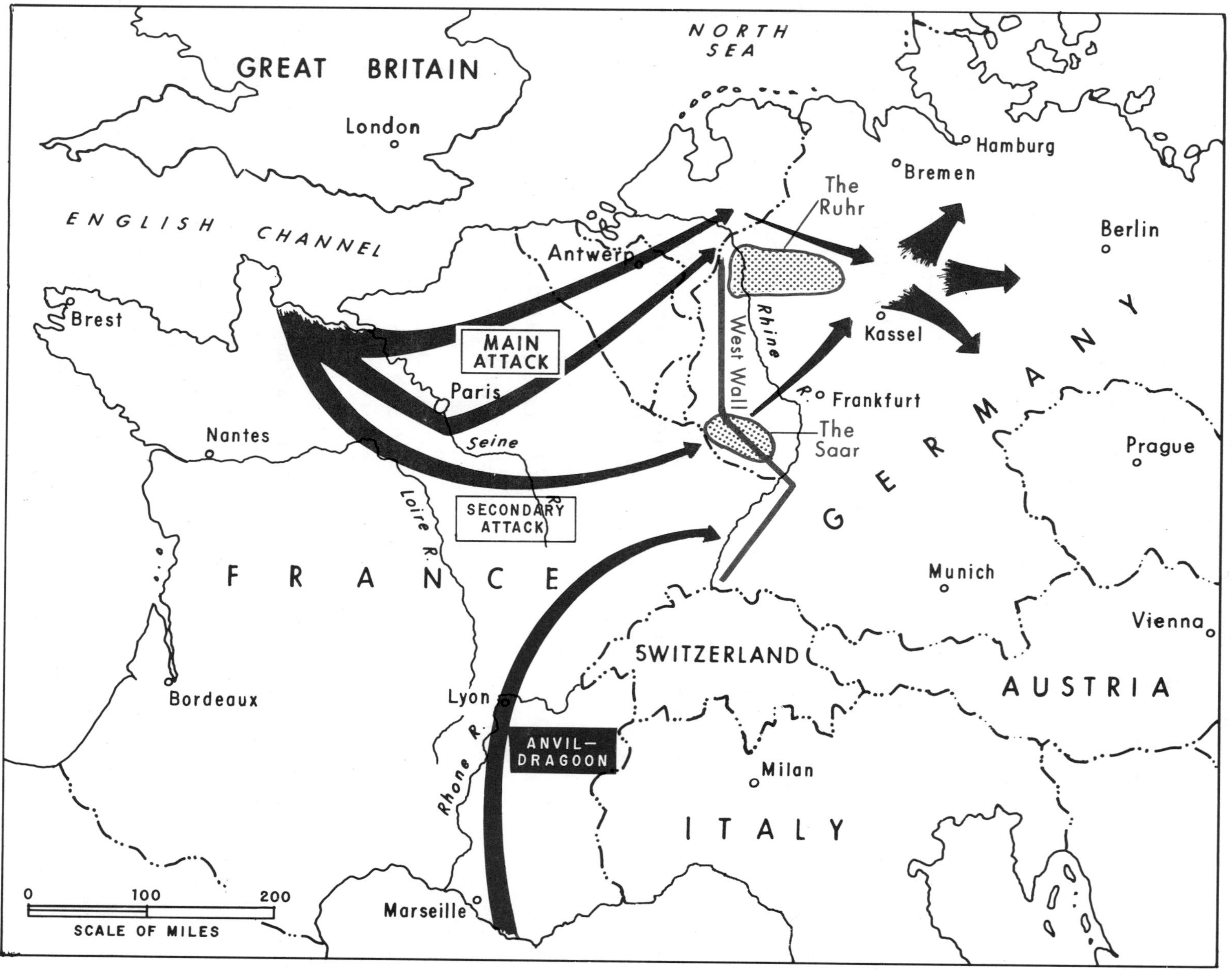

Allied General Plan

an army. Montgomery was to take the vital port of Antwerp as well as other Channel ports and, moving towards the Rhine, head for the north of the Ruhr industrial area, the site of much of the German munitions industry. Simultaneously, an American army group would assist Montgomery in the north while attacking toward the Saar farther to the south. This southern assault would link up with an invasion force which was to have landed in southern France. Following the juncture, many German troops in France would be cut off from their homeland, and France could be cleared rapidly. As a result of this operation, the Americans would open a supplemental line of communication through southern France to support their armies. Then the combined force, oriented to the east, could tackle the German defense of the West Wall and the Rhine River. The main attack across the Rhine would be a double envelopment of the Ruhr. When the pincers closed in the Kassel area, Germany would have lost any hope of winning. Virtually all that would remain would be a clearing operation. As the campaign ultimately developed, the Allies were able to proceed in a manner which was remarkably close to this general plan.[2]

One step had to be taken at a time, however, and the first step was the seizure of a beachhead. Two task forces would transport the Allied invasion force to France. *(See Map 54, in Atlas.)* The American First Army was to land on the west, with the VII Corps on Utah Beach and the V Corps on Omaha Beach. Between the two beaches lay the Vire River and the Carentan Estuary. Two U.S. airborne divisions, the 82nd and the 101st, were to be dropped behind Utah Beach to secure causeways leading inland from the beach. Once ashore, the VII Corps was to clear the Cotentin peninsula, including the port of Cherbourg, while the V Corps, after establishing a beachhead between the Vire River and Port en Bessin, was to drive inland toward Caumont and St. Lô. Farther to the east, on beaches Gold, Juno, and Sword, the British Second Army was to land with assistance from the British 6th Airborne Division; the Second Army was to take a beachhead stretching from Port en Bessin to Bayeux and Caen, then following the Orne River back to the Channel. An area east of the Orne, as well as some critical bridges, would be taken by the airborne troops.[3]

For many days prior to the actual sailing of the invasion force, men and supplies had been moving into areas near the ports of embarkation. Port space was at a premium, so some supply ships were never unloaded; they were, instead, kept as floating warehouses to be sent to France when needed. Almost 5,000 ships of all types had been gathered to transport and support the invasion force. Over 3.5 million men and more than 13,000 aircraft were stationed in England. Much materiel had been amassed, including almost 1,000 locomotives and about 20,000 cars; some said, with tongue in cheek, that if it were not for the barrage balloons, the British Isles would sink into the sea.[4]

Eisenhower's earlier designation of June 5 as D-Day had initiated a chain of events that was designed to insure the proper positioning of the entire invasion force for the assault. Following this schedule, the blockships, which were to be sunk off the Normandy coast to form artificial breakwaters, set sail on May 30 from ports in Scotland, where they had been readied to make their final journey. One of these multi-ship breakwaters—or Gooseberries, as they were called—was planned for each of the five invasion beaches. Plans specified that by the fifth day of the attack, all five would be set up. Next, in two of the areas, Omaha and Gold, the Gooseberries would be enlarged into Mulberry Harbors. *(See inset, Map 58, in Atlas.)*

These artificial harbors were a tribute to engineering ingenuity. Cylindrical floats (bombardons), linked together and anchored in deep water, would serve as a breakwater. Concrete caissons (phoenixes), some as high as six-story buildings, would be towed across the Channel and sunk in place to extend the Gooseberry breakwater. In the sheltered water, room was to be provided for the anchoring of ocean-going as well as coastal ships. Landing craft would carry the cargoes from the large ships, while the smaller vessels could discharge directly onto floating piers. The piers were tied by posts to the Channel floor, but had roadbeds that raised and lowered with the tide.[5]

These Mulberry Harbors were critically important to a sustained Allied war effort. As late as the end of May, Eisenhower felt that the Germans did not know that artificial ports would be used. The Supreme Commander had excellent intelligence from ULTRA intercepts as well as from other sources, while on the other side of the Channel the German leaders found themselves virtually blind. The last good photographs of any British ports had come in on May 24. Little was known about Allied

Mulberry at Omaha Beach

WACs at Work in the Communications Section of the Operations Room at an Army Air Force Station

intentions. Where and when the next invasion would come was still unknown. Allied deceptive efforts being conducted in Turkey, the Balkans, against southern France, on the Biscay Coast, in Scandinavia, and against the Pas de Calais were designed to maintain the uncertainty.[6]

The number of troops that would be able to take part in the assault and its follow-up had increased slightly as a result of the replacement of soldiers by members of the Women's Army Corps (WAC). Women served in both Army and Army Air Force units, and by D-Day there were 3,687 in Great Britain. Their jobs ranged from photo interpretation to secretarial work. So much in demand were expert typists and stenographers that the War Department notified the requesting officers in England that to fill European needs, male typists would have to replace women in the U.S. so that the women could be sent to England. It was thought that such a move would be embarrassing to all concerned. The ETO reply was that such embarrassment was no problem, and that the women should be sent. Although the general standard of performance of the WAC's was high, some soldiers—those who were relieved from clerical jobs and sent to perform combat tasks—were often less than happy to see the women arrive. Once the invasion began, the women were eager to accompany their units, which were generally higher headquarters, when they moved to France.[7]

Many others were itching to get closer to France. Among them was Prime Minister Churchill, who asked Admiral Ramsay to arrange for him to view the assault from one of the bombardment ships. Ramsay followed orders but also asked Eisenhower to try to dissaude the Prime Minister. Unsuccessful in this attempt, Eisenhower, as Supreme Commander, ordered Churchill to stay home. The Prime Minister still balked, claiming that he had the authority and responsibility to decide who was to sail as a member of the complement of a British ship. The King found out about Churchill's plan, initially decided that he too should go, and finally demurred. Only then did Sir Winston reluctantly back down. As the King said, this was no time to risk changing either Sovereign or Prime Minister.[8]

Another high-ranking individual who was eager to get into the fray was the man who would lead the Third Army once it was committed, Lieutenant General George S. Patton, Jr. Shortly before the invasion, Patton visited Bradley at the First Army headquarters, in Bristol. He arrived in a black Packard automobile equipped with silver flagstaffs and Greyhound bus horns. As First Army staff members knew that he liked fancy escorts, he was met by a group of military police on motorcycles. When told by Bradley's aide of the escort detail, a military policeman who was aware of Patton's earlier slapping difficulty in Sicily asked, "Should we have them wear boxing gloves?"[9]

Bradley was ready to go. At dinner on June 2 he appeared to be in extremely good humor, and commented that with all the planning complete, it was time "to climb aboard a ship and sail on our way to France." Early the next day, he did just that, wearing a pistol and steel helmet for the first time since he had worn them in Sicily. On the evening of the second, he briefed correspondents on what the First Army was about to do. There were, he said, three critical periods in the invasion: first, getting on shore; second, defeating the major counterattack that would probably come about D + 6; and third, breaking out of the initial lodgment area. Most difficult would probably be the defeat of the counterattack, which would be launched with all the reserves the enemy could muster.[10] Bradley well knew, however, that landing on a hostile shore was seldom easy; even as he spoke to the correspondents, his Supreme Commander was pondering the question of postponement.

The Loneliness and Pressure of Command

Considered by many to be a lucky commander due to his experiences in the Mediterranean, where the seas calmed in time for the invasion of North Africa and the storm which raged while the invasion force was en route to Sicily decreased in intensity before the troops landed, Eisenhower had tried to do all that he could to enhance his chances of making the proper decision. He intended to use the best available information as a basis for his choice. Weather briefings, presented weekly in early April, were increased to twice a week, and by June 1 were being presented three times each day. As an athlete tried to get in shape for a contest by training, Eisenhower had a weekly practice session regarding the decision. Each Monday he selected a test D-Day some 48 to 72 hours in the future. He then compared the actual weather to that which had been predicted. Through this process he was able to develop in his own mind the weight which he would accord to the weather forecasts that he received before the actual decision had to be made. These practice predictions had been quite good, but the ones that would affect the lives of thousands were yet to come.[11]

On May 29, Group Captain James M. Stagg, RAF, Eisenhower's chief weather man had predicted fairly good weather for the first week in June, and Eisenhower had released a message which indicated that D-Day would be the fifth. As factors affecting all services would have to be considered during the decision-making process, the Supreme Commander began daily meetings with his three top leaders on June 1. Sea conditions, for example, were important not only to Ramsay, who had to transport the invasion force and fire in its support, but to Montgomery as well. If the ground troops were violently seasick when they hit the beaches, their combat effectiveness would be impaired. Adequate visibility was important to all services, while a wind which blew inland off the Channel would tend to propel dust and smoke into the faces of the enemy.

With each passing day the strain on Eisenhower increased. He even told his doctor of a loud ringing in the ear, a typical physical sign of stress. Although Eisenhower tried to relax by playing bridge, much of his time was spent walking and thinking. On June 2, the weather forecast for D-Day did not look as favorable as it had previously; but Eisenhower, after meeting with his commanders, decided to allow the sailing of some of the most distantly-based bombardment ships. On the same day, two midget submarines which were to mark the British Juno and Sword Beaches, set out to sea. Once they found their proper locations, they were to submerge and wait on the bottom during daylight hours. Early on D-Day they would surface and use lights to guide the invasion force.[12]

Seas were rising and winds were blowing stronger when more bombardment ships sailed early June 3, but Eisenhower seemed determined to get the invasion under way, cabling Marshall that unless the forecasts turned much more pessimistic he would adhere to his schedule. He planned to announce his final decision at a meeting that night at 9:30 p.m. Fortunately for historians, that very morning the Supreme Commander prepared a memorandum in which he set forth his thoughts on several matters. Concerning weather, Eisenhower wrote:

> The weather in this country is practically unpredictable. For some days our experts have been meeting almost hourly and I have been holding Commander-in-Chief meetings once or twice a day to consider the reports and tentative predictions. While at this moment, the morning of June 3, it appears that the weather will not be so bad as to preclude landings and will possibly even permit reasonably effective gunfire support from the Navy, the picture from the air viewpoint is not so good.
>
> Probably no one that does not have to bear the specific and direct responsibility of making the final decision as to what to do, can understand the intensity of these burdens. The Supreme Commander, much more than any of his subordinates, is kept informed of the political issues involved, particularly the anticipated effect of delay upon the Russians. He likewise is in close touch with all the advice from his military subordinates and must face the issue even when technical advice as to weather is not unanimous from the several experts. Success or failure might easily hinge upon the effectiveness, for example, of airborne operations. If the weather is suitable for everything else, but unsuitable for airborne operations, the question becomes whether to risk the airborne movement anyway or to defer the whole affair in the hope of getting weather that is a bit better.
>
> My tentative thought is that the desirability for getting started on the next favorable tide is so great and the uncertainty of the weather is such that we could never anticipate really perfect weather coincident with proper tidal conditions, that we must go unless there is a real and very serious deterioration in the weather.[13]

As the hours before the moment of choice dragged by, units completed loading troops. Members of the assault force had trained hard for this operation and were impatient to begin their mission. Those left behind in England continued their normal work and training. One such was an apprentice teletype operator in the Associated Press Bureau who was practicing on her machine. Her practice message was: "URGENT PRESS ASSOCIATED NYK FLASH EISENHOWER'S HQ ANNOUNCED ALLIED LANDINGS IN FRANCE." Somehow her perforated tape was transmitted before the regular evening story from Russia. Although it was corrected thirty seconds later, the story caused quite a stir in the United States. It caused another type of commotion in the German Fifteenth Army headquarters located in France, where the message had been picked up by a German radio interception team.[14]

Since there were no reports of action from the front, the Fifteenth Army intelligence officer, Lieutenant Colonel Helmuth Meyer, did not alert the staff. Meyer also noted that the second half of a signal designed to alert the French Resistance Movement had not been sent. He had learned of this signal from the head of German intelligence back in January, when he received his orders to monitor all the many transmissions which would be sent to the underground. The first part was intercepted on the night of June 1 following the evening BBC news; if German intelligence was right, the second part would mean that the invasion would come within 48 hours. German intelligence had failed many times in the past, but it was correct regarding the meaning of the signal. Because previous intercepts of the first part of the message had resulted in a German reaction and no attack, however, Rundstedt had ordered that information from such messages would trigger an alert only if he personally gave approval. Although the messages were picked up on the nights of June 2 and 3, Rundstedt took no action because he felt that the adverse weather precluded the launching of an assault. Moreover, because the Allies had detected and destroyed German weather stations in the Arctic and on board ships sailing in the Atlantic, Rundstedt was deprived of the type of long-range weather information which was available to Eisenhower. As the hours passed, Meyer and his men waited with equipment so sophisticated that it could pick up the transmissions of jeep radios from England. On the other side of the Channel, the man whose decision would cause the second part of the message to be sent met with his senior commanders and his weather expert.[15]

Stagg told the Supreme Commander and his subordinates that the predicted weather would be worse than that described at earlier meetings. In addition, he stated that due to the unsettled nature of the weather he could reliably forecast only 24 hours in advance. Eisenhower decided to permit ships to sail according to the June 5 D-Day plan, but chose to defer his final decision for seven hours. The group was to meet again early on Sunday the fourth.[16]

The night sky was almost clear and the air close to calm when the leaders next met. They were told that due to unfavorable weather the air forces would not be able to support the attack. Sea conditions, however, would be a little better than had previously been thought. Still, high winds and waves would interfere with ship-to-shore movement and with the delivery of accurate naval gunfire. Eisenhower asked for opinions. Ramsay adopted a neutral attitude. He agreed that the accuracy of naval gunfire would suffer, but he thought that the landing force could be put ashore. Montgomery wanted to go ahead and attack without air support. Both Tedder and Leigh-Mallory favored postponement. Eisenhower then stated that as he did not have a large superiority over the enemy in ground forces, he felt that the invasion should not be launched without air support. He asked if anyone disagreed with his decision. When no one did, he ordered a 24-hour delay. D-Day would now be June 6. Prearranged messages were immediately dispatched to the ships at sea.[17]

During the day, while all waited for the next decision, Eisenhower sent his chief of staff to Portsmouth to see the troops who had returned to port. Smith later recalled: "It was heartbreaking to watch their faces. The eagerness had gone out of them, now that the edge of their expectation was dulled. I have never seen more unhappy soldiers."[18] But there was some news that raised the spirits of all who supported the Allied cause; on June 4, the day of delay, the U.S. Fifth Army entered Rome.

As if Eisenhower did not have enough on his mind, he also had to contend with the displeasure of General De Gaulle, the leader of the Free French, who arrived in England from Algiers on June 4.* DeGaulle had played a large part in the strengthening and unifying of the French resistance effort, whose groups the Allies had long been supplying and directing on sabotage missions. SHAEF intended to use the resistance units as part of the invasion effort, primarily to disrupt the movement of German reinforcements. DeGaulle, not politically recognized by the Allies as the French chief in exile and just now being apprised of OVERLORD plans, was not pleased with what he found in England.[19]

DeGaulle was incensed to learn that Allied troops would be issued francs which had not been printed by the French Committee of National Liberation, for he felt that as President of the Provisional Government he was the only one who could authorize the printing of money. A stormy conference with Churchill settled nothing. The Prime Minister took him to Portsmouth to see Eisenhower for a briefing on OVERLORD. There the Supreme Commander and DeGaulle stepped outside for a walk. Eisenhower showed his visitor a copy of a speech he had recorded; the recording would be broadcast to the French people on D-Day. DeGaulle strongly objected to much of what was contained in the speech. Neither he nor his government were mentioned, and while DeGaulle had reached no agreement concerning the use of French forces in OVERLORD, Eisenhower talked of having French troops under his command. It appeared to DeGaulle that the Allies were preparing to occupy—not liberate—France. He flatly refused to use a speech which had been prepared for him by the SHAEF Psychological Warfare Division. As it turned out, he finally agreed to address his countrymen on D-Day in his own words, stressing that, "The orders given by the French government and by the leaders which it had recognized must be followed precisely." While not using the exact words SHAEF preferred, the French leader had at least agreed to talk to his people. Allied forces would receive the assistance of the French Resistance Movement, and Allied leaders, for a time, put DeGaulle's complaints aside and concerned themselves with other problems.[20]

When Eisenhower and his commanders met again the evening of June 4, the wind was blowing hard and rain pounded on

*The complexity of the political relationship between French forces in exile and the Allies is beyond the scope of this text. Chapter 7 briefly alludes to this matter as regards 1942 to 1943. The issue, involving Eisenhower as it frequently did, serves to illustrate how, at the highest levels, political and military considerations are not mutually exclusive.

the windows of their meeting room. At about 9:30 P.M., Stagg came in with the latest weather forecast and predicted better weather for D-Day. Rain would stop in two to three hours, and the winds, then blowing at 25 to 31 knots, would lessen. These changes would herald a period of about three days of better weather. On D-Day, June 6, the clouds might be high enough so that at H-Hour naval guns could fire under observed conditions. As the day wore on, more clouds would gather and the weather would worsen. This cloudy condition was of great concern to airmen Tedder and Leigh-Mallory, but when Tedder remarked that medium and heavy bombers might not be able to get through the clouds, Eisenhower said that he had many fighter-bombers which would do the job. Ramsay spoke up and said that the decision could not be postponed for another weather report, for to be in position for the June 6 attack, sailing orders for the U.S. task force had to be issued within 30 minutes. Should this task force sail and a recall order be given later, the ships could not be readied in time to land the invasion force on June 7. A recall order, then, would have the effect of postponing the invasion to June 19, for due to light and tidal conditions, June 8 was not an acceptable alternative date.[21]

Such a recall would mean that the troops would have to be brought back, disembarked, and returned to their assembly areas, where they would join units of the follow-up force which had already moved into the camps. Conditions would be crowded and morale would surely suffer. Eisenhower felt that the secrecy of the invasion would be sacrificed because astute observers, both in England and the U.S., would be able to deduce that an invasion attempt had misfired. Such a delay would also result in sacrifice of a period of good campaigning weather, and this was important because normal stormy weather would preclude resupply over the beaches after September 1. Moreover, by the time an attack could be launched in mid-June, the enemy would have had extra time to stiffen its defenses on the coast and, if the Germans learned of the aborted attempt, to shift resources from other areas. Thanks to ULTRA, the Allies knew that 50 launching sites were ready for Hitler's "secret" weapons. If a number of these weapons were launched against the packed assembly areas of the harbors filled with the invasion fleet, all plans could be disrupted. There was also always the possibility that weather for the new date might be even worse than that now predicted for June 6. Finally, even if the invasion was launched in mid-June, the vital airborne drops would have to be made without the benefit of moonlight. For all these reasons, a decision to postpone was fraught with danger.[22]

Gordon A. Harrison, author of the U.S. official history, who based his account on the signed notes of a senior British officer, recorded what happened at the evening meeting. After Eisenhower had heard from Tedder, Leigh-Mallory, and Ramsay, he asked for Montgomery's opinion:

> "Do you see any reason for not going Tuesday?"
>
> "I would say—Go!" Montgomery replied.
>
> "The question," Eisenhower pointed out, "[is] just how long can you hang this operation on the end of a limb and let it hang there."
>
> The discussion continued a few more minutes.
>
> At 9:45 P.M., Eisenhower announced his decision. "I'm quite positive we must give the order . . . I don't like it, but there it is . . . I don't see how we can possibly do anything else."[23]

Eisenhower's decision meant that H-Hour for U.S. troops would be at 6:30 A.M. on June 6, while the British and Canadians, faced with different tidal conditions, would land about an hour later. As the invasion could still be cancelled, a final meeting was scheduled for 4:00 A.M., June 5. Within a few seconds of hearing Eisenhower's decision, the commanders started back to their command posts. When they stepped outside, they were greeted by heavy rain and high winds, far from prime invasion weather. Eisenhower was left alone in the room that would long be famous as the site of his momentous decision. Whereas but a short time previously he was the center of attention, now he was left alone with his thoughts—the OVERLORD plan had taken over.[24]

Smith later recalled that he drove to the 4:00 A.M. meeting through a chilly and windy night. A fire warmed the meeting room and hot coffee was available. Had Eisenhower not ordered the 24-hour postponement, H-Hour would have been but two hours away. When Stagg came in he reported that bad weather was hitting the coast of France. Reassuringly, this confirmed his earlier prediction. Next he reaffirmed his more optimistic prediction of the previous day. Better weather would arrive within a few hours, but rough seas might once again prevail on the Channel as early as June 7. This meant that it was conceivable that the Allies could land a couple of waves, and then have the remainder of the force cut off by high waves while the initial group was defeated in detail. Eisenhower listened to remarks made by both the weather experts and his commanders. Then, after thinking for a time, he confirmed the decision he had made a few hours previously by declaring, "O.K., let's go."[25]

The German Situation in France On the Eve of Invasion

As H-Hour drew nearer, Allied intelligence experts watched for any sign that the Germans had learned of the impending invasion. The news from ULTRA, passed to Tedder early the afternoon of June 5, was comforting—the Allies had intercepted no evidence of a German alert.

Rundstedt's order of battle for the coming campaign reflected 58 divisions. *(See Maps 53 and 54, in Atlas.)* Some of his infantry divisions were field types which were trained in mobile warfare, but others were static and were not schooled to operate in a fluid situation. A number of divisions were exhausted from fighting on the Russian Front, and several were just forming or were in the early stages of their training period. Moreover, many of Rundstedt's troops were natives of countries other than Germany. Somehow, the fact that the well-trained 352nd Infantry Division, a field division, had been moved up to defend the area encompassing Omaha and Gold Beaches had not been picked up by intelligence sources in time to be disseminated to the commanders who were to assault these beaches. *(See Map 54, in Atlas.)* Thus, the U.S. 1st Infantry Division was destined to attack not the single regiment of a static division spread out over a wide front, as had been anticipated, but elements of the 352nd.[26]

General der Artillerie Erich Marcks, commander of the German LXXXIV Corps, a part of the Seventh Army, led the troops stationed in Normandy and part of Brittany. On the coast, to the east of the 352nd, was the 716th Infantry Division, a static unit. To the west of the 352nd, on the Cotentin Peninsula, was the 709th infantry Division, which guarded the eastern coast of the peninsula. The 709th was an experienced static unit, but due to rapid rotation of personnel its combat effectiveness was declining. Also on the Cotentin Peninsula was the 91st Airlanding Division with an attached parachute regiment. It was the arrival of this division in the central part of the peninsula that had caused Bradley to move the drop zones of the U.S. 82nd Airborne Division. The mission of the 91st was to defend against airborne landings. Rounding out the Cotentin defense forces was the 243rd Infantry Division, which was being converted from a static to a field infantry unit. Most of the 243rd was located to the west or southwest of Cherbourg. Positioned in the corps area, but under army group control, was the 21st Panzer Division, composed of four infantry battalions and two tank battalions plus artillery and the normal division troops. Although the divisional headquarters was located southeast of Caen, some units had been placed on both sides of the Orne River between Caen and the Channel. Should the entire division be required, it would take some time to assemble all units. Other armored divisions, the 12th SS Panzer and the Panzer Lehr, were located at a greater distance from the invasion front and formed a part of the OKW reserve. In the air, the Germans were very weak. As of June 4, only 183 German day-fighters were stationed in France with about 160 of them being serviceable. Of this latter number 124 were shifted away from the coast on June 5 because they were coming under such severe Allied air attack. Supplies for these displaced planes were expected to arrive at the new bases on June 6 or 7. Finally, little German naval strength was available to contest the Allied movement across the Channel.[27]

Unknowingly, the Allies were to gain another advantage in that Rommel would be absent when the landings occurred. The German general felt that if the invasion were launched in June it would come during one of the two periods when moonlight, sunrise, and tidal conditions were favorable. These were June 5 to 7 and 12 to 14. Because the weather was bad on June 4 and the forecast was for a continuation of the stormy conditions for the next few days, Rommel decided to leave for Germany early on the fifth. He wanted to persuade Hitler to shift more *panzer* divisions to army group control so that they might be rapidly employed in a counterattack. While in Germany, Rommel planned to be with his wife on her birthday—June 6.[28]

Although Rommel was prepared to do his utmost to repel any invasion along his front, as early as February 1944 he had been contacted by the *Schwartze Kapelle* and had agreed to support that movement which was committed to overthrowing Hitler. Rommel hoped that the war with the western Allies could be concluded before an invasion was launched. In May, he had authorized the holding of a meeting of conspirators which took place in France on the fifteenth. There, all agreed that if an armistice could be arranged, the Nazi regime would be overturned and German troops would withdraw from all conquered territory in the West. As the *Schwartze Kapelle* had been deceived by FORTITUDE into thinking that the invasion was not near, the *coup d'état* was set for the middle of June.[29]

The anticipated stretch of bad weather which led Rommel to plan his trip at the worst possible time had other harmful effects on the German state of readiness. Because the chief meteorologist of the *Luftwaffe*, stationed in Paris, predicted weather so bad that Allied planes could not even fly, stand down orders were sent out to antiaircraft units. At the same time, because his men were tired and had been under stress, Generaloberst Friedrich Dollman, the commanding general of Seventh Army, lowered the alert status of all of his troops, including those guarding the shores of Normandy and Brittany. The Allies also would benefit from the large map exercise the Germans had scheduled to begin early on June 6 in Rennes. The scenario specified an Allied airborne attack to be followed by a seaborne invasion; General Marcks was to play the role of the Allied commander. By this fortunate coincidence, the Allies would be assured that at the time of the landing the commanders of divisions in Normany either would have departed for Rennes or would be preparing to do so. The chief of staff of one of these divisions, moreover, would be out hunting with his mistress at an unknown location. Finally, Rommel's operations officer and the OB West intelligence officer had also chosen this date to be in Germany, and the naval commander in the West would be en route to Bordeaux when Eisenhower's troops landed.[30]

Across the Channel the Allied Supreme Commander was spending the last few hours before the landings very differently. Responsible for the success or failure of the entire op-

Eisenhower Talks With Paratroopers

eration, Eisenhower sat down and penned a message which would be transmitted if he found it necessary to withdraw the invasion force. When he had finished, the Supreme Commander placed the note, mistakenly dated July rather than June, in his wallet. It read:

> Our landings in the Cherbourg-Havre area have failed to gain a satisfactory foothold and I have withdrawn the troops. My decision to attack at this time and place was based upon the best information available. The troops, the air and the navy did all that bravery and devotion to duty could do. If any blame or fault attaches to the attempt it is mine alone—July 5.[31]

As the hours passed during the day, no signs of breakdown in OVERLORD plans surfaced. At 6:00 P.M., the fidgety Supreme Commander left to visit the 101st Airborne Division. Many of the paratroopers had blackened their faces with charcoal and shaved their heads in the Iroquois style, leaving but a narrow band of hair which ran from front to back. Eisenhower walked among the troops and spoke to many of them. One soldier from Texas even offered him a postwar job. The commander of the division, Major General Maxwell D. Taylor, was going to jump with his men, and Eisenhower bid him farewell. Taylor, who had torn a ligament in his knee during an afternoon squash game, walked carefully away; he did not want his injury to show for fear of being pulled off the mission by the Supreme Commander. It was an emotional moment for Eisenhower. Over the strong objection of his air expert he had ordered the airborne drops on the Cotentin Peninsula. Perhaps he was wrong; in that case these men with whom he had been bantering but a few moments before were being sent to almost certain death. Red Mueller of NBC looked at Eisenhower after the takeoff as the formation of planes flew across the field and headed for France. Tears filled the Supreme Commander's eyes.[32]

Eisenhower and his party arrived back at camp about 1:15 A.M., June 6. For a time they sat in the office trailer in silence, then some went to bed. The Supreme Commander, after looking at the maps of the Cotentin again and reading a bit in a western novel, finally did the same. There was nothing more that he could do.

Business as Usual

Just before 9:00 P.M., June 5, over a dozen Allied minesweepers worked their way to within sight of the French coast. The Germans did not detect them even though they were so close that their crews could observe individual houses. When they had accomplished their sweeping mission, the ships headed back out into the Channel. One of their number, the *U.S.S. Osprey*, hit a mine and sank. Members of the crew of the *Osprey* were the first American OVERLORD casualties. No one reported the minesweeper activity to higher German headquarters.[33]

A flurry of excitement occurred around 10:15 P.M.[34] when

Paratrooper Enters Transport Plane

Lieutenant Colonel Meyer's men intercepted the second part of the pre-invasion message to the French Resistance Movement. This message meant to Meyer that the invasion would come in the 48-hour period which began one minute after midnight on June 5. Meyer rushed into the dining room where the Fifteenth Army commander and chief of staff were playing bridge. "General!" he said, "The message, the second part—it's here." After a pause to consider the situation, the army commander, Generaloberst Hans von Salmuth, ordered that the entire army be placed on alert. Meyer left and the general turned back to his cards, saying, "I'm too old a bunny to get too excited about this."[35]

While Meyer was interrupting the bridge game of the commander of the Fifteenth Army, the G3 of OB West was relaxing in the officers' mess. OB West listeners had also intercepted the critical message and one of the intelligence officers then informed the G3. The latter informed Rundstedt and his chief of staff, and passed the information to both higher and subordinate headquarters as well as to the *Luftwaffe*, Navy, and the military commanders of Brussels and Paris. If the Germans still did not know where the blow would be struck, they would, it appeared, at least not be caught completely off guard. Of course, if this were but another false alarm—and most who heard of the message thought just that because of the bad weather—all the excitement would be for nothing. The air duty officer knew that during the morning of June 5 a substantial amount of radio tuning had been detected in England, a sure indicator that large numbers of planes would be aloft during the night. He also noted the interception of a number of American weather intelligence broadcasts made at night—another sign of a night attack. This officer had read a German weather forecast, based on a statistical study of weather for the last 50 years, which noted that a short period of good weather might arrive on June 6. He weighed all available information and ordered a few night-fighters to take off on patrol. Fortunately for the Allies, the area he directed to be searched was about 100 miles east of the actual invasion fleet. Meanwhile, for some unknown reason, Seventh Army, holding the stretch of coast which was the target of the invasion, was not alerted. The map exercise at Rennes was not cancelled, and at the corps headquarters in St. Lô, members of the staff prepared for a 1:00 A.M. party which would honor the birthday of General Marcks. Such an hour was deemed to be necessary as the general had to depart early for Rennes.[36]

Just as several senior staff officers were about to enter the general's room, they heard the sound of antiaircraft fire. Running outside, they saw an Allied bomber plunging in flames toward the ground. This excitement over, they saluted the general on his birthday by drinking to his health. As they raised their glasses, Allied paratroopers were landing in France. D-Day had finally arrived.[37]

The Airborne Landings

Deception was an important part of the overall Allied plan regarding the use of airborne troops in the invasion, essentially because the extensive use of such forces could herald a subsequent major landing. Accordingly, the Allies simulated attacks up to brigade strength in size, using dummy paratroopers and firecrackers. One such "attack," designed to convince the Germans that the Pas de Calais was the target of an invasion, was made near Le Havre, about 20 miles inland. It was coupled with air and sea feints in the same vicinity and simulation of Allied troop movements immediately across the Channel in England. Meanwhile, the three airborne divisions were mounting the "real" assault behind the beachhead areas.[38]

The American airborne divisions were transported to the Normandy drop zones by a route which incorporated several turns, and thus provided an opportunity for pilot error. *(See Map 54, in Atlas.)* Pathfinders, landing shortly after midnight, preceded the main body and had only one hour to mark drop zones. Some did not make it because of dispersion in drops due to navigational error intensified by cloud cover and antiaircraft fire. The main body had the same problem, some loads dropping as far as 35 miles off target. *(See Map 56, in Atlas.)* One trooper, caught by his parachute on a church steeple in St. Mère-Eglise, feigned death for over two hours before the Germans took him prisoner. Others dropped in flooded areas and drowned, and some landed on German positions. But by 3:30 A.M., when the last trooper was down, units, or parts of them, were organizing as best they could and setting out toward objectives. The mission of the 101st Airborne Division was to seize the area behind Utah Beach, including causeways over flooded areas in order to facilitate the 4th Infantry Division advance; to capture a dominant six-gun battery at Varreville; and to defend the VII Corps southern boundary, prepared to attack to the south on order. *(See Map 56, in Atlas.)* The 82nd Airborne Division was to take St. Mère Eglise, establish and hold the northern and western edges of the airhead, and seize bridgeheads over the Merderet River to facilitate an attack to the west to cut the peninsula.[39]

Carrying out the details of their missions was not an easy task for the airborne units, who recognized that glider-borne reinforcements in need of landing zones were due at 4:00 A.M., to be followed a little over two hours later by the seaborne landing. To complicate matters, the troopers had to contend with hedgerows—earthen dikes almost four feet high and covered with hedges and trees; enclosing areas smaller than football fields, they made excellent defensive positions. Many little battles at close range took place, leading to a generally confused situation and little information being passed to higher headquarters.[40]

British Glider Landing Site Near Bridge Over Caen Canal

To the east, near the Orne River, members of the British Sixth Airborne Division began landing shortly after midnight. The division's mission was to seize two critical bridges over the Orne River and parallel Caen Canal, destroy other bridges, and hold the left flank of the beachhead. *(See Map 55, in Atlas.)* Encountering the same problems as their American counterparts, they, too, were widely dispersed on landing. One pathfinder team dropped onto the lawn in front of the headquarters of the German 711th Infantry Division and was promptly captured. Taken before the division commander and questioned, one paratrooper replied: "Awfully sorry, old man, but we simply landed here by accident."[41] To take the critical bridges, the British had created a special task force of volunteers which landed in six plywood gliders, all but one within 150 yards of the bridges. Capitalizing on surprise, the force captured the bridges in a few minutes and tenaciously held them against several German attacks throughout the next six hours. Thus the Allies were assured of blocking a major east-west route which the Germans needed in order to move reinforcements.[42] Elements of the division also captured a key German battery near Merville (protected by six feet of concrete and additional dirt) which could wreak havoc on the seaborne landing.

The confusion which plagued the Allied airborne elements was shared by their foe. The dispersion of the airborne drops actually contributed to German uncertainty. Reports of firing were coming in, but the Germans did not know the number of enemy troops involved. Perhaps the noise came from efforts of the French Resistance, or from crewmen who had parachuted from stricken bombers. Moreover, there had been many false alarms previously. But units sent out patrols—and waited. Subordinates did not awaken General Dollman (Seventh Army), and the commanding general of the 91st Air Landing Division left for the games at Rennes.[43]

By 2:00 A.M., if only tentatively, German commanders were beginning to react to the landings. Fifteenth Army, motivated by the scattering of some British paratroopers into its zone, asked that the 12th SS Panzer Division be moved forward. Shortly thereafter, Seventh Army put LXXXIV Corps on full alert and, having identified the airborne concentrations as being in the vicinity of St. Mère Eglise and near the mouth of the Orne, directed Corps to have the 91st Air Landing and 709th Divisions counterattack the American forces.* When German radar reported the presence of a landing force shortly before 3:00 A.M., Seventh Army, and particularly its chief of staff, Generalmajor Max Pemsel, became convinced that the invasion had begun. Dollman would sleep no more that night.[44]

If Seventh Army believed the Allies would land shortly, neither Rommel's chief of staff, Generaleutnant Hans Speidel, nor Rundstedt was yet convinced that a major operation was underway. They believed that this was a diversionary attack prior to the expected main assault against Fifteenth Army. Rundstedt was also concerned about prematurely committing *panzer* divisions in the wrong area. Around 3:30 A.M., however, when landing craft were reported heading toward the Orne estuary, Rundstedt decided that he must commit reserve units, correctly concluding that the only area where sea and airborne units could link up was on the beaches between Cotentin and the Orne. Although still not convinced that this was the main attack, he knew that if it succeeded, the Allies would quickly reinforce the assault and turn it into the major effort. Accordingly, Rundstedt ordered the 12th SS Panzer Division† to move toward Caen and alerted the Panzer Lehr Division, placing both under Army Group B.

The commander of OB West quickly discovered, however, that he would have to defend the French coast without complete freedom to move reserves. The two divisions he wanted to shift were more than "technically" in OKW reserve. They could not be moved without Hitler's approval, and the *Fuehrer* was asleep at Berchtesgaden; his attendants refused to awaken him. Bodo Zimmermann, a major general and Rundstedt's chief of operations (G3), recalled that the field marshal "was fuming with rage, red in the face, and his anger made his speech unintelligible." Much later, around 10:00 A.M., and

*Between 3:00 and 4:00 A.M., Generaleutnant Wilhelm Falley, commander of the 91st Air Landing Division, heard aircraft and bombing while he was en route to Rennes. He decided to return to his command post. American paratroopers killed him before he could reach it.[45]

†Rundstedt had declined to act on the earlier Fifteenth Army request to move this division. His cautiousness paid off, for had he acceded, that division would now have been in the wrong area for employment.

after many protests, OKW told OB West that the 12th SS Panzer Division could be moved forward but that it could not be used without the express approval of OKW. The Panzer Lehr Division was to stay where it was. As a field marshal, Rundstedt was authorized direct communication with the *Fuehrer*, but even on this most critical of occasions he could not lower himself to beg for Hitler's approval.[46]

Meanwhile, the Allied airborne units were organizing their positions and accomplishing most of their missions. By dawn, they had done well. The British paratroopers, in addition to capturing the bridges and enemy battery as described above, had destroyed bridges over the Dives River and occupied key defensive positions on the eastern flank of the proposed beachhead. Fifty miles to the west, American paratroopers had liberated their first French town, St. Mère Eglise. Flying over the village was the same U.S. flag that the conquering battalion of the 82nd Airborne Division had raised over Naples. By daybreak, the paratroopers had cut the main highway between St. Mère Eglise and Cherbourg and were preparing to repel counterattacks from the north. They were dug in and holding crossings over the Merderet and Douve Rivers, had taken the area immediately inland of Utah Beach, and were approaching the causeways. They had grown in strength with the arrival of reinforcements by glider shortly before dawn.[47]

On the "other side of the hill," German headquarters were receiving numerous reports of ship noises. Pemsel felt so sure a major attack was coming that about 5:00 A.M. he called Speidel at army group to argue his case. This call led to Speidel's decision to release to Seventh Army control of the 21st Panzer Division, the only *panzer* reserve unit in the vicinity which the German field commanders completely controlled. Much of the division (an artillery battalion, the antitank and antiaircraft battalions, and half of the infantry) was stationed along the east and west banks of the Orne, attached to the 716th Division which was defending the coast. Thus it was a small and weak unit that the division commander, Generaleutnant Edgar Feuchtinger, sent northward against the British. German fears were confirmed when in about a half hour the light of dawn revealed that the sea between the Cherbourg Peninsula and the Orne River was literally filled with ships. Shortly, the naval gunfire preparation began. Soon the sky filled with clouds of bombers and the beach defenses came under attack from both air and sea.[48]

The Assault From the Sea

While the Germans watched and waited for dawn, the immense Allied invasion fleet was traversing the Channel and naval parties were organizing the landing waves, all in response to the complex but carefully devised OVERLORD plans. Prior to sailing across the Channel, the ships assembled in an area off the Isle of Wight, nicknamed "Piccadilly Circus." There the five convoys, one per beach, were organized. They then set out along parallel lanes which had been swept of mines and marked by minesweepers and buoy layers. Antisubmarine and antisurface ship patrols operated on the flanks, while over-

Glider-Borne Reinforcements Landing in British 6th Airborne Division Area

head there were barrage balloons and swarms of night-fighters. As the convoys neared the coast, each split into two portions, with ships capable of maintaining a fast pace in one lane and the slower vessels in another. By 5:30 A.M., before the ships were even seen from the shore, the first wave of invaders had already traversed much of the ship-to-shore distance.[49]

Regardless of how meticulously a military plan is devised, inevitably unanticipated problems or natural difficulties arise in its execution. Human beings simply cannot eliminate Clausewitz's "friction." OVERLORD was no exception. Due to adverse weather, minesweepers had difficulty in doing their jobs; as a result, some ships in the following convoys hit mines that had been missed. Weather conditions also affected the embarked troops, for seasickness was rampant. The great effort made to serve good food to the troops during their journey unfortunately backfired, because many of them could not keep it down. Men, some of whom had been on board for a week, were packed tightly together. Many sanitary facilities could not take the load and malfunctioned, adding to the misery.[50] Other problems would surface later.

While the British were able to lower their landing craft only 7 miles from shore, due to the anticipated fire from enemy guns the Americans lowered some 11 miles out. This 11-mile distance meant that a three-hour ride in a landing craft on choppy seas had to be endured. There was a mixture of sounds as mother ships lowered landing craft by noisy chains, banging them into the steel sides of the ships as they went down. Leaders barked last-minute orders and gave pep talks. Men could be observed exchanging addresses before they left their ships so that if something happened to one, the other could contact the bereaved family. Many prayed. Due to the unsettled seas, a number of the assault troops were injured before they could even get into the boats. Once loaded, the craft circled in rendezvous areas until the order to head for the beaches was given.[51]

Weather conditions prevailing at the time of H-Hour (6:30 A.M. for U.S. beaches and about an hour later at British beaches, due to tidal fluctuations), were a little better than had been predicted, if far from ideal. The maximum wind was 15 knots and the visibility was 8 miles. Although the ceiling was 10,000-12,000 feet, scattered clouds from 3,000 to 7,000 feet covered approximately half of the Channel sky and became thicker over land. Due to overcast conditions, bombing was by instrument at Omaha Beach. To prevent bombs from falling on the initial waves of assault boats, Eisenhower, who had witnessed a short drop in practice, had approved an up-to-30 second delay in release time. This resulted in all bombs impacting inland of the coastal defensive positions. These bombs did detonate many minefields, which would be beneficial later, but that was of little comfort to the assault troops at this time. The bombing accuracy was better for the British beaches and quite good at Utah. While it achieved no great success in neutralizing positions, the heavy bombing attack did wonders for the morale of the men in the landing craft. So did the naval gunfire preparation which commenced at 5:30 A.M. on British beaches and 20 minutes later on Omaha and Utah Beaches. The big ships continued to fire until just before the troops landed, and then rocket ships and other close-support vessels took up the task. Meanwhile, shaken by concussion, the German coastal defense troops could peer through the dust and smoke and see the invasion fleet and a multitude of assault craft which were closing on their positions.[52]

German heavy caliber artillery fire and attack by aircraft on the invasion fleet or beaches was either lacking or ineffective. About 5:35 A.M., coastal guns began to fire, but they had little success. Only a few aircraft were based within range of the beaches. To make matters worse for the Germans, the massive aerial reinforcement called for in the German defensive plan was cancelled due to operations on the Eastern Front and conditions in Germany. Allied leaders, recalling the vicious German air attacks against beaches and shipping at Dunkirk, were pleasantly surprised at the lack of opposition. The first German planes, in fact the only enemy aircraft to attack the morning of D-Day, were two FW-190 fighters which did not reach the invasion area until after 9:00 A.M. Allied fighters intercepted later attempts by fighter bombers to get to the beachhead, and forced the attackers to drop their bombs early.[53]

The Allied plan called for elements of a corps to land on each of the two American beaches. *(See Map 55, in Atlas.)* Major General Leonard T. Gerow, one of the earlier planners of OVERLORD, commanded V Corps, which would land on Omaha Beach; Utah Beach would be assaulted by the VII Corps, commanded by Major General J. Lawton Collins, who had led the 25th Infantry Division at Guadalcanal. Later, the XIX Corps, commanded by Major General Charles H. Corlett, who had commanded the 7th Infantry Division in its seizure of Kwajalein Island in the Marshalls, would become operational in the sector between the V and VII Corps. An element of the XIX Corps, part of the 29th Infantry Division, accordingly, had been attached to the V Corps for the assault.

Generals Bradley, Gerow, Eisenhower and Collins

Utah Beach

The terrain at Utah Beach offered advantages to the German defenders who had emplaced 110 guns, varying in size from 75-mm to 170-mm caliber. Behind the beach lay a stretch of sand dunes 150 to 1,000 yards deep, and behind that barrier there was a one-to-two mile wide flooded area crossed only by causeways. Then came the hedgerow country and obstacles formed by the Merderet and Douve Rivers and the marshy ground adjacent to them. *(See Map 56, in Atlas.)* Aided by the airborne troops, elements of the 4th Infantry Division would have to cross and fight through this terrain in order to cut the Cotentin Peninsula and seize Cherbourg.[54]

The loss of a control ship, poor visibility due to smoke, and a strong current caused the assault elements to land 2,000 yards south of the planned point. As the invasion force moved toward the beaches, an undetected mine field took its toll: the control ship, an LCT loaded with tanks, and the destroyer, *U.S.S. Corry*, carrying Bernie Glisson who had listened to Axis Sally on June 4. Luckily, the off-course landing came in at a point less stoutly defended than the intended location. Brigadier General Theodore Roosevelt, the assistant division commander of the 4th Infantry Division, came ashore with the first wave; he decided to continue landing troops there rather than shifting them to the planned location.* Thanks in part to earlier actions taken by the airborne divisions, the assault elements encountered only light artillery fire; within an hour, they had cleared the beach obstacles, eliminated a few Germans in field works, and begun to move inland, supported by tanks.[55]

By 10:00 A.M., six infantry battalions were ashore and the beach was a hum of logistical activity. When troops in vehicles tried to move off the beaches, however, congestion resulted. Infantrymen could wade through the flooded area, but vehicles had to traverse the only open causeway. Worried about seizing a strong position from which to repel the expected German counterattack, Major General Raymond O. Barton, commander of the 4th Infantry Division, and Roosevelt stood on either side of the road to direct traffic so that it might flow smoothly across the causeway. One hour later, another causeway opened and tanks rapidly moved across it; advanced elements linked up with airborne troops shortly thereafter.[56]

*Tanks to accompany assault elements for all beaches had been equipped with an ingenious canvas flotation kit and duplex drive which enabled them to "swim" ashore after debarkation some distance off the beach.

American Troops Going Ashore on Utah Beach

Shingle on Omaha Beach

Omaha Beach

If enemy resistance was relatively light at Utah Beach, such was not the case at Omaha. There the 1st Infantry Division landed in the teeth of strong defenses manned by eight battalions of the well-trained German 352nd Infantry Division. The landing beach, flanked on east and west by cliffs, was about 7,000 yards wide. In terms of a profile, the assaulting troops first had to negotiate a tidal flat which was relatively firm but covered with man-made obstacles. *(See inset, Map 57, in Atlas.)* Behind that lay the shingle, a belt of heavy gravel of three-inch size which extended about 15 yards on an 8-foot incline; it was an obstacle to vehicular traffic. Assault troops next had to cross sand dunes (or a sea wall) and then a flat shelf on which there were some summer homes, marshy areas, barbed wire entanglements, and mine fields. Finally, 100- to 170-foot high bluffs had to be scaled before the troops were in relatively open country. The Germans had excellent observation from the bluffs and had studded these heights with interconnected strongpoints, walling in most of the artillery pieces so that they could fire on the beaches without their flashes being seen from the sea. Four valleys provided exits from the beaches, a fact well known to both attacker and defender.[57]

The 16th Regimental Combat Team (RCT) of the 1st Infantry Division, on the left, and the 116th RCT of the 29th Infantry Division, on the right, both under the command of Major General Clarence R. Huebner of the 1st Infantry Division, comprised the assault echelon at Omaha. Thirty or more men with all their equipment were packed into each of the flat-bowed landing craft which bounded their way toward shore while waves broke over bow and gunwales. Troops were cold and seasick, some so sick that they lay in the bilge water on the floor of the boat, not caring what transpired. Men threw up on themselves and on their buddies, and when no more vomit remained they continued to gag. In some boats the water got so deep that the troops had to bail. Occasionally, bailing was not enough and the boat went down. Orders specified that no boat in the assault wave was to stop, so the survivors of these sinkings had to await the rescue boats which were scheduled to follow the attackers.[58]

When the Allied naval bombardment began (600 rounds of 12- and 14-inch battleship shells and 3,000 rounds of 4- to 6-inch shells from cruisers and destroyers), the concussion was so great that men in the boats who had cheered the start of the firing began to tremble. Ernest Hemingway, riding in a small boat en route to Omaha, described the scene. Troops, Hemingway wrote, " . . . were watching the *Texas* with looks of surprise and happiness. Under their steel helmets they looked like pikemen of the Middle Ages to whose aid in battle had suddenly come a strange and unbelievable monster."[59]

As the landing craft closed, they were swept as much as 1,000 yards to the east of their planned landing points by a coastal current. No enemy fire was received until they were but 400 yards out. Then the Germans opened with a large volume that grew in intensity with the approach of the attackers. Artillery and mortar as well as automatic weapons fire was directed at the boats. Some were hit but many continued on. The sound of machine gun bullets striking the metal front ramps served as a harbinger of evil things to come. Friendly fire from light artillery pieces positioned on the decks of close support ships commenced, and when the first wave reached a point of 300 yards from shore, 9,000 rockets were fired. Men from sunken landing craft did their best to reach shore. Some made it.

Assault Landing at Omaha Beach

Omaha Beach on D-Day

Rather than face the machinegun fire when the ramp was dropped, a number of troops went over the side. Hundreds died in the surf or on the wide expanse of sand before they could reach the scant cover of the shingle or sea wall.[60]

Thirty-two duplex-drive tanks had been detailed to support each assaulting RCT. Due to the winds and waves, 27 of the 29 that were launched to move in with the 16th RCT sank. Two remained in the water and made it to shore. Three more, in a barge with a jammed ramp, were landed later. When those supervising the unloading of tanks for the 116th RCT saw what had happened, they decided to put theirs directly on the beach. Many tanks, however, fell prey to German artillery fire before they could do much good. A number of early casualties can be traced to the loss of support from tanks. Heavy seas also took a toll of artillery pieces which were being carried ashore in DUKW's (amphibious 2.5-ton trucks). Among the major losers was a battalion which landed with but one of its 105s, and another which reported six howitzers sunk.[61]

Men of the first wave sought whatever cover they could find. No bomb craters were available, and fire on the beach was intense. Naval guns were of no immediate help, for fire from the sea had been shifted to the backs of the beach so that no friendly casualties would be inflicted. Engineer demolition men braved the enemy fire to try to destroy the beach obstacles, but they were sometimes prevented from accomplishing their task by the presence of wounded Americans who huddled behind the obstacles. It appeared that the V Corps would never attain its mission of securing a beachhead and of making contact with the adjacent British and American units. In fact, conditions were so bad for the Americans at Omaha that throughout D-Day both German LXXXIV Corps and Seventh Army officers thought the attack had been halted.[62]

This first wave of 8 infantry companies (1,450 troops), 96 tanks (many already lost), 16 tank dozers, and 16 demolition teams was but the beginning of the large force which was to land according to a precise schedule. By H + 30 minutes, the rest of the two assault regiments and two Ranger battalions were to arrive; an hour after that, engineer and artillery special brigades were due to land.[63]

The units already ashore were fragmented due to the shifting effect of the coastal current and the heavy enemy fire. Pre-invasion briefings, which had concentrated on one specific beach area for each unit, no longer had meaning. Only 3 of the 16 tank dozers were working, and so many infantrymen were hiding behind one that it could not function properly. The minutes passed and with them the opportunity to blow many of the obstacles, because the rising water soon was too deep. Still the demolition men did what they could, and by 7:00 A.M. six gaps were open. Due to the loss of marking equipment, only one gap had been marked when the second wave arrived. So heroic were the demolition men in the face of enemy fire, that 15 of them were later awarded the Distinguished Service Cross (DSC). These feats of courage notwithstanding, the men in the second wave faced many of the problems the soldiers in the first had encountered.[64]

While infantrymen were struggling for a foothold at Omaha, west of that beach three Ranger companies were assaulting an artillery battery. Considered a vital target, it consisted of six partially casemated 155-mm guns (estimated range, 25,000 yards) and was supposed to be located on the top of the sheer 100-foot high Pointe du Hoc cliff.[65] *(See Map 55, in Atlas.)* These guns could fire on both the Omaha and Utah transport areas. General Bradley later described the mission:

> No soldier in my command has ever been wished a more difficult task than that which befell the 34 year-old commander of this Provisional Ranger Force. Lieutenant Colonel James E. Rudder, a rancher from Brady, Texas, was to take a force of 200 men, land on a shingled shelf under the face of a 100-foot cliff, scale the cliff, and there destroy an enemy battery of coastal guns.[66]

Rudder, who continued to lead his troops after being wounded twice, received the DSC. Due to the eastward coastal drift, the Rangers were also late in landing, and surf crashing against the rocks made the operation extremely difficult. The troops fired rockets containing grapnels with rope ladders and climbing ropes attached; while many fell short, some held. Then the Rangers began to climb. Although the enemy tried to repel them by cutting the ropes, dropping hand grenades, and firing over the edge, the Rangers, helped by shells from two destroyers, were over the top within five minutes of the time they landed.[67]

Quickly clearing the Germans from the trenches and gun emplacements, the Rangers found about 250 holes from shells fired by the 14-inch guns of the battleship *Texas*, but no artillery pieces. Later five weapons were found with ammunition, but without crews, in a clump of trees several hundred yards from the edge of the cliff. When the Rangers destroyed the gun breeches, their mission had been accomplished. They then made ready to repel the counterattacks that were sure to come. Rudder's force was not relieved until the morning of D+2. Due to continued German counterattacks during the intervening period, his effective strength dropped from 225 to 90 men.[68]

By the time the Rangers had reached the shore at Pointe du Hoc, the second wave was landing at Omaha Beach. Due to the failure to clear the beach, men and material from this and the succeeding waves piled up. Troops took cover everywhere, even behind the bodies of their comrades. The tide continued to rise, and the wounded were drowned as the width of sand between the water and the dune-seawall line narrowed. The order was given to suspend vehicle landings. Morale was low. Cover was scant, but standing fast seemed better than risking a dash through the barbed wire and minefields in full view of the enemy in an attempt to reach the bluffs. *(See Map 57, in Atlas.)* Still, here and there men moved forward.[69]

In times of dire stress men will often respond to inspired leadership, even while dreading the consequences. Colonel George Taylor, commander of the 16th RCT who was later promoted for his performance on D-Day, told his soldiers:[70] "The only people on the beach are the dead and those who are going to die—now let's get the hell out of here." In the sector of the 116th RCT, the assistant division commander of the 29th Infantry Division, Brigadier General Norman D. Cota, and the commander of the RCT, Colonel C. D. W. Canham, worked to get the men moving. Others, such as the unnamed sergeant who was heard yelling "Get your ass up that hill!", contributed to the forward movement.[71]

Up they went. Naval fire-support parties were now in operation, and highly accurate naval gunfire could be used to knock out troublesome enemy pockets. Destroyers—eight American and three British—were firing, sometimes coming within 800 yards of shore to provide more effective support. By 9:00 A.M., some Americans had reached the top of the bluffs and were moving to attack enemy defensive positions. Back on the beaches, landing craft commanders who could find no path through the maze of obstacles, bashed their way shoreward by brute force. Some craft were destroyed, but many made it and the build-up continued.[72]

Offshore on the *Augusta*, with his ears filled with cotton to block out the terrific noise created by the naval guns, Bradley anxiously awaited news of the landings. Appropriately enough, the first message he received from V Corps read, "Thank God for the U.S. Navy!"[73] All indications, however, were that the operation was falling behind schedule. A naval gunnery officer and Bradley's aide, who took a closer look in a PT boat, returned with a report of the confusion. V Corps messages indicated that this was a critical situation. Bradley considered diverting the Omaha follow-up forces of 25,000 men and 4,400 vehicles to other beaches where the landings had been more successful. It was almost 1:30 P.M. before he received the news that the troops were moving up the bluffs. It appeared that the situation at Omaha, while still serious, was improving. But if Omaha was to remain as a beachhead, enough resources had to be pushed ashore to hold against any counterattack. After visiting Gerow on his command ship, Bradley decided to land the follow-up force.[74] Unknowingly, he could be thankful that the divisional reaction force of the 352nd Infantry Division had been committed early in the morning against one of the deceptive (simulated) airborne raids. Not until mid-afternoon did it return to the invasion area, where half of it was employed at Omaha Beach. *(See Map 55, in Atlas.)*

Gold, Juno, and Sword Beaches

British and Commonwealth troops landed between 7:25 and 8:00 A.M. on three beaches, each approximately a mile wide. The 50th Infantry Division of XXX Corps came in at Gold, about 10 miles east of Omaha; one mile farther east, the Canadian 3rd Infantry Division landed at Juno; and five miles on up the coast at Sword Beach the British 3rd Infantry Division attacked. They landed accurately as a result of signal lights and radar beacons shown by two British midget submarines. These ships had been under water a total of 64 hours since leaving port. Most of this time was spent in position, resting on the bottom, waiting for the appointed time to rise and do their work. Frogmen, charged with destroying underwater obstacles, preceded the first wave by some 20 minutes.[75] The mission of the assault echelons was to link up with the British 6th Airborne Division, to join the three beachheads, and to seize the key road centers of Bayeux and Caen by the end of D-Day. The terrain these troops had to negotiate was more favorable to the attacker than it was in the American sector. The beaches had a gradual slope and there were no high bluffs, although there were sand dunes and low cliffs. Behind the beaches, hedgerow country extended for 40 miles inland. An open area, which was regarded as prime tank country, lay southeast of Caen. While part of Gold Beach was held by units of the German 352nd Infantry Division, the defense of most of the British beach area was left to elements of the 716th Infantry Division, a static unit which numbered many non-Germans, mostly eastern Europeans, in its ranks.[76]

The British prepared carefully for what they anticipated would be a difficult fight on landing. The invasion sites were bombed for two hours, followed 15 minutes later with a two-hour naval gunfire preparation. At dawn, swarms of fighter aircraft provided protective cover. The British, unlike the Americans, also devoted much effort to the development and planned employment of dual-drive tanks, flail tanks which would cut lanes through minefields, and other "funnies," as the specialized pieces of armored equipment were called. The effort paid dividends, although some infantrymen, eager to get off the fireswept beaches, ran ahead of the vehicles to neutralize enemy weapons positions. A bagpiper of the commandos, however, was in no great hurry to leave the beach. Although he had stepped out of his landing craft into armpit-high water, he piped his way to shore and once he got there continued piping as he walked up and down on the beach. His example was admired by some. "That's the stuff, Jock," called one as he ran by; but another chimed in, "Get down, you mad bugger."[77]

The landings went smoothly and the British and Canadian troops gained control of the beaches relatively quickly. Then they moved inland, tearing apart the 716th Infantry Division. Later in the afternoon, seaborne and airborne elements effected a link-up. But, unknown to the British, a golden opportunity had been missed. About 10:00 A.M., in the area of the 50th Infantry Division, a German strongpoint fell, completely opening the road to Bayeux. Later, the Germans rushed up forces to seal the gap which, unfortunately for the Allies, had not been exploited.[78]

The German Reaction

As the OVERLORD troops clawed their way on to and beyond the beaches, German leaders were trying to decide how to use their resources to destroy the invasion force. Reports of naval gunfire and of landings were pouring into German headquarters. Since the commander of the 352nd Division, responsible for Omaha Beach, reported that things looked fairly good, the critical area seemed to be that of the 716th Division, where British tanks had penetrated to the German artillery positions. A decision was made to divert the 21st Panzer Division for employment against the British landing forces. As noted above, much of that division was being used elsewhere, so only that portion which had been directed earlier to attack the British airborne units could be employed. Now, the division was ordered to cross the Orne and attack the advancing tanks.[79] It was this order changing the division's mission, which came from Germany and was intercepted by ULTRA, that led to the Allies learning that Rommel was not at his headquarters in France. The commander of Army Group B, who had been briefed by his chief of staff and had issued his initial instructions by telephone, did not physically reach his headquarters until 4:00 P.M.[80]

It will be recalled that Hitler, who was in Bavaria and surrounded by military assistants, had predicted that a deceptive attack would precede the main assault. As late as mid-morning of D-Day when Speer arrived for an appointment, he had not awakened. Several hours later, in a conference in a Berghof salon, the *Fuehrer* remarked that one of the many intelligence reports he had received had cited the exact time and place of the attack. Because what was happening fit the contents of this report so well, he knew that this initial assault was not the main attack. Later, around 3:30 P.M. and too late to affect the D-Day battle, he released from OKW reserve the 12th SS Panzer, 17th SS Panzer Grenadier, and Panzer Lehr Divisions. *(See Map 54, in Atlas.)* The 12th SS Panzer did not arrive until the next morning, while what was left of the Panzer Lehr, which was repeatedly hit by Allied air, arrived in the area on the ninth.[81]

What Rundstedt, and particularly Rommel, had told Hitler about the importance of early reaction and movement of reserves, was proving all too correct. Mist and fog, which might have helped cover the movement of the reserve *panzer* units had they been released in time, burned off by 11:00 A.M. Now the only cover would be darkness, still many hours away. During the day, a new plan for the use of the German units was prepared. Both the 12th SS Panzer and Panzer Lehr, as well as the 21st Panzer and 716th Divisions, would be placed under the 1st SS Panzer Corps which would take over the eastern portion of the LXXXIV Corps area (Bayeux-Orne) and then counterattack. The contemplated employment of the 716th Division, however, was not realistic, because by the end of D-Day the British had practically destroyed it—only 12 artillery pieces and about one infantry battalion remained. It should also be noted that the German leaders, still fearing a later major assault, could not bring themselves to order more reinforcements to Normandy. Rommel, for example, squelched the immediate movement of some troops from Brittany because of his concern for the possibility that the Allies might launch an airborne operation against targets on the peninsula.[82]

Early Consolidation of the Beachheads

Split into small groups in towns and fortified positions, many of the Germans on the Cotentin Peninsula were still confused about the situation. By 1:00 P.M., men of the 4th Infantry Division had made contact with paratroopers of the 101st Airborne. *(See Map 56, in Atlas.)* Both the 101st and the 82nd remained locked in combat with the Germans for the rest of D-Day. While communciation between units was not always adequate, while airborne units had yet to collect all of their scattered combat strength, and while all of the desired terrain had not been taken, the Utah force, although weak in some areas, appeared to be there to stay. Reinforcements, both sea- and glider-borne, continued to arrive. Virtually the entire 4th Infantry Division landed and prepared to continue the attack on June 7.[83]

At Omaha Beach, the situation was steadily improving, although it could still become critical. *(See Map 57, in Atlas.)* Reinforcements were arriving on a regular basis in spite of the way in which the beach was littered with the debris of war. Beach exits had been opened. American units, supported by air and naval gunfire, moved onto the plateau where the German-infested hedgerows awaited them. Fortunately for the attackers, no German reserves were available for an immediate counterattack. When the tide receded, the engineers once again set to work removing the beach obstacles, but by the end of the day only a third had been cleared. Although not originally scheduled to land until June 7, a regiment of the 29th Infantry Division arrived early to help hold the beachhead, which nowhere was more than a mile and a half deep. As the attackers struggled to reach areas where they could defend through the night, it appeared that if conditions were steadily improving, the battle on Omaha Beach could still go either way.[84]

To the east, British and Canadian troops had made significant gains during the day. *(See Map 55, in Atlas.)* Adjacent to the American sector, the British 50th Infantry Division stopped short of Bayeux for the night because the commander felt that although the opposition he was meeting was light, he could not occupy the city and establish a strong defense before

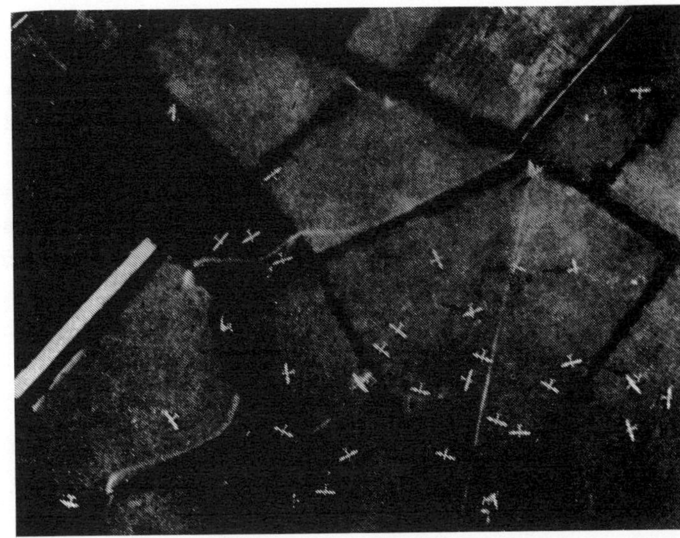

Gliders Among the Hedgerows (Crashes are Marked by Arrows)

dark. Next to the 50th Division, the 3rd Canadian Infantry Division moved three to six miles in from the coast and patrolled to a depth of nine miles. Farther east, the British 3rd Infantry Division reached positions within two miles of Caen, gateway to the excellent tank country which lay just beyond. Though neither Caen nor Bayeux had been taken, the Germans felt most severely threatened in the British sector, where a breakthrough could open up much of France. That was why they had ordered the 21st Panzer Division to that area.[85]

Allied reconnaissance aircraft picked up the movement of this reserve division during the morning, and beginning at 11:00 A.M. the unit came under virtually unceasing air attack. By noon, the division had reached Caen only to find a city with its streets filled with debris and civilians trying to flee with their belongings. Only one bridge over the Orne was usable. Rather than get involved in this maze from which he might never escape, the division commander countermarched his troops and went around Caen. Valuable hours were lost. When he attacked at 4:00 P.M., the British were ready. With the help of naval gunfire from three battleships, which destroyed 10 tanks in a few minutes, they smashed the attack, the only large counterattack of D-Day. The Germans dug in a few hundred yards ahead of their line of departure. A handful of troops slipped through to the coast, but all they could do was observe the mighty invasion force. Their presence had no real effect on the battle.[86]

About 5:00 P.M., in a colossal display of ignorance of the true situation, OKW cavalierly ordered Seventh Army to wipe out the beachheads that day. The officers who had to fight the battle had no reinforcements available and could only continue to plan for the attack by I SS Panzer Corps the next day with whatever troops could get in position. In addition to what has been mentioned above, they ordered a battle group to ferry across the Seine and with the 711th Division attack the British 6th Airborne Division. Another battle group from the south would move up to hit the Americans in the St. Lô area, and a division was started by rail from St. Nazaire toward Bayeux. Movement of these reserves, as Rommel knew from his African experience, would not be easy. Allied air power had inflicted much damage on troop and materiel targets, and no respite was in sight. Choke points, such as that created at Caen, were developing in other areas, and transportation targets of all types were hit as the Allies continued their effort to isolate the battle area from the remainder of France.[87]

Confidence and Relief in Higher Quarters

Back in England, Dwight D. Eisenhower eagerly awaited news of how the invasion was proceeding. At 7:00 A.M. he was in bed reading a western novel when Admiral Ramsay called to say that all seemed to be proceeding according to plan. Next, Eisenhower's aide, Commander Butcher, came in with a message from Air Marshal Leigh-Mallory in which the airman reported that the air drop had gone well, with less airplane losses than he had feared. One hour later, Eisenhower was dictating his first report to Marshall. Having first assured himself that the troops were ashore on all five beaches, he authorized the release of a message which was broadcast over BBC at 9:33 A.M. The message read: "Under the Command of General Eisenhower, Allied naval forces, supported by strong air forces, began landing Allied armies this morning on the northern coast of France."[88] After a short period of news about the landings, the speeches which the exiled heads of European governments had previously recorded were aired. These talks were designed to stress to the resistance movement that orders must be followed, and also to cause the Germans to misinterpret the actual Allied intention.[89]

Britons heard the good news at work, where some stopped and sang "God Save the King." In the United States, the first message came through at 3:33 A.M., eastern time. Work stopped for a moment in the war plants. In Philadelphia, joyful citizens rang the Liberty Bell. People who were not working that night were awakened by neighbors, and the news spread. Even American airmen in enemy prison camps listened in over small crystal sets designed either to look like pencils or to fit in toothbrush holders.[90]

Allied deception operations continued, while those who knew the real plan worked to implement it. Many senior American officers, not directly involved with the invasion at this stage, were stationed in England. To keep them up to date, the U.S. theater headquarters held a briefing at 11:00 A.M. Political leaders were also kept informed. Churchill, for example, received reports from Allied sources and ULTRA messages as well. At noon, he discussed the landing before the House of Commons. In support of the ongoing deception effort, he included a reference to this attack being but the first of a number which would be launched against the Continent. Before the day was over, Churchill had also informed Stalin of the assault, and the Russian leader had replied that his planned summer offensive would commence about mid-June in one area, and by July become a general attack. At the strategic level, there was an air of optimism. Perhaps the Allies had reached the beginning of the end.[91]

D-Day in Hindsight

During the 24-hour period that was D-Day, the *Luftwaffe* was able to manage some 500 sorties of all types, although many of these were flown in the Pas de Calais area. The Allies, enjoying complete air superiority, flew over 14,000. In fact, there were so many Allied planes in the air that controlling them became a problem. Ground troops on both sides rapidly realized what the true air situation was. German ground forces were practically devoid of air support. At dusk, some German planes attacked the invasion fleet, but they were met by a tremendous quantity of flak. Gunners had been watching the skies all day for such an opportunity. So excited was one of them that he shot down his own barrage balloon.[92]

Allied leaders were cautiously optimistic at the end of the day, even though some assigned objectives had not been taken and the tonnage of supplies landed was behind schedule. The latter was a little troubling, particularly if future weather deteriorated to such an extent as to adversely affect the build-up. Indeed, there was ample justification for the British official historian's later comment that the D-Day invasion was "a notable feat of arms." Some aspects, however, deserve further comment.[93]

Thanks to security, deception, and most of all to the weather, the Germans were surprised by the assault. For some time after the paratroopers landed, they were unsure concerning what was happening. Confusion caused by the widespread paratrooper drops assisted the Allies in the early stages of the attack; but by the end of D-Day, many troops had still not rejoined their units. Such dispersion was serious. Yet, as Major General Matthew B. Ridgway, commander of the 82nd Airborne Division, observed in a later report to SHAEF, the dispersion situation in Normandy was much better than that which had prevailed in the Sicilian invasion. With more training of the divisions, Ridgway felt that the improvement would continue. In OVERLORD, airborne troops had amply demonstrated their value in assisting a seaborne invasion force. No longer would invading troops, such as the British forces at Gallipoli, necessarily have to deal with both the beach defenders and local reserves; airborne forces, if capable of employment in strength, could engage the reserves before the attackers landed.[94]

The landings also confirmed the value and effectiveness of naval gunfire. Although all the beach defenses were not destroyed, large ships and destroyers, coming in close to shore, provided highly accurate fire support. The casualties suffered by the 21st Panzer Division during its abortive attack are an excellent example of superior battleship gunnery.[95]

The support which tanks provided, in spite of heavy losses in the early stages, was important. Yet, even with the tanks, had it not been for the inspired leadership of a few and the bravery of those who followed them, the assault, certainly at Omaha and possibly at the other beaches, would have failed.[96]

"The Normandy assault was perhaps as thoroughly planned as any battle in the history of war."[97] So wrote Gordon A. Harrison, the author of the U.S. official history. The careful preparation, under the leadership first of Morgan and then of Eisenhower, paid off when the plan was forcefully executed by a well-integrated ground, air, and naval force composed of men who could not only follow the plan but improvise as necessary.[98]

As the sun set that summer evening of June 6, 1944, it seemed that the Allies had successfully taken the German dare.

Notes

[1]Cornelius Ryan, *The Longest Day: June 6, 1944* (New York, 1959), pp. 39-41.

[2]Arthur W. Tedder, *With Prejudice: The War Memoirs of Marshal of the Royal Air Force Lord Tedder G. C. B.* (Boston, 1966), p. 549; Roland G. Ruppenthal, "Logistic Planning for OVERLORD in Retrospect," in *D-Day: The Normandy Invasion in Retrospect* (Lawrence, Kansas, 1971), p. 89; Dwight D. Eisenhower, *Crusade in Europe* (Garden City, 1948), pp. 225-229; L. F. Ellis, *Victory in the West*, I, *The Battle of Normandy* (London, 1962), pp. 82-83; Alfred D. Chandler (ed.), *The Papers of Dwight D. Eisenhower: The War Years* (5 vols.; Baltimore, 1970), III: No. 1732, Memorandum, June 3, 1944. The Eisenhower papers are hereinafter cited as *EP*.

[3]T. Dodson Stamps and Vincent J. Esposito (eds.), *A Military History of World War II* (2 vols.; West Point, N.Y., 1956), I, 375-385.

[4]Robert W. Coakley and Richard M. Leighton, *Global Logistics and Strategy, 1943-1945* (Washington, 1968), pp. 354-355; Ellis, *Normandy*, pp. 28-29; Charles B. MacDonald, *The Mighty Endeavor: American Armed Forces in the European Theater in World War II* (New York, 1969), p. 263.

[5]Material for the above two paragraphs is from: MacDonald, *Mighty Endeavor*, p. 263; Ellis, *Normandy*, pp. 88-89, 140; Roland G. Ruppenthal, *Logistical Support of the Armies* (2 vols.; Washington, 1953), I, 273-282.

[6]*EP*, III: No. 1719, Eisenhower to Combined Chiefs of Staff, May 30, 1944; F. W. Winterbotham, *The Ultra Secret* (New York, 1974), p. 129; George M. Elsey, "Naval Aspects of Normandy in Retrospect," in *D-Day: The Normandy Invasion in Retrospect* (Lawrence, Kansas, 1971), p. 179. Friederich Ruge, "The Invasion of Normandy," in Hans-Adolf Jacobsen and Jürgen Rohwer (eds.), *Decisive Battles of World War II: The German View* (London, 1965), p. 329; Bodo Zimmermann, MS#B-308: "OB WEST, Atlantic Wall to Siegfried Line, A Study in Command," in *OB WEST (Atlantic Wall to Siegfried Line), A Study in Command,* James F. Scoggin, Jr. (ed.) (Allendorf, Germany, 1946-1947), I, 69; Anthony Cave Brown, *Bodyguard of Lies* (New York, 1975), pp. 601-602, 612-613.

[7]Mattie E. Treadwell, *The Women's Army Corps* (Washington, 1954), pp. 383-385, 387.

[8]Winston S. Churchill, *Closing the Ring* (Boston, 1951), pp. 619-624; Stephen E. Ambrose, *The Supreme Commander: The War Years of General Dwight D. Eisenhower* (Garden City, 1969), pp. 407-408.

[9]Chester B. Hansen, "War Diary," Chester B. Hansen Papers, United States Army Military History Research Collection, Carlisle Barracks, Pa., entries of June 1-2, 1944. Quotation is from the June 2 entry.

[10]*Ibid.*, entries June 2 and 3, 1944; Omar N. Bradley, *A Soldier's Story* (New York, 1951), pp. 252, 255-257; MacDonald, *Mighty Endeavor*, pp. 263-264.

[11]Walter B. Smith, *Eisenhower's Six Great Decisions* (New York, 1956), pp. 41, 51; Ambrose, *Supreme Commander*, p. 406; Harry C. Butcher, *My Three Years with Eisenhower* (New York, 1946), p. 546; *EP*, III: editor's note accompanying No. 1728, p. 1653.

[12]Ambrose, *Supreme Commander*, p. 406; Smith, *Six Decisions*, p. 42; Cave Brown, *Bodyguard*, pp. 614, 624-626; Ellis, *Normandy*, pp. 140-141; Roger Parkinson, *A Day's March Nearer Home: The War History from Alamein to VE Day Based on the War Cabinet Papers of 1942 to 1945* (New York, 1974), p. 304.

[13]*EP*, III: No. 1732, Memorandum, June 3, 1944; No. 1731, Eisenhower to Marshall, June 3, 1944; Gordon A. Harrison, *Cross-Channel Attack* (Washington, 1951), p. 232.

[14]Ryan, *Longest Day*, pp. 30-31, 49-50; MacDonald, *Mighty Endeavor*, pp. 249-250 (message appears in *Mighty Endeavor*, p. 250).

[15]Ryan, *Longest Day*, pp. 30-34; Cave Brown, *Bodyguard*, pp. 262-267, 640.

[16]Harrison, *Cross-Channel*, p. 272; Ellis, *Normandy*, p. 141.

[17]Eisenhower, *Crusade in Europe*, pp. 249-250; Ellis, *Normandy*, p. 141; Ambrose, *Supreme Commander*, p. 415.

[18]Smith, *Six Decisions*, p. 52.

[19]Ambrose, *Supreme Commander*, p. 384; Ellis, *Normandy*, pp. 49, 51; Forrest C. Pogue, *The Supreme Command* (Washington, 1954), p. 156.

[20]Ambrose, *Supreme Commander*, pp. 384-387; Pogue, *Supreme Command*, pp. 149-232; Parkinson, *Day's March*, pp. 306-307; quotation is from Ambrose, *Supreme Commander*, p. 387.

[21]Ellis, *Normandy*, p. 143; Ambrose, *Supreme Commander*, pp. 415-416; Harrison, *Cross-Channel*, pp. 272-274; MacDonald, *Mighty Endeavor*, p. 265.

[22]Eisenhower, *Crusade in Europe*, p. 239; Winterbotham, *Ultra*, p. 121; Harrison, *Cross-Channel*, pp. 273-274; Pogue, *Supreme Command*, p. 168; Bradley, *Soldier's Story*, pp. 259-260.

[23]Harrison, *Cross-Channel*, p. 274.

[24]MacDonald, *Mighty Endeavor*, p. 265; Ellis, *Normandy*, p. 143; Ambrose, *Supreme Commander*, pp. 417-418.

[25]Ambrose, *Supreme Commander*, p. 417 (the quotation appears on this page); Smith, *Six Decisions*, pp. 52-53; Eisenhower, *Crusade in Europe*, p. 250.

[26]Winterbotham, *Ultra*, pp. 131-132; MacDonald, *Mighty Endeavor*, p. 260; Harrison, *Cross-Channel*, p. 319; Benjamin A. Dickson, "G-2 Journal Algiers to the Elbe" (Devon, Pa., n.d.), copy in Special Collections Division, U.S. Military Academy Library, p. 117.

[27]Ellis, *Normandy*, pp. 197-198, 553; Harrison, *Cross-Channel*, pp. 138, 186, 238, 252, 254, 260, 332; Ryan, *Longest Day*, pp. 28-83.

[28]Ryan, *Longest Day*, pp. 20-21, 30, 35-36; Cave Brown, *Bodyguard*, pp. 623, 637-638.

[29]Cave Brown, *Bodyguard*, pp. 430, 583-587.

[30]Ryan, *Longest Day*, pp. 78-82; Bodo Zimmermann, "France, 1944," in Seymour Freidin and William Richardson (eds.), *The Fatal Decisions* (New York, 1956), p. 211; Guenther Blumentritt, *Von Rundstedt: The Soldier and the Man* (London, 1952), p. 221; Ellis, *Normandy*, p. 130; Harrison, *Cross-Channel*, pp. 275-276; Cave Brown, *Bodyguard*, p. 639.

[31]*EP*, III: No. 1734, Note, June 5, 1944; editor's note with No. 1734, p. 1908.

[32]Butcher, *Three Years*, pp. 565-566; Peter Lyon, *Eisenhower: Portrait of a Hero* (Boston, 1974), p. 290; Ryan, *Longest Day*, pp. 97-99.

[33]MacDonald, *Mighty Endeavor*, p. 265; Ryan, *Longest Day*, p. 89; Friedrich Ruge, "German Naval Operations on D-Day," in *D-Day: The Normandy Invasion in Retrospect* (Lawrence, Kansas, 1971), p. 162.

[34]All times used are Double British Summer Time (DBST). The German Army operated on Central European Time, one hour behind DBST, thus German sources indicate the intercept was made at 9:15 P.M.

[35]Ryan, *Longest Day*, pp. 96-97 (quotations are from p. 96); Harrison, *Cross-Channel*, p. 275; MacDonald, *Mighty Endeavor*, pp. 261-262.

[36]Zimmermann, "France," p. 212; Blumentritt, *Rundstedt*, p. 221; Ryan, *Longest Day*, pp. 96-97; Harrison, *Cross-Channel*, pp. 275-276; Cave Brown, *Bodyguard*, pp. 649-650.

[37]Ryan, *Longest Day*, pp. 117-118.

[38]Forrest C. Pogue, "D-Day–1944," in *D-Day: The Normandy Invasion in Retrospect* (Lawrence, Kansas, 1971), p. 9; Ellis, *Normandy*, pp. 159-160; Alfred Goldberg, "Air Campaign OVERLORD: To D-Day," in *D-Day: The Normandy Invasion in Retrospect* (Lawrence, Kansas, 1971), p. 70; Cave Brown, *Bodyguard*, pp. 643, 648, 654.

[39]Ellis, *Normandy*, pp. 156-158; Smith, *Six Decisions*, p. 56; Ryan, *Longest Day*, pp. 86-87, 105-107, 135, 141; MacDonald, *Mighty Endeavor*, p. 266; *The Army Air Forces in World War II*, Vol. III, *Europe: ARGUMENT to VE Day January 1944 to May 1945* (Chicago, 1951), p. 188; Harrison, *Cross-Channel*, p. 280.

[40]Ryan, *Longest Day*, pp. 135, 138; Ellis, *Normandy*, p. 156.

[41]Ryan, *Longest Day*, pp. 105-106, 113, 120-124 (quotation is taken from p. 113); Ellis, *Normandy*, p. 156.

[42]Ryan, *Longest Day*, pp. 107-110; Ellis, *Normandy*, p. 150; MacDonald, *Mighty Endeavor*, p. 269.

[43]Harrison, *Cross-Channel*, p. 278; Ryan, *Longest Day*, pp. 116-117, 269.

[44]Blumentritt, *Rundstedt*, p. 224; MacDonald, *Mighty Endeavor*, pp. 266-267; Ryan, *Longest Day*, pp. 145, 150; Ellis, *Normandy*, pp. 150, 198-200; Ruge, "Naval Operations", p. 162; Stamps and Esposito, *Military History*, I, 386; Harrison, *Cross-Channel*, pp. 278-297.

[45]Ryan, *Longest Day*, pp. 149-150, 269.

[46]Ellis, *Normandy*, pp. 199-200; Bodo Zimmermann, MS#B-308: "A Study in Command," I, 72, 75; MacDonald, *Mighty Endeavor*, p. 269; Harrison, *Cross-Channel*, p. 333; Ryan, *Longest Day*, p. 256. (Quotation is from Ryan, *Longest Day*). Through ULTRA intercept, the Allies learned of the OB WEST request for the *panzer* divisions as soon as it was sent (Winterbotham, *Ultra*, p. 132).

[47]Ellis, *Normandy*, p. 149, 151, 154-156; Ryan, *Longest Day*, pp. 133-134, 154, 158-159, 181; Stamps and Esposito, *Military History*, I, 376-377; MacDonald, *Mighty Endeavor*, p. 269.

[48]Harrison, *Cross-Channel*, p. 332; Ryan, *Longest Day*, pp. 183, 189; MacDonald, *Mighty Endeavor*, p. 270.

[49]Ryan, *Longest Day*, pp. 90-91, 193; Bradley, *Soldier's Story*, p. 259; Ellis, *Normandy*, pp. 145-146.

[50]Elsey, "Naval," p. 179; Ryan, *Longest Day*, pp. 69, 94-95, 190-192.

[51]Ellis, *Normandy*, p. 166; Harrison, *Cross-Channel*, p. 300.

[52]Harrison, *Cross-Channel*, pp. 300-302, 320; Ellis, *Normandy*, pp. 161, 163, 166-167; Craven and Cate, *ARGUMENT*, pp. 190, 193; Tedder, *With Prejudice*, p. 548.

[53]Blumentritt, *Rundstedt*, p. 223; Ellis, *Normandy*, pp. 193-194; Ryan, *Longest Day*, pp. 270-271; Ruge, "Invasion," p. 335.

[54]Elsey, "Naval," p. 181; Stamps and Esposito, *Military History*, I, 374; Vincent J. Esposito (ed.), *The West Point Atlas of American Wars* (2 vols.; New York, 1959), II, Section 2, Chart A.

[55]Ellis, *Normandy*, p. 188; Elsey, "Naval," p. 187; Ryan, *Longest Day*, p. 234; MacDonald, *Mighty Endeavor*, p. 271; Stamps and Esposito, *Military History*, I, 377; Harrison, *Cross-Channel*, p. 304; Bradley, *Soldier's Story*, p. 255; and Ruge, "Naval Operations," p. 164. MacDonald and Ruge say that the *Corry* was sunk by fire from shore guns.

[56]Stamps and Esposito, *Military History*, I, 378; Ellis, *Normandy*, p. 190; Ryan, *Longest Day*, pp. 232-233, 285-286.

[57]MacDonald, *Mighty Endeavor*, pp. 271-272; Esposito, *West Point Atlas*, II, Section 2, Chart B; Bradley, *Soldier's Story*, p. 272; Cave Brown, *Bodyguard*, pp. 665-666; Stamps and Esposito, *Military History*, I, 379-380.

[58]MacDonald, *Mighty Endeavor*, p. 272; Ryan, *Longest Day*, pp. 202-207.

[59]Hemingway is quoted in Elsey, "Naval," p. 181. Other sources are Stamps and Esposito, *Military History*, I, 381; Don Whitehead, "A Correspondent's View of D-Day," in *D-Day: The Normandy Invasion in Retrospect* (Lawrence, Kansas, 1971), p. 49; Ryan, *Longest Day*, p. 198.

[60]Stamps and Esposito, *Military History*,I, 381; MacDonald, *Mighty Endeavor*, pp. 272-273.

[61]Ryan, *Longest Day*, pp. 205-206; Harrison, *Cross-Channel*, pp. 309, 313, 315.

[62]MacDonald, *Mighty Endeavor*, pp. 272-273; Stamps and Esposito, *Military History*, I, 379; Harrison, *Cross-Channel*, p. 305.

[63]Stamps and Esposito, *Military History*, I, 379-381.

[64]*Ibid.*, pp. 381-382; Harrison, *Cross-Channel*, pp. 313, 317.

[65]The correct name for this piece of terrain is Pointe du Hoc and this term is used here. Contemporary allied accounts called it Point de Hoe. (Elsey, "Naval," p. 197.)

[66]Bradley, *Soldier's Story*, p. 269.

[67]MacDonald, *Mighty Endeavor*, p. 274; Harrison, *Cross-Channel*, pp. 196, 308, 318, 322; Ryan, *Longest Day*, pp. 68, 237-238; Bradley, *Soldier's Story*, p. 270; Ellis, *Normandy*, p. 198.

[68]MacDonald, *Mighty Endeavor*, p. 274; Elsey, "Naval," pp. 181-182; Bradley, *Soldier's Story*, p. 270; Harrison, *Cross-Channel*, pp. 318, 322; Ryan, *Longest Day*, p. 239.

[69]Ryan, *Longest Day*, pp. 228-230; Stamps and Esposito, *Military History*, I, 381-383.

[70]Quoted in Pogue, "D-Day," p. 6.

[71]*Ibid.*; MacDonald, *Mighty Endeavor*, p. 275. (The sergeant's statement is quoted in MacDonald, *Mighty Endeavor*.)

[72]MacDonald, *Mighty Endeavor*, p. 275; Ellis, *Normandy*, pp. 166, 193; Elsey, "Naval," p. 186.

[73]Quoted in Bradley, *Soldier's Story*, p. 254.

[74]*Ibid.*, pp. 270-274; Ryan, *Longest Day*, p. 196.

[75]Stamps and Esposito, *Military History*, I, 386; Ellis, *Normandy*, pp. 160-161, 170-171; Ryan, *Longest Day*, pp. 182-183, 242-243.

[76]Ellis, *Normandy*, pp. 171, 197; Stamps and Esposito, *Military History*, I, 274; MacDonald, *Mighty Endeavor*, p. 276.

[77]Ellis, *Normandy*, pp. 163-169; Kenneth Macksey, *Tank Warfare: A History of Tanks in Battle* (New York, 1972), p. 226; Ryan, *Longest Day*, p. 242. (Quotations are from Ryan, *Longest Day*)

[78]MacDonald, *Mighty Endeavor*, p. 276; Harrison, *Cross-Channel*, p. 321.

[79]Ellis, *Normandy*, pp. 200-201.

[80]Winterbotham, *Ultra*, p. 132; Hans Speidel, MS#B-718: "Commentary on MS#B-308," in *OB WEST (Atlantic Wall to Siegfried Line), A Study in Command,* James F. Scoggin, Jr. (ed.) (Allendorf, Germany, 1946-1947), I, 78.

[81]Ryan, *Longest Day*, p. 296; Ruge, "Invasion," p. 334; Treusch von Buttlar, MS#B-672: "Commentary on MS#B-308," in *OB WEST (Atlantic Wall to Siegfried Line), A Study in Command*, James F. Scoggin, Jr. (ed.) (Allendorf, Germany, 1946-1947), II, 40-44; Albert Speer, *Inside the Third Reich* (New York, 1971), pp. 455-456.

[82]Zimmermann, "OB WEST," I, p. 76; Harrison, *Cross-Channel*, p. 334.

[83]Harrison, *Cross-Channel*, pp. 281-282, 286, 288-289, 328-329; Stamps and Esposito, *Military History*, I, 376-379; *EP*, III: editor's note with No. 1739, p. 1917.

[84]MacDonald, *Mighty Endeavor*, p. 278; Ellis, *Normandy*, pp. 213-215; Harrison, *Cross-Channel*, pp. 326-328.

[85]Harrison, *Cross-Channel*, p. 332.

[86]Ellis, *Normandy*, p. 223; MacDonald, *Mighty Endeavor*, pp. 276-277; Craven and Cates, *ARGUMENT*, p. 193; Ryan, *Longest Day*, p. 295; Harrison, *Cross-Channel*, pp. 332-333.

[87]Ellis, *Normandy*, pp. 216-217; Harrison, *Cross-Channel*, p. 378; Craven and Cates, *ARGUMENT*, pp. 193-194.

[88]Quotation is from Ryan, *Longest Day*, p. 279.

[89]*Ibid.*, pp. 278-279; Butcher, *Three Years*, pp. 566-567; Cave Brown, *Bodyguard*, p. 671.

[90]Ryan, *Longest Day*, pp. 279-283.

[91]John D. Horn, "War Diary," John D. Horn Papers, Darien, Conn., entry of June 6; Winterbotham, *Ultra*, p. 133; Parkinson, *Day's March*, pp. 308, 310; MacDonald, *Mighty Endeavor*, pp. 279-280; Tedder, *With Prejudice*, p. 549; Winston S. Churchill, *Triumph and Tragedy* (Boston, 1953), pp. 6-7.

[92]Stamps and Esposito, *Military History*, I, 373; Ellis, *Normandy*, pp. 212, 223; Goldberg, "Air Campaign," pp. 70-73; Dickson, "G-2 Journal," pp. 118-119.

[93]Ellis, *Normandy*, p. 217; MacDonald, *Mighty Endeavor*, pp. 278-279.

[94]Tedder, *With Prejudice*, p. 549; Stamps and Esposito, *Military History*, I, 404; Report, "82nd Airborne Division—Operation NEPTUNE," to SHAEF, July 25, 1944, World War II Personal Files, Matthew B. Ridgway Papers, Military History Research Collection, Carlisle, Pa.; Cave Brown, *Bodyguard*, p. 670.

[95]Ellis, *Normandy*, p. 187; Stamps and Esposito, *Military History*, I, 404.

[96]Stamps and Esposito, *Military History*, I, 404.

[97]Harrison, *Cross-Channel*, p. 274.

[98]*Ibid.*, pp. 274-275; Elsey, "Naval," p. 192.

A Business of Build-Up

13

. . . just as soon as we land this business becomes primarily a business of build-up. For you can almost always force an invasion—but you can't always make it stick.

*Omar N. Bradley**

First light on June 7 revealed that the five Allied beachheads in Normandy had survived the night. *(See Map 55, in Atlas.)* During the hours of darkness, however, the Germans had secured valuable information when they found a copy of the American VII Corps field order in a boat which had washed off Utah Beach and drifted into the mouth of the Vire. Moreover, that evening they would remove a copy of the V Corps order from the body of a fallen officer. Marked "Destroy before Embarkation," both orders revealed that the objectives of the U.S. First Army were St. Lô and Cherbourg, but they contained no hint concerning British operations nor reference to the projected American attack toward the Brittany ports.

Not knowing of ULTRA, and therefore marvelling at the accuracy with which the Allies had located their units prior to the invasion, the Germans pondered the captured orders in light of their own intelligence reports. Rundstedt and Rommel, believing that the British posed the most serious threat because they were near the excellent tank country just beyond Caen, decided to mass German strength in that sector.[1] Such a decision, however, was easier to make than it would be to execute in the face of overwhelming Allied aerial superiority and German doubts about Allied intentions—doubts which were still being sustained by the subtle deception plan. To add to these factors, there was the advantage ULTRA gave the Allies and the unpredictability and intransigence of Hitler. Accordingly, although there would be days of hard fighting ahead and the Allies could not predict the outcome of the invasion with certainty, the OVERLORD forces were in France to stay. In due time they would break out of Normandy in a devastating offensive, putting behind them the weeks of impatient waiting and frustratingly slow gains.

*From a press briefing by Lieutenant General Omar N. Bradley aboard the *USS Augusta* on June 3, 1944. Bradley's remarks are quoted in Omar N. Bradley, *A Soldier's Story* (New York, 1951), p. 256.

Linking of the Beaches

It was vital to deepen the beachhead quickly in order to provide room for the reinforcements and supplies, thus enabling the Allies to maintain the momentum of the invasion. Bradley could then take a measure of reassurance in the knowledge that at Omaha, in spite of D-Day bloodletting and the slippage in scheduled unloading, there were five regiments ashore at dawn on June 7. German artillery fire was still falling on the beach, but the German 352nd Infantry Division had been hard hit, and conditions were improving. To the west, Utah Beach seaborne and airborne forces had established contact.[2] The major concern of the senior commanders, however, was that German counterattacks might prove disastrous to the shallow American beachheads, particularly since they were not yet linked. Montgomery and Bradley discussed this point early the morning of the seventh, the former having sailed across the Channel late D-Day to set up a shipboard headquarters. *(See Map 55, in Atlas.)* The result was a change in plans whereby instead of concentrating on quickly cutting the Cotentin Peninsula, the VII Corps would seize Carentan and link up with V Corps forces, attacking westward from Omaha Beach. Eisenhower confirmed this decision later in the day during an off-shore tour by boat, at which time the enthusiastic boat commander managed to run his craft aground on a sandbar.[3]

Trained and accustomed to command, the senior leaders found June 6 and 7 to be frustrating days. They were chafing to get ashore and assume more active direction of overall operations. Like the ship carrying Eisenhower, the one transporting Montgomery went aground on D+1. He later recalled the incident:

> I was on the quarter deck with an A.D.C., and I sent him up to the bridge to ask if we were going to get any closer to the shore. This was not well received by the captain. Meanwhile, the facts were being explained to me on deck by the first lieutenant. When he told me we were aground I am reported to have said: "Splendid. Then the captain had got as close in as he possibly can. Now what about a boat to put me on shore?"[4]

Bradley was more successful later that same day, making the first leg of the trip in a Landing Craft, Mechanized (LCM) and then shifting to a DUKW (amphibious 2.5 ton truck) which put him ashore on Utah Beach. While he was there, two German fighter aircraft strafed the area. Everyone sought shelter—everyone, that is, except Bradley, who continued to walk around. American antiaircraft guns managed to down one of the planes.[5]

By the end of D+1, the overall status of the invaders looked better, but the situation was still serious in the American sector where the advance had not penetrated as deeply as in the British zone. More obstacles had been cleared and the snipers were less effective, although German artillery fire still reached the beach area. Many units were disorganized and the unloading of supplies was but 25 percent of that planned. Moreover, there were serious shortages in tanks, artillery, mortars, and automatic weapons. Still, as would become clear later, troop reinforcements were coming ashore faster than the Germans could shift reserves.[6]

While Bradley was visiting Omaha Beach on the next day (June 8), leaving in his wake several awe-stricken soldiers surprised to see him there, the American offensive to link the two beaches was underway. The task fell to elements of the 101st Airborne Division, driving on Carentan essentially across a single, well-defended causeway, and the 175th Regimental Combat Team of the 29th Infantry Division, attacking to the west from Omaha Beach. *(See Map 55, in Atlas.)* It was not an easy task, particularly for the paratroopers, who were largely canalized and vigorously opposed. Rommel, considering Carentan very important, charged its defenders accordingly and ordered the 17th SS Panzer Grenadier Division to move up from the vicinity of Tours. Elements of two American forces established contact northeast of Carentan on June 10; two days later, after a fierce fight, the 101st Airborne Division took Carentan and then dug in for the expected counterattack. Coming on the thirteenth and delayed by the difficulties the *panzer* grenadiers had in moving to the area, the counterattack almost dislodged the defenders who tenaciously held on the edge of town, admirably supported by naval gunfire and an armored division combat command which had been diverted from Omaha Beach. The link between beaches was tenuous, but it existed.[7]

To the east, the Americans made greater gains in the first few days after the landing. *(See Map 55, in Atlas.)* The 1st and 2nd Infantry Divisions, striking south out of the Omaha beachhead, slowly but steadily advanced through the difficult hedgerow country. Infantrymen from the 29th Infantry Division broke through to link up with the Rangers at Pointe du Hoc on June 8, and the next day, elements of the 1st Infantry Division made contact with British forces just to the west of Bayeux. On the eleventh and twelfth, the Allies, not realizing how weakly held the sector was, came close to rupturing the middle of the line at Caumont. Because Rommel accorded priority to the Carentan area, the Germans could only provide a reconnaissance battalion to defend the gap at Caumont. Just to the east, however, the British thrust was stopped, and the Americans, leery of the long anticipated counterattack, exercised caution. Hindsight reveals a clearer picture and the great opportunity which commanders on the spot, operating in the heat of war, were not privileged to know. Moreover, mindful of his major mission to cut the Cotentin and seize Cherbourg, Bradley called off the southward push toward St. Lô on June 13.[8]

In their zone, British and Canadian forces, fighting in terrain more open and favorable than the hedgerow country, took Bayeux and deepened the bridgehead everywhere. The Germans, however, concentrated what armor they could against Lieutenant General Miles Dempsey's divisions and resisted stubbornly. In the Caen area, Montgomery decided to dig in, reinforce, and then attack in overwhelming strength. Dempsey prepared a plan to envelop the city, but when he learned on June 12 of German preparations for a counterattack, he suspended his offensive and prepared to blunt the enemy thrust. So concerned was he that he told Lieutenant General J. T. Crocker, commanding the I British Corps, to mass his armor south of Douvres on high ground. "This bit of ground is the heart of the British empire," Dempsey said, "Don't move your armour from there!" He did not know that the previous evening the Royal Air Force had bombed the headquarters of the *panzer* unit which was to conduct the attack. As the German commander had not operated in a theater where his enemy had air dominance, he had neglected to camouflage his vehicles. Following the raid, the commander and what was left of his unit were withdrawn to Paris. A German attack ultimately was launched against Dempsey's troops, but it was weak and was easily contained.[9]

Meanwhile, as the combat divisions fought their way inland, the build-up of supplies on the beaches was slowly gaining momentum and the artificial harbors were being built. Among the troops landing in France there were many black

Lieutenant General Miles Dempsey

units, including artillery, port engineer, amphibious truck, ordnance ammunition, quartermaster service, and medical ambulance organizations. As the battle progressed, black artillery units would serve under white artillery group headquarters, while white units would work for the black group headquarters. Perhaps, in the heat of combat, some of the problems which had been evident in England could be forgotten.[10]

Across these beaches, on June 12, Eisenhower escorted the American Chiefs of Staff (Generals George C. Marshall and Henry H. Arnold and Admiral Ernest J. King). These high ranking dignitaries were on a trip to Europe to visit the battle zone. After a lunch of C-rations and biscuits at Bradley's headquarters, they talked to senior commanders and briefly toured part of the American sector. Undoubtedly relieved when the distinguished guests departed without mishap and set sail for England, the American field commanders returned to the task of directing operations against a German command which was desperately trying to piece together a defensive front which would hold.[11]

The View from the German Side

By D+2, Field Marshals Rundstedt and Rommel were convinced that the Allied invasion was a full-fledged and dangerous attack, if not necessarily the main assault. The captured American orders gave them something of the same advantage ULTRA provided the Allies and enabled more intelligent shifting of troops to critical points. The captured plans also gave Rundstedt some leverage to use on Hitler, who reluctantly agreed to release 17 divisions earmarked for Case Three, the plan under which German reserves would move to counterattack an invasion attempt. Rundstedt also ordered the use of a new code system on the assumption that the Allies had broken the *Wehrmacht* field code, which they had. While high level ULTRA information continued to reach Allied intelligence agencies, this code change snuffed out what had been an excellent lower level source of information.[12]

Allied leaders soon learned through ULTRA of Hitler's release of reserves and of orders to assemble them in Normandy. Knowing the necessity of using every means to discourage this assemblage of forces, they redoubled the deceptive measures, making everything point to an imminent invasion of the Pas de Calais. A valued double agent, for example, dutifully reported that Patton himself had said that the time was ripe to invade that area of France. This multiplicity of effort was really directed at one mind—that of Hitler. If he could be made to believe that a large force would soon land in the Pas de Calais, perhaps he would rescind the orders to move the reserves. As it turned out, the Allied scheme worked. At his midnight conference on June 9, the *Fuehrer* ordered the divisions en route from the Pas de Calais to be halted and the Fifteenth Army to be reinforced. When Rundstedt and Rommel learned of this order they realized that Germany was destined to lose the battle of the beachhead. Contrasted to the gloomy German reaction was the elation felt in London when Allied leaders learned via ULTRA that FORTITUDE had succeeded and that Hitler had cancelled Case Three.[13] Freed by this stroke of good fortune from having to contend with sizable reinforcements, the Allies could concentrate their devastating aerial attacks on those German forces closer to the battle zone.

Black Gun Crew in France

Air superiority proved to be an invaluable Allied asset in the early days of the invasion. Although ULTRA intercepts could reveal that Rommel had ordered troops to move from Brittany to the Cotentin or that armored units were to mass near Caen, it was airpower, combined when appropriate with naval gunfire, which took a heavy toll of units on the move and in assembly areas. When German reinforcements did arrive at the front, often tattered and torn by air attacks and in jumbled order due to the destruction of rail junctions and bridges, they usually were committed piecemeal to hold key positions (e.g., Caen which controlled the land communications link with the Fifteenth Army). Allied bombing, however, was not confined to bridges, railroads, roads, and units on the move; enemy night-fighter bases and early warning facilities were hit as well. Loss of these facilities would have a major effect on the air war over Germany, for if the American bombers had previously been winning their portion of the war, German night- fighters had been exacting such a heavy toll of the British bombers that Allied leaders were concerned. By the fall of the year, after the bombing of key facilities had taken effect, the night situation was much improved.[14]

The tremendous effect of Allied airpower on the German ability to resist is summed up in a sentence which appears in the report "Experiences from the Invasion Battles of Normandy," which Rundstedt submitted on June 20. He wrote:

> Within 2½ days, at a depth from the enemy bridgehead of about 65 miles, 29,000 enemy sorties were counted; of these, about 2,300 aircraft a day divebomb and strafe every movement on the ground, even a single soldier.[15]

In spite of the Allied air attacks, however, Rundstedt continued to plan counterattacks and to attempt to carry them out. An assault which would strike the Allied boundary, divide the national forces, and defeat them in detail was ordered, but it was cancelled when those forces which were to be in the attack, to include *panzer* units, had to be committed piecemeal. As had been the case near Caen, counterattacks started in other areas made little progress because the Allies simply had too much overall ground and air power.[16]

German commanders, although their plans were repeatedly frustrated, continued to counterattack as reinforcements trickled into the battle area. The travails of the 2nd SS Panzer Division, which took 12 days to traverse 350 miles, typifies the difficulties which had to be overcome. At the outset of the invasion, this division was located in a dispersed posture in the south of France, where it was carrying out operations against the French Resistance Movement. *(See Map 53, in Atlas.)* While its tanks were being loaded onto rail cars, the marshalling yard was bombed. Departure of the wheeled convoy was delayed by French citizens who were excited about the invasion and were elated to be seeing the last of the occupiers. Even though advance patrols preceded the convoy, attacks by resistance fighters and air strikes they called in frequently interrupted the movement. So frustrated did the SS troopers become that in a bestial display in the village of Oradour-sur-Glâne, they executed the men, then herded the women and children into the church and set it afire. In all, 642 French civilians died. After a four-day delay in loading, the rail convoy set out, but when it reached the Loire River all bridges but one had been closed by air strikes and the lone remaining structure was in such bad shape that the rail cars had to be towed across one at a time. By the time the division arrived at its destination it had suffered significant materiel damage and had lost about 4,000 dead and 400 captured.[17]

Allied naval gunfire also figured prominently in the early stages of the campaign. As there was but a slight German naval threat, a large proportion of the naval firepower could be devoted to supporting the ground troops. German observers were amazed at the range of the large naval batteries. A concentration of armor, some 17 miles inland from Sword Beach, for example, was broken up by shells fired by the *Rodney*, a British battleship. Both Rundstedt and Rommel remarked on the effectiveness of Allied naval gunfire. So devastating was it that on June 11 Rommel reported to Hitler, " . . . the effects of heavy naval bombardment are so powerful that an operation either with infantry or armoured formations is impossible in an area commanded by this rapid firing artillery."[18]

Considering the weight of Allied airpower, the ingenious fixing of much German strength in the Pas de Calais area, and the inevitable uncertainties of the battlefield, it appears that in simply giving ground slowly in Normandy, German troops performed extremely well. Their leaders, however, knew that wars are usually not won by the side which gives way slowly. Their attempts to improve this situation by using troops in the Pas de Calais seem to have been dominated by the spectre of Patton's army group poised for invasion. Generalmajor Treusch von Buttlar, Chief of Army Operations at OKW, recalled shortly after the war that reports on June 9 indicated that less than 20 percent of the Allied combat troops then believed to be based in England had been committed. In addition to this potential threat, another large force known to be in North Africa could probably be landed in southern France. These were only some of the thoughts which, with each passing day, caused Rundstedt to grow more and more frustrated. Why, he felt, should the Allies run the risks of launching other invasions if the first was going well? Militarily, it seemed better to reinforce success. Yet all his requests for significant transfers from Fifteenth Army were denied due to the hazy situation and Hitler's obsession. Almost every evening, Field Marshal Wilhelm Keitel, Chief of OKW, called *OB West* to reiterate the need for keeping Fifteenth Army up to strength and full alert.[19]

Allied Gains and German Frustration

With a linked beachhead relatively well established by June 13, Eisenhower's divisions now concentrated on carving out a lodgment area which could accommodate the landing of more troops and supplies and facilitate a breakout leading to a war of maneuver. The Germans had lost the battle for Carentan, but they were still capable of using the difficult terrain to make the seizure of Cherbourg and St. Lô expensive; and in front of Caen, the third major Allied objective, they were not incapable of reacting violently to Montgomery's offensive sallies. As noted above, on the thirteenth, Bradley shifted the American effort to the Cotentin, going essentially on the defensive on the St. Lô front.

On June 14, Major General J. Lawton Collins' VII Corps launched the attack which ultimately culminated in the capture of Cherbourg. *(See Map 58, in Atlas.)* The 9th Infantry Division, replacing the 90th Infantry Division which had had trouble making progress, had the mission of separating the Cotentin Peninsula from the rest of Normandy while the 82nd Airborne Division provided flank protection to the south. Mounted on narrow fronts with reserves in depth, the attack went well in spite of the difficult *bocage* country; the 9th Division reached the coast on June 18, and then turned north to join other elements of the VII Corps in the drive on Cherbourg. Meanwhile, Major General Troy H. Middleton's VIII Corps had become operational on June 15 and assumed responsibility for protection of the south flank. While Collins moved north to seize the important port, Middleton was to attack to the south to keep pressure on the Germans and to gain more favorable terrain (drier, less swampy) from which later attacks could be

A Mulberry Harbor Under Construction

U.S. Mulberry After the Storm of June 19-22, 1944

launched. As it turned out, a Channel storm so disrupted the logistical situation that Middleton's attack was cancelled in order to give Collins priority on the limited amount of supplies.[20]

On the morning of June 17, strong winds began to blow from the northeast, heralding the onset of a storm which came as a surprise and raged until June 22. Portions of the Mulberries, then under tow across the channel, were lost, and by noon unloading over the American beaches had practically ceased. Two British and two American divisions aboard ship could not land; the unhappy soldiers had to ride out the storm aboard the tossing transports. By the end of June 20, the Mulberry at Omaha Beach was beginning to come apart; when the storm ended two days later, it was in a shambles. (Because naval experts concluded that reconstruction was not feasible and had also discovered that LSTs could beach successfully, the artificial port was not rebuilt; replacement sections were shifted to the British Mulberry which had not suffered as much damage.) The storm tossed about 800 small ships and landing craft onto the beach above high-tide level; about 500 were destroyed.

With Allied aircraft restricted in operations during the storm, Eisenhower felt that the time was ripe for a German counterattack. However, none came. Enemy failure to capitalize on the act of nature can be attributed to several causes. Transportation arteries had been so devastated before the storm that reinforcements, although they were now free from the threat of air attack, were slow in arriving in Normandy. Even more important was the fact that the Germans did not really understand the Allied supply situation and the seriousness of the effect of the storm. The peak of enemy air activity, however, did occur on the night of June 19 when 116 German aircraft flew sorties over beaches and shipping lanes. Damage was minimal. When the storm finally ended, Bradley assessed the cost as being much greater than that which had been suffered on D-Day. Nevertheless, even without the Mulberry, by June 26 Omaha facilities were discharging cargo across the beaches at a rate greater than had been planned.[21]

In spite of the tremendous damage done in the storm, the Allies were able to compensate for the destruction, demonstrating once again the deep reservoir of logistical support on which Eisenhower could rely. The Supreme Commander, who was in his quarters in England when he heard of the onset of the storm, ordered a stiff scotch and water before inquiring into the destruction. He was able to reflect after he later visited the beach area:

> There was no sight in the war that so impressed me with the industrial might of America as the wreckage on the landing beaches. To any other nation the disaster would have been almost decisive; but so great was America's productive capability that the great storm occasioned little more than a ripple in the development of our buildup.[22]

Stagg, the British weatherman, reminded the Supreme Commander that had the invasion been postponed for 14 days, as Eisenhower had considered doing, D-Day would have been scheduled during the storm. Another postponement would no doubt have resulted, moving the invasion into July. Not only would a large number of good campaigning days have been lost, but the invasion force would have had to cope with the barrage of V-1 buzz-bombs which began to fall on the night of June 12. Had the Germans been able to turn these bombs against the ports full of invasion craft rather than on London, the effect could have been disastrous. The appropriateness of Eisenhower's note of June 23 to Stagg, ". . . thank the gods of war we went when we did!" is obvious.[23]

Given supply priority, the divisions of the VII Corps closed rapidly on Cherbourg. By the evening of June 21 they were up against the ring of strong field and permanent fortifications designed to protect the city. His superiors had repeatedly given Generalleutnant Karl Wilhelm von Schleiben orders to hold Cherbourg to the last. Indeed, Hitler had personally forbade withdrawal or evacuation. His shortage of field units and the length of his front, however, prevented Schleiben from fighting an effective delaying action back to his ring of fortifications. Perhaps partially for that reason, both Rommel and Hitler sent him messages of encouragement which were intercepted by ULTRA. Hoping that the German commander would consider alternatives, Collins broadcast an ultimatum to the defenders in German, Russian, Polish, and French, indicating that if the garrison did not surrender by 9:00 A.M., June 22, it would be annihilated. When the time came and went, Collins launched his assault.[24]

Preliminary to the ground attack, the IX Bomber Command (medium bombers) pounded the German positions in an attempt to demoralize the defenders. This massive air strike, begun with 20 minutes of fighter runs and followed by waves of medium and fighter bombers, did not wipe out the enemy defensive works, but it did adversely affect his will to resist. Unfortunately, some fighter bombers hit friendly troops due to misidentification, and for the rest of the war some elements of the 9th Infantry Division were hesitant to use friendly air support. Bradley, impressed by the air attack, worked far into the night on the application of saturation bombing to other problems that faced First Army.[25]

Collins's ground assault made progress slowly, finally penetrating the main defensive belt on June 26. Key positions, including the citadel of Fort du Roule which was situated on dominating terrain, however, were still in German hands. Coastal guns (180-mm) positioned at the fort could fire on both land and sea targets. Bradley asked for naval support, and even though the German batteries outranged those on board the ships, a fleet of three battleships, four cruisers, and eleven destroyers was detailed for the job. On June 25, under their covering fire, as well as that of field artillery, Collins attacked with all three divisions of VII Corps. Members of the French Resistance, who knew how to get through the fortifications, also assisted. Although the ships had to withdraw shortly due to enemy fire, infantrymen were able to climb up the cliffs at Fort du Roule and enter its defenses. By the evening of the twenty-fifth, the situation of the defenders was critical. On the twenty-sixth, Schlieben and 800 of his men were taken, and the next day the city fell. With its capture, the main OVERLORD objective of First Army had been accomplished. As soon as the diehards holding out on both sides of Cherbourg were defeated, Bradley could concentrate his efforts on the attack on St. Lô.[26]

Soon after Cherbourg was taken, the Americans captured an Axis agent who was transmitting from the city. As he was caught with his codes and schedules of broadcasting, his captors allowed him to continue his transmissions, knowing that German controllers would query him. This agent and others found later were used to deceive the Germans concerning Allied intentions. Moreover, by analyzing the questions asked, Allied intelligence experts could deduce much concerning German plans.[27]

When the mop-up operation terminated on June 30, engineers as well as naval representatives were studying the damage that the Germans had done to the port. Colonel Alvin G. Viney, responsible for the first rehabilitation plan, observed: "The demolition of the port of Cherbourg is a masterful job, beyond a doubt the most complete, intensive, and best planned demolition in history."[28] Mines of many types, including one with a new pressure device which was very difficult to sweep, had been sown throughout the harbor. These new mines could be set to explode after the pressure exerted by the passing of from one to twelve ships had been sensed—thus, twelve minesweeping passes were needed. Location of the minefields, obtained from captured German officers, was sent to minesweepers waiting off shore via a wooden sailboat which would not detonate magnetic mines and had too shallow a draft to hit other types. Many sunken ships and piles of masonry, which had been blown into the water, further restricted the movement of ships. Loading cranes were destroyed. Although he had been captured, the man responsible for the port destruction, *Konteradmiral* Walther Hennecke, was awarded the Knight's Cross by Hitler. It would be July 16 before the first cargo was landed across the beach, and August before large supply ships could unload onto the docks.[29]

The inability of the Germans to delay the capture of Cherbourg for any length of time was symptomatic of the frustration felt in German high command circles. Beginning shortly after the invasion, commanders in France, and even some senior military officials in Berlin, urged the acceptance of the risk of attack in the Pas de Calais and southern France sectors in order to concentrate forces in Normandy. Hitler, however, would not allow any significant troop transfers from the Fifteenth Army, although he did order a two-division SS *panzer* corps to move from the eastern front to France. Another *panzer* division was to come from Norway and, as noted above, the 2nd SS Panzer Division would move up from the south of France. Such moves were deemed to be inadequate by Rundstedt and Rommel, who wanted Hitler's approval to move any of their units they saw fit, even if it meant that at times withdrawals would have to be made. Hitler's philosophy, nurtured in Russia, dictated that all territory must be held and that no fallback positions could be prepared.

Feeling that an explanation of their position made to a senior OKW official might result in the granting of more authority, the field marshals requested that a meeting be held in France. Word came back that Hitler himself would attend. Rommel proposed that the conference convene at his headquarters. He is alleged to have planned to ask once again for the use of troops from Fifteenth Army and, if denied, to arrest the *Fuehrer*. Whatever the truth of the assertion, the opportunity did not materialize, for Hitler declined to meet at Rommel's command post, selecting instead *Wolfsschlucht II*, a concrete bunker located northeast of Paris at Margival and optimistically built in 1940 for use during the projected invasion of England. Later Hitler had said that at the time of an Allied invasion he would use the bunker and another to fight the battle for France. This, however, was the first time that the headquarters had been used. Hitler was accompanied by Jodl, Chief of the OKW Operations Staff, while Rundstedt and Rommel brought their respective chiefs of staff, Blumentritt and Speidel.[30]

The meeting began early the morning of June 17. Hitler, who appeared to be tired and ill, sat on a stool during the conference; both field marshals, never invited to sit, remained standing. They described the situation in detail to their leader and then outlined their recommendations. Rundstedt later recalled that they proposed that as the invasion had succeeded and the enemy could no longer be expelled, the German defense line should be shortened by the evacuation of southern France. Army Group B would be on the right and Army group G on the left on a line along the Seine and the upper Loire to the Swiss border. Behind this shortened and continuous front, reserves could be amassed and rearward positions constructed. This would permit a more flexible defense and the launching of counterattacks as appropriate.

Hitler responded by equating retrenchment ideas with defeatism. If troops such as those in the Cherbourg area were surrounded, they were to continue the battle in strongly defended positions called fortresses. These fortresses would fix the enemy units that were needed to attack them. While Rommel said that he thought the fortresses served no purpose, his remark fell on deaf ears. (Garrisoning the cities in the West that Hitler declared to be fortresses later cost the German army 200,000 troops and their equipment.) Hitler stressed the impact that the V-weapons and jet fighters would have on the battle. He felt that Rundstedt and Rommel could perform their mission with the resources they had available. Both field marshals, however, believed that political overtures should be made toward the Allies, and when Rommel remarked that Hitler should end the war, Hitler interrupted and said, "Don't you worry about the future course of the war, but rather about your own invasion front."[31]

Begun at 9:00 A.M., the meeting ended at 4:00 P.M. The only break was for lunch. Hitler took a number of pills and several types of medicine, and ate a dish of vegetables and rice—but only after the food had been tasted by another person. He was obviously concerned about his personal security, for the conference site was ringed with SS units and two SS men stood behind his chair throughout the meal. Both Rundstedt and Rommel wanted Hitler to see the front. German troops had learned of a trip made by Churchill; they thought a visit by Hitler would do much to raise morale. Also, the *Fuehrer* would get a better feel for the situation. Hitler planned to go, but later in the day several V-1s with defective steering mechanisms went east rather than west, and one crashed near the bunker. Although there were no casualties, the incident was enough for the already-concerned Hitler. With a heavy fighter escort, he flew back to Germany. After he arrived at Berchtesgaden he was heard to say, "Rommel has lost his nerve; he's become a pessimist. In these times only optimists can achieve anything."[32]

Virtually nothing had been accomplished at the conference, for Hitler had merely reiterated his earlier positions. The desire of his senior commanders to withdraw and the discussion of a political solution reinforced his distrust of the German officer corps. The one positive feature was soon nullified. Hitler had promised reinforcement for the Normandy front, particularly air units, but the Russian attack of June 23 against the German Army Group Center caused him to change his mind and send the reserves to the East.[33]

Rommel returned to his command post determined to do what he could to bring the war to a speedy end. He planned to have the larger SS units in the West engaged at the front on the day of the revolt being secretly planned by those in opposition to Hitler. That way they could not actively oppose it; as many army *panzer* units as could be spared would be held in reserve to counter any SS moves that did materialize. Once the fateful act was completed, Rommel would send six representatives through the lines to arrange an armistice and the subsequent withdrawal of German troops in the West. But before the coup was begun, Rommel wanted to see Hitler one more time. As it turned out, that meeting would take place near the end of the month, at a time when the British and Germans were engaged near Caen.[34]

As Rommel formulated his scheme, the war in the West continued. Commanders fought with what they had. On June 20, OKW ordered Runstedt to launch a counterattack with six *panzer* divisions toward Bayeux to split the beachhead. *(See Map 58, in Atlas.)* Although the storm spared the Germans from Allied air attacks for several days, only one of the divisions was ready. The others were either in contact in the line or had not yet arrived. In addition, insufficient ammunition was available to sustain such a large attack. Planning commenced, but it was disrupted by the British attack at Caen on June 25 to 26. Montgomery had temporarily relaxed his attempts to take Caen in view of strong German reactions, indicating that his purpose was equally well served if the British could draw German armor to the Caen area, thereby relieving pressure on U.S. forces. But now he renewed the drive, having planned the attack for the eighteenth and then postponed it because of the storm. Fierce *panzer* counterattacks stopped the British after an advance of five miles, but at a cost to the pending German offensive. When that attack came on June 29, it was made by only two *panzer* divisions. Due to an ULTRA intercept, the Allies learned of the location of the attack and that it was to begin at 7:00 A.M. Just before that hour, the 2nd Tactical Air Force struck. After a delay of seven hours, the German attackers finally moved, but they made only scant gains. As if the Germans had not suffered enough, on the previous day the commanding general of the Seventh Army, Generaloberst Friedrich Dollmann, had died of a heart attack. Generaloberst der Waffen-SS Paul Hausser, commander of the II SS Panzer Corps, was appointed to the command of Seventh Army.[35]

Neither Rundstedt nor Rommel was in France to follow the progress of the counterattack, for they had travelled to Berchtesgaden to meet with Hitler. Rundstedt had made the lengthy trip by automobile; after he had been kept waiting six hours past the appointment time, he remarked to Keitel that there should be no surprise if he, an old and sick man, should expire the same way as had Dollmann. The meeting on June 29 was attended by Hitler, Rundstedt, Rommel, Keitel, and Jodl. Both Rundstedt and Rommel briefed on the situation. Hitler remained adamant. All ground must be held; new planes, new weapons, and more troops would soon be on the way. The western commanders spoke again of a political solution, but Hitler gave no reply. He still expected a second invasion in the Pas de Calais area. Troops in Normandy had to prevent the Allies from exercising their advantage in mobility, because before long the German armored forces would have two attacks to repel. Thus, although in Normandy no large scale counterattack was now possible due to the Allied superiority in the air as well as to devastating effect that naval gunfire would have on such a move, the enemy had to be attrited and pushed back. Rundstedt and Rommel returned to France with none of their problems resolved. Once again Hitler had turned down all requests for either a political solution or a flexible defense. Rommel was determined that Hitler had to go. Rundstedt, although not privy to Rommel's intentions, was deeply concerned. After arriving at his headquarters, the commander of *OB WEST* had occasion to talk to Keitel on the telephone. When Keitel asked Rundstedt what he thought should be done about the German situation, the field marshal replied, "End the war, you fools!"[36] Hitler, of course, had no intention of doing that, continuing instead to place great hope in the new German weapons.

The Vengeance Weapons

German V-1s began to fall on London throughout the last half of June 1944. The first ten were launched on the night of June 12, and 244 were fired on the night of June 15. By the end of the month, 2,000 had been counted. Of these, 660 were knocked down and about 1,000 reached London. Although the death toll was but one per bomb launched, the psychological effect of the bombs was enormous. John Eisenhower, who was spending his West Point graduation leave with his father, arrived in London on June 13. The Supreme Commander had often said that he thought it a good idea to have a junior officer see how a major headquarters was run before he reported to his own unit. John later recalled that the Londoners found the V-1 onslaught hard to take; admittedly they had endured mcuh heavier losses during earlier enemy air raids, but those attacks had ceased. The Battle of Britain had been won, and the threat

V-1 Descending on London

from the air had seemingly been ended. Now when the putt-putt noise was heard—some said it sounded like an outboard motor, others, like a Model T Ford engine—an area would be hit, for even if the bomb were shot down, it exploded on impact. British troops in France and elsewhere were concerned for their loved ones, and Americans who had been billeted in England and who had made many friends worried about those they had left behind. By June 27, over 200,000 houses had been destroyed or damaged. The Home Minister expressed concern over the amount of window glass shattered and a fear that it could not be replaced before winter. If this situation materialized, much of England's labor force would become ill. Women, children, and the aged, as well as hospital patients, were evacuated from the target area, thus aggravating the already serious traffic control problem.[37]

Allied leaders were not surprised by the attack. Their intelligence sources had indicated that it would soon commence, and German controllers had told their most important agents to move out of London; but, nevertheless, Churchill and the War Cabinet were extremely concerned. They made every effort to lessen the aerial blow. Fast fighter aircraft were retained in England so that they could try to intercept the V1s; and antiaircraft weapons, then protecting the invasion forces from the *Luftwaffe*, were moved to counter the new threat. The senior British leaders even considered the retaliatory use of poison gas and bacteriological weapons, as well as the idea of bombing small German cities into obliteration. These ideas, however, did not get beyond the speculative atage.

Although by June 18 Churchill had told Eisenhower that London could take the damage and that the Supreme Commander should not change his overall strategic plan just to capture the V-1 launching sites, the Prime Minister asked that the bombing of the V-sites be put at the top of Eisenhower's target list. The Supreme Commander agreed, and stated that with the exception of support for the actual battle area, the suppression mission (Operation CROSSBOW) would take priority. Approximately 40 percent of the Allied bomber effort was used in this way, while the remainder supported the ground action, hit transportation targets, flew supply missions, trained for airborne drops, and bombed strategic targets deep inside Germany. The Allies also sent massive retaliatory raids against Berlin. Even though the strategic airmen felt that more of the effort, especially on days of good visibility, should be used on strategic targets, they wholeheartedly supported the CROSSBOW program. These bombings were of doubtful effectiveness because the Germans could build new sites faster than they could be destroyed by the numbers of airplanes employed in the operation. But—and this was important from the political and humane viewpoints—at least something was being done.[38]

Carving Out the Lodgment Area

After the capture of Cherbourg, the VII Corps became available to assist in Bradley's effort to gain suitable terrain from which to launch a breakout offensive. Before Cherbourg fell, Bradley had been working on plans for just such an offensive, which the Germans feared would be disastrous if successful because it would unhinge their line and allow the Caen

Hedgerow Fighting (Soldier is About to Fire a Rifle Grenade)

defenders to be attacked from the rear. *(See Map 58, in Atlas.)* But before any such grand plan could be implemented the divisions of the U.S. First Army had to drive south, off the marshy Carentan plain, and reach terrain suitable for mechanized warfare. That meant more fighting through the discouraging hedgerows and against German troops who, although lacking supplies, had surprisingly good morale and excellent terrain to defend.

Bradley's offensive to reach a suitable jump-off line for the coming major offensive got under way on July 3 with attacks by the VIII Corps on the western flank. *(See Map 59, page 000.)* Collins, who had been directed to be ready to attack with VII Corps five days after Cherbourg fell, joined in the offensive on the fourth, and a few days later the XIX Corps kicked off its attack in the vicinity of Lison. To celebrate the national holiday, Bradley ordered every artillery piece in the army, some 1,100, to be fired so that all rounds would impact on enemy targets at noon on the fourth. The salute was duly fired.[39] During this period Eisenhower was visiting the battle zone. He crossed the Channel in a P-51 Mustang, piloted by Major General Elwood R. Quesada, Commanding General of the IX Tactical Air Command, partially in order to have an opportunity to view the troublesome Normandy terrain. During the visit, Eisenhower's eagerness could have resulted in his capture. With but an aide and orderly for company, he took the wheel of his own jeep and proceeded to drive unknowingly behind enemy lines. Luckily nothing happened, and Eisenhower soon reached an American command post where he was told that he had been in German territory.[40]

The initial results of Bradley's offensive were disappointing to the senior commanders, who were becoming concerned about the growing strength of the German defenses. Everywhere the divisions of First Army met stubborn resistance. The Americans took heavy casualties and the gains were small. Moreover, the fighting in the hedgerows was turning into a grinding, slugging match. The author of the unit history of the 314th Infantry Regiment described the fighting:

> Over a stretch of such days, you become so dulled by fatigue that the names of the killed and wounded they checked off each night, the names of men who had been your best friends, might have come out of a telephone book for all you knew. All the old values were gone, and if there was a world beyond this tangle of hedgerows . . . you never expected to see it.[41]

This combat, apparently without end, had a deleterious effect on troop morale. Some men would do anything, even shoot themselves, to escape. The fact that morale was dipping was driven home to Eisenhower when he found in one of the hospitals in the lodgment area over 1,000 men who were there due to self-inflicted wounds.[42] In the heavy fighting then taking place, virtually anything which can give a force an edge was attempted. Psychological warfare was employed by both forces. For example, the psychological warfare officer of the 2nd Armored Division used a sound truck each evening to serenade the enemy with Strauss waltzes. He then spoke to the German soldier, reminded him of his prewar home, and concluded by saying:

> You have fought well and you have conducted yourself honorably before your countrymen. But there is no longer any reason for fighting. Our bombers have destroyed your cities. You are faced with overwhelming strength. Surrender now and return safely to the loved ones you left behind. If you don't surrender and come over we have no alternative but to give you more of this.[43]

The 2nd Armored Division Artillery then fired a 48-gun barrage into the German positions.

Although British forces continued to hold most of the German armor in the vicinity of Caen, Bradley's offensive forced Rommel to shift some *panzer* elements to the American sector. The tanks these troops were using, particularly the larger models, were giving First Army units considerable difficulty. American tank and antitank weapons (57-, 75-, and 76-mm guns, and 105-mm howitzers) could not penetrate the frontal armor of the 45-ton Mark V (Panther) tank. That model had not previously been encountered in Europe, but the Allies had met the 56-ton Mark VI (Tiger) tank in North Africa. Due to the limited maneuver area in the hedgerow country, it was difficult to move rapidly into firing positions to engage German tanks from the flank. Thus the speed and maneuverability of the 30-ton Sherman tanks of the Americans were largely negated by the terrain. On July 5, Eisenhower wrote Marshall to complain. A more powerful gun and better ammunition for the weapons already in use were needed quickly. The Supreme Commander noted that he understood that experimentation on new types of ammunition had been going on for quite some time. He concluded the letter to his boss by saying, "I cannot emphasize too strongly that what we must have now is effective ammunition at the earliest practicable date. We cannot wait for futher experimentation.:"[44]

The hedgerows also created problems for American tanks when used offensively. Perhaps because the Allies were optimistic about early success in the Caen area which would enable them to outflank the Cotentin Peninsula and make fighting there unnecessary, or perhaps due to neglect, no pre-invasion training had been conducted in hedgerow fighting; nor had techniques been developed to deal with special difficulties to be encountered. One such problem concerned tank vulnerability. When a tank climbed over a hedgerow, its lightly armored belly was exposed to enemy fire while its guns could not be depressed enough to provide protection. A member of a light tank unit, Sergeant Curtis G. Cullin, Jr., devised a sort of fork made of iron which could be attached to the front of a tank, thus enabling it to cut through a hedgerow rather than climb over it. A maintenance expert in Cullin's unit, the 102nd Cavalry Reconnaissance Squadron, worked on the technical aspects of the problem and built the fork out of salvaged iron bars which the Germans had used for beach obstacles. Soon the device was shown to the commanding general of the 2nd Infantry Division and Generals Gerow and Bradley. The latter immediately ordered that everything be done to equip as many tanks as possible with the device before the final breakout was attempted. (By the time that the attack would be launched, three of every five tanks which were to be involved had been modified.) Tankers also added sandbags to provide added protection against German shells. For his innovativness, Sergeant Cullin was awarded the Legion of Merit.[45]

Tanks and their problems were of great interest to the commander of the phantom 1st Army Group, Lieutenant General George S. Patton. On July 6, he appeared on the Continent. While his expertise might be helpful and his exposure to the battlefield conditions in Europe would aid him when he took over a part of the front with his Third Army, publicity concerning his presence in France could damage the carefully constructed deception plan. To insure that the secret did not leak, a First Army staff officer called the resident correspondents together and said: "I don't know whether any of you have seen what you took to be General Patton around here with his dog. You were mistaken. Good morning."[46]

But before too long Patton's army would be operational, and if the deception was to be preserved, a believable story concerning his transfer from the command of an army group to an army must be concocted. Eisenhower decided to make it known that Patton, due to his indiscretions, had been relieved from his army group and replaced by Lieutenant General Leslie J. McNair, commander of the Army Ground Forces and an officer who was well known to both friend and foe. A further leak would disclose that the next invasion had been delayed for a short time. This would preserve the deception, for if the date were left in doubt, the Germans would not have enough information to shift forces from the Pas de Calais with the certain knowledge that they could be returned before the McNair invasion was launched. In support of the Allied plan, McNair would be extremely visible and would travel about as if he were getting ready to move. At the same time, wood and canvas, or rubber, assault craft were put in place, rubber dummies were used to simulate a new tactical air force, and false radio traffic was aired. Reports of double agents reinforced the deception. The target date for the invasion was August 14.[47]

If the defense being mounted by German units seemed stiff to the Allied troops slugging it out on the line, the German higher commanders continued to be pessimistic. Upon their return to France from the June 29 meeting at Berchtesgaden, Rundstedt and Rommel had found Hitler's latest directive. It reiterated that units from Fifteenth Army could not be employed in the Seventh Army area. Available *panzer* divisions, accordingly, would have to be used to hold the line, thereby precluding their being massed for counterattack purposes.[48] The German commanders tried once more, however, to sway

Tank Equipped With Hedgerow Cutter

Hitler. A pessimistic estimate of the situation, prepared by the commanders of Seventh Army and Panzer Group West and endorsed by Rommel and Rundstedt, was forwarded to OKW on July 1. Once again they requested authority to withdraw and conduct a more flexible defense. Once again Hitler refused. But this report, although it gained nothing as far as the defensive philosophy was concerned, followed so close upon the meeting between Hitler and his generals that it brought differences to a head. On July 2, Hitler's adjutant came to Rundstedt's command post, presented the field marshal with the oak leaf to the Knight's Cross, and gave him a letter from Hitler in which Rundstedt was told that due to his age and health he was relieved of command. The commander of Panzer Group West was also replaced, and Rommel was supposed to have said, "I will be next."[49] In a postwar recollection, Rundstedt expressed surprise at his relief. His surprise is hard to believe, for twice within a period of a few days he had challenged the leadership of the *Fuehrer*. He had to go.[50]

Field Marshal Guenther von Kluge

On July 3, Generalfeldmarschall Guenther von Kluge assumed command of OB West. Kluge would face an Allied force which had already landed 929,000 men, 586,000 tons of supplies, and 177,000 vehicles; which had air and naval superiority; and which was pushing hard to force its way past the beachhead line that Hitler wanted so desperately to hold.[51] Initially, Kluge seemed sure that he could drive the invading forces back into the sea, but after completing a two-day inspection trip to the front, he began to appreciate the dire German situation. He came to sympathize with the conspiracy, and by the middle of July he and Rommel had agreed that when the time was ripe, fighting would cease and the British and American armies would be permitted to advance freely to the German border.[52]

As Bradley's offensive continued to meet stiff resistance, the commander of the First Army revised his thinking regarding seizing the Coutance-St. Lô-Caumont line as his prebreakout objective. *(See Map 50, in Atlas.)* It became clear that the cost in casualties to gain it would be prohibitive. Bradley, accordingly, began to contemplate the line Lessay-St. Lô as the objective, one which would still enable him to mass troops for the breakout. By July 13, after careful study of maps and discussions with subordinates, the idea had matured. The breakout plan, which would become Operation COBRA, was endorsed enthusiastically by Montgomery and Eisenhower. Meanwhile, there was still hard fighting ahead to gain even the newly designated line. St. Lô was a particularly tough nut to crack, extracting 11,000 casualties from the five divisions attacking the important communications center over a period of 12 days, before it finally fell on July 18.[53]

The difficult and costly fighting of the first two weeks in July led to reports hinting at stalemate and static war. Many who recalled the First World War were concerned lest the Normandy operation evolve into trench warfare. Eisenhower was determined this would not happen and encouraged his key subordinates in their offensives. This led to a delicate situation involving Montgomery, whose offensive at Caen in late June seems to have disappointed Eisenhower. His July 8 attack on that city also evoked disappointment. *(See Map 59, in Atlas.)* This offensive was preceded by a 470-heavy bomber attack which laid a 2,300-ton carpet, 4,000 yards wide and 1,500 yards deep. In addition, preparations were fired by ground and naval artillery. Due to weather conditions, the bombers went in early and the enemy had time to prepare for the ground attack. When it came, the attack was slowed, as the bombs used were 500- and 1,000-pounders, and the craters they made had to be filled in by bulldozers before the tanks could advance. By the time the attack stopped on July 9, however, all of Caen west of the Orne River was in British hands.[54]

Both Eisenhower, the Supreme Commander, and Montgomery, the temporary ground commander, had strong personalities. It was almost inevitable that there would be some misunderstandings, some disagreement between the two. Montgomery's use of the British Second Army in the attack on Caen is one aspect of the campaign which has been argued by participants and historians alike. Montgomery claimed that his intention was, and continued to be, to attack in such a manner that the mass of the German armor would be attracted to Caen and fixed there, thus enabling Bradley's First Army to move forward more rapidly. Tedder and others on Eisenhower's staff felt that Montgomery planned a British breakout, and that when he was not successful he fell back on his assertion that his attacks had been merely diversions. This disagreement was particularly evident in relation to Operation GOODWOOD, begun by the Second Army on July 18. *(See Map 59, in Atlas.)*

Tedder thought GOODWOOD would gain the space needed for Allied airfields, while Eisenhower believed it to be the eastern portion of a twin breakout offensive to be launched by the British Second and American First Armies. GOODWOOD was preceded by a naval gunfire preparation and another massive air carpet, which this time used fragmentation bombs in the sector to be traversed by armor. Montgomery's troops took that part of the city still in German hands, but they were halted short of a breakthrough after taking heavy losses in three days of tough fighting. Both Eisenhower and Tedder were disappointed with the results of the operation. Eisenhower wrote to Montgomery and urged him to be more aggressive.

It appears that a major part of the Eisenhower-Montgomery problem lay in a lack of understanding between the two men. While both were at fault, the ultimate responsibility in such situations lies with the senior officer. Complete concord between high level commanders of Allied nations, even if they both speak the same tongue, is inherently difficult. Eisenhower was reared in an American tradition wherein the subordinate commander is told what to do, then supported as he formulates his plan and carries it out. The British tradition, especially as it was practiced by Montgomery, called for much closer supervision. Thus Tedder, an Englishman, often urged Eisenhower to be more specific when the Supreme Commander wrote Montgomery to tell of his concern over the lack of progress. In this case, Bradley's coming COBRA breakout would nullify the incident, but there were to be more conflicts between Eisenhower and Montgomery before the war ended.[55]

If there were frustrations among Allied leaders regarding the July fighting, there was a much deeper sense of despair in the German command echelon. Within Hitler's restrictions, commanders attempted to move reinforcements into the battle area. Although the French had an excellent transportation system, it had been turned into a shambles both by Allied air strikes and forays of the French Resistance. During the hours of daylight in good weather, almost nothing moved for some 30 kilometers on the German side of the lines. In addition, when Allied aircraft were in the area, the use of German artillery markedly declined. Farther to the rear, a traffic jam of trains was formed on the Franco-German border, where an average of 1,800 trains were tied up. Special transportation procedures were instituted, but only 34 trains of a normal 210 were getting into the OB West area daily. Not only did this shortfall affect troop movements, but it also lowered the delivery of supplies. Men, however, can walk, and some marched all the way across France. As virtually no German air protected them, their morale had suffered greatly by the time they had finished their trek. Other replacements travelled by truck, but these motor movements cut deeply into the scant German gasoline stocks. Little in the way of gasoline resupply could be expected because not only was the rail distribution system in disarray, but Allied bombers which had been used to support the invasion were again striking the German fuel industry.[56]

On July 15, Rommel reported to Hitler that the situation was worsening each day. His casualty figures far exceeded the number of replacements arriving at the front. Due to shortages, the expenditure of artillery and mortar rounds was also being controlled. Rommel concluded that an Allied break-through must be expected at any time. It was late on this same day, the fifteenth, that American troops took the high ground which dominated the St. Lô-Périers road. On the seventeenth, without checking with higher headquarters, Rommel approved a request made by the Seventh Army commander to withdraw from St. Lô. Speidel, Rommel's chief of staff, told the army commander Hausser, "Just report to us afterward that the enemy penetrated your main line of resistance in several places and that you barely succeeded in re-establishing a new line to the rear."[57]

During a visit to the front on July 17, Rommel learned of the critical situation at St.Lô. While he was en route back to his headquarters, his car was attacked by several British fighter-bombers. Rommel's driver was killed and the field marshal suffered a skull fracture and concussion. He went home to Ulm to recover, and Kluge took over Army Group B while still retaining command of OB West.[58] A fellow conspirator and friend of Rommel wrote:

> The blow that felled Rommel on the Livarot road on 17 July 1944 deprived our plan of the only man strong enough to bear the terrible weight of war and civil war simultaneously, the only man who was straightforward enough to counter the frightful folly of the leaders in Germany. This was an omen which had only one interpretation.[59]

Rommel was injured only three days before the unsuccessful attempt on Hitler's life. When the fact that Rommel was involved in the conspiracy was discovered, Hitler's emissaries gave him the choice between trial for high treason and suicide. He took cyanide. Hitler ordered that he be given a state funeral as befitted a great leader who had died from wounds. Many others who were suspected of involvement died. Estimates of those killed ranged as high as 5,000, while some 20,000 went to concentration camps. Field Marshal Kluge, actually involved in the conspiracy, came under suspicion, but Hitler's agents took no action against him and he attended Rommel's funeral. When the turmoil died down, Nazis were in even better positions to control the armed forces as well as the government of Germany. Hitler, always, doubtful of the loyalty of his military subordinates, felt that he must personally take a more detailed interest in the fighting on all fronts. Restrictions on the prerogative of commanders would be even more stringent than

WACs Landing in Normandy, July 14, 1944

they had been previously, and in Germany the propaganda machine began an attack on the General Staff.[60]

As the last week in July arrived, troops and supplies continued to build up in the Allied beachhead. Soldiers were preparing to depart from England, and the billeting areas originally occupied by the invasion forces were filled and refilled. Bradley's aide observed during a trip to England that the "troops had gone but they had already been replaced by others and girls were simply hanging on to another set of arms in the same U.S. uniform."[61]

Some American women, members of the Women's Army Corps, began leaving England for the lodgment area. The first unit arrived on July 14. Their presence in France was proof of the resolution of a problem that had long been discussed. It was claimed that women should not go because, unlike nurses, they would not be given the privileges of officers if taken prisoner. Some even said that the effectiveness of the combat troops would be affected because they would be worrying so much about the safety of the female soldiers who were working in the rear area. But many staff officers protested that the women were needed to work in their offices on the Continent, and the women wanted to go. No evidence of an adverse effect on fighting effectiveness was observed, and more WACs went to the Continent.[62]

In the rear area where the WACs worked, many support installations had been erected. This was also the location of camps where prisoners of war were kept, pending evacuation from France. Among the prisoners were some Russians who had been fighting for the Germans. On July 13, several Russian generals came to First Army and visited the prisoners. At first they tried to say that no Russian would aid the Germans, but the Russians behind the wire were proof positive to the contrary. Then they spoke to a terrified prisoner who said that he had volunteered for a labor battalion to get out of a concentration camp; he had then been given a weapon and told to fight. A Russian general said that the prisoner was too weak to be a Russian and advised him not to return. They also questioned a captive German airborne captain. When asked what he thought would happen to Germany after the coming Allied victory, the captain said that he imagined his country would be divided into many small parts. In a serious tone, the Russian general said, "Not Germany, captain—Germans."[63]

Meanwhile, Bradley's troops were poised along the St. Lô-Périers line in readiness for their breakout attempt. Although the British Operation GOODWOOD, launched a few hours after Rommel was injured, had not achieved a break-through, two *panzer* divisions which were to have gone to the St. Lô area had been diverted to Caen, thus making Bradley's job a little easier. *(See Map 59, in Atlas.)* Moreover, the Germans had not been able to mount a single major counterattack. Admittedly, the Allies had only gained terrain to the line that they had expected to reach on D + 5, but men and equipment had flowed into the lodgment area at about the planned rate. The equivalent of 34 divisions was ashore. Many support units had also landed. Once a breakout was achieved, the Allies possessed the capability to make a rapid drive through France. Equally important, Hitler's Germany was also under intensive pressure on other European fronts. *(See Map 60, in Atlas.)*

On July 24, with a large beachhead area secure, the Normandy campaign officially ended. Operation COBRA would be next.

Notes

[1]Benjamin A Dickson, "G-2 Journal: Algiers to the Elbe" (Devon, Pa., n.d.), copy in Special Collections Division, U.S. Military Academy Library, p. 122; Charles B. MacDonald, *The Mighty Endeavor: American Armed Forces in the European Theater in World War II* (New York, 1969), pp. 281-282; Guenther Blumentritt, *Von Rundstedt: The Soldier and the Man* (London, 1952), p. 230.

[2]Omar N. Bradley, *A Soldier's Story* (New York, 1951), p. 278; Vincent J. Esposito (ed.), *The West Point Atlas of American Wars* (2 vols.; New York, 1959), II, Section 2, 49.

[3]Bernard Law Montgomery, *The Memoirs of Field Marshal the Viscount Montgomery of ALAMEIN, K.G.* (Cleveland, 1958), pp. 223, 225; Harry C. Butcher, *My Three Years with Eisenhower* (New York, 1946), pp. 568-573; Chester B. Hansen, "War Diary," Chester B. Hansen Papers, United States Army Military History Research Collection, Carlisle Barracks, Pa., entry of June 7, 1944; Alfred D. Chandler (ed.), *The Papers of Dwight D. Eisenhower: The War Years* (5 vols.; Baltimore, 1970), III: No. 1738, Eisenhower to Combined Chiefs of Staff, June 8, 1944 and editor's note accompanying No. 1739, p. 1918; Bradley, *Soldier's Story*, pp. 279-281; MacDonald, *Mighty Endeavor*, p. 283; Dwight D. Eisenhower, *Crusade in Europe* (Garden City, 1948), pp. 253-254; Stephen E. Ambrose, *The Supreme Commander: The War Years of General Dwight D. Eisenhower* (Garden City, 1969), p. 422. The Eisenhower Papers are herinafter referred to as *EP*.

[4]Quotation is from Montgomery, *Memoirs*, p. 226. Butcher, *Three Years*, p. 577, is an additional source.

[5]Hansen, "War Diary," entry of June 7, 1944; Bradley, *Soldier's Story*, p. 281.

[6]George M. Elsey, "Naval Aspects of Normandy in Retrospect" in *D-Day: The Normandy Invasion in Retrospect* (Lawrence, Kansas, 1971), p. 188; T. Dodson Stamps and Vincent J. Esposito (eds.), *A Military History of World War II* (2 vols.; West Point, N.Y., 1956), I, 388.

[7]Hansen, "War Diary," entry of June 8, 1944; Stamps and Esposito, *Military History*, I, 389-391; MacDonald, *Mighty Endeavor*, p. 284; Bradley, *Soldier's Story*, p. 282; Gordon A. Harrison, *Cross-Channel Attack* (Washington, 1951), pp. 357-364.

[8]Harrison, *Cross-Channel*, pp. 370-376.

[9]Dempsey is quoted in Chester Wilmot, *The Struggle for Europe* (London, 1952), p. 302; Also see: Stamps and Esposito, *Military History*, I, 391 and Ambrose, *Supreme Commander*, pp. 427-428.

[10]L. F. Ellis, *Victory in the West*, I, *The Battle of Normandy* (London, 1962), p. 263; Hansen, "War Diary," entry of June 12, 1944; Elsey, "Naval," p. 189; Ulysses Lee, *The Employment of Negro Troops* (Washington, 1966), pp. 592, 644, 654.

[11]Bradley, *Soldier's Story*, pp. 289-291; *EP*, III: No. 1754, editor's note, p. 1929; Eisenhower, *Crusade in Europe*, p. 254; Butcher, *Three Years*, pp. 578-579; Omar N. Bradley, Personal Interview conducted by Kitty Buhler, Omar N. Bradley Papers, U.S. Military Academy Library, p. 94; Forrest C. Pogue, *George C. Marshall: Organizer of Victory* (New York, 1973), pp. 395-396.

[12]Anthony Cave Brown, *Bodyguard of Lies* (New York, 1975), pp. 667, 680-681.

[13]*Ibid.*, pp. 681-687.

[14]Bodo Zimmermann, MS#B-308: "OB WEST, Atlantic Wall to Siegfried Line, A Study in Command," in *OB WEST (Atlantic Wall to Siegfried Line), A Study in Command*, James F. Scoggin, Jr. (ed.) (Allendorf, Germany, 1946-1947), I, 91-92; Alfred Goldberg, "Air Campaign OVERLORD: To D-Day," in *D-Day: The Normandy Invasion in Retrospect* (Lawrence, Kansas, 1971), p. 72; Stamps and Esposito, *Military History*, I, 392.

[15]Rundstedt's report is quoted in Arthur W. Tedder, *With Prejudice: The War Memoirs of Marshal of the Royal Air Force Lord Tedder G.C.B.* (Boston, 1966), pp. 578-579.

[16]Zimmermann, "OB WEST," I, 110; Zimmermann, "France, 1944," in Seymour Freidin and William Richardson (eds.), *The Fatal Decisions* (New York, 1956), p. 217; Blumentritt, *Rundstedt*, pp. 230-231.

[17]Fritz Ziegelmann, MS#B-022: *The Resistance Movement in France* (Headquarters United States Army Europe, 1946), p. 1; Wilmot, *Struggle for Europe*, pp. 305-306; MacDonald, *Mighty Endeavor*, p. 285.

[18]Elsey, "Naval," pp. 190-191 (Elsey quotes from Rommel's report); B. H. Liddell Hart (ed.), *The Rommel Papers* (New York, 1953), pp. 476-477; Liddell Hart, *The German Generals Talk* (New York, 1948), p. 244; Zimmermann, "France," p. 216; Tedder, *With Prejudice*, pp. 551-552.

[19]Treusch von Buttlar, MS#B-672: "Commentary on MS#B-308," in *OB WEST (Atlantic Wall to Siegfried Line), A Study in Command,* James F. Scoggin, Jr. (ed.) (Allendorf, Germany, 1946-1947), II, 42-44; Cave Brown, *Bodyguard*, p. 686; Blumentritt, *Rundstedt*, p. 229.

[20]Esposito, *West Point Atlas*, II, Section 2, 50; Stamps and Esposito, *Military History*, I, 393-394; Bradley, *Soldier's Story*, pp. 288-289, 298-299; Harrison, *Cross-Channel*, pp. 403-420.

[21]Stamps and Esposito, *Military History*, I, 394, 397; Bradley, *Soldier's Story*, pp. 296, 298-299, 302; MacDonald, *Mighty Endeavor*, pp. 288-289; *EP*, III: No. 1764, Eisenhower to Marshall and King, June 20, 1944; Montgomery, *Memoirs*, p. 231; Eisenhower, *Crusade in Europe*, p. 261; Friedrich Ruge, "German Naval Operations on D-Day: The Normandy Invasion in Retrospect," in *D-Day: The Normandy Invasion in Retrospect* (Lawrence, Kansas, 1971), p. 340; Harrison, *Cross-Channel*, pp. 422-426.

[22]Eisenhower, *Crusade in Europe*, p. 261.

[23]*EP*, III: editor's note with No. 1772, p. 1948; John S. D. Eisenhower, *Strictly Personal* (Garden City, 1974), p. 66; Bradley, *Soldier's Story*, p. 265.

[24]Gerd von Rundstedt, MS#B-633: "Commentary on MS#B-308," in *OB WEST (Atlantic Wall to Siegfried Line), A Study in Command,* James F. Scoggin, Jr. (ed.) (Allendorf, Germany, 1946-1947), I, 112; F. W. Winterbotham, *The Ultra Secret* (New York, 1974), p. 135; Bradley, *Soldier's Story*, pp. 301-303, 307; Stamps and Esposito, *Military History*, I, 394-397; Harrison, *Cross-Channel*, pp. 422, 428.

[25]Bradley, *Soldier's Story*, pp. 308, 309; Harrison, *Cross-Channel*, pp. 428-429; Stamps and Esposito, *Military History*, I, 394.

[26]Bradley, *Soldier's Story*, p. 312; Stamps and Esposito, *Military History*, I, 394; Elsey, "Naval," p. 191; Eisenhower, *Crusade in Europe*, p. 260; Hansen, "War Diary," entry of July 1, 1944; Harrison, *Cross-Channel*, pp. 434, 438; MacDonald, *Mighty Endeavor*, p. 289.

[27]Cave Brown, *Bodyguard*, pp. 730-731.

[28]Viney is quoted in Harrison, *Cross-Channel*, p. 441.

[29]Harrison, *Cross-Channel*, pp. 441-442; Butcher, *Three Years*,

pp. 596-598, 600; Stamps and Esposito, *Military History*, I, 394; Robin Higham, "Technology and D-Day," in *D-Day: The Normandy Invasion in Retrospect* (Lawrence, Kansas, 1971), p. 232; Esposito, *West Point Atlas*, II, Section 2, 50.

[30]MacDonald, *Mighty Endeavor*, pp. 285-286; Stamps and Esposito, *Military History*, I, 408; Buttlar, "Commentary," pp. 47-51; Cave Brown, *Bodyguard*, p. 705.

[31]Hitler is quoted in Hans Speidel, *Invasion 1944* (New York, 1968), p. 94; Harrison, *Cross-Channel*, pp. 411-413.

[32]Hitler is quoted in Albert Speer, *Inside the Third Reich* (New York, 1970), p. 458.

[33]Sources for the above five paragraphs are: Joachim C. Fest, *Hitler* (New York, 1973), p. 706; Speer, *Third Reich*, pp. 457-458; MacDonald, *Mighty Endeavor*, pp. 286-287; Ellis, *Normandy*, pp. 268-269; Harrison, *Cross-Channel*, pp. 412-413; Rundstedt, "Commentary," I, 112; Speidel, *Invasion*, pp. 89-95; Zimmermann, "OB WEST," I, 103; Zimmermann, "France," pp. 217-218; Friedrich Ruge, "The Invasion of Normandy," in Hans-Adolf Jacobsen and Jürgen Rohwer (eds.), *Decisive Battles of World War II: The German View* (London, 1965), p. 340; Peter Lyon, *Eisenhower: Portrait of a Hero* (Boston, 1974), p. 292; Liddell Hart, *Rommel Papers*, pp. 478-479; Esposito, *West Point Atlas*, II, Section 2, 50.

[34]Cave Brown, *Bodyguard*, pp. 706-707.

[35]MacDonald, *Mighty Endeavor*, pp. 289-290; Ruge, "Naval Operations," pp. 340-341; Ambrose, *Supreme Commander*, p. 431; Winterbotham, *Ultra*, p. 136; Harrison, *Cross-Channel*, pp. 444-445; Esposito, *West Point Atlas*, II, Section 2, 50.

[36]Rundstedt is quoted in Zimmermann, "France," p. 219; Harrison, *Cross-Channel*, pp. 445-446; Rundstedt, "Commentary," I, 115-117; MacDonald, *Mighty Endeavor*, pp. 290-291; Cave Brown, *Bodyguard*, p. 708.

[37]Bradley, *Soldier's Story*, p. 265; Wilmot, *Struggle for Europe*, pp. 317-318; Butcher, *Three Years*, pp. 582-583; J. Eisenhower, *Personal*, p. 58; MacDonald, *Mighty Endeavor*, p. 287; Eisenhower, *Crusade in Europe*, pp. 259-260; Cave Brown, *Bodyguard*, pp. 721-722.

[38]Sources for the above two paragraphs are: Wilmot, *Struggle for Europe*, p. 318; Lyon, *Eisenhower*, p. 292; Ambrose, *Supreme Commander*, pp. 442-444; *EP*, III: No. 1758, Eisenhower to Tedder, June 18, 1944; Tedder, *With Prejudice*, pp. 580-581; Butcher, *Three Years*, p. 588; Wesley F. Craven and James L. Cate (eds.), *The Army Air Forces in World War II*, Vol. III, *Europe: ARGUMENT to V-E Day, January 1944 to May 1945* (Chicago, 1951), p. 540; Cave Brown, *Bodyguard*, pp. 719-721, 725-727.

[39]Bradley, *Soldier's Story*, pp. 324-325; Hansen, "War Diary," entry of July 4, 1944.

[40]Hansen, "War Diary," entries of July 4-5, 1944; Butcher, *Three Years*, p. 604; Ambrose, *Supreme Commander*, p. 433.

[41]Quoted in Martin Blumenson, *Breakout and Pursuit* (Washington, 1961), p. 176.

[42]Cave Brown, *Bodyguard*, p. 713.

[43]Bradley, *Soldier's Story*, pp. 308-309.

[44]*EP*, III: No. 1791, Eisenhower to Marshall, July 5, 1944; editor's note with No. 1795, pp. 1970-1971; Blumenson, *Breakout*, pp. 44-45.

[45]*EP*, III: editor's note with No. 1794, p. 1969; Eisenhower, *Crusade in Europe*, pp. 268-269; Lida Mayo, *On Beachhead and Battlefront* (Washington, 1968), pp. 253-255; Blumenson, *Breakout*, pp. 206-207; MacDonald, *Mighty Endeavor*, p. 294; Bradley, *Soldier's Story*, pp. 341-342.

[46]The staff officer is quoted in Winterbotham, *Ultra*, p. 140; Hansen, "War Diary," entry of July 6, 1944; Blumenson, *Breakout*, p. 45.

[47]*EP*, III: No. 1803, Eisenhower to Marshall, July 6, 1944; No. 1814, Eisenhower to Smith, July 10, 1944; Cave Brown, *Bodyguard*, pp. 734-735.

[48]Cave Brown, *Bodyguard*, p. 708.

[49]Rommel is quoted in Harrison, *Cross-Channel*, p. 447.

[50]MacDonald, *Mighty Endeavor*, pp. 290-291; Ruge, "Naval Operations," p. 341; MacDonald, *Mighty Endeavor*, pp. 446-447.

[51]Harrison, *Cross-Channel*, p. 447.

[52]Cave Brown, *Bodyguard*, pp. 709-712. Peter Hoffmann, *The History of the German Resistance, 1933-1945* (Cambridge, Mass., 1977), p. 354, is less sure than Cave Brown that Kluge was so completely in agreement with Rommel, even if he was sympathetic.

[53]Bradley, *Soldier's Story*, pp. 294-295, 301-304, 309, 318-321, 329-332; Zimmermann, "OB WEST," I, 113-114; Hansen, "War Diary," entries of June 14, 24-25, 1944; *EP*, III: No. 1773, Eisenhower to Bradley, June 25, 1944; Stamps and Esposito, *Military History*, I, 393-399; Esposito, *West Point Atlas*, II, Section 2, 51.

[54]Eisenhower, *Crusade in Europe*, pp. 257, 263; Stamps and Esposito, *Military History*, I, 400; Esposito, *West Point Atlas*, II, Section 2, 51; MacDonald, *Mighty Endeavor*, pp. 292-293; Bradley, *Soldier's Story*, p. 339; Ambrose, *Supreme Commander*, p. 439.

[55]Sources for the above three paragraphs are: John Ehrman, *Grand Strategy*, V, *August 1943-September 1944* (London, 1956), p. 340; Esposito, *West Point Atlas*, II, Section 2, 50-51; Ambrose, *Supreme Commander*, pp. 428-429, 434-439; Tedder, *With Prejudice*, pp. 554, 557-563, 565-568; Eisenhower, *Crusade in Europe*, pp. 267-268; Bradley, *Soldier's Story*, p. 319; Stamps and Esposito, *Military History*, I, 399-400; *EP*, III: No. 1807, Eisenhower (E) to Montgomery (M), July 7, 1944; editor's note with No. 1807, p. 1983; No. 1813, E to M, July 10, 1944; editor's note with 1826, pp. 2002-2003; No. 1827, E to M, July 14, 1944; No. 1844, E to M, July 21, 1944; editor's note with No. 1844, p. 2019; Martin Blumenson, "Some Reflections on the Immediate Post-Assault Strategy," in *D-Day: The Normandy Invasion in Retrospect* (Lawrence, Kansas, 1971), pp. 204, 206-208, 211-213; MacDonald, *Mighty Endeavor*, pp. 296-297; Montgomery, *Memoirs*, pp. 226-229; Zimmermann, "France," p. 223.

[56]Stamps and Esposito, *Military History*, I, 400-403; Zimmermann, "OB WEST," I, 93-95; Speer, *Third Reich*, p. 449.

[57]Speidel's words appear in MacDonald, *Mighty Endeavor*, pp. 295-296; Liddell Hart, *Rommel Papers*, pp. 486-487.

[58]MacDonald, *Mighty Endeavor*, p. 296; Ruge, "Naval Operations," p. 344; Zimmermann, "OB WEST," I, 121-122.

[59]Juenger is quoted in Cave Brown, *Bodyguard*, p. 744.

[60]MacDonald, *Mighty Endeavor*, pp. 300-301; Stamps and Esposito, *Military History*, I, 400, 411; Cave Brown, *Bodyguard*, pp. 765-768, 799.

[61]Hansen, "War Diary," entry of July 9, 1944.

[62]Mattie E. Treadwell, *The Women's Army Corps* (Washington, 1954), pp. 385, 387-388.

[63]Hansen, "War Diary," entry of July 13, 1944.

[64]MacDonald, *Mighty Endeavor*, p. 298; Esposito, *West Point Atlas*, II, Section 2, 52; Stamps and Esposito, *Military History*, I, 402-403, 406; Cave Brown, *Bodyguard*, p. 744.

Planning and Implementing the Breakout: Operation COBRA

14

From the moment we started on OVERLORD planning, I was determined that we must avoid at all costs those pitfalls that might bog down our advance and lead us into the trench warfare of World War I. . . . to exploit [our] advantage in mobility it was essential that we break a hole through the enemy's defenses rather than heave him back. Only a breakout *would enable us to crash into the enemy's rear where we could fight a war of movement on our own best terms.*

*Omar N. Bradley**

On July 25, 1944, Omar Bradley launched his COBRA offensive, which had become the Allied bid to break out of the confining Normandy beachhead and restore maneuver to the battlefield. If the Allies were to exploit their tremendous advantage in mobile forces, they had to rupture the German defensive position, which stood roughly only at the planned D+5 line. *(See Map 53, in Atlas.)* Once this was done, a gigantic wheeling movement, pivoting on the British Second Army, could commence and lead first to the cutting off of the Brittany peninsula and the securing of its vital ports, and then to an advance to the Seine River and the Rhine beyond.[1]

During the exploration of strategies that could break the stalemate which seemed to be developing, SHAEF planners considered the use of amphibious and airborne forces to loosen up the German defenses and provide opportunities within the lodgment area. The resources required in ships, troops, and aircraft, however, made such alternatives (e.g., a landing on the Brittany peninsula) questionable at best; this became particularly clear in light of the potential of the earlier agreed-upon invasion of southern France. Thus the careful planning of a breakout from the Normandy area grew ever more important in Eisenhower's eyes as he sought to find a way to unleash the considerable combat power building up in the beachhead.

It was Omar Bradley, not SHAEF planners, however, who quietly worked away at the key plan while his First Army slugged its way through the hedgerow country. His concept, which he gradually expanded into the COBRA breakout plan, would lead to decisive results and the unhinging of the entire German defensive system in France.[2]

The Genesis of COBRA

Bradley conceived the outline of his plan in solitude. Since his operations maps filled the walls of the truck he used for his personal command post, he told his aide, Major Chester B. Hansen, to set up a planning tent nearby. There, sifting his thoughts of the past few weeks and working on a detailed map of the area with his colored pencils, he reduced his ideas to a broad concept suitable for discussion with subordinates. As noted previously,* Bradley settled for a jump-off position for the attack short of Coutances in the west. That position would need to be on dry ground, have suitable road nets on both sides of the line of contact to enable massing and later dispersing forces, be clearly discernible to airmen, and be in an area where German defenses were relatively weak. *(See Map 61, in Atlas.)* The St. Lô Périers line met these requirements and also would allow the maneuver units to exploit the ridge lines and valleys after the breakthrough to drive on Coutances.[3]

*Omar N. Bradley, *A Soldier's Story* (New York, 1951), pp. 317-318.

*See Chapter 13, p. 318.

Bradley experimented with various schemes of attack until he was satisfied. He chose "the nervy and ambitious Collins" to command the breakthrough,[4] envisioning that commander using his infantry to rupture the line and then mobile elements to exploit and seize objectives in the German rear. This maneuver would cut off German forces opposing Middleton's VIII Corps, get the Americans out of the difficult hedgerow country, and seize objectives which furthered sealing off Brittany. Although the Americans ultimately would convert COBRA into a decisive exploitation, it was originally designed to gain a limited terrain objective.[5]

In addition to artillery, Bradley's fire support plan placed great reliance on the use of both fighter and strategic bombers to lay a carpet of bombs. This not only would conserve artillery ammunition stocks, which were only slowly being built up, but would also capitalize on shock effect, as had been shown to be the case earlier at Cherbourg and Caen. He selected a 7,000 by 2,500 yard area, bounded on the north by the St. Lô-Périers road, for the carpet.[6]

Satisfied with his concept, Bradley first called in his deputy, Hodges, then his Chief of Staff, G3, and G2 to critique it. By July 12, he was ready to present it to his corps commanders. This would be an American show, and Bradley was naturally quite excited at the prospect. His aide recorded that the general said, "I've been wanting to do this . . . since we landed. When we pull it, I want it to be the biggest thing in the world. We want to smash right on through."[7]

Evolution of the Plan for COBRA

The First Army plan for COBRA consisted of three phases *(see Map: First Army Outline Plan, page 325)*. The object of the entire operation was to effect a "penetration of the enemy's defenses West of St. Lô by VII Corps and exploit this penetration with a strong armored and motorized thrust deep into the enemy's rear toward Coutances."[8] Collins' VII Corps would initiate the first phase on July 18, immediately after the carpet bombing, by making a three-mile breach and taking the towns of Marigny and St. Gilles. The second phase, or the exploitation, would begin when Collins ordered his one motorized and two armored divisions through the gap to seize Coutances, Brehal, and crossings over the Sienne River. Blocking positions to the south and east would also be established, and tactical air would destroy bridges around the perimeter of the operation. During the first two phases, the other American corps would also attack to hold Germans in position. In phase three, gains, including advances possible by the VIII and XIX Corps, would be consolidated along the Coutances-Caumont line, and the troops were to be ready to exploit German disorganization through further advances.[9]

In presenting the outline plan to his corps commanders on July 13, Bradley stressed that the operation must be bold and that by careful allocation of resources he would do all he could to ensure its success. In furtherance of this pledge, he gave VII Corps the only two armored divisions yet ashore, and transportation to motorize an infantry division. He also ensured that Collins used only combat-experienced divisions and that artillery support was weighted in favor of VII Corps. (Over 250 non-divisional pieces would fire in support of VII Corps, and that corps' artillery ammunition allocation for the five-day operation was 140,000 rounds, as compared to 27,000 for V Corps, for example.) In selecting Collins to implement the plan, Bradley was designating an aggressive commander in whom he had great confidence; they had served together before, were good friends, and worked together excellently as a team.[10]

Considering the short amount of time he had to prepare the important corps implementing plan, Collins had much work to do. His two breakthrough units, the 9th and 30th Infantry Divisions, were tired from previous fighting. When Major General Manton S. Eddy, commander of the 9th, complained of his width of front at a later planning conference, Bradley offered Collins the army reserve, the 4th Infantry Division. This swelled Collins' command to six divisions and made his corps virtually a small army. On the way back to his headquarters, Bradley remarked to his G3, "Gosh, I never thought I'd ever be in the position where I could give away a division so easily." This extra division gave Collins more flexibility in his planning.[11]

After studying the First Army outline plan, General Collins proposed modifications in the VII Corps part, particularly in the exploitation phase, which gave the plan a potential for greater results. *(See Map: VII Corps Modifications, page 326.)* In Bradley's plan, one armored division would encircle Coutances while the other penetrated to the coast and blocked German attempts to move reserves from the south or southeast; these divisions would be supported by the 1st Infantry Division. Collins accepted a greater risk of German movement of reinforcements to the area in order to seize Coutances promptly, emphasizing the quick defeat of enemy units facing VII and VIII Corps. Moreover, he left open a corridor on the west (between Cérences and the Gulf of St. Malo), not only to avoid a possible melée between VII and VIII Corps units but also to leave the opportunity for a spontaneous and greater exploitation to the south by VIII Corps. Under the modification proposed by Collins and accepted by Bradley, not only would Coutances be taken as Bradley desired, but the stage was also set for a more effective exploitation. Because in Bradley's

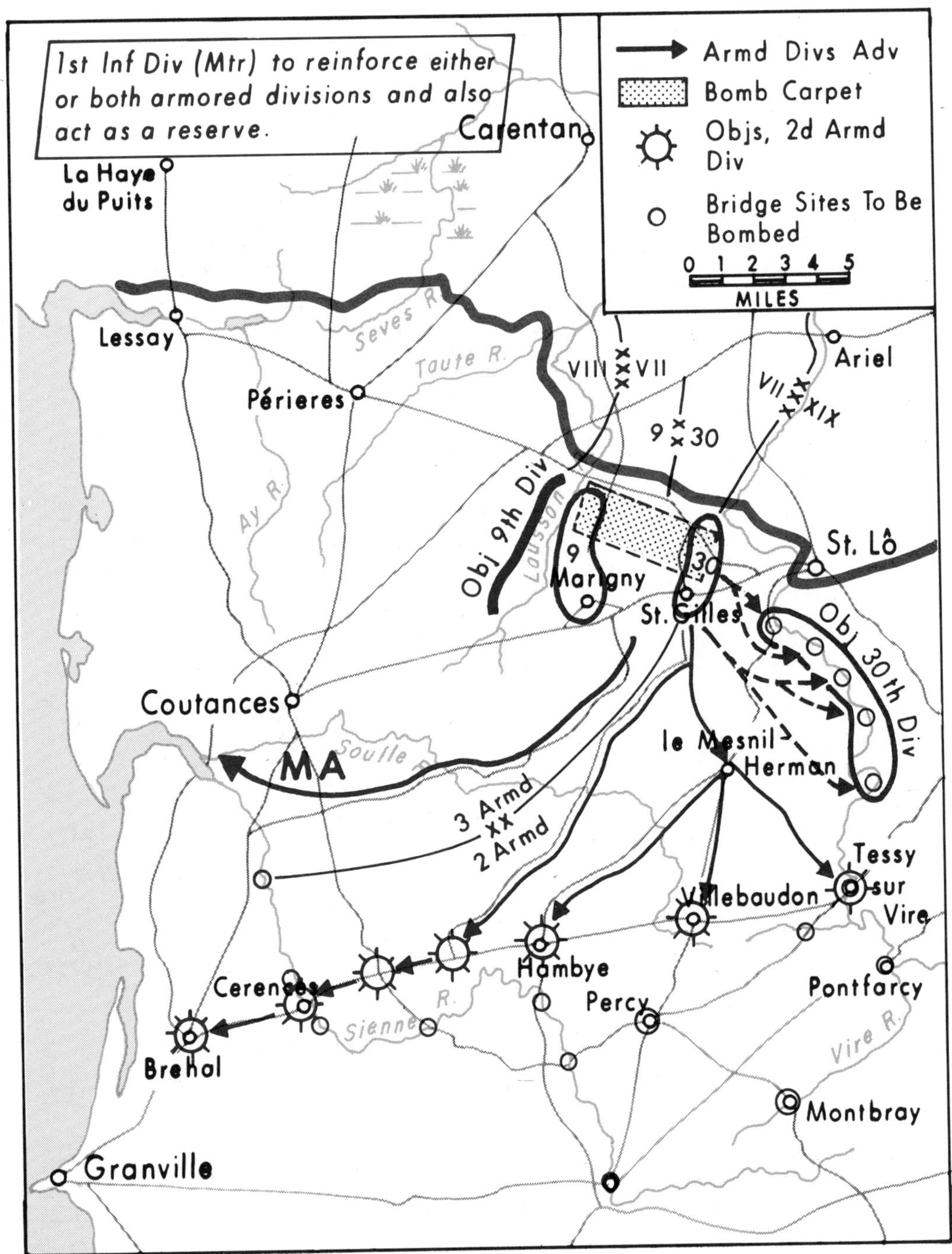

First Army Outline Plan for COBRA

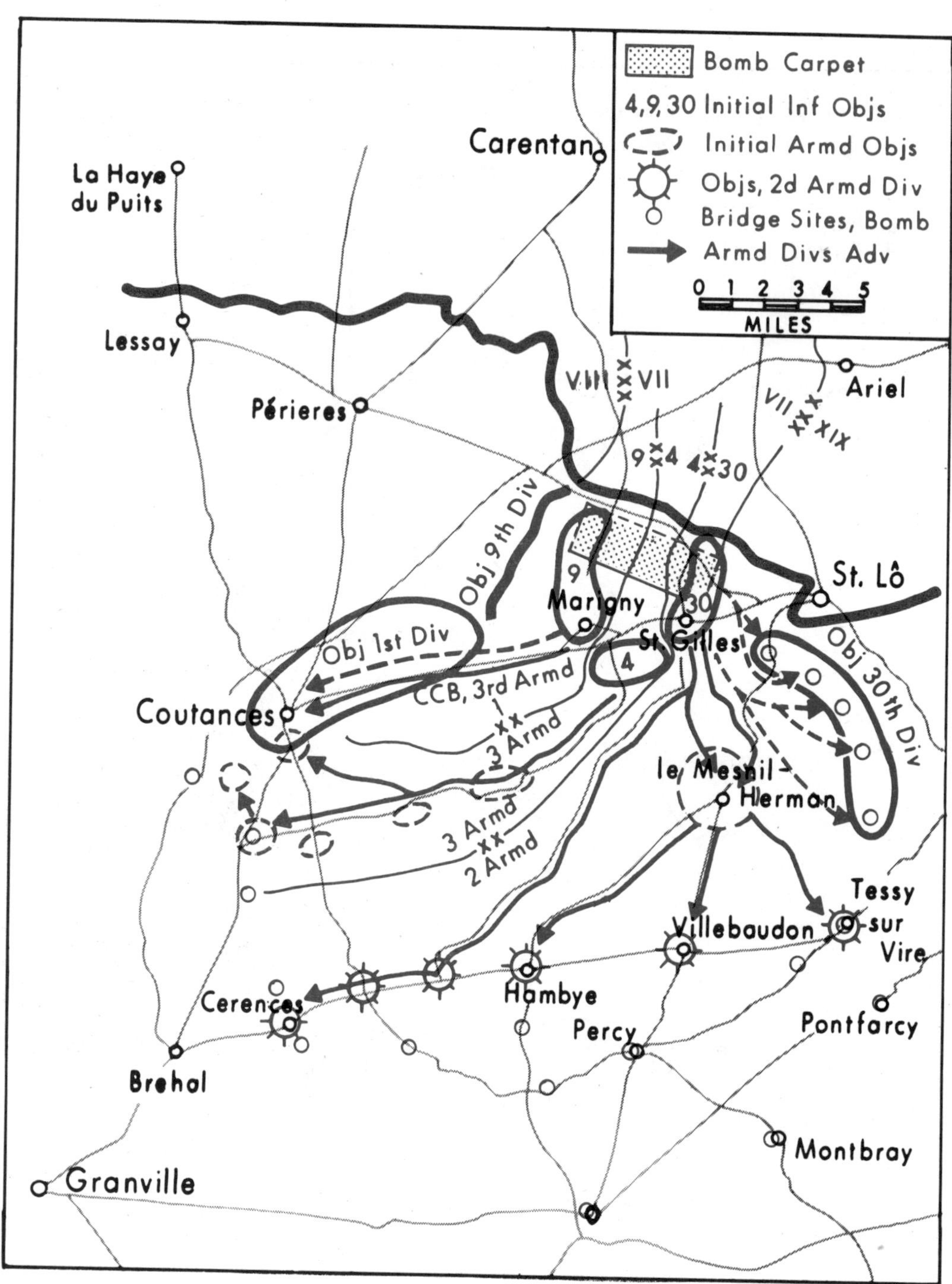

VII Corps Modifications to COBRA

overall army plan the corps adjacent to the VII were also to attack, COBRA now had the potential to turn into a large-scale breakout.[12]

Although with the benefit of hindsight it now appears that Bradley's army seemed assured of making a successful penetration and subsequent exploitation, in the days between the issuing of the army plan on July 13 and the actual beginning of COBRA, high-level commanders and staff officers were cautious in outlook. While all certainly wished for the greatest measure of success for the operation, perhaps even a rapid advance on Avranches, the basic COBRA plan still was designed to take the Coutances-Caumont line. Moreover, the failure in the week prior to COBRA of the 83rd and 90th Infantry Divisions of the VIII Corps to eliminate German strongpoints due to difficult terrain and poor leadership, among other factors, did little to encourage hopes for a decisive breakthrough.[13]

Air Support for COBRA

On July 19, the day the 1st Infantry Division moved into its assembly area behind the 9th Infantry Division, Bradley flew to England to discuss the air portion of the COBRA plan. Major General Elwood R. Quesada, Commander of the IX Tactical Air Command, which provided close air support for First Army, had been working on the details of that plan in coordination with Bradley's staff (his headquarters was co-located with that of First Army).[14] Bradley now wanted to confer with the senior airmen at SHAEF concerning certain details. The meeting took place in the office of the CINC, Allied Expeditionary Air Force, Air Chief Marshall Sir Trafford Leigh-Mallory. Tedder, Spaatz, and Lieutenant General Lewis H. Brereton, Commander of the U.S. Ninth Tactical Air Force, were also present.

Bradley explained his rationale concerning the air support. Familiar with the Caen experience, he wanted light bombs used to preclude excessive amounts of building rubble in villages and to prevent cratering of the ground over which his troops would advance. He also recommended that the planes fly an east-west route parallel to the front line when laying the bomb carpet. This would provide a better measure of safety for his troops, whom he wanted to withdraw only 800 yards from the forward edge of the carpet (i.e., the front line). He knew that this would require pilots to fly longer over enemy territory than if the bomb run were made at right angles, but he thought there was some compensation in coming at the target "out of the sun." (Bradley thought he had won his point, but when the attack actually came, he was surprised to see the aircraft coming at right angles. The airmen had later concluded that the Périers-St. Lô road was so visible that there would be no short drops, that enemy antiaircraft fire would prove too disruptive to aircraft flying the parallel route, and that there would be too much congestion with planes swarming at the narrow side of the target.) Concerned with the 800-yard safety factor, the airmen wanted 3,000 yards, but agreed to compromise with Bradley on 1,200.

Air command responsibilities were apportioned so that Tedder would supervise the entire air operation while Leigh-Mallory selected the time and date. Although Bradley had tentatively selected July 21 as the date for the attack, he decided to attack when Leigh-Mallory said that conditions were right for the air bombardment. Brereton was to plan the bomber attack while Quesada would coordinate air and ground troops.

Collins' troops would pull back one hour before the air attack was to start, leaving a screening force which would withdraw 20 minutes before the bombardment. Air strikes would start 80 minutes before the VII Corps assault, first with fighter-bombers attacking a 250-yard wide strip just south of the highway, and then with heavy bombers pounding the remainder of the target area. As an added safety measure, panel and star displays plus artillery red smoke rounds were to be used for marking purposes. The infantry assault would begin, supported by fighter-bombers again attacking the forward strip. After a 10-minute pause, medium bombers would strike the deeper part of the target. In all, about 2,500 planes would drop almost 5,000 tons of ordnance on an area of six square miles. In addition, artillery would be firing sizeable concentrations in support of the infantry. It should be noted regarding the carpet bombing plan, however, that although several safety measures had been instituted, there was no direct radio link between the heavy bombers and the ground troops. These large planes bombed from a high altitude and in groups, with the bombardier of the lead plane designating the point of release for about 11 others. Thus a single misidentification or error could result in serious casualties to the ground troops. Morale of those who were not hit but who realized casualties were being inflicted by friendly air would surely suffer.[15]

When Bradley returned to his headquarters from England, he first had dinner and then went to VII Corps, where he told Collins and Eddy about the air commitment. Collins listened quietly, but Eddy objected to withdrawing 1,200 yards because it would mean giving up hard-won ground that he feared his men would have to fight and die to regain. It was at this meeting, after Eddy had complained that the frontage of both his (9th) and the 30th Infantry Divisions was too great, that Bradley had offered the 4th Infantry Division. Collins could now make those adjustments to his plan that were discussed earlier. It was then late on July 19, and with COBRA tentatively slated for the twenty-first, much work remained to be done. The last few days, however, had been ones of purposeful preparation, not to mention ones for visiting dignitaries.[16]

Final Preparations and a False Start

Positioning the troops and building up the supplies for the attack, particularly in the VII Corps area, required careful planning and coordination. The ditches on the sides of the roads rapidly filled with communication wires and cables. On the sixteenth, the 3rd Armored Division moved into its assembly areas, while the 2nd Armored came in on July 17. Last-minute preparations, including maintenance of vehicles, were the order of the day. When the armor moved, it would have to go fast and hard; and the possibility of men becoming exhausted before their machines wore out was always present. To do all possible to guard against this happening, the physical fitness program was intensified. Men also had time to rest. Creature comforts such as showers, clean clothes, and hot meals were arranged. Yet the atmosphere of war was still evident, for the tankers were within range of enemy air and artillery. On the night of July 21, the 3rd Armored had a poison gas scare.[17] Although no gas was encountered, the enemy had the capability to employ this silent killer, and the possibility of its use was an ever-present threat. Any time a gas alarm was sounded, those who had discarded their gas masks as excess weight had a difficult few minutes until the "all clear" was heard.

Also alerted by gas alarms was Lieutenant General William H. Simpson, whose Ninth Army would later join Eisenhower's command. He had arrived on July 18, the original target date set for COBRA, to get a feel for the battle area and observe the start of the attack. A major operation seems to exert an irresistible pull on senior officers who can get away to observe it, and, of course, they can learn by watching their brother officers as they direct the battle. Thus, on July 17, Patton, whose Third Army was destined to become operational before Simpson's Ninth, came into the First Army headquarters to take a look. Secretary of War Henry L. Stimson also came on the seventeenth. Although he was then almost 77 years old, Stimson rode through the army in a reconnaissance car, accompanied by Bradley and Patton, and talked with patients in an evacuation hospital. The Secretary's tour included a drive along the invasion beach and a dinner of canned roast beef at Bradley's headquarters. Stimson's departure did not mark the end of the stream of high-ranking visitors, for Eisenhower came on July 20 and Lieutenant General Lesley J. McNair, who had replaced Patton as commander of the phantom 1st Army Group, arrived on the twenty-second. McNair planned to watch the kick-off of COBRA.[18]

Eisenhower's visit signified to some degree the Supreme Commander's anxiety over the seeming inability of the Allies to mount an offensive that would unravel the German defenses. He had held high hopes for the British attack, GOODWOOD, begun two days before his visit to France; but now he was already sensing that Dempsey's Second Army, in spite of the heavy casualties it was taking, would not break the tenaciously defended German lines in the vicinity of Caen.* (Montgomery had postponed that offensive one day because of bad weather, and on the twenty-first called it off after the British VIII Corps had taken over 4,000 casualties.) Hence, Bradley's offensive, which had already been postponed once from July 18 to 19 because American closure to the jump-off line had been slow, and a second time to July 21 so as to time it with GOODWOOD, took on increasing significance.[19]

Postponements were hard not only on the men who had mentally prepared themselves to move forward against the enemy lines and their leaders who had carefully prepared the attack while maintaining secrecy, but also on the war correspondents who were eager for news to flash back to their editors and readers. First, the attack of Middleton's VIII Corps toward Coutances had been cancelled on July 14 by Bradley after 12 days and only a 12,000-yard advance at a price of more than 10,000 casualties; then Bradley had delayed COBRA the first time; and, finally, Dempsey's Second Army could not achieve a breakthrough at Caen. To many reporters, the situation looked ominously like the stalemate of the First World War. As the days ticked off in mid-July, Bradley had kept his own counsel and had not informed reporters of COBRA, fearing that a leak would lead to a shift of German troops. The newsmen had become increasingly critical. Now, after Eisenhower's visit and with the attack due the next day, Bradley decided that

*See Chapter 13, pp. 318-319.

Jeep Splashes Through Flooded Road in Normandy

the time was right to brief the war correspondents. After supper he drove to the farmhouse where the newsmen were living. He outlined the plan and disclosed the numbers of aircraft that were scheduled to bomb. When asked if he planned to warn the French citizens who lived in the carpet area, he shook his head—no. Warning the civilians would alert the enemy, who might withdraw. In that event, the COBRA bombs would merely plow up empty fields.[20]

No bombs were destined to be dropped on fields or elsewhere on July 21, for due to adverse weather conditions the operation was again postponed. As noted above and according to the air plan, Leigh-Mallory had the responsibility for determining the date and time of the attack. About midnight a call from his headquarters announced the postponement. This choice proved to be a wise one as heavy rains fell on Friday, July 21. Nor was COBRA launched on either the twenty-second or twenty-third, and Bradley steadily became more concerned that the enemy would discern the American plan. As he looked at the sky that Sunday morning, Bradley told his chief of staff: "Dammit, I'm going to have to court-martial the chaplain if we have many more days like this."[21] Late that night the long-awaited call came in—the weather on the twenty-fourth would be clear enough for the COBRA bombing to start at noon. Word that the time had finally come was rapidly passed to the assault units.[22]

Although they had fought fiercely and given ground grudgingly, the German units which Eisenhower's troops faced were growing ever weaker under Allied pounding. Allied intelligence, of course, could not foretell exactly how the German commanders envisioned the situation. Dempsey's GOODWOOD offensive had just about exhausted the reserves available to Panzer Group West. OB WEST commander, Generalfeldmarschall Guenther von Kluge, felt that the next Allied blow would again come in the Caen area. He told his subordinate commanders on July 20, when GOODWOOD was about over, "We will hold and if no miracle weapons can be found to improve our basic situation, then we'll just die like men on the battlefield."[23] Kluge did not harangue his officers, for their troops had acquitted themselves well. German strength had been concentrated in the Caen area not only to keep the British forces from reaching favorable terrain but also because it appeared to the German leaders that this was the best area from which to launch a decisive stroke which would reach the sea and split the Allied forces. Now a holding action was all that Kluge could demand of his tired units.[24]

To the west, facing Bradley's army, the Germans had a relatively thin defensive line. *(See Map 61, in Atlas.)* To oppose Collins' VII Corps of six divisions, they had about 5,000 troops in or near the front line, or 30,000 in the area, if all reserves, supply, and headquarters personnel were included. German units had been in the line for long periods of time, since relief troops were not available. Replacements were far fewer than losses, supplies were short, and German leaders were expressing worry about a slackening in the aggressive spirit of their troops.

Concern for the Caen area, which was intensified by Operation GOODWOOD, had drawn high-level German attention away from the Cotentin, or German Seventh Army, front. Generaloberst Paul Hausser knew that his troops had fought hard under adverse circumstances. He did all he could to bolster the defense, and even went to the length of leaving two armored divisions, the 2nd SS Panzer Division and the Panzer Lehr Division, in the line when he could have replaced them with infantry divisions. Hausser reasoned that the armored units were more capable of resisting attack.

Hausser felt that a major American blow was sure to come, but because he thought that the terrain west of the Vire River was poor, he expected Bradley to strike east of the river. Thus, when on July 23 Generalleutnant Dietrich von Choltitz, who commanded the LXXXIV Corps opposite Collins, reported an armored concentration near the west coast of the Cotentin, it did not fit Hausser's conception, and Seventh Army Headquarters did not consider the information indicative of large-scale attack.[25] He would be surprised when Bradley's main effort struck just west of St. Lô.

Dawn on July 24 revealed a gray sky, and the atmosphere was heavy with mist. Leery of the forecasters' prediction that the weather would clear by noon, Leigh-Mallory personally flew to Normandy for a check. Clouds and an overcast sky confirmed his doubts, and he immediately radioed England, directing cancellation of the air strikes. He was too late, however, to stop many of the planes which had already taken off.

Six fighter-bomber groups, all based in France, were already in the air. Three of them got the word, but the other three attacked their targets, some of their strikes falling in friendly territory. When Leigh-Mallory's order reached England, 1,586 heavy bombers of the Eighth Air Force were already aloft, and only a few planes of the final formation received the postponement message before takeoff. Airmen on the ground, in France, tried to reach their comrades in the air, but as there was no direct ground-air link and no specified emergency frequency, contact could not be made. Due to poor weather conditions the first wave of 500 heavy bombers did not bomb. Of the second wave, 35 did drop, but only after three passes to be sure of the correct target identification. Unfortunately for the men on the ground, the weather had improved somewhat by the time the third wave arrived, and some 300 bombers released 135 tons of fragmentation bombs and 550 tons of high explosive. The medium bombers were still on the ground and were stopped in time.

The bombing created considerable confusion in the ground chain of command and resulted in friendly casualties due to bombing errors. Collins had received word of the postponement, but when the bombing began he was in a quandary. Was the attack on again? Determined that the enemy not take the hard-won ground he had given up for the safety zone, Collins ordered his troops to advance back to the road. He learned shortly that COBRA was definitely postponed, but he let the assault proceed to gain back the safety zone. German artillery fire and opposition from Germans who had moved forward took their toll, just as Eddy had predicted.

More regrettable, however, was the damage inflicted principally on the 30th Infantry Division by the bombing. Most of the casualties (25 killed and 131 wounded) came from the 1st Battalion, 120th Infantry, which had been selected to spearhead the attack of its regiment. A bombing error resulted when the bombardier aboard the lead plane of a heavy bomber formation encountered problems with his bomb release mechanism and dropped a portion of his bombs by mistake. Keying on him, the 15 planes behind dropped at the same point. Some fighter-bombers also hit friendly forces. Bradley's aide was escorting high-ranking officers present for the COBRA kickoff, when two planes turned toward their observation post, seemingly homing in on them. Major John D. Horn, Simpson's aide, recalled that as all hit the ground he saw three lieutenant generals trying to get under one jeep. None were wounded, but Quesada's airmen hit an adjacent ammunition dump which promptly exploded.

Bradley was shocked and not just a little angry when he learned of the short bombing because he believed that the attack would be executed parallel to the front. Quesada, whose fighter-bombers had bombed laterally, was also surprised. Both men complained. Late that evening, Leigh-Mallory called Bradley and told him that the planes had bombed perpendicularly to the road on purpose, and would bomb the same way the next day

Bradley's meeting with the airmen on July 19 had obviously made a different impression on the various participants. Whereas the airmen thought that Bradley realized the possibility of bombing error and had agreed to let them select the approach direction, Bradley recalled otherwise. The size of bombs to be used also proved to be a point of contention. Apparently the bomb size limitation, devised to prevent cratering, had never been agreed to by all parties, for some of the fighter-bombers carried bombs as large as 500 pounds.

In the midst of disagreement, Bradley had to decide what to do. If he insisted tht the approach route be changed, he feared that COBRA would be delayed while appropriate preparations were made. Each day of waiting increased the chance that Allied intentions would be discovered by the enemy. In addition, Bradley realized that his superiors wanted an attack. He finally decided to try to launch COBRA the next morning, July 25.[26]

Although the direction of the attack could not be changed on such short notice, some adjustments to the air plan were made. Before the waves of planes arrived, a special weather reconnaissance plane would check the area to ensure that the bombing targets could be seen from the air and that the atmospheric conditions were proper for the aerial attack. Moreover, heavy bomber formations were to come in as low as possible, and all targets north of the Périers-St. Lô highway which had previously been assigned to fighter-bombers were now given to artillery units.[27]

As the last hours ticked away, it appeared that everything conceivable had been done to prepare, yet the nagging possibility remained that the abbreviated bombing might have tipped Bradley's hand to his enemy. From the German point of view, however, a large American attack had been blunted. Coupled with the sound of thousands of airplane engines, the explosions of the bombs which did fall had had quite an effect. When the day was done, Generalleutnant Fritz Bayerlin, who commanded the Panzer Lehr Division, was pleased with the action of his troops. If he had lost men and equipment and much artillery ammunition had been expended, the Americans had been kept from crossing the Périers-St. Lô highway. They would probably attack again on the twenty-fifth, thought Bayerlin, but his command could handle them. Far from moving out of the carpet area, Bayerlin decided to thin his outpost line north of the road and shift most of the troops to the south, to the area that soon would become famous as the site of the COBRA carpet. Meanwhile Kluge, who still thought the next Allied push would be made by the British, planned to visit that sector on the twenty-fifth. Bradley's plan had not been compromised.[28]

Operation COBRA: Breakout

As he had on July 24, Bradley positioned himself at VII Corps Headquarters during the preparatory bombing on July 25 so as to be accessible should an army-level decision be required on short notice. He would have been pleased had he known that Kluge, worried about the Caen sector, had shifted the 2nd Panzer Division from the vicinity of Caumont to the Orne River valley. *(See Map 59, in Atlas.)* The move was completed the night of July 24, and, indeed, the shift seemed logical when early on the twenty-fifth the Canadian II Corps attacked south of Caen and by the end of the day drew a *panzer* group closer to the front line. It would be the morning of July 27, almost 48 hours after COBRA had begun, before Kluge began to shift armored units westward to oppose Bradley's forces. Meanwhile, the COBRA offensive had gained a sizeable head of steam.[29]

Allied air strikes began about 9:40 A.,M. and continued for some two and a half hours. An average of 10 bombs per acre was dropped on the target area. Though the first waves of bombers hit their target, accurate bombing was much more difficult for the planes which followed. Plans specified that bombs would be dropped from about 15,000 feet, but due to cloud cover the actual attack was made from as low as 12,000 feet. This decrease in altitude caused the bombardiers to recompute their data while aloft. German antiaircraft was also more effective at this lower height. When the target area was reached, the airmen found that the earlier bombing had thrown up clouds of smoke and dust, and red artillery markers could not be picked out amid the many flashes. Once-tight formations tended to spread. Acutely aware of the safety problem, the fliers attempted to insure that no bombs fell on friendly forces. Thus many were dropped long or to the flanks of the target.[30]

American ground troops waiting to assault cheered the demonstration of air might—cheered, that is, until once again they heard the ominous sound of bombs falling toward them. Then all dived for cover. A slight wind had blown the smoke and dust northward, and when a lead bombardier who had bomb-sight trouble released visually, his bombs hit friendly troops. Another lead pilot ordered the drop early, while a third misidentified critical landmarks. In all, 42 medium and 35 heavy bombers dropped bombs which killed 111 American troops, including Lieutenant General Lesley J. McNair, commander of the phantom 1st US Army Group and of the Army Ground Forces, who had been observing the drop. Wounded totaled 490.[31]

The company commander of Company B, 8th Infantry Regiment, 4th Infantry Division, when later interviewed, described his experience:

> The dive bombers came in beautifully and dropped their bombs right . . . where they belonged. Then the first group of heavies dropped them in the draw several hundred yards in front of us. . . . The next wave came in closer, the next one . . . still closer. The dust cloud was drifting back toward us. Then they came right on top of us. . . . We put on all the orange smoke we had but I don't think it did any good, they could not have seen it through the dust. . . . The shock was awful. A lot of the men were sitting around after the bombing in a complete daze. . . .[32]

Disorganization was rife in the affected areas. An infantry battalion had lost 30 soldiers killed or wounded, including its entire command group less the battalion commander. The battalion was replaced for the attack. An artillery battalion fire direction center was knocked out, and much damage was done to wire communications. Commanders were concerned for their men and tried to secure adequate medical treatment for the

Troops Dig Out After Bombs Fall Short

wounded, but virtually all units commenced the ground attack close to the appointed hour; within a short time the remaining units joined the assault.[33]

Conditions on the south side of the Périers-St. Lô highway made the American difficulties appear insignificant. *(See Map 61, in Atlas.)* When the attack began, the Panzer Lehr Division and a regiment of paratroopers were occupying positions in the carpet area. Roads along ridges which led back to Marigny and St. Gilles had been utilized to construct a tank defense in depth. Bayerlin thought his position was strong and he was optimistic about defending it, but he had not reckoned on being carpeted with bombs. He later described what it was like:

> The planes kept coming over, as if on a conveyor belt, and the bomb carpets unrolled in great rectangles. My flak had hardly opened its mouth, when the batteries received direct hits which knocked out half the guns and silenced the rest. After an hour I had no communications with anybody, even by radio. By noon nothing was visible but dust and smoke. My frontlines looked like the face of the moon and at least 70 percent of my troops were out of action—dead, wounded, crazed or numbed. All my forward tanks were knocked out, and the roads were practically impassable.[34]

Although it appeared to the German commander that his unit was destroyed, American infantrymen who were used to the bitter fighting of the hedgerow country were cautious. Many German defenders, some with automatic weapons, had lived through the onslaught, and their defensive efforts were often supported by artillery fire. The rate of advance in many areas was slow.[35]

By the end of the first day, July 25, Bradley and Collins were cautiously optimistic about the potential for sizeable

Infantrymen Advance Into Dust Raised by COBRA Bombardment

gains, but they could not predict with any certainty the successful outcome of COBRA. The higher-level commanders were convinced that the carpet bombing had provided a decisive impetus. The lower-level commanders, however, were less certain; they had expected too much, almost a cakewalk. They were disappointed, even though the day's advance was over a thousand yards, a significant accomplishment compared to the fighting in the previous weeks.[36] VII Corps had suffered about 1,000 casualties, and it was still short of the initial objectives. *(See Map: VII Corps Modifications to COBRA, page 326.)* Both Marigny and St. Gilles remained in enemy hands, and on the western edge of the penetration, pressure from German mechanized elements was beginning to be felt. Collins realized that if he committed his armor before German defenses had been sufficiently ruptured, it could become entangled in belts of defensive works and fall prey to armored counterattack. If he waited too long, however, a new defensive line could be established and reinforcements summoned. His decision was to commit part of his armor and motorized infantry on the twenty-sixth in the belief that this added weight would complete the rupture and lead to full-scale exploitation.[37]

By the end of the second day of COBRA, July 26, the initial crisis was over. That morning Collins committed his main attack force (1st Infantry Division plus Combat Command B, 3rd Armored Division) and the 2nd Armored Division. Meanwhile, his infantry divisions continued to advance slowly against occasional stiff resistance, particularly on the flanks. The 2nd Armored took St. Gilles in mid-afternoon and continued southward against little resistance. Although the lower-level leaders were still a bit pessimistic, it was becoming clearer that there was considerable confusion and only slight organized resistance behind the German main line of resistance, which had now been broken. Collins ordered his last exploiting force, the 3rd Armored Division (–), to attack the next morning. *(See Map 62, in Atlas.)*[38]

On July 27, with all of his exploiting forces in action, Collins broke open the front and assured the successful completion of COBRA. Hausser tried to hold by concentrating his defenses along main roads and at road junctions, but the American tanks, equipped with hedgerow-busting Rhino devices, were able to leave the roads and maneuver through the hedgerows to positions to the rear of the defenders. German tanks and antitank guns, which could not traverse the hedgerows, were repeatedly struck by fighter-bombers accompanying each advancing column. Destroyed and damaged equipment littered the area. It was the beginning of several days which the fliers would characterize as "a fighter-bomber's paradise." Particularly in the eastern part of the breakthrough zone, the German situation was so muddled that commanders talked in the clear over the radio to report that their disintegrating units were surrounded. In the west, however, conscious of the need to keep an escape route open, Choltitz pulled back his forces facing Middleton's VIII Corps and fought viciously to hold Coutances. Thus, while the VII Corps exploitation went well in the east, the 1st Infantry Division could not break through to take Coutances. That city ultimately fell, on July 28, to an VIII Corps armored column (4th Armored Division).[39]

In the three days following the commencement of COBRA, Kluge had been feeling pressure on both flanks. While Bradley's troops were chopping a hole in his western defenses, a realization he only gradually reached because of his concern with the Caen sector, the Canadian II Corps did its work well in the limited objective attack which attracted immediate German attention. Conscious of the gravity of the situation, Kluge asked for reinforcements; on July 27, Hitler gave him a *panzer* division from southern France and the next day finally began pulling troops (three divisions) from the Pas de Calais. If its usefulness was now about at an end, FORTITUDE had served its purpose well by deceiving Hitler this long. *(See Map 62, in Atlas.)* Late on the twenty-seventh, Kluge also ordered two *panzer* divisions to move from the Orne River area to Hausser's disintegrating front, but he refused Hausser's two requests in three days to make substantive withdrawals in the Seventh Army sector. He not only feared that this would un-

Tanks of the 4th Armored Division in Coutances

Hodges, Bradley and Patton

hinge his Caen defenses but also, perhaps more perceptively than Hausser, suspected that a withdrawal might become a rout. As it turned out, the two *panzer* divisions, hit repeatedly by air attacks during the move, could not stem Collins' exploitation; their thrusts were blunted primarily by the XIX Corps, which Bradley directed on July 27 to take over part of the VII Corps sector.[40]

German attempts to patch up a defensive line and hold the potent force Bradley had unleashed were doomed to failure. Kluge's troops simply lacked the firepower, strength, and mobility, all in the face of overwhelming Allied air superiority, to do much more than fight a delaying action, hoping for minimal losses. *(See Map 62, in Atlas.)* On July 28 and 29, both the VII and VIII Corps continued to make sizeable gains, driving in the direction of Avranches, the gateway to Brittany. The last two days of the month, VIII Corps armor really broke loose, spurred on by an impatient Patton who had finally entered the combat picture. *(See Map 63, in Atlas.)*

A week earlier, Eisenhower had authorized Bradley to regroup his divisions into two armies under an American 12th Army Group. Bradley would command the group, Hodges the First Army, and Patton the Third Army. Until Eisenhower assumed overall ground command personally, Montgomery would continue to control the ground battle. Bradley selected August 1 as the change date, and on the twenty-eighth told Hodges he was to keep the V, XIX, and VII Corps. Patton would get six divisions and the VIII Corps Headquarters. Other corps would join his army as the campaign continued. Although Patton would not officially assume command until August 1, Bradley told him to keep contact with and unofficially lead his units. As one of his first actions, Patton told Middleton to move his two armored divisions through his infantry and have the tankers lead the attack. This led to great gains the last two days of the month. Avranches fell to the 4th Armored Division on the thirtieth, and the next day divisional elements seized a bridgehead, complete with bridge, across the Sélune River. When German forces coming from St. Malo were not able to eliminate the bridgehead, the stage was set for an even greater exploitation and greater pressure all along the German line.[41]

As it became clear that Bradley's attack was succeeding, Montgomery, prodded by Eisenhower, ordered Dempsey to keep the pressure on German defenses near the American-British army boundary. Accordingly, Dempsey attacked on July 30, charged by Montgomery, as he told Eisenhower: "I have ordered Dempsey to throw all caution overboard and to take any risks he likes and to accept any casualties and to step on the gas for Vire." Dempsey's two corps encountered stiff opposition, but gained ground and held in that vicinity German armor which was desperately needed to the west.[42]

After so many days of dreary conflict in the hedgerows, it was hard to believe what had been accomplished in a single week. The German defensive line had been ruptured, many units were virtually destroyed, and the way to the Breton ports was open. Many prisoners filled Allied cages and the material destruction was great. Allied air claimed 362 tanks destroyed, over 200 damaged, and 1,337 other vehicles destroyed in the July 26-31 period alone. Credit belongs to both ground troops and airmen; but especially praiseworthy are Collins, who planned and executed the breakthrough, and Bradley, who devised the original plan and supervised its execution. Patton's summary was to the point: "Brad has really pulled a great show and should get credit for it."[43]

Into the Open

The news of Bradley's breakthrough could not have been heartening to Hitler, who seemed to grow more mystical and petulant with each passing day. After Avranches fell, Kluge told Generaloberst Alfred Jodl at OKW: "As a result of the

Knocked-Out American Tanks Near Avranches

breakthrough of the enemy armored spearheads, the whole western front has been ripped open. . . . The left flank has collapsed."[44] This news dominated Hitler's meeting with his advisors in East Prussia on July 31. Since the assassination attempt on July 20, the *Fuehrer* had grown even more distrustful of the high-level German professional military men and had decided that in the future he would select commanders on the basis of loyalty and aggressiveness, not seniority. For these reasons, but also because there appeared to be security leaks in the channel used to transmit plans to the West, he forbade sending any more than minimal information to Kluge. Hitler reiterated his instructions that ports should be transformed into fortresses and that the ground must be held in the West. Anything else would simply let Eisenhower build up strength faster and exploit the mobility advantage his forces had. The war, he said, could only end when one side was destroyed. After commenting on the situation facing Germany on other fronts—an evaluation noteworthy for its unrealistic view of events in the East—Hitler ended the meeting.

Upon the conclusion of the conference, Jodl's deputy, General der Artillerie Walter Warlimont, tried to get concrete guidance for Kluge. The *Fuehrer* replied:

> Tell Field Marshal von Kluge that he should keep his eyes riveted to the front and on the enemy without ever looking backward. If and when precautionary measures have to be taken in the rear of the theater of operations in the West, everything necessary will be done by OKW and OKW alone.[45]

In case there had been any doubt, Kluge would now know his place. Hitler continued to be oblivious to the critical situation the Germans faced in France.

Third Army Heads East

In that country, meanwhile, the Americans seized the opportunity COBRA had created. On August 1, the flamboyant but boldly imaginative Patton sent VIII Corps into the Britanny peninsula in keeping with earlier plans to capture Breton ports, which were believed necessary acquisitions if the Allies were to sustain the logistical build-up. *(See Map 64, in Atlas.)* As the map shows, Middleton's divisions quickly sealed off and overran the peninsula, assisted by the French Resistance; his divisions met little German opposition since most of the field units had been moved piecemeal to Normandy earlier.[46] Combat Command A, 4th Armored Division, advanced so rapidly that handling prisoners would have slowed the attack. Colonel Bruce C. Clarke, commander of CCA, ordered his subordinates to cause prisoners to throw their weapons on the road, and then have an American tank run over the weapons. Next the prisoners were to be told to walk to the rear with hands on heads. Clarke was sure that a follow-up unit would pick up these men.[47] Simultaneously, Patton (and Hodges to a lesser degree) was funneling divisions of his other corps through the Avranches gap to block for VIII Corps or take advantage of opportunities of the moment. Senior officers were positioned at the northern side of the opening to push the units through as quickly as possible. Division integrity was forgotten during the passage. At the exit, each division was assigned a road. Whatever came through was sorted out so that vehicles belonging to a particular division were sent down the proper road.[48] As these movements continued, Eisenhower's senior commanders and their planners began to reassess the strategic alternatives.

Capitalizing on Kluge's disintegrating situation, on August 4 Montgomery ordered the first major change in the original OVERLORD plan. Pre-invasion strategic thinking had been predicated on what was expected to be a vital need to capture the Breton ports, unless, when that time came, German resistance seemed to be collapsing. *(See Map 64, in Atlas.)* Now, in the last days of July, the planners sensed that that very disintegration was occurring, and projected a bolder strategic option—strike to the east in maximum strength and try to destroy Kluge's armies west of the Seine River. Bradley's August 3 decision, with which Montgomery concurred, to have Patton use *minimum* forces to clear Brittany triggered the major change in strategy. Eisenhower, visiting France that same day, agreed with the new scheme, and further directed Montgomery to consider using airborne forces near Chartres to assist the drive by ground elements. Under the new plan, most of Patton's army was to drive to the east, while protecting the Allied right flank (Loire River); his initial objective was the Mayenne River line. At the same time, Hodges would continue to attack in the Vire-Mortain area and make a tighter wheeling movement, the Canadians would attack toward Falaise, and the British would move on Argentan. The object was to try to encircle the Germans west of the Seine or, barring that, to herd them against the lower reaches of that river and destroy them there.[49] The plan de-emphasized the presumed logistical importance of Brittany, quite correctly as it later turned out when the chances of taking better ports improved and the area lost its importance. Middleton was told to contain Lorient and St. Nazaire. Brest, however, would have to be taken; on September 19, it was.[50]

Implementation of the new plan went well in the early days of August, particularly on the south flank where the aggressive Patton drove his exploiting corps hard. *(See Map 64, in Atlas.)* Collins' corps took Mortain, the hub about which the Allied forces pivoted, and established a strong blocking position there. This development simply highlighted the decision Hitler had made on August 2 to launch a major counterattack. The *Fuehrer* wanted Kluge to use eight of the nine *panzer* divisions in Normandy to attack in the Vire-Mortain area. He expected this armor-heavy force to drive to the sea, isolate Patton's army, and then turn north to crush the beachhead. He thought the operation "a unique, never recurring opportunity for a complete reversal of the situation."[51]

In ordering the counterattack, Hitler had accepted the offensive course of action of the two OKW devised. Withdrawal to the Seine, ultimately the West Wall, which would also entail evacuating southern France and pulling back in Italy, was more than he could stomach. This option meant giving up the recently operational V weapons sites, surrendering areas furnishing war materials, and, in Hitler's view, foreshortening Germany's ability to prolong the war. On the other hand, he reasoned, a full-blooded counterattack could force the battle back into the difficult Normandy terrain; perhaps it would also lead the war-weary British to negotiate, considered in conjunction with stepped-up V weapon attacks, and thereby fracture the coalition relationship. If it failed, however, it might become impossible for the Germans to withdraw formations across the Seine with any semblance of order. It was this last, ominous eventuality which bothered Kluge and Hausser, both of whom expected that the counterstroke, as Hitler envisioned it, would mean the end of Seventh Army.[52]

The manner in which the German attack toward Avranches was mounted highlighted the difference in conceptual thinking between Kluge, on the spot and aware of the true situation, and Hitler, sitting isolated and distrustful in East Prussia and completely out of touch with reality. Kluge, too, had seen the need for retaking Avranches, but simply as the anchor for a new line of defense in Normandy. He did not consider the situation hopeless and was not yet convinced of the need to withdraw to the Seine, but he was realistic about what was possible. Accordingly, because he thought it would take too long to assemble eight divisions, Kluge planned to employ only four *panzer* divisions for the attack, using three to penetrate and the fourth to pass through and seize Avranches. It would be a surprise attack, launched at night and without artillery preparation. When Hitler learned of the plan, one day before the attack, he objected, complaining that the force was too weak and would not accomplish the grand goals he sought, a fact of which Kluge was well aware. Grudgingly, however, the *Fuehrer* agreed to let the attack commence. From that time on, however, he would grant Kluge practically no flexibility in making command decisions in the West.[53]

German Vehicles Destroyed by Air Attack Near Mortain

Once again ULTRA provided advance information to the Allies by virtue of the monitoring of messages back and forth between Kluge and OKW. More details were filled in by reports from stay-behind agents.[54] Bradley thus was able to prepare a defense in depth, and Montgomery ordered British elements to attack the flank of the *panzer* force. When the attack came shortly after midnight on August 6, mounted by *panzer* elements massing only about 250 tanks, Kluge's units penetrated to a depth of three to seven miles before they were halted. *(See Map 64, in Atlas.)* Bradley plugged one hole with one of Patton's divisions, which he temporarily held back, and used his devastating air power and the 3rd Armored Division and 30th Infantry Division to good effect.[55]

The 2nd Battalion, 120th Infantry Regiment (30th Infantry Division) held a position from which it was possible to observe much of the VII Corps sector. Early in the attack, the Germans overran the battalion command post and took the command group prisoners. Under the command of Captain Reynold C. Erichson, the unit held throughout five days of repeated enemy attacks, during which food and ammunition were parachuted in and medical supplies arrived as loads in artillery projectiles, which normally carried propaganda leaflets. Throughout the period, observers on Hill 317 called artillery fire in on German units. When relieved, over 300 men walked out, but another 300 had been killed or wounded. Erichson and four others received the Distinguished Service Cross and the battalion was awarded the Presidential Unit Citation.[56]

By mid-afternoon of August 7, Kluge was convinced that his attack had failed, and he wanted to disengage. Hitler was furious and would have none of that. He berated Kluge for having attacked too soon and ordered him to bring in more *panzers* and continue the assault. Time was running out for the OB WEST commander, however, and the additional units he tried to pull together had to be diverted to oppose the Canadian attack toward Falaise which had begun on August 8. Allied pressure continued to build up all along the line, and as the distinct possibility of Patton turning north from Le Mans materialized, Kluge would have to postpone any effort to renew his assault. In effect, Hitler's gamble had failed, and now the Germans would have to fight desperately to get back to the Seine.[57]

The Falaise Pocket: A Killing Ground

On August 8, Bradley proposed a modification in the Allied plan, confident that First Army could hold at Mortain against the slackening German attack. He now suggested turning the flanking corps of First and Third Army north to meet the British and Canadians, thereby closing a trap on German troops in the salient Mortain-Argentan-Falaise. *(See Map 64, in Atlas.)* Taking advantage of the abortive German attack and Hitler's unwillingness to withdraw his forces, Bradley wanted to seize the opportunity to make a closer-in envelopment than the one the Allied plan envisioned occurring near the Seine. Eisenhower, who was at Bradley's command post, was enthused, and Montgomery, in charge of the overall battle, gave his approval telephonically.[58] When the latter issued a new directive on August 11, the day after XV Corps had turned north from Le Mans, he wrote: "Obviously if we can close the gap completely, we shall have put the enemy in a most awkward predicament."[59]

Montgomery felt that the Germans would be able to resist the advance of the Americans more readily than that of the Canadians, presumably because of more favorable defensive terrain. He knew that by August 9 the Canadian force had advanced nine miles, and was but seven more from Falaise. Accordingly, he drew the boundary between army groups a few miles south of Argentan and assigned that town as a Canadian objective. *(See Map 64, in Atlas.)* Thus, when the troops of Major General Wade H. Haislip's XV Corps reached the edge of Argentan on August 13, they had already crossed the army group boundary on the basis of Haislip's liberal interpretation of Patton's instructions to prepare for a further advance when his forces reached the boundary.[60]

Train Destroyed by Allied Bombing

The American advance had been amazingly rapid, not only since the turn north but, indeed, since the beginning of the month. Air support had been excellent and overwhelming. Pilots of tactical aircraft talked to men in tanks below so that their efforts could be coordinated. At the same time, as Map 64 shows, the air interdiction program was continued. German generals called the Seine-Chartres-Loire area a "traffic desert." Meanwhile, Allied supply trucks moved virtually bumper to bumper, 24 hours a day.[61] Consequently, Patton was surprised and disappointed when, on August 13, Bradley directed him to restrain Haislip, hold his position near Argentan, and build up strength there.[62]

Bradley's decision to halt at Argentan has become one of the most controversial of the war. Patton felt that he could have closed the gap, but the man responsible for the southern portion of the operation was Bradley. The 12th Army Group commander later wrote that as no plan of meeting had been agreed upon between American and Canadian forces, he feared that a continued attack could end in confusion and result in needless loss of life in both armies. Even if an easily identifiable terrain feature had been selected, Bradley felt that, while Patton might have reached Falaise, he would have been stretched too thin to hold against a determined enemy. Patton had but four divisions in the area, and they were already blocking several potential escape routes. If Patton's road block were to be extended to Falaise, it would stretch some 40 miles. Moreover, the XV Corps was operating with both flanks wide open and could become the object of encirclement.

As it was, the XV Corps had already passed the army group boundary. Boundaries are but lines on maps and can be changed, but this boundary had been established by Montgomery, who exercised overall control of the fluid ground situation. Bradley knew the Canadians were about to start another push, which all the leaders optimistically expected would reach Argentan. (The drive, made against stiff German resistance, finally took Falaise late on August 17.) A more audacious commander than Bradley might have tried to have the boundary changed and continue the attack. He later said, however, that he "preferred a solid shoulder at Argentan to the possibility of a broken neck at Falaise."[63] Yet, one day later, he would be daring enough to order Patton to send much of the XV Corps eastward toward the Seine, away from the "solid shoulder."

As Charles MacDonald points out, Montgomery shares the brunt of postwar criticism for the Allied failure to close the Falaise-Argentan gap. He did not reinforce the Canadian drive with extra available British divisions, and he kept the British Second Army attacking the side of the pocket, thereby driving Germans toward the exit where they needed strength. Nor did he apparently consider changing the army group boundary.[64]

It is quite likely that the fighting quality of German formations had more than a little to do with the Allied missed opportunity. In July, Hitler's divisions had fought well against difficult odds, and memories of those days were not forgotten by Allied leaders. Now, penned up inside a tightening pocket, they were still capable of putting up a stiff fight and, more important, they were desperate. ULTRA continued to give Bradley and Montgomery important information about German units, in many instances revealing vast confusion, supply shortages, and losses of men and machines.[65] In spite of this intelligence, the Allied leaders had a grudging respect for the wounded but still dangerous *panzers*. Bradley's caution, in particular, probably reflects that respect.

At any rate, the Allies did not close the gap at Argentan and, although they suffered heavy losses, the Germans managed to evacuate more men than the Allies would have liked before Americans and Poles (with the Canadian First Army) linked up 10 miles east at Chambois on August 19. (Montgomery reoriented the directions of the pincer attacks when the closer-in drives stalled.) In that interim, Kluge's trials, enduring repeated tongue-lashings from Hitler while trying to cope with the fluid situation, were enough to tax even the most capable of commanders.

The strained relationship in German command channels and the almost unbelievably detailed control by Hitler is difficult to imagine. From the time on August 7 when he proposed discontinuing the Mortain attack until he was relieved 10 days later, Kluge lived a nightmare as a senior commander. He did not want to renew the attack on August 9, but Hitler gave him no choice, sharply questioning almost every detail (including unit dispositions and locations of guns) and reserving the right to designate H-hour as well as who should lead the attack. Nevertheless, the worsening situation, and particularly the Canadian push, caused Kluge to delay the attack, thereby inviting the *Fuehrer*'s wrath and an order to attack on August 11. Kluge and his commanders quickly concluded that this would be impossible. They needed more time to assemble the requisite *panzers*; they had also concluded, in accordance with the advice of meteorologists, that August 20 was the earliest date when weather unfavorable to Allied air activity and offering suitable moonlit conditions would occur. Kluge, moreover, had grown very concerned over the threat posed to his southeastern flank by Patton's XV Corps; accordingly, on the tenth, he not only explained why Hitler's August 11 attack was infeasible, but also suggested the need to counter Haislip's northward advance. After much querying and lecturing, Hitler agreed to delay the renewed assault at Mortain and approved the attack on the XV Corps, but even then he gave instructions about how it should be mounted in greater strength and for more decisive objectives. Hitler was oblivious to how difficult it would be to mount even the relatively modest attack proposed by Kluge. As it turned out, the attack never came off because General Heinrich Eberbach had to commit piecemeal the troops he was trying to assemble as the strike force in order to stop the XV Corps on the edge of Argentan.

The operational situation was not the only problem vexing Kluge. He was haunted by the fear that Hitler would construe his protestations as signs of defeatism and that the *Fuehrer*'s agents, moreover, would connect him—quite correctly—with the July 20 assassination attempt. His disappearance for several hours on August 15, indeed, was interpreted by Hitler as an attempt by Kluge to reach and negotiate with Allied leaders. In truth, the OB West commander's staff car had been strafed and he had been forced to take to a ditch without an operational radio for most of the day. When he re-established communications, he bluntly told Jodl on August 16 that the attack to smash XV Corps, ordered on the fourteenth by Hitler, could not be mounted:

> No matter how many orders are issued, the troops cannot, are not able to, are not strong enough to defeat the enemy. It would be a fateful error to succumb to a hope that cannot be fulfilled, and no power in this world [can accomplish its will simply] through an order it may give. That is the situation.[66]

Kluge wanted to withdraw, and said so. By mid-afternoon that same day, Hitler could no longer ignore reality, and issued the order to withdraw from the pocket toward the Seine, gratuitously telling his field commanders how to hold the gap open. Meanwhile, the day before, he had decided to replace Kluge with Generalfeldmarschall Walter Model, a hard-bitten and ruthless favorite of Hitler. The new commander arrived on August 17, but he could do little more than carry out Kluge's withdrawal plans; later in the year, he, too, would be relieved. As for Kluge, he bit on a potassium cyanide capsule while en route back to Germany on August 19. Hitler found it convenient to tell party officials that the dead field marshal had admitted his guilt for the defeat in the West.[67]

Field Marshal Walter Model

German positions were falling rapidly as Model took over. By August 17, Orleans, Dreux, and St. Malo were gone, and at the end of the day the pocket, which contained 100,000 troops, measured only 20 miles wide by 10 miles deep, with a gap at the exit of but 6 miles. Model put Hausser in command of the entire pocket, and told him to pull back from the Orne to the Dives River. *(See Map 65, in Atlas.)* Exit roads were jammed; confusion reigned. The slaughter was tremendous. Allied artillerymen had only to fire their weapons into the pocket packed with men and equipment to hit a target. By the evening of August 19, the seal was in place at Chambois. Early on the twentieth, what remained of five *panzer* divisions tried to break out, and although the attack was frustrated in several places, one road was opened for six hours before it was closed for good. Among those who escaped was Hausser, who had been badly wounded, but the Allies took 50,000 prisoners in the pocket. About 10,000 German troops were killed, and much equipment as well as many horses were destroyed. Although from 20,000 to 40,000 men escaped, many were noncombat troops who had been ordered out early.[68]

Destruction within the pocket was so vast, it was virtually indescribable. Eisenhower later recalled his first visit to the area:

> Forty-eight hours after the closing of the gap I was conducted through it on foot, to encounter scenes that could be described only by Dante. It was literally possible to walk for hundreds of yards at a time, stepping on nothing but dead and decaying flesh.[69]

Eisenhower Changes the Basic Plan

On August 14, several days before the Allies completed the reduction of the Falaise pocket, Bradley initiated the deeper envelopment in the vicinity of the Seine by directing Patton to send two divisions from the Argentan area eastward. *(See Map 65, in Atlas.)* Patton also received authority to send the XII and XX Corps toward the Seine. These exploiting drives strained the logistical system, particularly in providing sufficient gasoline. Conditions were expected to improve, however, because the first PLUTO (cross-Channel pipeline) had been connected on August 12. Moreover, to ease the logistical strain, SHAEF directed that heavy bombers continue to operate from England so that the available tonnage of supplies could be used by the ground troops and short-range aircraft. Supply trucks were a scarce commodity, and their return to the dumps after unloading was essential if a continuous flow were to be maintained. Therefore, Patton's habit of keeping them forward to use in moving his troops faster, while it appealed to infantrymen, caused logisticians to fume.[70]

In spite of the rapid advance of his forces since the COBRA breakout, Eisenhower feared overconfidence. On August 15, the same day that another invasion force landed in southern France and that he cancelled a planned airborne operation for the Paris-Orleans gap so that the airlift could be used to carry gasoline to the ground troops near Le Mans, the Supreme Commander held a press conference. He thought that the newsmen were getting too optimistic and told them that, as Hitler knew that he would hang if he surrendered, the *Fuehrer* had nothing to lose by fighting to the last. A number of German armies would have to be defeated in the field before victory could be claimed.[71]

A few days later, on August 19, Eisenhower decided to change his pre-invasion plan in order to persist in defeating those armies before Hitler could stiffen German defenses.

The End of the Falaise Pocket

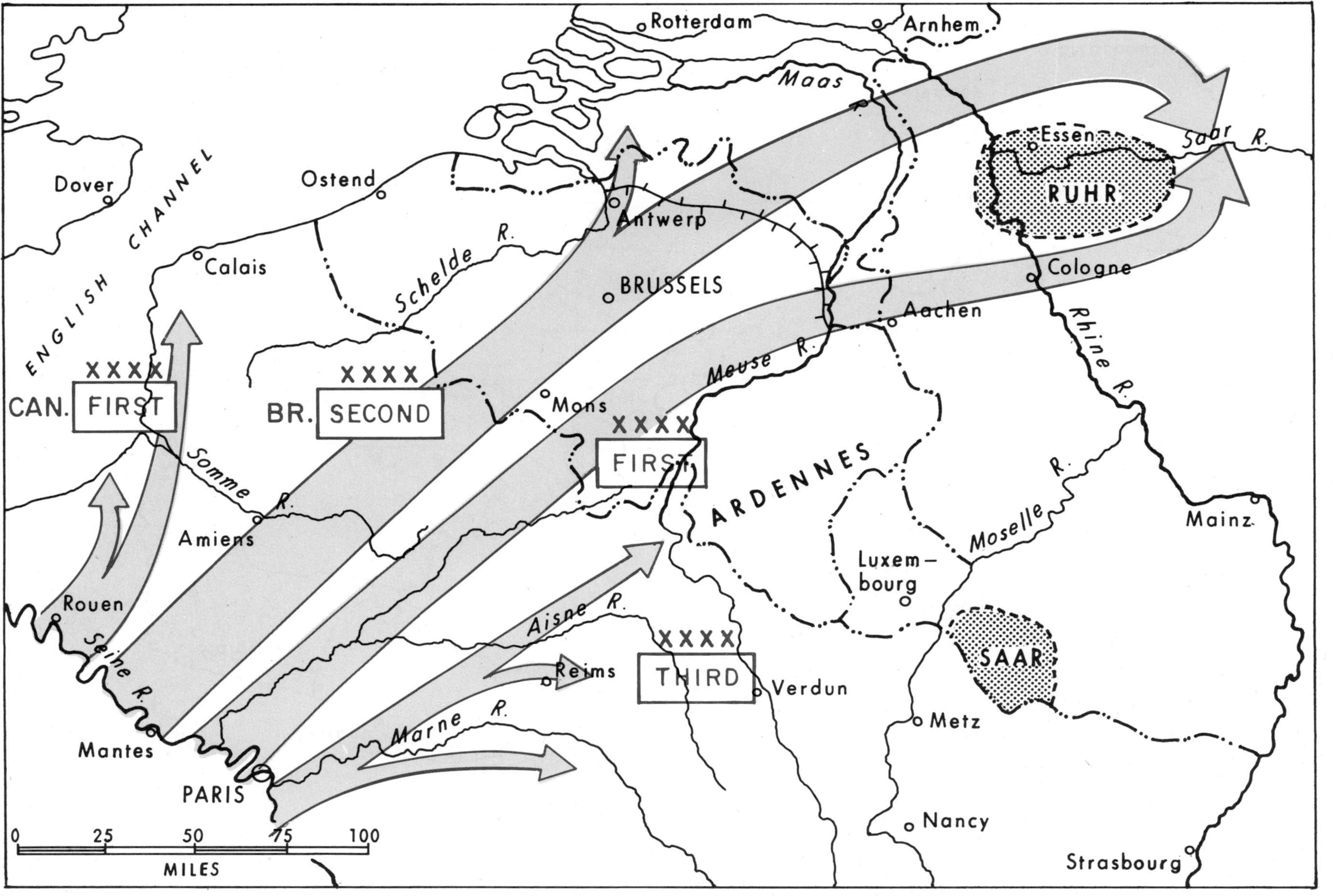

Montgomery's Plan: August 1944

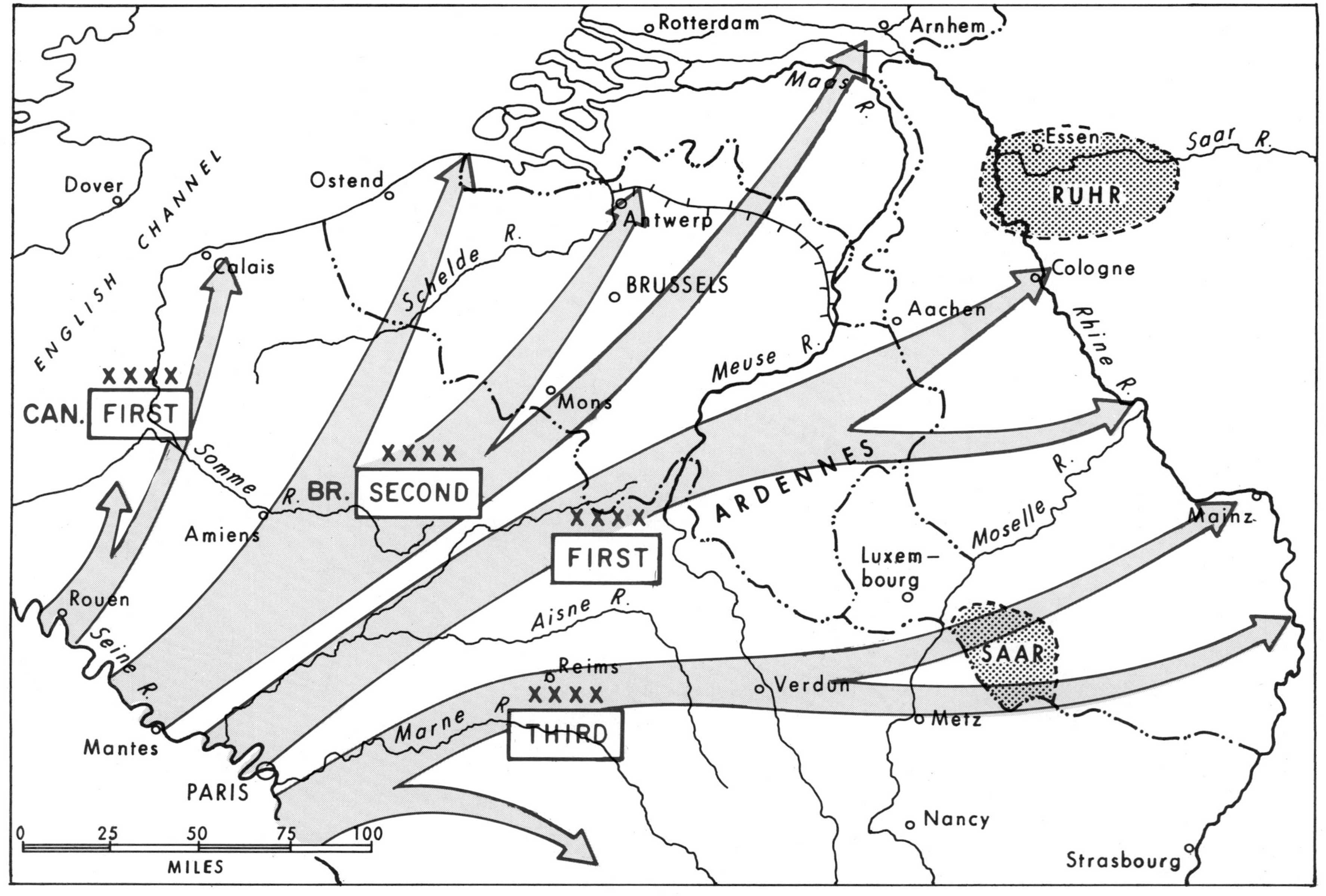

Eisenhower's Plan: August 1944

Rather than stopping to reorganize and build up along the Seine River line for three months, as had originally been anticipated, the Supreme Commander now decided to continue his attack across the river. By making this move he would defer improving his logistical situation in order to take advantage of a favorable tactical situation. The planned pause had been designed to open ports, build airfields, land support troops, and construct support installations. Forgoing it would entail accepting the risk that the offensive might run out of steam, but Eisenhower knew that a pursuit, once begun, should be pressed relentlessly. Hence, he decided to try to destroy as many German troops as he could to the west of the Seine, cross the river, and continue the attack toward Germany.[72]

Once the decision was made to cross the Seine, the method of advancing was also reconsidered. Prior to the invasion, planners had felt that the main objective should be the Ruhr industrial area, as Berlin was too far to the east.* To enable the Allies to shift troops to take advantage of favorable situations, to deceive the enemy, and to frustrate any plan to concentrate all counterattack forces in one area, however, the planners envisioned two thrusts. In addition to the advance by the 21st Army Group toward the Ruhr, a second one would be carried out by the 12th Army Group farther south, toward the Saar industrial region. It was that basic plan which Eisenhower intended now to implement, modified only by the reinforcement of Montgomery's army group with the First Allied Airborne Army, and perhaps a "minimum" of American ground troops.[73]

Eisenhower's decision initiated what would perhaps become the most heated and persistent argument over ground strategy between the two western Allies during the war. Introduced in this chapter, it will be covered in more detail in later chapters. On August 23, Montgomery proposed that the advance be made by a force of some 40 divisions on *one* front; both army groups would advance into Belgium and toward the Ruhr in such strength that nothing could stop them. (Montgomery's scheme came to known as the "Single Thrust"—*see Map: Montgomery's Plan, page 339.)* Acquiescing to some degree to Montgomery's arguments, the Supreme Commander decided to modify his plan by adding Hodge's First Army to the northern drive and, within Bradley's army group, by giving First Army priority over Patton's Third Army on gasoline stocks. (Eisenhower's scheme came to be known as the "Broad Front"—*see Map: Eisenhower's Plan, page 340.)*[74]

Eisenhower's American subordinates were not happy with this decision, which seemed to them to downgrade Patton's advance toward the Saar while splitting Bradley's command by the Ardennes forest. Eisenhower held firm, however, convinced that objectives in the north were vital. He was equally firm in refusing to adopt Montgomery's plan in total. The British leader felt that his scheme would bring the war to a speedy conclusion. Both the British economy and manpower situation were such that a quick end was greatly desired. Eisenhower, sure of eventual victory, would have to accept risks if he adopted Montgomery's scheme. Flexibility would be sacrificed, and should the enemy launch a large counterattack against the thrust, the distant and supply-short Third Army would have difficulty intervening. Eisenhower, moreover, also had a home front to consider. How could the War Department justify its force levels if divisions were idled in forward areas and new units which landed in France were kept from combat? Eisenhower felt that the American people would not countenance stopping Patton and converting his once rampaging Third Army into a flank guard while the other armies advanced.[75] Eisenhower's decision would stand, at least for the present. Meanwhile, the Allies still had to get to and across the Seine River, and in that process the capture of Paris proved to be more of political concern than military necessity.

Eisenhower hoped that he would be able to by-pass Paris on both the south and north, and thus avoid having to fight for the city. He did not relish the idea of prolonged combat in the streets, and he was concerned about the possible destruction of treasured monuments and buildings. Logistical considerations were also important, as it would take 4,000 tons of supplies a day—enough to support seven reinforced divisions—just to take care of the 2,000,000 inhabitants. As long as the city remained in German hands, the people would no doubt be short of food and fuel, but Eisenhower felt that the Parisians would accept temporary discomfort if it meant that the war would end sooner.

Eisenhower's plans were upset on the night of August 19 when resistance groups took over the heart of the city and sent out a call for an uprising. By the next morning, the German commander had asked for an armistice so that he could withdraw his troops from western Paris. He agreed to allow food convoys to enter the city and to recognize the members of the Resistance as belligerents. The offer of an armistice was accepted, with the expiration to be noon on August 23. Due to misunderstandings and the inability of Resistance leaders to control their troops, fighting soon erupted again, and Paris Radio, still controlled by the Germans, declared that the revolt would be smashed. This caused more fighting, and by the night of August 21 it appeared that the Germans might emerge victorious. The Resistance sent envoys to entreat the Allies to help them.

General Charles De Gaulle, who had recently arrived in France, was also urging action. He felt that it was imperative to

*See Map, p. 284.

Members of French Resistance in the Streets of Paris

move regular French troops into the city as soon as possible because Resistance forces, once victorious, would probably split into feuding factions. Communist influence was high, and it was known that a large group of resisters was preparing to oppose De Gaulle's government. On August 21, De Gaulle wrote Eisenhower that if the Supreme Commander would not dispatch troops to Paris, French units might be used on the authority of the head of the provisional government. Later that day, General de Division Jacque Philippe Leclerc, who had been denied permission to move on Paris by both the V Corps and US First Army commanders, ordered a unit forward.

By August 22, when exaggerated reports indicated that most of the city was in friendly hands, Eisenhower decided to reinforce the success of the Resistance, and ordered Leclerc to take the city. His division, some 100 miles from the capital, began to move on August 23. It travelled through throngs of well-wishing and wine-bearing Frenchmen, who filled the roads. Bradley, however, thought that Leclerc's division was moving too slowly as it partied its way toward Paris, so he ordered the 4th Infantry Division, also a part of V Corps, to enter the city. News of this order did wonders for the French rate of advance. Leclerc soon made his way into the city. By noon on August 25, elements of both the French 2nd Armored and U.S. 4th Infantry Divisions were in the heart of Paris.

The Germans surrendered and De Gaulle installed his government. On the next day, August 26, to demonstrate his control of the entire Resistance and of the government, De Gaulle relighted the flame at the Tomb of the Unknown Soldier and then led a triumphal parade down the Champs Elysees. A crowd of almost 2,000,000 people watched as De Gaulle marched. All knew that with the liberation of Paris, the battle for France had been won.[76]

Meanwhile, Model's situation was growing progressively worse. On August 19, the day that American troops seized a bridgehead across the Seine at Mantes, Montgomery, Dempsey, and Bradley met to discuss the immediate future. *(See Map 65, in Atlas.)* When Dempsey said that he could not spare two divisions to travel by truck through the Third Army area to the Seine for an attack down the left bank, Bradley proposed that American units be employed. Both Dempsey and Montgomery agreed to the move, which would cause U.S. troops to advance across the British front. Bradley's men reached Elbeuf on August 24, where a determined enemy delayed further advance for some two days. During this period, as many German troops as possible were transported across the river by ferries, rafts, pontoon bridges, and boats. Some even swam. Bad weather kept many Allied planes on the ground, and although much German equipment was left behind and many troops were killed or captured, most got away. Still, the German losses were enormous. Since the invasion, approximately one-half million casualties had been suffered, of which 210,000 were prisoners of war. Of the 2,300 German tanks and assault guns which were in Normandy, only 100 to 110 had been moved to the north bank of the Seine by the time that the last German troops crossed on August 29.[77]

When Eisenhower reported to the Combined Chiefs of Staff on the progress of the campaign from D-Day to August 25, he was ecstatic. Allied forces had defeated not only the German Seventh and Fifth Panzer Armies, but also many units drawn from the First and Fifteenth Armies. Ten *panzer* divisions and one *panzer* grenadier division had been destroyed or severely mauled, while 32 infantry divisions suffered the same fate. Two infantry divisions and a parachute division were encircled in Brittany fortresses, and another was in the Channel Islands.

General Charles de Gaulle Leads Parade in Paris. (General Leclerc is at Center Rear)

Enemy forces had lost heavily in the air as well; over 2,000 aircraft had been destroyed while aloft and over 1,000 more on the ground. Eisenhower lavished praise on all who had made the victory possible, including pre-invasion planners and airmen. He concluded, " . . . the greatest factor of all has been the fighting qualities of the soldiers, sailors and airmen of the United Nations. Their valor, stamina and devotion to duty have been beyond praise. They will continue to be."[78]

Leadership which did not seriously err and a great superiority in the implements of war, coupled with mobile forces and air superiority, had defeated the German armies in France. It would be an oversight, however, not to recognize that the way in which the great deception plan had been orchestrated was of considerable significance; perhaps of even more import was the impact of ULTRA. Considered in light of that sizeable intelligence advantage, it is difficult to see how the Allies might have lost the campaign; it is, moreover, understandable that the luster attached to Allied leadership dims a bit in those instances when a call for aggressive action was tempered by caution in spite of the secret knowledge of the enemy's situation. At the same time, our present knowledge of Hitler's incompetent directives and of the interception of his messages by the Allies makes us marvel at how effectively the German troop units and leadership managed to stem the advance as long as they did. Even so, in the final analysis the Normandy Campaign and the succeeding breakout resulted in a great Allied victory—one that Hitler could ill afford.

By August 25, though a few enemy pockets remained, the lodgment area between the Loire and Seine Rivers as envisaged in the OVERLORD plan had been secured. Tactically, as Allied troops crossed the Seine, they were ahead of schedule. Logistically, due to the recent rapid movements, the support capability was lagging. As the advance continued, this logistical shortage would become more and more the controlling factor in the campaign.[79]

Notes

[1]Dwight D. Eisenhower, *Crusade in Europe* (Garden City, 1948), pp. 266-267; Omar N. Bradley, *A Soldier's Story* (New York, 1951), pp. 317-318; Martin Blumenson, *Breakout and Pursuit* (Washington, 1961), pp. 179-180, 185-187, 197; T. Dodson Stamps and Vincent J. Esposito (eds.), *A Military History of World War II* (2 vols; West Point, NY, 1956), I, 412.

[2]Blumenson, *Breakout and Pursuit*, pp. 185-187; Bradley, *Soldier's Story*, pp. 329-332.

[3]Bradley, *Soldier's Story*, pp. 318, 329-330; Blumenson, *Breakout and Pursuit*, p. 214; Omar N. Bradley, Personal interview conducted by Kitty Buhler, 1966, Omar N. Bradley Papers, U.S. Military Academy Library, pp. 2-3, 6.

[4]Bradley, *Soldier's Story*, p. 332.

[5]Blumenson, *Breakout and Pursuit*, pp. 197, 214-215; Vincent J. Esposito (ed.), *The West Point Atlas of American Wars* (2 vols.; New York, 1959), II, Section 2, 53; Bradley, *Soldier's Story*, p. 330; Bradley interview with Buhler, p. 6.

[6]Bradley, *Soldier's Story*, pp. 330, 338-339; Blumenson, *Breakout and Pursuit*, p. 220.

[7]Bradley is quoted in Chester B. Hansen, "War Diary," Chester B. Hansen Papers, United States Army Military History Research Collection, Carlisle Barracks, Pa., entry of July 12, 1944. Also see Bradley, *Soldier's Story*, pp. 329-330.

[8]OUTLINE PLAN OPERATION "COBRA," dated July 13, 1944, a copy of which can be found in Hansen, "War Diary."

[9]*Ibid.*; Blumenson, *Breakout and Pursuit*, pp. 215, 217; First United States Army, "Report of Operations, 20 October, 1943-1 August, 1944," Book I, 97-98.

[10]Blumenson, *Breakout and Pursuit*, pp. 213-214, 219; "First Army Report," Book I, 98.

[11]Quotation from Hansen, "War Diary," entry of July 19, 1944; "First Army Report," Book I, 98; Blumenson, *Breakout and Pursuit*, p. 217.

[12]Blumenson, *Breakout and Pursuit*, pp. 217-219.

[13]*Ibid.*, pp. 198-204.

[14]Bradley, *Soldier's Story*, pp. 337-338.

[15]Discussion in the above four paragraphs is based on: Hansen, "War Diary," entry of July 19, 1944; Bradley, *Soldier's Story*, pp. 340-341, 346-347; Blumenson, *Breakout and Pursuit*, pp. 220-223; Robert L. Hewitt, *Work Horse of the Western Front: The Story of the 30th Infantry Division* (Washington, 1946), p. 35; Eisenhower, *Crusade in Europe*, p. 262; Wesley F. Craven and James L. Cate (eds.), *The Army Air Forces in World War II,* Volume III, *Europe: ARGUMENT to V-E Day, January 1944 to May 1945* (Chicago, 1951), pp. 228, 231-232.

[16]Hansen, "War Diary," entry of July 19, 1944.

[17]Frederick E. Pamp, "Normandy to the Elbe, XIX Corps" (n.p., 1945), p. 15; *Spearhead in the West 1941-45, The Third Armored Division* (Frankfurt, 1945), pp. 68-69; E. A. Trahan (ed.), *A History of the Second United States Armored Division 1940-1946* (Atlanta, 1946), Chapter V (n.p.); Blumenson, *Breakout and Pursuit*, p. 210.

[18]Hansen, "War Diary," entries of July 17, 18, and 22, 1944; "OUTLINE 'COBRA,'" Hansen Papers; Bradley, *Soldier's Story*, pp. 345, 355; John D. Horn, "War Diary," John D. Horn Papers, Darien, Conn., entry of July 18, 1944.

[19]L. F. Ellis, *Victory in the West*, I, *The Battle of Normandy* (London, 1962), p. 358; Blumenson, *Breakout and Pursuit*, pp. 188-194; Hansen, "War Diary," entry of July 21, 1944; Bradley, *Soldier's Story*, p. 343.

[20]Bradley, *Soldier's Story*, pp. 335, 345-346; Blumenson, *Breakout and Pursuit*, pp. 127-128.

[21]Bradley, *Soldier's Story*, p. 346.

[22]Bradley, *Soldier's Story*, pp. 343, 346; Hansen, "War Diary," entry of July 21, 1944; William C. Sylvan, "Personal Diary," William C. Sylvan Papers, United States Army Center for Military History, Washington, D.C., entry of July 21, 1944.

[23]Quoted in Blumenson, *Breakout and Pursuit*, p. 194.

[24]*Ibid.*, pp. 193-194; Blumenson, "Some Reflections on the Immediate Post-Assault Strategy," in *D-Day: The Normandy Invasion in Retrospect* (Lawrence, Kansas, 1971), p. 215; Anthony Cave Brown, *Bodyguard of Lies* (New York, 1975), p. 745.

[25]Discussion in the above three paragraphs is based on: Bodo Zimmermann, MS#B-308: "OB WEST Atlantic Wall to Siegfried Line, A Study in Command," in *OB WEST (Atlantic Wall to Siegfried Line), A Study in Command*, James F. Scoggin, Jr. (ed.) (Allendorf, Germany, 1946-1947), I, 128; Esposito, *West Point Atlas*, II, Section 2, 53; Blumenson, *Breakout and Pursuit*, pp. 181-182, 225-228.

[26]Discussion in the above seven paragraphs is based on: Bradley, *Soldier's Story*, pp. 346-348; Bradley, Personal interview conducted by Buhler, pp. 12, 79; Craven and Cate, *ARGUMENT*, pp. 228, 230-231; Hansen, "War Diary," entry of July 24, 1944; Hewitt, *Work Horse*, p. 36; Horn, "War Diary," entry of July 24, 1944; Sylvan, "Personal Diary," entry of July 24, 1944.

[27]Blumenson, *Breakout and Pursuit*, pp. 233-234; Craven and Cate, *ARGUMENT*, p. 232.

[28]Blumenson, *Breakout and Pursuit*, pp. 238-239; Cave Brown, *Bodyguard*, p. 773.

[29]Blumenson, *Breakout and Pursuit*, p. 228; Chester Wilmot, *The Struggle for Europe* (London, 1952), pp. 390-391; C. P. Stacey, *Official History of the Canadian Army in the Second World War:* Vol. III, *The Victory Campaign: The Operations in North-West Europe 1944-1945* (Ottawa, 1960), pp. 181-196; Bradley, *Soldier's Story*, p. 348; Charles B. MacDonald, *The Mighty Endeavor: American Armed Forces in the European Theater in World War II* (New York, 1969), pp. 303, 305.

[30]Blumenson, *Breakout and Pursuit*, pp. 234-235; MacDonald, *Mighty Endeavor*, p. 304.

[31]Blumenson, *Breakout and Pursuit*, pp. 235-236; MacDonald, *Mighty Endeavor*, p. 304.

[32]Quoted in Blumenson, *Breakout and Pursuit*, p. 237.

[33]*Ibid.*, pp. 236-237, 241; Hewitt, *Work Horse*, pp. 36-37.

[34]Bayerlin is quoted in Wilmot, *Struggle for Europe*, p. 391.

[35]*Mission Accomplished, the Story of the Campaigns of the VII Corps, United States Army in the War Against Germany, 1944-1945* (Leipzig, 1945), p. 24; MacDonald, *Mighty Endeavor*, p. 305; Stamps and Esposito, *Military History*, I, 414.

[36]Collins' feelings are detailed in Forrest C. Pogue, *The Supreme Command* (Washington, 1954), p. 199; Eisenhower's view is in Alfred D. Chandler (ed.), *The Papers of Dwight David Eisenhower: The War Years* (Baltimore, 1970) (hereinafter referred to as *EP*), III: No. 1854, Eisenhower to Bernard Law Montgomery, July 26, 1944; Bradley's assessment is in Bradley, *Soldier's Story*, p. 358. For lower-

level commanders' initial reaction, see Blumenson, *Breakout and Pursuit*, pp. 244-245.

[37]Bradley, *Soldier's Story*, p. 349; MacDonald, *Mighty Endeavor*, p. 305; Eisenhower, *Crusade in Europe*, p. 272; Wilmot, *Struggle for Europe*, p. 392; Harry C. Butcher, *My Three Years with Eisenhower* (New York, 1946), p. 625; Stamps and Esposito, *Military History*, I, 414; Blumenson, *Breakout and Pursuit*, p. 252.

[38]Wilmot, *Struggle for Europe*, p. 392; Blumenson, *Breakout and Pursuit*, pp. 249-250, 253-255, 264; MacDonald, *Mighty Endeavor*, pp. 305-306; *Mission Accomplished*, p. 24; Esposito, *West Point Atlas*, II, Section 2, 53; Bradley, *Soldier's Story*, p. 358.

[39]Stamps and Esposito, *Military History*, I, 414-415; Wilmot, *Struggle for Europe*, pp. 391-393; MacDonald, *Mighty Endeavor*, pp. 307-308; Blumenson, *Breakout and Pursuit*, pp. 266-271, 282-288; Hansen, "War Diary," entry of July 27, 1944.

[40]MacDonald, *Mighty Endeavor*, pp. 307-308; Pogue, *Supreme Command*, p. 201; Cave Brown, *Bodyguard of Lies*, pp. 775-776; Wilmot, *Struggle for Europe*, pp. 393-394; Blumenson, *Breakout and Pursuit*, pp. 248-249, 260-261.

[41]Hansen, "War Diary," entry of July 28, 1944; Wilmot, *Struggle for Europe*, p. 394; Esposito, *West Point Atlas*, II, Section 2, 53; Stamps and Esposito, *Military History*, I, 415; Pogue, *Supreme Command*, p. 204; MacDonald, *Mighty Endeavor*, pp. 308-309; Zimmermann, *OB WEST*, I, 129-130; Bradley, *Soldier's Story*, p. 358; Martin Blumenson (ed.), *The Patton Papers, 1940-1945* (Boston, 1974), pp. 490-493.

[42]Bernard Law Montgomery, *The Memoirs of Field Marshal the Viscount Montgomery of ALAMEIN, K.G.* (Cleveland, 1958), p. 253; Wilmot, *Struggle for Europe*, pp. 395-398; *EP*, IV: No. 1866, Eisenhower to Montgomery, July 28, 1944; Montgomery's letter to Eisenhower is quoted in editor's note with No. 1866, p. 2042.

[43]Blumenson, *Patton Papers*, p. 493: letter, Patton to Mrs. George Patton, 31 July 1944; *Mission Accomplished*, p. 25.

[44]Quoted in Wilmot, *Struggle for Europe*, pp. 394-395.

[45]Pogue, *Supreme Command*, pp. 201-203. Hitler is quoted on p. 203.

[46]Blumenson, "Reflections on Immediate Post-Assault Strategy," p. 207; Esposito, *West Point Atlas*, II, Section 2, 54; Bradley, *Soldier's Story*, p. 365; MacDonald, *Mighty Endeavor*, p. 310; Wilmot, *Struggle for Europe*, p. 458.

[47]Bruce C. Clarke, "Handling Prisoners During a Deep Penetration into Enemy Territory by Armor," no date, copy in Bruce C. Clarke Papers, United States Army Military History Research Collection, Carlisle Barracks, Pa.

[48]MacDonald, *Mighty Endeavor*, pp. 309-310; Pogue, *Supreme Command*, pp. 205-206.

[49]Stamps and Esposito, *Military History*, I, 420-421; Eisenhower, *Crusade in Europe*, p. 274; Pogue, *Supreme Command*, p. 206; MacDonald, *Mighty Endeavor*, p. 311; *EP*, IV: No. 1876, Eisenhower to Marshall and Combined Chiefs of Staff, August 2, 1944, and editor's note with No. 1882, p. 2055; Esposito, *West Point Atlas*, II, Section 2, 54; Blumenson, *Breakout and Pursuit*, pp. 430-432; Roland G. Ruppenthal, "Logistic Planning for OVERLORD in Retrospect," in *D-Day: The Normandy Invasion in Retrospect* (Lawrence, KS, 1971), p. 98.

[50]Eisenhower, *Crusade in Europe*, pp. 279-280; Bradley, *Soldier's Story*, pp. 365-367.

[51]Hitler is quoted in Pogue, *Supreme Command*, p. 207; Wilmot, *Struggle for Europe*, pp. 400-401.

[52]Treusch von Buttlar, MS#B-672: "Commentary on MS#B-308," in *OB WEST (Atlantic Wall to Siegfried Line), A Study in Command*, James F. Scoggin, Jr. (ed.) (Allendorf, Germany, 1946-1947), II, 55-59; Stamps and Esposito, *Military History*, I, 422-423; Cave Brown, *Bodyguard*, p. 777.

[53]MacDonald, *Mighty Endeavor*, p. 312; Wilmot, *Struggle for Europe*, p. 401; Blumenson, *Breakout and Pursuit*, pp. 457-460.

[54]F. W. Winterbotham, *The Ultra Secret* (New York, 1974), pp. 146-151; Cave Brown, *Bodyguard*, pp. 784-785.

[55]Wilmot, *Struggle for Europe*, p. 402; MacDonald, *Mighty Endeavor*, pp. 312-313; Stamps and Esposito, *Military History*, I, 423; *Mission Accomplished*, p. 26; Bradley, *Soldier's Story*, p. 372.

[56]Blumenson, *Breakout and Pursuit*, pp. 488-490; Bradley, *Soldier's Story*, p. 371; MacDonald, *Mighty Endeavor*, p. 313.

[57]Winterbotham, *Ultra*, pp. 152-153; Blumenson, *Breakout and Pursuit*, pp. 465, 479-482; Pogue, *Supreme Command*, p. 208.

[58]Bradley, *Soldier's Story*, pp. 374-375; Eisenhower, *Crusade in Europe*, p. 275; Stephen E. Ambrose, *The Supreme Commander: The War Years of General Dwight D. Eisenhower* (Garden City, New York, 1969), p. 473; Pogue, *Supreme Command*, p. 209; MacDonald, *Mighty Endeavor*, pp. 314-315; Blumenson, *Breakout and Pursuit*, p. 492.

[59]Quoted in Blumenson, *Breakout and Pursuit*, p. 495.

[60]*Ibid.*, pp. 494-501; Esposito, *West Point Atlas*, II, Section 2, 55.

[61]Bradley, *Soldier's Story*, p. 376; MacDonald, *Mighty Endeavor*, p. 315; Esposito, *West Point Atlas*, II, Section 2, 54; Stamps and Esposito, *Military History*, I, 418.

[62]Blumenson, *Breakout and Pursuit*, p. 505.

[63]Bradley, *Soldier's Story*, p. 377.

[64]Bradley, *Soldier's Story*, pp. 376-377; Bradley, Personal Interview conducted by Buhler, p. 58; MacDonald, *Mighty Endeavor*, pp. 315-316, 318; Esposito, *West Point Atlas*, II, Section 2, 54-55; Ambrose, *Supreme Commander*, p. 214; Eisenhower, *Crusade in Europe*, pp. 278-279; Blumenson, *Breakout and Pursuit*, pp. 506-509.

[65]Ronald Lewin, *Ultra Goes to War* (New York, 1978), pp. 342-344.

[66]Quoted in Blumenson, *Breakout and Pursuit*, p. 522.

[67]Discussion in the above three paragraphs is based upon Wilmot, *Struggle for Europe*, p. 421; Albert Speer, *Inside the Third Reich* (New York, 1971, paper edition), p. 503; MacDonald, *Mighty Endeavor*, pp. 314-319; Pogue, *Supreme Command*, pp. 210-213; Winterbotham, *Ultra*, p. 157; Cave Brown, *Bodyguard*, pp. 790-792; Blumenson, *Breakout and Pursuit*, pp. 481-486, 503-505, 515-523, 531, 535-536.

[68]Esposito, *West Point Atlas*, II, Section 2, 55; Stamps and Esposito, *Military History*, I, 427; Wilmot, *Struggle for Europe*, pp. 422-423; Pogue, *Supreme Command*, p. 215; *Mission Accomplished*, pp. 26-27; Blumenson, *Breakout and Pursuit*, pp. 537, 555-556, 663.

[69]Eisenhower, *Crusade in Europe*, p. 279; Blumenson, *Breakout and Pursuit*, p. 558.

[70]Blumenson, *Breakout and Pursuit*, pp. 523-524, 564-565; Bradley, *Soldier's Story*, pp. 378-379; Esposito, *West Point Atlas*, II, Section 2, 55; Stamps and Esposito, *Military History*, I, 426; Butcher, *Three Years*, pp. 641, 643.

[71]Pogue, *Supreme Command*, pp. 210, 213; Stamps and Esposito, *Military History*, I, 427-429; Ambrose, *Supreme Commander*, p. 477; Eisenhower, *Crusade in Europe*, p. 280.

[72]Esposito, *West Point Atlas*, II, Section 2, 55; MacDonald,

Mighty Endeavor, pp. 328-329; Pogue, *Supreme Command*, p. 215; Roland G. Ruppenthal, "Logistics and the Broad-Front Strategy," in Kent Robert Greenfield (ed.), *Command Decisions* (Washington, 1960), p. 476; Ambrose, *Supreme Commander*, p. 495.

[73]Blumenson, *Breakout and Pursuit*, pp. 657-658; MacDonald, *Mighty Endeavor*, p. 328; Ambrose, *Supreme Commander*, pp. 504-505.

[74]Pogue, *Supreme Command*, pp. 250-251; MacDonald, *Mighty Endeavor*, pp. 330-331; *EP*: IV, No. 1909, Eisenhower to Montgomery, August 24, 1944; Blumenson, *Breakout and Pursuit*, pp. 659-660.

[75]Montgomery, *Memoirs*, p. 243; *EP*: IV, editor's note with No. 1909, pp. 2091-2092; Wilmot, *Struggle for Europe*, p. 468; Stephen E. Ambrose, "Eisenhower as Commander: Single Thrust Versus Broad Front," in *EP*: V, p. 45.

[76]Discussion in the above six paragraphs is based on: Eisenhower, *Crusade in Europe*, pp. 296-297; Bradley, *Soldier's Story*, pp. 385-393; Wilmot, *Struggle for Europe*, pp. 429-430; Ambrose, *Supreme Commander*, pp. 480-486; *EP*, IV: No. 1907, Eisenhower to Combined Chiefs of Staff, August 22, 1944, editor's note with No. 1908, pp. 2089-2090.

[77]Esposito, *West Point Atlas*, II, Section 2, 55; Bradley, *Soldier's Story*, pp. 380-381; Wilmot, *Struggle for Europe*, pp. 433-434; MacDonald, *Mighty Endeavor*, pp. 318-319.

[78]*EP*, IV: No. 1922, Eisenhower to Combined Chiefs of Staff, August 30, 1944. The material contained in this message was released to the press on August 31.

[79]Bradley, *Soldier's Story*, p. 330; Eisenhower, *Crusade in Europe*, p. 302; Stamps and Esposito, *Military History*, I, 431, 440-441, 446.

The Tyranny of Logistics

15

The enemy forces immediately facing us are on the run. Our greatest difficulty at the moment except for the hard battle at Brest is maintenance. We have advanced so rapidly that further movement in large parts of the front even against very weak opposition is almost impossible. . . . The closer we get to the Siegfried Line the more we will be stretched administratively and eventually a period of relative inaction will be imposed upon us.

*Dwight D. Eisenhower**

After the defeat of the German forces in northwestern France during July and August, a spirit of optimism engulfed Allied leaders. Aware of the intense pressure Hitlerite Germany was feeling from the bombing of the homeland and from conditions on other fronts, some of those leaders began to foresee an end to the war in 1944. As noted earlier, Eisenhower warned against overconfidence, but even he hoped to advance to the Rhine, and perhaps across it, by the end of the year.

As the SHAEF armies crossed the Seine, a new invasion force drove northward up the Rhone Valley. Soon Eisenhower would add a third army group to his command. Equally important, that new force had captured Marseilles, a port of such capacity that it promised to go far toward overcoming the logistical shortcomings which were beginning to plague the Allies. The growing air of optimism, however, would prove to be ill-founded, primarily for two reasons. In the first place, the rate of Allied advance and consumption of supplies would be too great to be maintained. Second, the Germans would prove to be amazingly resilient and capable of putting up greater opposition west of the Rhine than had been expected. In southern France, however, the weakened German forces were no match for the Allied army, which landed on August 15.

*Alfred D. Chandler (ed.), *The Papers of Dwight D. Eisenhower: The War Years* (Baltimore, 1970), IV: No. 1934, Eisenhower to Marshall, September 4, 1944.

Planning the Southern French Invasion

The U.S. Seventh Army headquarters, located in Algiers, accomplished the detailed planning for DRAGOON, formerly called ANVIL. This army was commanded by Lieutenant General Alexander M. Patch, a veteran of the fighting in the Pacific. He assumed command of Seventh Army on March 2, 1944, after Patton had gone to England and after the brief interlude during which Mark Clark controlled the army headquarters while also commanding Fifth Army in Italy. As concerned planning the future operation, Patch faced an uncertain situation upon his arrival in the Mediterranean Theater. He knew neither the projected invasion date nor the size of the force he would eventually lead, because OVERLORD requirements and the situation in Italy had priority on Allied assets. Moreover, the southern France landing was a highly debated operation, causing considerable division among Allied strategic planners. Nevertheless, Patch's planners proceeded with the investigation of suitable landing sites, largely influenced by the realization that a sizeable port would need to be captured early in order to provide logistical support. *(See Map 66, in Atlas.)* They selected Marseilles, which could handle large tonnages, over Toulon and Sète, which could not. As for landing beaches, suitable ones were available only west of Sète, in an area beyond the range of land-based fighter support, or east of Toulon, where such cover could be provided. This consideration, supported by other factors, led to the selection of a landing site east of Toulon. The strategic controversy, meanwhile, continued to flare.[1]

The idea of landing on the French Mediterranean coast

Lieutenant General Alexander M. Patch

evoked hot argument between the British and Americans.* Ultimately, the controversy was elevated to the level of Churchill and Eisenhower, who held strongly opposing views. When DRAGOON was delayed until mid-August, the Supreme Commander could no longer argue that the Mediterranean assault was necessary to divert German attention from OVERLORD; but he could, and did, insist that the port of Marseilles would be vital to the logistical support of the Allied drive into Germany. Moreover, an Allied advance up the Rhone Valley could link up with the advancing OVERLORD forces, thereby cutting off German units in western and southwestern France and coincidentally providing security for the long southern flank of 12th Army Group. Churchill would not concede, however, and pursued his argument almost to the eve of the August 15 landing. He went over Eisenhower's head to Roosevelt, urging cancellation of the operation, and on August 5 he argued with Ike for over six hours. Although he had previously wanted to use the DRAGOON forces in Italy or the Balkans, Churchill now wanted to exploit German difficulties in western France by introducing these divisions through one of the Brittany ports. Eisenhower flatly disagreed. He was planning to use the Brittany ports, when they could be put in operating condition, to support other troops. Churchill then suggested a landing in the Bay of Biscay, but Eisenhower reiterated his position. The Supreme Commander even refused to waver on August 9 when the Prime Minister threatened to go to the King and resign. Eisenhower's case was strong because Roosevelt refused to intercede and many of the DRAGOON ships were set to sail on August 10. Troops and supplies were already aboard. To change landing sites at this point would mean that many of the ships would have to be unloaded and reloaded to adjust to the new mission and to the different sailing conditions which would be encountered in the Atlantic. Churchill, predicting great losses and claiming that he had been "dragooned" into the operation, finally backed down.[2]

Churchill was not the only leader concerned about the use of the Allied invasion force in an area other than southern France. German officers were also aware of this possibility, and it figured strongly in Hitler's decision to continue to defend southern France. Without such a defense on the coast, the Germans feared, the Allies would only employ French troops, both Regular and Resistance elements, while the remainder of the invasion force could go elsewhere.[3] Accordingly, Hitler left 10 divisions in southern France. Of these, two reserve infantry divisions and a corps headquarters were on the Atlantic coast. On the Mediterranean coast, the Nineteenth Army defended with three corps headquarters, and eight understrength infantry, coastal defense, and reserve divisions. The 11th Panzer Division, the strongest and most mobile unit in the area, was en route from Toulouse to the Nineteenth Army area and had reached a point just west of Avignon when the Allied attack came. While the German coastal defenses were in many ways similar to those found at Normandy, there were less troops to man them.[4]

The planning for DRAGOON was typical of the careful analysis the Allies had learned was necessary to mount complex amphibious operations. Assembling the invasion force and coordinating the supporting air and naval strikes was not simple. *(See Inset, Map 67, in Atlas.)* Much effort also went into the cover plan which was designed to convince the Germans that Genoa was the target. In Patch's favor, however, was the fact that, except for a few French units, all of the fighting elements had experienced considerable combat. All three assault divisions of Major General Lucian K. Truscott's VI Corps were withdrawn from combat in time to undergo three weeks of preinvasion training near Salerno. Truscott, who had extensive combat experience and would end the war as an army commander and one of America's most illustrious fighting leaders, was designated to command the assault until a beachhead had been established; then Patch would assume control. *(See Map 67, in Atlas.)* The French II Corps would comprise the follow-up force and the French I Corps would be the build-up force. After the latter corps landed, General Jean de Lattre de Tassigny would set up French Army B headquarters and be under Seventh Army control until an army group headquarters could be established. Patch's command also included the 1st Airborne Task Force, which numbered some 8,000 parachute and glider infantry and artillery, and the 1st Special Service Force (SSF), a composite unit made up of Americans and Canadians. The Western Task Force, 835 ships strong under Vice Admiral Henry K. Hewitt, would land and support the ground troops. Brigadier General Gordon P. Saville, commander of the XII Tactical Air Command, would control all aircraft in the assault area. He had some 1,100 planes based on

*See Chapter 11, p. 263, for general commentary.

Corsica, and would also direct 200 aircraft from carriers, as well as heavy bombers of the Fifteenth Air Force based at Foggia in Italy.[5]

Allied air attacks, which had begun sporadically in April, intensified during the period of August 5 to August 10 as aircraft struck at lines of communication, airfields, and submarine bases in the Genoa and Po Valley areas of Italy, as well as in the Marseilles-Toulouse region. By August 10, virtually all major routes into the invasion site had been blocked. Then, in the next four days, the airmen attacked large coastal batteries, radar sites and coastal defense troops from Sète to Genoa. Finally, in the four hours before the assault, swarms of aircraft hit the defenses in the landing areas. This carefully planned pre-assault bombing program, coupled with the fighting which was taking place in Italy, caused some German intelligence experts to think that Genoa was to be the site of the invasion.[6]

DRAGOON Exceeds Expectations

On the night of August 14, as the Falaise pocket was being closed far to the north, Hewitt's invasion force lay off the French coast. During the night, a number of measures calculated to confuse the enemy were executed. As had been the case in the Normandy invasion, west of Toulon the Allies dropped 500 dummy paratroopers complete with noisemakers which sounded like small arms fire. Naval demonstrations were also conducted between Marseilles and Toulon as well as between Cannes and Nice. *(See Map 67, in Atlas.)* The 1st SSF attacked Port Cos and Levant, where the target gun emplacements were found to be fakes, and French Commandos blocked the coastal road from Toulon.[7]

Members of a French demolition party which landed west of Cannes were discovered, and most were killed or captured. Although the demolition project largely failed, the airborne drop depicted on the map was a major success. No aircraft were downed by the enemy, and by 4:30 A.M. fully 85 percent of the force had landed in or near the correct drop zones. Some touched down in the midst of a German corps headquarters, an intrusion which did much to upset early coordination of German defense efforts.[8]

The main amphibious assault went extremely well. Air and naval preparations observed by Churchill, who was aboard a British destroyer, preceded the landing of Truscott's VI Corps at 8:00 A.M. Camel Force (the 36th Infantry Division) was the only element to encounter much resistance. By mid-day on August 17, the three infantry divisions had reached or crossed the beachhead line *(solid blue line on Map 67)*, and the follow-up French II Corps was landing. By the end of that day, over 86,000 men, 12,000 vehicles, and 46,000 tons of supplies were on shore. The French II Corps was slated to tackle Toulon and Marseilles while Truscott pushed VI Corps to the north in exploitation of the rapid gains made by the landing force. His plan was to use the 3rd and 45th Infantry Divisions as a direct pressure force, and a provisional organization, commanded by Brigadier General Frederick B. Butler and known as Task Force Butler, as an encircling force—all in an attempt to cut German withdrawal routes.[9]

Truscott's plan was being implemented at the same time that the Germans had decided to withdraw from southern France, while exacting as heavy a price as possible. Recognizing the power of Patch's invasion force while also suffering severe losses in the Argentan-Falaise area, Hitler reluctantly agreed to withdraw all troops from southern and western France, less those needed to defend the ports. The Alpine passes were to be blocked and the remainder of Nineteenth Army was to fall back to the Vosges Mountains in Alsace. The withdrawal order was monitored by ULTRA, but because of effective German counterattacks, an Allied shortage of artillery ammunition due to lengthening supply lines, and skillful German troop handling, Truscott was not able to seal the defile at Montelimar until August 28. Thus, although much equipment was destroyed and 57,000 Germans became prisoners, many of Hitler's troopers managed to evade the trap. That same day, August 28, Toulon and Marseilles fell to the French II Corps.[10]

Following the battle at Montelimar, Patch's troops continued driving northward against dwindling German opposition. *(See Map 66, in Atlas.)* DeLattre moved a corps on either side of VI Corps while the 1st Airborne Task Force, assisted by French elements, sealed the Italian and Swiss frontiers. A reconnaissance patrol from the French II Corps met a Third Army reconnaissance unit northwest of Dijon on September 12, and two days later firm contact was established between the two armies near Chaumont. That same day, Patch

Liberation Ceremony in Marseilles, August 1944: Minister of War André Diethelm and General Jean de Lattre de Tassigny Review Troops

directed the French II Corps to sideslip and go into line to the right of the French I Corps, both to come under DeLattre and his newly designated French First Army. The following day, September 15, Lieutenant General Jacob L. Devers' Sixth Army Group became operational, controlling the armies of Patch and DeLattre and subordinated to SHAEF.[11]

DRAGOON proved to be a major success. The invasion force had made a firm link-up with Eisenhower's right flank army a full two months earlier than the estimated time. In so doing, it not only eliminated the German presence in southern France, but also took about 70,000 prisoners, inflicted great equipment losses on Hitler's army, and seized the vitally important port of Marseilles. Total Allied casualties were slightly less than 14,000. Now new airbases could be constructed and a major supply line introduced into Metz from the south.[12] Eisenhower summed up the impact of DRAGOON by writing:

> There was no development of that period which added more decisively to our advantages or aided us more in accomplishing the final and complete defeat of the German forces than did the secondary attack coming up the Rhone Valley.[13]

Even the long-skeptical Churchill congratulated Eisenhower on the smooth start of DRAGOON. The Supreme Commander, recalling the many bitter arguments over the Mediterranean attack, confided to General Marshall that when he received the message he could not decide whether he should laugh or cry. Finally, he wired the Prime Minister that it appeared that as he had adopted the newborn baby, DRAGOON, it would surely grow and flourish.[14]

The landing in southern France proved to be very successful for several reasons. Certainly, the German opposition was less intense than had been the case in Normandy, and assistance from the French Resistance fighters was noteworthy, particularly during the exploitation phase. The smoothness with which the airborne operation came off, and the fact that the assault divisions were all combat-tested were also contributory factors. But, beyond those reasons, one of the most important considerations was the flexibility and aggressiveness of the high level leadership. In this regard, Devers exercised considerable influence as the army group commander designate. Moreover, as Commanding General, NATOUSA, he controlled the supporting logistical organization which was directed by imaginative and improvisatory leaders who drove it to accomplish herculean efforts, notwithstanding the ammunition problem mentioned earlier. Devers foresaw the need to be ready for rapid exploitation; taking care not to appear to be unduly meddling in the business of the designated commanders, he discussed the matter with Truscott in Italy, happily learning that the assault commander was already considering how to form Task Force Butler. On the beaches, he also gently suggested to Patch that it might be expedient to send the French II Corps up the west side of the Rhone, in modification of the basic plan. This type of leadership, in abundance among DRAGOON leaders, was a key ingredient in the success of the operation.[15]

Continued Debate Over Strategy

While optimistic reports about the success of DRAGOON had been raising Eisenhower's spirits, continued disagreements with Montgomery over the course of future strategy was having the opposite effect. It will be recalled* that pre-invasion planners had envisioned a dual thrust into Germany; Montgomery, however, favored a virtual cessation of operations in areas other than the north, while a huge force moved on the Ruhr, and eventually Berlin, under his direction. In the ongoing debate in late August, Eisenhower essentially compromised by reinforcing Montgomery and giving him supply priority, but he refused to halt Bradley's southern operations. Nevertheless, the British general continued to press his argument with an increasingly irritated Eisenhower, even though Montgomery's own chief of staff, Major General Francis de Guingand, felt that the plan would not work. The Supreme Commander held firm, however, and on August 29 issued a directive to his senior commanders.[16]

Eisenhower directed that Montgomery cross the Seine and, working with Bradley's left wing, attack to the north to take the Pas de Calais area, Antwerp, and the Belgian airfields. An additional asset for Montgomery would be the First Allied Airborne Army which could be employed to assist in the accomplishment of the 21st Army Group mission. Bradley was to assist Montgomery by crossing the Seine to destroy German forces between that river and the Somme River. On order, he would continue to attack to the northeast toward the West Wall. *(See cross-hatched red belt, Map 66.)* Bradley would also clear up the still-contested situation on the Brittany Peninsula, link up with the DRAGOON forces advancing from the south, protect the Allied right and southern flanks, and build up a force east of Paris. The order temporarily restrained Patton's Third Army, which could attack toward the Saar at a later date.[17]

The impact of Eisenhower's directive irritated his American subordinates, particularly Patton. That impatient leader, acting on Bradley's earlier orders, had sent his XX and XII Corps to the northeast on August 26. *(See Map 66, in Atlas.)* Chateau Thierry fell that day, Châlons on the twenty-eighth,

*See Chapter 14.

and Reims the next day. By the thirtieth, with spearheads across the Meuse and his eye on Metz, Patton received word that his low supply priority would cause a cessation of gasoline shipments. Aerial resupply, captured stocks and an all-out effort by truck units—the 616-mile round trip between Cherbourg and Verdun took five days—had kept Patton's tanks rolling. Now he was forced to stop. Angry and irritable over the turn of events, the Third Army commander voiced his protest when he met with Hodges, Eisenhower, and Bradley on September 2. But the situation was not as bad as it appeared. Although Hodges' First Army was short of gas, Eisenhower, who had assumed direct command of the ground battle on September 1, decided to allocate some of his critically limited supply to Patton. While 21st Army Group would still have the main attack, both American armies were to continue to move toward the Rhine. As Hodges advanced to the north, he would pinch out the British, so Eisenhower told him to shift his attack to the east with Cologne and Coblenz as his objectives. Moreover, since a gap had opened between First and Third Army, Hodges was also directed to send a corps through the Ardennes. This scheme, Eisenhower hoped, would pose so many threats to the enemy that Hitler would not be able to spare troops to organize and defend the West Wall positions properly.[18]

German Efforts to Stem the Tide

The northwestern arm of the Allied drive, starting a few days later than Patton's offensive, made equally rapid gains. Before he could attack on August 27, Hodges had to bring back the units he had earlier sent into the British zone in an attempt to encircle the withdrawing Germans. Although traffic control was complex, this shifting of units was successfully accomplished.[19] Montgomery, meanwhile, was readying the attack of his two armies for the twenty-ninth. Determined to move rapidly, he ordered that " . . . any tendency to be 'sticky' or cautious must be stamped on ruthlessly . . ."[20] Dempsey, to motorize two of the corps of his Second Army, stopped the third and most of his antiaircraft, heavy and medium artillery west of the Seine. Truck companies were diverted from unloading ships to carrying supplies to forward units, but the gain was largely nullified when it was discovered that defective pistons in 1,400 British three-ton trucks as well as in the replacement engines caused these vehicles to be inoperative.[21]

Although transportation and fuel were problems, and Hodges soon halted one of his three corps so the remaining two could advance, his army made notable progress. *(See Map 66, in Atlas.)* On the last day of August, General der Panzertruppen Eberbach was captured, along with the tactical command post of the German Seventh Army. By September 3, the British had Brussels. Concurrently the Canadian First Army was moving up the coast. On September 1, Dieppe fell to the Canadian 2nd Division, the same unit that had suffered such heavy casualties in the 1942 raid. The next day, St. Valery-en-Caux, west of Dieppe on the English Channel where in June of 1940 much of the British 51st (Highland) Division had been surrounded and captured, was liberated by the same unit. By the third, the Canadians had a bridgehead across the Somme.[22]

German Equipment on the South Bank of the Seine, August 1944

Meanwhile, Hodges' bagging of 25,000 Germans in the Mons pocket highlighted for both Allies and Germans the importance of signal security. ULTRA had provided information concerning the German concentration at Mons, thereby helping Hodges spring the trap. A concurrent stroke of luck had also contributed; the Allies captured a three months' supply of Enigma keys at Brest when the Germans air-dropped the keys along with a shipment of Iron Crosses in a parcel which fell within American lines.

After the Mons success, however, ULTRA information gradually became less valuable. For one thing, Hitler became ever more secretive in issuing instructions and information, feeding his deep suspicion of the senior Regular officers after the abortive assassination attempt. Then, too, as German armies fell back closer to their homeland, they began to rely, once again, on safe telephone and teletypewriter links. Finally, late in 1944—too late to do much good—the Germans modified the Enigma machine, thus creating problems for the Allied technicians.[23]

The rapid Allied advance, commencing with the crossing of the Seine, required planners to be extremely flexible. Should the Germans try to hold at a Belgian river line, Eisenhower intended to employ his airborne force in an attempt at encirclement. Among the possible targets was Tournai, located some 13 miles east of Lille. A plan was prepared over the objections of Bradley, who contended that ground troops would reach the area before the scheduled landing of the paratroopers on September 3. Transport aircraft were withdrawn from aerial resupply duties several days prior to the target date, but, as Bradley had predicted, ground troops beat the paratroopers to the objectives. Although Tournai lay some six miles within the 21st Army Group zone, Bradley ordered Hodges to take it, and on the morning of September 3, Hodges' troops were holding the city. When Montgomery complained that the American presence was blocking his way to Brussels, Hodges' units withdrew. While the airborne operation was cancelled, the tonnage lost due to the diversion of transport aircraft for some six days had had a serious effect on the movement of the Third Army, which had been receiving the aerial resupply.[24]

Fuel shortages were also having an adverse effect on German operations. Due to Allied bombing of the Rumanian oilfields, and the mining of the Danube which cut movement of oil barges on the river, the import of petroleum products slowed to a trickle. Repeated bombings of synthetic oil plants also took their toll, although during August the Germans were using the services of 150,000 workers to restore the damage. Once Allied reconnaissance revealed that a plant was back in operation, however, it was hit again. Aviation gas, produced in the last refining stage, was in particularly short supply because the bombers often returned before its production had been resumed. Compared to pre-bombing levels, August production was 10 percent and that of September was 5.5 percent. Lack of fuel not only affected the ability of the *Luftwaffe* to fight the air war, but also caused the training of new pilots to be modified so that they had but a fourth of the flight training hours considered normal for British and American pilots. To further save precious fuel, the Germans cut running-in time for new airplane engines by 75 percent. Allied factories were turning out new and improved aircraft models, but to keep production of new aircraft high, German plants basically stayed with the old designs. This resulted in inadequately trained pilots flying planes that were outdated and had engines which often failed.[25]

On the ground, the German situation was critical. Model, who Hitler called "the savior of the Eastern Front" and who had been shifted so often that he called himself "the *Fuehrer*'s fireman," did what he could to stem the tide of the Allied advance, but a continued withdrawal was inevitable. Even OKW recognized the need to pull back. Hitler, however, insisted that the fortress garrisons stay in place. The long-neglected West Wall would form the eventual defensive position, but much work still needed to be done to make it ready. Somehow, the Allies would have to be delayed to provide time to do that work. The line Breskens-Antwerp-Albert Canal-Maastricht-Meuse River-Nancy-Epinal-Swiss border was selected as an intermediate position for that purpose. General der Infanterie Gustav von Zangen came from Italy to take command of the Fifteenth Army; a new formation, the First Parachute Army under Generaloberst Kurt Student, was also organized and inserted between the Fifteenth and Seventh Armies. *(See Map 66, in Atlas.)* Student's force would initially consist of troops provided by Goering, including six parachute regiments (either being trained or re-equipped), two regiments of convalescents, and 10,000 men allotted from *Luftwaffe* ground crews and air staffs. Finally, on September 5, Rundstedt was recalled to reassume his position as Commander-in-Chief West, and Model was free to concentrate on the rebuilding task which faced him as commander of Army Group B.[26]

German leaders in the field were also concerned over increasing signs of panic and confusion within the withdrawing units. Morale was low, looting was noted, and resistance was generally spotty. Communications were poor. In some cases supplies were destroyed too early; in others the Allies captured entire dumps, undamaged. Frequently, bridges were found intact by the advancing Allied armored and infantry units which moved along the main highways, leaving the rest of the territory to be cleared by cavalry and French Resistance units. The advance seemed so easy that Allied soldiers began to discuss their chances of being deployed to another theater after the Germans were beaten, and staff officers talked of being home by Christmas.[27]

Eisenhower's forces seemed to be on the verge of total victory. On September 2, the same day that the Supreme Commander wrenched his knee when he was helping to move his light plane after he had been forced to land on a beach, Eisenhower wrote Marshall: "All reports show that the enemy is routed and running on our entire front."[28] Two days later he told his senior commanders: "Every resistance on the entire front shows signs of collapse."[29] Troops on all fronts, including Patton's, were to advance. Both the Saar and the Ruhr would be assaulted in the hope that the enemy would choose to defend these vital areas; Hitler's western armies could then be destroyed in one decisive struggle. Lack of logistical support seemed to be the only factor which might prevent an early Allied victory.[30]

By this time, Eisenhower's command had grown considerably since that day in June when elements of five divisions had landed in Normandy. Forces under SHAEF now numbered approximately twenty American divisions in France with six more in England; twelve British divisions in France; and three Canadian, one French, and one Polish division in France. Soon these troops would be joined by the DRAGOON invaders who were moving up from the south. Eisenhower could also call on some 4,035 heavy bombers; 1,720 light, medium and torpedo bombers; 5,000 fighters, and over 2,000 transport

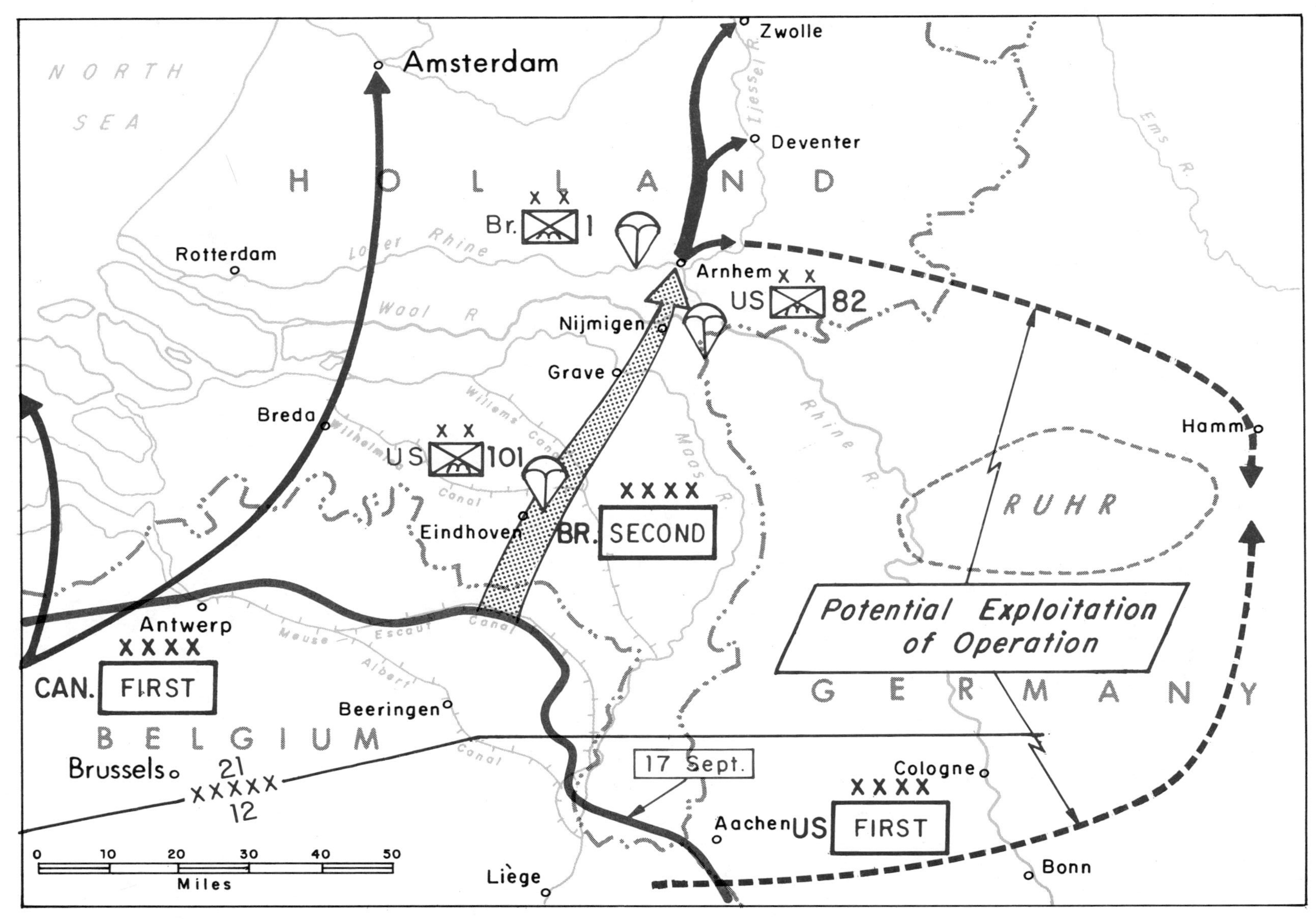

Plan for MARKET-GARDEN

planes. Although he would soon lose control of the strategic bombers to the Combined Chiefs of Staff, he would encounter no significant hindrance in the conduct of his operations, as his needs were accorded the highest priority for their use.[31]

The receipt of the news on September 4 that Dempsey had captured Antwerp served to heighten the optimistic outlook of the Allies. With the clearing of the Schelde, the waterway between Antwerp and the sea, it seemed that even the troublesome logistical problems would be resolved. Unfortunately, neither Dempsey nor Montgomery saw to it that troops were immediately dispatched to do the job. As a result, the Germans were granted a respite to establish defenses; it would not be until November 28, after a hard-fought clearing campaign, that the first ship anchored in the port of Antwerp.[32]

Strategy and Logistics

Montgomery now thought that, with Antwerp taken and the German front apparently split, conditions were perfect for his long cherished, major thrust to the Ruhr. He raised the subject again with Eisenhower. If only Patton were halted and all Allied resources concentrated, wrote the Field Marshal, the Ruhr and perhaps even Berlin were within reach. The next day, Eisenhower patiently replied that he did not feel resources were available for an attack on Berlin, and that while priority would still be given to Montgomery's northern thrust, the broad front advance using all major lines of communication would continue. Montgomery was not satisfied. At a meeting held in Eisenhower's plane on September 10 in Brussels, he spoke so strongly that Eisenhower finally said, as he put a restraining hand on the Field Marshal's knee, "Steady, Monty. You can't speak to me like that. I'm your boss."[33]

After apologizing, Montgomery continued to press his argument, but in a more restrained fashion. As he had been doing for some days, Eisenhower stressed his hope for the early opening of Antwerp and for the seizing of a line far enough beyond the port to cover it from enemy interference. Although he continued to favor the broad front approach, part of Montgomery's scheme appealed to him—the proposal to use airborne troops to project Allied forces across three large rivers, thereby seizing a bridgehead beyond the Rhine near Arnhem. *(See Map, page 353.)* This assault would cut off the German Fifteenth Army, outflank the West Wall, and seize the security line that Eisenhower desired. Of course, it would also put Montgomery in position for a stab at the Ruhr, should the Supreme Commander allow him to try. Eisenhower, glad for a chance to get a bridgehead before his troops lost their momentum and pleased to be able to use his airborne forces at last, approved this use of his theater reserve to exploit success. The tentative date of September 17 was set and the code name MARKET-GARDEN was assigned. MARKET was the name for the drop of three airborne divisions, while GARDEN signified the ground link-up drive which would require that one corps attack over 60 miles to Arnhem across seven large bridges hopefully held by the paratroopers.[34]

The MARKET-GARDEN proposal also seemed appealing because Allied progress was gradually becoming more difficult as supply lines stretched ever longer. German resistance, with the battle lines nearing the homeland, was stiffening, helped by the reinstatement of Rundstedt, a well-known figure about whom the troops might rally. At the same time, the *Fuehrer* moved to raise and equip 25 *volksgrenadier* divisions and 10 new *panzer* brigades. Men for the *volksgrenadier* divisions, named for the German people, were obtained by raising the maximum and lowering the minimum draft ages and by adding convalescents as well as troops gleaned from the *Luftwaffe* and Navy. With Rundstedt in charge to hold the enemy long enough for the new formations to arrive, German industry still producing reasonably well, and the hope that jet-propelled aircraft would soon take to the air, the German situation was not necessarily hopeless.[35]

The West Wall further bolstered the German position, at least in the minds of the rank and file. For them, the defensive line seemed to have an almost mystical significance. In reality, this fortified line, neglected for four years, was originally designed to halt an assault temporarily while mobile Reserve units were massed to defeat it. By September 1944, such units were not available. Although defenses were being improved as the fighting grew nearer, the wall was but a shadow of its former self. Much of its barbed wire and many of its guns and mines had been removed through the years. Even if new weapons could be obtained, some would not fit into the casemates. For example, many positions designed for emplacement of the 37-mm antitank gun, which could stop the armor of 1939, would not accommodate the larger guns needed in 1944. Even

Dragon's Teeth Located in the West Wall

though it had not been completely modernized, this obstacle—averaging some three miles in depth, composed of mutually supporting pillboxes connected in many places by field fortifications, and sporting bands of concrete "dragon's teeth" between natural antitank obstacles—could slow and, Hitler hoped, stop the Allied advance.[36]

While the Germans feverishly rushed preparations to stem the Allied advance, Eisenhower's troops closed in on key river lines, facing increasing resistance and slowed by fuel shortages. Patton managed to move some of his units across the Moselle River, however, and after the assignment of operations in Brittany to Simpson's Ninth Army on September 5, was able to devote his entire attention to the attack on Germany. *(See Map 66, in Atlas.)* As noted above, elements of Patton's army linked up with DRAGOON forces on the twelfth. Hodges, meanwhile, advanced to the German border, and tanks from his VII Corps crossed it 10 miles south of Aachen on September 13. Farther north, Montgomery's troops continued their advance, as shown, so that by September 14 the Second Army had reached, and in some places crossed, the Albert Canal. Units under Canadian command encountered resistance in port areas, but took Le Havre on September 12. Many of the sites from which the feared V-1's had been launched were captured, but on September 8 the first V-2 supersonic rocket impacted in a London suburb. Now, for several months, targets in both England and Belgium would have to sustain blows from this awesome new weapon.[37]

The logistical difficulties which were now becoming serious for the Allies can be better understood by comparing the planned and actual lines of advance. *(See Map 60, in Atlas.)* By D + 100, the actual advance was over 200 days ahead of the planned advance to which logistical support had been keyed. If in hindsight the planning appears to have been too conservative, one must also bear in mind that the amount of shipping, the availability of *operable* ports, and the means for forward movement of supplies were not unlimited. Actually, the supply system was beginning to break down by mid-September. Some 150 vessels were waiting to unload on September 1, and by October 20 the number would reach 240. In November, the War Department would have to cancel the sailing of ships slated to carry needed cargo to allow time to untangle this mess. For its part, the Communications Zone took control of key roads and instituted the Red Ball Express in an attempt to speed supplies forward. Trucks were stopped only to switch drivers, to load and unload, and to make repairs—they averaged 20 hours a day on the road. This constant service was hard on trucks and roads, but by the time the Red Ball Express service ended (November 13), it had moved 334,000 tons of supplies, many of which went to MARKET-GARDEN.[38]

The Allies Needed Antwerp's Port Capacity

Gasoline-Laden Convoy Traveling Along Red Ball Express Highway, September 1944

What had become clear in the early days of September 1944 was that logistics was slowly but inexorably dictating strategy. The senior commanders grudgingly came to understand this, but not wanting to accept it, bent every effort to break the logistical bottleneck. Failing in this, as was bound to be the case, Montgomery and Bradley (with an overt nudge from Patton) each tried to convince Eisenhower to establish supply priority for his front at the expense of the other's.

For reasons which have already been mentioned, Eisenhower was unwilling to adopt such a "single thrust" strategy, hoping that the Germans would remain off balance and disorganized and that he could keep the advance moving all along the front. His policy was to evaluate the overall situation continuously, shifting priorities to some degree, restraining here and then there, generally favoring Montgomery, but never completely stopping Bradley. Understandably, this proved frustrating to his two senior subordinates, particularly when the Germans began to recover. Montgomery seemed to believe that because the Supreme Commander indicated some

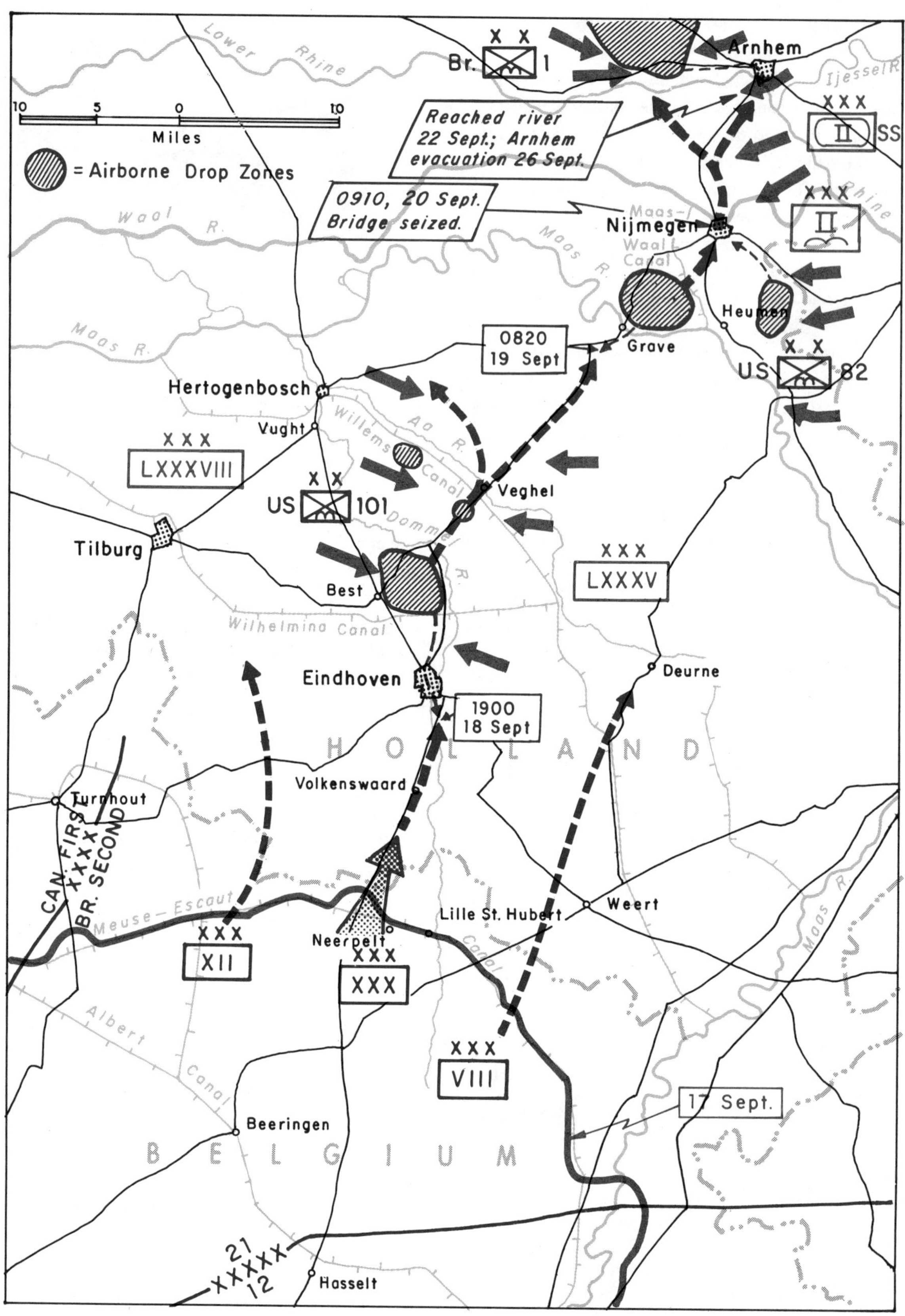

MARKET-GARDEN Operations, September 1944

priority to the north, he was in effect approving the Briton's proposed strategy; even after the September 10 meeting he held this view.[39] Under this interpretation of what had been decreed, Montgomery expressed irritation when Eisenhower, in a seeming contradiction, allowed Patton to continue to advance.* The British commander could not, or would not, understand that Eisenhower intended to direct operations personally, and that although he favored the north in terms of resources, Montgomery would not have *carte blanche* thereupon at the total expense of the southern armies. At the same time, the field marshal probably appreciated more than other leaders the crucial importance of time—the need to recognize what was possible before the Germans successfully regrouped.[40]

The strategic argument which ran its course in September and October 1944 was one of the most controversial of the war. It still continues among historians. Whether either Montgomery or Patton could have made decisive advances into Germany had he been given absolute priority on supplies and troops is at best a moot question. One can be sure that logistics were at the heart of the matter, however, and that a thorough analysis of this subject remains to be done. Nor can one ignore the amazing recuperative power of the German Army. In both of these areas the Allies were inclined to underestimate; but, paradoxically, recognition of the influence of both areas contributed greatly to Eisenhower's interest in and high hopes for MARKET-GARDEN.[41]

MARKET-GARDEN

When Eisenhower approved the MARKET-GARDEN operation on September 10, he realized that it would delay the launching of a major drive to clear the approaches to Antwerp. Certainly, the use of that port was important to him, but so was the possibility of quickly seizing a bridgehead over the Rhine. The operation would also provide a buffer zone for protection of the Antwerp port facilities. Moreover, like Montgomery, he expected the seizure of the approaches to the port to be a simple matter, although for two weeks he had emphasized the importance of the task more than had the British leader. Hopefully, the two operations could be completed quickly and then Montgomery, exploiting Antwerp's port capacity, could begin encircling the Ruhr.[42]

*For example, on September 13, Eisenhower told his army group commanders that Montgomery had priority—to drive across the Rhine and on the Ruhr; Patton would only hold bridgeheads over the Moselle and threaten the enemy. But two days later he hedged and indicated that if Montgomery was making progress and Hodges was getting sufficient supplies, there was no reason to restrain Patton. The latter needed no larger a loophole. See *EP*, IV: No. 1946, Eisenhower to Montgomery, Bradley, *et al.*, September 13, 1944; No. 1956, Eisenhower to Bradley, September 15, 1944.

On September 14, Montgomery's headquarters issued the orders to the British Second Army to carry out the MARKET-GARDEN operation. Prior discussions had been held, of course, not only with Dempsey but also with Lieutenant General Lewis H. Brereton and the staff of his First Airborne Army, which would carry out the MARKET part of the operation. The staff had only one week in which to plan the operation for September 17 after Eisenhower's approval, but the plan was very similar to the recently cancelled COMET operation upon which the planners had been working for some time. Moreover, German resistance was expected to be spotty, and a strong reason for using the airborne elements all along had been to exploit enemy disorganization.[43]

The airborne part of MARKET-GARDEN was designed to employ three divisions, placed under the direction of Lieutenant General F. A. M. Browning, Brereton's deputy and also commander of the British I Airborne Corps. *(See Map, page 353.)* On the first day of the operation, sufficient airlift would be available to deliver the three parachute regiments of both the U.S. 82nd and 101st Airborne Divisions. Each division had several tasks to perform, primarily associated with the seizure of bridges over the several rivers and canals and the securing of the major highway over which the link-up force would move. Brigadier General James M. Gavin, commander of the 82nd, had a difficult choice to make. As the middle division in the drop pattern, the 82nd had to be prepared to fight and hold for up to three days, awaiting ground link-up. Gavin had to seize six bridges, In addition, his sector contained the only high ground in the corridor area, ground which had to be held in order to defend against German counterattack. This high ground, Gavin believed, and Browning agreed, must take priority as an objective, even though it meant delaying the attempt to capture the bridge at Nijmegen. Major General R. E. Urquhart, commanding the third and northernmost assault element (British 1st Airborne Division), had sufficient airlift to move a parachute brigade, an air-landing brigade, and a regiment of air-landing artillery in the first lift. His drop zones were some six to eight miles from the primary objective, the Arnhem road bridge. On the second day, all three divisions would get some of their additional combat elements. On the third day, despite anticipated resupply requirements, the organic reinforcement would continue, and the 1st Polish Parachute Brigade would join the British division.[44]

The ground link-up mission was assigned by Dempsey to the XXX Corps. *(See Map: MARKET-GARDEN Operations, page 356.)* It would be assisted by the VIII Corps on the right and the XII Corps on the left. In theory, this attack by three corps looks impressive. However, the VIII Corps, which had been stopped at the Seine so that its vehicles could be used to support other British units, was not yet ready to attack, and the terrain in front of the XII Corps was marshy. Supplies, always a critical factor, would be even shorter with the loss of the VIII Corps vehicles; and even with Red Ball help, amounts would be available to support an immediate full-fledged thrust only of the XXX Corps. In the center, due to road limitations, LTG B. G. Horrocks' XXX Corps of some 20,000 vehicles would have to advance along the single route that was suitable for armor. No substantial help could be hoped for from the U.S. First Army, as Hodges' two northern corps were involved in operations near Aachen.[45]

Although Montgomery realized that his plan was very bold—indeed, some planners thought it was too risky—he was not disposed to make any changes. Alarmed by information that two *panzer* divisions were refitting in the Arnhem area, Eisenhower's chief of staff, Smith, tried to get Montgomery to reallocate his airborne resources, but the British leader lightly dismissed the information and suggestion.[46] The sending of a single corps along a narrow corridor, almost 80 miles over seven major bridges secured by paratroopers, during a season when weather is normally bad in northwest Europe, had to be predicated upon a belief that German resistance would be spotty. Such was the belief held by most of the planners and commanders. There was a predisposition to believe that the XXX Corps would have a fight breaking through the initial position, but that once that crust was shattered the Germans would not be able to concentrate troops to stem the advance; and Montgomery thought that the unprecedented deep, mass airborne assault would confuse the Germans and sufficiently slow their reactions, thereby allowing the Allies to accomplish their mission. This viewpoint, which also helped create overconfidence in Allied quarters, explains in large part how the Allies could discount information about *panzer* locations, confirmed by photo reconnaissance and ULTRA intercepts; an ULTRA intercept revealing that Model had his headquarters three miles west of Arnhem (in the heart of the drop area); and ULTRA information revealing German analysis of possible Allied actions, including a thrust toward Arnhem.[47] Yet, from another viewpoint, Allied operations in August and September, taken as a whole, were a gamble to exploit German disorganization and, many hoped, end the war. Seen in that light, and recognizing Montgomery's frustration at his inability to corral the resources which he felt would enable his army group to plunge deep into Germany, MARKET-GARDEN seemed a small enough risk to take.

German commanders did not anticipate Montgomery's MARKET-GARDEN operation. For three weeks prior to the air drops, they had been feverishly trying to reconstruct a line of defense, and speculating that the British effort would be concentrated on clearing the approaches to Antwerp. As noted earlier, Hitler's concern had led to Student's transfer to the area, as well as some piecemeal reinforcement. In analyzing Allied options, the Germans through Montgomery's attack would continue straight north from Antwerp to the coast, although they considered, and dismissed, the possibility of a drive toward Arnhem. The Allied delay in making this expected attack allowed Model to begin moving units of the Fifteenth Army eastward out of the feared area of entrapment. As for possible use of the Allied airborne reserve, German analysts believed it would be used soon, but they expected it would be employed either in a bold stroke as far as 50 miles east of the Rhine or in conjunction with an amphibious assault in northeastern Holland. Student, it is true, had off-handedly remarked that the Allies might try a closer-in vertical envelopment, but Model had replied: "Montgomery is a very cautious general, not inclined to plunge into mad adventures."[48] At the same time, on the eve of MARKET-GARDEN, the Germans had made amazing recuperative strides, salvaging from the chaos of just two weeks earlier a defensive system which was stronger than the Allies expected, if not yet nearly as strong or responsive as Model wanted. Moreover, they had the mauled, badly depleted, but still dangerous and fanatically committed 9th and 10th Panzer Divisions positioned in the vicinity of Arnhem. Finally, in a stroke of German good fortune, Student had his command post in Vught, just to the west of the 101st Airborne Division drop zones, and Model was headquartered practically in the British drop zone, just west of Arnhem. These two commanders would quickly size up the situation, move units promptly, and stall the Allied bid to jump the Rhine.[49]

MARKET-GARDEN was begun with great optimism. If all went well, the British XXX Corps would move along the corridor in which key defiles had been secured by airborne elements, reach Arnhem, seize the airfields there, and establish a bridgehead. Beginning the night of September 16, over a thousand bombers attacked German antiaircraft batteries along the flight routes and near the drop zones. Late the morning of the seventeenth, some 1,240 fighters swarmed aloft to protect the 1,545 troop carriers and 478 gliders which rose from 22 airfields in England en route to drop zones in Holland. So efficient was the flak suppression that the British lost no planes or gliders to the enemy, but the tow ropes of 38 gliders broke en route. The cost to the Americans was 35 planes and 13 gliders, far below the toll that had been predicted. At 2:00 P.M. on September 17, troops began landing. Within minutes some 16,500 paratroopers and 3,500 glidermen were on the ground. Their accuracy was very good.[50]

Farthest to the south, the 101st, although suffering casualties from the flak located near Eindhoven, took four of its assigned five bridges intact. *(See Map: MARKET-GARDEN Operations, page 356.)* The southern bridge was destroyed, but the paratroopers crossed the water barrier and by dawn were close to Eindhoven, where they were to meet the ground forces. To the north, the 82nd took the bridge at Grave and the

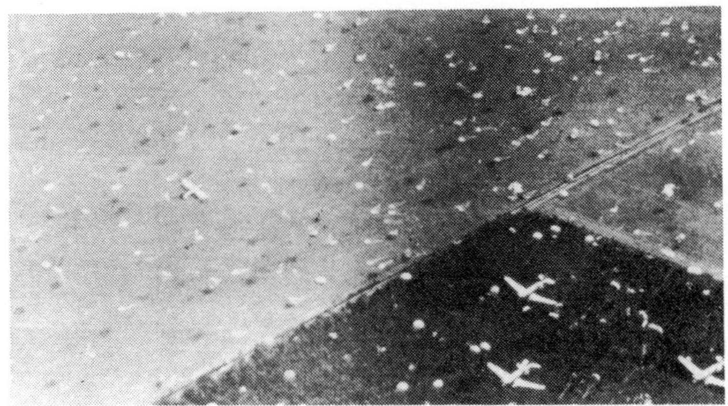

The British 1st Airborne Division Lands Near Arnhem, September 1944

critical high ground near Nijmegen, but by the time that troops moved to take the large highway bridge, the Germans had been able to form a defense. Farther north still, at Arnhem, members of the British 1st Airborne Division were having a tough go. LTC J. D. Frost and some 600 men of the 21st Parachute Battalion were able to move to the critical highway bridge located six to eight miles east of the drop zones, but they could only secure the northern end. The other bridge at Arnhem, a railroad span, had been destroyed.[51]

Meanwhile, at 2:25 P.M., the cannon of the XXX Corps artillery commenced firing a rolling barrage about one mile wide and five miles deep. The barrage was oriented on the only major road, soon to be christened "Hell's Highway," which led through the corridor. Swampy terrain on both sides of the road restricted movement. Swarms of aircraft provided constant overhead cover and immediately available fire support. By dusk, the leading elements of the corps were five miles south of Eindhoven. At this time, the end of the first day, key bridges at Nijmegen and Arnhem were still in enemy hands, and the ground forces had yet to link up with the southern airborne unit (Major General Maxwell D. Taylor's 101st Airborne Division). On the German side, a stroke of luck abetted by poor security had led to a captured copy of the Allied operations order being delivered to Student within two hours of the start of the operation. Knowing the Allied objectives and dispositions obviously aided the German commanders; Model promptly divided his defensive zone into three sectors, corresponding roughly to the areas of operation of the three Allied divisions.[52]

Bad weather, which set in on the morning of the eighteenth, delayed and often cancelled planned troop and supply flights. Effects were significant, for reinforcements of both men and supplies figured prominently in Allied plans. Also, when drops were delayed, vitally needed units had to be detailed to clearing and holding drop zones, and could not be used in attacks on vital objectives.[53]

The British XXX Corps, however, continued to advance on the second day, against increasing German resistance. Late that day, tankers from the Guards Armored Division established contact with Taylor's paratroopers just south of Eindhoven, and immediately set about replacing the blown bridge over the Wilhelmina Canal to the north of the city. The advance continued, and early on the nineteenth, Horrocks' men linked up with Gavin's troops just southwest of Grave; by noon they were in Nijmegen, but the key bridge over the Waal River was still in German hands. Paratroopers were ferried across the river so that simultaneous British-American attacks could be launched from both south and north. These assaults, made late on September 20, the fourth day, were successful, but Germans held out both below and in the superstructure of the bridge until the fifth day was almost over.[54]

Only 10 miles of road separated Horrocks' troops from Frost's paratrooper force, which by that time had been cut in strength to about 140 men while trying to hold the north end of the Arnhem bridge. These stalwarts were holding a shrinking perimeter, but their contribution had already been great, for they had stopped, until almost the end of September 21, German efforts to move tanks and artillery south. Then the British roadblock was blasted open. During that night, the Germans pushed as much as they could across the bridge. It was not until the seventh day, September 23, that an appreciable friendly force reached the area across from Frost's positions. Earlier attempts to reinforce Frost, made by the Polish Brigade which had dropped on September 21 south of the river, had been unsuccessful. Efforts made by the XXX Corps also largely failed. Consequently, during the night of September 25, the British airborne troops (both from Frost's detachment and from the other units of the 1st Airborne Division which, although still north of the river, had not been able to reach the bridge defense area) were withdrawn. It would be seven months before Montgomery's forces re-entered Arnhem.[55]

During the afternoon before the evacuation, a British signal officer, located in the headquarters of the 1st Airborne Division north of the river, released the last of the carrier pigeons which had been transported from England. One of the pigeons arrived at VIII Corps Headquarters with the message:

1. Have to release birds owing to shortage of food and water.
2. About eight tanks lying about in sub-unit areas, very untidy but not otherwise causing us any trouble.
3. Now using as many German weapons as we have British.
4. Dutch people grand but Dutch tobacco rather stringy.
5. Great beard growing competition on in our unit, but no time to check up on the winner.[56]

In terms of assessment by the yardstick of success or failure, MARKET-GARDEN has remained a controversial operation among historians. It was a relatively expensive operation, costing the Allies some 11,850 casualties, most of them within the airborne divisions. Of the approximately 9,000 men fighting north of the river near Arnhem, only about 2,400 were evacuated. The Allies *did* drive a salient some 65 miles deep into the German defensive line, jump two major rivers, seize valuable airfield sites, draw German strength from other sectors of the line, and gain a buffer to protect Antwerp. But, in terms of the more ambitious hopes, they did not seize a Rhine bridgehead and position Montgomery's armies for a drive on the Ruhr or cut off the German Fifteenth Army. In that sense, the operation was a failure.

From the tactical viewpoint, overly optimistic plans and friction in war played major roles. The airborne troops, perhaps dropping too far from objectives in some instances, did not seize key bridges (Zon, Nijmegen) soon enough; the XXX Corps advance, essentially restricted to a single road, fell behind schedule; and the British were unable to concentrate sufficient strength at the Arnhem bridge. The weather played havoc, both with regard to troop-reinforcement and supply drops. There were also intelligence failures, quite probably abetted by overconfidence, as has already been pointed out. But perhaps as crucial a factor as any was the speed, flexibility, and surprising strength of the German reaction, clearly aided by several of the considerations already mentioned. This reaction served to signal a resurgence of German strength in the West and a doggedness of defense which would continue to stall the Allies during the remainder of the year, as they set about clearing the Antwerp approaches and penetrating the West Wall.[57]

The Schelde and Continued Debate Over Strategy

In an effort to link strategy and logistics, Eisenhower invited additional commentary from his subordinates on September 15, two days before MARKET-GARDEN commenced. Assuming that Montgomery would get his Arnhem bridgehead and then attack toward the Ruhr while Bradley also took the Saar, the Supreme Commander now speculated on how Germany might be overrun. Implicit in his appreciation, also, was an operational port at Antwerp. This letter triggered correspondence, largely with Montgomery, and meetings until mid-October, during which time, unfortunately, little action was taken to clear the Schelde and open Antwerp.

The basic point of contention remained the "broad-front" strategy. Replying to Eisenhower on September 18, Montgomery chided the Supreme Commander for shifting the discussion to the final defeat of Germany when so much still remained to be done to get to that point. He reiterated his argument that resources should be clearly allocated to *one* area to enable a single powerful thrust—either in his area or that of Bradley. This decision needed to be made *now* while there was still time to exploit German disorganization, he argued. Messages flew back and forth, with Montgomery continuing to push for priority in his area, even after the failure of MARKET-GARDEN, and Eisenhower sharply prodding the field marshal to get on with clearing the approaches to Antwerp. At the same time, Patton fumed and Bradley showed discomfiture. Montgomery continued to be critical, now shifting to complaints about the lack of strategic control since Eisenhower had assumed direction of the ground effort. He even let his disgruntlement over this matter be known to Marshall during the latter's visit to the European Theater of Operations on October 8. The American Chief of Staff said little, but Montgomery clearly got the impression that Marshall disagreed. Finally, when Eisenhower wrote bluntly to him about command relationships and the possibility of elevating the dispute to a higher level, Montgomery backed off and accepted the *status quo*. In that same letter of October 13, the Supreme Commander indicated his decision, for the time being at least, to shift the major effort to Bradley's group (on Bradley's northern flank) so that Montgomery could devote his full attention to clearing the Schelde. This decision was confirmed at a meeting on October 18 as the stormy issues of command relationship and strategic priorities moderated.[58]

Almost a month and a half had elapsed since the fall of Antwerp, and still its cargo-handling facilities were denied to the Allies. Now Montgomery gave the clearing operation top priority, aided by Eisenhower's shifting of two American divisions to his operational control because of the increased front the MARKET-GARDEN salient had created. *(See Map 68, in Atlas.)*Although the Canadians had been trying to clear up the coastal situation since September 15, their efforts had been accorded low priority, and overall Allied progress was initially slow over the lowland terrain, made more difficult by the German opening of dikes and the resultant flooding.[59]

At Walcheren Island, however, the Allies turned the flooding weapon against the Germans. Deciding not to employ airborne troops, Eisenhower had made the area a high priority target for air strikes. Dikes were among the targets hit, and by mid-October 75 percent of the island was under water, leaving the garrison of about 8,000 troops split into five relatively dry areas. As they had elsewhere along the Schelde, German soldiers put up a stiff defense. Motivated by the knowledge that they were fighting to prevent the Allies from obtaining the supplies needed to attack the Fatherland, the men were also on notice that early surrender would be considered desertion. When the names of those who surrendered prematurely could be learned, a list would be sent back to Germany and published. From that time on, relatives of the "deserters" would be considered enemies of all loyal Germans. It took an amphibious operation, coupled with a ground attack, to clear the resistance on Walcheren. Fighting ended on November 8, but the waters of the Schelde still had to be cleared of mines before the first ship could dock. Meanwhile, elements of the British I and XII Corps fought their way northward to the Maas River, helping to flatten out the earlier salient. On November 28, almost three months after Antwerp had been taken, the first ship arrived at the port.[60]

Meanwhile, in the American sector, fighting continued in September and early October as Bradley and Devers closed on the West Wall and the former reorganized his forces. *(See Map 69, in Atlas.)* Bradley translated Eisenhower's guidance into a 12th Army Group directive which he issued on September 25. Because at this time Eisenhower was still according priority of effort to the north, Hodges was directed to protect Montgomery's right. In addition, when he had determined that his strength and logistical situation permitted, he was to attack toward the Rhine near Bonn and Cologne. As the First Army front was exceedingly broad, Ninth Army, its role on the Brittany Peninsula over now that Brest had fallen, would take over the southern portion of Hodges' zone. Initially, Simpson was to command only a single corps, but both Eisenhower and Bradley felt that risks could be taken in the rugged Ardennes sector so that the available troops could be massed for the upcoming attacks. Patton would have to wait for an improvement in the supply situation before embarking on a major attack. At the same time, Devers would mount an offensive with Sixth Army Group to seize Mulhouse and Strasbourg. His one-corps Seventh Army was enlarged by transferring Haislip's XV Corps from Patton's army, somewhat over the latter's objections. Clearly, very early in his thinking about employment of forces, Eisenhower had relegated Sixth Army Group to a purely subsidiary effort. He confided to Bradley that except for political reasons he would have assigned Seventh Army to 12th Army Group but that, in any event, Devers' forces would always be maneuvered to support Bradley's operations.[61] This fixation would have an impact later. At this time, however, Devers seemed to be in a good position to exploit the logistical capacity of Marseilles.

In spite of these carefully formulated plans, it was clear that major offensives were going to be increasingly influenced by logistical considerations. At the end of September, supply experts from the Communications Zone estimated that October deliveries would not meet daily needs, and that substantial reserve stocks could not be amassed in the forward areas until mid-November. Estimates were based on the port of Antwerp being operational by November 1. If it opened later, as it actually did, American troops would have to continue to rely on supply lines which stretched back to Normandy. Gasoline, ammunition, and spare parts seemed always to be in short supply. The probing of the German defenses as well as occasional limited attacks were about all that could be supported. During periods of inaction, maintenance was stressed.[62]

Stiffening German Opposition

While Eisenhower was trying to move to the Rhine on a broad front and giving priority to the north in an effort to jump that river quickly, Hitler was becoming concerned about the sector in which Patton was operating. Early in September, in orders which the Allies intercepted, the *Fuehrer* directed that a counterattack be made against Third Army in the Luneville-Nancy area. *(See Map 69, in Atlas.)* The Fifth Panzer Army headquarters, recuperating in Holland after the debacle in France and the withdrawal of its shattered units for rehabilitation, would direct the attack. General der Panzertruppen Hasso von Manteuffel—an energetic, young expert in armored warfare with a good record in the East and suitable political views—was hand-picked by Hitler to command the army. Although the target date for the attack was September 12, Patton's attacks forced commitment of some of the German units, and it took longer than anticipated for other units to be assembled. When it finally came on September 18, Manteuffel's attack was roughly handled by the U.S. 4th Armored Division. Hitler then replaced Blaskowitz with the allegedly more aggressive General der Panzertruppen Hermann Balck, who added the First Army to the attack, but still had little success. On September 29, Hitler agreed to call off the offensive and began moving most of his armor northward. Manteuffel's headquarters was shifted to the north in October where it became part of the elaborate deception scheme the Germans were implementing to hide headquarters and build up forces for their forthcoming Ardennes offensive.[63]

The German attack blunted, Patton resumed his limited offensive, and Devers continued to drive the Germans back into the Vosges Mountains. *(See Map 69, in Atlas.)* The XX Corps, attacking on October 3, took the upper part of Fort Driant, an important link in the defenses of Metz; but after 10 days of intense German artillery bombardment, during which the Germans were able to hold on to the underground portions of the fort, the Americans were obliged to withdraw. By November 7, these southern operations had made advances as shown on the map. However, bad weather, rough terrain, and a growing shortage of artillery ammunition were having an increasing impact on offensive operations.[64]

Eisenhower could have chosen to go on the defensive until both the weather and his logistical situation improved, but he continued to plan for the attack. At the end of September, he had 46 active divisions; 8 others were either in southern France or Normandy without transport to support them in a forward posture, and 6 were staging through the United Kingdom. Average frontage for the active divisions was over 12 miles in a straight line, or often a good deal more if the twists in the front line trace were considered. To make matters worse, infantry replacements were in short supply. Yet the Allied advantages over the enemy were considerable. Eisenhower's aircraft far outnumbered those that the Germans could put in the air to support Rundstedt. Tank superiority was 20 to 1, and the ratio of artillery pieces was 2.5 to 1. The Supreme Commander noted that many new and poorly trained German units were being encountered. If given a respite to prepare these formations for battle properly, however, German leaders might field a much tougher force. In addition, by spring, many jet-propelled aircraft would be in the air, and there was always the possibility of a German technological breakthrough (e.g., the production of the proximity fuse, up to that time possessed only by the Allies). Developments of this magnitude could significantly affect the upcoming battles. Both lives and time, Eisenhower believed, would be saved if he continued to press. He had the will, but the necessary supplies were still lacking. Hopefully, by the time the supply problem was resolved, all divisions could be supported at the front.[65] In the meantime, he would advance when and where he could.

In some of October's most vicious fighting, Hodges' VII and XIX Corps attacked through the West Wall in the vicinity of Aachen. To the Germans, Aachen, birthplace of Charlemagne, meant the First Reich, or Holy Roman Empire. Hitler had often compared his Thousand Year Reich to Charlemagne's Empire. Of great symbolic value to the Nazis, that city must be held. Hitler ordered a house-by-house defense. As far as Hodges was concerned, Aachen had to be taken, for when the full-fledged attack to the Rhine was executed, he would not have the resources both to contain the city and also to crack through the strong German defenses. The XIX Corps attacked on October 2, and by the sixteenth had made contact with the VII Corps. On October 21, after bitter fighting during which streetcars were painted with the number 13, filled with dynamite, and rolled down hills into the city, Aachen fell. The German commander said, "When the Americans start using 155s as sniper weapons, it is time to give up."[66] Between October 2 and 21, First Army sustained almost 10,000 casualties, but with Aachen captured, Hodges could turn virtually all his efforts to preparing the upcoming attack to the Rhine.[67]

Civilian Refugees Leave Aachen

Closing Toward the Rhine

As was pointed out above, following the round of controversial discussions on strategy in September and October, Eisenhower shifted the Allied main effort to 12th Army Group. *(See Map 70, in Atlas.)* As the plan evolved, Hodges, with a target date of November 5, would attack toward Cologne and Bonn, on the south of the Ruhr. At the same time, Simpson, his army now enlarged to two corps and moved to the north of First Army, would protect Hodges' left until the Roer River was crossed, and then turn northeast toward Krefeld. Secondary attacks were to be launched by Montgomery, east of Eindhoven toward the Ruhr, and by Patton. Eventually all armies would reach the Rhine and take bridgeheads; the main attack would then be shifted back to Montgomery.[68]

While supplies were stockpiled, replacements brought up, items of winter clothing issued, plans made, and even shower units established, Ninth Army headquarters made its move to Maastricht. As the newest of Bradley's three armies, the Ninth had earlier been placed in the Ardennes to hold, while the more experienced First and Third Armies attacked to the Rhine. Plans had since changed. Bradley now feared that American troops would eventually be given to Montgomery to strengthen his 21st Army Group. If his fears were to prove correct, Bradley did not want to lose his veteran First Army, so he inserted Simpson north of Hodges. Each army seemed to have its own personality: Bradley characterized the First as "temperamental," the Third as "noisy and bumptious," and the Ninth as "uncommonly normal."[69] Bradley later reflected that the new lineup, one which lasted for the duration of the war, functioned well since the Ninth Army worked better with Montgomery than either the First or Third would have done. Transfer of units from one American army to another, on the other hand, was fairly easy as most staff officers had had experience with the Army school system, had studied the same manuals, and spoke the same language.[70]

Lieutenant General William Simpson

It is well to remember that while his subordinate commanders were primarily involved in strategy and tactics, Eisenhower had to think about high-level political matters as well as military matters. Stability of the French Government had long been one of his concerns. In urging official recognition of the Provisional Government headed by De Gaulle, the Supreme Commander reasoned that recognition would give De Gaulle a firmer position from which to govern as he tried to establish control over the resistance fighters of the Free French of the Interior. Additionally, in the eyes of the French people, it would make their own government, not the Allied armed forces, responsible for the well-being of the civilian population during the winter to come. Eisenhower had enough to handle without having to worry about caring for French civilians. He was pleased, therefore, when on October 23 the United States, Russia, Great Britain, and five other nations recognized De Gaulle's government. The same day a proclamation was issued which stated that a French zone of interior under civilian authority would be established.[71]

Other problems continued to require Eisenhower's attention. For example, in late October he was called upon to approve the sending of food and medical supplies by ship to German-occupied areas of the Netherlands, where supplies were critically short. While he realized that the Germans would get some of the supplies, Eisenhower approved the mission. Unfortunately for the Dutch, due to the inability of the Netherlands Red Cross to distribute the materials, the goods were not sent and no real solution was found until the end of the war.[72]

Although demands on his time came from all quarters, Eisenhower tried to visit his troops as often as possible. While he realized that he could see but a small fraction of the men under his command, he knew that word of the visits would circulate and, hopefully, help to raise morale. By talking to the enlisted men, he consciously was trying to set the example for the officers who served under him. He often asked the men if they had new ideas and encouraged a feeling of partnership and trust between the leader and the led.[73]

Front-line troops usually have something about which to complain. The fact that frequent gripes about the lack of cigarettes seemed to have a sound foundation was revealed in a report which reached Eisenhower. An active black market in cigarettes and gasoline existed in Paris. Investigation revealed that a number of troops from one unit were involved. After their cases were heard and those found guilty were sentenced and their sentences published, Eisenhower offered the opportunity for a second chance to the enlisted men who would volunteer to serve at the front. Many accepted and eventually earned honorable discharges. No such second chance was offered to the officers involved.[74] Meanwhile, preparations for the November offensive proceeded apace.

As Bradley made his preparations, he recognized that the center of his army group area was thinly held. Both he and Eisenhower felt the risk was worth taking. *(See Map 70, in Atlas.)* Just to be sure, Bradley calculated the maximum penetration he thought the Germans could make if they attacked the VIII Corps; he then ensured that the very minimum number of supply installations were located in that area.[75] As the date for the offensive neared, a German attack near Eindhoven caused Montgomery to postpone returning an American division Bradley needed for his assault in the north. He thus delayed the attacks by Hodges and Simpson, but told Patton to go on November 5. Although counselled to delay his assault by Devers, who knew about the building high water in the streams from being positioned on the headwaters in the mountains, Patton restrained himself for only three days and then attacked in the rain on November 8.[76]

Patton's immediate goal was Metz. As this fortress city stood in the way of a Third Army advance to the Saar Valley and the West Wall, it had to be taken. Patton planned a double envelopment close to the fortress by the XX Corps, while the XII Corps attacked to the northeast and protected the south flank of the double envelopment. The weather continued to be generally unfavorable and flood waters repeatedly washed out bridges, but the two XX Corps forces finally managed to meet on November 18, thus encircling Metz. The city fell on November 22, but the last fort was not taken until December 13. Then the Third Army closed to the West Wall, seizing several small bridgeheads over the Saar River by December 15. Because the assault through West Wall defenses would require the expenditure of great quantities of heavy artillery ammunition, further offensive operations were postponed until the

U.S. Troops in Metz, November 1944

Infantrymen of the Seventh Army Advance Through Snow and Sleet

necessary stocks could be acquired.[77]

To the south, Devers' troops made the greatest gains of the period. *(See Map 70, in Atlas.)* Attacking in a driving snowstorm on November 13, Patch's troops took Saarebourg on the twentieth, outflanked and then cleared the Saverne Gap, and entered Strasbourg on the twenty-third. There they fought off a German counterattack and took the last of the forts around the city on November 27. Meanwhile, farther to the south, De Lattre's French First Army cleared the Belfort Gap, reached the Rhine on the twentieth, and captured Mulhouse on November 22. Documents captured in Strasbourg indicated that German scientists were behind in the race to develop atomic energy devices—news which was gratefully received by American leaders and scientists.[78]

On the Rhine, opposite the north edge of the Black Forest, Devers was in a position to exploit the most significant gain the Allies had made since crossing the Seine River. Devers wanted to cross the Rhine, but Eisenhower was skeptical. The Supreme Commander saw the primary objectives as being in the north, and knew that Devers had minimal strength; he was also concerned about the German pocket around Colmar, a situation which would continue to irritate him, although Devers seems to have judged its significance more correctly on the assumption that it could be contained and eliminated in due time.[79] Little thought seems to have been given to placing Patton's army under Devers, a logical choice considering how the situation had developed in the south. A speculative question which requires more scholarly research, particularly in the logistical area, is how a Devers' crossing of the Rhine might have affected events. Even reinforced, Seventh Army would have had rough going, but such an advance would have loosened up Patton's front and might very well have forced Hitler to unleash the forces he was readying for the Ardennes counteroffensive. At any rate, Eisenhower's decision was not to realign his strategy, but to allow Devers to move north along the west bank of the Rhine.

While these gains were being made in Alsace-Lorraine, Bradley's northern armies were launching the main attack. *(See Map 70, in Atlas.)* For a week, beginning on November 2, the 28th Infantry Division struggled southeast of Aachen in the Huertgen Forest, trying to take the high ground near the town of Schmidt. German leaders realized, as American commanders responsible for the attack apparently did not, that two large Roer River dams, dominated by the high ground near Schmidt, controlled waters which could be released so as to flood the Roer, washing out bridges and cutting off any force which had crossed to the east. Three divisions, one a *panzer* unit, were thrown in to oppose the 28th Infantry. The high ground remained in German hands. The cost to the Americans was some 6,000 casualties.[80]

North of the Huertgen Forest, Collins' VII Corps was preparing to make the main thrust of the combined First and Ninth Army attack. The XIX Corps would protect Collins' left. Supporting attacks were being delivered by Patton, and Dempsey attacked on November 14, clearing enemy opposition west of the Maas. Plenty of troops were available to the American commanders. At one time during the operation, 10 divisions were in action along a 24-mile front, with others in reserve. Due to the shortage in artillery ammunition, however, the preattack preparatory fires were to be delivered by heavy bombers. Many safety precautions had been planned for this, the largest close-support bombing attack of the war to date. Jeeps with radios which transmitted vertical beams marked the friendly front lines, and 90-mm antiaircraft guns fired colored flak along the front at an altitude 2,000 feet below the bombers. To insure the safety of the attackers, ground troops were positioned some two miles from the bombing targets. Good weather was essential and the bombardment, termed Operation QUEEN, was repeatedly postponed.[81]

On November 16, when the more than 10,000 bombs finally fell, the only bombing errors were caused by defective bomb racks, and only one minor casualty was sustained. Unfortunately for the attackers, the bombs had not blasted a hole in the enemy defenses. By the time the troops had recouped the two miles to the German positions, the bombing shock had worn off, and German defenses were tough. Each town became a strongpoint, and field works often connected these towns. Factories and coal mines had been turned into defensive works. Room to maneuver was limited, and frontal attacks often had to be launched. Bad weather conditions coupled with the tenacious German resistance allowed only slow progress. The few miles to the Roer River were crossed at great cost to both armies, as well as to the German defenders. First Army suffered, from November 16 to December 15, some 21,500 casualties, while the Ninth Army total was about 10,000. Bradley later estimated that German losses exceeded those suffered by the Americans by a ratio of at least 2 to 1. Ninth Army reached the Roer, a total advance of eight to twelve miles, on December 3, and First Army closed to the river by the middle of the month. Due to concern about the possible flooding of the river, there was no further advance until the dams could be taken.[82]

As American troops neared the Roer, fighting continued in the Huertgen Forest. Hodges sent unit after unit into the woods, while the casualty total mounted. Shell fragments tore into trees, concrete, bunkers, and human flesh. Mines seemed to be buried everywhere. Equipment, much of it stained with blood, littered the ground. Bodies lay in the open, their smell filling the battle area. Streams of wounded headed back past those who were moving up to the battle. Eight divisions had entered the grayness and all lost heavily. But by mid-December most of the forest had been taken. Casualties totalled over 24,000 killed, wounded, or taken prisoner, plus 5,000 who were lost due to respiratory illness, combat fatigue, or trench foot. German troops, who but a couple of months previously had appeared to be all but beaten, had fought well. By December 15, the Allied main attack had been stopped at the Roer and the critical dams still were in German hands.[83]

The Allied offensive in the West had spent itself by December 15. There would be no crossing of the Rhine or penetration of the German heartland in 1944. Eisenhower's broad front strategy had kept the Germans off balance all along the front, responding to a threat here, another there, never able to relax or seize a local initiative. It had been a conservative, safe strategy, one which did not risk a major, all-out effort in a single area in search of a decisive victory. It had also been a strategy dominated by logistical deficiencies and considerably influenced by the amazing and unexpected recuperative powers of the western German armies. Whether massing forces in great strength in the north or in Lorraine would have led to a decisive breakthrough and required the Germans to fall back across the Rhine we cannot know; whether Devers' opportunity to cross the Rhine at Strasbourg should have been exploited also is unanswered; and, finally, whether the Allies had sufficient command flexibility, adequate lateral communications, and logistical support to manage such changes in strategy is also a moot question. What we do know is that in spite of pressure all along the front and Allied closure to and in some instances penetration of the West Wall, Hitler and his generals managed to concentrate a force in secrecy in preparation for a major counteroffensive. That blow would fall viciously, and completely by surprise, on Bradley's center in the next two weeks.

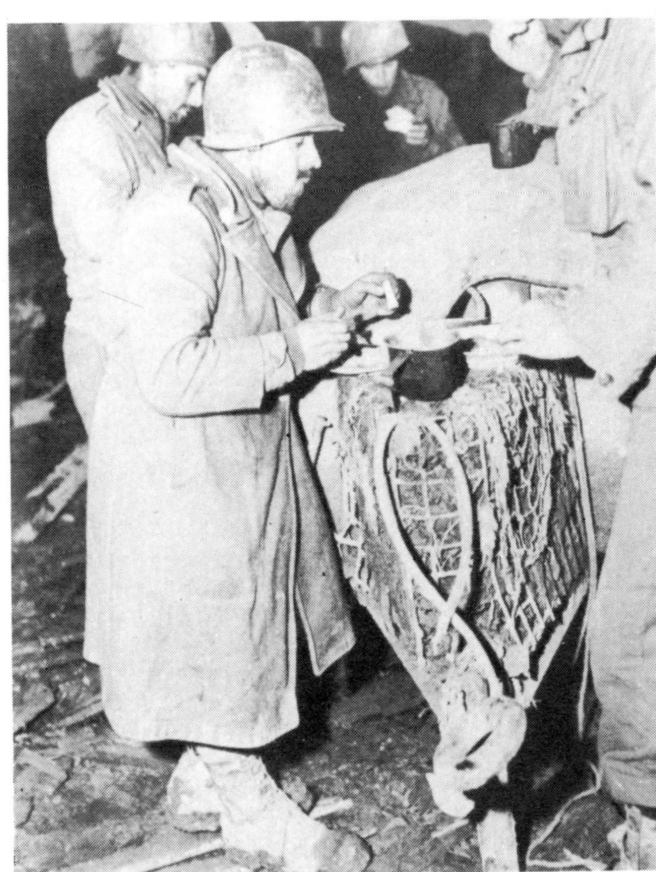

Infantrymen, Veterans of the Huertgen Forest Fight, Eat Their First Hot Meal in Days

Notes

[1]T. Dodson Stamps and Vincent J. Esposito (eds.), *A Military History of World War II* (2 vols.; West Point, 1956), I, 446-447. Vincent J. Esposito (ed.), *The West Point Atlas of American Wars* (2 vols.; New York, 1959), II, Section 2, 57.

[2]Charles B. MacDonald, *The Mighty Endeavor: American Armed Forces in the European Theater in World War II* (New York, 1969), pp. 320-321; Esposito, *West Point Atlas*, II, Section 2, 57; Alfred D. Chandler (ed.), *The Papers of Dwight D. Eisenhower: The War Years* (Baltimore, 1970), IV: No. 1883, Eisenhower to Marshall, August 5, 1944; No. 1884, Eisenhower memorandum, probably written on August 6 or 7, 1944; editor's notes with No. 1883, p. 2056, and No. 1891, p. 2066; Harry C. Butcher, *My Three Years with Eisenhower* (New York, 1946), pp. 635, 639; Chester Wilmot, *The Struggle for Europe* (London, 1952), p. 456; Dwight D. Eisenhower, *Crusade in Europe* (Garden City, 1948), pp. 281-283. Hereinafter the Eisenhower Papers are cited as *EP*.

[3]Treusch von Buttlar, MS#B-672: "Commentary on MS#B-308," in *OB WEST (Atlantic Wall to Siegfried Line) A Study in Command*, James F. Scoggin, Jr., ed. (Allendorf, Germany, 1946-1947), II, 60-61.

[4]Stamps and Esposito, *Military History*, I, 450; Esposito, *West Point Atlas*, II, Section 2, 57; MacDonald, *Mighty Endeavor*, p. 321.

[5]Esposito, *West Point Atlas*, II, Section 2, 57; Stamps and Esposito, *Military History*, I, 448-449.

[6]Stamps and Esposito, *Military History*, I, 449.

[7]Stamps and Esposito, *Military History*, I, 451-452; Esposito, *West Point Atlas*, II, Section 2, 57.

[8]Stamps and Esposito, *Military History*, I, 451; Esposito, *West Point Atlas*, II, Section 2, 57; Bodo Zimmerman, MS#B-308: "OB WEST, Atlantic Wall to Siegfried Line, A Study in Command," in *OB WEST (Atlantic Wall to Siegfried Line), A Study in Command*, James F. Scoggin, Jr., ed. (Allendorf, Germany, 1946-1947), I, 147.

[9]Esposito, *West Point Atlas*, II, Section 2, 57; Stamps and Esposito, *Military History*, I, 453-455; MacDonald, *Mighty Endeavor*, p. 321.

[10]Buttlar, "Commentary," II, 65; Zimmerman, "OB West," I, 156; MacDonald, *Mighty Endeavor*, p. 322; Stamps and Esposito, *Military History*, I, 455-457; F. W. Winterbotham, *The Ultra Secret* (New York, 1974), p. 158; Esposito, *West Point Atlas*, II, Section 2, 57.

[11]Stamps and Esposito, *Military History*, I, 458-459; Esposito, *West Point Atlas*, II, Section 2, 57; "Final Report, G-3 Section, Headquarters 6th Army Group," July 1, 1945, Heidelberg, Germany (unpublished MS) in General Jacob L. Devers Papers, Historical Society of York County, York, Pennsylvania, p. 7.

[12]Stamps and Esposito, *Military History*, I, 458-459; "G-3 Final Report, 6th Army Group," p. 8.

[13]Eisenhower, *Crusade in Europe*, pp. 294, 310, the quotation is taken from p. 294; Forrest C. Pogue, *George C. Marshall: Organizer of Victory* (New York, 1973), p. 415; Stamps and Esposito, *Military History*, I, 459.

[14]Winston S. Churchill, *Triumph and Tragedy* (Boston, 1953), pp. 96-100; *EP*, IV: No. 1910, Eisenhower to Marshall, August 24, 1944.

[15]Interview, Col. T. E. Griess with Gen. J. L. Devers, Washington, D.C., July 31, 1969.

[16]Stephen E. Ambrose, "Eisenhower as Commander: Single Thrust Versus Broad Front," in *EP*, V: pp. 42, 45-46; Eisenhower, *Crusade in Europe*, pp. 225-228; Charles B. MacDonald, "The Decision to Launch Operation MARKET-GARDEN," in Kent Roberts Greenfield (ed.), *Command Decisions* (Washington, 1960), p. 433; *EP*, IV: No. 1920, Eisenhower to Bertram Home Ramsay, *et al.*, August 29, 1944.

[17]*EP*, IV: No. 1902, Eisenhower to Bertram Home Ramsay, *et al.*, August 29, 1944.

[18]Stamps and Esposito, *Military History*, I, 434; Stephen E. Ambrose, *The Supreme Commander: The War Years of General Dwight D. Eisenhower* (Garden City, 1969), p. 508; Martin Blumenson, *The Patton Papers 1940-1945* (Boston, 1974), p. 528; Esposito, *West Point Atlas*, II, Section 2, 56; Omar N. Bradley, *A Soldier's Story* (New York, 1951), pp. 404, 410-411; Wilmot, *Struggle for Europe*, pp. 469, 472-473; Martin Blumenson, *Breakout and Pursuit* (Washington, 1961), pp. 685-686; MacDonald, *Mighty Endeavor*, p. 331.

[19]Bradley, *Soldier's Story*, p. 381.

[20]Montgomery's orders are quoted in Wilmot, *Struggle for Europe*, p. 470.

[21]Esposito, *West Point Atlas*, II, Section 2, 56; Stamps and Esposito, *Military History*, I, 435-436; Wilmot, *Struggle for Europe*, pp. 470-472.

[22]Ambrose, *Supreme Commander*, p. 508; Esposito, *West Point Atlas*, II, Section 2, 56; Stamps and Esposito, *Military History*, I, 435-436; Bradley, *Soldier's Story*, pp. 407-408; C. P. Stacey, *Official History of the Canadian Army in the Second World War*, Volume III, *The Victory Campaign: The Operations in North-West Europe 1944-1945* (Ottawa, 1960), p. 300.

[23]Ronald Lewin, *Ultra Goes to War* (New York, 1978), pp. 340, 345-346, 359-360.

[24]Bradley, *Soldier's Story*, pp. 401-403; Eisenhower, *Crusade in Europe*, pp. 302-303; Ambrose, *Supreme Commander*, p. 499.

[25]Albert Speer, *Inside the Third Reich* (New York, 1971), pp.. 449-450; Wilmot, *Struggle for Europe*, pp. 440-442.

[26]Wilmot, *Struggle for Europe*, pp. 435-436; Stamps and Esposito, *Military History*, I, 436-437, 479-480; Zimmerman, "OB WEST," I, 162.

[27]Blumenson, *Breakout and Pursuit*, pp. 688-689; Bradley, *Soldier's Story*, p. 407; Wilmot, *Struggle for Europe*, p. 474.

[28]*EP*, IV: No. 1930, Eisenhower to Marshall, September 2, 1944.

[29]*Ibid.*, IV: No. 1933, Eisenhower to Ramsay, *et al.*, September 4, 1944.

[30]*Ibid.*, IV: No. 1933, Eisenhower to Ramsay, *et al.*, September 4, 1944; No. 1934, Eisenhower to Marshall, September 4, 1944; editor's note with No. 1933, pp. 2117-2118; Eisenhower, *Crusade in Europe*, pp. 305-306; MacDonald, *Mighty Endeavor*, p. 332.

[31]Eisenhower, *Crusade in Europe*, pp. 289, 307; *EP*, IV: editor's note with No. 1931, p. 2113.

[32]Blumenson, *Breakout and Pursuit*, p. 699; MacDonald, *Mighty Endeavor*, pp. 332, 348; Esposito, *West Point Atlas*, II, Section 2, 56; Charles B. MacDonald, *The Siegfried Line Campaign* (Washington, 1963), pp. 207-215.

[33]Eisenhower is quoted in MacDonald, *Mighty Endeavor*, p. 339; Wilmot, *Struggle for Europe*, p. 476; Blumenson, *Breakout and Pursuit*, p. 687; *EP*, IV: No. 1935, Eisenhower to Montgomery, September 5, 1944; editor's note with No. 1935, p. 2120.

[34]Wilmot, *Struggle for Europe*, pp. 488-489; Eisenhower, *Crusade in Europe*, pp. 306-307; MacDonald, *Mighty Endeavor*, p. 339; MacDonald, "Operation MARKET-GARDEN," pp. 429-430, 438-

442; Stamps and Esposito, *Military History*, I, 469; L. F. Ellis, *Victory in the West*, Volume II, *The Defeat of Germany* (London, 1968), pp. 10, 16-18, 22.

[35]*EP*, IV: No. 1939, Eisenhower to Combined Chiefs of Staff, September 9, 1944; MacDonald, *Mighty Endeavor*, pp. 334-335.

[36]Zimmerman, "OB WEST," I, 181, 183-184; Wilmot, *Struggle for Europe*, p. 478; MacDonald, *Mighty Endeavor*, p. 333; MacDonald, *Siegfried Line*, pp. 30-35.

[37]Stamps and Esposito, *Military History*, I, 437-439; Esposito, *West Point Atlas*, II, Section 2, 56; MacDonald, *Mighty Endeavor*, pp. 287, 332; *EP*, IV: No. 1939, Eisenhower to Combined Chiefs of Staff, September 9, 1944; Bradley, *Soldier's Story*, pp. 412, 414-415.

[38]Stamps and Esposito, *Military History*, I, 460-463; Ambrose, *Supreme Commander*, p. 494; Roland G. Ruppenthal, "Logistics and the Broad Front Strategy," in Kent Roberts Greenfield (ed.), *Command Decisions* (Washington, 1960), pp. 422-424.

[39]Ellis, *Defeat of Germany*, pp. 23-24.

[40]*Ibid.*, pp. 77-79; Forrest C. Pogue, *The Supreme Command* (Washington, 1954), pp. 290-291.

[41]Background for the analysis in the above three paragraphs appears in Pogue, *Supreme Command*, pp. 256-260, 281, 288-293; Ellis, *Defeat of Germany*, pp. 8-10, 21-27, 70-73, 77-79; *EP*, IV: Nos. 1933, 1934, 1935, 1939, 1945, 1946, 1953, 1956, 1957.

[42]MacDonald, "MARKET-GARDEN," p. 440; Ruppenthal, "Logistics and the Broad Front Strategy," p. 425; *EP*, IV: editor's note with No. 1945, pp. 2134-2135; Esposito, *West Point Atlas*, II, Section 2, 58.

[43]MacDonald, *Siegfried Line*, pp. 119-120, 128-129.

[44]Stamps and Esposito, *Military History*, I, 470; Wilmot, *Struggle for Europe*, pp. 498-500; MacDonald, *Siegfried Line*, pp. 128-132, 154-157.

[45]Stamps and Esposito, *Military History*, I, 470; Wilmot, *Struggle for Europe*, pp. 491, 494-495, 500-501; MacDonald, *Siegfried Line*, p. 133.

[46]MacDonald, *Siegfried Line*, p. 122; Lewin, *Ultra*, p. 350.

[47]Wilmot, *Struggle for Europe*, pp. 500-501; MacDonald, *Mighty Endeavor*, p. 340; F. W. Winterbotham, *Ultra Secret*, pp. 165-166; Constantine FitzGibbon, "The 'Ultra' Secret: 'Enigma' in the War," *Encounter*, 44 (March, 1975), 84; Stamps and Esposito, *Military History*, I, 470; Lewin, *Ultra*, pp. 346-351.

[48]Model is quoted in Wilmot, *Struggle for Europe*, p. 502.

[49]Wilmot, *Struggle for Europe*, pp. 502-503; MacDonald, *Siegfried Line*, pp, 123-127, 134-136; Ellis, *Defeat of German*, p. 31; Pogue, *Supreme Command*, p. 284.

[50]Wilmot, *Struggle for Europe*, pp. 501-503; MacDonald, *Mighty Endeavor*, pp. 341-342; Stamps and Esposito, *Military History*, I, 470.

[51]MacDonald, *Mighty Endeavor*, pp. 343-344; Wilmot, *Struggle for Europe*, pp. 503-505.

[52]Wilmot, *Struggle for Europe*, pp. 506-508; MacDonald, *Mighty Endeavor*, pp. 343-344; MacDonald, *Siegfried Line*, pp. 141-142.

[53]Wilmot, *Struggle for Europe*, p. 509; MacDonald, *Mighty Endeavor*, p. 344.

[54]Wilmot, *Struggle for Europe*, p. 512; MacDonald, *Mighty Endeavor*, p. 344; MacDonald, *Siegfried Line*, pp. 148-150, 179-182.

[55]Wilmot, *Struggle for Europe*, pp. 521-522; MacDonald, *Mighty Endeavor*, pp. 344-345.

[56]Wilmot, *Struggle for Europe*, p. 521.

[57]MacDonald, *Siegfried Line*, pp. 197-201; Ellis, *Defeat of Germany*, pp. 50-58; Pogue, *Supreme Command*, pp. 287-288.

[58]Pogue, *Supreme Command*, pp. 290-298, 310; Ellis, *Defeat of German*, pp. 77-79, 84-91; *EP*, IV: Nos. 1957, 1975, 1979, 1989, 2031, 2032, and 2038.

[59]Bradley, *Soldier's Story*, pp. 423-425; Eisenhower, *Crusade in Europe*, 312; Esposito, *West Point Atlas*, II, Section 2, 58; MacDonald, *Mighty Endeavor*, p. 348.

[60]Wilmot, *Struggle for Europe*, pp. 545-548; Esposito, *West Point Atlas*, II, Section 2, 58; MacDonald, *Mighty Endeavor*, p. 348; *EP*, IV: No. 1977, Eisenhower to Montgomery, September 21, 1944.

[61]*EP*, IV: No. 1956, Eisenhower to Bradley, September 15, 1944.

[62]Ambrose, *Supreme Commander*, p. 495; Stamps and Esposito, *Military History*, I, 477; Ruppenthal, "Broad-Front Strategy," p. 427; Roland G. Ruppenthal, "Logistic Planning for OVERLORD in Retrospect," in *D-Day: The Normandy Invasion in Retrospect* (Lawrence, Kansas, 1971), pp. 98-99.

[63]Wilmot, *Struggle for Europe*, pp. 473, 536-538; Winterbotham, *Ultra*, pp. 162-163; MacDonald, *Mighty Endeavor*, pp. 336-338; Stamps and Esposito, *Military History*, I, 479-480; Esposito, *West Point Atlas*, II, Section 2, 59; Hugh M. Cole, *The Lorraine Campaign* (Washington, 1950), pp. 215-255; MacDonald, *Siegfried Line*, pp. 247, 394-396.

[64]Stamps and Esposito, *Military History*, I, 480, 486-487; Esposito, *West Point Atlas*, II, Section 2, 59; MacDonald, *Mighty Endeavor*, p. 349.

[65]Eisenhower, *Crusade in Europe*, pp. 322-323; MacDonald, *Mighty Endeavor*, pp. 347-348; Message, October 8, 1944, Eisenhower to Bradley, WW II Documents and Reports, Chester B. Hansen Papers, United States Army Military History Research Collection, Carlisle Barracks, Pennsylvania; Bradley, *Soldier's Story*, pp, 433-435.

[66]The German commander is quoted in Eisenhower, *Crusade in Europe*, p. 312.

[67]MacDonald, *Siegfried Line*, p. 280; Bradley, *Soldier's Story*, p. 426; Wilmot, *Struggle for Europe*, p. 540; Stamps and Esposito, *Military History*, I, 477-478; Esposito, *West Point Atlas*, II, Section 2, 59; G. Patrick Murray, "Courtney Hodges: Modest Star of WW II," *American History Illustrated*, VII (January, 1973), 20.

[68]Bradley, *Soldier's Story*, pp. 433-435; Esposito, *West Point Atlas*, II, Section 2, 59; Wilmot, *Struggle for Europe*, p. 562; MacDonald, *Mighty Endeavor*, p. 350; Pogue, *Supreme Command*, p. 310.

[69]Characterizations are from Bradley, *Soldier's Story*, p. 422.

[70]Characterizations are from Bradley, *Soldier's Story*, pp. 435-437; MacDonald, *Mighty Endeavor*, pp. 351-352; Bradley, Personal Interview Conducted by Kitty Buhler, 1966, Omar N. Bradley Papers, U. S. Military Academy Library, West Point, N.Y.

[71]Pogue, *Supreme Command*, pp. 325, 327-328; *EP*, IV: No. 1988, Eisenhower to Walter Bedell Smith, September 22, 1944; editor's note with No. 2039, pp. 2226-2227; Eisenhower, *Crusade in Europe*, pp. 318-319.

[72]Pogue, *Supreme Command*, pp. 334-336; *EP*, IV: No. 2079, Eisenhower to Combined Chiefs of Staff, October 29, 1944.

[73]Eisenhower, *Crusade in Europe*, pp. 313-314.

[74]*Ibid.*, p. 316.

[75]*Ibid.*, pp. 337-338.

[76]Wilmot, *Struggle for Europe*, p. 563; Bradley, *Soldier's Story*, p. 438.

[77]Stamps and Esposito, *Military History*, I, 482-484; Esposito, *West Point Atlas*, II, Section 2, 59.

[78]Stamps and Esposito, *Military History*, I, 487-488; Esposito, *West Point Atlas*, II, Section 2, 59; MacDonald, *Mighty Endeavor*, p. 353.

[79]Stamps and Esposito, *Military History*, I, 488-489; Esposito, *West Point Atlas*, II, Section 2, 59; MacDonald, *Mighty Endeavor*, pp. 353-354; Eisenhower, *Crusade in Europe*, pp. 331-332.

[80]MacDonald, *Mighty Endeavor*, p. 352.

[81]Eisenhower, *Crusade in Europe*, pp. 321, 324; Stamps and Esposito, *Military History*, I, 484; Bradley, *Soldier's Story*, p. 440.

[82]Stamps and Esposito, *Military History*, I, 485-486; MacDonald, *Mighty Endeavor*, pp. 354-355; Esposito, *West Point Atlas*, II, Section 2, 59; Wilmot, *Struggle for Europe*, pp. 567-569; Bradley, *Soldier's Story*, pp. 440-441; MacDonald, *Siegfried Line*, pp. 411-414.

[83]MacDonald, *Mighty Endeavor*, pp. 354-356.

A Rather Ambitious Counterattack

16

Yesterday morning the enemy launched a rather ambitious counterattack east of the Luxembourg area where we have been holding very thinly. In order to concentrate at vital points we have had divisions holding thirty mile fronts.

*Dwight D. Eisenhower**

Early on December 16, 1944, large number of gray-green coated German infantrymen, supported by tanks, attacked over the snow-covered ground of the heavily forested and rugged Ardennes, a sector which the Americans were holding thinly with units that were either battle weary or just entering combat. Artillery, mortar, and small arms fire could be plainly heard throughout the area. Occasionally a V-1 raced through the cold, early morning air. Although the Americans who met the initial onslaught had no time to contemplate the magnitude of the enemy attack, they were opposing the breakthrough force of a German counteroffensive which Hitler had designed to cross the Meuse River, seize Antwerp, and split the Allied front.[1]

Timed to commence during a period of bad weather which would minimize Allied air strikes, the vicious German attack completely surprised the Allies. Confident that Hitler's western armies were still seriously suffering the effects of the shattering defeat of the previous summer and also lacked fuel for an offensive, Allied commanders considered Rundstedt too sensible to contemplate undertaking a major offensive. Accordingly, they were willing to accept the risk of a thinly manned sector in the Ardennes in order to mass strength elsewhere. Thus, while Eisenhower continued to plan operations for closing to the Rhine and subsequent thrusts deep into Germany, Hitler readied and launched the December offensive. That surprisingly powerful attack would eventually be contained, after causing sizeable casulaties on both sides and shattering a few Allied misconceptions. In the end, however, it would be Hitler's last gasp in the West and would set the stage for a rapid allied closure to and jumping of the Rhine.

*Alfred D. Chandler (ed.), *The Papers of Dwight D. Eisenhower: The War Years* (Baltimore, 1970), IV: No. 2177, Eisenhower to Brehon Burke Somervell, December 17, 1944.

Allied View of Situation in December 1944 and Continued Dialogue Over Strategy

The situation in western Europe on the eve of the German attack seemingly was not one to evoke optimism among German leaders. *(See Map 71, in Atlas.)* The Allies had regained most of the territory formerly occupied by Germany, as Hitler tried to stave off armies which seemed to be advancing from virtually all sides. In the north, Montgomery was near the Rhine; but he occupied a long front and, more critically, he could count on receiving no more British or Commonwealth divisions unless they came from the Italian theater. To his right, although their attacks had been costly, the First and Ninth Armies were on the Roer River, preparing to renew the offensive. In the south, Patton was readying his army for a December 19 attack, and Devers, already across the German border on a 22-mile front, was pressing his fall offensive. American divisions continued to arrive on the Continent. Near Reims, Eisenhower's strategic reserve, the XVIII Airborne Corps (the 82nd and 101st Airborne Divisions), was refitting. Both divisions had sustained sizeable casualties during and after MARKET-GARDEN, having been left in the line long after they had jumped into Holland. By mid-December, moreover, the Allies were busy training for a Rhine crossing on rivers not far from the front lines. Landing craft, with naval crews, had been moved on tank-recovery vehicles from Antwerp and the Seine to these training sites.[2]

In the air, the German situation seemed a bit better, at least in a relative sense. *Luftwaffe* strength had increased to the point where several hundred sorties could be flown daily against Allied formations. Spaatz expressed concern over this apparent revitalization of the German air arm, and Doolittle warned that the Eighth Air Force might have to deemphasize strategic bombing and revert to direct attacks on the *Luftwaffe*. Taking the larger view, however, the Allied air forces still had a substantial edge over Goering's airmen. Each Allied army group was supported by a tactical air force, while a tactical air command or its equivalent worked with each army. *(See Map 71, in Atlas.)* When the Allied Expeditionary Air Force headquarters ceased operation on October 15, its staff shifted to SHAEF. Thereafter, the tactical air forces were controlled by Eisenhower's headquarters while strategic air was available to the Supreme Commander upon request.[3]

The slowing of the Allied advance along most of the line since October had given the logisticians a chance to improve the critical supply situation. With the repair of many of the railroad lines, most supplies were being transported by train to railheads located in the army areas. Antwerp was operational. Omaha and Utah Beaches were no longer handling cargo. Fuel and ammunition were arriving in more adequate quantities, thus enabling commanders to build up forward reserve stockages. All problems had not been resolved, however, for some troublesome deficiencies in such items as antifreeze, tires, and overshoes still remained.[4]

Communication Zone activities are shown on Map 71. The general organization was similar to that which had been developed for the Services of Supply in the First World War. The Advance Section (ADSEC) supported Bradley's 12th Army Group, while the Continental Advance Section supported Devers' 6th Army Group. Backing up ADSEC was the Oise Intermediate Section. Supplies entering the Continent passed through Base Sections, which were tasked with the responsibility of operating ports and base depots. With the help of a French Base Section (not shown), the southern sections served the French First Army. Approximately 45 percent of the port capacity of Antwerp was devoted to handling supplies destined for Montgomery's 21st Army Group.[5]

If the supply situation had improved as fall turned to winter, however, the growing shortage of infantry replacements was beginning to plague American commanders. There were four main reasons for this shortfall. First, in the fall of 1943, the Selective Service fell some 100,000 men short of its goal for inductees, and thus all manpower projections had to be recomputed. Though the director, Major General Lewis B. Hershey, had been working in the recruitment area since 1936, Secretary of War Henry L. Stimson and Chief of Staff George C. Marshall discussed the possibility of replacing him. Hershey stayed on, however, and continued to head the Selective Service for some years more. Also contributing to the shortage were plans based on the North African experience, which had caused too many troops to be trained for artillery, special troops, and armor at the expense of the infantry. The third reason was an early error in computing the vast number of soldiers that would be in the pipeline en route to their units at any one time. Finally, the nation's leaders had consistently pressured the War Department to keep manpower demands low.[6] Casualties suffered in the recent heavy fighting, frostbite, respiratory illnesses, and trenchfoot further aggravated the problem.

U.S. Locomotive Arrives in France, 1944

Eisenhower and his subordinates grappled with the problem and tried to find at least partial solutions which could be implemented within the theater. Able-bodied men in service units were replaced by limited duty or WAC personnel. Those so released were retrained and sent forward. Spaatz transferred 10,000 men from his air organizations, but still the ranks of infantry units were not filled. Eisenhower eagerly accepted Marshall's offer to send infantry regiments from trained divisions then in the United States ahead of the remainder of their units. As time passed, however, the overall shortage persisted. By December 15, the 31 divisions on the line in the 12th Army Group reported that they were short some 17,000 riflemen.[7]

It was this shortage of infantrymen which was the primary reason for Bradley being at Eisenhower's headquarters the day Hitler's Ardennes offensive began. The meeting was convened to discuss every possible solution to the problem, and it led to the effort to tap a new source of manpower—black Americans serving in service units. A call went out for volunteers. To qualify, men had to have had infantry training and either be in the grade of private or private first class, or agree to take a reduction in rank. Those chosen would be given a refresher course before they went to the front. Initially only 2,000 would be picked from those who had the highest qualifications, as that number was all that the Ground Force Replacement Command (GFRC) could handle. The first volunteers reported to the GFRC in January and early February. By March 1, the first 2,253 men, organized into 37 platoons, were ready to go forward. A second group of 16 platoons moved up later. In the 12th Army Group, where the platoons were usually assigned one per regiment and subsequently to a company as a fourth rifle platoon, the results were generally good. In the 6th Army Group, however, the black soldiers were organized and employed as provisional armored infantry companies. For troops who barely knew how to operate as squads and platoons, company operations presented great problems. Use of the black troops as platoons was scheduled to be discussed by the commanding general of the 12th Armored Division, the unit to which the replacements went, and the Seventh Army commander when the war ended. Thus it was that battlefield conditions caused Army leaders to reverse their decision that the armed services should not be used as an instrument for social change—a policy which had previously required that black soldiers be used in solely black units.[8]

The shortage of infantrymen was not the only problem nagging Eisenhower as November gave way to December. During Eisenhower's visit to Montgomery's headquarters on November 28, the Englishman returned to his time-worn argument for concentrating great strength in the north and putting a single commander in charge of it, the Field Marshal by implication. But, even worse, he believed he had convinced Eisenhower that the earlier Allied strategy had frittered away

Black Volunteers Being Trained for Infantry Duty, 1944

strength through lack of concentration and thus had led to a "strategic reverse." The Supreme Commander, Montgomery was sure, would "go to almost any length to succeed next time," and this meant effectively turning over "operational charge" to Monty, putting Bradley, leading a strong army group north of the Ardennes, under the Englishman's command, and relegating Devers to a purely holding role. This assessment Montgomery conveyed privately to the Chief of the Imperial General Staff, Field Marshal Lord Alanbrooke. Either because he had doubts about the discussion on the twenty-eighth or because he feared Eisenhower would be influenced by SHAEF or American arguments, however, he wrote to Ike on November 30, apparently to confirm his understanding of the agreement. In that letter he also proposed a meeting at Maastricht with Eisenhower and Bradley and their chiefs of staff, "who must not speak."[9]

Eisenhower did not take at all kindly to Montgomery's letter. Ruffled and hot under the collar, he fired back a December 1 reply which he dictated at Bradley's headquarters while en route back to SHAEF. Defending his broad-front strategy, he did not agree that the Allies had suffered a strategic reverse, although he acknowledged they had not achieved all they had hoped for. Nor would he stop Devers and Patton as long as they were making progress, for their gains would permit later concentrations for major attacks. He liked the army group boundary tied to the Ruhr, as he had placed it, leaving Bradley independent of Montgomery. He agreed to a December 7 meeting and would bring Smith if possible, but he would not insult him by forbidding him to speak. In the next two days, each man backed off a little, Montgomery stating that he did not mean to condemn all recent Allied efforts in Europe—just the failure to carry out the October 28 directive; and Eisenhower apologizing for assuming the worst about Montgomery's letter and charge. But the basic conflict in views still existed and would not go away.[10]

Churchill then entered the fray, very likely prodded by Brooke, and telegraphed Roosevelt on December 6, expressing disappointment that the Rhine had not been reached in the north. Three days later, the President answered that years previously he had bicycled over much of the area and had always felt that the advance to the Rhine would be a difficult one. He compared the roles of the two leaders to those of Commanders-in-Chief who had made their strategic plans, informed their commanders, and given them the resources to achieve the desired ends. Now the field commanders must be allowed to do their jobs. Roosevelt declared his confidence in the incumbent military leaders and said that he did not consider a meeting of the Combined Chiefs of Staff necessary.[11]

Meanwhile, the meeting at Maastricht had taken place. En route there, Eisenhower passed through the Ardennes and again asked Bradley about this thinly held portion of the line.

Bradley said that to secure the Ardennes he would have to draw from the forces which were to attack in the Roer and Saar. He believed that the risk of an enemy attack was acceptable, for he had placed no major supply installations east of the Meuse. Should an assault come, it could be attacked from both flanks and stopped short of the river.[12] At Maastricht, it quickly became clear that there was still a wide divergence of views on the proper strategy and organization. During the meeting with Bradley, Montgomery, Tedder, and Smith, Eisenhower stated that once Bradley had taken the Roer Dams, converging attacks from the Reichswald and Roer would clear the lower Rhineland to the river. The target date for these attacks was to be January 12. The major thrust across the Rhine would be north of the Ruhr, led by the 21st Army Group, and supported by a 10-division-strong U.S. army, the Ninth. American forces would launch a secondary attack to the south of the main thrust. When Montgomery raised the subject of putting all operations north of the Ardennes under one commander, Eisenhower declared once again that command boundaries were set according to what was to happen to the front, not to the rear. Thus he felt that the Ruhr should serve as the dividing line. Nor would he accede to Montgomery's request for the cessation of operations in the Third Army sector, as long as it appeared that Patton was making good progress.[13]

After the meeting, Montgomery wrote to Brooke: "I can do no more myself. . . . If we want the war to end within any reasonable period you have to get Eisenhower's hand taken off the land battle. I regret to say that in my opinion he just doesn't know what he is doing."[14] As Roosevelt's reply to Churchill's message had indicated that he would not interfere, the British Chiefs of Staff contemplated direct discussions with Eisenhower. When the Supreme Commander, upset after the Maastricht meeting, proposed to Churchill that he visit London to explain his views, a meeting was quickly arranged for December 12.[15]

At the meeting in London, Eisenhower explained his plan to Churchill and the British Chiefs. Brooke disagreed, saying that the Allies had insufficient force to mount two attacks across the Rhine. Moreover, he was unhappy with the projected date of May for a Rhine crossing and with Churchill's only lukewarm support of his arguments. Eisenhower refused to cancel the southern thrust, but he did consent to strengthen the northern attack by sending all incoming reinforcements to the First and Ninth Armies. As he told Marshall the next day, his main goal was to reach the Rhine from Bonn northward, while his secondary task was to ensure that troops would be ready to move on Frankfurt when the time was right to cross. Discouraged and upset, Brooke set in motion plans to request Eisenhower to submit to the Combined Chiefs of Staff a report of his recent operations and plans for the future. Within a week, the German offensive made the proposal academic.[16]

Meanwhile, in keeping with Eisenhower's plans, First Army launched an attack on December 13 to seize the Roer River dams. To the south, Patton prepared for his Saar offensive which was scheduled to begin on December 19. He made no secret of the fact that he expected to make speedy gains. Eisenhower and Bradley agreed, however, that if major progress was not made within a week, the attack would be stopped. Supplies could then go to nourish the force in the north, which would make the primary thrust. Hitler's *panzers* saw to it that Patton's claims were never tested.[17]

Hitler's Plan for a Counteroffensive

The proposal for the large counteroffensive that led to the cancellation of Patton's drive had been announced on September 16 to a small group of key advisors. The announcement was made after the routine situation briefing held in the Wolf's Lair, the *Fuehrer*'s East Prussian headquarters. After analyzing the situation, Hitler had decided to strike in the West. His armies would attack out of the Ardennes, with Antwerp, just over 100 miles away, the final objective. *(See Map: German Plan for Ardennes Offensive, page 373.)* Once he had taken Antwerp, Hitler could not only disrupt the flow of supplies to the Allies, but also might be able to destroy all enemy forces north of the line Bastogne-Brussels-Antwerp.[18]

Before selecting the Ardennes, Hitler had considered an attack on the Eastern Front. Distances were so great in the East, however, that limited German troop strength and gasoline supplies precluded the capture of a decisive objective. In the Ardennes, where German armies had twice previously surprised their enemies, the terrain was difficult. German forces, which would be quickly swallowed up in the vastness of the East, could have an amplified effect. Moreover, to the east of the lightly held American line lay the forests of the Eifel region, where large units could be secretly massed. If the attack could be conducted during a prolonged period of poor flying weather, a not uncommon occurrence in December, the Germans could be over the Meuse and en route to Brussels and Antwerp before the Allies could react. Hitler reasoned that the British were war weary and that because the Americans really had no desire to fight Germany, U.S. troop morale would plummet after a major defeat.[19]

When the operation was concluded, Hitler would not only have relieved the pressure on the Ruhr and eliminated a large portion of the enemy force, but also might have dealt a death blow to an already strained alliance. His hero, Frederick the Great, had persevered in the face of enemies attacking from all

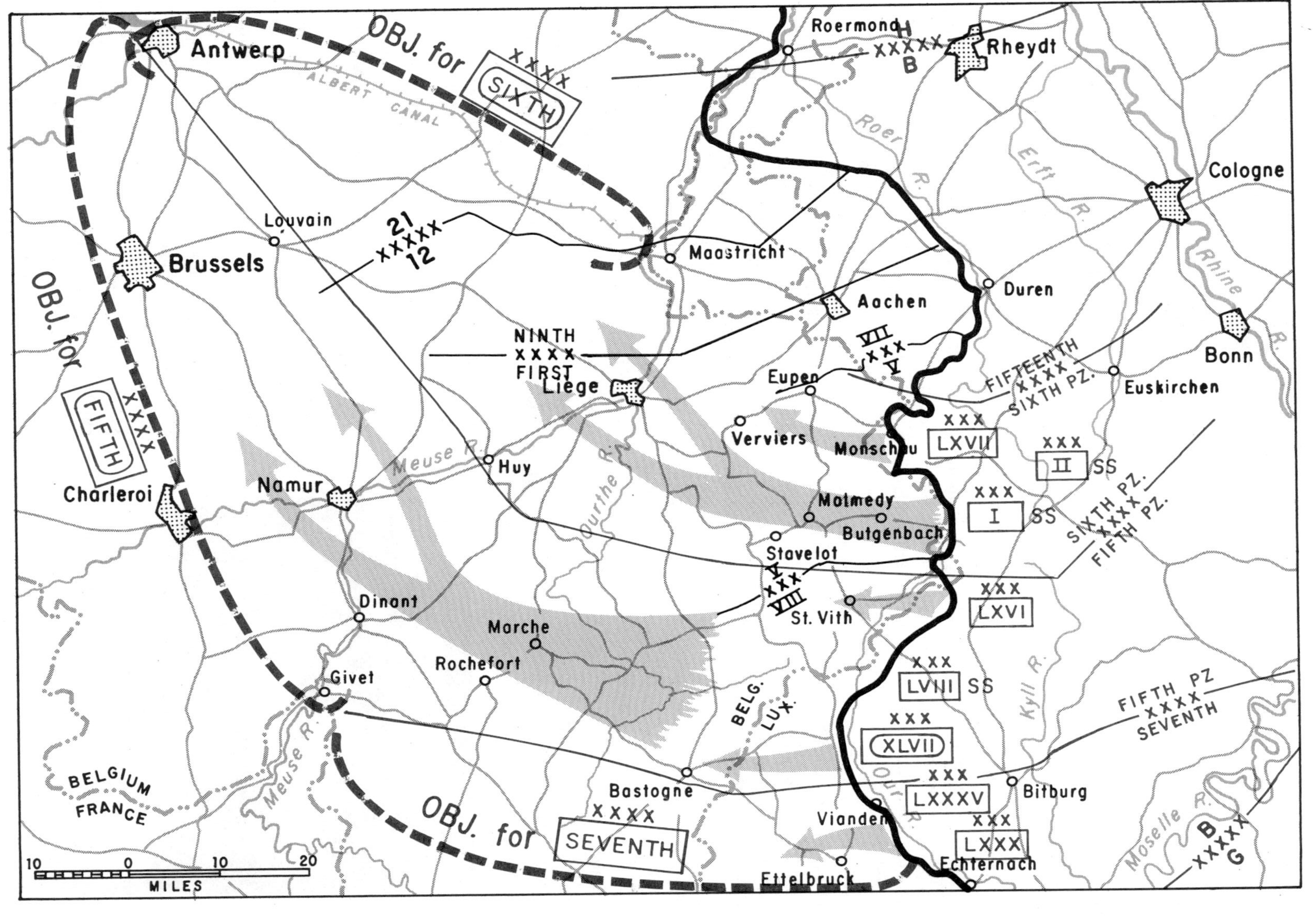

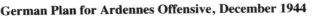

German Plan for Ardennes Offensive, December 1944

directions until the opposing alliance disintegrated. Perhaps that performance could be repeated. In any case, no matter what advice his conservative military leaders gave, Hitler was determined to act decisively while German industry was still producing the materials of war, morale at home was reasonably strong, and troops could be massed for an attack, thanks to the Roer River Dams and West Wall fortifications which were enabling the Germans to hold back their enemies with minimum strength. The alternative seemed to be a continued withdrawal. Even if the planned offensive was not completely successful, it would upset Eisenhower's timetable and gain time to rebuild war plants and produce more of the new jet-propelled aircraft and improved submarines.[20]

It was late October before Rundstedt and Model, the two German commanders who would execute Hitler's plan, learned of his intentions. Although the *Fuehrer* promised large reinforcements, gasoline, ammunition, and 1,500 fighter plans (including 100 jets), both field marshals though the plan was much too ambitious. They advocated a more limited offensive. While each had his own ideas, they both intended to use Hitler's reinforcements to cut off the 14 American divisions in the Aachen area and in the process take the large supply base of Liège. Although the Rundstedt-Model concept, eventually called the Small Solution, was presented to Hitler, he termed it a "Half Solution" and refused to discuss it. Even the added support of Generaloberst der Waffen SS Josef "Sepp" Dietrich and General der Panzertruppen Hasso von Manteuffel, who were to lead the Sixth Panzer and Fifth Panzer Armies respectively in the attack, was not sufficient to sway the *Fuehrer*. He felt that he could only achieve his ends if Germany gambled all on a chance for a major victory.[21] *(See Map, page 373.)*

General Sepp Dietrich

General Hasso von Manteuffel

Hitler's fully developed plan specified that Dietrich's Sixth Panzer Army of three corps would make the main attack. Hitler and Dietrich were old cronies. The ex-butcher, high in SS circles, had no qualifications for high level command, but because Hitler distrusted the German Regulars, Dietrich not surprisingly was selected to lead the SS-heavy army. His army, on the narrowest front of the three assaulting armies, was to penetrate between Eupen and Stavelot and enable three infantry divisions to advance to Eupen and Verviers where they would establish blocking positions. South of the infantry, the 1st and 12th SS Panzer Divisions of the I SS Panzer Corps were to attack through the gap at Butgenbach and take Malmedy and Stavelot. As rapidly as possible, this corps, followed by the II SS Panzer Corps, would cross the Meuse on both sides of Liège and head for Antwerp. Dietrich was to reach the Meuse in no more than 48 hours.

Meanwhile, to the south, Manteuffel's Fifth Panzer Army, also with three corps, would be attacking toward the key road junctions of St. Vith and Bastogne. Manteuffel's troops were then to cross the Meuse on both sides of Namur and head for Brussels and Antwerp, while at the same time protecting the exposed southern flank of the Sixth Panzer Army. Flank protection on the extreme south was to be provided by four infantry divisions from General der Panzertruppen Eric Brandenberger's Seventh Army, which would cross the Our River between Vianden and Echternach and block north of Luxembourg and Arlon.

In the initial assault, the Germans would be able to achieve a 2 to 1 superiority in tanks and a 6 to 1 ratio in troop strength at the critical points. To assist in the speedy crossing of the Meuse, a special brigade, commanded by Lieutenant Colonel Otto Skorzeny, was to be assembled. Skorzeny, who had achieved fame by his daring rescue of Mussolini, would use American equipment and dress his troops, 150 of whom spoke "American," in captured uniforms so that they might slip through American defenses, secure the Meuse bridges, and generally disrupt the American rear area. As a further help, a battalion of paratroopers would be dropped near Monschau to block a key road which led south from Aachen.

As it turned out, neither Skorzeny's brigade nor the paratrooper battalion lived up to expectations. Only a few of Skorzeny's men succeeded in reaching the American rear. While their presence did start a flock of rumors and caused activities to be slowed by frequent identity checks, they did not take the Meuse bridges and caused little physical damage. Due to the lack of gasoline for the trucks which were to carry the paratroopers to their planes, the airborne drop was postponed. When it was finally executed, early on December 17, one company landed behind German lines and the other paratroopers were so widely spread that they had little tangible effect and most were soon captured.

But at the time that the fully developed plan was disseminated to the senior commanders, the failure of both the paratroopers and Skorzeny's brigade lay in the future. If the offensive was to have any chance for success, the Allies must be surprised. To accomplish this feat, the Germans devised a detailed deception plan.[22]

Final German Preparations and Allied Reactions to Intelligence

The German deception plan deliberately capitalized upon the scale and success of the Allied November attacks, particularly those made east of Aachen in the closure to the Roer River. It was obvious to both sides that once the Roer dams were captured, the Allies would attack toward Cologne and Bonn. *(See Map 72, in Atlas.)* Thus Hitler's positioning of the Sixth Panzer Army headquarters just northwest of Cologne and his assignment thereto of several *panzer* divisions was logical—in anticipation of the counterattack this army would be ready to launch in response to the expected Allied drive to the Rhine. These preparations were paraded before the Allies, whose intelligence agencies picked up the concentration of *panzer* divisions and ultimately the existence of Sixth Panzer Army; moreover, the agencies accepted the deception scheme as to how this army would be employed. What the Allies did not guess was that at the last moment Dietrich's divisions would move secretly at night to the south, into the northern Eifel, to launch the main effort of the counteroffensive.

Meanwhile, and in extreme secrecy, the Fifth Panzer Army was to assemble in the heart of the heavily wooded Eifel. The Germans hoped that this assembly would go unnoticed, but recognized that some units might be identified by the Allies; accordingly, the cover plan called for a few weakened divisions to be positioned in the Eifel to counterattack the south flank of an American drive across the Roer. This also rationalized the build-up in the minds of Germans below army group command level, who were not privy to Hitler's offensive design until the last moment. The deception scheme also included masking headquarters' locations. Shortly after its transfer from Lorraine in late October to Army Group B control, Manteuffel's Fifth Panzer Army headquarters was secretly pulled into the Eifel and given a military police command designation. To replace it in the line, Fifteenth Army headquarters secretly came down from Holland—its designation was still retained in the north by another headquarters—and took command as Gruppe von Manteuffel.

Having devised this logical deception plan, the Germans bent every effort to make it plausible to the Allies. Even the code name Hitler selected for his offensive WACHT AM RHEIN (Watch on the Rhine) was designed to reinforce Allied beliefs that the Germans were doing all that they could to try to blunt a future American attack. Published orders and radio messages were filled with news of defensive preparations. Those few officers who knew of the real scheme were sworn to secrecy on pain of death. Special couriers were used when written material had to be transmitted. To preclude capture, no one with knowledge of the plan was allowed to fly west of the Rhine. Only those who had earned the trust of their superiors went on patrols, and foreigners were combed from front-line divisions to decrease the chance that a deserter would reveal the build-up. Units in the Eifel took special care to insure that camouflage discipline was maintained, and radio blackout was vigorously enforced. The method of designating the target date was changed from X–1, X–2, etc., to 0-Day as the target date with N being X–1, M being X–2, etc. If the Allies captured a document with the old designation and the intelligence expert was able to relate an event to a certain day, he could deduce the date of attack. With the new scheme and no mention made that the attack would be launched on 0-Day, the relation of an activity to a particular day would have much less value.

As the days in November passed, the Germans quickened the pace of marshalling troops and supplies for their counteroffensive, all of which followed a very carefully devised and intricate plan. The Allied attacks in Alsace-Lorraine and east of Aachen, which pinned down some units slated for use in the attack, led Hitler to cancel the November 25 target date. That day he designated December 10 as 0-Day, but later moved the date to the fifteenth and ultimately to December 16 because sufficient fuel had not been accumulated, and not all initial attack divisions were in their assembly areas. It was nip and tuck withdrawing divisions from the fighting along the Roer River, but the task was accomplished in time to allow the three nights required to make the final moves to the attack positions. On the nights of December 13 and 14, infantry divisions went into place, and on the night of the fourteenth, *panzer* units moved over icy roads to go into attack locations. Wheels were wrapped with straw and roads were covered with hay to muffle the sound of movement. Harassing artillery fire and planes flying over American listening posts also distracted the attention of Hodges' forces. The cloak of secrecy had been lifted by December 8 when corps and division commanders were briefed on the attack plans; Hitler personally talked to key commanders three days later.

On December 15, Rundstedt's intelligence staff nervously checked the American sector to try to determine if the build-up had been discovered. They could find no such sign, and communications intelligence detachments reported that continued American carelessness in the use of radio and commercial telephone indicated that no U.S. reinforcements were moving to the Ardennes area. The deception plan seemed to have worked. Weather conditions were also favorable. Rundstedt decided to go ahead and so notified OKW; Hitler's confirmation came back at 3:30 P..M. That night, as units moved to the line of departure, the troops first learned of the plan to attack the American sector at 5:30 A.M., December 16.[23]

The failure of Allied intelligence agencies to give warning of the Ardennes counteroffensive was the result of Hitler's deception scheme coupled with the Allies' own preconceptions, all of which worked to lull Allied leaders into a state of euphoria. American intelligence sources continued to report that German forces, steadily growing weaker, would merely react in response to new Allied offensives.

As was the case with the surprise attack of Pearl Harbor, there were a number of indicators which could have led analysts to a different conclusion about German capabilities and intentions in December 1944. Hindsight now enables the student to appreciate their significance more than the participant, wrapped in the fog of war, did then. An understanding of the Allied feeling about these indicators, however, can be instructive. Most of the intelligence items were either downgraded or passed to higher levels too late to prevent surprise, another indication of how good German security was.

One of the major factors contributing to the Allied intelligence failure was the almost total lack of ULTRA information. As noted earlier, German communications security was extremely strict, due at least in part to concern that the high level code had been broken. One air liaison officer with the Sixth Panzer Army, however, grew careless and in a message picked up by ULTRA referred to "the coming big operation." The intercept had no effect, probably because no other ULTRA information was available and because the analysts and commanders were mentally conditioned to expect only a German defensive effort. While the lack of ULTRA information might have alerted Allied intelligence officers, it seemed to have the opposite effect. Without confirmation by ULTRA, information received from other sources was generally discounted. In this regard, Ronald Lewin's observation is enlightening:

> In scientific studies it is sometimes possible to weigh the effect of a particular factor or element by examining what happens in a given situation when it is absent. The Ardennes affair illustrates the value of Ultra to battle-commanders in precisely this negative way. If we take Normandy as an example, it was not just the exact forewarning about a coming attack that mattered—as in the case of von Kluge's drive on Avranches. Perhaps even more important, in terms of the conduct of the battle *from day to day*, was the manner in which Ultra could confirm, reinforce, qualify or expand the existing ideas of the staffs and their generals. But the practical value of intelligence depends on the attitude of mind of its recipients. In Normandy, Montgomery and his team, committed to the broad concept of keeping the German armour concentrated on the British front, could read immediately the significance of those abundant signals that gave them the location, strength, equipment and leadership of the panzer divisions. It fitted into their mental picture. But this corroborative effect of Ultra was never more fatally absent than before the Ardennes offensive. Whether British or American, those officers who had to give critical advice or take critical decisions were looking at the wrong picture. They therefore failed to interpret correctly such evidence as was available to them from conventional sources, and there was no Ultra to shift their minds from a fixed position.[24]

The Allied leaders also placed too much stock in the belief that with Rundstedt in command the Germans would probably move to meet an American attack, or if they did counterattack, strike for a limited objective in the Aachen area. Of course, such a restricted attack was just what Rundstedt proposed in the Small Solution. Unfortunately, the assumption that Rundstedt was controlling events was erroneous. Hitler was really calling the tune, and he had decided on a major offensive.

For years after the war, arguments flew back and forth concerning who was responsible for the failure of Allied intelligence to predict the attack. The fact that intelligence failure occurred is evident, but the responsibility rests on many shoulders. The 12th Army Group intelligence summary of December 12, for example, included:

> It is now certain that attrition is steadily sapping the strength of German forces on the Western Front and that the crust of defenses is thinner, more brittle and more vulnerable than it appears on our G-2 maps or to the troops in the line.[25]

From First Army, about five days before the attack, came a report of indications of increased troop strength in the Eifel and of heightened morale among prisoners. Aerial reconnaissance on December 8, 10, 11, 14 and 15, picked up sizeable movements of troops and equipment both east and west of the Rhine. Intelligence experts, however, did not interpret this information to mean that an attack was coming. Also reported was a captured order which specified special training for German troops who spoke "American." Although hindsight reveals that the build-up was in preparation for the attack while the "American" speakers were wanted for Skorzeny's brigade, these bits of information, at the time, were not cause enough for American leaders to revise their plans, cancel their attacks, and order reserves to the Ardennes. The army G-2, who had predicted attacks before, continued to plan for his leave in Paris. He was there when the Germans struck.

There were other reports which today seem pregnant with implication. Several nights before the attack, both the 28th and 106th Infantry Divisions reported more vehicle noise than usual. As the 106th was a green unit, little weight was given to its report. The 28th, an experienced outfit, interpreted the noises simply to mean the relief of enemy units, similar to a relief which had taken place three weeks previously. This report also was discounted. On December 14, a woman who had crossed the lines told the commanding general of the 28th Infantry Division that German equipment literally filled the woods near Bitburg. She impressed both the division and corps G-2's, and was sent to First Army for interrogation; she arrived there on December 16. Four prisoners taken on December 15 said that new units were coming in and that an attack would be launched before Christmas. Two, both deserters, said the troops had been promised this before, but that no attack had come. The other two prisoners were wounded, but one impressed his questioners with the information he presented. As he had been given morphine, however, it was decided to wait to question him further. Of the seven incidents (four prisoners, the woman line-crosser, and the two reports of noise), only one was reported to 12th Army Group. One of the reports of noise, interpreted to mean that a unit had been relieved, was included in the commander's morning briefing on December 16. By then, the attack had been in progress for almost three hours.

Even if all of the incidents had been passed up the chain of command, it is doubtful that Bradley would have reacted strongly. Aerial reconnaisance had not revealed the build-up. The railroad lines which brought vehicles to detraining points opposite VIII Corps could also be used to bring reinforcements to areas threatened either by Patton's army in the south or by the forces on the Roer in the north. The interpretation was that the enemy was merely reinforcing to meet the expected American attacks.

German capabilities had been severely underrated. The author of the Army's official history of the Ardennes offensive, Hugh M. Cole, wrote: "Americans and British had looked in a mirror for the enemy and seen there only the reflection of their own intentions."[26]

WACHT AM RHEIN: *The German Onslaught*

The major American formations which were positioned in the area where Hitler's attack was to strike are shown on Map 72. In the V Corps zone, the 99th Infantry Division held a front of over 20 miles in difficult terrain. Through the southern portion of the division sector ran the main roads that were to be used by Dietrich's Sixth Panzer Army. At the time the German attack came, the experienced 2nd Infantry Division was attacking through the northern part of the sector of the 99th Division toward the Roer Dams. South of the 99th, in the VIII Corps zone, a light task force from the 14th Cavalry Group screened the Losheim Gap. Next came the green 106th Infantry Division which had completed the relief of the 2nd infantry Division just four days before the German attack. Two regiments of the 106th were positioned on the Schnee Eifel. The experienced but tired 28th Infantry Division occupied the center of the corps sector. Major General Norman D. Cota, the division commander, needed time to train and integrate reinforcements which had arrived to replace the men lost in recent battles in the Huertgen Forest. On the corps right, or south, flank were inexperienced elements of the 9th Armored Division; next to them stood the veteran 4th Infantry Division, which had recently sustained 5,000 battle and 2,500 non-battle casualties in the

German Soldier Moves Forward, December 1944

Huertgen Forest. Similar to the 28th Division, the 4th Division was resting and refitting in a quiet sector. At 5:30 a.m., December 16, the rest period ended.[27]

The cold stillness of the dark night was shattered by reports from 2,000 guns. Searchlights switched on. Their beams reflecting off clouds created artificial moonlight to illuminate American-held territory. On a front from Monschau to Echternach, German infantrymen moved forward across the snow-covered ground as Hitler's attempt to regain the initiative in western Europe began.[28]

German planners and commanders were well aware that the rough terrain in the Eifel-Ardennes area could hamper the employment of masses of armored and wheeled vehicles. But they also knew that the Americans had risked thinning sector defenses largely for that reason; and, in 1940, the terrain had not stopped them. Generally rolling and covered with forests with many steep valleys, the Ardennes was traversed by many roads, but few were in good shape. The best roads led to the southwest, a condition that was welcomed in 1940 but one which would cause problems in 1944. In their efforts to move northwest, the Germans would have to rely often on secondary roads which twisted and turned their way from village to village. Possession of the few main roads would be crucial because, with the exception of the Bastogne and St. Vith area, the terrain limited cross country mobility. The side which controlled key road junctions would have a distinct advantage. The critical communication centers were Bastogne, on the main Arlon-Liège highway; St. Vith, another important road junction; and Marche, on both the Sedan-Liège and Brussels-Luxembourg highways. *(See Map 72, in Atlas.)*

Once Hitler's forces had crossed the Our River, which marks the German border and flows along most of the front, they hoped to make rapid progress toward the Meuse, some 60 miles ahead. Several terrain features which could be used by the defense would have to be kept in mind. A ridge runs from Bastogne through St. Vith to the vicinity of Losheim. From Stavelot to past Monschau, and parallel to the Bastogne-Losheim Ridge, is the Hohes Venn, also high ground. East of the Hohes Venn, and on the access routes to Malmedy and Spa, is the Elsenborn Ridge. Between Elsenborn Ridge and another piece of high ground, the Schnee Eifel which lies to the south, is the Losheim Gap. To the west, the Ourthe and Amblève Rivers become obstacles as they near the Meuse.[29]

In the zone of the 99th Infantry Division, where in November members of the Hitler Youth had harassed rear area personnel by pouring sugar in gasoline tanks and stretching wires across roads to decapitate jeep passengers, the Germans encountered units which had been in positions for two months. At first, it appeared to the American defenders that the German attack was merely a reaction to thrusts being made in the north by the 2nd Infantry Division. In reality, they were encountering the initial elements of the Sixth Panzer Army, the main attack force. After the forward positions had been penetrated, Dietrich's forces were either to cross or go to the south of Elsenborn Ridge and attack toward the Meuse along four good roads. *(See Map 72, in Atlas.)*

Fighting raged throughout the day. Units of the 99th Infantry Division put up so fierce a defense that the Germans were forced to commit tanks which had been designated for the exploitation. When darkness came, although some ground had been lost, key American positions were still intact. Meanwhile, to the north, the 2nd Infantry Division had continued to attack. By the end of the day, it reported taking its first objectives. Gerow, commander of the V Corps, however, had decided that the battle being fought just to the south might result in the 2nd Division being left in a precarious position. Accordingly, that afternoon he had asked Hodges to suspend the 2nd Division's attack so that the unit might withdraw to a safer location on Elsenborn Ridge. Still believing that the Germans had merely launched a spoiling attack to interrupt the assault on the Roer dams, Hodges refused the request and directed that planning continue for the advance on December 17.

That evening the deputy corps commander, Major General Clarence R. Huebner, told Major General Walter M. Robertson, commander of the 2nd Infantry Division, to be ready to move his unengaged troops rapidly in case the plan changed. Change it did, for at 7:30 A.M., December 17, Hodges, realizing that the 99th Division needed help, told Gerow to handle his corps as he felt best. Gerow called off the 2nd Division attack and ordered that the main defensive battle be conducted on Elsenborn Ridge, some six miles to the rear of the current front. Robertson would take charge of the entire force (units from both divisions) and manage the withdrawal to what Gerow hoped would become a strong shoulder position. If the troops on Elsenborn Ridge held, the corps sector would be protected, at least to the front, and the penetration then taking place in the VIII Corps could grow no wider. Due to a decision made by Hodges later on December 16, Gerow also was to have the use of the lst Infantry Division; already en route, its first regiment to arrive would take positions not far from Butgenbach to block the key road which went to the west from Bullingen.

During the next few days Robertson fought what Eisenhower later termed "one of the brilliant divisional actions of the war in Europe."[30] He conducted his masterful withdrawal in two phases. First, using units of the 99th Division to cover, he withdrew his two regiments which had been conducting the attack toward the Roer dams. Robertson used these regiments to hold key positions while his third regiment and the less experienced troops of the 99th moved back. When elements of the 99th reached Elsenborn Ridge, they were released to their own commanding general, Major General Walter

Lauer, who organized the new position. On December 19, Robertson successfully withdrew the 2nd Division to Elsenborn Ridge.

Although the Germans tried to take the position, the 1st and 9th Infantry Divisions bolstered the defense, and the northern shoulder held. While the cost was high, the Americans held on to roads vital to the success of the German plan. On December 20, Model shifted the main German attack to the Fifth Panzer Army.[31]

Meanwhile, well to the south, the German Seventh Army, composed of the LXXXV and LXXX Corps, each with two *volksgrenadier* divisions, attacked a regiment of the 28th Infantry Division, an armored infantry battalion of the 9th Armored Division, and a regiment of the 4th Infantry Division. Once they had broken through, the German divisions were to turn south, one by one, to form a strong southern flank for the penetration. Although the attackers were able to make some gains on the first day, key strongpoints held. As the hours passed, the Germans made gains and crossed the Our River, especially to the north where most of the Seventh Army tanks and assault guns were employed against the regiment of the 28th Division. But the tenacious American defense had gained two valuable days. At the end of the third day, the regimental commander was faced with a choice of fighting to the death, pulling back to the west, or moving southwest to join the armored infantry battalion from the 9th Armored Division, now reinforced to combat command size. He chose to move southwest. On December 17, the 4th Infantry Division near Echternach, was reinforced by a combat command from the 10th Armored Divison, which had moved up from Third Army. Thus, by the end of the third day, the southern shoulder had taken shape, and, as in the north, the Germans could widen their penetration no farther. Luxembourg City, home for the advanced command posts of both the 12th Army Group and Ninth Air Force, appeared to be safe, although it was only about 12 miles west of the German lines.[32]

Between the two developing shoulders, areas of haven for American troops were few. The remaining two regiments of the 28th Division, located just south of the Schnee Eifel, bore the brunt of the Fifth Panzer Army's main attack, as Manteuffel sent two *panzer* corps against them. The southern regiment, the 110th under the command of Colonel Hurley Fuller, had only two battalions in line and was spread over a 10-mile front. The third battalion was some 10 miles to the rear in division reserve. Fuller, who had fought in the Argonne Forest in the First World War, established company-sized strongpoints at key road junctions across his front, and had a light screen of outposts forward. Hard fighting raged throughout the day, with the Germans suffering heavy casualties but succeeding in bypassing American strongpoints. Cota had issued orders to the 28th Division to hold at all costs, and with the help of cooks, clerks, artillerymen, and others, the strongpoints held. But the enemy continued to pound at them. Eventually, Colonel Gustin Nelson wheeled his 112th Infantry, the northern regiment of the division, to the north to join the defense which was forming around the important road junction of St. Vith.

Fuller did all he could to halt the enemy onslaught and keep the Germans from reaching the town of Clerf, located on a main road to Bastogne and the temporary home of the regimental command post. By the evening of December 17, however, Fuller was forced to withdraw, having defended the town with everything he had, including his headquarters troops. One of the last to try to leave, he was taken prisoner. The good road from Clerf to Bastogne was open.

Farther to the south, soldiers from the division headquarters, supplemented with such combat troops as could be gathered, fought to hold the town of Wiltz, on the southern route to Bastogne. Cota's men retained the town through the eighteenth, even as German units some 15 miles to their rear approached the outskirts of Bastogne. On the morning of December 19, the headquarters of the 28th Division left Wiltz for a position southwest of Bastogne where Cota hoped he could reorganize his division. Wiltz fell that night and the defenders withdrew in small groups. Although elements would continue to fight under other commanders, for the present the 28th Infantry Division no longer existed. Its sacrifice, however, had not been in vain, for the schedule of the XLVII Panzer Corps, charged with the capture of Bastogne, had been severely disrupted.[33]

The inexperienced 106th Infantry Division was in position to the north of the 28th Infantry Division, with two of its regiments on the Schnee Eifel and its command post at St. Vith. Two squadrons of the 14th Cavalry Group, which was attached to the 106th Division, were screening a 9,000-yard-wide sector in the Losheim Gap, just to the north. The cavalrymen came under attack from elements of both *panzer* armies, and were unable to prevent a penetration. Manteuffel's troops turned southwest of the Schnee Eifel to attack the artillery units which were supporting the forward American elements. To the north of the two American regiments, German units which formed the other wing of the pincer advanced about a mile.

Back at division headquarters, Major General Alan B. Jones and his staff began to realize by the evening of December 16 that the two forward regiments were in a precarious situation, even though they had not been surrounded during the first day of battle. Jones, whose son was serving in one of the forward regiments, decided to leave his men in place. He had already been reinforced by Combat Command B of the 9th Armored Division, which he sent to the south of the Schnee Eifel to restore the broken link to his third regiment. He also expected the 7th Armored Division to arrive in his area shortly. Jones had been told that one or two of its combat commands

German Tank Enroute to the Front Passes Captured American Troops, December 1944

could be used for a counterattack.

Unfortunately for the men of the 106th Division, the 7th Armored had to move some 60 miles parallel to the front over slippery roads which were clogged with traffic. Elements of the first combat command, led by recently promoted Brigadier General Bruce C. Clarke, did not arrive in St. Vith until about dusk on the seventeenth; they had been expected early that morning. In the meantime, the Germans had renewed their efforts on the seventeenth to encircle the two regiments on the Schnee Eifel. They were successful in this endeavor by about 9:00 A.M. When American attempts at breakout or relief failed, virtually all of the surrounded troops, low on ammunition and increasingly herded into tighter pockets, surrendered. Most of them capitulated on the nineteenth, but the last elements held out until December 21. It was a heavy blow to American prestige.[34]

Meanwhile, back at St. Vith, Jones essentially left the matter of command to Clarke, who organized a horseshoe defense of that vital position. His troops fought tenaciously to hold the village. Each hour that Manteuffel was denied access to this road junction not only further delayed the German advance and interfered with the resupply of units which had penetrated in the north, but also contributed to the massive German traffic jams building up to the east. Shortly before midnight on December 21, Clarke was forced out of St. Vith, but his force, which consisted of elements of many units, continued to delay the enemy advance until it withdrew across the Salm River late on December 23. The American defense had been costly, but the Germans had lost valuable time. Whereas Manteuffel had expected to seize St. Vith the second day, he could not take it until the fifth day. By the end of December 23, the Allies had capitalized on the delay imposed on the enemy by the dogged American defensive actions to reorganize, bring in reserves, and establish a 40-mile front from Monschau to the Salm River.[35]

While Clarke stubbornly held on to St. Vith, Colonel Joachim Peiper had led the armored spearhead of the 1st SS Panzer Division through the Losheim Gap deep into the American rear area. *(See Map 72, in Atlas.)* Finding gasoline, Peiper used American prisoners to refuel his tanks, then continued westward. Shortly after noon on the seventeenth, his leading element ran into a truck convoy, Battery B, 285th Field Artillery Observation Battalion. The Germans took the battery under fire. The artillerymen, heading south from Malmedy, dismounted and ran for the cover of woods and ditches. Peiper's main body pushed on, but some of his following troops captured the Americans, marched them into a field, and at a prearranged signal used machineguns and pistols to execute them. When the firing ceased, wounded soldiers who moved or made noises were shot in the head. Although a few escaped by pretending to be dead, at least 86 died. Earlier that day Peiper's men had killed 19 unarmed soldiers in one place and 50 at another.

By December 20, about 100 unarmed Belgian civilians and 350 American prisoners had been killed by Peiper's men in what proved to be the only systematic execution of prisoners by either side during the battle. Word of the killings quickly spread through the American units. Thereafter, German troops, especially SS, would find it difficult to surrender.

Peiper's advance was slowed by the determined opposition of small groups of defenders. He waited to attack Stavelot until dark on December 17 because he thought that trucks moving through the town were filled with troops, when in reality they were removing gasoline from a nearby depot. At that time only an engineer squad defended the town. When he did attack, the few reinforcements which had arrived joined in, putting up such a stiff defense that it took the Germans most of the morning to clear the village. In the confusion, a single platoon without antitank weapons withdrew toward the gasoline depot. An American major in charge of defending the dump found a road cut in a place where the German tanks could not maneuver, ordered it filled with gasoline, lit it, and had a 124,000-gallon roadblock. Peiper did not get the remainder of the gasoline. His troops continued their westerly movements, but they were often delayed. In one instance, a 57-mm antitank gun was able to get off one shot which stopped the lead tank. Although the gun was knocked out, the Germans had been delayed long enough for a key bridge to be destroyed. Peiper continued to advance, but he acted alone because, due to the limited capacity of the roads between Elsenborn Ridge and St. Vith, he could not be supported adequately. Soon American reinforcements stopped his drive, trapped him, and destroyed much of his force. Ultimately, only 800 of his original 2,000 men returned to German lines.[36]

Eisenhower's Reactions and Adjustments in Allied Defenses

Miles from the front, where the desperate and visceral slugging match was taking place, high-level commanders grappled with the meaning of the sudden flare-up along the Ardennes line. As is always the case in such situations, they hungered for accurate information on which to base crucial decisions, instinctively wanting a firsthand look at the battle in order to reinforce necessary judgments. Such was the case with Eisenhower and Bradley, who were in conference at SHAEF headquarters on December 16, discussing the infantry replacement problem. Apprised of small penetrations in the zones of the V and VIII Corps, Bradley thought the Germans had launched a spoiling attack; but Eisenhower felt that something bigger had begun. If the attack were just a small one, the Supreme Commander reasoned, it would be designed to draw Allied forces, while a major attack began somewhere else. This did not seem plausible because the Allies were so strong in all other sectors that a second attack would have no chance for success. Perhaps Rundstedt was trying to re-enact the 1940 success. Eisenhower decided that the VIII Corps would need reinforcement; the 10th Armored Division, out of the line in the Third Army sector, and the 7th Armored Division, from Ninth Army, were ordered to move to the threatened area. As has already been noted, it turned out that two combat commands of the 10th Armored shored up the defense of the 4th Infantry Division on the south shoulder while the 7th Armored was the deciding factor at St. Vith.[37]

The question of what other units were available for reinforcement purposes and the formation of reserves then occupied the two commanders and the SHAEF staff. There was no 12th Army Group reserve, because Bradley had given all of the divisions to his three armies for use in offensive actions. The closest sizeable unit to the battle area was the XVIII Airborne Corps, composed of the 82nd and 101st Airborne Divisions, then retraining near Reims. There was also an armored division which had recently landed on the continent, an airborne division which could be brought from England, and an infantry division which could be moved up. In addition, in the north Montgomery had the XXX Corps out of the line, resting and preparing it for an attack. Finally, divisions could be drawn from those areas of the front where the Germans had not attacked. SHAEF, accordingly, alerted army commanders that divisions might be ordered to move on short notice.[38]

Before Bradley returned to his headquarters on December 17, he and Eisenhower agreed on how the American battle would be waged if the German attack did turn into a major offensive. They were sure that they had the resources to stop any German drive, and decided that the penetration must be halted short of a line which ran forward of Luxembourg City and Sedan, along the Meuse River, and in front of Liège. Reserves would be committed to influence the battle—but not in a piecemeal fashion. So that all available combat units could be employed in the actual battle, engineers and support units from the Services of Supply were given the mission to defend and if necessary destroy the Meuse bridges.[39]

Weather conditions made flying impossible, so Bradley had to drive back to his Luxembourg headquarters. As he rolled into town, escorted by a machinegun jeep, he told his aide that he planned to keep the 12th Army Group Tactical Command Post in the city, even though German lines were nearby. Any rearward movement of such a major headquarters, Bradley thought, would not only create panic among the local civilians but also have an adverse effect on the morale of American troops.

That day, at Bradley's request, both the 82nd and 101st Airborne Divisions were released to 12th Army Group control, and other units were ordered up. By the end of the seventeenth, some 60,000 men and 11,000 vehicles were headed for the First Army sector. Many more, three times as many, were to move within the next eight days.[40] That evening, moreover, the airborne divisions were alerted to travel to Bastogne. From that town they could easily be moved to wherever they were needed. But the 82nd was told before it could start moving, to go to Werbomont where it could block Peiper's drive to the west. The division eventually formed a defense line which ran east and west, facing south, until it reached the Salm and then swung north along the river. It was through the positions of the 82nd that the defenders of St. Vith ultimately withdrew. The 101st went to Bastogne.[40]

December 18 was a critical day for the VIII Corps and for the formation of the defensive positions which ultimately secured Bastogne. On that morning, members of Middleton's corps headquarters were the only occupants of the city. They were receiving stragglers from the 28th Infantry Division and remained alerted for movement, orders for which came later in the day. About midnight of the seventeenth, Middleton had learned that he would probably be reinforced by the airborne divisions, but it was not until the next afternoon that he got permission to divert the 101st Airborne Division specifically to Bastogne to defend that key communications center. Meanwhile, he had pieced together from engineer units a delaying force which went into position east of the city. The commander of Manteuffel's XLVII Panzer Corps, General der Panzertruppen Heinrich Freiherr von Leuttwitz, had also learned on the night of the seventeenth, from an intercepted radio message, of the displacement of the American airborne units. Thus, for both sides, December 18 became a day in which events resolved themselves into a race to occupy the city in strength.

The Americans won the race. With the arrival of Combat Command B of the 10th Armored Division at about dusk, Middleton was able to reinforce his weak screening force, which continued to fight a desperate delaying action long enough to allow the 101st to reach Bastogne. The first elements detrucked at midnight, and by 9:00 a.m. December 19, all four regiments were there. Had Leuttwitz's columns been able to reach Bastogne early on the eighteenth, they could have taken it with ease, and the vital roads to Dinant and Namur would have been open. Now they would have to fight for the city.[41]

The fluid situation and rapid German advance north of Bastogne had the initial effect of working to the advantage of the defenders of that city. From Bastogne to near Werbomont, where the 82nd Airborne Division was taking up positions, there were no strong defense forces to bar the German advance. By the end of December 19, another day during which Allied air support was severely limited due to weather conditions, the Germans took Houffalize. Fortunately for the defenders of Bastogne, the troops which took Houffalize were from the LVIII Panzer Corps and had the mission of moving to the northwest. *(See Map 72, in Atlas.)* Thus they did not try to encircle Bastogne. Leuttwitz, however, continued his efforts to take it. By December 21, it had become evident that the city was indeed surrounded. Both Middleton and Bradley ordered that it be held at all costs. The defenders of Bastogne, under the command of Brigadier General Anthony C. McAuliffe, were the 101st Airborne Division, Combat Command B of the 10th Armored Division, and various artillery, engineer, and tank destroyer units. Major General Maxwell D. Taylor, the commander of the 101st, was on leave in the United States, and the assistant division commander was in England. Thus, McAuliffe, commanding general of the division artillery, had assumed temporary command and led the 101st into Bastogne and its rendezvous with history.[42]

Brigadier General Anthony C. McAuliffe

While the VIII Corps fought to contain the German penetrations, Eisenhower and his key subordinates were shaping the strategy to blunt and then destroy Hitler's rampaging columns. On December 18, Bradley directed Patton to suspend offensive actions in the Saar and call off his attack which was scheduled for the nineteenth. That same day, Eisenhower furnished Bradley and Devers with the contents of the directive he proposed issuing following the meeting he had scheduled for the next day with them and Patton at Verdun. Barring modifications stemming from the meeting, he indicated that 6th Army Group would cease offensive operations and take over a portion of the Third Army sector in order to enable Patton to mount a counterattack as soon as possible. Devers was also to eliminate the Colmar Pocket. While Bradley counterattacked, Montgomery was to regroup and then launch an attack southeastward from Nijmegen between the Meuse and the Rhine.[43]

When the commanders met at Verdun on December 19, they knew the general outline of Eisenhower's plan; only the details remained to be settled. As he began the conference, Eisenhower said, "The present situation is to be regarded as one of opportunity for us and not of disaster. There will be only cheerful faces at this conference table."[44] The situation was reviewed. Eisenhower stressed that the enemy was not to be allowed to cross the Meuse, and then further stated that as soon as a counterattack force could be readied, he planned to commit it. The amount of Devers' extension to his left was determined. Then Eisenhower turned to Patton and asked him when he could form a force and start an attack. Patton, who had already discussed such a move with his staff, said that he could begin on the morning of December 22. To insure that a strong force could be assembled, Eisenhower set the date for the attack, which was to be controlled by Third Army under 12th Army Group supervision, at no earlier than December 22 and not later than December 23. Patton would turn two of the three corps which comprised Third Army north, absorb VIII Corps, and strike for Bastogne. *(See Map 72, in Atlas.)* Once there, he was to prepare to continue the attack toward Houffalize. Before the meeting was adjourned, Eisenhower assured all present that he would provide plenty of air support as soon as the weather cleared. In addition, he stated that he would order a similar counterattack on the north flank when the German drive had been blunted. His immediate strategy, as he messaged Montgomery later in the day, was to seal the northern flank while he counterattacked in the south.[45]

When Eisenhower returned to his headquarters on the nineteenth, after the Verdun meeting, many reports awaited him. It appeared that Bastogne would soon be surrounded. To the north, although the position at St. Vith was still holding, continued occupation of that key communications center was doubtful. Should Bastogne be surrounded and St. Vith lost, the Germans would almost have split Bradley's army group in two. *(See Map 72, in Atlas.)* Eisenhower sat down to rethink the entire problem.[46]

As Eisenhower considered the Allied situation, Major General Sir John F. M. Whiteley, SHAEF Deputy G-3, and Major General Kenneth W. D. Strong, SHAEF G-2, also pondered developments. The German drive seemed to be aimed at Namur and beyond. How could Bradley, who would not shift his command post from Luxembourg City, attempt to control and supervise operations on the northern shoulder? It appeared to Whiteley, who was no real fan of Montgomery, that the British field marshal should be given command of the northern sector, including most of the First and all of the Ninth Army. Strong agreed. Whiteley called the SHAEF chief of staff, Lieutenant General Walter Bedell Smith, and asked to see him. Although he was initially enraged at the suggestion made by the two British officers, Smith called Eisenhower at about 11:00 P.M. and found him still in his office. Eisenhower decided to consider the suggestion.

Splitting the front would put major American formations under the command of a British officer, but Eisenhower could see much merit in the idea. Bradley's direct line to the army commanders in the north had been cut. Although he could still communicate through a system of relays, he was unable to exercise active supervision. He had only seen Hodges in person once since the attack began. Hodges and Middleton faced much the same problem on a smaller scale; they could not effectively control all the units of their dispersed commands. In addition, the only major reserve available for employment in the north was the British XXX Corps. If Montgomery took over in the north, he could use this reserve as he saw fit at the most critical point anywhere along his 250-mile front. Eisenhower decided to make the change. Before he retired for the night, he had Smith inform Bradley. Smith assured the 12th Army Group commander that the shift would be temporary. Bradley would have preferred to turn over to an American or a British soldier other than Montgomery, but he agreed to the change. The U.S. IX and XXIX Tactical Air Commands, which normally supported First and Ninth Armies, would be placed under the operational control of the British Second Tactical Air Force. First Army received news of the new command arrangement during the morning of the twentieth. At approximately 1:00 P.M., Field Marshal Montgomery made his first of what was to become a series of daily visits.[47]

As one of Montgomery's own officers put it, ". . . the Field-Marshal strode into Hodges' H.Q. like Christ come to cleanse the temple."[48] Ignoring the large First Army operations map, he chose to work from his own small sheet on which had been plotted information received from his liaison officers. He had brought a lunch box and thermos bottle and, though Hodges invited him to lunch, Montgomery, as was his usual practice, chose to dine alone. After some discussion, he approved the holding of the north shoulder at Elsenborn Ridge as well as Hodges' decision to put the 82nd Airborne Division along the Salm River and to the rear of the St. Vith position, which was still being held by the 7th Armored Division. This placement of the 82nd would not only provide an escape route for the St. Vith defenders, but would also cover the massing of a counterattack force. To lead that force, Montgomery wanted Collins, whom he felt was the most aggressive American corps commander. Collins was to pull his VII Corps headquarters from the line, but leave his divisions in place. Ninth Army would assume responsibility for the extra frontage. Collins would then form a counterattack force composed of both new and battle-tested divisions. He was to attack on Montgomery's orders, after the German drive had spent its strength.[49]

The Germans Lose the Initiative

On December 22, the situation still looked grim for the Allies. *(See Map 72, in Atlas.)* St. Vith was lost and Bastogne was surrounded. A German *panzer* division was regrouping at Houffalize, apparently ready to continue the drive to the west, and another was already beyond the Ourthe River, only 23 miles from the Meuse. Weather conditions still precluded the

Patton's Armor Heading for the Ardennes, December 1944

employment of Allied aircraft. But the Elsenborn Ridge position remained intact, thus restricting the advance of the Sixth Panzer Army to two of the planned four roads. One of the German-held roads was heavily interdicted by American artillery fire. So difficult had the traffic situation become, that on the twenty-first Rundstedt ordered two of Dietrich's SS *panzer* divisions transferred to Manteuffel's command. The Fifth Panzer Army henceforth would have the main attack. The tenacious defense at Elsenborn Ridge and St. Vith had paid off.[50]

But the tide was beginning to turn, even as Manteuffel's spearhead *panzer* divisions renewed the drive toward the Meuse. Patton, having quickly and brilliantly turned his forces to the north, also went into action on the twenty-second. He sent an infantry division to help hold the southern shoulder, and launched an armored division and second infantry division toward Bastogne. Progress was slow, initially because the Germans had learned through an intercepted radio message of Patton's plan to attack, but the drive to relieve Bastogne had begun. On that day, also, McAuliffe is alleged to have replied "Nuts!" to a German request to surrender, under the threat to annihilate all troops within Bastogne if the request were not honored within two hours. Word of McAuliffe's reply quickly spread and served to bolster morale, even if the defenders knew that difficult times lay ahead. Their spirits received a further boost when cold winds began to blow at dusk and the weather started to clear. It was a comforting thought to know that Allied aircraft would fill the skies in the morning.[51]

Fighter-bombers, medium bombers, and transports were all aloft on December 23. Supplies were dropped to the defenders in Bastogne, and bombers hit German columns throughout the area. Meanwhile, fighters strafed enemy targets. But the German 116th and 2nd Panzer Divisions continued to attack. Stopping them took not only an infantry division, which had been slated for the VII Corps counterattack force, but also the 2nd Armored Division. Although the 2nd Armored was scheduled to be a part of Montgomery's counterattack force, Hodges had not specifically forbidden an attack, so Collins authorized its employment. The attack of the 2nd Armored against the German 2nd Panzer began shortly after dawn on Christmas Day. With the help of British armor, American fighter-bombers, and empty German gasoline tanks, the German drive was stopped by December 26. German units had suffered heavy casualties. At its farthest point of advance, the 2nd Panzer Division had reached Celles, only four miles from the Meuse. To the east, on the northern edge of the Bulge on Christmas Day, the American 3rd Armored Division stopped the drive of the 2nd SS Panzer Division toward Namur.[52]

Meanwhile, the Germans continued to try to take Bastogne. At 3:00 A.M. on December 25, after the town had been bombed twice, a newly arrived *panzer* grenadier division launched a fierce attack from the northwest. *(See Map 72, in Atlas.)* American positions were penetrated, but all of the 18 tanks which had broken through were knocked out, and the breaches in the defenses were closed. The attack continued on the twenty-sixth, but at dusk a relief force from the 4th Armored Division reached American lines. When Captain William Dwight, commander of the two-company lead task force, reported to McAuliffe, the acting commander of the 101st understatedly said, "I am mighty glad to see you."[53]

With the siege of Bastogne broken, Allied spirits rose. During the darkest days of Hitler's offensive, however, both Churchill and Marshall had assured Eisenhower of their support, while Roosevelt neither made an effort to intervene nor questioned tha acts of his commander. The Supreme Commander tried to give the same support to his subordinates. He wrote to Hodges and Simpson, both of whom were serving under Montgomery's operational control, and urged them to "respond cheerfully and efficiently to every instruction he gives. The slogan is 'chins up.'"[54] Realizing that the shift of control of two armies could be interpreted to mean that he had lost confidence in Bradley, Eisenhower chose this time to recommend that Bradley be promoted to four-star rank.[55]

The lifting of the siege of Bastogne did not mean that the Germans, within the area of their Ardennes penetration, were not still fighting aggressively and demanding herculean efforts from the Allies. During the first nine days of battle, in a feat which Bradley later compared to that of the turning of Patton's Third Army to the north, First Army cleared 196 convoys of 48,000 vehicles which carried some 248,000 troops. Allied aircraft continued to take a heavy toll of German vehicles traveling on the few supply routes the enemy had been able to capture, while other planes hit German rear area lines of communication. *(See Map 73, in Atlas.)* There was much fighting in the Bastogne corridor, which in some places was less than 300 yards wide. On one occasion, the Germans launched a coordinated attack on Bastogne at the same time that Patton sent two new divisions into an assault. The American divisions ran into the flank of German units moving southeast to cut off Bastogne. Although the collision caused American plans to drive toward Houffalize and eventually St. Vith to be temporarily delayed, the German assault was stopped. Patton also stopped a German attack from the southeast which was timed to coincide with that of their comrades. Patton later termed December 30, ". . . the critical day of the operation as there was a concerted effort on the part of the Germans, using at least five divisions, to again isolate Bastogne."[56]

During this period, while Patton was aggressively attacking and the 2nd Armored Division had halted the German drive at Celles, Bradley and Hodges impatiently awaited Montgomery's northern offensive. For his part, Montgomery felt that the Germans would launch one more concerted effort. As soon as that had been defeated, he planned to attack. To strengthen his striking force, he moved the XXX British Corps into the Givet-Marche sector. After discussing the matter with him on December 28, Eisenhower agreed that Montgomery could delay his attack for a few days. If the German major assault had not materialized by January 3, however, Montgomery was to attack on that date.[57]

Hitler Concedes Failure

While the Allied commanders wrestled with the problem of repositioning troops and systematically squeezing out the salient, the German High Command also had crucial decisions to make. Hitler's attention was riveted on the Ardennes. Although his troops had not reached the Meuse, much less Antwerp, he had succeeded in disrupting Allied offensive plans. Toward the end of December his field commanders and Jodl recommended that he turn the *panzer* armies north, attack to the west of Liège, and strike Aachen from the rear—essentially the Small Solution. Hitler disagreed and ordered the additional attacks on Bastogne already described. He continued to believe that the capture of Antwerp was a possibility. Moreover, since Patton had moved so many divisions north and the Allied defenses in Alsace seemed weak, Hitler kept alive the projected operation he had directed be planned to strike Devers' forces.[58]

Wearing Snow Camouflage Capes, First Army Troops Move Up, January 1945

The situation continued to deteriorate, however, and Hitler was forced to face reality. Pessimistic reports continued to flow into his headquarters. Although the *Luftwaffe* scored something of a success on January 1, when 156 Allied aircraft (including Montgomery's personal plane) were destroyed in a surprise raid on airfields in Holland and Belgium, by early January even Hitler acknowledged that his offensive could not succeed. The final attack on Bastogne took place on January 3 and 4, 1945. When it was repulsed, Model ordered an SS *panzer* division north to defend against the attack of the First Army, which had begun as scheduled on January 3. *(See Map 73, in Atlas.)* On the eighth, Hitler authorized a withdrawal to the Ourthe River.[59]

Montgomery's January 3 assault was launched in weather that was cold, windy, and foggy and over terrain deeply covered with snow. Bad weather would continue to plague the Allied efforts during the next two weeks, as they received fighter-bomber support on but three days. Although the going was slow, Eisenhower's troops made progress in both the north and south, and on January 16 American patrols met in Houffalize. On January 17, Bradley regained control of the First Army, and by the twenty-eighth the Bulge had been completely cleared. *(See Map 73, in Atlas.)* Hitler, his try for a decisive success in the West stymied, had to turn his attention elsewhere, for on January 12 the Russians had launched a major offensive. As soon as it could get underway, the Sixth SS Panzer Army headed east.[60]

Allied Friction

As the Allies gradually curbed Hitler's offensive thrust and then set about reducing the huge salient, Eisenhower had some intra-family squabbles with which to cope. The first of these involved Montgomery and the old question of command and concentration of force, as well as the Briton's role in stopping the German offensive.

During Eisenhower's visit to his headquarters on December 28, Montgomery had reopened the question of his controlling ground operations of both the 21st and 12th Army Groups when the Allies took the offensive to cross the Rhine. Again he mistakenly assumed that his argument had won over Eisenhower to his viewpoint; he bluntly suggested in a letter the next day how the Supreme Commander's directive should unmistakably convey that Monty would be in control. Worn and under great pressure as a result of the German attack, Eisenhower reacted very negatively since he did *not* agree with Montgomery's argument. He was tired of the whole business, and, egged on by Smith, he decided that he would force a showdown by putting the matter in the hands of the Combined

Chiefs of Staff (CCS). Moreover, in the opinion of SHAEF, the British press had not helped matters by publishing stories which gave the impression that Montgomery had had to come to the rescue of an American command. Eisenhower feared that Bradley's position would become untenable. Marshall, too, was aware of the problem, and sent a message of support to Eisenhower on December 30 in which he said that Eisenhower should make no concessions, as such action would be resented in the United States.

De Guingand, Montgomery's chief of staff, proved to be the crucial actor in resolving the potential crisis. Learning of the bitterness at SHAEF and at 12th Army Group headquarters, he flew to Versailles to visit Eisenhower on December 30 and convinced the Supreme Commander to delay sending the message to the CCS for 24 hours, an interlude during which De Guingand could take action. Convinced that the whole affair was deplorable and debilitating to Allied unity of effort and that the only result would be the sacking of Montgomery, De Guingand convinced his chief, who was genuinely surprised at the uproar, to make amends. He also talked to members of the British press about their reporting styles. The upshot was Montgomery's telegram to Eisenhower on December 31, promising his full support and ending, "Very distressed that my letter may have upset you and I would ask you to tear it up." This did the trick, and Eisenhower junked his proposed message to the CCS. In retrospect, the Allies owed a great debt to De Guingand for the service he rendered their cause those last two days of December 1944. Unfortunately, there was some squabbling of a less critical nature still to occur.[61]

When the British press continued to carry stories critical of Eisenhower and the command arrangement, Montgomery held a press conference on January 7 to demonstrate his support of the Supreme Commander. He expressed his devotion to Eisenhower and praised the fighting qualities of the Americans. But, unfortunately, the tone of some of his remarks left the impression in the minds of some Americans that it was only after he had assumed control that the excellent fighting capability of American troops was properly employed. It seemed that Montgomery was trying to say that he had practically defeated the German thrust single-handedly. His remarks cast a cloud over the performance of the American commanders. Matters were made worse when German broadcasters cleverly used a BBC wavelength to air a distorted version of the press conference. Enraged because he saw Montgomery's remarks as a direct reflection on his own ability, Bradley thereupon held his own press conference and stated that the shift of a portion of his command to Montgomery was only temporary. Further, Bradley told Eisenhower that if he were asked to serve under Montgomery, he would request relief. Patton echoed Bradley's ultimatum. Eisenhower, who felt that Montgomery had not really meant to belittle the American leaders, later wrote: "This incident caused me more distress and worry than did any similar one of the war."[62]

Although both Eisenhower and Montgomery worked to restore good relations, the ruffled feelings of Americans were only soothed when Prime Minister Churchill gave unstinting praise to the American troops and commanders in a speech before the House of Commons on January 17. With this, the immediate incident was closed, but American commanders would not forget Montgomery's press conference.[63] The occurrence was an unfortunate one, but it illustrates that in coalition warfare even high-level commanders are human and are influenced by both personal and national interests which are at stake. Neither Montgomery nor Bradley acquitted himself with distinction in the exchange of press conferences; but Eisenhower, with Churchill's help, was able to calm all concerned.

Montgomery would never command the 12th Army Group, but he would be able to retain operational control of Simpson's Ninth Army, at least for a time. In a plan sent to Montgomery and Bradley on December 31, Eisenhower specified that after the Ardennes salient was reduced, the 21st Army Group, with Ninth Army, would continue to prepare to clear the area in the north up to the Rhine. When he continued relating his plans to the Combined Chiefs of Staff on January 20, Eisenhower still felt that before the river was crossed in strength he needed to reach an easily defensible line so that the maximum number of troops could be massed for a main attack north of the Ruhr, while a secondary attack would be made in the south. This supporting effort would allow the Allies to use available crossing sites and lines of communication, at the same time forcing the Germans to spread their steadily diminishing defensive resources. The British Chiefs of Staff, however, still believed that two attacks could not be supported. At Brooke's insistence, they got the question made a matter of discussion at a CCS February meeting on Malta, preparatory to the Yalta Conference. With strong support from the American chiefs, however, Eisenhower's concept prevailed.[64]

A Smaller German Attack in the South

The second intra-Allied difficulty which required Eisenhower's attention involved De Gaulle, and was occasioned by an offensive that Hitler directed his forces to mount in Alsace-Lorraine in early January.

For some time, Hitler had envisioned striking Devers' 6th Army Group, which had penetrated the West Wall in Lorraine. An attack there could exploit the existence of the Colmar Pocket and also keep the Allies off balance. *(See Maps 72 and 75a, in Atlas.)* Then, as the Ardennes offensive rolled westward, the *Fuehrer* saw the southern attack as both an opportunity to retain the initiative in the West and a chance to exploit Devers' sector, which had been weakened when Eisenhower extended the Sixth Army front westward and pulled troops from Devers for a SHAEF reserve and ultimate use to the north. To this end, Hitler ordered Operation NORWIND to be launched on New Year's Eve, having directed the preparations of plans only two weeks earlier and then dictated changes which specified exactly where the thrusts were to be made.

Devers was ready for the German attack when it came. The surprise the Germans achieved in the Ardennes had sobered and alerted Allied intelligence agencies to the realities of war. Patch and Devers had accurate information from their own intelligence sources, and it also seems likely that they profitted from ULTRA intercepts. But readying his defenses had not been easy for the 6th Army Group commander.

Devers had his hands full with multiple missions. Under considerable pressure from Eisenhower to free troops for Bradley's use to the north, he was also plagued by the Colmar Pocket. That salient irritated Ike, but it was difficult to eliminate because the First French Army units were worn, tired, and discouraged. Finally, he was responsible for clearing German pockets of resistance near Bordeaux, many miles from his front. Nor was he encouraged by the fact that SHAEF had given his army group the lowest priority on receipt of replacements and new units.

Devers' frustration and discouragement resulting from his having to take up a defensive posture when Seventh Army was partly through the West Wall are, accordingly, understandable. This is so, even though he understood how Hitler's Ardennes attack had dictated changes. What bothered Devers most, however, was Eisenhower's expressed view that he had better prepare to withdraw all the way to the Vosges Mountains in order to shorten his line and enable SHAEF to pull more troops out of the sector so that they could be used to the north. Devers made his plans accordingly, establishing three lines to which he would successively fall back if required, the first being the old Maginot Line (Sarreguemines-Bitch-Lembach-Hatten-Sessenheim; *see Map 75A, in Atlas.)* and the last being the eastern edge of the Vosges. He hoped, however, that SHAEF would give him flexibility, because he well appreciated the political and emotional significance that Strasbourg held for the French, and knew that it would be abandoned if Devers' armies fell back to the Vosges. He also believed that he could hold on a line short of that final position. The decision which triggered the political repercussions was made by Eisenhower on January 1, when he ordered Devers to pull his main forces back to the Vosges after learning of the German attack (NORWIND).[65]

De Gaulle immediately objected, and sent the Chief of Staff of the Ministry of Defense, General Alphonse Pierre Juin, to Eisenhower's headquarters to protest. Juin told Smith that to prevent the loss of Strasbourg, De Gaulle had ordered the commander of the French First Army, De Lattre, to defend the city. DeGaulle thus had not only directed the disobedience of official orders, but had also ordered the violation of an army boundary. Smith replied that if De Gaulle's wishes were executed, the French would receive no more American supplies. Juin retorted that the French might then not allow the Americans to use the French national railroads; perhaps they would even leave Eisenhower's command.

De Gaulle then requested a meeting with Eisenhower, which was set for January 3. Unknown to Ike, he also appealed to Roosevelt and Churchill; the former declined to interfere, but Churchill decided to speak to Eisenhower and was present at the January 3 meeting, although he stayed in the background. De Gaulle prophesied that the loss of Strasbourg might result in open revolt. Eisenhower realized that his troubles with the French leaders might adversely affect his ability to use the lines of communication which led through France as well as the conduct of the entire campaign. After a thorough discussion of the problem, Eisenhower decided to change the orders he had sent to Devers. Strasbourg would be defended by the French First Army. The boundary between the French and the American Seventh Army was shifted north, as is shown on Map 75a. De Gaulle left happy, and Churchill, who had observed the entire meeting but who had not spoken, remarked to Eisenhower, "I think you've done the wise and proper thing."[66]

The fighting associated with NORWIND turned out to be unspectacular. Neither side had sufficient troops to make major gains. Devers withdrew as he had wanted—when forced to, but in good order. *(See Map 75a, in Atlas.)* On January 5 the Germans sent a division across the Rhine, surprised the defenders, and took a bridgehead in the area of Drusenheim-Gambsheim. Although the attackers were stopped short of Strasbourg, the troublesome bridgehead remained. On January 7, the Germans attacked northward out of the Colmar Pocket at Rhinau, but they were halted at the last bridge before Strasbourg, some 13 miles to the south. Meanwhile, far to the north of the city, also on January 7, an assault in the vicinity of Hatten was launched by two divisions. After several days of heavy fighting and high casualties, the Germans abandoned their attempt to achieve a break-through. An attack that began on January 17 near Sessenheim, however, did link up with the force in the bridgehead. Although the Germans launched another attack near Haguenau on January 25, it was driven back on the twenty-sixth. By the end of January, Hitler had given up and had been forced to transfer at least three of the divisions in the area to the Eastern Front.[67]

An Armored Column Moves Through a Snowstorm Along a Slippery Road, January 1945

On January 20, as the fighting was dying down to the north, an Allied assault on the Colmar Pocket began. *(See Map 75a, in Atlas.)* Five French and one American divisions made little progress, so Devers added an American corps to the fight. When Hitler finally permitted withdrawal, some Germans managed to cross the Rhine, but the forces sustained heavy losses. By February 9, the pocket no longer existed. Allied troops south of Strasbourg had closed to the line of the Rhine.[68]

Far to the north, in the British sector, the XII SS Corps had two infantry divisions in a bridgehead west of the Roer River, south of Roermond. *(See Map 74, in Atlas.)* As this salient, called the Roermond Triangle, threatened the left flank of the Ninth Army, which would soon attack toward the Rhine, Montgomery directed its elimination. Between January 15 and 26, the XII Corps of the Second British Army cleared the area.[69]

Meanwhile, Bradley continued to keep pressure on the German troops in the Ardennes. He had been told by Eisenhower that as soon as it appeared that he did not have a chance of achieving a decisive success, he was to go on the defensive. Although Bradley's troops made some gains and penetrated the West Wall in some places, in early February Eisenhower ordered that all attacks by the Twelfth Army Group, less those against the critical Roer River dams, be stopped. A new phase of the war in Europe was about to begin.[70]

During December and January, the war in the West had taken a sudden turn as the Ardennes and Alsace-Lorraine exploded in the fury of close and desperate combat. The results were sobering to the Allies, but disastrous to Hitlerite Germany. By attacking in the Ardennes, Hitler had gambled on reaching Antwerp, and had lost. Although his last-gasp effort set back Allied operations some six weeks, the Germans paid a heavy price in men and equipment. Some 100,000 Germans became casualties while the Americans suffered about 81,000, including 19,000 killed and 15,000 taken prisoner. British casualties were 1,400. While Allied leaders had functioned well, with the exception of the intelligence failure, the real heroes of the Bulge were the American soldiers. Seemingly casual in dress and lacking in discipline, they appeared to the German High Command to be inferior fighters. But the Americans who held at Elsenborn Ridge, St. Vith, Bastogne, and Echternach soon rectified that theory. Their resourceful defense gave those who controlled the mighty Allied war machine the time that was needed to shift forces to stop and eventually defeat the assault. When the battle ended, the Anglo-American coalition remained intact, and 4,000,000 troops in three army groups were poised on the border of Germany.[71]

Notes

[1]Charles B. MacDonald, *The Mighty Endeavor: American Armed Forces in the European Theater in World War II.* (New York, 1969), pp. 356-359, 363, 367.

[2]Vincent J. Esposito (ed.), *The West Point Atlas of American Wars* (New York, 1959), II, Section 2, 60; MacDonald, *Mighty Endeavor,* p. 356; T. Dodson Stamps and Vincent J. Esposito (eds.), *A Military History of World War II* (2 vols.; West Point, 1953), I, 492, 496-497; Dwight D. Eisenhower, *Crusade in Europe* (Garden City, 1948), pp. 328, 340; Charles B. MacDonald, *The Siegfried Line Campaign* (Washington, 1963), p. 205.

[3]Stamps and Esposito, *Military History,* I, 491-492; Esposito, *West Point Atlas,* II, Section 2, 60.

[4]Alfred D. Chandler (ed.), *The Papers of Dwight D. Eisenhower: The War Years* (Baltimore, 1970), IV: No. 2148, Eisenhower to Combined Chiefs of Staff, December 3, 1944; Esposito, *West Point Atlas,* II, Section 2, 60; Stamps and Esposito, *Military History,* I, 492-495. The Eisenhower Papers are hereinafter cited as *EP*.

[5]Esposito, *West Point Atlas,* II, Section 2, 60; James A. Huston, *The Sinews of War: Army Logistics 1775-1953* (Washington, 1966), p. 530; Stamps and Esposito, *Military History,* I, 493-495.

[6]Forrest C. Pogue, *George C. Marshall: Organizer of Victory* (New York, 1973), pp. 490-491.

[7]Eisenhower, *Crusade in Europe,* pp. 332-334; Omar N. Bradley, *A Soldier's Story* (New York, 1951), p. 444; Ulysses Lee, *The Employment of Negro Troops* (Washington, 1966), p. 688; Stamps and Esposito, *Military History,* I, 496.

[8]Eisenhower, *Crusade in Europe,* p. 342; Forrest C. Pogue, *The Supreme Command* (Washington 1954), p. 391; Lee, *Negro Troops,* pp. 688-701; Pogue, *Organizer of Victory,* p. 499.

[9]J. F. Ellis, *Victory in the West, Volume II: The Defeat of Germany* (London, 1968), pp. 165-167; Arthur Bryant, *Triumph in the West: Based on the Diaries of Field Marshal Lord Alanbrooke* (Garden City, NY, 1959), pp. 258-261. Quotations are from Bryant.

[10]*EP,* IV: Nos. 2145 and 2146, Eisenhower to Montgomery, December 1 and 2, 1944.

[11]Francis L. Lowenheim, Harold D. Langley and Manfred Jones (eds.), *Roosevelt and Churchill: Their Secret Wartime Correspondence* (New York, 1975), No. 474: Churchill to Roosevelt, December 6, 1944 and No. 481: Roosevelt to Churchill, December 9, 1944; Esposito, *West Point Atlas,* II, Section 2, 60; Ellis, *Victory in the West,* p. 169.

[12]Chester Wilmot, *The Struggle for Europe* (London, 1953), pp. 573-574.

[13]Wilmot, *Struggle for Europe,* p. 573; Stephen E. Ambrose, *The Supreme Commander: The War Years of General Dwight D. Eisenhower* (Garden City, 1969), pp. 549-551; Pogue, *Supreme Command,* pp. 316-317; Ellis, *Victory in the West,* pp. 167-168.

[14]Montgomery is quoted in Bryant, *Triumph in the West,* p. 265.

[15]*Ibid.*; Ellis, *Victory in the West,* p. 169; *EP,* IV: No. 2159, Eisenhower to Churchill, December 8, 1944.

[16]Ambrose, *Supreme Commander* p. 550: *EP,* IV: No. 2163, Eisenhower to Marshall, December 13, 1944; editor's note with No. 2163, p. 2342; Bryant, *Triumph in the West,* pp. 266-267.

[17]MacDonald, *Siegfried Line,* p. 598; Eisenhower, *Crusade in Europe,* p. 340; Ambrose, *Supreme Commander,* p. 551.

[18]MacDonald, *Mighty Endeavor,* pp. 357-358; Charles V.P. von Luttichau, "The German Counteroffensive in the Ardennes," in Kent R. Greenfield (ed.), *Command Decisions* (Washington, 1960), pp. 444-445; Esposito, *West Point Atlas,* II, Section 2, 60.

[19]MacDonald, *Mighty Endeavor,* p. 358; Wilmot, *Struggle for Europe,* p. 560.

[20]MacDonald, *Mighty Endeavor,* pp. 357-358; Stamps and Esposito, *Military History,* I, 500; Pogue, *Organizer of Victory,* p. 485.

[21]Wilmot, *Struggle for Europe,* p. 576; MacDonald, *Mighty Endeavor,* pp. 359-360; Hasso von Manteuffel, "The Ardennes," in Seymour Freiden and William Richardson (eds.), *The Fatal Decisions* (New York, 1956), p. 258; Pogue, *Organizer of Victory,* p. 485.

[22]Material for the above five paragraphs, which deal with the German plan, is drawn from: MacDonald, *Mighty Endeavor,* pp. 365-367; Wilmot, *Struggle for Europe,* p. 581; Hugh M. Cole, *The Ardennes: Battle of the Bulge* (Washington, 1965), pp. 76-77, 174-175, 271.

[23]Material for the above five paragraphs which deal with the German deception plan is drawn from: MacDonald, *Mighty Endeavor,* pp. 360-361; Stamps and Esposito, *Military History,* I, 503; Bradley, *Soldier's Story,* pp. 460-461; Walter Schaufelberger, *Secrecy, Deception, Camouflage and Cover, as used by the German Forces During the Ardennes Offensive (Battle of the Bulge), 1944* (Zurich, n.d.), p. 16; Cole, *Ardennes,* pp. 49-50, 69-71, 73-74; John S. D. Eisenhower, *The Bitter Woods* (New York, 1969), p. 156; Manteuffel, "Ardennes," p. 262; MacDonald, *Siegfried Line,* pp. 393-395.

[24]Ronald Lewin, *Ultra Goes to War* (New York, 1978), p. 357.

[25]The intelligence summary is quoted in Cole, *Ardennes,* p. 57.

[26]Material for the above eight paragraphs on the allied intelligence failure is drawn from: Cole, *Ardennes,* pp. 56-63 (the mirror quotation appears on p. 63); MacDonald, *Mighty Endeavor,* pp. 364-365; Bradley, *Soldier's Story,* pp. 461-464; Esposito, *West Point Atlas,* II, Section 2, 61; Wilmot, *Struggle for Europe,* pp. 574-575; G. Patrick Murray, "Courtney Hodges: Modest Star of WW II," *American History Illustrated,* VII (January 1973), 20-21; F. W. Winterbotham, *The Ultra Secret (New York, 1974)*, pp. 177-179; Wesley F. Craven and James L. Cate (eds.), *The Army Air Forces in World War II,* Volume III, *Europe: ARGUMENT to VE Day January 1944 to May 1945* (Chicago, 1951), pp. 679-681; Anthony Cave Brown, *Bodyguard of Lies* (New York, 1975), p. 811; Lewin, *Ultra Goes to War,* pp. 355-359; Pogue, *Supreme Command,* pp. 361-372.

[27]J. Eisenhower, *Bitter Woods,* pp. 181-182, 204, 210; Cole, *Ardennes,* pp. 53-56; Esposito, *West Point Atlas,* II, Section 2, 61.

[28]Manteuffel, "The Ardennes," pp. 270-271; Wilmot, *Struggle for Europe,* p. 582; MacDonald, *Mighty Endeavor,* p. 367; Stamps and Esposito, *Military History,* I, 546-547; J. Eisenhower, *Bitter Woods,* p. 457.

[29]Stamps and Esposito, *Military History,* I, 505-506; Wilmot, *Struggle for Europe,* p. 580; MacDonald, *Mighty Endeavor,* p. 373.

[30]Eisenhower, *Crusade in Europe,* p. 347.

[31]Material for the above five paragraphs is drawn from: J. Eisenhower, *Bitter Woods,* pp. 193-195, 221-225; Cole, *Ardennes,* pp. 103-104, 135; MacDonald, *Mighty Endeavor,* pp. 367, 369-371; Murray, "Hodges," p. 21.

[32]J. Eisenhower, *Bitter Woods,* pp. 209-211; MacDonald, *Mighty*

Endeavor, pp. 371-373; Bradley, *Soldier's Story*, p. 433.

[33]Material for the above three paragraphs is drawn from: J. Eisenhower, *Bitter Woods*, pp. 209, 253-255, 305-306, 315-316; Cole, *Ardennes*, pp. 457-458; MacDonald, *Mighty Endeavor*, pp. 375-376; Manteuffel, "Ardennes," pp. 276-277.

[34]Material for the above three paragraphs is drawn from: MacDonald, *Mighty Endeavor*, pp. 373-375; Cole, *Ardennes*, pp. 148, 164, 168, 170, 274-277; J. Eisenhower, *Bitter Woods*, pp.195, 203, 227.

[35]J. Eisenhower *Bitter Woods*, pp. 228-235, 294-298, 303-304; MacDonald, *Mighty Endeavor*, p. 375; Cole, *Ardennes*, p. 406.

[36]Material for the above three paragraphs is drawn from: Cole, *Ardennes*, pp. 260-268; MacDonald, *Mighty Endeavor*, pp. 378-379, 384, 386-387; J. Eisenhower, *Bitter Woods*, pp. 237-238; Wilmot, *Struggle for Europe*, p. 584.

[37]Pogue, *Organizer of Victory*, p. 484; Bradley, *Soldier's Story*, pp. 449, 465; Eisenhower, *Crusade in Europe*, pp. 342-344; MacDonald, *Mighty Endeavor*, p. 379.

[38]Eisenhower, *Crusade in Europe*, p. 344; *EP*, IV: No. 2198, Memorandum, December 23, 1944; MacDonald, *Mighty Endeavor*, pp. 379-380; Bradley, *Soldier's Story*, p. 464.

[39]Eisenhower, *Crusade in Europe*, pp. 344-345, 348.

[40]*Ibid.*,pp. 348-349; Bradley, *Soldier's Story*, p. 466; Chester B. Hansen, "War Diary," Chester B. Hansen Papers, United States Army Military History Research Collection, Carlisle Barracks, Pa., entry of December 17, 1944; MacDonald, *Mighty Endeavor*, pp. 380, 386; Wilmot, *Struggle for Europe*, p. 590; Cole, *Ardennes*, p. 420; J. Eisenhower, *Bitter Woods*, p. 309.

[41]Wilmot, *Struggle for Europe*, pp. 585-586; MacDonald, *Mighty Endeavor*, p. 384; Cole, *Ardennes*, pp. 306-309.

[42]MacDonald, *Mighty Endeavor*, pp. 384-385; Cole, *Ardennes*, pp. 305, 460-461; *EP*, IV: editor's note with No. 2198, p. 2376; J. Eisenhower, *Bitter Woods*, pp. 310-311; Hansen, "War Diary," entry of December 19, 1944.

[43]Esposito, *West Point Atlas*, II, Section 2, 61; Wilmot, *Struggle for Europe*, p. 588; *EP*, IV: No. 2178, Eisenhower to Bradley and Devers, December 18, 1944.

[44]Eisenhower, *Crusade in Europe*, p. 350.

[45]*Ibid.*,pp. 350-351; J. Eisenhower, *Bitter Woods*, pp. 256-257; MacDonald, *Mighty Endeavor*, pp. 381-382; *EP*, IV: No. 2198, Memorandum, December 23, 1944; Wilmot, *Struggle for Europe*, p. 589; Martin Blumenson, *The Patton Papers, 1940-1945* (Boston, 1974), pp. 599-600.

[46]J. Eisenhower, *Bitter Woods*, p. 267.

[47]Material for the above two paragraphs is drawn from: Cole, *Ardennes*, pp. 423-426; Eisenhower, *Crusade in Europe*, p. 355; MacDonald, *Mighty Endeavor*, pp. 382-383; 404; Pogue, *Supreme Command*, p. 378; Bradley, *Soldier's Story*, pp. 476-477; J. Eisenhower, *Bitter Woods*, pp. 267-270.

[48]Quoted in Wilmot, *Struggle for Europe*, p. 592.

[49]MacDonald, *Mighty Endeavor*, pp. 383-384; Wilmot, *Struggle for Europe*, pp. 592-593; Cole, *Ardennes*, pp. 426-427.

[50]MacDonald, *Mighty Endeavor*, pp. 386-387; Cole, *Ardennes*, pp. 412-413.

[51]MacDonald, *Mighty Endeavor*, pp. 388-389; Cole, *Ardennes*, p. 468; J. Eisenhower, *Bitter Woods*, p. 328; Esposito, *West Point Atlas*, II, Section 2, 61.

[52]*EP*, IV: editor's note with No. 2198, p. 2376; MacDonald, *Mighty Endeavor*, pp. 389-392.

[53]J. Eisenhower, *Bitter Woods*, pp. 343-344 (quote appears on p. 344); Wilmot, *Struggle for Europe*, pp. 600-601; MacDonald, *Mighty Endeavor*, pp. 392-393.

[54]*EP*, IV, No. 2193, Eisenhower to Simpson, December 22, 1944.

[55]*Ibid.*, No. 2191, Eisenhower to Marshall, December 21, 1944 and editor's note with No. 2196, p. 2370; Pogue, *Organizer of Victory*, p. 488.

[56]Stamps and Esposito, *Military History*, I, 523-525 (Patton's comments appear on p. 525); Bradley, *Soldier's Story*, p. 478; Blumenson, *Patton Papers*, pp. 609-610; Esposito, *West Point Atlas*, II, Section 2, 62.

[57]Wilmot, *Struggle for Europe*, p. 604; Eisenhower, *Crusade in Europe*, p. 360; Stamps and Esposito, *Military History*, I, 528; MacDonald, *Mighty Endeavor*, pp. 393-394.

[58]Esposito, *West Point Atlas*, II, Section 2, 62; MacDonald, *Mighty Endeavor*, p. 393; Wilmot, *Struggle for Europe*, pp. 605-606; Albert Speer, *Inside the Third Reich* (New York, 1971-paper edition), p. 531.

[59]Esposito, *West Point Atlas*, II, Section 2, 62, 64; MacDonald, *Mighty Endeavor*, pp. 398-399.

[60]MacDonald, *Mighty Endeavor*, pp. 400-402; Esposito, *West Point Atlas*, II, Section 2, 62; Stamps and Esposito, *Military History*, I, 530; Manteuffel, "Ardennes," p. 288.

[61]Quotation is from Bernard Law Montgomery, *The Memoirs of Field Marshall the Viscount Montgomery of Alamein, K. G.* (Cleveland, 1958), p. 286. For background on the coverage in these two paragraphs also see: Pogue, *Organizer of Victory*, p. 487; Bryant, *Triumph in the West*, pp. 278-281, 286-287; J. Eisenhower, *Bitter Woods*, pp. 380-392; Ellis, *Victory in the West*, pp. 199-207; Pogue, *Supreme Command*, pp. 385-389.

[62]Eisenhower, *Crusade in Europe*, p. 356; Wilmot, *Struggle for Europe*, pp. 610-611; Hansen, "War Diary," entries of January 9-10, 1945; Pogue, *Organizer of Victory*, p. 510; MacDonald, *Mighty Endeavor*, pp. 403-404; *EP*, IV: editor's note with No. 2284, p. 2483.

[63]Bradley, *Soldier's Story*, p. 488; J. Eisenhower, *Bitter Woods*, p. 391; Pogue, *Supreme Command*, pp. 389, 435.

[64]Eisenhower, *Crusade in Europe*, pp. 370-374; *EP*, IV; No. 2210, Eisenhower to Montgomery, December 31, 1944; No. 2211, Eisenhower to Montgomery, December 31, 1944; No. 2232, Eisenhower to Marshall, January 10, 1945; editor's note with No. 2232, pp. 2424-2425; No. 2233, Eisenhower to Marshall, January 10, 1945; No. 2242, Eisenhower to Marshall, January 15, 1945; No. 2254, Eisenhower to Combined Chiefs of Staff, January 20, 1945; Ellis, *Victory in the West*, pp. 207-213; Bryant, *Triumph in the West*, pp. 287-288, 294, 297-302.

[65]Material for the above three paragraphs is drawn from: Winterbotham, *Ultra*, p. 180; MacDonald, *Mighty Endeavor*, pp. 394-396; Eisenhower, *Crusade in Europe*, p. 362; *EP*, IV: No. 2209, Eisenhower to Combined Chiefs of Staff, December 31, 1944; Esposito, *West Point Atlas*, II, Section 2, 64; J. Eisenhower, *Bitter Woods*, pp. 393-399; Jacob L. Devers, "Diary," Commanding General Sixth Army Group, Devers Papers, Historical Society of York County, Pa., entries of December 19, 21, 22, 26, 27, 28, 30, 31 and January 1, 1945.

[66]Material for the above two paragraphs is drawn from: Eisenhower, *Crusade in Europe*, pp. 362-363 (Churchill's words appear on p. 363); MacDonald, *Mighty Endeavor*, pp. 396-397; *EP*, IV: No. 2221, Eisenhower to De Gaulle, January 5, 1945; No. 2224,

Eisenhower to Marshall, January 6, 1945; No. 2237, Eisenhower to Marshall, January 12, 1945; J. Eisenhower, *Bitter Woods*, pp. 400-401.

[67]Esposito, *West Point Atlas*, II, Section 2, 64; Stamps and Esposito, *Military History*, I, 540-541; MacDonald, *Mighty Endeavor*, p. 398.

[68]Esposito, *West Point Atlas*, II, Section 2, 64; Stamps and Esposito, *Military History*, I, 541-543; MacDonald, *Mighty Endeavor*, p. 417.

[69]Stamps and Esposito, *Military History*, I, 537; Esposito, *West Point Atlas*, II, Section 2, 63.

[70]*EP*, IV: No. 2248, Eisenhower to Montgomery, Bradley, *et al.*, January 18, 1945; No. 2270, Eisenhower to Montgomery and Bradley, February 1, 1945; Esposito, *West Point Atlas*, II, Section 2, 63.

[71]MacDonald, *Mighty Endeavor*, pp. 406, 422; J. Eisenhower, *Bitter Woods*, pp. 462, 469.

Mission Fulfilled 17

The mission of this Allied force was fulfilled at 0241, local time, May 7th, 1945.

Eisenhower to Combined Chiefs of Staff
May 7, 1945

On January 20, 1945, Franklin D. Roosevelt was inaugurated President of the United States for the fourth time. Three days later, he and a number of advisors set sail for the Mediterranean aboard the cruiser *Quincy*. After a short meeting with Prime Minister Winston Churchill and his advisors on the island of Malta, both groups would journey to Yalta in the Crimea for a top-level American-British-Russian conference. In the interim, the American Joint Chiefs of Staff and Secretary of State Edward R. Stettinius, Jr., flew on to Malta ahead of the *Quincy* to meet with their British counterparts before the President arrived.[1]

There was a distinct air of optimism among the senior Allied leaders on the eve of the historic Yalta conference. Although the western Allies had been surprised by the German Ardennes offensive, they had successfully blunted Hitler's bid for a major reversal of the situation in the West and then turned the German initiative into a costly setback for the Reich. Stronger than ever in a relative sense, the Allies were now poised to renew the offensive, jump the Rhine, and subdue the German homeland in conjunction with the massive Russian war machine which was inexorably grinding up Hitler's armies in the East. There could no longer be much doubt that Germany was doomed, under attack as it was from all sides while being mercilessly hammered from the air. The Allied leaders knew this. Quite naturally, therefore, the high level conferences involved more political matters than those of a military nature.

The western Allies, however, still had a major barrier to cross. If Hitler allowed his generals to utilize the Rhine correctly, it could become a costly obstacle for Eisenhower's armies to breach. Aware of this, the western leaders had, for months, been planning tactically and logistically for the crossing of this major river, which had such real and psychological significance for both sides. In the end, it would prove to be easily negotiated, but Eisenhower and his generals could not know this four months before war's end. The immediate task facing them, however, was closing to the fabled Rhine. At the high level of command, moreover, strategic questions also remained to be settled.

High Level Policy and Strategy

Army Chief of Staff George C. Marshall stopped off at Marseilles, en route to Malta, to discuss future plans with Eisenhower. From correspondence in November and December, he was well aware of British dissatisfaction with Eisenhower's ideas on strategy and command arrangements. He therefore felt the need to discuss these matters firsthand before meeting with the British chiefs, who had insisted that the subject be on the agenda. Eisenhower's concept of advancing to the Rhine, then holding the river line with a minimum of force while massing for a main attack north of the Ruhr and a secondary attack in the Frankfurt area, continued to gain Marshall's endorsement. The two men also talked about the possibility of appointing Field Marshal Sir Harold R. L. G. Alexander, then Supreme Commander of the Mediterranean Theater, as Eisenhower's deputy; this would free his current deputy, Air Chief Marshal Sir Arthur W. Tedder, for reassignment to the Far East. Marshall feared that this British proposal was more designed to enable Alexander to become ground commander than it was to use Tedder's talents in Asia, and he was determined not to permit this change in the command structure. Since Eisenhower's assumption of command in the field in September 1944, the British had consistently advocated the appointment of a ground commander. The Chief of Staff was inalterably opposed to the move. So strong were Marshall's feelings that he told Eisenhower he would resign if a ground commander were named.[2].

When the American Chiefs of Staff met the British Chiefs on January 30, Marshall strongly supported Eisenhower's plan. Heated remarks were exchanged as the discussion continued in closed session the next day, for the British were worried that Eisenhower would not try to cross the Rhine, even if an opportunity arose, until he had cleared the entire west bank. When Eisenhower declared, via message on January 31, that he would cross the Rhine in the north with a maximum of strength as soon as possible, opposition died down. The British Chiefs were satisfied that there would be no weakening of forces in the north and that Montgomery would command this major effort, which would include a sizeable American army. The Supreme Commander's plan was accepted on February 2. While it was proposed at Malta that Alexander replace Tedder as Eisenhower's deputy, no action was taken. Later, in mid-February, Eisenhower said that he would accept Alexander, but that Alexander's role as deputy would be primarily political and economic; the establishment of any official or unofficial headquarters between Eisenhower and his army group commanders would not be permitted. Churchill, who had long advocated the change, finally acknowledged defeat on March 11. Although the alliance between the two great countries was probably the closest in the history of warfare, and despite the fact that Eisenhower's forces had moved from the coast of France to the German border in but a few months, the British leader had continued to advocate a major restructuring of the high-level command almost until the war in Europe ended.[3]

Churchill and Roosevelt flew in separate planes to Saki in the Crimea on February 3, and then drove to Yalta, where Stalin joined them the next day.* Victory was in the air, with both the Japanese and Germans being steadily pushed back. In mid-January, Eisenhower had stressed to Marshall the adverse impact that a weak Soviet offensive would have on the campaign in western Europe. Thus, at Yalta, both Marshall and Brooke, during their meetings with high-level representatives of the Russian Army, emphasized the importance of sustained Soviet pressure. General Alexi I. Antonov, First Deputy Chief of Staff, remarked that the Russian offensive would continue unless bad weather caused it to be temporarily interrupted. For their part, the Russians, now rapidly closing on the Oder River, pressed the western Allies to attack as soon as possible; otherwise, the Germans might transfer troops to the East and strike while the Russian armies near Berlin were refitting after their 300-mile advance.[4]

During the Yalta Conference, zones of occupation in a conquered Germany, which had been drawn previously by the European Advisory Commission, were approved, with the addition of a French zone in the southwestern part of the country. All participants agreed that these boundaries were not to affect military operations. Churchill later wrote that as the meeting ended, the conferees departed "not only as Allies but as friends facing a still mighty foe with whom all our armies were struggling in fierce and ceaseless battle."[5]

While the heads of state and their advisors were conferring at Yalta, Eisenhower's key subordinates were readying their troops for the offensive designed to carry Allied armies to the Rhine all along the line. *(See Map 75b, in Atlas.)* As briefly recounted in the previous chapter, Eisenhower allowed Bradley to continue his attacks in the cold and snowy Eifel until February 1, when the priority of effort, men, and supplies shifted northward to Montgomery. While Hodges' V Corps was to continue attacks to seize the Roer dams, Bradley's and Devers' army groups' offensive operations elsewhere were to cease. Patton was to be on the "active defense," pinning down German troops, and Bradley had already begun to reinforce Simpson's Ninth Army so that it numbered three corps, totaling three armored and seven infantry divisions. As Eisenhower had promised earlier, Simpson's army would be under Montgomery's control and would form the southern pincer of an offensive designed to close to the Rhine in the north.[6]

As conceived by the planners, Montgomery's offensive would be the first and most power-packed attack in a series of drives consecutively unfolding down the line from north to south. *(See Map 75b, in Atlas.)* In Montgomery's sector, where ULTRA had revealed that the Germans expected an attack opposite the Ruhr, the British Second Army would maintain pressure while the Canadian First Army would attack no later than February 8, in Operation VERITABLE. By February 10, Ninth Army would attack to the northeast in Operation GRENADE. Once Montgomery had reached the Rhine, where he would prepare to launch the SHAEF main effort across the river (Operation PLUNDER), Bradley was to attack once again in the Eifel in Operation LUMBERJACK. Next would come Operation UNDERTONE, an offensive by elements of Devers' Sixth Army Group. Although Eisenhower had promised the Chiefs of Staff at Malta that he would not necessarily wait to cross the Rhine until the entire west bank had been cleared of German troops, successful completion of VERITABLE, GRENADE, LUMBERJACK, and UNDERTONE would enable him to hold at the river with a minimum force while he massed for his crossing attempts.[7]

Montgomery's assault crossing of the Rhine (Operation

*See Chapter 8, p. 198, for a discussion of the Yalta Conference.

PLUNDER) would be executed in the Wesel-Emmerich area by the British Second Army and the American Ninth Army. Airborne troops (Operation VARSITY) were to be dropped in support of that attack. Later, the 12th and 6th Army Groups would make secondary crossings of the river. As Eisenhower's plan evolved, the two major avenues of approach into the heart of the Reich would be north of the Ruhr across the North German Plain and along the Frankfurt-Kassel corridor. When forces advancing along these two axes met, the industrial area of the Ruhr, replete with blast furnaces, factories, and coal mines, would be cut off from the remainder of Germany. In late January, the Russians were already nearing the eastern Silesian industrial complex. Loss of both of these critical areas would constitute a serious, if not fatal, blow to the German war effort. Not only the Allies, but the Germans as well, could see this. This consideration, accordingly, reinforced Hitler's refusal to allow any ground to be surrendered voluntarily, and strengthened his fanatical determination to defend the area west of the Rhine.[8]

Closing to the Rhine

The importance that the Germans attached to the Ruhr influenced the way they positioned troops for the defense. The German strategy, however, did not include plans for an evacuation of the west bank. Although an evacuation would have allowed for a more effective defense of the river line, Hitler simply refused to consider such a proposal. *(See Map 76a, in Atlas.)* Given these circumstances, the commanders placed most of the best troops remaining in the West, including the First Parachute Army, opposite Montgomery's forces. Because they also expected the major Allied drive on the Ruhr to be made in the Duren area, they strengthened the Fifteenth Army. Nor was the importance of the Roer dams underestimated. Those structures held back water which, if loosed after some Americans had crossed the river, could cut off elements of the Ninth and First Armies and make them vulnerable to a German counterattack. Although Allied airmen had tried to destroy the dams with bombs as large as the British 12,000-pound "blockbuster," the massive structures remained virtually intact. The Germans intended to fight hard to retain them against units of Gerow's V Corps, which set out to seize them on February 2.[9]

To the north, Montgomery was readying the First Canadian Army for Operation VERITABLE. Lieutenant General H. D. G. Crerar's normal complement of forces had been increased by the addition of a number of British units, including armor and artillery. *(See Map 76a, in Atlas.)* The main attack would be made by the British XXX Corps. Once it achieved a breakthrough, the Canadian II Corps would assume control of some of the divisions of XXX Corps and attack south along the Rhine. Because the Germans had weakened the defenses in the area in order to reinforce the Duren sector, initially only one division opposed the XXX Corps; but the impact of this division was multiplied by the defenses it could use. Even though the West Wall did not extend to the Reichswald, the Germans had made good use of five months of relative calm to prepare the wooded area for defense in some depth. They had also flooded territory to restrict vehicular movement, and had fortified the towns of Cleves and Goch. A third defensive position extended from Geldern to Rees. Lieutenant General Brian G. Horrocks, commander of the British XXX Corps, planned to slash through the Reichswald defenses and reach the wider area of the lower Rhineland before German reserves could be moved to stop him.[10]

Preliminary air attacks focused on ferries and bridges in an attempt to isolate the battle area. Cleves and Goch, as well as key installations in the German rear, were hit hard during the night before the attack. Early on February 8, over a thousand guns began a five-and-a-half hour artillery preparation during which more than 500,000 shells were fired along the seven-mile front. At 10:30 A.M., Horrocks launched his attack force which included eleven regiments of specialized armor (equipped with vehicles designed to get through fortified positions), most of five infantry divisions, and three regular armored brigades. Although there were only two good roads into the German position, the British troops made significant progress. They reached Cleves on the afternoon of February 9, the day prior to the scheduled start of Operation GRENADE. Unfortunately for the 15th Scottish Division, which was leading the attack, British bombers had hit Cleves the night before the attack began, using high explosive bombs rather than incendiaries, and the streets were filled with rubble and bomb craters. The advance ground to a halt.[11]

As the Scots neared Cleves, Simpson was trying to decide if it was prudent to launch Operation GRENADE on schedule. The German defenses were thin on the east bank of the Roer, so once the Americans reached the far shore they should have little difficulty. The key Roer dams, however, were still in enemy hands. Simpson knew that even a relatively small force of Germans could destroy his advance elements if rising water cut them off before adequate support could be moved across the river. To compound the problem, he had received several reports of increased water levels early on February 9. Realizing that if he did not attack, the Germans could mass their reserves against VERITABLE, he also had to be concerned about losing a major portion of his army. Troubled, Simpson sought advice from the commanders of the two corps which were to participate in the crossing. While one recommended an attack, the other advised caution. H-hour had been scheduled for 5:30 A.M. on February 10; but a field army is a large organization,

Schwammenauel Dam

and to insure that a stop order could be disseminated to all elements in time, Simpson would have to make his decision by 4:45 P.M. on the ninth. The army engineer felt that the reported rise in the water level stemmed from German manipulation, but he could not be certain. Nor was the information from First Army encouraging. Although V Corps elements were nearing their objective, they had not seized the dams. The Germans still retained the flood weapon. Simpson later recalled, "so here I sat, you see . . . it just seemed like 4:30 was just rolling at me rapidly . . . ."[12]

More reports of rising water were received, and at about 4:00 p.m. Simpson spoke again with his corps commanders. Their advice was the same—one favored the attack and the other recommended a delay. Simpson recalled, "I was awfully anxious to go ahead and the question was: well what the hell, let's take a chance; or shall I call it off?"[13]

Finally, just before the deadline, Simpson decided to postpone the crossing. When the massive Schwammenauel Dam was finally taken early on February 10, Simpson's decision was proven to be correct, for the departing Germans had so damaged the discharge valves and control machinery that the Roer rose rapidly, flooding its banks. It would be two weeks before Simpson could cross.[14]

While Ninth Army waited, German reserve divisions were committed against the Canadian First Army. *(See Map 76a, in Atlas.)* Rain, floods, and a tenacious defense slowed the advance, but by February 23 Crerar had overcome the first two German positions and was regrouping to strike the third.[15]

Simpson wanted to attack as soon as possible. Although the estimates were that the water level would not be back to normal until February 24, he chose to move early on the twenty-third. He had prepared two plans for use once the water barrier was crossed. Should the ground be passable for vehicles and the enemy opposition relatively light, he would quickly loose his armor to exploit any advantage gained. On the other hand, if the enemy put up great resistance, Simpson would root out the German defenders with his infantry. He was well equipped with units of both arms. Eleven divisions, three of them armored, formed the core of his army, which numbered over 300,000 troops. On his right was the VII Corps of the First Army, another 75,000 men, which would attack along with Ninth Army. In support were over 2,000 artillery pieces (one per ten yards of front), almost 1,400 tanks, 375 fighter-bombers from the XXIX Tactical Air Command, and various other units with tank destroyers, mortars, and antiaircraft guns. Five hundred C-47 transport aircraft were loaded and standing by in case the army required an emergency supply run. Ammunition dumps, as well as supply depots, had been moved well forward, and a gasoline pipeline terminated at Maastricht, the site of Ninth Army headquarters.[16]

As darkness fell on February 22, all was in readiness for what was to be one of the last American set-piece battles of the war. Speaking quietly so that their movement was not detected, men moved to assault positions near the edge of the water. Engineers brought up bridging equipment and assault boats. At 2:45 A.M. the artillery barrage began. For 45 minutes the ground shook and the sky blazed a dirty orange. Then the first wave of infantry began to cross. Although the swift current caused the boats to land as far as 125 yards away from their planned targets, the crossing was a success. Bridging operations were difficult, but as the day progressed, fighter-bombers substituted for tanks and successfully broke up German counterattacks. By the end of the first day only three foot bridges had been completed, but 28 battalions had managed to cross the river; Simpson's troops held bridgeheads from two to four miles deep. The early crossing, made while the river was still flooding, surprised the Germans. Casualties for the entire Ninth Army on February 23 amounted to 92 killed, 913 wounded, and 61 missing; in the VII Corps, 66 were killed, 280 were wounded, and 35 were missing. While many boats and much bridging equipment had been destroyed, the toll in lives was light. Simpson's crossing of the last water barrier before the Rhine was a huge success.[17]

Early on the twenty-fourth, engineers opened vehicular bridges, and machines of war began to stream across. On the twenty-fifth and twenty-sixth, Simpson, having decided to employ his armor, started to wheel to the northeast so that he could effect a link-up with the VERITABLE forces. On the twenty-seventh, his armored divisions passed through the infantry and advanced at an average of a mile an hour. *(See Map 76a, in Atlas.)* Though the Germans exchanged the headquarters of the Fifth Panzer Army for that of the Fifteenth Army so that a headquarters experienced in mobile warfare could oppose the American drive, there were two few troops to stem Simpson's attack. As early as February 25, Rundstedt had asked Hitler for new directives to allow more flexibility and permit the forming of a cohesive defensive force—meaning a withdrawal across the Rhine, if necessary. *(See Map 76a, in Atlas.)* He was worried not only about the Crerar-Simpson offensive, but also about the gains that Patton was making in the south. Hitler refused the request. Finally, on the twenty-eighth, he authorized the lesser withdrawal Rundstedt had pleaded for twice—from the salient near Roermond, formed by the Maas and Roer Rivers. The Germans got out of the salient just ahead of the northward drive by the XVI Corps, which went all the way to Venlo. The Germans were being squeezed into an ever smaller area, between the advancing divisions of Crerar and Simpson. Ninth Army troops reached the Rhine north of Neuss on March 2 and linked up with British troops near Geldern on the third. The army boundary had been shifted northward on March 1 to allow full play of the exploitation by Simpson's rampaging columns. By March 5 all that remained in German hands was the Wesel bridgehead, and that was cleared by the tenth. *(See Map 76a, in Atlas.)* As in Normandy, Montgomery's forces had fixed the enemy reserves while the Americans penetrated and then raced across the countryside. Now, with his forces on the Rhine, Montgomery could prepare to cross that river.[18]

While Ninth Army divisions were racing for the Rhine, all Allied leaders from Eisenhower on down yearned for the capture of a usable bridge over the river. At Neuss, the 83rd Infantry Division found all three bridges destroyed, but its mobile columns tried again a few miles down river at Oberkassel. A task force, with Sherman tanks disguised as German vehicles and German-speaking soldiers aboard each tank, approached the village under the cover of darkness. So good was the disguise that German troops moving the opposite way on foot on the same road seemed to notice no problem. Just as it appeared that the ruse might work, a German soldier raised the alarm. Throwing caution to the winds and firing as they went, the tankers tried to get to the bridge in time, but just as they reached the western end the Germans set off the prepared explosive charges.[19]

At Uerdingen, even farther downstream, the XIX Corps made another attempt. Here the Americans got to the bridge; but due to a crater the tanks could not get on it, and small arms fire coupled with the bursts of mortar shells prevented a successful infantry attack. After dark, a small engineer patrol crossed and cut the demolition wires, but the Germans rewired the bridge and demolished it. The Germans also destroyed two bridges at Rheinhausen, six miles downstream from Uerdingen, before elements of the 95th Infantry Division could seize them.[20]

Simpson had Rhine fever. Although all bridges in his sector had been destroyed, he still harbored thoughts of crossing. He later stated that had he been under American command he would have crossed the river to follow up his victory on the west bank, but as he was under Montgomery's operational control he asked permission to execute a crossing south of Uerdingen. Simpson felt that the German commanders who had fought so hard west of the Rhine would have little strength to resist a crossing attempt if it were begun immediately. Once across, he planned to advance to the north along the east bank until he reached the area north of the Ruhr from which an attack along the northern edge of that industrial area could be launched.[21]

Montgomery said no. Such an attack, he declared, would cause Simpson to become entangled in the industrial Ruhr. Although Montgomery obviously had overestimated the enemy strength, members of Simpson's staff saw the refusal as an indication of Montgomery's concern lest anything detract from his planned major assault. Whatever Montgomery's reasoning, there is little doubt that Simpson could have succeeded in crossing in early March.[22]

While Simpson was dashing to the Rhine, Hodges and Patton were preparing for Operation LUMBERJACK. *(See Map 76a, in Atlas.)* In the First Army zone, elements of the VII Corps which had advanced to protect Simpson's right flank, turned toward Cologne. Patton, emphasizing the "active" aspect of his "active defense" mission, had clawed his way through the West Wall, taking an average of 1,000 prisoners a day from the German Seventh Army. LUMBERJACK called for the bulk of the First Army to drive southeast toward the point at which the Ahr River flows into the Rhine. Once at the Rhine, Hodges would swing south to meet Patton, who would be attacking to the northeast through the Eifel. Hopefully, the twin drives would bag a sizeable group of Germans.[23]

Rapid progress characterized LUMBERJACK. *(See Map 76b, in Atlas.)* Collins' VII Corps entered Cologne on March 5, the same day that Patton unleashed his armor. As Third Army advanced up the north bank of the Moselle River, German troops scrambled to escape either to the south bank or across the Rhine. Although the German Seventh Army, under its new commander, General der Infanterie Hans Felber—Hitler had relieved Brandenberger for defeatism—moved south of the Moselle, the move was virtually ineffective. This left the rear of Army Group G, which was holding the Saar industrial region, practically defenseless.[24]

Thus far, although they had reached the Rhine in many areas, the attempts of Allied troops to cross had been frustrated either by blown bridges or by disapproval at higher headquarters. As his III Corps neared the waterway, Major General John Millikin hoped that he could succeed where others had failed. Millikin's major thrust was toward Bonn, while elements of the 9th Armored Division were detailed to comply with the mission of reaching the Ahr River to link up with

Third Army.[25]

Most of the 9th Armored Division headed directly for the Ahr, but a small task force, commanded by Lieutenant Colonel Leonard Engeman, advanced on Remagen, the site of the Ludendorff railroad bridge. German defenses were disorganized, and when the leading elements of the task force reached a bluff overlooking the bridge they could see that the structure was still standing. Engeman quickly organized an attack, but as the leading tanks neared the western approach to the bridge an explosion occurred, throwing rocks and dirt in the faces of the tankers. When the dust settled the bridge was still standing. The German charge had only been designed to deny tanks access to the bridge.

Now, in feverish haste, the Germans attempted to demolish the bridge itself under a hail of rifle and tank fire. They had an intricate, electrically activated demolition plan; but apparently the circuit was broken by the American fire. A volunteer moved out on the bridge to detonate the charges by igniting primer cord. When the charges finally exploded, the planking over the railroad tracks was destroyed, but the bridge itself only lifted slightly and then settled back on its foundations. Although damaged, the bridge was still intact and the side walkways were usable. American infantrymen dashed across and began to climb the cliff from which they could command the bridge approaches. Close behind came engineers who severed all wires and cables which might still be connected to remaining German explosives. American troops had crossed the Rhine. The date was March 7, 1945.

When the news was passed up the chain of command, both the division and corps commanders ordered the immediate reinforcement of the bridgehead. An excited Bradley called Eisenhower. While the Supreme Commander still planned his main attack for the north, he authorized Bradley to push five divisions across. During the next few days, the Germans tried by every conceivable means, including the use of V-2 rockets and the "Karl Howitzer" (a gun which fired a 4,400-pound projectile), to destroy the bridge. At the same time, however, American forces steadily strengthened the bridgehead. German ground forces, drawn from anywhere they could be found, were committed piecemeal and steadily repulsed. By the time that the bridge finally collapsed on March 17, the Americans had built ponton bridges; these, with the help of ferries, could carry the required traffic. In fact, when it fell, the Ludendorff bridge had been closed for repairs since March 13.

The Ludendorff Railroad Bridge at Remagen (Note Damaged Area at Center of Picture)

The same day, Eisenhower told Bradley that he was to secure the Remagen bridgehead as a possible jumping-off area for an attack on Frankfurt, but that it was also to be used to draw enemy units from the areas opposite the planned 21st Army Group attack in the north and the 6th Army Group attack in the south. The degree to which Bradley could reinforce the bridgehead would have to be limited, because 10 or more divisions of First Army might be called upon to exploit Montgomery's crossing in the north. Acting on this order, Bradley held down the expansion of the bridgehead. Hodges, advancing about 1,000 yards a day, could enlarge it to a size of about 25 miles wide and 10 miles deep. Chafing at this restriction, Hodges impatiently awaited the instructions which, when they finally came, told him to be ready to break out to the southeast and link up with Third Army any time after March 23. His First Army attack, which was permitted on the twenty-fifth, once again launched Hodges into a period of mobile warfare.

While the Remagen operation won fame for Major General John W. Leonard and the men of his Ninth Armored Division, it resulted in the sacking of two other generals. Rundstedt once again was relieved by Hitler. This time he was replaced by Generalfeldmarschall Albert Kesselring, who had been Commander-in-Chief South, in charge of operations in Italy. On the American side, Hodges, who had been unhappy with the performance of Millikin, replaced him with Major General James A. Van Fleet, commander of the 90th Infantry Division.

The capture of the bridge at Remagen was a spectacular achievement, and it dealt a blow to German morale; but it is doubtful that it had a major effect on the length of the war. German military capabilities in the West were already low, and even if the bridgehead had not drawn forces from other areas, the subsequent crossings would have succeeded.[26]

With the success of Operation LUMBERJACK, the stage was set for the start of Operation UNDERTONE. The speed with which Bradley's armies had advanced, however, led to a modification of the original plan for the latter operations. *(See Map 77a, in Atlas.)* Under the revised plan, Patton would attack southeastward across the Moselle, sweep along the west bank of the Rhine and cut German communications, and at the same time attack out of the Trier bridgehead to help loosen up the West Wall defenses facing Sixth Army Group. Although this modification offered a promise of trapping the German First and Seventh Armies, Bradley and Patton also saw it as a way to commit Third Army troops so that divisions would not be transferred to Montgomery or Devers. For his part, Eisenhower hoped that UNDERTONE would draw German strength from the north. In his pre-attack orders to Bradley and Devers, the Supreme Commander specified that Devers' mission included the establishment of bridgeheads across the Rhine in the Mainz-Mannheim area.[27]

The fact that Eisenhower authorized only Devers to seize Rhine bridgeheads did not sit well with an impatient Patton, who was literally busting at the seams to cross the river. Guessing that the Germans were on the verge of collapse from the earlier Eifel drives, Patton expected from the first to make a quick breakthrough and then exploit beyond the Moselle to the Rhine. Surely he could find a place to jump the Rhine, and if he had to cross the army group boundary in so doing, so be it. He orally advised his corps commanders that the boundary *(See Map 77a)* should impose no restrictions on their maneuvers.

Before UNDERTONE began, German field commanders realized that without reinforcements the situation was hopeless. Hausser pointed out the danger facing the two German armies, but Kesselring, abiding by Hitler's orders, refused to allow either a withdrawal or a delaying action. The troops of the Seventh and First Armies must defend in place. Hausser did manage to provide a few substandard reinforcements, and First Army did have strong positions in the West Wall, an area which Devers had partially penetrated before the Ardennes debacle and its aftermath necessitated his withdrawal. *(See Map 77a.)* But Patton's attacks along the Moselle on March 13 and 14 triggered a German disaster. The Third Army commander was initially unhappy with the progress of the XX Corps, which he expected to draw German attention and set up the later thrust to the Rhine by the XII Corps. Part of his concern, he wrote in his diary, was apprehension that Patch would beat him to the Rhine. He need not have worried, for the infantry divisions of both the XX and XII Corps made sufficient progress on the next day to allow both corps commanders to commit their armored divisions on March 15 and 16 in an exploitation phase. In the process, Patton was able to convince Eisenhower to transfer one of Devers' armored divisions to Third Army, the day after Patch launched the Seventh Army attack into the West Wall defenses on March 15.[29]

March 17 was a pivotal day for commanders on both sides. That day Kesselring left an opening in an order which Hausser seized upon to order Seventh Army to pull back behind the Nahe River. *(See Map 77A.)* The OB West commander, while directing retention of present positions, also warned his subordinates not to allow encirclement and annihilation of the main body of troops—and that is just what Patton's exploiting columns were about to do to the German Seventh Army. On the seventeenth also, Devers, Patton, and Patch met with Eisenhower to discuss ways of exploiting the fluid situation. Devers and Patch agreed to Patton's driving south across the army group boundary on the basis, as Devers put it, that "we were out to win the war and whoever was there first would go on." The boundary was adjusted southward *(See Map 77a)*, but even that would not restrain Patton's armor in his quest to bag more Germans, or stop him from creating the opportunity for his cherished Rhine crossing. Devers was privately piqued, as apparently the race for the Rhine had become something of a personal contest with Patton. Concerned from the first about entangling two American armies, Devers now harbored a suspicion that "Patton was up to his old tricks . . . and I believe is willing to go to some lengths to cross us up." He was correct in that Patton yearned for a quick and spectacular crossing of the Rhine, a desire which Bradley furthered on the nineteenth by telling Patton to take the river on the run. Eisenhower confirmed this authority in a message two days later, which modified his March 8 directive and ordered *both* Seventh and Third Armies to be alert for Rhine crossing opportunities.[30]

After March 19, the German situation disintegrated rapidly. On the twentieth, Seventh Army was finally authorized to withdraw its shattered remnants, mostly headquarters elements, across the Rhine. First Army, under attack from front and rear, used Kesselring's qualification in his March 17 order to pull back into an ever-shrinking bridgehead on the Rhine. *(See Map 77a, in Atlas.)* On the twenty-third, the army was finally allowed to cross its battered units. On March 24, the Allied helf the west bank of the Rhine from Switzerland to the English Channel.[31]

The Rhineland Campaign was one of Hitler's greatest defeats. *(See Map 77b.)* Eisenhower's armies captured approximately a quarter million Germans and killed or wounded about 60,000 more. The campaign practically destroyed the German army in the West, and left little in the way of an effective force to defend the Rhine. Hitler's policy of forbidding a planned withdrawal across the river early enough so that such action might be more orderly and equipment and manpower be salvaged for a later, more effective defense, was disastrous. His field commanders and decimated units fought as well as they could in the face of overwhelming Allied ground and aerial strength. Understanding these conditions, one marvels at the ability of those units of the *Wehrmacht* in the south to fight a skillful delaying action against Patton and Patch long enough to extricate some of their units. Although this German accomplishment is a tribute to the discipline and steadfastness of the men in ranks, as well as to the flexibility of leaders in the field, it also raises the question of whether the Americans pushed hard enough driving south and north along the Rhine to pinch off the salient. Future bridgeheads may have been too tempting. Whatever one's judgment, it is clear that for the Germans the die was cast. Hitler's forces, disorganized and depleted behind the Rhine, were on their last legs.[32]

Crossing the Rhine in Force

The campaign in the Palatinate created the opportunity for Patton to make his long harbored crossing of the Rhine. One day after Eisenhower's directive had alerted Third Army to be opportunistic, Patton turned the 5th Infantry Division to the east from its southward drive and directed it to make a surprise crossing at Oppenheim. *(See Map 79, in Atlas.)* The crossing, begun the night of March 22 without an artillery preparation and under intense pressure from Patton, was an instant success. The German Seventh Army, which was responsible for the area of the crossing, was pathetically weak and trying to reorganize after the Palatinate disaster. As the first infantry elements to cross the river carved out a shallow beachhead, Patton's engineers started bridge construction, using equipment which had been held in dumps for weeks, its transference to the river having begun on the twentieth. Navy landing craft were also used to speed the crossing of infantry. By the end of the twenty-third, one heavy bridge was passable and most of the 5th Division had crossed. The next day, the corps commander, Major General Manton S. Eddy, pushed two additional divisions across, including the tough, ubiquitous 4th Armored Division, which at once began exploiting the crossing to the northeast. German counterattacks were feeble and ineffectual. An elated Patton had his Rhine bridgehead.

Bradley announced the news to a startled press late on the evening of March 23. The timing of the announcement was obviously aimed at twitting Montgomery, who was just then beginning "the first assault crossing of the Rhine in modern times," after extensive aerial and artillery bombardments and with the help of two airborne divisions. Bradley's news release also stressed that American troops were capable of crossing the Rhine as they pleased, without aerial or airborne support. To punctuate that boast, Patton's VIII Corps made two more crossings on March 24 and 25 at Boppard and St. Goar, upstream from Coblenz. On the twenty-sixth, moreover, Patch's Seventh Army joined the club by staging two crossings near Worms, against stiffer but still disorganized German resistance.[33]

Navy Landing Craft Loads Troops for Rhine Crossing, March 1945

To almost everyone but Hitler, on the eve of the Rhine crossings it was clear that the Allies were rapidly reducing Germany to a state of impotence. *(See Map 78, in Atlas.)* Eisenhower alone commanded 4,000,000 men, and his was but one of several commands pressing the Reich. Since mid-February, the Russians had been building up on the Oder. Their attack on Berlin could begin at any time. And in Italy, although the Germans had been fighting well, the Allies seemed to be close to breaking through the last defense line south of the Po Valley. Allied bombers were ranging over Germany, striking mostly fuel plants, transportation, and industrial areas. The Ruhr had been particularly hard hit, and was practically isolated from the rest of Germany. By February, total production in Germany had fallen to a fifth of that of the summer of 1944. German war plants were relying heavily on already existing parts, and stocks of these were diminishing. Troop losses had been staggering in the West alone—over 2,000,000 killed, wounded, missing, or captured since the Normandy invasion. Many of the remaining troops lacked adequate training, and their units were short of weapons, ammunition, and gasoline.[34]

Hitler, with defeat staring him in the face, was determined not to surrender. A technological breakthrough in weaponry was not to be; nor would the Allied coalition fall apart, as he had hoped. But he would continue to fight. On March 19, over the strongly voiced protest of Minister of Armaments and War Production Albert Speer, Hitler had decreed that "the battle should be conducted without consideration of our own population."[35] Anything which might be of use to the enemies of Germany was to be destroyed. Speer immediately set to work to convince industrialists and politicians that Hitler's decree should not be obeyed, thereby preventing much last-minute destruction.[36] Meanwhile, the Allies continued to pound the Reich, well-supported by a streamlined Communications Zone and engineer construction effort, which kept the tactical airfields operational close behind the front. For three days prior to Montgomery's assault, bombers struck airfields, railyards, and communication centers in preparation for the long-heralded crossing in the north.

Montgomery's preparations for crossing the Rhine were detailed, meticulous, and calculated to bring overwhelming power to bear. He controlled over a million men, including the British Second Army (nine divisions), the American Ninth Army (twelve divisions), the First Allied Airborne Army (two divisions), and the First Canadian Army (eight divisions). The first three armies would be in the assault, and the latter would follow up to expand the bridgehead to the north. To support the attack, Montgomery had over 300,000 tons of stock-piled supplies, 5,500 artillery tubes, and massive air support. An elaborate deception plan was used to deceive the enemy as to the crossing sites. Simpson's and Dempsey's armies were designated to launch the ground assault at night, while the airborne divisions would jump the next morning near Wesel (Operation VARSITY). *(See Map 79, in Atlas.)* The latter units would cut communications and then link up with the bridgehead troops; there would not be another Arnhem, for the airborne troops were to land within artillery-supporting distance. To oppose this mighty force, the Germans had only about 85,000 demoralized troops in the immediate vicinity; 35 tanks, termed a *panzer* corps, were in reserve.[37]

After a final weather check on the afternoon of March 23, Montgomery directed that the attack be made that night. The tempo of artillery fire picked up at 6:00 P.M., and the first infantry assault crossing commenced three hours later. Churchill, Brooke, and Eisenhower were present to observe the spectacle. The Supreme Commander and Simpson initially watched events from a church tower; later they joined a group of infantrymen and walked with them toward the river.[38]

German opposition to the ground crossing was relatively light. The massive artillery preparation kept German infantry huddled in their riverline holes and cut communications between artillery forward observers and their batteries. Fog and smoke blanketed the area and interfered with the vision of the defenders. Dempsey's troops encountered the stiffest opposition, but on the whole the outcome of the operation was never in doubt. *(See Map 79.)* By the end of the first day (March 24), Simpson's assault corps had a bridgehead nine miles wide and from three to six miles deep; Dempsey's enclave was slightly smaller. Within the two bridgeheads, which were linked on the twenty-fifth, there were four American and five British divisions. Earlier, by the evening of the twenty-fourth, the airborne troops had established contact with ground elements.[39]

Operation VARSITY was a resounding success, but the necessity for this airborne operation can be questioned. At 10:00 A.M. on March 24, an air fleet of 1,696 transports and 1,348 gliders began to land the 21,680 assault troops of Major General Matthew B. Ridgway's XVIII Airborne Corps. The troop carriers were escorted by 889 fighters, while 240 bombers, loaded with supplies rigged for airdrop, followed closely behind. Antiaircraft fire was intense; the Germans, anticipating the use of Allied airborne elements, had selected the area north

Operation VARSITY: American Paratrooper Caught in a Tree

of Wesel as a likely drop zone, and massed mobile antiaircraft pieces from throughout Army Group H. Largely due to fire from these weapons, the Allied force lost 44 transports, over 50 gliders, and 15 of the resupply bombers. In the 17th Airborne Division alone, 159 were killed, 522 wounded, and 840 missing on the first day. To these figures must be added the losses of the British 6th Airborne Division and the losses of the various air organizations which participated. In stark contrast were the losses sustained by the two American ground assault divisions, the 50th and 79th Infantry Divisions, in which there were 41 killed, 450 wounded, and 7 missing. It is true that the airborne assault aided Dempsey's divisions. The objectives Ridgway's troops seized, however, were within the capability of ground troops, considering the weakness of the defenders, a condition not entirely unknown to the Allies. Moreover, the airborne assault did not speed up heavy bridge construction nor appreciably expand the depth of the bridgehead beyond what the 30th Division accomplished. The airborne elements also crowded the bridgehead, a condition frustrating to Simpson who initially sought unsuccessfully for a way to insert his other corps and break out in the exploitation. Montgomery, however, had the responsibility for Operation PLUNDER, and he was determined that, unlike MARKET-GARDEN, it would not fail. He believed that he needed the airborne divisions to speed his crossing, the prelude to his long-anticipated drive across the North German Plain toward Berlin. It is difficult to refrain from speculating, however, about how many lives and how much time and materiel might have been saved had the Field Marshal allowed Simpson to make a surprise crossing early in March.[40]

On March 25, the same day that Churchill crossed the Rhine and created considerable uneasiness among senior commanders concerned for his safety, Bradley allowed Hodges to break out of the Remagen bridgehead.[41] *(See Map 79, in Atlas.)* Model commander of Army Group B, expected that Hodges would attack to the north, and had arranged his dispositions to counter such a move. Hodges, however, sent a portion of his force to the south to link up with Patton, while the remainder moved first to the east, and then northeast to encircle the Ruhr from the south. German resistance was sporadic, and breakthroughs were achieved on March 26. Hodges released his armored divisions to exploit the advantage. Meanwhile, Patton's Third Army was also making rapid gains. Even farther south, De Lattre, prodded by De Gaulle, who wanted a Rhine bridgehead to solidify French claims on an occupation zone, obtained an expanded frontage from Devers and crossed the Rhine near Speyer on March 31.[42] *(See Map 80, in Atlas.)* The Rhine was no longer an obstacle to Eisenhower's armies, all of which had firm footholds on the east bank and were already beginning drives to the east. Nor had there been, for some time, much German opposition to the strategic bombing campaign conducted by the overpowering Allied air forces. That campaign, only briefly mentioned previously, played an important role in the defeat of Germany. However, before doctrine emerged and technology improved, it encountered many difficulties.

The Strategic Bombing of Germany

In spite of Dowding, Watson-Watt and Inskip, the 1939 Air Staff of the Royal Air Force (RAF) remained convinced that the bomber would get through.* They had ordered a great fleet of heavy four-engine bombers before war broke out, and they were waiting only for the delivery of these great aircraft before implementing the theories of Hugh Trenchard. Using two-engine bombers in the first winter of the war, however, the RAF discovered that daylight bombing was a very expensive proposition; accordingly, by April 1940, the Bomber Command had adopted the night offensive for the sake of security. This necessarily entailed a violation of the principle of mass, as it spread the firepower of the Bomber Command far and wide across western Europe. Night navigation and bombing were simply too primitive to permit the destruction of the enemy's *ability* to fight through the bombing of its industrial facilities. Thus, the limits of technology forced the abandonment of precision bombing, favoring instead the tactics of area bombing. This strategy was based on Giulio Douhet's theory that civilian morale is a decisive, legitimate, and vulnerable target.

Instead of destroying the factory in which the German worker labored, the Bomber Command would destroy his *will* to work by burning the city in which he lived. Although a 1000-plane raid was launched against Cologne in May 1942, the early results of the night offensive were disappointing. Gradually, through electronics and pathfinder tactics, the British were once more able to implement the principle of mass. But, at the same time, the *Luftwaffe* was eroding the security of the British bomber force through the improvement of the German air defense system. During the early part of 1944, the situation had reached a point where British losses at night were exceeding those of the Americans in their daylight operations against Germany. The campaign reached its zenith with the 1945 raids on the city of Dresden—many have argued that 135,000 people died there. However that may be, the Bomber Command never did succeed in breaking the morale of the German worker. The power of Germany's totalitarian government over its people, the force of habit, and the worker's need to continue making a living had been underestimated.[43]

The attempted American solution to the dilemma of security versus mass was quite the opposite to that of the RAF. Rather than go over to the night offensive for the sake of the immediate gain in security and then gradually work to improve the mass of firepower, the Eighth Air Force chose to retain accurate daylight bombing methods and to work to improve the security of the force in daylight. From the outset, this was done in the face of opposition from the experienced hands of the RAF's Air Staff. The RAF said it couldn't be done, but the American "big bomber" men said that it could. The newcomers thought that the "lessons" of history did not apply to them because they had a better bomber (a true "battleplane") and because they had the Norden bombsight which would direct the missiles into a "pickle barrel" from high altitude. Further, the theories of Billy Mitchell and the Americans' view of their own humanitarian superiority impelled the Eighth Air Force in the direction of a strategy which would assault the German *ability*—as opposed to *will*—to wage war. That is to say, the Americans would not be so barbaric as to "cook" the German worker in his slumber; rather, they would surgically remove his machine tools from his industrial centers without disturbing anything else.

The Boeing B-17 (Flying Fortress) was believed capable of doing this with impunity. If any of the German defenders managed to reach its domain in the upper fringes of the atmosphere, they would be met with a storm of defensive fire. In its final version, the B-17 carried 13 caliber .50 machineguns which were further massed by grouping the aircraft into tremendous formations which could spout fire in any direction. The American bomber men were confident that no German fighter aircraft could penetrate such formations.

*See Chapter 3 for a brief discussion of the doubts about the bomber's invulnerability which were held by Fighter Command and some scientists.

The initial tests of American daylight bombing techniques seemed promising. The first raid was flown against the rail yards of Rouen in the summer of 1942. The results were thought to be encouraging, and the losses were not prohibitive. So it continued throughout 1942 and well into 1943.

Then came the disasters of Ploesti and Schweinfurt. The first named raid, launched on August 1, 1943, departed with 178 aircraft. Sixty-one of these never made it back to Bengazi—a loss rate of 34 percent. Of those aircraft that did return, many were so badly damaged that hardly more than 30 ever flew again.[44] The Second Schweinfurt Raid was not much better. Two hundred and ninety-one airplanes flew; 60 of those never came back. The loss ratio was 23 percent. Picture the psychology of the new, young tail gunner just arriving in his Eighth Air Force unit. He knows not of Munich, Buchenwald, or the Nazi ideology. He knows only that he wants to get back to the homeland with a whole body. The magic figure that will permit his return to America is 25 missions. Yesterday's raid, according to his buddies in the mess hall, lost a quarter of its strength—in only one mission. Even with average luck, our gunner would go down on his fifth mission. What are the prospects for completing 25 missions?

After Schweinfurt, the leaders of Eighth Air Force knew that changes were essential. They still did not want to go over to the night attack because that would fly in the face of their fundamental perception of what their campaign was all about. To do so would be to change the objective from the destruction of the German *ability* to resist (destruction of armament factories, etc.) to the breaking of the Teutonic *will* to resist (ruination of civilian morale though the burning of their homes). Another method to improve the security of the force would have to be found.[45]

The first reaction to the horrendous losses of the early fall was to discontinue the deep penetration raids in favor of attacks on the German periphery. Fortunately, another, better solution was waiting in the wings. Douhet had insisted that there was no future for escort fighters, but Mitchell had allowed that such aircraft might be useful under some circumstances. The American theorists of the 1930s could not imagine a fighter which could carry enough fuel to make the round trip with their bombers, so an attempt to overcome this problem early in the campaign was to take the basic B-17 airframe and replace the weight of the bombs and bombing systems with machineguns and ammunition. This heavily armed craft would be placed in the most vulnerable parts of the combat formations and add so much to the firepower of the force that the Germans presumably would not brave the storm of lead. When the idea was tried, it was found that the new machine gun-carrying airplanes became a burden on the rest of the formation after the bomb run. The standard B-17s substantially reduced their gross weight and, consequently, increased their air-speed, when they released their bombs. But the weight and speed of the gunships remained the same. The bomber pilots were most reluctant to throttle back in the hostile skies of Germany to wait for the tardy gunships. Yet, if the latter straggled, they would become sitting ducks for the German fighters.

The better solution was a single-engine fighter. In a stroke of good luck, the North American Mustang, which had earlier been rejected by the U.S. Army Air Force (USAAF), was put into production on the orders of the British. In its original version, the rather mediocre engine caused its performance to be substandard. However, once it was re-equipped with a Rolls Royce engine, it could outperform any of the German propeller-driven aircraft used in World War II. But, equally important, the engine was quite efficient, and workable drop tanks were tardily developed which finally allowed the P-51 (later the F-51) to fly farther than the B-17 could.

The new, high performance, long-range Mustangs began to appear in numbers in Europe during the last weeks of 1943, and their impact was immediate and dramatic. In February, Eighth Air Force, now emboldened to return to the deep penetration raids, began a concerted effort to destroy the *Luftwaffe*. The offensive came to be known as "Big Week." By March, air superiority had been won. Douhet had held that command of the air had to be won by an attack on the enemy air force on the ground; however, Mitchell, and to some extent Trenchard as well, thought that it had to be done partly with an attack on th ground resources and partly with a battle in the air. In the final analysis, all were agreed that air superiority had to be somehow won before the enemy's *will* or *ability* to resist could be directly assaulted. Eighth Air Force had long been trying to destroy German airpower on the ground *a la* Douhet, without much success. In fact, German fighter production continued to grow dramatically until the month of October 1944. What really destroyed enemy airpower was the killing of fighter pilots. After the Mustangs appeared on the scene, the experienced hands of the *Luftwaffe* began to fall in droves, not only to the fire of the P-51s, but also to the guns of the bomber force. The average level of experience of the defending flyers began a decided decline—so much so that, before the end, many youths were going into the fight with a total flying time of about 40 hours. (At the same time, USAAF fighter pilots were being given a minimum of 325 hours of flying time—at least 125 of which were in fighter aircraft—before flying an operational mission.) Thus, command of the air had been achieved by March, and the time to turn to the exploitation phase had arrived.[46]

The leaders of the strategic bombing forces, however, were to suffer further frustration before they could turn to the "surgical" destruction of the German war economy. As previously stated, in April the Combined Chiefs of Staff gave operational control of the big bombers to Eisenhower so that he could use them in support of OVERLORD.* He retained that control throughout most of the summer, and although he often allowed the bomber commanders to select their objectives, he sometimes ordered them to fly in direct support of ground force operations. The carpet bombings at St. Lô and Caen are examples of such a use. Strategic bombing enthusiasts have argued that this use of the bombers was a violation of the principle of the objective in that it employed strategic forces against unsuitable tactical objectives—much as Goering had attempted to achieve strategic objectives with his tactical support instrument in the Battle of Britain. Be that as it may, the leaders of the strategic air forces were given their heads late in the summer when the CCS reclaimed operational control of the big bombers.

By the time the OVERLORD diversion was over, the strategic bombing planners had finally settled their target selection priorities. The daylight forces had long been directed against targets such as the submarine pens and aircraft factories. Now, very late in the game, it was decided to mass the attack against the German petroleum and transportation industries. From the fall of 1944 onwards, the effects of this attack were impressive. Fully three quarters of the bomb weight used against Germany in World War II was dropped *after* the D-Day landings.[47] Before the western armies had crossed the Rhine in force, Albert Speer had gone to the *Fuehrer* and insisted that, because of the denial of movement and petroleum, the complete collapse of the German economy in a matter of weeks was inevitable.[48] One of the objectives of the German offensive in the Battle of the Bulge had been the capture of Allied oil stocks so that the offensive itself could be continued. That objective was not achieved, and a good many German vehicles had to be abandoned on the battlefield for the want of fuel. About 2,000 of the jet ME 262s were produced before the war ended. These would have certainly been decisive against the Combined Bomber Offensive and against the Normandy landings had they appeared two years earlier; coming on the line in numbers late in 1944, however, fewer than half of them ever flew at all—and those which did fly were sometimes manned by inexperienced pilots who had been restricted in flying time largely because of the dire lack of fuel for training purposes. In short, after many trials and tribulations, the bomber offensive against Germany was probably one of the decisive factors in ending Hitler's dream of conquest.

As far as the American part of the air campaign against Germany is concerned then, the objective was probably both attainable and decisive. The United States Army Air Force was not sufficiently attentive, at first, to the need to conquer the enemy's main battle force (the *Luftwaffe*) before working on the German economy. When the German air defenses forcibly brought themselves to the attention of the American decision makers, a somewhat fortuitous solution to the security problem was at hand. The P-51, along with the bombers, solved that problem early in 1944 and, after helping out with the invasion, the force wrecked the German economy. Thus, the strategic bombing effort in Europe suffered from some misdirection, but was effective on the whole.

*See Chapter 11, pp. 265-266.

The Final Offensive

With his forces streaming across the Rhine and making rapid gains out of initial bridgeheads, Eisenhower reassessed the strategic situation and made a decision, the merits of which have been debated by historians ever since. He decided to shift the main effort from the north to Bradley's army group in the center. Once the 12th and 21st Army Groups had isolated the Ruhr, Ninth Army was to revert to Bradley's control; the American commander would then use his increased force to reduce the Ruhr, and also to attack eastward along the Erfurt-Leipzig-Dresden axis. *(See Map 80, in Atlas.)* Montgomery was to protect Bradley's north flank, while Devers would protect the south. Both the 12th and 21st Army Groups were to advance to the Elbe and be prepared to cross and continue east on order. Devers was to be ready to advance down the Danube valley to meet the Russians.[49]

Montgomery, who had just told the British Second and American Ninth Armies to drive hard for the Elbe, was surprised to learn of the change in plans. He had had no warning that Eisenhower was considering deemphasizing the drive toward Berlin, which had previously been accorded priority in Allied plans. Nor did he like losing Ninth Army, fearing that this detachment would hamper "the great movement which is now beginning to develop." He asked that Simpson at least remain under his control until the Elbe was reached, but Eisenhower denied the request.[50]

The basis for Eisenhower's change in strategy was his judgment that Berlin could no longer be classed as a decisive military objective for the western Allies. His intelligence sources had revealed that not only was much of the city in ruins from years of bombing, but also that the government ministries were in the process of leaving. Moreover, he knew that the Russians were only 30 miles from the German capital while the British and Americans were about 200 miles away. Germany had already been politically divided into zones which would be occupied by the various Allies after hostilities had ceased. Berlin, which itself was to be divided, lay deep in the Russian zone. Eisenhower realized that territory captured in an attack on Berlin—perhaps at a not inconsiderable cost in American lives—would later have to be given to the Russians. Thus if he decided to attack Berlin, American soldiers would die in an attempt to seize a city which he no longer considered to be of primary military importance and which the forces of an Allied nation could easily capture.

Eisenhower thought that central Germany, on the other hand, offered more military advantages for the movement of his armies. The terrain favored an advance in the center, where the plateau which ran from Kassel to Leipzig could be traversed and rivers flowing toward the North Sea could be crossed near their sources. The spring run-off would swell these rivers to a width that would make them easily defendable obstacles in Montgomery's zone. An advance by Bradley in the center could be expected to link up quickly with the Russians, and split Germany in half. The capture of Leipzig would also eliminate much of the remaining German manufacturing capability. Once the Leipzig area was reached, the Supreme Commander planned to consolidate his position along the easily recognizable lines of the Elbe and Mulde Rivers, where contact with the Russians would be made. Hopefully the meeting would occur without incident due to the mutually understood and clearly visible line selected. When the consolidation was completed, Eisenhower might return Ninth Army to British operational control to aid in clearing the north German coast west to Lubeck. Allied capture of Lubeck *(See Map 82, in Atlas.)* would cut off German troops stationed in Denmark.

Another factor which Eisenhower had to consider was the possibility that even after most of Germany and Austria were overrun, there might be considerable resistance stemming from the National Redoubt, a mountainous area in southern Bavaria, western Austria, and northern Italy. Although this threat would later be proved to be hollow and one based on faulty intelligence, Eisenhower had to act on what SHAEF intelligence presently indicated. Reports received over a period of weeks indicated that many units would withdraw, according to plan, into the redoubt, where weapons, supplies, and even aircraft production plants had already been located. When the German order of battle was consulted, it tended to confirm this, for a number of SS divisions were located in the south on both the eastern and western fronts. This threat was too serious to ignore. If a major force did reach the redoubt area and the mountain passes were blocked, much time would be lost and many lives expended before German opposition was completely crushed. By weighting his center, Eisenhower would not only sever north-south movement but would also be in a position to send major elements quickly toward the redoubt area.

Finally, in Eisenhower's view, weighting the drive through central Germany would not only end the war quickly and with the least cost, but would also preserve maximum strength for speedy redeployment. The war against Japan was still raging, and troops would need to be shipped out of Europe as soon as possible. Each mile of advance into the Russian zone meant an additional mile that would have to be traversed when the troops withdrew to the ports.[51]

Eisenhower's revelation of a change in plans perturbed Churchill and the British Chiefs of Staff. Whereas Eisenhower believed that he had always left open the option of shifting the main effort to the Frankfurt area, the British interpreted his new orders as reneging on the agreement reached at Malta. They also objected to his having communicated the new plan to Stalin before having notified the Combined Chiefs of Staff. Churchill, for his part, stressed the importance of Berlin as a political objective, and sharply questioned the Supreme Commander; but after subsequent discussions with Eisenhower, he pressed his argument no further, particularly when the American Chiefs strongly supported the Supreme Commander.[52]

Since 1945 and the end of the war, many authors have speculated on what would have happened had Eisenhower tried to take Berlin. Like a similar speculation regarding the potential effect of an Allied advance through the Balkans from Italy, discussions of this effort, although intriguing, depend largely on supposition and imagination. In all probability the Russians, located much closer to the city, would have accelerated their timetable and still have been the first to enter the city. But even if Eisenhower's forces had somehow managed to capture Berlin, it is difficult to see how the postwar situation would have appreciably changed. American policy was that of cooperation with Russia. As the zones of occupation had already been drawn and accepted by all parties concerned, the western Allies no doubt would have retained their portions of the city and then, as they did elsewhere, withdrawn to their own sectors.

The western Allies made rapid progress from March 29 to April 4, 1945, in their implementation of Eisenhower's new directive. *(See Map 80.)* On March 30, the 3rd Armored Division of First Army moved over 90 miles. So disorganized was the German defense that the commander of CCB of the 2nd Armored Division, advancing north of the Ruhr, used existing telephone facilities to call from one town to the next to demand surrender. Although the southern advance, designed to seal the Ruhr, was temporarily delayed by the resistance offered by the instructors and students at the *panzer* training center in Padeborn, elements of First and Ninth Armies met at Lippstadt on April 1, thereby completing the encirclement of the Ruhr. Model's Army Group B had been herded into a 4,000-square mile pocket.[53]

On April 4, Ninth Army returned to 12th Army Group control. Bradley planned, at least initially, to use four of his corps to reduce the Ruhr, while seven would be free to attack to the east; another, as part of the new Fifteenth Army, which was responsible for an extensive area west of the Rhine, would be positioned along that river. Bradley's total command, the largest purely American field command that had ever been assembled, included 4 armies, 12 corps, and 48 divisions.[54]

To the north of the main attack, in Montgomery's 21st Army Group, the First Canadian Army was advancing northward in an effort to cut off the German troops in The Netherlands. Dempsey's Second British Army was moving across the North German Plain, although German demolitions restricted progress to some degree. Devers, in the south, advanced to the east and south. The Germans put up stiff resistance at Heilbronn, but on April 4 the French First Army took Karlsruhe.[55]

As German prospects for contesting Allied initiatives faded, Hitler, who seemed oblivious to reality, continued to order attacks. When Blaskowitz requested permission to withdraw sufficient forces from The Netherlands to link with Model in the Ruhr pocket and establish a front along the Weser River, the *Fuehrer* denied it. Commanders in all areas were told to hold and resist to the last. In the south, Army Group G maintained a front, but continued to withdraw. Although the Seventh Army, in the center, was but a shadow of its former self, it still existed—under yet another general. Felber had been relieved for failure to hold on the Rhine, and General der Infanterie Hans von Obstfelder had assumed command. Claiming that Germany would somehow be delivered from defeat, Hitler declared that the Germans could stymie the Russians on the Oder and Niesse Rivers if the advances of the western Allies could be at least temporarily halted. Kesselring did not even know how many troops he controlled, but he was told to delay while a reserve, the Eleventh Army, was formed in the Harz Mountains. This reserve army would then attack to relieve Model in the Ruhr. Meanwhile, the German people, both in and out uniform, continued to suffer. Millions of refugees sought places of safety.[56]

There was no sanctuary in the Ruhr Pocket, where American forces continued to hammer the German defenders. Realizing that he could not escape, but determined to hold out as long as his efforts diverted Allied troops from the thrust to the east, Model continued to resist. *(See Map 81, in Atlas.)* On April 14 troops of the 8th Infantry Division from the south and the 79th Infantry Division from the north met on the Ruhr River, splitting the pocket. Still Model would not surrender, although he could see that the end was near. Wanting to avoid the useless loss of German lives, he decided to dissolve Army Group B, for an organization that was no longer in being could not surrender. Then, believing that a field marshal should never capitulate and satisfied that he had done all he could, Model drove into the forest and, like Samsonov at Tannenberg, committed suicide. German surrenders mounted. The final tally for the Ruhr reached a total of 317,000.[57] With the fall of this industrial complex, the German field commands were reorganized. *(See Map 81, in Atlas.)* Army Group H was dissolved, and Blaskowitz, as Commander-in-Chief Netherlands, activated Army Group Netherlands. Generalfeldmarschall Ernst Busch, commanding Army Group Northwest, took control of First Parachute Army and various fragments of units which were opposing Montgomery. In the south, Kesselring was trying to control Army Group G, now commanded by General der Infanterie Friedrich Schulz, and various other units which had withdrawn in that direction.

All the while, Eisenhower's armies afforded no respite for the decimated and hard-pressed *Wehrmacht*. Armored divisions and infantry divisions, the latter motorized by dint of trucks furnished by quartermaster battalions or corps artillery units, pressed Hitler's forces relentlessly. Plentifully supported with fuel and other supplies from the logisticians, they raced through the countryside and towns, many of which were decked with white flags. The hastily formed Eleventh Army put up a brief fight, but it could only slightly delay the inevitable as armored units quickly bypassed and then encircled the force. On April 11, after travelling 73 miles that day, the 2nd Armored Division of Ninth Army reached the Elbe; the next day, the 83rd Infantry Division from that same army also arrived at the river. By the end of April 18, there was little of Germany left under Hitler's nominal control, except in Bavaria. *(See Map 81.)* In the north, the Canadians had cut off the Germans in Holland and were driving on Emden-Wilhemshaven against stiffer resistance. Dempsey's forces were nearing the Elbe, and Bradley's armies were on that river and the Mulde, or close to it; Patton was also close to the Czech frontier. In the south, Devers' armies were picking up momentum, although the Germans were fanatically defending Nuremburg. To compound Hitler's problems, the Allies had attacked in Italy on April 14, and two days later the Russians had launched their final offensive. That same day, April 16, Spaatz had told the United States Strategic Air Forces in Europe that, as no strategic targets remained in Germany, the Combined Bomber Offensive was over.[58]

Eisenhower tried to keep up with the rapidly changing front by visiting his commanders. On April 12, with Bradley and Patton, he visited some Third Army units, then inspected a salt mine where about $250,000,000 in gold bars (virtually the entire German gold reserve) as well as gold coins, gold and silver plate, and piles of currency had been discovered. That same day he viewed the first concentration camp captured by the western Allies. Patton vomited and Eisenhower paled at the sights they saw. The Supreme Commander looked everywhere so that he could speak with authority in case he should later have to testify about the conditions in the camp. That evening he sent messages to London and Washington in which he urged that legislators and newspaper editors be sent to Germany so they could tell the story to the British and American people.[59]

Redeployment to the Pacific was the main topic of conversation as Eisenhower, Bradley, and Patton talked far into the night on April 12. Patton's watch had stopped, so after his two friends had retired he listened to the radio to get a time signal. While waiting, he heard the news of President Roosevelt's death. He immediately awakened Bradley, and the two went to Eisenhower's room where they discussed the impact that the death of their President would have on the conduct of the war. They agreed that while they all felt a personal loss there would be no pause in their efforts to end the war in Europe promptly.[60]

Hitler, deep in the *Fuehrerbunker* under the garden of his Chancellory to which he had moved during an air attack, learned of Roosevelt's death by telephone from his propaganda chief, Josef Goebbels. Goebbels, who had been reading Thomas Carlyle's *History of Freidrich II of Prussia,* likened Roosevelt's demise to that of the Russian Czarina Elizabeth during the Seven Years War. Then, Prussia had fought alone against a coalition, but with the Czarina's death, Russia withdrew. The historical parallel, Goebbels felt, was obvious. Friday, April 13, would be the turning point of the war. After he had finished talking with Hitler, Goebbels ordered champagne for all present in the Ministry of Propaganda.[61]

For all of Goebbels' wishful thinking, there would be no turning back on the part of any of the Allies. The day after Roosevelt's death, Simpson's 83rd Infantry Division established a bridgehead across the Elbe,and held it. *(See Map 81, in Atlas.)* Simpson believed that with two days of preparation(to bring up supplies and ready airfields for tactical aircraft) he could drive on Berlin. On April 15, he proposed as much to Bradley, who then called Eisenhower. After Bradley explained the situation, he was heard to say, "All right, Ike, that's what I thought. I'll tell him." American troops were not to attack Berlin. The decision was Eisenhower's to make. His choice, as he explained in a message to Marshall on the day he denied Simpson's request, was to assume a defensive line along an easily identifiable terrain feature in the center while devoting his attention to reaching Lubeck in the north and taking care of the redoubt area in the south. This, in his opinion, was the best way to use the resources available to him. Bradley later wrote that as Berlin was at that time roughly between the American and Russian armies, an American force probably could have reached the city had Eisenhower decided to take the resulting casualties. Although the outcome of a race between the two armies will never be known, the Russians had had several months to prepare, while the Americans had just completed driving 250 miles in two weeks. In any case, numerous American casualties would have resulted, and the problems of controlling the converging armies within the urban area would have been enormous.[62]

As attention was riveted on the Elbe, the First Canadian Army was advancing to the north, and on April 16 it reached the North Sea. Conditions for the civilian population within the German-occupied portion of The Netherlands were steadily worsening. Because Montgomery felt that further attacks would only result in more suffering among the Dutch, many of whom were already reduced to eating tulip bulbs in order to survive, he recommended that offensive action cease. Eisenhower agreed. The German commander, however, refused to capitulate as long as an effective government existed in Germany; he did agree, if the Allies would halt their advance, to refrain from flooding more territory and to allow the entrance of food shipments. In early May, food began to be air-dropped and trucked into the area.[63]

Meanwhile, in the *Fuehrerbunker* on April 20, Hitler, now visibly sick, celebrated his 56th birthday. To all the high ranking leaders who came to wish him well, the *Fuehrer* proclaimed that the Russians would soon be defeated east of Berlin. When warned that all escape routes from the city would soon be severed, he stated that he would stay but that the others could leave. Many did.[64]

In the few remaining days of the war, the greatest Allied advances were made in the south. *(See Map 82, in Atlas.)* Patton had been directed to take over part of the Sixth Army Group front and drive down the Danube. He pushed his commanders hard and on May 4 captured Linz, Austria. Devers, meanwhile, was clearing out the area erroneously supposed to contain the redoubt. The French caused him as much trouble as the Germans, as the Allied squabbles were more in evidence with victory assured. De Gaulle wanted to be sure that France had an occupation zone and so instructed De Lattre, thereby causing the latter to disobey Devers' orders on at least two occasions. The seizure and occupation of Stuttgart led to one imbroglio, which ultimately involved Eisenhower and the new President, Harry Truman. De Lattre was also determined to reenact Napoleon's victorious entry into Ulm, and did so, blatantly disobeying Devers' orders and causing the army group commander to comment that "the act was that of an unbalanced man."[65]

To the north, the British made good progress, and patrols from the V Corps of First Army established contact with the Russians at Torgau on April 25. *(See Map 82.)* That same day, the Russians surrounded Berlin, thereby easing Stalin's concern that the Americans were trying to get there first.* Montgomery, reinforced by the XVIII Airborne Corps, crossed the Elbe and on May 2 reached the Baltic, just two hours before the Russians arrived. Although Montgomery's advance had cut off the German troops in Denmark and also denied the Russians access to that country, Eisenhower was uncertain concerning the German reaction. Should the forces of occupation

*See Chapter 6, p. 158.

choose to fight, he was prepared to launch an airborne attack across the Kiel Canal.[66]

Meanwhile, Russian artillery pounded the city of Berlin as Stalin's troops closed in. By April 30, Hitler realized that the end was near. He had prepared a will in which he named Grossadmiral Karl Doenitz as head of state and Supreme Commander of the Armed Forces. After saying farewell to members of his personal staff, he went to his suite in the bunker. With him was his long-time mistress and now wife of a few hours, Eva Braun. Eva bit on a cyanide capsule. Hitler shot himself. Their bodies were carried into the garden, doused with gasoline, and burned. It was more than 24 hours before the news was generally released, but when word reached German troops in the field, resistance virtually ceased.[67]

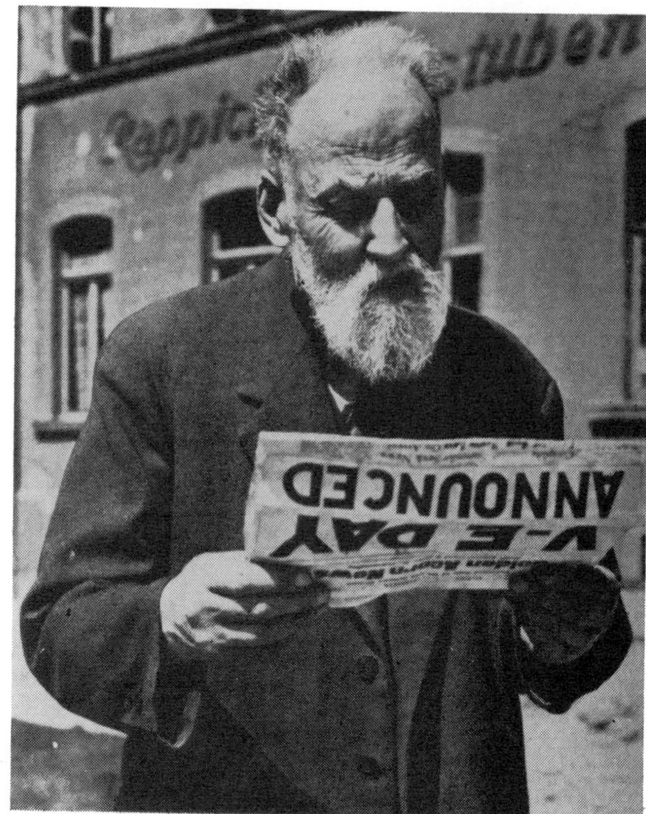

German Civilian Reads About the Surrender, May 1945

War's End

German troops in Italy surrendered on May 2, the same day that Berlin capitulated. On the following day, German emissaries arrived at Montgomery's headquarters and offered to surrender military forces, including two armies which were then fighting the Russians. Montgomery had received permission from Eisenhower to accept the surrender of those forces which were opposing him, but he could not take the surrender of entire units engaged on the Russian front. On the next day, the western Allies accepted the unconditional surrender of German troops in The Netherlands, northwest Germany, and Denmark; Montgomery accepted the surrender of the units opposing his forces. While units then fighting the Russians could not surrender, Montgomery said he would accept the surrender of individual soldiers. German troops, fearing the vengeance of their Russian conquerors, had been streaming through British and American lines for days. In the zone of Simpson's Ninth Army alone, almost 100,000 Germans entered American territory. Meanwhile, in the south, Army Group G surrendered unconditionally to Devers.[68]

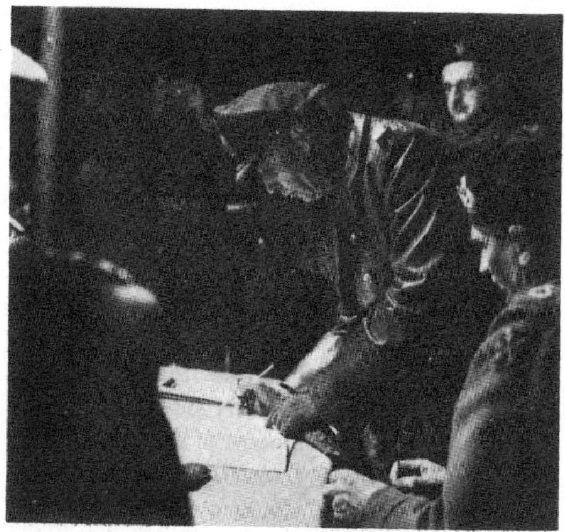

Montgomery Accepts the German Surrender at Lunebürg Heath, May 1945

Doenitz wanted to prolong the surrender procedure as long as possible in order to permit the maximum number of Germans to flee to the West. On May 5, his representative arrived at Eisenhower's headquarters in Reims. The Supreme Commander saw through the stalling tactics and demanded the unconditional surrender of all German forces left in the field. Doenitz's representative, Generaladmiral Hans Georg von Friedeburg, commander of the German Navy, said that such a surrender exceeded his authority, and asked Doenitz for further instructions. The next day, Generaloberst Alfred Jodl arrived. The fact that the German emissaries were still delaying was obvious. Eisenhower reacted by stating that if an agreement for unconditional surrender was not rapidly concluded, he would seal the western front and allow no further movement through western lines. Jodl telegraphed Doenitz and secured permission to surrender. Documents of capitulation were signed in Eisenhower's War Room at 2:41 A.M. May 7, 1945, with the surrender to be effective at 11:01 P.M. May 8.[69]

The war in Europe was over. After pictures had been taken and Eisenhower had made a short recording for newsreels and radio, members of his staff tried to compose a message to send to the Combined Chiefs of Staff. Eisenhower listened to a number of proposals, rejected all of them, and then dictated:[70] "The mission of this Allied force was fulfilled at 0241, local time, May 7, 1945."

A later announcement from both London and Washington designated May 8 as Victory in Europe (V-E) Day. After the Russians held a second surrender ceremony in Berlin late on the eighth, an announcement was issued in Moscow. Europe rejoiced. Headlights were turned on and blackout curtains were taken down. Fireworks filled the air. Soldiers could once more light cigarettes at night without worrying about sniper fire. There was many a wild celebration.[71]

But the end of the fighting did not mean a termination of the problems which faced Allied military leaders. German troops, many stationed outside their homeland, had to be disarmed and shipped home. Suspected war criminals, high ranking officers, Nazi party leaders, weapons technicians and scientists were detained for questioning. Displaced persons, released slave laborers, and former Allied prisoners of war had to be cared for and moved to the proper locations. In one camp alone, near Le Havre, as many as 47,000 released American prisoners were gathered. And at the same time that prisoners and displaced persons were being transported, units had to be redeployed for service in the Far East. All of these problems were very real to the senior leaders. Devers, for example, had for weeks been mentioning in letters to his wife his deep concern about how a war-shocked Europe, particularly a prostrate Germany, could be revived. The day he accepted the surrender of Army Group G, he wrote in his diary about his discouragement over the tremendous destruction and waste in Germany with which the occupiers would have to cope; he was discouraged over the problem the Allies faced with regard to feeding the people.[72]

While the initial aspects of these problems of movement and feeding were being dealt with by the appropriate authorities, a moving human drama was being played out before the front lines of the western Allies. After the surrender agreement became effective, British and American troops were told to turn back any Germans who attempted to enter their lines. Many soldiers killed their families and then committed suicide rather than surrender to the Russians.[73]

It was not until July 1 that American and British forces began to withdraw to their predetermined zones of occupation. *(See Map 83, in Atlas.)* There were some awkward moments in negotiations, but the representatives of the coalition members persevered, at least outwardly. At the same time, the sectors within the jointly administered cities of Berlin and Vienna were occupied. Unfortunately, the western Allies did not ensure control of surface communications between their zones and Berlin, a situation which would lead to later heartache. In those times of heady optimism, however, this did not seem partcularly significant. What mattered to most people was that victory had been achieved.[74]

With the signing of the surrender documents on May 7 and 8, the Allied countries achieved the unequivocal goal their leaders had set for their military forces—unconditional surrender of the German armed forces. The victory was costly in terms of lives and national treasury. As already noted, the toll in Russian lives and destruction was tremendous, far exceeding American and British costs. But in the West, the cost was also significant; between D-Day and V-E Day, Allied casualties in western Europe totaled 766,294, which included almost 200,000 dead. While the Germans lost three million dead during the entire war, their casualties in the West during the last year, excluding prisoners, were about the same, or a little higher, than those of the western Allies. Since 1945, some critics have contended that had the Allies not demanded unconditional surrender, the war might have ended sooner and with less cost. The argument has merit, particularly when considered within the framework of Clausewitz's dictum that war is an instrument of policy—policy which must be farseeing and recognize that the ultimate goal of war is a better peace. At the same time, the critic must not ignore the strong hold Hitler had over the German populace. Had he been killed, either by Allied bombing or by the Germans who conspired against him, a policy of less than unconditional surrender would have been entirely reasonable. But Hitler was not killed. To the last, his control over Germany was all-pervasive, and his determination to continue the war bordered on the fanatical. Whether an Allied overture offering alternatives could have swayed him, or weakened his control, must remain speculative.[75]

From the military viewpoint, the strategy which Eisenhower used to fight the campaign achieved a crushing and complete victory in the West in a little less than a year. Yet, as has been noted throughout this narrative, that strategy—indeed the entire Allied performance—has not been without its critics. In some respects, the historian is among them, for it is his task to recount and assess. The Allied victory in the West, not unlike other great victories, was attained by a force superior in numbers and resources. The leadership which guided the way to that victory was generally conservative and cautious; with the vast resources upon which it could call, there was no need to take great chances. In another respect, there was little likelihood that the war could be lost, once the lodgment in Normandy proved successful. From that time, the Germans were engaged in a two-front war which was beyond their capacity to win. It then became a question of how best to apply the resources to win in the shortest time and at least cost, honestly recognizing that the bulk of the *Wehrmacht* was being destroyed in the East. To some degree that cost depended upon how skillfully German leadership directed the defensive efforts of their forces. In any assessment of that consideration, one cannot avoid concluding that Hitler's influence was detrimental on the whole. In spite of this, the Germans fought well.

In the final analysis, Eisenhower headed what was perhaps the most successful coalition in history. There were Allied intelligence failures, and the degree to which ULTRA gave Eisenhower's forces an inestimable advantage still remains to be analyzed thoroughly. The fact is that, blessed with a common language and heritage and influenced by Eisenhower's continued emphasis on unity, the British and American forces worked admirably together to defeat a German foe which fought tenaciously to the end. Confident in the justice of the cause for which they fought, as Charles MacDonald, the official historian of the final offensive, notes:

> . . . few if any who fought in it could have entertained any doubts as to the right of their cause—they had seen at Buchenwald, Belsen, Dachau, and at a dozen other places, including little Ohrdruf, what awful tyranny man can practice on his fellow man. To erase those cruel monuments to evil was reason enough for it all, from bloody OMAHA Beach to that bridgehead to nowhere over the Elbe.[76]

Eisenhower's "Crusade in Europe" ended with the crushing of Hitlerite Germany. As had the Allied powers in 1815, so now too would the victorious Allies set about trying to construct a viable peace and bind up European wounds. The devastation was enormous, the toll in personal tragedy almost beyond comprehension. Thoughtful, compassionate, and great-hearted men and women, sharing a trust and common goal, would be taxed to the limit to rebuild the community of European nations. Unfortunately, the commonality of purpose and trust was shortlived. Driven together in the cauldron of war, the victorious Allied coalition began to disintegrate in the aftermath of peace. A new era dawned.

Notes

[1]Forrest C. Pogue, *George C. Marshall: Organizer of Victory* (New York, 1973), p. 507.

[2]*Ibid.*, pp. 508-512; Forrest C. Pogue, *The Supreme Command* (Washington, 1954), p. 413; Charles B. MacDonald, *The Last Offensive* (Washington, 1973), p. 5; Alfred D. Chandler (ed.), *The Papers of Dwight D. Eisenhower: The War Years* (Baltimore, 1970), IV: No. 2264, Conference Notes, January 28, 1944. The Eisenhower papers are hereinafter cited as *EP*.

[3]Pogue, *Organizer of Victory*,pp. 513-514, 516; *EP*,IV: No. 2268, Eisenhower to Walter Bedell Smith, January 31, 1945; No. 2284, Eisenhower to Alan Francis Brooke, February 16, 1945; Pogue, *Supreme Command*, pp. 413-414; Arthur W. Tedder, *With Prejudice: The War Memoirs of Marshal of the Royal Air Force Lord Tedder, G. C. B.* (Boston, 1966), pp. 663-664; Bernard Law Montgomery, *The Memoirs of Field Marshal The Viscount Montgomery of Alamein, K. G.* (Cleveland, 1958), p. 292; L.F. Ellis, *Victory in the West*, Volume II, *The Defeat of Germany* (London, 1968), pp. 209-213.

[4]Francis L. Lowenheim, Harold D. Langley, Manfred Jonas (eds.), *Roosevelt and Churchill: Their Secret Wartime Correspondence* (New York, 1975), p. 654; Pogue, *Organizer of Victory*, pp. 508-509, 540; *EP*, IV: No. 2242, Eisenhower to Marshall, January 15, 1945; Stephen E. Ambrose, *Eisenhower and Berlin, 1945: The Decision to Halt at the Elbe* (New York, 1967), p. 44.

[5]Winston S. Churchill, *Trumph and Tragedy* (Boston, 1953), p. 510; Lowenheim, *Roosevelt and Churchill*, p. 654.

[6]Charles B. MacDonald, *The Mighty Endeavor: American Armed Forces in the European Theater in World War II* (New York, 1969), pp. 414-416; Dwight D. Eisenhower, *Crusade in Europe* (Garden City, 1948); pp. 364, 375; *EP*, IV: No. 2270, Eisenhower to Montgomery and Bradley, February 1, 1945; Pogue, *Supreme Command*, p. 417.

[7]F. W. Winterbotham, *The Ultra Secret* (New York, 1974), p. 181; T. Dodson Stamps and Vincent J. Esposito (eds.), *A Military History of World War II* (2 vols., West Point, 1953), I, 554-555; *EP*, IV: No. 2268, Eisnhower to Smith, January 31, 1945; No. 2270, Eisenhower to Montgomery and Bradley, February 1, 1945.

[8]Stamps and Esposito, *Military History*, I, 549, 555-556; MacDonald, *Last Offensive*, pp. 18, 208, 298.

[9]Eisenhower, *Crusade in Europe*, p. 375; Stamps and Esposito, *Military History*, I, 558.

[10]Stamps and Esposito, *Military History*, I,. 556; Chester Wilmot, *The Struggle for Europe* (London, 1952), p. 671; Vincent J. Esposito (ed.), *The West Point Atlas of American Wars* (2 vols., New York, 1959), II, Section 2, 65.

[11]Stamps and Esposito, *Military History*, I, 557; Wilmot, *Struggle for Europe*, pp. 671-672; Esposito, *West Point Atlas*, II, Section 2, 65; Ellis, *Defeat of Germany*, pp. 256-263.

[12]Statement by General William H. Simpson, Personal Interview conducted by Thomas R. Stone, April 22, 1971.

[13]*Ibid.*

[14]Material for the above three paragraphs is drawn from: Thomas R. Stone, "1630 Comes Early on the Roer," *Military Review*, LIII (October 1973), 17-19; MacDonald, *Mighty Endeavor*, p. 419.

[15]Wilmot, *Struggle for Europe*, pp.672-673; Esposito, *West Point Atlas*, II, Section 2, 65.

[16]MacDonald, *Mighty Endeavor*, pp. 420-421; Stamps and Esposito, *Military History*, I, 560.

[17]MacDonald, *Mighty Endeavor*, pp. 421-422; MacDonald, *Last Offensive*, p. 162; Stamps and Esposito, *Military History*, I, 562.

[18]MacDonald, *Mighty Endeavor*, pp. 422-423. Stamps and Esposito, *Military History*, I, 562-563; *EP*, IV: No. 2302, Eisenhower to Marshall, February 27, 1945; MacDonald, *Last Offensive*, pp. 166-168, 171, 175, 183.

[19]MacDonald, *Mighty Endeavor*, p. 424.

[20]MacDonald, *Last Offensive*, pp. 177-178.

[21]MacDonald, *Mighty Endeavor*, p. 425; MacDonald, *Last Offensive*, p. 178.

[22]*Ibid.*; R. W. Thompson, *Montgomery the Field Marshal: The Campaign in North-West Europe, 1944-45* (New York, 1969), p. 285; Wilmot, *Struggle for Europe*, p. 677.

[23]Esposito, *West Point Atlas*, II, Section 2, 65; Stamps and Esposito, *Military History*, I, 565-567; Omar N. Bradley, *A Soldier's Story* (New York, 1951), p. 508; MacDonald, *Mighty Endeavor*, p. 426.

[24]MacDonald, *Mighty Endeavor*, pp. 427, 438.

[25]*Ibid.*, pp. 427-428.

[26]Material for the above six paragraphs on the Remagen operation is drawn from: MacDonald, *Mighty Endeavor*, pp. 428, 432-437; MacDonald, *Last Offensive*, pp. 216-217, 222, 229, 231-235; Esposito, *West Point Atlas*, II, Section 2, 65-66; *EP*, IV: No. 2319, Eisenhower to Combined Chiefs of Staff and British Chiefs of Staff, March 8, 1945; No. 2334, Eisenhower to Bradley, March 13, 1945; G. Patrick Murray, "Courtney Hodges: Modest Star of WW II," *American History Illustrated*, VII (January 1973), 22-24; Stamps and Esposito, *Military History*, I, 570-573.

[27]*EP*, IV: No. 2321, Eisenhower to Bradley and Devers, March 8, 1945; Esposito, *West Point Atlas*, II, Section 2, 66; MacDonald, *Last Offensive*, pp. 238-240.

[28]MacDonald, *Last Offensive*, p. 241.

[29]*Ibid.*, pp. 241-244, 246, 249; Stamps and Esposito, *Military History*, I, 384; Martin Blumenson (ed.), *The Patton Papers, 1940-1945* (Boston, 1974), p. 655 (Diary entry, March 14, 1945); MacDonald, *Mighty Endeavor*, pp. 438-441.

[30]Quotations are from Jacob L. Devers, "Diary, Commanding General Sixth Army Group," Devers Papers, Historical Society of York County, Pa., entry of March 17, 1945; *EP*, IV: No. 2348, Eisenhower to Devers, Bradley and Brereton, March 21, 1945; MacDonald, *Last Offensive*, pp. 257-258, 266.

[31]MacDonald, *Last Offensive*, pp. 259-264.

[32]*Ibid.*, pp. 264-265; Esposito, *West Point Atlas*, II, Section 2, 66.

[33]Esposito, *West Point Atlas*, II, Section 2, 68; Bradley, *Soldier's Story*, pp. 518-522; Winterbotham, *Ultra*, p. 185; MacDonald, *Mighty Endeavor*, pp.442-444, 449-450; MacDonald, *Last Offensive*, pp. 267-279, 285-289.

[34]Stamps and Esposito, *Military History*, I, 578-579, 581; Wilmot, *Struggle for Europe*, p. 660; Esposito, *West Point Atlas*, II, Section 2, 68.

[35]Hitler is quoted in Wilmot, *Struggle for Europe*, p.679.

[36]*Ibid.*, pp. 663, 679; Albert Speer, *Inside the Third Reich* (New York, 1971—paper edition), pp. 551-552; MacDonald, *Last Offensive*, p. 337.

[37]MacDonald, *Mighty Endeavor*, pp. 444-446; MacDonald, *Last Offensive*, p. 301; Stamps and Esposito, *Military History, I, 587.*

[38]*MacDonald, Mighty Endeavor*, p. 446; MacDonald, *Last Offensive*, 303; Eisenhower, *Crusade in Europe*, p. 389.

[39]MacDonald, *Mighty Endeavor*, p. 447; Stamps and Esposito, *Military History*, I, 591.

[40]Esposito, *West Point Atlas*, II, Section 2, 68; Stamps and Esposito, *Military History*, I, 589-590; MacDonald, *Last Offensive*, pp. 313-314, 318-319; MacDonald, *Mighty Endeavor*, p. 448.

[41]For accounts of Churchill's crossing of the Rhine see: Arthur Bryant, *Triumph in the West: Based on the Diaries of Field Marshal Lord Alanbrooke* (Garden City, N.Y., 1959), pp. 333-334; Statement by General William H. Simpson, Personal Interview conducted by Thomas R. Stone, January 27, 1972; Churchill, *Triumph and Tragedy*, pp. 415-417.

[42]Stamps and Esposito, *Military History*, I, 583-585; Bradley, *Soldier's Story*, pp. 524, 526; Esposito, *West Point Atlas*, II, Section 2, 68; *EP*, IV: No. 2355, Eisenhower to Marshall, March 26, 1945; MacDonald, *Last Offensive*, pp. 321-322.

[43]Peter Calvocoressi and Guy Wint, *Total War: The Story of World War II* (New York, 1972), pp. 464-482, provides a concise and fairly accurate summary of the campaign. The classical work on the British bomber offensive is Sir Charles Webster and Noble Frankland, *The Strategic Air Offensive Against Germany* (London, 1961). A recent, less favorable, one-volume work is Anthony Verrier, *The Bomber Offensive* (London, 1968). Sir Arthur Harris gives his version of things in *Bomber Offensive* (New York, 1947).

[44]Popular treatments of Ploesti include John Sweetman, *Ploesti Oil Strike* (New York, 1974) and James Deigan and Carroll Stewart, *Ploesti* (New York, 1962). A short scholarly treatment of the same subject is: Wesley Frank Craven and James Lea Cate, *The Army Air Forces in World War II*, Vol. II, *Europe: Torch to Pointblank* (Chicago, 1949), pp. 477-484. The authoritative work on the origins of U.S. theory is Robert Futrell, *Ideas, Concepts and Doctrine: A History of Basic Thinking in the United States Air Force, 1904-1964* (2 vols.; Aerospace Studies Institute, Air University, 1971). The most recent scholarly book on Mitchell is Alfred Hurley, *Billy Mitchell* (New York, 1964). William Mitchell's own works are *Skyways* (New York, 1930) and *Winged Defenses* (New York, 1925).

[45]Craven and Cate, *Torch to Pointblank*, Chap 21, is a good, scholarly version of Schweinfurt. The popular version is Martin Caidin, *Black Thursday* (New York, 1960).

[46]An excellent, concise treatment of the struggle for command of the air in early 1944 is William R. Emerson, *Operation Pointblank*, Harmond Memorial Lecture, USAF Academy, 1962.

[47]Franklin D'Olier (Chairman) *The United States Strategic Bombing Survey, Over-all Report* [European War] September 30, 1945, p. 6. This 109-page document was written by a group of scholars and military men partially to gain ideas for what was thought to be the coming assault against Japan and partially, one suspects, to sustain Henry Arnold in his argument for the coming struggle for an independent air force. The document should be required reading for any military historian or professional soldier no matter what his views on airpower. Many of the participants in the survey (e.g., George W. Ball, John K. Galbraith, Paul H. Nitze) are sufficiently prestigious as to command a hearing in their own right. The favorite line of the strategic bombing enthusiasts is on page 107: "The German experience suggests that even a first-class military power—rugged and resilient as Germany was—cannot live long under full-scale and free exploitation of air weapons over the heart of its territory." The survey also published *Summary Report: Pacific War*, 1946.

[48]At the time the Remagen Bridge was taken, Speer was preparing a memorandum for Hitler which stated that "the final collapse of the German economy" could be expected "with certainty" within four to eight weeks, and that afterward the war "could not be continued on the military plane." Albert Speer, *Inside the Third Reich* (New York, 1970), p. 436.

[49]Esposito, *West Point Atlas*, II, Section 2, 68; Stamps and Esposito, *Military History*, I, 597-598; *EP*, IV: No. 2354, Eisenhower to Devers, Bradley and Montgomery, March 25, 1945; No. 2364, Eisenhower to Montgomery, March 28, 1945.

[50]Stamps and Esposito, *Military History*, I, 597; Ellis, *Defeat of Germany*, pp. 297-300. Quotation is from Ellis, p. 298.

[51]Material for the above four paragraphs is drawn from: John Ehrman, *Grand Strategy*, Volume VI, *October 1944-August 1945* (London, 1956), pp. 133-134; MacDonald, *Mighty Endeavor*, pp. 466-467; Eisenhower, *Crusade in Europe*, pp. 396-398; Pogue, *Organizer of Victory*, pp. 539, 555, 574-575; Stamps and Esposito, *Military History*, I, 597; MacDonald, *Last Offensive*, p. 480; Bradley, *Soldier's Story*, pp. 536-537; Ambrose, *Eisenhower and Berlin*, p. 96; *EP*, IV: No. 2373, Eisenhower to Marshall, March 30, 1945; No. 2401, Eisenhower to Marshall, April 7, 1945; Esposito, *West Point Atlas*, II, Section 2, 70; Forrest C. Pogue, "The Decision to Halt at the Elbe," in Kent R. Greenfield (ed.), *Command Decisions* (Washington, 1960), p. 492; John S. D. Eisenhower, *The Bitter Woods* (New York 1969), p. 468.

[52]*EP*, IV: Nos. 2372 and 2373, Eisenhower to Marshall, both dated March 30, 1945; No. 2374, Eisenhower to Churchill, March 30, 1945 and editor's notes thereto; No. 2401, Eisenhower to Marshall, April 7, 1945; Pogue, *Organizer of Victory*, pp. 557-578; Ellis, *Defeat of Germany*, pp. 301-304.

[53]Material for the above two paragraphs is drawn from: Stamps and Esposito, *Military History*, I, 593-594; Esposito, *West Point Atlas*, II, Section 2, 69; Eisenhower, *Crusade in Europe*, p. 396; Letter, Sidney R. Hinds to I. D. White, July 27, 1967, Sidney R. Hinds Papers, U.S. Army Military History Research Collection, Carlisle Barracks, Pa.

[54]Stamps and Esposito, *Military History*, I, 533, 593-594; Eisenhower, *Crusade in Europe*, p. 396; MacDonald, *Mighty Endeavor*, p. 476.

[55]Esposito, *West Point Atlas*, II, Section 2, 69; Stamps and Esposito, *Military History*, I, 594-595.

[56]Esposito, *West Point Atlas*, II, Section 2, 69; MacDonald, *Mighty Endeavor*, p. 452, 454-457.

[57]MacDonald, *Mighty Endeavor*, pp. 472-474; Esposito, *West Point Atlas*, II, Section 2, 70.

[58]MacDonald, *Mighty Endeavor*, pp. 462-464, 480-481; Stamps and Esposito, *Military History*, I, 599-601; Esposito, *West Point Atlas*, II, Section 2, 70.

[59]Eisenhower, *Crusade in Europe*, pp. 407-409; MacDonald, *Mighty Endeavor*, pp. 477-478.

[60]Eisenhower, *Crusade in Europe*, p. 409; MacDonald, *Mighty Endeavor*, p. 484.

[61]Cornelius Ryan, *The Last Battle* (New York, 1966), pp. 259, 318-319; Wilmot, *Struggle for Europe*, pp. 698-699.

[62]Bradley's words are quoted in MacDonald, *Last Offensive*, p. 399; MacDonald, *Mighty Endeavor*, pp. 481-486; Ryan, *Last Battle*, pp. 314-317, 319-320; Bradley, *Soldier's Story*, p. 537; Ambrose, *Eisenhower and Berlin*, pp. 93-94; *EP*, IV: No. 2418, Eisenhower to Marshall, April 15, 1945.

[63]*EP*, IV: editor's notes with No. 2431, p. 2631; No. 2439, Eisenhower to Combined Chiefs of Staff, April 23, 1945; Eisenhower, *Crusade in Europe*, pp. 412, 416-417; MacDonald, *Mighty Endeavor*, p. 475.

[64]MacDonald, *Mighty Endeavor*, pp.503-504.

[65]Esposito, *West Point Atlas*, II, Section 2, 71; "Devers Diary," entries of April 27 and May 6, 1945; MacDonald, *Last Offensive*, pp. 427-433; *EP*, IV: No. 2457, Eisenhower to De Gaulle, April 28, 1945. Devers' quotation appears in his note placed on letter, De Lattre to Devers, April 24, 1945, Devers Papers, Historical Society of York County, Pa.

[66]MacDonald , *Mighty Endeavor*, pp. 493-496, 508; Esposito, *West Point Atlas*, II, Section 2, 70-71; Eisenhower, *Crusade in Europe*, p. 415.

[67]MacDonald, *Mighty Endeavor*, pp. 505-507; Ryan, *Last Battle*, pp. 497-498.

[68]Pogue, *Organizer of Victory*, p. 582; Stamps and Esposito, *Military History*, I, 606; *EP*, IV: No. 2474, Eisenhower to British Chiefs of Staff and Combined Chiefs of Staff, May 3, 1945; MacDonald, *Mighty Endeavor*, pp. 508-510.

[69]MacDonald, *Mighty Endeavor*, pp. 510-511; MacDonald, *Last Offensive*, p. 475; Pogue, *Organizer of Victory*, pp. 582, 583.

[70]Message is in *EP*, IV: No. 2499, Eisenhower to Combined Chiefs of Staff and British Chiefs of Staff, May 7, 1945; editor's note with No. 2498, p. 2696.

[71]MacDonald, *Mighty Endeavor*, pp. 511-512.

[72]*Ibid.*, p. 512; Eisenhower, *Crusade in Europe*, p. 420; Esposito, *West Point Atlas*, II, Section 2, 72; "Devers Diary," entry of May 5, 1945.

[73]MacDonald, *Mighty Endeavor*, p. 512.

[74]Esposito, *West Point Atlas*, II, Section 2, 72.

[75]MacDonald *Last Offensive*, pp. 478, 481; George A. Lincoln, "Commentary," in Monte D. Wright and Lawrence J. Paszek (eds.), *Soldiers and Statesmen: The Proceedings of the 4th Military History Symposium United States Air Force Academy, 22-23 October, 1970* (Washington, 1973), p. 117.

[76]MacDonald, *Last Offensive*, p. 481.

Selected Bibliography

General

Baldwin, Ralph B. *The Deadly Fuze: Secret Weapon of World War II*. San Rafael, California, 1979. Science at war.

Brown, Anthony Cave. *Bodyguard of Lies*. New York, 1975. Popular work on Allied counterintelligence, deception plans, and the application of special intelligence (especially ULTRA) to the Allied war effort. Not admired by the official historians who are preparing their documented versions.

Carsten, Francis L. *The Reichswehr and Politics, 1919–1933*. Oxford, 1966. Comprehensive study of civil-military relations in Germany and the development of the Army from the end of World War I until the advent of Hitler.

Cecil, Robert. *Hitler's Decision to Invade Russia*. London, 1975. A small book, but one done with scholarly attention to detail. Authoritative.

Churchill, Winston. *The Second World War*. 6 vols. Boston, 1953. Detailed history of World War II. At times self-serving, but provides insights into strategic planning and compromise.

Colby, Benjamin. *'Twas a Famous Victory*. New Rochelle, New York, 1974. A thoroughly bad-tempered, but uncomfortably accurate restudy of Allied propaganda, foreign and domestic, in World War II.

Craig, Gordon A. *The Politics of the Prussian Army, 1640–1945*. New York, 1970. Standard work on the role of the German Army in German society. Gives excellent analysis of interwar transformation of the Army and officer corps, along with detailed discussion of the political relationship between Hitler and the High Command.

Cruickshank, Charles. *Deception in World War II*. Oxford, 1979. Scholarly, well-documented.

Deakin, F. W. *The Brutal Friendship: Mussolini, Hitler and the Fall of Italian Fascism*. New York, 1962.

Deane, John R. *The Strange Alliance: The Story of Our Efforts at Wartime Cooperation with Russia*. New York, 1947. A blunt tale of lend-lease aid to Russia, told by a frustrated American who played a major role.

De Gaulle, Charles. *The Army of the Future*. Philadelphia, 1941. Originally published in 1934, this book advances De Gaulle's doctrinal and organizational proposals for the French Army in order to transform it into a compact, professional force capable of waging a *blitzkrieg*-style war.

Deutsch, Harold C. *Hitler and His Generals*. Minneapolis, 1974. Thorough analysis of the German Army, the Blomberg-Fritsch affairs, and the root of the anti-Hitler military conspiracy.

Feis, Herbert. *Churchill, Roosevelt, Stalin*. Princeton, 1957. The story of the Allied coalition, the ideas and purposes which motivated its members, its successes, and its ultimate collapse.

Gordon, Don E. *Electronic Warfare*. New York, 1981. Science at war.

Greenfield, Kent Roberts. *American Strategy in World War II: A Reconsideration*. Baltimore, 1963. Collection of short lectures concerning American and British strategy, coalition warfare, airpower, and Franklin D. Roosevelt's role as Commander-in-Chief.

———. (ed.). *Command Decisions*. Washington, 1960. Excellent sampler of critical United States decisions made during the war.

Harriman, W. Averell and Elie Abel. *Special Envoy to Churchill and Stalin, 1941–1946*. An outstanding history of the dirty work at the crossroads of Allied diplomacy.

Herring, George C. *Aid to Russia 1941–1946: Strategy, Diplomacy, and the Origins of the Cold War*. New York, 1973. Covers lend-lease aid to USSR, both in its military and political aspects.

Hickey, Michael. *Out of the Sky: A History of Airborne Warfare*. New York, 1979. The story of all aspects of airborne operations, from their beginnings to the present.

Hoffmann, Peter. *The History of the German Resistance*. Trans. Richard Barry. Cambridge, Massachusetts, 1977. A massive book which traces the story of the opposition to Hitler. Detailed, difficult to read, but authoritative.

Hogg, Ian V. *British and American Artillery of World War 2*. London, 1978. Complete and detailed.

Hunnicutt, E. P. *Sherman: A History of the American Medium Tank*. Belmont, California, 1978. Lavishly illustrated and detailed history of the development of American World War II medium tanks and other armored combat vehicles.

Huston, James A. *The Sinews of War: Army Logistics 1775–1953*. Washington, 1966. Part IV covers World War II. Emphasis is on lend-lease, industrial mobilization, and transportation of supplies. A U.S. Army official history.

Jacobsen, Jans and Jurgen Rohwer (eds.). *Decisive Battles of World War II: The German View*. London, 1965. Analysis by German scholars of critical battles of the war.

Kenneth, Lee. *A History of Strategic Bombing*. New York, 1982. A recent, somewhat revisionist work.

Klein, Burton H. *Germany's Economic Preparations for War*. Cambridge, 1959. Offers detailed analysis of Germany's economic status prior to the outbreak of war in 1939.

Langer, William L. and S. Everett Gleason. *The Undeclared War, 1940–1941*. New York, 1953. A well-written account of how the U.S. gradually found itself at war. Though highly sympathetic to President Roosevelt's aims, it does not conceal the various maneuvers by which he involved the United States in an undeclared shooting war in the Atlantic months before Pearl Harbor.

Lewin, Ronald. *Ultra Goes to War*. New York, 1978. First story of ULTRA that is based on British wartime documents.

Michel, Henri. *The Second World War*. Trans. Douglas Parmee. New York, 1975. One of the best single-volume summaries of the war.

———. *The Shadow War*. Trans. Richard Barry. New York, 1972. A thoughtful account of the development of resistance movements in Europe from 1939–1945.

Morison, Samuel E. *Strategy and Compromise*. Boston, 1958. Part I deals with the European war and emphasizes problems of developing strategy in a coalition war.

Murphy, Robert. *Diplomat Among Warriors*. New York, 1964. Murphy was the State Department representative with the American forces in Europe.

O'Donnell, James P. *The Bunker: The History of the Reich Chancellory Group*. Boston, 1978. An excellent presentation of the last days of Hitler.

Parkinson, Roger. *A Day's March Nearer Home: The War History from Alamein to VE Day Based on the War Cabinet Papers of 1942 to 1945*. New York, 1974. Excellent source of material on British high-level decisions.

Scheibert, von Horst, and Ulrich Elfrath. *Panzer in Russland*. Dorheim, 1971. A splendidly illustrated history of German/Russian armored warfare, from 1941 to 1944. The text is in both German and English.

Shirer, William L. *The Rise and Fall of the Third Reich: A History of Nazi Germany*. New York, 1960. Classic history of Nazi Germany. Chapters 17 to 31 cover wartime Germany.

Smith, Gaddis. *American Diplomacy During the Second World War, 1941–1945*. New York, 1967. Short but excellent summary of American wartime diplomacy.

Speer, Albert. *Inside the Third Reich*. New York, 1971. Prejudiced but enlightening view of German wartime governmental operations.

Tolstoy, Nikolai. *The Secret Betrayal, 1944–1947*. New York, 1977. The grim, secret aftermath of Allied victory—the forcible return of millions of eastern Europeans to Soviet captivity.

Wilmot, Chester. *The Struggle for Europe*. London, 1952. Emphasis on planning and conduct of Normandy invasion. British perspective. Lots of detail and some bias.

Winterbotham, F. W. *The Ultra Secret*. New York, 1974. The first of several books published in the last decade which deal with ULTRA. Primarily autobiographical in nature, it provides general background and some campaign detail. Based on the suthor's recollections from his wartime work with the intelligence community.

Wouk, Herman. *War and Remembrance*. Boston, 1978. Wouk's fictional account of the war from 1941 to 1945.

———. *The Winds of War*. Boston, 1971. Fictional account of World War II through December 1941. Very readable.

Wright, Gordon. *The Ordeal of Total War, 1939–1945*. New York, 1968. Synthesis of economic, psychological, scientific, diplomatic, and military elements of the war.

Battles and Campaigns

Ambrose, Stephen E. *Eisenhower and Berlin, 1945: The Decision to Halt at the Elbe*. New York, 1967. Short analysis of the decision to halt at the Elbe. Designed to refute revisionist charges that Eisenhower is solely responsible for the postwar division of Germany.

Ansel, Walter. *Hitler and the Middle Sea*. Durham, North Carolina, 1972. An analysis of the place of the Mediterranean in the formulation of German strategy.

Armstrong, John A. (ed.). *Soviet Partisans in World War II*. Madison, 1964. Study based on case histories which emphasizes the political and psychological value of Soviet partisans.

Baldwin, Hanson, *Battles Lost and Won*. New York, 1966. Case studies of several major battles in the European and Pacific theaters. Baldwin' style is crisp and his analysis forthright.

Baumbach, Werner. *The Life and Death of the Luftwaffe*. New York, 1960. A good general history of the German Air Force.

Bekker, Cajus. *The Luftwaffe War Diaries*. Garden City, 1968. A mostly-operational history of the German Air Force.

Bennett, Ralph. *Ultra in the West: The Normandy Campaign 1944–45*. London, 1980. Written by a Cambridge historian and wartime participant in the ULTRA experience, this book cites official ULTRA intercepts and examines the 1944–1945 campaigns in a new and careful light. Very useful and readable.

Blau, George E. *The German Campaign in Russia: Planning and Operations, 1940–1941*. Washington, 1955. Study by U.S. Army official historian of German preparation and conduct of BARBAROSSA. Focuses almost exclusively on German sources and issues.

———. *The German Campaign in the Balkans*. Washington, 1953. A U.S. Army official operational history with good maps and order-of-battle information. Based on German sources.

Blumenson, Martin. *Anzio: The Gamble That Failed*. New York, 1963. Thorough account of the Allied attempt to envelop the German line of defense in Italy by amphibious assault.

———. *Breakout and Pursuit*. Washington, 1961. Allied breakout operations from the Normandy lodgment area (July–September 1944). The U.S. Army official history.

———. *Kasserine Pass*. Cambridge, 1967. The most accurate and readable book devoted solely to the American defeat in North Africa.

———. *Salerno to Cassino*. Washington, 1969. A U.S. Army official history which covers American participation in the war in Italy with excellent insight and analysis.

Caidin, Martin. *The Tigers are Burning*. New York, 1974. Account of Battle of Kursk told principally from the Soviet viewpoint.

Carse, Robert A. *A Cold Corner of Hell: The Story of the Murmansk Convoys, 1941–1945*. New York, 1969. Realistic portrayal of an important logistical link.

Chew, Allen F. *The White Death: The Epic of the Soviet-Finnish Winter War*. Lansing, 1971. Thorough book, slightly pro-Finnish, detailing the Winter War and Finland's subsequent alignment with Germany in 1941.

Chuikov, Vasili. *The Battle for Stalingrad*. New York, 1964. Good personal insights into the conduct of the battle for Stalingrad. Propagandic-heroic style not as onerous here as in some other Soviet works.

———. *The Fall of Berlin*. New York, 1968. These memoirs of the commander of the 8th Guards Army during the Soviet drive on

Berlin are surprisingly frank, even occasionally critical of Soviet strategy.

Coakley, Robert W. and Richard M. Leighton. *Global Logistics and Strategy*, 1943–1945. Washington, 1968. Examination of the effects of logistical constraints on Allied strategy. Another of the U.S. Army official histories.

Cole, Hugh M. *The Ardennes: Battle of the Bulge*. Washington, 1965. The U.S. Army official history. Accurate and detailed.

Collier, Basil. *The Battle of Britain*. New York, 1962. Scholarly and through account of Battle of Britain by the author of the British official history.

———. *Defence of the United Kingdom*. London, 1957. A British official history which constitutes the leading authoritative source on the British side of air defense in World War II.

Craig, William. *Enemy at the Gates: The Battle for Stalingrad*. New York, 1973. A somewhat popularized account of the Battle of Stalingrad, told largely through personal accounts by participants on both sides.

Craven, Wesley Frank and James Lee Cate (eds.). *The Army Air Forces in World War II*, Vol. III, *Europe: Argument to V-E Day, January 1944 to May 1945*. Chicago, 1951. U.S. Air Force official history.

D-Day: The Normandy Invasion in Retrospect. Lawrence, Kansas, 1971. Collection of excellent retrospective articles by experts in the field. Published by the Eisenhower Presidential Library.

Djilas, Milovan. *Wartime*. New York, 1977. The story of the Communist-directed resistance movement in Yugoslavia, by one of Tito's close associates.

Ehrmann, John. *Grand Strategy*. Vols. V and VI. London, 1956. British official history of strategic planning during World War II, from 1943 to 1945.

Eisenhower, John S. D. *The Bitter Woods*. New York, 1969. Written by the Supreme Commander's son and conceived as a study of the high command relationships, this book provides a detailed examination of the "Battle of the Bulge" at all levels. Well-written and documented; useful, but not many new insights.

Ellis, Lionel F. *Victory in the West*. 2 vols. London, 1968. British official history of operations in western Europe from 1944 to 1945.

———. *The War in France and Flanders, 1939-40*. London, 1953. Standard operational account of the German victory in France, told by a British official historian.

Erickson, John. *The Road to Stalingrad*. New York, 1975. Probably the best available English-language source on Soviet operations from 1941 to 1942.

Esposito, Vincent J. (ed.). *The West Point Atlas of American Wars*. 2 vols. New York, 1959. Outstanding operational history and maps of campaigns. The European war appears in Volume II.

Esseme, H. *The Battle for Germany*. New York, 1969. The British side of the campaigns in northwest Europe, 1944–1945, presented by an infantry brigadier who admired good soldiers of any nation.

Fisher, Ernest F. *Cassino to the Alps*. Washington, 1977. The final volume in the U.S. Army official history of the war in Italy.

Fleming, Peter. *Operation Sea Lion*. New York, 1957. Standard popular account of the German plans and preparations for a cross-Channel attack on Great Britain in 1940.

Foertsch, Hermann. *The Army of Modern War*. New York, 1940. An excellent summary of the theories of warfare held by the German Army on the eve of World War II. Written by a German General Staff officer.

Frankland, Noble. *The Bombing Offensive Against Germany*. London, 1961. Good account of RAF night-bombing offensive against Germany.

Friedin, Seymour. *The Fatal Decisions*. New York, 1956. Analysis of German strategy in World War II, based on interviews with former German officers.

Frost, John. *A Drop Too Many*. London, 1980. A British airborne officer describes his service in North Africa, Sicily, and northwest Europe. His critique of the Arnhem operation is acute.

Goure, Leon. *The Siege of Leningrad*. Stanford, 1962. A detailed, factual account of the 900-day investment of the Soviet second city. Also available as a McGraw Hill paperback.

Goutard, Colonel A. *The Battle of France, 1940*. Trans. Captain A. R. P. Burgess. London, 1958. An enlightened account of the fall of France by a French soldier and participant.

The Great Patriotic War of the Soviet Union, 1941-45. Moscow, 1974. A one-volume condensation of the longer official Soviet history. While its propagandic-heroic style and statistical distortions weaken its scholarship, this work contains much detail in regard to Soviet order-of-battle and personalities not readily available elsewhere.

Harrison, Gordon A. *Cross-Channel Attack*. Washington, 1951. The U.S. Army official history of the planning for and conduct of the Normandy invasion.

Hechler, Ken. *The Bridge at Remagen*. New York, 1957. A splendid retelling of one of World War II's most dramatic actions.

Horne, Alistair. *To Lose a Battle: France, 1940*. Boston, 1969. Thorough discussion of French strategic, economic, political, and social weaknesses contributing to the 1940 military defeat. Includes detailed account of military operations in France, May-June 1940.

Howarth, David. *We Die Alone*. London, 1957. Commando operations in Norway.

Howe, George F. *Northwest Africa: Seizing the Initiative in the West*. Washington, 1957. The U.S. Army official history of American participation in the North African campaign.

Huston, James A. *Out of the Blue: U.S. Army Airborne Operations in World War II*. West Lafayette, Indiana, 1972. A concise, impartial review.

Infield, Glenn B. *The Poltava Affair*. New York, 1973. The carefully researched explanation of an odd episode in American-Russian wartime relations, involving one of the worst defeats the U.S. Army Air Force suffered.

Jackson, W. F. G. *The Battle for Italy*. New York, 1967. Perhaps the best single-volume survey of the Sicilian and Italian campaigns.

———. *The Battle for North Africa*. New York, 1975. One of the better campaign histories. British viewpoint, but generally impartial.

Kennedy, Robert M. *The German Campaign in Poland, 1939*. Washington, 1956. Although based primarily on German sources, this is the best available English-language account of the German invasion of Poland.

Killen, John. *A History of the Luftwaffe*. Garden City, 1964. A handy summary of the history of the *Luftwaffe*. Basically sound, easy to ready, and available in paperback.

Leach, Barry A. *German Strategy Against Russia, 1939–1941*. Oxford, England, 1973. Best single source on origins of the BARBAROSSA Plan and the constraints imposed on German operations by logistical limitations.

Lee, Ulysses. *The Employment of Negro Troops*. Washington, 1966. Focuses on development of Army policies on the use of blacks and the problems these policies caused at home and abroad. A U.S. Army official history.

Leighton, Richard M. and Robert W. Coakley. *Global Logistics and Strategy, 1940–1943*. Washington, 1955. Detailed examination of the effect of logistics on world-wide strategy. Another U.S. Army official history.

Lord, Walter. *The Miracle at Dunkirk*. New York, 1983. A fresh, well-researched look at the evacuation of the British Army.

Lucas, James and James Barker. *The Battle of Normandy: The Falaise Gap*. New York, 1978. A new, somewhat critical analysis of a pivotal battle.

MacDonald, Charles B. *The Mighty Endeavor: American Armed Forces in the European Theater in World War II*. New York, 1969. A well-written, accurate, and popular account by one of the Army's official historians. Particularly fine in its treatment of the campaigns in France and Germany.

———. *The Last Offensive*. Washington, 1973. The U.S. Army official history of Allied offensives, January–May 1945.

MacIntyre, Donald. *The Naval War Against Hitler*. New York, 1971. Good general history of the war at sea in the Atlantic and Mediterranean.

Majdalamy, Fred. *The Battle of Cassino*. Boston, 1957. One of the finest battle studies of World War II.

———. *The Fall of Fortress Europe*. London, 1968. A rousing yet studious account of Hitler's accelerating downfall from November 1941 to August 1944.

Mason, Francis K. *Battle Over Britain*. New York, 1970. A commemorative volume which contains a host of fascinating details on the day-to-day events during the Battle of Britain.

Matloff, Maurice and Edwin M. Snell. *Strategic Planning for Coalition Warfare, 1941–1942*. Washington, 1953. Balanced examination of problems in developing Allied and American strategy. Another of the U.S. Army official histories.

———. *Strategic Planning for Coalition Warfare, 1943–1944*. Washington, 1959. Extends analysis of earlier volume (on 1941–1942). Another U.S. Army official history.

Meretskov, K. A. *Serving the People*. Trans. David Fidlon. Moscow, 1971. Meretskov spent most of the war on the Finnish front, without distinction until late 1944. Mendacious and strictly according to the party line; but the best Russian source for those operations.

Mitchell, Donald W. *A History of Russian and Soviet Sea Power*. New York, 1974. Invaluable coverage of Russian naval operations through World War II and Murmansk lend-lease convoy operations.

Morison, Samuel E. *The Battle of the Atlantic, September 1939–May 1943*. Boston, 1948. Authoritative account of American naval operations in the Atlantic from 1939 to 1943.

———. *Sicily-Salerno-Anzio*. Boston, 1964. Good general reference on these amphibious operations by an eminent scholar of the naval history of World War II.

Parotkin, Ivan. *The Battle of Kursk*. Moscow, 1974. Russian analysis of the greatest tank battle in World War II. Propagandistic, but useful.

Petrow, Richard, *The Bitter Years*. New York, 1974. Thorough discussion of German invasion and occupation of Denmark and Norway. Contains useful information on various underground movements, OSS and British Commando operations, and the role of the Scandinavian governments-in-exile in Allied strategy. Actual extent of underground activities is probably exaggerated.

Piekalkiewicz, Janusz. *Arnhem, 1944*. New York, 1976. An expertly illustrated account of the last major German victory of World War II.

Playfair, I. S. O., et. al. *The Mediterranean and Middle East*. 4 vols. London, 1954, 1956, 1960, 1966. Thorough British official history of the war in the African and Mediterranean theaters.

Pogue, Forrest C. *The Supreme Command*. Washington, 1953. The U.S. Army official history of SHAEF from 1944 to 1945. Excellent on coverage of strategic decisions.

Richards, Denis and Hilary St. George Saunders. *The Royal Air Force, 1939–1945*. 3 vols. London, 1953-54. British official history.

Roskill, S. W. *The War at Sea*. 3 vols. London, 1954. The British official history of the war at sea during World War II.

Ruppenthal, Roland G. *Logistical Support of Armies*. 2 vols. Washington, 1953. Relates logistics to tactical plans and operations in Normandy and the drive across western Europe. A U.S. Army official history.

Ryan, Cornelius. *A Bridge Too Far*. New York, 1974. Highly personalized popular account of the MARKET-GARDEN operation.

———. *The Last Battle*. New York, 1966. Good account of German, Soviet, and Anglo-American plans and operations leading to the capture of Berlin. Despite heavy emphasis on personal narrative, provides useful operational discussion.

———. *The Longest Day: June 6, 1944*. New York, 1959. Ryan's popularized account of D-Day.

Salisbury, Harrison E. *The 900 Days: The Siege of Leningrad*. New York, 1969. A detailed story of the epic World War II siege, based largely on eye-witness accounts. Interestingly told, but drags somewhat.

Schroeter, Heinz. *Stalingrad*. Trans. Constantine Fitzgibbon. New York, 1958. Account of the battle for Stalingrad and the destruction of the German Sixth Army. Viewpoint mostly German.

Seaton, Albert. *The Battle for Moscow, 1941–1942*. London, 1971. Balanced, thorough account of the unsuccessful German attack on Moscow and the Soviet counteroffensives in 1941 and 1942.

———. *The Russo-German War, 1941–1945*. New York, 1971. Best English-language history of the Eastern Front during World War II. Massive and full of detail.

Shtemenko, S. M. *The Last Six Months*. Trans. Guy Daniels. New York, 1977. Despite political dogmatism, thorough and frank operational discussion of concluding Soviet drives against Germany.

Stacy, G. P. *Official History of the Canadian Army in the Second World War:* III, *The Victory Campaign: The Operations in North-West Europe, 1944–1945*. Ottawa, 1960. Presents the Canadian viewpoint.

Stein, George H. *The Waffen SS, 1939–1945*. Ithaca, New York, 1966. Scholarly treatment of the origin, organization, ideology, and recruiting of German SS combat units.

Steward, Ian McDougall. *The Struggle for Crete, 20 May–June 1941*. Oxford, England, 1966. The best general account of the German attack on Crete.

Sweet, John T. *Mounting the Threat: The Battle of Bourquebus Ridge*. San Rafael, California, 1978. Montgomery's great battle north of Caen.

Townsend, Peter. *Duel of Eagles*. New York, 1971. Despite being written by a participant, this work is fair-minded and reflects extensive scholarly research. Perhaps the best general account of the Battle of Britain.

Treadwell, Mattie E. *The Women's Army Corps*. Washington, 1954.

U.S. Army official history of the Women's Army Corps in World War II.

Turney, Alfred. *Disaster at Moscow*. London, 1971. Analysis of Field Marshal Fedor von Bock's offensive to capture Moscow in 1941.

Werth, Alexander. *Russia at War, 1941–1945*. London, 1964. Based on journalist's firsthand observations of Soviet wartime activities.

Whaley, Barton. *Codeword Barbarossa*. Boston, 1973. Analysis of intelligence indicators available to Soviets prior to German attack in June, 1941.

Ziemke, Earl F. *The German Northern Theater of Operations, 1940–1945*. Washington, 1959. A U.S. Army study of German operations in Finland and Norway during World War II.

———. *Stalingrad to Berlin*. Washington, 1968. U.S. Army official history of Russian victory in the East. Relies largely on German sources, but strives for impartiality.

Personalities

Alexander, Harold R. L. G. *The Alexander Memoirs, 1940–1945*. Ed. by John North. New York, 1961. Memoirs of British general concerning the Mediterranean theater from 1942 to 1945. He was the theater commander for the last two years of the war. Includes his opinion of controversial American and British generals.

Arnold, Henry. *Global Mission*. New York, 1949. Memoirs of U.S. Army Air Force Chief of Staff.

Barnett, Corelli. *The Desert Generals*. London, 1964. This study of the North African campaign covers only British figures. Very unflattering in its treatment of Montgomery. A revised, enlarged edition appeared in 1982.

Bialer, Seweryn (ed.). *Stalin and his Generals: Soviet Military Memoirs of World War II*. New York, 1969. Excellent compilation of Soviet memoir material, including many less well-known military figures.

Blumenson, Martin. *The Patton Papers*. 2 vols. Boston, 1974. Gives excellent insights into Patton's thinking during World War II.

Blumentritt, Guenther. *Von Rundstedt: The Soldier and the Man*. London, 1952. Biography of Rundstedt by his Chief of Staff.

Bradley, Omar. *A Soldier's Story*. New York, 1951. Bradley's folksy account of campaigns in Europe and the Mediterranean.

Bradley, Omar N., and Clay Blair. *A General's Life*. New York, 1983. An egocentric book, full of bitterness toward other—and possibly abler—generals, now dead. Covers a long reach of American military history.

Bryant, Arthur. *Triumph in the West: Based on the Diaries of Field Marshal Lord Alanbrooke*. Garden City, New York, 1959. The somewhat biased account by the British Army Chief of Staff of the last two years of the war.

Buell, Thomas B. *Master of Sea Power: A Biography of Fleet Admiral Ernest J. King*. Boston, 1980. The most recent study of the American wartime Chief of Naval Operations.

Burns, James MacGregor. *Roosevelt, The Soldier of Freedom*. New York, 1970. Balanced biography of Roosevelt as a wartime leader.

Butcher, Harry C. *My Three Years with Eisenhower*. New York, 1946. Wartime diary of Eisenhower's aide.

Chandler, Alfred D. (ed.). *The Papers of Dwight D. Eisenhower: The War Years*. 5 vols. Baltimore, 1970. Reprint of Eisenhower's personal papers and official messages.

Collins, J. Lawton. *Lightning Joe: An Autobiography*. Baton Rouge, Louisiana, 1979. Memoirs of American wartime division and corps commander—later Army Chief of Staff. Informative and direct.

Cunningham, Andrew Browne. *A Sailor's Odyssey*. London, 1951. Memoirs of the British Mediterranean Fleet commander. Rich in color and operational details.

De Gaulle, Charles. *The War Memoirs of Charles de Gaulle*. Trans. Richard Howard. 3 vols. New York, 1958–1960. Presents the French viewpoint.

De Guingand, Sir Francis W. *Operation VICTORY*. London, 1947. Memoirs of Montgomery's Chief of Staff.

De Lattre de Tassigny, Marshal Jean. *The History of the French First Army*. Trans. Malcolm Barnes. London, 1952. The story of the French contribution to the invasion and liberation of southern France. De Lattre, the French First Army commander, was a gallant and capable soldier, but frequently a major trial to his allies.

Eisenhower, Dwight D. *Crusade in Europe*. New York, 1948. Eisenhower's description of the problems of planning and executing coalition warfare.

Esseme H. *Patton: A Study in Command*. New York, 1974. An excellent biography, written by a British combat veteran.

Fest, Joachim C. *Hitler*. New York, 1973. The best biography of Hitler. Parts VI-VIII cover his preparation and conduct of the war.

Fraser, David. *Alanbrooke*. London, 1982. An authoritative biography, which also describes the "machinery of government by which the war was waged."

Galland, Adolf. *The First and the Last*. New York, 1954. Memoirs by the chief of the *Luftwaffe* fighter group.

Gavin, James M. *On to Berlin: Battles of an Airborne Commander, 1943–1946*. New York, 1978. Memoirs of one of America's two most experienced high-level airborne commanders in World War II. Useful, but opinionated.

Guderian, Heinz. *Panzer Leader*. Trans. Constantine Fitzgibbon. New York, 1952. Valuable, if personalized, account of the creation of the German armored force and its use during the various campaigns in which the author participated. Treatment of the campaign in Poland provides interesting insights into early German command flexibility and doctrinal flaws.

Hamilton, Nigel. *Monty: The Making of a General*. New York, 1981. An exhaustive study of Montgomery's development as a commander. It does not make him lovable, but it does bring out his tough competence.

Horrocks, Brian. *Corps Commander*. New York, 1978. Memoirs of a distinguished British commander. Thoroughly honest and blunt. Very useful.

———. *Escape to Action*. New York, 1961. Memoirs of British XXX Corps commander.

Irving, David. *The Trail of the Fox*. New York, 1977. The story of Erwin Rommel, with emphasis on the campaigns in North Africa. Readable and detailed, but without specific documentation.

Jackson, W. G. F. *Alexander of Tunis as a Military Commander*. New York, 1971. An excellent biography of an Anglo-Irish aristocrat-at-arms who could lead troops of all nations.

Kesselring, Albert. *A Soldier's Story*. New York, 1954. Though occasionally presenting elements of self-justification, this work covers the career of the *Luftwaffe* Field Marshal who participated in early air campaigns (Battle of Britain) and later commanded German forces in Italy.

Lee, Asher. *Goering: Air Leader*. New York, 1972. Superb account of the chief of the *Luftwaffe*.

Lewin, Ronald. *Rommel as Military Commander*. London, 1968. An authoritative and readable account of Germany's most publicized general.

Lowenheim, Francis L., Harold D. Langley and Manfred Jones (eds.). *Roosevelt and Churchill: Their Secret Wartime Correspondence*. New York, 1975. Reprint of recently declassified documents.

Liddell Hart, Sir Basil H. *The Other Side of the Hill*. London, 1948. Compilation based on Liddell Hart's postwar interviews with various German officers. Published in the United States in abridged form under the title, *The German Generals Talk*.

———. (ed.). *The Rommel Papers*. New York, 1953. Rommel's highly accurate appraisal of the lessons of his campaigns.

MacDonald, Charles B. *Company Commander*. Washington, 1947. An American infantry company commander's story. Captures the atmosphere of battle and the weight of responsibility which a small-unit commander must carry.

Macksey, Kenneth J. *Guderian: Creator of the Blitzkrieg*. New York, 1976. Biography of Guderian by noted authority on tanks and armored warfare.

Manstein, Erich von. *Lost Victories*. Chicago, 1958. Memoirs and campaign analyses by Germany's finest strategist during World War II.

Mellenthin, Friederich W. von. *Panzer Battles*. Norman, Oklahoma, 1956. Highly insightful account of German armored operations by former general staff officer who served in all major theaters.

Montgomery of Alamein, Field Marshal the Viscount. *Memoirs*. Cleveland, 1958. Memoirs of the controversial British general. Self-serving and occasionally contains factual inaccuracies. Much personal detail.

Patton, George S., Jr. *War As I Knew It*. Boston, 1947. Patton's account, from his diary, of his role in World War II.

Pogue, Forrest C. *George C. Marshall: Ordeal and Hope, 1939–1942*. New York, 1966. Preparing for war.

———. *George C. Marshall: Organizer of Victory*. New York, 1973. A detailed and readable account of Marshall during the last two years of the war.

Ryan, Stephan. *Petain the Soldier*. New York, 1969. A comprehensive biography of the French soldier, which also deals extensively with the development of the French Army during the interwar period.

Smith, Walter B. *Eisenhower's Six Great Decisions*. New York, 1956. Analysis of Eisenhower's leadership at SHAEF by his wartime Chief of Staff.

Tedder, Arthur W. *With Prejudice: The War Memoirs of Marshal of the Royal Air Force, Lord Tedder G. C. B.* Boston, 1966. Memoirs by Eisenhower's deputy at SHAEF.

Truscott, Lucian K., Jr. *Command Decisions*. New York, 1954. Memoirs of American generals' service in Africa, Sicily, and Italy. One of the better memoirs.

Weigley, Russell F. *Eisenhower's Lieutenants*. Bloomington, Indiana, 1981. A scholarly study of the 1944 to 1945 Allied high-level command in western Europe, written by one of America's premier military historians. Carefully and thoughtfully researched, the book presents a new, less complimentary assessment of American generalship.

Young, Desmond. *Rommel: The Desert Fox*. New York, 1950. Old, somewhat uncritically admiring, but the one Anglo-American biography of Rommel that embodies the smell and feel of combat.

Index